# Critics' Choice

New York Drama Critics' Circle
Prize Plays 1935-55

*For dramatic critics I have the same admiration that I have for Alpine climbers, channel swimmers, novelists and all those people who can do marvelous feats which I cannot even imagine myself attempting. . . . For what I want from the dramatic critic . . . is to know the immediate, one might almost say instantaneous, mark that the play makes on a sensitive plate, on the mind of a man who loves the theatre, and who is so experienced that he can form an opinion simultaneously of the play itself, its construction and its language and the verisimilitude of the personages, and of the merits and defects of producer, cast and designer (and perhaps couturier as well), without having any more previous knowledge of play or production than the rest of the first-night audience.*

T. S. Eliot

# Critics' Choice

## New York Drama Critics' Circle Prize Plays 1935-55

*edited by*

JACK GAVER

*Play Anthology Reprint Series*

 BOOKS FOR LIBRARIES PRESS

FREEPORT, NEW YORK

INTERNATIONAL STANDARD BOOK NUMBER:
0-8369-8221-5


LIBRARY OF CONGRESS CATALOG CARD NUMBER:
70-173622


PRINTED IN THE UNITED STATES OF AMERICA
BY
NEW WORLD BOOK MANUFACTURING CO., INC.
HALLANDALE, FLORIDA 33009

For CLAUDIA
who is not yet old enough to
realize that one does not love
a drama critic

# Contents

NOTE: No plays are included for the seasons of 1938–39, 1941–42, 1943–44 and 1945–46 because no awards were made for those particular seasons.

# Twenty Years
# in the American Theatre

1. *A Good Season*

In the autumn of 1935 the American drama was about as vigorous from the standpoint of quality, playwriting ability and vitality as it ever had been, and none of the twenty seasons since, although they brought the inevitable changes in style and taste that tend to muddle definitive comparison, has been markedly, if at all, superior.

The late Burns Mantle, annual chronicler of the seasons from 1919–20 through 1946–47 in *The Best Plays* series published by Dodd, Mead and Company, was moved to write of the 1935–36 season in praiseful terms such as he did not use afterwards; nor have the two subsequent editors of the series to this date.

"It is quite generally admitted," Mantle wrote of 1935–36, "by those familiar with the situation that this theatrical season has been the most exciting and the most satisfying of any New York has enjoyed since the years preceding the crash of '29. I see no particular reason why we should stop at '29. Except in the matter of those statistics that boast the number of plays produced it would be possible to go back even farther without coming upon a record of plays more satisfying or more worthy of enthusiastic endorsement."

The playwrights who did so much to raise the level of the American drama in the decade immediately after World War I were still in robust form in the early 1930's— Robert E. Sherwood, Sidney Howard, Samson Raphaelson, Marc Connelly, Maxwell Anderson, John van Druten, George S. Kaufman, Philip Barry, Elmer Rice, S. N. Behrman. Eugene O'Neill, the bellwether, had embarked in 1935 on a theatrical sabbatical of uncertain duration to write a cycle of nine dramas dealing with the American scene over the centuries.

Perhaps even more important was the fact that there were a number of younger dramatists just beginning to make an impression—Paul Green, Sidney Kingsley, Lynn Riggs, Lillian Hellman, Moss Hart, John Wexley, Clifford Odets, Edward Chodorov, Clare Boothe Brokaw (Luce), Paul Osborn. John Patrick was heard from for the first time at this period, but almost a decade was to pass before this highly important playwright of today was to appear with a second play and begin to gain real recognition.

So, it cannot be argued successfully that the New York Drama Critics' Circle was born out of any desperate need to "save" or "revive" or "raise the level of" American drama. Even if there had been such a need, it is doubtful whether critics, individually or organized, possess any such sure-fire magic at any time. Such power simply cannot be proven. Argue, if you wish, that the critics can proclaim extraordinary merit in a new dramatist and "push" him into initial widespread public inspection. The fact abides that they cannot keep him atop the heap unless the paying customers, rightly or wrongly, warm to him sufficiently of their own accord. They may go to see him once out of curiosity piqued by the critics, but, after that, the stuff they want had better be there or all of the critics in the world can't make them go.

9

The case of William Saroyan is a prime example. His *Love's Old Sweet Song* was at least as good as *The Time of Your Life,* and some critics were passionate about *The Beautiful People*. But the public would have nothing to do with these two successors to his only really popular work.

Why do Ibsen, Shaw, Shakespeare or the French and Greek classics succeed on the American stage today—on the not too frequent occasions when they do? Not, certainly, because the critics might urge that such productions be seen simply because they involve classics. Such successes are based almost wholly on a combination of acting personalities and arresting productions, with a heavy accent on the personalities. Even the critics themselves do not automatically enjoy just any production of a classic.

"There were giants in those days" is a fallible bromide that applies to the field of dramatic criticism as well as to any other. Bernard Shaw, the critic who preceded the playwright, did not, contrary to popular belief, engineer whatever success the Norwegian Henrik Ibsen was to have in the English-speaking world. Ibsen was the right storm shaking the trees at the right time. Nor did any critic make Bernard Shaw, the playwright, a success; rather, a good argument could be made that some of them hindered him. And if you will examine the casts of the successful British and American productions of Shaw's plays over the decades, you'll find a veritable *Who's Who* of popular acting personalities providing box-office magic in his behalf. Playwright Shaw may have felt he was writing classics, but he was taking no chances on the critics' efforts to help "sell" them on that basis alone.

## 2. *The Atmosphere*

This year of 1935, when the New York Drama Critics' Circle was organized, was part of a period of social ferment on the domestic scene and of political tensions internationally. These were reflected in the drama of the time, although not as much as you might think in recalling now how momentous was the decade of 1930–40. Nor did these reflections in themselves leave a deep or widespread impression on the drama from a creative standpoint.

The shadow of the Great Depression had not been completely obliterated—lamentably, the steadily gathering war clouds had to burst on the United States some five years later before this was to be accomplished.

It was a time, for example, when a producing organization called Theatre Union, Inc., was a leader in the then semi-popular game of belaboring the bosses with the bladder of proletarian contempt while indiscriminately pinning the wings of righteous unionism to the shoulders of all workers through the production of such dubious dramatic fare as *Mother, Stevedore* and *Black Pit* in the Civic Repertory Theatre on Fourteenth Street. Uptown, on Broadway, John Howard Lawson was being accorded a certain amount of misguided deference as an important (if not financially successful) playwright. To their credit, it must be said that only occasionally did the critics nod in the matter of separating the propaganda chaff from the dramatic wheat.

At the same time, the critics were quite properly applauding the advent of Clifford Odets, who, regardless of the special pleading of his earlier dramas, was sufficiently astute to create in terms of authentic character and effective dramatic content. (Lack of critical encouragement certainly cannot be blamed for the fact that Odets seemed to part at his playwriting seams about five years later.)

It was a time also when Adolf Hitler began getting his dramatic lumps through an increasing number of largely undistinguished anti-Nazi plays that seemed to make no impression whatever on the Third Reich. Oddly enough, the playwrights had managed to avoid the rather obvious fact that similar material with a Russian accent had been available all along. When Moscow did infrequently draw dramatic attention, it was usually in a serio-comic vein of implied benevolence that ignored the true situation.

The almost single exception came rather late in the game, in the spring of 1940, when Robert E. Sherwood's highly effective *There Shall Be No Night* dealt with Russia's inexcusable invasion of Finland. But it will be everlastingly to his discredit that within two years—after the original run of the play and because Russia had become a wartime ally—he had revised the script for stock library purposes to deal with the Nazi invasion of Greece. In this connection, it is impossible to avoid the ironic observation that no group does more screaming about integrity of idea and script than do playwrights, who usually profess to regard expediency as a dirty word.

The Federal Theatre Project of the Works Progress Administration got into full swing in 1935 for its three-year career that proved to be a very mixed blessing of an experiment in state theatre. It nurtured a few worthwhile careers at a precarious time, offered a few exciting experimental productions as well as a spate of amateurish claptrap, and supported a vast number of persons whose theatrical qualifications were long on desire and short on talent.

The season of the Circle's birth may have been high in quality, but it saw a continuation of the downward trend in the number of productions that actually began a year before the 1929 Wall Street crash.

Broadway production hit an all-time peak of approximately 270 shows in 1927–28, a figure that some astute theatre people felt was too high for the theatre's own good. After that, the trend was downward, slowly at first, then more rapidly as the full impact of inexpensive talking pictures and mushrooming radio combined with the economic recession to make the theatre more of a luxury item than ever before.

In 1935–36, the production total barely got over the 100 mark, and, two decades later, 70 productions would be regarded as constituting a big season. If, by some miracle, 270 productions—or even half that number—should suddenly become available now, they could not possibly be accommodated. There were some eighty legitimate theatres in 1927–28; the number now fluctuates narrowly around the 28 mark, and even a 60 or 70 show season can cause an occasional booking jam.

Coinciding with this shrinkage in productions and theatres was the rise of the phenomenon of the long long-run. In 1935, the records showed just 34 productions in the history of the American stage that had played 500 or more performances in New York. The economics had been such that a play that ran for nine months, roughly 300 performances, in New York could generally be considered a big hit. Given good business for 100 performances, most productions were considered to have escaped financial failure.

Of the over-500 group in mid-1935, only *Tobacco Road* was still current. A year later, two more productions had made the list, and from then on the acceleration was even more rapid. Today there are 124 shows on the list, of which eighteen are over the 1,000 mark and fourteen others have had more than 800 performances.

Drama critics, naturally, have never been in danger of being voted "most popular," but these economic changes in the theatre have been responsible more than anything else for the fact that the first twenty years of the Circle's life have seen more—and more bitter—attacks against play reviewers than ever before.

As the number of productions shrank—and, consequently, employment of actors and outlets for playwrights and technicians—and production costs soared astronomically, the modest success and the show that could afford to hang on in an effort to "find its audience" virtually disappeared. Generally, it is now a case of a quick hit or a quick closing, and the quick hit has to have an emphatic majority of "rave" or, at least, "provocative" reviews. "Bucking the notices" is economic suicide except in the rarest cases.

Thus the critics, without any desire on their part to have such power, have been forced into the position of seeming to be the enemies of everyone in the theatre when they don't turn out a set of notices that can be used to box-office advantage. It is only human that resentment should well up in certain quarters from time to time. It is also only human—and right—that the critics should continue to hew to the line of their individual opinions without consideration of any factor aside from how any given production strikes their assorted fancies.

The Circle, of course, was not organized for mutual protection of beleaguered critics any more than it was to "save" the American drama.

11

## 3. The Inspiration

He was never to know his responsibility, but the late Joseph Pulitzer, Sr., noted newspaper publisher, laid the foundation for the New York Drama Critics' Circle 'way back in 1904 when he drew up his will and provided the Pulitzer prizes for journalism and the arts. In regard to the drama, his instruction was:

"For the original American play, performed in New York, which shall best represent the educational value and power of the stage in raising the standard of good morals, good taste and good manners. ($1,000)."

The first such award was made in 1918 to *Why Marry?* by Jesse Lynch Williams. The seventeenth, made in the spring of 1935—there was no award in 1919—to *The Old Maid* by Zoë Akins, proved to be more offensive to the critics than so vulgar a gesture as organizing to make their own annual award, and the Circle quickly came into being.

Of course, *The Old Maid* alone might not have been enough to spark such action. But there had been several advance temblors. The first of note came when the prize for the 1923–24 season was assigned to Hatcher Hughes' *Hell-bent fer Heaven* instead of to the highly regarded George Kelly play, *The Show-off*. The late Professor William Lyon Phelps revealed that the drama jury was unanimous for Kelly's play but that the Advisory Board had shelved the choice in favor of Hughes, a lecturer on the drama at Columbia University, which administers the Pulitzer prizes. Furthermore, it was widely rumored that the late Professor Brander Matthews, then doyen of the drama at Columbia, had pressured this reversal of the jury.

The matter of a board being able to overrule the decision of the drama jury—or any of the Pulitzer selection groups for that matter—has stuck in many a craw over the years. It has done more than even an occasional errant selection to cause observers in the various arts and journalism divisions to be skeptical of Pulitzer winners at times. The feeling, and it seems a reasonable one, is that the members of the juries are professionals in their fields and are better qualified to make deserving choices than is a large, conglomerate board that may have other things in mind besides pure merit.

George Jean Nathan, for one, deplored such selections as *They Knew What They Wanted* and *Craig's Wife*. When the 1927 award went to *In Abraham's Bosom,* the late Alexander Woollcott observed: "I think an acrid critic might describe it as the work of a serious man who had achieved the prodigious, the almost incredible, feat of writing a play about four Negroes and making them all uninteresting characters."

There wasn't much to grouse about during the next three years as *Strange Interlude, Street Scene* and *The Green Pastures* were honored, although there was some technical discussion as to whether Marc Connelly's masterpiece properly filled the Pulitzer requirement of being an "original" play since *The Green Pastures* was an adaptation of the collection of stories by Roark Bradford, *Ol' Man Adam an' His Chillun.* However, the overlooking of such a technicality could, in view of the excellence of the work in this case, only redound to the credit of the Pulitzer people.

But it was painful to watch the prize go in 1931 to *Alison's House* when such works as Maxwell Anderson's *Elizabeth the Queen,* Philip Barry's *Tomorrow and Tomorrow* and Lynn Riggs's *Green Grow the Lilacs* were available.

There were enough good plays in the 1931–32 season to supply half a dozen seasons with a prize-winner, but no one could really fault the Pulitzer award to *Of Thee I Sing.* In fact, this was a courageous and laudable award, marking, as it did, the first time a musical had received it. And, in 1933, *Both Your Houses* was a quite acceptable selection in a season that did not offer much.

The giving of the prize in 1934 to Sidney Kingsley, a freshman playwright, was not particularly objectionable in itself, but there was some discussion of the fact that the Advisory Board again had overruled the play jury in giving the award to *Men in White.* The jury had recommended *Mary of Scotland* by Maxwell Anderson, the winning playwright of the previous year.

At this particular time, the board apparently had become sensitive to grumblings about repeaters. O'Neill had won three drama prizes. Louis Untermeyer, poet and critic, had commented, in 1928 when Edward Arlington Robinson won his third prize for poetry, that "acknowledged leaders acclaimed by the masses" were monopolizing the prizes. Besides Anderson, O'Neill and Sidney Howard were previous winners who had plays in the 1933–34 season with as much merit as *Men in White*. The overruling action prompted Walter Prichard Eaton, then a professor of playwriting at Yale University, to comment:

"They don't want dramatic experts any more—they want office boys. No self-respecting, intelligent critic would serve on such a jury."

Thus was the stage set on May 3, 1935, when the critical roof fell in on the quite innocent head of Miss Akins, who really never intended to rile anyone. The least of the barbs leveled at *The Old Maid* was that, like *The Green Pastures*, it was not an original play; it was adapted from a novel by Edith Wharton.

The announcement of Miss Akins' victory was still warm when Clayton Hamilton, a Pulitzer play jury member for sixteen years, planted himself in front of an N.B.C. microphone that same night and declared:

"The mountain has labored and brought forth a mouse. The award was made in defiance of the conditions expressly stipulated in the will of the late Joseph Pulitzer. He decreed that a prize of $1,000 be given for the original American play, produced in New York, which shall best represent the educational value and power of the stage. . . . There was no dearth of original American dramas—*The Children's Hour, The First Legion, Awake and Sing, Stevedore* and *Accent on Youth*."

The greatest critical indignation was over the fact that *The Children's Hour*, Lillian Hellman's first produced play, had been passed over. Hamilton might well have mentioned Robert E. Sherwood's *The Petrified Forest* and Maxwell Anderson's *Valley Forge* rather than a couple of those on his list, but he did get across the idea that there was no lack of candidates without having to dig *The Old Maid* out of the dramatic attic.


## 4. *The Organization*

There had been two earlier attempts to get the drama critics organized, but those efforts of 1925 and 1932 were short-lived. The failures contributed to the popular belief that the reviewers were so allergic to each other or to organization *per se* that any such effort was foredoomed to failure. However, in 1935, a woman decided it was time something was done, and the poor male critics had little choice but to accept their destiny.

This distaff inspiration was provided by a charming and talented theatrical press agent named Helen Deutsch, who, for her pains, received the dubious privilege of serving as the Circle's executive secretary in its early years.

"It occurred to me," Miss Deutsch has explained, "that the only really qualified voters for a best play award were the drama critics of the New York papers. I therefore wrote a letter to about twelve of the major critics. I asked them if they were willing to meet just once (I knew how difficult it was to get those boys together) to vote on the best play of the season. I was surprised at the enthusiasm and success of the first meeting. They decided to form the Critics' Circle and subsequently invited several others to join, swelling the ranks to seventeen."

It is almost forgotten now, but Miss Deutsch's spadework in getting the Circle started fell under suspicion in some quarters during its very first season because it developed that the first winner of a Circle award was Maxwell Anderson's *Winterset,* and she happened to be its press agent.

"There was some disagreement, of course, over the choice of the play," she recalled. "One man who did not agree with the choice (I think it was Robert Garland) made a few remarks about the fact that I had an interest in the play (I owned a tiny piece of it). A couple of years later a columnist (I think it was Lucius Beebe of the *Herald Tribune*) implied that I had started the Circle and influenced all of those men in their voting in order to publicize *Winterset*. It was naughty of Garland and Beebe to hint at such a thing. When the rumor appeared in print, the boys were angry. Several of them wrote columns about it."

The seventeen original members of the Circle were:

Kelcey Allen of *Women's Wear Daily*, John Anderson of the *Journal*, Brooks Atkinson of the *Times*, Robert Benchley of the *New Yorker*, Whitney Bolton of the *Morning Telegraph*, John Mason Brown of the *Post*, Rowland Field of the *Times-Union* (Brooklyn), Gilbert Gabriel of the *American*, Robert Garland of the *World-Telegram*, Percy Hammond of the *Herald Tribune*, Joseph Wood Krutch of the *Nation*, Richard Lockridge of the *Sun*, Burns Mantle of the *Daily News*, George Jean Nathan of the *American Mercury* and other magazines, Arthur Pollock of the *Eagle* (Brooklyn), Walter Winchell of the *Daily Mirror* and Stark Young of the *New Republic*. Young had to resign as a member of the Pulitzer play jury in order to join.

Of this group, Allen, Anderson, Benchley, Gabriel, Hammond and Mantle are now dead. So are the *Times-Union,* the *Eagle* and the *Sun,* and the *American* has been merged with the *Journal* to form the *Jo. nal-American*. Only Atkinson, Bolton, Brown and Nathan still were members in 1955; only Atkinson and Bolton were still with their original publications; and all four were out of the Circle at various times during its first twenty years. Krutch, Pollock and Young are now listed as members emeritus. Atkinson was the first president and served through two seasons.

The Circle made its formal bow at a meeting on October 22, 1935, in a room in the Algonquin Hotel which has accommodated its sessions ever since. The constitution adopted once was described in the *Times* by Atkinson as having been "written gaily, over beer and sandwiches, in the home of Whitney Bolton." The original preamble to the constitution read:

"The purpose of the Circle is the fostering and rewarding of merit in the American theatre, and the awarding of a prize, to be known as the Drama Critics' Prize, for the best new play by an American playwright produced in New York during the theatrical season."

Apparently, it was decided later, the Bolton hospitality had been so beguiling that the drafters hadn't applied themselves as thoroughly to the preamble as they had to the refreshments, so a somewhat more elaborate constitutional preface was adopted at a meeting on December 4, 1936, as follows:

"The purpose of the Critics' Circle is to provide a means by which an association of professional dramatic critics of New York may use their combined influence to promote the welfare of the American theatre, to encourage native talent through the awarding of an annual prize to the best play by an American author, produced each season in New York, and to maintain the prestige and dignity of dramatic criticism."

The Circle had rather grandiose ideas about a "prize" during the early months. Probably with an eye to beggaring the $1,000 which then was the amount of the Pulitzer drama award (it has been $500 since 1941), the Circle members talked in terms of a $1,500 purse at their first meeting. Since they lacked the financial resources of a Pulitzer, it was proposed that this money be donated by "an acceptable person."

That dream did not last long. The Circle either discovered that "appropriate persons" with $1,500 to give to playwrights had been withdrawn from circulation or it came belatedly to proper evaluation of its own sterling worth with the realization that any accolade from the critics should be above and beyond the crassness of cash.

Anyway, at the meeting on February 6, 1936, well before the decision on the first prize play, it was decided, quite sensibly, to accept the offer of the noted artist, Henry Varnum Poor, to supply a design for a silver plaque to be given each winning playwright. The design was a handsome one depicting a scene from a performance in the old John Street Theatre, a Manhattan playhouse in the latter part of the eighteenth century. It was voted that each member contribute $10 to help pay for the first plaque and for other Circle expenses. The Circle's dues, incidentally, are $10 annually, with an occasional modest special assessment.

## 5. *Some Changes Are Made*

The first plaque, of course, went to Maxwell Anderson for *Winterset,* which Guthrie McClintic produced and directed so masterfully. The playwright was given his award at a dinner in the Algonquin Hotel on April 5, 1936, with this citation:

"The Circle's decision is based on the conviction that in *Winterset* the author accomplished the notably difficult task of interpreting a valid and challenging contemporary theme dealing with the pursuit of human justice in terms of unusual poetic force, realizing a drama of rich meaning and combining high literary distinction with compelling theatrical effect."

There was a dissenting voice, of course, as there is always bound to be where the Circle is concerned. Percy Hammond, one of three who voted for Robert E. Sherwood's *Idiot's Delight,* remarked of *Winterset* that "it is spinach, smothered with juicy, rich gravies, but still spinach."

In his speech of acceptance, Anderson said:

"Except for the theatre critics of New York no body of men in the country is qualified by training, education and professional experience to render judgment on a season's plays. I am, I assure you seriously, much more interested in that aspect of the ceremony than the fact that the first award goes to *Winterset.* Anybody with the requisite cash can offer a prize for excellence in the theatre, but in order to encourage excellence it is necessary to know when it appears, and a knowledge of what is excellent is more difficult to obtain than cash. I have never been greatly impressed with the Pulitzer Prize for the best play of the year because the final authority for its presentation rests with a committee which is aware only dimly and at second-hand of most of what occurs in the theatres of Broadway. It follows that in so far as the Pulitzer Prize has had an influence on our theatre, it has been a confusing and misleading influence, an encouragement to mediocrity, a gift passed out to a lucky winner by authorities who possess in this field neither standards nor information. But neither ignorance nor lack of standards can be charged against the Critics' Circle. The critics know very definitely what they are for and why they are for it, and whatever their faults of judgment may be, they earn their knowledge of the plays offered during any year by an undeviating attention to what can be seen and heard from the aisle seats of Manhattan playhouses, an attention which amounts on some occasions to sheer martyrdom. I have, in my time, contributed to that martyrdom, and learned by stinging comments in the next day's papers that the boys knew what they were about. I have had both praise and blame in stimulating quantities, and have learned —perhaps unequally—from both."

(Within a little less than ten years Anderson was to prove to be considerably less happy with the critics, but more of that later.)

Eugene O'Neill, whose peculiar career chronology gave the Circle only one chance to vote on a work of his—*The Iceman Cometh* in 1947—and he didn't win then, saluted the foundation of the Circle in the following letter:

"It is a terrible, harrowing experience for a playwright to be forced to praise critics for anything. There is something morbid and abnormal about it, something destructive to the noble tradition of correct conduct for dramatists. Nevertheless, conscience drives me to reiterate that I think the Critics' Circle award a damned fine idea. Prizes in themselves are neither good nor bad. They have no meaning except that which derives from the recognized authority of the awarders of the prizes as judges of true merit. The Critics' Circle possesses that recognized authority, and so I am sure that its awards will deservedly have a significant and growing effect in helping to shape public opinion and in directing the future course of our drama. It is my hope that these yearly awards will direct the attention of the public to the fact that our theatre is now adult and fully capable of standing adult comparison with that of any country in the world today; that it is no longer purely a showshop and an amusement racket, but has grown to be a place where Art may exist."

The organization of the Circle would seem to have had one immediate effect on the Pulitzer people. They quickly decided to drop the idea of discriminating against past winners. Their 1936 prize went to Sherwood for *Idiot's Delight*. Sherwood was not a former Pulitzer winner, so was not involved, but he announced at the time that he would not have accepted the award had the restriction remained in force.

Except that the losers probably resented the Circle's choices just as much as the also-rans always deplored the Pulitzer winners, the critics' organization moved serenely through selection of Anderson's *High Tor* in 1937 and Steinbeck's *Of Mice and Men* in 1938. In the latter year, incidentally, the Circle instituted the policy of giving "an honorary citation to the best new foreign play presented in English during the season in New York" and pinned the first such honor on Paul Vincent Carroll's *Shadow and Substance*.

Then, in 1939, the Circle found itself impaled on its own rules, failing to select a winner in a season rich with candidates, and nine years of varied changes in the voting procedure ensued before arriving at the present simple system whereby the play with the most votes wins, or, in case of a tie, there are two winners.

The original provision was that the winner had to receive a three-fourths majority. After the 1939 impasse, this was changed so that if such a majority was not forthcoming in five ballots, a simple majority would determine the winner, if three-fourths of the members agreed to the switch. Even this modification failed to make a selection possible for the season of 1941–42, and the rule was changed again, in 1943, to provide for a single ballot and a simple majority. But this didn't prevent a third stalemate in 1944 and a fourth in 1946. It was in the latter year that the Circle gave its first citation to a musical, the Rodgers-Hammerstein *Carousel*, and agreed to make such recognition an annual event if the members first voted to consider musicals.

The day after the 1946 failure, John Chapman of the *Daily News* resigned with the declaration that "I do feel and have always felt that the Critics' Circle should select a play for the award." This dramatized a difference of viewpoint within the organization. Some felt that the Circle, if it stood for anything, stood for a high standard of playwriting, and that it was quite proper in any season when the quality was low to refuse to vote for anything. "No choice" votes had been largely responsible for three of the Circle's failures to select a winner.

Chapman and some others felt, however, that if the Circle couldn't decide on a play, it was not fulfilling its purpose. To them "the awarding of an annual prize to the best play by an American author" meant exactly that; in any season, no matter how poor, there should be one work that could be called the best of the lot. Since there are as many critical standards as there are members of the Circle, whose standard, they asked quite reasonably, could be used as the yardstick of quality?

As a result, the members voted on September 23, 1946, to make the award mandatory "without regard to any absolute critical standard" and adopted "the Shipley plan" of voting, named after Joseph T. Shipley, critic for the *New Leader*.

This involved plan called for a proportional vote if no play received a simple majority on the first ballot. All of the plays receiving votes the first time around would be rated in the order of choice for a point score. This worked successfully in 1947 for the selection of Arthur Miller's *All My Sons*, but there was much dissatisfaction with the involved procedure. George Jean Nathan referred to the scheme as a "swindle" and vowed he'd never vote by that method again. One trouble with it was that any proxy vote — of which there are a few at each meeting — had to be thrown out on the preferential ballot because no one could guess how the absent member would want to rate the candidates.

The result was adoption of the present plurality system that makes it impossible not to select a winner — or two — on the very first ballot. Through 1955 there had been no ties.

The closest race came in that year when *Cat on a Hot Tin Roof* received one more vote than did *Bus Stop*.

## 6. *The Informal Touch*

The years since the plurality rule went into effect have been quiet ones for the Circle. The fall organizational meetings and the award sessions each spring are as routine and short as possible. A committee arranges a slate of officers each year, and there is never any fuss about an election.

The members seem to want to get the business over with and get out; there is little "shop talk." No one wants to hear the minutes of the last meeting, which is just as well. They might not be available.

The Circle, to an organizational expert, would seem like a slaphappy group badly in need of education in the proper way to go about being a responsible body. Practically everyone seems to be hazy at some time or other on the exact stipulations of the constitution. In 1952, the members blithely voted the revival of the ten-year-old *Pal Joey* as the best musical. They didn't realize, until someone checked the record afterwards, that the citation has to be for a "new musical." Anyway, it was new in the sense that the Circle wasn't considering musical shows at the time of the original production of *Pal Joey*. No sleep was lost over this *faux pas*.

No one fretted in 1942 when it was discovered that most of the original records of the Circle had been lost. Its books disappeared in a general housecleaning at the Algonquin Hotel, where they had been kept. A new set of records was pieced out from the files of members. In 1952, writing in the *Times* of the loss of the original copy of the constitution and the matrix for the Poor plaque, whose use had been discontinued in the war years anyway, Atkinson commented:

"The loss of the constitution . . . may, in fact, be just the thing the Circle has been trying to achieve ever since it originally coagulated. For criticism is a form of anarchy; and when the members of the Circle finally forget what they think the constitution contained they will be completely happy. . ."

The members can reverse themselves from one year to the next without a blush. Take the case of Harold Clurman, who was in the Circle for a few years as the critic for the *New Republic*. Clurman, of course, had been a noted stage director for years, and one of his jobs was on Carson McCullers' *The Member of the Wedding*, which was a leading candidate for honors in 1950. The Circle decided that it wouldn't be cricket for Clurman to vote in this case. It turned out that his vote wouldn't have made the least difference; *Wedding* received 13 more votes than its closest competitor.

Again, in 1951, Clurman was the director of another candidate, Lillian Hellman's *Autumn Garden*. This time he was authorized to cast a vote, but again it didn't make any difference. *Autumn Garden* finished a bad fourth in a field of five.

There is really only one matter that crops up regularly to keep the meetings from being even shorter than they are. And it is an important matter, dealing with the Circle's basic function under the present rules, which is to give its principal award to an American play.

Those who want a change feel that the Circle would be doing itself and the theatre in general a genuine service by choosing a "best play" without regard to nationality. They feel that, in the haste of original organization, there was thoughtless aping of the Pulitzer concern with the native drama; that an organization of critics should operate with an international viewpoint; that the American drama no longer needs special favors because it has been able to command respect in open competition for some thirty years. Furthermore, they argue, in the rare event of a foreign victory, a special vote could be taken to give a citation to the best American play.

The matter has come up at almost every Circle session since Atkinson introduced it at the September 23, 1947, meeting. Tabled at that time, Atkinson's proposal was defeated a few weeks later. The next serious attempt to make the change came at the meeting of September 28, 1949, when Atkinson, Chapman, Gabriel and Kappo Phelan pushed the proposition. But again it failed to pass, although thirteen members backed it in the vote on December 6. This total was short of the necessary three-fourths majority.

There is strong, determined backing for the change, and it is entirely likely that, what with shifting opinions and membership, the required majority may be obtained in the not too distant future. The subject was put over to the Circle's 1955–56 agenda in April, 1955, when Chapman reported with something like alarm that the Pulitzer people had stolen a march on the Circle by revising their staunchly American viewpoint after thirty-seven years to stipulate that the winning play be "preferably American." Such phrasing, of course, would make it possible for a foreign work to win, but Chapman had been given the wrong information or had wrongly interpreted information.

What the Pulitzer committee did in 1955 was simply to change the drama award text from "For the original American play, etc." to "For the American play, preferably original, etc." This was the eighth textual change for the Pulitzer drama award, and there may be more in years to come, but it is highly unlikely that its strictly American flavor ever will be altered.

This in itself is something of an argument for the Circle to increase the scope of its major award; the Pulitzer is insurance that American playwrights won't be neglected. Furthermore, the critics are called upon in their daily routine to rule on foreign plays, which are in competition with the native product for the public's attention, and it would seem only natural for them to take the international view in choosing the best play of a season.

## 7. *The Crisis*

The Circle, in its second decade, went right down the scale in the matter of social activities without a complaint from members or public. In the early years, there was always a dinner at the Algonquin for the winners. Later, the winners had to be content with a cocktail party presentation. This, too, was abandoned, although a public presentation of some sort still is arranged. The 1955 winners, for example, received their official scrolls from the Circle's president between acts at a performance of *Cat on a Hot Tin Roof* in the Morosco Theatre.

Also, in the beginning, the Circle usually had a couple of meetings annually besides the fall and spring sessions, and it even managed a Christmas party or two for the members. These gradually were abandoned. A few years ago Robert Coleman of the *Mirror* suggested at a meeting that the Circle hold a luncheon every month and swap trade talk with some theatrical personalities, but this danger-fraught proposal was howled down as though it were sedition.

The Poor plaque was shelved for the first time in 1942 when it was voted to donate the money it would have cost to British war relief and to the American Theater Wing. In 1944, it was decided permanently to substitute scrolls for the plaque. The practice of phrasing flowery citations to go along with the plaques (or scrolls) was voted out in the spring of 1948, an act which caused Kappo Phelan of *Commonweal* to lament in a letter to the *Times*:

". . . In their refusal to make even an abstract superficial citation with the award this year, it seems to me that the Drama Critics' Circle (of which I am a member) is guilty of refusing the very function of criticism. If it says nothing else, criticism says why."

All of this does not indicate a lack of interest among the members in the organization and its primary purpose. It simply means that, by a process of elimination through the years, they have reduced the mechanism of their function to the minimum of inconvenience to themselves, and they are quite happy about it.

The only time the Circle was in real danger was the fall of 1943. John Anderson, in office as president less than a year, died that July. Four other founding members were out of circulation — John Mason Brown and Richard Lockridge were in the Navy, Brooks Atkinson had become a war correspondent, Burns Mantle had retired. And Richard Watts, Jr., who had replaced Percy Hammond for the *Herald Tribune*, also had turned war reporter.

Shortly before the annual organizational meeting on October 12, it was learned that George Jean Nathan, Wolcott Gibbs of the *New Yorker* and Stark Young had submitted their resignations; also that Joseph Wood Krutch had advised he would be out of action for a year because he was taking a leave of absence from the *Nation*. Nathan's only public comment on the matter, then or later, was: "I prefer to remain in absentia until such time as the Circle recaptures its original ideal of merit and dignity."

A few hours before the Circle convened, editions of the *World-Telegram* were on the street carrying this past-tense comment by Burton Rascoe, critic for that newspaper and a then rather recent Circle member:

"The Drama Critics' Circle has gone down the drain. And good riddance, too. It was a presumptuous, unrepresentative and exclusive social club from which certain metropolitan drama critics were excluded for no fathomable reason, and it had no excuse even as a social club, for it engaged in no social activities except an annual dinner at which an award was made (or not made) to some playwright who a simple majority of the votes of the critics had decided had written the best play of the year. . . . The very name, Circle, was enough to condemn us in the eyes of the public, for we're not even a union."

At the meeting, the resignations of Nathan, Gibbs and Young were accepted. Young wrote that the war had brought disruption of the theatre in general, that this naturally included the critics, and he didn't believe the Circle could function properly for the time being.

Rascoe, who had been a successful and happy maverick in the literary field for years and whose play reviews for the *World-Telegram* had raised numerous ires and eyebrows, showed up at the meeting. He moved that the Circle's constitution be changed to broaden the scope of membership to include more newspaper and magazine reviewers and the critics for the wire services, failing which the Circle should be dissolved. His proposal was defeated, getting only two votes besides his own. Lewis Nichols of the *Times* and Louis Kronenberger of *Time* magazine supported dissolution on the grounds that the Circle was serving no great purpose at the moment. Kronenberger said he felt there was little prospect of any outstanding plays in wartime; besides, he didn't like the Circle's voting method because he felt it had no integrity.

When the vote went against him, Rascoe submitted his resignation. It was promptly accepted, and he donned his homburg and left. He never came back although he did not leave his *World-Telegram* post until the spring of 1946.

The Circle, of course, did not go down the drain. The remaining members elected as president Howard Barnes, who had replaced Watts on the *Herald Tribune,* at a meeting in November, 1943. Early in 1944, Gibbs returned to the Circle without fanfare. Nathan and Young were re-elected to membership on November 12, 1946, at their request.

Although Rascoe's proposal to broaden the membership failed, it is a fact that in the next few years there was a gradual acceptance of some critics who previously had not been invited to join. However, there continued to be a rejection or two a year on various grounds until October, 1953, when the Circle adopted a revision of its membership clause to make it apply only to critics for newspapers and magazines "that are published in English and have their editorial offices in New York." The members resisted a suggestion that the phrasing be ". . . published in *good* English . . ." on the grounds that it was "impractical" to demand such perfection even of New York writers and editors. The change was designed to discourage once and for all the annual applications for membership in behalf of persons working for foreign-language publications, or English publications in the metropolitan area but actually outside New York City, and fringe publications with dubious claim to effective communion with the theatre.

## 8. *Critical Fun*

The Circle, as an organization, takes no cognizance of the various embroilments in which critics become involved during occasional seasons because someone takes exception to a review or reviews. It is not an instrument for defending critics or for disciplining or regimenting them. No critic would want to be hampered by an organizational defense that might rob him of the fun of first-hand tilting with his detractors — in print, of course.

The only time the Circle did speak up was in November, 1946, when this impotent resolution was addressed to the show-business trade papers, *Variety* and *The Billboard*:

"The New York Drama Critics' Circle would appreciate it if *Variety* and *The Billboard* would in future omit the critics' box scores which have for some years been features of their publications. The Circle would like to go on record as protesting against these scores. It finds they are not only detrimental to the theatre's best interest but utterly alien to the purpose and intenion of criticism.

"Feeling that criticism and the box office are completely unrelated, and being convinced that the critic's function is to appraise the merits of productions rather than to prophesy the length of runs, we would, as a body, be grateful for the discontinuance of such irrelevant and harmful scores."

Critics were graded as to whether their approval or disapproval of a play coincided with its estimated commercial success or failure. If a critic liked a play that didn't make money, he had erred, and vice versa. Actually, the box scores involved but a minority of the Circle because only the critics of the New York daily newspapers were included in the listings.

*Variety* pointed out that it had started the box scores in 1923 because managers were fed up with too many "no opinion" notices, and it claimed that the policy did result in critics being much more careful to take a definite stand in their reviews. Developments in recent years would indicate that producers would be happy to trade a bad notice for one of no opinion. Needless to say, the two publications refused to drop the box scores.

But whatever they do, the critics are found to wind up in someone's doghouse periodically. A little less than ten years after Maxwell Anderson spoke all those kind words about them when he received the award for *Winterset,* he was voicing that classic denunciation of them as "the Jukes family of journalism." The reference was to the fictional name given by sociologists to a real upstate New York family notorious for generations of shiftless poverty, mental vagrancy and general wretchedness.

This firecracker was set off by the critics' failure to appreciate one of Anderson's less effective efforts, *Truckline Café,* which opened February 27, 1946. Anderson's producers, Harold Clurman (not yet in the Circle), Elia Kazan and the Playwrights' Company, were responsible for two newspaper advertisements which assailed the critics as exercising an unwarranted dictatorship over what the public shall or shall not see and accused them of "intemperance," "vindictiveness," "vituperation" and "a violation of decent critical standards."

Needless to say, there were no denunciatory advertisements the very next season when the Circle gave its award to *All My Sons,* which was produced by Clurman, Kazan and Walter Fried, and the critics wrote generally favorable notices for Anderson's *Joan of Lorraine.*

It is a never-ceasing wonder that anyone can think that anything can be gained by attacking the critics. Yet someone is always entering the lists against them, and they range from newcomer producers who know no better to the most experienced, such as J. J. Shubert.

On November 1, 1948, this younger brother of the dynasty that owns or controls most of the nation's legitimate theatres sent a letter to newspaper editors in which he said he wanted something done about the power of the critics to control "the very life of our business." His plea was on a purely economic basis. The publishers figured that they had economic problems of their own and paid no attention to the plea. The Shuberts, of course, have not been suffering since 1948.

Playwright Irwin Shaw let loose at the critics as a result of their failure to appreciate his *The Assassins* in 1945, introducing something of a novelty by putting matters on a social plane. In the introduction of the printed version of his play, he wrote: "I would no more think of sitting down to dinner with certain of the critics of the New York papers than I would think of breaking bread with the master of Buchenwald," referring to the then fresh memory of a notorious German concentration camp.

About two years later, Shaw was briefly a member of the Circle as critic for the *New Republic*. During that period, *The Survivors,* which he wrote in collaboration, opened. The critics thumbed it down, and Shaw himself wrote that midway in rehearsals, when it was too late to remedy matters, they discovered they had approached the writing of the play in the wrong manner.

When there was no enthusiasm along the aisles for a Ben Hecht—Charles MacArthur collaboration, *Swan Song,* in 1946, the authors (Hecht is a veteran critic-baiter) had one of the actors make a curtain speech at each performance, urging the customers to stir up enthusiasm for the play to turn it into a hit that would disconcert the critics and "might even kill them." There were twenty-two performances; the critics proved more durable.

Producer Herman Shumlin once rapped the reviewers on the grounds that they are lenient with plays meant only to entertain but pick on tiny flaws in serious and socially conscious works. A Negro weekly in Harlem, *The People's Voice,* and the *Daily Worker* once accused the critics of racial bias, a preposterous charge.

One of the silliest of all of these periodic, futile arguments occurred in the spring of 1955 when a musical comedy entitled *Ankles Aweigh* arrived at the Mark Hellinger Theatre. This was a peculiar affair, too, because it did not follow the usual pattern of producer or actor or backer versus critic.

The critics didn't like it and said so in varying degrees of disapproval, although most of them acknowledged the comical abilities of the two leading players, sisters Betty and Jane Kean. The controversy was touched off before the ink was dry on the reviews by a newspaper colleague, Walter Winchell, gossip and cosmic columnist of the *Daily Mirror,* who went all out in a damn-the-critics, praise-the-show campaign he pursued daily for weeks.

Oddly enough, the other gossip and night-club columnists of the newspapers took a similar stand; "oddly" because the history of New York columning is filled with intramural feuds which more often than not have involved Winchell. The result was something of a nine-day wonder as to whether the critics or the columnists were more powerful in influencing the public regarding a show.

Any such argument, of course, isn't worth the hot air involved in conducting it. The critics, right or wrong, not only must say whether they like or dislike an attraction, but also they must examine it in detail and analyze its good and bad points. The "why" is all-important. The columnists, accustomed to the back-patting, non-critical "reviewing" of night-club shows, are under no such compulsion. The Keans, justifiably, have been favorites of theirs for several years through their night-club work, and, when they are having themselves a high old time in a Broadway musical, the natural thing is to urge the public to go see them and never mind the rest of the proceedings.

One of the most ridiculous aspects of the *Ankles Aweigh* affair was the implication, especially by Winchell, that this was unprecedented and that at last someone was going to set the critics down hard for the first time. But the record books are full of evidence that many shows have persisted to prosperity in the face of adverse reviews—and where there was no issue of critics versus columnists involved. It would be a rare case indeed when the critics begrudged such triumph. They take no delight in the closing of shows; they know that the theatre's prosperity is important to them. They don't mind if an attraction they don't like runs forever, so long as they don't have to sit through it a second time.

Winchell apparently can never forget—and I suppose there's no reason he should—that, back in 1938, his steady plugging was a vital factor in building Olsen and Johnson's musical nonesuch, *Hellzapoppin,* into a long-run success. He tried to duplicate that feat several times thereafter—*Small Wonder* in 1948 comes quickly to mind—but never was able to do it. Nor did he succeed with *Ankles Aweigh*, which managed to hang on for twenty-two weeks but lost an estimated $300,000.

It was noted earlier that Winchell was one of the charter members of the Circle. He seems to have attended no more than the first two or three meetings, if the minutes can be relied upon. As early as 1938 he was passing up the annual award voting because he hadn't seen enough plays to be competent to make a choice. Robert Coleman was doing most of the reviewing. Winchell finally resigned from the Circle in 1945 after further feelers from the Circle about his intentions, and Coleman became the *Daily Mirror's* representative in the Circle in the fall of 1946. However, Winchell said he was holding on to the title of drama critic. He hasn't written a formal review in many seasons, but he still exercises a sort of emeritus liberty. When he feels strongly enough, one way or another, about a new show whose premiere he chances to attend, his capsule comment in the staccato Winchell style will be appended to Coleman's review, which may or may not jibe with it. They were not quite in harmony on *Ankles Aweigh*.

In an argument such as the *Ankles Aweigh* imbroglio, the public gets a distorted view of the Circle's members and their operations. Not that the critics mind particulary. They are human (they are so!) enough to relish a little attention, and they enjoy dodging verbal brickbats if for no other reason than it gives them something to write about on otherwise dull days. A season in which some St. George doesn't joust with them in a major way is a dull one indeed.

There is probably less "shop" communication among critics than in any other group of persons engaged in a common line of work. Richard Watts once wrote in the *Post*—possibly only partly in jest—that "the melancholy truth is that most of them don't really like each other." They are, perhaps, the last of the rugged individualists.

What the public is in no position to learn at first hand is the fact that the most devastating, the most virulent critics of all are theatre workers—actors, directors, producers and such. They may applaud heartily, they may go backstage to congratulate members of a company, but listen to them when there is no need to put up a front and often you'll hear comments that would make a critic blush. By comparison, the critic is the personification of kindness and restraint.

And, now, let the plays begin!

JACK GAVER
*June 5, 1955*
*New York City*

# 1935-36

*Winterset* achieved the honor of becoming the first prize play of the New York Drama Critics' Circle on March 26, 1936. Twenty years later, despite a steady stream of dramas from Maxwell Anderson, many still consider it his best work, or at least on a par with two others, *Elizabeth the Queen* and *Mary of Scotland*.

This tragedy of vengeance in the wake of a miscarriage of justice, frankly inspired by the Massachussetts Sacco-Vanzetti case, won the necessary majority—fourteen of the seventeen votes—on the fifth ballot. In the final cast, the three other votes, those of John Anderson, Robert Garland and Percy Hammond, were given to Robert E. Sherwood's *Idiot's Delight*.

Other plays considered in the early ballots were S. N. Behrman's *End of Summer*, Sidney Kingsley's *Dead End, First Lady* by Katharine Dayton and George S. Kaufman, and *Ethan Frome* by Owen and Donald Davis.

This was the season that also saw the original production of the Gershwin-Heyward *Porgy and Bess*, Helen Hayes in *Victoria Regina*, Rudy Vallee as a star in a production of George White's *Scandals*, Jimmy Durante, Paul Whiteman and an elephant in a gigantic musical, *Jumbo*, at the old Hippodrome, and Katharine Cornell in her fine revival of Shaw's *Saint Joan*.

Those who saw *Winterset* will never forget the poignant, exciting playing of Burgess Meredith and Margo in the leading roles, nor the haunting set with the great bridge in the background designed by Jo Mielziner.

*Winterset* achieved 179 performances in its first engagement and played 16 in a return visit.

# Winterset

## By MAXWELL ANDERSON

Presented by Guthrie McClintic at the Martin Beck Theatre, New York City, September 25, 1935, with the following cast:

| | |
|---|---|
| TROCK | *Eduardo Ciannelli* |
| SHADOW | *Harold Johnsrud* |
| LUCIO | *Morton L. Stevens* |
| PINY | *Fernanda Eliscu* |
| MIRIAMNE | *Margo* |
| GARTH | *Theodore Hecht* |
| ESDRAS | *Anatole Winogradoff* |
| 1st GIRL | *Eva Langbord* |
| 2nd GIRL | *Ruth Hammond* |
| HOBO | *John Philliber* |
| JUDGE GAUNT | *Richard Bennett* |
| CARR | *Billy Quinn* |
| MIO | *Burgess Meredith* |
| SAILOR | *St. John Terrell* |
| RADICAL | *Abner Biberman* |
| POLICEMAN | *Anthony Blair* |
| SERGEANT | *Harold Martin* |
| TWO YOUNG MEN | *Stanley Gould* |
| | *Walter Holbrook* |

## SCENE

Act   I—Scenes 1 and 3—Under a bridge. Scene 2—In a tenement.

Act   II—In the tenement.

Act   III—Under the bridge.

# WINTERSET

## ACT ONE

### SCENE I

SCENE: *The scene is the bank of a river under a bridgehead. A gigantic span starts from the rear of the stage and appears to lift over the heads of the audience and out to the left. At the right rear is a wall of solid supporting masonry. To the left an apartment building abuts against the bridge and forms the left wall of the stage with a dark basement window and a door in the brick wall. To the right, and in the foreground, an outcropping of original rock makes a barricade behind which one may enter through a cleft. To the rear, against the masonry, two sheds have been built by waifs and strays for shelter. The river bank, in the foreground, is black rock worn smooth by years of trampling. There is room for exit and entrance to the left around the apartment house, also around the rock to the right. A single street lamp is seen at the left—and a glimmer of apartment lights in the background beyond. It is an early, dark December morning.*

*Two* YOUNG MEN IN SERGE *lean against the masonry, matching bills.* TROCK ESTRELLA *and* SHADOW *come in from the left.*

TROCK. Go back and watch the car. (*The* TWO YOUNG MEN *go out.* TROCK *walks to the corner and looks toward the city.*)
You roost of punks and gulls! Sleep it off,
whatever you had last night, get down in warm,
one big ham-fat against another—sleep,
cling, sleep and rot! Rot out your pasty guts
with diddling, you had no brain to begin.
If you had
there'd be no need for us to sleep on iron
who had too much brains for you.

SHADOW. Now look, Trock, look,
what would the warden say to talk like that?

TROCK. May they die as I die!
By God, what life they've left me
they shall keep me well! I'll have that out of them—
these pismires that walk like men!

SHADOW. Because, look, chief,
it's all against science and penology
for you to get out and begin to cuss that way
before your prison vittles are out of you.
Hell,
you're supposed to leave the pen full of high thought,
kind of noble-like, loving toward all mankind,
ready to kiss their feet—or whatever parts
they stick out toward you. Look at me!

TROCK. I see you.
And even you may not live as long as you think.

You think too many things are funny. Well, laugh.
But it's not so funny.

SHADOW. Come on, Trock, you know me.
Anything you say goes, but give me leave
to kid a little.

TROCK. Then laugh at somebody else!
It's a lot safer! They've soaked me once too often
in that vat of poisoned hell they keep upstate
to soak men in, and I'm rotten inside, I'm all
one liquid puke inside where I had lungs
once, like yourself! And now they want to get me
and stir me in again—and that'd kill me—
and that's fine for them. But before that happens to me
a lot of these healthy boys'll know what it's like
when you try to breathe and have no place to put air—
they'll learn it from me!

SHADOW. They've got nothing on you, chief.

TROCK. I don't know yet. That's what I'm here to find out.
If they've got what they might have
it's not a year this time—
no, nor ten. It's screwed down under a lid.—
I can die quick enough, without help.

SHADOW. You're the skinny kind
that lives forever.

25

TROCK. He gave me a half a year,
the doc at the gate.

SHADOW. Jesus.

TROCK. Six months I get,
and the rest's dirt, six feet. (LUCIA, *the
street-piano man, comes in right from behind the rock and goes to the shed where
he keeps his piano.* PINY, *the apple woman,
follows and stands in the entrance.* LUCIA
*speaks to Estrella, who still stands facing
Shadow.*)

LUCIA. Morning. (TROCK *and* SHADOW *go out
round the apartment house without speaking.*)

PINY. Now what would you call them?

LUCIA. Maybe someting da river washed up.

PINY. Nothing ever washed him—that black
one.

LUCIA. Maybe not, maybe so. More like his
pa and ma raise-a heem in da cellar .(*He
wheels out the piano.*)

PINY. He certainly gave me a turn. (*She
lays a hand on the rock.*)

LUCIA. You don' live-a right, ol' gal. Take
heem easy. Look on da bright-a side. Never
say-a die. Me, every day in every way I getta
be da regular heller. (*He starts out.*)

CURTAIN

# SCENE II

SCENE: *A cellar apartment under the apartment building, floored with cement and
roofed with huge boa constrictor pipes that run slantwise from left to right, dwarfing
the room. An outside door opens to the left and a door at the right rear leads to the
interior of the place. A low squat window to the left. A table at the rear and a few
chairs and books make up the furniture.* GARTH, *son of* ESDRAS, *sits alone, holding a
violin upside down to inspect a crack at its base. He lays the bow on the floor and runs
his fingers over the joint.* MIRIAMNE *enters from the rear, a girl of fifteen.* GARTH *looks
up, then down again.*

MIRIAMNE. Garth—

GARTH. The glue lets go. It's the steam, I
guess.
It splits the hair on your head.

MIRIAMNE. It can't be mended?

GARTH. I can't mend it.
No doubt there are fellows somewhere
who'd mend it for a dollar—and glad to
do it.
That is if I had a dollar.—Got a dollar?
No, I thought not.

MIRIAMNE. Garth, you've sat at home here
three days now. You haven't gone out at all.
Something frightens you.

GARTH. Yes?

MIRIAMNE. And father's frightened.
He reads without knowing where. When a
shadow falls
across the page he waits for a blow to follow
after the shadow. Then in a little while
he puts his book down softly and goes out
to see who passed.

GARTH. A bill collector, maybe.
We haven't paid the rent.

MIRIAMNE. No.

GARTH. You're a bright girl, sis.—
You see too much. You run along and cook.
Why don't you go to school?

MIRIAMNE. I don't like school.
They whisper behind my back.

GARTH. Yes? About what?

MIRIAMNE. What did the lawyer mean
that wrote to you?

GARTH (*rising*). What lawyer?

MIRIAMNE. I found a letter
on the floor of your room. He said, "Don't
get me wrong,
but stay in out of the rain the next few days,
just for instance."

GARTH. I thought I burned that letter.

MIRIAMNE. Afterward you did. And then
what was printed
about the Estrella gang—you hid it from me,

you and father. What is it—about this murder—?

GARTH. Will you shut up, you fool!

MIRIAMNE. But if you know
why don't you tell them, Garth?
If it's true—what they say—
you knew all the time Romagna wasn't
guilty,
and could have said so—

GARTH. Everybody knew
Romagna wasn't guilty! But they weren't
listening
to evidence in his favor. They didn't want it.
They don't want it now.

MIRIAMNE. But was that why
they never called on you?—

GARTH. So far as I know
they never'd heard of me—and I can assure
you
I knew nothing about it—

MIRIAMNE. But something's wrong—
and it worries father—

GARTH. What could be wrong?

MIRIAMNE. I don't know. (*A pause.*)

GARTH. And I don't know. You're a good
kid, Miriamne,
but you see too many movies. I wasn't
mixed up
in any murder, and I don't mean to be.
If I had a dollar to get my fiddle fixed
and another to hire a hall, by God I'd fiddle
some of the prodigies back into Sunday
School
where they belong, but I won't get either,
and so
I sit here and bite my nails—but if you
hoped
I had some criminal romantic past
you'll have to look again!

MIRIAMNE. Oh, Garth, forgive me—
But I want you to be so far above such
things
nothing could frighten you. When you seem
to shrink
and be afraid, and you're the brother I
love,
I want to run there and cry, if there's any
question
they care to ask, you'll be quick and glad
to answer,
for there's nothing to conceal!

GARTH. And that's all true—

MIRIAMNE. But then I remember—
how you dim the lights—
and we go early to bed—and speak in
whispers—
and I could think there's a death somewhere
behind us—
an evil death—

GARTH (*hearing a step*). Now for God's
sake, be quiet! (ESDRAS, *an old rabbi with
a kindly face, enters from the outside. He
is hurried and troubled.*)

ESDRAS. I wish to speak alone with someone
here
if I may have this room. Miriamne—

MIRIAMNE (*turning to go*). Yes, father.
(*The outer door is suddenly thrown open.*
TROCK *appears.*)

TROCK (*after a pause*). You'll excuse me
for not knocking. (SHADOW *follows* TROCK
*in.*)
Sometimes it's best to come in quiet. Sometimes
it's a good way to go out. Garth's home,
I see.
He might not have been here if I made a
point
of knocking at doors.

GARTH. How are you, Trock?

TROCK. I guess
you can see how I am.
(*To* MIRIAMNE). Stay here. Stay where you
are.
We'd like to make your acquaintance.
—If you want the facts
I'm no better than usual, thanks. Not
enough sun,
my physician tells me. Too much close con-
finement.
A lack of exercise and an overplus
of beans in the diet. You've done well, no
doubt?

GARTH. I don't know what makes you think
so.

TROCK. Who's the family?

GARTH. My father and my sister.

TROCK. Happy to meet you.
Step inside a minute. The boy and I
have something to talk about.

ESDRAS. No, no—he's said nothing—
nothing, sir, nothing!

TROCK. When I say go out, you go—

ESDRAS (*pointing to the door*). Miriamne—

GARTH. Go on out, both of you!

ESDRAS. Oh, sir—I'm old—
old and unhappy—

GARTH. Go on! (MIRIAMNE *and* ESDRAS *go inside.*)

TROCK. And if you listen
I'll riddle that door! (SHADOW *shuts the door behind them and stands against it.*)
I just got out, you see,
and I pay my first call on you.

GARTH. Maybe you think
I'm not in the same jam you are.

TROCK. That's what I do think.
Who started looking this up?

GARTH. I wish I knew,
and I wish he was in hell! Some damned
professor
with nothing else to do. If you saw his
stuff
you know as much as I do.

TROCK. It wasn't you
turning state's evidence?

GARTH. Hell, Trock, use your brain!
The case was closed. They burned Romagna
for it
and that finished it. Why should I look for
trouble
and maybe get burned myself?

TROCK. Boy, I don't know,
but I just thought I'd find out.

GARTH. I'm going straight, Trock.
I can play this thing, and I'm trying to make
a living.
I haven't talked and nobody's talked to me.
Christ—it's the last thing I'd want!

TROCK. Your old man knows.

GARTH. That's where I got the money that
last time
when you needed it. He had a little saved
up,
but I had to tell him to get it. He's as
safe
as Shadow there.

TROCK (*looking at Shadow*). There could
be people safer
than that son-of-a-bitch.

SHADOW. Who?

TROCK. You'd be safer dead
along with some other gorillas.

SHADOW. It's beginning to look
as if you'd feel safer with everybody dead,
the whole god-damn world.

TROCK. I would. These Jesus-bitten
professors! Looking up their half-ass cases!
We've got enough without that.

GARTH. There's no evidence
to reopen the thing.

TROCK. And suppose they called on you
and asked you to testify?

GARTH. Why then I'd tell 'em
that all I know is what I read in the papers.
And I'd stick to that.

TROCK. How much does your sister know?

GARTH. I'm honest with you, Trock. She read
my name
in the professor's pamphlet, and she was
scared
the way anybody would be. She got nothing
from me, and anyway she's go to the chair
herself before she'd send me there.

TROCK. Like hell.

GARTH. Besides, who wants to go to trial
again
except the radicals?—You and I won't spill
and unless we did there's nothing to take to
court
as far as I know. Let the radicals go on howling
about getting a dirty deal. They always
howl
and nobody gives a damn. This professor's
red—
everybody knows it.

TROCK. You're forgetting the judge.
Where's the damn judge?

GARTH. What judge?

TROCK. Read the morning papers.
It says Judge Gaunt's gone off his nuts. He's
got

that damn trial on his mind, and been going round

proving to everybody he was right all the time

and the radicals were guilty—stopping people

in the street to prove it—and now he's nuts entirely

and nobody knows where he is.

GARTH. Why don't they know?

TROCK. Because he's on the loose somewhere! They've got the police of three cities looking for him.

GARTH. Judge Gaunt?

TROCK. Yes. Judge Gaunt.

SHADOW. Why should that worry you?
He's crazy, ain't he? And even if he wasn't he's arguing on your side. You're jittery, chief.
God, all the judges are looney. You've got the jitters,
and you'll damn well give yourself away some time
peeing yourself in public. (TROCK *half turns toward* SHADOW *in anger.*)
Don't jump the gun now,
I've got pockets in my clothes, too. (*His hand is in his coat pocket.*)

TROCK. All right. Take it easy. (*He takes his hand from his pocket, and* SHADOW *does the same.*) (*To* GARTH)
Maybe you're lying to me and maybe you're not.
Stay at home a few days.

GARTH. Sure thing. Why not?

TROCK. And when I say stay at home I mean stay home.
If I have to go looking for you you'll stay a long time
wherever I find you. (*To* SHADOW)
Come on. We'll get out of here. (*To* GARTH)
Be seeing you. (SHADOW *and* TROCK *go out. After a pause* GARTH *walks over to his chair and picks up the violin. Then he puts it down and goes to the inside door, which he opens.*)

GARTH. He's gone. (MIRIAMNE *enters,* ESDRAS *behind her.*)

MIRIAMNE (*going up to* GARTH.) Let's not stay here. (*She puts her hands on his arms.*)

I thought he'd come for something—horrible.
Is he coming back?

GARTH. I don't know.

MIRIAMNE. Who is he, Garth?

GARTH. He'd kill me if I told you who he is, that is, if he knew.

MIRIAMNE. Then don't say it—

GARTH. Yes, and I'll say it! I was with a gang one time
that robbed a pay roll. I saw murder done, and Trock Estrella did it. If that got out
I'd go to the chair and so would he—that's why
he was here today—

MIRIAMNE. But that's not true—

ESDRAS. He says it
to frighten you, child.

GARTH. Oh, no I don't! I say it
because I've held it in too long! I'm damned
if I sit here forever, and look at the door, waiting for Trock with his sub-machine gun, waiting
for police with a warrant!—I say I'm damned, and I am,
no matter what I do! These piddling scales on a violin—first position, third, fifth, arpeggios in E—and what I'm thinking
is Romagna dead for the murder—dead while I sat here
dying inside—dead for the thing Trock did while I looked on—and I could have saved him, yes—
but I sat here and let him die instead of me because I wanted to live! Well, it's no life, and it doesn't matter who I tell, because
I mean to get it over!

MIRIAMNE. Garth, it's not true!

GARTH. I'd take some scum down with me if I died—
that'd be one good deed—

ESDRAS. Son, son, you're mad—
someone will hear—

GARTH. Then let them hear! I've lived with ghosts too long, and lied too long. God damn you
if you keep me from the truth!—(*He turns away.*)

Oh, God damn the world!
I don't want to die! (*He throws himself
down.*)

ESDRAS. I should have known.
I thought you hard and sullen,
Garth, my son. And you were a child, and
   hurt
with a wound that might be healed.
—All men have crimes,
and most of them are hidden, and many
   are heavy
as yours must be to you. (GARTH *sobs.*)
They walk the streets
to buy and sell, but a spreading crimson
   stain
tinges the inner vestments, touches flesh,
and burns the quick. You're not alone.

GARTH. I'm alone
in this.

ESDRAS. Yes, if you hold with the world that
   only
those who die suddenly should be revenged.
But those whose hearts are cancered, drop
   by drop
in small ways, little by little, till they've
   borne
all they can bear, and die—these deaths will
   go
unpunished now as always. When we're
   young
we have faith in what is seen, but when
   we're old
we know that what is seen is traced in air
and built on water. There's no guilt under
   heaven,
just as there's no heaven, till men believe it—
no earth, till men have seen it, and have a
   word
to say this is the earth.

GARTH. Well, I say there's an earth,
and I say I'm guilty on it, guilty as hell.

ESDRAS. Yet till it's known you bear no guilt
   at all—
unless you wish. The days go by like film,
like a long written scroll, a figured veil
unrolling out of darkness into fire
and utterly consumed. And on this veil,
running in sounds and symbols of men's
   minds

reflected back, life flickers and is shadow
going toward flame. Only what men can see
exists in that shadow. Why must you rise
   and cry out:
That was I, there in the ravelled tapestry,
there, in that pistol flash, when the man was
   killed.
I was there, and was one, and am bloodstained!
Let the wind
and fire take that hour to ashes out of time
and out of mind! This thing that men call
   justice,
this blind snake that strikes men down in
   the dark,
mindless with fury, keep your hand back
   from it,
pass by in silence—let it be forgotten, forgotten!—
Oh, my son, my son—have pity!

MIRIAMNE. But if it was true
and someone died—then it was more than
   shadow—
and it doesn't blow away—

GARTH. Well, it was true.

ESDRAS. Say it if you must. If you have heart
   to die,
say it, and let them take what's left—there
   was little
to keep, even before—

GARTH. Oh, I'm a coward—
I always was. I'll be quiet and live. I'll live
even if I have to crawl. I know. (*He gets
up and goes into the inner room.*)

MIRIAMNE. Is it better
to tell a lie and live?

ESDRAS. Yes, child. It's better.

MIRIAMNE. But if I had to do it—
I think I'd die.

ESDRAS. Yes, child. Because you're young.

MIRIAMNE. Is that the only reason?

ESDRAS. The only reason.

CURTAIN

# SCENE III

SCENE: *Under the bridge, evening of the same day. When the curtain rises* MIRIAMNE *is sitting alone on the ledge at the rear of the apartment house. A spray of light fall on her from a street lamp above. She shivers a little in her thin coat, but sits still as if heedless of the weather. Through the rocks on the other side a* TRAMP *comes down to the river bank, hunting a place to sleep. He goes softly to the apple-woman's hut and looks in, then turns away, evidently not daring to preempt it. He looks at* MIRIAMNE *doubtfully. The door of the street-piano man is shut. The vagabond passes it and picks carefully among some rags and shavings to the right.* MIRIAMNE *looks up and sees him but makes no sign. She looks down again, and the man curls himself up in a makeshift bed in the corner, pulling a piece of sacking over his shoulders. Two* GIRLS *come in from round the apartment house.*

FIRST GIRL. Honest, I never heard of anything so romantic. Because you never liked him.

SECOND GIRL. I certainly never did.

FIRST GIRL. You've got to tell me how it happened. You've got to.

SECOND GIRL. I couldn't. As long as I live I couldn't. Honest, it was terrible. It was terrible.

FIRST GIRL. What was so terrible?

SECOND GIRL. The way it happened.

FIRST GIRL. Oh, please—not to a soul, never.

SECOND GIRL. Well, you know how I hated him because he had such a big mouth. So he reached over and grabbed me, and I began all falling to pieces inside, the way you do—and I said, "Oh no you don't, mister," and started screaming and kicked a hole through the windshield and lost a shoe, and he let go and was cursing and growling because he borrowed the car and didn't have money to pay for the windshield, and he started to cry, and I got so sorry for him I let him, and now he wants to marry me.

FIRST GIRL. Honest, I never heard of anything so romantic! (*She sees the sleeping* Tramp.) My God, what you won't see! (*They give the Tramp a wide berth, and go out right. The* TRAMP *sits up looking about him.* JUDGE GAUNT, *an elderly, quiet man, well dressed but in clothes that have seen some weather, comes in uncertainly from the left. He holds a small clipping in his hand and goes up to the* HOBO.)

GAUNT (*tentatively*). Your pardon, sir. Your pardon, but perhaps you can tell me the name of this street.

HOBO. Huh?

GAUNT. The name of this street?

HOBO. This ain't no street.

GAUNT. There, where the street lamps are.

HOBO. That's the alley.

GAUNT. Thank you. It has a name, no doubt?

HOBO. That's the alley.

GAUNT. I see. I won't trouble you. You wonder why I ask, I daresay.—I'm a stranger.— Why do you look at me? (*He steps back.*) I—I'm not the man you think. You've mistaken me, sir.

HOBO. Huh?

JUDGE. Perhaps misled by a resemblance. But you're mistaken—I had an errand in this city. It's only by accident that I'm here—

HOBO (*muttering*). You go to hell.

JUDGE (*going nearer to him, bending over him*). Yet why should I deceive you? Before God, I held the proofs in my hands. I hold them still. I tell you the defense was cunning beyond belief, and unscrupulous in its use of propaganda—they gagged at nothing—not even—(*He rises.*) No, no— I'm sorry—this will hardly interest you. I'm sorry. I have an errand. (*He looks toward the street.* ESDRAS *enters from the basement and goes to* MIRIAMNE. *The* JUDGE *steps back into the shadows.*)

ESDRAS. Come in, my daughter. You'll be cold here.

MIRIAMNE. After a while.

ESDRAS. You'll be cold. There's a storm coming.

MIRIAMNE. I didn't want him to see me crying. That was all.

ESDRAS. I know.

MIRIAMNE. I'll come soon. (ESDRAS *turns reluctantly and goes out the way he came.* MIRIAMNE *rises to go, pausing to dry her eyes.* MIO *and* CARR, *road boys of seventeen or so, come round the apartment house. The* JUDGE *has disappeared.*)

CARR. Thought you said you were never coming east again.

MIO. Yeah, but—I heard something changed my mind.

CARR. Same old business?

MIO. Yes. Just as soon not talk about it.

CARR. Where did you go from Portland?

MIO. Fishing—I went fishing. God's truth.

CARR. Right after I left?

MIO. Fell in with a fisherman's family on the coast and went after the beautiful mackerel fish that swim in the beautiful sea. Family of Greeks—Aristides Marinos was his lovely name. He sang while he fished. Made the pea-green Pacific ring with his bastard Greek chanties. Then I went to Hollywood High School for a while.

CARR. I'll bet that's a seat of learning.

MIO. It's the hind end of all wisdom. They kicked me out after a time.

CARR. For cause?

MIO. Because I had no permanent address, you see. That means nobody's paying school taxes for you, so out you go. (*To* MIRIAMNE.) What's the matter, kid?

MIRIAMNE. Nothing. (*She looks up at him and they pause for a moment.*) Nothing.

MIO. I'm sorry.

MIRIAMNE. It's all right. (*She withdraws her eyes from his and goes out past him. He turns and looks after her.*)

CARR. Control your chivalry.

MIO. A pretty kid.

CARR. A baby.

MIO. Wait for me.

CARR. Be a long wait? (MIO *steps swiftly out after* MIRIAMNE, *then returns.*) Yeah?

MIO. She's gone.

CARR. Think of that.

MIO. No, but I mean—vanished. Presto—into nothing—prodigioso.

CARR. Damn good thing, if you ask me. The homely ones are bad enough, but the lookers are fatal.

MIO. You exaggerate, Carr.

CARR. I doubt it.

MIO. Well, let her go. This river bank's loaded with typhus rats, too. Might as well die one death as another.

CARR. They say chronic alcoholism is nice but expensive. You can always starve to death.

MIO. Not always. I tried it. After the second day I walked thirty miles to Niagara Falls and made a tour of the plant to get the sample of shredded wheat biscuit on the way out.

CARR. Last time I saw you you couldn't think of anything you wanted to do except curse God and pass out. Still feeling low?

MIO. Not much different. (*He turns away, then comes back.*) Talk about the lost generation, I'm the only one fits that title. When the State executes your father and your mother dies of grief, and you know damn well he was innocent, and the authorities of your home town politely inform you they'd consider it a favor if you lived somewhere else—that cuts you off from the world—with a meat-axe.

CARR. They asked you to move?

MIO. It came to that.

CARR. God, that was white of them.

MIO. It probably gave them a headache just to see me after all that agitation. They knew as well as I did my father never staged a hold-up. Anyway, I've got a new interest in life now.

CARR. Yes—I saw her.

MIO. I don't mean the skirt.—No, I got wind of something, out west, some college professor investigating the trial and turning up new evidence. Couldn't find anything he'd written out there, so I beat it east and arrived on this blessed island just in time to find the bums holing up in the public library for the winter. I know now what the unemployed have been doing since the depression started. They've been catching up on their reading in the main reference room. Man, what a stench! Maybe I stank, too, but a hobo has the stench of ten because his shoes are poor.

CARR. Tennyson.

MIO. Right. Jeez, I'm glad we met up again! Never knew anybody else that could track me through the driven snow of Victorian literature.

CARR. Now you're cribbing from some half-forgotten criticism of Ben Jonson's Roman plagiarisms.

MIO. Where did you get your education, sap?

CARR. Not in the public library, sap. My father kept a news-stand.

MIO. Well, you're right again. (*There is a faint rumble of thunder.*) What's that? Winter thunder?

CARR. Or Mister God, beating on His little tocsin. Maybe announcing the advent of a new social order.

MIO. Or maybe it's going to rain coffee and doughnuts.

CARR. Or maybe it's going to rain.

MIO. Seems more likely. (*Lowering his voice.*) Anyhow, I found Professor Hobhouse's discussion of the Romagna case. I think he has something. It occurred to me I might follow it up by doing a little sleuthing on my own account.

CARR. Yes?

MIO. I have done a little. And it leads me to somewhere in that tenement house that backs up against the bridge. That's how I happen to be here.

CARR. They'll never let you get anywhere with it, Mio. I told you that before.

MIO. I know you did.

CARR. The State can't afford to admit it was wrong, you see. Not when there's been that much of a row kicked up over it. So for all practical purposes the State was right and your father robbed the pay roll.

MIO. There's still such a thing as evidence.

CARR. It's something you can buy. In fact, at the moment I don't think of anything you can't buy, including life, honor, virtue, glory, public office, conjugal affection and all kinds of justice, from the traffic court to the immortal nine. Go out and make yourself a pot of money and you can buy all the justice you want. Convictions obtained, convictions averted. Lowest rates in years.

MIO. I know all that.

CARR. Sure.

MIO. This thing didn't happen to you.
They've left you your name
and whatever place you can take. For my
  heritage
they've left me one thing only, and that's
  to be
my father's voice crying up out of the earth
and quicklime where they stuck him. Electrocution
doesn't kill, you know. They eviscerate them
with a turn of the knife in the dissecting
  room.
The blood spurts out. The man was alive.
  Then into
the lime pit, leave no trace. Make it short
  shrift
and chemical dissolution. That's what they
  thought
of the man that was my father. Then my
  mother—
I tell you these county burials are swift
and cheap and run for profit! Out of the
  house
and into the ground, you wife of a dead dog.
  Wait,
here's some Romagna spawn left.
Something crawls here—
something they called a son. Why couldn't
  he die
along with his mother? Well, ease him out
  of town,
ease him out, boys, and see you're not too
  gentle.
He might come back. And, by their own
  living Jesus,

I will go back, and hang the carrion
around their necks that made it!
Maybe I can sleep then.
Or even live.

CARR. You have to try it?

MIO. Yes.
Yes. It won't let me alone. I've tried to live
and forget it—but I was birthmarked with
hot iron
into the entrails. I've got to find out who
did it
and make them see it till it scalds their eyes
and make them admit it till their tongues
are blistered
with saying how black they lied! (HERMAN,
*a gawky shoe salesman, enters from the left.*)

HERMAN. Hello. Did you see a couple of girls
go this way?

CARR. Couple of girls? Did we see a couple
of girls?

MIO. No.

CARR. No. No girls. (HERMAN *hesitates, then
goes out right.* LUCIA *comes in from the
left, trundling his piano.* PINY *follows him,
weeping.*)

PINY. They've got no right to do it—

LUCIA. All right, hell what, no matter, I
got to put him away, I got to put him away,
that's what the hell! (TWO STREET URCHINS
*follow him in.*)

PINY. They want everybody on the relief
rolls and nobody making a living?

LUCIA. The cops, they do what the big boss
says. The big boss, that's the mayor, he says
he heard it once too often, the sextette—

PINY. They want graft, that's all. It's a new
way to get graft—

LUCIA. Oh, no, no, no! He's a good man,
the mayor. He's just don't care for music,
that's all.

PINY. Why shouldn't you make a living on
the street? The National Biscuit Company
ropes off Eighth Avenue—and does the
mayor do anything? No, the police hit you
over the head if you try to go through!

LUCIA. You got the big dough, you get the
pull, fine. No big dough, no pull, what the
hell, get off the city property! Tomorrow I

start cooking chestnuts . . . (*He strokes
the piano fondly. The* TWO GIRLS *and* HER-
MAN *comes back from the right.*) She's a
good little machine, this baby. Cost plenty—
and two new records I only played twice.
See, this one. (*He starts turning the crank,
talking while he plays.*) Two weeks since
they play this one in a picture house. (A
SAILOR *wanders in from the left. One of
the* STREET URCHINS *begins suddenly to
dance a wild rumba, the others watch.*)
Good boy—see, it's a lulu—it itches in the
feet! (HERMAN, *standing with his girl, tosses
the boy a penny. He bows and goes on dancing; the other* URCHIN *joins him. The* SAILOR
*tosses a coin.*)

SAILOR. Go it, Cuba! Go it! (LUCIA *turns the
crank, beaming.*)

SECOND GIRL. Oh, Herman! (*She throws her
arms round* HERMAN *and they dance.*)

FIRST URCHIN. Hey, pipe the professionals!

FIRST GIRL. Do your glide, Shirley! Do your
glide!

LUCIA. Maybe we can't play in front, maybe
we can play behind! (*The* HOBO *gets up from
his nest and comes over to watch. A* YOUNG
RADICAL *wanders in.*) Maybe you don't
know, folks! Tonight we play good-bye to
the piano! Good-bye forever! No more
piano on the streets! No more music! No
more money for the music-man! Last time,
folks! Good-bye to the piano—good-bye
forever! (MIRIAMNE *comes out the rear
door of the apartment and stands watching. The* SAILOR *goes over to the* FIRST GIRL
*and they dance together.*) Maybe you don't
know, folks! Tomorrow will be sad as
hell, tonight we dance! Tomorrow no more
Verdi, no more rumba, no more good time!
Tonight we play good-bye to the piano,
good-bye forever! (*The* RADICAL *edges up
to* MIRIAMNE, *and asks her to dance. She
shakes her head and he goes to* PINY, *who
dances with him. The* HOBO *begins to do
a few lonely curvets on the side above.*)
Hoy! Hoy! Pick 'em up and take 'em
around! Use the head, use the feet! Last
time forever! (*He begins to sing to the air.*)

MIO. Wait for me, will you?

CARR. Now's your chance. (MIO *goes over to
MIRIAMNE and holds out a hand, smiling.
She stands for a moment uncertain, then*

*dances with him.* ESDRAS *comes out to watch.* JUDGE GAUNT *comes in from the left. There is a rumble of thunder.*)

LUCIA. Hoy! Hoy! Maybe it rains tonight, maybe it snows tomorrow! Tonight we dance good-bye. (*He sings the air lustily. A* POLICEMAN *comes in from the left and looks on. Two or three* PEDESTRIANS *follow him.*)

POLICEMAN. Hey you! (LUCIA *goes on singing.*)Hey, you!

LUCIA (*still playing*). What you want?

POLICEMAN. Sign off!

LUCIA. What you mean? I get off the street!

POLICEMAN. Sign off!

LUCIA (*still playing*). What you mean? (*The* POLICEMAN *walks over to him.* LUCIA *stops playing and the* DANCERS *pause.*)

POLICEMAN. Cut it.

LUCIA. Is this a street?

POLICEMAN. I say cut it out. (*The* HOBO *goes back to his nest and sits in it, watching.*)

LUCIA. It's the last time. We dance good-bye to the piano.

POLICEMAN. You'll dance good-bye to something else if I catch you cranking that thing again.

LUCIA. All right.

PINY. I'll bet you don't say that to the National Biscuit Company!

POLICEMAN. Lady, you've been selling apples on my beat for some time now, and I said nothing about it—

PINY. Selling apples is allowed—

POLICEMAN. You watch yourself—(*He takes a short walk around the place and comes upon the* HOBO.) What are you doing here? (*The* HOBO *opens his mouth, points to it, and shakes his head.*) Oh, you are, are you? (*He comes back to* LUCIA.) So you trundle your so-called musical instrument to wherever you keep it, and don't let me hear it again. (*The* RADICAL *leaps on the base of the rock at right. The* FIRST GIRL *turns away from the* SAILOR *toward the* SECOND GIRL *and* HERMAN.)

SAILOR. Hey, captain, what's the matter with the music?

POLICEMAN. Not a thing, admiral.

SAILOR. Well, we had a little party going here—

POLICEMAN. I'll say you did.

SECOND GIRL. Please, officer, we want to dance.

POLICEMAN. Go ahead. Dance.

SECOND GIRL. But we want music!

POLICEMAN (*turning to go*). Sorry. Can't help you.

RADICAL. And there you see it, the perfect example of capitalistic oppression! In a land where music should be free as air and the arts should be encouraged, a uniformed minion of the rich, a guardian myrmidon of the Park Avenue pleasure hunters, steps in and puts a limit on the innocent enjoyments of the poor! We don't go to theatres! Why not? We can't afford it! We don't go to night clubs, where women dance naked and the music drips from saxophones and leaks out of Rudy Vallee—we can't afford that either!—But we might at least dance on the river bank to the strains of a barrel organ—! (GARTH *comes out of the apartment and listens.*)

POLICEMAN. It's against the law!

RADICAL. What law? I challenge you to tell me what law of God or man—what ordinance—is violated by this spontaneous diversion? None! I say none! An official whim of the masters who should be our servants!—

POLICEMAN. Get down! Get down and shut up!

RADICAL. By what law, by what ordinance do you order me to be quiet?

POLICEMAN. Speaking without a flag. You know it.

RADICAL (*pulling out a small American flag*). There's my flag! There's the flag of this United States which used to guarantee the rights of man—the rights of man now violated by every third statute of the commonweal—

POLICEMAN. Don't try to pull tricks on me!
I've seen you before! You're not making any
speech, and you're climbing down—

JUDGE GAUNT (*who has come quietly forward*). One moment, officer. There is some
difference of opinion even on the bench as to
the elasticity of police power when applied
in minor emergencies to preserve civil order.
But the weight of authority would certainly
favor the defendant in any equable court,
and he would be upheld in his demand to be
heard.

POLICEMAN. Who are you?

JUDGE GAUNT. Sir, I am not accustomed to
answer that question.

POLICEMAN. I don't know you.

GAUNT. I am a judge of some standing, not
in your city, but in another with similar
statutes. You are aware, of course, that the
bill of rights is not to be set aside lightly by
the officers of any municipality—

POLICEMAN (*looking over* GAUNT's *somewhat
bedraggled costume*). Maybe they understand you better in the town you come from,
but I don't get your drift.— (*To the*
RADICAL.) I don't want any trouble, but
if you ask for it you'll get plenty. Get
down!

RADICAL. I'm not asking for trouble, but I'm
staying right here. (*The* POLICEMAN *moves
toward him.*)

GAUNT (*taking the policeman's arm, but
shaken off roughly*). I ask this for yourself,
truly, not for the dignity of the law nor the
maintenance of precedent. Be gentle with
them when their threats are childish—be
tolerant while you can—for your harsh word
will return on you in the night—return in
a storm of cries!—(*He takes the* POLICEMAN's
*arm again.*) Whatever they may have said
or done, let them disperse in peace! It is
better that they go softly, lest when they are
dead you see their eyes pleading, and their
outstretched hands touch you, fingering cold
on your heart!—I have been harsher than
you. I have sent men down that long corridor into blinding light and blind darkness!
(*He suddenly draws himself erect and
speaks defiantly.*) And it was well that I
did so! I have been an upright judge! They
are all liars! Liars!

POLICEMAN (*shaking* GAUNT *off so that he
falls*). Why, you fool, you're crazy!

GAUNT. Yes, and there are liars on the force!
They came to me with their shifty lies! (*He
catches at the* POLICEMAN, *who pushes him
away with his foot.*)

POLICEMAN. You think I've got nothing
better to do than listen to a crazy fool?

FIRST GIRL. Shame, shame!

POLICEMAN. What have I got to be ashamed
of? And what's going on here, anyway?
Where in hell did you all come from?

RADICAL. Tread on him! That's right! Tread
down the poor and the innocent! (*There is
a protesting murmur in the crowd.*)

SAILOR (*moving in a little*). Say, big boy,
you don't have to step on the guy.

POLICEMAN (*facing them, stepping back*).
What's the matter with you? I haven't stepped on anybody!

MIO (*at the right, across from the* POLICE-
MAN). Listen now, fellows, give the badge
a chance.
He's doing his job, what he gets paid to do,
the same as any of you. They're all picked
men,
these metropolitan police, hand picked
for loyalty and a fine up-standing pair
of shoulders on their legs—it's not so easy
to represent the law. Think what he does
for all of us, stamping out crime!
Do you want to be robbed and murdered in
your beds?

SAILOR. What's eating you?

RADICAL. He must be a capitalist.

MIO. They pluck them fresh
from Ireland, and a paucity of headpiece
is a prime prerequisite. You from Ireland,
buddy?

POLICEMAN (*surly*). Where are you from?

MIO. Buddy, I tell you flat
I wish I was from Ireland, and could boast
some Tammany connections. There's only
one drawback
about working on the force. It infects the
brain,
it eats the cerebrum. There've been cases
known,

fine specimens of manhood, too, where
autopsies,
conducted in approved scientific fashion,
revealed conditions quite incredible
in policemen's upper layers. In some, a trace,
in others, when they've swung a stick too
long,
there was nothing there!—but nothing! Oh,
my friends,
this fine athletic figure of a man
that stands so grim before us, what will
they find
when they saw his skull for the last inspection?
I fear me a little puffball dust will blow
away
rejoining earth, our mother—and this same
dust,
this smoke, this ash on the wind, will represent
all he had left to think with!

THE HOBO. Hooray! (*The* POLICEMAN *turns
on his heels and looks hard at the* HOBO, *who
slinks away.*)

POLICEMAN. Oh, yeah?

MIO. My theme
gives ears to the deaf and voice to the dumb!
But now
forgive me if I say you were most unkind
in troubling the officer. He's a simple man
of simple tastes, and easily confused
when faced with complex issues. He may
reflect
on returning home, that is, so far as he
is capable of reflection, and conclude
that he was kidded out of his uniform pants,
and in his fury when this dawns on him
may smack his wife down!

POLICEMAN. That'll be about enough from
you, too, professor!

MIO. May I say that I think you have
managed this whole situation rather badly,
from the beginning?—

POLICEMAN. You may not! (TROCK *slips in
from the background. The* TWO YOUNG MEN
IN SERGE *come with him.*)

MIO. Oh, but your pardon, sir! It's apparent
to the least competent among us that you
should have gone about your task more
subtly—the glove of velvet, the hand of iron,
and all that sort of thing—

POLICEMAN. Shut that hole in your face!

MIO. Sir, for that remark I shall be satisfied
with nothing less than an unconditional
apology! I have an old score to settle with
policemen, brother, because they're fools
and fat-heads, and you're one of the most
fatuous fat-heads that ever walked his feet
flat collecting graft! Tell that to your
sergeant back in the booby-hatch.

POLICEMAN. Oh, you want an apology, do
you? You'll get an apology out of the other
side of your mouth! (*He steps toward* MIO.
CARR *suddenly stands in his path.*) Get out
of my way! (*He pauses and looks round
him; the crowd looks less and less friendly.
He lays a hand on his gun and backs to a
position where there is nobody behind him.*)
Get out of here, all of you! Get out! What
are you trying to do—start a riot?

MIO. There now, that's better! That's in the
best police tradition. Incite a riot yourself
and then accuse the crowd.

POLICEMAN. It won't be pleasant if I decide
to let somebody have it! Get out! (*The on-
lookers begin to melt away. The* SAILOR *goes
out left with the* GIRLS *and* HERMAN. CARR
*and* MIO *go out right,* CARR *whistling "The
Star Spangled Banner." The* HOBO *follows
them. The* RADICAL *walks past with his head
in the air.* PINY *and* LUCIA *leave the piano
where it stands and slip away to the left. At
the end the* POLICEMAN *is left standing in the
center, the* JUDGE *near him.* ESDRAS *stands in
the doorway.* MIRIAMNE *is left sitting half
in shadow unseen by* ESDRAS.)

JUDGE GAUNT (*to the* POLICEMAN). Yes, but
should a man die, should it be necessary that
one man die for the good of many, make not
yourself the instrument of death, lest you
sleep to wake sobbing! Nay, it avails nothing
that you are the law—this delicate ganglion
that is the brain, it will not bear these
things—! (*The* POLICEMAN *gives the* JUDGE
*the once-over, shrugs, decides to leave him
there and starts out left.* GARTH *goes to his
father—a fine sleet begins to fall through the
street lights.* TROCK *is still visible.*)

GARTH. Get him in here, quick.

ESDRAS. Who, son?

GARTH. The Judge, damn him!

ESDRAS. Is it Judge Gaunt?

GARTH. Who did you think it was? He's crazy as a bedbug and telling the world. Get him inside! (*He looks round.*)

ESDRAS (*going up to* GAUNT). Will you come in, sir?

GAUNT. You will understand, sir. We old men know how softly we must proceed with these things.

ESDRAS. Yes, surely, sir.

GAUNT. It was always my practice—always. They will tell you that of me where I am known. Yet even I am not free of regret— even I. Would you believe it?

ESDRAS. I believe we are none of us free of regret.

GAUNT. None of us? I would it were true. I would I thought it were true.

ESDRAS. Shall we go in, sir? This is sleet that's falling.

GAUNT. Yes. Let us go in. (ESDRAS *and* GARTH *enter the basement and shut the door.* TROCK *goes out with his men. After a pause* MIO *comes back from the right, alone. He stands at a little distance from* MIRIAMNE.)

MIO. Looks like rain. (*She is silent.*) You live around here? (*She nods gravely.*) I guess you thought I meant it—about waiting here to meet me. (*She nods again.*) I'd forgotten about it till I got that winter across the face. You'd better go inside. I'm not your kind. I'm nobody's kind but my own. I'm waiting for this to blow over. (*She rises.*) I lied. I meant it— I meant it when I said it—but there's too much black whirling inside me—for any girl to know. So go on in. You're somebody's angel child and they're waiting for you.

MIRIAMNE. Yes. I'll go. (*She turns.*)

MIO. And tell them when you get inside where it's warm, and you love each other, and mother comes to kiss her darling, tell them to hang on to it while they can, believe while they can it's a warm safe world, and Jesus finds his lambs and carries them in his bosom.—I've seen some lambs that Jesus missed. If they ever want the truth tell them that nothing's guaranteed in this climate except it gets cold in winter, nor on this earth except you die sometime. (*He turns away.*)

MIRIAMNE. I have no mother. And my people are Jews.

MIO. Then you know something about it.

MIRIAMNE. Yes.

MIO. Do you have enough to eat?

MIRIAMNE. Not always.

MIO. What do you believe in?

MIRIAMNE. Nothing.

MIO. Why?

MIRIAMNE. How can one?

MIO. It's easy if you're a fool. You see the words in books. Honor, it says there, chivalry, freedom, heroism, enduring love—and these are words on paper. It's something to have them there. You'll get them nowhere else.

MIRIAMNE. What hurts you?

MIO. Just that. You'll get them nowhere else.

MIRIAMNE. Why should you want them?

MIO. I'm alone, that's why. You see those lights, along the river, cutting across the rain—? those are the hearths of Brooklyn, and up this way the love-nests of Manhattan—they turn their points like knives against me—outcast of the world, snake in the streets.—I don't want a hand-out. I sleep and eat.

MIRIAMNE. Do you want me to go with you?

MIO. Where?

MIRIAMNE. Where you go. (*A pause. He goes nearer to her.*)

MIO. Why, you god-damned little fool—
what made you say that?

MIRIAMNE. I don't know.

MIO. If you have a home
stay in it. I ask for nothing. I've schooled
myself
to ask for nothing, and take what I can get,
and get along. If I fell for you, that's my
look-out,
and I'll starve it down.

MIRIAMNE. Wherever you go, I'd go.

MIO. What do you know about loving?
How could you know?
Have you ever had a man?

MIRIAMNE (*after a slight pause*). No. But I
know.
Tell me your name.

MIO. Mio. What's yours?

MIRIAMNE. Miriamne.

MIO. There's no such name.

MIRIAMNE. But there's no such name as Mio!
M.I.O. It's no name.

MIO. It's for Bartolomeo.

MIRIAMNE. My mother's name was Miriam,
so they called me Miriamne.

MIO. Meaning little Miriam?

MIRIAMNE. Yes.

MIO. So now little Miriamne will go in
and take up quietly where she dropped them
all
her small housewifely cares.—When I first
saw you,
not a half-hour ago, I heard myself saying,
this is the face that launches ships for me—
and if I owned a dream—yes, half a dream—
we'd share it. But I have no dream. This
earth
came tumbling down from chaos, fire and
rock,
and bred up worms, blind worms that sting
each other
here in the dark. These blind worms of the
earth
took out my father—and killed him, and set
a sign
on me—the heir of the serpent—and he was
a man
such as men might be if the gods were
men—

but they killed him—
as they'll kill all others like him
till the sun cools down to the stabler mole-
cules,
yes, till men spin their tent-worm webs to
the stars
and what they think is done, even in the
thinking,
and they are the gods, and immortal, and
constellations
turn from them all like mill wheels—still
as they are
they will be, worms and blind. Enduring
love,
oh gods and worms, what mockery!—And
yet
I have blood enough in my veins. It goes
like music,
singing, because you're here. My body turns
as if you were the sun, and warm. This men
called love
in happier times, before the Freudians
taught us
to blame it on the glands. Only go in
before you breathe too much of my atmosphere
and catch death from me.

MIRIAMNE. I will take my hands
and weave them to a little house, and there
you shall keep a dream—

MIO. God knows I could use a dream
and even a house.

MIRIAMNE. You're laughing at me, Mio!

MIO. The worms are laughing.
I tell you there's death about me
and you're a child! And I'm alone and
half mad
with hate and longing. I shall let you love
me
and love you in return, and then, why then
God knows what happens!

MIRIAMNE. Something most unpleasant?

MIO. Love in a box car—love among the
children.
I've seen to much of it. Are we to live
in this same house you make with your two
hands
mystically, out of air?

MLRIAMNE. No roof, no mortgage!
Well, I shall marry a banker out in Flatbush,
it gives hot bread in the morning! Oh, Mio,
Mio,
in all the unwanted places and waste lands

that roll up into the darkness out of sun
and into sun out of darkness, there should
  be one empty
for you and me.

MIO. No.

MIRIAMNE. Then go now and leave me.
I'm only a girl you saw in the tenements,
and there's been nothing said.

MIO. Miriamne. (*She takes a step toward
him.*)

MIRIAMNE. Yes. (*He kisses her lips lightly.*)

MIO. Why, girl, the transfiguration on the
  mount
was nothing to your face. It lights from
  within—
a white chalice holding fire, a flower in
  flame,
this is your face.

MIRIAMNE. And you shall drink the flame
and never lessen it. And round your head
the aureole shall burn that burns there now,
forever. This I can give you. And so forever
the Freudians are wrong.

MIO. They're well-forgotten
at any rate.

MIRIAMNE. Why did you speak to me
when you first saw me?

MIO. I knew then.

MIRIAMNE. And I came back
because I must see you again. And we
  danced together
and my heart hurt me. Never, never, never,
though they should bind me down and tear
  out my eyes,
would I ever hurt you now. Take me with
  you, Mio,
let them look for us, whoever there is to
  look,
but we'll be away. (MIO *turns away toward
the tenement.*)

MIO. When I was four years old
we climbed through an iron gate, my mother
  and I,
to see my father in prison. He stood in the
  death-cell
and put his hand through the bars and said,
  My Mio,
I have only this to leave you, that I love you,
and will love you after I die. Love me then,
  Mio,

when this hard thing comes on you, that you
  must live
a man despised for your father. That night
  the guards,
walking in flood-lights brighter than high
  noon,
led him between them with his trousers slit
and a shaven head for the cathodes. This
  sleet and rain
that I feel cold here on my face and hands
will find him under thirteen years of clay
in prison ground. Lie still and rest, my
  father,
for I have not forgotten. When I forget
may I lie blind as you. No other love,
time passing, nor the spaced light-years of
  suns
shall blur your voice, or tempt me from the
  path
that clears your name—
till I have these rats in my grip
or sleep deep where you sleep. (*To* MIR-
IAMNE.)
I have no house,
nor home, nor love of life, nor fear of death,
nor care for what I eat, or who I sleep with,
or what color of calcimine the Government
will wash itself this year or next to lure
the sheep and feed the wolves. Love somewhere else,
and get your children in some other image
more acceptable to the State! This face of
  mine
is stamped for sewage! (*She steps back, sur-
mising.*)

MIRIAMNE. Mio—

MIO. My road is cut
in rock, and leads to one end. If I hurt you,
  I'm sorry.
One gets over hurts.

MIRIAMNE. What was his name—
your father's name?

MIO. Bartolomeo Romagna.
I'm not ashamed of it.

MIRIAMNE. Why are you here?

MIO. For the reason
I've never had a home. Because I'm a cry
out of a shallow grave, and all roads are
  mine
that might revenge him!

MIRIAMNE. But Mio—why here—why here?

MIO. I can't tell you that.

MIRIAMNE. No—but—there's someone
lives here—lives not far—and you mean to
see him—
you mean to ask him—(*She pauses.*)

MIO. Who told you that?

MIRIAMNE. His name
is Garth—Garth Esdras—

MIO (*after a pause, coming nearer*). Who are
you then? You seem
to know a good deal about me.—Were you
sent
to say this?

MIRIAMNE. You said there was death about
you! Yes,
but nearer than you think! Let it be as
it is—
let it all be as it is, never see this place
nor think of it—forget the streets you came
when you're away and safe! Go before
you're seen
or spoken to!

MIO. Will you tell me why?

MIRIAMNE. As I love you
I can't tell you—and I can never see you—

MIO. I walk where I please—

MIRIAMNE. Do you think it's easy for me
to send you away? (*She steps back as if to
go.*)

MIO. Where will I find you then
if I should want to see you?

MIRIAMNE. Never—I tell you
I'd bring you death! Even now. Listen!

(SHADOW *and* TROCK *enter between the
bridge and the tenement house.* MIRIAMNE
*pulls* MIO *back into the shadow of the rock
to avoid being seen.*)

TROCK. Why, fine.

SHADOW. You watch it now—just for the
record, Trock—
you're going to thank me for staying away
from it
and keeping you out. I've seen men get that
way,
thinking they had to plug a couple of guys
and then a few more to cover it up, and then
maybe a dozen more. You can't own all
and territory adjacent, and you can't
slough all the witnesses, because every man
you put away has friends—

TROCK. I said all right.
I said fine.

SHADOW. They're going to find this judge,
and if they find him dead it's just too bad,
and I don't want to know anything about
it—
and you don't either.

TROCK. You all through?

SHADOW. Why sure.

TROCK. All right.
We're through, too, you know.

SHADOW. Yeah? (*He becomes wary.*)

TROCK. Yeah, we're through.

SHADOW. I've heard that said before, and
afterwards
somebody died. (TROCK *is silent.*)
Is that what you mean?

TROCK. You can go.
I don't want to see you.

SHADOW. Sure, I'll go.
Maybe you won't mind if I just find out
what you've got on you. Before I turn my
back
I'd like to know. (*Silently and expertly he
touches* TROCK's *pockets, extracting a gun.*)
Not that I'd distrust you,
but you know how it is. (*He pockets the
gun.*)
So long, Trock.

TROCK. So long.

SHADOW. I won't talk.
You can be sure of that.

TROCK. I know you won't.

(SHADOW *turns and goes out right, past the
rock and along the bank. As he goes the*
TWO YOUNG MEN IN BLUE SERGE *enter from
the left and walk slowly after* SHADOW. *They
look toward* TROCK *as they enter and he
motions with his thumb in the direction
taken by* SHADOW. *They follow* SHADOW *out
without haste.* TROCK *watches them disappear, then slips out the way he came.* MIO
*comes a step forward, looking after the* TWO
MEN. *Two or three shots are heard, then
silence.* MIO *starts to run after* SHADOW.)

MIRIAMNE. Mio!

MIO. What do you know about this?

MIRIAMNE. The other way,
Mio—quick! (CARR *slips in from the right,
in haste.*)

CARR. Look, somebody's just been shot.
He fell in the river. The guys that did the
shooting
ran up the bank.

MIO. Come on.

(MIO *and* CARR *run out right.* MIRIAMNE
*watches uncertainly, then slowly turns and
walks to the rear door of the tenement. She
stands there a moment, looking after* MIO,
*then goes in, closing the door.* CARR *and* MIO
*return.*)

CARR. There's a rip tide past the point. You'd
never find him.

MIO. No.

CARR. You know a man ought to carry insurance living around here.—God, it's easy,
putting a fellow away. I never saw it done
before.

MIO (*looking at the place where* MIRIAMNE
*stood*). They have it all worked out.

CARR. What are you doing now?

MIO. I have a little business to transact in this
neighborhood.

CARR. You'd better forget it.

MIO. No.

CARR. Need any help?

MIO. Well, if I did I'd ask you first. But I
don't see how it would do any good. So
you keep out of it and take care of yourself.

CARR. So long, then.

MIO. So long, Carr.

CARR (*looking down-stream*). He was drift.
ing face up. Must be halfway to the island
the way the tide runs. (*He shivers.*) Good,
it's cold here. Well—

(*He goes out to the left.* MIO *sits on the edge
of the rock.* LUCIA *comes stealthily back from
between the bridge and the tenement, goes
to the street-piano and wheels it away.* PINY
*comes in. They take a look at* MIO, *but say
nothing.* LUCIA *goes into his shelter and*
PINY *into hers.* MIO *rises, looks up at the
tenement, and goes out to the left.*)

CURTAIN

# ACT TWO

SCENE: *The basement as in Scene 2 of Act One. The same evening.* ESDRAS *sits at the
table reading,* MIRIAMNE *is seated at the left, listening and intent. The door of the inner
room is half open and* GARTH'S *violin is heard. He is playing the theme from the third
movement of Beethoven's Archduke Trio.* ESDRAS *looks up.*

ESDRAS. I remember when I came to the end
of all the Talmud said, and the commen-
taries,
then I was fifty years old—and it was time
to ask what I had learned. I asked this
question
and gave myself the answer. In all the Talmud
there was nothing to find but the names of
things,
set down that we might call them by those
names
and walk without fear among things known.
Since then
I have had twenty years to read on and on
and end with Ecclesiastes. Names of names,
evanid days, evanid nights and days

and words that shift their meaning. Space
is time,
that which was is now—the men of tomorrow
live, and this is their yesterday. All things
that were and are and will be, have their
being
then and now and to come. If this means
little
when you are young, remember it. It will
return
to mean more when you are old.

MIRIAMNE. I'm sorry—I
was listening for something.

ESDRAS. It doesn't matter.
It's a useless wisdom. It's all I have,

but useless. It may be there is no time,
but we grow old. Do you know his name?

MIRIAMNE. Whose name?

ESDRAS. Why, when we're young and listen
    for a step
the step should have a name—(MIRIAMNE,
*not hearing, rises and goes to the window.*
GARTH *enters from within, carrying his
violin and carefully closing the door.*)

GARTH (*as* ESDRAS *looks at him*). Asleep.

ESDRAS. He may
sleep on through the whole night—then in
    the morning
we can let them know.

GARTH. We'd be wiser to say nothing—
let him find his own way back.

ESDRAS. How did he come here?

GARTH. He's not too crazy for that. If he
    wakes again
we'll keep him quiet and shift him off to-
    morrow.
Somebody'd pick him up.

ESDRAS. How have I come
to this sunken end of a street, at a life's
    end—?

GARTH. It was cheaper here—not to be
    transcendental—
So—we say nothing—?

ESDRAS. Nothing.

MIRIAMNE. Garth, there's no place
in this whole city—not one—
where you wouldn't be safer
than here—tonight—or tomorrow.

GARTH (*bitterly*). Well, that may be.
What of it?

MIRIAMNE. If you slipped away and took
a place somewhere where Trock couldn't
find you—

GARTH. Yes—
using what for money? and why do you
    think
I've sat here so far—because I love my home
so much? No, but if I stepped round the
    corner
it'd be my last corner and my last step.

MIRIAMNE. And yet—
if you're here—they'll find you here—
Trock will come again—
and there's worse to follow—

GARTH. Do you want to get me killed?

MIRIAMNE. No.

GARTH. There's no way out of it. We'll wait
and take what they send us.

ESDRAS. Hush! You'll wake him.

GARTH. I've done it.
I hear him stirring now. (*They wait quietly.*
JUDGE GAUNT *opens the door and enters.*)

GAUNT (*in the doorway*). I beg your
    pardon—
no, no, be seated—keep your place—I've
    made
your evening difficult enough, I fear;
and I must thank you doubly for your kind-
    ness,
for I've been ill—I know it.

ESDRAS. You're better, sir?

GAUNT. Quite recovered, thank you. Able,
    I hope,
to manage nicely now. You'll be rewarded
for your hospitality—though at this moment
(*He smiles*)
I'm low in funds. (*He inspects his billfold.*)
Sir, my embarrassment
is great indeed—and more than monetary,
for I must own my recollection's vague
of how I came here—how we came to-
    gether—
and what we may have said. My name is
    Gaunt,
Judge Gaunt, a name long known in the
    criminal courts,
and not unhonored there.

ESDRAS. My name is Esdras—
and this is Garth, my son. And Miriamne,
the daughter of my old age.

GAUNT. I'm glad to meet you.
Esdras. Garth Esdras. (*He passes a hand
over his eyes.*)
It's not a usual name.
Of late it's been connected with a case—
a case I knew. But this is hardly the man.
Though it's not a usual name. (*They are
silent.*)
Sir, how I came here,
as I have said, I don't well know. Such
    things
are sometimes not quite accident.

ESDRAS. We found you
outside our door and brought you in.

GAUNT. The brain
can be overworked, and weary, even when
  the man
would swear to his good health. Sir, on my
  word
I don't know why I came here, nor how,
  nor when,
nor what would explain it. Shall we say the
  machine
begins to wear? I felt no twinge of it.—
You will imagine how much more than
  galling
I feel it, to ask my way home—and where
  I am—
but I do ask you that.

ESDRAS. This is New York City—
or part of it.

GAUNT. Not the best part, I presume? (*He
smiles grimly.*)
No, not the best.

ESDRAS. Not typical, no.

GAUNT. And you—(*To* GARTH.)
you are Garth Esdras?

GARTH. That's my name.

GAUNT. Well, sir, (*to* ESDRAS)
I shall lie under the deepest obligation
if you will set an old man on his path,
for I lack the homing instinct, if the truth
were known. North, east and south mean
  nothing to me
here in this room.

ESDRAS. I can put you in your way.

GARTH. Only you'd be wiser to wait a while—
if I'm any judge.—

GAUNT. It happens I'm the judge—(*with
stiff humor*)
in more ways than one. You'll forgive me
  if I say
I find this place and my predicament
somewhat distasteful. (*He looks round
him.*)

GARTH. I don't doubt you do;
but you're better off here.

GAUNT. Nor will you find it wise
to cross my word as lightly as you seem
inclined to do. You've seen me ill and
  shaken—
and you presume on that.

GARTH. Have it your way.

GAUNT. Doubtless what information is required
we'll find nearby.

ESDRAS. Yes, sir—the terminal,—
if you could walk so far.

GAUNT. I've done some walking—
to look at my shoes. (*He looks down, then
puts out a hand to steady himself.*)
That—that was why I came—
never mind—it was there—and it's gone.
(*To* GARTH.)
Professor Hobhouse—
that's the name—he wrote some trash about
  you
and printed it in a broadside.
—Since I'm here I can tell you
it's a pure fabrication—lacking facts
and legal import. Senseless and impudent,
written with bias—with malicious intent
to undermine the public confidence
in justice and the courts. I knew it then—
all he brings out about this testimony
you might have given. It's true I could have
  called you,
but the case was clear—Romagna was
  known guilty,
and there was nothing to add. If I've en-
  dured
some hours of torture over their attacks
upon my probity—and in this torture
have wandered from my place, wandered
  perhaps
in mind and body—and found my way to
  face you—
why, yes, it is so—I know it—I beg of you
say nothing. It's not easy to give up
a fair name after a full half century
of service to a state. It may well rock
the surest reason. Therefore I ask of you
say nothing of this visit.

GARTH. I'll say nothing.

ESDRAS. Nor any of us.

GAUNT. Why, no—for you'd lose, too.
You'd have nothing to gain.

ESDRAS. Indeed we know it.

GAUNT. I'll remember you kindly. When I've
  returned,
there may be some mystery made of where
  I was—
we'll leave it a mystery?

GARTH. Anything you say.

GAUNT. Why, now I go with much more
peace of mind—
if I can call you friends.

ESDRAS. We shall be grateful
for silence on your part, Your Honor.

GAUNT. Sir—
if there were any just end to be served
by speaking out, I'd speak! There is none.
No—
bear that in mind!

ESDRAS. We will, Your Honor.

GAUNT. Then—
I'm in some haste. If you can be my guide,
we'll set out now.

ESDRAS. Yes, surely. (*There is a knock at
the door. The four look at each other with
some apprehension.* MIRIAMNE *rises.*) I'll
answer it.

MIRIAMNE. Yes. (*She goes into the inner
room and closes the door.* ESDRAS *goes to the
outer door. The knock is repeated. He opens
the door.* MIO *is there.*)

ESDRAS. Yes, sir.

MIO. May I come in?

ESDRAS. Will you state your business, sir?
It's late—and I'm not at liberty—

MIO. Why, I might say
that I was trying to earn my tuition fees
by peddling magazines. I could say that,
or collecting old newspapers—paying cash—
highest rates—no questions asked—(*He
looks round sharply.*)

GARTH. We've nothing to sell.
What do you want?

MIO. Your pardon, gentlemen.
My business is not of an ordinary kind,
and I felt the need of this slight introduction
while I might get my bearings. Your name is
Esdras,
or they told me so outside.

GARTH. What do you want?

MIO. Is that the name?

GARTH. Yes.

MIO. I'll be quick and brief.
I'm the son of a man who died many years
ago
for a pay roll robbery in New England. You

should be Garth Esdras, by what I've heard.
You have
some knowledge of the crime, if one can
believe
what he reads in the public prints, and it
might be
that your testimony, if given, would clear
my father
of any share in the murder. You may not
care
whether he was guilty or not. You may not
know.
But I do care—and care deeply, and I've
come
to ask you face to face.

GARTH. To ask me what?

MIO. What do you know of it?

ESDRAS. This man Romagna,
did he have a son?

MIO. Yes, sir, this man Romagna,
as you choose to call him, had a son, and I
am that son, and proud.

ESDRAS. Forgive me.

MIO. Had you known him,
and heard him speak, you'd know why I'm
proud, and why
he was no malefactor.

ESDRAS. I quite believe you.
If my son can help he will. But at this
moment,
as I told you—could you, I wonder, come
tomorrow,
at your own hour?

MIO. Yes.

ESDRAS. By coincidence
we too of late have had this thing in mind—
there have been comments printed, and
much discussion
which we could hardly avoid.

MIO. Could you tell me then
in a word?—What you know—
is it for him or against him?—
that's all I need.

ESDRAS. My son knows nothing.

GARTH. No.
The picture-papers lash themselves to a fury
over any rumor—make them up when
they're short
of bedroom slops.—This is what happened. I
had known a few members of a gang one
time

up there—and after the murder they picked
    me up
because I looked like someone that was seen
in what they called the murder car. They
    held me
a little while, but they couldn't identify me
for the most excellent reason I wasn't there
when the thing occurred. A dozen years
    later now
a professor comes across this, and sees red
and asks why I wasn't called on as a witness
and yips so loud they syndicate his picture
in all the rotos. That's all I know about it.
I wish I could tell you more.

ESDRAS. Let me say too
that I have read some words your father said,
and you were a son fortunate in your father,
whatever the verdict of the world.

MIO. There are few
who think so, but it's true, and I thank you.
    Then—
that's the whole story?

GARTH. All I know of it.

MIO. They cover their tracks well, the inner
    ring
that distributes murder. I came three thou-
    sand miles
to this dead end.

ESDRAS. If he was innocent
and you know him so, believe it, and let
    the others
believe as they like.

MIO. Will you tell me how a man's
to live, and face his life, if he can't believe
that truth's like a fire,
and will burn through and be seen
though it takes all the years there are?
While I stand up and have breath in my
    lungs
I shall be one flame of that fire;
it's all the life I have.

ESDRAS. Then you must live so.
One must live as he can.

MIO. It's the only way
of life my father left me.

ESDRAS. Yes? Yet it's true.
the ground we walk on is impacted down
and hard with blood and bones of those who
    died
unjustly. There's not one title to land or life,
even your own, but was built on rape and
    murder,

back a few years. It would take a fire indeed
to burn out all this error.

MIO. Then let it burn down,
all of it!

ESDRAS. We ask a great deal of the world
at first—then less—and then less.
We ask for truth
and justice. But this truth's a thing unknown
in the lightest, smallest matter—and as for
    justice,
who has once seen it done? You loved your
    father,
and I could have loved him, for every word
    he spoke
in his trial was sweet and tolerant, but the
    weight
of what men are and have, rests heavy on
the graves of those who lost. They'll not
    rise again,
and their causes lie there with them.

GAUNT. If you mean to say
that Bartolomeo Romagna was innocent,
you are wrong. He was guilty.
There may have been injustice
from time to time, by regrettable chance, in
    our courts,
but not in that case, I assure you.

MIO. Oh, you assure me!
You lie in your scrag teeth, whoever you
    are!
My father was murdered!

GAUNT. Romagna was found guilty
by all due process of law, and given his
    chance
to prove his innocence.

MIO. What chance? When a court
panders to mob hysterics, and the jury
comes in loaded to soak an anarchist
and a foreigner, it may be due process of law
but it's also murder!

GAUNT. He should have thought of that
before he spilled blood.

MIO. He?

GAUNT. Sir, I know too well
that he was guilty.

MIO. Who are you? How do you know?
I've searched the records through, the trial
    and what
came after, and in all that million words
I found not one unbiased argument
to fix the crime on him.

GAUNT. And you yourself,
were you unprejudiced?

MIO. Who are you?

ESDRAS. Sir,
this gentleman is here, as you are here,
to ask my son, as you have asked, what
ground
there might be for this talk of new evidence
in your father's case. We gave him the same
answer
we've given you.

MIO. I'm sorry. I'd supposed
his cause forgotten except by myself. There's
still
a defense committee then?

GAUNT. There may be. I
am not connected with it.

ESDRAS. He is my guest,
and asks to remain unknown.

MIO (*after a pause, looking at* GAUNT). The
judge at the trial
was younger, but he had your face. Can it be
that you're the man?—Yes—Yes.—The jury
charge—
I sat there as a child and heard your voice,
and watched that Brahminical mouth. I
knew even then
you meant no good to him. And now you're
here
to winnow out truth and justice—the
fountain-head
of the lies that slew him! Are you Judge
Gaunt?

GAUNT. I am.

MIO. Then tell me what damnation to what
inferno
would fit the toad that sat in robes and lied
when he gave the charge, and knew he lied!
Judge that,
and then go to your place in that hell!

GAUNT. I know and have known
what bitterness can rise against a court
when it must say, putting aside all weakness,
that a man's to die. I can forgive you that,
for you are your father's son, and you think
of him
as a son thinks of his father. Certain laws
seem cruel in their operation; it's necessary
that we be cruel to uphold them. This
cruelty
is kindness to those I serve.

MIO. I don't doubt that.
I know who it is you serve.

GAUNT. Would I have chosen
to rack myself with other men's despairs,
stop my ears, harden my heart, and listen
only
to the voice of law and light, if I had hoped
some private gain for serving? In all my
years
on the bench of a long-established common-
wealth
not once has my decision been in question
save in this case. Not once before or since.
For hope of heaven or place on earth, or
power
or gold, no man has had my voice, nor will
while I still keep the trust that laid on me
to sentence and define.

MIO. Then why are you here?

GAUNT. My record's clean. I've kept it so.
But suppose
with the best intent, among the myriad
tongues
that come to testify, I had missed my way
and followed a perjured tale to a lethal end
till a man was forsworn to death? Could
I rest or sleep
while there was doubt of this,
even while there was question in a layman's
mind?
For always, night and day,
there lies on my brain like a weight, the
admonition:
see truly, let nothing sway you; among all
functions
there's but one godlike, to judge. Then see
to it
you judge as a god would judge, with clarity,
with truth, with what mercy is found con-
sonant
with order and law. Without law men are
beasts,
and it's a judge's task to lift and hold them
above themselves. Let a judge be once
mistaken
or step aside for a friend, and a gap is made
in the dykes that hold back anarchy and
chaos,
and leave men bond but free.

MIO. Then the gap's been made,
and you made it.

GAUNT. I feared that too. May you be a judge
sometime, and know in what fear,

through what nights long
in fear, I scanned and verified and compared
the transcripts of the trial.

MIO. Without prejudice,
no doubt. It was never in your mind to prove
that you'd been right.

GAUNT. And conscious of that, too—
that that might be my purpose—watchful
  of that,
and jealous as his own lawyer of the rights
that should hedge the defendant!
And still I found no error,
shook not one staple of the bolts that linked
the door to the deed! Still following on
from step to step, I watched all modern
  comment,
and saw it centered finally on one fact—
Garth Esdras was not called. This is Garth
  Esdras,
and you have heard him. Would his deposi-
tion
have justified a new trial?

MIO. No. It would not.

GAUNT. And there I come, myself. If the man
  were still
in his cell, and waiting, I'd have no faint
  excuse
for another hearing.

MIO. I've told you that I read
the trial from beginning to end. Every word
  you spoke
was balanced carefully to keep the letter
of the law and still convict—convict, by
  Christ,
if it tore the seven veils! You stand here now
running cascades of casuistry, to prove
to yourself and me that no judge of rank
  and breeding
could burn a man out of hate! But that's
  what you did
under all your varnish!

GAUNT. I've sought for evidence,
and you have sought. Have you found it?
  Can you cite
one fresh word in defence?

MIO. The trial itself
was shot full of legerdemain, prearranged
  to lead
the jury astray—

GAUNT. Could you prove that?

MIO. Yes!

GAUNT. And if
the jury were led astray, remember it's
the jury, by our Anglo-Saxon custom,
that finds for guilt or innocence. The judge
is powerless in that matter.

MIO. Not you! Your charge
misled the jury more than the evidence,
accepted every biased meaning, distilled
the poison for them!

GAUNT. But if that were so
I'd be the first, I swear it, to step down
among all men, and hold out both my hands
for manacles—yes, publish it in the streets,
that all I've held most sacred was defiled
by my own act. A judge's brain becomes
a delicate instrument to weigh men's lives
for good and ill—too delicate to bear
much tampering. If he should push aside
the weights and throw the beam, and say,
  this once
the man is guilty, and I will have it so
though his mouth cry out from the ground,
and all the world
revoke my word, he'd have a short way to go
to madness. I think you'd find him in the
  squares,
stopping the passers-by with arguments,—
see, I was right, the man was guilty there—
this was brought in against him, this— and
  this—
and I was left no choice! It's no light thing
when a long life's been dedicated to one end
to wrench the mind awry!

MIO. By your own thesis
you should be mad, and no doubt you are.

GAUNT. But my madness
is only this—that I would fain look back
on a life well spent—without one stain—
  one breath
of stain to flaw the glass—not in men's
  minds
nor in my own. I take my God as witness
I meant to earn that clearness, and believe
that I have earned it. Yet my name is
  clouded
with the blackest, fiercest scandal of our age
that's touched a judge. What I can do to
  wipe
that smutch from my fame I will. I think
  you know
how deeply I've been hated, for no cause
that I can find there. Can it not be—and I
  ask this
quite honestly—that the great injustice lies

on your side and not mine? Time and time
again
men have come before me perfect in their
lives,
loved by all who knew them, loved at home,
gentle, not vicious, yet caught so ripe red-
handed
in some dark violence there was no denying
where the onus lay.

MIO. That was not so with my father!

GAUNT. And yet it seemed so to me. To other
men
who sat in judgment on him. Can you be
sure—
I ask this in humility—that you,
who were touched closest by the tragedy,
may not have lost perspective—may have
brooded
day and night on one theme—till your eyes
are tranced
and show you one side only?

MIO. I see well enough.

GAUNT. And would that not be part of the
malady—
to look quite steadily at the drift of things
but see there what you wish—not what is
there—
not what another man to whom the story
was fresh would say is there?

MIO. You think I'm crazy.
Is that what you meant to say?

GAUNT. I've seen it happen
with the best and wisest men. I but ask the
question.
I can't speak for you. Is it not true wherever
you walk, through the little town where
you knew him well,
or flying from it, inland or by the sea,
still walking at your side, and sleeping only
when you too sleep, a shadow not your own
follows, pleading and holding out its hands
to be delivered from shame?

MIO. How you know that
by God I don't know.

GAUNT. Because one spectre haunted you and
me—
and haunts you still, but for me it's laid to
rest
now that my mind is satisfied. He died
justly and not by error. (*A pause.*)

MIO (*stepping forward*). Do you care to
know

you've come so near to death it's miracle
that pulse still beats in your splotchy throat?
Do you know
there's murder in me?

GAUNT. There was murder in your sire,
and it's to be expected! I say he died
justly, and he deserved it!

MIO. Yes, you'd like too well
to have me kill you! That would prove your
case
and clear your name, and dip my father's
name
in stench forever! You'll not get that from
me!
Go home and die in bed, get it under cover,
your lux-et-lex putrefaction of the right
thing,
you man that walks like a god!

GAUNT. Have I made you angry
by coming too near the truth?

MIO. This sets him up,
this venomous slug, this sets him up in a
gown,
deciding who's to walk above the earth
and who's to lie beneath! And giving
reasons!
The cobra giving reasons; I'm a god,
by Buddha, holy and worshipful my fang,
and can I sink it in! (*He pauses, turns as if
to go, then sits.*)
This is no good.
This won't help much. (*The* JUDGE *and*
ESDRAS *look at each other.*)

GAUNT. We should be going.

ESDRAS. Yes. (*They prepare to go.*)
I'll lend you my coat.

GAUNT (*looking at it with distaste*). No,
keep it. A little rain
shouldn't matter to me.

ESDRAS. It freezes as it falls,
and you've a long way to go.

GAUNT. I'll manage, thank you. (GAUNT *and*
ESDRAS *go out,* ESDRAS *obsequious, closing the
door.*)

GARTH (*looking at* MIO's *back*). Well?

MIO (*not moving*). Let me sit here a
moment.

(GARTH *shrugs his shoulders and goes toward
the inner door.* MIRIAMNE *opens it and comes
out.* GARTH *looks at her, then at* MIO, *then*

*lays his fingers on his lips. She nods.* GARTH
*goes out.* MIRIAMNE *sits and watches* MIO.
*After a little he turns and sees her.*)

MIO. How did you come here?

MIRIAMNE. I live here.

MIO. Here?

MIRIAMNE. My name is Esdras. Garth
is my brother. The walls are thin.
I heard what was said.

MIO (*stirring wearily*). I'm going. This is
no place for me.

MIRIAMNE. What place
would be better?

MIO. None. Only it's better to go.
Just to go. (*She comes over to him, puts her
arm round him and kisses his forehead.*)

MIRIAMNE. Mio.

MIO. What do you want?
Your kisses burn me—and your arms. Don't
offer
what I'm never to have! I can have nothing.
They say
they'll cross the void sometime to the other
planets
and men will breathe in that air.
Well, I could breathe there,
but not here now. Not on this ball of mud.
I don't want it.

MIRIAMNE. They can take away so little
with all their words. For you're a king
among them.
I heard you, and loved your voice.

MIO. I thought I'd fallen
so low there was no further, and now a pit
opens beneath. It was bad enough that he
should have died innocent, but if he were
guilty—
then what's my life—what have I left to
do—?
The son of a felon—and what they spat on
me
was earned—and I'm drenched with the
stuff.
Here on my hands
and cheeks, their spittle hanging! I liked
my hands
because they were like his. I tell you I've
lived
by his innocence, lived to see it flash
and blind them all—

MIRIAMNE. Never believe them, Mio,
never. (*She looks toward the inner door.*)

MIO. But it was truth I wanted, truth—
not the lies you'd tell yourself, or tell a
woman,
or a woman tells you! The judge with his
cobra mouth
may have spat truth—and I may be mad!
For me—
your hands are too clean to touch me. I'm
to have
the scraps from hotel kitchens—and instead
of love
those mottled bodies that hitch themselves
through alleys
to sell for dimes or nickels. Go, keep yourself chaste
for the baker bridegroom—baker and son
of a baker,
let him get his baker's dozen on you!

MIRIAMNE. No—
say once you love me—say it once; I'll never
ask to hear it twice, nor for any kindness,
and you shall take all I have! (GARTH *opens
the inner door and comes out.*)

GARTH. I interrupt
a love scene, I believe. We can do without
your adolescent mawkishness. (*To* MIRI-
AMNE)
You're a child.
You'll both remember that.

MIRIAMNE. I've said nothing to harm you—
and will say nothing.

GARTH. You're my sister, though,
and I take a certain interest in you. Where
have you two met?

MIRIAMNE. We danced together.

GARTH. Then
the dance is over, I think.

MIRIAMNE. I've always loved you
and tried to help you, Garth. And you've
been kind.
Don't spoil it now.

GARTH. Spoil it how?

MIRIAMNE. Because I love him.
I didn't know it would happen. We danced
together.
And the world's all changed. I see through
a mist,
and our father, too. If you brought this to
nothing
I'd want to die.

GARTH (*to* MIO). You'd better go.

MIO. Yes, I know. (*He rises. There is a trembling knock at the door.* MIRIAMNE *goes to it. The* HOBO *is there shivering.*)

HOBO. Miss, could I sleep under the pipes tonight, miss?
Could I, please?

MIRIAMNE. I think—not tonight.

HOBO. There won't be any more nights—
if I don't get warm, miss.

MIRIAMNE. Come in. (*The* HOBO *comes in, looks round deprecatingly, then goes to a corner beneath a huge heating pipe, which he crawls under as if he's been there before.*)

HOBO. Yes, miss, thank you.

GARTH. Must we put up with that?

MIRIAMNE. Father let him sleep there—
last winter.

GARTH. Yes, God, yes.

MIO. Well, good night.

MIRIAMNE. Where will you go?

MIO. Yes, where? As if it mattered.

GARTH. Oh, sleep here, too.
We'll have a row of you under the pipes.

MIO. No, thanks.

MIRIAMNE. Mio, I've saved a little money.
It's only
some pennies, but you must take it. (*She shakes some coins out of a box into her hand.*)

MIO. No, thanks.

MIRIAMNE. And I love you.
You've never said you love me.

MIO. Why wouldn't I love you
when you're clean and sweet,
and I've seen nothing sweet or clean
this last ten years? I love you. I leave you that
for what good it may do you. It's none to me.

MIRIAMNE. Then kiss me.

MIO (*looking at* GARTH). With that scowling over us? No.
When it rains, some spring

on the planet Mercury, where the spring comes often,
I'll meet you there, let's say. We'll wait for that.
It may be some time till then.
(*The outside door opens and* ESDRAS *enters with* JUDGE GAUNT, *then, after a slight interval,* TROCK *follows.* TROCK *surveys the interior and its occupants one by one, carefully.*)

TROCK. I wouldn't want to cause you inconvenience,
any of you, and especially the Judge.
I think you know that. You've all got things to do—
trains to catch, and so on. But trains can wait.
Hell, nearly anything can wait, you'll find,
only I can't. I'm the only one that can't
because I've got no time. Who's all this here?
Who's that? (*He points to the* HOBO.)

ESDRAS. He's a poor half-wit, sir,
that sometimes sleeps there.

TROCK. Come out. I say come out,
whoever you are. (*The* HOBO *stirs and looks up.*)
Yes, I mean you. Come out. (*The* HOBO *emerges.*)
What's your name?

HOBO. They mostly call me Oke.

TROCK. What do you know?

HOBO. No, sir.

TROCK. Where are you from?

HOBO. I got a piece of bread. (*He brings it out, trembling.*)

TROCK. Get back in there! (*The* HOBO *crawls back into his corner.*)
Maybe you want to know why I'm doing this.
Well, I've been robbed, that's why—
robbed five or six times;
the police can't find a thing—so I'm out for myself—
if you want to know. (*To* MIO.)
Who are you?

MIO. Oh, I'm a half-wit,
came in here by mistake. The difference is
I've got no piece of bread.

TROCK. What's your name?

MIO. My name?
Theophrastus Such. That's respectable.
You'll find it all the way from here to the
coast
on the best police blotters.
Only the truth is we're a little touched in
the head,
Oke and me. You'd better ask somebody
else.

TROCK. Who is he?

ESDRAS. His name's Romagna. He's the son.

TROCK. Then what's he doing here? You
said you were on the level.

GARTH. He just walked in. On account of
the stuff in the papers. We didn't ask him.

TROCK. God, we are a gathering. Now if
we had Shadow we'd be all here, huh?
Only I guess we won't see Shadow. No,
that's too much to ask.

MIO. Who's Shadow?

TROCK. Now you're putting questions.
Shadow was just nobody, you see. He blew
away. It might happen to anybody. (*He
looks at* GARTH.) Yes, anyone at all.

MIO. Why do you keep your hand in your
pocket, friend?

TROCK. Because I'm cold, punk. Because I've
been outside and it's cold as the tomb of
Christ. (*To* GARTH.) Listen, there's a car
waiting up at the street to take the Judge
home. We'll take him to the car.

GARTH. That's not necessary.

ESDRAS. No.

TROCK. I say it is, see? You wouldn't want
to let the Judge walk, would you? The Judge
is going to ride where he's going, with a
couple of chauffeurs, and everything done
in style. Don't you worry about the Judge.
He'll be taken care of. For good.

GARTH. I want no hand in it.

TROCK. Anything happens to me happens
to you too, musician.

GARTH. I know that.

TROCK. Keep your mouth out of it then.
And you'd better keep the punk here to-

night, just for luck. (*He turns toward the
door. There is a brilliant lightning flash
through the windows, followed slowly by
dying thunder.* TROCK *opens the door. The
rain begins to pour in sheets.*) Jesus, somebody tipped it over again! (*A cough racks
him.*) Wait till it's over. It takes ten days
off me every time I step into it. (*He closes
the door.*) Sit down and wait. (*Lightning
flashes again. The thunder is fainter.* ESDRAS,
GARTH *and the* JUDGE *sit down.*)

GAUNT. We were born too early. Even you
who are young
are not of the elect. In a hundred years
man will put his finger on life itself, and
then
he will live as long as he likes. For you and
me
we shall die soon—one day, one year more
or less,
when or where, it's no matter. It's what we
call
an indeterminate sentence. I'm hungry.
(GARTH *looks at* MIRIAMNE.)

MIRIAMNE. There was nothing left
tonight.

HOBO. I've got a piece of bread. (*He breaks
his bread in two and hands half to the
JUDGE.*)

GAUNT. I thank you, sir. (*He eats.*)
This is not good bread. (*He rises.*)
Sir, I am used
to other company. Not better, perhaps, but
their clothes
were different. These are what it's the
fashion to call
the underprivileged.

TROCK. Oh, hell! (*He turn toward the door.*)

MIO (*to* TROCK). It would seem that you and
the Judge know each other. (TROCK *faces
him.*)

TROCK. I've been around.

MIO. Maybe you've met before.

TROCK. Maybe we have.

MIO. Will you tell me where?

TROCK. How long do you want to live?

MIO. How long? Oh, I've got big ideas about
that.

TROCK. I thought so. Well, so far I've got nothing against you but your name, see? You keep it that way. (*He opens the door. The rain still falls in torrents. He closes the door. As he turns from it, it opens again, and* SHADOW, *white, bloodstained and dripping, stands in the doorway.* GARTH *rises.* TROCK *turns.*)

GAUNT (*to the* HOBO). Yet if one were careful of his health, ate sparingly, drank not at all, used himself wisely, it might be that even an old man could live to touch immortality. They may come on the secret sooner than we dare hope. You see? It does no harm to try.

TROCK (*backing away from* SHADOW). By God, he's out of his grave!

SHADOW (*leaning against the doorway, holding a gun in his hands*). Keep your hands where they belong, Trock.
You know me.

TROCK. Don't! Don't! I had nothing to do with it! (*He backs to the opposite wall.*)

SHADOW. You said the doctor gave you six months to live—
well, I don't give you that much. That's what you had,
six months, and so you start bumping off your friends
to make sure of your damn six months. I got it from you.
I know where I got it.
Because I wouldn't give it to the Judge.
So he wouldn't talk.

TROCK. Honest to God—

SHADOW. What God?
The one that let you put three holes in me when I was your friend? Well, He let me get up again
and walk till I could find you. That's as far as I get,
but I got there, by God! And I can hear you even if I can't see! (*He takes a staggering step forward.*)
A man needs blood
to keep going.—I got this far.—And now I can't see!
It runs out too fast—too fast—
when you've got three slugs
clean through you.
Show me where he is, you fools! He's here! I got here! (*He drops the gun.*)

Help me! Help me! Oh, God! Oh, God! I'm going to die! Where does a man lie down?
I want to lie down!

(MIRIAMNE *starts toward* SHADOW. GARTH *and* ESDRAS *help him into the next room,* MIRIAMNE *following.* TROCK *squats in his corner, breathing hard, looking at the door.* MIO *stands, watching* TROCK. GARTH *returns, wiping his hand with a handkerchief.* MIO *picks up and pockets the gun.* MIRIAMNE *comes back and leans against the door jamb.*)

GAUNT. You will hear it said that an old man makes a good judge, being calm, clear-eyed, without passion. But this is not true. Only the young love truth and justice. The old are savage, wary, violent, swayed by maniac desires, cynical of friendship or love, open to bribery and the temptations of lust, corrupt and dastardly to the heart. I know these old men. What have they left to believe, what have they left to lose? Whorers of daughters, lickers of girls' shoes, contrivers of nastiness in the night, purveyors of perversion, worshippers of possession! Death is the only radical. He comes late, but he comes at last to put away the old men and give the young their places. It was time. (*He leers.*) Here's one I heard yesterday:
Marmaduke behind the barn
  got his sister in a fix;
he says damn instead of darn;
  ain't he cute? He's only six!

THE HOBO. He, he, he!

GAUNT. And the hoot-owl hoots all night,
    and the cuckoo cooks all day,
  and what with a minimum grace of God
    we pass the time away.

THE HOBO. He, he, he—I got ya! (*He makes a sign with his thumb.*)

GAUNT (*sings*). And he led her all around
    and he laid her on the ground
    and he ruffled up the feathers of her
      cuckoo's nest!

HOBO. Ho, ho, ho!

GAUNT. I am not taken with the way you laugh. You should cultivate restraint. (ESDRAS *reënters.*)

TROCK. Shut the door.

ESDRAS. He won't come back again.

TROCK. I want the door shut! He was dead, I tell you! (ESDRAS *closes the door.*) And Romagna was dead, too, once! Can't they keep a man under ground?

MIO. No. No more! They don't stay under ground any more, and they don't stay under water! Why did you have him killed?

TROCK. Stay away from me! I know you!

MIO. Who am I, then?

TROCK. I know you, damn you! Your name's Romagna!

MIO. Yes! And Romagna was dead, too, and Shadow was dead, but the time's come when you can't keep them down, these dead men! They won't stay down! They come in with their heads shot off and their entrails dragging! Hundreds of them! One by one— all you ever had killed! Watch the door! See!—It moves!

TROCK (*looking, fascinated, at the door*). Let me out of here! (*He tries to rise.*)

MIO (*the gun in his hand*). Oh, no! You'll sit there and wait for them! One by one they'll come through that door, pulling their heads out of the gunny-sacks where you tied them—glauming over you with their rotten hands! They'll see without eyes and crawl over you—Shadow and the paymaster and all the rest of them—putrescent bones without eyes! Now! Look! Look! For I'm first among them!

TROCK. I've done for better men than you! And I'll do for you!

GAUNT (*rapping on the table*). Order, gentlemen, order! The witness will remember that a certain decorum is essential in the court-room!

MIO. By God, he'll answer me!

GAUNT (*thundering*). Silence! Silence! Let me remind you of courtesy toward the witness! What case is this you try?

MIO. The case of the state against Bartolomeo Romagna for the murder of the paymaster!

GAUNT. Sir, that was disposed of long ago!

MIO. Never disposed of, never, not while I live!

GAUNT. Then we'll have done with it now! I deny the appeal! I have denied the appeal before and I do so again!

HOBO. He, he!—He thinks he's in the moving pictures! (*A flash of lightning.*)

GAUNT. Who set that flash! Bailiff, clear the court! This is not Flemington, gentlemen! We are not conducting this case to make a journalistic holiday! (*The thunder rumbles faintly.* GARTH *opens the outside door and faces a solid wall of rain.*) Stop that man! He's one of the defendants! (GARTH *closes the door.*)

MIO. Then put him on the stand!

GARTH. What do you think you're doing?

MIO. Have you any objection?

GAUNT. The objection is not sustained. We will hear the new evidence. Call your witness.

MIO. Garth Esdras!

GAUNT. He will take the stand!

GARTH. If you want me to say what I said before, I'll say it!

MIO. Call Trock Estrella then!

GAUNT. Trock Estrella to the stand!

TROCK. No, by God!

MIO. Call Shadow, then! He'll talk! You thought he was dead, but he'll get up again and talk!

TROCK (*screaming*). What do you want of me?

MIO. You killed the paymaster! You!

TROCK. You lie! It was Shadow killed him!

MIO. And now I know! Now I know!

GAUNT. Again I remind you of courtesy toward the witness!

MIO. I know them now!
Let me remind you of courtesy toward the
   dead!
He says that Shadow killed him! If Shadow
   were here
he'd say it was Trock! There were three
   men involved
in the new version of the crime for which
my father died! Shadow and Trock Estrella

as principals in the murder—Garth as witness!—
Why are they here together?—and you—
the Judge—
why are you here? Why, because you were
all afraid
and you drew together out of that fear to
arrange
a story you could tell! And Trock killed
Shadow
and meant to kill the Judge out of that same
fear—
to keep them quiet! This is the thing I've
hunted
over the earth to find out, and I'd be blind
indeed if I missed it now! (*To* GAUNT.)
You heard what he said:
It was Shadow killed him! Now let the night
conspire
with the sperm of hell! It's plain beyond
denial
even to this fox of justice—and all his
words
are curses on the wind! You lied! You lied!
You knew this too!

GAUNT (*low*). Let me go. Let me go!

MIO. Then why
did you let my father die?

GAUNT. Suppose it known,
but there are things a judge must not believe
though they should head and fester underneath
and press in on his brain. Justice once ren-
dered
in a clear burst of anger, righteously,
upon a very common laborer,
confessed an anarchist, the verdict found
and the precise machinery of law
invoked to know him guilty—think what
furor
would rock the state if the court then flatly
said;
all this was lies—must be reversed? It's
better,
as any judge can tell you, in such cases,
holding the common good to be worth more
than small injustice, to let the record stand,
let one man die. For justice, in the main,
is governed by opinion. Communities
will have what they will have, and it's quite
as well,
after all, to be rid of anarchists. Our rights
as citizens can be maintained as rights
only while we are held to be the peers

of those who live about us. A vendor of fish
is not protected as a man might be
who kept a market. I own I've sometimes
wished
this was not so, but it is. The man you
defend
was unfortunate—and his misfortune bore
almost as heavily on me.—I'm broken—
broken across. You're much too young to
know
how bitter it is when a worn connection
chars
and you can't remember—can't remember.
(*He steps forward.*)
You
will not repeat this? It will go no further?

MIO. No.
No further than the moon takes the tides—
no further
than the news went when he died—
when you found him guilty
and they flashed that round the earth. Wherever men
still breathe and think, and know what's
done to them
by the powers above, they'll know. That's
all I ask.
That'll be enough. (TROCK *has risen and
looks darkly at* MIO.)

GAUNT. Thank you. For I've said some
things
a judge should never say.

TROCK. Go right on talking.
Both of you. It won't get far, I guess.

MIO. Oh, you'll see to that?

TROCK. I'll see to it. Me and some others.
Maybe I lost my grip there just for a minute.
That's all right.

MIO. Then see to it! Let it rain!
What can you do to me now when the
night's on fire
with this thing I know? Now I could almost
wish
there was a god somewhere—I could almost
think
there was a god—and he somehow brought
me here
and set you down before me here in the rain
where I could wring this out of you! For it's
said,
and I've heard it, and I'm free! He was as I
thought him,
true and noble and upright, even when
he went

to a death contrived because he was as he
was
and not your kind! Let it rain! Let the night
speak fire
and the city go out with the tide, for he was
a man
and I know you now, and I have my day!
(*There is a heavy knock at the outside door.*
MIRIAMNE *opens it, at a glance from* GARTH.
*The* POLICEMAN *is there in oilskins.*)

POLICEMAN. Evening. (*He steps in, followed
by a* SERGEANT, *similarly dressed.*) We're
looking for someone
might be here. Seen an old man around
acting a little off? (*To* ESDRAS.)
You know the one
I mean. You saw him out there. Jeez! You've
got
a funny crowd here! (*He looks round. The*
HOBO *shrinks into his corner.*)
That's the one I saw.
What do you think?

SERGEANT. That's him. You mean to say
you didn't know him by this pictures? (*He
goes to* GAUNT.)
Come on, old man.
You're going home.

GAUNT. Yes, sir. I've lost my way.
I think I've lost my way.

SERGEANT. I'll say you have.
About three hundred miles. Now don't you
worry.
We'll get you back.

GAUNT. I'm a person of some rank
in my own city.

SERGEANT. We know that. One look at you
and we'd know that.

GAUNT. Yes, sir.

POLICEMAN. If it isn't Trock!
Trock Estrella. How are you, Trock?

TROCK. Pretty good,
Thanks.

POLICEMAN. Got out yesterday again, I hear?

TROCK. That's right.

SERGEANT. Hi'ye, Trock?

TROCK. O.K.

SERGEANT. You know we got orders
to watch you pretty close. Be good now,
baby.

or back you go. Don't try to pull anything,
not in my district.

TROCK. No, sir.

SERGEANT. No bumping off.
If you want my advice quit carrying a gun.
Try earning your living for once.

TROCK. Yeah.

SERGEANT. That's an idea.
Because if we find any stiffs on the river
bank
we'll know who to look for.

MIO. Then look in the other room!
I accuse that man of murder! Trock Estrella!
He's a murderer!

POLICEMAN. Hello. I remember you.

SERGEANT. Well, what murder?

MIO. It was Trock Estrella
that robbed the pay roll thirteen years ago
and did the killing my father died for!
You know
the Romagna case! Romagna was innocent,
and Trock Estrella guilty!

SERGEANT (*disgusted*). Oh, what the hell!
That's old stuff—the Romagna case.

POLICEMAN. Hey, Sarge! (*The* SERGEANT *and*
POLICEMAN *come closer together.*)
The boy's a professional kidder. He took me
over
about half an hour ago. He kids the police
and then ducks out!

SERGEANT. Oh, yeah?

MIO. I'm not kidding now.
You'll find a dead man there in the next
room
and Estrella killed him!

SERGEANT. Thirteen years ago?
And nobody smelled him yet?

MIO (*pointing*). I accuse this man
of two murders! He killed the paymaster
long ago
and had Shadow killed tonight. Look, look
for yourself!
He's there all right!

POLICEMAN. Look boy. You stood out there
and put the booby sign on the dumb police
because they're fresh out of Ireland. Don't
try it twice.

SERGEANT (*to* GARTH). Any corpses here?

GARTH. Not that I know of.

SERGEANT. I thought so. (MIO *looks at* MIRI-AMNE.)

(*To* MIO.)
Think up a better one.

MIO. Have I got to drag him
out here where you can see him? (*He goes
toward the inner door.*)
Can't you scent a murder
when it's under your nose? Look in!

MIRIAMNE. No, no—there's no one—there's
no one there!

SERGEANT (*looking at* MIRIAMNE). Take a
look inside.

POLICEMAN. Yes, sir. (*He goes into the inside
room. The* SERGEANT *goes up to the door.
The* POLICEMAN *returns.*)
He's kidding, Sarge. If there's a cadaver
in here I don't see it.

MIO. You're blind then! (*He goes into the
room, the* SERGEANT *following him.*)

SERGEANT. What do you mean? (*He comes
out,* MIO *following him.*)
When you make a charge of murder it's
better to have
the corpus delicti, son. You're the kind puts
in
fire alarms to see the engine!

MIO. By God, he was there!
He went in there to die.

SERGEANT. I'll bet he did.
And I'm Haile Selassie's aunt! What's your
name?

MIO. Romagna. (*To* GARTH).
What have you done with him?

GARTH. I don't know what you mean.

SERGEANT (*to* GARTH). What's he talking
about?

GARTH. I wish I could tell you.
I don't know.

SERGEANT. He must have seen something.

POLICEMAN. He's got
the Romagna case on the brain. You watch
yourself,
chump, or you'll get run in.

MIO. Then they're in it together!
All of them! (*To* MIRIAMNE.)
Yes, and you!

GARTH. He's nuts, I say.

MIRIAMNE (*gently*). You have dreamed
something—isn't it true?
You've dreamed—
But truly, there was no one—(MIO *looks at
her comprehendingly.*)

MIO. You want me to say it. (*He pauses.*)
Yes, by God, I was dreaming.

SERGEANT (*to* POLICEMAN). I guess you're
right.
We'd better be going. Haven't you got a
coat?

GAUNT. No, sir.

SERGEANT. I guess I'll have to lend you mine.
(*He puts his oilskins on* GAUNT.)
Come on, now. It's getting late. (GAUNT, *the*
POLICEMAN *and the* SERGEANT *go out.*)

TROCK. They're welcome to him.
His fuse is damp. Where is that walking
fool
with the three slugs in him?

ESDRAS. He fell in the hall beyond
and we left him there.

TROCK. That's lucky for some of us. Is he
out this time
or is he still butting around?

ESDRAS. He's dead.

TROCK. That's perfect. (*To* MIO.)
Don't try using your firearms, amigo baby,
the Sarge is outside. (*He turns to go.*)
Better ship that carrion
back in the river! The one that walks when
he's dead;
maybe he'll walk the distance for you.

GARTH. Coming back?

TROCK. Well, if I come back,
you'll see me. If I don't, you won't. Let the
punk
go far as he likes. Turn him loose and let
him go.
And may you all rot in hell. (*He pulls his
coat around him and goes to the left.* MIR-
IAMNE *climbs up to look out a window.*)

MIRIAMNE. He's climbing up to the street, along the bridgehead. (*She turns.*) Quick, Mio! It's safe now! Quick!

GARTH. Let him do as he likes.

MIRIAMNE. What do you mean? Garth! He means to kill him! You know that!

GARTH. I've no doubt Master Romagna can run his own campaign.

MIRIAMNE. But he'll be killed!

MIO. Why did you lie about Shadow? (*There is a pause.* GARTH *shrugs, walks across the room, and sits.*) You were one of the gang!

GARTH. I can take a death if I have to! Go tell your story, only watch your step, for I warn you, Trock's out gunning and you may not walk very far. Oh, I could defend it but it's hardly worth while. If they get Trock they get me too. Go tell them. You owe me nothing.

ESDRAS. This Trock you saw, no one defends him. He's earned his death so often there's nobody to regret it. But his crime, his same crime that has dogged you, dogged us down from what little we had, to live here among the drains, where the waterbugs break out like a scrofula on what we eat—and if there's lower to go we'll go there when you've told your story. And more that I haven't heart to speak—

MIO (*to* GARTH). My father died in your place. And you could have saved him! You were one of the gang!

GARTH. Why, there you are. You certainly owe me nothing.

MIRIAMNE (*moaning*). I want to die. I want to go away.

MIO. Yes, and you lied! And trapped me into it!

MIRIAMNE. But Mio, he's my brother. I couldn't give them my brother.

MIO. No. You couldn't. You were quite right. The gods were damned ironic tonight, and they've worked it out.

ESDRAS. What will be changed if it comes to trial again? More blood poured out to a mythical justice, but your father lying still where he lies now.

MIO. The bright, ironical gods! What fun they have in heaven! When a man prays hard for any gift, they give it, and then one more to boot that makes it useless. (*To* MIRIAMNE.*) You might have picked some other stranger to dance with!

MIRIAMNE. I know.

MIO. Or chosen some other evening to sit outside in the rain. But no, it had to be this. All my life long I've wanted only one thing, to say to the world and prove it: the man you killed was clean and true and full of love as the twelve-year-old that stood and taught in the temple. I can say that now and give my proofs—and now you stick a girl's face between me and the rites I've sworn the dead shall have of me! You ask too much! Your brother can take his chance! He was ready enough to let an innocent man take certainty for him to pay for the years he's had. That parts us, then, but we're parted anyway, by the same dark wind that blew us together. I shall say what I have to say. (*He steps back.*) And I'm not welcome here.

MIRIAMNE. But don't go now! You've stayed too long! He'll be waiting!

MIO. Well, is this any safer? Let the winds blow, the four winds of the world, and take us to the four winds.

(*The three are silent before him. He turns and goes out.*)

**CURTAIN**

# ACT THREE

SCENE: *The river bank outside the tenement, a little before the close of the previous act. The rain still falls through the street lamps. The* TWO NATTY YOUNG MEN IN SERGE AND GRAY *are leaning against the masonry in a ray of light, concentrating on a game of chance. Each holds in his hand a packet of ten or fifteen crisp bills. They compare the numbers on the top notes and immediately a bill changes hands. This goes on with varying fortune until the tide begins to run toward the* FIRST GUNMAN, *who has accumulated nearly the whole supply. They play on in complete silence, evidently not wishing to make any noise. Occasionally they raise their heads slightly to look carefully about. Luck begins to favor the* SECOND GUNMAN, *and the notes come his way. Neither evinces the slightest interest in how the game goes. They merely play on, bored, half-absorbed. There is a slight noise at the tenement door. They put the bills away and watch.* TROCK *comes out, pulls the door shut and comes over to them. He says a few words too low to be heard, and without changing expression the* YOUNG MEN *saunter toward the right.* TROCK *goes out to the left, and the* SECOND PLAYER, *catching that out of the corner of his eye, lingers in a glimmer of light to go on with the game. The* FIRST, *with an eye on the tenement door, begins to play without ado, and the bills again shift back and forth, then concentrate in the hands of the* FIRST GUNMAN. *The* SECOND *shrugs his shoulders, searches his pockets, finds one bill, and playing with it begins to win heavily. They hear the door opening, and putting the notes away, slip out in front of the rock.* MIO *emerges, closes the door, looks round him and walks to the left. Near the corner of the tenement he pauses, reaches out his hand to try the rain, looks up toward the street, and stands uncertainly a moment. He returns and leans against the tenement wall.* MIRIAMNE *comes out.* MIO *continues to look off into space as if unaware of her. She looks away.*

MIO. This rather takes one off his high horse.—What I mean, tough weather for a hegira. You see, this is my sleeping suit, and if I get it wet—basta!

MIRIAMNE. If you could only hide here.

MIO. Hide?

MIRIAMNE. Lucia would take you in. The street-piano man.

MIO. At the moment I'm afflicted with claustrophobia. I prefer to die in the open, seeking air.

MIRIAMNE. But you could stay there till daylight.

MIO. You're concerned about me.

MIRIAMNE. Shall I ask him?

MIO. No. On the other hand there's a certain reason in your concern. I looked up the street and our old friend Trock hunches patiently under the warehouse eaves.

MIRIAMNE. I was sure of that.

MIO. And here I am, a young man on a cold night, waiting the end of the rain.

Being read my lesson by a boy, a blind boy—you know the one I mean. Knee-deep in the salt-marsh, Miriam, bitten from within, fought.

MIRIAMNE. Wouldn't it be better if you came back in the house?

MIO. You forget my claustrophobia.

MIRIAMNE. Let me walk with you, then. Please. If I stay beside you he wouldn't dare.

MIO. And then again he might.—We don't speak the same language, Miriamne.

MIRIAMNE. I betrayed you. Forgive me.

MIO. I wish I knew this region. There's probably a path along the bank.

MIRIAMNE. Yes. Shadow went that way.

MIO. That's true, too. So here I am, a young man on a wet night, and blind in my weather eye. Stay and talk to me.

MIRIAMNE. If it happens—it's my fault.

MIO. Not at all, sweet. You warned me to keep away. But I would have it. Now I have to find a way out. It's like a chess game.

If you think long enough there's always
a way out.—For one or the other.—I wonder
why white always wins and black always
loses in the problems. White to move and
mate in three moves. But what if white
were to lose—ah, what then? Why, in that
case, obviously black would be white and
white would be black.—As it often it.—
As we often are.—Might makes white.
Losers turn black. Do you think I'd have
time to draw a gun?

MIRIAMNE. No.

MIO. I'm a fair shot. Also I'm fair game.
(*The door of the tenement opens and* GARTH
*comes out to look about quickly. Seeing
only* MIO *and* MIRIAMNE *he goes in and
comes out again almost immediately carrying one end of a door on which a body lies
covered with a cloth. The* HOBO *carries the
other end. They go out to the right with
their burden.*)
This is the burial of Shadow, then;
feet first he dips, and leaves the haunts of
  men.
Let us make mourn for Shadow, wetly
  lying,
in elegiac stanzas and sweet crying.
Be gentle with him, little cold waves and
  fishes;
nibble him not, respect his skin and tissues—

MIRIAMNE. Must you say such things?

MIO. My dear, some requiem is fitting over
  the dead, even
for Shadow. But the last rhyme was bad.
Whittle him not, respect his dying wishes.
That's better. And then to conclude:
His aromatic virtues, slowly rising
will circumnamb the isle, beyond disguising.
He clung to life beyond the wont of men.
Time and his silence drink us all. Amen.
How I hate these identicals. The French
allow them, but the French have no principles anyway. You know, Miriamne, there's
really nothing mysterious about human life.
It's purely mechanical, like an electric ap-
pliance. Stop the engine that runs the
generator and the current's broken. When
we think the brain gives off a small electric discharge—quite measurable, and constant within limits. But that's not what
makes your hair stand up when frightened.

MIRIAMNE. I think it's a mystery.

MIO. Human life? We'll have to wear veils
if we're to keep it a mystery much longer.

Now if Shadow and I were made up into
sausages we'd probably make very good
sausages.

MIRIAMNE. Don't—

MIO. I'm sorry. I speak from a high place,
far off, long ago, looking down. The
cortège returns. (GARTH *and the* HOBO *return, carrying the door, the cloth lying
loosely over it.*) I hoped you placed an obol
in his mouth to pay the ferry-man? Even
among the Greeks a little money was prerequisite to Elysium. (GARTH *and the* HOBO
*go inside, silent.*) No? It's grim to think
of Shadow lingering among lesser shades
on the hither side. For lack of a small
gratuity. (ESDRAS *comes out the open door
and closes it behind him.*)

ESDRAS. You must wait here, Mio, or go
  inside. I know
you don't trust me, and I haven't earned
  your trust.
You're young enough to seek truth—
and there is no truth;
and I know that—
but I shall call the police and see that you
get safely off.

MIO. It's a little late for that.

ESDRAS. I shall try.

MIO. And your terms? For I daresay you
  make terms?

ESDRAS. No.

MIO. Then let me remind you what will
  happen.
The police will ask some questions.
When they're answered
they'll ask more, and before they're done
  with it
your son will be implicated.

ESDRAS. Must he be?

MIO. I shall not keep quiet. (*A pause.*)

ESDRAS. Still, I'll go.

MIO. I don't ask help, remember. I make no
  truce.
He's not on my conscience, and I'm not
  on yours.

ESDRAS. But you
could make it easier, so easily.
He's my only son. Let him live.

MIO. His chance of survival's
better than mine, I'd say.

ESDRAS. I'll go.

MIO. I don't urge it.

ESDRAS. No. I put my son's life in your hands.
When you're gone,
that may come to your mind.

MIO. Don't count on it.

ESDRAS. Oh,
I count on nothing. (*He turns to go.* MIRI-
AMNE *runs over to him and silently kisses
his hands.*)
Not mine, not mine, my daughter!
They're guilty hands. (*He goes out.* GARTH's
*violin is heard within.*)

MIO. There was a war in heaven
once, all the angels on one side, and all
the devils on the other, and since that time
disputes have raged among the learned,
    concerning
whether the demons won, or the angels.
    Maybe
the angels won, after all.

MIRIAMNE. And again, perhaps
there are no demons or angels.

MIO. Oh, there are none.
But I could love your father.

MIRIAMNE. I love him. You see,
he's afraid because he's old. The less one has
to lose the more he's afraid.

MIO. Suppose one had
only a short stub end of life, or held
a flashlight with the batteries run down
till the bulb was dim, and knew that he
    could live
while the glow lasted. Or suppose one knew
that while he stood in a little shelter of time
under a bridgehead, say, he could live, and
    then,
from then on, nothing. Then to lie and turn
with the earth and sun, and regard them not
    in the least
when the bulb was extinguished or he
    stepped beyond
his circle into the cold? How would he live
that last dim quarter-hour, before he went,
minus all recollection, to grow in grass
between cobblestones?

MIRIAMNE. Let me put my arms round you,
    Mio.
Then if anything comes, it's for me, too.
(*She puts both arms round him.*)

MIO. Only suppose
this circle's charmed! To be safe until he
    steps
from this lighted space into dark! Time
    pauses here
and high eternity grows in one quarter-hour
in which to live.

MIRIAMNE. Let me see if anyone's there—
there in the shadows. (*She looks toward
the right.*)

MIO. It might blast our eternity—
blow it to bits. No, don't go. This is for-
    ever,
here where we stand. And I ask you,
    Miriamne,
how does one spend a forever?

MIRIAMNE. You're frightened?

MIO. Yes.
So much that time stands still.

MIRIAMNE. Why didn't I speak—
tell them—when the officers were here? I
    failed you
in that one moment!

MIO. His life for mine? Oh, no.
I wouldn't want it, and you couldn't give it.
And if I should go on living we're cut
    apart
by that brother of yours.

MIRIAMNE. Are we?

MIO. Well, think about it.
A body lies between us, buried in quick-
    lime.
Your allegiance is on the other side of that
    grave
and not to me.

MIRIAMNE. No, Mio! Mio, I love you!

MIO. I love you, too, but in case my life
    went on
beyond that barrier of dark—then Garth
would run his risk of dying.

MIRIAMNE. He's punished, Mio.
His life's been torment to him. Let him go,
for my sake, Mio.

MIO. I wish I could. I wish
I'd never seen him—or you. I've steeped too
    long
in this thing. It's in my teeth and bones. I
    can't
let go or forget. And I'll not add my lie
to the lies that cumber his ground. We live
    our days
in a storm of lies that drifts the truth too
    deep
for path or shovel; but I've set my foot on
    a truth
for once, and I'll trail it down! (*A silence.*
MIRIAMNE *looks out to the right.*)

MIRIAMNE. There's someone there—
I heard—(CARR *comes in from the right.*)

MIO. It's Carr.

CARR. That's right. No doubt about it.
Excuse me.

MIO. Glad to see you. This is Miriamne.
Carr's a friend of mine.

CARR. You're better employed
than when I saw you last.

MIO. Bow to the gentleman,
Miriamne. That's meant for you.

MIRIAMNE. Thank you, I'm sure.
Should I leave you, Mio? You want to talk?

MIO. Oh, no,
we've done our talking.

MIRIAMNE. But—

CARR. I'm the one's out of place—
I wandered back because I got worried about
    you,
that's the truth.—Oh—those two fellows
    with the hats
down this way, you know, the ones that ran
after we heard the shooting—they're back
    again,
lingering or malingering down the bank,
revisiting the crime, I guess. They may
mean well.

MIO. I'll try to avoid them.

CARR. I didn't care
for the way they looked at me.—No luck, I
    suppose,
with that case history? The investigation
**you** had on hand?

MIO. I can't say. By the way,
the stiff that fell in the water and we saw
    swirling
down the eddy, he came trudging up, later
    on,
long enough to tell his name. His name was
    Shadow,
but he's back in the water now. It's all in an
    evening.
These things happen here.

CARR. Good God!

MIO. I know.
I wouldn't believe it if you told it.

CARR. But—
the man was alive?

MIO. Oh, not for long! He's dunked
for good this time. That's all that's hap-
    pened.

CARR. Well,
if you don't need me—

MIRIAMNE. You had a message to send—
have you forgotten—?

MIO. I?—Yes, I had a message—
but I won't send it—not now.

MIRIAMNE. Then I will—!

MIO. No.
Let it go the way it is! It's all arranged
another way. You've been a good scout,
    Carr,
the best I ever knew on the road.

CARR. That sounds
like making your will.

MIO. Not yet, but when I do
I've thought of something to leave you. It's
    the view
of Mt. Rainier from the Seattle jail,
snow over cloud. And the rusty chain in my
    pocket
from a pair of handcuffs my father wore.
    That's all
the worldly goods I'm seized of.

CARR. Look, Mio—hell—
if you're in trouble—

MIO. I'm not. Not at all. I have
a genius that attends me where I go,
and guards me now. I'm fine.

CARR. Well, that's good news.
He'll have his work cut out.

MIO. Oh, he's a genius.

CARR. I'll see you then.
I'll be at the Grand Street place. I'm lucky tonight,
and I can pay. I could even pay for two.

MIO. Thanks, I may take you up.

CARR. Good night.

MIO. Right, Carr.

CARR (*to* MIRIAMNE). Good night.

MIRIAMNE (*after a pause*). Good night.
(CARR *goes out to the left.*)
Why did you do that? He's your genius, Mio,
and you let him go.

MIO. I couldn't help it.

MIRIAMNE. Call him.
Run after him and call him!

MIO. I tried to say it
and it strangled in my throat. I might have known
you'd win in the end.

MIRIAMNE. Is it for me?

MIO. For you?
It stuck in my throat, that's all I know.

MIRIAMNE. Oh, Mio,
I never asked for that! I only hoped
Garth could go clear.

MIO. Well, now he will.

MIRIAMNE. But you—
It was your chance!

MIO. I've lost
my taste for revenge if it falls on you. Oh, God,
deliver me from the body of this earth
I've dragged behind me all these years!
  Miriamne!
Miriamne!

MIRIAMNE. Yes!

MIO. Miriamne, if you love me
teach me a treason to what I am, and have been,
till I learn to live like a man! I think I'm waking
from a long trauma of hate and fear and death

that's hemmed me from my birth—and glimpse a life
to be lived in hope—but it's young in me yet, I can't
get free, or forgive! But teach me how to live
and forget to hate!

MIRIAMNE. He would have forgiven.

MIO. He?

MIRIAMNE. Your father. (*A pause.*)

MIO. Yes. (*Another pause.*)
You'll think it strange, but I've never remembered that.

MIRIAMNE. How can I help you?

MIO. You have.

MIRIAMNE. If I were a little older—if I knew
the things to say! I can only put out my hands
and give you back the faith you bring to me
by being what you are. Because to me
you are all hope and beauty and brightness drawn
across what's black and mean!

MIO. He'd have forgiven—
Then there's no more to say—I've groped long enough
through this everglades of old revenges— here
the road ends.—Miriamne, Miriamne,
the iron I wore so long—it's eaten through
and fallen from me. Let me have your arms.
They'll say we're children—Well—the world's made up
of children.

MIRIAMNE. Yes.

MIO. But it's too late for me.

MIRIAMNE. No. (*She goes into his arms, and they kiss for the first time.*)
Then we'll meet again?

MIO. Yes.

MIRIAMNE. Where?

MIO. I'll write—
or send Carr to you.

MIRIAMNE. You won't forget?

MIO. Forget?
Whatever streets I walk, you'll walk them, too,

from now on, and whatever roof or stars
I have to house me, you shall share my roof
and stars and morning. I shall not forget.

MIRIAMNE. God keep you!

MIO. And keep you. And this to remember!
if I should die, Miriamne, this half-hour
is our eternity. I came here seeking
light in darkness, running from the dawn,
and stumbled on a morning.

(*One of the* YOUNG MEN IN SERGE *strolls in
casually from the right, looks up and down
without expression, then, seemingly having
forgotten something, retraces his steps and
goes out.* ESDRAS *comes in slowly from the
left. He has lost his hat, and his face is bleeding from a slight cut on the temple. He
stands abjectly near the tenement.*)

MIRIAMNE. Father—what is it? (*She goes
towards* ESDRAS.)

ESDRAS. Let me alone. (*He goes nearer to*
MIO.)
He wouldn't let me pass.
The street's so icy up along the bridge
I had to crawl on my knees—he kicked
  me back
three times—and then he held me there—
  I swear
what I could do I did! I swear to you
I'd save you if I could.

MIO. What makes you think
that I need saving?

ESDRAS. Child, save yourself if you can!
He's waiting for you.

MIO. Well, we knew that before.

ESDRAS. He won't wait much longer. He'll
  come here—
he told me so. Those damned six months
  of his—
he wants them all—and you're to die—
  you'd spread
his guilt—I had to listen to it—

MIO. Wait—(*He walks forward and looks
casually to the right, then returns.*)
There must be some way up through the
  house and out
across the roof—

ESDRAS. He's watching that. But come in—
and let me look.—

MIO. I'll stay here, thanks. Once in
and I'm a rat in a deadfall—Ill stay here—
look for me if you don't mind.

ESDRAS. Then watch for me—
I'll be on the roof—(*He goes in hurriedly.*)

MIO (*looking up*). Now all you silent powers
that make the sleet and dark, and never yet
have spoken, give us a sign, let the throw
  be ours
this once, on this longest night, when the
  winter sets
his foot on the threshold leading up to spring
and enters with remembered cold—let fall
some mercy with the rain. We are two lovers
here in your night, and we wish to live.

MIRIAMNE. Oh, Mio—
if you pray that way, nothing good will
  come!
You're bitter, Mio.

MIO. How many floors has this building?

MIRIAMNE. Five or six. It's not as high as
  the bridge.

MIO. No, I thought not. How many pome-
  granate seeds
did you eat, Persephone?

MIRIAMNE. Oh, darling, darling,
if you die, don't die alone.

MIO. I'm afraid I'm damned
to hell, and you're not damned at all. Good
  God,
how long he takes to climb!

MIRIAMNE. The stairs are steep. (*A slight
pause.*)

MIO. I'll follow him.

MIRIAMNE. He's there—at the window—
  now.
He waves you to go back, not to go in.
Mio, see, that path between the rocks—
they're not watching that—they're out at
  the river—
I can see them there—they can't watch
  both—
it leads to a street above.

MIO. I'll try it, then.
Kiss me. You'll hear. But if you never
  hear—
then I'm the king of hell, Persephone,
and I'll expect you.

MIRIAMNE. Oh, lover, keep safe.

MIO. Good-bye. (*He slips quickly between the rocks. There is a quick machine gun rat-tat. The violin stops,* MIRIAMNE *runs toward the path.* MIO *comes back slowly, a hand pressed under his heart.*)
It seems you were mistaken.

MIRIAMNE. Oh, God, forgive me! (*She puts an arm round him. He sinks to his knees.*)
Where is it, Mio? Let me help you in!
  Quick, quick,
let me help you!

MIO. I hadn't thought to choose—this—
  ground—
but it will do. (*He slips down.*)

MIRIAMNE. Oh, God, forgive me!

MIO. Yes?
The king of hell was not forgiven then,
Dis is his name, and Hades is his home—
and he goes alone—

MIRIAMNE. Why does he bleed so? Mio, if
  you go
I shall go with you.

MIO. It's better to stay alive.
I wanted to stay alive—because of you—
I leave you that—and what he said to me
  dying:
I love you, and will love you after I die.
Tomorrow, I shall still love you, as I've
  loved
the stars I'll never see, and all the mornings
that might have been yours and mine. Oh,
  Miriamne,
you taught me this.

MIRIAMNE. If only I'd never seen you
then you could live—

MIO. That's blasphemy—Oh, God,
there might have been some easier way of it.
You didn't want me to die, did you,
  Miriamne—?
You didn't send me away—?

MIRIAMNE. Oh, never, never—

MIO. Forgive me—kiss me—I've got blood
  on your lips—
I'm sorry—it doesn't matter—I'm sorry—
(ESDRAS *and* GARTH *come out.*)

MIRIAMNE. Mio—
I'd have gone to die myself—you must hear
  this, Mio,

I'd have died to help you—you must listen,
  sweet,
you must hear it—(*She rises.*)
I can die, too, see! You! There!
You in the shadows!—You killed him to
  silence him! (*She walks toward the path.*)
But I'm not silenced! All that he knew I
  know,
and I'll tell it tonight! Tonight—
tell it and scream it
through all the streets—that Trock's a murderer
and he hired you for this murder!
Your work's not done—
and you won't live long! Do you hear?
You're murderers, and I know who you are!
(*The machine gun speaks again. She sinks
to her knees.* GARTH *runs to her.*)

GARTH. You little fool! (*He tries to lift her.*)

MIRIAMNE. Don't touch me! (*She crawls
toward* MIO.)
Look, Mio! They killed me, too. Oh, you
  can believe me
now, Mio. You can believe I wouldn't hurt
  you,
because I'm dying! Why doesn't he answer
  me?
Oh, now he'll never know! (*She sinks down,
her hand over her mouth, choking.* GARTH
*kneels beside her, then rises, shuddering.
The* HOBO *comes out.* LUCIA *and* PINY *look
out.*)

ESDRAS. It lacked only this.

GARTH. Yes. (ESDRAS *bends over* MIRIAMNE,
*then rises slowly.*)
Why was the bastard born? Why did he
  come here?

ESDRAS. Miriamne—Miriamne—yes, and
  Mio,
one breath shall call you now—forgive us
  both—
forgive the ancient evil of the earth
that brought you here—

GARTH. Why must she be a fool?

ESDRAS. Well, they were wiser than you and
  I. To die
when you are young and untouched, that's
  beggary
to a miser of years, but the devils locked in
  synod
shake and are daunted when men set their
  lives

at hazard for the heart's love, and lose. And
   these,
who were yet children, will weigh more
   than all
a city's elders when the experiment
is reckoned up in the end. Oh, Miriamne,
and Mio—Mio, my son—know this where
   you lie,
this is the glory of earth-born men and
   women,
not to cringe, never to yield, but standing,
take defeat implacable and defiant,
die unsubmitting. I wish that I'd died so,
long ago; before you're old you'll wish
that you had died as they have. On this star,
in this hard star-adventure, knowing not
what the fires mean to right and left, nor
   whether
a meaning was intended or presumed,

man can stand up, and look out blind, and
   say:
in all these turning lights I find no clue,
only a masterless night, and in my blood
no certain answer, yet is my mind my own,
yet is my heart a cry toward something dim
in distance, which is higher than I am
and makes me emperor of the endless dark
even in seeking! What odds and ends of life
men may live otherwise, let them live, and
   then
go out, as I shall go, and you. Our part
is only to bury them. Come, take her up.
They must not lie here.

(LUCIA *and* PINY *come near to help.* ESDRAS
*and* GARTH *stoop to carry* MIRIAMNE.)

CURTAIN

# 1936-37

*High Tor* was something of a change of pace for Maxwell Anderson whose work had been on a down-to-earth, factual plane even when couched in poetic terms. The Circle's citation was indicative of this:

". . . In its decision, the Circle celebrates the advent of the first distinguished fantasy by an American in many years. Imaginative and as comic as it is poetic in both spirit and expression, *High Tor* is a singular accomplishment, giving rare grace to this theatrical season in New York."

Again Anderson won with fourteen votes, but this time there were eighteen voting members. The struggle was more prolonged, with victory not coming until the eleventh ballot on March 28, 1937. The runner-up on the last ballot was Paul Green's unusual *Johnny Johnson* with three votes. One vote was given to Robert Turney's *Daughters of Atreus.*

Plays that fell by the wayside during the eleven ballots were *The Wingless Victory* and *The Masque of Kings,* also by Anderson; *You Can't Take It with You* by Moss Hart and George.S. Kaufman, *Yes, My Darling Daughter* by Mark Reed, *Having Wonderful Time* by Arthur Kober and *Marching Song* by John Howard Lawson.

The season also was notable for Maurice Evans' Napoleon in *St. Helena* by R. C. Sherriff and Jeanne De Casalis, and for the same star's work in the title role of Shakespeare's *Richard II;* for two productions of *Hamlet,* starring John Gielgud and Leslie Howard, respectively; Noel Coward's nine short plays bearing the over-all title of *Tonight at 8:30,* in which he starred with Gertrude Lawrence, and *The Women* by a future ambassadress, Clare Boothe Luce.

Burgess Meredith scored another triumph in *High Tor.* The young man was reaching his peak as an actor. He was expected to be *the* Hamlet of 1940. Unfortunately, this never came about.

*High Tor* ran for 171 performances.

# High Tor

## By MAXWELL ANDERSON

Presented by Guthrie McClintic at the Martin Beck Theatre, New York City, January 5, 1937, with the following cast:

| | |
|---|---|
| THE INDIAN | *Harry Irvine* |
| VAN VAN DORN | *Burgess Meredith* |
| JUDITH | *Mab Maynard* |
| ART. J. BIGGS | *Harold Moffet* |
| JUDGE SKIMMERHORN | *Thomas W. Ross* |
| LISE | *Peggy Ashcroft* |
| CAPTAIN ASHER | *Byron McGrath* |
| PIETER | *John Philliber* |
| 1st SAILOR | *William Casamo* |
| 2nd SAILOR | *Will Archie* |
| 3rd SAILOR | *Harold Grau* |
| DeWITT | *Charles D. Brown* |
| DOPE | *Leslie Gorall* |
| ELKUS | *Hume Cronyn* |
| BUDDY | *John Drew Colt* |
| PATSY | *Charles Forrester* |
| A.B. SKIMMERHORN | *John M. Kline* |
| BUDGE | *Jackson Halliday* |

---

## SCENE

Acts I, II and III—Sections near and at the summit of High Tor

---

# HIGH TOR

## ACT ONE

### SCENE I

SCENE: *A section of the broad flat trap-rock summit of High Tor, from which one looks out into sky and from which one might look down a sheer quarter mile to the Tappan Zee below. A cluster of hexagonal pillared rocks masks the view to the left and a wind-tortured small hemlock wedges into the rock floor at the right. Light from the setting sun pours in from the left, and an ancient* INDIAN, *wearing an old greatcoat thrown round him like a blanket, stands in the rays from a cleft, making his prayer to the sunset.*

THE INDIAN. I make my prayer to you, the falling fire,
bearing in mind the whisper in my ears
from the great spirit, talking on the wind,
whispering that a young race, in its morning,
should pray to the rising sun, but a race that's old
and dying, should invoke the dying flame
eaten and gulfed by the shark-toothed mountain-west,
a god that dies to live. As we have died,
my race of the red faces and old ways,
and as we hope to rise. I give you thanks
for light, for the coming summer that will warm
my snake's blood, cold and crawling; for the rain
that fed the ripe May apples in the woods
in secret for me; for the waterfall
where the trout climb and pause under my hand,
taken in silence; for quiet on the hills
where the loud races dare not walk for fear
lest they be lost, where their blind hunters pass
peering with caps and guns, but see no game,
and curse as they go down, while the raccoon waits,
the woodchuck stands erect to catch the wind,
the partridge steps so lightly over leaves
the listening fox hears nothing, the possum hangs
head down, looking through his hands, and takes no breath,
the gray squirrel turns to stone against the rock,
watching the owl, the rabbit holds his ears
steady above the trembling of his heart
and the crow mocks down the shellbark. I am fed
and sheltered on this mountain where their hands
are helpless. But I am old as my race is old;
my eyes hunt day and night along the ground
the grave where I shall lie; my ears have heard
dead women calling upward from the earth,
mother and wife and child: "You are welcome here;
you are no longer welcome where you walk,
but here you are most welcome." I shall go,
and lie and sleep, and I shall give you thanks,
O God that dies, that my last night is dark
and long, for I am tired, but yet I ask
one summer more, that I may be warm again
and watch the nestlings grown upon the crag,
and hear the wild geese honking south by night,
if this may be, but if it may not be
then is my prayer, that when I lie to sleep
I may lie long, sleep soundly, hear no step,
hear only through the earth your step in spring,
O God of the dying fire!
(VAN DORN *and* JUDITH *come in from the right.*)

VAN DORN. Evening, John.

THE INDIAN. Evening.

VAN DORN. Had any luck so far?

THE INDIAN. Yes. Plenty of luck.

VAN DORN. Found it?

THE INDIAN. Yes.

VAN DORN. O.K., John, let me know. Let me know in time.

THE INDIAN. I will. Good night.

VAN DORN. Good night. (*The* INDIAN *slips away through the rocks to the left.*)

JUDITH. Who is it, Van?

VAN. Just an Indian.

JUDITH. Are there Indians?
I didn't know there were any Indians left.

VAN. Well, there's one. There's not much left of him,
and he's the last around here.

JUDITH. He's hunting something?
You asked him if he's found it.

VAN. Um—yes, you see,
he's looking for a place to make his grave,
and he's kind of captious about it—folks get that way
along toward the end, wanting their bones done up
in some particular fashion. Maybe because
that's all you've got to leave about that time
and you want it the way you want it.

JUDITH. Did he tell you this?

VAN. We've got an understanding. When he feels it
coming over him he's going to die
he'll let me know, and I'll go dig him in
so the crows and foxes can't get at him. See,
he's all alone in the world. We fixed this up
a couple of years ago.

JUDITH. But you couldn't, Van,
without a permit. A burial permit.

VAN. Oh,
I guess you could. This getting old and dying
and crawling into the ground, that was invented
back before medical examiners
and taxes and all that. The old boy's clean.
He'll go right back to dirt.

JUDITH. But, Van, you can't!
People can't die that way!

VAN. I guess they can.
What the hell good's being wrapped in cellophane?
You don't keep anyway.

JUDITH. You're impossible
to live with! Why do you say such things? If I
should die—you'd get a pine box!—

VAN. If you should die
the old boy that drives the sun around up there,

he'd unhitch, and put the cattle out
to grass, and give it up. He'd plumb lose interest
if you should die. Maybe I would myself,
I don't say. Maybe I would.—Fetch out that supper.
We want to see what we eat.

JUDITH (opening a lunch box). It's dinner, Van,
not supper.

VAN. That's what I said. Fetch out that dinner.
When it gets a little darker what's black's pepper
and what's green's parsley; still you can't be sure.
It might be ants.

JUDITH. Just the same we'll quarrel.
We'll always quarrel.

VAN. Oh, no, We've both got sense.
What's the sense fighting? (He looks at a paper that was round the lunch.)

JUDITH. And you shouldn't read at table.

VAN. I never do. The Nanuet bank's been robbed.
My God, there's not enough money in Nanuet
to buy their gas for a get-away. One night
pap and me sat in on a poker game
in Nanuet and took twenty-seven dollars
out of town. Next day they couldn't do business.
The place was clean.

JUDITH. There were troopers at the train
tonight, and sirens going through Haverstraw,
but the robbers got away.

VAN. They took twenty-five thousand.
How'd twenty-five thousand get to Nanuet?
It's against nature.

JUDITH. It didn't stay there long.

VAN. No—I understand that.
But just to have it there in passing, just
to look at, just to fool the customers,
how do they do it?

JUDITH. Maybe it wasn't real.

VAN. Federal money, that's it. Some of the stuff

Jim Farley prints in Washington with the stamps
to pay you for voting straight. Only now you see it
and now you don't.

JUDITH. They say it buys as much
as if you earned it.

VAN. Bad for the stomach, though,
to live on humble pie.

JUDITH. I'd rather work.

VAN. Well, as I said, don't work if you don't feel like it.
Any time you want to move up in the hills
and sleep with me, it's a bargain.

JUDITH. Van!

VAN. Why not?
We'll get married if that's what you mean.

JUDITH. You haven't any job. And you make it sound
like animals.

VAN. I'm fond of animals.

JUDITH. You shoot them all the time.

VAN. Well, I get hungry.
Any man's liable to get hungry.

JUDITH. Van,
I want to talk to you seriously.

VAN. Can't be done.
Listen, things get serious enough
without setting out to do it.

JUDITH. Van, this spring
you had three weeks' work, laying dry wall.
You could have had more, but you didn't take it.
You're an expert mason—

VAN. I'm good at everything.

JUDITH. But you work three weeks in the year—

VAN. That's all I need—

JUDITH. And all the rest of the year you hunt or fish
or sleep, or God knows what—

VAN. Ain't it the truth?

JUDITH. Last fall I came looking for you once, and you

were gone—gone to Port Jervis hunting—deer,
you said on the postcard—

VAN. Sure, I was hunting deer—
didn't I bring you half a venison?

JUDITH. But not a word to me till I got the postcard
ten days later—

VAN. Didn't have a minute—

JUDITH. Then last winter there's a note nailed to a tree
and you're in Virginia, down in the Dismal Swamp
tracking bear. Now, for God's sake, Van,
it's no way to live.

VAN. Jeez, it's a lot of fun.

JUDITH. Maybe for you.

VAN. You want me to take that job.

JUDITH. Why don't you, Van?

VAN. Porter in a hotel, lugging up satchels,
opening windows, maybe you get a dime.
I'd choke to death.

JUDITH. I'd see you every day.

VAN. Yeah, I could see you on the mezzanine,
taking dictation from the drummer boys,
all about how they can't get home. You can stand it,
a woman stands that stuff, but if you're a man
I say it chokes you.

JUDITH. We can't live in your cabin
and have no money, like the Jackson Whites
over at Suffern.

VAN. Hell, you don't need money.
Pap worked that out. All you need's a place to sleep
and something to eat. I've never seen the time
I couldn't find a meal on the mountain here,
rainbow trout, jugged hare, something in season
right around the zodiac.

JUDITH. You didn't like
the Chevrolet factory, either?

VAN .(*walking toward the cliff edge*). Look at it, Judy.
That's the Chevrolet factory, four miles down,

and straight across, that's Sing Sing. Right
from here
you can't tell one from another; get inside,
and what's the difference? You're in there,
and you work,
and they've got you. If you're in the factory
you buy a car, and then you put in your time
to pay for the goddam thing. If you get in
a hurry
and steal a car, they put you in Sing Sing
first,
and then you work out your time. They
graduate
from one to the other, back and forth, those
guys,
paying for cars both ways. But I was smart.
I parked at a polis station and rung the bell
and took to the woods. Not for your Uncle
Dudley.
They plugged the dice.

JUDITH. But one has to have a car.

VAN. Honest to God now, Judy, what's the
hurry?
Where in hell are we going?

JUDITH. If a man works hard,
and has ability, as you have, Van,
he takes a place among them, saves his
money,
works right out of the ruck and gets above
where he's safe and secure.

VAN. I wouldn't bet on it much.

JUDITH. But it's true.

VAN. All right, suppose it's true. Suppose
a man saves money all his life, and works
like hell about forty years, till he can say:
good-bye, I'm going, I'm on easy street
from now on. What's he do?

JUDITH. Takes a vacation.

VAN. Goes fishing, maybe? I'm on vacation
now.
Why should I work forty years to earn
time off when I've got it?

JUDITH. It's not always easy,
you know it's not. There was that time last
winter
when I helped you out.

VAN. Why, sure, you helped me out.
Why wouldn't you? But if you didn't help
me
I'd get along.

JUDITH. Yes, you would. I know you would.
But you don't even seem to want money.
You won't take it
when they bring it to you.

VAN. When did they bring me any?

JUDITH. And what if there was a child?

VAN. Why, he'd be fine—
the less they have the better they like it.—
Oh,
you mean the trap-rock company, wanting
to buy
High Tor? They offered seven hundred
dollars—
and they offered pap ten thousand before
he died,
and he wouldn't sell.

JUDITH. He wouldn't?

VAN. They wanted to chew
the back right off this mountain, the way
they did
across the clove there. Leave the old palisades
sticking up here like billboards, nothing left
but a false front facing the river. Not for
pap,
and not for me. I like this place.

JUDITH. But, Van Van Dorn!
Ten thousand dollars!

VAN. Well, it's Federal money.
Damn stuff evaporates. Put it in a sock
along with moth balls, and come back next
year,
and there's nothing left but the smell. Look,
Judy, its
a quarter mile straight down to the Tappan
Zee
from here.—You can see fifteen miles of
river
north and south. I grew up looking at it.
Hudson came up that river just about
three hundred years ago, and lost a ship
here in the Zee. They say the crew climbed
up
this Tor to keep a lookout for the fleet
that never came. Maybe the Indians got
them.
Anyway on dark nights before a storm,
they say you sometimes see them.

JUDITH. Have you seen them?

VAN. The Dutchmen? Maybe I have. You
can't be sure.
It's pretty wild around here when it storms.

That's when I like it best. But look at it now.
There was a Jaeger here from Switzerland
last year. He took one squint at this and said
they could keep their Alps, for all him.
Look at the willows
along the far breakwater.

JUDITH. It's beautiful.

VAN. Every night I come back here like the
Indian
to get a fill of it. Seven hundred dollars
and tear it down? Hell, no. (BIGGS *and* SKIM-
MERHORN *come in from the right, a bit bedraggled, and wiping their brows.* SKIMMER-
HORN *carries a brief-case. It is growing
darker.*)

BIGGS. Hey listen, Mac, any houses round
here?

VAN. Guess you're off the beat, buddy; never
heard of any houses on the mountain.

SKIMMERHORN. Come on, Art; we're doing
well if we're down at the road before dark.

BIGGS. Look, Mac, maybe you can help us
out. You familiar with this region, at all?

VAN. I've been around here some.

BIGGS. Well, we're all afternoon hunting a
cabin that's somewhere along the ridge. Ever
hear of it?

VAN. Anybody live in it?

BIGGS. Fellow named Van Dorn.

VAN. Oh, yes, sure.

BIGGS. You know where it is?

VAN. Sure. You climb down the face of the
cliff here and keep left along the ledge about
a hundred yards, then you turn sharp left
through a cleft up the ridge. Follow the trail
about half a mile and there you are.

SKIMMERHORN. Down the face of the cliff?

VAN. Down through the rocks there, then
turn left—

SKIMMERHORN. A monkey couldn't go down
there, hanging on with four hands and a
tail!

VAN. Well, you can always walk along back
toward Little Tor, and cut down from there
through the gulch. There's a slough at the

bottom of the ravine, but if you get through
that you can see the cabin up on the side-
hill. About four miles that way.

SKIMMERHORN. Yeah, we'll set right out. I
always did want to get lost up here and
spend a night in the hills.

VAN. Oh, you'll get lost, all right.

BIGGS. Any snakes?

VAN. No, you might see a copperhead, or a
timber rattler.

SKIMMERHORN. Coming back down?

BIGGS. Yeah, we'd better go down. Thanks.

VAN. Don't mention it. (BIGGS *and* SKIMMER-
HORN *go out to the right.*)

JUDITH. But they were looking for you?

VAN. Yeah.

JUDITH. Why didn't you tell them?

VAN. What?

JUDITH. Who you were!

VAN. They didn't ask about that.

JUDITH. But out of common courtesy!

VAN. Well, you see, I know who they are.

JUDITH. Who are they?

VAN. Art J. Biggs, Junior, and Skimmerhorn,
Judge Skimmerhorn.

JUDITH. But why not talk to them?

VAN. Oh, we communicate by mail. I've got
a dozen letters stacked up from the firm:
Skimmerhorn, Skimmerhorn, Biggs and
    Skimmerhorn,
and maybe two or three Skimmerhorns I left
    out
printed across the top. They're realtors,
whatever that is, and they own the trap-rock
    company,
and one of the Skimmerhorns, he's probate
    judge,
and goes around condemning property
when they want to make a rake-off. Take
    a letter:
Dear Skimmerhorn—

JUDITH. But they're the trap-rock men!

VAN. That's what I said.

JUDITH. I'll call them!

VAN. Oh, no; oh, no!
I've got nothing to say to those two buzzards
except I hope they break their fat-back necks
on their own trap-rock.

JUDITH. You take a lot for granted.

VAN. Do I?

JUDITH. You think, because I said I loved
   you once,
that's the end; I'm finished.

VAN. Oh, far from it.

JUDITH. Oh, yes—you think because a girl's
   been kissed
she stays kissed, and after that the man
does her thinking for her.

VAN. Hell, it's all I can do
to handle my own thinking.

JUDITH. If we're married
I'll have to live the way you want to live.
You prefer being a pauper!

VAN. Get it straight!
I don't take money nor orders, and I live
as I damn well please.

JUDITH. But we'd live like paupers!
And you could have a fortune!

VAN. Seven hundred dollars?

JUDITH. You could get more!

VAN. I don't mean to sell at all.

JUDITH. You see; it's your place, and your
   thinking! You decide,
but I'd have to stand it with you!

VAN. What do you want?

JUDITH. Something to start on; and now,
   you see, we could have it,
only you won't!

VAN. I can't, Judy, that's the truth.
I just can't.

JUDITH. They'll get it anyway.
They've worked right up to where your land
   begins,
and they won't stop for you. They'll just
   condemn it
and take it.

VAN. They'll be in trouble.

JUDITH. You can't make trouble
for companies. They have a dozen lawyers
and ride right over you. I've worked for
   them.
It's never any use.

VAN. Well, I won't sell.

JUDITH. We'll call it off then.

VAN. What?

JUDITH. Between you and me.

VAN. Only you don't mean it.

JUDITH. I know I do, though.
You haven't thought about it, and so you
   think
I couldn't do it. But it's better now
than later.

VAN. You don't know what it means to me
if you can say it.

JUDITH. It means as much to me,
but I look ahead a little.

VAN. What do you see?

JUDITH. Two people growing old
and having children, running wild in the
   woods
with nothing.

VAN. There's no better place to run.
But I've been counting on you. More than
   you know.
More than—Judy, this is the kind of night
we've been in love most.

JUDITH. Yes, we could be in love,
but that's not everything.

VAN. Well, just about.
What else do we get?

JUDITH. I think I'd better go.
It's getting dark.

VAN. You could find your way by the beacon.

JUDITH. I'd better go. (BIGGS and SKIMMER-
HORN come back from the right.)

BIGGS. Listen, Mac, would you do something
for us?

VAN. I don't know.

BIGGS. Could you take a paper round to Van
Dorn and leave it with him?

VAN. A summons?

BIGGS. A sort of notice.

VAN. Yeah, a notice to appear. No, I couldn't.

BIGGS. It's worth a dollar to me.

VAN. I'd be cheating you.

SKIMMERHORN. Make it two dollars.

VAN. You'd be throwing away money.

SKIMMERHORN. Never mind that part of it. Will you do it?

VAN. You'll take a running jump over the edge of the cliff and think things over on the way down before I serve any papers for you.

BIGGS. What's the matter with us?

VAN. Might be hoof and mouth disease, for all I know. You certainly brought an awful stench up here with you.

SKIMMERHORN. Not much on manners, these natives.

VAN. My rule in life is keep away from skunks.

BIGGS. You'll get the tar kicked out of you one of these days.

VAN. Make it today.

JUDITH. If you gentlemen care to know, this is Mr. Van Dorn.

BIGGS. Say, are you Van Dorn?

VAN. Sure I am.

BIGGS (*extending a hand*). Oh, in that case, forget it—you're the fellow we want to see!— Boy, we apologize—(*He uncovers.*) and to the lady, too! Listen, I don't know what to say but you've got us all wrong. We want to buy this place!

VAN. You like the view, I suppose?

BIGGS. Certainly is a view.

VAN. You wouldn't spoil it, of course? You wouldn't move in with a million dollars' worth of machinery and cut the guts out of the mountain, would you?

SKIMMERHORN. We always leave the front— the part you see from the river.

VAN. But you take down all the law allows.

SKIMMERHORN. Well, we're in business.

VAN. Not with me.

JUDITH. Do you mind if I ask how much you're offering?

BIGGS. We said seven hundred, but I'll make it a thousand right here and now.

SKIMMERHORN. As a matter of fact, we'll make it two thousand.

BIGGS. Yeah, all right. Two thousand for the hundred and seven acres.

JUDITH. But you offered Mr. Van Dorn's father ten thousand before he died.

SKIMMERHORN. His father had a clear title, right down from the original Dutch patroon to the original Van Dorn. But unfortunately the present Mr. Van Dorn has a somewhat clouded claim to the acreage.

VAN. My father's title was clear, and he left it to me.

SKIMMERHORN. The truth is he should have employed a lawyer when he drew his will, because the instrument, as recorded, is faulty in many respects. It was brought before me in my capacity as probate judge at Ledentown.

VAN. And in your capacity as second vice-president of the trap-rock company you shot it full of holes.

SKIMMERHORN. Sir, I keep my duties entirely separate.

VAN. Sure, but when your left hand takes money your right hand finds out about it. And when there's too much to carry away in both hands you use a basket. You're also vice-president of the power company, and you stole right-of-ways clear across the country north and south—

SKIMMERHORN. We paid for every foot of land—

VAN. Yes, at your own price.

BIGGS. Let's not get in an argument, Mr. Van Dorn, because the fact that your father's will was improperly drawn means he died intestate and the land goes to his heirs. Now we've found twenty-seven Van Dorns living at Blauvelt, all claiming relationship and all willing to sign away their rights for a consideration.

VAN. The best you can do you'll need my name in your little paper, and you won't have it.

SKIMMERHORN. To put it straight, you'll take three thousand dollars, and I'll hold the will valid.

VAN. Oh, it's three thousand, now?

BIGGS. You'll say that's crooked, but it's not. It's perfectly legal—and it's what you get.

VAN. I'm still waiting to hear what you do about my signature.

SKIMMERHORN. It's quite possible you'll be held incompetent by the court and a guardian appointed.

VAN. Me, incompetent.

SKIMMERHORN. But I've got the validation in my pocket, naming you executor, if you'll sell.

BIGGS. And by God, anybody that won't take money when it's offered to him is incompetent! And you'll take it now or not at all! I don't go mountain-climbing every day with a blank check in my pocket! (*A pause.*) Come on: It's bad enough sliding down that trail by daylight.

VAN. Well, I wouldn't want to make you nervous,
a couple of eminent respectables
like you two—but a dog won't bite a Dutchman—
maybe you've heard that—and the reason is
a Dutchman's poison when he don't like you. Now,
I'm Dutch and I don't like you.

SKIMMERHORN. That's a threat?

VAN. Not at all. Only don't try to eat me or you'll curl up. I'm poison to a hound-dog, and you're both sons-of-bitches.

BIGGS. Come on. (*The daylight is now gone. The airplane beacon lights the scene from the right.*)

VAN. What's more
there's something funny about this mountain-top.
It draws fire. Every storm on the Tappan Zee
climbs up here and wraps itself around

High Tor, and blazes away at what you've got,
airplane beacon, steam-shovels, anything
newfangled. It smashed the beacon twice. It blew
the fuses on your shovel and killed a man
only last week. I've got a premonition
something might happen to you.

BIGGS. God, he's crazy.

SKIMMERHORN. Yeah, let him talk. (*There is a sudden rumbling roar of falling rock.*)

BIGGS. What's that?

VAN. That's nothing much.
That's just a section of the cliff come down
across the trail. I've been expecting it
this last two years. You'd better go down this way.

BIGGS. This way?

VAN. Yeah.

BIGGS. No, thanks.

VAN. Just as you say.
But there's something definitely hostile here
toward you two pirates. Don't try that trail in the dark.
Not if you want to be buried in your vaults
in Mount Repose. Your grieving families
might have to move two thousand tons of rock
to locate your remains. You think High Tor's
just so much raw material, but you're wrong.
A lot of stubborn men have died up here
and some of them don't sleep well. They come back
and push things round, these dark nights. Don't blame me
if anything falls on you.

SKIMMERHORN. Oh, what the hell!
Let's get out of here. (*Another long rumble of falling rock.*)

VAN. Another rock-fall.
Once they start there's likely to be more.
Something hanging round in the dark up here
doesn't like you boys. Not only me.
Better go down this way.

BIGGS. Thanks. (BIGGS *and* SKIMMERHORN *go out to the right.*)

JUDITH. What do you mean?

VAN. I don't know.

JUDITH. They'll say you threatened them. Good-bye, Van.

VAN. You'll be up tomorrow?

JUDITH. No. (*She steps down into a cleft.*)

VAN. You'd better let me see you down.

JUDITH. Oh, no.
I can climb. Stay here and guard your rock—
you think so much of it.

VAN. When will I see you?

JUDITH. Never.
We'll forget about it. You had a choice
and you chose High Tor. You're in love with
   your mountain.
Well, keep your mountain.

VAN. All right.

JUDITH. Good night.

VAN. Good night.
(*She disappears down the rocks.* VAN *sits in
the shadows, looking into darkness. After
a moment a barely perceptible* FIGURE *enters
from the gloom at the right and crosses the
stage toward the rocks at the left. At the foot
of the climb he pauses and his face is caught
in the light of the beacon. He is seen to be
young or middle-aged, bearded, and wearing
the costume of a Dutch sailor of the sixteen
hundreds. He climbs the rocks, and* ANOTHER
SAILOR, *a small cask strapped to his shoulders, follows.* THREE MORE *cross the stage
similarly, then the* CAPTAIN *and* HIS WIFE
*pause, like the others, in the light of the
beacon. The* CAPTAIN *is like his men, only
younger perhaps;* HIS WIFE *is a tiny figure,
with a delicate girlish face looking out from
under the Dutch bonnet. They too pass up
the rocks, and are followed by a rolling*
SILENUS *in the same garments. As they
vanish* VAN *rises, looking after them.*)
Uh—huh—going to rain.

CURTAIN

## SCENE II

SCENE: *The curtain goes up on complete darkness enfolding the summit of the Tor.
There is a long cumbrous rolling, as of a ball going down a bowling alley, a flash of white
light, a crackling as of falling pins and a mutter dying into echo along the hills. The flash
reveals the outline of the Tor, black against the sky, and on it the figures of the* DUTCH
CREW. *Again the roll, the flash, the break and the dying away. The beam of the airplane
beacon steals into the scene sufficiently to suggest the bowlers, some of them standing,
some sitting about the keg, the* CAPTAIN's WIFE *a little apart from the rest. Beyond the
peak is a moving floor, the upper side of blown cloud.*

THE CAPTAIN'S WIFE. I'm weary of it, Martin!
   When you drink
there should be one on guard to watch the
   river
lest the ship come, and pass, and we must
   haunt
the dark another year!

THE CAPTAIN. To humor her,
Pieter, old son, climb down and post the Zee,
and mind you keep good lookout.

PIETER. Ships, aye, ships—
when the ball's rolling and there's gin in
   hand
I go to post. My luck!

THE CAPTAIN. When you shipped with me
you signed the voyage.

PIETER. Is this sea or land?
I'm no foot soldier!

THE CAPTAIN. March!

PIETER. Aye, aye. I'm going. (PIETER *detaches
himself from the group and goes down the
rocks.*)

THE CAPTAIN. Are you content?

THE CAPTAIN'S WIFE. When the *Half Moon*
   returns
and we have boarded her, and the wind
   scuds fair
into the east—yes, when we see the wharves
of Texel town across the Zuyder Zee,
with faces waiting for us, hands and cries
to welcome our returning, then perhaps
I shall be content.

A SAILOR. Now God, for Texel town.

ANOTHER SOLDIER (*rising*). I'll drink no
more.

DEWITT (*the Silenus*). Drink up, lads, and
forget.
It's a long way to the Texel. Drink your
drink
and play your play.

THE CAPTAIN. Drink up and play it out.

THE CAPTAIN'S WIFE. Have you forgotten how
the cobbled street
comes down by cranks and turns upon the
quay,
where the *Onrust* set sail? The traders' doors
under the blowing signs, bright colors hung
to catch unwary eyes? The bakers' ovens
and the long, hot brown loaves? The red-
coal fires
and silver under candles? There your wives
wait for you, their sharp roofs in Amsterdam
cut on a rainy sky.

THE CAPTAIN. Be quiet, Lise.
You were so much in love you must come
with me;
you were so young that I was patient with
you,
but now day long, night long you carp and
quarrel,
a carping wife.

LISE. We stay so long—so long;
Asher, at first the days were years, but now
the years are days; the ship that set us down
to watch this river palisades becomes
alike with supper-stories round a hearth
when we were children. Was there this ship
at all,
was there a sailor-city, Amsterdam,
where the salt water washed the shallow
piers
and the wind went out to sea? Will the ship
return,
and shall I then see the Netherlands once
more,
with sabots clattering homeward from the
school
on winter evenings?

ASHER. Aye, there was a ship,
and we wait here for her, but she's long
away,
somewhere up-river.

LISE. And now you drink and drink,
distill your liquor on the mountain-top
and bowl against the light. But when you
break it
these new strange men come build it up
again;
and giant shovels spade the mountain down,
and when you break them still the new
strange men
rig them afresh and turn them on the rock,
eating the pillored stone. We must go back.
There's no safety here.

A SAILOR. We must go back.

ASHER. These muttering fools!

LISE. Oh, Asher, I'm afraid!
For one thing I have known, and never told
lest it be true, lest you be frightened, too,
lest we be woven of shadow! As the years
have gone, each year a century, they seem
less real, and all the boundaries of time,
our days and nights and hours, merge and
are one,
escaping me. Then sometimes in a morning
when all the crew come down the rocks together,
holding my breath, I see you in the light,
and back of you the gray rock bright and
hard,
seen through figures of air! And you, and
you,
and you were but cloud-drift walking,
pierced by the light,
translucent in the sun.

DEWITT. Now damn the woman!

LISE. Love, love, before our blood
be shadow only, in a dark fairyland
so far from home, we must go back, go back
where earth is earth, and we may live again
and one day be one day!

ASHER. Why, then, I knew it,
and I have known it, now that you know it,
too.
But the old Amsterdam of our farewells
lies in another world. The land and sea
about us on this dark side of the earth
is thick with demons, heavy with enchantment,
cutting us off from home.

LISE. Is it enchantment?
Yes, it may be. At home there were tulips
growing
along my bordered path, but here the flowers

are strange to me, not one I knew, no trace
of any flower I knew; no, seedling set
upon a darkened, alien outer rim
of sea, blown here as we were blown, en-
    chanted,
drunken and blind with sorcery.

ASHER. And yet
what we're to have we shall have here.
    Years past
the demons of this air palsied our hands,
fixed us upon one pinnacle of time,
and on this pinnacle of stone, and all
the world we knew slid backward to the
    gulf,
stranding us here like seaweed on the
    shingle,
remembering the sea. In Texel town
new houses have gone up, after new
    fashions;
the children of the children of our days,
lying awake to think of what has been,
reach doubtfully beyond the clouds of years
back to our sailing out of Texel. Men
are like the gods, work miracles, have power
to pierce the walls with music. Their beacon
    light
destroys us. You have seen us in the sun,
wraithlike, half-effaced, the print we make
upon the air thin tracery, permeable,
a web of wind. They have changed us. We
    may take
the fire-balls of the lightning in our hands
and bowl them down the level floor of cloud
to wreck the beacon, yet there was a time
when these were death to touch. The life we
    keep
is motionless as the center of a storm,
yet while we can we keep it; while we can
snuff out to darkness their bright sweeping
    light,
melt down the harness of the slow machines
that hew the mountain from us. When it
    goes
we shall go too. They leave us this place,
    High Tor,
and we shall have no other. You learn it last.
A long while now we've known.

A SAILOR. Aye, aye, a long while.

ASHER. Come, we'll go down. (*The* CAPTAIN
*and his* MEN *go out, leaving only* DEWITT
*with* LISE.)

LISE. That's why they drink.

DEWITT. It's enough to drive a sailor-man
to drink, by the great jib boom, marooned

somewhere on the hinder parts of the earth
and degenerating hourly to the status of
a flying Dutchman, half-spook and half God-
knows-what. Maps and charts we have, compass and sextant, but the ship these days are
bewitched like ourselves, spanking up and
down the Mauritius with sails struck, against
wind and tide, and on fire from below.
Drink? Why wouldn't we drink? A pewter
flagon of Hollands gin puts manhood into
the remnants and gives a sailor courage to
look out on these fanciful new devils that
ride sea, land and air on a puff of blue
smoke. They're all witches and mermaids,
these new-world devils, dancing around on
bubbles, speaking a language God never
heard, and nothing human about them except when they fall they break like the rest
of us.

LISE. If I had known. It's too late. The sun
still rises in the east and lays a course
toward the old streets and days. These are
    my hands
as when I was a child. Some great magician,
binding a half-world in his wiles, has laid
a spell here. We must break it and go home.
I see this clearly.

DEWITT. Lise, little heart, the devils are too
much for us. God knows it's a hard thing
to say, and I'd help you if I could help myself, but all hell wouldn't know where we
are nor where we ought to go. The very
points of the compass grow doubtful these
latter years, partly because I'm none too
sober and partly because the great master
devil sits on top of the world stirring up
north and south with a long spoon to confuse poor mariners. I've seen him at it, a
horned bull three times the size of Dunden-
berg and with more cloven feet than the
nine beasts in Revelations. Very clearly I saw
him, too, as clear as you see the east and a
path across the waters.

LISE. Are we to wait till all the color steals
from flower and cloud, before our eyes; till
    a wind
out of the morning from the Tappan Zee
lifts us, we are so light, for all our crying,
and takes us down the valleys toward the
    west,
and all we are becomes a voiceless cry
heard on the wind?

DEWITT. We'll see the time, if they continue
to work on us, when we'll be apparent in a

strong light only by the gin contained in our interior piping. The odor itself, along with that of church-warden tobacco, should be sufficient to convince a magistrate of our existence.—You tremble, little Lise, and you weep, but look now, there's a remedy I've had in mind. Fall in love with one of them. Fall in love with one of these same strange new-world magicians. I shall choose me out one of their female mermaid witches, and set my heart on her, and become a man again. And for God's sake let her love me strongly and hold on, lest I go down the brook like a spring freshet in the next pounding rain.

LISE. I gave my love long ago, and it's no help.
I love enough.

DEWITT. Aye, but he's in a worse case than you are, the Captain. Saving his captaincy, there's not enough belief in him to produce half a tear in a passion of sobbing. You'll make me weep, little one, and what tears I have I shall need, lest my protestation turns out to be a dry rain.
LISE. Aye, we were warned before we came away
against the cabalistic words and signs
of those who dwell along these unknown waters;

never to watch them dance nor hear them sing
nor draw their imprecations—lest their powers
weave a weird medicine throughout the air, chilling the blood, transfixing body and mind
and we be chained invisibly, our eyes darkened,
our wrists and breasts pulseless, anchored in time
like birds blown back in a wind. But we have listened,
and we are stricken through with light and sound,
empty as autumn leaves, empty as prayers that drift in a godless heaven. Meaningless, picked clean of meaning, stripped of bone and will,
the chrysalids of locust staring here
at one another.

DEWITT. If it's true it's enough to make a man weep for himself, Lise, and for all lost mariners, wherever they are, and for us more than any, here on these spellbound rocks, drawing up water from time past—the well growing deeper, and the water lower, till there be none. (*He turns to go down the path.*)

CURTAIN

## SCENE III

SCENE: *Another section of the Tor, in darkness save for the airplane beacon. A large steam shovel reaches in from an adjacent excavation and hangs over the rock, the control cables dangling.* VAN *is alone on the stage looking at the machinery. He reaches up, catches a cable, and swings the shovel a little.* BIGGS *and* SKIMMERHORN *enter from the right.*

BIGGS. Hey, what are you doing with that shovel?

VAN. Did you know you're trespassing? Also when a man owns land he owns the air above it and the rock below. That means this damn shovel of yours is also trespassing.

BIGGS. Oh, it's Van Dorn. We'll have that moved tomorrow, Mr. Van Dorn. Somebody's made a miscue and left it hanging over the line.

SKIMMERHORN. By the way, that trail's gone out completely, Mr. Van Dorn; there's a fifty foot sheer drop there now, where it was.

Now we've got to get off, if you can think of any way to manage it.

VAN. I'm not worrying about it. Spend the night. No charge.

SKIMMERHORN. The truth is I have to be in court early tomorrow, and a man needs his sleep.

VAN. Afraid you'd doze off on the bench and somebody else might take a trick? Oh, you'd wake up before they got far with anything. The Skimmerhorns are automatic that way.

BIGGS. You don't know any other trail down?

van. I showed you the one I knew, and you both turned green looking at it. What am I supposed to do now? Pin wings on you? (*He goes out to the right.*)

skimmerhorn. I think I'll swear out a warrant for the squirt. He's too independent by half.

biggs. On what ground?

skimmerhorn. He threatened us, didn't he?

biggs. And where'll that get us?

skimmerhorn. He might be easier to talk to in jail.

biggs. That's true.

skimmerhorn (*sitting on a rock*). This is a hell of a mess.

biggs. You're explaining to me?

skimmerhorn. What did we ever come up here for?

biggs. Twenty-two thousand dollars.

skimmerhorn. Will we get it?

biggs. It'll look all right on the books.

skimmerhorn. It's not good enough, though.

biggs. What are you grousing about?

skimmerhorn. Because I want my dinner, damn it! And because I'm tired of taking forty per cent and giving you sixty on all the side bets! I want half!

biggs. You're a damn sight more likely to get your dinner. You're overpaid already.

skimmerhorn. The will's perfectly good. I could find holes in it, but I've probated plenty much the same.

biggs. What of it?

skimmerhorn. A judge has some conscience, you know. When he sets a precedent he likes to stick to it.

biggs. I never knew your conscience to operate except on a cash basis. You want half.

skimmerhorn. Yes, I want half.

biggs. Well, you don't get it. Any other judge I put in there'd work for nothing but the salary and glad of the job. You take a forty per cent cut and howl for more. The woods are full of shyster lawyers looking for probate judgeships and I'll slip one in at Ledentown next election.

skimmerhorn. Oh, no, you won't, Art; oh, no, you won't. You wouldn't do that to an old friend like me; because if you did, think what I'd do to an old friend like you.

biggs. Well, maybe I wouldn't. Not if you're reasonable. Look, what's the difference between forty per cent and fifty per cent? Practically nothing!

skimmerhorn. Then why don't you give it to me?

biggs. Because, try and get it!—

skimmerhorn. Damn it, I'm hungry.—I ought to telephone my wife, too.

biggs. Why don't you?

skimmerhorn. Maybe it's fun for you— nothing to eat, no place to sleep, cold as hell, black as Tophet and a storm coming up! Only I'm not used to it!

biggs. You're pulling down forty per cent of twenty-two thousand dollars for the night's work. I say it's worth it.

skimmerhorn. Think we could slide down one of those cables?

biggs. Maybe you could, Humpty-Dumpty, but not me.

skimmerhorn. I'm going to look at it. (*He goes out left,* biggs *following. After a moment* THREE MEN *climb in through the rocks at the right, one of them carrying a small zipper satchel. They throw themselves down wearily on the rock. They are, in brief, the Nanuet bank robbers,* ELKUS, DOPE *and* BUDDY.)

dope. God, I got no wind. (*A siren is heard faintly, far down on the road.*)

elkus. Sons a' bitches a' troopers.

dope. What'd you want to wreck the car for?

elkus. Want to get caught with the stuff on you?

buddy. We'll get four hundred years for this

elkus. Shut up!

DOPE. You didn't need to wreck the car, though.

ELKUS. Didn't you hear the trooper slam on the brakes when he went by? You'd be wearing bracelets right now if I hadn't dumped the old crate over the embankment! The way it is he thinks he's following us, and he'll blow that fire alarm all the way to Bear Mountain Bridge. Only hope he meets something solid head-on at ninety miles an hour.

DOPE. What I want to know is where we go from here.

ELKUS. Down the other side and pick up a car. (*The siren is heard receding.*)

BUDDY. We'll get four hundred years for this.

ELKUS. What do you think you are, a chorus? Go on back to St. Thomas's and sing it to the priest. You're about as much help as a flat tire.

BUDDY. I never wanted to be in it. I was only lookout—you're both witness to that.

ELKUS. What good do you think that does you, you poor fish? Brace up and take it like a man. There's twenty-five thousand in that bag and some of it's yours.

DOPE. How do you know it's twenty-five thousand?

ELKUS. It's the Orangeburg pay roll. (BUDDY *looks off left.*)

BUDDY. Before God, it's Judge Skimmerhorn!

ELKUS. What? Where?

BUDDY. There. Coming round the rocks. Judge Skimmerhorn of Ledentown.

ELKUS. Does he know you?

BUDDY. Sure, he knows me.

ELKUS. We're out climbing, see? Hikers, see? On a picnic. (*They stand.* ELKUS *holds the satchel behind him casually.* BIGGS *and* SKIMMERHORN *come in.*)

BIGGS. Hello.

ELKUS. How are you?

BIGGS. Out walking?

ELKUS. That's right. Climbed up on a bet.

SKIMMERHORN. Isn't that Buddy?

BUDDY. Yes, sir. Evening, Judge.

SKIMMERHORN. You're a long way from home.

BUDDY. Yes, sir.

BIGGS. Think you could show us a way down? We're stuck up here.

BUDDY. There's a path down the cliff. Yes, sir.

SKIMMERHORN. No, thanks. I saw that one. Going to camp here?

ELKUS. Might as well. Sure.

SKIMMERHORN. Bring anything to eat?

ELKUS. Matter of fact, we didn't. (*He sets the satchel down behind the rock, unobtrusively.*)

SKIMMERHORN. Not a thing?

ELKUS. Not a thing.

SKIMMERHORN. That's funny. Camping wtih nothing to eat.

ELKUS. Yeah, it is kinda funny.

DOPE. We ate before we started. (*He smiles cunningly.*)

ELKUS. That's right. The Dope's right for once. We ate before we started.

SKIMMERHORN. Wish I had.

BUDDY. You—you staying up here tonight, sir?

SKIMMERHORN. Seems that way. We came up looking for somebody.

ELKUS. Looking for somebody?

SKIMMERHORN. That's what I said.

ELKUS. Who was it?

BIGGS. That's our business.

ELKUS. I see.

SKIMMERHORN (*coming near the three*). Listen, Buddy, you're young and ambitious. Would you do something for me if you got well paid?

BUDDY. I guess so, Judge.

SKIMMERHORN (*sitting on the rock and incidentally over the satchel*). We're done in, traipsing around the rocks. Would you climb down the Tor and get to Haverstraw and telephone my wife I can't come home?

BUDDY. I guess so, wouldn't I, Elkus?

ELKUS. Up to you.

SKIMMERHORN. And while you're there will you buy a dozen sandwiches and some beer?

BUDDY. Yes, sir.

SKIMMERHORN. There's another thing you could do. Call up the state troopers for me, and tell them I'm here and I want them to ome up and make an arrest.

BUDDY. You—want to arrest somebody?

SKIMMERHORN. You get it. What do you say?

BUDDY. I—I guess so. Is it all right, Elkus?

DOPE. Oh—no. Oh—no.

ELKUS. Sure it's O.K. Why not?

BUDDY. It'd take about five hours—to get down and back.

SKIMMERHORN. Damn it—I'll starve to death.

DOPE. What do you want to make an arrest for?

BIGGS. That's our business.

BUDDY. All right. I'll go.

SKIMMERHORN. Here's five dollars for you. And another when you get back. And make it fast, will you?

BUDDY. Yes, sir. (*He starts out right.*)

ELKUS. Just a minute, Bud. (ELKUS *and* DOPE *follow* BUDDY *out to converse with him.*)

BIGGS. You might have made it two dozen sandwiches.

SKIMMERHORN. I guess I will. (*He starts to rise, places his hand on the satchel, and jumps.*) Christ, what's that? (*He kicks the satchel, then flips it up into the rocks.*)

BIGGS. Yeah?

SKIMMERHORN. I thought it was a snake. Somebody's mouldy luggage. People are always throwing truck around. (*He calls.*) Say, for God's sake, get started, will you?

BUDDY (*outside*). Yes, sir. Right away. (ELKUS *and* DOPE *return.*)

ELKUS. I guess we'll all go. (*He looks nonchalantly where the satchel was.*)

SKIMMERHORN. Fine. Will you make it two dozen sandwiches?

ELKUS. What the hell's going on here?

SKIMMERHORN. We're hungry, that's all.

ELKUS. Are you two finnegling with us? Because if you are—!

BIGGS. What are you looking for?

ELKUS. Nothing. Who said I was looking for anything?

DOPE. Hey, Elkus! They got the troopers up here!
(DEWITT's *broad Dutch hat appears above the rocks in the rear, looking, for the moment, remarkably like that of a state trooper.* ELKUS *and* DOPE *freeze, looking at it.*)

ELKUS (*drawing a gun*). Why, you fat pimps! (DEWITT *disappears.*)

DOPE. Beat it, you fool! (ELKUS *and* DOPE *scatter out to the right.*)

BIGGS (*looking at the rocks*). What was all that about?

SKIMMERHORN. I hope they bring those sandwiches. (*He also stares toward the rear.*)

BIGGS. Sandwiches? They're not bringing sandwiches for anybody, those two. (*He calls.*) Hey! Hey, you! Anybody there?— What did he mean by troopers?

SKIMMERHORN. Want to take a look?

BIGGS. I'm plenty unhappy, right where I am. (SKIMMERHORN *climbs up on the rocks.*)

SKIMMERHORN. Wish to God I did see a trooper.

BIGGS. Nobody there?

SKIMMERHORN. Not a thing. Hey! Hey, you! (*A silence.*) Nope. Nobody.

BIGGS. Looks to me as if we just missed being stuck up by a couple of lunatics.

SKIMMERHORN. If I can't eat I'm going to sleep.

BIGGS. Maybe you've never tried adjusting yourself to igneous limestone.

SKIMMERHORN. I'm about to try it now.

BIGGS. You have my sympathy. (SKIMMERHORN *stretches out on the rock, takes off his coat for a pillow and lies down.*)

SKIMMERHORN. Thanks.

BIGGS. Beautiful shape you have. A lot of slop tied up with a piece of string.

SKIMMERHORN (*sitting up*). God it's cold.. Listen, we could use one coat for a pillow and put the other one over us.

BIGGS. What other one?

SKIMMERHORN. Yours.

BIGGS. A proposition, huh?

SKIMMERHORN. You going to sit up all night?

BIGGS. In some ways it might be preferable.

SKIMMERHORN. You can't prop yourself on end forever, like a duck on a rock.

BIGGS. Pull yourself together, then. You stick out behind like a bump on a duck. All right. Move over.

SKIMMERHORN. Your coat's bigger than mine. (*They pull* BIGG's *coat around them and lie down.*)

BIGGS. Just a couple of perfect forty-nines. Where the hell am I supposed to put my hip bone?

SKIMMERHORN. You juggle your own hip bones. (DEWITT *appears on the rocks at the rear, looking down.*)

BIGGS. If you snore, you probate judge, I'll have you disbarred.

SKIMMERHORN. Go to sleep.

BIGGS. Wish I thought I could. On bed rock. Wake me early, mother dear.

SKIMMERHORN. Shut up.

(DEWITT *meanwhile has opened the satchel and now brings it down into the light to examine the contents. He sits down, takes out five packets of bills, shakes the satchel, then begins to go through the inner pockets. He finds a roll of pennies, which he breacks open into his hands.*)

DEWITT. Copper pieces, by the great jib boom, enough to purchase a new wig, if a man ever got back to a place where money was useful to him. A counting-house full of them wouldn't buy a ship from one of these semi-demi-demi-semi-devils, so that's no good. (*Two snores rise in concert from* BIGGS *and* SKIMMERHORN. DEWITT *goes over to them, dropping the money.*) What kind of demi-semi-devil do you think you are, with four legs and two faces, both looking the same direction? Jesu Maria, it's a kind of centaur, as big one way as another, no arms, and feet the size of dishpans.

BIGGS. What's that?

DEWITT (*backing away*). It's the rear end that talks, evidently, the front being fast asleep in the manner of a figure-head.

BIGGS. Who's there? Did somebody speak?

DEWITT. None too clear in the back thinker, I should say, which would be a natural result of lugging two sets of brains, fore and aft. I'd incline to communicate with the front end, but if necessary I'll converse with the posterior.

BIGGS (*sitting up, looking at* DEWITT). Skimmerhorn!

SKIMMERHORN. What's the matter?

BIGGS. I'm damned if I know.

SKIMMERHORN. Go to sleep, then.

BIGGS. Do you believe in apparitions?

SKIMMERHORN. No.

BIGGS. Well, there's a figure of fun sitting talking to me, right out of a masquerade ball.

SKIMMERHORN. You been drinking?

BIGGS. What would I find to drink?

DEWITT. If the forecastle wakes now I shall play both ends against the middle, like a marine auctioneer. I want to buy a boat.

BIGGS. You've come to the wrong shop, sailor. I'm in the real-estate business, and it's a long mile down to sea level. (SKIMMERHORN *sits up suddenly.*)

DEWITT. You have no boats?

BIGGS. No boats.

SKIMMERHORN. What in the hell?—

BIGGS. I told you I'm damned if I know.

DEWITT. And the front end has no boats?

BIGGS. You're the front end, see. He wants to know if you've got boats.

SKIMMERHORN. No, stranger, no boats.

DEWITT. Ah. (*He shakes his head mournfully, turns him about and goes to the right, still muttering.*) The great plague on them, the lying, two-headed fairies out of a witch's placket. What chance has an honest man against a two-faced double-tongued beast, telling the same tale — (*He disappears through the rocks.*)

BIGGS. Did you see what I saw?

SKIMMERHORN. Not if you saw what I saw. What I saw wasn't possible.—Did you fake that thing?

BIGGS. Fake it? I saw it.

SKIMMERHORN. Oh, no—! Nobody saw that —what I saw. I didn't either. I've got a family to support. They aren't going to put me away anywhere.

BIGGS. Whatever it was, it left a calling card. Looks as if he ate his lunch here, supposing a thing like that eats lunch. Maybe he left some for us.

SKIMMERHORN. I don't want any of that.

BIGGS (*rising and turning the package over with his foot*). There's something in it.

SKIMMERHORN. Help yourself.

BIGGS (*opening a package, tossing the cover away*). You know what this is?

SKIMMERHORN. Probably a sheaf of contracts with the devil, all ready to sign.

BIGGS. No, it's money.

SKIMMERHORN. Money! (*He leaps to his feet.*)

BIGGS. Fives and tens. (*He opens another package.* SKIMMERHORN *does the same.*)

SKIMMERHORN. Well, bless the poor little Dutchman's heart—after all we said about him, too!

BIGGS. Think he left it?

SKIMMERHORN. It wasn't there before.

BIGGS. No.

SKIMMERHORN. Were you born with a caul, or anything?

BIGGS. Always before I had to work for it, or steal it. Never till tonight have I been waked up by a little man in a big hat, fetching it to me in packages.

SKIMMERHORN. Are you asleep?

SKIMMERHORN. If you're dreaming, you're dreaming that I found money.

BIGGS. Oh, you found it now?

SKIMMERHORN. Fifty-fifty.

BIGGS. Wait a minute. You know what money this is?

SKIMMERHORN. No. (BIGGS *picks up a discarded envelope.*)

BIGGS. It came out of the Nanuet bank. (SKIMMERHORN *takes the envelope from him.*)

SKIMMERHORN. If that little guy's a bank robber he's certainly careless with the proceeds.

BIGGS. That's where it came from.

SKIMMERHORN. In that case we ought to give it back. For the reward.

BIGGS. No reward offered yet.

SKIMMERHORN. Maybe we ought to give it back anyway.

BIGGS. Think so?

SKIMMERHORN. Might be marked bills.

BIGGS. No, it's not. I was talking with the president of the bank on the 'phone. Made up for a pay roll. No marks on any of it.

SKIMMERHORN. It ought to be returned, though.

BIGGS. Sure, it should. Question is, will it be?

SKIMMERHORN. I think so, don't you?

BIGGS. I'm inclined to think so. Bank robbing's away out of my line.

SKIMMERHORN. Mine, too, as a matter of fact. The president of the bank's a friend of yours?

BIGGS. Yes, he is, in a way. Oh, he's gypped me a couple of times, same as you would.

SKIMMERHORN. He wouldn't lose anything.

BIGGS. Oh, no, he's insured.

SKIMMERHORN. Has it occurred to you the little Dutchman that was here might not mean any good to us?

BIGGS. Did you see a little Dutchman?

SKIMMERHORN. I thought I did, there for a minute.

BIGGS. I don't believe that any more.

SKIMMERHORN. Certainly doesn't sound very likely.

BIGGS. We'd better count it. Man never ought to carry money around without knowing how much it is.

SKIMMERHORN. Yeah, let's count it. It said twenty-five thousand in the paper.

BIGGS. You know, nobody in the world would ever know who had it?

SKIMMERHORN. No, they wouldn't.

BIGGS. What do you say?

SKIMMERHORN. I say fifty-fifty.

BIGGS. Damn you, Skimmerhorn, if I hadn't been in business with you for twenty years I'd say you were a crook!

SKIMMERHORN. If I wasn't a crook after twenty years with you I'd be slow in the head and hard of hearing!

BIGGS. What's fifty per cent of twenty-five thousand? Twelve thousand five hundred? And what's forty per cent? Ten thousand! Are you going to hold up the deal for two thousand five hundred?

SKIMMERHORN. I certainly am.

BIGGS. All right, take it. Fifty-fifty on this one deal.

SKIMMERHORN. And on the Van Dorn deal, too.

BIGGS. Why, you fat louse—(VAN DORN *comes in from the right out of the shadows.*)

VAN. Sorry to bother you, gentlemen, but—

BIGGS (*as they stuff the bills into their pockets*). Where the hell did you come from?

VAN. Why, you re not friends of mine, but there's a storm blowing in and it occurred to me I might show you where you could keep dry under a ledge.

BIGGS. Thanks. Much obliged.

VAN. Want me to go with you?

BIGGS. No, thanks—Let's get a little nearer the light.

SKIMMERHORN. Good idea.
(BIGGS *and* SKIMMERHORN *go out right.* VAN *looks after them, then picks up one of the discarded envelopes and studies it. He sits.* LISE *comes up the rocks in the rear and stands looking out to the river, shading her eyes from the beacon.*)

LISE. You who have watched this river in the past
till your hope turned bitterness, pity me now,
my hope gone, but no power to keep my eyes
from the mocking water. The hills come down like sand,
and the long barges bear them off to town,
to what strange market in what stranger town,
devouring mountains? but never, in all days,
never, though I should watch here without rest,
will any ship come downward with the tide
flying the flag we knew. (VAN *rises.* LISE *draws back an instant, then comes down a step toward him.*)
Do you hear my voice?

VAN. Yes, lady.

LISE. Do you see me in the light,
as I see you?

VAN. Yes.

LISE. You are one of those
the earth bears now, the quick, fierce wizard men
who plow the mountains down with steel, and set
new mountains in their sky. You've come to drive
machines through the white rock's heart.

VAN. Not I. I haven't.
I hate them all like poison.

LISE. You're against them—
the great machines?

VAN. I'd like to smash the lot,
and the men that own them.

LISE. Oh, if there were a friend
among so many enemies! I wish
I knew how to make you friend. But now
  my voice
shrinks back in me, reluctant, a cold thing,
fearing the void between us.—I have seen
  you.
I know you. You are kind.

VAN. How do you know?

LISE. When I have been most lonely in the
  spring,
the spring rain beating with my heart, I
  made
a wild flower garden; none of these I knew,
for none I knew are here, flowers of the
  woods,
little and lovely, nameless. One there was
like a pink moccasin, another low
with blotted leaves, wolf-toothed, and many
  more
rooted among the fern. I saw you then
come on this garden, secret as the tears
wept for lost days, and drew my breath in
  dread
that you should laugh and trample it. You
  smiled
and then went on. But when I came again
there was a new flower growing with the
  rest,
one I'd not seen. You brought and placed
  it there
only for love of gardens, ignorant whose
the garden you enriched. What was this
  flower?

VAN. Wild orchid. It was your garden?

LISE. Yes. You know
the names of all the flowers?

VAN. Yes.

LISE. But then
you'd teach them to me?

VAN. Yes.

LISE. Teach me the names.
What is the tall three-petaled one that's black
almost, the red's so dark?

VAN. That's trillium.
Speaking of flowers, tell me your name.

LISE. It's Lise,
or used to be.

VAN. Not now?

LISE. I'm weary of it,
and all things that I've been. You have a
  lover?
She'll be angry?

VAN. She's angry now. She's off
and gone. She won't come back.

LISE. Love me a little,
enough to save me from the dark. But if
you cannot give me love, find me a way!
The seas lie black between your harbor
  town
and mine, but your ships are quick. If I
  might see
the corner where the three streets come to
  an end
on sundial windows, there, a child by a
  fire—
no, but it's gone!

VAN. I've seen you on the hills
moving with shadows. But you're not
  shadow.

LISE. No.
Could one live and be shadow?

VAN. Take my hand.

LISE. I dare not.

VAN. Come, let me see your garden.

LISE. No.
I dare not. It is your race that thins our
  blood
and gathers round, besieging us with charms
to stay the feet of years. But I know you
  kind.—
Love me a little. Never put out your hand
to touch me, lest some magic in your blood
reach me, and I be nothing. What I am
I know not, under these spells, if I be cloud
or dust. Nor whether you dream of me, or I
make you of light and sound. Between this
  stone
and the near constellations of the stars
I go and come, doubting now whence I
  come
or when I go. Cling to me. Keep me still.
Be gentle. You were gentle with the
  orchid—

VAN. You're cold.

LISE. Yes.

VAN. Here on the Tor
the sun beats down like murder all day long
and the wind comes up like murder in the
night.
I'm cold myself.

LISE. How have I slipped so far
from the things you have? I'm puzzled
here and lost.
Is it so different for you? Keep my hand
and tell me. In these new times are all men
shadow?
All men lost?

VAN. Sometimes I stand here at night
and look out over the river when a fog
covers the light. Then if it's dark enough
and I can't see my hands or where the rock
leaves off against the cloud, and I'm alone,
then, well I'm damned if I know who I am,
staring out into that black. Maybe I'm cloud
and maybe I'm dust. I might be old as time.
I'd like to think I knew. A man gets that
way
standing staring at darkness.

LISE. Then—you do know.
It's better now.—Somewhere along a verge
where your life dips in dusk and my gray
days
lift to the light a moment, we walk there
and our eyes meet.—Look, when the wizards
come
to tear the mountain down, I'll have no
place.
I'll be gone then.

VAN. Child, they won't get our mountain!
Not if I have to shoot them as they come
they won't get our mountain! The mountain's mine,
and you're to make your garden where you
like;
their feet won't step across it! All their
world's
made up of fat men doing tricks with laws
to manage tides and root up hills. The hills
can afford to laugh at them. A race of grubs
bred down from men!

LISE. Is it the light I feel
come flooding back in me? Light or their
charms
broken here, seeing your face?

VAN. Your hands are warm.

LISE. I'm not cold now; for an instant I'm
not cold,
seeing your face. This is your wizardry.
Let me stand here and see you.

ELKUS (outside). Somewhere around here
it was. Over toward the crane.

DOPE (outside). What's you go and put
down the satchel for?

ELKUS (outside). How did I know he'd sit
on top of it? (VAN and LISE slip out through
the rocks at the rear. ELKUS and DOPE come
in furtively from the right.)

DOPE. That's where. Under that rock.

ELKUS. Keep your eye peeled. They're probably beating the woods for us.

DOPE. What's that? (He picks up an envelope.)

ELKUS. They got it.

DOPE. God damn the rotten business! Now
we will get four hundred years.

ELKUS. Now you're saying it—

DOPE. What are we going to do?

ELKUS. I'm going to send Buddy back with
sandwiches to see if the Judge got the
money. If he did we'll stick him up.

DOPE. Hey, how about the troopers?

ELKUS. If that was troopers I'm Admiral
Dewey. Troopers would a' used the artillery.
Come on.

DOPE. O.K. Some pennies here.

ELKUS. To hell with 'em. (DOPE flings the
pennies to the left along the ledge.)

DOPE. Get going. (ELKUS and DOPE go out
right. BIGGS and SKIMMERHORN come in along
the ledge.)

BIGGS. Now it's raining money. I got the
price of a morning paper square in the eye.

SKIMMERHORN. I've got two thousand five
hundred in a breast pocket, five thousand
in a side pocket, and five thousand in the
billfold. (He slaps his rear.) How do I look?

BIGGS. No different. Just a lot of slop tied
up with string. I've got five thousand in
each side pocket and two thousand five
hundred in the back. How do I look?

SKIMMERHORN. You? All you need now's a pair of wings.

BIGGS. Wish I could find the little guy with the big heart that gave us the money. Maybe he'd help us down off this devil's belfry.

SKIMMERHORN. How about that shovel? Any possibility of making it pick us up and set us down below there?

BIGGS. Well—if anybody was running it, sure. If it swung us over on that dump we could slide the rest of the way. You might wear out that last five thousand of yours, the five thousand that's bringing up the rear there.

SKIMMERHORN. When do they come to work in the morning?

BIGGS. They won't come to work tomorrow. They can't do any more till we buy this land.

SKIMMERHORN. That's fine. That's just dandy.

BIGGS. Nice idea though. Somebody might come along that could run the engine.

SKIMMERHORN. You don't think that boy's coming back with the sandwiches?

BIGGS. No, I don't.

SKIMMERHORN. The way I feel inside I may never live to spend the money.

BIGGS. Who you going to leave it to?

SKIMMERHORN. Yeah?

BIGGS. Oh, all right. Nothing personal. (*They sit facing the audience. The* CAPTAIN *and* HIS CREW, *including* DEWITT, *seep in through the rocks about them and stand quietly looking on.*) There was something in that—what you said about needing a pair of wings.

SKIMMERHORN. I should say that wings was the last thing likely to grow on you. You might grow horns, or a cloven hoof, or a tail, but wings, no. Not unless somebody slipped up behind you and bashed you over the head.

BIGGS. You know, you'd murder me for what I've got in my pockets?

SKIMMERHORN. You thought of it first. Who am I going to leave it to, you said.

BIGGS. Just the same I wouldn't feel right if you were standing behind me with a rock in your hand. (*The* CREW *move in a little.*)

SKIMMERHORN. You wouldn't?

BIGGS. No. At the moment I wouldn't like to think anybody was creeping up behind me. (*He stiffens.*) And by God there is somebody behind me.

SKIMMERHORN (*without turning*). What makes you think so?

BIGGS (*running a hand over his hair*). I just feel it. Turn around, will you? Take a look.

SKIMMERHORN (*shivering*). I will not.—Now you've got me worried.—Or else I'm getting light-headed for lack of food.

(BIGGS *ducks suddenly, as if from an imaginary blow.* SKIMMERHORN *dodges in sympathy, and with their heads drawn in like turtles they creep forward on hands and knees.*)

BIGGS. See anything?

SKIMMERHORN. There's nothing there, you ass! What are you dodging? Want to scare me to death? Go on, turn around and face it like a man!

BIGGS. Now!

SKIMMERHORN. Now! (*They whirl in concert, on their knees, facing the* CREW. *They look at each other.*)

BIGGS. You're crazy!

SKIMMERHORN. I certainly am. And so are you.

BIGGS. That isn't there at all. There's nothing there.

SKIMMERHORN. All right, you go up and hit it. I'll stay right here, and you go punch it in the nose. (BIGGS *stands up.*)

BIGGS. Uh—how do you do?—Maybe you—wanted to give us something, huh? (*To* DEWITT.) Uh—I see you brought your friends with you.—If you want the money back you can have it, you know. We don't want the money. (*He sticks a hand in his pocket.*) How much was it now? (*The* CREW *look at each other gravely, tapping their foreheads.*

SKIMMERHORN *rises.*) Anything we could do, you know, we'd be glad to do. We're just trying to get down off here.

SKIMMERHORN. You know what it is, Art; it's a moving picture company. And have they got the laugh on us? Thinking they're real. It's all right, boys, we're onto you.

BIGGS. Is that so? Say, I guess that's so. Was that moving picture money, you gave us, you fellows? We thought that was real. Ha ha! That's a good one. I guess you must have thought we were pretty funny, backing up that way and jumping around. You had us scared stiff! (*The* CREW *shake their heads at each other.*)

SKIMMERHORN. Come on, now, you aren't bluffing us at all. We've seen the pictures work over at Suffern. We were right out on location there with actors and producers and everything. Some of those girls didn't care whether they wore clothes or not. You're probably used to that where you come from, but I certainly got a kick out of pictures. Fifty chorus girls changing clothes in the bushes over there. (*A silence.* DEWITT *goes over to the* CAPTAIN *and whispers in his ear.*)

ASHER. Lay a hand to it. (DEWITT *catches hold of the dangling cable.*)

DEWITT. Lay a hand to it, lads. Heave. (*The* CREW *catch the rope and haul on it, sailorfashion. The shovel begins to descend.*)

THE CREW (*pulling down*). Heave! Heave! Heave! Heave!
Coming a blow, coming a blow;
Sea runs black; glass runs low;
Heave! Heave!
Yardarm dips; foam's like snow!
Heave! (*The shovel touches ground.*)

BIGGS. Say, that's an act if I ever saw one. What kind of picture you putting on? (*The* CAPTAIN *points to the interior of the shovel, looking at* BIGGS *and* SKIMMERHORN.) What's up, anyway? Want us to go aboard? You know, we were just saying if somebody could run that thing we might get across to the dump and slide down out of here. Think you could swing it across there? (*The* SAILORS *maneuver behind the two, edging them into the machine.*) You might haul us up there and not be able to get us down, you know. It's mighty friendly of you to try it, but you'll have your work

cut out. Sure, I'll get in. I'll try anything once. (*He steps in,* SKIMMERHORN *follows reluctantly. The* CAPTAIN *and* DEWITT *guard their retreat. The* SAILORS *catch hold of the cable.*) Take it easy, now.

THE CREW. Hoist! Hoist! Hoist! Hoist!
Tar on a rope's end, man on a yard.
Wind through an eye-bolt, points on a card;
Hoist! Hoist!
Weevil in the biscuit, rats in the lard,
Hoist!

(*They haul the two up as far as seems necessary, and swing the crane out over the abyss. Then they stop to contemplate their handiwork.*)

BIGGS. I'll tell you what—if you catch that line over there some of you can hold back while the rest pull and that'll swing it around.—If that don't work you'd better pull it down again and we'll just wait till morning. (*The* CREW *continue to stare silently.*)

SKIMMERHORN. I'm getting sick at my stomach, boys; you better make it snappy. It gives me the megrims to look down this way. (*He draws his feet up suddenly.*)

BIGGS. Hey, don't rock the boat, you fool! It's a thousand miles straight down!

SKIMMERHORN. I'm going to be sick.

BIGGS. You better take us down, fellows. It's no good. You can't make it.

DEWITT. How about a game of bowls? (*The* CAPTAIN *nods.*)

PIETER. Aye, a game of bowls. (*Led by the* CAPTAIN, *the* CREW *begin to file out.*)

BIGGS. Hey, you wouldn't leave us up here, would you? Hey, listen! You! You can have that money back, you know! We don't want the money! What in the name of time?— Listen, what did we ever do to you?— A joke's a joke, after all, but this thing might let go any minute! What's more you're responsible if anything happens to us! There's such a thing as laws in this country! (*But they have all gone.*)

SKIMMERHORN. I'm sick.

BIGGS. You'll be sicker before you're out of this mess.—What do you think they meant by that?

SKIMMERHORN. I don't know.—Quit kicking me, will you? I'm sick.

BIGGS. Well, keep it to yourself.

SKIMMERHORN. I wish I thought I could.

BIGGS. Help, somebody! Help! We're stuck up here!

SKIMMERHORN. What good's that going to do?

BIGGS. You don't think they'll leave us here, do you?

SKIMMERHORN. I don't know. I don't care. I wish I was dead!—Say, keep away from me, will you? What are you trying to do, pick my pocket?

BIGGS. Pick your pocket, you fish? All I ask is keep your feet out of my face.

SKIMMERHORN. Well, where in hell's my billfold?

BIGGS. How do I know? Do you think I took it?

SKIMMERHORN. Come on, now. Where is it? (*He searches his clothes frantically.*)

BIGGS. You're probably sitting on it.—You are sitting on it. There it is.

SKIMMERHORN (*finding it*). Jeez, I might have lost it.

BIGGS. Now you'd better count it. Just to make sure it's good.

SKIMMERHORN. I think I will. (*He begins to count the bills.*) It's good money, Art. Look at it.

BIGGS. Not a bad idea, either. (*He takes out money and counts it. There is a flash, a long roll and a crash of thunder. Then another and another.*) Isn't that coming pretty close?

SKIMMERHORN. What?

BIGGS. The lightning, you fool! Put your money away before you get it wet. You know what I think?

SKIMMERHORN. No.

BIGGS. There's something up there taking pot shots at us.

SKIMMERHORN. There's one thing about money you find. You don't have to pay income tax on it.

BIGGS. That's true. (*There is a terrific flash, a crash, and the stage is in darkness.*) That one got the beacon! (*Another flash runs right down the crane.*) Good God, will you quit that? That's close enough!—Say, do you know any prayers?

SKIMMERHORN. I know one.

BIGGS. Say it, will you?

SKIMMERHORN. Matthew, Mark, Luke and John,
Bless the bed that I lie on.

BIGGS. That's not much good, that one.

SKIMMERHORN. It's the only one I know.— Hey, catch it—hey!

BIGGS. What? (*The lightning is now an almost perpetual illumination, the thunder a constant roll.*)

SKIMMERHORN. I dropped fourteen ten dollar bills!

BIGGS. Do you know we're going to die here?

SKIMMERHORN. We're going to what?

BIGGS. Will you quit counting money? We're going to be killed! We're going to die right here in our own steam shovel!

SKIMMERHORN. Oh, no. I can't die now. I'm not ready to die!

BIGGS. I wish you'd put up your money, then, and pray!

SKIMMERHORN. I don't know how to pray. (*A crash.*)

BIGGS (*on his knees*). Oh, God, I never did this before, and I don't know how, but keep me safe here and I'll be a better man! I'll put candles on the altar, yes, I'll get that Spring Valley church fixed up, the one that's falling down! I can do a lot for you if you let me live! Oh, God—(*A crash.*)

SKIMMERHORN (*on his knees, his hands full of money*). Oh, God, you wouldn't do a thing like that, hang us up in our own steam shovel, wet through, and then strike us with lightning! Oh, God, you've been kind to us tonight, and given us things we never expected to get so easy; don't spoil it now!—God damn it, there goes another batch of bills! (*He snatches at the falling money, and is hauled back by* BIGGS.) I don't know how to pray! What makes you think there's anybody up there, anyway? (*Another crash.*)

BIGGS. Say the one you know then, for God's sake—say it!

SKIMMERHORN. Matthew, Mark, Luke and John,
Bless the bed that I lie on!

BIGGS. Matthew, Mark, Luke and John,
Bless the bed—Oh, God, I've got an old

mother dependent on me; please let me live! Why don't you tell him you'll give the money back?

SKIMMERHORN. Because I won't! And you won't, either! (*A crash.*)

BIGGS. Now you've done it! Can't you keep anything to yourself? There's such a thing as being politic, even when you're talking to God Almighty! (*Thunder again.*)

CURTAIN

# ACT TWO

## SCENE I

SCENE: *The Tor and the steam shovel as before, only five or six hours later. It's still pitch dark, and* BIGGS *and* SKIMMERHORN *are still in the shovel. They are, however, fast asleep in much the same postures they took formerly on the ground. Under the shovel sits* DEWITT, *picking up and smoothing on his knee a few bills which he has found blowing loose on the rock. The beacon light flashes into the scene.*

DEWITT. There comes on the light again, too, the sweeping light that withers a body's entrails. No sooner out than lit again.—(*Two snores rise from the sleeping pair.*) Aye, take your ease and rest, you detachable Doppelgangers, swollen with lies, protected by the fiends, impervious to lightning, shedding rain like ducks—and why wouldn't you shed rain? your complexions being pure grease and your insides blubber? You can sleep, you can rest. You of the two-bottoms. You make nothing of the lightning playing up and down your backbones, or turning in on cold iron, but a poor sailor out of Holland, what rest has he?—(*He smooths a bill.*) These will be tokens and signs, these will, useful in magic, potent to ward off evil or put a curse on your enemies. Devil's work or not, I shall carry them on me, and make myself a match for these fulminating latter-day spirits. (*He pouches the bills.*) I'm hanged if it's not noticeable at once, a sort of Dutch courage infused into the joints and tissues from the mere pocketing up of their infernal numbered papers. (*He takes out a bill and looks at it.*) That's sorcery, that's witchcraft, that's black art for you— that's a trick after the old one's heart; why, this stuff would make a man out of a cocked hat and a pair of crutches! (*He slaps his

chest.*) Now I shall face destiny and take it like a pinch of snuff! Which reminds me I could use a pinch of snuff. (*He takes out his snuffbox.*) Snuff? When have I reached for snuff? It would seem to me I haven't gone after snuff in something like two hundred years! (*He ladles into both nostrils and sneezes violently.*) Aha, DeWitt! You're a man and a devil! And what shall we wish for now that we have wishing papers in the pockets of our pantaloons? What but a woman, one of these new female furies of theirs, wearing pants like a man, and with nothing to indicate her sex but the general conformation! (*He draws out bills.*) Let my woman appear, god of the numbered papers, and let her wear what she likes, so long as a man can make out how she's made. Let her appear within this next three minutes, for God knows how long this mood will last in an old man! (*He takes another pinch of snuff.*)Aha! Destiny, present occasions! (BUDDY *enters carrying beer and sandwiches.*)

BUDDY. Hello.

DEWITT. What answer would a man make to that now? That's a strange greeting.

BUDDY. Seen a couple of old fat men around anywhere?

DEWITT. Boy, I have seen nothing else all night.

BUDDY. Where are they?

DEWITT. You wish to find a couple of old fat men?

BUDDY. That's right.

DEWITT. I begin to doubt the supernal powers of these new angel-demons. Here he stands in their presence and asks very foolishly if old DeWitt has seen them.

BUDDY. What's foolish about that?

DEWITT. A very cheap, witless little cabin boy unless all signs fail. One who carries packages and lives very badly by the day on half a skilling. A cabin boy.

BUDDY. What's the matter with you?

DEWITT. What do you carry in the bag?

BUDDY. That's my business.

DEWITT. He has a business then. He is not perhaps so witless as he appears.

BUDDY. Are you going to tell me where those two are or do you want me to blow your brains out?

DEWITT. Is my carcass so thin you think to puff my brains out with a breath? Look, 'prentice devil, I am one of you. I bear your signs and symbols. Here you see your own countersign, a cabalistic device of extreme rarity and force. What have you in the bag?

BUDDY. Nothing but sandwiches. What do you mean, you're one of us?

DEWITT (*waving a sheaf of bills*). You should recognize the insignium.

BUDDY. Where'd you get it?

DEWITT. It blew away from these same two fat men, 'prentice devil, but now I have it, and it's mine and I obtain power over you. Let me see these sandwiches.

BUDDY. It blew away from the fat men, huh? All right, that's what I want to know. It's mine, see? Hand it over.

DEWITT. You reveal yourself a very young and tender 'prentice.

BUDDY. Hand it over or I'll fill you full of holes. (*He sets down his packages and draws a gun, but* DEWITT *is beforehand with two flintlock pistols.*)

DEWITT. You will drop your child's armory on the ground, cabin boy, or I shall pull both triggers at once and blast you halfway to the water. (BUDDY *drops the gun.*) I tell you I am now a great devil and violent. When I wish merely I have my way.

(BUDDY *suddenly takes to his heels.* DEWITT *pulls the triggers one after another; the hammers click but there is no explosion.*) Why, this new world is not so bad. I am left in possession of the field. (*He picks up the automatic and the bag and retreats to his rock.*) They fight with the weapons of children. Why, this new world begins to be mine, to do as I please with. Whatever kind of witch a sandwich may be come out and let me interrogate you. (*He takes out sandwiches.*) If it be food eaten by witches and wizards so much the better, for I am now a wizard myself, and by the great jib boom I haven't tasted food in God knows when. (*He eats.*) A sweet and excellent morsel, very strong with garlic and salami, medical for the veins and bladder. (*He looks at his pistols.*) A little glazed powder in the priming now, and these two will speak with more authority if it becomes necessary to defend my position. (*He opens his powder horn and renews the priming.*) We have seen the time, these blunderbusses and myself, when we could defend a crow's nest against a whole crew in mutiny. (*He pushes away the beer bottles with his foot.*) I will eat your rations, cabin boy out of the new age, and I will master you all, men and maids, now that my strength comes back, but I will not drink your drink. As Pastor Van Dorf observed very wisely before we sailed; you may eat the food of the salvages, said he, when you have voyaged to the new lands overseas; you may share their rations, you may even make up to their females after the fashion of sailors when the flesh is weak, but drink none of their drink, said he, lest it prove to be Circe's liquor and turn you all to hogs. (*He eats.*) Now I have small inclination to be a hog, but a man I will be, and a very good man, too, of the fieriest model. (*He hears* JUDITH's *step.*) Take care now, take care! I'm an armed man and a man of blood! (JUDITH *enters.*)

JUDITH (*at some distance*). I beg your pardon, sir—

DEWITT. A woman, by the great tropical cross, a salvage woman, come in answer to my unspoken desires. (*He rises.*) Your humblest servant, lady salvage; don't run away, please. I'm a poor lost little man, wouldn't hurt a fly.

JUDITH. Who are you?

DEWITT. I'm a ˙poor bosun, ma'am, but grown, God knows how, to something of a person this last quarter hour.

JUDITH. Are you lost?

DEWITT. Completely adrift, ma'am, on my own mountain.

JUDITH. I don't think I've seen you before.

DEWITT. That may be, though I'm by way of being one of the earliest inhabitants, not counting Indians and Patagonians.

JUDITH. You live on the mountain?

DEWITT. I maintain a residence here, though the situation eludes me at the moment.

JUDITH. Then you are acquainted with Van—Van Dorn?

DEWITT. I have seen him about.

JUDITH. Have you seen him tonight? I want to find him.

DEWITT. A mere blind, I should say, a maidenly defense, not to be too forthright; but sent by the talisman she is.

JUDITH. You have seen him?

DEWITT. God help him, I have, and in none too sanctified an attitude, saving your ladyship, for the lad was obviously a bit taken with the captain's wife, and she a married woman of some years' standing, young though she appear.

JUDITH. Where was he? (*She takes a step nearer to him.*)

DEWITT. I was never one to break in on a budding romance, sweetheart, and out of sheer delicacy I looked the other way.

JUDITH. No, but where was he, please? I can show you the path.

DEWITT. If you hunt out a very pretty little mistress in a bonnet somewhat behind the fashion, and look under the bonnet, you may chance to find him there.

JUDITH. Who are you?

DEWITT. Alpheus DeWitt, your most humble, bosun in the King's navy.

JUDITH. Forgive me—I shall look elsewhere—

DEWITT. Oh, but I assure you the lad's head over ears, ma'am, and loathe you'd be to interrupt him. Now a pretty lass like yourself should have no trouble replacing one sailor man with another in these stirring times. They come and go like a run of salmon.

JUDITH. Thank you.

DEWITT. I am myself a notionable lad. Salt tears have been wept for me by one and another.

JUDITH. No doubt.

DEWITT. I'm a blunt man, but constant and of considerable substance on my own wharf. Could you find it in your heart to love me?

JUDITH. I'm sorry, no.

DEWITT. To save a sad and desperate man from such a death as the lines of frost on a window? This is a kindly face, this of mine, and a kindly heart under a worn jerkin. These are real tears on my cheek, too, and I weep them for you, lady.

JUDITH. I've never seen you till this moment.

DEWITT. Yet you could save me from their sorcery, with one touch of your hand. I waited here for you, and you came.

JUDITH. You're horrible. Your face is horrible!

DEWITT. Is it, truly?

JUDITH. Ancient and terrible and horrible!— Tell me where he is. I must know.

DEWITT. I don't know where he is.—You will think better of it. You need only pity me a little at first, or even laugh at me— so you do it kindly—

JUDITH. I'm in no mood for laughing, though you're ridiculous enough in that get-up.

DEWITT. It's not the latest, I know. And I'm a sad and broken man, lady, lost here among the lesser known peaks on the west side of the world, and looking only for a hand to help me.

JUDITH. I don't think you're lost at all.

DEWITT. Yes, lady, quite lost.—Nevertheless they run from me! You should have seen the lad run when I snapped my pistols at him.

JUDITH (*stepping back*). I should think he would.—Isn't there someone coming there now? (*She points to the right.* DEWITT *faces about, reaching for his pistols.* JUDITH *slips away left.*)

DEWITT. If there be, watch what soldierly stand old DeWitt makes in defense of a lady! Come out, children of the new Satan, show yourselves in the light! (ELKUS *and* DOPE *appear at right.*)

ELKUS. Stick 'em up, bo! (*They train automatics on him.*)

DEWITT. More toys! Stand back, you cheap new devils!

ELKUS. Keep your hands down or I'll let you have it!

DEWITT. Watch now how a man holds off the fiends. (*He lifts his pistols.*)

ELKUS. Give it to him! (*They fire a fusillade at* DEWITT, *who stands unmoved.*)

DEWITT. Firecrackers! You think me a devil like yourselves, to be exorcised with firecrackers?

ELKUS. Give it to him! (*They fire once more.*)

DEWITT. Look, you puny devils, I'm a patient man, but in one moment I shall blow you both into the Tappan Zee!

ELKUS (*stepping up and pouring bullets into him*). Too bad about you! (*To* DOPE.) Take the money off him.

DOPE. There's something funny about this guy! I can see right through him!

ELKUS. No wonder. He's full of holes as a tennis racket.

DOPE. No, by God, I can see through him! Look! (*They step back together.*)

ELKUS. What kind of a thing are you?

DEWITT. I'm not a man to be daunted by loud noises and firecrackers, Beelzebub! Go seek your place with the new father of hell before I send you there! Wizards!

ELKUS. Where's the money?

DEWITT. I have a talisman and I ate a sandwich, devils!

DOPE. Look, he's a moving picture! He's a regular church window! Look!

DEWITT. Disperse or I fire!

ELKUS. Keep out of the way of that sawed-off shotgun! (DOPE *suddenly runs in and shoots* DEWITT *through the head, then retreats.*)

DEWITT. I warn you I begin to be annoyed!

DOPE. It's no use, chief. I blew his brains out, and he's standing right there!

BIGGS (*looking over the side of the shovel*). It's a war.

ELKUS. Who said that?

DOPE. Damned if I know.

ELKUS. Beat it.

DOPE. Yeah, beat it. Let the money hang. I'm for Canada.

ELKUS. You said it. (*They turn tail. As they are going* DEWITT *fires his pistols in the air.*)

DEWITT. Now am I master of the world of things,
a buccaneer, a devil and a rake!
Women love mastery, and they ran from me;
they ran, these minor devils, ran from De-
Witt!
Look where they go there, sweetheart! (*He turns.*)
God, she's gone!
Lady! New-world lady! Are you lost? (*He follows her.*)
Look now, I've dispersed them, brats and
wizards,
spawn out of hell, they ran! I'm master here,
I'm master of the world! Look, lady! (*He goes out left.*)

SKIMMERHORN. Are you awake?

BIGGS. I hope not. I hope this is a nightmare and I wake up at home in bed.

SKIMMERHORN. How did we get here?

BIGGS. It must have been something we ate.

SKIMMERHORN. I didn't eat anything.

BIGGS. There's a bag of sandwiches down there on the ground.

SKIMMERHORN. That's a pleasant thought.

BIGGS. Look for yourself.

SKIMMERHORN. You're right. It's a bag of sandwiches.

BIGGS. Didn't we send somebody for sandwiches and beer, away back there before all this started?

SKIMMERHORN. I don't know. I'm all wet, and I'm stuck to the shovel.

BIGGS. You do seem to be kind of going to pieces. What's the matter with your toupee?

SKIMMERHORN. The glue must have melted. (*He takes off his wig.*)Now I'll catch cold.

BIGGS. If any of your constituency sees you in that condition you're out of office for good.

SKIMMERHORN. I don't even care if I fall out. I feel terrible.

BIGGS. Might be more comfortable for me if you did fall out. (*He shifts his weight.*)

SKIMMERHORN. Sit down! Quit rocking the boat!

BIGGS. I've got a cramp. Ouch!

SKIMMERHORN. Don't shove me! (*He pushes* BIGGS.)

BIGGS (*pushing back*). You want to pitch me overboard?

SKIMMERHORN. Hey! You know I might have gone out?

BIGGS. What do you care?

SKIMMERHORN. I'll show you what I care! (*They lock in a deadly struggle on the verge.*)

BIGGS. Wait, Skimmer, look now! If one of us goes down the other goes too. Look at the drop. You don't want to splash on those rocks and I don't either.

SKIMMERHORN. Let go then.

BIGGS. I'll let go when you do. I'll count three and we'll both let go.

SKIMMERHORN. All right.

BIGGS. One—two—three. (*They let go and catch the ropes over the swinging basket.*) That's better. Now take it easy, buddy. You woke up feeling like poison this morning. After this you count ten when you get an impulse to push anybody.

SKIMMERHORN. Same to you.

BIGGS. Fine. (*They sit down cautiously.*)

SKIMMERHORN. How in hell did those sandwiches get there?

BIGGS. How in hell did we get here?

SKIMMERHORN. You haven't got a fishing hook on you, have you?

BIGGS. No, I haven't. (*They sit gloomily looking at the sandwiches.* LISE *and* VAN *come in from the left.*)

VAN. Nothing in all the woods
is silent as the owl; you see his shadow
but never hear his wings. The partridge
   now,
every time he takes off he creaks and cranks
like an old Ford. You never heard such a
   fuss;
but he's quiet on the ground.

LISE. And is there a squirrel
that flies, bird-fashion?

VAN. Well, there's a flying squirrel,
but he's more the glider type. No engine,
   see,
but he'll do thirty yards. He's on the way
to be a bat if he's not careful.

LISE. How?

VAN. He'll leave off tail and put on wings
   until
he's mostly wing. No doubt the bat was once
some kind of flying mouse.

LISE. Some men have wings.
I've seen them overhead.

VAN. That's all put on.
They've no more wings than a goat. When
   they come down.

LISE. I've hoped that it was true that men
had wings.

VAN. Why?

LISE. Oh, they've lived so long, and tried so hard,
and it all comes to nothing.

VAN. Having wings,
would that be something?

LISE. Yes, it seems so. And yet
a bird has wings.

VAN. And he gets nowhere.

LISE. Yes.
Nothing but just to be a bird, and fly,
and then come down. Always the thing itself
is less than when the seed of it in thought
came to a flower within, but such a flower
as never grows in gardens.

BIGGS. Eh—Van Dorn!

VAN (*looking up*). What are you doing on
the roost, you birds?
Building a nest?

BIGGS. We can't get down.

VAN. I'd say
it ought to be just as easy to get down
as it was to get up there.

SKIMMERHORN. Will you help us out?

VAN. You look all right to me. What happened to you?

BIGGS. Everything.

VAN. How did you get there?

BIGGS. God,
it's a long story.

VAN. You've been there all night?

BIGGS. Yes, all night.

VAN. I wouldn't want to spoil it.
It's too good to be true. You see those two,
Lise, there in the scoop?

LISE. They're pitiful.
Shouldn't you help them?

VAN. No. Since time began
there haven't been two fat-guts that deserved
a hoisting like those two. In their own machine—
that makes it perfect.

LISE. What have they done?

VAN. They've been
themselves, that's all. Two thieves, a probate judge
and a manipulator, hand and glove
to thieve what they can get. They've got High Tor
among other things, and mean to carve it down,
at three cents a square yard.

LISE. These poor old men?

VAN. Yes, these poor old men.

LISE. Let them hang there then!

VAN. They'll hang there for all me. (LISE *and* VAN *turn to go.*)

SKIMMERHORN. I'll tell you what,
Van Dorn, I'll let you have the validation
if you'll help me down.

VAN. That means I'd own the land?

SKIMMERHORN. Yes, you'd own it.

VAN. Only you'd cancel it,
once you got down.

SKIMMERHORN. To tell the truth I couldn't,
not if you had the paper.

VAN. Toss it over;
I'd like to see it. (SKIMMERHORN *gets out an envelope and throws it to* VAN.)

BIGGS. You're a simple judge!
Now the land's his.

VAN. There's a bond goes with this,
a bond signed by the court. Oh, I looked it up.
I've read that much law.

SKIMMERHORN. Yes, I'll keep the bond
till we're on your level.

VAN. Then I'd advise you both
to make yourself a nest with two-three sticks,
like a couple of crows, and settle down to see
what you can hatch—or maybe lay an egg—
you'll have plenty of time.

BIGGS. Come now, Van Dorn,
we're in a bad way. It drops off straight down
a thousand feet here, and Judge Skimmerhorn

has vertigo. Why, just to save a life,
out of common humanity, lean on that cable
and pull us in.

VAN. This one? (*He pulls. The shovel dips.*)

BIGGS. Oh, no, no! God,
do you want to dump us out!

VAN. You said to pull it.

BIGGS. Not that one! This! Pull up on that
again!
We're sliding!

VAN. Sure. (*He rights the shovel.*)
Now you know how it feels
when you kick out the props from under
men
and slide 'em on the relief rolls. Ever think
how that might feel?

BIGGS. You don't know what we've both
been through, Van Dorn. Rained on and
struck by lightning,
no dinner; we're half-crazy; we've had nightmares,
funny people in hats; that's how we got
here,
one of those nightmares!

VAN. You sound disconnected.
Maybe you've lost your minds; still I'm not
melting
down in my shoes with compunction. The
fact is
he's clinging to the bond, Judge Skimmerhorn;
he's not too sunk for that. Now here's my
bargain:
You're hanging onto life by one steel cable,
but that's much safer than the spider web
most men have to trust to. Toss me the bond,
Judge Skimmerhorn, or I'll give this line a
yank
and you won't even hang.

SKIMMERHORN. You wouldn't do it.

VAN. Oh, wouldn't I? For a two-cent lollipop
I'd pull the chain right now!

SKIMMERHORN. You wouldn't do it!

VAN. Hang on, then! Just for a taste, how's
the incline now?
A little steep? (*He pulls the line. The shovel
tips as before.*)

BIGGS. Pull it up! Take the God damn
bond!—
throw it to him!

SKIMMERHORN. I will not!

VAN. Try this then. (*He tips the shovel
further.*)

BIGGS. Give him his bond! I'm slipping!

SKIMMERHORN. I will not!

BIGGS. I say you will! What good's the money
to you
if you're bologny?

SKIMMERHORN. What money?

BIGGS. You know what money!

SKIMMERHORN. Straighten it up.

VAN. Do I get the bond?

SKIMMERHORN. Hell, yes! (VAN *restores their
equilibrium.*)
You get the bond if you agree to accept
five thousand for your claim. (*He brings out
a paper.*)

VAN. Don't stall with me!
I'll never have a chance like this again,
and it's hard to resist!

SKIMMERHORN. I'm offering you five thou
sand!
Five thousand! Cash!

VAN (*leaping to the rope*). Keep it!

BIGGS. Give him his bond! (*He wrenches the
paper from* SKIMMERHORN *and sails it to
VAN.*)
And now you've got it how's five thousand
sound?
You settle for it?

VAN. Bid against them, Lise. It's a game.
What would you say, Lise?
They offer me five thousand.

LISE. Pieces of silver?

VAN. Pieces of silver.

LISE (*smiling*). But I'll give you more!
Only five thousand for this crag at dawn
shedding its husk of cloud to face a sunrise
over the silver bay? For silver haze
wrapping the crag at noon, before a storm
cascading silver levin? For winter rains
that run in silver down the black rock's face
under a gray-sedge sky? For loneliness
here on this crag? I offer you nine thousand!
To be paid in silver!

VAN. You hear? I've got nine thousand;
what am I offered?

BIGGS. Make it ten thousand—
and let us down in the bargain!

VAN. Yes? Ten thousand?
A mountain for ten thousand? Hear them,
Lise,
In their despair they lift it by a grand!
Should it go for ten?

SKIMMERHORN. We'll never get it back—
but that's all right.

VAN. Yes, Lise?

LISE. Will they pay
no more then for the piling of this stone,
set in its tall hexagonals by fire
before men were? Searching a hundred king-
doms
men will not find a site for lodge or tower
more kingly! A hundred thousand, sir, in
silver,
this is my offer!

VAN. Come now, meet it boys—
I have a hundred thousand!

BIGGS. She's a fraud!
She's no dealer; she's a ringer, primed
to put the price up! What do you mean by
silver?
She won't pay silver!

VAN. Coinage of the moon,
but it's current here!

SIMMERHORN. Ten thousand, cash, and that's
the last. Five thousand out of my pocket, see,
and five from Biggs! (*He pulls out a bundle
of bills.* BIGGS *does the same.*)
Take a good look at cash,
see how that operates! (*He tosses down the
roll.* BIGGS *follows suit.*)

VAN. You go well-heeled
when you go mountain-climbing. Is it real?

SKIMMERHORN. Well, look it over. Count it.
(VAN *takes up one packet, then another.*)

VAN. Where did this come from?

SKIMMERHORN. Where would you think?

VAN. I'll say I got a shock. (*He studies the
bills again.*)
I don't want your money.

BIGGS. What's wrong with it?

VAN. Didn't I tell you I had a hundred thousand?
Take the stuff back. We reckon in moonlight here!
Put up your mitts! (*He tosses the bundles
back.*)

BIGGS. It's yours if you want it.

VAN. No,
oh, no, I thank you. It's no sale. What's more
I never meant to sell. The auctioneer's
about to take a walk.

BIGGS. Well, look, we're sitting
right where we were.

VAN. You sit there for your health,
and think it over.

SKIMMERHORN. You won't do that, Van
Dorn,
just leave us here.

VAN. Watch me, if you don't think so. (*He
gives an arm to* LISE.)
Let me tell you about those babes in the
wood,
did I say they were thieves? (*They start
out.*)

BIGGS. Make it fifteen!

VAN. Go to sleep.

SKIMMERHORN. Well, twenty! and let us
down!

VAN. Sweet dreams.

SKIMMERHORN. We'll run you out of the
state, Van Dorn!

VAN. You'll have to get down first!

SKIMMERHORN. Is he going away
and leave us sitting?

BIGGS. Looks like it. (VAN *and* LISE *move
off.*)

SKIMMERHORN. Say, Van Dorn,
will you pitch us up a sandwich?

VAN. Sure; they're soggy,
lying out in the rain. (*He returns and tosses
sandwiches to them.*)

BIGGS. Thanks.

VAN. Don't mention it. (*He goes out right
with* LISE. BIGGS *and* SKIMMERHORN *unwrap
sandwiches.*)

SKIMMERHORN. He got away with that bond.

BIGGS. Yeah.

SKIMMERHORN. Looks as if we wouldn't make anything on Van Dorn.

BIGGS. That's what it looks like.

SKIMMERHORN. Christ.

BIGGS. Well, we've still got the windfall.

SKIMMERHORN. Yeah, we've got that.

BIGGS. And here he comes again.

SKIMMERHORN. Who?

BIGGS. Our mascot, little rabbit's foot, little good-luck token, little knee-high with the big heart.

(DEWITT *comes in from the left, looks at the place where the sandwiches were and then at the two in the shovel. He mutters.*)

DEWITT. Magic again! More devil's work!
And the woman
gone, slipped round a turn, and the scent was cold
for an old dog like me. By the mizzen yards,
it's wearing to the temper of a man
even if he's not choleric!—And those two,
those buzzards of evil omen, brooding there
on how they'll cut the mountain like a pie
and sell it off in slices! (*He looks at his pistols.*)

One apiece.
It should be just enough, and it's a wonder
I never thought of it. (*He lifts his pistols, the two drop their sandwiches into the void, and cower down; he clicks the hammers.*)
Damp again! Well, boys,
we'll fix that. (*He sits down to freshen the priming.*)
They'll brood over us no more,
those two sea-lions. Damn the rain and mist;
it penetrates the priming! Damn the flint,
and damn the spring! A brace of fine horse-
   pistols,
that's what the Jew said back in Amsterdam;
it takes a horse to cock 'em. Now then, damn
   you,
blow 'em off their perch! (*As he rises his eye catches something out on the Zee. He stands transfixed for a moment, watching.*)
It can't be there!
It's there! It's gone! I saw it! Captain Asher!
Captain! Captain! Captain! Captain Asher!
(BIGGS *and* SKIMMERHORN *have ducked down again.* DEWITT *rushes out to the right, firing his pistols in the air in his excitement.* BIGGS *sits up, then* SKIMMERHORN).

SKIMMERHORN. Am I hurt? Do you see blood anywhere?

BIGGS. It seems there was nothing there.
(*They contemplate the place where* DEWITT *stood.*)

**CURTAIN**

# SCENE II

SCENE: *Another part of the Tor.* LISE *is sitting high up on a ledge, looking out over the Zee.* VAN *stands near her, looking at her as she speaks. She has his old felt hat in her lap and has woven a wreath of dandelions around the brim. The beacon light strikes athwart her face.*

LISE. But nobody likes this flower?

VAN. I like it now.
I used to think it was a weed, but now,
well, it's a flower now.

LISE. The dandelion.
Where will you find another prodigal
so merry or so golden or so wasteful,
pouring out treasure down the sides of hills
and cupping it in valleys?

VAN. Buttercups
and touch-me-nots. The touch-me-not's a
   shoe,

a tiny golden shoe, with a hair-spring latchet
for bees to loosen.

LISE. When did you part from Judith?

VAN. Judith?

LISE. When did she go away?

VAN. Last evening.
But it seems longer.

LISE. Why?

VAN. Why, a lot's happened.—
It's almost morning.

LISE. How do you know? (*He steps up to the ledge.*)

VAN. See that star,
that heavy red star back in the west? When that
goes down, then look for the morning star across
Long Island Sound, and after that the lights
dim down in the gray.

LISE. You loved her, very much?

VAN. Yes.

LISE. I loved someone too. I love him still.

VAN. No, you're mine now. (*He sits beside her.*)

LISE. See the great gulf that lies
between the heavy red star down the west
and the star that comes with morning? It's a long way.
There's that much lies between us.

·VAN. Not for me.

LISE. Even for you.—You're weary?

VAN. Well, the truth is
I sometimes sleep at night.

LISE. Put your head down.
I'll hold you. (*He lays his head on her knees and stretches out.*)
Now I'll wish that I could sing
and make you sleep. Somehow they're all forgotten,
the old songs. Over and over when the birds
begin at morning I try hard to catch
one tune of theirs. There's one that seems to say:
  Merrily, merrily, chirr, chirr,
  Lueté, lueté, stee—
  Merrily, merrily, chirr, lueté,
  Chirr, lueté, stee.
That's only what it says; for what it sings
you'll have to ask the bird.

VAN. I know it, though.
That's the song sparrow.

LISE. Have I come so near?

VAN. Say it again.

LISE. I can't. May I ask you something?

VAN. Yes.

LISE. There's so much that's changed now
  men can fly
and hear each other across seas, must men
still die—do they die still?

VAN. Oh yes, they die.
Why do you ask?

LISE. Because I'm still so young,
and yet I can't remember all the years
there must have been.—In a long night
  sometimes
I try to count them, but they blow in clouds
across the sky, the dancing firefly years,
incredible numbers.—Tell me how old you
  are
before you go to sleep.

VAN. Lying here now
there's not much logic in arithmetic.
Five, or six, maybe. Five or six thousand,
  maybe.
But when I'm awake I'm twenty-three.

LISE. No more?

VAN. No more.

LISE. Tell me why it is I am as I am
and not like you?

VAN. I don't know, Lise.

LISE. But tell me.
Have I been enchanted here? I've seen
the trap-rock men, there in the shovel, seeming
so stupid and so pitiful. Could these
use charms and rites to hold wrecked
  mariners
forever in a deep cataleptic spell
high on a mountain-fringe?

VAN. The trap-rock men?
They're no more wizards than I am. They
  buy
and sell, and when they've had their fill
  of dust
they die like the rest of us.

LISE. But they laid spells
about us?

VAN. There are no wizards and no spells.
Just men and women and money and the
  earth
the way it always was. The trap-rock men
don't know you're here.

LISE. It's not sorcery then. If I had died
and left my bones here on the mountain-top
but had no memory of it, and lived on
in dreams, it might be as it is. As children
sure we were told of living after death,
but there were angels there, and onyx stone
paving an angel city, and they sang
eternally, no darkness and no sun,
nothing of earth. Now can it be men die
and carry thence no memory of death,
only this curious lightness of the hands,
only this curious darkness of the mind,
only to be still changeless with the winters
passing; not gray, not lined, not stricken
  down,
but stamped forever on the moving air,
an echo and an image? Restless still
with the old hungers, drifting among men,
till one by one forgotten, fading out
like an old writing, undecipherable,
we lose our hold and go? Could it be true?
Could this be how men die?

VAN (*half asleep*). It may be, Lise.
I love you when you speak.

LISE. And I love you.
But I am dead, and all the crew is dead;
all of the *Onrust* crew—and we have clung
beyond our place and time, on into a world
unreal as sleep, unreal as this your sleep
that comes upon you now. Oh, you were
  cruel
to love me and to tell me I am dead
and lie here warm and living! When you
  wake
we shall be parted—you will have a world
but I'll have none! There's a chill falls on
  me,
the night-dew gathering, or my mind's death
  chill—
knowing at last I know.—You haven't
  heard.
You told me this in a half-dream. You've
  been kind.
You never thought to hurt me. Are you
  asleep?

VAN. I think I was.

LISE. Sleep, sleep. There was once a song,
if only I could call back air and words,
about a king who watched a goblet rising
and falling in the sea. It came to land
and on the rim the king's name was in-
  scribed
with a date many years before. Oh, many
  years,

a hundred or three hundred. Then he knew
that all his life was lived in an old time,
swept out, given to the waters. What remained
was but this goblet swimming in the sea,
touching his dust by chance.— But he's
  asleep.
And very well he might be with dull stories
out of old songs.—Sleep, sweet; let me have
your head here on my knees, only this nighr,
and your brown hair round my finger.
(*A girl's shadowy figure comes in from the
right, walking lightly, pauses, as if at seeing
them, and turns to go, the face still unre-
vealed.*)
Are you Judith?

JUDITH. Yes.

LISE. The lad's asleep, but when he wakes
you'll have him back.

JUDITH. Do you dispose of him
just as you please?

LISE. No. It's not what I please.
It's what will happen.

JUDITH. I don't know who you are.

LISE. I'm but a friend of his. You left him
  bitter
going away so lightly. I was bitter—
and so we tried to play at being lovers,
but it won't do. He'll wake, and he'll be
  yours,
all as it was. Only if I may hold him
while he lies here asleep, it helps a little
and I'll be happier.

JUDITH. You'll keep him then
after he wakes.

LISE. No.

JUDITH. Then why are you crying?

LISE. Am I crying?
Well, they're not for him, nor you, these
  tears;
something so far away, so long ago,
so hopeless, so fallen, so lost, so deep in dust
the names wash from the urns, summons
  my tears,
not love or longing. Only when you have
  him,
love him a little better for your sake,
for your sake, knowing how bitterly
I cried, for times past and things done.

JUDITH. You're strange—
the dress you wear's strange, too.—Who are
  you then?
I'm—afraid of you!

LISE. Afraid of tears
and a voice out of long ago? It's all I have.

JUDITH. No—no—I'm not afraid. Only for
  him.
I've done my crying, too.—Shall I come
  back?

LISE. Don't wake him now. Come back at
  dawn. You'll find him
here alone.
(TWO *or* THREE SAILORS *appear on the rocks
at the rear, looking out over the Zee.*)

PIETER. Look for yourself.

A SAILOR. Aye.

PIETER. Do you make her out?

THE SAILOR. She's the square top-yards.

ANOTHER SAILOR. Now, God, if it were she!

PIETER. It's the brigantine! The *Onrust* from
  up-river
tacking this way!

ASHER (*outside*). Lise! Lise! Lise! (*The*
CAPTAIN *comes in at the rear with* DEWITT.)
Lise, the ship's on the river! Quick, there's
  haste!
She must catch the tide down-stream!

LISE. Hush! Hush! You'll wake him!

ASHER. But look across the Zee! The *Onrust's*
  in
and waiting for us!

LISE. But you say it, Asher,
only to comfort me. There is no ship,
nor are we caught in spells here, or enchanted,
but spectres of an old time. The life we live
is but a lingering, a clinging on,
our dust remembering. There is no ship,
only a phantom haunting down the Zee
as we still haunt the heights.

ASHER. Look! The *Onrust!*
Look, Lise!

LISE. Yes, I see it.

ASHER. Will you come?

LISE. Why would I stay? Why would I go?
  For go
or stay we're phantoms still.

ASHER. But will you come?
Who is this lad?

LISE. Her lad. But he was hurt
and fell asleep. (VAN *wakes and lifts his
head.*)

ASHER. Come quickly!

LISE. Yes, for his sake
it's better I should go.

VAN. Where must you go? (*She rises.*)

LISE. The *Onrust's* on the river
and we must catch the tide.

VAN. Would you leave me now?

LISE. Yes, I must leave you.

VAN. You'll go back with him?

LISE. Yes.

VAN. And was nothing meant of all we said?

LISE. What could we mean, we two? Your
  hurt's quite cured
and mine's past curing.

VAN. Let me go with you then.

LISE. I should have told you if I'd only
  known
how we stood at the tangent of two worlds
that touched an instant like two wings of
  storm
drawn out of night; touched and flew off,
  and, falling,
fall now asunder through a wide abyss,
not to touch again. (*She steps back among
the rocks.*)

VAN. Let them go if they like!
What do I care about worlds? Any world
  you have
I'll make it mine!

LISE. You told me in your sleep.
There is no witchcraft. Men are as they
  were;
we're parted now.

VAN. Give me your hand again!
They dare not take you from me, dare not
  touch you

no matter who they are, or where they come
from—
they have no hold on us!

LISE. If I could stay!
If I could stay with you. And tend my
garden
only a little longer!

VAN. Put out your hand!

LISE. There were too many, many, many
years.

VAN. I'll be alone here—

LISE. No, not alone. When you must walk
the air,
as all must walk it sometime, with a tread
that stirs no leaf, and breathe here with a
breath
that blows impalpable through smoke or
cloud,
when you are as I am, a bending wind
along the grain, think of me sometimes then
and how I clung to earth. The earth you
have
seems now so hard and firm, with all its
colors
sharp for the eye, as a taste's sharp to the
tongue,
you'll hardly credit how its outlines blur
and wear out as you wear. Play now with fire
while fire will burn, bend down the bough
and eat
before the fruit falls. For there comes a time
when the great sun-lit pattern of the earth
shakes like an image under water, darkens,
dims, and the clearest voices that we knew
are sunken bells, dead sullen under sea,
receding. Look in her eyes. (VAN *looks at*
JUDITH.)

ASHER. Come!

LISE. See, the dawn
points with one purple finger at a star
to put it out. When it has quite gone out
then we'll be gone. (VAN *looks at the dawn,
then turns back towards* LISE.)

VAN. Lise! Lise! (*But even as he speaks* LISE
*and the* CREW *have disappeared.*)

LISE (*unseen*). This is your age, your dawn,
your life to live.
The morning light strikes through us, and
the wind
that follows after rain tugs at our sails—
and so we go.

DEWITT (*still half-seen*). And welcome you
are to the age, too, an age of witches
and sandwiches, an age of paper, an age of
paper money
and paper men, so that a poor Dutch wraith's
more man
than the thickest of you! (*He steps back and
vanishes. It is now dawn.*)

VAN. She never said good-bye.

JUDITH. There is a ship.

VAN. Yes?

JUDITH. Tiny, with black, square sails;
low and small.

VAN (*still looking after* LISE). She'll be a
phantom too
like all the rest. The canvas casts no shadow;
the light sifts through the spars. A moonlight
rig
no doubt they call it.

JUDITH. I think I hear their voices
as they go down the crag.

VAN. But you won't see them.
No matter what you hear.

THE SAILORS (*a wisp of chantey in the
distance*). Coming a blow, coming a blow,
sea runs black, glass runs low.

VAN. Just voices down the wind.
Why, then they were all mist, a fog that
hangs
along the crevices of hills, a kind
of memory of things you read in books,
things you thought you'd forgotten. She was
here,
and she was real, but she was cloud, and
gone,
and the hill's barren of her.

JUDITH. There are no ghosts.

VAN. I know—but these were ghosts or I'm
a ghost,
and all of us. God knows where we leave off
and ghosts begin. God knows where ghosts
leave off
and we begin.

JUDITH. You were in love with her.

VAN. She leaves the mountain barren now
she's gone.
And she was beautiful.

JUDITH. I came to tell you
that I was wrong—I mean about the land—
what you have here is better than one buys
down in the towns. But since I come too late
I'll say it and then go.—Your was was best.
I think it always would be.—So, good night,
  Van—
or, rather, it's good morning.

VAN. Yes, it's morning.—
Is it too late?

JUDITH. Oh, Van, I think it is.
It was for Lise you were calling, not
for Judith. I can't say I blame you much,
because she is more beautiful. And yet
you love her, and not me. You'll say they're
  ghosts
and won't come back. Perhaps. I'm not so
  certain
about the way of ghosts. She may come back.
And you still love her.

VAN. There's no ship at all.
It faded in the dawn. And all the mists
that hung about the Tor, look how they lift,
pouring downstream with the wind. Whatever it was,
was said, or came between us, it's all gone
now it's daylight again.

JUDITH. I came to say
if only I could keep you, you should keep
the Tor, or what you wished. I'm sorry I
went.
I'm sorry this has happened. But it has.
And so—

VAN. Should I keep the Tor?

JUDITH. Yes, if you like.

VAN. God knows they haven't left me much
of it.
Look, where the new road winds along the
ledge.
Look at the jagged cut the quarries make
down to the south, and there's a boy scout
  trail
running along the ridge Mount Ivy way,

where they try out their hatchets. There's
  the light,
and steps cut into stone the linesmen blew
for better climbing. The crusher underneath
dumps road rock into barges all day long
and sometimes half the night. The West
  Shore tunnel
belches its trains above the dead lagoons
that line the brickyards. Their damned
  shovel hangs
across my line, ready to gouge the peak
we're standing on. Maybe I'm ghost myself
trying to hold an age back with my hands;
maybe we're all the same, these ghosts of
  Dutchmen
and one poor superannuated Indian
and one last hunter, clinging to his land
because he's always had it. Like a wasp
that tries to build a nest above your door—
and when you brush it down he builds again,
then when you brush it down he builds
  again—
but after a while you get him.

JUDITH. Then you'll sell?

VAN. I guess if you were with me then we'd
  sell
for what we could, and move out farther
  west
where a man's land's his own. But if I'm
  here
alone, I'll play the solitary wasp
and sting them till they get me.

JUDITH. If it's your way
then it's your way.

VAN. I'll sell it if you'll stay.
Won't you stay with me, Judith?

JUDITH. I think I'd always hear you calling
  Lise
while I was standing by. I took a wrong
  turning
once, when I left you and went down the
  hill,
and now it may not ever be the same.
(*She turns.*)

**CURTAIN**

# ACT THREE

SCENE: *The shovel still hangs over the verge, and* BIGGS *and* SKIMMERHORN *still occupy it. The rising sun sends level rays across the rock, lighting their intent faces as they stare downward.* BIGGS *has torn a handkerchief into strips and tied them together into a string. He appears to be fishing for something which lies below the ledge, out of view of the audience. Over and over he tries his cast.*

SKIMMERHORN. Little to the left.

BIGGS. You don't say?

SKIMMERHORN. Little to the right.

BIGGS. Put it to a tune and sing it, why don't you?

SKIMMERHORN. There! Almost!

BIGGS. I don't need any umpire.

SKIMMERHORN. Let me try it.

BIGGS. Oh, no. You always were a butter-fingers. (*The string tightens.*) By Golly!

SKIMMERHORN. It's on!

BIGGS. You're explaining to me? (*He pulls up. A bottle of beer emerges from below.*)

SKIMMERHORN. Fifty per cent!

BIGGS. What? (*He pauses, the bottle in air.*)

SKIMMERHORN. You tore up my handker-chief! Fifty per cent. That's the natural division between capital and labor.

BIGGS. Oh, now I'm labor and you're capital. (*He pulls up carefully.*)

SKIMMERHORN. Fifty per cent!

BIGGS. I get the first pull at it. That's all I ask. (*The string parts, and the bottle descends silently into the void.*) That's that.

SKIMMERHORN. You should 'a let me handle it.

BIGGS. Yeah. No doubt.

SKIMMERHORN. Am I thirsty?

BIGGS. Wait till the sun gets up a little. We'll be pan-fried in this thing.

SKIMMERHORN. Look! (*He points down the rocks.*)

BIGGS. If it's more of those little people I give up.

SKIMMERHORN. It's a trooper.

BIGGS. What do you know? Up early for a trooper, too. Listen, about that stuff in our pockets?

SKIMMERHORN. Yeah?

BIGGS. Do we say anything about it?

SKIMMERHORN. Do you?

BIGGS. Do you?

SKIMMERHORN. No.

BIGGS. Neither do I, then.

SKIMMERHORN. Beautiful morning.

BIGGS. I always say it's worth while being up early just to catch the sunrise. (*A* TROOPER *climbs in followed by* SKIMMERHORN SENIOR.)

THE TROOPER. Hello!

BIGGS. Hello, Patsy.

PATSY. Say, you boys had the wives worried down in Ledentown. Been looking for you all night. There they are, Mr. Skimmerhorn.

SKIMMERHORN, SR. (*winded*). Good God! (*He sits, a hand to his heart.*) And I climbed up here. We thought you were under that rock slide.

SKIMMERHORN. I guess you're disappointed.

SENIOR. The next time you two go on a bat and spend a night up a tree you can stay there and sober up.

SKIMMERHORN. We haven't been drinking.

SENIOR (*pointing to a bottle*). What's that?

SKIMMERHORN. Beer. But we didn't have a drop to drink. I'd certainly appreciate a swallow of that now.

PATSY (*tossing up bottle*). Here you are. Hair of the dog that bit you.

BIGGS. We're not drunk. We're dry. We didn't have a drop to drink nor a bite to eat.

PATSY. All right. All right. Only the ground's covered with beer and sandwiches.

BIGGS. You tell 'em how it was, Skimmer.

SKIMMERHORN. You tell 'em.

BIGGS. Well, you see, the whole thing's pretty complicated.

PATSY. I know. I've been through it. You wake up in the morning and you can't believe it yourself.

BIGGS. I don't mean that. I'm sober as a judge.

PATSY. Yeah, what judge? (*He hauls at a cable.*) Can you lend me a hand with this, A.B.?

SENIOR. Give me a minute. (*The shovel tips.*)

BIGGS. Hey, not that one! The other one!

PATSY. Sorry. Not much of a mechanic.

BIGGS. Straighten it up again. (PATSY *does so.*)

SKIMMERHORN. Are we never getting off this? My legs are paralyzed sitting here.

BIGGS. So are mine.

PATSY (*hauling down*). It's too much for me alone.

SKIMMERHORN. Got your wind yet, A.B.?

SENIOR. I don't know whether I want you down yet. You had your good time, now you can put in a few minutes paying for it.

SKIMMERHORN. Oh, we had a good time, did we?

SENIOR. What were you doing? You came up here to buy Van Dorn's property; you're gone all night, and the whole damn town's up all night hunting for you! And we find you up in a steam shovel enjoying a hang-over!

PATSY. And now I know what a hang-over looks like.

BIGGS. I tell you we didn't even have a drink of water!

SENIOR. I believe that!

BIGGS. And we're thirsty! Have you got an opener?

PATSY. No, I haven't.

SENIOR. Before you open anything tell me what you were doing last night. Did you see Van Dorn?

SKIMMERHORN. Sure we saw him.

SENIOR. Well, what did he say?

SKIMMERHORN. He said no.

SENIOR. And I suppose that took all night?

SKIMMERHORN. We had an argument.

SENIOR. And then he chased you up the crane, I suppose?

SKIMMERHORN. No.

SENIOR. Well, how did you get up there?

SKIMMERHORN. We were hauled up.

SENIOR. All right. Who hauled you up?

SKIMMERHORN. You tell him, Art.

BIGGS. Oh, no. You tell him.

SKIMMERHORN. As a matter of fact, I don't think it happened.

SENIOR. You're there, aren't you?

SKIMMERHORN. Yes, we're here.

SENIOR. Well, if you weren't drunk how did you get there?

SKIMMERHORN. Well, you see, first we tried to negotiate with Van Dorn.

SENIOR. And he wouldn't take the money?

SKIMMERHORN. That's right.

SENIOR. Did you tell him he didn't really own the land? Till the will was validated?

SKIMMERHORN. Yes, we told him that.

SENIOR. And he still wouldn't talk business?

SKIMMERHORN. He's stubborn. Stubborn as a mule.

SENIOR. Did you tell him you could take the land away from him?

SKIMMERHORN. Oh, yes.

SENIOR. And you offered him the twenty-five thousand?

BIGGS. We offered him a fair price.

SENIOR. You were authorized to say twenty-five thousand.

BIGGS. We didn't quite get to that. We offered ten.

SKIMMERHORN. You see, we thought we'd save the company some money.

SENIOR. I'll bet you did. You thought you'd make a little on the side, and I'd never know.

SKIMMERHORN. Oh, no.

BIGGS. Oh, no.

SENIOR. All right, you offered ten and he wouldn't take it. Then what happened?

SKIMMERHORN. Well, we couldn't get down because of the slide, so some sailors offered to let us down in this thing.

SENIOR. Sailors—up here?

SKIMMERHORN. Little men, in big hats.

BIGGS. Might have been a moving picture company.

SENIOR. Yeah? Any elephants? Or snakes?

SKIMMERHORN. We're trying to tell you the truth!

PATSY. Certainly sounds like delirium tremens, boys.

SENIOR. Never mind, you were hauled up by pink elephants, and then what?

SKIMMERHORN. Van Dorn came along and started to dump us down the cliff.

SENIOR. What's Van Dorn look like? Kind of an octopus, with long feelers?

SKIMMERHORN. Are you going to let us down out of this basket?

SENIOR. No. Not till you come across with what's been going on.

SKIMMERHORN. All right. I'll talk when I'm down.

SENIOR. Can a grown man get pie-eyed on beer?

PATSY. Must have been something stronger. (VAN DORN comes in from the right.)

SENIOR. Who are you?

VAN. Oh, I'm nobody. I just own the property.

SENIOR. What property?

VAN. This.

SENIOR. Are you Van Dorn?

VAN. I am.

SENIOR. I'm A. B. Skimmerhorn, Mr. Van Dorn, president of Igneous Trap rock, and I'm glad to meet you. (He put out a hand.)

VAN (ignoring the hand). Are these friends of yours?

SENIOR. One's a nephew and one's a partner. Why?

VAN. Because any friend of theirs is no friend of mine. (JUDITH and THE INDIAN enter at the rear. She is leading him.)

PATSY. Who do you think you're talking to?

VAN. A. B. Skimmerhorn, of Skimmerhorn, Skimmerhorn, Biggs and Skimmerhorn, small-time crooks and petty thieving done. Cheap.

SENIOR. Now, to be frank, there may have been some misunderstanding, Mr. Van Dorn. Those two were hardly in condition to negotiate. But I can offer you a fair price for your land, and if you don't take it we may have to push you a little, because we want this acreage and we intend to have it.

SKIMMERHORN. He's got the validation papers.

SENIOR. You gave him the validation papers?

BIGGS. We had to. He started to trip the machine.

SENIOR. That puts us in a sweet mess, that does. Will you take twenty-five thousand?

VAN. No.

SENIOR. Will you take fifty thousand?

VAN. No.

SENIOR. Then, we go home, and the machinery can rust here. That's the best I can do.

VAN. Fine. Let it rust.

JUDITH. Van?

VAN. Yes, Judith.

JUDITH. There's someone here to see you.

VAN. You want to see me, John?

THE INDIAN. But I can wait. I have time
enough.

VAN. I'll be right with you.

JUDITH. I had to bring him, Van, because
he said
his eyes were bad. He couldn't see the way.

VAN. Thanks, Judith.

SENIOR. Look, Van Dorn, you know the
saying,
every man has his price. I've heard it said
God has his price, if you'll go high enough.
Set a figure.

VAN. I'm not thinking of prices.
I don't want to sell. Hell, fifty thousand's
too much money for me.

SENIOR. We'll give you less.

VAN. I don't want less or more. It's not a
matter of money.

SENIOR. Will you take a partnership
in the company?

VAN. No.

SSENIOR. Good God, what do you want?

VAN. I want to have it back the way it was
before you came here. And I won't get that.
I know
what kind of fool I look to all of you,
all but old John there. But I'll be a fool
along with John, and keep my own, before
I let you have an inch. John, fifty thousand
or this old hill-top. Is it worth keeping?

THE INDIAN. No.

VAN. No?

THE INDIAN. It's gone already. Not worth
keeping.

VAN. I thought you'd say it was. I counted on
you
to be my friend in that.

THE INDIAN. It's an old question,
one I heard often talked of round the fire
when the hills and I were younger. Then as
now
the young braves were for keeping what was
ours

whatever it cost in blood. And they did try,
but when they'd paid their blood, and still
must sell,
the price was always less than what it was
before their blood was paid.

VAN. Well, that may be.

THE INDIAN. I wish now I had listened when
they spoke
their prophecies, the sachems of the tents;
they were wiser than I knew. Wisest of all,
Iachim, had his camp here on this Tor
before the railroad came. I saw him stand
and look. out toward the west, toward the
sun dying,
and say, "Our god is not the setting sun,
and we must follow it. For other races,
out of the east, will live here in their time,
one following another. Each will build
its cities and its monuments to gods
we dare not worship. Some will come with
ships,
and some with wings, and each will de-
secrate
the altars of the people overthrown,
but none will live forever. Each will live
its little time, and fly before the feet
of those who follow after." Let them come
in
despoiling, for a time is but a time
and these will not endure. This little hill,
let them have the little hill, and find your
peace
beyond, for there's no hill worth a man's
peace
while he may live and find it. But they
fought it out
and died, and sleep here.

SENIOR. Why, this is a wise Indian.
A little pessimistic about the aims
of civilization, but wise anyway.
What do you say, Van Dorn?

THE INDIAN. You too will go
like gnats on the wind. An evening and a
day, but still you have your day. Build
monuments
and worship at your temples. But you too
will go.

SENIOR. You're on my side, so I don't mind,
but you have a damned uncomfortable way
of speaking. I'm a Republican myself,
but I don't go that far! What do you say,
Van Dorn?
Can we do business?

VAN. Judith?

JUDITH. I'm out of it.
It's your decision. I'd say keep it though
if you want to keep it.

VAN. I'll sell it. Fifty thousand.
On one condition. There's a burying grouna
I want to keep.

SENIOR. Sure. That can be arranged.
It's settled, then. Come down to Ledentown
tomorrow and get your money.

VAN. Yes, I'll come.

SENIOR. Why, three cheers, boys. We're out
of the woods. Take hold,
Van Dorn, and swing these topers off the
limb.
Then they can sign the pledge. (*A* TROOPER
*appears with* ELKUS *and* DOPE.)

BUDGE (THE TROOPER). Help me keep an eye
on these two, will you, Patsy? I've got a
confession out of them on the Nanuet bank
robbery, and they say the money's up here.

PATSY. Up here? Whereabouts?

BUDGE. They left it in a satchel.

PATSY. There's the satchel, all right. (*He
examines it.*) Empty.

BUDGE. Looks like a stall, you guys. You
buried it.

ELKUS. Didn't keep a cent, officer. Somebody
up here got it.

BUDGE. Well, who?

ELKUS. Last time I saw it one of those birds
sat down on it. (*He points to* BIGGS *and*
SKIMMERHORN.)

PATSY. You know who they are? That's
Judge Skimmerhorn of the Probate Court,
and Arthur Biggs of the Trap-rock Company.

ELKUS. Well, one of them sat down on it.

BUDGE. Why didn't he pick it up?

ELKUS. I don't know whether he saw it.

DOPE. And then there was a little guy in a
big hat that had some of it.

PATSY. Yeah? Who?

BUDGE. That's right. Buddy said something
about a little guy in a big hat.

PATSY. You think he got away with it?

ELKUS. He had some of it, and we haven't
got a cent.

BUDGE. So now we have to look for a little
guy in a big hat. Any other description?

ELKUS. Short and fat, had two sawed-off
shotguns, and wore knee-pants.

DOPE. And you could see right through him.
(BUDGE *is writing in a notebook.*)

PATSY. What?

DOPE. You could see right through him.

BUDGE. I'm beginning to think I can see
right through you.

PATSY. Check on that. Elkus, you saw him.
Could you see through him?

ELKUS. Certainly was a funny-looking guy.
Looked as if you could see right through
him.

BUDGE. You expect me to send that out
over the country: "Look for a short, fat man
with a big hat and two sawed-off shotguns.
Dangerous. You can see right through
him."?

PATSY. They buried the money, Budge. Or
else they're screwy.

ELKUS. I thought I was screwy. You couldn't
hurt him with a gun.

BUDGE. What do you mean?

DOPE. We bored him full of holes and he
wouldn't even sit down.

BUDGE. You mean he kept on running?

DOPE. Running? He just stood there and let
us shoot him. Like shooting through a window.

BUDGE. Must have been wearing a vest.

DOPE. I shot him through the head! Two feet
away! And it just made him mad!

PATSY. Take 'em away, Budge. They're nuts.

ELKUS. But he had the money! Buddy saw
him with the money!

PATSY. They're all three nuts.

BUDGE. I never heard a line like that before.

PATSY. Who lives around here?

VAN. I guess I'm the only one that lives near-by.

PATSY. Did you hear any shooting last night?

VAN. Plenty of it.

PATSY. Did you take a look round?

VAN. Yes, I did.

PATSY. Did you see a little guy in a big hat?

VAN. Six or seven of them.

BUDGE. What!

VAN. Six or seven of them.

BUDGE. I suppose you could see right through them?

VAN. Once in a while.

BUDGE. I'm going to quit writing this down. There's enough here to get me fired already.

PATSY. If you saw six or seven where did they go?

VAN. Down the river.

PATSY. In a car?

VAN. In a ship.

PATSY. Sounds like a motor-boat gang. Well, that's something. They went down the river.

VAN. But I can tell you where there's thirty dollars of the money.

BUDGE. Where?

VAN. On the ledge there below the shovel. (BUDGE *and* PATSY *step over to look.*)

BUDGE. There it is. Three ten dollar bills. How did it get there?

VAN. I don't know. I just happened to see it.

BUDGE. Did you try to get it?

VAN. No, I thought it probably belonged to the gentlemen up there in the scoop.

PATSY. Did one of you drop some money, Judge?

SKIMMERHORN. I don't think so. Not me.

BIGGS. Not me.

PATSY. Did either of you see a little man in a big hat? (*The two look at each other.*)

SKIMMERHORN. Why, yes, we did. (PATSY *and* BUDGE *look at each other.*)

BUDGE. Well, if they say so he must have been here.

PATSY. What was he doing?

SKIMMERHORN. He was fighting with those two. (*He points to* ELKUS *and* DOPE.)

BIGGS. A regular war.

PATSY. Say, listen to that.

BUDGE. Do you know if he took anything out of the satchel?

SKIMMERHORN. Yes, I think he did. He had the satchel.

BUDGE. Now we're getting somewhere.

PATSY. You don't know where they went?

SKIMMERHORN. No.

PATSY. If you saw anything else that might give us a clue—?

SKIMMERHORN. No, not a thing.

PATSY. It beats me.

VAN. Want me to suggest a question?

PATSY. What?

VAN. Ask the Judge if he gained any weight during the night.

PATSY. What's the matter with you?

VAN. Looks to me like he picked up a good deal.

PATSY. I'll think up my own questions, thanks. Might as well trundle the yeggs back to pail, Budge. Whoever got the stuff it's gone.

BUDGE. That's what it looks like.

VAN. Aren't you going to help the Judge down before you go?

BIGGS. Oh, don't bother. We'll get down.

SKIMMERHORN. No hurry. We're all right. You take care of your prisoners.

PATSY. Might as well lend a hand while we're here.

BIGGS. Run along, boys. We're all right. Don't worry about us.

PATSY (*to* BUDGE). Want to wait a minute?

BUDGE. Well, I'm due back, if they can make it themselves.

BIGGS. Sure.

VAN. Oh, don't leave those poor fellows up. on that crane! They've been there all night!

SKIMMERHORN. We're fine. You run along.

BUDGE. Well, take a drag on the rope, Patsy. I'll wait. (PATSY *and* VAN *haul the shovel down.*)

SKIMMERHORN. No need to go to all this trouble.

PATSY. No trouble at all.

VAN. A pleasure. Why, you were asking me all night to get you out of this. (*The shovel touches ground. The two sit still.*)

PATSY. What's the matter?

SKIMMERHORN. Guess my legs are asleep.

BIGGS. Mine too.

PATSY. I'll help you up. (*They are pulled to their feet, staggering. Their pockets are very obvious.*)

BUDGE. How about it? O.K.?

PATSY. All set. Say, you are loaded down. Carried plenty of lunch, I guess?

BIGGS. Oh, we brought plenty.

VAN (*tapping* BIGG's *pocket*). I told you they gained weight. Something in the air up here.

ELKUS. Couldn't be money, could it?

BIGGS. As a matter of fact, some of it is. We were carrying cash to pay Van Dorn for his farm.

PATSY. Cash?

BIGGS. Yeah, cash.

PATSY. How much?

BIGGS. Just what we were authorized to pay. Twenty-five thousand.

VAN. Funny thing, too. It's got the Orangeburg pay roll stamp on it.

BIGGS. Well, hardly.

PATSY. What makes you think so?

VAN. I saw it. They offered me ten thousand.

PATSY. Just for the record, I'd better look at it, Judge.

SKIMMERHORN. I wouldn't if I were you. I'm hardly under suspicion of bank robbery.

PATSY. I'll take a look at it. (*He holds out a hand.* BIGGS *passes him a package.*)

SENIOR. I don't get this at all.

PATSY. It's got the Orangeburg stamp on it, all right.

SKIMMERHORN. Must be some mistake. They must have got the money mixed at the bank.

PATSY. Sure. Well, if that's all we can easy check on that.

VAN. Sure. You'd better check on it.

SKIMMERHORN. Are you under the impression that we robbed the bank?

VAN. You explain it. I can't.

SENIOR. You say you drew the money to pay Van Dorn?

SKIMMERHORN. That's right, A.B.

SENIOR. And it's got the Orangeburg label on it?

SKIMMERHORN. That's what they say.

SENIOR. I'll have something to say to the bank about that.

SKIMMERHORN. Oh, I'll take care of it. Just a clerical error.

PATSY. I'm afraid I'll have to take the money, though. Oh, you'll get your own money back, but if this is the Orangeburg money—

BIGGS. Sure, take it. (*They unload.*)

PATSY. And I guess I really ought to put you both under arrest.

BIGGS. What? Under arrest?

PATSY. Wouldn't you say so, Budge?

BUDGE. Don't see any way out of it. Doesn't mean anything. Just an examination.

SKIMMERHORN. I'd like to keep it out of the papers, if possible, of course. An examination might be very embarrassing—you see, I have political enemies.

BIGGS. Always ready to think the worst of a man, and print it, too.

PATSY. Still, I guess we'll have to have an examination. Just for the record.

SKIMMERHORN. You know who we are, of course?

PATSY. Yes, sir.

SKIMMERHORN. I won't submit to an examinaton! It's preposterous!

PATSY. I don't see how we can get out of it, though. Because we had a robbery, and here's the money, and we've got to explain it somehow.

SKIMMERHORN. I won't submit to it!

PATSY. You got an extra pair of handcuffs there, Budge?

BUDGE. Yeah.

SKIMMERHORN. All right. I'll go.

BIGGS. Sure. We'll go. And we'll make a lot of people sorry!

PATSY. Go on ahead, Budge. (BUDGE *starts out with his prisoners.*)

DOPE. But how about the little guy with the big hat? How about him?

BUDGE. I'll tell you about him. It's entirely possible there wasn't any little guy in a big hat.

DOPE. But we all saw him!

BUDGE. Oh, no, you didn't see him. You saw right through him. And the reason was he wasn't there. (BUDGE, ELKUS *and* DOPE *go out.*)

BIGGS. You don't think we made that up, about the man in the big hat?

PATSY. Well, you have to admit it doesn't sound exactly plausible. (PATSY, BIGGS *and* SKIMMERHORN *go out.*)

SENIOR (*as he goes*). It shakes a man's faith in evidence. (*To* VAN.) See you tomorrow.

VAN. I'll be there. (SKIMMERHORN SENIOR *goes out.*) So now—I've sold the Tor.

THE INDIAN. Yes, but it's better.

VAN. Better than living on a grudge, I guess. It might come down to that.

THE INDIAN. There's wilder land,
and there are higher mountains, in the west.

VAN. Out Port Jervis way.

THE INDIAN. Perhaps. You'll find them.

JUDITH. He came to tell you, Van—this is his death-day.
I'll go now.

VAN. All right, John.

THE INDIAN. Could I keep it?
The hand I held? It's a new thing, being blind,
when you've had an Indian's eyes. (JUDITH *returns and gives him her hand again.*)

JUDITH. I'll stay a while.

THE INDIAN. When I had lost the path
halfway along the ridge, there at my feet
I heard a woman crying. We came on
together, for she led me. There'll be time
for crying later. Take her west with you.
She'll forget the mountain.

VAN. Will you come?

JUDITH. I'd remember Lise!

VAN. Was there a Lise?
I think she was my dream of you and me
and how you left the mountain barren once
when you were gone. She was my dream of you
and how you left the Tor. Say you'll come with me.

JUDITH. Yes.

THE INDIAN. It's a long day's work to dig a grave
in stony ground. But you're young and have good shoulders.
It should be done tonight.

VAN. I'll have it done
even if you don't need it. Tell me the place.

THE INDIAN. There's still an Indian burying
   ground that lies
behind the northern slope. Beneath it runs
a line of square brown stones the white
   men used
to mark their dead. Below still, in a ring,
are seven graves, a woman and six men,
the Indians killed and laid there. In the
   freshet,
after the rain last night, the leaf-mould
   washed,
and the seven looked uncovered at the sky,
white skeletons with flintlocks by their sides,
and on the woman's hand a heavy ring
made out of gold. I laid them in again.

VAN. Seven graves—a woman and six
   men—
Maybe they'll rest now.

THE INDIAN. Dig them in deeper, then.
They're covered only lightly.

VAN. I'll dig them deeper.

THE INDIAN. But you must make my grave
   with my own people,
higher, beneath the ledge, and dig it straight,
and narrow. And you must place me in the
   fashion
used by the Indians, sitting at a game,
not fallen, not asleep, And set beside me
water and food. If this is strange to you,
think only I'm an Indian with strange ways,
but I shall need them.

VAN. Don't worry. You shall have it
just the way you want it.

THE INDIAN. Shall we go?

VAN. One last look at the rock. It's too late
to hold out on the bargain. Think of the
   gouge
they'll make across these hills.

JUDITH. If it's for me
you sell, we'll have enough without it, Van.
We'll have each other.

VAN. Oh, but you were right.
When they wash over you, you either swim
or drown. We won't be here.

THE INDIAN. And there's one comfort.
I heard the wise Iachim, looking down
when the railroad cut was fresh, and the
   bleeding earth
offended us. There is nothing made, he said,
and will be nothing made by these new men,
high tower, or cut, or buildings by a lake
that will not make good ruins.

JUDITH. Ruins? This?

THE INDIAN. Why, when the race is gone, or
   looks aside
only a little while, the white stone darkens,
the wounds close, and the roofs fall, and
   the walls
give way to rains. Nothing is made by men
but makes, in the end, good ruins.

VAN. Well, that's something.
But I can hardly wait.

CURTAIN

# 1937-38

John Steinbeck's *Of Mice and Men* did not have too much trouble winning on April 18, 1938, the latest date on which the Circle had voted. The balloting in subsequent years was to remain roughly at mid-April.

The winner was decided on the fourth ballot, with twelve votes this time representing the majority necessary to decide. Whitney Bolton and Walter Winchell did not ballot because they had not seen enough shows.

The runner-up throughout the four ballots was Thornton Wilder's sceneryless *Our Town,* and it seems amazing in retrospect that it didn't win easily. Other plays that received votes were *The Cradle Will Rock* by Marc Blitzstein, *Golden Boy* by Clifford Odets, and E. P. Conkle's *Prologue to Glory,* which, incidentally, was a production of the then flourishing WPA Federal Theatre.

The citation for *Of Mice and Men* read:

"For its direct force and perception in handling a theme genuinely rooted in American life; for its bite into the strict quality of its material; for its refusal to make the study of tragic loneliness and frustration either cheap or sensational, and finally for its simple, intense and steadily rising effect on the stage."

It was this year that the decision was made to give an honorable-mention citation to the best new foreign play, and the winner was Paul Vincent Carroll's *Shadow and Substance* which received a unanimous vote on the fourth ballot.

The season also was memorable for presenting George M. Cohan as the President of the United States in the George S. Kaufman–Moss Hart–Richard Rodgers–Lorenz Hart musical comedy, *I'd Rather Be Right,* the Lunts in the delightful Giraudoux *Amphitryon 38,* the modern-dress sceneryless *Julius Caesar* of Orson Welles' imaginative Mercury Theatre group, Paul Osborn's funny and heart-tugging fantasy, *On Borrowed Time,* and a new Sidney Howard drama, *The Ghost of Yankee Doodle,* which was to be the outstanding playwright's last Broadway production. He was tragically killed at forty-eight the following year.

*Of Mice and Men* had two notable performances from Wallace Ford and Broderick Crawford and provided the latter with the first real recognition he had received. It ran 207 performances.

# Of Mice and Men

## By JOHN STEINBECK

Presented by Sam H. Harris at the Music Box Theatre, New York City, November 23, 1937, with the following cast:

| | |
|---|---|
| GEORGE | *Wallace Ford* |
| LENNIE | *Broderick Crawford* |
| CANDY | *John F. Hamilton* |
| THE BOSS | *Thomas Findlay* |
| CURLEY | *Sam Byrd* |
| CURLEY'S WIFE | *Claire Luce* |
| SLIM | *Will Geer* |
| CARLSON | *Charles Slattery* |
| WHIT | *Walter Baldwin* |
| CROOKS | *Leigh Whipper* |

---

## SCENE

Act I—Scene 1—Sandy bank of the Salinas River, Thursday night. Scene 2—Interior of a bunkhouse, late Friday morning.

Act II—Scene 1—Same as Act I, Scene 2, about 7:30 Friday evening. Scene 2—Room of the stable buck, a lean-to, 10 o'clock Saturday evening.

Act III—Scene 1—One end of a great barn, mid-afternoon, Sunday. Scene 2—Same as Act I, Scene 1, Sunday night.

Time: The present.

Place: An agricultural valley in Central California.

---

# OF MICE AND MEN

## ACT ONE

### SCENE I

*Thursday night.*
*A sandy bank of the Salinas River sheltered with willows—one giant sycamore right, upstage.*
*The stage is covered with dry leaves. The feeling of the stage is sheltered and quiet. Stage is lit by a setting sun.*
*Curtain rises on an empty stage. A sparrow is singing. There is a distant sound of ranch dogs barking aimlessly and one clear quail call. The quail call turns to a warning call and there is a beat of the flock's wings. Two figures are seen entering the stage in single file, with* GEORGE, *the short man, coming in ahead of* LENNIE. *Both men are carrying blanket rolls. They approach the water. The small man throws down his blanket roll, the large man follows and then falls down and drinks from the river, snorting as he drinks.*

GEORGE (*irritably*). Lennie, for God's sake, don't drink so much. (*Leans over and shakes* LENNIE.) Lennie, you hear me! You gonna be sick like you was last night.

LENNIE (*dips his whole head under, hat and all. As he sits upon the bank, his hat drips down the back*). That's good. You drink some, George. You drink some too.

GEORGE (*kneeling and dipping his finger in the water*). I ain't sure it's good water. Looks kinda scummy to me.

LENNIE (*imitates, dipping his finger also*). Look at them wrinkles in the water, George. Look what I done.

GEORGE (*drinking from his cupped palm*). Tastes all right. Don't seem to be runnin' much, though. Lennie, you oughtn' to drink water when it ain't running. (*Hopelessly.*) You'd drink water out of a gutter if you was thirsty. (*He throws a scoop of water into his face and rubs it around with his hand, pushes himself back and embraces his knees.* LENNIE, *after watching him, imitates him in every detail.*)

GEORGE (*beginning tiredly and growing angry as he speaks*). God damn it, we could just as well of rode clear to the ranch. That bus driver didn't know what he was talkin' about. "Just a little stretch down the highway," he says. "Just a little stretch"—damn near four miles. I bet he didn't want to stop at the ranch gate. . . . I bet he's too damn lazy to pull up. Wonder he ain't too lazy to stop at Soledad at all! (*Mumbling.*) Just a little stretch down the road.

LENNIE (*timidly*). George?

GEORGE. Yeh . . . what you want?

LENNIE. Where we goin', George?

GEORGE (*jerks down his hat furiously*). So you forgot that already, did you? So I got to tell you again! Jeez, you're a crazy bastard!

LENNIE (*softly*). I forgot. I tried not to forget, honest to God, I did!

GEORGE. Okay, okay, I'll tell you again. . . . (*With sarcasm.*) I ain't got nothin' to do. Might just as well spen' all my time tellin' you things. You forgit 'em and I tell you again.

LENNIE (*continuing on from his last speech*). I tried and tried, but it didn't do no good. I remember about the rabbits, George!

GEORGE. The hell with the rabbits! You can't remember nothing but them rabbits. You remember settin' in that gutter on Howard Street and watchin' that blackboard?

LENNIE (*delightedly*). Oh, sure! I remember that . . . but . . . wha'd we do then? I remember some girls come by, and you says—

GEORGE. The hell with what I says! You remember about us goin' in Murray and Ready's and they give us work cards and bus tickets?

LENNIE (*confidently*). Oh, sure, George . . . I remember that now. (*Puts his hand into his side coat-pocket; his confidence vanishes. Very gently.*) . . . George?

GEORGE. Huh?

LENNIE (*staring at the ground in despair*). I ain't got mine. I musta lost it.

GEORGE. You never had none. I got both of 'em here. Think I'd let you carry your own work card?

LENNIE (*with tremendous relief*). I thought I put it in my side pocket. (*Puts his hand in his pocket again.*)

GEORGE (*looking sharply at him; and as he looks*, LENNIE *brings his hand out of his pocket.*) Wha'd you take out of that pocket?

LENNIE (*cleverly*). Ain't a thing in my pocket.

GEORGE. I know there ain't. You got it in your hand now. What you got in your hand?

LENNIE. I ain't got nothing, George! Honest!

GEORGE. Come on, give it here!

LENNIE (*holds his closed hand away from* GEORGE). It's on'y a mouse!

GEORGE. A mouse? A live mouse?

LENNIE. No . . . just a dead mouse. (*Worriedly.*) I didn't kill it. Honest. I found it. I found it dead.

GEORGE. Give it here!

LENNIE. Leave me have it, George.

GEORGE (*sternly*). Give it here! (LENNIE *reluctantly gives him the mouse.*) What do you want of a dead mouse, anyway?

LENNIE (*in a propositional tone*). I was petting it with my thumb while we walked along.

GEORGE. Well, you ain't pettin' no mice while you walk with me. Now let's see if you can remember where we're going. (GEORGE *throws it across the water into the brush.*)

LENNIE (*looks startled and then in embarrassment hides his face against his knees*). I forgot again.

GEORGE. Jesus Christ! (*Resignedly.*) Well, look, we are gonna work on a ranch like the one we come from up north.

LENNIE. Up north?

GEORGE. In Weed!

LENNIE. Oh, sure I remember—in Weed.

GEORGE (*still with exaggerated patience*). That ranch we're goin' to is right down there about a quarter mile. We're gonna go in and see the boss.

LENNIE (*repeats as a lesson*). And see the boss!

GEORGE. Now, look! I'll give him the work tickets, but you ain't gonna say a word. You're just gonna stand there and not say nothing.

LENNIE. Not say nothing!

GEORGE. If he finds out what a crazy bastard you are, we won't get no job. But if he sees you work before he hears you talk, we're set. You got that?

LENNIE. Sure, George . . . sure, I got that.

GEORGE. Okay. Now when we go in to see the boss, what you gonna do?

LENNIE (*concentrating*). I . . . I . . . I ain't gonna say nothing . . . jus' gonna stand there.

GEORGE (*greatly relieved*). Good boy, that's swell! Now say that over two or three times so you sure won't forget it.

LENNIE (*drones softly under his breath*). I ain't gonna say nothing . . . I ain't gonna say nothing. . . . (*Trails off into a whisper.*)

GEORGE. And you ain't gonna do no bad things like you done in Weed neither.

LENNIE (*puzzled*). Like I done in Weed?

GEORGE. So you forgot that too, did you?

LENNIE (*triumphantly*). They run us out of Weed!

GEORGE (*disgusted*). Run us out, hell! We run! They was lookin' for us, but they didn't catch us.

LENNIE (*happily*). I didn't forget that, you bet.

GEORGE (*lies back on the sand, crosses his hands under his head. And again* LENNIE *imitates him*). God, you're a lot of trouble! I could get along so easy and nice, if I didn't have you on my tail. I could live so easy!

LENNIE (*hopefully*). We gonna work on a ranch, George.

GEORGE. All right, you got that. But we're gonna sleep here tonight, because . . . I want to. I want to sleep out. (*The light is going fast, dropping into evening. A little wind whirls into the clearing and blows leaves. A dog howls in the distance.*)

LENNIE. Why ain't we goin' on to the ranch to get some supper? They got supper at the ranch.

GEORGE. No reason at all. I just like it here. Tomorrow we'll be goin' to work. I seen thrashing machines on the way down; that means we'll be buckin' grain bags. Bustin' a gut liftin' up them bags. Tonight I'm gonna lay right here an' look up! Tonight there ain't a grain bag or a boss in the world. Tonight, the drinks is on the . . . house. Nice house we got here, Lennie.

LENNIE (*gets up on his knees and looks down at* GEORGE, *plaintively*). Ain't we gonna have no supper?

GEORGE. Sure we are. You gather up some dead willow sticks. I got three cans of beans in my bindle. I'll open 'em up while you get a fire ready. We'll eat 'em cold.

LENNIE (*companionably*). I like beans with ketchup.

GEORGE. Well, we ain't got no ketchup. You go get the wood, and don't you fool around none. Be dark before long. (LENNIE *lumbers to his feet and disappears into the brush.* GEORGE *gets out the bean cans, opens two of them, suddenly turns his head and listens. A little sound of splashing comes from the direction that* LENNIE *has taken.* GEORGE *looks after him; shakes his head.* LENNIE *comes back carrying a few small willow sticks in his hand.*) All right, give me that mouse.

LENNIE (*with elaborate pantomime of innocence*). What, George? I ain't got no mouse.

GEORGE (*holding out his hand*). Come on! Give it to me! You ain't puttin' nothing over. (LENNIE *hesitates, backs away, turns and looks as if he were going to run. Coldly*). You gonna give me that mouse or do I have to take a sock at you?

LENNIE. Give you what, George?

GEORGE. You know goddamn well, what! I want that mouse!

LENNIE (*almost in tears*). I don't know why I can't keep it. It ain't nobody's mouse. I didn' steal it! I found it layin' right beside the road. (GEORGE *snaps his fingers sharply, and* LENNIE *lays the mouse in his hand.*) I wasn't doin' nothing bad with it. Just stroking it. That ain't bad.

GEORGE (*stands up and throws the mouse as far as he can into the brush, then he steps to the pool, and washes his hands*). You crazy fool! Thought you could get away with it, didn't you? Don't you think I could see your feet was wet where you went in the water to get it? (LENNIE *whimpers like a puppy.*) Blubbering like a baby. Jesus Christ, a big guy like you! (LENNIE *tries to control himself, but his lips quiver and his face works with an effort.* GEORGE *puts his hand on* LENNIE's *shoulder for a moment.*) Aw, Lennie, I ain't takin' it away just for meanness. That mouse ain't fresh. Besides, you broke it pettin' it. You get a mouse that's fresh and I'll let you keep it a little while.

LENNIE. I don't know where there is no other mouse. I remember a lady used to give 'em to me. Ever' one she got she used to give it to me, but that lady ain't here no more.

GEORGE. Lady, huh! . . . Give me them sticks there. . . . Don't even remember who that lady was. That was your own Aunt Clara. She stopped givin' 'em to you. You always killed 'em.

LENNIE (*sadly and apologetically*). They was so little. I'd pet 'em and pretty soon they bit my fingers and then I pinched their head a little bit and then they was dead . . . because they was so little. I wish we'd get the rabbits pretty soon, George. They ain't so little.

GEORGE. The hell with the rabbits! Come on, let's eat. (*The light has continued to go out of the scene so that when* GEORGE *lights the fire, it is the major light on the stage.* GEORGE *hands one of the open cans of beans to* LENNIE.) There's enough beans for four men.

LENNIE (*sitting on the other side of the fire, speaks patiently*). I like 'em with ketchup.

GEORGE (*explodes*). Well, we ain't got any. Whatever we ain't got, that's what you want. God Almighty, if I was alone, I could live so easy. I could go get a job of work and no trouble. No mess . . . and when the end of the month come, I could take my fifty bucks and go into town and get whatever I want. Why, I could stay in a cat-house all night. I could eat any place I want. Order any damn thing.

LENNIE (*plaintively, but softly*). I didn't want no ketchup.

GEORGE (*continuing violently*). I could do that every damn month. Get a gallon of whiskey or set in a pool room and play cards or shoot pool. (LENNIE *gets up to his knees and looks over the fire, with frightened face.*) And what have I got? (*Disgustedly.*) I got you. You can't keep a job and you lose me every job I get!

LENNIE (*in terror*). I don't mean nothing, George.

GEORGE. Just keep me shovin' all over the country all the time. And that ain't the worst—you get in trouble. You do bad things and I got to get you out. It ain't bad people that raises hell. It's dumb ones. (*He shouts.*) You crazy son-of-a-bitch, you keep me in hot water all the time. (LENNIE *is trying to stop* GEORGE's *flow of words with his hands. Sarcastically.*) You just wanta feel that girl's dress. Just wanta pet it like it was a mouse. Well, how the hell'd she know you just wanta feel her dress? How'd she know you'd just hold onto it like it was a mouse?

LENNIE (*in panic*). I didn't mean to, George!

GEORGE. Sure you didn't mean to. You didn't mean for her to yell bloody hell, either. You didn't mean for us to hide in the irrigation ditch all day with guys out lookin' for us with guns. Alla time it's something you didn't mean. God damn it, I wish I could put you in a cage with a million mice and let them pet *you*. (GEORGE's *anger leaves him suddenly. For the first time he seems to see the expression of terror on* LENNIE's *face. He looks down ashamedly at the fire, and maneuvers some beans onto the blade of his pocket-knife and puts them into his mouth.*)

LENNIE (*after a pause*). George! (GEORGE *purposely does not answer him.*) George?

GEORGE. What do you want?

LENNIE. I was only foolin', George. I don't want no ketchup. I wouldn't eat no ketchup if it was right here beside me.

GEORGE (*with a sullenness of shame*). If they was some here you could have it. And if I had a thousand bucks I'd buy ya a bunch of flowers.

LENNIE. I wouldn't eat no ketchup, George. I'd leave it all for you. You could cover your beans so deep with it, and I wouldn't touch none of it.

GEORGE (*refusing to give in from his sullenness, refusing to look at* LENNIE.) When I think of the swell time I could have without you, I go nuts. I never git no peace!

LENNIE. You want I should go away and leave you alone?

GEORGE. Where the hell could you go?

LENNIE. Well, I could . . . I could go off in the hills there. Some place I could find a cave.

GEORGE. Yeah, how'd ya eat? You ain't got sense enough to find nothing to eat.

LENNIE. I'd find things. I don't need no nice food with ketchup. I'd lay out in the sun and nobody would hurt me. And if I found a mouse—why, I could keep it. Wouldn't nobody take it away from me.

GEORGE (*at last he looks up*). I been mean, ain't I?

LENNIE (*presses his triumph*). If you don't want me, I can go right in them hills, and find a cave. I can go away any time.

GEORGE. No. Look! I was just foolin' ya. 'Course I want you to stay with me. Trouble with mice is you always kill 'em. (*He pauses.*) Tell you what I'll do, Lennie. First chance I get I'll find you a pup. Maybe you wouldn't kill it. That would be better than mice. You could pet it harder.

LENNIE (*still avoiding being drawn in*). If you don't want me, you only gotta say so. I'll go right up on them hills and live by myself. And I won't get no mice stole from me.

GEORGE. I want you to stay with me. Jesus Christ, somebody'd shoot you for a coyote if you was by yourself. Stay with me. Your Aunt Clara wouldn't like your runnin' off by yourself, even if she is dead.

LENNIE. George?

GEORGE. Huh?

LENNIE (*craftily*). Tell me—like you done before.

GEORGE. Tell you what?

LENNIE. About the rabbits.

GEORGE (*near to anger again*). You ain't gonna put nothing over on me!

LENNIE (*pleading*). Come on, George . . . tell me! Please! Like you done before.

GEORGE. You get a kick out of that, don't you? All right, I'll tell you. And then we'll lay out our beds and eat our dinner.

LENNIE. Go on, George. (*Unrolls his bed and lies on his side, supporting his head on one hand.* GEORGE *lays out his bed and sits cross-legged on it.* GEORGE *repeats the next speech rhythmically, as though he had said it many times before.*)

GEORGE. Guys like us that work on ranches is the loneliest guys in the world. They ain't got no family. They don't belong no place. They come to a ranch and work up a stake and then they go in to town and blow their stake. And then the first thing you know they're poundin' their tail on some other ranch. They ain't got nothin' to look ahead to.

LENNIE (*delightedly*). That's it, that's it! Now tell how it is with us.

GEORGE (*still almost chanting*). With us it ain't like that. We got a future. We got somebody to talk to that gives a damn about us. We don't have to sit in no barroom blowin' in our jack, just because we got no place else to go. If them other guys gets in jail, they can rot for all anybody gives a damn.

LENNIE (*who cannot restrain himself any longer. Bursts into speech*). But not us! And why? Because . . . because I got you to look after me . . . and you got me to look after you . . . and that's why! (*He laughs.*) Go on, George!

GEORGE. You got it by heart. You can do it yourself.

LENNIE. No, no. I forget some of the stuff. Tell about how it's gonna be.

GEORGE. Some other time.

LENNIE. No, tell how it's gonna be!

GEORGE. Okay. Some day we're gonna get the jack together and we're gonna have a little house, and a couple of acres and a cow and some pigs and . . .

LENNIE (*shouting*). And live off the fat of the land! And have rabbits. Go on, George! Tell about what we're gonna have in the garden. And about the rabbits in the cages. Tell about the rain in the winter . . . and about the stove and how thick the cream is on the milk, you can hardly cut it. Tell about that, George!

GEORGE. Why don't you do it yourself—you know all of it!

LENNIE. It ain't the same if I tell it. Go on now. How I get to tend the rabbits.

GEORGE (*resignedly*). Well, we'll have a big vegetable patch and a rabbit hutch and chickens. And when it rains in the winter we'll just say to hell with goin' to work. We'll build up a fire in the stove, and set around it and listen to the rain comin' down on the roof—Nuts! (*Begins to eat with his knife.*) I ain't got time for no more. (*He falls to eating.* LENNIE *imitates him, spilling a few beans from his mouth with every bite.* GEORGE, *gesturing with his knife.*) What you gonna say tomorrow when the boss asks you questions?

LENNIE (*stops chewing in the middle of a bite, swallows painfully. His face contorts with thought*). I . . . I ain't gonna say a word.

GEORGE. Good boy. That's fine. Say, maybe you're gittin' better. I bet I can let you tend the rabbits . . . specially if you remember as good as that!

LENNIE (*choking with pride*). I can remember, by God!

GEORGE (*as though remembering something, points his knife at* LENNIE's *chest*). Lennie, I want you to look around here. Think you can remember this place? The ranch is 'bout a quarter mile up that way. Just follow the river and you can get here.

LENNIE (*looking around carefully*). Sure, I can remember here. Didn't I remember 'bout not gonna say a word?

GEORGE. 'Course you did. Well, look, Lennie, if you just happen to get in trouble, I want you to come right here and hide in the brush.

LENNIE (*slowly*). Hide in the brush.

GEORGE. Hide in the brush until I come for you. Think you can remember that?

LENNIE. Sure I can, George. Hide in the brush till you come for me!

GEORGE. But you ain't gonna get in no trouble. Because if you do I won't let you tend the rabbits.

LENNIE. I won't get in no trouble. I ain't gonna say a word.

GEORGE. You got it. Anyways, I hope so. (GEORGE *stretches out on his blankets. The light dies slowly out of the fire until only the faces of the two men can be seen.* GEORGE *is still eating from his can of beans.*) It's gonna be nice sleeping here. Lookin' up . . . and the leaves . . . Don't build no more fire. We'll let her die. Jesus, you feel free when you ain't got a job—if you ain't hungry. (*They sit silently for a few moments. A night owl is heard far off. From across the river there comes the sound of a coyote howl and on the heels of the howl all the dogs in the country start to bark.*)

LENNIE (*from almost complete darkness*). George?

GEORGE. What do you want?

LENNIE. Let's have different color rabbits, George.

GEORGE. Sure. Red rabbits and blue rabbits and green rabbits. Millions of 'em!

LENNIE. Furry ones, George. Like I seen at the fair in Sacramento.

GEORGE. Sure. Furry ones.

LENNIE. 'Cause I can jus' as well go away, George, and live in a cave.

GEORGE (*amiably*). Aw, shut up.

LENNIE (*after a long pause*). George?

GEORGE. What is it?

LENNIE. I'm shutting up, George. (*A coyote howls again.*)

CURTAIN

# SCENE II

*Late Friday morning.*
*The interior of a bunkhouse.*
*Walls, white-washed board and bat. Floors unpainted.*
*There is a heavy square table with upended boxes around it used for chairs. Over each bunk there is a box nailed to the wall which serves as two shelves on which are the private possessions of the working men.*
*On top of each bunk there is a large noisy alarm clock ticking madly.*
*The sun is streaking through the windows. Note: Articles in the boxes on wall are soap, talcum powder, razors, pulp magazines, medicine bottles, combs, and from nails on the sides of the boxes a few neckties.*
*There is a hanging light from the ceiling over the table, with a round dim reflector on it.*
*The curtain rises on an empty stage. Only the ticking of the many alarm clocks is heard.*
CANDY, GEORGE *and* LENNIE *are first seen passing the open window of the bunkhouse.*

CANDY. This is the bunkhouse here. Door's around this side. (*The latch on the door rises and* CANDY *enters, a stoop-shouldered old man. He is dressed in blue jeans and a denim coat. He carries a big push broom in his left hand. His right hand is gone at the wrist. He grasps things with his right arm between arm and side. He walks into the room followed by* GEORGE *and* LENNIE. *Conversationally.*) The boss was expecting you last night. He was sore as hell when you wasn't here to go out this morning. (*Points with his handless arm.*) You can have them two beds there.

GEORGE. I'll take the top one . . . I don't want you falling down on me. (*Steps over to the bunk and throws his blankets down. He looks into the nearly empty box shelf over it, then picks up a small yellow can.*) Say, what the hell's this?

CANDY. I don't know.

GEORGE. Says "positively kills lice, roaches and other scourges." What the hell kinda beds you givin' us, anyway? We don't want no pants rabbits.

CANDY (*shifts his broom, holding it between his elbow and his side, takes the can in his left hand and studies the label carefully*). Tell you what . . . last guy that had this bed was a blacksmith. Helluva nice fellow. Clean a guy as you'd want to meet. Used to wash his hands even *after* he et.

GEORGE (*with gathering anger*). Then how come he got pillow-pigeons? (LENNIE *puts his blankets on his bunk and sits down, watching* GEORGE *with his mouth slightly open.*)

CANDY. Tell you what. This here blacksmith, name of Whitey, was the kinda guy that would put that stuff around even if there wasn't no bugs. Tell you what he used to do. He'd peel *his* boiled potatoes and take out every little spot before he et it, and if there was a red splotch on an egg, he'd scrape it off. Finally quit about the food. That's the kind of guy Whitey was. Clean. Used to dress up Sundays even when he wasn't goin' no place. Put on a necktie even, and then set in the bunkhouse.

GEORGE (*skeptically*). I ain't so sure. What da' ya say he quit for?

CANDY (*puts the can in his pocket, rubs his bristly white whiskers with his knuckles*). Why . . . he just quit the way a guy will. Says it was the food. Didn't give no other reason. Just says "give me my time" one night, the way any guy would. (GEORGE *lifts his bed tick and looks underneath, leans over and inspects the sacking carefully.* LENNIE *does the same with his bed.*)

GEORGE (*half satisfied*). Well, if there's any grey-backs in this bed, you're gonna hear from me! (*He unrolls his blankets and puts his razor and bar of soap and comb and bottle of pills, his liniment and leather wristband in the box.*)

CANDY. I guess the boss'll be out here in a minute to write your name in. He sure was burned when you wasn't here this morning. Come right in when we was eatin' breakfast and says, "Where the hell's them new men?" He give the stable buck hell, too. Stable buck's a nigger.

GEORGE. Nigger, huh!

CANDY. Yeah. (*Continues.*) Nice fellow **too.** Got a crooked back where a horse kicked him. Boss gives him hell when he's mad. But the stable buck don't give a damn about that.

GEORGE. What kinda guy is the boss?

CANDY. Well, he's a pretty nice fella for a boss. Gets mad sometimes. But he's pretty nice. Tell you what. Know what he done Christmas? Brung a gallon of whiskey right in here and says, "Drink hearty, boys, Christmas comes but once a year!"

GEORGE. The hell he did! A whole gallon?

CANDY. Yes, sir. Jesus, we had fun! They let the nigger come in that night. Well, sir, a little skinner name Smitty took after the nigger. Done pretty good too. The guys wouldn't let him use his feet so the nigger got him. If he could a used his feet Smitty says he would have killed the nigger. The guys says on account the nigger got a crooked back Smitty can't use his feet. (*He smiles in reverie at the memory.*)

GEORGE. Boss the owner?

CANDY. Naw! Superintendent. Big land company. . . . Yes, sir, that night . . . he comes right in here with a whole gallon . . . he set right over there and says, "Drink hearty, boys," . . . he says. . . . (*The door opens. Enter the* BOSS. *He is a stocky man, dressed in blue jean trousers, flannel shirt, a black unbuttoned vest and a black coat. He wears a soiled brown Stetson hat, a pair of high-heeled boots and spurs. Ordinarily he puts his thumbs in his belt.* CANDY, *shuffling towards the door, rubbing his whiskers with his knuckles as he goes.*) Them guys just come. (CANDY *exits and shuts the door behind him.*)

BOSS. I wrote Murray and Ready I wanted two men this morning. You got your work slips?

GEORGE (*digs in his pockets, produces two slips, and hands them to the* BOSS). Here they are.

BOSS (*reading the slips*). Well, I see it wasn't Murray and Ready's fault. It says right here on the slip, you was to be here for work this morning.

GEORGE. Bus driver give us a bum steer. We had to walk ten miles. That bus driver says we was here when we wasn't. We couldn't thumb no rides. (GEORGE *scowls meaningly at* LENNIE *and* LENNIE *nods to show that he understands.*)

BOSS. Well, I had to send out the grain teams short two buckers. It won't do any good to go out now until after dinner. You'd get lost. (*Pulls out his time book, opens it to where a pencil is stuck between the leaves. Licks his pencil carefully.*) What's your name?

GEORGE. George Milton.

BOSS. George Milton. (*Writing.*) And what's yours?

GEORGE. His name's Lennie Small.

BOSS. Lennie Small. (*Writing.*) Le's see, this is the twentieth. Noon the twentieth . . . (*Makes positive mark. Closes the book and puts it in his pocket.*) Where you boys been workin'?

GEORGE. Up around Weed.

BOSS (*to* LENNIE). You too?

GEORGE. Yeah. Him too.

BOSS (*to* LENNIE). Say, you're a big fellow, ain't you?

GEORGE. Yeah, he can work like hell, too.

BOSS. He ain't much of a talker, though, is he?

GEORGE. No, he ain't. But he's a hell of a good worker. Strong as a bull.

LENNIE (*smiling*). I'm strong as a bull. (GEORGE *scowls at him and* LENNIE *drops his head in shame at having forgotten.*)

BOSS (*sharply*). You are, huh? What can you do?

GEORGE. He can do anything.

BOSS (*addressing* LENNIE). What can you do? (LENNIE, *looking at* GEORGE, *gives a high nervous chuckle.*)

GEORGE (*quickly*). Anything you tell him. He's a good skinner. He can wrestle grain bags, drive a cultivator. He can do anything. Just give him a try.

BOSS (*turning to* GEORGE). Then why don't you let *him* answer? (LENNIE *laughs.*) What's he laughing about?

GEORGE. He laughs when he gets excited.

BOSS. Yeah?

GEORGE (*loudly*). But he's a goddamn good worker. I ain't saying he's bright, because he ain't. But he can put up a four hundred pound bale.

BOSS (*hooking his thumbs in his belt*). Say, what you sellin'?

GEORGE. Huh?

BOSS. I said what stake you got in this guy? You takin' his pay away from him?

GEORGE. No. Of course I ain't!
BOSS. Hell, I never seen one guy take so much trouble for another guy. I just like to know what your percentage is.

GEORGE. He's my . . . cousin. I told his ole lady I'd take care of him. He got kicked in the head by a horse when he was a kid. He's all right. . . . Just ain't bright. But he can do anything you tell him.

BOSS (*turning half away*). Well, God knows he don't need no brains to buck barley bags. (*He turns back.*) But don't you try to put nothing over, Milton. I got my eye on you. Why'd you quit in Weed?

GEORGE (*promptly*). Job was done.

BOSS. What kind of job?

GEORGE. Why . . . we was diggin' a cesspool.

BOSS (*after a pause*). All right. But don't try to put nothing over 'cause you can't get away with nothing. I seen wise guys before. Go out with the grain teams after dinner. They're out pickin' up barley with the thrashin' machines. Go out with Slim's team.

GEORGE. Slim?

BOSS. Yeah. Big, tall skinner. You'll see him at dinner. (*Up to this time the* BOSS *has been full of business. He has been calm and suspicious. In the following lines he relaxes, but gradually, as though he wanted to talk but felt always the burden of his position. He turns toward the door, but hesitates and allows a little warmth into his manner.*) Been on the road long?

GEORGE (*obviously on guard*). We was three days in 'Frisco lookin' at the boards.

BOSS (*with heavy jocularity*). Didn't go to no night clubs, I 'spose?

GEORGE (*stiffly*). We was lookin' for a job.

BOSS (*attempting to be friendly*). That's a great town if you got a little jack, Frisco.

GEORGE (*refusing to be drawn in*). We didn't have no jack for nothing like that.

BOSS (*realizes there is no contact to establish; grows rigid with his position again*). Go out with the grain teams after dinner. When my hands work hard they get pie and when they loaf they bounce down the road on their can. You ask anybody about me. (*He turns and walks out of bunkhouse.*)

GEORGE (*turns to* LENNIE). So you wasn't gonna say a word! You was gonna leave your big flapper shut. I was gonna do the talkin'. . . . You goddamn near lost us the job!

LENNIE (*stares hopelessly at his hands*). I forgot.

GEORGE. You forgot. You always forget. Now, he's got his eye on us. Now, we gotta be careful and not make no slips. You keep your big flapper shut after this.

LENNIE. He talked like a kinda nice guy towards the last.

GEORGE (*angrily*). He's the boss, ain't he? Well, he's the boss first an' a nice guy afterwards. Don't you have nothin' to do with no boss, except do your work and draw your pay. You can't never tell whether you're talkin' to the nice guy or the boss. Just keep your goddamn mouth shut. Then you're all right.

LENNIE. George?

GEORGE. What you want now?

LENNIE. I wasn't kicked in the head with no horse, was I, George?

GEORGE. Be a damn good thing if you was. Save everybody a hell of a lot of trouble!

LENNIE (*flattered*). You says I was your cousin.

GEORGE. Well, that was a goddamn lie. And I'm glad it was. Why, if I was a relative of yours—(*He stops and listens, then steps to the front door, and looks out.*) Say, what the hell you doin', listenin'?

CANDY (*comes slowly into the room. By a rope, he leads an ancient drag-footed, blind sheep dog. Guides it from running into a table leg, with the rope. Sits down on a box, and presses the hind quarters of the old dog down*). Naw . . . I wasn't listenin'. . . . I was just standin' in the shade a minute, scratchin' my dog. I jest now finished swamping out the washhouse.

GEORGE. You was pokin' your big nose into our business! I don't like nosey guys.

CANDY (*looks uneasily from* GEORGE *to* LENNIE *and then back*). I jest come there . . . I didn't hear nothing you guys was sayin'. I ain't interested in nothing you was sayin'. A guy on a ranch don't never listen. Nor he don't ast no questions.

GEORGE (*slightly mollified*). Damn right he don't! Not if the guy wants to stay workin' long. (*His manner changes*). That's a helluva ole dog.

CANDY. Yeah. I had him ever since he was a pup. God, he was a good sheep dog, when he was young. (*Rubs his cheek with his knuckles.*) How'd you like the boss?

GEORGE. Pretty good! Seemed all right.

CANDY. He's a nice fella. You got ta take him right, of course. He's runnin' this ranch. He don't take no nonsense.

GEORGE. What time do we eat? Eleven-thirty? (CURLEY *enters. He is dressed in working clothes. He wears brown high heeled boots and has a glove on his left hand.*)

CURLEY. Seen my ole man?

CANDY. He was here just a minute ago, Curley. Went over to the cookhouse, I think.

CURLEY. I'll try to catch him. (*Looking over at the new men, measuring them. Unconsciously bends his elbow and closes his hand and goes into a slight crouch. He walks gingerly close to* LENNIE.) You the new guys my ole man was waitin' for?

GEORGE. Yeah. We just come in.

CURLEY. How's it come you wasn't here this morning?

GEORGE. Got off the bus too soon.

CURLEY (*again addressing* LENNIE). My ole man got to get the grain out. Ever bucked barley?

GEORGE (*quickly*). Hell, yes. Done a lot of it.

CURLEY. I mean him. (*To* LENNIE.) Ever bucked barley?

GEORGE. Sure he has.

CURLEY (*irritatedly*). Let the big guy talk!

GEORGE. 'Spose he don't want ta talk?

CURLEY (*pugnaciously*). By Christ, he's gotta talk when he's spoke to. What the hell you shovin' into this for?

GEORGE (*stands up and speaks coldly*). Him and me travel together.

CURLEY. Oh, so it's that way?

GEORGE (*tense and motionless*). What way?

CURLEY (*letting the subject drop*). And you won't let the big guy talk? Is that it?

GEORGE. He can talk if he wants to tell you anything. (*He nods slightly to* LENNIE.)

LENNIE (*in a frightened voice*). We just come in.

CURLEY. Well, next time you answer when you're spoke to, then.

GEORGE. He didn't do nothing to you.

CURLEY (*measuring him*). You drawin' cards this hand?

GEORGE (*quietly*). I might.

CURLEY (*stares at him for a moment, his threat moving to the future*). I'll see you get a chance to ante, anyway. (*He walks out of the room.*)

GEORGE (*after he has made his exit*). Say, what the hell's he got on his shoulder? Lennie didn't say nothing to him.

CANDY (*looks cautiously at the door*). That's the boss's son. Curley's pretty handy. He done quite a bit in the ring. The guys say he's pretty handy.

GEORGE. Well, let 'im be handy. He don't have to take after Lennie. Lennie didn't do nothing to him.

CANDY (*considering*). Well . . . tell you what, Curley's like a lot a little guys. He hates big guys. He's alla time pickin' scraps with big guys. Kinda like he's mad at 'em because *he* ain't a big guy. You seen little guys like that, ain't you—always scrappy?

GEORGE. Sure, I seen plenty tough little guys. But this here Curley better not make no mistakes about Lennie. Lennie ain't handy, see, but this Curley punk's gonna get hurt if he messes around with Lennie.

CANDY (*skeptically*). Well, Curley's pretty handy. You know, it never did seem right to me. 'Spose Curley jumps a big guy and licks him. Everybody says what a game guy Curley is. Well, 'spose he jumps 'im and gits licked, everybody says the big guy oughta pick somebody his own size. Seems like Curley ain't givin' nobody a chance.

GEORGE (*watching the door*). Well, he better watch out for Lennie. Lennie ain't no fighter. But Lennie's strong and quick and Lennie don't know no rules. (*Walks to the square table, and sits down on one of the boxes. Picks up scattered cards and pulls them together and shuffles them.*)

CANDY. Don't tell Curley I said none of this. He'd slough me! He jus' don't give a damn. Won't ever get canned because his ole man's the boss!

GEORGE (*cuts the cards. Turns over and looks at each one as he throws it down*). This guy Curley sounds like a son-of-a-bitch to me! I don't like mean little guys!

CANDY. Seems to me like he's worse lately. He got married a couple of weeks ago. Wife lives over in the boss's house. Seems like Curley's worse'n ever since he got married. Like he's settin' on a ant-hill an' a big red ant come up an' nipped 'im on the turnip. Just feels so goddanm miserable he'll strike at anything that moves. I'm kinda sorry for 'im.

GEORGE. Maybe he's showin' off for his wife.

CANDY. You seen that glove on his left hand?

GEORGE. Sure I seen it!

CANDY. Well, that glove's full of vaseline.

GEORGE. Vaseline? What the hell for?

CANDY. Curley says he's keepin' that hand soft for his wife.

GEORGE. That's a dirty kind of a thing to tell around.

CANDY. I ain't quite so sure. I seen such funny things a guy will do to try to be nice. I ain't sure. But you jus' wait till you see Curley's wife!

GEORGE (*begins to lay out a solitaire hand, speaks casually*). Is she purty?

CANDY. Yeah. Purty, but—

GEORGE (*studying his cards*). But what?

CANDY. Well, she got the eye.

GEORGE (*still playing at his solitaire hand*). Yeah? Married two weeks an' got the eye? Maybe that's why Curley's pants is fulla ants.

CANDY. Yes, sir, I seen her give Slim the eye. Slim's a jerkline skinner. Hell of a nice fella. Well, I seen her give Slim the eye. Curley never seen it. And I seen her give a skinner named Carlson the eye.

GEORGE (*pretending a very mild interest*). Looks like we was gonna have fun!

CANDY (*stands up*). Know what I think? (*Waits for an answer.* GEORGE *doesn't answer.*) Well, I think Curley's married himself a tart.

GEORGE (*casually*). He ain't the first. Black queen on a red king. Yes, sir . . . there's plenty done that!

CANDY (*moves towards the door, leading his dog out with him*). I got to be settin' out the wash basins for the guys. The teams'll be in before long. You guys gonna buck barley?

GEORGE. Yeah.

CANDY. You won't tell Curley nothing I said?

GEORGE. Hell, no!

CANDY (*just before he goes out the door, he turns back*). Well, you look her over, mister. You see if she ain't a tart! (*He exits.*)

GEORGE (*continuing to play out his solitaire. He turns to* LENNIE). Look, Lennie, this here ain't no set-up. You gonna have trouble with that Curley guy. I seen that kind before. You know what he's doin'. He's kinda feelin' you out. He figures he's got you scared. And he's gonna take a sock at you, first chance he gets.

LENNIE (*frightened*). I don't want no trouble. Don't let him sock me, George!

GEORGE. I hate them kind of bastards. I seen plenty of 'em. Like the ole guy says: "Curley don't take no chances. He always figures to win." (*Thinks for a moment.*) If he tangles with you, Lennie, we're goin' get the can. Don't make no mistake about that. He's the boss's kid. Look, you try to keep away from him, will you? Don't never speak to him. If he comes in here you move clear to the other side of the room. Will you remember that, Lennie?

LENNIE (*mourning*). I don't want no trouble. I never done nothing to him!

GEORGE. Well, that won't do you no good, if Curley wants to set himself up for a fighter. Just don't have nothing to do with him. Will you remember?

LENNIE. Sure, George . . . I ain't gonna say a word. (*Sounds of the teams coming in from the fields, jingling of harness, croak of heavy laden axles, men talking to and cussing the horses. Crack of a whip and from a distance a voice calling.*)

SLIM'S VOICE. Stable buck! Hey! Stable buck!

GEORGE. Here come the guys. Just don't say nothing.

LENNIE (*timidly*). You ain't mad, George?

GEORGE. I ain't mad at you. I'm mad at this here Curley bastard! I wanted we should get a little stake together. Maybe a hundred dollars. You keep away from Curley.

LENNIE. Sure I will. I won't say a word.

GEORGE (*hesitating*). Don't let 'im pull you in—but—if the son-of-a-bitch socks you—let him have it!

LENNIE. Let him have what, George?

GEORGE. Never mind. . . . Look, if you get in any kind of trouble, you remember what I told you to do.

LENNIE. If I get in any trouble, you ain't gonna let me tend the rabbits?

GEORGE. That's not what I mean. You remember where we slept last night. Down by the river?

LENNIE. Oh, sure I remember. I go there and hide in the brush until you come for me.

GEORGE. That's it. Hide till I come for you. Don't let nobody see you. Hide in the brush by the river. Now say that over.

LENNIE. Hide in the brush by the river. Down in the brush by the river.

GEORGE. If you get in trouble.

LENNIE. If I get in trouble.
(*A brake screeckes outside and a call: "Stable buck, oh, stable buck!" "Where the hell's that goddamn nigger?" Suddenly* CURLEY'S WIFE *is standing in the door. Full, heavily rouged lips. Wide-spaced, made-up eyes, her fingernails are bright red, her hair hangs in little rolled clusters like sausages. She wears a cotton house dress and red mules, on the insteps of which are little bouquets of red ostrich feathers.* GEORGE *and* LENNIE *look up at her.*)

CURLEY'S WIFE. I'm lookin' for Curley!

GEORGE (*looks away from her*). He was in here a minute ago but he went along.

CURLEY'S WIFE (*puts her hands behind her back and leans against the door frame so that her body is thrown forward*). You're the new fellas that just come, ain't you?

GEORGE (*sullenly*). Yeah

CURLEY'S WIFE (*bridles a little and inspects her fingernails*). Sometimes Curley's in here.

GEORGE (*brusquely*). Well, he ain't now!

CURLEY'S WIFE (*playfully*). Well, if he ain't, I guess I'd better look some place else. (LENNIE *watches her, fascinated.*)

GEORGE. If I see Curley I'll pass the word you was lookin' for him.

CURLEY'S WIFE. Nobody can't blame a person for lookin'.

GEORGE. That depends what she's lookin' for.

CURLEY'S WIFE (*a little wearily, dropping her coquetry*). I'm jus' lookin' for somebody to talk to. Don't you never jus' want to talk to somebody?

SLIM (*offstage*). Okay! Put that lead pair in the north stalls.

CURLEY'S WIFE (*to* SLIM, *offstage*). Hi, Slim!

SLIM (*voice offstage*). Hello.

CURLEY'S WIFE. I—I'm trying to find Curley.

SLIM'S VOICE (*offstage*). Well, you ain't tryin' very hard. I seen him goin' in your house.

CURLEY'S WIFE. I—I'm tryin' to find Curley. *and* LENNIE). I gotta be goin'! (*She exits hurriedly.*)

GEORGE (*looking around at* LENNIE). Jesus, what a tramp! So, that's what Curley picks for a wife. God Almighty, did you smell that stink she's got on? I can still smell her. Don't have to see *her* to know she's around.

LENNIE. She's purty!

GEORGE. Yeah. And she's sure hidin' it. Curley got his work ahead of him.

LENNIE (*still staring at the doorway where she was*). Gosh, she's purty!

GEORGE (*turning furiously at him*). Listen to me, you crazy bastard. Don't you even look at that bitch. I don't care what she says or what she does. I seen 'em poison before, but I ain't never seen no piece of jail bait worse than her. Don't you even smell near her!

LENNIE. I never smelled, George!

GEORGE. No, you never. But when she was standin' there showin' her legs, you wasn't lookin' the other way neither!

LENNIE. I never meant no bad things, George. Honest I never.

GEORGE. Well, you keep away from her. You let Curley take the rap. He let himself in for it. (*Disgustedly.*) Glove full of vaseline. I bet he's eatin' raw eggs and writin' to patent-medicine houses.

LENNIE (*cries out*). I don't like this place. This ain't no good place. I don't like this place!

GEORGE. Listen—I don't like it here no better than you do. But we gotta keep it till we get a stake. We're flat. We gotta get a stake. (*Goes back to the table, thoughtfully.*) If we can get just a few dollars in the poke we'll shove off and go up to the American River and pan gold. Guy can make a couple dollars a day there.

LENNIE (*eagerly*). Let's go, George. Let's get out of here. It's mean here.

GEORGE (*shortly*). I tell you we gotta stay a little while. We gotta get a stake. (*The sounds of running water and rattle of basins are heard.*) Shut up now, the guys'll be comin' in! (*Pensively.*) Maybe we ought to wash up. . . . But hell, we ain't done nothin' to get dirty.

SLIM (*enters. He is a tall, dark man in blue jeans and a short denim jacket. He carries a crushed Stetson hat under his arm and combs his long dark damp hair straight back. He stands and moves with a kind of majesty. He finishes combing his hair. Smoothes out his crushed hat, creases it in the middle and puts it on. In a gentle voice*). It's brighter'n a bitch outside. Can't hardly see nothing in here. You the new guys?

GEORGE. Just come.

SLIM. Goin' to buck barley?

GEORGE. That's what the boss says.

SLIM. Hope you get on my team.

GEORGE. Boss said we'd go with a jerk-line skinner named Slim.

SLIM. That's me.

GEORGE. You a jerk-line skinner?

SLIM (*in self-disparagement*). I can snap 'em around a little.

GEORGE (*terribly impressed*). That kinda makes you Jesus Christ on this ranch, don't it?

SLIM (*obviously pleased*). Oh, nuts!

GEORGE (*chuckles*). Like the man says, "The boss tells you what to do. But if you want to know how to do it, you got to ask the mule skinner." The man says any guy that can drive twelve Arizona jack rabbits with a jerk line can fall in a toilet and come up with a mince pie under each arm.

SLIM (*laughing*). Well, I hope you get on my team. I got a pair a punks that don't know a barley bag from a blue ball. You guys ever bucked any barley?

GEORGE. Hell, yes. I ain't nothin' to scream about, but that big guy there can put up more grain alone than most pairs can.

SLIM (*looks approvingly at* GEORGE). You guys travel around together?

GEORGE. Sure. We kinda look after each other. (*Points at* LENNIE *with his thumb.*) He ain't bright. Hell of a good worker, though. Hell of a nice fella too. I've knowed him for a long time.

SLIM. Ain't many guys travel around together. I don't know why. Maybe everybody in the whole damn world is scared of each other.

GEORGE. It's a lot nicer to go 'round with a guy you know. You get used to it an' then it ain't no fun alone any more. (*Enter* CARLSON. *Big-stomached, powerful man. His head still drips water from scrubbing and dousing.*)

CARLSON. Hello, Slim! (*He looks at* GEORGE *and* LENNIE.)

SLIM. These guys just come.

CARLSON. Glad to meet ya! My name's Carlson.

GEORGE. I'm George Milton. This here's Lennie Small.

CARLSON. Glad to meet you. He ain't very small. (*Chuckles at his own joke.*) He ain't small at all. Meant to ask you, Slim, how's your bitch? I seen she wasn't under your wagon this morning.

SLIM. She slang her pups last night. Nine of 'em. I drowned four of 'em right off. She couldn't feed that many.

CARLSON. Got five left, huh?

SLIM. Yeah. Five. I kep' the biggest.

CARLSON. What kinda dogs you think they gonna be?

SLIM. I don't know. Some kind of shepherd, I guess. That's the most kind I seen around here when she's in heat.

CARLSON (*laughs*). I had an airdale an' a guy down the road got one of them little white floozy dogs, well, she was in heat and the guy locks her up. But my airedale, named Tom he was, he et a woodshed clear down to the roots to get to her. Guy come over one day, he's sore as hell, he says, "I wouldn't mind if my bitch had pups, but Christ Almighty, this morning she slang a litter of Shetland ponies. . . ." (*Takes off his hat and scratches his head.*) Got five pups, huh! Gonna keep all of 'em?

SLIM. I don' know, gotta keep 'em awhile, so they can drink Lulu's milk.

CARLSON (*thoughtfully*). Well, looka here, Slim, I been thinkin'. That dog of Candy's is so goddamn old he can't hardly walk. Stinks like hell. Every time Candy brings him in the bunkhouse. I can smell him two or three days. Why don't you get Candy to shoot his ol' dog, and give him one of them pups to raise up? I can smell that dog a mile off. Got no teeth. Can't eat. Candy feeds him milk. He can't chew nothing else. And leadin' him around on a string so he

don't bump into things . . . (*The triangle outside begins to ring wildly. Continues for a few moments, then stops suddenly.*) There she goes! (*Outside there is a burst of voices as a group of men go by.*)

SLIM (*to LENNIE and GEORGE*). You guys better come on while they's still somethin' to eat. Won't be nothing left in a couple of minutes. (*Exit SLIM and CARLSON, LENNIE watches GEORGE excitedly.*)

LENNIE. George!

GEORGE (*rumpling his cards into a pile*). Yeah, I heard 'im, Lennie . . . I'll ask 'im!

LENNIE (*excitedly*). A brown and white one.

GEORGE. Come on, let's get dinner. I don't know whether he's got a brown and white one.

LENNIE. You ask him right away, George, so he won't kill no more of 'em!

GEORGE. Sure! Come on now—le's go. (*They start for the door.*)

CURLEY (*bounces in, angrily*). You seen a girl around here?

GEORGE (*coldly*). 'Bout half an hour ago, mebbe.

CURLEY. Well, what the hell was she doin'?

GEORGE (*insultingly*). She *said* she was lookin' for you.

CURLEY (*measures both men with his eyes for a moment*). Which way did she go?

GEORGE. I don't know. I didn't watch her go. (*CURLEY scowls at him a moment and then turns and hurries out the door.*) You know, Lennie, I'm scared I'm gonna tangle with that bastard myself. I hate his guts! Jesus Christ, come on! They won't be a damn thing left to eat.

LENNIE. Will you ask him about a brown and white one? (*They exeunt.*)

**CURTAIN**

# ACT TWO

## SCENE I

*About seven-thirty Friday evening.*
*Same bunkhouse interior as in last scene.*
*The evening light is seen coming in through the window, but it is quite dark in the interior of the bunkhouse.*
*From outside comes the sound of a horseshoe game. Thuds on the dirt and occasional clangs as a shoe hits the peg. Now and then voices are raised in approval or derision: "That's a good one." . . . "Goddamn right it's a good one." . . . "Here goes for a ringer. I need a ringer." . . . "Goddamn near got it, too."*
SLIM *and* GEORGE *come into the darkening bunkhouse together.* SLIM *reaches up and turns on the tin-shaded electric light. Sits down on a box at the table.* GEORGE *takes his place opposite.*

SLIM. It wasn't nothing. I would of had to drown most of them pups anyway. No need to thank me about that.

GEORGE. Wasn't much to you, mebbe, but it was a hell of a lot to him. Jesus Christ, I don't know how we're gonna get him to sleep in here. He'll want to stay right out in the barn. We gonna have trouble keepin' him from gettin' right in the box with them pups.

SLIM. Say, you sure was right about him. Maybe he ain't bright—but I never seen such a worker. He damn near killed his partner buckin' barley. He'd take his end of that sack (*a gesture*) pretty near kill his partner. God Almighty, I never seen such a strong guy.

GEORGE (*proudly*). You just tell Lennie what to do and he'll do it if it don't take no figuring. (*Outside the sound of the horseshoe game goes on: "Son of a bitch if I can win a goddamn game." . . . "Me neither. You'd think them shoes was anvils."*)

SLIM. Funny how you and him string along together.

GEORGE. What's so funny about it?

SLIM. Oh, I don't know. Hardly none of the guys ever travels around together. I hardly never seen two guys travel together. You know how the hands are. They come in and get their bunk and work a month and then they quit and go on alone. Never seem to give a damn about nobody. Jest seems kinda funny. A cuckoo like him and a smart guy like you traveling together.

GEORGE. I ain't so bright neither or I wouldn't be buckin' barley for my fifty and found. If I was bright, if I was even a little bit smart, I'd have my own place and I'd be bringin' in my own crops 'stead of doin' all the work and not gettin' what comes up out of the ground. (*He falls silent for a moment.*)

SLIM. A guy'd like to do that. Sometimes I'd like to cuss a string of mules that was my own mules.

GEORGE. It ain't so funny, him and me goin' round together. Him and me was both born in Auburn. I knowed his aunt. She took him when he was a baby and raised him up. When his aunt died Lennie jus' come along with me, out workin'. Got kinda used to each other after a little while.

SLIM. Uh huh.

GEORGE. First I used to have a hell of a lot of fun with him. Used to play jokes on him because he was too dumb to take care of himself. But, hell, he was too dumb even to know when he had a joke played on him. (*Sarcastically.*) Hell, yes, I had fun! Made me seem goddamn smart alongside of him.

SLIM. I seen it that way.

GEORGE. Why, he'd do any damn thing I tole him. If I tole him to walk over a cliff, over he'd go. You know that wasn't so damn much fun after a while. He never got mad about it, neither. I've beat hell out of him and he could bust every bone in my body jest with his hands. But he never lifted a finger against me.

SLIM (*braiding a bull whip*). Even if you socked him, wouldn't he?

GEORGE. No, by God! I tell you what made me stop playing jokes. One day a bunch of guys was standin' aroun' up on the Sacramento river. I was feelin' pretty smart. I turns to Lennie and I says, "Jump in."

SLIM. What happened?

GEORGE. He jumps. Couldn't swim a stroke. He damn near drowned. And he was so nice to me for pullin' him out. Clean forgot I tole him to jump in. Well, I ain't done nothin' like that no more. Makes me kinda sick tellin' about it.

SLIM. He's a nice fella. A guy don't need no sense to be a nice fella. Seems to be sometimes it's jest the other way round. Take a real smart guy, he ain't hardly ever a nice fella.

GEORGE (*stacking the scattered cards and getting his solitaire game ready again*). I ain't got no people. I seen guys that go round on the ranches alone. That ain't no good. They don't have no fun. After a while they get mean.

SLIM (*quietly*). Yeah, I seen 'em get mean. I seen 'em get so they don't want to talk to nobody. Some ways they got to. You take a bunch of guys all livin' in one room an' by God they got to mind their own business. 'Bout the only private thing a guy's got is where he come from and where he's goin'.

GEORGE. 'Course Lennie's a goddamn nuisance most of the time. But you get used to goin' round with a guy and you can't get rid of him. I mean you get used to him an' you can't get rid of bein' used to him. I'm sure drippin' at the mouth. I ain't told nobody all this before.

SLIM. Do you want to git rid of him?

GEORGE. Well, he gets in trouble all the time. Because he's so goddamn dumb. Like what happened in Weed. (*He stops, alarmed at what he has said.*) You wouldn't tell nobody?

SLIM (*calmly*). What did he do in Weed?

GEORGE. You wouldn't tell?—No, 'course you wouldn't.

SLIM. What did he do?

GEORGE. Well, he seen this girl in a red dress. Dumb bastard like he is he wants to touch everything he likes. Jest wants to feel of it. So he reaches out to feel this red dress. Girl lets out a squawk and that gets Lennie all mixed up. He holds on 'cause that's the only thing he can think to do.

SLIM. The hell!

GEORGE. Well, this girl squawks her head off. I'm right close and I hear all the yellin', so I comes a-running. By that time Lennie's scared to death. You know, I had to sock him over the head with a fence picket to make him let go.

SLIM. So what happens then?

GEORGE (*carefully building his solitaire hand*). Well, she runs in and tells the law she's been raped. The guys in Weed start out to lynch Lennie. So there we sit in an irrigation ditch, under water all the rest of that day. Got only our heads stickin' out of water, up under the grass that grows out of the side of the ditch. That night we run outa there.

SLIM. Didn't hurt the girl none, huh?

GEORGE. Hell, no, he jes' scared her.

SLIM. He's a funny guy.

GEORGE. Funny! Why, one time, you know what that big baby done! He was walking along a road—(*Enter* LENNIE *through the door. He wears his coat over his shoulder like a cape and walks hunched over.*) Hi, Lennie. How do you like your pup?

LENNIE (*breathlessly*). He's brown and white jus' like I wanted. (*Goes directly to his bunk and lies down. Face to the wall and knees drawn up.*)

GEORGE (*puts down his cards deliberately*). Lennie!

LENNIE (*over his shoulder*). Huh? What you want, George?

GEORGE (*sternly*). I tole ya, ya couldn't bring that pup in here.

LENNIE. What pup, George? I ain't got no pup. (GEORGE *goes quickly over to him, grabs him by the shoulder and rolls him over. He picks up a tiny puppy from where* LENNIE *has been concealing it against his stomach.*)

LENNIE (*quickly*). Give him to me, George.

GEORGE. You get right up and take this pup to the nest. He's got to sleep with his mother. Ya want ta kill him? Jes' born last night and ya take him out of the nest. Ya take him back or I'll tell Slim not to let you have him.

LENNIE (*pleadingly*). Give him to me, George. I'll take him back. I didn't mean no bad thing, George. Honest I didn't. I jus' want to pet him a little.

GEORGE (*giving the pup to him*). All right, you get him back there quick. And don't you take him out no more. (LENNIE *scuttles out of the room.*)

SLIM. Jesus, he's just like a kid, ain't he?

GEORGE. Sure he's like a kid. There ain't no more harm in him than a kid neither, except he's so strong. I bet he won't come in here to sleep tonight. He'll sleep right alongside that box in the barn. Well, let him. He ain't doin' no harm out there. (*The light has faded out outside and it appears quite dark outside. Enter* CANDY *leading his old dog by a string.*)

CANDY. Hello, Slim. Hello, George. Didn't neither of you play horseshoes?

SLIM. I don't like to play every night.

CANDY (*goes to his bunk and sits down, presses the old blind dog to the floor beside him*). Either you guys got a slug of whiskey? I got a gut ache.

SLIM. I ain't. I'd drink it myself if I had. And I ain't got no gut ache either.

CANDY. Goddamn cabbage give it to me. I knowed it was goin' to before I ever et it. (*Enter* CARLSON *and* WHIT.)

CARLSON. Jesus, how that nigger can pitch shoes!

SLIM. He's plenty good.

WHIT. Damn right he is.

CARLSON. Yeah. He don't give nobody else a chance to win. (*Stops and sniffs the air. Looks around until he sees* CANDY's *dog.*) God Almighty, that dog stinks. Get him outa here, Candy. I don't know nothing that stinks as bad as ole dogs. You got to get him outa here.

CANDY (*lying down on his bunk, reaches over and pats the ancient dog, speaks softly*).

I been round him so much I never notice how he stinks.

CARLSON. Well, I can't stand him in here. That stink hangs round even after he's gone. (*Walks over and stands looking down at the dog.*) Got no teeth. All stiff with rheumatism. He ain't no good to you, Candy. Why don't you shoot him?

CANDY (*uncomfortably*). Well, hell, I had him so long! Had him since he was a pup. I herded sheep with him. (*Proudly.*) You wouldn't think it to look at him now. He was the best damn sheep dog I ever seen.

GEORGE. I knowed a guy in Weed that had an airedale that could herd sheep. Learned it from the other dogs.

CARLSON (*sticking to his point*). Lookit, Candy. This ole dog jus' suffers itself all the time. If you was to take him out and shoot him—right in the back of the head . . . (*Leans over and points.*) . . . right there, why he never'd know what hit him.

CANDY (*unhappily*). No, I couldn't do that. I had him too long.

CARLSON (*insisting*). He don't have no fun no more. He stinks like hell. Tell you what I'll do. I'll shoot him for you. Then it won't be you that done it.

CANDY (*sits up on the bunk, rubbing his whiskers nervously, speaks plaintively*). I had him from a pup.

WHIT. Let 'im alone, Carl. I ain't a guy's dog that matters. It's the way the guy feels about the dog. Hell, I had a mutt once I wouldn't a traded for a field trial pointer.

CARLSON (*being persuasive*). Well, Candy ain't being nice to him, keeping him alive. Lookit, Slim's bitch got a litter right now. I bet you Slim would give ya one of them pups to raise up, wouldn't ya, Slim?

SLIM (*studying the dog*). Yeah. You can have a pup if you want to.

CANDY (*helplessly*) Mebbe it would hurt. (*After a moment's pause, positively.*) And I don't mind taking care of him.

CARLSON. Aw, he'd be better off dead. The way I'd shoot him he wouldn't feel nothin'. I'd put the gun right there. (*Points with his toe.*) Right back of the head.

WHIT. Aw, let 'im alone, Carl.

CARLSON. Why, hell, he wouldn't even quiver.

WHIT. Let 'im alone. (*He produces a magazine.*) Say, did you see this? Did you see this in the book here?

CARLSON. See what?

WHIT. Right there. Read that.

CARLSON. I don't want to read nothing. . . . It'd be all over in a minute, Candy. Come on.

WHIT. Did you see it, Slim? Go on, read it. Read it out loud.

SLIM. What is it?

WHIT. Read it.

SLIM (*reads slowly*). "Dear Editor: I read your mag for six years and I think it is the best on the market. I like stories by Peter Rand. I think he is a whing-ding. Give us more like the Dark Rider. I don't write many letters. Just thought I would tell you I think your mag is the best dime's worth I ever spen'." (*Looks up questioningly.*) What you want me to read that for?

WHIT. Go on, read the name at the bottom.

SLIM (*reading*). "Yours for Success, William Tenner." (*Looks up at* WHIT.) What ya want me to read that for?

CARLSON. Come on, Candy—what you say?

WHIT (*taking the magazine and closing it impressively. Talks to cover* CARLSON). You don't remember Bill Tenner? Worked here about three months ago?

SLIM (*thinking*). Little guy? Drove a cultivator?

WHIT. That's him. That's the guy.

CARLSON (*has refused to be drawn into this conversation*). Look, Candy. If you want me to, I'll put the old devil outa his misery right now and get it over with. There ain't nothing left for him. Can't eat, can't see, can't hardly walk. Tomorrow you can pick one of Slim's pups.

SLIM. Sure . . . I got a lot of 'em.

CANDY (*hopefully*). You ain't got no gun.

CARLSON. The hell, I ain't. Got a Luger. It won't hurt him none at all.

CANDY. Mebbe tomorrow. Let's wait till tomorrow.

CARLSON. I don't see no reason for it. (*Goes to his bunk, pulls a bag from underneath, takes a Luger pistol out.*) Let's get it over with. We can't sleep with him stinking around in here. (*He snaps a shell into the chamber, sets the safety and puts the pistol into his hip pocket.*)

SLIM (*as* CANDY *looks toward him for help*). Better let him go, Candy.

CANDY (*looks at each person for some hope.* WHIT *makes a gesture of protest and then resigns himself. The others look away, to avoid responsibility. At last, very softly and hopelessly*). All right. Take him.
(*He doesn't look down at the dog at all. Lies back on his bunk and crosses his arms behind his head and stares at the ceiling.* CARLSON *picks up the string, helps the dog to its feet.*)

CARLSON. Come, boy. Come on, boy. (*To* CANDY, *apologetically.*) He won't even feel it. (CANDY *does not move nor answer him.*) Come on, boy. That's the stuff. Come on. (*He leads the dog toward the door.*)

SLIM. Carlson?

CARLSON. Yeah.

SLIM (*curtly*). Take a shovel.

CARLSON. Oh, sure, I get you.
(*Exit* CARLSON *with the dog.* GEORGE *follows to the door, shuts it carefully and sets the latch.* CANDY *lies rigidly on his bunk. The next scene is one of silence and quick staccato speeches.*)

SLIM (*loudly*). One of my lead mules got a bad hoof. Got to get some tar on it. (*There is a silence.*)

GEORGE (*loudly*). Anybody like to play a little euchre?

WHIT. I'll lay out a few with you. (*They take places opposite each other at the table but* GEORGE *does not shuffle the cards. He ripples the edge of the deck. Everybody looks over at him. He stops. Silence again.*)

SLIM (*compassionately*). Candy, you can have any them pups you want. (*There is no answer from* CANDY. *There is a little gnawing noise on the stage.*)

GEORGE. Sounds like there was a rat under there. We ought to set a trap there. (*Deep silence again.*)

WHIT (*exasperated*). What the hell is takin' him so long? Lay out some cards, why don't you? We ain't gonna get no euchre played this way.
(GEORGE *studies the backs of the cards. And after a long silence there is a shot in the distance. All the men start a bit, look quickly at* CANDY. *For a moment he continues to stare at the ceiling and then rolls slowly over and faces the wall.* GEORGE *shuffles the cards noisily and deals them.*)

GEORGE. Well, let's get to it.

WHIT (*still to cover the moment*). Yeah . . . I guess you guys really come here to work, huh?

GEORGE. How do you mean?

WHIT (*chuckles*). Well, you come on a Friday. You got two days to work till Sunday.

GEORGE. I don't see how you figure.

WHIT. You do if you been round these big ranches much. A guy that wants to look over a ranch comes in Saturday afternoon. He gets Saturday night supper, three meals on Sunday and he can quit Monday morning after breakfast without turning a hand. But you come to work on Friday noon. You got ta put in a day and a half no matter how ya figure it.

GEORGE (*quietly*). We're goin' stick around awhile. Me and Lennie's gonna roll up a stake. (*Door opens and the Negro stable buck puts in his head. A lean-faced Negro with pained eyes.*)

CROOKS. Mr. Slim.

SLIM (*who has been watching* CANDY *the whole time*). Huh? Oh, hello, Crooks, what's the matter?

CROOKS. You tole me to warm up tar for that mule's foot. I got it warm now.

SLIM. Oh, sure, Crooks. I'll come right out and put it on.

CROOKS. I can do it for you if you want, Mr. Slim.

SLIM (*standing up*). Naw, I'll take care of my own team.

CROOKS. Mr. Slim.

SLIM. Yeah.

CROOKS. That big new guy is messing round your pups in the barn.

SLIM. Well, he ain't doin' no harm. I give him one of them pups.

CROOKS. Just thought I'd tell ya. He's takin' 'em out of the nest and handling 'em. That won't do 'em no good.

SLIM. Oh, he won't hurt 'em.

GEORGE (*looks up from his cards*). If that crazy bastard is foolin' round too much jus' kick him out. (SLIM *follows the stable buck out.*)

WHIT (*examining his cards*). Seen the new kid yet?

GEORGE. What kid?

WHIT. Why, Curley's new wife.

GEORGE (*cautiously*). Yeah, I seen her.

WHIT. Well, ain't she a lulu?

GEORGE. I ain't seen that much of her.

WHIT. Well, you stick around and keep your eyes open. You'll see plenty of her. I never seen nobody like her. She's just workin' on everybody all the time. Seems like she's even workin' on the stable buck. I don't know what the hell she wants.

GEORGE (*casually*). Been any trouble since she got here? (*Obviously neither man is interested in the card game.* WHIT *lays down his hand and* GEORGE *gathers the cards in and lays out a solitaire hand.*)

WHIT. I see what you mean. No, they ain't been no trouble yet. She's only been here a couple of weeks. Curley's got yellow jackets in his drawers, but that's all so far. Every time the guys is around she shows up. She's lookin' for Curley. Or she thought she left somethin' layin' around and she's lookin' for that. Seems like she can't keep away from guys. And Curley's runnin' round like a cat lookin' for a dirt road. But they ain't been no trouble.

GEORGE. Ranch with a bunch of guys on it ain't no place for a girl. Specially like her.

WHIT. If she's give you any ideas you ought to come in town with us guys tomorrow night.

GEORGE. Why, what's doin'?

WHIT. Just the usual thing. We go in to old Susy's place. Hell of a nice place. Old Susy is a laugh. Always cracking jokes. Like she says when we come up on the front porch last Saturday night: Susy opens the door and she yells over her shoulder: "Get your coats on, girls, here comes the sheriff." She never talks dirty neither. Got five girls there.

GEORGE. What does it set you back?

WHIT. Two and a half. You can get a shot of whiskey for fifteen cents. Susy got nice chairs to set in too. If a guy don't want to flop, why, he can just set in them chairs and have a couple or three shots and just pass the time of day. Susy don't give a damn. She ain't rushin' guys through, or kicking them out if they don't want to flop.

GEORGE. Might go in and look the joint over.

WHIT. Sure. Come along. It's a hell of a lot of fun—her crackin' jokes all the time. Like she says one time, she says: "I've knew people that if they got a rag rug on the floor and a kewpie doll lamp on the phonograph they think they're runnin' a parlor house." That's Gladys's house she's talkin' about. And Susy says: "I know what you boys want," she says: "My girls is clean," she says. "And there ain't no water in my whiskey," she says. "If any you guys want to look at a kewpie doll lamp and take your chance of gettin' burned, why, you know where to go." She says: "They's guys round here walkin' bowlegged because they liked to look at a kewpie doll lamp."

GEORGE. Gladys runs the other house, huh?

WHIT. Yeah. (*Enter* CARLSON. CANDY *looks at him.*)

CARLSON. God, it's a dark night. (*Goes to his bunk; starts cleaning his pistol.*)

WHIT. We don't never go to Gladys's. Gladys gits three bucks, and two bits a shot and she don't crack no jokes. But Susy's place is clean and she got nice chairs. A guy can set in there like he lived there. Don't let no Manila Goo-Goos in, neither.

GEORGE. Aw, I don't know. Me and Lennie's rollin' up a stake. I might go in and set and have a shot, but I ain't puttin' out no two and a half.

WHIT. Well, a guy got to have some fun sometimes. (*Enter* LENNIE. LENNIE *creeps to his bunk and sits down.*)

GEORGE. Didn't bring him back in, did you, Lennie?

LENNIE. No, George, honest I didn't. See?

WHIT. Say, how about this euchre game?

GEORGE. Okay. I didn't think you wanted to play. (*Enter* CURLEY *excitedly.*)

CURLEY. Any you guys seen my wife?

WHIT. She ain't been here.

CURLEY (*looks threateningly about the room*). Where the hell's Slim?

GEORGE. Went out in the barn. He was goin' put some tar on a split hoof.

CURLEY. How long ago did he go?

GEORGE. Oh, five, ten minutes. (CURLEY *jumps out the door.*)

WHIT (*standing up*). I guess maybe I'd like to see this. Curley must be spoilin' or he wouldn't start for Slim. Curley's handy, goddamn handy. But just the same he better leave Slim alone.

GEORGE. Thinks Slim's with his wife, don't he?

WHIT. Looks like it. 'Course Slim ain't. Least I don't think Slim is. But I like to see the fuss if it comes off. Come on, le's go.

GEORGE. I don't want to git mixed up in nothing. Me and Lennie got to make a stake.

CARLSON (*finishes cleaning gun, puts it in his bag and stands up*). I'll look her over. Ain't seen a good fight in a hell of a while. (WHIT *and* CARLSON *exeunt.*)

GEORGE. You see Slim out in the barn?

LENNIE. Sure. He tole me I better not pet that pup no more, like I said.

GEORGE. Did you see that girl out there?

LENNIE. You mean Curley's girl?

GEORGE. Yeah. Did she come in the barn?

LENNIE (*cautiously*). No—anyways I never seen her.

GEORGE. You never seen Slim talkin' to her?

LENNIE. Uh-uh. She ain't been in the barn.

GEORGE. Okay. I guess them guys ain't gonna see no fight. If they's any fightin', Lennie, ya get out of the way and stay out.

LENNIE. I don't want no fight. (GEORGE *lays out his solitaire hand.* LENNIE *picks up a face card and studies it. Turns it over and studies it again.*) Both ends the same. George, why is it both ends the same?

GEORGE. I don't know. That jus' the way they make 'em. What was Slim doin' in the barn when you seen him?

LENNIE. Slim?

GEORGE. Sure, you seen him in the barn. He tole you not to pet the pups so much.

LENNIE. Oh. Yeah. He had a can of tar ·and a paint brush. I don't know what for.

GEORGE. You sure that girl didn't come in like she come in here today?

LENNIE. No, she never come.

GEORGE (*sighs*). You give me a good whore-house every time. A guy can go in and get drunk and get it over all at once and no messes. And he knows how much it's goin' set him back. These tarts is jus' buckshot to a guy. (LENNIE *listens with admiration, moving his lips, and* GEORGE *continues.*) You remember Andy Cushman, Lennie? Went to grammar school same time as us?

LENNIE. The one that his ole lady used to make hot cakes for the kids?

GEORGE. Yeah. That's the one. You can re-member if they's somepin to eat in it. (*Scores up some cards in his solitaire playing.*) Well, Andy's in San Quentin right now on ac-count of a tart.

LENNIE. George?

GEORGE. Huh?

LENNIE. How long is it goin' be till we git that little place to live on the fat of the land?

GEORGE. I don't know. We gotta get a big stake together. I know a little place we can get cheap, but they ain't givin' it away. (CANDY *turns over and watches* GEORGE.)

LENNIE. Tell about that place, George.

GEORGE. I jus' tole you Jus' last night.

LENNIE. Go on, tell again.

GEORGE. Well, it's ten acres. Got a windmill. Got a little shack on it and a chicken run. Got a kitchen orchard. Cherries, apples, peaches, 'cots and nuts. Got a few berries. There's a place for alfalfa and plenty water to flood it. There's a pig pen. . . .

LENNIE (*breaking in*). And rabbits, George?

GEORGE. I could easy build a few hutches. And you could feed alfalfa to them rabbits.

LENNIE. Damn right I could. (*Excitedly.*) You goddamn right I could.

GEORGE (*his voice growing warmer*). And we could have a few pigs. I'd build a smoke-house. And when we kill a pig we could smoke the hams. When the salmon run up the river we can catch a hundred of 'em. Every Sunday we'd kill a chicken or rabbit. Mebbe we'll have a cow or a goat. And the cream is so goddamn thick you got to cut it off the pan with a knife.

LENNIE (*watching him with wide eyes, softly*). We can live off the fat of the land.

GEORGE. Sure. All kinds of vegetables in the garden and if we want a little whiskey we can sell some eggs or somethin'. And we wouldn't sleep in no bunkhouse. Nobody could can us in the middle of a job.

LENNIE (*begging*). Tell about the house, George.

GEORGE. Sure. We'd have a little house. And a room to ourselves. And it ain't enough land so we'd have to work too hard. Mebbe six, seven hours a day only. We wouldn't have to buck no barley eleven hours a day. And when we put in a crop, why we'd be there to take that crop up. We'd know what come of our planting.

LENNIE (*eagerly*). And rabbits. And I'd take care of them. Tell how I'd do that, George.

GEORGE. Sure. You'd go out in the alfalfa patch and you'd have a sack. You'd fill up the sack and bring it in and put it in the rabbit cages.

LENNIE. They'd nibble and they'd nibble, the way they do. I seen 'em.

GEORGE. Every six weeks or so them does would throw a litter. So we'd have plenty rabbits to eat or sell. (*Pauses for inspiration.*) And we'd keep a few pigeons to go flying round and round the windmill, like they done when I was a kid. (*Seems entranced.*) And it'd be our own. And nobody could can us. If we don't like a guy we can say: "Get to hell out," and by God he's got to do it. And if a friend come along, why, we'd have an extra bunk. Know what we'd say? We'd say, "Why don't you spen' the night?" And by God he would. We'd have a setter dog and a couple of striped cats. (*Looks sharply at* LENNIE.) But you gotta watch out them cats don't get the little rabbits.

LENNIE (*breathing hard*). You jus' let 'em try. I'll break their goddamn necks. I'll smash them cats flat with a stick. I'd smash 'em flat with a stick. That's what I'd do. (*They sit silently for a moment.*)

CANDY (*at the sound of his voice, both* LEN-NIE *and* GEORGE *jump as though caught in some secret*). You know where's a place like that?

GEORGE (*solemnly*). S'pose I do, what's that to you?

CANDY. You don't need to tell me where it's at. Might be any place.

GEORGE (*relieved*). Sure. That's right, you couldn't find it in a hundred years.

CANDY (*excitedly*). How much they want for a place like that?

GEORGE (*grudgingly*). Well, I could get it for six hundred bucks. The ole people that owns it is flat bust. And the ole lady needs medicine. Say, what's it to you? You got nothing to do with us!

CANDY (*softly*). I ain't much good with only one hand. I lost my hand right here on the ranch. That's why they didn't can me. They give me a job swampin'. And they give me two hundred and fifty dollars 'cause I lost my hand. An' I got fifty more saved up right in the bank right now. That's three hundred. And I got forty more comin' the end of the month. Tell you what . . . (*He leans forward eagerly.*) S'pose I went in with you guys? That's three hundred and forty bucks I'd put in. I ain't much good, but I could cook and tend the chickens and hoe the garden some. How'd that be?

GEORGE (*his eyes half closed, uncertainly*). I got to think about that. We was always goin' to do it by ourselves. Me an' Lennie. I never thought of nobody else.

CANDY. I'd make a will. Leave my share to you guys in case I kicked off. I ain't got no relations nor nothing. You fellas got any money? Maybe we could go there right now.

GEORGE (*disgustedly*). We got ten bucks between us. (*He thinks.*) Say, look. If me and Lennie work a month and don't spend nothing at all, we'll have a hundred bucks. That would be four forty. I bet we could swing her for that. Then you and Lennie could go get her started and I'd get a job and make up the rest. You could sell eggs and stuff like that. (*They look at each other in amazement. Reverently.*) Jesus Christ, I bet we could swing her. (*His voice is full of wonder.*) I bet we could swing 'er.

CANDY (*scratches the stump of his wrist nervously*). I got hurt four years ago. They'll can me pretty soon. Jest as soon as I can't swamp out no bunkhouses they'll put me on the county. Maybe if I give you guys my money, you'll let me hoe in the garden, even when I ain't no good at it. And I'll wash dishes and little chicken stuff like that. But hell, I'll be on our own place. I'll be let to work on our own place. (*Miserably.*) You seen what they done to my dog. They says he wasn't no good to himself nor nobody else. But when I'm that way nobody'll shoot me. I wish somebody would. They won't do nothing like that. I won't have no place to go and I can't get no more jobs.

GEORGE (*stands up*). We'll do 'er! God damn, we'll fix up that little ole place and we'll go live there. (*Wonderingly.*) S'pose they was a carnival, or a circus come to town or a ball game or any damn thing. (CANDY *nods in appreciation.*) We'd just go to her. We wouldn't ask nobody if we could. Just say we'll go to her, by God, and we would. Just milk the cow and sling some grain to the chickens and go to her.

LENNIE. And put some grass to the rabbits. I wouldn't forget to feed them. When we gonna to do it, George?

GEORGE (*decisively*). In one month. Right squack in one month. Know what I'm gonna do? I'm goin' write to them ole people that owns the place that we'll take 'er. And Candy'll send a hundred dollars to bind her.

CANDY (*happily*). I sure will. They got a good stove there?

GEORGE. Sure, got a nice stove. Burns coal or wood.

LENNIE. I'm gonna take my pup. I bet by Christ he likes it there. (*The window, center backstage, swings outward.* CURLEY'S WIFE *looks in. They do not see her.*)

GEORGE (*quickly*). Now don't tell nobody about her. Jus' us three and nobody else. They'll liable to can us so we can't make no stake. We'll just go on like we was a bunch of punks. Like we was gonna buck barley the rest of our lives. And then all of a sudden, one day, bang! We get our pay and scram out of here.

CANDY. I can give you three hundred right now.

LENNIE. And not tell nobody. We won't tell nobody, George.

GEORGE. You're goddamn right we won't. (*There is a silence and then* GEORGE *speaks irritably.*) You know, seems to me I can almost smell that carnation stuff that goddamn tart dumps on herself.

CURLEY'S WIFE (*in the first part of the speech by* GEORGE *she starts to step out of sight but at the last words her face darkens with anger. At her first words everybody in the room looks around at her and remains rigid during the tirade*). Who you callin' a tart! I come from a nice home. I was brung up by nice people. Nobody never got to me before I was married. I was straight. I tell you I was good. (*A little plaintively.*) I was. (*Angrily again.*) You know Curley. You know he wouldn't stay with me if he wasn't sure. I tell you Curley is sure. You got no right to call me a tart.

GEORGE (*sullenly*). If you ain't a tart, what you always hangin' round guys for? You got a house an' you got a man. We don't want no trouble from you.

CURLEY'S WIFE (*pleadingly*). Sure I got a man. He ain't never home. I got nobody to talk to. I got nobody to be with. Think I can just sit home and do nothin' but cook for Curley? I want to see somebody. Just see 'em an' talk to 'em. There ain't no women. I can't walk to town. And Curley don't take me to no dances now. I tell you I jus' want to talk to somebody.

GEORGE (*boldly*). If you're just friendly what you givin' out the eye for an' floppin' your can around?

CURLEY'S WIFE (*sadly*). I just wanta be nice. (*The sound of approaching voices: "You don't have to get mad about it, do you?"* ... *"I ain't mad, but I just don't want no more questions, that's all. I just don't want no more questions."*)

GEORGE. Get goin'. We don't want no trouble. (CURLEY'S WIFE *looks from the window and closes it silently and disappears. Enter* SLIM, *followed by* CURLEY, CARLSON *and* WHIT. SLIM'S *hands are black with tar.* CURLEY *hangs close to his elbow.*)

CURLEY (*explaining*). Well, I didn't mean nothing, Slim. I jus' ast you.

SLIM. Well, you been askin' too often. I'm gettin' goddamn sick of it. If you can't look after your own wife, what you expect me to do about it? You lay off of me.

CURLEY. I'm jus' tryin' to tell you I didn't mean nothing. I just thought you might of saw her.

CARLSON. Why don't you tell her to stay to hell home where she belongs? You let her hang around the bunkhouses and pretty soon you're goin' to have somethin' on your hands.

CURLEY (*whirls on* CARLSON). You keep out of this 'less you want ta step outside.

CARLSON (*laughing*). Why you goddamn punk. You tried to throw a scare into Slim and you couldn't make it stick. Slim throwed a scare into you. You're yellow as a frog's belly. I don't care if you're the best boxer in the country, you come for me and I'll kick your goddamn head off.

WHIT (*joining in the attack*). Glove full of vaseline!

CURLEY (*glares at him, then suddenly sniffs the air, like a hound*). By God, she's been in *here.* I can smell— By God, she's been in here. (*To* GEORGE.) You was here. The other guys was outside. Now, God damn you— you talk.

GEORGE (*looks worried. He seems to make up his mind to face an inevitable situation. Slowly takes off his coat, and folds it almost daintily. Speaks in an unemotional monotone*). Somebody got to beat the hell outa you. I guess I'm elected. (LENNIE *has been watching, fascinated. He gives his high, nervous chuckle.*)

CURLEY (*whirls on him*). What the hell you laughin' at?

LENNIE (*blankly*). Huh?

CURLEY (*exploding with rage*). Come on, you big bastard. Get up on your feet. No big son-of-a-bitch is gonna laugh at me. I'll show you who's yellow.

(LENNIE *looks helplessly at* GEORGE. *Gets up and tries to retreat upstage.* CURLEY *follows slashing at him. The others mass themselves in front of the two contestants:* "That ain't no way, Curley—he ain't done nothing to you." . . . "Lay off him, will you, Curley. He ain't no fighter." . . . "Sock him back, big guy! Don't be afraid of him!" . . . "Give him a chance, Curley. Give him a chance.")

LENNIE (*crying with terror*). George, make him leave me alone, George.

GEORGE. Get him, Lennie. Get him! (*There is a sharp cry. The gathering of men opens and* CURLEY *is flopping about, his hand lost in* LENNIE's *hand.*) Let go of him, Lennie. Let go! ("He's got his hand!" . . . "Look at that, will you?" . . . "Jesus, what a guy!" LENNIE *watches in terror the flopping man he holds.* LENNIE's *face is covered with blood.* GEORGE *slaps* LENNIE *in the face again and again.* CURLEY *is weak and shrunken.*) Let go his hand, Lennie. Slim, come help me, while this guy's got any hand left. (*Suddenly* LENNIE *lets go. He cowers away from* GEORGE.)

LENNIE. You told me to, George. I heard you tell me to. (CURLEY *has dropped to the floor.* SLIM *and* CARLSON *bend over him and look at his hand.* SLIM *looks over at* LENNIE *with horror.*)

SLIM. We got to get him to a doctor. It looks to me like every bone in his hand is busted.

LENNIE (*crying*). I didn't wanta. I didn't wanta hurt 'im.

SLIM. Carlson, you get the candy wagon out. He'll have to go into Soledad and get his hand fixed up. (*Turns to the whimpering* LENNIE.) It ain't your fault. This punk had it comin' to him. But Jesus—he ain't hardly got no hand left.

GEORGE (*moving near*). Slim, will we git canned now? Will Curley's ole man can us now?

SLIM. I don't know. (*Kneels down beside* CURLEY.) You got your sense enough to listen? (CURLEY *nods.*) Well, then you listen. I think you got your hand caught in a machine. If you don't tell nobody what happened, we won't. But you jest tell and try to get this guy canned and we'll tell everybody. And then will you get the laugh! (*Helps* CURLEY *to his feet.*) Come on now. Carlson's goin' to take you in to a doctor. (*Starts for the door, turns back to* LENNIE.) Le's see your hands. (LENNIE *sticks out both hands.*) Christ Almighty!

GEORGE. Lennie was just scairt. He didn't know what to do. I tole you nobody ought never to fight him. No, I guess it was Candy I tole.

CANDY (*solemnly*). That's just what you done. Right this morning when Curley first lit into him. You says he better not fool with Lennie if he knows what's good for him. (*They all leave the stage except* GEORGE *and* LENNIE *and* CANDY.)

GEORGE (*to* LENNIE, *very gently*). It ain't your fault. You don't need to be scairt no more. You done jus' what I tole you to. Maybe you better go in the washroom and clean up your face. You look like hell.

LENNIE. I didn't want no trouble.

GEORGE. Come on—I'll go with you.

LENNIE. George?

GEORGE. What you want?

LENNIE. Can I still tend the rabbits, George? (*They exeunt together, side by side, through the door of the bunkhouse.*)

**CURTAIN**

# SCENE II

*Ten o'clock Saturday evening.*
*The room of the stable buck, a lean-to off the barn. There is a plank door upstage center; a small square window center right. On one side of the door a leather working bench with tools racked behind it, and on the others racks with broken and partly mended harnesses, collars, hames, traces, etc. At the left upstage Crooks' bunk. Over it two shelves. On one a great number of medicines in cans and bottles. And on the other a number of tattered books and a big alarm clock. In the corner right upstage a single-barreled shotgun and on the floor beside it a pair of rubber boots. A large pair of gold spectacles hang on a nail over Crooks' bunk.*
*The entrance leads into the barn proper. From that direction and during the whole scene come the sounds of horses eating, stamping, jingling their halter chains and now and then whinnying.*
*Two empty nail kegs are in the room to be used as seats. Single unshaded small-candle-power carbon light hanging from its own cord.*
*As the curtain rises, we see* CROOKS *sitting on his bunk rubbing his back with liniment. He reaches up under his shirt to do this. His face is lined with pain. As he rubs he flexes his muscles and shivers a little.*
*LENNIE appears in the open doorway, nearly filling the opening. Then* CROOKS, *sensing his presence, raises his eyes, stiffens and scowls.*
*LENNIE smiles in an attempt to make friends.*

CROOKS (*sharply*). You got no right to come in my room. This here's my room. Nobody got any right in here but me.

LENNIE (*fawning*). I ain't doin' nothing. Just come in the barn to look at my pup, and I seen your light.

CROOKS. Well, I got a right to have a light. You go on and get out of my room. I ain't wanted in the bunkhouse and you ain't wanted in my room.

LENNIE (*ingenuously*). Why ain't you wanted?

CROOKS (*furiously*). 'Cause I'm black. They play cards in there. But I can't play because I'm black. They say I stink. Well, I tell you all of you stink to me.

LENNIE (*helplessly*). Everybody went into town. Slim and George and everybody. George says I got to stay here and not get into no trouble. I seen your light.

CROOKS. Well, what do you want?

LENNIE. Nothing . . . I seen your light. I thought I could jus' come in and set.

CROOKS (*stares at* LENNIE *for a moment, takes down his spectacles and adjusts them over his ears; says in a complaining tone*). I don't know what you're doin' in the barn anyway. You ain't no skinner. There's no call for a bucker to come into the barn at all. You've got nothing to do with the horses and mules.

LENNIE (*patiently*). The pup. I come to see my pup.

CROOKS. Well, God damn it, go and see your pup then. Don't go no place where you ain't wanted.

LENNIE (*advances a step into the room, remembers and backs to the door again*). I looked at him a little. Slim says I ain't to pet him very much.

CROOKS (*the anger gradually going out of his voice*). Well, you been taking him out of the nest all the time. I wonder the ole lady don't move him some place else.

LENNIE (*moving into the room*). Oh, she don't care. She lets me.

CROOKS (*scowls and then gives up*). Come on in and set awhile. Long as you won't get out and leave me alone, you might as well set down. (*A little more friendly.*) All the boys gone into town, huh?

LENNIE. All but old Candy. He jus' sets in the bunkhouse sharpening his pencils. And sharpening and figurin'.

CROOKS (*adjusting his glasses*). Figurin'? What's Candy figurin' about?

LENNIE. 'Bout the land. 'Bout the little place.

CROOKS. You're nuts. You're crazy as a wedge. What land you talkin' about?

LENNIE. The land we're goin' to get. And a little house and pigeons.

CROOKS. Just nuts. I don't blame the guy you're traveling with for keeping you out of sight.

LENNIE (*quietly*). It ain't no lie. We're gonna do it. Gonna get a little place and live on the fat of the land.

CROOKS (*settling himself comfortably on his bunk*). Set down. Set down on that nail keg.

LENNIE (*hunches over on the little barrel*). You think it's a lie. But it ain't no lie. Ever' word's the truth. You can ask George.

CROOKS (*puts his dark chin on his palm*). You travel round with George, don't you?

LENNIE (*proudly*). Sure, me and him goes ever' place together.

CROOKS (*after a pause, quietly*). Sometimes he talks and you don't know what the hell he's talkin' about. Ain't that so? (*Leans forward.*) Ain't that so?

LENNIE. Yeah. Sometimes.

CROOKS. Just talks on. And you don't know what the hell it's all about.

LENNIE. How long you think it'll be before them pups will be old enough to pet?

CROOKS (*laughs again*). A guy can talk to you and be sure you won't go blabbin'. A couple of weeks and them pups will be all right. (*Musing.*) George knows what he's about. Just talks and you don't understand nothing. (*Mood gradually changes to excitement.*) Well, this is just a nigger talkin' and a busted-back nigger. It don't mean nothing, see. You couldn't remember it anyway. I seen it over and over—a guy talking to another guy and it don't make no difference if he don't hear or understand. The thing is they're talkin'. (*He pounds his knee with his hand.*) George can tell you screwy things and it don't matter. It's just the talkin'. It's just bein' with another guy, that's all. (*His voice becomes soft and malicious.*) S'pose George don't come back

no more? S'pose he took a powder and just ain't comin' back. What you do then?

LENNIE (*trying to follow* CROOKS). What? What?

CROOKS. I said s'pose George went into town tonight and you never heard of him no more. (*Presses forward.*) Just s'pose that.

LENNIE (*sharply*). He won't do it. George wouldn't do nothing like that. I been with George a long time. He'll come back to-night. . . . (*Doubt creeps into his voice.*) Don't you think he will?

CROOKS (*delighted with his torture*). Nobody can tell what a guy will do. Let's say he wants to come back and can't. S'pose he gets killed or hurt so he can't come back.

LENNIE (*in terrible apprehension*). I don't know. Say, what you doin' anyway? It ain't true. George ain't got hurt.

CROOKS (*cruelly*). Want me to tell you what'll happen? They'll take you to the booby hatch. They'll tie you up with a collar like a dog. Then you'll be jus' like me. Livin' in a kennel.

LENNIE (*furious, walks over towards* CROOKS). Who hurt George?

CROOKS (*recoiling from him with fright*). I was just supposin'. George ain't hurt. He's all right. He'll be back all right.

LENNIE (*standing over him*). What you supposin' for? Ain't nobody goin' to s'pose any hurt to George.

CROOKS (*trying to calm him*). Now set down. George ain't hurt. Go on now, set down.

LENNIE (*growling*). Ain't nobody gonna talk no hurt to George.

CROOKS (*very gently*). Maybe you can see now. You got George. You know he's comin' back. S'pose you didn't have nobody. S'pose you couldn't go in the bunkhouse and play rummy, 'cause you was black. How would you like that? S'pose you had to set out here and read books. Sure, you could play horseshoes until it got dark, but then you got to read books. Books ain't no good. A guy needs somebody . . . to be near him. (*His tone whines.*) A guy goes nuts if he ain't got nobody. Don't make no difference who it is as long as he's with you. I tell you a guy gets too lonely, he gets sick.

LENNIE (*reassuring himself*). George gonna come back. Maybe George come back already. Maybe I better go see.

CROOKS (*more gently*). I didn't mean to scare you. He'll come back. I was talkin' about myself.

LENNIE (*miserably*). George won't go away and leave me. I know George won't do that.

CROOKS (*continuing dreamily*). I remember when I was a little kid on my ole man's chicken ranch. Had two brothers. They was always near me, always there. Used to sleep right in the same room. Right in the same bed, all three. Had a strawberry patch. Had an alfalfa patch. Used to turn the chickens out in the alfalfa on a sunny morning. Me and my brothers would set on the fence and watch 'em—white chickens they was.

LENNIE (*interested*). George says we're gonna have alfalfa.

CROOKS. You're nuts.

LENNIE. We are too gonna get it. You ask George.

CROOKS (*scornfully*). You're nuts. I seen hundreds of men come by on the road and on the ranches, bindles on their back and that same damn thing in their head. Hundreds of 'em. They come and they quit and they go on. And every damn one of 'em is got a little piece of land in his head. And never a goddamn one of 'em gets it. Jus' like heaven. Everybody wants a little piece of land. Nobody never gets to heaven. And nobody gets no land.

LENNIE. We are too.

CROOKS. It's jest in your head. Guys all the time talkin' about it, but it's jest in your head. (*The horses move restlessly. One of them whinnies.*) I guess somebody's out there. Maybe Slim. (*Pulls himself painfully upright and moves toward the door. Calls.*) That you, Slim?

CANDY (*from outside*). Slim went in town. Say, you seen Lennie?

CROOKS. You mean the big guy?

CANDY. Yes. Seen him around any place?

CROOKS (*goes back to his bunk and sits down, says shortly*). He's in here.

CANDY (*stands in the doorway, scratching his wrist. Makes no attempt to enter*). Look, Lennie, I been figuring something out. About the place.

CROOKS (*irritably*). You can come in if you want.

CANDY (*embarrassed*). I don't know. 'Course if you want me to.

CROOKS. Oh, come on in. Everybody's comin' in. You might just as well. Gettin' to be a goddamn race track. (*He tries to conceal his pleasure.*)

CANDY (*still embarrassed*). You've got a nice cozy little place in here. Must be nice to have a room to yourself this way.

CROOKS. Sure. And a manure pile under the window. All to myself. It's swell.

LENNIE (*breaking in*). You said about the place.

CANDY. You know, I been here a long time. An' Crooks been here a long time. This is the first time I ever been in his room.

CROOKS (*darkly*). Guys don't come in a colored man's room. Nobody been here but Slim.

LENNIE (*insistently*). The place. You said about the place.

CANDY. Yeah. I got it all figured out. We can make some real money on them rabbits if we go about it right.

LENNIE. But I get to tend 'em. George says I get to tend 'em. He promised.

CROOKS (*brutally*). You guys is just kiddin' yourselves. You'll talk about it a hell of a lot, but you won't get no land. You'll be a swamper here until they take you out in a box. Hell, I seen too many guys.

CANDY (*angrily*). We're gonna do it. George says we are. We got the money right now.

CROOKS. Yeah. And where is George now? In town in a whorehouse. That's where your money's goin'. I tell you I seen it happen too many times.

CANDY. George ain't got the money in town. The money's in the bank. Me and Lennie and George. We gonna have a room to ourselves. We gonna have a dog and chickens. We gonna have green corn and maybe a cow.

CROOKS (*impressed*). You say you got the money?

CANDY. We got most of it. Just a little bit more to get. Have it all in one month. George's got the land all picked out too.

CROOKS (*exploring his spine with his hands*). I've never seen a guy really do it. I seen guys nearly crazy with loneliness for land, but every time a whorehouse or a blackjack game took it away from 'em. (*Hesitates and then speaks timidly.*) If you guys would want a hand to work for nothin'—just his keep, why I'd come and lend a hand. I ain't so crippled I can't work like a son-of-a-bitch if I wanted to.

GEORGE (*strolls through the door, hands in pockets, leans against the wall, speaks in a half-satiric, rather gentle voice*). You couldn't go to bed like I told you, could you, Lennie? Hell, no—you got to get out in society an' flap your mouth. Holdin' a convention out here.

LENNIE (*defending himself*). You was gone. There wasn't nobody in the bunkhouse. I ain't done no bad things, George.

GEORGE (*still casually*). Only time I get any peace is when you're asleep. If you ever get walkin' in your sleep I'll chop off your head like a chicken. (*Chops with his hand.*)

CROOKS (*coming to* LENNIE's *defense*). We was jus' settin' here talkin'. Ain't no harm in that.

GEORGE. Yeah. I heard you. (*A weariness has settled on him.*) Got to be here ever' minute, I guess. Got to watch ya. (*To* CROOKS.) It ain't nothing against you, Crooks. We just wasn't gonna tell nobody.

CANDY (*tries to change subject*). Didn't you have no fun in town?

GEORGE. Oh! I set in a chair and Susy was crackin' jokes an' the guys was startin' to raise a little puny hell. Christ Almighty—I never been this way before. I'm jus' gonna set out a dime and a nickel for a shot an' I think what a hell of a lot of bulk carrot seed you can get for fifteen cents.

CANDY. Not in them damn little envelopes—but bulk seed—you sure can.

GEORGE. So purty soon I come back. I can't think of nothing else. Them guys slingin' money around got me jumpy.

CANDY. Guy got to have *some* fun. I was to a parlor house in Bakersfield once. God Almighty, what a place. Went upstairs on a red carpet. They was big pitchers on the wall. We set in big sof' chairs. They was cigarettes on the table—an' they was *free*. Purty soon a Jap come in with drinks on a tray an' them *drinks* was free. Take all you want. (*In a reverie.*) Purty soon the girls come in an' they was jus' as polite an' nice an' quiet an' purty. Didn't seem like hookers. Made ya kinda scared to ask 'em. . . . That was a long time ago.

GEORGE. Yeah? An' what'd them sof' chairs set you back?

CANDY. Fifteen bucks.

GEORGE (*scornfully*). So ya got a cigarette an' a whiskey an' a look at a purty dress an' it cost ya twelve and a half bucks extra. You shot a week's pay to walk on that red carpet.

CANDY (*still entranced with his memory*). A week's pay? Sure. But I worked weeks all my life. I can't remember none of them weeks. But . . . that was nearly twenty years ago. And I can remember that. Girl I went with was named Arline. Had on a pink silk dress.

GEORGE (*turns suddenly and looks out the door into the dark barn, speaks savagely*). I s'pose ya lookin' for Curley? (CURLEY's WIFE *appears in the door.*) Well, Curley ain't here.

CURLEY'S WIFE (*determined now*). I know Curley ain't here. I wanted to ast Crooks somepin'. I didn't know you guys was here.

CANDY. Didn't George tell you before—we don't want nothing to do with you. You know damn well Curley ain't here.

CURLEY'S WIFE. I know where Curley went. Got his arm in a sling an' he went anyhow. I tell ya I come out to ast Crooks somepin'.

CROOKS (*apprehensively*). Maybe you better go along to your own house. You hadn't ought to come near a colored man's room.

I don't want no trouble. You don't want to ask me nothing.

CANDY (*rubbing his wrist stump*). You got a husband. You got no call to come foolin' around with other guys, causin' trouble.

CURLEY'S WIFE (*suddenly angry*). I try to be nice an' polite to you lousy bindle bums—but you're too good. I tell ya I could of went with shows. An'—an' a guy wanted to put me in pitchers right in Hollywood. (*Looks about to see how she is impressing them. Their eyes are hard.*) I come out here to ast somebody somepin' an'—

CANDY (*stands up suddenly and knocks his nail keg over backwards, speaks angrily*). I had enough. You ain't wanted here. We tole you, you ain't. Callin' us bindle stiffs. You got floozy idears what us guys amounts to. You ain't got sense enough to see us guys ain't bindle stiffs. S'pose you could get us *canned*—s'pose you *could*. You think we'd hit the highway an' look for another two-bit job. You don't know we got our own ranch to go to an' our own house an' fruit trees. An' we got friends. That's what we got. Maybe they was a time when we didn't have nothing, but that ain't so no more.

CURLEY'S WIFE. You damn ol' goat. If you had two bits, you'd be in Soledad gettin' a drink an' suckin' the bottom of the glass.

GEORGE. Maybe she could ask Crooks what she come to ask an' then get the hell home. I don't think she come to ask nothing.

CURLEY'S WIFE. What happened to Curley's hand? (CROOKS *laughs.* GEORGE *tries to shut him up.*) So it wasn't no machine. Curley didn't act like he was tellin' the truth. Come on, Crooks—what happened?

CROOKS. I wasn't there. I didn't see it.

CURLEY'S WIFE (*eagerly*). What happened? I won't let on to Curley. He says he caught his han' in a gear. (CROOKS *is silent.*) Who done it?

GEORGE. Didn't nobody do it.

CURLEY'S WIFE (*turns slowly to* GEORGE). So *you* done it. Well, he had it comin'.

GEORGE. I didn't have no fuss with Curley.

CURLEY'S WIFE (*steps near him, smiling*). Maybe now you ain't scared of him no more. Maybe you'll talk to me sometimes now. Ever'body was scared of him.

GEORGE (*speaks rather kindly*). Look! I didn't sock Curley. If he had trouble, it ain't none of our affair. Ask Curley about it. Now listen. I'm gonna try to tell ya. We tole you to get the hell out and it don't do no good. So I'm gonna tell you another way. Us guys got somepin' we're gonna do. If you stick around you'll gum up the works. It ain't your fault. If a guy steps on a round pebble an' falls an' breaks his neck, it ain't the pebble's fault, but the guy wouldn't of did it if the pebble wasn't there.

CURLEY'S WIFE (*puzzled*). What you talkin' about pebbles? If you didn't sock Curley, who did? (*She looks at the others, then steps quickly over to* LENNIE.) Where'd you get them bruises on your face?

GEORGE. I tell you he got his hand caught in a machine.

LENNIE (*looks anxiously at* GEORGE, *speaks miserably*). He caught his han' in a machine.

GEORGE. So now get out of here.

CURLEY'S WIFE (*goes close to* LENNIE, *speaks softly and there is a note of affection in her voice*). So . . . it was you. Well . . . maybe you're dumb like they say . . . an' maybe . . . you're the only guy on the ranch with guts. (*She puts her hand on* LENNIE'S *shoulder. He looks up in her face and a smile grows on his face. She strokes his shoulder.*) You're a nice fella.

GEORGE (*suddenly leaps at her ferociously, grabs her shoulder and whirls her around*). Listen . . . you! I tried to give you a break. Don't you walk into nothing! We ain't gonna let you mess up what we're gonna do. You let this guy alone an' get the hell out of here.

CURLEY'S WIFE (*defiant but slightly frightened*). You ain't tellin' me what to do. (*The* BOSS *appears in the door, stands legs spread, thumbs hooked over his belt.*) I got a right to talk to anybody I want to.

GEORGE. Why, you—(GEORGE, *furiously, steps close—his hand is raised to strike her. She cowers a little.* GEORGE *stiffens, seeing* BOSS, *frozen in position. The others see* BOSS *too. Girl retreats slowly.* GEORGE'S *hand drops slowly to his side—he takes two slow backward steps. Hold the scene for a moment.*)

CURTAIN

# ACT THREE

## SCENE I

*Mid-afternoon Sunday.*

*One end of a great barn. Backstage the hay slopes up sharply against the wall. High in the upstage wall is a large hay window. On each side are seen the hay racks, behind which are the stalls with the horses in them. Throughout this scene the horses can be heard in their stalls, rattling their halter chains and chewing at the hay.*

*The entrance is downstage right.*

*The boards of the barn are not close together. Streaks of afternoon sun come between the boards, made visible by dust in the air. From outside comes the clang of horseshoes on the playing peg, shouts of men encouraging or jeering.*

*In the barn there is a feeling of quiet and humming and lazy warmth. Curtain rises on* LENNIE *sitting in the hay, looking down at a little dead puppy in front of him. He puts out his big hand and strokes it clear from one end to the other.*

LENNIE (*softly*). Why do you got to get killed? You ain't so little as mice. I didn' bounce you hard. (*Bends the pup's head up and looks in its face.*) Now maybe George ain't gonna let me tend no rabbits if he finds out you got killed. (*He scoops a little hollow and lays the puppy in it out of sight and covers it over with hay. He stares at the mound he has made.*) This ain't no bad thing like I got to hide in the brush. I'll tell George I found it dead. (*He unburies the pup and inspects it. Twists its ears and works his fingers in its fur. Sorrowfully.*) But he'll know. George always knows. He'll say: "You done it. Don't try to put nothin' over on me." And he'll say: "Now just for that you don't get to tend no—you-know-whats." (*His anger rises. Addresses the pup.*) God damn you. Why do you got to get killed? You ain't so little as mice. (*Picks up the pup and hurls it from him and turns his back on it. He sits bent over his knees moaning to himself.*) Now he won't let me. . . . Now he won't let me. (*Outside there is a clang of horseshoes on the iron stake and a little chorus of cries.* LENNIE *gets up and brings the pup back and lays it in the hay and sits down. He mourns.*) You wasn't big enough. They tole me and tole me you wasn't. I didn' know you'd get killed so easy. Maybe George won't care. This here goddamn little son-of-a-bitch wasn't nothin' to George.

CANDY (*voice from behind the stalls*). Lennie, where you at? (LENNIE *frantically buries the pup under the hay.* CANDY *enters excitedly.*) Thought I'd find ya here. Say . . . I been talkin' to Slim. It's okay. We ain't gonna get the can. Slim been talkin' to the boss. Slim tol' the boss you guys is good buckers. The boss got to move that grain. 'Member what hell the boss give us las' night? He tol' Slim he got his eye on you an' George. But you ain't gonna get the can. Oh! an' say. The boss give Curley's wife hell, too. Tole her never to go near the men no more. Give her worse hell than you an' George. (*For the first time notices* LENNIE's *dejection.*) Ain't you glad?

LENNIE. Sure.

CANDY. You ain't sick?

LENNIE. Uh-uh!

CANDY. I got to go tell George. See you later. (*Exits.* LENNIE, *alone, uncovers the pup. Lies down in the hay and sinks deep in it. Puts the pup on his arm and strokes it.* CURLEY'S WIFE *enters secretly. A little mound of hay conceals* LENNIE *from her. In her hand she carries a small suitcase, very cheap. She crosses the barn and buries the case in the hay. Stands up and looks to see whether it can be seen.* LENNIE *watching her quietly tries to cover the pup with hay. She sees the movement.*)

CURLEY'S WIFE. What—what you doin' here?

LENNIE (*sullenly*). Jus' settin' here.

CURLEY'S WIFE. You seen what I done.

LENNIE. Yeah! you brang a valise.

CURLEY'S WIFE (*comes near to him*). You won't tell—will you?

LENNIE (*still sullen*). I ain't gonna have nothing to do with you. George tole me. I ain't to talk to you or nothing. (*Covers the pup a little more.*)

CURLEY'S WIFE. George give you all your orders?

LENNIE. Not talk nor nothing.

CURLEY'S WIFE. You won't tell about that suitcase? I ain't gonna stay here no more. Tonight I'm gonna get out. Come here an' get my stuff an' get out. I ain't gonna be run over no more. I'm gonna go in pitchers. (*Sees* LENNIE's *hand stroking the pup under the hay.*) What you got there?

LENNIE. Nuthing. I ain't gonna talk to you. George says I ain't.

CURLEY'S WIFE. Listen. The guys got a horse-shoe tenement out there. It's on'y four o'clock. Them guys ain't gonna leave that tenement. They got money bet. You don't need to be scared to talk to me.

LENNIE (*weakening a little*). I ain't supposed to.

CURLEY'S WIFE (*watching his buried hand*). What you got under there?

LENNIE (*his woe comes back to him*). Jus' my pup. Jus' my little ol' pup. (*Sweeps the hay aside.*)

CURLEY'S WIFE. Why! He's dead.

LENNIE (*explaining sadly*). He was so little. I was jus' playin' with him—an' he made like he's gonna bite me—an' I made like I'm gonna smack him—an'—I done it. An' then he was dead.

CURLEY'S WIFE (*consoling*). Don't you worry none. He was just a mutt. The whole country is full of mutts.

LENNIE. It ain't that so much. George gonna be mad. Maybe he won't let me—what he said I could tend.

CURLEY'S WIFE (*sits down in the hay beside him, speaks soothingly*). Don't you worry. Them guys got money bet on that horseshoe tenement. They ain't gonna leave it. And tomorra I'll be gone. I ain't gonna let them run over me. (*In the following scene it is apparent that neither is listening to the other*

*and yet as it goes on, as a happy tone increases, it can be seen that they are growing closer together.*)

LENNIE. We gonna have a little place an' raspberry bushes.

CURLEY'S WIFE. I ain't meant to live like this. I come from Salinas. Well, a show come through an' I talked to a guy that was in it. He says I could go with the show. My ol' lady wouldn't let me, 'cause I was on'y fifteen. I wouldn't be no place like this if I had went with that show, you bet.

LENNIE. Gonna take a sack an' fill it up with alfalfa an'—

CURLEY'S WIFE (*hurrying on*). 'Nother time I met a guy an' he was in pitchers. Went out to the Riverside Dance Palace with him. He said he was gonna put me in pitchers. Says I was a natural. Soon's he got back to Hollywood he was gonna write me about it. (*Looks impressively at* LENNIE.) I never got that letter. I think my ol' lady stole it. Well, I wasn't gonna stay no place where they stole your letters. So I married Curley. Met *him* out to the Riverside Dance Palace too.

LENNIE. I hope George ain't gonna be mad about this pup.

CURLEY'S WIFE. I ain't tol' this to nobody before. Maybe I oughtn' to. I don't like Curley. He ain't a nice fella. I might a stayed with him but last night him an' his ol' man both lit into me. I don't have to stay here. (*Moves closer and speaks confidentially.*) Don't tell nobody till I get clear away. I'll go in the night an' thumb a ride to Hollywood.

LENNIE. We gonna get out a here purty soon. This ain't no nice place.

CURLEY'S WIFE (*ecstatically*). Gonna get in the movies an' have nice clothes—all them nice clothes like they wear. An' I'll set in them big hotels and they'll take pitchers of me. When they have them openings I'll go an' talk in the radio . . . an' it won't cost me nothing 'cause I'm in the pitcher. (*Puts her hand on* LENNIE's *arm for a moment.*) All them nice clothes like they wear . . . because this guy says I'm a natural.

LENNIE. We gonna go way . . . far away from here.

CURLEY'S WIFE. 'Course, when I run away from Curley, my ol' lady won't never speak to me no more. She'll think I ain't decent. That's what she'll say. (*Defiantly.*) Well, we really ain't decent, no matter how much my ol' lady tries to hide it. My ol' man was a drunk. They put him away. There! Now I told.

LENNIE. George an' me was to the Sacramento Fair. One time I fell in the river an' George pulled me out an' saved me, an' then we went to the Fair. They got all kinds of stuff there. We seen long-hair rabbits.

CURLEY'S WIFE. My ol' man was a sign-painter when he worked. He used to get drunk an' paint crazy pitchers an' waste paint. One night when I was a little kid, him an' my ol' lady had an awful fight. They was always fightin'. In the middle of the night he come into my room, and he says, "I can't stand this no more. Let's you an' me go away." I guess he was drunk. (*Her voice takes on a curious wondering tenderness.*) I remember in the night—walkin' down the road, and the trees was black. I was pretty sleepy. He picked me up, an' he carried me on his back. He says, "We gonna live together. We gonna live together because you're my own little girl, an' not no stranger. No arguin' and fightin'," he says, "because you're my little daughter." (*Her voice becomes soft.*) He says, "Why you'll bake little cakes for me, and I'll paint pretty pitchers all over the wall." (*Sadly.*) In the morning they caught us . . . an' they put him away. (*Pause.*) I wish we'd a' went.

LENNIE. Maybe if I took this here pup an' throwed him away George wouldn't never know.

CURLEY'S WIFE. They locked him up for a drunk, and in a little while he died.

LENNIE. Then maybe I could tend the rabbits without no trouble.

CURLEY'S WIFE. Don't you think of nothing but rabbits? (*Sound of horseshoe on metal.*) Somebody made a ringer.

LENNIE (*patiently*). We gonna have a house and a garden, an' a place for alfalfa. And I take a sack and get it all full of alfalfa, and then I take it to the rabbits.

CURLEY'S WIFE. What makes you so nuts about rabbits?

LENNIE (*moves close to her*). I like to pet nice things. Once at a fair I seen some of them long-hair rabbits. And they was nice, you bet. (*Despairingly.*) I'd even pet mice, but not when I could get nothin' better.

CURLEY'S WIFE (*giggles*). I think you're nuts.

LENNIE (*earnestly*). No, I ain't. George says I ain't. I like to pet nice things with my fingers. Soft things.

CURLEY'S WIFE. Well, who don't? Everybody likes that. I like to feel silk and velvet. You like to feel velvet?

LENNIE (*chuckling with pleasure*). You bet, by God. And I had some too. A lady give me some. And that lady was—my Aunt Clara. She give it right to me. . . . (*Measuring with his hands.*) 'Bout this big a piece. I wish I had that velvet right now. (*He frowns.*) I lost it. I ain't seen it for a long time.

CURLEY'S WIFE (*laughing*). You're nuts. But you're a kinda nice fella. Jus' like a big baby. A person can see kinda what you mean. When I'm doin' my hair sometimes I jus' set there and stroke it, because it's so soft. (*Runs her fingers over the top of her head.*) Some people got kinda coarse hair. You take Curley, his hair's just like wire. But mine is soft and fine. Here, feel. Right here. (*Takes* LENNIE's *hand and puts it on her head.*) Feel there and see how soft it is. (LENNIE's *fingers fall to stroking her hair.*) Don't you muss it up.

LENNIE. Oh, that's nice. (*Strokes harder.*) Oh, that's nice.

CURLEY'S WIFE. Look out now, you'll muss it. (*Angrily.*) You stop it now, you'll mess it all up. (*She jerks her head sideways and* LENNIE's *fingers close on her hair and hang on. In a panic.*) Let go. (*She screams.*) You let go. (*She screams again. His other hand closes over her mouth and nose.*)

LENNIE (*begging*). Oh, please don't do that. George'll be mad. (*She struggles violently to be free. A soft screaming comes from under* LENNIE's *hand. Crying with fright.*) Oh, please don't do none of that. George gonna say I done a bad thing. (*He raises his hand from her mouth and a hoarse cry escapes. Angrily.*) Now don't. I don't want you to yell. You gonna get me in trouble just like George says you will. Now don't you do that. (*She struggles more.*) Don't you go yellin'. (*He shakes her violently. Her neck snaps sideways and she lies still. Looks down at her and cautiously removes his hand from over her mouth.*) I don't wanta hurt you. But George will be mad if you yell. (*When she doesn't answer he bends closely over her. He lifts her arm and lets it drop. For a moment he seems bewildered.*) I done a bad thing. I done another bad thing. (*He paws up the hay until it partly covers her. The sound of the horseshoe game comes from the outside. And for the first time* LENNIE *seems conscious of it. He crouches down and listens.*) Oh, I done a real bad thing. I shouldn't a did that. George will be mad. And . . . he said . . . and hide in the brush till he comes. That's what he said. (*He picks up the puppy from beside the girl.*) I'll throw him away. It's bad enough like it is.

(*He puts the pup under his coat, creeps to the barn wall and peers out between the cracks and then he creeps around to the end of the manger and disappears. The stage is vacant except for* CURLEY'S WIFE. *She lies in the hay half covered up and she looks very young and peaceful. Her rouged cheeks and red lips make her seem alive and sleeping lightly. For a moment the stage is absolutely silent. Then the horses stamp on the other side of the feeding rack. The halter chains clink and from outside men's voices come loud and clear.*)

CANDY (*offstage*). Lennie! Oh, Lennie, you in there? (*He enters.*) I been figurin' some more, Lennie. Tell you what we can do. (*Sees* CURLEY'S WIFE *and stops. Rubs his white whiskers.*) I didn't know you was here. You was tol' not to be here. (*He steps near her.*) You oughn't to sleep out here. (*He is right beside her and looks down.*) Oh, Jesus Christ! (*Goes to the door and calls softly.*) George, George! Come here . . . George!

GEORGE (*enters*). What do you want?

CANDY (*points at* CURLEY'S WIFE). Look.

GEORGE. What's the matter with her? (*Steps up beside her.*) Oh, Jesus Christ! (*Kneels beside her and feels her heart and her wrist.*

*Finally stands up slowly and stiffly. From this time on through the rest of the scene* GEORGE *is wooden.*)

CANDY. What done it?

GEORGE (*coldly*). Ain't you got any ideas? (CANDY *looks away.*) I should of knew. I guess way back in my head I did.

CANDY. What we gonna do now, George? What we gonna do now?

GEORGE (*answering slowly and dully*). Guess . . . we gotta . . . tell . . . the guys. Guess we got to catch him and lock him up. We can't let him get away. Why, the poor bastard would starve. (*He tries to reassure himself.*) Maybe they'll lock him up and be nice to him.

CANDY (*excitedly*). You know better'n that, George. You know Curley's gonna want to get him lynched. You know how Curley is.

GEORGE. Yeah. . . . Yeah . . . that's right. I know Curley. And the other guys too. (*He looks back at* CURLEY'S WIFE.)

CANDY (*pleadingly*). You and me can get that little place, can't we, George? You and me can go there and live nice, can't we? Can't we? (CANDY *drops his head and looks down at the hay to indicate that he knows.*)

GEORGE (*shakes his head slowly*). It was somethin' me and him had. (*Softly.*) I think I knowed it from the very first. I think I knowed we'd never do her. He used to like to hear about it so much. I got fooled to thinkin' maybe we would. (CANDY *starts to speak but doesn't.*)

GEORGE (*as though repeating a lesson*). I'll work my month and then I'll take my fifty bucks. I'll stay all night in some lousy cathouse or I'll set in a pool room until everybody goes home. An' then—I'll come back an' work another month. And then I'll have fifty bucks more.

CANDY. He's such a nice fellow. I didn't think he'd a done nothing like this.

GEORGE (*gets a grip on himself and straightens his shoulders*). Now listen. We gotta tell the guys. I guess they've gotta bring him in. They ain't no way out. Maybe they won't hurt him. I ain't gonna let 'em hurt Lennie.

(*Sharply.*) Now you listen. The guys might think I was in on it. I'm gonna go in the bunkhouse. Then in a minute you come out and yell like you just seen her. Will you do that? So the guys won't think I was in on it?

CANDY. Sure, George. Sure, I'll do that.

GEORGE. Okay. Give me a couple of minutes then. And then you yell your head off. I'm goin' now. (GEORGE *exits.*)

CANDY (*watches him go, looks helplessly back at* CURLEY'S WIFE; *his next words are in sorrow and in anger*). You goddamn tramp. You done it, didn't you? Everybody knowed you'd mess things up. You just wasn't no good. (*His voice shakes.*) I could of hoed in the garden and washed dishes for them guys. . . . (*Pauses for a moment and then goes into a sing-song repeating the old words.*) If there was a circus or a baseball game . . . we would o' went to her . . . just said to hell with work and went to her. And they'd been a pig and chickens . . . and in the winter a little fat stove. An' us jus' settin' there . . . settin' there. . . . (*His eyes blind with tears and he goes weakly to the entrance of the barn. Tries for a moment to break a shout out of his throat before he succeeds.*) Hey, you guys! Come here! Come here!
(*Outside the noise of the horseshoe game stops. The sound of discussion and then the voices come closer: "What's the matter?" . . . "Who's that?" . . . "It's Candy." . . . "Something must have happened." Enter* SLIM *and* CARLSON, *Young* WHIT *and* CURLEY, CROOKS *in the back, keeping out of attention range. And last of all* GEORGE. GEORGE *has put on his blue denim coat and buttoned it. His black hat is pulled down low over his eyes. "What's the matter?" . . . "What's happened?"*)
(*A gesture from* CANDY. *The men stare at* CURLEY'S WIFE. SLIM *goes over to her, feels her wrist and touches her cheek with his fingers. His hand goes under her slightly twisted neck.* CURLEY *comes near. For a moment he seems shocked. Looks around helplessly and suddenly he comes to life.*)

CURLEY. I know who' done it. That big son-of-a-bitch done it. I know he done it. Why, everybody else was out there playing horseshoes. (*Working himself into a fury.*) I'm gonna get him. I'm gonna get my shotgun. Why, I'll kill the big son-of-a-bitch myself.

I'll shoot him in the guts. Come on, you guys. (*He runs out of the barn.*)

CARLSON. I'll go get my Luger. (*He runs out too.*)

SLIM (*quietly to* GEORGE). I guess Lennie done it all right. Her neck's busted. Lennie could o' did that. (GEORGE *nods slowly. Half-questioning.*) Maybe like that time in Weed you was tellin' me about. (GEORGE *nods. Gently.*) Well, I guess we got to get him. Where you think he might o' went?

GEORGE (*struggling to get words out*). I don't know.

SLIM. I guess we gotta get him.

GEORGE (*stepping close and speaking passionately*). Couldn't we maybe bring him in and lock him up? He's nuts, Slim, he never done this to be mean.

SLIM. If we could only keep Curley in. But Curley wants to shoot him. (*He thinks.*) And s'pose they lock him up, George, and strap him down and put him in a cage, that ain't no good.

GEORGE. I know. I know.

SLIM. I think there's only one way to get him out of it.

GEORGE. I know.

CARLSON (*enters running*). The bastard stole my Luger. It ain't in my bag.

CURLEY (*enters carrying a shotgun in his good hand. Officiously*). All right, you guys. The nigger's got a shotgun. You take it, Carlson.

WHIT. Only cover around here is down by the river. He might have went there.

CURLEY. Don't give him no chance. Shoot for his guts, that'll double him over.

WHIT. I ain't got a gun.

CURLEY. Go in and tell my old man. Get a gun from him. Let's go now. (*Turns suspiciously on* GEORGE.) You're comin' with us, fella!

GEORGE. Yeah. I'll come. But listen, Curley, the poor bastard's nuts. Don't shoot him, he didn't know what he was doin'.

CURLEY. Don't shoot him! He's got Carlson's Luger, ain't he?

GEORGE (*weakly*). Maybe Carlson lost his gun.

CARLSON. I seen it this morning. It's been took.

SLIM (*looking down at* CURLEY'S WIFE). Curley, maybe you better stay here with your wife. (*The light is fading into evening.* CURLEY *hesitates. Seems almost to weaken, then he hardens again.*)

CURLEY. Naw, I'm gonna shoot the guts out of that big bastard, I'm gonna get him myself. Come on, you guys.

SLIM (*to* CANDY). You stay here then, Candy. The rest of us better get goin'. (*They walk out,* SLIM *and* GEORGE *last. Exeunt all but* CANDY. *He squats in the hay, watching the face of* CURLEY'S WIFE.)

CANDY. Poor bastard.

CURTAIN

# ACT THREE

## SCENE II

*Evening.*
*The river bank again.*
*Light from the setting sun shines on the low brown hills. Among the trees by the river, the shade is deep with evening feeling.*
*Sounds: distant barking of dogs and the quiet call of quail.*
*The curtain rises on an empty stage.*
*There is a sudden whistle of evening wind that stirs the trees and scuds the leaves on the ground.*
*The stage is still again.* LENNIE *enters as silently as a bear. He is bent over and wary. On stage he looks behind him. Then he takes from under his coat the dead pup, lays it on the ground and, going to the river, lies on his stomach and drinks.*
*He returns to the dead pup, sits down beside it.*

LENNIE. George gonna give me hell . . . I bet. I . . . won't tell him. I'll bury him. (*Begins to scoop a hole in the sand in front of him. Softly.*) But I didn't forget, you bet. I come right here. Hide in the brush an' wait for George. (*Works carefully at his little grave, shaping the hole. At last he picks up the pup and lays it in the hole. Mourning.*) He gonna give me hell. He gonna wish he was alone. (*Adjusts the puppy in the hole, turning it around to make it fit better. Defiantly.*) Well . . . I can go right up in the hills an' find a cave. 'Course I wouldn't never have no ketchup. (*Begins packing sand down carefully about the pup, patting it as he does in beat with his words.*) I'll— go—away—go- -away. (*Every word a pat. Fills the grave carefully, smooths the sand over it.*) There now. (*Gathers leaves and scatters them over the place. Gets up on his knees and cocks his head to inspect the job.*) Now. I won't never tell George. (*Sinks back to a sitting position.*) He'll know. He always knows.

(*Far off sound of voices approaching. They come closer during the scene. Suddenly there is the clicking warning of a cock-quail and then the drum of the flock's wings.* GEORGE *enters silently, but hurriedly.*)

GEORGE (*in a hoarse whisper*). Get in the tules—quick.

LENNIE. I ain't done nothing, George. (*The voices are very close.*)

GEORGE (*frantically*). Get in the tules—damn you. (*Voices are nearly there.* GEORGE *half pushes* LENNIE *down among the tules. The tops rustle showing his crawling progress.*)

WHIT (*offstage*). There's George. (*Enters.*) Better not get so far ahead. You ain't got a gun. (*Enter* SLIM, CARLSON, BOSS, CURLEY, *and three other ranch hands. They are armed with shotguns and rifles.*)

CARLSON. He musta come this way. Them prints in the sand was aimed this way.

SLIM (*has been regarding* GEORGE). Now look. We ain't gonna find him stickin' in a bunch this way. We got to spread out.

CURLEY. Brush is pretty thick here. He might be lying in the brush. (*Steps toward the tules.* GEORGE *moves quickly after him.*)

SLIM (*Seeing the move speaks quickly*). Look—(*pointing*)—up there's the county road an' open fields an' over there's the highway. Le's spread out an' cover the brush.

BOSS. Slim's right. We got to spread.

SLIM. We better drag up to the roads an' then drag back.

CURLEY. 'Member what I said—shoot for his guts.

SLIM. Okay, move out. Me an' George'll go up to the county road. You guys gets the highway an' drag back.

BOSS. If we get separated, we'll meet here. Remember this place.

CURLEY. All I care is getting the bastard. (*The men move offstage right, talking.* SLIM *and* GEORGE *move slowly upstage listening to the voices that grow fainter and fainter.*)

SLIM (*softly to* GEORGE). Where is he? (GEORGE *looks him in the eyes for a long moment. Finally trusts him and points with his thumb toward the tules.*)

SLIM. You want—I should—go away? (GEORGE *nods slowly, looking at the ground.* SLIM *starts away, comes back, tries to say something, instead puts his hand on* GEORGE's *shoulder for a second, and then hurries off upstage.*)

GEORGE (*moves woodenly toward the bank and the tule clump and sits down*). Lennie! (*The tules shiver again and* LENNIE *emerges dripping.*)

LENNIE. Where's them guys goin'? (*Long pause.*)

GEORGE. Huntin'.

LENNIE. Whyn't we go with 'em? I like huntin'. (*Waits for an answer.* GEORGE *stares across the river.*) Is it 'cause I done a bad thing?

GEORGE. It don't make no difference.

LENNIE. Is that why we can't go huntin' with them guys?

GEORGE (*woodenly*). It don't make no difference. . . . Sit down, Lennie. Right there. (*The light is going now. In the distance there are shouts of men.* GEORGE *turns his head and listens to the shouts.*)

LENNIE. George!

GEORGE. Yeah?

LENNIE. Ain't you gonna give me hell?

GEORGE. Give ya hell?

LENNIE. Sure. . . . Like you always done before. Like—"If I didn't have you I'd take my fifty bucks . . ."

GEORGE (*softly as if in wonder*). Jesus Christ, Lennie, you can't remember nothing that happens. But you remember every word I say!

LENNIE. Well, ain't you gonna say it?

GEORGE (*reciting*). "If I was alone I—could live—so easy. (*His voice is monotonous.*) I could get a job and not have no mess. . . ."

LENNIE. Go on, go on! "And when the end of the month come . . ."

GEORGE. "And when the end of the month come, I could take my fifty bucks and go to—a cat-house. . . ."

LENNIE (*eagerly*). Go on, George, ain't you gonna give me no more hell?

GEORGE. No!

LENNIE. I can go away. I'll go right off in the hills and find a cave if you don't want me.

GEORGE (*speaks as though his lips were stiff*). No, I want you to stay here with me.

LENNIE (*craftily*). Then tell me like you done before.

GEORGE. Tell you what?

LENNIE. 'Bout the other guys and about us!

GEORGE (*recites again*). "Guys like us got no families. They got a little stake and then they blow it in. They ain't got nobody in the world that gives a hoot in hell about 'em!"

LENNIE (*happily*). "But not *us.*" Tell about us now.

GEORGE. "But not us."

LENNIE. "Because . . ."

GEORGE. "Because I got you and . . ."

LENNIE (*triumphantly*). "And I got you. We got each other," that's what, that gives a hoot in hell about us. (*A breeze blows up the leaves and then they settle back again. There are the shouts of men again. This time closer.*)

GEORGE (*takes off his hat; shakily*). Take off your hat, Lennie. The air feels fine!

LENNIE (*removes his hat and lays it on the ground in front of him*). Tell how it's gonna be. (*Again the sound of men. *GEORGE *listens to them.*)

GEORGE. Look acrost the river, Lennie, and I'll tell you like you can almost see it. (LENNIE *turns his head and looks across the river.*) "We gonna get a little place . . . (*Reaches in his side pocket and brings out* CARLSON's *Luger. Hand and gun lie on the ground behind* LENNIE's *back. He stares at the back of* LENNIE's *head at the place where spine and skull are joined. Sounds of men's voices talking offstage.*)

LENNIE. Go on! (GEORGE *raises the gun, but his hand shakes and he drops his hand on to the ground.*) Go on! How's it gonna be? "We gonna get a little place. . . ."

GEORGE (*thickly*). "We'll have a cow. And we'll have maybe a pig and chickens—and down the flat we'll have a . . . little piece of alfalfa. . . ."

LENNIE (*shouting*). "For the rabbits!"

GEORGE. "For the rabbits!"

LENNIE. "And I get to tend the rabbits?"

GEORGE. "And you get to tend the rabbits!"

LENNIE (*giggling with happiness*). "And live on the fat o' the land!"

GEORGE. Yes. (LENNIE *turns his head. Quickly.*) Look over there, Lennie. Like you can really see it.

LENNIE. Where?

GEORGE. Right acrost that river there. Can't you almost see it?

LENNIE (*moving*). Where, George?

GEORGE. It's over there. You keep lookin', Lennie. Just keep lookin'.

LENNIE. I'm lookin', George. I'm lookin'.

GEORGE. That's right. It's gonna be nice there. Ain't gonna be no trouble, no fights. Nobody ever gonna hurt nobody, or steal from 'em. It's gonna be—nice.

LENNIE. I can see it, George. I can see it! Right over there! I can see it! (GEORGE *fires.* LENNIE *crumples; falls behind the brush. The voices of the men in the distance.*)

**CURTAIN**

# 1938-39

This season provided the Circle with some of its richest material, but it was because of this fact that the group couldn't pick a winner, what with the three-fourths majority being needed. Two groups stuck staunchly with their favorites and no play came close to getting the necessary twelve out of fifteen votes on April 18.

On the tenth and final ballot there were six votes for Lillian Hellman's *The Little Foxes,* in which Tallulah Bankhead had her best role and gave the best performance of her long career, and five for Robert E. Sherwood's *Abe Lincoln in Illinois.* Two votes stayed with Clifford Odets' *Rocket to the Moon* and two with William Saroyan's initial Broadway production, *My Heart's in the Highlands.*

Paul Vincent Carroll, the Irish playwright, again won the citation for a foreign work, this time with *The White Steed.* It was a unanimous decision.

In retrospect it is obvious that the season was chiefly notable for marking the debut of the Playwrights' Company as a producing organization. After twenty years, it is going stronger than ever. The original members were Maxwell Anderson, Elmer Rice, Sidney Howard, S. N. Behrman and Robert E. Sherwood, all of whom cut their ties with the Theatre Guild to seek some production freedom with the result that the Guild sank to a low estate in the ensuing five years before being rescued by *Oklahoma!* Abe *Lincoln in Illinois* (it won Sherwood his second Pulitzer Prize), the Maxwell Anderson–Kurt Weill musical play, *Knickerbocker Holiday,* and Behrman's *No Time for Comedy* were all successes of this first season. Anderson, Rice and Sherwood are still active in the organization.

This was the season in which Philip Barry had two outstanding plays, *The Philadelphia Story,* a big hit, and *Here Come the Clowns,* a respected flop; *Hellzapoppin* began its long career, Robert Morley was so good in the title role of *Oscar Wilde,* and Maurice Evans gave New York its first full-length text *Hamlet,* playing the title role, of course. It ran four hours, with a dinner intermission. He also did an excellent Falstaff in *Henry IV (Part I).*

This was the last season for the WPA Federal Theatre which succumbed to official liquidation.

*Abe Lincoln in Illinois* had 472 performances; *The Little Foxes,* 410.

# 1939-40

*The Time of Your Life* was the first winner under the first revision of the voting rule whereby it became possible for a decision to be reached on a simple majority vote if three-fourths of the members approved the step after five ballots had failed to produce a victor under the original three-quarter majority stipulation. The date was May 3, 1940.

William Saroyan's delightfully unorthodox play could not make it on the first five ballots, but it won on the sixth when only a simple majority was needed. At that time it received eleven votes to four for Robert E. Sherwood's *There Shall Be No Night*, two for Maxwell Anderson's *Key Largo* and one for George S. Kaufman's and Moss Hart's *The Man Who Came to Dinner*. This was the citation:

"To William Saroyan whose *The Time of Your Life* is an exhilarating demonstration of the fresh, original and imaginative talent he has brought into the American theatre, for the provocation of the play's unconventionality and for the depth of its honest joy."

There was no foreign play citation, it being deemed that none of the imports was worth consideration.

Memorable data of the season:

*Life with Father* began its marathon career on November 8, 1939; Laurence Olivier and Vivien Leigh, who could make money with any old vehicle today, were dismal flops in *Romeo and Juliet*; John Barrymore was pathetic in his last time around in an atrocious play entitled *My Dear Children;* the Theatre Guild put on Ernest Hemingway's only produced play, *The Fifth Column;* an unknown named Danny Kaye was to be seen briefly in a makeshift show, *The Straw Hat Revue,* which, incidentally, was produced and masterminded by the equally unknown Max Liebman, today's master of the television "spectacular"; *The Male Animal* proved to be one of the more delightful comedies of the modern stage thanks to the writing of James Thurber and Elliott Nugent and the playing of the latter, and the veteran producer Earl Carroll, after an absence of several seasons, tried Broadway for the last time and had to close his *Vanities* revue after twenty-five performances.

Aside from the play itself, the most memorable thing about *The Time of Your Life* was the playing of Eddie Dowling, its co-producer, in the pivotal role. The play was good for 185 performances.

*The Time of Your Life* was the first play to win both the Critics' Circle and Pulitzer awards.

# The Time of Your Life

### By WILLIAM SAROYAN

Presented by The Theatre Guild in association with Eddie Dowling at the Booth Theatre, New York City, October 25, 1939, with the following cast:

| | |
|---|---|
| NEWSBOY | *Ross Bagdasarian* |
| DRUNK | *John Farrell* |
| WILLIE | *Will Lee* |
| JOE | *Eddie Dowling* |
| NICK | *Charles De Sheim* |
| TOM | *Edward Andrews* |
| KITTY DUVAL | *Julie Haydon* |
| DUDLEY | *Curt Conway* |
| HARRY | *Gene Kelly* |
| WESLEY | *Reginald Beane* |
| LORENE | *Nene Vibber* |
| BLICK | *Grover Burgess* |
| ARAB | *Houseley Stevens, Sr.* |
| MARY L | *Celeste Holme (Holm)* |
| KRUPP | *William Bendix* |
| McCARTHY | *Tom Tully* |
| KIT CARSON | *Len Doyle* |
| NICK'S MA | *Michelette Burani* |
| SAILOR | *Randolph Wade* |
| ELSIE | *Cathie Bailey* |
| A KILLER | *Evelyn Geller* |
| HER SIDE KICK | *Mary Cheffey* |
| A SOCIETY LADY | *Eva Leonard Boyne* |
| A SOCIETY GENTLEMAN | *Ainsworth Arnold* |
| FIRST COP | *Randolph Wade* |
| SECOND COP | *John Farrell* |

## SCENE

Act  I—Nick's Pacific Street saloon, restaurant and entertainment palace at the foot of the Embacadero, San Francisco.

Act II—Scenes 1 and 3, same as Act I. Scene 2—Room in the New York Hotel, San Francisco.

Act III—Same as Act I.

Time: Afternoon and night of a day in October, 1939.

# THE TIME OF YOUR LIFE

## ACT ONE

*In the time of your life, live—so that in that good time there shall be no ugliness or death for yourself or for any life your life touches. Seek goodness everywhere, and when it is found, bring it out of its hiding-place and let it be free and unashamed. Place in matter and in flesh the least of the values, for these are the things that hold death and must pass away. Discover in all things that which shines and is beyond corruption. Encourage virtue in whatever heart it may have been driven into secrecy and sorrow by the shame and terror of the world. Ignore the obvious, for it is unworthy of the clear eye and the kindly heart. Be the inferior of no man, nor of any man be the superior. Remember that every man is a variation of yourself. No man's guilt is not yours, nor is any man's innocence a thing apart. Despise evil and ungodliness, but not men of ungodliness or evil. These, understand. Have no shame in being kindly and gentle, but if the time comes in the time of your life to kill, kill and have no regret. In the time of your life, live—so that in that wondrous time you shall not add to the misery and sorrow of the world, but shall smile to the infinite delight and mystery of it.*

*Nick's is an American place: a San Francisco waterfront honky-tonk. At a table,* JOE: *always calm, always quiet, always thinking, always eager, always bored, always superior. His expensive clothes are casually and youthfully worn and give him an almost boyish appearance. He is thinking. Behind the bar,* NICK: *a big red-headed young Italian-American with an enormous naked woman tattooed in red on the inside of his right arm. He is studying* The Racing Form. *The* ARAB, *at his place at the end of the bar. He is a lean old man with a rather ferocious old-country mustache, with the ends twisted up. Between the thumb and forefinger of his left hand is the Mohammedan tattoo indicating that he has been to Mecca. He is sipping a glass of beer. It is about eleven-thirty in the morning.* SAM *is sweeping out. We see only his back. He disappears into the kitchen. The* SAILOR *at the bar finishes his drink and leaves, moving thoughtfully, as though he were trying very hard to discover how to live. The* NEWSBOY *comes in.*

NEWSBOY *(cheerfully).* Good-morning, everybody. *(No answer. To* NICK.*)* Paper, Mister? *(*NICK *shakes his head, no. The* NEWSBOY *goes to* JOE.*)* Paper, Mister?

*(*JOE *shakes his head, no. The* NEWSBOY *walks away, counting papers.)*

JOE *(noticing him).* How many you got?

NEWSBOY. Five.

*(*JOE *gives him a quarter, takes all the papers, glances at the headlines with irritation, throws them away.)*

*(The* NEWSBOY *watches carefully, then goes.)*

ARAB *(picks up paper, looks at headlines, shakes head as if rejecting everything else a man might say about the world).* No foundation. All the way down the line.

*(The* DRUNK *comes in. Walks to the telephone, looks for a nickel in the chute, sits down at* JOE's *table.)*

*(*NICK *takes the* DRUNK *out. The* DRUNK *returns.)*

DRUNK *(champion of the Bill of Rights).* This is a free country, ain't it?

*(*WILLIE, *the marble-game maniac, explodes through the swinging doors and*

157

*lifts the forefinger of his right hand com-
ically, indicating one beer. He is a very
young man, not more than twenty. He is
wearing heavy shoes, a pair of old and
dirty corduroys, a light green turtle-neck
jersey with a large letter "F" on the chest,
an oversize two-button tweed coat, and a
green hat, with the brim up.* NICK *sets out
a glass of beer for him, he drinks it,
straightens up vigorously, saying Aaah,
makes a solemn face, gives* NICK *a one-
finger salute of adieu, and begins to leave,
refreshed and restored in spirit. He walks
by the marble game, halts suddenly, turns,
studies the contraption, gestures as if to
say, Oh, no. Turns to go, stops, returns to
the machine, studies it, takes a handful of
small coins out of his pants pocket, lifts a
nickel, indicates with a gesture, One game,
no more. Puts the nickel in the slot, pushes
in the slide, making an interesting noise.)*

NICK. You can't beat that machine.

WILLIE. Oh, yeah?

*(The marbles fall, roll, and take their
place. He pushes down the lever, placing
one marble in position. Takes a very deep
breath, walks in a small circle, excited at
the beginning of great drama. Stands
straight and pious before the contest. Himself vs. the machine. Willie vs. Destiny.
His skill and daring vs. the cunning and
trickery of the novelty industry of America,
and the whole challenging world. He is
the last of the American pioneers, with
nothing more to fight but the machine,
with no other reward than lights going
on and off, and six nickels for one. Before
him is the last champion, the machine.
He is the last challenger, the young man
with nothing to do in the world.* WILLIE
*grips the knob delicately, studies the situa-
tion carefully, draws the knob back, holds
it a moment, and then releases it. The first
marble rolls out among the hazards, and
the contest is on. At the very beginning
of the play "The Missouri Waltz" is coming from the phonograph. The music ends
here.)*

*(This is the signal for the beginning of
the play.)*

*(*JOE *suddenly comes out of his reverie.
He whistles the way people do who are
calling a cab that's about a block away,*

*only he does it quietly.* WILLIE *turns
around, but* JOE *gestures for him to return to his work.* NICK *looks up from The
Racing Form.)*

JOE *(calling).* Tom. *(To himself.)* Where
the hell is he, every time I need him?
*(He looks around calmly: the nickel-in-
the-slot phonograph in the corner; the
open public telephone; the stage; the marble-game; the bar; and so on. He calls
again, this time very loud.)* Hey, Tom.

NICK *(with morning irritation).* What
do you want?

JOE *(without thinking).* I want the boy
to get me a watermelon, that's what *I*
want. What do *you* want? Money, or
love, or fame, or what? You won't get
them studying The Racing Form.

NICK. I like to keep abreast of the times.

*(*TOM *comes hurrying in. He is a great
big man of about thirty or so who appears
to be much younger because of the child-
like expression of his face: handsome,
dumb, innocent, troubled, and a little bewildered by everything. He is obviously
adult in years, but it seems as if by all
rights he should still be a boy. He is defensive as clumsy, self-conscious, over-
grown boys are. He is wearing a flashy
cheap suit.* JOE *leans back and studies him
with casual disapproval.* TOM *slackens his
pace and becomes clumsy and embarrassed,
waiting for the bawling-out he's pretty
sure he's going to get.)*

JOE *(objectively, severely, but a little
amused).* Who saved your life?

TOM *(sincerely).* You did, Joe. Thanks.

JOE *(interested).* How'd I do it?

TOM *(confused).* What?

JOE *(even more interested).* How'd I do
it?

TOM. Joe, you know how you did it.

JOE *(softly).* I want you to answer me.
How'd I save your life? I've forgotten.

TOM *(remembering, with a big sorrowful
smile).* You made me eat all that chicken
soup three years ago when I was sick and
hungry.

JOE *(fascinated)*. Chicken soup?

TOM *(eagerly)*. Yeah.

JOE. Three years? Is it that long?

TOM *(delighted to have the information)*. Yeah, sure. 1937. 1938. 1939. This is 1939, Joe.

JOE *(amused)*. Never mind what year it is. Tell me the whole story.

TOM. You took me to the doctor. You gave me money for food and clothes, and paid my room rent. Aw, Joe, you know all the different things you did.

*(JOE nods, turning away from TOM after each question.)*

JOE. You in good health now?

TOM. Yeah, Joe.

JOE. You got clothes?

TOM. Yeah, Joe.

JOE. You eat three times a day. Sometimes four?

TOM. Yeah, Joe. Sometimes five.

JOE. You got a place to sleep?

TOM. Yeah, Joe.

*(JOE nods. Pauses. Studies TOM carefully.)*

JOE. Then, where the hell have you been?

TOM *(humbly)*. Joe, I was out in the street listening to the boys. They're talking about the trouble down here on the waterfront.

JOE *(sharply)*. I want you to be around when I need you.

TOM *(pleased that the bawling-out is over)*. I won't do it again. Joe, one guy out there says there's got to be a revolution before anything will ever be all right.

JOE *(impatient)*. I know all about it. Now, here. Take this money. Go up to the Emporium. You know where the Emporium is?

TOM. Yeah, sure, Joe.

JOE. All right. Take the elevator and go up to the fourth floor. Walk around to the

back, to the toy department. Buy me a couple of dollars' worth of toys and bring them here.

TOM *(amazed)*. Toys? What *kind* of toys, Joe?

JOE. Any kind of toys. Little ones that I can put on this table.

TOM. What do you want toys for, Joe?

JOE *(mildly angry)*. *What?*

TOM. All right, all right. You don't have to get sore at *everything*. What'll people think, a big guy like me buying toys?

JOE. *What people?*

TOM. Aw, Joe, you're always making me do crazy things for you, and *I'm* the guy that gets embarrassed. You just sit in this place and make me do all the dirty work.

JOE *(looking away)*. Do what I tell you.

TOM. O.K., but I wish I knew *why*. *(He makes to go.)*

JOE. Wait a minute. Here's a nickel. Put it in the phonograph. Number seven. I want to hear that waltz again.

TOM. Boy, I'm glad *I* don't have to stay and listen to it. Joe, what do you hear in that song anyway? We listen to that song ten times a day. Why can't we hear number six, or two, or nine? There are a lot of other numbers.

JOE *(emphatically)*. Put the nickel in the phonograph. *(Pause.)* Sit down and wait till the music's over. Then go get me some toys.

TOM. O.K. O.K.

JOE *(loudly)*. Never mind being a martyr about it either. The cause isn't worth it.

*(TOM puts the nickel into the machine, with a ritual of impatient and efficient movement which plainly shows his lack of sympathy or enthusiasm. His manner also reveals, however, that his lack of sympathy is spurious and exaggerated. Actually, he is fascinated by the music, but is so confused by it that he pretends he dislikes it.)*

*(The music begins. It is another variation of "The Missouri Waltz," played dreamily and softly, with perfect orchestral form, and with a theme of weeping in the horns repeated a number of times.)*

*(At first* TOM *listens with something close to irritation, since he can't understand what is so attractive in the music to* JOE, *and what is so painful and confusing in it to himself. Very soon, however, he is carried away by the melancholy story of grief and nostalgia of the song.)*

*(He stands, troubled by the poetry and confusion in himself.)*

*(*JOE, *on the other hand, listens as if he were not listening, indifferent and unmoved. What he's interested in is* TOM. *He turns and glances at* TOM.*)*

*(*KITTY DUVAL, *who lives in a room in The New York Hotel, around the corner, comes beyond the swinging doors, quietly, and walks slowly to the bar, her reality and rhythm a perfect accompaniment to the sorrowful American music, which is her music, as it is Tom's. Which the world drove out of her, putting in its place brokenness and all manner of spiritually crippled forms. She seems to understand this, and is angry. Angry with herself, full of hate for the poor world, and full of pity and contempt for its tragic, unbelievable, confounded people. She is a small powerful girl, with that kind of delicate and rugged beauty which no circumstance of evil or ugly reality can destroy. This beauty is that element of the immortal which is in the seed of good and common people, and which is kept alive in some of the female of our kind, no matter how accidently or pointlessly they may have entered the world.* KITTY DUVAL *is somebody. There is an angry purity, and a fierce pride, in her.)*

*(In her stance, and way of walking, there is grace and arrogance.* JOE *recognizes her as a great person immediately. She goes to the bar.)*

KITTY. Beer.

*(*NICK *places a glass of beer before her mechanically.)*

*(She swallows half the drink, and listens to the music again.)*

*(*TOM *turns and sees her. He becomes dead to everything in the world but her. He stands like a lump, fascinated and undone by his almost religious adoration for her.* JOE *notices* TOM.*)*

JOE *(gently).* Tom. *(*TOM *begins to move toward the bar, where* KITTY *is standing. Loudly.)* Tom. *(*TOM *halts, then turns, and* JOE *motions to him to come over to the table.* TOM *goes over. Quietly.)* Have you got everything straight?

TOM *(out of the world).* What?

JOE. What do you mean, what? I just gave you some instructions.

TOM *(pathetically).* What do you want, Joe?

JOE. I want you to come to your senses.

*(He stands up quietly and knocks Tom's hat off.* TOM *picks up his hat quickly.)*

TOM. I got it, Joe. I got it. The Emporium. Fourth floor. In the back. The toy department. Two dollars' worth of toys. That you can put on a table.

KITTY *(to herself).* Who the hell is he to push a big man like that around?

JOE. I'll expect you back in a half hour. Don't get side-tracked anywhere. Just do what I tell you.

TOM *(pleading).* Joe? Can't I bet four bits on a horse race? There's a long shot— Precious Time—that's going to win by ten lengths. I got to have money.

*(*JOE *points to the street.* TOM *goes out.* NICK *is combing his hair, looking in the mirror.)*

NICK. I thought you wanted him to get you a watermelon.

JOE. I forgot. *(He watches* KITTY *a moment. To* KITTY, *clearly, slowly, with great compassion.)* What's the dream?

KITTY *(moving to* JOE, *coming to).* What?

JOE *(holding the dream for her).* What's the dream, *now?*

KITTY *(coming still closer).* What dream?

JOE. What dream! The dream you're dreaming.

NICK. Suppose he did bring you a watermelon? What the hell would you do with it?

JOE (*irritated*). I'd put it on this table. I'd look at it. Then I'd eat it. What do you *think* I'd do with it, sell it for a profit?

NICK. How should i know what *you'd* do with *anything*? What I'd like to know is, where do you get your money from? What work do you do?

JOE (*looking at* KITTY). Bring us a bottle of champagne.

KITTY. Champagne?

JOE (*simply*). Would you rather have something else?

KITTY. What's the big idea?

JOE. I thought you might like some champagne. I myself am very fond of it.

KITTY. Yeah, but what's the big idea? You can't push *me* around.

JOE (*gently but severely*). It's not in my nature to be unkind to another human being. I have only contemp. for wit. Otherwise I might say something obvious there fore cruel, and perhaps un ue.

KITTY. You be areful what you think about me.

JOE (*slowly, not looking at her*). I have only the noblest thoughts for both your person, and your spirit.

NICK (*having listened carefully and not being able to make it out*). What are you talking about?

KITTY. You shut up. You—

JOE. He owns this place. He's an important man. All kinds of people come to him looking for work. Comedians. Singers. Dancers.

KITTY. I don't care. He can't call me names.

NICK. All right, sister. I know how it is with a two-dollar whore in the morning.

KITTY (*furiously*). Don't you dare call me names. I used to be in burlesque.

NICK. If you were ever in burlesque, I used to be Charlie Chaplin.

KITTY (*angry and a little pathetic*). I *was* in burlesque. I played the burlesque circuit from coast to coast. I've had flowers sent to me by European royalty. I've had dinner with young men of wealth and social position.

NICK. You're dreaming.

KITTY (*to* JOE). *I was in burlesque.* Kitty Duval. That was my name. Life-size photographs of me in costume in front of burlesque theaters all over the country.

JOE (*gently, coaxingly*). I believe you. Have some champagne.

NICK (*going to table, with champagne bottle and glasses*). There he goes again.

JOE. Miss Duval?

KITTY (*sincerely, going over*). That's not my *real* name. That's my *stage* name.

JOE. I'll call you by your stage name.

NICK (*pouring*). All right, sister, make up your mind. Are you going to have champagne with him, or not?

JOE. Pour the lady some wine.

NICK. O.K., Professor. Why you come to this joint instead of one of the high-class dumps uptown is more than I can understand. Why don't you have champagne at the St. Francis? Why don't you drink with a lady?

KITTY (*furiously*). Don't you call me names—you dentist.

JOE. Dentist?

NICK (*amazed, loudly*). What kind of cussing is that? (*Pause. Looking at* KITTY, *then at* JOE, *bewildered.*) This guy doesn't belong here. The only reason I've got champagne is because *he* keeps ordering it all the time. (*To* KITTY.) Don't think you're the only one he drinks champagne with. He drinks with *all* of them. (*Pause.*) He's crazy. Or something.

JOE (*confidentially*). Nick, I think you're going to be all right in a couple of centuries.

NICK. I'm sorry, I don't understand your English.

(JOE *lifts his glass.*)

(KITTY *slowly lifts hers, not quite sure of what's going on.*)

JOE *(sincerely).* To the spirit, Kitty Duval.

KITTY *(beginning to understand, and very grateful, looking at him).* Thank you.

*(They drink.)*

JOE *(calling).* Nick.

NICK. Yeah?

JOE. Would you mind putting a nickel in the machine again? Number—

NICK. Seven. I know. I know. I don't mind at all, Your Highness, although, personally, I'm not a lover of music. *(Going to the machine.)* As a matter of fact I think Tchaikowsky was a dope

JOE. Tchaikowsky? Where'd you ever hear of Tchaikowsky.

NICK. He was a dope.

JOE. Yeah. Why?

NICK. They talked about him on the radio one Sunday morning. He was a sucker. He let a woman drive him crazy.

JOE. I see.

NICK. I stood behind that bar listening to the God damn stuff and cried like a baby. *None but the lonely heart!* He was a dope.

JOE. What made you cry?

NICK. What?

JOE *(sternly).* What made you cry, Nick?

NICK *(angry with himself).* I don't know.

JOE. I've been underestimating you, Nick. I lay number seven.

NICK. They get everybody worked up. They give everybody stuff they shouldn't have.

*(NICK puts the nickel into the machine and the Waltz begins again. He listens to the music. Then studies The Racing Form.)*

KITTY *(to herself, dreaming).* I like champagne, and everything that goes with it. Big houses with big porches, and big rooms with big windows, and big lawns, and big trees, and flowers growing everywhere, and big shepherd dogs sleeping in the shade.

NICK. I'm going next door to Frankie's to make a bet. I'll be right back.

JOE. Make one for me.

NICK *(going to JOE).* Who do you like?

JOE *(giving him money).* Precious Time.

NICK. *Ten dollars?* Across the board?

JOE. No. On the nose.

NICK. O.K. *(He goes.)*

*(DUDLEY R. BOSTWICK, as he calls himself, breaks through the swinging doors, and practically flings himself upon the open telephone beside the phonograph.)*

*(DUDLEY is a young man of about twenty-four or twenty-five, ordinary and yet extraordinary. He is smallish, as the saying is, neatly dressed in bargain clothes, overworked and irritated by the routine and dullness and monotony of his life, apparently nobody and nothing, but in reality a great personality. The swindled young man. Educated, but without the least real understanding. A brave, dumb, salmon-spirit struggling for life in weary, stupefied flesh, dueling ferociously with a banal mind which has been only irritated by what it has been taught. He is a great personality because, against all these handicaps, what he wants is simple and basic: a woman. This urgent and violent need, common yet miraculous enough in itself, considering the unhappy environment of the animal, is the force which elevates him from nothingness to greatness. A ridiculous greatness, but in the nature of things beautiful to behold. All that he has been taught, and everything he believes, is phony, and yet he himself is real, almost super-real, because of this indestructible force in himself. His face is ridiculous. His personal rhythm is tense and jittery. His speech is shrill and violent. His gestures are wild. His ego is disjointed and epileptic. And yet deeply he possesses the same wholeness of spirit, and directness of energy, that is in all species of animals. There is little innate or cultivated spirit in him, but there is no absence of innocent animal force. He is a young man who has been taught that he has a chance, as a person, and believes it. As a matter of fact, he hasn't a chance in the world, and should have been told by somebody, or should not have had his natural and valuable ignorance spoiled by education, ruining an otherwise perfectly good and charming member of the human race.)*

*(At the telephone he immediately begins to dial furiously, hesitates, changes his mind, stops dialing, hangs up furiously, and suddenly begins again.)*

*(Not more than half a minute after the firecracker arrival of* DUDLEY R. BOSTWICK, *occurs the polka-and-waltz arrival of* HARRY.*)*

*(*HARRY *is another story.)*

*(He comes in timidly, turning about uncertainly, awkward, out of place everywhere, embarrassed and encumbered by the contemporary costume, sick at heart, but determined to fit in somewhere. His arrival constitutes a dance.)*

*(His clothes don't fit. The pants are a little too large. The coat, which doesn't match, is also a little too large, and loose.)*

*(He is a dumb young fellow, but he has ideas. A philosophy, in fact. His philosophy is simple and beautiful. The world is sorrowful. The world needs laughter.* HARRY *is funny. The world needs* HARRY. HARRY *will make the world laugh.)*

*(He has probably had a year or two of high school. He has also listened to the boys at the pool room.)*

*(He's looking for Nick. He goes to the* ARAB, *and says, Are you Nick? The* ARAB *shakes his head. He stands at the bar, waiting. He waits very busily.)*

HARRY *(as* NICK *returns).* You Nick?

NICK *(very loudly).* I am Nick.

HARRY *(acting).* Can you use a great comedian?

NICK *(behind the bar).* Who, for instance?

HARRY *(almost angry).* Me.

NICK. You? What's funny about you?

*(*DUDLEY *at the telephone, is dialing. Because of some defect in the apparatus the dialing is very loud.)*

DUDLEY. Hello. Sunset 7349? May I speak to Miss Elsie Mandelspiegel?

*(Pause.)*

HARRY *(with spirit and noise, dancing).* I dance and do gags and stuff.

NICK. In costume? Or are you wearing your costume?

DUDLEY. All I need is a cigar.

KITTY *(continuing the dream of grace).* I'd walk out of the house, and stand on the porch, and look at the trees, and smell the flowers, and run across the lawn, and lie down under a tree, and read a book. *(Pause.)* A book of poems, maybe.

DUDLEY *(very, very clearly).* Elsie Mandelspiegel. *(Impatiently.)* She has a room on the fourth floor. She's a nurse at the Southern Pacific Hospital. Elsie Mandelspiegel. She works at night. Elsie. Yes. *(He begins waiting again.)*

*(*WESLEY, *a colored boy, comes to the bar and stands near* HARRY, *waiting.)*

NICK. Beer?

WESLEY. No, sir. I'd like to talk to you.

NICK *(to* HARRY). All right. Get funny.

HARRY *(getting funny, an altogether different person, an actor with great energy, both in power of voice, and in force and speed of physical gesture).* Now, I'm standing on the corner of Third and Market. I'm looking around. I'm figuring it out. There it is. Right in front of me. The whole city. The whole world. People going by. They're going somewhere. I don't know where, but they're going. I ain't going *anywhere.* Where the hell can you go? I'm figuring it out. All right, I'm a citizen. A fat guy bumps his stomach into the face of an old lady. They were in a hurry. Fat and old. *They bumped.* Boom. I don't know. It may mean war. *War.* Germany. England. Russia. I don't know for sure. *(Loudly, dramatically, he salutes, about faces, presents arms, aims, and fires.)* WAAAAAR. *(He blows a call to arms.* NICK *gets sick of this, indicates with a gesture that* HARRY *should hold it, and goes to* WESLEY.*)*

NICK. What's on *your* mind?

WESLEY *(confused).* Well—

NICK. Come on. Speak up. Are you hungry, or what?

WESLEY. Honest to God, I ain't hungry. All I want is a job. I don't want no charity.

NICK. Well, what can you do, and how good are you?

WESLEY. I can run errands, clean up, wash dishes, anything.

DUDLEY (*on the telephone, very eagerly*). Elsie? Elsie, this is Dudley. Elsie, I'll jump in the bay if you don't marry me. Life isn't worth living without you. I can't sleep. I can't think of anything but you. All the time. Day and night and night and day. Elsie, I love you. I love you. What? (*Burning up.*) Is this Sunset 7-3-4-9? (*Pause.*) 7943? (*Calmly, while* WILLIE *begins making a small racket.*) Well, what's *your* name? *Lorene?* Lorene Smith? I thought you were Elsie Mandelspiegel. What? Dudley. Yeah. Dudley R. Bostwick. Yeah. R. It stands for Raoul, but I never spell it out. I'm pleased to meet *you,* too. What? There's a lot of noise around here. (WILLIE *stops hitting the marble-game.*) Where am I? At Nick's, on Pacific Street. I work at the S. P. I told them I was sick and they gave me the afternoon off. Wait a minute. I'll ask them. I'd like to meet *you,* too. Sure. I'll ask them. (*Turns around to* NICK.) What's this address?

NICK. Number 3 Pacific Street, you cad.

DUDLEY. Cad? You don't know how I've been suffering on acount of Elsie. I take things too ceremoniously. I've got to be more lackadaisical. (*Into telephone.*) Hello, Elenore? I mean, Lorene. It's number 3 Pacific Street. Yeah. Sure. I'll wait for you. How'll you know me? You'll *know* me. I'll recognize you. Good-bye, now. (*He hangs up.*)

HARRY (*continuing his monologue, with gestures, movements, and so on*). I'm standing there. I didn't do anything to anybody. Why should *I* be a soldier? (*Sincerely, insanely.*) BOOOOOOOOOM. WAR! O.K. War. *I* retreat. *I* hate war. I move to Sacramento.

NICK (*shouting*). All right, Comedian. Lay off a minute.

HARRY (*broken-hearted, going to* WILLIE). Nobody's got a sense of humor any more. The world's dying for comedy like never before, but nobody knows how to *laugh.*

NICK (*to* WESLEY). Do you belong to the union?

WESLEY. What union?

NICK. For the love of Mike, where've you been? Don't you know you can't come into a place and ask for a job and get one and go to work, just like that. You've got to belong to one of the unions.

WESLEY. I didn't know. I got to have a job. Real soon.

NICK. Well, you've got to belong to a union.

WESLEY. I don't want any favors. All I want is a chance to earn a living.

NICK. Go on into the kitchen and tell Sam to give you some lunch.

WESLEY. Honest, I ain't hungry.

DUDLEY (*shouting*). What I've gone through for Elsie.

HARRY. I've got all kinds of funny ideas in my head to help make the world happy again.

NICK (*holding* WESLEY). No, he isn't hungry.

(WESLEY *almost faints from hunger.* NICK *catches him just in time. The* ARAB *and* NICK *go off with* WESLEY *into the kitchen.*)

HARRY (*to* WILLIE). See if you think this is funny. It's my own idea. I created this dance myself. It comes after the monologue.

(HARRY *begins to dance.* WILLIE *watches a moment, and then goes back to the game. It's a goofy dance, which* HARRY *does with great sorrow, but much energy.*)

DUDLEY. Elsie. Aw, gee, Elsie. What the hell do I want to see Lorene Smith for? Some girl I don't know.

(JOE *and* KITTY *have been drinking in silence. There is no sound now except the soft shoe shuffling of* HARRY, *the Comedian.*)

JOE. What's the dream now, Kitty Duval?

KITTY (*dreaming the words and pictures*). I dream of home. Christ, I always dream of home. I've no *home.* I've no place. But I always dream of all of us together again. We had a farm in Ohio. There was nothing good about it. It was always sad. There was always trouble. But I always dream about it as if I could go back and Papa would be there and Mamma and Louie and my little brother Stephen and my sister Mary. I'm Polish. Duval! My name isn't Duval, it's Koranovsky. Katerina Koranovsky. We lost everything. The house, the farm, the trees, the horses, the cows, the chickens. Papa died. He was old. He was thirteen years older than Mamma. We moved to Chicago. We tried to work. We tried to stay together. Louie got into trouble. The fellows he was with killed him for something. I don't know what. Stephen ran away from home. Seventeen years old. I don't know where he is. Then Mamma died. *(Pause.)* What's the dream? I dream of home.

*(NICK comes out of the kitchen with WESLEY.)*

NICK. Here. Sit down here and rest. That'll hold you for a *while*. Why didn't you tell me you were hungry? You all right now?

WESLEY *(sitting down in the chair at the piano)*. Yes, I am. Thank you. I didn't know I was *that* hungry.

NICK. Fine. *(To HARRY who is dancing.)* Hey. What the hell do you think you're doing?

HARRY *(stopping)*. That's my own idea. I'm a natural-born dancer and comedian.

*(WESLEY begins slowly, one note, one chord at a time, to play the piano.)*

NICK. You're no good. Why don't you try some other kind of work? Why don't you get a job in a store, selling something? What do you want to be a comedian for?

HARRY. I've got something for the world and they haven't got sense enough to let me give it to them. Nobody knows me.

DUDLEY. Elsie. Now I'm waiting for some dame I've never seen before. Lorene Smith. Never saw her in my life. Just happened to get the wrong number. She turns on the personality, and I'm a cooked Indian. Give me a beer, please.

HARRY. Nick, you've got to see my act. It's the greatest thing of its kind in America. All I want is a chance. No salary to begin. Let me try it out tonight. If I don't wow 'em, O.K., I'll go home. If vaudeville wasn't dead, a guy like me would have a chance.

NICK. You're not funny. You're a sad young punk. What the hell do you want to try to be funny for? You'll break every-

body's heart. What's there for you to be funny about? You've been poor all your life, haven't you?

HARRY. I've been poor all right, but don't forget that some things count more than some other things.

NICK. What counts more, for instance, than what else, for instance?

HARRY. Talent, for instance, counts more than money, for instance, that's what, and I've got talent. I get new ideas night and day. Everything comes natural to me. I've got style, but it'll take me a little time to round it out. That's all.

*(By now WESLEY is playing something of his own which is very good and out of the world. He plays about half a minute, after which HARRY begins to dance.)*

NICK *(watching)*. I run the lousiest dive in Frisco, and a guy arrives and makes me stock up with champagne. The whores come in and holler at me that they're ladies. Talent comes in and begs me for a chance to show itself. Even society people come here once in a while. I don't know what for. Maybe it's liquor. Maybe it's the location. Maybe it's my personality. Maybe it's the crazy personality of the joint. The old honky-tonk. *(Pause.)* Maybe they can't feel at home anywhere else.

*(By now WESLEY is really playing, and HARRY is going through a new routine. DUDLEY grows sadder and sadder.)*

KITTY. Please dance with me.

JOE *(loudly)*. I never learned to dance.

KITTY. Anybody can dance. Just hold me in your arms.

JOE. I'm very fond of you. I'm *sorry*. I *can't* dance. I wish to God I could.

KITTY. Oh, please.

JOE. Forgive me. I'd like to very much.

*(KITTY dances alone. TOM comes in with a package. He sees KITTY and goes ga-ga again. He comes out of the trance and puts the bundle on the table in front of JOE.)*

JOE *(taking the package)*. What'd you get?

TOM. Two dollars' worth of toys. That's what you sent me for. The girl asked me what I wanted with toys. I didn't know what to tell her. *(He stares at* KITTY, *then back at* JOE.) Joe? I've got to have some money. After all you've done for me, I'll do anything in the world for you, but, Joe, you got to give me some money once in a while.

JOE. What do you want it for?

*(*TOM *turns and stares at* KITTY *dancing.)*

JOE *(noticing).* Sure. Here. Here's five. *(Shouting.)* Can you dance?

TOM *(proudly).* I got second prize at the Palomar in Sacramento five years ago.

JOE *(loudly, opening package).* O.K., dance with her.

TOM. You mean *her?*

JOE *(loudly).* I mean Kitty Duval, the burlesque queen. I mean the queen of the world burlesque. Dance with her. She wants to dance.

TOM *(worshipping the name Kitty Duval, helplessly).* Joe, can I tell you something?

JOE *(he brings out a toy and winds it).* You don't have to. I know. You love her. You *really* love her. I'm not blind. I know. But take care of yourself. Don't get sick that way again.

NICK *(looking at and listening to* WESLEY *with amazement).* Comes in here and wants to be a dish-washer. Faints from hunger. And then sits down and plays better than Heifetz.

JOE. Heifetz plays the violin.

NICK. All right, don't get careful. He's good, ain't he?

TOM *(to* KITTY). Kitty.

JOE *(he lets the toy go, loudly).* Don't *talk.* Just *dance.*

*(*TOM *and* KITTY *dance.* NICK *is at the bar, watching everything.* HARRY *is dancing.* DUDLEY *is grieving into his beer.* LORENE SMITH, *about thirty-seven, very overbearing and funny-looking, comes to the bar.)*

NICK. What'll it be, lady?

LORENE *(looking about and scaring all the young men).* I'm looking for the young man I talked to on the telephone. Dudley R. Bostwick.

DUDLEY *(jumping, running to her, stopping, shocked).* Dudley R. *(Slowly.)* Bostwick? Oh, yeah. He left here ten minutes ago. You mean Dudley Bostwick, that poor man on crutches?

LORENE. Crutches?

DUDLEY. Yeah. Dudley Bostwick. That's what he *said* his name was. He said to tell you not to wait.

LORENE. Well. *(She begins to go, turns around.)* Are you sure *you're* not Dudley Bostwick?

DUDLEY. Who—me? *(Grandly.)* My name is Roger Tenefrancia. I'm a French-Canadian. I never saw the poor fellow before.

LORENE. It seems to me your voice is like the voice I heard over the telephone.

DUDLEY. A coincidence. An accident. A quirk of fate. One of those things. Dismiss the thought. That poor cripple hobbled out of here ten minutes ago.

LORENE. He said he was going to commit suicide. I only wanted to be of help. *(She goes.)*

DUDLEY. Be of help? What kind of help could she be, of? *(*DUDLEY *runs to the telephone in the corner.)* Gee whiz, Elsie. Gee whiz. I'll never leave you again. *(He turns the pages of a little address book.)* Why do I always forget the number? I've tried to get her on the phone a hundred times this week and I still forget the number. She won't come to the phone, but I keep trying anyway. She's out. She's not in. She's working. I get the wrong number. Everything goes haywire. I can't sleep. *(Defiantly.)* She'll come to the phone one of these days. If there's anything to true love at all, she'll come to the phone. Sunset 7349.

*(He dials the number, as* JOE *goes on studying the toys. They are one big mechanical toy, whistles, and a music box.* JOE *blows into the whistles, quickly, by way of getting casually acquainted with them.)*

*(*TOM *and* KITTY *stop dancing.* TOM *stares at her.)*

DUDLEY. Hello. Is this Sunset 7349? May I speak to Elsie? Yes. *(Emphatically, and bitterly.)* No, this is *not* Dudley Bostwick. This is Roger Tenefrancia of Montreal,

Canada. I'm a childhood friend of Miss Mandelspiegel. We went to kindergarten together. *(Hand over phone.)* God damn it. *(Into phone.)* Yes. I'll wait, thank you.

TOM. I love you.

KITTY. You want to go to my room? *(TOM can't answer.)* Have you got two dollars?

TOM *(shaking his head with confusion)*. I've got *five* dollars, but I *love* you.

KITTY *(looking at him)*. You want to spend *all* that money?

*(TOM embraces her. They go. JOE watches. Goes back to the toy.)*

JOE. Where's that longshoreman, McCarthy?

NICK. He'll be around.

JOE. What do you think he'll have to say today?

NICK. Plenty, as usual. I'm going next door to see who won that third race at Laurel.

JOE. Precious Time won it.

NICK. That's what you think. *(He goes).*

JOE *(to himself)*. A horse named McCarthy is running in the sixth race today.

DUDLEY *(on the phone)*. Hello. Hello, Elsie? Elsie? *(His voice weakens; also his limbs.)* My God. She's come to the phone. Elsie, I'm at Nick's on Pacific Street. You've got to come here and talk to me. Hello. Hello, Elsie? *(Amazed.)* Did she hang up? Or was I disconnected?

*(He hangs up and goes to bar.)*

*(WESLEY is still playing the piano. HARRY is still dancing. JOE has wound up the big mechanical toy and is watching it work.)*

*(NICK returns.)*

NICK *(watching the toy)*. Say. That's some gadget.

JOE. How much did I win?

NICK. How do you know you *won*?

JOE. Don't be silly. He said Precious Time was going to win by ten lengths, didn't he? He's in love, isn't he?

NICK. O.K. I don't know why, but Precious Time won. You got eighty for ten. How do you do it?

JOE *(roaring)*. Faith. Faith. How'd he win?

NICK. By a nose. Look him up in The Racing Form. The slowest, the cheapest, the worst horse in the race, and the worst jockey. What's the matter with my luck?

JOE. How much did you lose?

NICK. Fifty cents.

JOE. You should never gamble.

NICK. Why not?

JOE. You always bet fifty cents. You've got no more faith than a flea, that's why.

HARRY *(shouting)*. How do you like this, Nick? *(He is really busy now, all legs and arms.)*

NICK *(turning and watching)*. Not bad. Hang around. You can wait table. *(To WESLEY.)* Hey. Wesley. Can you play that again tonight?

WESLEY *(turning, but still playing the piano)*. I don't know for sure, Mr. Nick. I can play *something*.

NICK. Good. *You* hang around, too. *(He goes behind the bar.)*

*(The atmosphere is now one of warm, natural, American ease; every man innocent and good; each doing what he believes he should do, or what he must do. There is deep American naïveté and faith in the behavior of each person. No one is competing with anyone else. No one hates anyone else. Every man is living, and letting live. Each man is following his destiny as he feels it should be followed; or is abandoning it as he feels it must, by now, be abandoned; or is forgetting it for the moment as he feels he should forget it. Although everyone is dead serious, there is unmistakable smiling and humor in the scene; a sense of the human body and spirit emerging from the world-imposed state of stress and fretfulness, fear and awkwardness, to the more natural state of casualness and grace. Each person belongs to the environment, in his own person, as himself: WESLEY is playing better than ever. HARRY is hoofing better than ever. NICK is behind the bar shining glasses. JOE is smiling at the toy and studying it. DUDLEY, although still troubled, is at least calm now and full of melancholy poise. WILLIE, at the*

*marble-game, is happy. The* ARAB *is deep in his memories, where he wants to be.)*

*(Into this scene and atmosphere comes* BLICK.*)*

*(*BLICK *is the sort of human being you dislike at sight. He is no different from anybody else physically. His face is an ordinary face. There is nothing obviously wrong with him, and yet you know that it is impossible, even by the most generous expansion of understanding, to accept him as a human being. He is the strong man without strength—strong only among the weak—the weakling who uses force on the weaker.)*

*(*BLICK *enters casually, as if he were a customer, and immediately* HARRY *begins slowing down.)*

BLICK *(oily, and with mock-friendliness).* Hello, Nick.

NICK *(stopping his work and leaning across the bar).* What do you want to come here for? You're too big a man for a little honky-tonk.

BLICK *(flattered).* Now, Nick.

NICK. Important people never come here. *Here.* Have a drink. *(Whiskey bottle.)*

BLICK. Thanks, I don't drink.

NICK *(drinking the drink himself).* Well, why don't you?

BLICK. I have responsibilities.

NICK. You're head of the lousy Vice Squad. There's no vice here.

BLICK *(sharply).* Street-walkers are working out of this place.

NICK *(angry).* What do you want?

BLICK *(loudly).* I just want you to know that it's got to stop.

*(The music stops. The mechanical toy runs down. There is absolute silence, and a strange fearfulness and disharmony in the atmosphere now.* HARRY *doesn't know what to do with his hands or feet.* WESLEY'S *arms hang at his sides.* JOE *quietly pushes the toy to one side of the table eager to study what is happening.* WILLIE *stops playing the marble-game, turns around and begins to wait.* DUDLEY *straightens up very, very vigorously, as if to say: "Nothing can scare me. I know love is the only*

*thing." The* ARAB *is the same ພ, ever, but watchful.* NICK *is arrogantly aloof. There is a moment of this silence and tension, as though* BLICK *were waiting for everybody to acknowledge his presence. He is obviously flattered by the acknowledgment of Harry, Dudley, Wesley, and Willie, but a little irritated by Nick's aloofness and unfriendliness.)*

NICK. Don't look at me. I can't tell a street-walker from a lady. You married?

BLICK. You're not asking *me* questions. *I'm* telling *you.*

NICK *(interrupting).* You're a man of about forty-five or so. You *ought* to know better.

BLICK *(angry).* Street-walkers are working out of this place.

NICK *(beginning to shout).* Now, don't start any trouble with me. People come here to drink and loaf around. I don't care who they are.

BLICK. Well, I do.

NICK. The only way to find out if a lady is a street-walker is to walk the streets with her, go to bed, and make sure. You wouldn't want to do that. You'd *like* to, of course.

BLICK. Any more of it, and I'll have your joint closed.

NICK *(very casually, without ill-will).* Listen. I've got no use for you, or anybody like you. You're out to change the world from something bad to something worse. Something like yourself.

BLICK *(furious pause, and contempt).* I'll be back tonight. *(He begins to go.)*

NICK *(very angry but very calm).* Do yourself a big favor and don't come back tonight. Send somebody else. I don't like your personality.

BLICK *(casually, but with contempt).* Don't break any laws. I don't like yours, either.

*(He looks the place over, and goes.)*

*(There is a moment of silence. Then* WILLIE *turns and puts a new nickel in the slot and starts a new game.* WESLEY *turns to the piano and rather falteringly begins to play. His heart really isn't in it.* HARRY *walks about, unable to dance.* DUDLEY *lapses*

*into his customary melancholy, at a table.* NICK *whistles a little: suddenly stops.* JOE *winds the toy.)*

JOE *(comically).* Nick. You going to kill that man?

NICK. I'm disgusted.

JOE. Yeah? Why?

NICK. Why should I get worked up over a guy like that? Why should I hate *him?* He's nothing. He's nobody. He's a mouse. But every time he comes into this place I get burned up. He doesn't want to drink. He doesn't want to sit down. He doesn't want to take things easy. Tell me one thing?

JOE. Do my best.

NICK. What's a punk like *that* want to go out and try to change the world for?

JOE *(amazed).* Does *he* want to change the world, too?

NICK *(irritated).* You know what I mean. What's he want to bother people for? He's *sick.*

JOE *(almost to himself, reflecting on the fact that* BLICK *too wants to change the world).* I guess he wants to change the world at that.

NICK. So I go to work and hate him.

JOE. It's not him, Nick. It's everything.

NICK. Yeah, *I know.* But I've still got no use for him. He's no good. You know what I mean? He hurts little people. *(Confused.)* One of the girls tried to commit suicide on account of him. *(Furiously.)* I'll break his head if he hurts anybody around here. This is *my* joint. *(Afterthought.)* Or anybody's *feelings,* either.

JOE. He may not be so bad, deep down underneath.

NICK. I know all about him. He's no good.

*(During this talk* WESLEY *has really begun to play the piano, the toy is rattling again, and little by little* HARRY *has begun to dance.* NICK *has come around the bar, and*

now, *very much like a child—forgetting all his anger—is watching the toy work. He begins to smile at everything: turns and listens to* WESLEY: *watches* HARRY: *nods at the* ARAB: *shakes his head at* DUD-LEY: *and gestures amiably about* WILLIE. *It's his joint all right.)*

*(It's a good, low-down, honky-tonk American place that lets people alone.)*

NICK. I've got a good joint. There's nothing wrong here. Hey. Comedian. Stick to the dancing tonight. I think you're O.K. Wesley? Do some more of that tonight. That's fine!

HARRY. Thanks, Nick. Gosh, I'm on my way at last. *(On telephone.)* Hello, Ma? Is that you, Ma? Harry. I got the job. *(He hangs up and walks around, smiling.)*

NICK *(watching the toy all the time).* Say, that really is something. What is that, anyway?

*(*MARY L. *comes in.)*

JOE *(holding it toward* NICK, *and* MARY L.*).* Nick, this is a toy. A contraption devised by the cunning of man to drive boredom, or grief, or anger out of children. A noble gadget. A gadget, I might say, infinitely nobler than any other I can think of at the moment.

*(Everybody gathers around* JOE's *table to look at the toy. The toy stops working.* JOE *winds the music box. Lifts a whistle: blows it, making a very strange, funny and sorrowful sound.)*

Delightful. Tragic, but delightful.

*(*WESLEY *plays the music-box theme on the piano.* MARY L. *takes a table.)*

NICK. Joe. That girl, Kitty. What's she mean, calling me a dentist? I wouldn't hurt anybody, let alone a tooth.

*(*NICK *goes to* MARY L.'s *table.* HARRY *imitates the toy. Dances. The piano music comes up, the light dims slowly, while the piano solo continues.)*

CURTAIN

# ACT TWO

*An hour later. All the people who were at Nick's when the curtain came down are still there.* JOE *at his table, quietly shuffling and turning a deck of cards, and at the same time watching the face of the woman, and looking at the initials on her handbag, as though they were the symbols of the lost glory of the world. The* WOMAN, *in turn, very casually regards* JOE *occasionally. Or rather senses him; has sensed him in fact the whole hour. She is mildly tight on beer, and* JOE *himself is tight, but as always completely under control; simply sharper. The others are about, at tables, and so on.*

JOE. Is it Madge—Laubowitz?

MARY. Is what *what?*

JOE. Is the name Mabel Lepescu?

MARY. What name?

JOE. The name the initials M. L. stand for. The initials on your bag.

MARY. No.

JOE *(after a long pause, thinking deeply what the name might be, turning a card, looking into the beautiful face of the woman).* Margie Longworthy?

MARY *(all this is very natural and sincere, no comedy on the part of the people involved: they are both solemn, being drunk).* No.

JOE *(his voice higher-pitched, as though he were growing alarmed).* Midge Laurie? *(*MARY *shakes her head.)* My initials are J. T.

MARY *(Pause).* John?

JOE. No. *(Pause.)* Martha Lancaster?

MARY. No. *(Slight pause.)* Joseph?

JOE. Well, not exactly. That's my first name, but everybody calls me Joe. The last name is the tough one. I'll help you a little. I'm Irish. *(Pause.)* Is it just plain Mary?

MARY. Yes, it is. I'm Irish, too. At least on my father's side. English on my mother's side.

JOE. I'm Irish on both sides. Mary's one of my favorite names. I guess that's why I didn't think of it. I met a girl in Mexico City named Mary once. She was an American from Philadelphia. She got married there. In Mexico City, I mean. While I was *there.* We were in love, too. At least *I* was. You never know about anyone else. They were engaged, you see, and her

mother was with her, so they went through with it. Must have been six or seven years ago. She's probably got three or four children by this time.

MARY. Are you still in love with her?

JOE. Well—no. To tell you the truth, I'm not sure. I guess I am. I didn't even knew she was engaged until a couple of days before they got married. I thought *I* was going to marry her. I kept thinking all the time about the kind of kids we would be likely to have. My favorite was the third one. The first two were fine. Handsome and fine and intelligent, but that third one was different. Dumb and goofy-looking. I liked *him* a lot. When she told me she was going to be married, I didn't feel so bad about the first two, it was that dumb one.

MARY *(after a pause of some few seconds).* What do you do?

JOE. Do? To tell you the truth, nothing.

MARY. Do you always drink a great deal?

JOE *(scientifically).* Not *always.* Only when I'm awake. I sleep seven or eight hours every night, you know.

MARY. How nice. I mean to drink when you're awake.

JOE *(thoughtfully).* It's a privilege.

MARY. Do you really *like* to drink?

JOE *(positively).* As much as I like to *breathe.*

MARY *(beautifully).* Why?

JOE *(dramatically).* Why do I like to drink? *(Pause.)* Because I don't like to be gypped. Because I don't like to be dead most of the time and just a little alive every once in a long while. *(Pause.)* If I don't drink, I become fascinated by unimportant things—like everybody else. I get busy. Do things. All kinds of little stupid things, for all kinds of little stupid reasons. Proud, selfish, *ordinary* things. I've done them. Now I don't do anything. *I live all the time.* Then I go to sleep. *(Pause.)*

MARY. Do you sleep well?

JOE *(taking it for granted)*. Of course.

MARY *(quietly, almost with tenderness)*. What are your plans?

JOE *(loudly, but also tenderly)*. Plans? I haven't *got* any. *I just get up.*

MARY *(beginning to understand everything)*. Oh, yes. Yes, of course.

*(DUDLEY puts a nickel in the phonograph.)*

JOE *(thoughtfully)*. Why do I drink? *(Pause, while he thinks about it. The thinking appears to be profound and complex, and has the effect of giving his face a very comical and naïve expression.)* That question calls for a pretty complicated answer. *(He smiles abstractly.)*

MARY. Oh, I didn't mean—

JOE *(swiftly, gallantly)*. No. No. I *insist*. I *know* why. It's just a matter of finding words. Little ones.

MARY. It really doesn't matter.

JOE *(seriously)*. Oh, yes, it does. *(Clinically.)* Now, why do I drink? *(Scientifically.)* No. Why does *anybody* drink? *(Working it out.)* Every day has twenty-four hours.

MARY *(sadly, but brightly)*. Yes, that's true.

JOE. Twenty-four hours. Out of the twenty-four hours at *least* twenty-three and a half are—my God, I don't know why—dull, dead, boring, empty, and murderous. Minutes on the clock, *not time of living.* It doesn't make any difference who you are or what you do, twenty-three and a half hours of the twenty-four are spent *waiting.*

MARY. Waiting?

JOE *(gesturing, loudly)*. And the more you wait, the less there is to wait for.

MARY *(attentively, beautifully his student)*. Oh?

JOE *(continuing)*. That goes on for days and days, and weeks and months and years, and years, and the first thing you know *all* the years are dead. All the minutes are dead. You yourself are dead.

There's nothing to wait for any more. Nothing except *minutes* on the *clock*. No time of life. Nothing but minutes, and idiocy. Beautiful, bright, intelligent idiocy. *(Pause.)* Does that answer your question?

MARY *(earnestly)*. I'm afraid it does. Thank you. You shouldn't have gone to all the trouble.

JOE. No trouble at all. *(Pause.)* You have children?

MARY. Yes. Two. A son and a daughter.

JOE *(delighted)*. How swell. Do they look like you?

MARY. Yes.

JOE. Then why are you sad?

MARY. I was always sad. It's just that after I was married I was allowed to drink.

JOE *(eagerly)*. Who are you waiting for?

MARY. No one.

JOE *(smiling)*. I'm not waiting for anybody, either.

MARY. My husband, of course.

JOE. Oh, sure.

MARY. He's a lawyer.

JOE *(standing, leaning on the table)*. He's a great guy. I like him. I'm very fond of him.

MARY *(listening)*. You have responsibilities?

JOE *(loudly)*. *One,* and *thousands.* As a matter of fact, I feel responsible to everybody. At least to everybody I met. I've been trying for three years to find out if it's possible to live what I think is a civilized life. I mean a life that can't hurt any other life.

MARY. You're famous?

JOE. Very. Utterly unknown, but very famous. Would you like to dance?

MARY. All right.

JOE *(loudly)*. I'm *sorry.* I don't dance. I didn't think you'd like to.

MARY. To tell you the truth, I don't like to dance at all.

JOE *(proudly. Commentator)*. I can hardly walk.

MARY. You mean you're tight?

JOE *(smiling).* No. I mean *all* the time.

MARY *(looking at him closely).* Were you ever in Paris?

JOE. In 1929, and again in 1934.

MARY. What month of 1934?

JOE. Most of April, all of May, and a little of June.

MARY. I was there in November and December that year.

JOE. We were there almost at the same time. You were married?

MARY. Engaged. *(They are silent a moment, looking at one another. Quietly and with great charm.)* Are you *really* in love with me?

JOE. Yes.

MARY. Is it the champagne?

JOE. Yes. Partly, at least. *(He sits down.)*

MARY. If you don't see me again will you be very unhappy?

JOE. Very.

MARY *(getting up).* I'm so pleased. *(JOE is deeply grieved that she is going. In fact, he is almost panic-stricken about it, getting up in a way that is full of furious sorrow and regret.)* I must go now. Please don't get up. *(JOE is up, staring at her with amazement.)* Good-by.

JOE *(simply).* Good-by.

*(The WOMAN stands looking at him a moment, then turns and goes. JOE stands staring after her for a long time. Just as he is slowly sitting down again, the NEWSBOY enters, and goes to Joe's table.)*

NEWSBOY. Paper, Mister?

JOE. How many you got this time?

NEWSBOY. Eleven.

*(JOE buys them all, looks at the lousy headlines, throws them away.)*

*(The NEWSBOY looks at JOE, amazed. He walks over to NICK at the bar.)*

NEWSBOY *(troubled).* Hey, Mister, do you own this place?

NICK *(casually but emphatically).* I own this place.

NEWSBOY. Can you use a great lyric tenor?

NICK *(almost to himself).* Great lyric tenor? *(Loudly.)* Who?

NEWSBOY *(loud and the least bit angry).* Me. I'm getting too big to sell papers. I don't want to holler headlines all the time. I want to *sing.* You can use a great lyric tenor, can't you?

NICK. What's lyric about you?

NEWSBOY *(voice high-pitched, confused).* My voice.

NICK. Oh. *(Slight pause, giving in.)* All right, then—sing!

*(The NEWSBOY breaks into swift and beautiful song: "When Irish Eyes Are Smiling." NICK and JOE listen carefully: NICK with wonder, JOE with amazement and delight.)*

NEWSBOY *(singing).*
When Irish eyes are smiling,
Sure 'tis like a morn in Spring.
In the lilt of Irish laughter,
You can hear the angels sing.
When Irish hearts are happy,
All the world seems bright and gay.
But when Irish eyes are smiling—

NICK *(loudly, swiftly).* Are you Irish?

NEWSBOY *(speaking swiftly, loudly, a little impatient with the irrelevant question).* No. I'm Greek. *(He finishes the song, singing louder than ever.)*

Sure they steal your heart away.

*(He turns to NICK dramatically, like a vaudeville singer begging his audience for applause. NICK studies the boy eagerly. JOE gets to his feet and leans toward the BOY and NICK.)*

NICK. Not bad. Let me hear you again about a year from now.

NEWSBOY *(thrilled).* Honest?

NICK. Yeah. Along about November 7th, 1940.

NEWSBOY *(happier than ever before in his life, running over to JOE).* Did you hear it too, Mister?

JOE. Yes, and it's great. What part of Greece?

NEWSBOY. Salonica. Gosh, Mister. Thanks.

JOE. Don't wait a year. Come back with some papers a little later. You're a great singer.

NEWSBOY (*thrilled and excited*). Aw, thanks, Mister. So long. (*Running, to* NICK.) Thanks, Mister.

(*He runs out.* JOE *and* NICK *look at the swinging doors.* JOE *sits down.* NICK *laughs.*)

NICK. Joe, people are so wonderful. Look at that kid.

JOE. Of course they're wonderful. Every one of them is wonderful.

(MC CARTHY *and* KRUPP *come in, talking.*)

(MC CARTHY *is a big man in work clothes, which make him seem very young. He is wearing black jeans, and a blue workman's shirt. No tie. No hat. He has broad shoulders, a lean intelligent face, thick black hair. In his right back pocket is the longshoreman's hook. His arms are long and hairy. His sleeves are rolled up to just below his elbows. He is a casual man, easy-going in movement, sharp in perception, swift in appreciation of charm or innocence or comedy, and gentle in spirit. His speech is clear and full of warmth. His voice is powerful, but modulated. He enjoys the world, in spite of the mess it is, and he is fond of people, in spite of the mess they are.*)

(KRUPP *is not quite as tall or broadshouldered as* MC CARTHY. *He is physically encumbered by his uniform, club, pistol, belt, and cap. And he is plainly not at home in the role of policeman. His movement is stiff and unintentionally pompous. He is a naïve man, essentially good. His understanding is less than McCarthy's, but he is honest and he doesn't try to bluff.*)

KRUPP. You don't understand what I mean. Hi-ya, Joe.

JOE. Hello, Krupp.

MC CARTHY. Hi-ya, Joe.

JOE. Hello, McCarthy.

KRUPP. Two beers, Nick. (*To* MC CARTHY.) All I do is carry out orders, carry out orders. I don't know what the idea is behind the order. Who it's for, or who it's against, or why. All I do is carry it out.

(NICK *gives them beer.*)

MC CARTHY. You don't read enough.

KRUPP. I do read. I read *The Examiner* every morning. *The Call-Bulletin* every night.

MC CARTHY. And carry out orders. What are the orders now?

KRUPP. To keep the peace down here on the waterfront.

MC CARTHY. Keep it for who? (*To* JOE.) Right?

JOE (*sorrowfully*). Right.

KRUPP. How do I know for who? The peace. Just keep it.

MC CARTHY. It's got to be kept for somebody. Who would you suspect it's kept for?

KRUPP. For citizens!

MC CARTHY. I'm a citizen!

KRUPP. All right, I'm keeping it for you.

MC CARTHY. By hitting me over the head with a club? (*To* JOE.) Right?

JOE (*melancholy, with remembrance*). I don't know.

KRUPP. Mac, you know I never hit you over the head with a club.

MC CARTHY. But you will if you're on duty at the time and happen to stand on the opposite side of myself, on duty.

KRUPP. We went to Mission High together. We were always good friends. The only time we ever fought was that time over Alma Haggerty. Did you marry Alma Haggerty? (*To* JOE.) Right?

JOE. Everything's right.

MC CARTHY. No. Did you? (*To* JOE.) Joe, are you with me or against me?

JOE. I'm with everybody. One at a time.

KRUPP. No. And that's just what I mean.

MC CARTHY. You mean neither one of us is going to marry the thing we're fighting for?

KRUPP. *I don't even know what it is.*

MC CARTHY. You don't read enough, I tell you.

KRUPP. Mac, you don't know what you're fighting for, either.

MC CARTHY. It's so simple, it's fantastic.

KRUPP. All right, what are you fighting for?

MC CARTHY. For the rights of the inferior. Right?

JOE. Something like that.

KRUPP. The who?

MC CARTHY. The inferior. The world is full of Mahoneys who haven't got what it takes to make monkeys out of everybody else, near by. The men who were created equal. Remember?

KRUPP. Mac, you're not inferior.

MC CARTHY. I'm a longshoreman. And an idealist. I'm a man with too much brawn to be an intellectual, exclusively. I married a small, sensitive, cultured woman so that my kids would be sissies instead of suckers. A strong man with any sensibility has no choice in this world but to be a heel, or a *worker*. I haven't the heart to be a heel, so I'm a worker. I've got a son in high school who's already thinking of being a writer.

KRUPP. I wanted to be a writer once.

JOE. Wonderful. *(He puts down the paper, looks at* KRUPP *and* MC CARTHY.*)*

MC CARTHY. They *all* wanted to be writers. Every maniac in the world that ever brought about the murder of people through war started out in an attic or a basement writing poetry. It stank. So they got even by becoming important heels. And it's still going on.

KRUPP. Is it really, Joe?

JOE. Look at today's paper.

MC CARTHY. Right now on Telegraph Hill is some punk who is trying to be Shakespeare. Ten years from now he'll be a senator. Or a communist.

KRUPP. Somebody ought to do something about it.

MC CARTHY *(mischievously, with laughter in his voice).* The thing to do is to have more magazines. Hundreds of them. *Thousands.* Print everything they write, so they'll believe they're immortal. That way keep them from going haywire.

KRUPP. Mac, you ought to be a writer yourself.

MC CARTHY. I hate the tribe. They're mischief-makers. Right?

JOE *(swiftly).* Everything's right. Right and wrong.

KRUPP. Then why do you read?

MC CARTHY *(laughing).* It's relaxing. It's soothing. *(Pause.)* The lousiest people born into the world are writers. Language is all right. It's the people who use language that are lousy. *(The* ARAB *has moved a little closer, and is listening carefully.) (To the* ARAB.*)* What do you think, Brother?

ARAB *(after making many faces, thinking very deeply).* No foundation. All the way down the line. What. What-not. Nothing I go walk and look at sky. *(He goes.)*

KRUPP. What? What-not? *(To* JOE.*)* What's that mean?

JOE *(slowly, thinking, remembering).* What? What-not? That means this side, that side. Inhale, exhale. What: birth. What-not: death. The inevitable, the astounding, the magnificent seed of growth and decay in all things. Beginning, and end. That man, in his own way, is a prophet. He is one who, with the help of *beer,* is able to reach that state of deep understanding in which what and what-not, the reasonable and the unreasonable, are one.

MC CARTHY. Right.

KRUPP. If you can understand that kind of talk, how can you be a longshoreman?

MC CARTHY. I come from a long line of McCarthys who never married or slept with anything but the most powerful and quarrelsome flesh. *(He drinks beer.)*

KRUPP. I could listen to you two guys for hours, but I'll be damned if I know what the hell you're talking about.

MC CARTHY. The consequence is that all the McCarthys are too great and too strong to be heroes. Only the weak and unsure perform the heroic. They've *got* to. The more heroes you have, the worse the history of the world becomes. Right?

JOE. Go outside and look at it.

KRUPP. You sure can philos—philosoph— Boy, you can talk.

MC CARTHY. I wouldn't talk this way to anyone but a man in uniform, and a man who couldn't understand a word of what I was saying. The party I'm speaking of, my friend, is *YOU.*

*(The phone rings.)*

*(*HARRY *gets up from his table suddenly and begins a new dance.)*

KRUPP *(noticing him, with great authority).* Here, here. What do you think you're doing?

HARRY *(stopping).* I just got an idea for a new dance. I'm trying it out. Nick. Nick, the phone's ringing.

KRUPP *(to* MC CARTHY*).* Has he got a right to do that?

MC CARTHY. The living have danced from the beginning of time. I might even say, the dance and the life have moved along together, until now we have— *(To* HARRY.*)* Go into your dance, son, and show us what we have.

HARRY. I haven't got it worked out *completely* yet, but it starts out like this. *(He dances.)*

NICK *(on phone).* Nick's Pacific Street Restaurant, Saloon, and Entertainment Palace. Good afternoon. Nick speaking. *(Listens.)* Who? *(Turns around.)* Is there a Dudley Bostwick in the joint?

*(*DUDLEY *jumps to his feet and goes to phone.)*

DUDLEY *(on phone).* Hello. Elsie? *(Listens.)* You're coming down? *(Elated. To the saloon.)* She's coming down. *(Pause.)* No. I won't drink. Aw, gosh, Elsie.

*(He hangs up, looks about him strangely, as if he were just born, walks around touching things, putting chairs in place, and so on.)*

MC CARTHY *(to* HARRY.*)* Splendid. Splendid.

HARRY. Then I go into this little routine.

*(He demonstrates.)*

KRUPP. Is that good, Mac?

MC CARTHY. It's awful, but it's honest and ambitious, like everything else in this great country.

HARRY. Then I work along into this. *(He demonstrates.)* And *this* is where I *really* get going. *(He finishes the dance.)*

MC CARTHY. Excellent. A most satisfying demonstration of the present state of the American body and soul. Son, you're a genius.

HARRY *(delighted, shaking hands with* MC CARTHY*).* I go on in front of an audience for the first time in my life tonight.

MC CARTHY. They'll be delighted. Where'd you learn to dance?

HARRY. Never took a lesson in my life. I'm a natural-born dancer. And *comedian,* too.

MC CARTHY *(astounded).* You can make people *laugh?*

HARRY *(dumbly).* I can be funny, but they won't laugh.

MC CARTHY. That's odd. Why not?

HARRY. I don't know. They just won't laugh.

MC CARTHY. Would you care to be funny now?

HARRY. I'd like to try out a new monologue I've been thinking about.

MC CARTHY. Please do. I promise you if it's funny I shall *roar* with laughter.

HARRY. This is it. *(Goes into the act, with much energy.)* I'm up at Sharkey's on Turk Street. It's a quarter to nine, daylight saving. Wednesday, the eleventh. What I've got is a headache and a 1918 nickel. What I *want* is a cup of coffee. If I buy a cup of coffee with the nickel, I've got to walk home. I've got an eight-ball problem. George the Greek is shooting a game of snooker with Pedro the Filipino. *I'm in rags.* They're wearing thirty-five dollar suits, made to order. I haven't got a cigarette. They're smoking Bobby Burns panatelas. I'm thinking it over, like I always do. George the Greek is in a tough spot. If I buy a cup of coffee, I'll want another cup. What happens? My *ear* aches! My ear. George the Greek takes the cue. Chalks it. Studies the table. Touches the cue-ball delicately. Tick. What happens? He makes the three-ball! What do I do. I get confused. *I go out and buy a morning paper.* What the hell do I want with a morning paper? What I *want* is a cup of coffee, and a good used car. I go out and buy a morning paper. Thursday, the twelfth. Maybe the headline's about *me*. I take a quick look. *No. The headline is not about me.* It's about Hitler. Seven thousand miles away. I'm here. Who the hell is Hitler? Who's behind the eight-ball? I turn around. *Everybody's behind the eight-ball!*

*(Pause.* KRUPP *moves toward* HARRY *as if to make an important arrest.* HARRY *moves to the swinging doors.* MC CARTHY *stops* KRUPP.*)*

MC CARTHY *(to* HARRY*).* It's the funniest thing I've ever heard. Or *seen,* for that matter.

HARRY *(coming back to* MC CARTHY*).* Then, why don't you laugh?

MC CARTHY. I don't know, *yet.*

HARRY. I'm always getting funny ideas that nobody will laugh at.

MC CARTHY *(thoughtfully).* It may be that you've stumbled headlong into a new kind of comedy.

HARRY. Well, what good is it if it doesn't make anybody laugh?

MC CARTHY. There are *kinds* of laughter, son. I must say, in all truth, that I *am* laughing, although not *out loud.*

HARRY. I want to *hear* people laugh. *Out loud.* That's why I keep thinking of funny things to say.

MC CARTHY. Well. They may catch on in time. Let's go, Krupp. So long, Joe. *(*MC CARTHY *and* KRUPP *go.)*

JOE. So long. *(After a moment's pause.)* Hey, Nick.

NICK. Yeah.

JOE. Bet McCarthy in the last race.

NICK. You're crazy. That horse is a double-crossing, no-good—

JOE. Bet everything you've got on McCarthy.

NICK. I'm not betting a nickel on him. *You* bet everything you've got on McCarthy.

JOE. I don't need money.

NICK. What makes you think McCarthy's going to win?

JOE. McCarthy's name's McCarthy, isn't it?

NICK. Yeah. So what?

JOE. The *horse* named McCarthy is going to win, *that's all.* Today.

NICK. Why?

JOE. You do what I tell you, and everything will be all right.

NICK. McCarthy likes to talk, that's all. *(Pause.)* Where's Tom?

JOE. He'll be around. He'll be miserable, but he'll be around. Five or ten minutes more.

NICK. You don't believe that Kitty, do you? About being in burlesque?

JOE *(very clearly).* I believe dreams sooner than statistics.

NICK *(remembering).* She sure is somebody. Called me a dentist.

*(*TOM, *turning about, confused, troubled, comes in, and hurries to Joe's table.)*

JOE. What's the matter?

TOM. Here's your five, Joe. I'm in trouble again.

JOE. If it's not organic, it'll cure itself. If it is organic, science will cure it. What is it, organic or non-organic?

TOM. Joe, I don't know— *(He seems to be completely broken-down.)*

JOE. What's eating you? I want you to go on an errand for me.

TOM. It's Kitty.

JOE. What about her?

TOM. She's up in her room, crying.

JOE. Crying?

TOM. Yeah, she's been crying for over an hour. I been talking to her all this time, but she won't stop.

JOE. What's she crying about?

TOM. I don't know. I couldn't understand anything. She kept crying and telling me about a big house and collie dogs all around and flowers and one of her brother's dead and the other one lost somewhere. Joe, I can't stand Kitty crying.

JOE. You want to marry the girl?

TOM (*nodding*). Yeah.

JOE (*curious and sincere*). Why?

TOM. I don't know why, exactly, Joe. (*Pause.*) Joe, I don't like to think of Kitty out in the streets. I guess I love her, that's all.

JOE. She's a nice girl.

TOM. She's like an angel. She's not like those other street-walkers.

JOE (*swiftly*). Here. Take all this money and run next door to Frankie's and bet it on the nose of McCarthy.

TOM (*swiftly*). All this money, Joe? Mc-Carthy?

JOE. Yeah. Hurry.

TOM (*going*). Ah, Joe. If McCarthy wins we'll be rich.

JOE. Get going, will you?

(TOM *runs out and nearly knocks over the* ARAB *coming back in.* NICK *fills him a beer without a word.*)

ARAB. No foundation, anywhere. Whole world. No foundation. All the way down the line.

NICK (*angry*). McCarthy! Just because you got a little lucky this morning, you have to go to work and throw away eighty bucks.

JOE. He wants to marry her.

NICK. Suppose she doesn't want to marry *him?*

JOE (*amazed*). Oh, yeah (*Thinking*). Now, why wouldn't she want to marry a nice guy like Tom?

NICK. She's been in burlesque. She's had flowers sent to her by European royalty. She's dined with young men of quality and social position. She's above Tom.

(TOM *comes running in.*)

TOM (*disgusted*). They were running when I got there. Frankie wouldn't take the bet. McCarthy didn't get a call till the stretch. I thought we were going to save all this money. Then McCarthy won by two lengths.

JOE. What'd he pay, fifteen to one?

TOM. Better, but Frankie wouldn't take the bet.

NICK (*throwing a dish towel across the room*). Well, for the love of Mike.

JOE. Give me the money.

TOM (*giving back the money*). We would have had about a thousand five hundred dollars.

JOE (*bored, casually, inventing*). Go up to Schwabacher-Frey and get me the biggest Rand-McNally map of the nations of Europe they've got. On your way back stop at one of the pawn shops on Third Street, and buy me a good revolver and some cartridges.

TOM. She's up in her room crying, Joe.

JOE. Go get me those things.

NICK. What are you going to do, study the map, and then go out and shoot some-body?

JOE. I want to read the names of some European towns and rivers and valleys and mountains.

NICK. What do you want with the re-volver?

JOE. I want to study it. I'm interested in things. Here's twenty dollars, Tom. Now go get them things.

TOM. A big map of Europe. And a revolver.

JOE. Get a good one. Tell the man you don't know anything about firearms and you're trusting him not to fool you. Don't pay more than ten dollars.

TOM. Joe, you got something on your mind. Don't go fool with a revolver.

JOE. Be sure it's a good one.

TOM. Joe.

JOE (*irritated*). What, Tom?

TOM. Joe, what do you send me out for crazy things for all the time?

JOE (*angry*). They're not crazy, Tom. Now, get going.

TOM. What about Kitty, Joe?

JOE. Let her cry. It'll do her good.

TOM. If she comes in here while I'm gone, talk to her, will you, Joe? Tell her about me.

JOE. O.K. Get going. Don't load that gun. Just buy it and bring it here.

TOM *(going)*. You won't catch me loading any gun.

JOE. Wait a minute. Take these toys away.

TOM. Where'll I take them?

JOE. Give them to some kid. *(Pause.)* No. Take them up to Kitty. Toys stopped me from crying once. That's the reason I had you buy them. I wanted to see if I could find out *why* they stopped me from crying. I remember they seemed awfully stupid at the time.

TOM. Shall I, Joe? Take them up to Kitty? Do you think they'd stop *her* from crying?

JOE. They might. You get curious about the way they work and you forget whatever it is you're remembering that's making you cry. That's what they're for.

TOM. Yeah. Sure. The girl at the store asked me what I wanted with toys. I'll take them up to Kitty. *(Tragically.)* She's like a little girl. *(He goes.)*

WESLEY. Mr. Nick, can I play the piano again?

NICK. Sure. Practice all you like—until I tell you to stop.

WESLEY. You going to pay me for playing the piano?

NICK. Sure. I'll give you enough to get by on.

WESLEY *(amazed and delighted)*. Get money for playing the piano?

*(He goes to the piano and begins to play quietly.* HARRY *goes up on the little stage and listens to the music. After a while he begins a soft shoe dance.)*

NICK. What were you crying about?

JOE. My mother.

NICK. What about her?

JOE. She was dead. I stopped crying when they gave me the toys.

*(*NICK's MOTHER, *a little old woman of sixty or so, dressed plainly in black, her face shining, comes in briskly, chattering loudly in Italian, gesturing.* NICK *is delighted to see her.)*

NICK's MOTHER *(in Italian)*. Everything all right, Nickie?

NICK *(in Italian)*. Sure, Mamma.

*(*NICK's MOTHER *leaves as gaily and as noisily as she came, after half a minute of loud Italian family talk.)*

JOE. Who was that?

NICK *(to* JOE, *proudly and a little sadly)*. My mother. *(Still looking at the swinging doors.)*

JOE. What'd she say?

NICK. Nothing. Just wanted to see me. *(Pause.)* What do you want with that gun?

JOE. I study things, Nick.

*(An old man who looks as if he might have been Kit Carson at one time walks in importantly, moves about, and finally stands at Joe's table.)*

KIT CARSON. Murphy's the name. Just an old trapper. Mind if I sit down?

JOE. Be delighted. What'll you drink?

KIT CARSON *(sitting down)*. Beer. Same as I've been drinking. And thanks.

JOE *(to* NICK*)*. Glass of beer, Nick.

*(*NICK *brings the beer to the table,* KIT CARSON *swallows it in one swig, wipes his big white mustache with the back of his right hand.)*

KIT CARSON *(moving in)*. I don't suppose you ever fell in love with a midget weighing thirty-nine pounds?

JOE *(studying the man)*. Can't say I have, but have another beer.

KIT CARSON *(intimately)*. Thanks, thanks. Down in Gallup, twenty years ago. Fellow by the name of Rufus Jenkins came to town with six white horses and two black ones. Said he wanted a man to break the horses for him because his left leg was wood and he couldn't do it. Had a meeting at Parker's Mercantile Store and finally came to blows, me and Henry Walpal. Bashed his head with a brass cuspidor and ran away to Mexico, but he didn't die.

Couldn't speak a word. Took up with a cattle-breeder named Diego, educated in California. Spoke the language better than you and me. Said, Your job, Murph, is to feed them prize bulls. I said, Fine, what'll I feed them? He said, Hay, lettuce, salt, beer, and aspirin.

Came to blows two days later over an

accordion he claimed I stole. I had *borrowed* it. During the fight I busted it over his head; ruined one of the finest accordions I ever saw. Grabbed a horse and rode back across the border. Texas. Got to talking with a fellow who looked honest. Turned out to be a Ranger who was looking for me.

JOE. Yeah. You were saying, a thirty-nine-pound midget.

KIT CARSON. Will I ever forget that lady? Will I ever get over that amazon of small proportions?

JOE. Will you?

KIT CARSON. If I live to be sixty.

JOE. Sixty? You look more than sixty now.

KIT CARSON. That's trouble showing in my face. Trouble and complications. I was fifty-eight three months ago.

JOE. That accounts for it, then. Go ahead, tell me more.

KIT CARSON. Told the Texas Ranger my name was Rothstein, mining engineer from Pennsylvania, looking for something worth while. Mentioned two places in Houston. Nearly lost an eye early one morning, going down the stairs. Ran into a six-footer with an iron-claw where his right hand was supposed to be. Said, You broke up my home. Told him I was a stranger in Houston. The girls gathered at the top of the stairs to see a fight. Seven of them. Six feet and an iron claw. That's bad on the nerves. Kicked him in the mouth when he swung for my head with the claw. Would have lost an eye except for quick thinking. He rolled into the gutter and pulled a gun. Fired seven times. I was back upstairs. Left the place an hour later, dressed in silk and feathers, with a hat swung around over my face. Saw him standing on the corner, waiting. Said, Care for a wiggle? Said he didn't. I went on down the street and left town. I don't suppose you ever had to put a dress on to save your skin, did you?

JOE. No, and I never fell in love with a midget weighing thirty-nine pounds. Have another beer?

KIT CARSON. Thanks. *(Swallows glass of beer.)* Ever try to herd cattle on a bicycle?

JOE. No. I never got around to that.

KIT CARSON. Left Houston with sixty cents in my pocket, gift of a girl named Lucinda. Walked fourteen miles in fourteen hours. Big house with barb-wire all around, and big dogs. One thing I never could get around. Walked past the gate, anyway, from hunger and thirst. Dogs jumped up and came for me. Walked right into them, growing older every second. Went up to the door and knocked. Big negress opened the door, closed it quick. Said, On your way, white trash.

Knocked again. Said, On your way. Again. On your way. Again. This time the old man himself opened the door, ninety, if he was a day. Sawed-off shotgun, too.

Said, I ain't looking for trouble, Father. I'm hungry and thirsty, name's Cavanaugh.

Took me in and made mint juleps for the two of us.

Said, Living here alone, Father?

Said, Drink and ask no questions. Maybe I am and maybe I ain't. You saw the lady. Draw your own conclusions.

I'd heard of that, but didn't wink out of tact. If I told you that old Southern gentleman was my grandfather, you wouldn't believe me, would you?

JOE. I might.

KIT CARSON. Well, it so happens he wasn't. Would have been romantic if he had been, though.

JOE. Where did you herd cattle on a bicycle?

KIT CARSON. Toledo, Ohio, 1918.

JOE. Toledo, Ohio? They don't herd cattle in Toledo.

KIT CARSON. They don't anymore. They did in 1918. One fellow did, leastaways. Bookkeeper named Sam Gold. Straight from the East Side, New York. Sombrero, lariats, Bull Durham, two head of cattle and two bicycles. Called his place The Gold Bar Ranch, two acres, just outside the city limits.

That was the year of the War, you'll remember.

JOE. Yeah, I remember, but how about herding them two cows on a bicycle? How'd you do it?

KIT CARSON. Easiest thing in the world. Rode no hands. Had to, otherwise couldn't lasso the cows. Worked for Sam Gold till the cows ran away. Bicycles scared them. They went into Toledo. Never saw hide nor hair of them again. Advertised in every paper, but never got them back. Broke his heart. Sold both bikes and returned to New York.

Took four aces from a deck of red cards and walked to town. Poker. Fellow in the game named Chuck Collins, liked to gamble. Told him with a smile I didn't suppose he'd care to bet a hundred dollars I wouldn't hold four aces the next hand. Called it. My cards were red on the blank side. The other cards were blue. Plumb forgot all about it. Showed him four aces. Ace of spades, ace of clubs, ace of diamonds, ace of hearts. I'll remember them four cards if I live to be sixty. Would have been killed on the spot except for the hurricane that year.

JOE. Hurricane?

KIT CARSON. You haven't forgotten the Toledo hurricane of 1918, have you?

JOE. No. There was no hurricane in Toledo in 1918, or any other year.

KIT CARSON. For the love of God, then what do you suppose that commotion was? And how come I came to in Chicago, dream-walking down State Street?

JOE. I guess they scared you.

KIT CARSON. No, that wasn't it. You go back to the papers of November 1918, and I think you'll find there was a hurricane in Toledo. I remember sitting on the roof of a two-story house, floating northwest.

JOE (seriously). Northwest?

KIT CARSON. Now, son, don't tell me *you* don't believe me, either?

JOE (pause. Very seriously, energetically and sharply). Of course I believe you. Living is an art. It's not bookkeeping. It takes a lot of rehearsing for a man to get to be himself.

KIT CARSON (thoughtfully, smiling, and amazed). You're the first man I've ever met who believes me.

JOE (seriously). Have another beer.

(TOM comes in with the Rand-McNally book, the revolver, and the box of cartridges. KIT goes to bar.)

JOE (to TOM). Did you give her the toys?

TOM. Yeah, I gave them to her.

JOE. Did she stop crying?

TOM. No. She started crying harder than ever.

JOE. That's funny. I wonder why.

TOM. Joe, if I was a minute earlier, Frankie would have taken the bet and now we'd have about a thousand five hundred dollars. How much of it would you have given me, Joe?

JOE. If she'd marry you—*all* of it.

TOM. Would you, Joe?

JOE (opening packages, examining book first, and revolver next). Sure. In this realm there's only one subject, and you're it. It's my duty to see that my subject is happy.

TOM. Joe, do you think we'll ever have eighty dollars for a race sometime again when there's a fifteen-to-one shot that we like, weather good, track fast, they get off to a good start, our horse doesn't get a call till the stretch, we think we're going to lose all that money, and then it wins, by a nose?

JOE. I didn't quite get that.

TOM. You know what I mean.

JOE. You mean the impossible. No, Tom, we won't. We were just a little late, that's all.

TOM. We might, Joe.

JOE. It's not likely.

TOM. Then how am I ever going to make enough money to marry her?

JOE. I don't know, Tom. Maybe you aren't.

TOM. Joe, I got to marry Kitty. (Shaking his head.) You ought to see the crazy room she lives in.

JOE. What kind of a room is it?

TOM. It's little. It crowds you in. It's bad, Joe. Kitty don't belong in a place like that.

JOE. You want to take her away from there?

TOM. Yeah. I want her to live in a house where there's room enough to live. Kitty ought to have a garden, or something.

JOE. You want to take care of her?

TOM. Yeah, sure, Joe. I ought to take care of somebody good that makes me feel like *I'm* somebody.

JOE. That means you'll have to get a job. What can you do?

TOM. I finished high school, but I don't know what I can do.

JOE. Sometimes when you think about it, what do you think you'd like to do?

TOM. Just sit around like you, Joe, and have somebody run errands for me and drink champagne and take things easy and never be broke and never worry about money.

JOE. That's a noble ambition.

NICK (*to* JOE). How do you do it?

JOE. I really don't know, but I think you've got to have the full co-operation of the Good Lord.

NICK. I can't understand the way you talk.

TOM. Joe, shall I go back and see if I can get her to stop crying?

JOE. Give me a hand and I'll go with you.

TOM (*amazed*). What! You're going to get up already?

JOE. She's crying, isn't she?

TOM. She's crying. Worse than ever now.

JOE. I thought the toys would stop her.

TOM. I've seen you sit in one place from four in the morning till two the next morning.

JOE. At my best, Tom, I don't travel by foot. That's all. Come on. Give me a hand. I'll find some way to stop her from crying.

TOM (*helping* JOE). Joe, I never did tell you. You're a different kind of guy.

JOE (*swiftly, a little angry*). Don't be silly. I don't understand things. I'm trying to understand them.

(JOE *is a little drunk. They go out together. The lights go down slowly, while* WESLEY *plays the piano, and come up slowly on:*)

# ACT THREE

*A cheap bed in Nick's to indicate room 21 of The New York Hotel, upstairs, around the corner from Nick's. The bed can be at the center of Nick's or up on the little stage. Everything in Nick's is the same, except that all the people are silent, immobile and in darkness, except* WESLEY *who is playing the piano softly and sadly.* KITTY DUVAL, *in a dress she has carried around with her from the early days in Ohio, is seated on the bed, tying a ribbon in her hair. She looks at herself in a hand mirror. She is deeply grieved at the change she sees in herself. She takes off the ribbon, angry and hurt. She lifts a book from the bed and tries to read. She begins to sob again. She picks up an old picture of herself and looks at it. Sobs harder than ever, falling on the bed and burying her face. There is a knock, as if at the door.*

KITTY (*sobbing*). Who is it?

TOM'S VOICE. Kitty, it's me. Tom. Me and Joe.

(JOE, *followed by* TOM, *comes to the bed quietly.* JOE *is holding a rather large toy carousel.* JOE *studies* KITTY *a moment.*)

(*He sets the toy carousel on the floor, at the foot of Kitty's bed.*)

TOM (*standing over* KITTY *and bending down close to her*). Don't cry any more, Kitty.

KITTY (*not looking, sobbing*). I don't like this life.

(JOE *starts the carousel which makes a strange, sorrowful, tinkling music. The music begins slowly, becomes swift, gradually slows down, and ends.* JOE *himself is interested in the toy, watches and listens to it carefully.*)

TOM (*eagerly*). Kitty. Joe got up from his chair at Nick's just to get you a toy and come here. This one makes music. We rode all over town in a cab to get it. Listen.

(KITTY *sits up slowly, listening, while* TOM *watches her. Everything happens slowly and somberly.* KITTY *notices the photograph of herself when she was a little girl. Lifts it, and looks at it again.*)

TOM (*looking*). Who's that little girl, Kitty?

KITTY. That's me. When I was seven.

(KITTY *hands the photo to* TOM.)

TOM (*looking, smiling*). Gee, you're pretty, Kitty.

(JOE *reaches up for the photograph, which* TOM *hands to him.* TOM *returns to* KITTY *whom he finds as pretty now as she was at seven.* JOE *studies the photograph.* KITTY *looks up at* TOM. *There is no doubt that they really love one another.* JOE *looks up at them.*)

KITTY. Tom?

TOM (*eagerly*). Yeah, Kitty.

KITTY. Tom, when you were a little boy what did you want to be?

TOM (*a little bewildered, but eager to please her*). What, Kitty?

KITTY. Do you remember when you were a little boy?

TOM (*thoughtfully*). Yeah, I remember sometimes, Kitty.

KITTY. What did you want to be?

TOM (*looks at* JOE. JOE *holds Tom's eyes a moment. Then* TOM *is able to speak*). Sometimes I wanted to be a locomotive engineer. Sometimes I wanted to be a policeman.

KITTY. I wanted to be a great actress. (*She looks up into Tom's face.*) Tom, didn't you ever want to be a doctor?

TOM (*looks at* JOE. JOE *holds Tom's eyes again, encouraging Tom by his serious expression to go on talking*). Yeah, now I remember. Sure, Kitty. I wanted to be a doctor—*once.*

KITTY (*smiling sadly*). I'm so glad. Because I wanted to be an actress and have a young doctor come to the theater and

see me and fall in love with me and send me flowers.

(JOE *pantomimes to* TOM, *demanding that he go on talking.*)

TOM. I would do that, Kitty.

KITTY. I wouldn't know who it was, and then one day I'd see him in the street and fall in love with him. I wouldn't know *he* was the one who was in love with me. I'd think about him all the time. I'd dream about him. I'd dream of being near him the rest of my life. I'd dream of having children that looked like him. I wouldn't be an actress all the time. Only until I found him and fell in love with him. After that we'd take a train and go to beautiful cities and see the wonderful people everywhere and give money to the poor and whenever people were sick he'd go to them and make them well again.

(TOM *looks at* JOE, *bewildered, confused, and full of sorrow.* KITTY *is deep in memory, almost in a trance.*)

JOE (*gently*). Talk to her, Tom. Be the wonderful young doctor she dreamed about and never found. Go ahead. Correct the errors of the world.

TOM. Joe. (*Pathetically.*) I don't know what to say.

(*There is rowdy singing in the hall. A loud young* VOICE *sings:* "*Sailing, sailing, over the bounding main.*")

VOICE. Kitty. Oh. Kitty! (KITTY *stirs, shocked, coming out of the trance.*) Where the hell are you? Oh, Kitty.

(TOM *jumps up, furiously.*)

WOMAN'S VOICE (*in the hall*). Who you looking for, Sailor Boy?

VOICE. The most beautiful lay in the world.

WOMAN'S VOICE. Don't go any further.

VOICE (*with impersonal contempt*). You? No. Not you. Kitty. You stink.

WOMAN'S VOICE (*rasping, angry*). Don't you dare talk to me that way. You pickpocket.

VOICE (*still impersonal, but louder*). Oh, I see. Want to get tough, hey? Close the door. Go hide.

WOMAN'S VOICE. You pickpocket. All of you.

*(The door slams.)*

VOICE *(roaring with laughter which is very sad).* Oh—Kitty.

Room 21. Where the hell is that room?

TOM *(to* JOE*).* Joe, I'll kill him.

KITTY *(fully herself again, terribly frightened).* Who is it?

*(She looks long and steadily at* TOM *and* JOE. TOM *is standing, excited and angry.* JOE *is completely at ease, his expression full of pity.* KITTY *buries her face in the bed.)*

JOE *(gently).* Tom. Just take him away.

VOICE. Here it is. Number 21. Three naturals. Heaven. My blue heaven. The west, a nest, and you. Just Molly and me. *(Tragically.)* Ah, to hell with everything.

*(A young* SAILOR, *a good-looking boy of no more than twenty or so, who is only drunk and lonely, comes to the bed, singing sadly.)*

SAILOR. Hi-ya, Kitty. *(Pause.)* Oh. Visitors. Sorry. A thousand apologies. *(To* KITTY*.)* I'll come back later.

TOM *(taking him by the shoulders, furiously).* If you do, I'll kill you.

*(*JOE *holds* TOM. TOM *pushes the frightened boy away.)*

JOE *(somberly).* Tom. You stay here with Kitty. I'm going down to Union Square to hire an automobile. I'll be back in a few minutes. We'll ride out to the ocean and watch the sun go down. Then we'll ride down the Great Highway to Half Moon Bay. We'll have supper down there, and you and Kitty can dance.

TOM *(stupefied, unable to express his amazement and gratitude).* Joe, you mean you're going to go on an errand for me? You mean you're not going to send me?

JOE. That's right.

*(He gestures toward* KITTY, *indicating that* TOM *shall talk to her, protect the innocence in her which is in so much danger when* TOM *isn't near, which* TOM *loves so deeply.* JOE *leaves.* TOM *studies* KITTY, *his face becoming child-like and somber. He sets the carousel into motion, listens, watching* KITTY, *who lifts herself slowly, looking only at* TOM. TOM *lifts the turning carousel and moves it slowly toward* KITTY, *as though the toy were his heart. The piano music comes up loudly and the lights go down, while* HARRY *is heard dancing swiftly.)*

BLACKOUT

# ACT FOUR

*A little later.*
WESLEY, *the colored boy, is at the piano.*
HARRY *is on the little stage, dancing.*
NICK *is behind the bar.*
*The* ARAB *is in his place.*
KIT CARSON *is asleep on his folded arms.*
*The* DRUNKARD *comes in. Goes to the telephone for the nickel that might be in the return-chute.* NICK *comes to take him out. He gestures for* NICK *to hold on a minute. Then produces a half dollar.* NICK *goes behind the bar to serve the* DRUNKARD *whiskey.*

THE DRUNKARD. To the old, God bless them. *(Another.)* To the new, God love them. *(Another.)* To—children and small animals, like little dogs that don't bite. *(Another. Loudly.)* To reforestation. *(Searches for money. Finds some.)* To—President Taft. *(He goes out.)*

*(The telephone rings.)*

KIT CARSON *(jumping up, fighting).* Come on, *all* of you, if you're looking for trou-ble. I never asked for quarter and I always gave it.

NICK *(reproachfully).* Hey, Kit Carson.

DUDLEY *(on the phone).* Hello. Who? Nick? Yes. He's here. *(To* NICK.*)* It's for you. I think it's important.

NICK *(going to the phone).* Important! *What's* important?

DUDLEY. He sounded like big-shot.

NICK. Big *what*? *(To* WESLEY *and* HARRY.*)* Hey, you. Quiet. I want to hear this important stuff.

*(*WESLEY *stops playing the piano.* HARRY *stops dancing.* KIT CARSON *comes close to* NICK.*)*

KIT CARSON. If there's anything I can do, name it. I'll do it for you. I'm fifty-eight years old; been through three wars; married four times; the father of countless children whose *names* I don't even know. I've got no money. I live from hand to mouth. But if there's anything I can do, name it. I'll do it.

NICK *(patiently)*. Listen, Pop. For a moment, please sit down and go back to sleep—for me.

KIT CARSON. I can do that, too.

*(He sits down, folds his arms, and puts his head into them. But not for long. As* NICK *begins to talk, he listens carefully, gets to his feet, and then begins to express in pantomime the moods of each of Nick's remarks.)*

NICK *(on phone)*. Yeah? *(Pause.)* Who? Oh, I see. *(Listens.)* Why don't you leave them alone? *(Listens.)* The church-people? Well, to hell with the church-people. I'm a Catholic myself. *(Listens.)* All right. I'll send them away. I'll tell them to lay low for a couple of days. Yeah, I know how it is. *(Nick's daughter* ANNA *comes in shyly, looking at her father, and stands unnoticed by the piano.)* What? *(Very angry.)* Listen. I don't like that Blick. He was here this morning, and I told him not to come back. I'll keep the girls out of here. You keep Blick out of here. *(Listens.)* I know his brother-in-law is important, but I don't want him to come down here. He looks for trouble everywhere, and he always finds it. I don't break any laws. I've got a dive in the lousiest part of town. Five years nobody's been robbed, murdered, or gypped. I leave people alone. Your swanky joints uptown make trouble for you every night. *(*NICK *gestures to* WESLEY—*keeps listening on the phone—puts his hand over the mouthpiece. To* WESLEY *and* HARRY.*)* Start playing again. My ears have got a headache. Go into your dance, son. *(*WESLEY *begins to play again.* HARRY *begins to dance.* NICK *into mouthpiece.)* Yeah. I'll keep them out. Just see that Blick doesn't come around and start something. *(Pause.)* O.K. *(He hangs up.)*

KIT CARSON. Trouble coming?

NICK. That lousy Vice Squad again. It's that gorilla Blick.

KIT CARSON. Anybody at all. You can count on me. What kind of a gorilla is this gorilla Blick?

NICK. Very dignified. Toenails on his fingers.

ANNA *(to* KIT CARSON, *with great warm, beautiful pride, pointing at* NICK*)*. That's my father.

KIT CARSON *(leaping with amazement at the beautiful voice, the wondrous face, the magnificent event)*. Well, bless your heart, child. Bless your lovely heart. I had a little daughter point me out in a crowd once.

NICK *(surprised)*. Anna. What the hell are you doing here? Get back home where you belong and help Grandma cook me some supper.

*(*ANNA *smiles at her father, understanding him, knowing that his words are words of love. She turns and goes, looking at him all the way out, as much as to say that she would cook for him the rest of her life.* NICK *stares at the swinging doors.* KIT CARSON *moves toward them, two or three steps.* ANNA *pushes open one of the doors and peeks in, to look at her father again. She waves to him. Turns and runs.* NICK *is very sad. He doesn't know what to do. He gets a glass and a bottle. Pours himself a drink. Swallows some. It isn't enough, so he pours more and swallows the whole drink.)*

*(To himself.)* My beautiful, beautiful baby. Anna, she is you again. *(He brings out a handkerchief, touches his eyes, and blows his nose.* KIT CARSON *moves close to* NICK, *watching Nick's face.* NICK *looks at him. Loudly, almost making* KIT *jump.)* You're broke, aren't you?

KIT CARSON. Always. Always.

NICK. All right. Go into the kitchen and give Sam a hand. Eat some food and when you come back you can have a couple of beers.

KIT CARSON (*studying* NICK). Anything at all. I know a good man when I see one.

(*He goes.*)

(ELSIE MANDELSPIEGEL *comes into Nick's. She is a beautiful, dark girl, with a sorrowful, wise, dreaming face, almost on the verge of tears, and full of pity. There is an aura of dream about her. She moves softly and gently, as if everything around her were unreal and pathetic.* DUDLEY *doesn't notice her for a moment or two. When he does finally see her, he is so amazed, he can barely move or speak. Her presence has the effect of changing him completely. He gets up from his chair, as if in a trance, and walks toward her, smiling sadly.*)

ELSIE (*looking at him*). Hello, Dudley.

DUDLEY (*broken-hearted*). Elsie.

ELSIE. I'm sorry. (*Explaining.*) So many people are sick. Last night a little boy died. I love you, but— (*She gestures, trying to indicate how hopeless love is. They sit down.*)

DUDLEY (*staring at her, stunned and quieted*). Elsie. You'll never know how glad I am to see you. Just to *see* you. (*Pathetically.*) I was afraid I'd never see you again. It was driving me crazy. I didn't want to live. Honest. (*He shakes his head mournfully, with dumb and beautiful affection.* TWO STREETWALKERS *come in, and pause near* DUDLEY, *at the bar.*) I know. You **to**ld me before, but I can't help it, Elsie. I love you.

ELSIE (*quietly, somberly, gently, with great compassion*). I know you love me, and I love you, but don't you see love is impossible in this world?

DUDLEY. Maybe it isn't, Elsie.

ELSIE. Love is for birds. They have wings to fly away on when it's time for flying. For tigers in the jungle because they don't know their end. We know *our* end. Every night I watch over poor, dying men. I hear them breathing, crying, talking in their sleep. Crying for air and water and love, for mother and field and sunlight. *We* can never know love or greatness. We *should* know both.

DUDLEY (*deeply moved by her words*). Elsie, I love you.

ELSIE. You want to live. *I* want to live, too, but where? Where can we escape our poor world?

DUDLEY. Elsie, we'll find a place.

ELSIE (*smiling at him*). All right. We'll try again. We'll go together to a room in a cheap hotel, and dream that the world is beautiful, and that living is full of love and greatness. But in the morning, can we forget debts, and duties, and the cost of ridiculous things?

DUDLEY (*with blind faith*). Sure, we can, Elsie.

ELSIE. All right, Dudley. Of course. Come on. The time for the new pathetic war has come. Let's hurry, before they dress you, stand you in line, hand you a gun, and have you kill and be killed.

(ELSIE *looks at him gently, and takes his hand.* DUDLEY *embraces her shyly, as if he might hurt her. They go, as if they were a couple of young animals. There is a moment of silence. One of the* STREETWALKERS *bursts out laughing.*)

KILLER. Nick, what the hell kind of a joint are you running?

NICK. Well, it's not out of the world. It's on a street in a city, and people come and go. They bring whatever they've got with them and they say what they must say.

THE OTHER STREETWALKER. It's floozies like her that raise hell with our racket.

NICK (*remembering*). Oh, yeah. Finnegan telephoned.

KILLER. That mouse in elephant's body?

THE OTHER STREETWALKER. What the hell does *he* want?

NICK. Spend your time at the movies for the next couple of days.

KILLER. They're all lousy. (*Mocking.*) All about love.

NICK. Lousy or not lousy, for a couple of days the flat-foots are going to be romancing you, so stay out of here, and lay low.

KILLER. I always was a pushover for a man in uniform, with a badge, a club and a gun.

(KRUPP *comes into the place. The girls put down their drinks.*)

NICK. O.K., get going.

(*The* GIRLS *begin to leave and meet* KRUPP.)

THE OTHER STREETWALKER. We was just going.

KILLER. We was formerly models at Magnin's. (*They go.*)

KRUPP (*at the bar*). The strike isn't enough, so they've got to put us on the tails of the girls, too. I don't know. I wish to God I was back in the Sunset holding the hands of kids going home from school, where I belong. I don't like trouble. Give me a beer.

(NICK *gives him a beer. He drinks some.*) Right now, McCarthy, my best friend, is with sixty strikers who want to stop the finks who are going to try to unload the *Mary Luckenbach* tonight. Why the hell McCarthy ever became a longshoreman instead of a professor of some kind is something I'll never know.

NICK. Cowboys and Indians, cops and robbers, longshoremen and finks.

KRUPP. They're all guys who are trying to be happy; trying to make a living; support a family; bring up children; enjoy sleep. Go to a movie; take a drive on Sunday. They're all good guys, so out of nowhere, comes trouble. All they want is a chance to get out of debt and relax in front of a radio while Amos and Andy go through their act. What the hell do they always want to make trouble for? I been thinking everything over, Nick, and you know what I think?

NICK. No. What?

KRUPP. I think we're all crazy. It came to me while I was on my way to Pier 27. All of a sudden it hit me like a ton of bricks. A thing like that never happened to me before. Here we are in this wonderful world, full of all the wonderful things— here we are—all of us, and look at us. Just look at us. We're crazy. We're nuts. We've got everything, but we always feel lousy and dissatisfied just the same.

NICK. Of course we're crazy. Even so, we've got to go on living together. (*He waves at the people in his joint.*)

KRUPP. There's no hope. I don't suppose it's right for an officer of the law to feel the way I feel, but, by God, right or not right, that's how I feel. Why are we all so lousy? This is a good world. It's wonderful to get up in the morning and go out for a little walk and smell the trees and see the streets and the kids going to school and the clouds in the sky. It's wonderful just to be able to move around and whistle a song if you feel like it, or maybe try to sing one. This is a nice world. So why do they make all the trouble?

NICK. I don't know. Why?

KRUPP. We're crazy, that's why. We're no good any more. All the corruption everywhere. The poor kids selling themselves. A couple of years ago they were in grammar school. Everybody trying to get a lot of money in a hurry. Everybody betting the horses. Nobody going quietly for a little walk to the ocean. Nobody taking things easy and not wanting to make some kind of a killing. Nick, I'm going to quit being a cop. Let somebody else keep law and order. The stuff I hear about at headquarters. I'm thirty-seven years old, and I still can't get used to it. The only trouble is, the wife'll raise hell.

NICK. Ah, the wife.

KRUPP. She's a wonderful woman, Nick. We've got two of the swellest boys in the world. Twelve and seven years old. (*The* ARAB *gets up and moves closer to listen.*)

NICK. I didn't know that.

KRUPP. Sure. But what'll I do? I've wanted to quit for seven years. I wanted to quit the day they began putting me through the school. I didn't quit. What'll I do if I quit? Where's money going to be coming in from?

NICK. That's one of the reasons we're all crazy. We don't know where it's going to be coming in from, except from wherever it happens to be coming in from at the time, which we don't usually like.

KRUPP. Every once in a while I catch myself being mean, hating people just because they're down and out, broke and hungry, sick or drunk. And then when I'm with the stuffed shirts at headquarters, all of a sudden I'm nice to them, trying to make an impression. On who? People I don't like. And I feel disgusted. (*With finality.*) I'm going to quit. That's all. Quit. Out.

I'm going to give them back the uniform and the gadgets that go with it. I don't want any part of it. This is a good world. What do they want to make all the trouble for all the time?

ARAB (*quietly, gently, with great understanding*). No foundation. All the way down the line.

KRUPP. What?

ARAB. No foundation. No foundation.

KRUPP. I'll say there's no foundation.

ARAB. All the way down the line.

KRUPP (*to* NICK). Is that all he ever says?

NICK. That's all he's been saying *this* week.

KRUPP. What is he, anyway?

NICK. He's an Arab, or something like that.

KRUPP. No, I mean what's he do for a living?

NICK (*to* ARAB). What do you do for a living, brother?

ARAB. Work. Work all my life. All my life, work. From small boy to old man, work. In old country, work. In new country, work. In New York. Pittsburgh. Detroit. Chicago. Imperial Valley. San Francisco. Work. No beg. Work. For what? Nothing. Three boys in old country. Twenty years, not see. Lost. Dead. Who knows? What. What-not. No foundation. All the way down the line.

KRUPP. What'd he say last week?

NICK. Didn't say anything. Played the harmonica.

ARAB. Old country song, I play. (*He brings a harmonica from his back pocket.*)

KRUPP. Seems like a nice guy.

NICK. Nicest guy in the world.

KRUPP (*bitterly*). But crazy. Just like all the rest of us. Stark raving mad.

(WESLEY *and* HARRY *long ago stopped* *playing and dancing. They sat at a table together and talked for a while; then began playing casino or rummy. When the* ARAB *begins his solo on the harmonica, they stop their game to listen.*)

WESLEY. You hear that?

HARRY. That's *something*.

WESLEY. That's crying. That's crying.

HARRY. I want to make people laugh.

WESLEY. That's deep, deep crying. That's crying a long time ago. That's crying a thousand years ago. Some place five thousand miles away.

HARRY. Do you think you can play to that?

WESLEY. I want to *sing* to that, but I can't *sing*.

HARRY. You try and play to that. I'll try to dance.

(WESLEY *goes to the piano, and after closer listening, he begins to accompany the harmonica solo.* HARRY *goes to the little stage and after a few efforts begins to dance to the song. This keeps up quietly for some time.*)

(KRUPP *and* NICK *have been silent, and deeply moved.*)

KRUPP (*softly*). Well, anyhow, Nick.

NICK. Hmmmmmmm?

KRUPP. What I said. Forget it.

NICK. Sure.

KRUPP. It gets me down once in a while

NICK. No harm in talking.

KRUPP (*the* POLICEMAN *again, loudly*) Keep the girls out of here.

NICK (*loud and friendly*). Take it easy.

(*The music and dancing are now at their height.*)

CURTAIN

# ACT FIVE

*That evening. Fog-horns are heard throughout the scene. A man in evening clothes and a woman, also in evening clothes, are entering.*
WILLIE *is still at the marble-game.* NICK *is behind the bar.* JOE *is at his table, looking at the book of maps of the countries of Europe. The box containing the revolver and the box containing the cartridges are on the table, beside his glass. He is at peace, his hat tilted back on his head, a calm expression on his face.* TOM *is leaning against the bar, dreaming of love and Kitty. The* ARAB *is gone.* WESLEY *and* HARRY *are gone.* KIT CARSON *is watching the boy at the marble-game.*

LADY. Oh, come on, please.

*(The gentleman follows miserably.)*

*(The* SOCIETY MAN *and* WIFE *take a table.* NICK *gives them a menu.)*

*(Outside, in the street, the Salvation Army people are playing a song. Big drum, tambourines, cornet and singing. They are singing "The Blood of the Lamb." The music and words come into the place faintly and comically. This is followed by an old sinner testifying. It is the* DRUNKARD. *His words are not intelligible, but his message is unmistakable. He is saved. He wants to sin no more. And so on.)*

DRUNKARD *(testifying, unmistakably drunk).* Brothers and sisters. I was a sinner. I chewed tobacco and chased women. Oh, I sinned, brothers and sisters. And then I was saved. Saved by the Salvation Army, God forgive me.

JOE. Let's see now. Here's a city. Pribor. Czecho-slovakia. Little, lovely, lonely Czecho-slovakia. I wonder what kind of a place Pribor was? *(Calling.)* Pribor! Pribor! *(*TOM *leaps.)*

LADY. What's the matter with him?

MAN *(crossing his legs, as if he ought to go to the men's room).* Drunk.

TOM. Who you calling, Joe?

JOE. Pribor.

TOM. Who's Pribor?

JOE. He's a Czech. And a Slav. A Czecho-slovakian.

LADY. How interesting.

MAN *(uncrosses legs).* He's drunk.

JOE. Tom. Pribor's a city in Czecho-slo-vakia.

TOM. Oh. *(Pause.)* You sure were nice to her, Joe.

JOE. Kitty Duval? She's one of the finest people in the world.

TOM. It sure was nice of you to hire an automobile and take us for a drive along the ocean-front and down to Half Moon Bay.

JOE. Those three hours were the most delightful, the most somber, and the most beautiful I have ever known.

TOM. Why, Joe?

JOE. Why? I'm a student. *(Lifting his voice.)* Tom. *(Quietly.)* I'm a student. I study all things. All. All. And when my study reveals something of beauty in a place or in a person where by all rights only ugliness or death should be revealed, then I know how full of goodness this life is. And that's a good thing to know. That's a truth I shall always seek to verify.

LADY. Are you *sure* he's drunk?

MAN *(crossing his legs).* He's either drunk, or just naturally crazy.

TOM. Joe?

JOE. Yeah.

TOM. You won't get sore or anything?

JOE *(impatiently).* What is it, Tom?

TOM. Joe, where do you get all that money? You paid for the automobile. You paid for supper and the two bottles of champagne at the Half Moon Bay Restaurant. You moved Kitty out of the New York Hotel around the corner to the St. Francis Hotel on Powell Street. I saw you pay her rent. I saw you give her money for new clothes. Where do you get all that money, Joe? Three years now and I've never asked.

JOE *(looking at* TOM *sorrowfully, a little*

*irritated, not so much with* TOM *as with the world and himself, his own superiority. He speaks clearly, slowly and solemnly).* Now don't be a fool, Tom. Listen carefully. If anybody's got any money—to hoard or to throw away—you can be sure he stole it from other people. Not from rich people who can spare it, but from poor people who can't. From their lives and from their dreams. I'm no exception. I *earned* the money I throw away. I stole it like everybody else does. I hurt people to get it. Loafing around this way, I *still* earn money. The money itself earns *more.* I *still* hurt people. I don't know who they are, or where they are. If I did, I'd feel worse than I do. I've got a Christian conscience in a world that's got no conscience at all. The world's trying to get some sort of a *social* conscience, but it's having a devil of a time trying to do *that.* I've got money. I'll always have money, as long as this world stays the way it is. I don't work. I don't make anything. *(He sips.)* I drink. I worked when I was a kid. I worked *hard.* I mean hard, Tom. People are supposed to enjoy living. I got tired. *(He lifts the gun and looks at it while he talks.)* I decided to get even on the world. Well, you can't enjoy living unless you work. Unless you do something. I don't do anything. I don't *want* to do anything any more. There isn't anything I can do that won't make me feel embarrassed. Because I can't do simple, good things. I haven't the patience. And I'm too smart. Money is the guiltiest thing in the world. It stinks. Now, don't ever bother me about it again.

TOM. I didn't mean to make you feel bad, Joe.

JOE *(slowly).* Here. Take this gun out in the street and give to to some worthy hold-up man.

LADY. What's he saying?

MAN *(uncrosses legs).* You wanted to visit a honky-tonk. Well, *this* is a honky-tonk. *(To the world.)* Married twenty-eight years and she's still looking for adventure.

TOM. How should I know who's a hold-up man?

JOE. Take it away. Give it to somebody.

TOM *(bewildered).* Do I *have* to *give* it to somebody?

JOE. Of course.

TOM. Can't I take it back and get some of our money?

JOE. Don't talk like a business man. Look around and find somebody who appears to be in need of a gun and give it to him. It's a good gun, isn't it?

TOM. The man said it was, but how can I tell who needs a gun?

JOE. Tom, you've seen good people who needed guns, haven't you?

TOM. I don't remember. Joe, I might give it to the wrong kind of guy. He might do something crazy.

JOE. All right. I'll find somebody myself. *(*TOM *rises.)* Here's some money. Go get me this week's *Life, Liberty, Time,* and six or seven packages of chewing gum.

TOM *(swiftly, in order to remember each item). Life, Liberty, Time,* and six or seven packages of chewing gum?

JOE. That's right.

TOM. All that chewing gum? What kind?

JOE. Any kind. Mix 'em up. All kinds.

TOM. Licorice, too?

JOE. Licorice, by all means.

TOM. Juicy Fruit?

JOE. Juicy Fruit.

TOM. Tutti-frutti?

JOE. Is there such a gum?

TOM. I think so.

JOE. All right. Tutti-frutti, too. Get *all* the kinds. Get as many kinds as they're selling.

TOM. *Life, Liberty, Time,* and all the different kinds of gum. *(He begins to go.)*

JOE *(calling after him loudly).* Get some jelly beans too. All the different colors.

TOM. All right, Joe.

JOE. And the longest panatela cigar you can find. Six of them.

TOM. Panatela. I got it.

JOE. Give a news-kid a dollar.

TOM. O.K., Joe.

JOE. Give some old man a dollar.

TOM. O.K., Joe.

JOE. Give them Salvation Army people in the street a couple of dollars and ask them to sing that song that goes— *(He sings loudly.)* Let the lower lights be burning, send a gleam across the wave.

TOM *(swiftly)*. Let the lower lights be burning, send a gleam across the wave.

JOE. That's it. *(He goes on with the song, very loudly and religiously.)* Some poor, dying, struggling seaman, you may rescue, you may save. *(Halts.)*

TOM. O.K., Joe. I got it. *Life, Liberty, Time,* all the kinds of gum they're selling, jelly beans, six panatela cigars, a dollar for a news-kid, a dollar for an old man, two dollars for the Salvation Army. *(Going.)* Let the lower lights be burning, send a gleam across the wave.

JOE. That's it.

LADY. He's absolutely insane.

MAN *(wearily crossing legs)*. You asked me to take you to a honky-tonk, instead of to the Mark Hopkins. You're *here* in a honky-tonk. I can't help it if he's crazy. Do you want to go back to where people *aren't* crazy?

LADY. No, not just yet.

MAN. Well, all right then. Don't be telling me every minute that he's crazy.

LADY. You needn't be huffy about it.

*(MAN refuses to answer, uncrosses legs.)*

*(When JOE began to sing, KIT CARSON turned away from the marble-game and listened. While the man and woman are arguing he comes over to Joe's table.)*

KIT CARSON. Presbyterian?

JOE. I attended a Presbyterian Sunday School.

KIT CARSON. Fond of singing?

JOE. On occasion. Have a drink?

KIT CARSON. Thanks.

JOE. Get a glass and sit down.
*(KIT CARSON gets a glass from NICK, returns to the table, sits down, JOE pours him*

*a drink, they touch glasses just as the Salvation Army people begin to fulfill the request. They sip some champagne, and at the proper moment begin to sing the song together, sipping champagne, raising hell with the tune, swinging it, and so on. The* SOCIETY LADY *joins them, and is stopped by her* HUSBAND.*)*
Always was fond of that song. Used to sing it at the top of my voice. Never saved a seaman in my life.

KIT CARSON *(flirting with the* SOCIETY LADY *who loves it)*. I saved a seaman once. Well, he wasn't exactly a seaman. He was a darky named Wellington. Heavy-set sort of a fellow. Nice personality, but no friends to speak of. Not until I came along, at any rate. In New Orleans. In the summer of the year 1899. No. Ninety-eight. I was a lot younger of course, and had no mustache, but was regarded by many people as a man of means.

JOE. Know anything about guns?

KIT CARSON *(flirting)*. All there is to know. Didn't fight the Ojibways for nothing. Up there in the Lake Takalooca Country, in Michigan. *(Remembering.)* Along about in 1881 or two. Fought 'em right up to the shore of the Lake. Made 'em swim for Canada. One fellow in particular, an Indian named Harry Daisy.

JOE *(opening the box containing the revolver)*. What sort of a gun would you say this is? Any good?

KIT CARSON *(at sight of gun, leaping)*. Yep. That looks like a pretty nice hunk of shooting iron. That's a six-shooter. Shot a man with a six-shooter once. Got him through the palm of his right hand. Lifted his arm to wave to a friend. Thought it was a bird. Fellow named, I believe, Carroway. Larrimore Carroway.

JOE. Know how to work one of these things? *(He offers KIT CARSON the revolver, which is old and enormous.)*

KIT CARSON *(laughing at the absurd question)*. Know how to work it? Hand me that little gun, son, and I'll show you all about it. *(JOE hands KIT the revolver.)* *(Importantly.)* Let's see now. This is probably a new kind of six-shooter. After my time. Haven't nicked an Indian in years. I believe this here place is supposed to move out. (He fools around and get the barrel out for loading.) That's it. There it is.

JOE. Look all right?

KIT CARSON. It's a good gun. You've got a good gun there, son. I'll explain it to you. You see these holes? Well, that's where you put the cartridges.

JOE (taking some cartridges out of the box). Here. Show me how it's done.

KIT CARSON (a little impatiently). Well, son, you take 'em one by one and put 'em in the holes, like this. There's one. Two. Three. Four. Five. Six. Then you get the barrel back in place. Then cock it. Then all you got to do is aim and fire.

(He points the gun at the LADY and GEN-TLEMAN who scream and stand up, scaring KIT CARSON into paralysis.)

(The gun is loaded, but uncocked.)

JOE. It's all set?

KIT CARSON. Ready to kill.

JOE. Let me hold it.

(KIT hands JOE the gun. The LADY and GENTLEMAN watch, in terror.)

KIT CARSON. Careful, now, son. Don't cock it. Many a man's lost an eye fooling with a loaded gun. Fellow I used to know named Danny Donovan lost a nose. Ruined his whole life. Hold it firm. Squeeze the trigger. Don't snap it. Spoils your aim.

JOE. Thanks. Let's see if I can unload it.

(He begins to unload it.)

KIT CARSON. Of course you can.

(JOE unloads the revolver, looks at it very closely, puts the cartridges back into the box.)

JOE (looking at gun). I'm mighty grateful to you. Always wanted to see one of those things close up. Is it really a good one?

KIT CARSON. It's a beaut, son.

JOE (aims the empty gun at a bottle on the bar). Bang!

WILLIE (at the marble-game, as the machine groans). Oh, Boy! (Loudly, triumph-antly.) There you are, Nick. Thought I couldn't do it, hey? Now, watch. (The machine begins to make a special kind of

noise. Lights go on and off. Some red, some green. A bell rings loudly six times.) One. Two. Three. Four. Five. Six. (An American flag jumps up. WILLIE comes to attention. Salutes.) Oh, boy, what a beau-tiful country. (A loud music-box version of the song "America." JOE, KIT, and the LADY get to their feet.) (Singing.) My country, 'tis of thee, sweet land of liberty, of thee I sing. (Everything quiets down. The flag goes back into the machine. WILLIE is thrilled, amazed, delighted. EVERYBODY has watched the performance of the defeated machine from wherever he happened to be when the performance began. WILLIE, looking around at every-body, as if they had all been on the side of the machine.) O.K. How's that? I knew I could do it. (To NICK.) Six nickels.

(NICK hands him six nickels. WILLIE goes over to JOE and KIT.) Took me a little while, but I finally did it. It's scientific, really. With a little skill a man can make a modest living beating the marble-games. Not that that's what I want to do. I just don't like the idea of anything getting the best of me. A machine or anything else. Myself, I'm the kind of a guy who makes up his mind to do something, and then goes to work and does it. There's no other way a man can be a success at anything.

(Indicating the letter "F" on his sweater.)

See that letter? That don't stand for some little-bitty high school somewhere. That stands for me. Faroughli. Willie Faroughli. I'm an Assyrian. We've got a civilization six or seven centuries old, I think. Some-where along in there. Ever hear of Osman? Harold Osman? He's an Assyrian, too. He's got an orchestra down in Fresno.

(He goes to the LADY and GENTLEMAN.)

I've never seen you before in my life, but I can tell from the clothes you wear and the company you keep (Graciously indi-cating the LADY.) that you're a man who looks every problem straight in the eye, and then goes to work and solves it. I'm that way myself. Well. (He smiles beau-tifully, takes GENTLEMAN's hand furiously.) It's been wonderful talking to a nicer type of people for a change. Well. I'll be seeing you. So long. (He turns, takes two steps, returns to the table. Very politely and se-riously.) Good-bye, lady. You've got a good man there. Take good care of him.

(WILLIE *goes, saluting* JOE *and the world.*)

KIT CARSON *(to* JOE*)*. By God, for a while there I didn't think that young Assyrian was going to do it. That fellow's got something.

(TOM *comes back with the magazines and other stuff.*)

JOE. Get it all?

TOM. Yeah. I had a little trouble finding the jelly beans.

JOE. Let's take a look at them.

TOM. These are the jelly beans.

(JOE *puts his hand into the cellophane bag and takes out a handful of the jelly beans, looks at them, smiles, and tosses a couple into his mouth.*)

JOE. Same as ever. Have some. *(He offers the bag to* KIT.*)*

KIT CARSON *(flirting)*. Thanks! I remember the first time I ever ate jelly beans. I was six, or at the most seven. Must have been in *(Slowly.)* eighteen—seventy-seven. Seven or eight. Baltimore.

JOE. Have some, Tom. (TOM *takes some.*)

TOM. Thanks, Joe.

JOE. Let's have some of that chewing gum.

(He *dumps all the packages of gum out of the bag onto the table.*)

KIT CARSON *(flirting)*. Me and a boy named Clark. Quinton Clark. Became a Senator.

JOE. Yeah. Tutti-frutti, all right. *(He opens a package and folds all five pieces into his mouth.)* Always wanted to see how many I could chew at one time. Tell you what, Tom. I'll bet I can chew more at one time than you can.

TOM *(delighted)*. All right. *(They both begin to fold gum into their mouths.)*

KIT CARSON. I'll referee. Now, one at a time. How many you got?

JOE. Six.

KIT CARSON. All right. Let Tom catch up with you.

JOE *(while* TOM's *catching up)*. Did you give a dollar to a news-kid?

TOM. Yeah, sure.

JOE. What'd he say?

TOM. Thanks.

JOE. What sort of a kid was he?

TOM. Little, dark kid. I guess he's Italian.

JOE. Did he seem pleased?

TOM. Yeah.

JOE. That's good. Did you give a dollar to an old man?

TOM. Yeah.

JOE. Was he pleased?

TOM. Yeah.

JOE. Good. How many you got in your mouth?

TOM. Six.

JOE. All right. I got six, too. *(Folds one more in his mouth.* TOM *folds one too.)*

KIT CARSON. Seven. Seven each. *(They each fold one more into their mouths, very solemnly, chewing them into the main hunk of gum.)* Eight. Nine. Ten.

JOE *(delighted)*. Always wanted to do this. *(He picks up one of the magazines.)* Let's see what's going on in the world. *(He turns the pages and keeps folding gum into his mouth and chewing.)*

KIT CARSON. Eleven. Twelve. (KIT *continues to count while* JOE *and* TOM *continue the contest. In spite of what they are doing, each is very serious.)*

TOM. Joe, what'd you want to move Kitty into the St. Francis Hotel for?

JOE. She's a better woman than any of them tramp society dames that hang around that lobby.

TOM. Yeah, but do you think she'll feel at home up there?

JOE. Maybe not at first, but after a couple of days she'll be all right. A nice big room. A bed for sleeping in. Good clothes. Good food. She'll be all right, Tom.

TOM. I hope so. Don't you think she'll get lonely up there with nobody to talk to?

JOE *(looking at* TOM *sharply, almost with admiration, pleased but severe)*. There's nobody *anywhere* for *her* to talk to—except *you.*

TOM *(amazed and delighted)*. Me, Joe?

JOE (*while* TOM *and* KIT CARSON *listen carefully,* KIT *with great appreciation*). Yes, you. By the grace of God, you're the other half of that girl. Not the angry woman that swaggers into this waterfront dive and shouts because the world has kicked her around. *Anybody* can have *her*. You belong to the little kid in Ohio who once dreamed of living. Not with her carcass, for *money,* so she can have food and clothes, and pay rent. With *all* of her. I put her in that hotel, so she can have a chance to gather herself together again. She can't do that in the New York Hotel. You saw what happens there. There's nobody anywhere for her to talk to, except you. They all make her talk like a whore. After a while, she'll *believe* them. Then she won't be able to remember. She'll get lonely. Sure. People can get lonely for *misery,* even. I want her to go on being lonely for *you,* so she can come together again the way she was meant to be from the beginning. Loneliness is good for people. Right now it's the only thing for Kitty. Any more licorice?

TOM (*dazed*). What? Licorice? (*Looking around busily.*) I guess we've chewed all the licorice in. We still got Clove, Peppermint, Doublemint, Beechnut, Teaberry, and Juicy Fruit.

JOE. Licorice used to be my favorite. Don't worry about her, Tom, she'll be all right. You really want to marry her, don't you?

TOM (*nodding*). Honest to God, Joe. (*Pathetically.*) Only, I haven't got any money.

JOE. Couldn't you be a prize-fighter or something like that?

TOM. Naaaah. I couldn't hit a man if I wasn't sore at him. He'd have to do something that made me hate him.

JOE. You've got to figure out something to do that you won't mind doing very much.

TOM. I wish I could, Joe.

JOE (*thinking deeply, suddenly*). Tom, would you be embarrassed driving a truck?

TOM (*hit by a thunderbolt*). Joe, I never thought of that. I'd like that. Travel. Highways. Little towns. Coffee and hot cakes. Beautiful valleys and mountains and streams and trees and daybreak and sunset.

JOE. There *is* poetry in it, at that.

TOM. Joe, that's just the kind of work I *should* do. Just sit there and travel, and look, and smile, and bust out laughing. Could Kitty go with me, sometimes?

JOE. I don't know. Get me the phone book. Can you drive a truck?

TOM. Joe, you know I can drive a truck, or any kind of thing with a motor and wheels. (TOM *takes* JOE *the phone book.* JOE *turns the pages.*)

JOE (*looking*). Here! Here it is. Tuxedo 7900. Here's a nickel. Get me that number. (TOM *goes to telephone, dials the number.*)

TOM. Hello.

JOE. Ask for Mr. Keith.

TOM (*mouth and language full of gum*). I'd like to talk to Mr. Keith. (*Pause.*) Mr. Keith.

JOE. Take that gum out of your mouth for a minute. (TOM *removes the gum.*)

TOM. Mr. Keith. Yeah. That's right. Hello, Mr. Keith?

JOE. Tell him to hold the line.

TOM. Hold the line, please.

JOE. Give me a hand, Tom. (TOM *helps* JOE *to the telephone. At phone, wad of gum in fingers delicately.*) Keith? Joe. Yeah. Fine. Forget it. (*Pause.*) Have you got a place for a good driver? (*Pause.*) I don't think so. (*To* TOM.) You haven't got a driver's license, have you?

TOM (*worried*). No. But I can get one, Joe.

JOE (*at phone*). No, but he can get one easy enough. To hell with the union. He'll join later. All right, call him a Vice-President and say he drives for relaxation. Sure. What do you mean? Tonight? I don't know why not. San Diego? All right, let him start driving without a license. What the hell's the difference? Yeah. Sure. Look him over. Yeah. I'll send him right over. Right. (*He hangs up.*) Thanks. (*To telephone.*)

TOM. Am I going to get the job?

JOE. He wants to take a look at you.

TOM. Do I look all right, Joe?

JOE (*looking at him carefully*). Hold up your head. Stick out your chest. How do you feel? (TOM *does these things.*)

TOM. Fine.

JOE. You *look* fine, too.

(JOE *takes his wad of gum out of his mouth and wraps* Liberty *magazine around it.*)

JOE. You win, Tom. Now, look. (*He bites off the tip of a very long panatela cigar, lights it, and hands one to* TOM, *and another to* KIT.) Have yourselves a pleasant smoke. Here. (*He hands two more to* TOM.) Give those slummers each one. (*He indicates the* SOCIETY LADY *and* GENTLEMAN.)

(TOM *goes over and without a word gives a cigar each to the* MAN *and the* LADY.)

(*The* MAN *is offended; he smells and tosses aside his cigar. The* WOMAN *looks at her cigar a moment, then puts the cigar in her mouth.*)

MAN. What do you think you're doing?

LADY. Really, dear. I'd like to.

MAN. Oh, this is too much.

LADY. I'd *really*, really like to, dear. (*She laughs, puts the cigar in her mouth. Turns to* KIT. *He spits out tip. She does the same.*)

MAN (*loudly*). The mother of five grown men, and she's still looking for *romance*. (*Shouts as* KIT *lights her cigar.*) No. I forbid it.

JOE (*shouting*). What's the matter with you? Why don't you leave her alone? What are you always pushing your women around for? (*Almost without a pause.*) Now, look, Tom. (*The* LADY *puts the lighted cigar in her mouth, and begins to smoke, feeling wonderful.*) Here's ten bucks.

TOM. Ten bucks?

JOE. He may want you to get into a truck and begin driving to San Diego tonight.

TOM. Joe, I got to tell Kitty.

JOE. I'll tell her.

TOM. Joe, take care of her.

JOE. She'll be all right. Stop worrying about her. She's at the St. Francis Hotel. Now, look. Take a cab to Townsend and Fourth. You'll see the big sign. Keith Motor Transport Company. He'll be waiting for you.

TOM. O.K., Joe. (*Trying hard.*) Thanks, Joe.

JOE. Don't be silly. Get going.

(TOM *goes.*)

(LADY *starts puffing on cigar.*)

(*As* TOM *goes,* WESLEY *and* HARRY *come in together.*)

NICK. Where the hell have you been? We've got to have some entertainment around here. Can't you see them fine people from uptown? (*He points at the* SOCIETY LADY *and* GENTLEMAN.)

WESLEY. You said to come back at ten for the second show.

NICK. Did I say that?

WESLEY. Yes, sir, Mr. Nick, that's exactly what you said.

HARRY. Was the first show all right?

NICK. That wasn't a show. There was no one here to see it. How can it be a show when no one sees it? People are afraid to come down to the waterfront.

HARRY. Yeah. We were just down to Pier 27. One of the longshoremen and a cop had a fight and the cop hit him over the head with a blackjack. We saw it happen, didn't we?

WESLEY. Yes, sir, we was standing there looking when it happened.

NICK (*a little worried*). Anything else happen?

WESLEY. They was all talking.

HARRY. A man in a big car came up and said there was going to be a meeting right away and they hoped to satisfy everybody and stop the strike.

WESLEY. Right away. *Tonight.*

NICK. Well, it's about time. Them poor cops are liable to get nervous and—shoot somebody. (*To* HARRY, *suddenly.*) Come back here. I want you to tend bar for a while. I'm going to take a walk over to the pier.

HARRY. Yes, sir.

NICK (*to the* SOCIETY LADY *and* GENTLE-MAN). You society people made up your minds yet?

LADY. Have you champagne?

NICK (*indicating* JOE). What do you think he's pouring out of that bottle, water or something?

LADY. Have you a chilled bottle?

NICK. I've got a dozen of them chilled. He's been drinking champagne here all day and all night for a month now.

LADY. May we have a bottle?

NICK. It's six dollars.

LADY. I think we can manage.

MAN. I don't know. I *know* I don't know.

(NICK *takes off his coat and helps* HARRY *into it.* HARRY *takes a bottle of champagne and two glasses to the* LADY *and the* GEN-TLEMAN, *dancing, collects six dollars, and goes back behind the bar, dancing.* NICK *gets his coat and hat.*)

NICK (*to* WESLEY). Rattle the keys, a little, son. Rattle the keys.

WESLEY. Yes, sir, Mr. Nick. (NICK *is on his way out. The* ARAB *enters.*)

NICK. Hi-ya, *Mahmed.*

ARAB. No foundation.

NICK. All the way down the line. (*He goes.*)

(WESLEY *is at the piano, playing quietly. The* ARAB *swallows a glass of beer, takes out his harmonica, and begins to play.* WESLEY *fits his playing to the Arab's.*)

(KITTY DUVAL, *strangely beautiful, in new clothes, comes in. She walks shyly, as if she were embarrassed by the fine clothes, as if she had no right to wear them. The* LADY *and* GENTLEMAN *are very impressed.* HARRY *looks at her with amazement.* JOE *is read-ing* Time *magazine.* KITTY *goes to his table.* JOE *looks up from the magazine, without the least amazement.*)

JOE. Hello, Kitty.

KITTY. Hello, Joe.

JOE. It's nice seeing you again.

KITTY. I came in a cab.

JOE. You been crying again? (KITTY *can't answer. To* HARRY.) Bring a glass. (HARRY *comes over with a glass.* JOE *pours* KITTY *a drink.*)

KITTY. I've got to talk to you.

JOE. Have a drink.

KITTY. I've never been in burlesque. We were just poor.

JOE. Sit down, Kitty.

KITTY (*sits down*). I tried other things.

JOE. Here's to you, Katerina Koranovsky. Here's to you. And Tom.

KITTY (*sorrowfully*). Where *is* Tom?

JOE. He's getting a job tonight driving a truck. He'll be back in a couple of days.

KITTY (*sadly*). I told him I'd marry him.

JOE. He wanted to see you and say good-by.

KITTY. He's too good for me. He's like a little boy. (*Wearily.*) I'm— Too many things have happened to me.

JOE. Kitty Duval, you're one of the few truly innocent people I have ever known. He'll be back in a couple of days. Go back to the hotel and wait for him.

KITTY. That's what I mean. I can't stand being alone. I'm no good. I tried very hard. I don't know what it is. I miss— (*She gestures.*)

JOE (*gently*). Do you really want to come back here, Kitty?

KITTY. I don't know. I'm not sure. Every-thing *smells* different. I don't know how to feel, or what to think. (*Gesturing pa-thetically.*) I know I don't belong there. It's what I've wanted all my life, but it's too *late.* I try to be happy about it, but all I can do is remember everything and cry.

JOE. I don't know what to tell you, Kitty. I didn't mean to hurt you.

KITTY. You haven't hurt me. You're the only person who's ever been good to me. I've never known anybody like you. I'm not sure about love any more, but I know I love you, and I know I love Tom.

JOE. I love you too, Kitty Duval.

KITTY. He'll want babies. I know he will. I know *I* will, too. Of course I will. I can't— (*She shakes her head.*)

JOE. Tom's a baby himself. You'll be very happy together. He wants you to ride with him in the truck. Tom's good for you. You're good for Tom.

KITTY *(like a child)*. Do you want me to go back and wait for him?

JOE. I can't *tell* you what to do. I think it would be a good idea, though.

KITTY. I wish I could tell you how it makes me feel to be alone. It's almost worse.

JOE. It might take a whole week, Kitty. *(He looks at her sharply, at the arrival of an idea.)* Didn't you speak of reading a book? A book of poems?

KITTY. I didn't know what I was saying.

JOE *(trying to get up)*. Of course you knew. I think you'll like poetry. Wait here a minute, Kitty. I'll go see if I can find some books.

KITTY. All right, Joe. *(He walks out of the place, trying very hard not to wobble.)*

*(Fog-horn. Music. The NEWSBOY comes in. Looks for JOE. Is broken-hearted because JOE is gone.)*

NEWSBOY *(to SOCIETY GENTLEMAN)*. Paper?

MAN *(angry)*. No.

*(The NEWSBOY goes to the ARAB.)*

NEWSBOY. Paper, Mister?

ARAB *(irritated)*. No foundation.

NEWSBOY. What?

ARAB *(very angry)*. No foundation. *(The NEWSBOY starts out, turns, looks at the ARAB, shakes head.)*

NEWSBOY. No foundation? How do you figure?

*(BLICK and TWO COPS enter.)*

NEWSBOY *(to BLICK)*. Paper, mister?

*(BLICK pushes him aside. The NEWSBOY goes.)*

BLICK *(walking authoritatively about the place, to HARRY)*. Where's Nick?

HARRY. He went for a walk.

BLICK. Who are you?

HARRY. Harry.

BLICK *(to the ARAB and WESLEY)*. Hey, you. Shut up. *(The ARAB stops playing the harmonica, WESLEY the piano.)*

BLICK *(studies KITTY)*. What's your name, sister?

KITTY *(looking at him)*. Kitty Duval. What's it to you?

*(KITTY's voice is now like it was at the beginning of the play: tough, independent, bitter and hard.)*

BLICK *(angry)*. Don't give me any of your gutter lip. Just answer my questions.

KITTY. You go to hell, you.

BLICK *(coming over, enraged)*. Where do you live?

KITTY. The New York Hotel. Room 21.

BLICK. Where do you work?

KITTY. I'm not working just now. I'm look-for work.

BLICK. What kind of work? *(KITTY can't answer.)* What kind of work? *(KITTY can't answer.)* *(Furiously.)* WHAT KIND OF WORK? *(KIT CARSON comes over.)*

KIT CARSON. You can't talk to a lady that way in *my* presence. *(BLICK turns and stares at KIT. The COPS begin to move from the bar.)*

BLICK *(to the COPS)*. It's all right, boys. I'll take care of this. *(To KIT.)* *What'd you say?*

KIT CARSON. You got no right to hurt people. Who are *you?*

*(BLICK, without a word, takes KIT to the street. Sounds of a blow and a groan. BLICK returns, breathing hard.)*

BLICK *(to the COPS)*. O.K., boys. You can go now. Take care of him. Put him on his feet and tell him to behave himself from now on. *(To KITTY again.)* Now answer my question. What kind of work?

KITTY *(quietly)*. I'm a whore, you son of a bitch. You know what kind of work I do. And I know what kind you do.

MAN *(shocked and really hurt)*. Excuse me, officer, but it seems to me that your attitude—

BLICK. Shut up.

MAN *(quietly)*. —is making the poor child say things that are not true.

BLICK. Shut up, I said.

LADY. Well. *(To the* MAN.*)* Are you going to stand for such insolence?

BLICK *(to* MAN, *who is standing)*. Are you?

MAN *(taking the* WOMAN's *arm)*. I'll get a divorce. I'll start life all over again. *(Pushing the* WOMAN*)*. Come on. Get the hell out of here!

*(The* MAN *hurries his* WOMAN *out of the place,* BLICK *watching them go.)*

BLICK *(to* KITTY*)*. Now. Let's begin again, and see that you tell the truth. What's your name?

KITTY. Kitty Duval.

BLICK. Where do you live?

KITTY. Until this evening I lived at the New York Hotel. Room 21. This evening I moved to the St. Francis Hotel.

BLICK. Oh. To the St. Francis Hotel. Nice place. Where do you work?

KITTY. I'm looking for work.

BLICK. What kind of work do you do?

KITTY. I'm an actress.

BLICK. I see. What movies have I seen you in?

KITTY. I've worked in burlesque.

BLICK. You're a liar.

*(WESLEY *stands, worried and full of dumb resentment.)*

KITTY *(pathetically, as at the beginning of the play)*. It's the truth.

BLICK. What are you doing here?

KITTY. I came to see if I could get a job here.

BLICK. Doing what?

KITTY. Singing—and—dancing.

BLICK. You can't sing or dance. What are you lying for?

KITTY. I can. I sang and danced in burlesque all over the country.

BLICK. You're a liar.

KITTY. I said lines, too.

BLICK. So you danced in burlesque?

KITTY. Yes.

BLICK. All right. Let's see what you did.

KITTY. I can't. There's no music, and I haven't got the right clothes.

BLICK. There's music. *(To* WESLEY*)*. Put a nickel in that phonograph. *(WESLEY *can't move.)* Come on. Put a nickel in that phonograph. *(WESLEY *does so. To* KITTY*)*. All right. Get up on that stage and do a hot little burlesque number. *(KITTY *stands. Walks slowly to the stage, but is unable to move.* JOE *comes in, holding three books.)* Get going, now. Let's see you dance the way you did in burlesque, all over the country. *(KITTY *tries to do a burlesque dance. It is beautiful in a tragic way.)*

BLICK. All right, start taking them off!

*(KITTY *removes her hat and starts to remove her jacket.* JOE *moves closer to the stage, amazed.)*

JOE *(hurrying to* KITTY*)*. Get down from there. *(He takes* KITTY *into his arms. She is crying. To* BLICK.*)* What the hell do you think you're doing!

WESLEY *(like a little boy, very angry)*. It's that man, Blick. *He* made her take off her clothes. He beat up the old man, too.

*(BLICK *pushes* WESLEY *off, as* TOM *enters.* BLICK *begins beating up* WESLEY.*)*

TOM. What's the matter, Joe? What's happened?

JOE. Is the truck out there?

TOM. Yeah, but what's happened? Kitty's crying again!

JOE. You driving to San Diego?

TOM. Yeah, Joe. But what's he doing to that poor colored boy?

JOE. Get going. Here's some money. Everything's O.K. *(To* KITTY.*)* Dress in the truck. Take these books.

WESLEY's VOICE. You can't hurt me. You'll get yours. You wait and see.

TOM. Joe, he's hurting that boy. I'll kill him!

JOE *(pushing* TOM*)*. Get out of here! Get married in San Diego. I'll see you when you get back. *(*TOM *and* KITTY *go.* NICK *enters and stands at the lower end of the bar.* JOE *takes the revolver out of his pocket. Looks at it.)* I've always wanted to kill somebody, but I never knew who it should be. *(He cocks the revolver, stands real straight, holds it in front of him firmly and walks to the door. He stands a moment watching* BLICK, *aims very carefully, and pulls trigger. There is no shot.)*

*(*NICK *runs over and grabs the gun, and takes* JOE *aside.)*

NICK. What the hell do you think you're doing?

JOE *(casually, but angry).* That dumb Tom. Buys a six-shooter that won't even shoot once.

*(*JOE *sits down, dead to the world.)*

*(*BLICK *comes out, panting for breath.)*

*(*NICK *looks at him. He speaks slowly.)*

NICK. Blick! I told you to stay out of here! Now get out of here. *(He takes* BLICK *by the collar, tightening his grip as he speaks, and pushing him out.)* If you come back again, I'm going to take you in that room where you've been beating up that colored boy, and I'm going to murder you—slowly—with my hands. Beat it! *(He pushes* BLICK *out. To* HARRY.) Go take care of the colored boy. *(*HARRY *runs out.)* *(*WILLIE *returns and doesn't sense that anything is changed.* WILLIE *puts another nickel into the machine, but he does so very violently. The consequence of this violence is that the flag comes up again.* WILLIE, *amazed, stands at attention and salutes. The flag goes down. He shakes his head.)*

WILLIE *(thoughtfully).* As far as I'm concerned, this is the *only* country in the world. If you ask me, *nuts* to Europe! *(He is about to push the slide in again when the flag comes up again. Furiously, to* NICK, *while he salutes and stands at attention, pleadingly.)* Hey, Nick. This machine is out of order.

NICK *(somberly).* Give it a whack on the side.

*(*WILLIE *does so. A hell of a whack. The result is the flag comes up and down, and* WILLIE *keeps saluting.)*

WILLIE *(saluting).* Hey, Nick. Something's wrong.

*(The machine quiets down abruptly.* WILLIE *very stealthily slides a new nickel in, and starts a new game.)*

*(From a distance two pistol shots are heard, each carefully timed.)*

*(*NICK *runs out.)*

*(The* NEWSBOY *enters, crosses to Joe's table, senses something is wrong.)*

NEWSBOY *(softly).* Paper, Mister?

*(*JOE *can't hear him.)*

*(The* NEWSBOY *backs away, studies* JOE, *wishes he could cheer* JOE *up. Notices the phonograph, goes to it, and puts a coin in it, hoping music will make* JOE *happier.)*

*(The* NEWSBOY *sits down. Watches* JOE. *The music begins.* "The Missouri Waltz.")

*(The* DRUNKARD *comes in and walks around. Then sits down.* NICK *comes back.)*

NICK *(delighted).* Joe, Blick's dead! Somebody just shot him, and none of the cops are trying to find out who. *(*JOE *doesn't hear.* NICK *steps back, studying* JOE.)

NICK *(shouting).* Joe.

JOE *(looking up).* What?

NICK. Blick's dead.

JOE. Blick? Dead? Good! That God damn gun wouldn't go off. I *told* Tom to get a good one.

NICK *(picking up gun and looking at it).* Joe, you wanted to kill that guy! *(*HARRY *returns.* JOE *puts the gun in his coat pocket.)* I'm going to buy you a bottle of champagne.

*(*NICK *goes to bar.* JOE *rises, takes hat from rack, puts coat on. The* NEWSBOY *jumps up, helps* JOE *with coat.)*

NICK. What's the matter, Joe?

JOE. Nothing. Nothing.

NICK. How about the champagne?

JOE. Thanks. *(Going.)*

NICK. It's not eleven yet. Where you going, Joe?

JOE. I don't know. Nowhere.

NICK. Will I see you tomorrow?

JOE. I don't know. I don't think so.

*(KIT CARSON enters, walks to JOE. JOE and KIT look at one another knowingly.)*

JOE. Somebody just shot a man. How are you feeling?

KIT. Never felt better in my life. *(Loudly, bragging, but somber.)* I shot a man once. In San Francisco. Shot him two times. In 1939, I think it was. In October. Fellow named Blick or Glick or something like that. Couldn't stand the way he talked to ladies. Went up to my room and got my old pearl-handled revolver and waited for him on Pacific Street. Saw him walking, and let him have it, two times. Had to throw the beautiful revolver into the Bay.

*(HARRY, NICK, the ARAB and the DRUNKARD close in around him.)*

*(JOE searches his pockets, brings out the revolver, puts it in Kit's hand, looks at him with great admiration and affection. JOE walks slowly to the stairs leading to the street, turns and waves. KIT, and then one by one everybody else, waves, and the marble-game goes into its beautiful American routine again: flag, lights, and music. The play ends.)*

CURTAIN

# 1940-41

*Watch on the Rhine* won for Lillian Hellman the award that escaped her in 1938–39 when her *The Little Foxes,* a better play, led in the voting but couldn't meet the inflexible three-fourths rule then in force.

This time she again failed to get a three-fourths majority in the first five ballots, but the simple majority switch was then invoked and her drama won on the seventh ballot. It received twelve final votes to six for William Saroyan's *The Beautiful People* and one for *Native Son* by Paul Green and Richard Wright.

The votes were widely scattered during the early ballots at this meeting on April 21, 1941. Others that figured briefly were *The Talley Method* by S. N. Behrman, *Flight to the West* by Elmer Rice, *Arsenic and Old Lace* by Joseph Kesselring, *Claudia* by Rose Franken, and *Lady in the Dark* by Moss Hart.

The citation described *Watch on the Rhine* as "a vital, eloquent and compassionate play about an American family suddenly awakened to the danger threatening its liberty." It was in the spirit of the times, with the world in the early stages of World War II.

The citation for a foreign play was won by Emlyn Williams' *The Corn Is Green* without trouble. It received sixteen votes. It was distinguished by Ethel Barrymore's illuminating performance.

Both the American and foreign winners were produced by Herman Shumlin, the only solo producer to achieve the "double" in the Circle's first twenty years. The Theatre Guild participated in producing both winners in the 1952–53 season, but in each case it had a different co-producer. Shumlin had the added distinction of having directed both of his winners.

An oddity of the season was that all three of the plays given final consideration by the Circle for the prize arrived within less than four weeks of the meeting date, which was purposely set at April 22 so *The Beautiful People,* which opened the night before, could be considered.

The season brought Al Jolson's last appearance in a Broadway musical, *Hold On to Your Hats;* the revival of *Charley's Aunt* that really got José Ferrer started on his sensational acting career, and the end (May 31, 1941) of the record long run of *Tobacco Road* whose 3,182 performances supplanted the mark of 2,327 set by *Abie's Irish Rose* when it closed in 1927.

*Watch on the Rhine* ran for 378 performances. Among those in the original cast were Anne Blyth, a child actress then who is a motion picture star today, and John Lodge (of the famous Massachusetts family) who later quit acting and entered politics to become governor of Connecticut.

# Watch on the Rhine

## *By* LILLIAN HELLMAN

Presented by Herman Shumlin at the Martin Beck Theatre, New York City, April 1, 1941, with the following cast:

| | |
|---|---|
| ANISE | *Eda Heinemann* |
| JOSEPH | *Frank Wilson* |
| FANNY FARRELLY | *Lucile Watson* |
| DAVID FARRELLY | *John Lodge* |
| MARTHE de BRANCOVIS | *Helen Trenholme* |
| TECK de BRANCOVIS | *George Coulouris* |
| SARA MUELLER | *Mady Christians* |
| JOSHUA MUELLER | *Peter Fernandez* |
| BODO MUELLER | *Eric Roberts* |
| BABETTE MUELLER | *Anne Blyth* |
| KURT MUELLER | *Paul Lukas* |

## SCENE

Living room of the Farrelly country house, about twenty miles from Washington. The time is late spring, 1940.

Act I—Early on a Wednesday morning.

Act II—Ten days later.

Act III—A half-hour later.

# WATCH ON THE RHINE

## ACT ONE

Scene: *The living-room of the Farrelly house, about twenty miles from Washington, D. C., on a warm July morning.*

*Center stage are large French doors leading to an elevated open terrace. On the terrace are chairs, tables, a large table for dining. Some of this furniture we can see: most of it is on the left side of the terrace, beyond our sight. L. stage is an arched entrance, leading to the oval reception hall. R. stage is a door leading to a library. The Farrelly house was built in the early 19th century. It has space, simplicity, style. The living-room is large. Upstage L., a piano, downstage L., a couch, downstage R., a couch and chairs, upstage a few smaller chairs. Four or five generations have furnished this room and they have all been people of taste. There are no styles, no periods, the room has never been refurnished. Each careless aristocrat has thrown into the room what he or she brought home when grown-up. Therefore the furniture is of many periods: the desk is English, the couch is Victorian, some of the pictures are modern, some of the ornaments French. The room has too many things in it: vases, clocks, miniatures, boxes, china animals. On the L. wall is a large portrait of a big kind-faced man in an evening suit of 1900. On another wall is a large, very ugly landscape. The room is crowded. But it is cool and clean and its fabrics and woods are in soft colors.*

*At Rise:* Anise, *a thin Frenchwoman of about sixty, in a dark housekeeper's dress, is standing at a table, sorting mail. She takes the mail from a small basket, holds each letter to the light, reads each postal card, then places them in piles. On the terrace,* Joseph, *a tall middle-aged Negro butler, wheels a breakfast wagon. As he appears,* Fanny Farrelly *comes on from the hall. She is a handsome woman of about sixty-three. She has on a fancy, good-looking dressing-gown.*

FANNY (*stops to watch* ANISE. *Sees* JOSEPH *moving about on terrace. Calls*). Joseph!

JOSEPH. Yes'm.

FANNY (*to* ANISE). 'Morning.

ANISE (*continues examining mail*). Good morning, Madame.

JOSEPH (*comes to terrace door*). Yes'm?

FANNY. Everybody down?

JOSEPH. No'm. Nobody. I'll get your tea. (*Starts off* R. *on terrace. He returns to breakfast wagon on terrace.*)

FANNY (*calling off* R.). Mr. David isn't down yet? (*Coming into room toward* ANISE, *crosses to sofa* L. *–sits* L. *end.*) But he knows he is to meet the train.

JOSEPH (*comes in from terrace with cup of tea. To top of step* R. *of* FANNY). He's got plenty of time, Miss Fanny. The train ain't in till noon.

FANNY. Breakfast is at nine o'clock in this house and will be until the day after I die. Ring the bell.

JOSEPH (*goes* D. L. *to* FANNY; *gives her tea*). But it ain't nine yet, Miss Fanny. It's eight-thirty.

FANNY. Well, put the clocks up to nine and ring the bell.

JOSEPH (*crosses* U. C. *toward door*). Mr. David told me not to ring it any more. He says it's got too mean a ring, that bell. It disturbs folks. (*Stops at sound of her voice and turns.*)

FANNY. That's what it was put there for. I like to disturb folks.

JOSEPH. Yes'm. (*Goes* U. S. *through terrace door and off* R.)

FANNY. You slept well, Anise. You were asleep before I could dismantle myself.

ANISE. I woke several times during the night.

FANNY. Did you? Then you were careful not to stop snoring. We must finally get around (ANISE *brings letters to* FANNY.) to rearranging your room. (ANISE *hands her three or four letters.* FANNY *puts down tea.*) Even when you don't snore, it irritates me.

(ANISE *crosses* D. L., *sits in armchair, opens and reads French newspaper.* FANNY *begins to open mail, to read it. After a moment.*) What time is it?

ANISE. It is about eight-thirty. Joseph just told you.

FANNY. I didn't hear him. I'm nervous. Naturally. (*Continues to read.*) My mail looks dull. (*Looking at letter in her hand. Still reading.*) Jenny always tells you a piece of gossip three times, as if it grew fresher with the telling. Did you put flowers in their rooms?

ANISE. Certainly.

FANNY. David ought to get to the station by eleven-thirty.

ANISE (*patiently*). The train does not draw in until ten minutes past noon.

FANNY. But it might come in early. (*Irritably.*) It might. Don't argue with me about everything. What time is it?

ANISE (*looking at watch*). It's now twenty-seven minutes before nine. It will be impossible to continue telling you the time every three minutes from now until Miss Sara arrives. I think you are having a nervous breakdown. Compose yourself.

FANNY. It's been twenty years. Any mother would be nervous. If your daughter were coming home and you hadn't seen her, and a husband, *and* grandchildren—

ANISE. I do not say that it is wrong to be nervous. I, too, am nervous. I say only that you are.

FANNY. Very well. I heard you. *I* say that I am. (*She taps her fingers on the chair, goes back to reading her letter. Looks up.*) Jenny's still in California. She's lost her lavalliere again. Birdie Chase's daughter is still faire l'amouring with that actor. Tawdry, Jenny says it is. An actor. Fashions in sin change. In my day, it was Englishmen. I don't understand infidelity. (*Puts down letters beside her and picks up teacup.*) If you love a man, then why? If you don't love him, then why stay with him? (*Without turning, she points over her head to* JOSHUA FARRELLY'S *portrait over mantel. Sips tea.*) Thank God, I was in love. I thought about Joshua last night. Three grandchildren. He would have liked that. I hope I will. (*Sips tea again and puts*

down cup. *Points to other letters.*) Anything in anybody else's mail?

ANISE. Advertisements for Mr. David, and legal things. For our Count and Countess, there is nothing but what seems an invitation to a lower-class Embassy tea, and letters asking for bills to get paid.

FANNY. That's every morning. (*Thoughtfully.*) In the six weeks the Balkan nobility has been with us, they seem to have run up a great many bills.

ANISE (FANNY *picks up tea*). Yes. I told you that. Then, there was a night-letter for Mr. David.

(*A very loud, very unpleasant bell begins to ring.*)

FANNY (*through the noise*). Really? From whom?

ANISE. From her. I took it on the telephone, and—

(*Bell drowns out her voice.*)

FANNY. Who is "her"? (*Bell becomes very loud.*) Go tell him to stop that noise—

ANISE (*crosses to terrace, calling off* R.). Joseph! Stop that bell. Miss Fanny says to stop it. (*She crosses back to chair* D. L. *and sits.*)

JOSEPH (*calls*). Miss Fanny said to start it.

FANNY (*shouts out to him*). I didn't tell you to hang yourself with it.

JOSEPH (*appears on terrace from* R.). I ain't hung. Your breakfast is ready. (*Disappears off* R.)

FANNY (*to* ANISE). Who is "her"?

ANISE. That Carter woman from Lansing, Michigan.

FANNY. Oh, my. Is she back in Washington again? What did the telegram say?

ANISE. It said the long sickness of her dear Papa had terminated in full recovery.

FANNY. That's too bad.

ANISE. She was returning, and would Mr. David come for dinner a week from Thursday? "Love," it said, "to you and your charming mother." (*To* FANNY.) That's you. I think Miss Carter from Lansing, Michigan, was unwise in attending the illness of her Papa.

FANNY. I hope so. Why?

ANISE *(shrugs)*. There is much winking of the eyes going on between our Countess and Mr. David.

FANNY *(eagerly)*. I know that. Anything new happen?

ANISE *(too innocently)*. Happen? I don't know what you mean.

FANNY. You know damned well what I mean.

ANISE. That? Oh, no, I don't think that.

JOSEPH *(appears at terrace door)*. The sausage cakes is shrinking.

FANNY *(rises, shrieks, crosses R. taking letters)*. I want everybody down here immediately. *(To JOSEPH.)* Is the car ready? *(JOSEPH nods. To ANISE.)* Did you order a good dinner? *(At hall door.)* David! *(DAVID FARRELLY, a pleasant-looking young man of thirty-nine, comes in from the entrance hall.)* Oh!

DAVID *(crossing the room. Crosses to mail table)*. Good morning, everybody.

ANISE *(to FANNY)*. Everything is excellent. You have *(JOSEPH crosses D. L. to sofa, picking up teacup.)* been asking the same questions for a week. You have made the kitchen very nervous.

*(FANNY crosses behind sofa R. to U. R. C.)*

DAVID *(examining mail. To JOSEPH)*. Why did you ring that air raid alarm again?

JOSEPH *(crosses U. R. C., crossing DAVID)*. Ain't me, Mr. David. I don't like no noise. Miss Fanny told me. *(Exits through terrace door U. R. C.)*

FANNY *(crosses to DAVID)*. Good morning, David.

DAVID *(calls to JOSEPH, who has gone)*. Tell Fred to leave the car. I'll drive to the station. *(To FANNY, half amused, half annoyed. Begins to read his mail.)* Mama, I think we'll fix up the chicken house for you as a playroom. We'll hang the room with bells and you can go into your second childhood in the proper privacy. *(He kisses her cheek and turns back to his mail.)*

FANNY. I find it very interesting. You sleep soundly, you rise at your usual hour —although your sister, whom you haven't seen in years, is waiting at the station—

DAVID. She is not waiting at the station. The train does not come in until ten minutes past twelve.

FANNY *(airily)*. It's almost that now.

ANISE *(turns to look at her)*. Really, Miss Fanny, contain yourself. It is twenty minutes before nine.

DAVID. And I have *not* slept soundly. And I've been up since six o'clock.

FANNY *(turns up and R.)*. Really? The Balkans aren't down yet. Where are they?

DAVID. I don't know.

ANISE *(picks up bag, crosses R.)*. There is nothing in your mail, Mr. David, only the usual advertisements.

DAVID. And for me, that is all that is ever likely to come—here.

ANISE *(stops R. before sofa. Haughtily, as she starts toward hall)*. I cannot, of course, speak for Miss Fanny. *(Crosses R. to door and stops.)* I have never opened a letter in my life.

DAVID. I know. You don't have to. For you, they fly open.

FANNY *(giggles)*. It's true. *(Two steps toward ANISE to back of chair R. C.)* You're a snooper, Anise. *(ANISE exits R. FANNY talks as ANISE moves out. Turns to DAVID.)* I rather admire it. It shows an interest in life. *(She looks up at JOSHUA's portrait.)* You know, I've been lying awake most of the night: wondering what Papa would have thought about Sara *(DAVID looks at her.)* and— He'd have been very pleased, wouldn't he? I always find myself wondering what Joshua would have felt—

DAVID. Yes. But maybe it would be just as well if you didn't expect me to be wondering about it, too. *(DAVID takes letters, crosses R., puts them on secretary, U. R.)* I wasn't married to him, Mama. He was just my father.

FANNY. My. You got up on the wrong side of the bed. *(She moves to mail table, points to mail.)* The *bills* are for our noble guests. Interesting—how *(Crosses R. to DAVID.)* many there are every morning. How much longer are they going to be with us?

DAVID *(without looking at her)*. I don't know.

FANNY. It's been six weeks. Now that Sara and her family are coming, even this house might be a little crowded— *(Starts L. He looks up at her. Quickly.)* I know I invited them. I felt sorry for Marthe, *(Moves to R. of piano keyboard.)* and Teck rather amused me. He plays good cribbage, and he tells good jokes. But that's not enough for a lifetime guest. If you've been urging her to stay, I wish you'd stop it. *(Turns to DAVID.)* They haven't any money; all right, lend them some—

DAVID. I have been urging them to stay?

FANNY. I'm not so old I don't recognize flirting when I see it.

DAVID. But you're old enough not to be silly.

FANNY. I'm not silly. I'm charming.

*(MARTHE DE BRANCOVIS, an attractive woman of thirty-one or two, enters from R.)*

MARTHE. Good morning, Fanny. 'Morning, David.

FANNY *(U. C. at terrace door)*. Good morning, Marthe.

DAVID *(warmly)*. Good morning.

MARTHE *(crosses U. R. to R. of FANNY)*. Fanny, darling, couldn't you persuade yourself to let me have a tray in bed and some cotton for my ears?

DAVID *(steps up to doorstep)*. Certainly not. My father ate breakfast at nine, and whatever my father did—

FANNY *(in U. C. door. Carefully, to DAVID)*. There was a night-letter for you from that Carter woman in Lansing, Michigan. She is returning and you are to come to dinner next Thursday. *(As she exits on terrace.)* C-A-R-T-E-R. *(Pronounces it carefully.)* Lansing, Michigan.

DAVID *(laughs)*. I know how to spell Carter, but thank you. *(FANNY exits through terrace door and off U. R. DAVID looks up at MARTHE.)* Do you understand my mother?

MARTHE *(crosses C.)*. Sometimes.

DAVID. Miss Carter was done for your benefit.

MARTHE *(smiles)*. That means she has guessed that I would be jealous. And she has guessed right.

DAVID *(looks at her)*. Jealous?

MARTHE *(gaily)*. I know I have no right to be but I am. And Fanny knows it.

DAVID *(carelessly)*. Don't pay any attention to Mama. *(Crosses below MARTHE to liquor table U. R. C.)* She has a sure instinct for women I like, and she begins to hammer away early. Marthe— *(Goes to decanter on side table.)* I'm going to have a drink. I haven't had a drink before breakfast since the day I took my bar examination. *(Pours himself a drink, gulps it down.)* What's it going to be like to stand on a station platform and see your sister after all these years—I'm afraid, I guess.

MARTHE. Why?

DAVID. I don't know. Afraid she won't like me— *(Shrugs.)* We were very fond of each other, but it's been a long time.

MARTHE. I remember Sara. Mama brought me one day when your Father was stationed in Paris. I was about six and Sara was about fifteen and you were—

DAVID *(two steps toward L.)*. You were a pretty little girl.

MARTHE. Do you really remember me? You never told me before. Mama and Fanny went off to gossip, and you and Sara and Anise and I sat stiffly in the garden; and I felt much too young. And then your Mama began to yell at my Mama—

FANNY *(yelling from terrace off R.)*. David! Come to breakfast.

DAVID *(as if he had not been listening)*. You know, I've never met Sara's husband. Mama did. I think the first day Sara met him, in Munich. Mama didn't like the marriage much in those days—and Sara didn't care, and Mama didn't like Sara not caring. Mama cut up about it, bad.

MARTHE. Why?

DAVID. Probably because they didn't let her arrange it. Why does Mama ever act badly? She doesn't remember ten minutes later.

MARTHE. Wasn't Mr. Muller poor?

DAVID. Oh, Mama wouldn't have minded that. If only they'd come home and let her fix their lives for them— *(Smiles.)* But Sara didn't want it that way.

MARTHE *(crosses to mail table,* U. L. C.*).* You'll have a house full of refugees—us and—

DAVID *(smiles).* Are you and Teck refugees? *(More toward her.)* I'm not sure I know what you're refugees from.

MARTHE *(turns to* DAVID*).* From Europe.

DAVID. From what Europe?

MARTHE *(smiles, shrugs).* I don't know. I don't know myself, really. Just Europe. *(Steps toward* DAVID*. Quickly, comes to him.)* Sara will like you. I like you. *(Laughs.)* That doesn't make sense, does it?

*(On her speech,* TECK DE BRANCOVIS *appears in hall,* R. *He is a good-looking man of about forty-five. She stops quickly.)*

TECK *(to* MARTHE *and* DAVID*).* Good morning.

*(The bell gives an enormous ring.)*

DAVID *(goes to terrace).* Good morning, Teck. For years I've been thinking they were coming for Mama with a net. I'm giving up hope. I may try catching her myself. *(Disappears, calling.)* Mama! Stop that noise. *(Exits through terrace door, goes off* R.*)*

*(*MARTHE *crosses to* R. C. *above chair.)*

TECK. I wonder if science has a name for women who enjoy noise. *(Goes to table, picks up his mail.)* Many mistaken people, Marthe, seem to have given you many charge accounts.

MARTHE *(crosses toward him, extends hand for mail).* The Countess de Brancovis. That still does it. It would be nice to be able to pay bills again— *(Crosses to front of sofa* L.*)*

TECK. Do not act as if I refuse to pay them, Marthe. *(Crosses to* R. *end of sofa* L.*)* I did not sleep well last night. I was worried. *(*MARTHE *sits on sofa* L.*)* We have eighty-seven dollars in American Express checks. *(Pleasantly, looking at her.)* That's all we have.

MARTHE *(shrugs, opening and reading letters).* Maybe something will turn up. It's due.

TECK *(carefully).* David? *(Then, as she turns to look at him.)* The other relatives will arrive this morning? *(Crosses* R. *to* U. C.*)*

MARTHE. Yes.

TECK *(*U. C.*—looks out on terrace).* I think Madame Fanny and Mr. David may grow weary of accents and charity guests. Or is the husband *(Turns to her.)* of the sister a rich one?

MARTHE. No. He's poor. He had to leave Germany in '33. *(*MARTHE *reads mail throughout this exchange.)*

TECK. A Jew?

MARTHE. No. I don't think so.

TECK. Why did he have to leave Germany?

MARTHE *(still reading).* Oh, I don't know, Teck. He's an anti-Nazi.

TECK. A political?

MARTHE. No, I don't think so. He was an engineer. I don't know. I don't know much about him.

TECK *(crosses to* R. *end of sofa* L.*).* Did you sleep well?

MARTHE. Yes. Why not?

TECK. Money does not worry you?

MARTHE. It worries me very much. But I just lie still now and hope. I'm glad to be here. *(Shrugs.)* Maybe something good will happen. *(Looks at* TECK.*)* We've come to the end of a road. That's been true for a long time. Things will have to go one way or the other. Maybe they'll go well, for a change.

TECK. I have not come to the end of any road.

MARTHE *(looks at him, smiles).* No? *(Rises, crosses front of* TECK *toward window* U. R. C.*)* I admire you.

TECK. I'm going into Washington tonight. Phili has a poker game every Wednesday evening. He has arranged for me to join it.

MARTHE *(after a pause).* Have you been seeing Phili?

TECK. Once or twice. Why not? Phili and I are old friends. He may prove useful. I do not want to stay in this country forever.

MARTHE (*crosses to* TECK). You can't leave them alone. Your favorite dream, isn't it, Teck, that they will let you play with them again. I don't think they will and I don't think you should be seeing Phili or that you should be seen at the Embassy.

TECK (*smiles*). You have political convictions now?

MARTHE. I don't know what I have. I've never liked Nazis, as you know, and you should have had enough of them. They seem to have had enough of you, God knows. It would be just as well to admit they are smarter than you are, and let them alone.

TECK (*looking at her carefully, after a minute*). That is interesting.

MARTHE. What is interesting?

TECK. I think you are trying to say something to me. What is it?

MARTHE. That you ought not to be at the Embassy, and that it's insane to play cards in a game with Von Seitz with eighty-seven dollars in your pocket. I don't think he'd like your not being able to pay up. Suppose you lose?

TECK. I shall try not to lose.

MARTHE. But if you do lose and can't pay, it will be all over Washington in an hour. (*Points to terrace.*) They'll find out about it, and we'll be out of here when they do.

TECK. I think I want to be out of here. I find that I do not like the picture of you and our host.

MARTHE (D. S. *few steps to back of chair* c. *Carefully*). There is no picture, as you put it, to like or dislike.

TECK. Not yet? I am glad to hear that. (*Comes slowly toward her. Crosses* R. *to* L. *of* MARTHE.) Marthe, you understand that I am not really a fool? You understand that it is unwise to calculate me that way?

MARTHE (*slowly, as if it were an effort*). Yes, I understand that. And I understand that I am getting tired. Just plain tired. The whole thing's too much for me. I've always meant to ask you, since you play on so many sides, why we don't come out any better. I've always wanted to ask you how it happened. (*Sharply.*) I'm tired, see? And I just want to sit down. Just to sit down in a chair and stay.

TECK (*carefully.*) Here?

MARTHE. I don't know. Any place—

TECK. You have thus arranged it with David?

MARTHE. I've arranged nothing.

TECK. But you are trying, eh? I think no. I would not like that. Do not make any arrangements, Marthe, I may not allow you to carry them through. (*Smiles.*) Come to breakfast now. (*He passes her, disappears on terrace. She stands still and thoughtful. Then she, too, moves to terrace, disappears.*)

(JOSEPH *appears on terrace, carrying a tray toward the unseen breakfast table. The stage is empty. After a minute there are sounds of footsteps in the hall.* SARA MULLER *appears in the doorway, comes toward the middle of the room as if expecting to find somebody, stops, looks around, begins to smile. Behind her in the doorway are three* CHILDREN; *behind them,* KURT MULLER. *They stand waiting, watching* SARA. SARA *is forty-one or two, a good-looking woman, with a well-bred, serious face. She is very badly dressed. Her dress is too long, her shoes were bought a long time ago and have no relation to the dress, and the belt of her dress has become untied and is hanging down. She looks clean and dowdy. As she looks around the room, her face is gay and surprised. Smiling, without turning, absently, she motions to the children and* KURT. *Slowly, the children come in.* BODO MULLER, *a boy of nine, comes first. He is carrying coats. Behind him, carrying two cheap valises, is* JOSHUA MULLER, *a boy of fourteen. Behind him is* BABETTE MULLER, *a pretty little girl of twelve. They are dressed for a much colder climate. They come forward, look at their mother, then move to a couch. Behind them is* KURT MULLER, *a large, powerful, German-looking man of about forty-three. He is carrying a shabby valise and a briefcase. He stands watching* SARA. JOSHUA *puts down the valises, goes to his father, takes the valise from* KURT, *puts it neatly near his, and puts the briefcase near* KURT. BABETTE *goes to* SARA, *takes a package from her, places it near the valise. Then she turns to* BODO, *takes the coats he is carrying, puts them neatly on top of the valises. After a second,* KURT *sits down. As he does so, we see that his movements are slow and careful, as if they are made with effort.)*

BABETTE *(points to a couch near which they are standing. She has a slight accent.)* Is it allowed?

KURT *(*SARA *crosses* L. *Smiles. He has an accent)*. Yes. It is allowed.

*(*KURT *sits on couch* S. L. BABETTE *sits stiffly* R. *end of settee, motions to* JOSHUA *and* BODO. BODO *on her left.* JOSHUA *stands* R. *of settee.)*

JOSHUA *(nervously. He has a slight accent)*. But we did not sound the bell—

SARA *(crosses* R. *Idly, as she wanders around room, her face excited)*. The door isn't locked. It never was. Never since I can remember.

BODO *(softly, puzzled)*. The entrance of the home is never locked! So.

KURT *(looks at him)*. You find it curious to believe there are people who live and do not need to watch, eh, Bodo?

BODO. Yes, Papa.

KURT *(smiles)*. You and I.

JOSHUA *(smiles)*. It is strange. But it must be good, I think.

*(*SARA *to back of settee* R.*)*

KURT. Yes.

SARA. Sit back. Be comfortable. *(Calls softly.)* I wonder where Mama and David— *(Delighted, sees portrait of* JOSHUA FARRELLY, *points to it.)* And that was my Father. *(Turns to them.)* That was the famous Joshua Farrelly. *(They all look up at it. She wanders around the room. Turns to* R. *look at room.)* My goodness, isn't it a fine room? I'd almost forgotten— *(Turns to mantel* L.*)* And this was my grandmother. *(Giggles.)* An unpleasant woman with great opinions. *(Very nervously.* U. *to* L. *of* KURT.*)* Shall I go and say we're here? They'd be having breakfast, I think. Always on the side terrace in nice weather. I don't know. Maybe— *(Up to piano. Picks up another picture from* D. *end of piano.)* "To Joshua

and Fanny Farrelly. With admiration. Alfonso. May 7, 1910." *(Moves behind piano to keyboard upstage.)* I had an ermine boa and a pink coat. I was angry because it was too warm in Madrid to wear it.

BODO. Alfons von Spanien? Der hat immer Bilder von sich verschenkt. Ein Schlechtes Zeichen für einen Mann.

JOSHUA *(crosses* D. R. *to chair* D. R.*)*. Mama told you it is good manners to speak the language of the country you visit. Therefore, speak in English.

BODO *(turns to* JOSHUA*)*. I said he seemed always to give his photograph. I said that is a bad flag on a man. Grow fat on the poor people and give pictures of the face.

*(*JOSHUA *sits* D. C.*)*

SARA *(to* KURT*)*. I remember a big party and cakes and a glass of champagne for me. *(Crosses* R. *to* R. *of terrace door* R. *and looks at pictures on that wall.)* I was ten, I guess— *(Suddenly laughs.)* That was when Mama said the first time a king got shot as he was a romantic, but the fifth time he was a comedian. And when Father gave his lecture in Madrid, he repeated it—right in Madrid. It was a great scandal. *(Turns to* CHILDREN.*)* You know, Alfonso was always getting shot at or bombed. *(*SARA *crosses to secretary, picks up small object, examines it and presses it to her cheek.)*

BODO *(shrugs)*. Certainement!

JOSHUA. Certainement? As-tu perdu la tete?

BABETTE. Speak in English, please.

KURT *(without turning)*. You are a terrorist, Bodo?

BODO *(slowly)*. No.

JOSHUA. Then since when has it become *natural* to shoot upon people?

*(*SARA *replaces small object in secretary.)*

BODO. Do not give me lessons. It is neither right nor natural to shoot upon people. I know that. *(Leans to* BABETTE.*)*

SARA *(to* R. *to* U. R. *table and places handbag on it. Looks at* BABETTE, *thoughtfully)*. An ermine boa. A boa is a scarf. I should like to have one for you, Babbie. *(Touches her hair.)* Once— *(Crosses* C. *to* U. R. *of*

R. C. *table—touching desk in passing.*)
in Prague, I saw a pretty one. I wanted
to buy it for you. But we had to pay our
rent. *(Laughs.)* But I almost bought it.

*(Crosses to* C.*)*

BABETTE. Yes, Mama. Thank you. Fix
your sash, Mama.

SARA *(thoughtfully).* Almost twenty years.

*(Looks down at carpet. Laughs de-
lightedly.)*

BODO. You were born here, Mama?

SARA. Upstairs. And I lived here until I
went to live with your Father. *(Looks
out beyond terrace.* U. C. *to terrace step.)*
Your Uncle David and I used to have a
garden, behind the terrace. I wonder if
it's still there. I like a garden. I've always
hoped we'd have a house some day and
settle down— *(Stops nervously, turns to
stare at* KURT, *who is looking at her.*
D. S. *to table* L. C.*)* I am talking so foolish. Sentimental. At my age. Gardens and
ermine boas. I haven't wanted anything—

KURT *(comes toward her, takes her hand).*
Sara, stop it. This is a fine room. A fine
place to be. Everything is so pleasant and
full of comfort; this will be a good piano
on which to play again. And it is all so
clean. I like that. You shall not be a baby.
You must enjoy your house, and not be
afraid that you hurt me with it. Yes?

BABETTE. Papa, fix Mama's sash, please.

SARA *(shyly smiles at him as* KURT *turns
SARA around, ties sash).* Yes, of course.
It's strange, that's all. We've never been
in a place like this together— *(Turns to
him.)*

KURT. That does not mean, and should
not mean, that we do not remember how
to enjoy what comes our way. We are on
a holiday.

JOSHUA. A holiday? But for how long?
And what plans for afterwards?

KURT *(crosses* D. L. *to* L. *end of sofa* L.
*Quietly).* We will have plans when the
hour arrives to make them.

*(SARA is facing terrace.* ANISE *comes down
stairs, stops, stares, amazed, a little frightened. She comes toward room, stares at
children. The* MULLERS *have not seen her.
As* SARA *turns,* ANISE *speaks.)*

ANISE *(to above table* D. R. *Looking at*
JOSHUA.*)* What? What?

*(*CHILDREN *rise.)*

SARA *(softly).* Anise, it's me. It's Sara.

ANISE *(coming forward slowly. Then as
she approaches* SARA, *she begins to run
toward her).* Miss Sara! Miss Sara! *(They
reach each other, both laugh happily.* SARA
*kisses* ANISE.*)* I would have known you.
Yes, I would. I would have known. *(Excited, bewildered, nervous, looks toward*
KURT. BODO *moves to* R. *of table* R. C.
JOSHUA *comes to* C. *of desk behind sofa*
R.*)* How do you do, sir? How do you do?
*(Turns toward* CHILDREN.*)* How do you
do?

JOSHUA. Thank you, Miss Anise. We are
in good health.

SARA *(happily).* You look the same. I think
you look the same. Just the way I've always remembered. *(To* OTHERS. *They step
down a bit.* SARA *holds* ANISE *throughout
this scene.)* This is the Anise I've told
you about. She was here before I was born.

*(*JOSHUA *crosses to behind table* R. C.*)*

ANISE. But how—did you just come in?
What a way to come home! And after
all the plans we've made. But you were
to come on the twelve o'clock train and
Mr. David was to meet you—

BABETTE *(steps* L.*).* The twelve o'clock
train was most expensive. We could not
have come with that train. We liked the
train we came on. It was most luxurious.

ANISE *(very nervous, rattled).* But Madame Fanny will have a fit. *(Turns to
SARA.)* I will call her— She will not be
able to contain herself. *(Starts up.)*

SARA *(softly. Stopping* ANISE*).* I wanted a
few minutes. I am nervous about coming
home, I guess.

BODO *(conversationally).* You are French,
Madame Anise?

ANISE. Yes. I am from the Bas Rhin. *(She
moves front and just past* SARA, *and bobs
her head idiotically at* KURT.*)* Sara's husband. That is nice. That is nice.

BODO. Yes, your accent is from the north. That is fine country. We were in hiding there once—

(BABETTE *touches his shoulder to silence him.*)

ANISE. Hiding? You— (*Turns nervously to* KURT.) But here we stand and talk. You have not had your breakfast, sir!

BABETTE (*simply*). It would be nice to have breakfast.

ANISE (*crosses* SARA *to* C). Yes, of course. I will go and order it.

SARA (*to* CHILDREN). What would you like for breakfast?

BABETTE. What would we like? Why, Mama, we will have anything that can be spared. If eggs are not too rare or too expensive—

ANISE (*amazed*). Expensive! Why—oh—I —I—must call Miss Fanny now. (*Crosses up to* C. *terrace door.*) It is of a necessity. Miss Fanny! Miss Fanny! (*Turns back to* SARA.) Have you forgotten your Mama's nature? She cannot bear not knowing things. Miss Fanny! What a way to come home. (BABETTE *sits* R. *end of sofa* R.) After twenty years. And nobody at the station.

FANNY'S VOICE (*off* R.). Don't yell at me. What is the matter with you?

ANISE (*excitedly, as* FANNY *draws near*). She's here. They're here. Miss Sara. She's here, I tell you.

(FANNY *comes up to her, entering from* U. R. *Stops at step, stares at her, stares at* BODO *and* JOSHUA *on the floor, looks slowly around until she sees* SARA. ANISE U. R. *as* FANNY *enters.*)

SARA (*softly*). Hello, Mama.

FANNY (*after a long pause, softly, coming toward her*). Sara. Sara, darling. You're here. (*Crosses down to* R. *of* SARA.) You're really here. (*She reaches her, takes her arms, kisses her, stares at her, smiles.*) Welcome. Welcome. Welcome to your house. (*After a second, looks at* SARA.) You're not young, Sara.

SARA (*smiles*). No, Mama. I'm forty-one.

FANNY (*softly*). Forty-one. Of course. (*Presses her arms again.*) Oh. Sara, I'm—

(*Then quickly.*) You look more like Papa now. That's good. The years have helped you. (*Embraces her. Turns to look at* KURT.) Welcome to this house, sir.

KURT (*warmly*). Thank you, Madame.

FANNY (*turns to look at* SARA *again, nervously pats her arm. Nods, turns again to stare at* KURT. *She is nervous and chatty. Crosses* D. L. *to* KURT). You are a good-looking man, for a German. I didn't remember you that way. I like a good-looking man. (*Shakes his hand.*) I always have.

KURT (*smiles*). I like a good-looking woman. I always have.

FANNY. Good. That's the way it should be.

BODO (*from* R. *of table* R. C., *who is just rising from floor, to* SARA). Ist das Grossmama? (*Crosses to* C.)

FANNY (*looks down*). Yes. I am your grandmother. Also, I speak German, so do not talk about me. I speak languages very well. But there is no longer anybody to speak with. Anise has half-forgotten her French, which was always bad; and I have nobody with whom to speak my Italian or German or— Oh, Sara— (SARA *down to* FANNY.) it's good to have you home. I'm chattering away, I—

JOSHUA. Now you have us, Madame. We speak ignorantly, but fluently, in German, French, Italian, Spanish—

KURT. And boastfully, in English.

JOSHUA (*softly*). I am sorry, Papa. You have right.

BODO (*to* JOSHUA). There is never a need for boasting. If we are to fight for the good of all men, it is to be accepted that we must be among the most advanced. (*Crosses to below table* R. C.)

ANISE (D. S. *a bit from* U. C.). My God.

FANNY (*to* SARA). Are these your *children*? Or are they dressed up midgets?

SARA (*laughs*). These are my children, Mama. This, Babette. (BABETTE *bows.*) This, Joshua. (JOSHUA D. S. *two steps, bows.*) This is Bodo. (BODO *bows.*)

FANNY (*crosses to* JOSHUA). Joshua was named for Papa. You wrote me. (*Kisses him. Indicates picture of* JOSHUA FAR-

RELLY.) You bear a great name, young man.

JOSHUA (*smiles, indicates his father*). My name is Muller.

FANNY (*looks at him, laughs*). Yes. You look a little like your grandfather. (*To* BABETTE. *Crosses* R. *to* BABETTE, *above* BODO.) And so do you. You are a nice looking girl. (*To* BODO.) You look like nobody.

BODO (*proudly*). I am not beautiful.

FANNY (*laughs*). Well, Sara, well. (BABETTE *on* R. *end of sofa* R.) Three children. You have done well. (*To* KURT, *crosses* L. *to* KURT.) You, too, sir, of course. Are you quite recovered? Sara wrote that you were in Spain and—

BODO. Did Mama write that Papa was a great hero? He was brave, he was calm, he was expert, he was resourceful, he was—

KURT (*laughs*). My biographer. And as unprejudiced as most of them.

SARA (D. *to* R. *of* FANNY). Where is David? I am so anxious— Has he changed much? Does he—

FANNY (*to* ANISE). Don't stand there. (*Crosses* U. *to* ANISE; SARA *moves* L. *to* R. *of* KURT.) Go and get him right away. (*Peers in the basket.*) Go get David. (JOSHUA *crosses up to door* U. R. *and looks out at terrace. As* ANISE *exits.*) He's out having breakfast with the titled folk. (D. S. *to* R. *of* SARA.) Do you remember Marthe Randolph? I mean, do you remember Hortie Randolph, her mother, who was my friend? Can you follow what I'm saying? I'm not speaking well today.

SARA (*laughs*). Of course I remember Marthe and Hortie. You and she used to scream at each other.

(JOSHUA *leaves the window and goes to secretary* R., *picks up book.*)

FANNY (*takes* SARA's *arm, brings her to settee, they sit,* FANNY R. *of* SARA). Well, Marthe, her daughter, married Teck de Brancovis. *Count* de Brancovis. He was fancy when she married him. Not so fancy now, I suspect. Although still chic and tired. You know what I mean, the way they are in Europe. Well, they're here—

(JOSHUA *looks at pages in book through this.*)

SARA. What's David like now? I—

FANNY. Like? Like? I don't know. He's a lawyer. You know that. Papa's firm. He's never married. You know that, too—

SARA. Why hasn't he married?

FANNY. Really, I don't know. I don't think he likes his own taste. Which is very discriminating of him. He's had a lot of girls, of course, one more ignorant and silly than the other— (*Grins to* KURT. *Goes toward terrace, begins to scream.*) And where is he? David! David— (*Goes* U. C. *to door;* BODO *follows her.*)

ANISE'S VOICE (*from* U. R.). He's coming, Miss Fanny. He's coming. Contain yourself. He was down at the garage getting ready to leave—

FANNY. I don't care where he is. Tell him to come. His sister comes home after twenty years— David! I'm getting angry.

BODO. You must not get angry. We never do. Anger is protest. And so you must direction it to the proper channels and then harness it for the good of other men. That is correct, Papa?

FANNY (*crosses* R. *to* BODO. *Peers down at him*). If you grow up to talk like that, and stay as ugly as you are, you are going to have one of those successful careers on the lecture platform.

(JOSHUA *and* BABETTE *laugh.*)

JOSHUA. Oh. It is a great pleasure to hear Grandma talk with you.

(KURT *has wandered to the piano. Standing, he touches the keys in the first bars of Mozart's Rondo in D Major.* DAVID *comes in from entrance hall* R. *At door, he stops and stares at* SARA. *Piano stops* —KURT *rises.*)

DAVID (*to* SARA). Sara. Darling—

SARA (*wheels, goes running toward him. She moves into his arms. He leans down, kisses her with great affection*). David. David. (*Crosses* R. *to* DAVID, *who has stopped above chair* L. *of table* D. R.)

(BABETTE *takes two steps* R. *to front of* L. *end of sofa.* JOSHUA *crosses to* L. *of table* R. C. KURT *crosses* D. *to* C.)

DAVID *(softly).* It's been a long, long time. I got to thinking it would never happen. *(He leans down, kisses her hair. After a minute he smiles, presses her arm.)*

SARA *(excited).* David, I'm excited. Isn't it strange? To be here, to see each other— But I'm forgetting— This is my husband and these are my children. Babette, Joshua, Bodo.

(JOSHUA D. L. *of* BODO, *who is* L. *of* BABETTE.)

ALL THREE. How do you do, Uncle David?

*(The* BOYS *move forward to shake hands.* BODO, *followed by* JOSHUA, *crosses. They shake hands and go to stand* R. *of their mother.)*

DAVID *(as he shakes hands with* JOSHUA). Boys can shake hands. But so pretty a girl must be kissed. *(He kisses her. She smiles, very pleased.)*

BABETTE. Thank you. *(She crosses front to* R. *then to above* SARA.*)* Fix your hairpin, Mama.

*(*SARA *shoves back a falling pin.* DAVID *and* KURT *move to meet front of table* R. C. FANNY *sits* R. *end of sofa* L.*)*

DAVID *(to* KURT). I'm happy to meet you, sir, and to have you here.

KURT. Thank you. Sara has told me so much from you. You have a devoted sister.

*(*SARA *crosses to* DAVID'S R. *and takes his arm.* ANISE *sticks her head in from the hall.)*

ANISE *(enters from* R., *crosses to* C.). Your breakfast is coming. Shall I wash the children, Miss Sara?

JOSHUA (D. R. *two steps. Amazed).* Wash us? Do people wash each other?

SARA. No, but the washing is a good idea. *(*ANISE *crosses* R. *to door, turns.)* Go along now, and hurry. *(All* THREE *start for hall.)* And then we'll all have a fine big breakfast again.

*(The* CHILDREN *exit* R.*)*

FANNY. Again? Don't you usually have a good breakfast?

KURT *(smiles, sits* D. L.*).* No, Madame. Only sometimes.

SARA *(laughs).* Oh, we do all right, usually. *(Sees* DAVID *staring at her, puts her hands in his affectionately. Very happily, very gaily.)* Ah, it's good to be here. We were kids. Now we're all grown up! I've got children, you're a lawyer, and a fine one, I bet—

FANNY. The name of Farrelly on the door didn't, of course, hurt David's career.

DAVID *(smiles).* Sara, you might as well know that Mama thinks of me only as a monument to Papa, and a not very well-made monument at that. I am not the man Papa was.

SARA *(to* FANNY, *smiles).* How do you know he's not?

FANNY *(carefully).* I beg your pardon. That is the second time you have spoken disrespectfully of your father. *(*SARA *and* DAVID *laugh.* FANNY *turns to* KURT.*)* I hope you will like me.

KURT. I hope so.

SARA *(pulls him to couch, sits down with him).* And I want to hear about you, David. *(Looks at him, laughs.)* I'm awfully nervous about seeing you. Are you about me?

DAVID. Yes, I certainly am.

SARA *(looks around).* I'm like an idiot. I want to see everything right away. The lake, and my old room, and the nursery, and is the asparagus-bed where it used to be, and I want to talk and ask questions—

KURT *(laughs).* More slow, Sara. It is most difficult to have twenty years in a few minutes.

SARA. Yes, I know, but— Oh, well. Kurt's right. We'll say it all slowly. It's just nice being back. Haven't I fine children?

DAVID. Very fine. You're lucky. I wish I had them.

FANNY. How could you have them? All the women you like are too draughty, if you know what I mean. I'm sure that girl from Lansing, Michigan, would be sterile. Which is as God in his wisdom would have it.

SARA. Oh. So you have a girl?

DAVID. I have no girl. This amuses Mama.

FANNY *(to* KURT*).* He's very attractive to some women. *(Points to* DAVID*.)* He's flirting with our Countess now, Sara. You will see for yourself.

DAVID *(sharply).* You are making nervous jokes this morning, Mama. And they're not very good ones.

FANNY *(gaily.)* I tell the truth. If it turns out to be a joke, all the better.

SARA *(affectionately).* Ah, Mama hasn't changed. And that's good, too.

FANNY. Don't mind me, Sara. I, too, am nervous about seeing you. *(To* KURT*.)* You'll like it here. You are an engineer?

KURT. Yes, Madame.

FANNY. Do you remember the day we met in Muenchen? The day Sara brought you to lunch? I thought you were rather a clod, and that Sara would have a miserable life. I think I was wrong. *(To* DAVID*.)* You see? I always admit when I'm wrong.

DAVID. You are a woman who is noble in all things, at all times.

FANNY. Oh, you're mad at me. *(To* KURT*.)* As I say, you'll like it here. I've already made some plans. The new wing will be for you and Sara. The old turkey-house we'll fix up for the children. A nice, new bathroom, and we'll put in their own kitchen, and Anise will move in with them—

SARA. That's kind of you, Mama. But— *(Very quietly.)* We won't make any plans for a while—a good, long vacation; God knows Kurt needs it—

FANNY *(to* SARA*).* A vacation? *(To* KURT*.)* You'll be staying here, of course. You don't have to worry about work. . . . Engineers can always get jobs, David says, and he's already begun to inquire—

KURT. I have not worked as an engineer since many years, Madame.

DAVID. Haven't you? I thought— Didn't you work for Dornier?

KURT. Yes. Before '33.

FANNY. But you have worked in other places. A great many other places, I should say. Every letter of Sara's seemed to have a new postmark.

KURT *(smiles).* We move most often.

DAVID. You gave up engineering?

KURT. I gave it up? *(Smiles.)* Well, one could say it that way.

FANNY. What do you do?

SARA. Mama, we—

KURT. It is difficult to explain.

DAVID *(after a slight pause, a little stiffly).* If you'd rather not . . .

FANNY. No. I—I'm trying to find out something. *(To* KURT*.)* May I ask it, sir?

KURT. Let me help you, Madame. You wish to know whether not being an engineer buys adequate breakfasts for my family. It does not. I have no wish to make a mystery of what I have been doing: it is only that it is awkward to place neatly. *(Smiles, motions with his hand.)* It sounds so big: it is so small. I am an anti-Fascist. And that does not pay well.

FANNY. Do you mind questions?

SARA. Yes.

KURT *(sharply).* Sara. *(To* FANNY*.)* Perhaps I shall not answer them. But I shall try.

FANNY. Are you a radical?

KURT. You would have to tell me first what that word means to you, Madame.

FANNY *(after a slight pause).* That is just. Perhaps we all have private definitions. We all are anti-Fascists, for example—

SARA. Yes. But Kurt works at it, Mama.

FANNY. What kind of work?

KURT. Any kind. Anywhere.

FANNY *(sharply).* I will stop asking questions.

SARA *(very sharply).* That would be sensible, Mama.

DAVID. Darling, don't be angry. We've been worried about you, naturally. We knew so little, except that you were having a bad time.

SARA. I didn't have a bad time. We never—

KURT. Do not lie for me, Sara.

SARA *(rises).* I'm not lying. *(Crosses to* C. *toward* FANNY.) I didn't have a bad time, the way they mean. I—

FANNY *(slowly.* SARA *hesitates* C., *moves* U. C. *a few steps).* You had a bad time just trying to live, didn't you? That's obvious, Sara, and foolish to pretend it isn't. Why wouldn't you take money from us? What kind of nonsense—

SARA *(slowly to* FANNY). We've lived the way we wanted to live. *(To* DAVID *and* FANNY.) I don't know the language of rooms like this any more. And I don't want to learn it again.

KURT. Do not bristle about it.

SARA. I'm not bristling. *(She moves toward* FANNY.) I married because I fell in love. You can understand that.

FANNY *(slowly).* Yes.

SARA *(sits* R. *of* FANNY). For almost twelve years Kurt went to work every morning and came home every night, and we lived modestly, and happily— *(Sharply.)* As happily as people could in a starved Germany that was going to pieces—

KURT. You're angry, Sara. Please. I do not like it that way. I will try to find a way to tell you with quickness. . . . Yes. *(To* FANNY *and* DAVID.) I was born in a town called Feurth. There is a holiday in my town. We call it Kirchweih. It was a gay holiday with games and music and a hot white sausage to eat with the wine. I grow up, I move away, to school, to work,—but always I come back for Kirchweih. For me, it is the great day of the year. *(Slowly.)* But, after the war, that day begins to change. The sausage is now made from bad stuff, the peasants come in without shoes, the children are now too sick— *(Carefully.)* It is bad for my people, those years, but always I have hope. But in the festival of August, 1931, one year before the storm, I give up that hope. On that day I saw twenty-seven men murdered in a Nazi street fight. I say, I cannot just stand by now and watch. My time has come to move. *(Looks down, smiles.)* I say with Luther, "Here I stand. I can do nothing else. God help me. Amen."

SARA. It doesn't pay well to fight for what you believe in. But I wanted it, the way Kurt wanted it. *(Shrugs.)* They don't like us in Europe: I guess they never did, So Kurt brought us home. You've always said you wanted us. If you don't, I will understand.

DAVID. Darling—of course we want you—

FANNY. I am old. And made of dry cork. And bad-mannered. *(Rises, turns to* KURT.) Please forgive me.

SARA *(rises, goes quickly to* FANNY, *puts her hands on* FANNY's *shoulders and turns her).* Shut up, Mama. We're all acting like fools. I'm glad to be home. That's all I know. So damned glad.

*(*FANNY *kisses her.)*

DAVID. And we're damned glad to have you. So that's settled. *(Stretches his hand out to her. She comes to him.)* Come on. Let's walk to the lake. We've made it bigger and planted the island with blackberries. *(She smiles. Together they move out hall entrance.)*

FANNY *(after a silence).* They've always liked each other. *(*KURT D. S. *to* R. *of* FANNY.) We're going to have Zwetschgen-Knoedel for dinner. You like them?

KURT. Indeed.

FANNY. I hope you like decent food.

KURT. I do.

FANNY. That's a good sign in a man.

MARTHE *(coming in from terrace from* U. R. *Stops in doorway).* Oh, I'm sorry, Fanny. We were waiting. *(Crosses* D. *to* C. R. *of mail table.)* I didn't want to interrupt the family reunion. I—

FANNY. This is my son-in-law, Herr Muller. The Countess de Brancovis—

KURT *and* MARTHE *(together.* KURT *crosses up to* L. *of* MARTHE). How do you do?

MARTHE. And how is Sara, Mr. Muller? I haven't seen her since I was a little girl. She probably doesn't remember me at all. *(*TECK *comes in from hall. She turns.)* This is my husband, Herr Muller.

*(Brings him down from door, crosses* R. *three steps.* TECK *at* R. *of* KURT.)

TECK. How do you do, sir? *(*KURT *bows. They shake hands.)* Would it be impertinent for one European to make welcome another?

KURT (*smiles*). I do not think so. It would be friendly.

BODO (*at door* R.). Papa! Oh! (MARTHE D. S. *to back of table.* TECK *follows, during speech. Sees* TECK *and* MARTHE, *bows, crosses to* R. *of table* R. C.) Good morning. Miss Anise says you are the Count and Countess de Brancovis.

TECK (*laughs*). How do you do?

(KURT *crosses to* R. *of sofa* L.)

MARTHE (*laughs*). What's your name?

BODO. My name is Bodo. It's a strange name. No? (BODO *crosses to* KURT.) This is the house of great wonders. Each has his bed, each has his bathroom. The arrangement of it, that is splendorous.

FANNY (*laughs*). You are a fancy talker, Bodo.

KURT. Oh, yes. In many languages.

BODO (*to* FANNY). Please to correct me when I am wrong. Papa, the plumbing is such as you have never seen. Each implement is placed on the floor, and all are simultaneous in the same room. (KURT *is amused.*) You will therefore see that being placed most solidly on the floor allows of no rats, rodents and crawlers, and is most sanitary. (*To* OTHERS.) Papa will be most interested. He likes to know how each thing of everything is put together. And he is so fond of being clean.

KURT (*laughs. To* FANNY). I am a hero to my children. It bores everybody but me.

TECK. It is most interesting, Herr Muller. I thought I had a good ear for the accents of your country. But yours is most difficult to place. Yours is Bayerisch—or is it—

BODO. That's because Papa has worked in so many . . .

KURT (*quickly placing hand on* BODO's *shoulder and moving him up*). German accents are the most difficult to identify. I, myself, when I try, am usually incorrect. It would be of a particular difficulty with me. I speak other languages. Yours would be Rumanian, would it not?

(BODO *to behind mail table.*)

MARTHE (*laughs*). My God, is it that bad?

KURT (*smiles*). I am showing off. I knew the Count de Brancovis is Rumanian.

TECK (*heartily*). So? We have met before? I thought so, but I cannot remember—

KURT. No, sir. We have not met before. I read your name in the newspapers.

TECK (*to* KURT). Strange. I was sure I had met you. I was in the Paris Legation for many years, and I thought perhaps we met there—

KURT. No. If it is possible to believe, I am the exile who is not famous. (*He turns to* FANNY.) I have been thinking with pleasure, Madame Fanny, of breakfast on your porch. (*Points to the portrait of* JOSHUA FARRELLY.) Your husband once wrote: "I am getting older and Europe seems far away. Fanny and I will have an early breakfast on the porch— (*Points to the terrace.*) and then I shall drive the bays into Washington." And then he goes on saying, "Henry Adams tells me he has been reading Karl Marx. I shall have to tell him my father made me read Marx many years ago, and that, since he proposes to exhibit himself to impress me, will spoil Henry's Sunday."

FANNY (*laughs delightedly. She rises, takes* KURT's *arm*). And so it did. I had forgotten that. I am pleased with you. I shall come and serve your food myself. I had forgotten Joshua ever wrote it.

(*They start out the terrace door together.*)

KURT (*as they disappear*). I try to impress you. I learned it last night. (*She laughs, they disappear.*)

TECK (*smiles*). He is a clever man. A quotation from Joshua Farrelly. That is the sure road to Fanny's heart. (*He has turned to look at* KURT's *valise.*) Where did you say Herr Muller came from?

MARTHE. Germany.

TECK. I know that. (*Has gone to table where valise has been placed, leans over, stares at it, pushes it, looks at labels, opens and closes lock.*) What part of Germany?

MARTHE (*taking cigarette and lighting it*). I don't know. And I never knew you were an expert on accents.

TECK (*going to where* JOSHUA *has placed* KURT's *briefcase*). I never knew it either. Are you driving into Washington with David this morning?

MARTHE (*crosses to front of sofa* L.). I was going to. But he may not be going to the office, now that Sara's here. I was to have lunch with Sally Tyne. (*Sits* R. *end of sofa.* TECK *has picked up the briefcase and is trying the lock.*) What are you doing?

TECK. Wondering why luggage is unlocked, and a shabby briefcase is so carefully locked.

MARTHE. You're very curious about Herr Muller.

TECK. Yes. And I do not know why. Something far away— I am curious about a daughter of the Farrellys who marries a German who has bullet scars on his face and broken bones in his hands.

MARTHE (*sharply*). Has he? There are many of them now, I guess.

TECK (*looks at her*). So there are. But this one is in (*Crosses* D. L. *to bell pull.*) this house.

MARTHE. It is—is he any business of yours?

TECK (*pulls bell, then crosses to* U. C. *looking at luggage* R.). What is my business? Anything might be my business now.

MARTHE. Yes—unfortunately. (*Sharply as he presses the catch of valise, it opens, he closes it.*) You might inquire from your friend, Von Seitz. They always know their nationals.

TECK (*pleasantly, ignoring the sharpness with which she has spoken*). Oh, yes, I will do that, of course. But I do not like to ask questions without knowing the value of the answers.

MARTHE (*rises, crosses to* TECK). This man is a little German Sara married years ago. I remember Mama talking about it. He was nothing then, and he isn't now. They've had a tough enough time already without . . .

TECK. Have you— Have you been sleeping with David?

MARTHE (*stops, stares at him, then simply*). No. I have not been. (*Turns away, crosses* L. *and puts out cigarette in ashtray on mail table.*) And that hasn't been your business for a good many years now.

TECK. You like him?

MARTHE (*nervously. Steps toward* TECK). What's this for, Teck?

TECK. Answer me, please.

MARTHE. I— (*She stops.*)

TECK. Yes? Answer me.

MARTHE. I do like him.

TECK. What does he feel about you?

MARTHE. I don't know.

(*There is a pause.*)

TECK. But you are trying to find out. You have made any plans with him?

MARTHE. Of course not. I—

TECK. But you will try to make him have plans. I have recognized it. Well, we have been together a long time. (JOSEPH *enters* L. TECK *stops, crosses to* R. *end of sofa* L.) Joseph, Miss Fanny wishes you to take the baggage upstairs.

JOSEPH (*crosses* R. *to baggage*). Yes, sir. I was going to. (*He begins to pick up baggage.*)

(MARTHE *has turned sharply and is staring at* TECK. *Then she rises, crosses to back of chair* R. C., *watches* JOSEPH *pick up baggage, turns again to look at* TECK.)

TECK. As I was saying. It is perhaps best that we had this talk.

MARTHE. I— (*She stops, waits for* JOSEPH *to move off. He exits, carrying valises.*) Why did you do that? Why did you tell Joseph that Fanny wanted him to take the baggage upstairs?

TECK (*has risen*). Obviously, it is more comfortable to look at baggage behind closed doors. (*Crosses her, continuing to door* R.)

MARTHE (*very sharply*). What kind of silliness is this now? (*Crosses* R., *grabs his arm and turns him. They are behind table* D. R.) Leave these people alone— (*As he starts to exit.*) I won't let you—

TECK. What? (*As he moves again, she comes after him.*)

MARTHE. I said, I won't let you. You are not—

TECK (*grabs her wrist and twists it*). How many times have you seen me angry?

(MARTHE *looks up, startled.*) You will not wish to see another. *(Releases her wrist.)* Run along now and have lunch with something you call Sally Tyne. But do not make plans with David. You will not be able to carry them out. You will go with me, when I am ready to go. You understand. *(He exits during his speech. The last words come as he goes through door, and as . . .)*

THE CURTAIN FALLS

# ACT TWO

SCENE: *The same as Act I, about ten days later. It is beginning to grow dark, the evening is warm, and the terrace doors are open.*

AT RISE: SARA *is sitting on couch, crocheting.* FANNY *and* TECK *are sitting at a small table playing cribbage.* BODO *is sitting near them, at a large table, working on a heating pad. The cord is torn from the bag, the bag is ripped open.* ANISE *sits next to him anxiously watching him. Outside on the terrace,* JOSHUA *is going through baseball motions, coached by* JOSEPH. *From time to time, they move out of sight, reappear, move off again.*

FANNY *(playing a card)*. One.

BODO *(pulling wires from heating pad. To* ANISE, *then to* TECK*)*. The arrangement of this heating pad grows more complex.

TECK *(smiles, moves on cribbage board)*. And the more wires you remove, the more complex it will grow.

BODO *(points to bag)*. Man has learned to make man comfortable. Yet all cannot have the comforts. *(To* ANISE.*)* How much did this cost you?

ANISE. It cost me ten dollars. And you have made a ruin of it.

BODO. That is not yet completely true. *(Turns to* FANNY.*)* Did I not install for you a twenty-five cent button-push for your radio?

FANNY. Yes, you're quite an installer.

TECK *(playing a card)*. Two and two.

BODO *(to* TECK*)*. As I was wishing to tell you, Count de Brancovis, comfort and plenty exist. Yet all cannot have it. Why?

TECK. I do not know. It has worried many men. Why?

ANISE *(to* BODO*)*. Yes—why?

BODO *(takes a deep breath, raises his finger as if about to lecture)*. Why? *(Considers a moment, then deflates himself.)* I am not as yet sure.

ANISE. I thought not.

FANNY *(calling. Turns to look at* JOSHUA *and* JOSEPH *on terrace)*. Would you mind doing that dancing some place else?

JOSEPH *(looking in)*. Yes'm. That ain't dancing. I'm teaching Josh baseball.

FANNY. Then maybe he'd teach you how to clean the silver.

JOSEPH *(crosses down to above table* C. JOSHUA *stands in door* U. C.*)*. I'm a good silver-cleaner, Miss Fanny.

FANNY. But you're getting out of practice.

JOSEPH *(after a moment's thought)*. Yes'm. I see what you mean. *(He exits* L.*)*

FANNY *(playing a card)*. Three.

JOSHUA *(crosses* D. *to* U. C., *tossing ball and catching it)*. It is my fault. I'm crazy about baseball.

BODO. Baseball players are among the most exploited people in this country. I read about it. . . .

FANNY. You never should have learned to read.

BODO *(*JOSHUA *crosses* R. *to* BODO, *moving above sofa* R.*)*. Their exploited condition is foundationed on the fact that—

JOSHUA *(bored)*. All right, all right. I still like baseball. *(He turns back to* U. C., *but stops and turns at* FANNY'S VOICE.*)*

TECK *(playing a card)*. Five and three.

SARA. Founded, Bodo, not foundationed.

JOSHUA *(crosses* U. R. *of table of sofa* R.*).* He does it always. He likes long words. In all languages.

TECK. How many languages do you children speak?

BODO. Oh, we do not really know any very well, except German and English. We speak bad French and—

SARA. And bad Danish and bad Czech.

TECK *(turns to* SARA*).* You seem to have stayed close to the borders of Germany. Did Herr Muller have hopes, as so many did, that National Socialism would be overthrown on every tomorrow?

*(*JOSHUA *crosses behind sofa to above table* C.*)*

SARA. We have not given up that hope. Have you, Count de Brancovis?

TECK *(turns back to game).* I never had it.

JOSHUA *(pleasantly).* Then it must be most difficult for you to sleep.

TECK. I beg your pardon?

*(*JOSHUA *starts to reply.)*

SARA. Schweig doch, Joshua!

FANNY *(to* TECK*).* Sara told Joshua to shut up. *(Playing card.)* Twelve.

TECK. I have offended you, Mrs. Muller. I am most sorry.

SARA *(pleasantly).* No, sir, you haven't offended me. I just don't like polite political conversations any more.

TECK *(nods).* All of us, in Europe, had too many of them.

SARA. Yes. Too much talk. By this time all of us must know where we are, and what we have to do. *(*TECK *turns back to game.)* It's an indulgence to sit in a room and discuss your beliefs as if they were a juicy piece of gossip.

FANNY *(*JOSHUA *comes* D. *to behind table* C.*).* You know, Sara, I find it very pleasant that Kurt, considering his background, doesn't make platform speeches. He hasn't tried to convince anybody of anything.

SARA *(smiles).* Why should he, Mama? You are quite old enough to have your own convictions—or Papa's.

FANNY *(turns to look at her).* I am proud to have Papa's convictions.

SARA. Of course. But it might be well to have a few new ones, now and then.

FANNY *(peers over her).* Are you criticizing me?

SARA *(smiles).* Certainly not.

TECK *(to* JOSHUA, *who is looking down at cribbage game).* I didn't know your Father was a politician.

*(*BABETTE *enters* L., *runs to behind table* C., *carrying a plate and fork. She pushes* JOSHUA *out of his way to* R.*)*

JOSHUA *(looks at him for a second, then pleasantly).* He wasn't, Count de Brancovis.

BABETTE *(she has on an apron and she is carrying a plate. She goes to* FANNY*).* Eat it while it's hot, Grandma.

*(*BODO *rises and quickly goes to* FANNY's R. ANISE *follows and stands behind* BODO. FANNY *peers down, takes fork, begins to eat.* ANISE *and* BODO *both rise, move to* FANNY, *inspect the plate.)*

FANNY *(to them).* Go away.

ANISE. It is a potato pancake. *(Crosses back to behind table* R. *and looks at dismantled heating pad.)*

FANNY *(irritably).* And it's the first good one I've eaten in many, many years. I love a good potato pancake.

BODO *(moving closer to* FANNY*).* I, likewise.

*(*FANNY *nudges him away with her elbow.)*

BABETTE. I am making a great number for dinner.

TECK *(playing a card).* Fifteen and two.

BABETTE. Move away, Bodo.

*(*BODO *goes to* R. *behind table* R.*)*

ANISE *(as* BODO *comes to her).* You have ruined it! I shall sue you. *(She sits in chair* R. *of table* R.*)*

JOSHUA. I told you not to let him touch it.

SARA *(laughs).* I remember you were always saying that, Anise—that you were going to sue. That's very French. I was sick once in Paris, and Babbie *(*BABETTE

*crosses to chair* U. R. C. *taking off apron.*
*She takes sewing material and sewing*
*basket from bag on chair, leaving apron*
*there.)* finished a dress I was making for
a woman on the Rue Jacob. The woman
admitted the dress was well done, but
said she was going to sue because I hadn't
done it all. Fancy that.

(BABETTE *crosses* R. *around sofa* R. *and sits*
*beside* FANNY *and sews.)*

FANNY *(slowly).* You sewed for a living?

SARA. Not a very good one. But Babbie
and I made a little something now and
then. Didn't we, darling?

FANNY *(sharply).* Really, Sara, were these
—these things necessary, Sara? Why
couldn't you have written?

SARA *(laughs).* Mama, you've asked me
that a hundred times in the last week.

JOSHUA *(gently).* I think it is only that
Grandma feels sorry for us. Grandma has
not seen much of the world.

FANNY. Now, don't you start giving me
lectures, Joshua. I'm fond of you. And of
you too, Babbie. *(To* ANISE.) Are there
two desserts for dinner? And are they
sweet?

ANISE. Yes.

FANNY *(turns to* BODO). I wish I were fond
of you.

BODO. You are. *(Happily.)* You are very
fond of me.

FANNY *(playing a card).* Twenty-five.

TECK *(playing last card).* Twenty-eight
and one.

(JOSHUA *goes to secretary to get a book.*
*He crosses to chair* U. C., *examines light*
*from window, sits, and reads.)*

FANNY *(counting score).* A sequence and
three, a pair and five. *(To* TECK, *as they*
*finish cribbage game.)* There. That's two
dollars off. I owe you eighty-fifty.

(BODO *sits* L. *of table* R.)

TECK. Let us carry it until tomorrow. You
shall give it to me as a going-away token.

FANNY *(too pleased).* You're going away?

TECK *(laughs).* Ah, Madame Fanny. Do
not sound *that* happy.

FANNY. Did I? That's rude of me. When
are you going?

TECK. In a few days, I think. *(Turns to*
*look at* SARA.) We're too many refugees,
eh, Mrs. Muller?

SARA *(pleasantly).* Perhaps.

TECK. Will you be leaving, also?

SARA. I beg your pardon.

TECK. I thought perhaps you, too, would
be moving on. Herr Muller does not give
me the feeling of a man who settles down.
Men who have done his work seldom
leave it. Not for a quiet country house.

*(All three* CHILDREN *look up.)*

SARA *(very quietly).* What work do you
think my husband has done, Count de
Brancovis?

TECK. Engineering?

SARA *(slowly, nods).* Yes. Engineering.

FANNY *(very deliberately to* TECK. JOSHUA
*back to book,* BABETTE *to sewing).* I don't
know what you're saying. They shall certainly not be leaving—ever. Is that understood, Sara?

SARA. Well, Mama—

FANNY. There are no wells about it. You've
come home to see me *die* and you will
wait until I'm ready.

(CHILDREN *look at* FANNY.)

SARA *(laughs).* Really, Mama, that isn't
the reason I came home.

FANNY. It's a good reason. I shall do a
fine death. I intend to be a great deal of
trouble to everybody.

(CHILDREN *smile and go back to what*
*they were doing.)*

ANISE. I daresay.

FANNY. I shall take to my bed early, and
stay for years. In great pain.

ANISE. I am sure of it. You will duplicate
the disgrace of the birth of Miss Sara.

SARA *(laughs).* Was I born in disgrace?

ANISE (FANNY *becomes interested in* BAB-
ETTE's *work).* It was not your fault. But it
was disgusting. Three weeks before you
were to come—all was excellent, of course,

in so healthy a woman as Madame Fanny —a great dinner was given here, and, most unexpectedly, attended by a beautiful lady from England.

FANNY. Do be still. You are dull and fanciful—

ANISE. Mr. Joshua made the great error of waltzing the beauty for two dances, Madame Fanny being unfitted for the waltz, and under no circumstances being the most graceful of dancers.

FANNY *(her voice rising)*. Are you crazy? I danced magnificently. I—

ANISE. It is well you thought so. A minute did not elapse between the second of the waltzes, and a scream from Madame Fanny. She was in labor. *(FANNY turns to table and puts cards in box.)* Two hundred people, and if we had left her alone, she would have remained in the ballroom—

FANNY. How you invent! How you invent!

ANISE. Do not call to me that I am a liar. For three weeks you are in the utmost agony—

FANNY. And so I was. I remember it to this day—

ANISE *(to SARA, angrily. FANNY continues to straighten table)*. Not a pain. Not a single pain. She would lie up there in state, stealing candy from herself. Then, when your Papa would rest himself for a minute at the dinner or with a book, a scream would dismantle the house—it was revolting. *(Spitefully to FANNY.)* And now, the years have passed, and I may disclose to you that Mr. Joshua knew you were going through the play-acting—

FANNY *(rises)*. He did not. You are a malicious, miserable—

ANISE. Once he said to me, "Anise, it is well that I am in love. This is of a great strain, and her great-uncle Freddie was not right in the head, neither."

FANNY *(rises. Screaming)*. You will leave this house— You are a liar, *(ANISE rises.)* a thief, a woman of—

SARA. Mama, sit down.

ANISE *(moves below table toward FANNY)*. I will certainly leave this house. I will—

*(Picks up wool she has dropped at her feet.)*

SARA *(sharply)*. Both of you. Sit down. And be still.

ANISE. She has intimated that I lie—

FANNY *(screaming)*. Intimate! Is that what I was doing— *(ANISE begins to leave the room.)* Very well! I beg your pardon. I apologize.

*(ANISE turns.)*

SARA. Both of you. You are acting like children.

BODO. Really, Mama. You insult us.

ANISE *(crosses to chair R. of table D. R.)*. I accept your apology. Seat yourself.

*(They both sit down at same time.)*

FANNY *(after a silence)*. I am unloved.

BABETTE. I love you, Grandma.

FANNY. Do you, Babbie?

JOSHUA. And I.

FANNY *(nods, very pleased. To BODO)*. And you?

BODO. *I* loved you the primary second I saw you.

FANNY. You are a charlatan.

ANISE. As for me, I am fond of all the living creatures. It is true, the children cause me greater work, which in turn more greatly inconveniences my feet, however I do not complain. I believe in children.

FANNY. Rather like believing in the weather, isn't it? *(DAVID and KURT come in from terrace. Both are in work clothes, their sleeves rolled up. DAVID enters door U. L., crosses to secretary to fill pipe there.)* Where have you been?

DAVID. We've been helping Mr. Chabeuf spray the fruit trees.

ANISE. Mr. Chabeuf says that Herr Muller has the makings of a good farmer. From a Frenchman that is a large thing to say.

KURT *(rolling down sleeves, putting on coat as he comes D. C. He has looked around room, looked at TECK, strolled over to BODO)*. Mr. Chabeuf and I have an excellent time exchanging misinformation. *(To* TECK, *in passing.)* My father was a farmer. I have a wide knowledge of farmers' misinformation.

FANNY. This is good farm land. Perhaps, in time—

*(DAVID crosses to back of* TECK's *chair.)*

DAVID *(laughs)*. Mama would give you the place, Kurt, if you guaranteed that your great-grandchildren would die here.

KURT *(at behind table* D. R.—*Smiles)*. I would like to so guarantee.

TECK. A farmer. That is very interesting. Abandon your ideals, Mr. Muller?

KURT. Ideals? *(Carefully.)* Sara, heist es auf Deutsch "Ideale"?

SARA. Yes.

KURT. Is that what I have now? I do not like the word. It gives to me the picture of a small, pale man at a seaside resort. *(To* BODO.*)* What are you doing?

BODO. Preparing an elderly electric pad for Miss Anise. I am confused.

KURT *(wanders toward piano)*. So it seems.

BODO. Something has gone wrong with the principle on which I have been working. It is probable that I will ask your assistance.

KURT *(bows to him, standing behind keyboard)*. Thank you. *(Begins to pick out notes with one hand.)* Whenever you are ready! *(*KURT *sits at piano and plays Haydn Minuet in A Major—six bars and a chord ending.)*

FANNY. We shall have a little concert tomorrow evening. In honor of Babbie's birthday. *(To* KURT.*)* Kurt, you and I will play the Clock Symphony. Then Joshua and I will play the duet we've learned, and Babbie will sing. And I shall finish with a Chopin Nocturne.

DAVID *(laughs)*. I thought you'd be the last on the program.

*(*PIANO *stops.* DAVID *crosses behind sofa toward* R.*)*

TECK. Where is Marthe?

FANNY. She'll be back soon. She went into town to do an errand for me. *(To* DAVID.*)* Did you buy presents for everybody?

DAVID. I did. *(*DAVID *comes* D. *to behind table* D. R.*)*

SARA *(smiles, to* BABETTE*)*. We always did that here. If somebody had a birthday, we all got presents. *(*KURT *plays again with one hand, improvisation.)* Nice, isn't it?

DAVID *(to* ANISE—*looks closely at pad* BODO *is "repairing")*. I shall buy you an electric pad. You will need it.

ANISE. Indeed.

FANNY. Did you buy me a good present?

DAVID. Pretty good. *(Crosses to behind* R. *end of sofa* R. *Pats* BABETTE's *head.)* The best present goes to Babbie: it's *her* birthday.

FANNY. Jewelry?

DAVID. No, not jewelry.

FANNY. Oh. Not jewelry.

DAVID. Why? Why should you want jewelry? You've got too many bangles now.

FANNY. I didn't say I wanted it. I just asked you.

TECK *(gets up)*. It was a natural mistake, David. You see, Mrs. Mellie Sewell told your mother that she had seen you and Marthe in Barstow's. And your mother said you were probably buying her a present, or one for Babbie.

DAVID *(too sharply)*. Yes.

TECK *(laughs)*. Yes what?

DAVID *(slowly)*. Just yes. *(*DAVID *crosses* U. *to window* U. R. C.*)*

FANNY *(too hurriedly)*. Mellie gets everything wrong. She's very anxious to meet Marthe because she used to know Francis Cabot, her aunt. Marthe's aunt, I mean, not Mellie's.

SARA *(too hurriedly)*. She really came to inspect Kurt and me. *(*KURT *plays irregularly and abstractedly, listening to conversation.)* But I saw her first. *(She looks anxiously at* DAVID *who has turned his back on the room and is facing the terrace)*. You were lucky to be out, David.

*(*DAVID *crosses to beside table* U. L. C.*)*

DAVID. Oh, she calls every Saturday afternoon, to bring Mama all the Washington gossip of the preceding week. She gets it all wrong, you understand, but that doesn't make any difference to either Mama or her. Mama then augments it, wits it up, Papa used to say—

FANNY. Certainly. I sharpen it a little. Mellie has no sense of humor.

DAVID. So Mama sharpens it a little, and delivers it tomorrow afternoon to old lady Marcy down the road. Old lady Marcy hasn't heard a word in ten years, so she unsharpens it again, and changes the names. By Wednesday afternoon—

TECK (*smiles. Turns in chair and interrupts* DAVID). By Wednesday afternoon (KURT *stops playing.*) it will not be you who (DAVID *crosses* D. C. *to be on level with* TECK.) were in Barstow's, and it will be a large diamond pin with four sapphires delivered to Gaby Delys.

DAVID (*looks at him*). Exactly.

FANNY (*very nervously*). Francis Cabot is (DAVID *crosses in front of sofa* L. *and* U. L. *to* D. *end of piano.*) Marthe's aunt, you understand— (*To* KURT.) Kurt, did you ever know Paul von Seitz, a German?

KURT. I have heard of him.

FANNY (*speaking very rapidly*). Certainly. He was your Ambassador to somewhere. I've forgotten. Well, Francie Cabot married him. I could have. Any American, not crippled, whose father had money . . . He was crazy about me. I was better looking than Francie. Well, years later when he was your Ambassador—my father was, too, as you probably know— not your Ambassador, of course, ours— but I am talking about Von Seitz.

DAVID (*laughs to* KURT). You can understand how it goes. Old lady Marcy is not entirely to blame.

(KURT *plays Mozart Minuet in B Flat Major with one hand.*)

FANNY. Somebody asked me if I didn't regret not marrying him. I said, "Madame, je le regrette tous les jours et j'en suis heureuse chaque soir." (FANNY *turns to* DAVID. TECK *turns to look at* KURT *at piano.*) That means I regret it every day and am happy about it every night. You

understand what I meant, by *night? Styles* in wit change so.

DAVID. I understood it, Mama.

JOSHUA. We, too, Grandma.

BABETTE (*approvingly*). It is most witty.

BODO. I do not know that I understood. You will explain to me, Grandma?

SARA. Later.

(KURT *continues to play, now both hands.*)

FANNY (*turns to look at* TECK). You remember the old Paul von Seitz?

TECK (*turns to* FANNY. *Nods*). He was stationed in Paris when I first was there.

FANNY. Of course. I always forget you were a diplomat.

TECK. It is just as well.

FANNY. There's something insane about a Roumanian diplomat. Pure insane. (TECK *turns back to* KURT.) I knew another one, once. At least he said he was a Roumanian. He wanted to marry me, too.

SARA (*laughs*). All of Europe.

FANNY. Not all. Some. Naturally. I was rich, I was witty, my family was of the best. I was handsome, unaffected—

DAVID. And noble and virtuous and kind and elegant and fashionable and simple— it's hard to remember everything you were. I've often thought it must have been boring for Papa to have owned such perfection.

FANNY (*shrieks*). What! Your father bored with me! Not for a second of our life—

DAVID (*laughs. Crosses* D. *to front of sofa* L. *and sits* L. *of* SARA). Oh God, when will I learn?

BODO. Do not shriek, Grandma. It is an unpleasant sound for the ear.

(JOSHUA *rises, crosses to secretary, takes another book, stands there reading and listening.*)

SARA. Why, Mama! A defect in you has been discovered.

FANNY. Where was I? Oh, yes. What I started out to say was— (*She turns, carefully to* TECK.) Mellie Sewell told me, when you left the room, that she had heard from Louis Chandler's child's governess that you had won quite a bit of money in a poker game with Sam Chandler and some Germans at the Embassy and— (KURT *stops playing sharply, hitting a discord as his hands fall on keys.* TECK *turns to look at him.*) And *that's* how I thought of Von Seitz. His nephew Philip was in on the game.

DAVID (*looks at* TECK, *leans forward, elbow on knees*). It must have been a big game. Sam Chandler plays in big games.

TECK. Not big enough.

DAVID. Have you known Sam long?

TECK. For years. (*Looks at* KURT.) Every Embassy in Europe knew him.

DAVID (*sharply*). Sam and Nazis must make an unpleasant poker game.

(KURT *starts to play piano. Soldiers' Song.*)

TECK (*who has not looked away from* KURT). I do not play poker to be amused.

DAVID (*irritably*). What's Sam selling now?

TECK. Bootleg munitions. He always has.

DAVID. You don't mind?

TECK. Mind? I have not thought about it.

(BODO *puts heating pad cover behind him, testing its size against his back.*)

FANNY. Well, you ought to think about it. Chandler has always been a scoundrel. All the Chandlers are. They're cousins (BODO *rises and crosses to behind* ANISE *and tests cover against her back.*) of mine. Mama used to say they never should have learned to walk on two feet. (TECK *turns in chair to look at* KURT. BABETTE *starts to hum song* KURT *plays,* JOSHUA *joins in.*) They would have been more comfortable on four.

TECK (*to* KURT, *who has started to play again*). Do you know the young Von Seitz, Herr Muller? He was your military attaché in Spain.

KURT. He was the German government attaché in Spain. I know his name, of course. He is a famous artillery expert. But the side on which I fought was not where he was stationed, Count de Brancovis.

ANISE (BODO *has come around in back of her, and is trying to fit electric pad to her back.* BABETTE and JOSHUA *begin to hum song* KURT *is playing.* SARA *begins to hum.*) It is time for the bath and the change of clothes. I will give you five more minutes—

(BODO *returns to his chair* L. *of table* D. R.)

FANNY. What is the song?

TECK. It was a German soldiers' song. They sang it as they straggled back in '18. I remember hearing it in Berlin. Were you there then, Herr Muller?

KURT (*the playing and singing continue*). I was not in Berlin.

TECK (*rises, crosses* U. *to* R. *of* KURT). But you were in the war, of course?

KURT. Yes. I was in the war.

FANNY. You didn't think then you'd live to see another war.

KURT. Many of us were afraid we would.

FANNY. What are the words?

SARA. The Germans in Spain, in Kurt's Brigade, wrote new words for it.

(*Humming stops.*)

KURT. This is the way you heard it in Berlin in 1918. (*Begins to sing in German.*)

"Wir zieh'n Heim, wir zieh'n Heim,
Mancher kommt nicht mit,
Mancher ging verschütt,
Aber freunde sind wir stets."

(*In English.*)

"We come home. We come home.
Some of us are gone, and some of us are lost, but we are friends:
Our blood is on the earth together.
Some day. Some day we shall meet again. Farewell."

(*Stops singing.*) At a quarter to six on the morning of November 7th, 1936, eighteen years later, five hundred Germans walked through the Madrid streets on their way to defend the Manzanares River. We felt good that morning. You know how it is to be good when it is needed to be good? So we had need of new words to say that. I translate with awkwardness, you understand. (*Begins to sing again in English.*)

"And so we have met again.
The blood on the earth did not have time
   to dry.
We lived to stand and fight again.
This time we fight for people.
This time the bastards—
Will keep their hands away.
Those who sell the blood of other men,
   this time,
They keep their hands away.
For us to stand.
For us to fight.
This time, no farewell, no farewell."

*(Music dies out. There is silence for a minute. Then* KURT *looks up.)* We did not win. *(Looks up, gently.)* It would have been a different world if we had.

SARA. Papa said so years ago. Do you remember, Mama? "For every man who lives without freedom, the rest of us must face the guilt."

*(*KURT *leans on piano, head in hand.)*

FANNY. "Yes, we are liable in the conscience-balance for the tailor in Lodz, the black man in our South, the peasant in—" *(Turns to* TECK. *Unpleasantly.)* Your country, I think.

*(*TECK *crosses* D. *a step, smiling at* FANNY.)*

ANISE *(rises).* Come. Baths for everybody. *(To* BODO.*)* Gather the wires. You have wrecked my cure.

*(*KURT *turns on stool to window.)*

BODO. If you allow me a few minutes more—

ANISE *(crosses to door* R., *stands above it).* Come along. I have been duped for long enough. Come, Joshua. Babette. Baths.

JOSHUA *(he takes book with him. Rises, crosses front to door, exits up stairs. Starts out after* ANISE. BABETTE *begins to gather up her sewing).* My tub is a thing of glory. But I do not like it so prepared for me and so announced by Miss Anise. *(He exits. As he passes* BABETTE *rises, crosses* L. *and* U. *to chair* U. R. C., *leaves sewing material there.)*

BODO *(who has gathered his tools and heating pad, standing above table* R. *To* ANISE*).* You are angry about this. I do not blame you with my heart or my head. I admit I have failed. But Papa will repair it, Anise. Will you not, Papa? *(*TECK *crosses to* BODO.*)* In a few minutes—

TECK *(to* BODO*).* Your father is an expert electrician?

BODO. Oh, yes, sir.

TECK. And as good with radio—

*(*BODO *begins to nod.)*

KURT *(rises. Sharply).* Count de Brancovis, make your questions to me, please. Not to my children.

*(*OTHERS *look up, surprised.)*

TECK *(pleasantly, crosses front to* L. *in front of fireplace and sits in armchair).* Very well, Mr. Muller.

ANISE *(as she exits with* BODO*).* Nobody can fix it. You have made a pudding of it.

BODO *(as he follows her).* Do not worry. In five minutes tonight you will have a pad far better— *(As* BODO *reaches door, he bumps into* MARTHE *who is carrying a large dress box.)* Oh. Your pardon. Oh, hello. *(He disappears.)*

MARTHE *(gaily).* Hello. *(To* FANNY.*)* I waited for them. I was afraid they wouldn't deliver this late in the day. *(To* SARA.*)* Come on, Sara. I can't wait to see them.

SARA. What?

MARTHE *(standing just on* R.*).* Dresses. From Fanny. A tan linen, and a dark green with wonderful buttons, a white *net* for Babbie, (BABETTE *crosses to back of* R. *end of sofa* R.*)* and a suit for you, and play dresses for Babbie, and a dinner dress in gray to wear for Babbie's birthday—gray should be good for you, Sara— *(*SARA *rises.)* all from Savitt's. We sneaked the measurements, Anise and I—

SARA *(crosses to above table* C. *to* FANNY*).* How nice of you, Mama. How very kind of you. And of you, Marthe, to take so much trouble— *(*KURT *comes to* R. *end of piano.* SARA *goes toward* FANNY. *She leans down, kisses* FANNY.*)* You're a sweet woman, Mama.

DAVID *(crosses to* MARTHE*).* That's the first time Mama's heard that word. *(He takes boxes from* MARTHE, *puts them on table near door.* MARTHE *smiles at him and touches his hand as* TECK *watches them.)*

FANNY (*as* DAVID *is crossing*). I have a bottom sweetness, if you understand what I mean.

DAVID. I've been too close to the bottom to see it.

FANNY. That should be witty. I don't know why it isn't.

(BABETTE *comes over to stare at boxes.* DAVID *opens boxes and lets* BABETTE *peek during next speeches.*)

SARA (*to* FANNY). From Savitt's. Extravagant of you. They had such lovely clothes. I remember my coming out dress. (*She goes to* KURT.) Do you remember the black suit, with the braid, the first day we met? Well, that was from Savitt's. (*She is close to him.*) Me, in an evening dress. Now, you'll have to take me into Washington. I want to show off. (*She caresses his shoulder not looking at him. He looks to* TECK.) Next week, and we'll dance, maybe— (*Sees he is not looking at her.*) What's the matter, darling? (*No answer. Slowly he turns to look at her.*) What's the matter, Kurt? Is it bad for me to talk like this? What have I done? It isn't that dresses have ever mattered to me, it's just that—

KURT. Of course they have mattered to you. As they should. I do not think of the dress. (*Draws her to him.*) How many years have I loved that face?

SARA (*her face is very happy*). So?

KURT. So. (*He leans down, kisses her, as if it were important.*)

SARA (*pleased, unembarrassed*). There are other people here.

MARTHE (*slowly*). And good for us to see.

TECK. Nostalgia?

MARTHE. No. Nostalgia is for something you have known.

(FANNY *coughs.*)

BABETTE (*comes to* FANNY). Grandma—it is allowed to look at my dresses?

FANNY. Of course, child. Run along.

BABETTE (*picks up the boxes.* DAVID *helps her.* SARA *crosses to* L. *of chair* U. C. *She goes to* R. *end of sofa* R.). I love dresses. I have a great fondness for materials and colors. Thank you, Grandma. (*She runs out of the room.*)

(JOSEPH *appears in the door* L.)

JOSEPH. There's a long distance operator with a long distance call for Mr. Muller. She wants to talk with him on the long distance phone.

KURT (*as he goes* L.). Excuse me, please.

(KURT *crosses* L. *quickly.* SARA *turns sharply to look at him.* TECK *looks up.* KURT *goes quickly out.* TECK *watches him go.* SARA *stands staring after him.*)

MARTHE (*laughs. As* KURT *passes sofa* L.). I feel the same way as Babbie. Come on, Sara. Let's try them on.

(SARA *does not turn.*)

TECK. You also have a new dress?

MARTHE (*looks at him*). Yes. Fanny was kind to me, too.

TECK (*takes two steps away from fireplace*). You are a very generous woman, Madame Fanny. Did you also give her a sapphire bracelet from Barstow's?

(MARTHE *crosses* D. *to chair* D. R.)

FANNY. I beg your—

DAVID (*slowly*). No. I gave Marthe the bracelet. And I understand that it is not any business of yours.

(FANNY *rises.* SARA *turns.*)

FANNY. Really, David—

DAVID. Be still, Mama.

TECK (*rises, crosses to* L. C. *After a second*). Did you tell him that, Marthe?

MARTHE. Yes.

TECK (*looks up at her*). I shall not forgive you for that. (*Looks at* DAVID.) It is a statement which no man likes to hear from another man. You understand that? (*Playfully.*) That is the sort of thing about which we used to play at duels in Europe.

(SARA *crosses* U. *to behind piano keyboard.*)

DAVID (*comes toward him*). We are not so musical comedy here. (*Crosses* U. *to behind sofa table* R.) And you are not in Europe.

TECK *(crosses* U C.*)*. Even if I were, I would not suggest any such action. I would have reasons for not wishing it.

DAVID *(crosses to behind chair* C.*)*. It would be well for you not to suggest *any* action. And the reason for *that* is, you might get hurt.

TECK *(slowly)*. That would not be my reason. *(Turns to* MARTHE—*crosses* D. R. *to her—stops and speaks.)* Your affair has gone far enough—

MARTHE *(sharply)*. It is not an affair—

*(*FANNY *crosses* L. *to front of* L. *end of sofa* L.*)*

TECK. I do not care what it is. The time has come to leave here. Go upstairs and pack your things. *(She stands where she is.* DAVID *crosses to below table* L. C.*)* Go on, Marthe.

MARTHE *(crosses* L. *to sofa table* R.*;  to* DAVID. TECK *does not turn)*. I am not going with him. I told you that.

DAVID. I don't want you to go with him.

FANNY *(carefully)*. Really, David, aren't you interfering in this a good deal—

DAVID *(looks to* FANNY. *Carefully)*. Yes, Mama. I am.

TECK *(turns to* MARTHE*)*. When you are speaking to me, please say what you have to say to me.

MARTHE *(comes to him, stands in front of the table)*. You are trying to frighten me. But you are not going to frighten me any more. *(Crosses* D. R. *to* TECK.*)* I will say it to you: I am not going with you. I am never going with you again.

TECK *(softly)*. If you do not fully mean what you say, or if you might change your mind, you are talking unwisely, Marthe.

MARTHE. I know that.

TECK. Shall we talk about it alone?

MARTHE. You can't make me go, can you, Teck?

TECK. No, I can't make you.

MARTHE. Then there's no sense talking about it.

TECK. Are you in love with him?

MARTHE. Yes.

FANNY *(sharply, taking steps* R.*)*. Marthe! What is all this?

MARTHE *(sharply)*. I'll tell *you* about it in a minute.

DAVID *(crosses to* D. C. *chair)*. You don't have to explain anything to anybody.

TECK *(ignores him)*. Is he in love with with you?

MARTHE. I don't think so. You won't believe it, because you can't believe anything that hasn't got tricks to it, but David hasn't much to do with this. I told you I would *(*DAVID *turns up and crosses to above chair* U. C., *turns back and watches scene* R.*)* leave some day, and I remember where I said it— *(Slowly.)* and why I said it.

TECK. I also remember. But I did not believe you, Marthe. I have not had much to offer you these last few years, but if we now had a little money and could go back . . .

MARTHE. No. I don't like you, Teck. I never have.

TECK. And I have always known it.

FANNY *(stiffly)*. I think your lack of affection should be discussed with more privacy.

*(*DAVID *turns sharply to* FANNY.*)*

DAVID. Mama!

*(*FANNY *crosses to sofa* L. *and sits.)*

MARTHE *(turning to* FANNY*)*. There's nothing to discuss. *(Turns to* TECK. FANNY *moves to* L. *ends of sofa* L.*)* Strange. I've talked to myself about this scene for almost fifteen years. I knew a lot of things to say to you, and I used to lie awake at night, or walk along the street and say them. Now I don't want to. I guess you only want to talk that way when you're not sure what you can do. When you're sure, then what's the sense of saying it? "This is why and this is why and this—" *(Very happily.)* But when you know you can do it, you don't have to say anything: you can just go. And I am going. There's nothing you can do. I would like you to believe that now.

TECK. Very well, Marthe. I think I made a mistake. I should not have brought you here. I believe you now. *(He moves up to decanter table.)*

MARTHE *(after a pause, she looks to* DAVID. *Crosses to* C*.).* I'll move into—Washington, and—

DAVID *(comes down to meet her* C. SARA *follows close behind* DAVID *on his* L*.).* Yes. Later, but I'd like you to stay here for a while with us, if you don't mind.

SARA. It would be better for you, Marthe—

FANNY. It's very interesting that I am not being consulted about this. *(To* MARTHE, *as she goes to stand in front of sofa* L*.)* I have nothing against you, Marthe. I am sorry for you, but I don't think— *(*FANNY *sits* L. *end of sofa* L*.)*

MARTHE. Thank you, Sara, David. But I'd rather move in now. *(Comes toward* FANNY*.)* But, perhaps, I have something against you. Do you remember my wedding?

FANNY. Yes.

MARTHE *(sits* R. *of* FANNY*).* Do you remember how pleased Mama was with herself? Brilliant Mama, handsome Mama— *(*FANNY *rises, steps* L*.)*—everybody thought so, didn't they? A seventeen year old daughter marrying a pretty good title, about to secure herself in a world that Mama liked.—She didn't ask me what I liked. And the one time I tried to tell her, she frightened me. *(Looks up.)* Maybe I've always been frightened. All my life.

TECK. Of course.

MARTHE *(to* FANNY, *as if she had not heard* TECK*).* I remember Mama's face at the wedding—it was *her* wedding, really, not mine.

FANNY *(sharply).* You are very hard on your mother.

MARTHE. 1925. No, I'm not hard on her. I only tell the truth. She wanted a life for me, I suppose. It just wasn't the life I wanted for myself. *(Rises—sharply facing* FANNY.*)* And that's what you tried to do. With your children. In another way. Only Sara got away. And that made you angry—until so many years went by that you forgot.

FANNY. I don't usually mind people saying anything they think, but I find that—

MARTHE. I don't care what you mind or don't mind. I'm in love with your son—

*(*TECK *turns head away* R*.)*

FANNY *(very sharply).* That's unfortunate—

MARTHE. And I'm sick of watching you try to make him into his father. I don't think you even know you do it any more, and I don't think he knows it any more, either. And that's what's most dangerous about it.

*(*TECK *turns back to scene.)*

FANNY *(steps* D. L. *Very angrily).* I don't know what you are talking about.

DAVID. I think you do. *(Smiles.)* You shouldn't mind hearing the truth—and neither should I. *(Turns* R. *and crosses up to* U. C. *chair.)*

FANNY *(worried, sharply. Crosses below* MARTHE *to* DAVID*).* David! What does all this nonsense mean? I—

*(*TECK *crosses* D. R. *to above chair* D. R*.)*

MARTHE *(to* FANNY*).* Look. That pretty world Mama got me into was a tough world, see? I'm used to trouble. So don't try to interfere with me, because I won't let you. *(She goes to* DAVID*.)* Let's just have a good time. *(He leans down, takes both her hands, kisses them. Then slowly she turns away, starts to exit, crosses to* TECK*.)* You will also be going today?

TECK. Yes.

MARTHE. Then let us make sure we go in different directions, and do not meet again. Good-bye, Teck.

TECK. Good-bye, Marthe. You will not believe me, but I tried my best, and I am now most sorry to lose you.

MARTHE. Yes. I believe you. *(She moves out.)*

*(Silence for a moment.)*

FANNY *(crosses to* C. *and sits in chair* D. R. C*.).* Well, a great many things have been said in the last few minutes.

DAVID *(crosses to bell cor* l. *To* TECK*).* I will get Joseph to pack for you.

TECK. Do not bother. I will ring for him when I am ready. (*KURT comes in from the study door. SARA turns, stares at him, crosses to back of chair U. C. He does not look at her.*) It will not take me very long. (*Looking at KURT.*)

(*KURT crosses to below R. end of sofa L.*)

SARA (*crosses to C.*). What is it, Kurt?

KURT. It is nothing of importance, darling— (*He looks quickly at TECK.*)

SARA (*crosses to KURT*). Don't tell me it's nothing. I know the way you look when—

KURT (*sharply*). I said it was of no importance. I must get to California for a few weeks. That is all.

SARA. I—

TECK (*turns, crosses up to get newspaper from secretary*). It is in the afternoon paper, Herr Muller. (*Points to paper.*) I was waiting to find the proper moment to call it to your attention. (*He moves toward table behind sofa R., as they all turn to watch him. He begins to read.*) "Zurich, Switzerland: The Zurich papers today reprinted a despatch from the Berliner Tageblatt—on the capture of Colonel Max Freidank. Freidank is said (*Small sharp sound from SARA. SARA moves to KURT.*) to be the chief of the Anti-Nazi Underground Movement. Colonel Freidank has long been an almost legendary figure. The son of the famous General Freidank, he was a World War officer, and a distinguished physicist before the advent of Hitler." (*Throws paper on desk behind sofa R.*) That is all—

SARA (*crying it out*). Max—

KURT. Be still, Sara.

TECK (*crosses above desk to L. end of it*). They told me of it at the Embassy last night. They also told me that with him they had taken a man who called himself Ebber, and a man who called himself Triste. They could not find a man called Gotter. (*He starts again toward the door, moving R. slowly, above desk.*) I shall be a lonely man without Marthe. I am also a very poor one. I should like to have ten thousand dollars before I go.

DAVID (*taking step toward TECK. Carefully*). You will make no loans in this house.

TECK (*at R. of table D. R. Turns to DAVID*). I was not speaking of a loan.

FANNY (*carefully*). God made you not only a scoundrel but a fool. That is a dangerous combination.

DAVID (*suddenly starts toward TECK*). Damn you . . . (*Crosses toward TECK.*)

KURT. Leave him alone. (*Tries to intercept DAVID.*) David! Leave him alone!

DAVID (*pushing past KURT. Angrily to KURT*). Keep out of it. (*Starts toward TECK again.*) I'm beginning to see what Marthe meant. Blackmailing with your wife— You—

KURT (*very sharply*). He is not speaking of his wife. (*DAVID turns to KURT.*) O you. He means me. (*Looks at TECK.*) Is that correct?

(*SARA moves toward KURT. DAVID draws back, bewildered. FANNY comes toward them, staring at TECK.*)

TECK. Good. (*Crosses above DAVID to R. end of sofa R.*) It was necessary for me to hear you say it. You understand that?

KURT. I understand it.

SARA (*crosses to L. of KURT. Frightened, softly*). Kurt—

DAVID. What is all this about? What the hell are you talking about?

TECK (*sharply for the first time*). Be still. (*DAVID starts for TECK, restrains himself—crosses up to L. end of table U. R. To KURT, looks down at him.*) At your convenience. Your hands are shaking, Mr. Muller.

KURT (*quietly*). My hands were broken: they are bad when I have fear.

(*SARA crosses slowly to front of L. end of sofa L.*)

TECK. I am sorry. I can understand that. It is not pleasant. (*Motions toward FANNY and DAVID.*) Perhaps you would like a little time to—I will go and pack, and be ready to leave. We will all find that more comfortable, I think. You should get yourself a smaller gun, Herr Muller. That pistol you have been carrying is big, and awkward. (*Crosses R. toward door R.*)

KURT. You saw the pistol when you examined my briefcase?

TECK (*smiles, turns back to* KURT). You know that?

KURT. Oh, yes. Because I have the careful eye, through many years of needing it. And then you have not the careful eye. The pistol was lying to the left of a paper package, and when you leave, it is to the right of the package.

SARA (*steps toward* KURT). Kurt! Do you mean that—

KURT (*sharply*). Please, darling, do not do that.

TECK (*puts his hand on* KURT's *hip pocket, pats it*). It is a German Army Luger?

KURT. Yes.

TECK. Keep it in your pocket, Herr Muller. You will have no need to use it. And, in any case, I am not afraid of it. You understand that?

KURT (*slowly, crosses to* TECK). Yes, I understand that you are not a man of fears. That is strange to me, because I am a man who has so many fears.

TECK (*laughs, as he exits*). Are you? That is most interesting. (*He exits* R.)

DAVID (*softly. Crosses* D. *to* L. *of* KURT). What is this about, Kurt?

KURT. He knows who I am and what I do, and what I carry with me. (KURT *crosses* U. *and* L. *to behind table back of sofa* R.)

SARA (*carefully—steps* U. C.). What about Max?

KURT (*crosses to her, speaks when there*). The telephone was from Mexico. Ilse received a cable. Early on the morning of Monday they caught Ebber and Triste; an hour after, they took Max, in Berlin. (*She looks up at him, begins to shake her head. He presses her arm.*) Yes. It is hard. (KURT *turns away from her.*)

FANNY (*softly*). You said he knew who you were and what you carried with you. I don't understand.

(SARA *crosses to behind piano keyboard.*)

KURT (*crosses to* L. *of* FANNY). I am going to tell you: I am a German outlaw. I have been working with many others in an illegal organization. I have so worked for seven years. I am on what is called the Desired List. But I did not know I was worth ten thousand dollars. My price has risen.

DAVID (*slowly*). And what do you carry with you?

KURT. Twenty-three thousand dollars. It has been gathered from the pennies and the nickels of the poor who do not like Fascism, and who believe in the work we do. (*Crosses slowly to below* L. *end of sofa* L.) I came here to bring Sara home, and to get the money. I had hopes to rest here for a while, and then—

SARA (*slowly*). And I had hopes someone else would take it back, and you would stay with us— (*Shakes her head, then.*) Max is not dead?

KURT. No. The left side of his face is dead. (*Crosses* D. L. *Softly.*) It was a good face.

SARA (*to* FANNY *and* DAVID, *as if she were going to cry*). It was a very good face. He and Kurt— (*A small move to* C.) In the old days . . . (*To* KURT.) After so many years. (*Steps toward* KURT.) If Max got caught, then nobody has a chance. Nobody. (*She suddenly turns and goes to sit* R. *end of sofa* L.)

DAVID (*steps* L. *toward* KURT). He wants to sell what he knows to you? Is that right?

KURT. Yes.

FANNY. Wasn't it careless of you to leave twenty-three thousand dollars lying around to be seen?

KURT. No, it was not careless of me. It is in a locked briefcase. I have thus carried money for many years. There seemed no safer place than Sara's home. It was careless of you to have in your house a man who opens baggage and blackmails.

DAVID (*sharply*). Yes. It was very careless.

FANNY. But you said you knew he'd seen it—

KURT. The first day we arrived. What was I to do about it? He is not a man who steals. This is a safer method. I knew it would come some other way. I have been waiting to see what the way would be That is all I could do.

DAVID *(to* FANNY*).* What's the difference? It's been done. *(To* KURT.*)* If he wants to sell to you, he must have another buyer. Who?

KURT. The Embassy. Von Seitz, I think.

DAVID. You mean he has told Von Seitz about you and—

KURT. No. I do not think he has told him anything. As yet. It would be foolish of him. He has probably only asked most guarded questions.

DAVID. But you're here. You're in this country. They can't do anything to you. They wouldn't be crazy enough to try it. Is your passport all right?

KURT. Not quite.

FANNY. Why not? Why isn't it?

KURT *(crosses to* U. C. *Wearily, as if he were bored).* Because people like me are not given visas with such ease. And I was in a hurry to bring my wife and my children to safety. *(Turns—comes to* L. *of* FANNY. *Sharply.)* Madame Fanny, you must come to understand it is no longer the world you once knew.

DAVID. It doesn't matter. You're a political refugee. We don't turn back people like you. People who are in danger. You will give me your passport and tomorrow morning I'll *(Turns, crosses* R. *to* R. *of* R. *end of sofa* R.*)* see Barens. We'll tell him the truth— *(Points to door.)* Tell de Brancovis to go to hell. There's not a damn thing he or anybody else can do.

SARA *(looks up at* KURT, *who is staring at her).* You don't understand, David.

DAVID. There's a great deal I don't understand. But there's nothing to worry about.

SARA *(*KURT *crosses to* SARA. *Still looking at* KURT*).* Not much to worry about as long as Kurt is in this house. But he's not going to—

KURT. The Count has made the guess that—

SARA. That you will go back to get Ebber and Triste and Max out? Is that right, Kurt? Is that right?

KURT. Yes, darling, I must try. They were taken to Sonnenburg. Guards can be bribed. It has been done once before at Sonnenburg. We will try for it again. I must get back, Sara. I must start.

SARA *(she gets up, comes to him. He holds her, puts his face in her hair. She stands holding him, trying to speak without crying).* Of course you must go back. I guess I was trying to think it wouldn't come. But— *(To* FANNY *and* DAVID.*)* Kurt's got to go back. He's got to go home. He's got to try to buy them out. He'll do it, too. You'll see. *(She stops, breathes.)* It's hard enough to get back. Very hard. *(Rises.)* But if they knew he was coming— They want Kurt bad. Almost as much as they wanted Max— And then there are hundreds of others, too— *(Crosses quickly to* KURT. *She puts her face down on his head.)* Don't be scared, darling. You'll get back. You'll see. You've done it before —you'll do it again. Don't be scared. You'll get Max out all right. *(Gasps.)* And then you'll do his work, won't you? That's good. That's fine. You'll do a good job, the way you've always done. *(She holds his shoulder hard with her* L. *arm. She is crying very hard. To* FANNY.*)* Kurt doesn't feel well. He was wounded and he gets tired. *(To* KURT.*)* You don't feel well, do you? *(Slowly, she is crying too hard now to be heard clearly.)* Don't be scared, darling. You'll get home. Don't worry, you'll get home. Yes, you will. *(She is holding his head close to her as the)*

CURTAIN FALLS

# ACT THREE

SCENE: *The same. A half hour later.*

AT RISE: FANNY *is pacing from* L. *to* R. KURT *is at piano, his head resting on one hand. He is playing softly with the other.* SARA *is sitting very quietly on the* R. *end of couch* R. DAVID *is pacing on the terrace.* FANNY *crosses from* L. *to entry hall, back to* C., *then up to terrace door.*

FANNY (*to* DAVID, *on the terrace*). David, would you stop that pacing, please? (*To* KURT.) And would you stop that one-hand piano playing? Either play, or get up.

(KURT *gets up, crosses to* L. *of* SARA, *sits.* SARA *looks at him, gets up, crosses to the decanters, begins to make a drink.* FANNY *crosses to* R. *end of piano keyboard, leans on piano.*)

SARA (*to* DAVID). A drink?

DAVID (*comes in, closes door*). What? Please. (*To* KURT. DAVID *crosses to back of chair* R. C., *leans on it.*) Do you intend to buy your friends out of jail?

KURT. I intend to try.

FANNY (*crosses* D. *to* D. L. C.). It's all very strange to me. I thought things were so well run that bribery and—

KURT (*smiles*). What a magnificent work Fascists have done in convincing the world that they are men from legends.

DAVID. They have done very well for themselves—unfortunately.

KURT. But not by themselves. Does it not make us all uncomfortable to remember that they came in on the shoulders of the most powerful men in the world? Of course. And so we would prefer to believe they are men from the planets. They are not. Let me reassure you. They are smart, they are sick, and they are cruel. But given men who know what they fight for— (*Shrugs.*) You saw it in Spain. (FANNY *moves* L., *stops when he speaks. Laughs.*) I will console you: a year ago last month, at three o'clock in the morning, Freidank and I, with two elderly pistols, raided the home of the Gestapo chief in Konstanz, got what we wanted and the following morning Freidank was eating his breakfast three blocks away, and I was over the Swiss border.

FANNY (*slowly*). You are brave men.

KURT. I do not tell you the story to prove we are remarkable, but to prove they are not.

(SARA *is behind sofa* R. SARA *brings him a drink. Gives one to* DAVID. FANNY *crosses to sofa* L. *and sits* R. *end.* DAVID *crosses* L. *to* R. *of mail table* U. L. C.)

SARA (*softly, touching* KURT's *shoulder*). Kurt loves Max. I've always been a little jealous.

KURT (*puts his hand on hers*). Always, since I came here, I have a dream: that he will walk in this room some day. How he would like it here, eh, Sara? (*To* FANNY.) He loves good food and wine, and you have books— (*Laughs happily.*) He is fifty-nine years of age. And when he was fifty-seven he carried me on his back seven miles across the border. I had been hurt— That takes a man, does it not?

FANNY (*to* KURT). You look like a sick man to me.

KURT. No. I am only tired. I do not like to wait. It will go.

SARA (*sharply*). Oh, it's more than that. (*Crosses* R. *end of sofa* R.) This is one of the times you wonder why everything has to go against you. Even a holiday, the first in years—

KURT. Waiting. It is waiting that is bad.

DAVID. Damn him, he's doing it deliberately.

KURT. It is then the corruption begins. Once in Spain I waited for two days until the planes would exhaust themselves. I think then why must our side fight always with naked hands? The spirit and the hands. All is against us but ourselves. Sometimes, it was as if you must put up your hands and tear the wings from the planes—and then it is bad.

SARA (*to* D. R. *end of sofa* R.). You will not think that when the time comes. It will go.

KURT. Of a certainty.

FANNY. But does it have to go on being your hands?

KURT. For each man, his own hands. (*Looks at his hands*). He has to sleep with them.

DAVID (*uncomfortably, as if he did not like to say it*). That's right. I guess it's the way all of us should feel. But— (DAVID *steps* R. *to* C.) but you have a family. Isn't there somebody else who hasn't a wife and children—?

KURT. Each could have his own excuse. Some love for the first time, some have bullet holes, some have fear of the camps, some are sick, many are getting older. (*Shrugs.*) Each could find a reason. And many find it. My children are not the only children in the world, even to me.

FANNY. That's noble of you, of course. But they are your children, nevertheless. And Sara, she—

SARA (*softly*). Mama—

KURT (*after a slight pause.* SARA *crosses* U. *and* L. *to behind* C. *of desk behind sofa* R.). One means always in English to insult with that word noble?

FANNY. Of course not, I—

KURT. It is not noble. It is the way I must live. Good or bad, it is what I am. (*Turns deliberately to look at* FANNY.) And what I am is not what you wanted for your daughter, twenty years ago or now.

FANNY. You are misunderstanding me.

KURT. For our girl, too, we want a safe and happy life. And it is thus I try to make it for her. We each have our way. I do not convert you to mine.

DAVID (*crosses to back of chair* R. C.). You are very certain of your way.

KURT (*smiles*). I seem so to you? Good.

(JOSEPH *appears in hall doorway. He is carrying valises, overcoats, and two small bags.*)

JOSEPH (*to above table* D. R.). What'll I do with these. Miss Fanny?

(SARA *crosses to decanter table.*)

FANNY. They're too large for eating, aren't they? What were you thinking of doing with them?

JOSEPH. I mean, it's Fred's day off.

DAVID. All right. You drive him into town. (*Crosses to* L. *end of desk behind sofa* R., *puts down glass.*)

JOSEPH. Then who's going to serve at dinner?

FANNY (*impatiently*). Belle will do it alone tonight.

JOSEPH (*crosses toward* FANNY, *stops* R. *of sofa* L.). No, she can't. Belle's upstairs packing with Miss Marthe. My, there's quite a lot of departing, ain't there?

(DAVID *crosses up to* U. L. C.)

FANNY (*very impatiently*). All right, then cook can bring in dinner.

JOSEPH. I wouldn't ask her to do that, if I were you. She's mighty mad: the sink pipe is leaking. You just better wait for dinner 'til I get back from Washington.

(*Crosses* FANNY *to* L. *end of sofa.*)

FANNY (*shouting*). We are not cripples and we were eating dinner in this house before you arrived to show us how to use the knife and fork. (JOSEPH *smiles.*) Go on. Put his things in the car. I'll ring for you when he's ready.

JOSEPH. You told me the next time you screamed to remind you to ask my pardon.

FANNY. You call that screaming?

JOSEPH. Yes'm.

FANNY. All right. I ask your pardon. Oh, go on. Go on.

JOSEPH. Yes'm. (*Exit* L., *closing door.*)

(TECK *appears in door. He is carrying his hat and the briefcase we have seen in Act I.* SARA, *seeing briefcase, looks startled, looks quickly at* KURT. KURT *watches* TECK *as he comes toward him.* TECK *throws his hat on a chair, comes to table at which* KURT *is sitting, puts briefcase on table.* KURT *puts out his hand, puts it on briefcase, leaves it there.*)

TECK (*crosses to* R. *of* KURT, *to put briefcase on table* D. *of* KURT. KURT *reaches for case and holds it on table. Smiles at gesture.)* Nothing has been touched, Mr. Muller. I brought it from your room, for your convenience.

FANNY *(angrily)*. Why didn't you steal it? Since you don't seem to—

TECK *(crosses to c.)* That would have been very foolish of me, Madame Fanny.

KURT. Very.

TECK *(turns to KURT)*. I hope I have not kept you waiting too long. I wanted to give you an opportunity to make any explanations—

DAVID *(crosses to L. of TECK. Angrily)*. Does your price include listening to this tony conversation?

TECK *(turns to look at him)*. My price will rise if I have to spend the next few minutes being interrupted by your temper. I will do my business with Mr. Muller. And you will understand I will take from you no interruptions, no exclamations, no lectures, no opinions of what I am or what I am doing.

KURT *(quietly)*. You will not be interrupted.

TECK *(sits down at table with KURT)*. I have been curious about you, Mr. Muller. Even before you came here. Because Fanny and David either knew very little about you, which was strange, or would not talk very much about you, which was just as strange. Have you ever had come to you one of those insistent half-memories of some person or some place?

*(SARA slowly moves to sit R. end of sofa R.)*

KURT *(quietly, without looking up)*. You had such a half-memory of me?

TECK *(DAVID crosses to chair U. L. C., turns and listens to TECK)*. Not even a memory, but something. The curiosity of one European for another, perhaps.

KURT. A most sharp curiosity. You lost no time examining— *(Pats case.)* this. You are an expert with locks?

TECK. No, indeed. Only when I wish to be.

FANNY *(rises. Angrily to TECK)*. I would like you out of this house as quickly as—

TECK *(turns to her)*. Madame Fanny, I just asked Mr. David not to do that. I must now ask you. *(Leans forward to KURT.)* Herr Muller, I got the Desired List from Von Seitz without, of course, revealing anything to him. As you probably know it is quite easy for anybody to get. I simply told him that we refugees move in small circles and I might come across somebody on it. If, however, I have to listen to any more of this from any of you, I shall go immediately to him.

KURT *(to DAVID and FANNY)*. Please allow the Count to do this in his own way. It will be best.

*(FANNY sits again.)*

TECK *(takes sheet of paper from pocket)*. There are sixty-three names on this list. I read them carefully, I narrow the possibilities and under "G" I find Gotter. *(Begins to read.)* "Age: forty to forty-five. About six feet. One hundred seventy pounds. Birthplace unknown to us. Original occupation unknown to us, although he seems to know Munich and Dresden. Schooling unknown to us. Family unknown to us. No known political connections. No known trade union connections. Many descriptions; few of them in agreement, and none of them of great reliability. Equally unreliable, though often asked for, were Paris, Copenhagen, Brussels police descriptions. Only points on which there is agreement: married to a foreign woman, *(SARA's hand grasps KURT's.)* either American or English; three children; has used name of Gotter, Thomas Bodmer, Karl Francis. Thought to have left Germany in 1933, and to have joined Max Freidank shortly after. Worked closely with Freidank, perhaps directly under his orders. Known to have crossed border in 1934—February, May, June, October." *(SARA begins to rise from table. KURT puts his hand over hers. She sits down again.)* "Known to have again crossed border with Max Freidank in 1935 —August, twice in October, November, January—"

KURT *(smiles)*. The report is unreliable. It would have been impossible for God to have crossed the border that often.

TECK *(looks up. Then looks back at list)*. Yes? "In 1934, outlaw radio station, announcing itself as Radio European, begins to be heard. Station was located in Dusseldorf; the house of a restaurant waiter was searched, and nothing was found. Radio heard during most of 1934 and 1935. In an attempt to locate it, two probable Communists killed in the toolhouse of a farm near Bonn. In three of the broadcasts, Gotter known to have crossed border immediately before and after. Radio again became active in early part of 1936. Active attempt made to locate Freidank. Gotter believed to have then appeared in Spain with Madrid Government army, in one of the German brigades, and to be a brigade commander under previously used name of Bodmer. Known to have stayed in France the first months of 1938. Again crossed German border some time during week when Hitler's Hamburg radio speech interrupted and went off the air." *(Looks up.)* That was a daring deed, Herr Muller. It caused a great scandal. I remember. It amused me.

KURT. It was not done for that reason.

TECK. No? "Early in 1939, informer in Konstanz reported Gotter's entry, carrying money which had been exchanged in Paris and Brussels. Following day, Konstanz Gestapo raided for spy list by two men—" *(*KURT *turns to look at* FANNY *and* DAVID, *smiles.)* My God, Mr. Muller, that job took two good men.

SARA *(angrily)*. Even you admire them.

TECK. Even I. Now, I conclude, a week ago, that you are Gotter, Karl Francis—

KURT. Please. Do not describe me to myself again.

TECK. And that you will be traveling home *(Points to briefcase.)*—with this. But you seem in no hurry, and so I must wait. Last night when I hear that Freidank has been taken, I guess that you will now be leaving. Not for California. I will tell you, free of charge, Herr Muller, that they have got no information from Freidank or the others.

KURT. Thank you. But I was sure they would not. I know all three most well. They will take—what will be given them.

TECK *(looks down. Softly)*. There is a deep sickness in the German character, Herr Muller. A pain-love, a death-love—

DAVID *(very angrily)*. Oh, for God's sake, spare us your moral judgments.

FANNY *(very sharply)*. Yes. They are sickening. Get on!

KURT. Fanny and David are Americans and they do not understand our world —as yet. *(Turns to* DAVID *and* FANNY.*)* All Fascists are not of one mind, one stripe. There are those who give the orders, those who carry out the orders, those who watch the orders being carried out. Then there are those who are half in, half hoping to come in. They are made to do the dishes and clean the boots. Frequently, they come in high places and wish now only to survive. They came late; some because they did not jump in time, some because they were stupid, some because they were shocked at the crudity of the German evil, and preferred their own evils, and some because they were fastidious men. For those last, we may well some day have pity. They are lost men, their spoils are small, their day is gone. *(To* TECK.*)* Yes?

TECK *(slowly)*. Yes. *(*DAVID *moves to front of chair* U. L. C.*)* You have the understanding heart. It will get in your way some day.

KURT *(smiles)*. I will watch it.

*(*DAVID *sits in chair* U. L. C.*)*

TECK. We are both men in trouble, Herr Muller. The world, ungratefully, seems to like your kind even less than it does mine. *(Leans forward.)* Now. Let us do business. You will not get back if Von Seitz knows you are going.

KURT. You are wrong. Instead of crawling a hundred feet an hour in deep night, I will walk across the border with as little trouble as if I were a boy again on a summer walking trip. There are many men they would like to have. I would be allowed to walk directly to them, if I were so big a fool, or if I found it necessary— until they had all the names, and all the addresses— *(*FANNY *rises.)* Roumanians* would pick me up ahead of time. *Germans* would not.

TECK *(smiles)*. Still the national pride?

KURT. Why not? For that which is good.

FANNY *(comes over, very angrily, to* TECK*).* I have not often in my life felt what I feel now. Whatever you are, and however you became it, the picture of a man selling the lives of other men—

TECK. Is very ugly, Madame Fanny. I do not do it without some shame, and I must therefore sink my shame in large money. *(*FANNY *slaps him with her handkerchief.* TECK *rises.* DAVID *rises.* FANNY *crosses to mail table and drops handkerchief on it.* TECK *turns to* KURT. *Violently, pointing to briefcase.)* The money is here. *(*TECK *sits.)* For ten thousand dollars you go back to save your friends; nobody will know that you are gone. *(Slowly, deliberately,* KURT *begins to shake his head.* TECK *waits, then carefully.)* What?

KURT. This money is going home with me. It was not given to me to save my life, and I shall not so use it. It is to save the lives and further the work of more than I. It is important to me to carry on that work: it is important to me to save the lives of three valuable men, and to do that with all possible speed. And, *(Sharply.)* Count de Brancovis, the first morning we arrived in this house my children wanted their breakfast with great haste. That is because the evening before we had been able only to buy milk and buns for them. If I would not touch this money for them, I would not touch it for you. *(Very sharply.)* It goes back with me. The way it is. And if it does not get back, it is because I will not get back.

*(There is a long pause.)*

TECK. Then I do not think you will get back, Herr Muller. You are a brave one, but you will not get back.

KURT *(as if he were very tired).* I will send to you a postal card, and tell you about my bravery.

DAVID *(coming toward* KURT*).* Is it true that if this swine talks you and the others will be—

SARA *(very softly).* Caught and killed. Of course. If they're lucky enough to get killed quickly. *(Quietly, points to the table.)* You should have seen those hands in 1935. *(Turns* R. *and rises. Crosses to* R. *end of sofa* R., *facing upstage.)*

FANNY *(violently, to* DAVID*).* We'll give him the money. For God's sake, let's give it to him and get him out of here.

DAVID *(crosses to* SARA*).* Do you want him to go back?

SARA. Yes. *(*KURT *looks up to her.)* I do.

DAVID. All right. *(Goes to her, arm around her.)* You're a good girl, Sara.

KURT. That is true. Brave and good, my Sara. She is everything. Handsome and gay and— *(Puts his hand over his eyes.)*

*(*SARA *turns away.)*

DAVID *(around desk to* L. *of* TECK. *After a second, comes to stand near* TECK*).* If we give you the money, what is to keep you from selling to Von Seitz?

TECK. I do not like your thinking I would do that. But—

DAVID *(tensely).* Look here. I'm sick of what you'd like or wouldn't like. And I'm sick of your talk. We'll get this over with now, without any more fancy talk from you, or as far as I am concerned you can get out of here without my money and sell to any buyer you can find. I can't take much more of you, at any cost.

TECK *(smiles).* It is your anger which delays us. I was about to say that I understood your fear that I would go to Von Seitz, and I would suggest that you give me a small amount of cash now, and a check dated a month from now. In a month, Herr Muller should be nearing home, and he can let you know. If you should not honor the check because Herr Muller is already in Germany, Von Seitz will pay a little something for a reliable description. I will take my chance on that. You will now say that I can do that in any case—and that is the chance you will take.

DAVID *(crosses up to behind table* R. C. *Looks at* KURT, *who does not look up).* Is a month enough? For you to get back?

KURT. I do not know!

DAVID *(to* TECK*).* Two months from today. How do you want the cash and how do you want the check?

TECK. *One month from today.* That I will not discuss. One month. Please decide now.

DAVID (*sharply*). All right. (*To* TECK.) How do you want it?

TECK. Seventy-five hundred dollars in a check. Twenty-five hundred in cash.

DAVID. I haven't anywhere near that much cash in the house. (*Turns, crosses* L.) Leave your address, and I'll send it to you in the morning.

TECK (DAVID *turns back. Laughs.*) Address? I have no address, and I wish it now. Madame Fanny has some cash in her sitting-room safe.

FANNY. Have you investigated that, too?

TECK (*laughs*). No. You once told me you always kept money in the house.

DAVID (*to* FANNY). How much have you got upstairs?

FANNY. I don't know. About fifteen or sixteen hundred.

TECK. Very well. That will do. Make the rest in the check.

DAVID. Get it, Mama, please. (*He starts toward library door.*)

FANNY (*looks carefully at* TECK). Years ago somebody said that being Roumanian was not a nationality, but a profession. The years have brought no change. (*Starts for the hall exit* R. DAVID *closes door* L. FANNY *stops as* KURT *speaks.*)

KURT (*softly*). Being a Roumanian *aristo-crat* is a profession.

(FANNY *exits. After her exit, there is silence.* KURT *does not look up,* SARA *does not move.*)

TECK (*awkwardly*). The new world has left the room. (*Looks up at them.*) I feel less discomfort with you. We are Euro-peans, born to trouble, and understand-ing it.

KURT. My wife is not a European.

TECK. Almost. (*Points upstairs*). They are young. The world has gone well for most of them. For us— (*Smiles.*) the three of us—we are like peasants watching the big frost. Work, trouble, ruin— (*Shrugs.*) But no need to call curses at the frost. There it is, there it will be again, always —for us.

SARA (*gets up, moves to the window, looks out*). You mean my husband and I do not have angry words for you. What for? We know how many there are of you. They don't yet. My mother and brother feel shocked that you are in their house. For us—we have seen you in so many houses. (*Crosses* U. L. *to terrace window* L.)

TECK. I do not say you *want* to under-stand me, Mrs. Muller. I say only that you do.

SARA. Yes. You are not difficult to under-stand.

KURT (*slowly gets up, stands stiffly, as if to adjust his back. Then he moves toward decanter table*). Whiskey?

TECK. No, thank you. (*He turns his head to watch* KURT *move. He turns back.*)

KURT (*picks up sherry decanter*). Sherry?

TECK (*nods*). Thank you, I will.

KURT (*as he pours. Removes decanter top*). You, too, wish to go back to Europe? (*Pours sherry.*)

TECK. Yes.

KURT. But they do not much want you. Not since the Budapest oil deal of '31. (*Puts down decanter and glass.*)

TECK. You seem as well informed about me as I am about you.

(KURT *moves to upstage side of decanter table.*)

KURT. That must have been a conference of high comedy, that one. Everybody try-ing to guess whether Kessler was work-ing for Fritz Thyssen, and what Thyssen *really* wanted—and whether this "Na-tional Socialism" was a smart blind of Thyssen's, and where was Wolff— (*Picks up whiskey decanter and glass.*) I should like to have seen you and your friends. It is too bad: you guessed an inch off, eh?

TECK. More than an inch.

(KURT *pours whiskey.*)

KURT. And Kessler has a memory? (*Puts down decanter, picks up syphon and adds soda. Almost playfully.*) I do not think Von Seitz would pay you money for a description of a man who has a month to travel. But I think he would pay you in a visa, and a cable to Kessler. I think you want a visa almost as much as you want money. Therefore, I conclude you will try for the money here, and the visa from Von Seitz. *(He stirs whiskey and soda.)* I cannot get anywhere near Germany in a month and you know it. *(He picks up sherry glass and comes toward table.)* I have been bored with this talk of paying you money. If they are willing to try you on this fantasy, I am not. Whatever made you think I would take such a chance? *(Puts down whiskey glass.)* Or *any* chance? You're a gambler. *(Offers* TECK *sherry glass.)* But you should not gamble with your life. *(Throws sherry glass to floor.* TECK *has turned to stare at him, made a half-motion as if to rise. As he does so, and on the words, "gamble with your life,"* KURT *upsets the glass. With his free left arm, he presses down on* TECK's *left arm, begins to move his right hand to hit* TECK's *jaw. As he does so,* TECK *makes a violent effort to rise.* KURT *throws himself on* TECK, *pressing him to the chair.* KURT *continues to punch* TECK *on the side jaw and head, and pushes him away. The chair turns over, and goes to the floor.* KURT *leans down, begins to lift* TECK *from the floor. As he does so* JOSHUA *appears in the hall entrance. He is washed and ready for dinner. As he reaches the door, he stops, sees the scene, stands quietly as if he were waiting for orders.* KURT *begins to balance* TECK, *to balance himself.* KURT, *to* JOSHUA, *in German.)* Mach die Tür auf! *(*JOSHUA *runs toward doors, opens them, stands waiting.)* Bleibt da. Mach die Tür zu. *(*KURT *begins to move out through terrace. When he is outside the doors,* JOSHUA *closes them quickly, stands looking at his mother.)*

SARA *(leans on chair* U. L. C.*)* There's trouble.

JOSHUA. Do not worry. I will go up now. I will pack. In ten minutes all will be ready. I will say nothing. I will get the children ready— *(He starts quickly for hall, turns for a second to look toward terrace doors. Then, almost with a sob.)* This was a nice house— *(Starts* R. *suddenly.)*

SARA *(softly.* JOSHUA *stops at* SARA's *VOICE).* We're not going this time, darling. There's no need to pack.

JOSHUA *(to* R. *end of sofa* R. *Stares at her, puzzled).* But Papa—

SARA. Go upstairs, Joshua. Take Babbie and Bodo in your room, and close the door. Stay there until I call you. *(He looks at her, then slowly starts toward the steps.* SARA *slowly sits in chair* U. L. C.*)* There's nothing to be frightened of, darling. Papa is all right. *(Then very softly, childishly.)* Papa is going home.

JOSHUA. Home? To Germany?

SARA. Yes.

JOSHUA. Oh. Alone?

SARA. Alone. *(very softly).* Don't say anything to the children. He will tell them himself.

JOSHUA. I won't.

SARA *(as he hesitates).* I'm all right. Go upstairs now. *(He moves slowly out* R., *she watches him, he disappears. For a moment she sits quietly. Then she gets up, moves to terrace doors, stands with her hands pressed against them. Then she crosses, picks up chair, places it behind table, picks up glass, puts it on table. As if without knowing what she is doing, she wipes table with her handkerchief.)*

*(After a second,* DAVID *comes in from* L. *followed by* FANNY, *who comes in from hall* R. DAVID *stops, puzzled.)*

DAVID *(to* L. *end of sofa* L.*).* Where— Is he upstairs?

SARA. They went outside.

FANNY *(*DAVID *to* R. *end of sofa* L.*).* Outside? They went outside? What are they doing, picking a bouquet together? *(*FANNY *goes to* R. *of table* D. R.*)*

SARA *(without turning).* They just went outside.

*(*DAVID *stands looking at her.)*

DAVID. What's the matter, Sara?

*(*SARA *goes to secretary and looks for a number in phone book.)*

FANNY *(counts some bills).* Eleven hundred, eleven hundred and fifty, twelve, twelve-fifty—

DAVID *(crosses toward* FANNY*).* For God's sake stop counting that money.

FANNY. All right. *(She sits* R. *of table.)* I'm nervous. And I don't like to think of giving him too much.

SARA *(dialing).* That's very kind of you and Mama. All that money— Hello. What time is your next plane? Oh, to—South. To El Paso, or Brownsville—yes.

DAVID *(to* FANNY. *Puts check on table* D. R.*).* Is Joseph ready?

FANNY. I don't know. I'd told him I'd call him.

*(*DAVID *begins to cross to bell cord.)*

SARA. To Brownsville? Yes. Yes. That's all right. At what time? Yes. No. The ticket will be picked up at the airport. *(She looks up.)* No. David. Don't call Joseph. *David! Please!* (*He draws back, stares at her. Looking at him, she goes on with the conversation.*) Ritter. R-i-t-t-e-r. From Chicago. Yes. Yes. *(She hangs up.)*

DAVID *(crosses to* C.*).* Sara! What's happening? What is all this? *(She does not answer.)* Where is Kurt? What— *(He starts for terrace door.)*

SARA. David. (*Stopping him* U. C. FANNY *rises.)* Don't go out.

FANNY (SARA *crosses to chair* U. L. C. *and leans against it).* Sara! What's happening—

SARA. For seven years now, day in, day out, men have crossed the German border. They are always in danger. And they always may be going in to die. Did you ever see the face of a man who never knows if this day will be the last day? *(Softly.)* Don't go out on the terrace, David. Leave Kurt alone.

FANNY *(softly).* Sara! What is it?

SARA *(quietly).* For them, it may be torture and it may be death. Some day, when it's all over, maybe there'll be a few of them left to celebrate. There aren't many of Kurt's age left. He couldn't take a chance on them. They wouldn't have liked it. *(Suddenly, violently.)* He'd have had a bad time trying to explain to them that because of this house, and this nice town, and my mother and my brother, he took chances with their work and with their lives. *(Quietly.)* Sit down, Mama. I think it's all over now. *(To* DAVID.*)* There's

nothing you can do about it. It's the way it had to be.

DAVID *(quietly).* God!

FANNY *(sits slowly).* Do you mean what I think you—?

SARA *(she turns, looks out toward doors. After a pause).* He's going away tonight, and he's never coming back any more. *(In a sing-song.)* Never, never, never. *(She looks down at her hands, as if she were very interested in them.)* I don't like to be alone at night. I guess everybody in the world's got a time in the day they don't like. Me, it's right before I go to sleep. And now it's going to be for always. All the rest of my life. *(She looks up as* KURT *comes in from terrace.* KURT *stands looking at her.)* I've told them. There is an eight-thirty plane going as far south as Brownsville. I've made you a reservation in the name of Ritter.

KURT *(he comes down to her. He puts his hand on her shoulder, she bends her head to touch it).* Liebe Sara! *(Then he goes to table at which* FANNY *is sitting. To* FANNY.*)* It is hard for you, eh? *(He pats her hand.)* I am sorry.

FANNY *(without knowing why, she takes her hand away).* Hard? I don't know. I—I don't—I don't know what I want to say.

KURT. Before I come in, I stand and think. I say, I will make Fanny and David understand. I say, How can I? Does one understand a killing? No. To hell with it, I say. I do what must be done. I have long sickened of words, when I see the men who live by them. What do you wish to make them understand? I ask myself. Stand here. Just stand here. What are you thinking? Say it to them as it comes to you. And this is how it came to me: when you kill in a war it is not so lonely; and I remember a cousin I have not seen for many years; and a melody comes back and I begin to make it with my fingers; a staircase in a house in Bonn years ago; Sara in a hundred places. Shame on us. Thousands of years and we cannot yet make a world. I have stopped a man's life. *(Points to place on couch where he was sitting opposite* TECK.*)* I sit here. I listen to him. You will not believe—but I pray I will not have to touch him. Then I know I will have to. I know that if I do not, it's only that I pamper myself, and risk the lives of others. I want you from the room. I know what I must do. *(Loudly.)* All right. Shall I now pretend sorrow? Shall I now pretend that it is not I who act thus? No! I do it. I have done it. And I will do it again. And I will keep my hope that we may make a world where all men can die in bed. I have great hate for the violent: they are the sick of the world. *(He sinks to sofa, softly.)* Maybe I am sick now, too.

SARA. You aren't sick. Stop that. It's late. You must go soon.

KURT *(looks up at her).* Maybe all that I ever wanted is a land that would let me have you. *(Then without looking away from her, he puts out his hands and takes hers. She sits beside him quickly. Rises.)* I will say good-bye now to my children. *(Turns up to DAVID.)* Then I am going to take your car. *(Motions with his head.)* I will take him with me. After that, it is up to you. Two ways: you can let me go and keep silent. I believe I can hide him and the car. At the end of two days, if they have not been found, you will call the police. You will tell as much of the truth as is safe for you to say. Tell them the last time you saw us we were on our way to Washington. You did not worry at the absence, we might have rested there. Two crazy foreigners fight, one gets killed, you know nothing of the reason. I will have left the gun, there will be no doubt who did the killing. If you will give me those two days, I think I will be far enough away from here. If the car is found before then— *(Shrugs.)* I will still try to move with speed. *(Turns to FANNY.)* And all that will make you, for yourselves, part of a murder. For the world, I do not think you will be in bad trouble. *(He pauses. Crosses down to FANNY.)* Then there is another way. You can call your police now. You can tell them the truth. I will not get home. *(To SARA.)* I wish to see the children now. *(She goes out into hall. After a second, KURT goes to L. to chair L.)*

*(There is silence. After a second, FANNY begins to speak.)*

FANNY. What are you thinking, David?

DAVID. I don't know.

FANNY. I was thinking about my Joshua. I was thinking that a few months before he died we were sitting out there. *(Points to terrace.)* "Fanny," he said, "the Renaissance American is dying, the Renaissance man is dying." I said, "What do you mean?" although I knew what he meant, I always knew. "Renaissance man," he said, "is a man who wants to know. He wants to know how fast a bird will fly, how thick is the crust of the earth, what made Iago evil, how to plough a field. He knows there is no dignity to a mountain, if there is no dignity to man. *(KURT turns to look at her.)* You cannot put that in a man, but once it is *really* there, and he will fight for it, you can put your trust in him."

DAVID *(looks at FANNY).* You're a smart woman sometimes. *(Rises, crosses to KURT.)* Don't worry about things here. My soul doesn't have to be so nice and clean. *(SARA and JOSHUA come down stairs.)* I'll take care of it. You'll have your two days. And good luck to you.

FANNY. You go with my blessing, too. I like you.

SARA *(to R. end of sofa R.).* See? I come from good stock.

*(KURT has looked at DAVID. Then he begins to smile. Nods to DAVID. Turns, smiles at FANNY.)*

FANNY. Do you like me?
*(On her speech, BODO comes in from hall.)*

KURT *(crosses to D. L. C.).* Very much, Madame.

FANNY. Would you be able to cash that check?

KURT *(laughs).* Oh, no.

FANNY. Then take the cash. I, too, would like to contribute—to your work.

KURT *(slowly).* Thank you.

BODO *(to KURT).* You like Grandma? *(Moves to FANNY.)* I thought you would, with time. I like her, too. Sometimes she dilates with screaming, but— Dilates is correct?

*(JOSHUA stands away from others, looking at KURT. KURT turns to look at him.)*

JOSHUA. Alles in Ordnung?

(BABETTE *comes in from the hall.*)

KURT. Alles in Ordnung.

BODO (*crosses to* KURT). What? What does that mean—all is well?

(KURT *crosses up to front of chair* U. L. C. *There is an awkward silence.*)

BABETTE (*to above and* L. *of* FANNY. *As if she sensed it*). We are all clean for dinner. But nobody else is clean. And I have on Grandma's dress to me—

FANNY (*rises, crosses behind* BABETTE *to* KURT *and gives him money*). Of course. And you look very pretty. You're a pretty little girl, Babbie. (FANNY *goes to behind desk, behind sofa* R., *tears check, sits.*)

(KURT *sits in chair* U. L. C.)

BODO (*looks around the room*). What is the matter? Everybody is acting like such a ninny. (*Crosses up to* KURT.) I got that word from Grandma.

KURT. Come here. . . . Come. (*They look at him. Then slowly* BABETTE *comes toward him, followed by* JOSHUA, *to stand at side of* KURT's *chair.* KURT *takes* BODO *on his lap,* BABETTE *to his* L., JOSHUA *to his* R.) We have said many good-byes to each other, eh? We must now say another. (SARA *moves up to* R. *of desk. As they stare at him, he smiles, slowly, as if it were difficult.*) This time I leave you with good people to whom I believe you, also, will be good. (*Half-playfully.*) Would you allow me to give away my share in you until I come back?

BABETTE (*slowly*). If you would like it.

KURT. Good! To Mama, her share. My share to Fanny and David. It is all and it is the most I have to give. (*Laughs.*) There. I have made a will, eh? Now. We will not joke. I have something to say to you. It is important for me to say it.

JOSHUA (*softly*). You are talking to us as if we were children.

KURT (*turns to look at him*). Am I, Joshua? I wish you were children. I wish I could say, Love your mother, do not eat too many sweets, clean your teeth . . . (*Draws* BODO *to him.*) I cannot say these things. You are not children. I took it all away from you.

BABETTE. We have had a most enjoyable life, Papa.

KURT (*smiles, pats her hand and holds it to his cheek*). You are a gallant little liar. And I thank you for it. I have done something bad today—

FANNY (*shocked, sharply*). Kurt—

SARA. Don't, Mama.

(BODO *and* BABETTE *have looked at* FANNY *and* SARA, *puzzled. Then they have turned again to look at* KURT.)

KURT. It is not to frighten you. In a few days, your mother and David will tell you.

BODO. You could not do a bad thing.

BABETTE (*proudly*). You could not.

KURT (*shakes his head*). Now let us get straight together. The four of us. Do you remember when we read *Les Miserables*? Do you remember that we talked about it afterwards, and Bodo got candy on Mama's bed?

BODO. I remember.

KURT. Well. He stole bread. The world is out of shape, we said, when there are hungry men. And until it gets in shape, men will always steal and lie and— (*A little more slowly.*) kill. But for whatever reason it is done, and whoever does it— you understand me—it is all bad. I want you to remember that. Whoever does it, it is bad. (*Then very gaily.*) But you will live to see the day when it will not have to be. All over the world, in every place and every town, there are men who are going to make sure it will not have to be. They want what I want: a childhood for every child. For my children, and I, for theirs. (*He picks* BODO *up, rises, moves toward hall, followed by* BABETTE *and* JOSHUA.) Think of that. It will make you happy. In every town and every village and every mud hut in the world, there is always a man who loves children, who will fight to make a good world for them. And now good-bye. Wait for me. I shall try to come back for you. (*He is above table* D. R.) Or you shall come to me. At Hamburg, the boat will come in. It will be a fine, safe land—I will be waiting on the dock. And there will be the three of you and Mama and Fanny and David. And I will have ordered an extra big dinner and we will show them what my Germany can be like— *(He has put* BODO *down. He leans down, presses his face in* BABETTE'S *hair. Tenderly, as her mother has done earlier, she touches his hair.)*

JOSHUA *(slowly).* Of course. That is the way it will be. Of course. But—but if you should find yourself delayed . . . *(Very slowly).* Then I will come to you. Mama.

SARA *(she has turned away).* I heard you, Joshua.

KURT *(he kisses* BABETTE*).* Gute Nacht, Liebling!

BABETTE. Gute Nacht, Papa. Mach's gut! *(*BABETTE *goes up steps.)*

KURT *(leans to kiss* BODO*).* Good night, Baby.

BODO. Good night, Papa. Mach's gut! *(*BODO *follows* BABETTE *slowly.)*

KURT *(kisses* JOSHUA*).* Good night, son.

JOSHUA. Good night, Papa. Mach's gut! *(He begins to climb the steps.)*

*(*KURT *stands watching them, smiling. When they disappear, he turns to* DAVID.*)*

KURT *(*FANNY *rises, crosses to* U. R. C. *Crosses to* DAVID*).* Good-bye, and thank you.

DAVID. Good-bye, and good luck.

KURT *(he moves up to* FANNY, *he offers his hand).* Good-bye. I have five children, eh?

FANNY. Yes, you have. *(He bends and kisses her hand.* FANNY *goes to behind desk.)*

*(*SARA *comes to* KURT.*)*

KURT *(slowly).* Men who wish to live have the best chance to live. I wish to live. I wish to live with you.

SARA. For twenty years. It is as much for me today— *(Takes his arms.)* Just once, and for all my life. *(She nods.)* Come back for me, darling. If you can.

KURT *(simply).* I will try. *(He pulls her toward him. They kiss. She breaks away, reaches for his briefcase and gives it to*

him. *He takes it and turns.)* Good-bye to you all. *(He exits.)*

*(*SARA *sits down, looks up at* DAVID, *smiles. He comes to her, kisses her, moves away again. After a second, there is the sound of a car starting. They sit listening to it. Gradually the noise begins to go off into the distance. A second later* JOSHUA *appears.)*

JOSHUA. Mama. *(She looks up. He is very tense.)* Bodo cries. Babette looks very queer. I think you should come.

SARA *(gets up, slowly).* I'm coming. *(And goes up stairs.)*

JOSHUA *(to* FANNY *and* DAVID. *Still very tense).* Bodo talks so fancy, we forget sometimes he is a baby. *(He goes up stairs.)*

*(*FANNY *and* DAVID *watch them.)*

FANNY *(after a minute).* Well, here we are. We're shaken out of the magnolias, eh?

DAVID *(laughs).* Yes, so we are.

FANNY. Tomorrow will be a hard day. But we'll have Babbie's birthday dinner. And we'll have music afterwards. You can be the audience. You'd better go up to Marthe now. Be as careful as you can. She'd better stay here for a while. I dare say I can stand it.

DAVID *(turns, smiles).* Even your graciousness is ungracious, Mama.

FANNY. I do my best. Well, I think I shall go and talk to Anise. *(Rises, starts* R.*)* I like Anise best when I don't feel well. *(She begins to move off.)*

DAVID. Mama. *(She turns.)* We are going to be in for trouble. You understand that?

FANNY. I understand it very well. We will manage. You and I. I'm not put together with flour paste. And neither are you—I am happy to learn.

DAVID *(he begins to laugh).* Good night, Mama.
*(As she moves out . . .)*

THE CURTAIN FALLS

# 1941-42

A look at the record shows that this season offered less for the consideration of the Circle than any other in its first twenty years. And this was reflected in the second failure of the organization to choose a winner of the main award at the meeting on April 16, 1942.

It was no ordinary failure after a struggle either. On the very first ballot ten of the seventeen voting had no choice, with four votes going to John Steinbeck's *The Moon Is Down* and three to *In Time to Come*, the drama about Woodrow Wilson by Howard Koch and John Huston, who later became the noted motion picture director.

Later this was switched to four for *In Time to Come* and two for *The Moon Is Down* as the Circle went on record by a vote of eleven to six to discontinue the effort to pick a winner. An official statement said that although the Circle was organized "to encourage native playwrights and honor native dramatists, it had also the third obligation of maintaining the standards of the theatre and of dramatic criticism, and that it felt it would cause a serious confusion of standards if it merely made a selection from a group of plays, none of which seemed up to the standards of the previous awards."

There was no such trouble with the foreign citation. Noel Coward's frothy *Blithe Spirit* received twelve votes to one for Patrick Hamilton's superlative thriller, *Angel Street*. There were three no-decision ballots. The citation to the winner read:

"To Noel Coward, for the skill and adroitness with which he has concocted a farce comedy of gayety and wit."

For the first time since the Circle was formed there also was no Pulitzer prize. This was only the second time the Pulitzer people had passed up a drama award and the first time in twenty-three years.

*In Time to Come* gave forty performances; *The Moon Is Down*, seventy-one.

# 1942-43

The Circle saw fit to honor Sidney Kingsley for the first time in the case of his historical play, *The Patriots,* dealing with the early years of our republic and the clash of personalities and ideas between Jefferson and Hamilton. The flavor is decidedly Jeffersonian, as a number of reviewers pointed out.

The award to *The Patriots* cited "its dignity of material, its thoughtful projection of a great American theme, its vigorous approach to the characters portrayed and, in spite of certain limitations, its driving final effect on the stage."

The work bears the Kingsley imprint of scholarly attention to detail, but this reviewer found it dull as a theatre piece, much preferring Thornton Wilder's exciting and offbeat *The Skin of Our Teeth,* which won the Pulitzer prize.

*The Patriots* won on the seventh ballot after failing to get a three-fourths majority on the first five. It received thirteen votes on the final call as against four for *The Skin of Our Teeth* and one for *This is the Army* at the meeting on April 13, 1943.

Others that figured in the early voting were *The Eve of St. Mark* by Maxwell Anderson, *Harriet* by Florence Ryerson and Colin Clements, in which Helen Hayes created one of her unforgettable portraits as Harriet Beecher Stowe, and *Oklahoma!*

There was no award for a foreign play.

The most important event of the season, of course, was the production of *Oklahoma!* It set a new pattern for the musical comedy or musical play and brought ballet to the fore as an integral part of the popular theatre; it gave a new lease on life to the veteran Theatre Guild, which was on its last financial legs and barely was able to get the production on; and it was the first joint work of Richard Rodgers, composer, and Oscar Hammerstein II, lyricist and librettist, who went on from there to become one of the greatest teams of collaborators in theatrical history, certainly the most successful financially in their own lifetimes.

*The Patriots* played 173 performances; *The Skin of Our Teeth,* 359; *This is the Army,* 113; *The Eve of St. Mark,* 307; *Harriet,* 377, and *Oklahoma!* went on and on to set a long-run record for musicals of 2,248 performances.

# The Patriots

## By SIDNEY KINGSLEY

Presented by The Playwrights' Company and Rowland Stebbins at the National Theatre, New York City, January 29, 1943, with the following cast:

| | |
|---|---|
| CAPTAIN | Byron Russell |
| THOMAS JEFFERSON | Raymond Edward Johnson |
| PATSY | Madge Evans |
| MARTHA | Frances Reid |
| JAMES MADISON | Ross Matthew |
| ALEXANDER HAMILTON | House Jameson |
| GEORGE WASHINGTON | Cecil Humphreys |
| SERGEANT | Victor Southwick |
| COLONEL HUMPHREY | Francis Compton |
| JACOB | Thomas Dillon |
| NED | George Mitchell |
| MAT | Philip White |
| JAMES MONROE | Judson Laire |
| MRS. HAMILTON | Peg La Centra |
| HENRY KNOX | Henry Mowbray |
| BUTLER | Robert Lance |
| MR. FENNO | Ronald Alexander |
| JUPITER | Juano Hernandez |
| MRS. CONRAD | Leslie Bingham |
| FRONTIERSMAN | John Stephen |
| THOMAS JEFFERSON RANDOLPH | Billy Nevard |
| ANNE RANDOLPH | Hope Lange |
| GEORGE WASHINGTON LAFAYETTE | Jack Lloyd |

## SCENE

Prologue: The deck of a schooner. 1790.

Act I—New York, 1790. Scene 1—The Presidential mansion. Scene 2—A smithy of an inn on the outskirts of New York.

Act II—Philadelphia, 1791–1793. Scene 1—Hamilton's home. Scene 2—Jefferson's rooms. Scene 3—The same, a few days later.

Act III—Washington, 1800. Scene 1—Jefferson's rooms at Conrad's boarding house. Scene 2—The Senate Chamber.

# THE PATRIOTS

## PROLOGUE

*1790. A section of the deck of a schooner. A star-lit night, wind in the sails, rushing water, the creak of tackle.*

*A middle-aged man and a girl lean on the ship's rail and gaze out over the ocean: JEFFERSON and his daughter, PATSY. He is tall and thin, his face too sensitive, a gentleness almost womanish written on it. He has dispensed with the wig of the period. His hair, ruffled by the winds, is reddish, streaked with gray. The girl is in her late teens, vibrant, lithe, handsome. Above them a helmsman, in shadow, steers the ship.*

*The CAPTAIN approaches them.*

CAPTAIN. Evening, sir.

JEFFERSON. Good evening, Captain.

PATSY. Are we nearing land, Captain?

CAPTAIN. If we hold to our course. Gittin' impatient?

*(PATSY laughs.)*

JEFFERSON. Tell me, does the voyage home always take forever?

CAPTAIN. Longer'n that, sometime. *(Looks at the sky.)* May blow up a bit, sir. Better think a goin' below. *(He salutes, goes off.* PATSY *and* JEFFERSON *stare out over the ocean.)*

PATSY. I wonder will the house be the way I remember it.

JEFFERSON. Not as large, perhaps. You were only a little lady when we left.

PATSY. How long ago that seems!

JEFFERSON. Doesn't it?

*(She sighs.* JEFFERSON *looks at her, smiles.)*

PATSY. Are we going to New York first?

JEFFERSON *(shakes his head)*. Direct to Monticello.

PATSY. I thought you might want to see President Washington at once.

JEFFERSON. We'll go home first and arrange your wedding.

PATSY. Won't the President be waiting your answer?

JEFFERSON. Not particularly—no.

*(Pause.)*

PATSY. Papa?

JEFFERSON. Yes, dear?

PATSY. I've been wondering.

JEFFERSON. What?

PATSY. Do you think we should put it off? My wedding?

JEFFERSON. Put it off?

PATSY. If you accept the President's offer, you'll have to live in New York. You'll be alone for the first time in your life. You'll be utterly miserable. I know you too well.

JEFFERSON. But I have no intention of accepting.

PATSY. You haven't?

JEFFERSON. He's given me the option of refusal. And I certainly mean to take advantage of it.

PATSY *(vastly relieved)*. Why didn't you tell me?

JEFFERSON. It never occurred to me. *(Pause.)* You see, dearest, I discovered a long time ago that Nature didn't make me for public office. I accepted the French post only because—at the time—your mother's death had left me so blank. . . . I fancied a change of scene would . . . *(He breaks off.)*

PATSY. I know, Father. *(A long pause as they both stare into space.)* Strange out there.

JEFFERSON. Time and space seem to disappear.

PATSY. I wish she were waiting for us at home.

JEFFERSON. Your mother?

PATSY. Yes. I never think of Monticello without thinking of her. She used to love to tell me about *your* wedding night.

JEFFERSON. Did she?

PATSY. In the garden cottage, midst such a clutter of your drawings and your books and your inventions, you could hardly move about.

JEFFERSON *(smiles)*. That's right.

PATSY. And how you lit a fire, and found half a bottle of wine a workman had left behind some books. And mother played the pianoforte and you your violin, and you sang old songs.

*(The wind rises.* JEFFERSON *draws his cloak tighter.)*

JEFFERSON. It is blowing up a bit. Excuse me. *(He starts off.)*

PATSY. Where are you going?

JEFFERSON. I want to take a look at your sister.

PATSY. She's asleep, Father.

JEFFERSON. She'll have kicked off her blanket. She might catch a chill. We don't want her coming home with the sniffles. *(He goes off.)*

PATSY *(calls after him)*. Father!

JEFFERSON *(off)*. Yes?

PATSY. I'll go. You wait here.

JEFFERSON. All right, dear. *(Re-enters.)*

PATSY. I'll be right back.

*(*PATSY *goes.* JEFFERSON *stares off toward the horizon. The hypnotic surge of the water. . . . The moonlight fades until he and the ship become a single silhouette in the night. Soft music dimly heard. . . . Slowly, dancing as if on the ocean, the exterior of an enchanting house material-izes.* Monticello! *Snow is falling and has piled deep around it.)*

*(Laughter is heard offstage.* TOM JEFFER-SON, *a young man, and* MARTHA, *a young woman, radiantly beautiful, appear, shak-ing the snow off their cloaks.)*

MARTHA. Was there ever such a wedding night? I declare, Tom Jefferson, those last few miles the horses fairly flew through the snow.

JEFFERSON *(points to the house)*. There it is, Martha.

*(*MARTHA *turns, gasps.)*

MARTHA. Oh, Tom!

JEFFERSON. You like it?

MARTHA. I never dreamed it would . . . You really designed this, yourself?

JEFFERSON. For you, Martha. *(Takes her hand.)*

MARTHA. It's incredibly lovely.

JEFFERSON. Your hand is like ice. Come!

MARTHA. No! I want to stand here and look at it a minute more. Please!

JEFFERSON. It'll be ready for us to move into by April. Till then we'll use the garden cottage. *(Apologetically.)* It's only one room.

MARTHA *(laughs)*. Like a couple of dor-mice. We won't stir till Spring. *(Looks about, enchanted. Points offstage.)* Your Blue Ridge Mountains are out there?

JEFFERSON *(nods)*. There's one peak, Martha, the sun tips with pure gold. And from here Nature spreads a magic carpet below—rocks, rivers, mountains, for-ests . . .

MARTHA. I can't wait for morning.

JEFFERSON. When stormy weather's brew-ing, you can look down into her work-shop and see her fabricating clouds and hail and snow and lightning—at your feet.

MARTHA. Tom, dearest?

JEFFERSON. Yes, Martha?

MARTHA. I can't tell you what you've done for me.

JEFFERSON. What I've done for you?

MARTHA. Before I met you, circumstances and the intolerance of little men had be-gun to make me lose faith. The earth had begun to shrink. Living had become some-thing quite unimportant. Then, the night we met, after the gay chatter, when you began to talk gravely, I suddenly fell in love, not only with you. I fell in love with the possibilities of the whole race of man.

*(She stops short. He is gazing at her, laughing.)* Now, what are *you* laughing at, Mr. Jefferson?

JEFFERSON. If I live to be a thousand and close my eyes—this is the way I'll see you, my love. With snow on your face and your eyes shining!

MARTHA. Oh, Tom, I'm only trying to say I'm happy.

JEFFERSON. Are you?

MARTHA. And I want to be bussed.

*(He kisses her tenderly.)*

JEFFERSON.
"When we dwell on the lips of the lass we
    adore,
Not a pleasure in nature is missing.
May his soul be in Heaven
He deserved it, I'm sure,
Who was first the inventor of kissing."

*(She laughs. They embrace.)*

MARTHA. Will you love me so forever, Tom?

JEFFERSON. Forever and ever—and ever . . . *(She shivers.)* You shivered? You are cold.

*(The light begins to fade.)*

MARTHA. A bit!

JEFFERSON. Come, Mrs. Jefferson. *(He sweeps her up in his arms.)* We'll light a fire that will warm you to the end of time! *(He carries her off. Suddenly the roar of a rising wind. Men's voices far off.)*

CAPTAIN's VOICE *(offstage)*. Port quarter! *(Monticello fades and vanishes. CAPTAIN enters, approaches the dreaming silhouette of JEFFERSON.)*

CAPTAIN. Runnin' into a patch of ugly weather. Better go below, sir. *(The sudden roar of wind. The wheel spins.)* Watch the helm, Higgins! Bring the wind on the port quarter!

*(VOICE offstage: "Aye, sir." Many voices offstage. Exit CAPTAIN. The babble of men's voices raised in argument.)*

*(Another vision appears in space. Young JEFFERSON, seated at a desk, a manuscript before him. As the voices are heard, he looks from one antagonist to another.)*

FIRST VOICE. Georgia votes nay.

SECOND VOICE. This document is a mass of glittering generalities.

THIRD VOICE. Carolina votes nay. I move to strike out the clause condemning the slave traffic. It has no place here. Georgia and Carolina object.

FOURTH VOICE. Motion to strike out clause condemning the slave traffic. Hands! For? *(JEFFERSON looks about, dismayed, counting the votes.)* Against? *(JEFFERSON raises his hand.)* Motion carried. You will please strike out that clause.

*(JEFFERSON bitterly scratches out the offending clause.)*

REID's VOICE. That second sentence. Don't like it.

JEFFERSON. But this is the heart of it, man. Are we going to have to creep up on liberty, inch by inch?

VOICE. Where does this lead? No wonder we're driving all our men of property into the arms of the loyalists.

JEFFERSON. I was asked to write the declaration and I wrote it. I haven't tried to be original. This is a simple expression of the American mind. Our people want this.

REID's VOICE. From a legalistic viewpoint . . .

JEFFERSON. The men who migrated to America, who built it with their sweat and blood were laborers, not lawyers.

REID's VOICE. Plague on't, boy! You want some precedent. Where can you show me anything like this in history?

JEFFERSON. Where in history do we see anything like this new world or the man of this new world? Where have we ever seen a land so marked by destiny to build a new free society based on the rights of man? Precedent? Let's make precedent! Better to set a good example, than follow a bad one.

REID's VOICE. Are you aware, sir, of the consequences?

JEFFERSON *(controls his emotion, rises, steps from behind the desk, appeals to the assembly)*. There is not a man in the whole empire who wished conciliation more than I. But, by the God that made me, I would have sooner ceased to exist than yield my freedom. And, in this, I know I speak for America. I am sorry to find a bloody campaign is decided on. But, since it is forced on us, we must drub the enemy and drub him soundly. We must teach the sceptered tyrant we are not brutes to kiss the hand that scourges us. But this is not enough. We are now deciding everlastingly our future and the future of our innocent posterity. Our people have already been fighting a year—for what? *(He picks up the document.)* For this. Let us give it to them—in writing—now. Now is the time to buttress the liberty we're fighting for. It can't be too strongly emphasized! *Now,* while men are bleeding and dying. Tomorrow they may grow tired and careless, and a new despot may find in the old laws an instrument to rob their liberty again. Now is the time to build a free society. Now! Not later.

REID's VOICE. I'll debate this point all day.

JEFFERSON *(fiercely)*. No member of this Congress is more eager than I to settle the business on hand and go home. My wife is ill and bearing me a child, and while I stay here she's doing all my work at home. I'm half mad with anxiety, but I'll stay on all summer, if necessary, to fight for this one sentence.

*(Pause.)*

REID's VOICE. Well—er—Read it again. Let's examine it again!

JEFFERSON *(sits. Reads from the document, his voice rich with deep emotion)*. We hold these truths to be self-evident: that all men are created equal; that they are endowed by their Creator with certain inalienable rights; that among these are life, liberty, and the pursuit of happiness; that to secure these rights, governments are instituted among men, deriving their just powers from the consent of the governed.

*(The Liberty Bell begins to peal. Young* JEFFERSON's *face is transfigured by an almost sacred light, which grows brighter, then fades and vanishes. Total darkness obscures even the shadowy ship and the* dreaming silhouette of JEFFERSON. In the darkness the Liberty Bell peals louder and louder, then fades off—Soft, sweet, ghostly music. . . . The image of MARTHA appears, smiling sadly. The dreamer on the ship becomes visible again. He reaches out his hand.)*

JEFFERSON *(murmurs)*. Forgive me, Martha! It was such a price to ask of you. Forgive me! I wanted a happy world—for us; and, reaching for it, I lost you. *(The ghost of* MARTHA *smiles sadly and shakes her head.)* Oh, my darling, in every picture I ever painted of the future you were the foreground. Without you, there's no picture. There's . . .

PATSY's VOICE *(off)*. Father!

*(The ghost of* MARTHA *reaches out her hand, then fades and vanishes.* PATSY *appears.)*

PATSY. Father! *(The light comes on slowly. The ship again.* PATSY *is at his side.)* Maria's all right. Father.

JEFFERSON. Hm?

PATSY. She's sound asleep—Maria.

JEFFERSON. Oh! Good. Did she kick off the blanket?

PATSY. Yes, but I tucked her in again. Tight.

JEFFERSON. Good.

PATSY. You were so deep in meditation. What were you thinking?

JEFFERSON. Oh—nothing, dear. Just thinking.

*(From above, the watch suddenly cries out, "Land ho!" The cry is repeated below. From above, "Two points to the starboard! Land ho!")*

PATSY. Father! There it is! Do you see?

JEFFERSON. No. Where, Patsy? Where?

PATSY. That light! There!

JEFFERSON *(peering off, his face working with emotion)*. Yes, yes, it's land! It's America, Patsy.

PATSY. We're home, again.

# ACT ONE

## SCENE I

SCENE: *New York, Spring 1790. The MacComb mansion on lower Broadway, the Presidential residence.* PRESIDENT WASHINGTON, *tight-lipped and grave, is listening to scholarly, prematurely wizened* JAMES MADISON *and* ALEXANDER HAMILTON, *a short, handsome, young man of flashing personality and proud carriage.* COLONEL HUMPHREYS, *foppish and affected, stands by, his face a mirror reflecting* HAMILTON'S *lightning changes of mood.*

MADISON *(vehemently).* If Colonel Hamilton's treasury bill is re-introduced, Congress will kill it again.

HAMILTON *(dryly).* Mr. Madison, I am tempted to seize your Congress by their separate heads and knock them together into a collective jelly.

MADISON. What would that achieve?

HAMILTON. Unity! Of some kind.

MADISON. Yes, but what kind? That's the question.

HAMILTON. You cry, "Speculation!" That's not the issue at all, and you know it.

MADISON. I know nothing of the sort. On the contrary.

HAMILTON. You deny your South is afraid the North will profit a little more?

MADISON. And will they? Will they?

HAMILTON. That's beside the point. Yes, they will. What of it? *(He turns to* WASHINGTON, *pleading.)* The crying need of this infant government *now* is confidence in its financial policy.

MADISON. Exactly. And is this the way to achieve it?

HAMILTON. Question? Can the wise and learned Congressman from Virginia propose any better plan?

MADISON. Colonel Hamilton! Personalities are not the . . .

WASHINGTON. Gentlemen! Gentlemen! Thank you, Mr. Madison, for your views. Of course it is not in this office to interfere with the people's legislature.

MADISON. Thank you!

HAMILTON. But, Mr. President! You . . .

WASHINGTON. Congress must decide the merits of your bill.

MADISON. Good day, Mr. President. *(Bows to* HAMILTON, *who is almost bursting with fury.)* Colonel Hamilton.

HAMILTON. My congratulations! You've won a noble victory over unity and honor. *(*MADISON *smiles, shakes his head, goes.* HAMILTON *turns to* WASHINGTON.*)* I warn you, sir . . .

WASHINGTON. Slow, Colonel. Slow but sure. That must be our political maxim.

HAMILTON. I'm afraid I may have to resign.

WASHINGTON. Now, my boy!

HAMILTON. I can't build a treasury out of thin air.

WASHINGTON. I know, my boy. I know. *(He hands* HAMILTON *some papers.)* Check these figures for me. *(He ruffles some other documents.)* These we'll go over this evening. Mrs. Washington is expecting you and your lady.

HAMILTON. Mrs. Hamilton is confined to bed.

WASHINGTON. She is? Anything wrong?

HAMILTON. On the contrary.

WASHINGTON. Another?

HAMILTON. On the way.

WASHINGTON. By God! You little men! My congratulations.

HAMILTON *(laughs).* Thank you, sir. I'll check these, now. Is there anything else?

WASHINGTON. No. *(*HAMILTON *turns to go. A sergeant enters.)*

SERGEANT. His Excellency's Ambassador to the Court of France, Mr. Jefferson!

WASHINGTON. Oh! Good! Show him in.

SERGEANT. Yes, sir. (SERGEANT exits. HAMILTON wheels around.)

HAMILTON. Mr. Jefferson in New York?

HUMPHREYS. He arrived last night. (HAMILTON glares at him. HUMPHREYS whines.) I thought you knew, Alec. . . . I . . .

HAMILTON (suddenly very excited, to the President). Providence is with us. Mr. Jefferson could easily persuade the South to vote for my treasury bill. I have never met him, so if you'd speak to him . . .

WASHINGTON. I can't do that.

HAMILTON. Why not?

WASHINGTON (groans). Again? Must we go over the ground again, and again, and again, and again, and again?

HAMILTON. It seems nothing but a catastrophe will make any impression. (Sweetly.) But I am optimistic. I expect very shortly we will see a colossal catastrophe. (He smiles ironically, bows, and goes. COLONEL HUMPHREYS follows. WASHINGTON stares after him, a shadow of a smile on his grim face. JEFFERSON enters.)

JEFFERSON. General Washington!

WASHINGTON (rises). Mr. Jefferson! Welcome home. Let me look at you. (The two men study each other.) Six years!

JEFFERSON. Six. A long time.

WASHINTON (sighs). Yes. How was Patsy's wedding?

JEFFERSON. Beautiful. (He hands WASHINGTON some parcels.) For Mrs. Washington. For you.

WASHINGTON. Oh! You shouldn't have. (Goes to his desk, picks up a knife, slits the seals of the parcels and opens them.)

HUMPHREYS (entering). Jefferson, mon vieux!

JEFFERSON. Billy Humphreys! How are you?

HUMPHREYS. Assez bien! Assez bien! Et notre charmante Paris? Comment va-t-elle?

JEFFERSON. Changed. Everybody in Paris now talks politics. And you know how the French love to talk.

HUMPHREYS. Ha! (Laughs—a high, affected cackle.) Et la chere reine? Et le roi? How are they? (Daintily pinches some snuff into his nostrils.)

JEFFERSON. The King hunts one half the day, drinks the other half.

HUMPHREYS (slyly). La! La!

JEFFERSON. The Queen weeps, but sins on.

HUMPHREYS. Ho, ho! Mechante . . .

WASHINGTON (opens his package, takes out some lily bulbs). By God! Lily bulbs!

JEFFERSON. The loveliest species I've ever seen. Magnificent flower. Found them in the south of France.

WASHINGTON. And rice seed.

JEFFERSON. Italy!

WASHINGTON. Beautiful grain.

JEFFERSON. Look at the size!

WASHINGTON. Mm. Beautiful! Sit here! (Moves a chair for him.)

JEFFERSON. Thank you. (Sits.)

WASHINGTON (crosses to a cabinet, takes out decanter and glasses, pours wine). And you found Virginia?

JEFFERSON. Ah!

WASHINGTON. Mm!

JEFFERSON. Yes!

WASHINGTON. Crops?

JEFFERSON. Rye's splendid. Wheat's good. It's going to be an excellent harvest.

WASHINGTON (sighs). So I hear.

JEFFERSON. Of course, my own lands are almost ruined.

WASHINGTON. These damnable overseers! Ignorant. Careless. (Hands him a glass of wine.)

JEFFERSON. Mine complained the rabbits always ate the outside row of cabbages.

WASHINGTON. Humph! What'd you tell him?

JEFFERSON. Told him to remove the outside row.

WASHINGTON (laughs). Good! (He draws up a chair and sits close to JEFFERSON.)

HUMPHREYS. Your Excellency, I believe you have an appointment. . . .

WASHINGTON *(dismisses* HUMPHREYS *with a gesture).* All right, Colonel Humphreys, later.

HUMPHREYS. *Monsieur l'Ambassadeur!* Your Excellency! *(He makes several exaggerated bows and backs off.)*

JEFFERSON *(stares after* HUMPHREYS, *amused).* Tell me, don't the little boys in the street run after him?

*(*WASHINGTON *looks after* HUMPHREYS, *turns to* JEFFERSON, *nods gravely.* JEFFERSON *laughs. They raise their glasses.)*

WASHINGTON. The Republic! *(They drink.* JEFFERSON *sips the wine appreciatively, holds it up to examine the color.)* Recognize it? *(*JEFFERSON *nods.)* Excellent Madeira!

JEFFERSON. Patsy and I shopped all over Paris for it.

WASHINGTON. Mr. Adams is very pleased with the wines you sent him. But—er— *(He looks gravely at* JEFFERSON.*)* his daughter is disappointed in the purchase you made for her.

JEFFERSON. Mrs. Smith? Now, what did she . . . ? The Paris corset? *(*WASHINGTON *nods.)* It didn't fit?

WASHINGTON. No! *(He gestures with his hands, indicating the outlines of an ample ·bosom.)*

JEFFERSON. Oh, what a tragedy!

WASHINGTON. It's very pretty, too. Mrs. Adams showed it to Mrs. Washington. Pink ribbons. The ladies are heartbroken.

JEFFERSON. They mustn't despair. Tell Mrs. Smith to put it aside. After all, there are ebbs as well as flows in this world. When the mountain didn't go to Mohamet, Mohamet went to the mountain.

WASHINGTON *(smiles, drains his glass, puts it on the sideboard).* So Lafayette is trying to establish a republic in France?

JEFFERSON. Slowly, by constitutional reform. In my rooms in Paris he drew up the first bill of rights for France. The people are all looking to our experiment. It's a heart-warming thought that in work-ing out the pattern of our own happiness, we are inadvertently working for oppressed people everywhere. There's a great danger there, though. I toured France, incognito. Visited the peasants in their hovels. The poverty and ignorance! Appalling! If they should ever lose Lafayette . . . *(Shakes his head, finishes his drink.)*

WASHINGTON. Anarchy?

JEFFERSON. Yes.

WASHINGTON *(sighs heavily).* Yes.

JEFFERSON *(studying him).* Mr. President, you look tired.

WASHINGTON *(rising).* I'm not accustomed to this indoor life. I need activity.

JEFFERSON. Long walks. The best exercise.

WASHINGTON. It's not permitted. The dignity of the State forbids it, I'm told. When we lived on Cherry Street, I couldn't go down the street without a parade. But I can tell you since we moved here to Broadway, it's a Godsend. Now, occasionally, I can steal out that door to the back yard, across the meadow and down to the river.

JEFFERSON. What do you do down at the river?

WASHINGTON. Go fishing.

JEFFERSON. Ah!

WASHINGTON *(rises, fetches a dish of biscuits).* I've had two attacks of illness this year. I doubt if I'd survive a third. Oh, well, tomorrow or twenty years from now, we are all in the hands of a Good Providence. Try one of these biscuits.

JEFFERSON. Thank you.

WASHINGTON *(goes to his desk).* I'm organizing the ministers of the various departments into a cabinet to advise me. As our Secretary of State, you're . . .

JEFFERSON. General Washington.

WASHINGTON. Mm?

JEFFERSON. In your letter you did give me the option of refusal.

WASHINGTON. You can't mean to refuse?

JEFFERSON. I must.

WASHINGTON. Why?

JEFFERSON. I've been away so long. I know none of the duties of this office. I may bungle it. I have forebodings.

WASHINGTON. We're all groping. This will be a government of accommodation.

JEFFERSON (*shakes his head*). I'm sorry. I want you to understand. Whatever spice of political ambition I may have had as a young man has long since evaporated. (*He rises, places the half-nibbled biscuit on a dish.*) I believe every man should serve his turn. I think I've done my share. Now I want to go home. I must complete my house. Twenty years it's waited. Patsy and her husband have come to stay with me at Monticello. The truth of the matter is, I've lived with my children so long, I've come to depend on their affection and comfort.

WASHINGTON. Tom, have you ever thought of marrying again?

JEFFERSON. No.

WASHINGTON. She was a wonderful woman, your Martha.

JEFFERSON. Yes. (*Pause.*) When I came home—she was in every room. (*Pause.*) I've learned one thing. For me there's no peace anywhere else in the world but Monticello. You understand why I must refuse your offer?

(HUMPHREYS *enters.*)

HUMPHREYS. Excuse me, sire.

WASHINGTON. Yes, Humphreys?

HUMPHREYS. The theatre box and guard of honor are arranged.

WASHINGTON (*dryly*). Good.

HUMPHREYS. And I've discovered the Ambassador of the Sultan of Turkey is going to be present.

WASHINGTON (*with a notable lack of enthusiasm*). Mm, mm.

HUMPHREYS. A suggestion, Excellency?

WASHINGTON. Yes?

HUMPHREYS. Wouldn't it be advisable to return to six horses on the coach?

WASHINGTON. I thought we compromised on four.

HUMPHREYS. When I was at the court of Louis . . .

WASHINGTON (*slowly, making a great effort to contain his impatience*). Colonel Humphreys, I recognize the importance of these forms to the dignity of a state, particularly one so young as ours. Understand, I know nothing of these matters. I've never been to the courts of Europe. I'm just an old soldier. I leave the ceremonies in your hands. (*The impatience wears thin and he growls.*) But it seems to me four horses and that canary coach with the pink and gilt angels will be enough to impress even the Ambassador of the Sultan of Turkey.

HUMPHREYS. But, sire . . .

WASHINGTON. Four will do—that's final. (*He ruffles some papers, frowns.*) On second thought, I won't be free to go to the theatre tonight. Cancel it!

HUMPHREYS. Sire, if I may . . .

WASHINGTON (*rises, thundering*). Don't sire me! How many times must I tell you? By the Eternal! I am not a King! I am the elected head of our people. This is a republic. Can you get that through your skull? (*He controls himself. Wearily.*) All right! Go!

HUMPHREYS. Very well, Mr. President. (*He goes.* WASHINGTON *sighs heavily.*)

WASHINGTON. I was offered the crown.

JEFFERSON. The crown!

WASHINGTON. Twice. (*Pause.*) I don't want to be a king, Tom. (*He crosses to the cabinet, takes up a pipe, fills it with tobacco from a jug.*)

JEFFERSON. I know you don't, Mr. President.

WASHINGTON. You've no idea. (*He touches a taper to the flame of a burning candle.*) Every eye is on this office. A number of our people suspect me. As God is my judge, I would rather live and die on my farm than be emperor of the world. (*He lights his pipe, puffing angrily.*)

JEFFERSON (*pause*). I know. And yet—since I've been back—particularly here in New York—I find alarming yearnings. Our fashionable folk appear to be looking wishfully for a king and a court of our own.

WASHINGTON. Yes. I suppose so. *(He sighs, exhales a huge puff of smoke, extinguishes the taper.)* On the other hand, there is equal danger of anarchy. We came close to it while you were away! *(He puffs nervously at his pipe.)* We walk between those two pitfalls. Our people don't take to discipline. But, without it—we shall be lost. We've yet to see how large a dose of freedom men can be trusted with. Tom, from the earliest days in Virginia, you were close to them, you seemed always to understand them. In this office I find myself far removed from direct contact with them. I need your agency. I need their faith in you. This is the last great experiment for promoting human happiness. I need the hand that wrote, "All men are created equal." I can't let you go home yet! I need you here.

*(A long pause.* JEFFERSON *turns to the desk, pours back the rice-seed he has been fondling, turns to* WASHINGTON.*)*

JEFFERSON. It's for you to marshal us as you see fit.

WASHINGTON *(goes to him, grips his shoulder).* Good!

JEFFERSON. It's a great honor. I hope I can be worthy of it.

*(*HUMPHREYS *enters.)*

HUMPHREYS. Mr. President?

WASHINGTON. I don't wish to be disturbed. . . .

HUMPHREYS. His Excellency, the Minister of Spain is arrived to pay his respects. It had already been arranged, sir. Just the courtesies!

WASHINGTON. All right. *(Sighs. Beckons to the reception room.)* I'll see him. *(To* JEFFERSON.*)* You'll excuse me? It will be a few minutes. There are some journals.

JEFFERSON *(holds up his portfolio).* I have my tariff reports to study.

*(*WASHINGTON, *escorted by* HUMPHREYS, *goes up corridor.* HAMILTON *drifts into the room, some papers in his hand. The two men look at each other.)*

HAMILTON. You're Jefferson?

JEFFERSON. Yes.

HAMILTON. I'm Hamilton.

JEFFERSON. The Hamilton?

HAMILTON *(bows).* Alexander.

JEFFERSON. Your servant.

HAMILTON. Yours.

JEFFERSON. I read your Federalist papers while I was in France. Brilliant! You've given me a great deal of pleasure.

HAMILTON. Thank you. *(*HAMILTON *looks at his papers, groans, shakes his head, throws the papers on the President's desk.)*

JEFFERSON. Troubles?

HAMILTON *(groans again).* God! Yes. You have a pleasant voyage home?

JEFFERSON. It seemed forever.

HAMILTON *(smiles).* Of course. *(He arranges papers on desk.)* Have you accepted the Secretary of State?

JEFFERSON. Yes.

HAMILTON. My congratulations. We must work in concert.

JEFFERSON. I'm such a stranger here, I shall lean on you.

HAMILTON. No, I'm afraid—it's—I who need your help. *(Suddenly agitated, emotional.)* Mr. Jefferson, it's enough to make any man who loves America want to cry. Forgive me! I really shouldn't burden you with this. It's a matter of my own department.

JEFFERSON. If I can be of any assistance . . . ?

HAMILTON. It's often been remarked that it's given to this country here to prove once and for all whether men can govern themselves by reason, or whether they must forever rely on the accident of tyranny. An interesting thought, Mr. Jefferson.

JEFFERSON. God, yes. We live in an era perhaps the most important in all history.

HAMILTON. An interesting thought! An awful thought! For, if it is true, then we dare not fail.

JEFFERSON. No.

HAMILTON. But we are failing. The machinery is already breaking down. *(He snaps his fingers.)* We haven't that much foreign credit. The paper money issued by the States is worthless. We are in financial chaos. *(He paces to and fro.)* The galling part is I have a remedy at hand. The solution is so simple. A nation's credit, like a merchant's, depends on paying its promissory notes in full. I propose to pay a hundred cents on the dollar for all the paper money issued by the States. Our credit would be restored instantaneously.

JEFFERSON *(worried)*. Mr. Madison spoke to me very briefly of your bill last night. It seems there's been some speculation in this paper, and he fears . . .

HAMILTON. Madison! I loved that man. I thought so high of that man. I swear I wouldn't have taken this office—except I counted on his support. And now, he's turned against me.

JEFFERSON. Mr. Madison has a good opinion of your talents. But this speculation . . .

HAMILTON. I don't want his good opinion. I want his support. Will you use your influence?

JEFFERSON. You understand I've been away six years. I've gotten out of touch here. I'll need time to study the facts.

HAMILTON. There is no time.

JEFFERSON. Well, three or four weeks.

HAMILTON. Three or four . . . ? For God's sake, man, can't you understand what I'm trying to tell you? The North is about to secede!

JEFFERSON. Secede?

HAMILTON. Hasn't the President told you?

JEFFERSON. No.

HAMILTON. Unless my bill is passed there is every prospect the Union will dissolve.

JEFFERSON. I'm aware there's a great deal of tension here, but . . .          .

HAMILTON. Walk in on a session of Congress tomorrow.

JEFFERSON. I see evils on both sides. *(A long pause.)* However, it seems to me —if the Union is at stake—reasonable men sitting about a table discussing this coolly should arrive at some compromise. *(He comes to a sudden decision.)* Have dinner with me tomorrow night?

HAMILTON. Delighted.

JEFFERSON. I'll invite a friend or two.

HAMILTON. Mr. Madison?

JEFFERSON. I can't promise anything. He's bitterly opposed to your plan.

HAMILTON. I have a way to sweeten the pill. The cost of living in New York has become so unreasonable there's talk of moving the capital.

JEFFERSON. Yes.

HAMILTON. It's already been promised temporarily to Philadelphia. Give me my bill and I can promise Madison the nation's capital will go to the South. Permanently. I was born in the West Indies—I have no local preference. However, for the sake of the Great Man, I'd like to see it go to Virginia.

JEFFERSON *(pause)*. Well, I'll bring you together, and sit at the table to see you don't shoot each other.

HAMILTON *(laughs)*. Fair enough.

JEFFERSON *(takes out his fan-shaped notebook, jots down the appointment)*. You see, Colonel Hamilton, we must never permit ourselves to despair of the republic.

HAMILTON. My dear Jefferson, if I haven't despaired of this republic till now, it's because of my nature, not my judgment. *(JEFFERSON laughs.)* Your address?

JEFFERSON. Twenty-three Maiden Lane.

HAMILTON. Twenty-three Maiden Lane. At seven?

JEFFERSON. Make it seven-thirty.

*(WASHINGTON enters.)*

WASHINGTON. You two gentlemen have met?

HAMILTON. Yes. What impression did the Spanish Ambassador leave with you?

WASHINGTON. Like all the rest. They regard us as a contemptuous joke.

HAMILTON. Well . . . (*Looks at* JEFFERSON, *smiles.*) we shan't despair. Seven-thirty? (*He bows to* WASHINGTON.) Excellency. (*He goes.*)

JEFFERSON. Remarkable young man.

WASHINGTON. They call him the Little Lion.

JEFFERSON. Little Lion! I can see it. (*Picks up his portfolio.*) Shall I review my report on the French Tariff situation?

WASHINGTON. Yes, yes, do.

JEFFERSON. Just before I left France, I had conversations with Monsieur Neckar on the matter of fishing rights. During the last year, some 23,000 francs . . . (WASHINGTON *heaves a huge sigh.* JEFFERSON *looks up. The* PRESIDENT *is staring out the window.*) Nice day out, isn't it?

WASHINGTON (*distracted, turns*). Hm? Oh, yes—yes.

JEFFERSON (*grins*). Have you a fishing pole for me?

WASHINGTON (*looks at* JEFFERSON, *goes to a closet, takes out two fishing poles*). How'd you know? (*Hands one to* JEFFERSON.) You don't mind, now?

JEFFERSON (*laughs*). I can't think of a better way to discuss the affairs of a republic.

(WASHINGTON *removes his jacket, takes an old one from the closet, calls gruffly:*)

WASHINGTON. Sergeant! (JEFFERSON *helps him on with the jacket.*) Sergeant!

(SERGEANT *enters.*)

SERGEANT. Yes, sir?

WASHINGTON. I'm not to be disturbed. By anyone. I'm in conference with my Secretary of State.

SERGEANT (*knowingly*). Yes, sir. (*Exits.*)

WASHINGTON (*whispers to* JEFFERSON). If Humphreys caught me in these clothes, I'd never hear the end. (WASHINGTON *removes his wig, sets it on a stand, claps on a disreputable battered old hat, picks up his pole and some documents, opens the door, starts out, sees someone off, draws back, signaling* JEFFERSON *to wait.*) One of the servants.

JEFFERSON. Don't they approve of democracy?

WASHINGTON (*looks at* JEFFERSON, *shakes his head sadly*). No! (*He peers out again. The coast is clear, now. He signals* JEFFERSON *to follow him.*) Come! (*Stealthily, they exit.*)

## SCENE II

SCENE: *The smithy of an inn in New York. Through the large open door a glimpse of the courtyard of the inn.* JACOB, *the smith, is hammering out a horseshoe.* MAT, *his apprentice, is pumping the bellows. Burst of laughter and men's voices from the inn courtyard.* POTBOY *crosses doorway clutching several foaming tankards.*

JACOB. Pump her, Mat!

(*His hammer comes down with a clang.* MAT *pumps the bellows. The fire glows.* NED THE POTBOY *enters.*)

POTBOY. Colonel Hamilton wants his horse saddled right off.

JACOB. He in a hurry?

(*Clang.*)

POTBOY. Yep.

JACOB. Leavin' his party? So soon?

POTBOY. Yep.

MAT. Why, they ain't hardly started a-belchin' yet.

JACOB. Fire's gettin' cold, Mat.

MAT. I'm a-pumpin'!

POTBOY. Wants her saddled right off, he said.

MAT. We heard you.

POTBOY (*irritably*). I'm only tellin' yuh what . . .

MAT (*sharply*). Awright.

JACOB. Here! Kinda techy, you two, to-day. Ain't you?

*(Pause. He looks at them both, shakes his head, hammers away at the horse-shoe.)*

POTBOY *(apologetically)*. Standin' by, listenin' to that Tory talk out there! Gets me mad.

JACOB. Git the saddle on, Mat!

MAT. Awright. *(Fetches saddle.)*

POTBOY. Braggin' about the millions they made in paper money! I keep thinkin' of my sister.

MAT. And me! Don't fergit me! Three hundred dollars—whish!—right out-a me pocket. *(Laughter off. He spits.)*

POTBOY. Know what one was a-sayin'? President ain't a good title for the head of the United States. Ain't got enough distingay.

MAT. French words!

POTBOY. 'At's what he said. There are presidents of cricket clubs and fire companies, he said.

MAT. What the plague do they want? Royal Highness?

POTBOY. Yep. That's it.

*(JACOB looks up, a frown on his face.)*

JACOB. You mean that?

POTBOY. 'At's what they said.

MAT. Fer cripes sake!

*(He goes. Just outside the door he greets newcomers, "Good afternoon, sir." JEFFERSON'S voice: "Afternoon, Mat." JEFFERSON enters with MONROE and MADISON.)*

JEFFERSON *(to MADISON)*. You tell my children they're to write me more often, will you, Jemmy?

MADISON. I'll do that.

JEFFERSON. I want to hear about everything at Monticello from Patsy to Grizzle.

MONROE. Who's Grizzle?

JEFFERSON. Our pet pig.

*(MONROE and MADISON laugh.)*

JACOB. Afternoon, Mr. Jefferson!

JEFFERSON. How are you today, Jacob?

JACOB. Middlin'. I forged them fittin's you ordered. They're right over there on that tool bench.

JEFFERSON. Fine.

MONROE. Smith, my horse is limpin' on the off-front foot.

JACOB. Picked up a pebble?

MONROE. May have.

JEFFERSON. Looks to me as if she's sprung a shoe, James.

MONROE. Think so?

JACOB. Find out fer yuh in a minute.

MADISON. Give my nag a good going over too, will you, smith? I'm off on a long journey.

JACOB. Where to, Mr. Madison?

MADISON. Home.

JEFFERSON *(sits on a keg examining the fittings)*. Virginia.

JACOB. Oh! Nice weather.

MADISON. Ideal.

JEFFERSON. The lilacs'll be in full bloom and the golden willows and the almond trees.

JACOB. Not so early.

JEFFERSON. Oh, yes. In Virginia.

JACOB. That so?

*(A burst of laughter, offstage.)*

MADISON. A festive board out there!

JACOB. Some a Colonel Hamilton's friends givin' him a party.

MONROE. Celebrating the passage of his bill, I suppose.

JACOB. Yep. *(He goes off.)*

MONROE *(bitterly)*. Yes.

JEFFERSON. Now, James.

MONROE. Well, plague on it, Mr. Jefferson!

MADISON. I have to agree with Mr. Jefferson. *Ad necessitatus rei.*

MONROE. No matter how many fine Latin names you call it—"a pig is a pig."

MADISON. This was the lesser of two evils.

MONROE. You honestly think so?

MADISON *(without conviction)*. I do. Yes.

MONROE. And you, Mr. Jefferson?

JEFFERSON *(doubtfully)*. I don't know. I—hope so. I'm . . .

*(Laughter offstage.* MONROE *growls in disgust.* JEFFERSON *looks up at him, smiles wryly at* MADISON, *picks up the fittings* JACOB *has forged for him, examines them.)*

MONROE. You've seen the newspapers, of course?

JEFFERSON. Yes, I've seen them.

MAT *(enters. To* MADISON*)*. Wants a feedin', your mare does. She's askin' for it.

MADISON. All right. Some oats, please.

*(*MAT *pours some oats in a bag.)*

MAT. Senator Monroe?

MONROE *(looks at his watch)*. Yes. It's her dinnertime.

MAT. Mr. Jefferson?

JEFFERSON *(rises)*. I just fed my horse, Mat, thank you. A couple of carrots, though. So he doesn't feel neglected.

MAT *(laughs)*. Got some in the kitchen. *(Hands* MADISON *and* MONROE *bags of oats.* MADISON *exits with bag of oats.* MAT *exits.* JACOB *enters, holding a horseshoe in his nippers.)*

JACOB. Sprung it, awright.

MONROE. Did, hm? Shoe he˗ at once, will you, smith?

JACOB. Yes, sir.

*(*MONROE *exits with bag of oats.* JACOB *puts the horseshoe in the furnace and proceeds to pump the bellows.* JEFFERSON *examines the metal fittings* JACOB *has forged for him.)*

JEFFERSON. You've done an excellent job on these.

JACOB. They awright?

JEFFERSON. Good. You know your craft!

JACOB. Ought to. Twenty years a-doin' it. *(*JEFFERSON *places some of the metal bits together.)* Makin' another one of your inventions, are you?

JEFFERSON. A "convenience."

JACOB. What is it this time?

JEFFERSON *(crosses to Jacob)*. A sort of closet on pulleys that will come up from the kitchen to the dining room—carry the food hot and the wine cold right in, without people running up and down stairs.

JACOB. Now, say, that's a purty good invention.

JEFFERSON. You think so?

JACOB. Told my wife about the collapsible buggy top you invented. Kinda useful idea, she said. But this'll catch her fancy. What do you call this here invention?

JEFFERSON *(smiles)*. A "dumbwaiter."

JACOB. Dumbwaiter? *(He puzzles it out.)* Oh, yeah! *(Gets it.)* Oh, yeah! *(Roars with laughter.)* A dumbwaiter. Purty good. *(*JACOB, *chuckling, extracts a horseshoe from the fire and begins to shape it on the anvil.)*

JEFFERSON. Jacob!

JACOB *(intent on his work)*. Yes?

JEFFERSON. I need your advice.

JACOB. What about?

JEFFERSON. This money bill we've just passed.

JACOB. Oh! *(Looks up for a moment.)*

JEFFERSON. What do you think of it?

JACOB. Don't like it much.

JEFFERSON. You don't?

JACOB. Nope. *(Frowns, hammers the shoe.)*

JEFFERSON. Because of the speculators?

JACOB. Yep.

JEFFERSON. I see. Still, it's done the country considerable good?

JACOB. Mebbe.

JEFFERSON. What do your friends think of it, generally?

JACOB. Don't like it much.

JEFFERSON. I see.

(POTBOY *pokes in his head.*)

NED. Saddled yet? He's waitin'!

JACOB. Tell Mr. Jefferson, Ned. He's askin' about the money bill.

NED. A blood-suckin' swindle, Mr. Jefferson. *(He is suddenly all aflame.)* Look at my sister! Her husband was killed at the battle of Saratoga. Left her two little ones and some paper money they paid him. She's been savin' that for years. Two months ago the speculators told her it would be years more before she got anything on it, if ever. Got her to sell it for forty dollars. Six hundred dollars' worth! 'N they got Jacob's savin's.

(MAT *enters.*)

JEFFERSON. They did?

JACOB. Nine hundred.

NED. From the Revolution. His pay.

JACOB. That ain't what we fit the Revolution fer.

JEFFERSON *(rises, restlessly).* No.

MAT. I tell you it's gettin' time we . . .

(HAMILTON *enters.*)

HAMILTON. Is my horse ready, Jacob? Mr. Jefferson! I thought I saw you in the courtyard. I've some very good reports for you.

(NED *exits.*)

JEFFERSON. Splendid.

JACOB. Mat?

MAT. She's ready. *(Exits.)*

JACOB. Your horse is ready, Colonel Hamilton.

HAMILTON. Thank you! Fine day, Jacob!

JACOB *(grunts).* Yep. *(Exits.)*

HAMILTON *(to* JEFFERSON*).* A little soured this morning, isn't he? Liver?

JEFFERSON *(shakes his head).* Speculators.

HAMILTON. Jacob? *(*JEFFERSON *nods.)* A shame.

JEFFERSON. And Mat. And the potboy.

HAMILTON. Why didn't they hold on to their paper?

JEFFERSON. Apparently they did. For almost seven years.

HAMILTON. Tch! Too bad. They should have had more faith in their government.

JEFFERSON. They had no way of knowing the bill was about to redeem that paper. I'm very disturbed by this.

HAMILTON. You are?

JEFFERSON. Very. Apparently a handful of speculators, many of them in high places, have taken advantage of their knowledge of the bill to feather their own nests.

HAMILTON. Oh, now! Don't paint it worse than it is.

JEFFERSON. There's a good deal of bitter talk.

HAMILTON. Idle gossip!

JEFFERSON. Hardly.

HAMILTON. The treasury can't ask every man who submits a paper note how he came by it. At least in this way these people received something.

JEFFERSON. There must have been a means to avert this speculation.

HAMILTON. Look here—I don't quite understand your attitude. *(Burst of laughter, offstage.)* If we want to develop this country we've got to create great personal fortunes. Those men out there are building manufactories and industry. They're building America!

JEFFERSON. Good. Let's encourage them! But not at the expense of the people!

HAMILTON. You and Madison! The people whisper—you tremble.

(MONROE *and* MADISON *enter, stand silently listening.*)

JEFFERSON. That's as it should be, isn't it?

HAMILTON. I am determined this country's happiness shall be established on a firm basis. I think its only hope now lies in a moneyed aristocracy to protect it from the indiscretions of the people.

JEFFERSON. I see. And this bill is to lay the foundation for such an aristocracy?

HAMILTON. Exactly.

JEFFERSON. I wasn't aware of that. You said nothing of that to me. I must be quite honest with you. I regret that I have been made a party to your bill.

HAMILTON. Made? Made, you say? You've been in politics twenty-one years. Don't play the innocent with me! Are you dissatisfied with your bargain? Is that it?

JEFFERSON. Bargain?

HAMILTON. The capital of the nation is going to *your* state—not mine.

JEFFERSON. Oh, for God's sake!

HAMILTON. Frankly, these alarms smell of hypocrisy. One minute you say you know nothing of Treasury matters; the next you set yourself up as an authority.

MONROE. What do you suppose, Colonel? Shall we scrap the Constitution at once?

HAMILTON (*turns, sees* MONROE *and* MADISON, *murmurs, in disgust*). The Constitution!

JEFFERSON. You supported it.

HAMILTON (*flaring*). I had no choice. I couldn't stand by and see the country go down in convulsions and anarchy. (*Pause. He controls himself.*) I must confess it's my opinion this government won't last five years. However, since we've undertaken this experiment, I'm for giving it a fair trial. But, be certain of this: while it lasts it will be an aristocratic republic. If any man wants a democracy, let him proceed to the confines of some other government. Good day, gentlemen. (*He goes.*)

JEFFERSON (*to* MONROE). My apologies. I was wrong. (*To* MADISON.) Forgive me, Jemmy. I shouldn't have asked you to compromise.

MADISON. Tom, we can't escape it. He's trying to administer the Constitution into something it was never intended to be.

MONROE. I have a statement from a man who swears that Hamilton gave him money out of the public treasury to speculate with.

JEFFERSON. That I don't believe.

MONROE. There are also some letters in Hamilton's hand.

JEFFERSON. Don't believe it! He's personally honest. I'll vouch for that.

MONROE. Will you at least confront him with these letters? Ask him to explain them?

JEFFERSON. I can't.

MONROE. Why not?

JEFFERSON. Oh, for God's sake, James!

MONROE. You fight fire with fire.

JEFFERSON. I'm no salamander. Fire's not my element.

MONROE. His bill has made the fortunes of half the prominent men in the Federalist Party. It's a ring he's put through their nose. And it's clear enough, God knows, where he intends to lead them. You can't allow that. You've got to fight him. You've got to wrest the leadership of the Federalist Party away from him!

JEFFERSON (*a surge of revulsion*). If there's one thing makes me sick to death—it's the whole spirit of party politics. James, if the only way I could enter heaven was on the back of a political party, I'd rather burn in purgatory.

(JACOB *appears in the doorway, adjusting saddle.*)

JACOB. Your horse is ready, Mr. Jefferson.

JEFFERSON (*looks at him, pauses*). Oh, thank you, Jacob.

JACOB. Ready your horses, gentlemen?

MADISON. Yes, please.

(JACOB *exits.*)

JEFFERSON (*staring after Jacob, his voice harsh and lifeless*). You're wrong about the letters, James. For the rest, his bill has values. But it's hurt our people. Through it, he's created a corrupt squadron. Naturally, if he does try to pervert the Constitution, I shall oppose him. But I must do it in my own way. I'm not a brawler; I'm not a politician. (*Crosses to* MADISON.) Say howdya to all my neighbors for me. (MADISON *nods.*) The matter I spoke to you of . . . ? (*Hands a paper to* MADISON.)

MADISON (*nods*). I'll tend to this first thing on my arrival.

JEFFERSON. Thanks, Jemmy.

MADISON. I know how important it is to you.

JEFFERSON. Very. Pleasant journey, Jemmy. Hurry back. (*To* MONROE, *gently.*) A game of chess tonight? (MONROE *nods.* JEFFERSON *goes.*)

MONROE (*looking after him*). Blast it! This isn't the Jefferson we knew.

MADISON. No.

MONROE. The country's red hot. It's being shaped, *now.* What does it need to wake him again.

MADISON. The tears Christ wept before the tomb of Lazarus.

MONROE. You talk of Tom as if he were dead.

MADISON (*holds up the paper Jefferson gave him*). He asked me to order a new stone for Martha's grave. (*Unfolds paper.*) Do you understand Greek?

MONROE. No. Translate it!

MADISON (*translates*). Roughly . . .
"If in the shades below,
  The fires of friends and lovers cease to glow,
  Yet mine, mine alone
  Will burn on through death, itself."

MONROE. After nine years?

MADISON. After nine years!

(JACOB *and* MAT *enter, go to hearth.*)

JACOB. Horses ready!

MONROE. Thank you, Jacob.

(NED *enters.* MADISON *and* MONROE *exit.*)

NED (*raging as he tears off his apron*). I'll be damned if I'll serve on them any more! Know what they're saying now? Dukes and Lords we oughta have!

MAT. Dukes and Lords?

NED. Ay! The blood-suckin' swindlers!

JACOB. Pump her, Mat! Pump her!

MAT. What do they want to do? Make serfs outa us?

NED. Is that what we fought Lexington and Bunker Hill for? Is this the freedom my brother and my sister's husband died for? Where's your goddamn revolution now?

JACOB (*between his teeth, grimly*). Pump her, Mat! Come on, pump her! (MAT *pumps. The forge glows, high-lighting the taut and angry faces.* JACOB *hammers the hot iron with mighty, ringing blows.*)

# ACT TWO

## SCENE I

SCENE: HAMILTON's *home. Candlelight.* HAMILTON, HUMPHREYS *and* KNOX *are having coffee.* MRS. HAMILTON *is pouring coffee.* HAMILTON *is opening a package of cigars.*

MRS. HAMILTON (*seated on sofa*). When I think of Louis and Marie in jail!

HUMPHREYS. I haven't slept a wink since the palace fell. Dreadful! Did you read Fenno's piece in the *Gazette* today?

MRS. HAMILTON. I never miss Fenno. Brilliant, wasn't it?

HUMPHREYS. *Un chef-d'oeuvre!*

MRS. HAMILTON. Veritable!

KNOX. The situation seems to be growing worse, too. What do you think, Alec, of this French Republic?

HAMILTON. Dangerous. Highly dangerous. I'm particularly disturbed by the effect it may have on some of our inflammables. (*He places the cigars on a tray.*)

HUMPHREYS. You certainly lashed Mr. Jefferson on that score! *Ma foi!* Gave it to him. But proper!

MRS. HAMILTON (*to* KNOX). Sugar?

KNOX. Please.

MRS. HAMILTON. Mr. Jefferson isn't really one of these filthy Democrats?

HAMILTON. I'm afraid so, my dear.

MRS. HAMILTON. Does he *really believe* every man is as good as every other man?

HAMILTON. Even better.

*(They laugh.* HUMPHREYS *applauds.)*

MRS. HAMILTON. Cream?

KNOX. Please.

HAMILTON. And our people seem so convinced of it. They can't wait to cut each other's throats. *(Offers cigars to* KNOX.*)* Try one of these.

KNOX. Yes. You saw it so clearly during the war. In the army.

HAMILTON. Army? *(He offers cigars to* HUMPHREYS*).* Colonel Humphreys?

HUMPHREYS *(takes a cigar, examines it apprehensively).* So this is one of these new "cigars"?

HAMILTON *(crosses to table, sets down cigars, lights a taper).* From the Spanish Islands. . . . Army? It was no army, it was a mob. Only one man held it together. *(He holds the lighted taper to* KNOX's *cigar.)*

KNOX. The Chief. *(Lights his cigar with huge puffs.)*

HAMILTON *(nods).* Washington. *(Lights* HUMPHREYS' *cigar.)*

KNOX *(examines his cigar).* Very interesting leaf.

HUMPHREYS *(puffing away).* Mm! Good! Good!

HAMILTON *(to* KNOX*).* I hope you like them, Henry. I've ordered a packet for you.

KNOX. Why, thank you, Alec.

HAMILTON. Not at all. *(Selects and lights a cigar for himself.)*

KNOX. Yes. The Chief made an army out of a rabble, all right. There's no doubt of that.

HAMILTON. Ah! But to accomplish it, even he had to resort to the gallows and the lash. As with an army, so with a nation. You need one strong man.

KNOX. The Chief's getting old, though.

HAMILTON. Exactly. Sometimes I lay awake nights wondering how we can ever hold this country together, when he's gone.

KNOX. Personally, I think it's his character alone that does it. I wouldn't give a penny for the Constitution without him.

HAMILTON *(sits).* Well, it's real value is as a stepping-stone. *(Purring over his cigar.)* Wonderful flavor?

KNOX. Mm!

HUMPHREYS *(wryly).* A bit strongish. *(They laugh. He disposes of his cigar in tray beside chair.)* I agree with Alec. A monarchy would have been our best salvation.

MRS. HAMILTON. Only today I was talking to some of the ladies of our court on this subject. You go out in the streets. It's frightening. We're all agreed, the time is ripening for us to have a *real* king.

BUTLER *(entering).* Senator Monroe is calling, sir.

HAMILTON. Monroe? What's he want? *(Rises.)* Show him in.

BUTLER. Yes, sir. *(BUTLER exits.)*

HUMPHREYS *(rises).* Now, there's a country bumpkin! James Monroe. *Pas d'élégance!*

KNOX. He's a good soldier! Fought in almost every important battle of the war.

HAMILTON. The soul of a clerk, though. I can't abide that.

HUMPHREYS. He was, you know. He was a clerk in Jefferson's law office ten years ago.

HAMILTON. Still is, as far as I'm concerned. *(They laugh.)* I'll wager ten to one he's here on some errand for Mr. Jefferson! Mark! You'll see!

*(BUTLER enters.)*

BUTLER. Colonel Monroe.

MONROE *(enters, bows).* Gentlemen! Colonel Hamilton.

*(KNOX rises, bows briefly, and sits again.)*

HAMILTON. Colonel Monroe. This is an unexpected pleasure. You've met my lady.

MONROE. Mrs. Hamilton. *(He bows.)* I was reluctant to intrude on you in your home.

HAMILTON *(crosses to pick up tray of cigars)*. Quite all right.

MONROE. However, I've been trying to make an appointment with you at your office for several weeks.

HAMILTON *(crosses to* MONROE, *offers him cigars)*. My office has been so busy. . . . The new taxes. Cigar?

MONROE. No, thanks.

HAMILTON. From the Spanish Islands.

MONROE. No, thanks. I should like to speak with you alone, if I may.

MRS. HAMILTON. My dear, it sounds ominous.

KNOX *(rises)*. Well—er . . .

HUMPHREYS. I have an engagement with my wig-maker.

HAMILTON *(restrains them)*. No. Stay, gentlemen. Pray. *(To* MONROE.*)* What's on your mind?

MONROE *(grimly)*. I said alone.

HAMILTON *(curbs his annoyance, smiles)*. I'm sorry. I've had an exhausting day. I refuse to discuss business now. I'll see you at my office. Tomorrow at four-thirty, if you wish.

MONROE. I'm seeing the President at four.

HAMILTON. Next week, perhaps.

MONROE. I'm seeing him on a matter that concerns you.

HAMILTON. Me? Indeed! Well, I wish you luck. You're sure you won't have one of these cigars—to smoke on the way?

MONROE. No, thanks.

HAMILTON. You'll excuse us, I'm sure. *(To* BUTLER, *who is waiting at the door.)* Chandler!

BUTLER *(steps forward)*. Yes, sir.

MONROE. Very well. I have some papers I intend to submit to the President. I wanted to give you a chance to explain.

HAMILTON. Give me a chance to . . . ? I don't like your tone. I don't like it at all.

MONROE. I think you should be informed. There have been charges leveled against you.

HAMILTON. What charges?

MONROE. Of appropriating treasury funds.

HAMILTON. What? *(Moves toward* MONROE.*)* You dare to come into my house and accuse me of . . . ?

MONROE. *I'm* not accusing you. I'm inquiring into the facts.

HAMILTON. General Knox, will you act as my second?

KNOX. Your servant.

HAMILTON. Sir, you will name your friend to this gentleman. They can arrange weapons, time, and place. Good night.

MONROE. I'll be very happy to oblige you.

HAMILTON *(to* SERVANT*)*. Show him out.

MONROE *(takes some letters out of his pocket)*. But I must first demand you explain these letters. . . .

HAMILTON *(raging—moves down, facing* MONROE*)*. Any man who dares call me thief . . .

MONROE. To Mr. Reynolds.

HAMILTON *(stops short)*. Reynolds?

MONROE. Yes.

HAMILTON. I see. May I . . . ? *(He .puts out his hand.* MONROE *gives him one of the letters. He glances at it, returns it.)*

MONROE. Is that your writing?

HAMILTON. It is. This puts the matter on a different footing. I have no objection to a fair inquiry. And I think you are entitled to a frank answer.

KNOX. We'll go, Alec. *(*KNOX *starts to go,* HAMILTON *restrains him.)*

HAMILTON. I want you as a witness to this.

KNOX. Of course.

HAMILTON *(to* MONROE*)*. If you will be at my office tomorrow evening, I . . .

MONROE *(stubbornly)*. I'm seeing the President at *four*.

HAMILTON. In the morning, then. It happens, fortunately, I can supply you with all the letters and documents in this instance.

MONROE. Mr. Reynolds charges you gave him money from the public treasuries to speculate with in your behalf.

HAMILTON. Where is Mr. Reynolds now?

MONROE. I've no idea.

HAMILTON. He's in jail. Subornation of perjury in a fraud case. You take the word of such a character?

MONROE. Did you give him this money?

HAMILTON. I did. But it was my own.

MONROE. And why did you give money to such a character?

*(A long pause.)*

HAMILTON. He was blackmailing me.

MRS. HAMILTON. Alec!

MONROE. What for?

HAMILTON. A personal matter which has nothing to do with the treasury. I'll prove that to your full satisfaction.

MONROE. Under any circumstances, I shall ask for an accounting to Congress.

HAMILTON. As a Senator that is your privilege. And I shall oblige you. I will invite all America to look into the window of my breast and judge the purity of my political motives. Not one penny of the public funds have I ever touched. I would sooner pluck out my eye by the roots.

*(MONROE remains stonily unmoved. HAMILTON's smile becomes cynical.)*

MONROE. At your office. Tomorrow at ten.

HAMILTON. Ten will do.

MONROE. If it's as you say, the matter will, of course, be kept confidential.

HAMILTON *(ironically)*. Yes, I'm sure it will. *(MONROE bows, turns to go.)* Tell him for me, Colonel Monroe, it would have been more manly, at least, to have come here, himself.

MONROE. Who are you referring to?

HAMILTON. Who sent you, Colonel Monroe?

MONROE. No one sent me, Colonel Hamilton.

HAMILTON. No one?

MONROE. No one! *(MONROE goes.)*

HUMPHREYS. *Quelle folie!*

HAMILTON. Henry! Humphreys! Will you gentlemen . . . ?

KNOX. Of course, Alec. We were just leaving. If there's anything we can do? Anything at all, call on us. All your friends will be at your disposal.

HAMILTON. Thank you. It's not as serious as that, believe me.

HUMPHREYS. Ridiculous, of course. A bagatelle! When I was at the court, there was such an incident. . . .

KNOX. Come, Humphreys!

HUMPHREYS. Hm? Oh, yes, yes! *(Bows.)* Your servant, my lady. *(To HAMILTON.)* *Votre cher ami,* Colonel.

KNOX. Mrs. Hamilton! Alec!

HAMILTON. Betsy, I tried to spare you this.

MRS. HAMILTON *(rises)*. We'll go to father. He'll help you, darling. I know he will. You mustn't worry.

HAMILTON. It's not a question of money. Good God, Betsy, do *you* think I'm an embezzler?

MRS. HAMILTON. I only know you're in trouble and I want to help you.

HAMILTON. Thank you, my dear. Thank you. *(He kisses her.)* You've been a wonderful wife, Betsy. Far better than I deserve.

MRS. HAMILTON. What was this man blackmailing you for? What have you done, Alec?

HAMILTON. I've been very foolish, Betsy.

MRS. HAMILTON. Please, Alec. Tell me!

HAMILTON. When I wooed you, do you remember I said I wanted a wife who would love God but hate a saint?

MRS. HAMILTON. Don't jest with me now, Alec.

HAMILTON. I'm not.

MRS. HAMILTON. What was this man blackmailing you for?

HAMILTON. Philandering with his wife.

MRS. HAMILTON. Oh! I see. *(Turns away —sits, controlling herself.)* Who is she? Do I know her?

HAMILTON. No. It was a game they were playing together. She and her husband. He suddenly appeared one night, claimed I'd ruined his life, and threatened to inform you, unless I gave him a thousand dollars. He's been bleeding me dry ever since. Now, he's gotten himself in jail, and wants me to use my influence to release him. I refused. This is his revenge. *(Contritely.)* Forgive me, dearest. I would do anything . . . *(He sits beside her.)*

MRS. HAMILTON. Let's not discuss that, Alec. The question is, what shall we do now to clear you?

HAMILTON. My accounts will do that, Betsy. Congress will clear me.

MRS. HAMILTON. Oh! *(Pause.)* Good, then. *(She turns to HAMILTON.)* Why didn't you tell me this before?

HAMILTON. I didn't want to hurt you.

MRS. HAMILTON *(suddenly rises, moves away)*. Then I wish to Heaven you hadn't told me at all.

HAMILTON *(rises)*. I'm forced to it, Betsy. Jefferson obviously wants to destroy my position as leader of the party. As long as these letters in his hands go unexplained —by insinuation, he could undermine belief in my honesty. I must be prepared to *publish* the facts, if necessary. *(He goes to her, takes her arm.)* Betsy . . .

MRS. HAMILTON *(drawing arm away)*. Please, Alec!

HAMILTON. You understand, don't you?

MRS. HAMILTON. Oh, yes.

HAMILTON. Believe me, I love you.

MRS. HAMILTON *(her indignation explodes with an icy blast)*. And slept with a harlot! Don't insult me, Alec! You never loved me.

HAMILTON. Why did I marry you?

MRS. HAMILTON. Was it because my father was General Schuyler?

HAMILTON *(flaring)*. And I the illegitimate son of a Scotch peddler? I married you for your wealth and your position! Is that what you believe?

MRS. HAMILTON *(wearily)*. I don't know what to believe.

*(BUTLER enters.)*

BUTLER. Excuse me, sir. Mr. Fenno calling on you, sir.

HAMILTON. Tell him to go away!

MRS. HAMILTON. Show him in, Chandler. *(The BUTLER hesitates.)* Show him in!

BUTLER. Yes, Ma'am. *(Exits.)*

HAMILTON. Betsy, I want to talk this out with you.

MRS. HAMILTON *(presses her fingers to her temples)*. I don't care to discuss this any more.

HAMILTON *(takes her by shoulders)*. Listen to me, Betsy! You must listen . . .

MRS. HAMILTON. Alec, please! *(She draws away from him.)* I don't care to hear any more, now. I'm—tired.

*(As she turns and goes, her handkerchief falls to the floor. He stares after her a moment, sees the handkerchief, picks it up.)*

BUTLER. Mr. Fenno.

*(Enter MR. FENNO, a dandified gentleman; at the moment, however, he is in a lather of perspiration.)*

FENNO. My dear Alec. I had to rush here and tell you. We have just received some shocking news. I- -I'm trembling so, I can hardly talk.

*(The BUTLER exits.)*

HAMILTON *(turning to FENNO, wearily)*. What is it, Fenno?

FENO. The King and Queen of France have been executed.

HAMILTON. They've . . . ?

FENNO. Guillotined.

HAMILTON. Monstrous!

FENNO *(sinks into a chair, mops his forehead with his kerchief)*. The mobs in France are utterly out of hand. Burning, looting, killing. A blood bath! Unbelievable, isn't it? Simply unbelievable!

HAMILTON. I was afraid of this.

FENNO. Worse. I've heard ugly rumors here. I passed a house yesterday, and I heard a group of men down in the cellar, singing "Ça Ira"! Rufus King told me he'd heard open threats against us. Even against General Washington.

HAMILTON. I've no doubt of it.

FENNO. I fear this is going to spread like the smallpox.

HAMILTON. Yes. And who've we to thank? Jefferson! Jefferson!

FENNO. Oh, no, I don't think he would dare . . .

HAMILTON (*pacing furiously*). I tell you, yes! The man's a lunatic. He's been encouraging our people to all sorts of wild illusions. Bill of rights! Freedom! Liberty! License! Anarchy! This is the fruit of his disordered imagination. That man will stop at nothing to achieve chaos. But there'll be no more of him here! I promise you. I will see to it. (*Looks at* BETSY's *handkerchief, smooths it, a note of savage heartbreak in his voice.*) There's no longer any room in this country—in this world, for both me and that—fanatic!

## SCENE II

SCENE: *The wild strains of "Ça Ira." As the music fades away, the harsh, discordant voices of a crowd chanting it are heard.*
*Philadelphia. 1793. Evening.*
*A room in a house rented by* JEFFERSON. *A mist hangs outside the window. Under the window, on the table, a row of potted plants. On a large table in the center of the room, books and papers piled high; a vise, some tools, a machine in process of construction. A kettle of water on a Franklin stove. The noise of the crowd in the street faintly heard.*
JEFFERSON *enters, hat in hand. He goes to the window, looks out. The sound of the crowd fades. He strikes flint and tinder and lights an oil lamp. Its light only serves to reveal the cheerlessness of the room. He extracts a journal from his pocket, sits, studying it, frowning.*
JUPITER, *his body servant, enters. A Negro with a good, intelligent face.*

JUPITER. Evenin', Mister Tom!

JEFFERSON. Good evening, Jupiter.

JUPITER (*goes about lighting the lamps*). You come in so quiet. Didn't hardly hear you. We have a busy day, Mister Tom?

JEFFERSON. Mm, hm.

JUPITER. Supper's ready soon as you say.

JEFFERSON. I'm not very hungry, Jupiter.

JUPITER. But yuh got to tuck sumpin' in yuh.

JEFFERSON. Later, perhaps. (*With an exclamation of disgust,* JEFFERSON *rises, throws the newspaper on the chair.* JUPITER *looks up, surprised at this unusual outburst.* JEFFERSON *walks over to the potted plants, examines them.* JUPITER *picks up the newspaper, looks at it quizzically, places it on the table.* JEFFERSON *examines the potted plants, nips off a few dead leaves.*)

JUPITER (*wheedles*). Good supper. We got basted puddin' an' chicken.

JEFFERSON (*shakes his head*). Thanks. (*Picks up a little watering pot near by and waters the plants.*)

JUPITER. You just come fum one a dem cabinet meetin's?

JEFFERSON (*nods, smiles*). Yes!

JUPITER. Mm, mm! (*Nods knowingly.*) Funny weather outside. Sticky! That yeller fog hanging all over Philadelphia. I heard today ten white folk died o' the fever.

JEFFERSON. More than that.

JUPITER. Don't like it none. (*Turns to go.* JEFFERSON *notices* JUPITER's *hand is roughly bandaged with a bloodstained handkerchief.*)

JEFFERSON. What's happened to your hand?

JUPITER. Oh, it's nothin'.

JEFFERSON. Let me look at it! Come here. *(He removes the bandage.)* A nasty gash. Sit over here! *(JUPITER sits. JEFFERSON goes to the stove, pours some water into a cup, selects a bottle of wine and cruet of oil from the cupboard.)* How did you do that, Jupiter?

JUPITER. When I do my marketin' this afternoon, Mister Tom.

*(JEFFERSON sets the cup, the wine and the oil on the table, opens a drawer, and takes out some cloth. He opens JUPITER's hand, examines it.)*

JEFFERSON. This is going to sting a bit. *(Tears cloth into strips.)*

JUPITER. That's all right, Mister Tom.

JEFFERSON *(dips the cloth in the water and starts to clean the wound. He soaks the cloth with wine, dabs the wound. JUPITER winces).* Hurt you? *(JUPITER stoically shakes his head.)* How did you do this?

JUPITER. Down outside Bainbridge Market. Just as I came out.

JEFFERSON. Yes?

JUPITER. Three men was talkin'. "Mr. Jefferson's a devil," they say. Colonel Hamilton tell dem you gonna bring the French Revolution here. Murder everybody. I don't like that. I told them that ain't true. "Ain't you Jefferson's nigger?" they say. They say they was gonna kill me. One of 'em tried to hit me on the head with a stick. I put my hand up. The stick had a nail in it.

JEFFERSON. Oh, Jupiter! Haven't you learned yet?

JUPITER. They talk bad about you. What I'm gonna do?

JEFFERSON. When an angry bull stands in your path, what do you do?

JUPITER. What I do?

JEFFERSON. A man of sense doesn't dispute the road with such an animal. He walks around it. *(He smiles. JUPITER laughs and nods.)*

JUPITER. Yeah, I guess so.

JEFFERSON. What happened then, Jupiter?

JUPITER. Then a crowd came down the street, yellin'! Dey's a lot a crowds in de street, Mister Tom.

JEFFERSON. I know.

JUPITER. De men see dat crowd. Dey get scared an' run away. Mister Tom—dem crowds in de street—dey're talkin' wild. Yellin' "Kill de aristocrats! Break dere windows! Burn dere houses!" Singin' French songs.

JEFFERSON *(he bandages the hand).* Hurt? Too tight?

JUPITER *(shakes his head).* Dey talkin' bad about President Washington.

JEFFERSON. Washington?

JUPITER. Yes, Mister Tom. *(JEFFERSON frowns as he bandages the hand.)* Dat get me all mixed up. I know he fight for liberty. I remind me you tell me General Washington try to free my people.

JEFFERSON. That's right. He did.

JUPITER. I remind me, how you try, Mister Tom. I like to see my little Sarah free some day. An' I remind me how you say we gotta some day open all that land in the Northwest and ain't gonna be no slaves there. An' how we gotta git my people education, an' we gotta git 'em land, an' tools.

JEFFERSON. Some day, Jupiter. It's written in the book of fate. Your people will be free.

JUPITER. Mister Tom. Dat crowd. Git me mixed up. Git me all mixed up. I don't like it. Dey jus' gonna make trouble.

JEFFERSON. I'm afraid you're right, Jupiter. You see, the men who beat you— they're Monarchists. They want a king here. The others—the crowd—they're mixed up. It's what's happening in France now. It's gone wild. *(Finishes bandaging JUPITER's hand.)* How's that feel?

JUPITER. Fine, Mister Tom. *(He tries his hand.)* Fine.

JEFFERSON. Don't use that hand for a while.

JUPITER. No, Mister Tom.

*(The bell tinkles.)*

JEFFERSON. The door-pull!

(JUPITER *goes to answer it.* JEFFERSON *picks up the wine, returns it to cupboard.*)

JUPITER (*appears in the doorway, excited and laughing*). Mister Tom! Looka here! Look who's here. (PATSY *enters.*)

PATSY. Father!

JEFFERSON. Patsy? Darling.

(*They rush to each other and embrace.*)

PATSY. Oh, Father. It's so good to see you.

JEFFERSON. My dearest. What in the world . . . ?

PATSY. I wanted to surprise you.

JEFFERSON. It's a wonderful surprise. Jupiter, kill the fatted calf! Two for supper.

JUPITER. It's chicken.

(*They laugh.*)

JEFFERSON. Kill it, anyway.

JUPITER (*laughs*). He got his appetite back! Looka his face. You shore good medicine, Mrs. Patsy.

JEFFERSON. Where's your trunk?

PATSY. The coachman left it outside.

JUPITER. I get it right away. (*Starts off.*)

JEFFERSON. I'll fetch it, Jupiter. Your hand is . . .

JUPITER (*holds up his good hand*). That's all right, Mister Tom. I kin manage.

PATSY (*goes to* JUPITER). Your wife sends you her love, Jupiter. And Sarah.

JUPITER (*stops, and turns*). Dey all right?

PATSY (*nods*). I've brought you some presents they made for you.

JUPITER. Thanks, Mrs. Patsy! It's sure good to have you here, Mrs. Patsy! (*He exits.*)

JEFFERSON. How's little Jeff, and my sweet Anne, and Maria? And Mr. Randolph? Here! Give me your cloak. (JEFFERSON *takes her cloak, places it on a chair.*)

PATSY. Jeff has two new teeth.

JEFFERSON. Two? Wonderful!

PATSY. He's beginning to talk. Anne's growing so. You'd hardly recognize her.

JEFFERSON. Does she still remember me, Patsy?

PATSY. Of course. She's always playing that game you taught her—I love my love with an A. She's forever chattering about you. "Where's grandpapa? When's grandpapa coming home? What presents is grandpapa going to bring me?"

JEFFERSON (*chuckles*). Mm, hm!

PATSY. Maria sends love, squeezes and kisses. We both adored the hats and veils.

JEFFERSON. Did they fit?

PATSY. Perfectly. And the cloaks were beautiful.

JEFFERSON. The style was all right?

PATSY. Oh, yes.

JEFFERSON. And how's your good husband?

PATSY. Mr. Randolph's well, working hard. Doing the best he can with the overseer. . . . Is it always so close in Philadelphia?

JEFFERSON. This is very bad weather. A contagious fever's broken out here.

PATSY (*looks about*). So this is where you live?

JEFFERSON. Do you like my quarters?

PATSY. A little gloomy, isn't it?

JEFFERSON (*laughs*). You must be exhausted. A glass of sherry?

PATSY. I'd love it. (JEFFERSON *crosses to wine cabinet.*) Father! Coming here—the coach had to stop. There was such a crowd of people up the street.

JEFFERSON. The French Ambassador's been haranguing them lately. There have been some disorders. This epidemic of fever here seems to bring a moral contagion with it. (*He selects several bottles, holds them up.*) Dry or sweet?

PATSY. Dry, please. (*She toys with a mechanical device on the table.*) What's this? Another "convenience" of yours?

JEFFERSON. That's a copying machine. Very handy. It makes duplicate copies of letters. I'll show you how it works.

PATSY (*laughs*). Oh, Father. You and your inventions! Sometimes I . . . (*Her eye is caught by the journal on the table. She stops laughing, frowns, picks it up, reads it. Her face sets in anger.)*

JEFFERSON *(pouring sherry).* Has Maria learned to baste a pudding yet? In her last letter she said Aunt Eppes was teaching her . . .

PATSY. Father!

JEFFERSON. Hm? *(Turns, sees her with the newspaper.)* Oh! You don't want to read that! *(Crosses to take it from her.)*

PATSY. Oh, my God!

JEFFERSON. Now don't get upset, dear!

PATSY. What sort of a newspaper is this?

JEFFERSON. The "court" journal. The snobs nibble it for breakfast. Here, drink your sherry.

PATSY. I'd heard what they were doing to you here, but this is worse than I could have possibly imagined.

JEFFERSON. It's very flattering. Especially that bit about the harem! A harem! At my age! Pretty good. . . .

PATSY. I don't see any humor in it! You'll answer these charges?

JEFFERSON. Answer one lie, they print twenty new ones.

PATSY. Then what are you going to do?

JEFFERSON. Let's ignore it, dear, hm?

PATSY. Who wrote it? Who's Pacificus?

JEFFERSON. I don't know. It's a pseudonym.

PATSY *(pauses. She looks at him, almost in tears; finally, very bitterly).* You must enjoy being the Secretary of State very much to put up with such abuse.

JEFFERSON. It's my job, dear.

PATSY. Job? *(Rises, walks to the window, agitated.)* Father?

JEFFERSON. Yes, dear?

PATSY. Don't you think you've sacrificed enough?

JEFFERSON. I haven't suffered anything.

PATSY. You haven't?

JEFFERSON. No.

*(Pause.)*

PATSY. A few weeks ago I found a pamphlet Mother had written during the Revolution to the Women of Virginia on the necessity for them *(Bitterly.)* to make sacrifices to help win the war. I remember Mother so ill she could hardly walk, doing ten men's work at home. I remember, after she died, sitting on the cold floor outside your door, listening to you sob till I thought you, too, must die. I remember hearing you cry out, you'd sacrificed her to the Revolution.

JEFFERSON *(sinks into a chair).* Patsy.

PATSY. The morning and afternoon of your life you sacrificed. Wasn't that enough?

JEFFERSON. Patsy, dear! Please!

PATSY. No. If you won't think of yourself, what of us? A child of twelve and a baby of four, torn from our home, from all we loved, taken to a foreign land, seeing you only on occasion, longing always for home and security and . . . Why? For what? Is there no end . . . ?

JEFFERSON. Patsy, I beg of you?

PATSY. Don't you owe anything to yourself? Don't you owe anything to us? I tell you, Father, everything at home is going to pieces. If you don't come back soon, there'll be nothing left. Nothing!

JEFFERSON *(rises, in agony).* Patsy! Will you, for God's sake, stop!

PATSY *(crosses to him, overcome with remorse).* Father! Oh, Father, I didn't mean to . . .

JEFFERSON *(takes her in his arms).* I know. I know.

PATSY. Forgive me.

JEFFERSON. Of course.

PATSY. I've been so confused and unhappy. I had to come and talk it out with you.

JEFFERSON. Of course you did. I should have been very hurt if you hadn't.

PATSY. It's the business of running Monticello and the farms. We try! Lord knows we try! But Mr. Randolph has no talent for it. And his failure makes him irritable. And I worry so. I'm afraid you may lose everything you own.

JEFFERSON. I see, my dear. I see. *(He strokes her hair.)* I haven't been altogether insensible to this. It's weighed on me very heavily, the trouble I put your good husband to.

PATSY. I shouldn't have said anything. I know what your work here means to you.

JEFFERSON (*a sudden surge of bitterness*). I have never loathed anything as much in my life. You've no idea, Patsy, of the rank and malignant hatreds here. Politics destroy the happiness of every being in this city! I'm surrounded here by hate and lies. Lately I've seen men who once called themselves my friends go so far as to cross the street to avoid tipping their hats to me.

PATSY. You of all people! Why?

JEFFERSON. There are a gang of king-jobbers here who are bent on changing our principle of government—by force, if necessary. Since Mr. Madison and Mr. Monroe have left, I'm alone against them. I can't contend with them, Patsy.

PATSY. What of the President?

JEFFERSON. Only his strength and his stubborn purity oppose them. But he's old, and he's sick. (*Sits.*) I work from morning till night. They undo everything. This isn't spending one's life here. It's getting rid of it.

PATSY. Oh, my poor father! (PATSY *goes to him, kneels at his feet. He draws out a locket hanging around his neck.*)

JEFFERSON. Do you know, dear, my only pleasure? For an hour or so every evening I sit and dream of Monticello. I find myself more and more turning to the past and to those I loved first. Your mother . . . (*He opens the locket, studies it.*) She was a beautiful person, Patsy. She loved you all so dearly. (*Closes the locket.*) You're right, Patsy. If I hadn't neglected my duties at home during the war, she would have been alive today. It's true. I sacrificed your mother to the Revolution. And now I'm doing the same to you. Darling, your happiness is more important to me than my life. And, like a fool, I've been jeopardizing it. For the privilege of being (*Rises, picks up the newspaper.*) called in the public prints "lecher, liar, thief, hypocrite!" (*He throws down the newspaper.*) But no

more! You mustn't worry, dearest. Everything's going to be all right. I promise you. I'm tending to my own from now on. (*Grim-faced, he takes down a portable writing-desk from the mantelpiece, sits, places it on his lap, opens it, extracts paper and pen, and begins to write furiously.*) Patsy!

PATSY. Yes.

JEFFERSON. Will you ring for Jupiter? The bell-pull's there. (PATSY *pulls the cord. A tinkle is heard, offstage.*) I have a job for you tomorrow.

PATSY. Good. What is it?

JEFFERSON (*as he writes*). I want you to help me select what furniture and articles suit Monticello, and pack and ship them to Richmond.

PATSY. To Richmond?

JEFFERSON. I'll be busy here the next few weeks, but we'd better get them off at once while the shipping lanes are still seaworthy. (*He sands the letter, blows it, reads it a moment.* JUPITER *enters.*)

JUPITER. Yes, Mister Tom?

JEFFERSON. You know where the President's home is?

JUPITER. Yes.

JEFFERSON. Please deliver this letter there at once.

JUPITER. After supper?

JEFFERSON (*rises*). No, now, Jupiter.

JUPITER. My supper's gonna get spoiled

JEFFERSON. At once, Jupiter. (*To* PATSY.) We're going home, together. To stay, Patsy. I'm resigning. (*He places the open portable desk on the table.*)

JUPITER. You goin' home, Mister Tom?

PATSY. Yes, Jupiter.

(JUPITER *stares at* JEFFERSON.)

JUPITER. Mister Tom goin' home . . . ?

PATSY. Oh! I'm so happy, Father, I . . .

(*The faint noise of a crowd outside.* PATSY *breaks off, listens. The noise grows.*)

JEFFERSON. The crowd again. (*He crosses to the window and looks out.*) This is good fuel for the Federalists!

*(The chanting of the mob suddenly be-comes loud and ominous.)*

PATSY. What are they chanting?

JEFFERSON. I can't make it out.

*(The chanted words: "Down with . . ." become distinguishable.)*

PATSY. Down with—who?

JEFFERSON *(as the last word becomes clearly "Washington").* Washington? Wash—! *(He and* PATSY *look at each other. A moment of shocked silence.)* He's

all that stands between them and their enemies. *(Pause.)* Patsy! When all our names are sponged from the records, his will burn brighter, wherever men fight for freedom. *(Irritably, to* JUPITER *who is standing there as if rooted to the spot.)* All right, Jupiter. Run along! What are you waiting for? *(*JUPITER *goes.* PATSY *looks at* JEFFERSON *questioningly.)* No, darling. It isn't going to make any dif-ference. If our people won't deserve their liberty, no one can save it for them. I'm going home. *(He picks up the portable desk, slams it shut, and places it back on the mantel.)*

## SCENE III

SCENE: *The same, a few days later. Most of the furnishings are now gone, leaving noticeably naked areas in the room. There are several bundles of books, etc., on the floor.* PATSY *is wrapping pictures and the more fragile articles in several layers of cloth, and packing them carefully in a barrel.* JEFFERSON, *sitting at his desk, is writing furi-ously, disposing rapidly of a great mass of documents piled before him. Clouds of smoke hang over the room, fed by several braziers.*

JUPITER *enters, his face sick with apprehension. He picks up a bundle of books, starts to take them out. The ominous rumbling of a cart is heard outside.* PATSY, JEFFERSON *and* JUPITER *straighten up, listening.*

JUPITER. De death cart! *(He goes to the window.)* It's piled full, Mister Tom . . . *(He crosses to the braziers.)* Dis yellow fever everywhere! White folks droppin' like flies, Mister Tom! *(He pours some nitre into the braziers. Fresh ribbons of smoke spiral up.)*

JEFFERSON *(to* PATSY*).* You hear that?

*(*PATSY *stubbornly continues her wrap-ping.)*

JUPITER. I never seen nuttin' like dis.

JEFFERSON. Jupiter! Take Mrs. Randolph at once to Germantown.

PATSY. I shan't go.

*(The door-pull tinkles.* JUPITER *goes to answer it.)*

JEFFERSON. Patsy! I'll pick you up there in a few days, and then we'll go on home together.

PATSY. I shan't leave you here alone.

JEFFERSON. I have work to finish.

PATSY. Then I'll stay, too.

JEFFERSON. You're a stubborn child.

PATSY. I come by it honestly.

*(Enter* JUPITER *and* HAMILTON.*)*

JUPITER. Mister Tom, you have a visitor.

JEFFERSON *(rises).* Colonel Hamilton.

HAMILTON. Has the President arrived yet? *(*JUPITER *exits.)*

JEFFERSON. Not yet. My daughter, Mrs. Randolph. Colonel Hamilton.

*(*PATSY *curtsies.* HAMILTON *bows.)*

HAMILTON. He asked me to meet him here. I'll wait in my carriage.

JEFFERSON. You're welcome to sit here.

HAMILTON. Thank you!

PATSY. Excuse me, Father! Colonel Hamil-ton! *(She curtsies, goes.)*

HAMILTON. There's a fellow lying on the sidewalk dead of the plague. *(*JEFFERSON *goes to the window.)* Not a pleasant sight. I sent my driver to fetch the death cart.

JEFFERSON. A bad business!

HAMILTON. Getting worse by the minute. *(Looks about.)* You moving?

JEFFERSON. Yes. You'll have to pardon our appearance. (*Sits, picks up his pen.*) Excuse me! I . . . (*Indicates his work.*)

HAMILTON. Quite all right. Please! Don't let me disturb you.

(JEFFERSON *goes back to his writing.*)

JEFFERSON. The President should have left the city immediately.

HAMILTON. You may be sure I ordered him out. The great man's a stubborn warrior, though. Can't budge him. Never could. (JEFFERSON *concentrates on his writing.* HAMILTON *glances at several magazines on table near his chair, selects one with great surprise, glances toward* JEFFERSON *with uplifted brows, then, smiling mischievously.*) The Gazette?

(JEFFERSON *looks up from his work, searches* HAMILTON *with a cold glance, murmurs dryly.*)

JEFFERSON. Yes.

HAMILTON. I notice an article referring to you. Have you read it?

JEFFERSON (*stops writing, looks up*). I have. (*There is a pause. He goes back to his writing.*)

HAMILTON (*smiles, enjoying the game immensely*). Well-phrased.

JEFFERSON. Brilliantly. And thoroughly untrue, Colonel Hamilton. Thoroughly.

HAMILTON. Oh, come now, Mr. Jefferson —you do well with the ladies.

JEFFERSON (*writes on*). So I see in *The Gazette.*

HAMILTON. When I read this article I . . .

JEFFERSON. Read it? It's commonly supposed, Mr. Hamilton, that you wrote it.

HAMILTON. It's written by some person called— (*Peers at journal mockingly.*) Pa—ci—fi—cus.

JEFFERSON (*savoring the irony, smiles wryly*). Pacificus. Peaceful! A proper pen name. Colonel Hamilton, almost since our first cabinet meeting—you and I have been thrown at each other like cocks in a pit. The cock fight is over. Peaceful will soon have the cabinet to himself.

HAMILTON. How is that?

JEFFERSON. Hasn't the President informed you?

HAMILTON. No.

JEFFERSON. I've resigned.

HAMILTON. Oh! I'm sorry to hear that.

JEFFERSON. I'm not. I'm very happy, Colonel.

HAMILTON (*rises, moves to window*). In that event I rejoice with you.

JEFFERSON. Colonel Hamilton, you're going to your home in the country, now, to wait out the plague?

HAMILTON. Yes.

JEFFERSON. I, too, will be gone in a few days. We may never see each other again.

(*Crosses to mantel; places portable writing-desk on it.*)

HAMILTON. Quite probably we won't.

JEFFERSON. I should like to ask you as man to man, without rancour or warmth— (*He picks up the newspaper.*) is this fitting to the dignity of a Minister of State?

HAMILTON (*bitterly*). Was it fitting the dignity of your high office to send your henchmen prying into my private life?

JEFFERSON. I never did that.

HAMILTON. You thought I would keep silent, did you? You thought sooner than risk my personal happiness I'd let you call me thief? Well! You see what you've done? Congress has cleared my public name, and I'm all the stronger for it! I didn't run away! However, in your case, I think it wise for you to go home and sit on your mountain-top. The philosophic experiment is over. Your Democracy is finished.

JEFFERSON. You really think that?

HAMILTON. I know it. I knew it six years ago. (*The bell-pull tinkles.*) My God, aren't the omens clear enough, even to a Utopian? What do you think of your people now? Your fellow dreamer, Lafayette, in irons, rotting in a German jail, his only refuge from the very ones he sought to free. At that he's lucky. If he hadn't escaped in time, even now his head would be lying in the basket, his blood flowing in the gutters רמניזע into a

river of the noblest blood of France—for
your drunken swine, the people, to swill
in. I tell you—it nauseates me to the very
heart. And now, the same rioting mobs
here, and next the same terror!

JUPITER *(enters)*. General Washington.

WASHINGTON *(enters)*. Gentlemen! *(He is
getting very old. His face is tired and
bewildered, but a bulwark of grim, stubborn determination.* JUPITER *exits.)*

JEFFERSON. Mr. President. *(Moves to
WASHINGTON; takes his hat and stick.)*

HAMILTON. No asafoetida pad? *(Produces
a spare pad and hands it to the* PRESIDENT.*)*
In these times, Mr. President, we can't
afford to lose you. I beg of you!

WASHINGTON. Very well. *(Accepts pad.)*
Thank you. *(Sits down heavily, silent for
a moment, as he broods, all the while
tapping the arm of the chair as if it were
a drum. The death cart outside rumbles
by.)* More than two thousand dead already. This plague is worse than a hundred battles of cannon. *(Sighs, taps.)*

HAMILTON. You should have left the city
immediately, sir.

WASHINGTON. I think I almost prefer to
be in my grave than in the present situation. *(Taps, sighs heavily. A long pause.)*
What does it mean? *(Silence; taps.)* Incredible. Aren't men fit to be free? Is that
the answer? Have you spoken to the
French minister?

JEFFERSON. Yes. One can't reason with
him. He's a lunatic! I've demanded his
recall.

WASHINGTON. They're all lunatics. Lafayette fleeing for his life! Lafayette! And
here now, mobs rioting! What does this
mean? *(Pause.)* We must do what we
can to help Lafayette.

JEFFERSON. I've already despatched a letter
to Ambassador Morris, uring him to make
every solicitation in his power.

WASHINGTON. I don't know if it'll help. I
doubt it. *(*WASHINGTON *nervously picks up*
The Gazette, *glances quickly at* JEFFER-
SON. *To* HAMILTON, *with a touch of stern-
ness.)* Do you mind waiting below? I
should like to talk with you.

HAMILTON *(glances a bit guiltily at* JEF-
FERSON, *then smiles ironically)*. I'll wait
in your carriage. *(*WASHINGTON *nods.)*
Your servant, Mr. Jefferson.

JEFFERSON. Mr. Hamilton.

*(*HAMILTON *goes.)*

WASHINGTON. I shall have to speak to him
again. He's very difficult. He's always been
that way, though. Once, during the war,
when he was my aide, he kept me waiting two hours. When I rebuked him, he
resigned. Sulked like a little boy. *(Softens,
with evident love of* HAMILTON.*)* Finally
I gave him what he wanted—a command
in the field. He was a very good soldier.
Led his troops in the first assault on York-
town. He's an invaluable man. Why can't
you two work together?

JEFFERSON. Our principles are as separate
as the poles.

WASHINGTON. Coalesce them!

JEFFERSON. It can't be done.

WASHINGTON. Let me be the mediator.

JEFFERSON. You've tried before.

WASHINGTON. Let me try again.

JEFFERSON. It's no use. Believe me. Neither
of us could honestly sacrifice his belief
to the other.

WASHINGTON *(sighs, taps)*. Well, I'm ordered back home. Any messages to Albe-
marle County?

JEFFERSON *(sits next to* WASHINGTON*)*. My
best regards to Mr. Madison. And you
might look at my new threshing machine.
If it interests you, the millwright's in
Richmond now. He'd be very happy for
any new commissions. You get eight bush-
els of wheat an hour out of two horses.

WASHINGTON. Hm! I'll certainly examine
it.

JEFFERSON. Tell Madison next spring we'll
be planting our gardens together.

WASHINGTON. No, Tom. I'm afraid you
won't.

JEFFERSON. Why not?

WASHINGTON *(rises. Takes out a paper, lays
it on desk)*. Your resignation. I can't accept it.

JEFFERSON *(rises)*. I'm sorry, Mr. President. You'll have to.

WASHINGTON. Where can I find anyone to replace you?

JEFFERSON. I don't flatter myself on that score. I've failed.

WASHINGTON. Let me be the judge of that.

JEFFERSON. I've spent twenty-four years in public life. I'm worn down with labors that I know are as fruitless to you as they are vexatious to me. My personal affairs have been abandoned too long. They are in utter chaos. I must turn to them and my family.

WASHINGTON. And the good esteem of your fellowmen?

JEFFERSON *(moves away)*. There was a time when that was of higher value to me than anything in the world. Now I prefer tranquillity. Here, for everything I hate, you ask me to give up everything I love. I'm sorry, no! I want a little peace in my lifetime.

WASHINGTON. I know. I know. I'm sick, Tom, and I'm getting old, and I catch myself dreaming of the Potomac and Mount Vernon. *(He almost shouts.)* Don't you think I hate this, too? Don't you think I yearn for the peace of my own farm? Don't you think all this—all this . . . *(Controls himself. There is a long silence. He murmurs.)* Peace in our life? Where . . . ? *(His memories turn back as he searches for the phrase.)* Oh, yes. . . . Paine wrote it. Was it in *The Crisis?* "These are the times that try men's souls. The summer soldier and the sunshine patriot will in this crisis shrink . . ." *(JEFFERSON sinks into a chair; unwittingly, the PRESIDENT has dealt him a stunning blow.)* How that brings back the picture! As if it were yesterday. My men starved, naked, bleeding. I read Paine's essay. You know, it lent me new strength. I had it read to my men through trumpets. Nailed it on trees for them to read. It helped them. Gave them sore-needed courage. Do you remember the passage on the Tory innkeeper who was opposed to the war because . . . *(He finds the phrase he's been searching for.)* that's it— "He wanted peace in his lifetime?" And Paine looked down at the innkeeper's children crawling on the floor and thought, "Were this

Tory a man, he would say: If there must be conflict with tyranny, let it come in my time. Let there be peace and freedom in my children's time." Yes. That's the answer, I suppose. The only answer. *(Suddenly, desperately, he grips JEFFERSON's arm.)* Tom! The fabric is crumbling. Our Republic is dying. We must bolster it, somehow—some way. *(Fiercely, a grim, stubborn warrior fighting a ghost. He pounds the table.)* It must have a chance. It will, I say. It will, it will, it will! I'll defend its right to a chance with the last drop of my blood. *(The fierceness vanishes. Again he becomes a tired, sick, old man.)* You'll stay on a few days more? Till I find someone else?

JEFFERSON. Yes.

WASHINGTON. Good! You see, I'm like a man about to be hanged. Even a few days' reprieve makes me rejoice. *(Sighs heavily, starts to go, turns.)* I wouldn't stay here. Take your papers, go to the country. You can work there. *(Bows.)* Mr. Jefferson.

JEFFERSON *(rises)*. Mr. President.

*(WASHINGTON goes. Outside, the death cart rumbles by. JEFFERSON, torn and tortured, drops back into his chair. JUPITER enters, pours more nitre into the braziers. PATSY enters, holding up a music box.)*

PATSY. Father! Look! I found this little music box inside. May I . . . Father! You're not ill?

JEFFERSON. No, Patsy.

PATSY. You look so pale. Are you sure, Papa?

JEFFERSON. Yes, dear.

PATSY. Can I get you something? A drink of water?

JEFFERSON. No, dear. I'm all right.

*(Pause. JUPITER exits.)*

PATSY. May I take this home to Anne?

JEFFERSON. Yes, dear.

*(She turns a knob. The music box plays a tinkling melody.)*

PATSY. Anne will love it. Can't you just see her face?

JEFFERSON. Mm.

(Pause.)

PATSY. Did the President accept your resignation?

JEFFERSON. Yes.

PATSY. I spoke to him in the hallway. He looks so old, doesn't he? (JEFFERSON *nods.* PATSY *shuts off the music box.*) Oh, Father, please! Please don't torment yourself so!

JEFFERSON (*rises*). He's a dying man, Patsy. He's dying. And, when he's gone, they'll take the reins. And that'll be the end, Patsy. That'll be the end of the Republic.

PATSY. Perhaps we weren't ready for it, Father.

JEFFERSON (*moves about, restlessly*). If not here and now, where then? Where will men ever have such a chance again? This was my dream, Patsy! From my earliest youth.

PATSY. You've done your best, Father.

JEFFERSON. Not good enough, apparently. Summer soldier. (*Pause.*) It was seventeen years ago, *here in Philadelphia,* I wrote the Declaration of Independence. That's how I dreamed of America, Patsy. A beacon for all mankind. (*Pause.*) Patsy! It's not our people who've failed us. It's we who've failed them. Yes. I see that now. (*Paces about the room.*) These fermentations are a healthy sign. Our people are groping. They're jealous of their rights? Good! They want a larger share in their government. Most of them today haven't even the privilege of voting. It would take so little education to make them understand these disorders are not to their advantage. That's where we've failed them, Patsy. It's not enough to create the form of a Republic. We must *make* it work. We must see that our people get the right to vote. We must educate them to use it and be worthy of it. We must give them free schools, and universities and a liberal press. Only an enlightened people can really be free. Till now, the genius of the common people has been buried in the rubbish heap. We must rescue that! I'm convinced of it! We must make war on ignorance and poverty. We must go into the streets and the squares and the smithies. . . .

JUPITER (*entering*). Mister Tom.

(HAMILTON *appears in the doorway.*)

HAMILTON. I beg your pardon. I didn't mean to . . .

(JEFFERSON *faces* HAMILTON. JUPITER *exits.*)

JEFFERSON. It's quite all right. Come in!

HAMILTON. The President asked me to speak to you. He's greatly distressed.

JEFFERSON. Yes, I know he is.

HAMILTON. He asked me to make an effort to coalesce our differences. There's no reason why we shouldn't.

JEFFERSON. You think we can?

HAMILTON. If you will only stop regarding the Constitution as something handed down from Mount Sinai.

JEFFERSON. I see.

HAMILTON. If we're to work together, you'll . . .

JEFFERSON. We're not!

HAMILTON. Oh!

JEFFERSON. We are natural enemies.

HAMILTON. Well, I offered peace.

JEFFERSON. The wolves offered the sheep peace.

HAMILTON. You don't flatter me!

JEFFERSON. It is not an American art.

HAMILTON. I am an American by choice, not by accident.

JEFFERSON. Yet you bring here a lie bred out of the vices and crimes of the old world.

HAMILTON. Lie?

JEFFERSON. The lie that the masses of men are born with saddles on their backs, and a chosen few booted and spurred to ride them legitimately, by the grace of God.

HAMILTON. It's laughable! You, born to wealth and land and slaves, driveling about the common people!

JEFFERSON. Search your own birth, Mr. Hamilton, and you'll . . .

HAMILTON. Don't say it! (*Trembling with rage.*) I must warn v...

JEFFERSON. Say what? That you as a boy were poor? That you came to this country and it gave you honor and wealth? I believe every boy in this land must have that opportunity.

HAMILTON. Why do you think I want the country strong?

JEFFERSON. It can only be strong if its people govern it.

HAMILTON. You think the peasants on my farm can make it strong?

JEFFERSON. There are no peasants in America.

HAMILTON. Words! What do I care for them! Call them yeomen! Call them what you will! Men cannot rule themselves.

JEFFERSON. Can they then rule others? Have we found angels in the forms of kings and dictators to rule them?

HAMILTON. I've made my last gesture. Go! Run back to your hill! From here on, I promise you, you will never again dare raise your head in this party.

JEFFERSON. I hate party. But if that's the only way I can fight you—then I'll create another party. I'll create a people's party.

HAMILTON. Now it comes out. You want two parties! You want blood to flow! At heart you, too, are a Jacobin murderer.

JEFFERSON. That's another lie you believe because you wish to believe it. It gives you the excuse you need to draw your sword! I'm sick to death of your silencing every liberal tongue by calling "Jacobin murderer."

HAMILTON. Well, aren't you? Confess it!

JEFFERSON. Go on! Wave the raw head and the bloody bones! Invent your scares and plots! We were asleep after the first labors, and you tangled us and tied us, but we have only to awake and rise and snap off your Lilliputian cords.

HAMILTON. Very well. Let it be a fight, then. But make it a good one. And, when you stir up the mobs, remember—we who really own America are quite prepared to take it back for ourselves, from your great beast, "The People."

JEFFERSON. And I tell you, when once our people have the government securely in their hands, they will be strong as a giant. They will sooner allow the heart to be torn out of their bodies than their freedom to be wrested from them by a Caesar!

HAMILTON (*bows*). Good day, Mr. Jefferson.

JEFFERSON. Good day, Colonel Hamilton. (HAMILTON *exits.* JEFFERSON *turns to* PATSY.) Patsy, this is a fight that may take the rest of my life. . . .

PATSY. Yes.

JEFFERSON. But I have to! I hate it, but I have to, Patsy. I want Anne and Jeff and their children to grow up in a free republic. I have to, Patsy.

PATSY. Of course you do. (*Rises. Crosses to* JEFFERSON.) Of course you do, Father. (*She takes his hand impulsively, kisses it.*)

# ACT THREE

## SCENE I

SCENE: *The new city of Washington, 1801.* JEFFERSON's *rooms in Conrad's Boarding House.*

JEFFERSON *seated at his desk, writing. His grandchildren, a little boy and a girl, playing on the floor at his feet.* PATSY *seated, crocheting. Outside, in the hallway, the excited babble of many voices.* JUPITER *is placing a tray on the desk. Prominently set on the mantel is a marble bust of* WASHINGTON.

*A knock at the door.* PATSY *starts up.* JUPITER *turns to the door.*

PATSY. I'll take it, Jupiter.

(*She hurries to the door, opens it. A*

MESSENGER *hands her a message. A crowd of boarders surrounds him, asking questions.*)

MESSENGER. Twenty-seventh ballot just come up.

PATSY. Thank you. *(The crowd assails her with questions.)* In a minute. *(She hands the message to her father.* JEFFERSON *reads it, while she waits anxiously.* JEFFERSON *crumples it, throws it away, smiles, shakes his head.)*

JEFFERSON. The same.

PATSY. Oh, dear! *(She goes to the door.)* No. I'm sorry. Congress is still deadlocked.

*(The crowd in the hallway becomes persistent.)*

FIRST MAN. We heard Mr. Burr lost a vote to your father.

PATSY. That's not true, as far as I know.

MESSENGER *(shakes his head)*. No. I told them. *(To others.)* I told you. *(He goes.)*

SECOND MAN. We elected Mr. Jefferson to be President. What's Congress fiddling around for, anyway? What are they up to, Mrs. Randolph?

THIRD MAN. Is it true the Feds are going to try and just make one of their own men President?

PATSY. I can't say. . . .

*(Suddenly a high-pitched voice is heard and a little lady comes pushing through the crowd. She is* MRS. CONRAD, *the proprietress of the boarding house.)*

MRS. CONRAD. In the parlor, please! All my boarders. Downstairs! In the parlor! You'll get the returns there as soon as you will up here. Now, stop a-pesting Mr. Jefferson! Give a man a little privacy, will you? Downstairs in the parlor! *(She enters, apologetically, in a whisper.)* Everybody's so worked up, you know.

PATSY. It's all in the family.

MRS. CONRAD. Well, I can't have the other boarders disturbing your father at a time like this.

PATSY. Thank you.

*(A husky voice is heard singing "Outa my way." "One side!" The boarders are tumbled aside. A man in frontier outfit, armed to the teeth, appears in door.)*

FRONTIERSMAN. Tom Jefferson here?

PATSY. What is it?

FRONTIERSMAN. Message from Governor Monroe of Virginia.

JEFFERSON. Here!

FRONTIERSMAN. You're Tom Jefferson?

JEFFERSON. Yes.

FRONTIERSMAN *(hands him message)*. Governor Monroe said to deliver it to you personal.

JEFFERSON. Thank you! *(Opens it. Reads it.)* Sit down.

FRONTIERSMAN. Don't mind astandin'. Rid my horse hard ali a way from Richmond. She's got a mean jog. Governor's waitin' on your answer.

JEFFERSON. No answer, yet.

FRONTIERSMAN. Nothing settled yet on the election?

JEFFERSON. No. You'd better stand by.

FRONTIERSMAN. Yep.

JEFFERSON. Mrs. Conrad, will you see this gentleman gets something warm to eat? Jupiter, will you saddle a fresh horse?

JUPITER. Yes, Mr. Tom. *(Exits.)*

MRS. CONRAD. I'll tend to it right away, Mr. Jefferson. *(Goes to door, calls.)* Nathan!

VOICE *(offstage)*. Yes, Mrs. Conrad.

MRS. CONRAD. Fix up some vittles right off!

PATSY. Perhaps you'd like a drink?

FRONTIERSMAN. Why, thank you, Ma'am. Now that's a Christian thought.

*(PATSY smiles, fetches brandy bottle.* MRS. CONRAD *returns.)*

BOY. Gramp! Play with me.

PATSY *(pouring drink)*. Jeff, Grandpapa's busy.

BOY. Come on, Gramp . . .

JEFFERSON. Later, Jeff. I've a new game to teach you.

BOY. A new one?

JEFFERSON. A good one.

BOY. Is it like riding a horse to market?

GIRL. Oh, goody, Grandpapa! Shall I get the broom?

PATSY *(hands drink to the Frontiersman).* Children! Go inside.

JEFFERSON. No, no. They don't disturb me. I want them here.

*(PATSY beckons the children away from the desk, seats them in the corner by her side.)*

FRONTIERSMAN *(tosses down the drink).* Hm! That washes the dust down!

*(A knock at the door. PATSY hurries to it. MADISON is there. Crowded behind him in the hall is the group of boarders. They are asking him questions. MR. MADISON is saying, "That's the latest balloting. I've just come from the Capitol.")*

MADISON *(enters, worn, breathless, almost crumbling with fatigue).* I've just come from the House of Representatives. I had to push my way here. The streets are jammed with people. I've never seen so many human beings.

JEFFERSON. Jemmy, you look like a dead one.

MADISON *(sits and groans).* I am. The twenty-seventh ballot came up.

JEFFERSON. We just got the message.

MADISON. You should see Congress! What a spectacle! They fall asleep in their chairs, on their feet. Red-eyed, haggard!

JEFFERSON. Mr. Nicholson's fever any better?

MADISON. Worse. He's resting in a committee-room. He has about enough strength to sign his ballot.

JEFFERSON. Who's attending him?

MADISON. His wife's by his side, giving him medicine and water.

JEFFERSON. He should be removed to a hospital.

MADISON. He won't budge. Insists he'll vote for you till he dies. I doubt whether he'll survive another night. *(JEFFERSON shakes his head.)* Tom, there's an ugly rumor going around. The crowds are getting angry.

JEFFERSON. Yes, I know. May be more than a rumor, I'm afraid. *(He hands MADISON a communication.)*

MADISON. Gad! How's this going to end?

MRS. CONRAD. I been talkin' to my husband, Mrs. Randolph, and we both decided the whole way of votin' now just ain't right.

MADISON. Agreed. Agreed.

MRS. CONRAD. Take my husband. He wanted your father for President, Mr. Burr for Vice-President. Well, he should be allowed to put that down on the ballot instead of just the two names and lettin' Congress decide. Stands to reason, don't it? See what happens? We beat the Federalists, and then the old Congress, most of 'em Feds themselves, don't know who to pick. Deadlocked six days now. They might like as not go on being deadlocked four years, and we'll have no President at all. Now, I say, it's deliberate. Everybody's sayin' that!

JEFFERSON. They are?

MRS. CONRAD. Stands to reason. *(She nods vigorously and scurries off, having said her piece.)*

MADISON. We should have foreseen this difficulty. We certainly bungled the electoral system.

FRONTIERSMAN. Constitution's gotta be changed so a man can put down who he wants for President.

JEFFERSON. Well, it can be amended. That's the great virtue of the Constitution. It can grow.

MADISON. If we ever have the chance to amend it. I'm worried sick by this, Tom.

*(A YOUNG MAN appears in the doorway.)*

YOUNG MAN. Does Monsieur Jefferson live here?

MRS. CONRAD *(appears).* In the parlor! Down in the parlor!

PATSY. It's all right, Mrs. Conrad.

MRS. CONRAD. Oh, excuse me. I thought he was one a my boarders. *(She goes.)*

YOUNG MAN. Monsieur Jefferson?

JEFFERSON. Yes, young man.

YOUNG MAN. You do not remember me? Twelve years ago, Paris?

JEFFERSON. You're .. ? Of course, you're Lafayette's boy.

YOUNG MAN (nods). Your servant.

JEFFERSON. I was expecting you. I'd heard you were in America. You remember Patsy? (To PATSY.) George Washington Lafayette.

PATSY. Of course.

(LAFAYETTE bows and PATSY curtsies.)

LAFAYETTE. She has not changed one little bit. Only more beautiful, if possible.

PATSY (laughs). He's Lafayette's son, all right.

JEFFERSON. He has the gift. And these are my grandchildren.

PATSY (proudly). My daughter, Miss Anne Randolph.

ANNE (curtsies). Monsieur Lafayette.

LAFAYETTE (bows). Miss Randolph.

PATSY. Monsieur George Washington Lafayette . . . (Brings the little boy forward.) My son . . . (Proudly.) Thomas Jefferson Randolph.

(The little boy makes a deep bow. LAFA-YETTE smiles at JEFFERSON, who beams.)

JEFFERSON. My friend, Mr. Madison.

LAFAYETTE. The father of your immortal Constitution? (Bows.) My veneration!

MADISON (dryly). Immortal? It's running a high fever now. The next few days, the next few hours, may tell whether it's going to live at all, or die in hemorrhage. (To JEFFERSON.) Tom! I'm as nervous as a cat. I haven't slept a wink in three nights.

JEFFERSON. Lie down inside.

MADISON. No, no.

JEFFERSON. Go on! Patsy, make up the bed for Jemmy.

MADISON. No! I couldn't. Please! Just let me sit here. (Sits.)

JEFFERSON (moves chair for Lafayette). We're passing through a terrible storm here.

LAFAYETTE (sits). I am sorry to come in the midst of all this, but as soon as I arrive I hurry to you.

JEFFERSON (to LAFAYETTE). Tell me! How is your father?

LAFAYETTE. He is out of prison now.

JEFFERSON. I'd heard. I haven't written him because things here, too, have been so bad these last years, my letter would never have reached him. (Pause.) How does he look?

LAFAYETTE. Six years in prison.

JEFFERSON. They didn't break his spirit?

LAFAYETTE. That they will never break.

JEFFERSON. No.

LAFAYETTE. He asked me to explain he dare not write. Bonaparte watches him. He is only free on—a string.

JEFFERSON (sighs). I had hoped at first Bonaparte would value the real glory of a Washington as compared to that of a Caesar. (He glances at bust of WASHINGTON.)

LAFAYETTE (follows his glance). When we heard he died, my father wept like a child.

(Pause.)

JEFFERSON. A great man fell that day. America now must walk alone.

LAFAYETTE. Here—forgive me. This isn't the America I expected. This is like when Bonaparte came to us.

JEFFERSON. There is an ominous note in this dissension. You've sensed it. Our own little Bonaparte may step in with his comrades at arms and force salvation on us in his way.

LAFAYETTE (rises). That must not be. This is the message my father asked me to deliver. Tell Jefferson, he says to me, tell him the eyes of all suffering humanity are looking to America. It is their last hope on earth.

(A knock at the door. JEFFERSON opens the door. A COURIER stands there.)

COURIER. Mr. Jefferson?

JEFFERSON. Yes?

COURIER. Message!

JEFFERSON. Thank you! (COURIER *goes.* JEFFERSON *takes message, opens it, reads it, becomes grave.*)

MADISON (*rises*). What is it, Tom?

JEFFERSON. A group of the Federalists are meeting tonight.

MADISON. To set aside the election?

JEFFERSON. Possibly. (*Hands the message to* MADISON. MADISON *reads it, groans.*)

FRONTIERSMAN. Like hell they will! Nobody's gonna take my Republic from me.

JEFFERSON (*to the* FRONTIERSMAN). That's right, my friend. (*He crosses to his desk, picks up the letter he has been writing, folds it.*) I'm afraid there's no time for that meal now. Will you see if your horse is ready?

FRONTIERSMAN. Yep. (*Goes.*)

JEFFERSON (*seals letter. To* PATSY). I think you had better plan on going home.

PATSY. Very well, Father.

JEFFERSON. I don't know how long this will keep up. I don't know how it will end.

(FRONTIERSMAN *returns.*)

FRONTIERSMAN. Horse is saddled and out front.

JEFFERSON (*hands letter to him*). To Governor Monroe, with my compliments.

FRONTIERSMAN. Yes, sir.

JEFFERSON. Give your horse the spur!

FRONTIERSMAN. Ride him like the wind, Mr. Jefferson. No fear! (*He goes.*)

PATSY. When do you want us to leave?

JEFFERSON. Now. (*Looks at his watch.*) After dinner.

PATSY. So soon?

JEFFERSON. Please.

PATSY. There's going to be serious trouble?

JEFFERSON. I don't know, Patsy.

PATSY. General Hamilton? Again? Is there no end to that man's malevolence?

LAFAYETTE. Hamilton? (*He looks about at a loss.*) But, during the war, he was my father's friend, too. My father often speaks of him.

PATSY. People changed here after the war, Monsieur Lafayette. The real revolution has been fought in the last six years.

MADISON. And our people have won, Monsieur Lafayette. Through the ballot they've taken the government into their own hands. But now the Federalists intend to drag everything down with them, rather than admit defeat.

(*There is a knock at the door.*)

PATSY. They've turned President Adams completely against my father—one of his oldest friends!

LAFAYETTE. This shocks me. I cannot believe it.

PATSY. Do you know *why* he didn't write your father all these years? He couldn't! They opened his mail! They twisted phrases he used in his letters, and printed them against him.

(*The knock is repeated.*)

JEFFERSON. These are things, Patsy, that are best forgotten.

PATSY. Father, there are men in the streets with guns. They're expecting Hamilton and his troops. They say there'll be shooting.

(*The doors open.* HAMILTON *stands there. A long, stunned silence.*)

HAMILTON. Mr. Jefferson.

JEFFERSON. General Hamilton.

PATSY. You dare . . . !

JEFFERSON. Pat! Go inside, please.

PATSY. Yes, Father. Come, children! (*She steers the children off.*)

JEFFERSON. General Hamilton, Monsieur George Washington Lafayette.

HAMILTON. Lafayette? You're his son?

LAFAYETTE. Yes.

HAMILTON. Of course. I knew your father well. He was my friend.

LAFAYETTE. He often speaks of you. He was yours.

MADISON (*picks up his hat and starts to leave*). Gentlemen!

LAFAYETTE. I go with you, if I may.

MADISON. Come along.

JEFFERSON. You'll dine with us? (LAFAYETTE *nods.* JEFFERSON *looks at his watch.*) In twenty-three minutes.

LAFAYETTE. Twenty-three.

JEFFERSON. On the dot. Mrs. Conrad runs her boarding house along democratic lines. The early birds get the choice cuts.

(LAFAYETTE *smiles, turns to* HAMILTON, *bows.*)

LAFAYETTE. Monsieur Hamilton.

(HAMILTON *bows.* LAFAYETTE *goes.* JEFFERSON *and* HAMILTON *survey each other.*)

JEFFERSON. What can I do for you, General Hamilton?

HAMILTON. Nothing! But I can do something for you. I'm not going to equivocate, Mr. Jefferson. My sentiments toward you are unchanged. I still despise you and everything you represent.

JEFFERSON (*moves to desk. Indicates a chair*). Chair, General?

HAMILTON. Is that understood?

JEFFERSON. I think pretty widely. (*Points to chair.*) Chair?

HAMILTON (*sits.*) Thank you. (*Pause. They survey each other.*) You've grown leaner.

JEFFERSON. And you stouter.

HAMILTON. Not at all. It's this waistcoat. ... A few pounds, perhaps. (*Pause.* HAMILTON *glances out the window.*) So this is your city of Washington. A mud hole.

JEFFERSON. A few trees and some sidewalks and it will do.

HAMILTON. The first day we met this was born.

JEFFERSON. Yes.

HAMILTON. You remember?

JEFFERSON. Oh, yes.

HAMILTON. The Presidential Mansion appears not bad.

JEFFERSON. Not bad.

HAMILTON. Large enough.

JEFFERSON. Large enough for two emperors and a rajah.

HAMILTON. Who's it to be—Aaron Burr or you?

JEFFERSON. Congress will decide.

HAMILTON (*rises*). I have some friends in that body. I can influence this decision for or against you, I believe.

JEFFERSON. I'm certain of that.

HAMILTON. Certain? I'm not. You'd be astonished, Mr. Jefferson, at the number of gentlemen who, no matter what I counsel, would vote for the devil himself in preference to you.

JEFFERSON. Yes. That's quite probable.

HAMILTON. Not that I approve of it. I don't. I deplore it. In the matter of the public good, men must consult their reason, not their passions. I believe I can swing Congress over to you, *if* you accede to certain conditions.

JEFFERSON. I see.

HAMILTON (*moves to desk*). One: I want your solemn assurance that you will continue all my friends in the offices they now fill. Two: I want . . .

JEFFERSON (*smiles, shakes his head*). I'm sorry.

HAMILTON. You refuse?

JEFFERSON. This time no bargains. I appreciate your motives . . .

HAMILTON (*in a rage, shouting*). Bargains? What puny channels your mind runs in!

JEFFERSON. No need to shout, General.

HAMILTON (*pacing furiously*). I'll raise the roof if I please.

JEFFERSON (*nods toward the next room*). My grandchildren . . .

HAMILTON. Excuse me.

JEFFERSON. This is like old times, General.

HAMILTON. Do you realize how dangerous this situation has become?

JEFFERSON. Yes.

HAMILTON. I came here to compromise. I hoped to avert the more drastic alternative.

But the years have made you even more pig-headed, if possible. I might have spared myself this trouble.

JEFFERSON. I couldn't enter the Presidency with my hands tied.

HAMILTON. Don't concern yourself. You won't enter it at all! My friends are meeting tonight. You oblige them to act to set aside this election altogether and choose their own man.

JEFFERSON *(grimly)*. They would be smashing the Constitution.

HAMILTON. Stretching it!

JEFFERSON *(rises)*. Smashing it, I say. *(HAMILTON shrugs his shoulders, turns to go.)* Have you seen the crowds about the Capitol Building?

HAMILTON. A pistol-shot and they'd disperse.

JEFFERSON. Don't deceive yourself! Our people will not be *"put aside."* *(Hands him a letter.)* From Maryland. Fifteen hundred men met last night. Resolved: If anyone dares usurp the Presidency, they will come here in a body and assassinate him. *(He picks up several letters.)* From Governor McKean of Pennsylvania . . . From Governor Monroe of Virginia. Their militia are ready to march at a moment's notice. If you put aside this election tonight, tomorrow morning there will be blood in the streets.

HAMILTON. I am an old soldier, Mr. Jefferson. If you give us no alternative . . .

JEFFERSON. But you have an alternative. End this deadlock at once! Use your influence with your friends. I shall use mine. Make Aaron Burr President.

HAMILTON. Aren't you being whimsical?

JEFFERSON. No. I should honestly prefer that.

HAMILTON. So you want Aaron Burr to be President?

JEFFERSON. He's a superior man, energetic, sharp, believes in our people.

HAMILTON. God! You're gullible! I know the man. He despises your Democracy more than I. Yet he has chimed in with all its absurdities. Why? Because he is cunning, and audacious, and absolutely without morality—possessed of only one principle, to get power by any means and keep it by all.

JEFFERSON. That's an opinion.

HAMILTON. That's a fact. He has said it to me to my face. A dozen times.

JEFFERSON. He has sworn the contrary to me.

HAMILTON. Burr has been bankrupt for years. Yet he spent vast sums of money on this campaign. Where do they come from?

JEFFERSON. I don't know.

HAMILTON. What do you think has been the sole topic of conversation at his dinner table? To whom are the toasts drunk? Can you guess?

JEFFERSON. No.

HAMILTON. The man who supplies his funds, the man with whose agents he is is in daily conference.

JEFFERSON. What man?

HAMILTON. Bonaparte.

JEFFERSON. Bonaparte? I can hardly . . .

HAMILTON *(extracts some documents from his pocket and places them on the desk.)* Proofs, if you wish them. Burr is the Cataline of America. He'll dare anything. You may as well think to bind a giant by cobwebs as his ambition by promises. Once President, he'd destroy all our institutions. Usurp for himself complete and permanent power. Make himself dictator.

JEFFERSON. I know you have no faith in them, but do you think the American people would stand idly by?

HAMILTON. No, I have no faith in them. But they'd fight. I grant you that. There'd be bloody civil war! And that's all Bonaparte would need. He would swoop down on us— *(Slams his fist on the desk.)* Like that! *(Long pause.* JEFFERSON *picks up the "proofs," studies them.)* Now you know my motive. I'm afraid, I'm profoundly afraid for the happiness of this country. *(HAMILTON examines the bust of WASHINGTON.)* Currachi?

JEFFERSON *(looks up from the "proofs")*. Yes.

HAMILTON. Excellent! I've commissioned him to sculp one of the Great Man for me. (JEFFERSON *looks up, sighs.*) Well? (JEFFERSON *lays down the papers. He is tired and confused.*) You've been duped, my friend.

JEFFERSON (*smiles feebly*). I suspected only you.

HAMILTON. Of what?

JEFFERSON. Planning to be our Bonaparte.

HAMILTON. When Washington died, I could have. Why didn't I?

JEFFERSON. Why?

HAMILTON. Burr asked me that question. Contemptuously. This may be difficult for you, but try to grasp it. I happen to love this country, too. I have fought for it in field and council. Above every small selfish personal desire, I want to see it peaceful and prosperous and strong. (*Triumphant.*) Well? Will you meet my terms?

(*Pause.*)

JEFFERSON (*miserably*). I can't.

HAMILTON (*moves to desk*). My conscience is clear. I know how to proceed.

JEFFERSON. If you do this, it can only lead to the very thing you condemn.

HAMILTON (*reaches for papers*). Perhaps. Perhaps that is the only hope for us in a world of Bonapartes and Burrs.

JEFFERSON. Then what will we have gained?

HAMILTON. Good day, Mr. Jefferson. (*Goes to the door.*)

JEFFERSON (*rising*). I warn you, there will be bloodshed tomorrow.

HAMILTON. Oh, no, there won't. You see, I'm counting on you. You will prevent it.

JEFFERSON (*with sudden new-born fierceness*). You're wrong, my friend.

HAMILTON (*pauses, turns*). You'd condone it?

JEFFERSON (*crosses to* HAMILTON). I'd be a part of it.

HAMILTON. You?

JEFFERSON (*growls*). I.

HAMILTON (*returns, looks at him, surprised*). You really mean it.

JEFFERSON. By the God that made me, I mean it. I'd open my veins and yours in a second.

HAMILTON. You amaze me.

JEFFERSON. Why? Isn't the blood of patriots and tyrants the natural manure for liberty?

HAMILTON. You've become a tough old man.

JEFFERSON. Who made me tough?

HAMILTON (*laughs ironically*). Then I haven't lived in vain.

JEFFERSON. That's right. (HAMILTON *is staring at* JEFFERSON.) Listen to me, Hamilton!

HAMILTON. This is a strange . . .

JEFFERSON. Listen to me! I know you love this country. But you have never understood it. You're afraid of Bonaparte? Well, there's no need to be. Bonaparte will die and his tyrannies will die, and we will be living, and we will be free. You're afraid of Burr? If Burr tries any quixotic adventures, he will smash himself against the rocks of our people. You see, this is the mistake you have always made. You have never properly estimated the character of the American people. You still don't understand them. At this moment.

(*There is a long silence.*)

HAMILTON. I confess it. I don't. (*Sits.*)

JEFFERSON (*standing over him. Gently*). This is not the way, Hamilton. Believe me. If you really love this country, this isn't the way. Our people who fought the Revolution from a pure love of liberty, who made every sacrifice and met every danger, did not expend their blood and substance to change this master for that. (*His voice grows strong.*) But to take their freedom in their own hands so that never again would the corrupt will of one man oppress them. You'll not make these people hold their breath at the caprice, or submit to the rods and the hatchet of a dictator. You cannot fix fear in their hearts, or make fear their principle of government. I know them. I place my faith in them. I have no fears for their ultimate victory.

HAMILTON (*wavering*). I wish I had such faith. (*Shakes his head.*) I don't know. I frankly don't know. I find *myself lost here.* Day by day, I am becoming more foreign to this land.

JEFFERSON. Yet you helped build it.

HAMILTON. There is a tide here that sweeps men to the fashioning of some strange destiny, even against their will. I never believed in this—and yet, as you say, I helped build it. Every inch of it. (*Pause. He rises.*) And still, I must admit it has worked better than I thought. If it could survive—if . . .

JEFFERSON. It can. And it will. This tide is irresistible. You cannot hold it back. This is the rising flood of man's long lost freedom. Try as you will, you cannot stop it. You may deflect it for a moment. But in the end you will lose. Try the old way of tyranny and usurpation and you *must* lose. Bonapartes may retard the epoch of man's deliverance, they may bathe the world in rivers of blood yet to flow, and still, still, in the end, they will fall back exhausted in their own blood, leaving mankind to liberty and self-government. No, General Hamilton, this way you lose. Believe me. (*He crosses to his desk, crisp*

and final.) I shall not compromise, General Hamilton. You do whatever you choose. I cannot compromise on this.

HAMILTON (*holds out his hand. It is shaky*). Since the fever took me, I can't hit the side of a barn with a pistol. Burr is cool as a snake, and one of the best shots in America. I've fought him for five years now. If I cross him in *this*—he will challenge me. I have no doubt of that. I am a dead man already. But at least you are honest. I shall urge my friends to break the deadlock. You will be President. Your victory is complete.

JEFFERSON. There is no personal victory in this for me. I didn't *want* this for myself. I still don't. If it will give you any satisfaction, my own affairs have been neglected so long . . . In another office, with time to mend them, I might have saved myself from bankruptcy. As President, I am certain to lose everything I possess, including Monticello, where my wife and four of my children lie. Where all the dreams of my youth lie. No matter! I thank you—for a glorious misery.

(HAMILTON *bows, goes.* JEFFERSON *turns, stares at the statue of* WASHINGTON.)

# SCENE II

SCENE: *The interior of the Senate Chamber.*
JEFFERSON, *hand raised, is taking the oath of office from* CHIEF JUSTICE MARSHALL.

JEFFERSON. I do solemnly swear that I will faithfully execute the office of President of the United States, and will, to the best of my ability, preserve, protect, and defend the Constitution of the United States.

(JUSTICE MARSHALL *waves* JEFFERSON *to assembled audience. Nervously, hesitantly,* JEFFERSON *steps forward to the audience, looks about. His glance rests on* PATSY, *standing proudly with* ANNE *and* JEFF. PATSY *smiles and nods.* JEFFERSON *faintly smiles. He turns to the audience, begins to speak in a voice hesitant and uncertain.*)

JEFFERSON. Friends and fellow citizens: Called upon to undertake the duties of the first executive of our country, I will avail myself of the presence of that portion of my fellow citizens which is here

assembled to express my grateful thanks for the favor with which they have been pleased to look upon me. A rising nation spread over a wide and fruitful land, advancing rapidly to destinies beyond the reach of mortal eye—when I contemplate these transcendent objects and see the honor, the happiness and the hopes of this beloved country committed to the issue of this day, I—I shrink before the magnitude of the undertaking. Utterly, indeed, should I despair if not for the presence of many whom I see here. To you, then, I look for that guidance and support which may enable us to steer with safety the vessel in which we are all embarked amid the conflicting elements of a troubled world.

This is the sum of good government. Equal and exact justice to all men, of whatever state or persuasion, a jealous care of the right of election, absolute acquiescence to the decisions of the majority, the vital principle of republics, from which is no appeal but to *force*, the vital principle and parent of despotism . . . Freedom of religion, freedom of press, freedom of person, and trial by juries impartially selected. These form the bright constellation which has gone before us and which has guided us in an age of revolution and reformation. The wisdom of our sages, and the blood of our heroes have attained them for us. They are the creed of our political faith, the touchstone of our public servants. Should we wander from them in moments of error or alarm, let us hasten to retrace our steps and to regain this road which alone leads to peace, liberty and safety. During the present throes and convulsions of the ancient world, during these agonizing spasms of blood and slaughter abroad, it was not strange that the agitation of the billows should reach even this distant and peaceful shore. That this should be more felt and feared by some than by others. I know, indeed, that some honest men fear that a republic cannot be strong, that this government is not strong enough. But would the honest patriot in the full tide of successful experiment, abandon a government which has so far kept us free and firm, on the theoretic fear that it may possibly want energy to preserve itself? I trust not. I believe this, on the contrary, the only government where every man would fly to the standard and meet invasions of the public order as his own personal concern. I believe this the strongest government on earth. I believe, indeed, I know, this government is the world's best hope . . .

# 1943-44

The new voting rule under which a simple majority was to determine the winner on a single ballot failed to get the desired result. For the third time there was no selection, and for the second time Lillian Hellman saw a play of hers lead the pack but fail to get the required number of votes.

This was *The Searching Wind,* a drama dealing with idealism and expediency in a World War II atmosphere. It needed eight votes to win, but received only seven. *The Voice of the Turtle* by John van Druten received two votes and one was given to *Tomorrow the World* by James Gow and Arnaud d'Usseau. Four critics made no choice, which is a fair indication that the season's quality was not high. There also was no Pulitzer award this season.

The foreign play citation went to *Jacobowsky and the Colonel* by Franz Werfel which reached the stage in an adaptation by S. N. Behrman. Five of the critics failed to make a choice in this category. The meeting was held on April 25, 1944.

A few reasons for remembering the season might be: Mary Martin's introduction as a leading lady in the musical comedy *One Touch of Venus;* Moss Hart's rather spectacular *Winged Victory,* produced by the U. S. Army Air Forces for Army emergency relief with a gigantic cast of Air Forces personnel, including such temporary soldiers as Red Buttons, Edmond O'Brien, Kevin McCarthy, Don Taylor, Gary Merrill, Ray Middleton and Lee Cobb, to name only a few of the show business folk, and Billy Rose's production of Oscar Hammerstein's splendid *Carmen Jones,* an adaptation in terms of the American Negro of Bizet's opera, *Carmen.* This was Hammerstein's second big success within a year, definitely putting an end to a decade of failure that had followed his first ten prosperous years in the theatre.

*The Searching Wind* had a run of 318 performances. *The Voice of the Turtle* eventually registered 1,310 performances.

# 1944-45

Ten days after Tennessee Williams made his bow as a Broadway playwright with the presentation of *The Glass Menagerie* at The Playhouse, the Circle selected it as its prize play on April 10, 1945.

The system of the preliminary trial ballot was now in use, and *The Glass Menagerie* received a clear majority of eight on that and a total of nine on the official signed ballot that followed. Fourteen members participated. Mary Chase's delightful *Harvey* received two votes, and one each went to John van Druten's *I Remember Mama* and Paul Osborn's *A Bell for Adano*. One member did not vote.

There was no award for a foreign play.

Williams had waited four and a half years for this Broadway break. It made up for his first adventure in the theatre at the end of 1940 when the Theatre Guild tried out his *Battle of Angels* in Boston. For a number of reasons, the première there was a fiasco and the play was abandoned.

*The Glass Menagerie* opened in Chicago at the end of 1943 to excellent notices. However, the customers stayed away for the first three weeks; then, suddenly, it became the thing to see. It played thirteen weeks in Chicago and could have stayed many more, but the producers wanted to get it onto a New York stage in time for it to be considered by both the Circle and the Pulitzers. They just made the Pulitzer deadline by opening on March 31. The Pulitzer prize, incidentally, went to *Harvey*.

A notable feature of the Williams play was the acting of Laurette Taylor, one of the truly great actresses of the American stage whose career had many ups and downs. Her role in this one put her back on top and ended her career on a high note. She died in December, 1946.

It was a lively and interesting season. Some of the memorable productions in addition to those mentioned above were *Ten Little Indians, Catherine Was Great*, by and with the inimitable Mae West, *Anna Lucasta, On the Town, Bloomer Girl, Dear Ruth, The Hasty Heart, Dark of the Moon* and *The Late George Apley*. Beatrice Lillie was back for the first time since the war began, starring in the *Seven Lively Arts* revue. Tucked away in the record was a play entitled *The Man Who Had All the Luck*, which was withdrawn after only four performances. It was Arthur Miller's first Broadway production.

One of the more publicized incidents of the season involved a play entitled *Trio*, by Dorothy and Howard Baker. It played 67 performances before the producer finally closed it under pressure from License Commissioner Paul Moss, who said there had been various complaints from church sources and others because of the drama's Lesbian theme. The commissioner actually had no power as a censor, but he did control the licensing of the theatre, and its owners did not wish to invite a padlock on some building code violation technicality. On the trial ballot, Wolcott Gibbs of the *New Yorker* voted for *Trio* as a gesture of protest against Moss.

*The Glass Menagerie* ran 561 performances; *Harvey* didn't close until January 15, 1949, after 1,775 performances.

# The Glass Menagerie

### By TENNESSEE WILLIAMS

Presented by Eddie Dowling and Louis J. Singer at The Playhouse, New York City, March 31, 1945, with the following cast:

| | |
|---|---|
| THE MOTHER | *Laurette Taylor* |
| HER SON | *Eddie Dowling* |
| HER DAUGHTER | *Julie Haydon* |
| THE GENTLEMAN CALLER | *Anthony Ross* |

---

## SCENE

An alley in St. Louis.

Part I—Preparation for a Gentleman Caller.

Part II—The Gentleman calls.

Time—Now and the Past.

---

# THE GLASS MENAGERIE

## SCENE I

*The Wingfield apartment is in the rear of the building, one of those vast hive-like conglomerations of cellular living-units that flower as warty growths in overcrowded urban centers of lower middle-class population and are symptomatic of the impulse of this largest and fundamentally enslaved section of American society to avoid fluidity and differentiation and to exist and function as one interfused mass of automatism.*

*The apartment faces an alley and is entered by a fire-escape, a structure whose name is a touch of accidental poetic truth, for all of these huge buildings are always burning with the slow and implacable fires of human desperation. The fire-escape is included in the set—that is, the landing of it and steps descending from it.*

*The scene is memory and is therefore nonrealistic. Memory takes a lot of poetic license. It omits some details; others are exaggerated, according to the emotional value of the articles it touches, for memory is seated predominantly in the heart. The interior is therefore rather dim and poetic.*

*At the rise of the curtain, the audience is faced with the dark, grim rear wall of the Wingfield tenement. This building, which runs parallel to the footlights, is flanked on both sides by dark, narrow alleys which run into murky canyons of tangled clotheslines, garbage cans and the sinister lattice-work of neighboring fire-escapes. It is up and down these side alleys that exterior entrances and exits are made, during the play. At the end of* Tom's *opening commentary, the dark tenement wall slowly reveals (by means of a transparency) the interior of the ground floor Wingfield apartment.*

*Downstage is the living room, which also serves as a sleeping room for* Laura, *the sofa unfolding to make her bed. Upstage, center, and divided by a wide arch or second proscenium with transparent faded portieres (or second curtain), is the dining room. In an old-fashioned what-not in the living room are seen scores of transparent glass animals. A blown-up photograph of the father hangs on the wall of the living room, facing the audience, to the left of the archway. It is the face of a very handsome young man in a doughboy's First World War cap. He is gallantly smiling, ineluctably smiling, as if to say, "I will be smiling forever."*

*The audience hears and sees the opening scene in the dining room through both the transparent fourth wall of the building and the transparent gauze portieres of the dining-room arch. It is during this revealing scene that the fourth wall slowly ascends, out of sight. This transparent exterior wall is not brought down again until the very end of the play, during* Tom's *final speech.*

*The narrator is an undisguised convention of the play. He takes whatever license with dramatic convention as is convenient to his purposes.*

Tom *enters dressed as a merchant sailor from alley, stage left, and strolls across the front of the stage to the fire-escape. There he stops and lights a cigarette. He addresses the audience.*

TOM. Yes, I have tricks in my pocket, I have things up my sleeve. But I am the opposite of a stage magician. He gives you illusion that has the appearance of truth. I give you truth in the pleasant disguise of illusion.

To begin with, I turn back time. I reverse it to that quaint period, the thirties, when the huge middle class of America was matriculating in a school for the blind. Their eyes had failed them, or they had failed their eyes, and so they were having their fingers pressed forcibly down on the fiery Braille alphabet of a dissolving economy.

In Spain there was revolution. Here there was only shouting and confusion.

In Spain there was Guernica. Here there were disturbances of labor, sometimes pretty violent, in otherwise peaceful cities such as Chicago, Cleveland, Saint Louis . . .

This is the social background of the play.

(MUSIC.)

The play is memory.

Being a memory play, it is dimly lighted, it is sentimental, it is not realistic.

In memory everything seems to happen to music. That explains the fiddle in the wings.

I am the narrator of the play, and also a character in it.

The other characters are my mother, Amanda, my sister, Laura, and a gentleman caller who appears in the final scenes. He is the most realistic character in the play, being an emissary from a world of reality that we were somehow set apart from.

But since I have a poet's weakness for symbols, I am using this character also as a symbol; he is the long delayed but always expected something that we live for.

There is a fifth character in the play who doesn't appear except in this larger-than-life-size photograph over the mantel.

This is our father who left us a long time ago.

He was a telephone man who fell in love with long distances; he gave up his job with the telephone company and skipped the light fantastic out of town . . .

The last we heard of him was a picture post-card from Mazatlan, on the Pacific coast of Mexico, containing a message of two words—

"Hello— Good-bye!" and no address.

I think the rest of the play will explain itself. . . .

(AMANDA's *voice becomes audible through the portieres.*)

(LEGEND ON SCREEN: "OU SONT LES NEIGES.") (*He divides the portieres and enters the upstage area.*)

(AMANDA *and* LAURA *are seated at a dropleaf table. Eating is indicated by gestures without food or utensils.* AMANDA *faces the audience.* TOM *and* LAURA *are seated in profile.*)

(*The interior has lit up softly and through the scrim we see* AMANDA *and* LAURA *seated at the table in the upstage area.*)

AMANDA (*calling*). Tom?

TOM. Yes, Mother.

AMANDA. We can't say grace until you come to the table!

TOM. Coming, Mother. (*He bows slightly and withdraws, reappearing a few moments later in his place at the table.*)

AMANDA (*to her son*). Honey, don't *push* with your *fingers*. If you have to push with something, the thing to push with is a crust of bread. And chew—chew! Animals have sections in their stomachs which enable them to digest food without mastication, but human beings are supposed to chew their food before they swallow it down. Eat food leisurely, son, and really enjoy it. A well-cooked meal has lots of delicate flavors that have to be held in the mouth for appreciation. So chew your food and give your salivary glands a chance to function!

(TOM *deliberately lays his imaginary fork down and pushes his chair back from the table.*)

TOM. I haven't enjoyed one bite of this dinner because of your constant directions on how to eat it. It's you that makes me rush through meals with your hawk-like attention to every bite I take. Sickening—spoils my appetite—all this discussion of —animals' secretion—salivary glands—mastication!

AMANDA (*lightly*). Temperament like a Metropolitan star! (*He rises and crosses downstage.*) You're not excused from the table.

TOM. I'm getting a cigarette.

AMANDA. You smoke too much.

(LAURA *rises.*)

LAURA. I'll bring in the blanc mange.

(*He remains standing with his cigarette by the portieres during the following.*)

AMANDA (*rising*). No, sister, no, sister—you be the lady this time and I'll be the darky.

LAURA. I'm already up.

AMANDA. Resume your seat, little sister— I want you to stay fresh and pretty—for gentlemen callers!

LAURA. I'm not expecting any gentlemen callers.

AMANDA *(crossing out to kitchenette. Airily).* Sometimes they come when they are least expected! Why, I remember one Sunday afternoon in Blue Mountain—

*(Enters kitchenette.)*

TOM. I know what's coming!

LAURA. Yes. But let her tell it.

TOM. Again?

LAURA. She loves to tell it.

*(AMANDA returns with bowl of dessert.)*

AMANDA. One Sunday afternoon in Blue Mountain—your mother received—*seventeen!*—gentlemen callers! Why, sometimes there weren't chairs enough to accommodate them all. We had to send the nigger over to bring in folding chairs from the parish house.

TOM *(remaining at portieres).* How did you entertain those gentlemen callers?

AMANDA. I understood the art of conversation!

TOM. I bet you could talk.

AMANDA. Girls in those days *knew* how to talk, I can tell you.

TOM. Yes?

*(IMAGE: AMANDA AS A GIRL ON A PORCH, GREETING CALLERS.)*

AMANDA. They knew how to entertain their gentlemen callers. It wasn't enough for a girl to be possessed of a pretty face and a graceful figure—although I wasn't slighted in either respect. She also needed to have a nimble wit and a tongue to meet all occasions.

TOM. What did you talk about?

AMANDA. Things of importance going on in the world! Never anything coarse or common or vulgar. *(She addresses TOM as though he were seated in the vacant chair at the table though he remains by portieres. He plays this scene as though he held the book.)* My callers were gentlemen—all! Among my callers were some of the most prominent young planters of the Mississippi Delta—planters and sons of planters!

*(TOM motions for music and a spot of light on AMANDA.)*

*(Her eyes lift, her face glows, her voice becomes rich and elegiac.)*

*(SCREEN LEGEND: "OU SONT LES NEIGES.")*

There was young Champ Laughlin who later became vice-president of the Delta Planters Bank.

Hadley Stevenson who was drowned in Moon Lake and left his widow one hundred and fifty thousand in Government bonds.

There were the Cutrere brothers, Wesley and Bates. Bates was one of my bright particular beaux! He got in a quarrel with that wild Wainwright boy. They shot it out on the floor of Moon Lake Casino. Bates was shot through the stomach. Died in the ambulance on his way to Memphis. His widow was also well-provided for, came into eight or ten thousand acres, that's all. She married him on the rebound —never loved her—carried my picture on him the night he died!

And there was that boy that every girl in the Delta had set her cap for! That beautiful, brilliant young Fitzhugh boy from Greene County!

TOM. What did he leave his widow?

AMANDA. He never married! Gracious, you talk as though all of my old admirers had turned up their toes to the daisies!

TOM. Isn't this the first you've mentioned that still survives?

AMANDA. That Fitzhugh boy went North and made a fortune—came to be known as the Wolf of Wall Street! He had the Midas touch, whatever he touched turned to gold!

And I could have been Mrs. Duncan J. Fitzhugh, mind you! But—I picked your *father!*

LAURA *(rising).* Mother, let me clear the table.

AMANDA. No, dear, you go in front and study your typewriter chart. Or practice your shorthand a little. Stay fresh and pretty!—It's almost time for our gentlemen callers to start arriving. *(She flounces girlishly toward the kitchenette.)* How many do you suppose we're going to entertain this afternoon?

*(TOM throws down the paper and jumps up with a groan.)*

LAURA (*alone in the dining room*). I don't believe we're going to receive any, Mother.

AMANDA (*reappearing, airily*). What? No one—not one? You must be joking! (LAURA *nervously echoes her laugh. She slips in a fugitive manner through the half-open portieres and draws them gently behind her. A shaft of very clear light is thrown on her face against the faded tapestry of the curtains.* MUSIC: "THE GLASS MENAGERIE" UNDER FAINTLY. *Lightly.*) Not one gentleman caller? It can't be true! There must

be a flood, there must have been a tornado!

LAURA. It isn't a flood, it's not a tornado, Mother. I'm just not popular like you were in Blue Mountain. . . . (TOM *utters another groan.* LAURA *glances at him with a faint, apologetic smile, her voice catching a little.*) Mother's afraid I'm going to be an old maid.

THE SCENE DIMS OUT WITH "GLASS MENAGERIE" MUSIC

# SCENE II

*"Laura, Haven't You Ever Liked Some Boy?"*
*On the dark stage the screen is lighted with the image of blue roses.*
*Gradually* LAURA's *figure becomes apparent and the screen goes out.*
*The music subsides.*
LAURA *is seated in the delicate ivory chair at the small claw-foot table.*
*She wears a dress of soft violet material for a kimono—her hair tied back from her forehead with a ribbon.*
*She is washing and polishing her collection of glass.*
AMANDA *appears on the fire-escape steps. At the sound of her ascent,* LAURA *catches her breath, thrusts the bowl of ornaments away and seats herself stiffly before the diagram of the typewriter keyboard as though it held her spellbound.*
*Something has happened to* AMANDA. *It is written in her face as she climbs to the landing: a look that is grim and hopeless and a little absurd.*
*She has on one of those cheap or imitation velvety-looking cloth coats with imitation fur collar. Her hat is five or six years old, one of those dreadful cloche hats that were worn in the late twenties and she is clasping an enormous black patent-leather pocketbook with nickel clasps and initials. This is her full-dress outfit, the one she usually wears to the D.A.R.*
*Before entering she looks through the door.*
*She purses her lips, opens her eyes very wide, rolls them upward and shakes her head.*
*Then she slowly lets herself in the door. Seeing her mother's expression* LAURA *touches her lips with a nervous gesture.*

LAURA. Hello, Mother, I was— (*She makes a nervous gesture toward the chart on the wall.* AMANDA *leans against the shut door and stares at* LAURA *with a martyred look.*)

AMANDA. Deception? Deception? (*She slowly removes her hat and gloves, continuing the sweet suffering stare. She lets the hat and gloves fall on the floor—a bit of acting.*)

LAURA (*shakily*). How was the D.A.R. meeting? (AMANDA *slowly opens her purse and removes a dainty white handkerchief which she shakes out delicately and delicately touches to her lips and nostrils.*) Didn't you go to the D.A.R. meeting, Mother?

AMANDA (*faintly, almost inaudibly*). —No. —No. (*Then more forcibly.*) I did not have the strength—to go to the D.A.R. In fact, I did not have the courage! I wanted to find a hole in the ground and hide myself in it forever! (*She crosses slowly to the wall and removes the diagram of the typewriter keyboard. She holds it in front of her for a second, staring at it sweetly and sorrowfully—then bites her lips and tears it in two pieces.*)

LAURA (*faintly*). Why did you do that, Mother? (AMANDA *repeats the same procedure with the chart of the Gregg Alphabet.*) Why are you—

AMANDA. Why? Why? How old are you, Laura?

LAURA. Mother, you know my age.

AMANDA. I thought that you were an adult; it seems that I was mistaken. (She crosses slowly to the sofa and sinks down and stares at LAURA.)

LAURA. Please don't stare at me, Mother.

(AMANDA closes her eyes and lowers her head. Count ten.)

AMANDA. What are we going to do, what is going to become of us, what is the future? (Count ten.)

LAURA. Has something happened, Mother? (AMANDA draws a long breath and takes out the handkerchief again. Dabbing process.) Mother, has—something happened?

AMANDA. I'll be all right in a minute, I'm just bewildered— (Count five.) —by life. . . .

LAURA. Mother, I wish that you would tell me what's happened!

AMANDA. As you know, I was supposed to be inducted into my office at the D.A.R. this afternoon. (IMAGE: A SWARM OF TYPEWRITERS.) But I stopped off at Rubicam's business college to speak to your teachers about your having a cold and ask them what progress they thought you were making down there.

LAURA. Oh. . . .

AMANDA. I went to the typing instructor and introduced myself as your mother. She didn't know who you were. Wingfield, she said. We don't have any such student enrolled at the school!

I assured her she did, that you had been going to classes since early in January.

"I wonder," she said, "if you could be talking about that terribly shy little girl who dropped out of school after only a few days' attendance?"

"No," I said, "Laura, my daughter, has been going to school every day for the past six weeks!"

"Excuse me," she said. She took the attendance book out and there was your name, unmistakably printed, and all the dates you were absent until they decided that you had dropped out of school.

I still said, "No, there must have been some mistake! There must have been some mix-up in the records!"

And she said, "No—I remember her perfectly now. Her hands shook so that she couldn't hit the right keys! The first time we gave a speed-test, she broke down completely—was sick at the stomach and almost had to be carried into the wash-room! After that morning she never showed up any more. We phoned the house but never got any answer—while I was working at Famous and Barr, I suppose, demonstrating those— Oh!"

I felt so weak I could barely keep on my feet!

I had to sit down while they got me a glass of water!

Fifty dollars' tuition, all of our plans—my hopes and ambitions for you—just gone up the spout, just gone up the spout like that.

(LAURA draws a long breath and gets awkwardly to her feet. She crosses to the victrola and winds it up.)

What are you doing?

LAURA. Oh! (She releases the handle and returns to her seat.)

AMANDA. Laura, where have you been going when you've gone out pretending that you were going to business college?

LAURA. I've just been going out walking.

AMANDA. That's not true.

LAURA. It is. I just went walking.

AMANDA. Walking? Walking? In winter? Deliberately courting pneumonia in that light coat? Where did you walk to, Laura?

LAURA. All sorts of places—mostly in the park.

AMANDA. Even after you'd started catching that cold?

LAURA. It was the lesser of two evils, Mother. (IMAGE: WINTER SCENE IN PARK.) I couldn't go back up. I—threw up—on the floor!

AMANDA. From half past seven till after five every day you mean to tell me you walked around in the park, because you wanted to make me think that you were still going to Rubicam's Business College?

LAURA. It wasn't as bad as it sounds. I went inside places to get warmed up.

AMANDA. Inside where?

LAURA. I went in the art museum and the bird-houses at the Zoo. I visited the penguins every day! Sometimes I did without lunch and went to the movies. Lately I've been spending most of my afternoons in the Jewel-box, that big glass house where they raise the tropical flowers.

AMANDA. You did all this to deceive me, just for deception? *(LAURA looks down.)* Why?

LAURA. Mother, when you're disappointed, you get that awful suffering look on your face, like the picture of Jesus' mother in the museum!

AMANDA. Hush!

LAURA. I couldn't face it.

*(Pause. A whisper of strings.)*

(LEGEND: "THE CRUST OF HUMILITY.")

AMANDA *(hopelessly fingering the huge pocketbook)*. So what are we going to do the rest of our lives? Stay home and watch the parades go by? Amuse ourselves with the glass menagerie, darling? Eternally play those worn-out phonograph records your father left as a painful reminder of him?

We won't have a business career—we've given that up because it gave us nervous indigestion! *(Laughs wearily.)* What is there left but dependency all our lives? I know so well what becomes of unmarried women who aren't prepared to occupy a position. I've seen such pitiful cases in the South—barely tolerated spinsters living upon the grudging patronage of sister's husband or brother's wife!—stuck away in some little mouse-trap of a room—encouraged by one in-law to visit another— little birdlike women without any nest— eating the crust of humility all their life! Is that the future that we've mapped out for ourselves?

I swear it's the only alternative I can think of!

It isn't a very pleasant alternative, is it?

Of course—some girls *do marry.*

*(LAURA twists her hands nervously.)*

Haven't you ever liked some boy?

LAURA. Yes. I liked one once. *(Rises.)* I came across his picture a while ago.

AMANDA *(with some interest)*. He gave you his picture?

LAURA. No, it's in the year-book.

AMANDA *(disappointed)*. Oh—a high-school boy.

(SCREEN IMAGE: JIM AS HIGH-SCHOOL HERO BEARING A SILVER CUP.)

LAURA. Yes. His name was Jim. *(LAURA lifts the heavy annual from the claw-foot table.)* Here he is in *The Pirates of Penzance.*

AMANDA *(absently)*. The what?

LAURA. The operetta the senior class put on. He had a wonderful voice and we sat across the aisle from each other Mondays, Wednesdays and Fridays in the Aud. Here he is with the silver cup for debating! See his grin?

AMANDA *(absently)*. He must have had a jolly disposition.

LAURA. He used to call me—Blue Roses.

(IMAGE: BLUE ROSES.)

AMANDA. Why did he call you such a name as that?

LAURA. When I had that attack of pleurosis —he asked me what was the matter when I came back. I said pleurosis—he thought that I said Blue Roses! So that's what he always called me after that. Whenever he saw me, he'd holler, "Hello, Blue Roses!" I didn't care for the girl that he went out with. Emily Meisenbach. Emily was the best-dressed girl at Soldan. She never struck me, though, as being sincere . . . It says in the Personal Section—they're engaged. That's—six years ago! They must be married by now.

AMANDA. Girls that aren't cut out for business careers usually wind up married to some nice man. *(Gets up with a spark of revival.)* Sister, that's what you'll do!

*(LAURA utters a startled, doubtful laugh. She reaches quickly for a piece of glass.)*

LAURA. But, Mother—

AMANDA. Yes? *(Crossing to photograph.)*

LAURA (*in a tone of frightened apology*). I'm—crippled!

(IMAGE: SCREEN.)

AMANDA. Nonsense! Laura, I've told you never, never to use that word. Why, you're not crippled, you just have a little defect— hardly noticeable, even! When people have some slight disadvantage like that, they cultivate other things to make up for it— develop charm—and vivacity—and— charm! That's all you have to do! (*She turns again to the photograph.*) One thing your father had *plenty of*—was *charm!*

(TOM *motions to the fiddle in the wings.*)

THE SCENE FADES OUT WITH MUSIC

## SCENE III

LEGEND ON SCREEN: "AFTER THE FIASCO—"
TOM *speaks from the fire-escape landing.*

TOM. After the fiasco at Rubicam's Business College, the idea of getting a gentleman caller for Laura began to play a more and more important part in Mother's calculations.

It became an obsession. Like some archetype of the universal unconscious, the image of the gentleman caller haunted our small apartment. . . .

(IMAGE: YOUNG MAN AT DOOR WITH FLOWERS.)

An evening at home rarely passed without some allusion to this image, this sceptre, this hope. . . .

Even when he wasn't mentioned, his presence hung in Mother's preoccupied look and in my sister's frightened, apologetic manner—hung like a sentence passed upon the Wingfields!

Mother was a woman of action as well as words.

She began to take logical steps in the planned direction.

Late that winter and in the early spring— realizing that extra money would be needed to properly feather the nest and plume the bird—she conducted a vigorous campaign on the telephone, roping in subscribers to one of those magazines for matrons called *The Home-maker's Companion,* the type of journal that features the serialized sublimations of ladies of letters who think in terms of delicate cup-like breasts, slim, tapering waists, rich, creamy thighs, eyes like wood-smoke in autumn, fingers that soothe and caress like strains of music, bodies as powerful as Etruscan sculpture.

(SCREEN IMAGE: GLAMOR MAGAZINE COVER.)

(AMANDA *enters with phone on long extension cord. She is spotted in the dim stage.*)

AMANDA. Ida Scott? This is Amanda Wingfield!

We *missed* you at the D.A.R. last Monday! I said to myself: She's probably suffering with that sinus condition! How is that sinus condition?

Horrors! Heaven have mercy!—You're a Christian martyr, yes, that's what you are, a Christian martyr!

Well, I just now happened to notice that your subscription to the *Companion's* about to expire! Yes, it expires with the next issue, honey!—just when that wonderful new serial by Bessie Mae Hopper is getting off to such an exciting start. Oh, honey, it's something that you can't miss! You remember how *Gone With the Wind* took everybody by storm? You simply couldn't go out if you hadn't read it. All everybody *talked* was Scarlett O'Hara. Well, this is a book that critics already compare to *Gone With the Wind*. It's the *Gone With the Wind* of the post-World War generation!—What?—Burning?— Oh, honey, don't let them burn, go take a look in the oven and I'll hold the wire! Heavens—I think she's hung up!

DIM OUT

(LEGEND ON SCREEN: "YOU THINK I'M IN LOVE WITH CONTINENTAL SHOEMAKERS?")

(*Before the stage is lighted, the violent voices of* TOM *and* AMANDA *are heard.*)

(*They are quarrelling behind the portieres. In front of them stands* LAURA *with clenched hands and panicky expression.*)

*(A clear pool of light on her figure throughout this scene.)*

TOM. What in Christ's name am I—

AMANDA *(shrilly)*. Don't you use that—

TOM. Supposed to do!

AMANDA. Expression! Not in my—

TOM. Ohhh!

AMANDA. Presence! Have you gone out of your senses?

TOM. I have, that's true, *driven* out!

AMANDA. What is the matter with you, you —big—big—IDIOT!

TOM. Look!—I've got *no thing,* no single thing—

AMANDA. Lower your voice!

TOM. In my life here that I can call my OWN! Everything is—

AMANDA. Stop that shouting!

TOM. Yesterday you confiscated my books! You had the nerve to—

AMANDA. I took that horrible novel back to the library—yes! That hideous book by that insane Mr. Lawrence. *(*TOM *laughs wildly.)* I cannot control the output of diseased minds or people who cater to them— *(*TOM *laughs still more wildly.)* BUT I WON'T ALLOW SUCH FILTH BROUGHT INTO MY HOUSE! No, no, no, no, no!

TOM. House, house! Who pays rent on it, who makes a slave of himself to—

AMANDA *(fairly screeching)*. Don't you DARE to—

TOM. No, no, *I* mustn't say things! *I've* got to just—

AMANDA. Let me tell you—

TOM. I don't want to hear any more! *(He tears the portieres open. The upstage area is lit with a turgid smoky red glow.)*

*(*AMANDA's *hair is in metal curlers and she wears a very old bathrobe, much too large for her slight figure, a relic of the faithless Mr. Wingfield.)*

*(An upright typewriter and a wild disarray of manuscripts is on the drop-leaf table. The quarrel was probably precipitated by* AMANDA's *interruption of his creative labor.*

*A chair is lying overthrown on the floor.)*

*(Their gesticulating shadows are cast on the ceiling by the fiery glow.)*

AMANDA. You *will* hear more, you—

TOM. No, I won't hear more, I'm going out!

AMANDA. You come right back in—

TOM. Out, out, out! Because I'm—

AMANDA. Come back here, Tom Wingfield! I'm not through talking to you!

TOM. Oh, go—

LAURA *(desperately)*. —Tom!

AMANDA. You're going to listen, and no more insolence from you! I'm at the end of my patience!

*(He comes back toward her.)*

TOM. What do you think I'm at? Aren't I supposed to have any patience to reach the end of, Mother? I know, I know. It seems unimportant to you, what I'm *doing*— what I *want* to do—having a little *difference* between them! You don't think that—

AMANDA. I think you've been doing things that you're ashamed of. That's why you act like this. I don't believe that you go every night to the movies. Nobody goes to the movies night after night. Nobody in their right minds goes to the movies as often as you pretend to. People don't go to the movies at nearly midnight, and movies don't let out at two A.M. Come in stumbling. Muttering to yourself like a maniac! You get three hours' sleep and then go to work. Oh, I can picture the way you're doing down there. Moping, doping, because you're in no condition.

TOM *(wildly)*. No, I'm in no condition!

AMANDA. What right have you got to jeopardize your job? Jeopardize the security of us all? How do you think we'd manage if you were—

TOM. Listen! You think I'm crazy *about* the *warehouse? (He bends fiercely toward her slight figure.)* You think I'm in love with the Continental Shoemakers? You think I want to spend fifty-five *years* down there in that—*celotex interior!* with— *fluorescent—tubes!* Look! I'd rather somebody picked up a crowbar and battered out my brains—than go back mornings! I *go!*

Every time you come in yelling that God damn *"Rise and Shine!" "Rise and Shine!"* I say to myself, "How *lucky dead* people are!" But I get up. I *go!* For sixty-five dollars a month I give up all that I dream of doing and being *ever!* And you say self—*self's* all I ever think of. Why, listen, if self is what I thought of, Mother, I'd be where he is—GONE! *(Pointing to father's picture.)* As far as the system of transportation reaches! *(He starts past her. She grabs his arm.)* Don't grab at me, Mother!

AMANDA. Where are you going?

TOM. I'm going to the *movies!*

AMANDA. I don't believe that lie!

TOM *(crouching toward her, overtowering her tiny figure. She backs away, gasping).* I'm going to opium dens! Yes, opium dens, dens of vice and criminals' hang-outs, Mother. I've joined the Hogan gang, I'm a hired assassin, I carry a tommy-gun in a violin case! I run a string of cat-houses in the Valley! They call me Killer, Killer Wingfield, I'm leading a double-life, a simple, honest warehouse worker by day, by night a dynamic *czar* of the *underworld,* Mother. I go to gambling casinos, I spin away fortunes on the roulette table! I wear a patch over one eye and a false mustache, sometimes I put on green whiskers. On those occasions they call me—*El Diablo!* Oh, I could tell you things to make you sleepless! My enemies plan to dynamite this place. They're going to blow us all sky-high some night! I'll be glad, very happy, and so will you! You'll go up,

up on a broomstick, over Blue Mountain with seventeen gentlemen callers! You ugly —babbling old—*witch.* . . . *(He goes through a series of violent, clumsy movements, seizing his overcoat, lunging to the door, pulling it fiercely open. The women watch him, aghast. His arm catches in the sleeve of the coat as he struggles to pull it on. For a moment he is pinioned by the bulky garment. With an outraged groan he tears the coat off again, splitting the shoulder of it, and hurls it across the room. It strikes against the shelf of* LAURA's *glass collection, there is a tinkle of shattering glass.* LAURA *cries out as if wounded.)*

(MUSIC. LEGEND: "THE GLASS MENAGERIE.")

LAURA *(shrilly).* My glass!—menagerie. . . . *(She covers her face and turns away.)*

*(But* AMANDA *is still stunned and stupefied by the "ugly witch" so that she barely notices this occurrence. Now she recovers her speech.)*

AMANDA *(in an awful voice).* I won't speak to you—until you apologize! *(She crosses through portieres and draws them together behind her.* TOM *is left with* LAURA. LAURA *clings weakly to the mantel with her face averted.* TOM *stares at her stupidly for a moment. Then he crosses to shelf. Drops awkwardly on his knees to collect the fallen glass, glancing at* LAURA *as if he would speak but couldn't.)*

*("The Glass Menagerie" steals in as)*

THE SCENE DIMS OUT

## SCENE IV

*The interior is dark. Faint light in the alley.*
*A deep-voiced bell in a church is tolling the hour of five as the scene commences.*
TOM *appears at the top of the alley. After each solemn boom of the bell in the tower, he shakes a little noise-maker or rattle as if to express the tiny spasm of man in contrast to the sustained power and dignity of the Almighty. This and the unsteadiness of his advance makes it evident that he has been drinking.*
*As he climbs the few steps to the fire-escape landing light steals up inside.* LAURA *appears in night-dress, observing* TOM's *empty bed in the front room.*
TOM *fishes in his pockets for door-key, removing a motley assortment of articles in the search, including a perfect shower of movie-ticket stubs and an empty bottle. At last he finds the key, but just as he is about to insert it, it slips from his fingers. He strikes a match and crouches below the door.*

TOM *(bitterly).* One crack—and it falls through!

*(LAURA opens the door.)*

LAURA. Tom! Tom, what are you doing?

TOM. Looking for a door-key.

LAURA. Where have you been all this time?

TOM. I have been to the movies.

LAURA. All this time at the movies?

TOM. There was a very long program. There was a Garbo picture and a Mickey Mouse and a travelogue and a newsreel and a preview of coming attractions. And there was an organ solo and a collection for the milk-fund—simultaneously—which ended up in a terrible fight between a fat lady and an usher!

LAURA (innocently). Did you have to stay through everything?

TOM. Of course! And, oh, I forgot! There was a big stage show! The headliner on this stage show was Malvolio the Magician. He performed wonderful tricks, many of them, such as pouring water back and forth between pitchers. First it turned to wine and then it turned to beer and then it turned to whiskey. I know it was whiskey it finally turned into because he needed somebody to come up out of the audience to help him, and I came up—both shows! It was Kentucky Straight Bourbon. A very generous fellow, he gave souvenirs. (He pulls from his back pocket a shimmering rainbow-colored scarf.) He gave me this. This is his magic scarf. You can have it, Laura. You wave it over a canary cage and you get a bowl of gold-fish. You wave it over the gold-fish bowl and they fly away canaries. . . . But the wonderfullest trick of all was the coffin trick. We nailed him into a coffin and he got out of the coffin without removing one nail. (He has come inside.) There is a trick that would come in handy for me—get me out of this 2 by 4 situation! (Flops onto bed and starts removing shoes.)

LAURA. Tom—Shhh!

TOM. What're you shushing me for?

LAURA. You'll wake up Mother.

TOM. Goody, goody! Pay 'er back for all those "Rise an' Shines." (Lies down, groaning.) You know it don't take much intelligence to get yourself into a nailed-up coffin, Laura. But who in hell ever got himself out of one without removing one nail?

(As if in answer, the father's grinning photograph lights up.)

SCENE DIMS OUT

(Immediately following: The church bell is heard striking six. At the sixth stroke the alarm clock goes off in AMANDA's room, and after a few moments we hear her calling: "Rise and Shine! Rise and Shine! Laura, go tell your brother to rise and shine!")

TOM (sitting up slowly). I'll rise—but I won't shine.

(The light increases.)

AMANDA. Laura, tell your brother his coffee is ready.

(LAURA slips into front room.)

LAURA. Tom!—It's nearly seven. Don't make Mother nervous. (He stares at her stupidly. Beseechingly.) Tom, speak to Mother this morning. Make up with her, apologize, speak to her!

TOM. She won't to me. It's her that started not speaking.

LAURA. If you just say you're sorry she'll start speaking.

TOM. Her not speaking—is that such a tragedy?

LAURA. Please—please!

AMANDA (calling from kitchenette). Laura, are you going to do what I asked you to do, or do I have to get dressed and go out myself?

LAURA. Going, going—soon as I get on my coat! (She pulls on a shapeless felt hat with nervous, jerky movement, pleadingly glancing at TOM. Rushes awkwardly for coat. The coat is one of AMANDA's, inaccurately made-over, the sleeves too short for LAURA.) Butter and what else?

AMANDA (entering upstage). Just butter. Tell them to charge it.

LAURA. Mother, they make such faces when I do that.

AMANDA. Sticks and stones can break our bones, but the expression on Mr. Garfinkel's face won't harm us! Tell your brother his coffee is getting cold.

LAURA (at door). Do what I asked you, will you, will you, Tom?

(He looks sullenly away.)

AMANDA. Laura, go now or just don't go at all!

LAURA (*rushing out*). Going—going! (*A second later she cries out.* TOM *springs up and crosses to door.* AMANDA *rushes anxiously in.* TOM *opens the door.*)

TOM. Laura?

LAURA. I'm all right. I slipped, but I'm all right.

AMANDA (*peering anxiously after her*). If anyone breaks a leg on those fire-escape steps, the landlord ought to be sued for every cent he possesses! (*She shuts door. Remembers she isn't speaking and returns to other room.*)

(*As* TOM *enters listlessly for his coffee, she turns her back to him and stands rigidly facing the window on the gloomy gray vault of the areaway. Its light on her face with its aged but childish features is cruelly sharp, satirical as a Daumier print.*)

(MUSIC UNDER: "AVE MARIA.")

(TOM *glances sheepishly but sullenly at her averted figure and slumps at the table. The coffee is scalding hot; he sips it and gasps and spits it back in the cup. At his gasp,* AMANDA *catches her breath and half turns. Then catches herself and turns back to window.*)

(TOM *blows on his coffee, glancing sidewise at his mother. She clears her throat.* TOM *clears his. He starts to rise. Sinks back down again, scratches his head, clears his throat again.* AMANDA *coughs.* TOM *raises his cup in both hands to blow on it, his eyes staring over the rim of it at his mother for several moments. Then he slowly sets the cup down and awkwardly and hesitantly rises from the chair.*)

TOM (*hoarsely*). Mother. I—I apologize, Mother. (AMANDA *draws a quick, shuddering breath. Her face works grotesquely. She breaks into childlike tears.*) I'm sorry for what I said, for everything that I said, I didn't mean it.

AMANDA (*sobbingly*). My devotion has made me a witch and so I make myself hateful to my children!

TOM. *No, you don't.*

AMANDA. I worry so much, don't sleep, it makes me nervous!

TOM (*gently*). I understand that.

AMANDA. I've had to put up a solitary battle all these years. But you're my right-hand bower! Don't fall down, don't fail!

TOM (*gently*). I try, Mother.

AMANDA (*with great enthusiasm*). Try and you will SUCCEED! (*The notion makes her breathless.*) Why, you—you're just *full* of natural endowments! Both of my children—they're *unusual* children! Don't you think I know it? I'm so—*proud!* Happy and—feel I've—so much to be thankful for but— Promise me one thing, Son!

TOM. What, Mother?

AMANDA. Promise, Son, you'll never be a drunkard!

TOM (*turns to her grinning*). I will never be a drunkard, Mother.

AMANDA. That's what frightened me so, that you'd be drinking! Eat a bowl of Purina!

TOM. Just coffee, Mother.

AMANDA. Shredded wheat biscuit?

TOM. No. No, Mother, just coffee.

AMANDA. You can't put in a day's work on an empty stomach. You've got ten minutes—don't gulp! Drinking too-hot liquids makes cancer of the stomach. . . . Put cream in.

TOM. No, thank you.

AMANDA. To cool it.

TOM. No! No, thank you, I want it black.

AMANDA. I know, but it's not good for you. We have to do all that we can to build ourselves up. In these trying times we live in, all that we have to cling to is—each other. . . . That's why it's so important to— Tom, I— I sent out your sister so I could discuss something with you. If you hadn't spoken I would have spoken to you. (*Sits down.*)

TOM (*gently*). What is it, Mother, that you want to discuss?

AMANDA. *Laura!*

(TOM *puts his cup down slowly.*)

(LEGEND ON SCREEN: "LAURA.")

(MUSIC: "THE GLASS MENAGERIE.")

TOM. —Oh.—Laura . . .

AMANDA (*touching his sleeve*). You know how Laura is. So quiet but—still water runs deep! She notices things and I think she—broods about them. *(*TOM *looks up.)* A few days ago I came in and she was crying.

TOM. What about?

AMANDA. You.

TOM. Me?

AMANDA. She has an idea that you're not happy here.

TOM. What gave her that idea?

AMANDA. What gives her any idea? However, you do act strangely. I—I'm not criticizing, understand *that!* I know your ambitions do not lie in the warehouse, that like everybody in the whole wide world- -you've had to—make sacrifices, but—Tom—Tom—life's not easy, it calls for Spartan endurance! There's so many things in my heart that I cannot describe to you! I've never told you but I—*loved* your father. . . .

TOM *(gently)*. I know that, Mother.

AMANDA. And you—when I see you taking after his ways! Staying out late—and—well, you *had* been drinking the night you were in that—terrifying condition! Laura says that you hate the apartment and that you go out nights to get away from it! Is that true, Tom?

TOM. No. You say there's so much in your heart that you can't describe to me. That's true of me, too. There's so much in my heart that I can't describe to *you!* So let's respect each other's—

AMANDA. But, why—*why,* Tom—are you always so *restless?* Where do you *go* to, nights?

TOM. I—go to the movies.

AMANDA. Why do you go to the movies so much, Tom?

TOM. I go to the movies because—I like adventure. Adventure is something I don't have much of at work, so I go to the movies.

AMANDA. But, Tom, you go to the movies *entirely* too *much!*

TOM. I like a lot of adventure.

*(*AMANDA *looks baffled, then hurt. As the familiar inquisition resumes he becomes hard and impatient again.* AMANDA *slips back into her querulous attitude toward him.)*

(IMAGE ON SCREEN: SAILING VESSEL WITH JOLLY ROGER.)

AMANDA. Most young men find adventure in their careers.

TOM. Then most young men are not employed in a warehouse.

AMANDA. The world is full of young men employed in warehouses and offices and factories.

TOM. Do all of them find adventure in their careers?

AMANDA. They do or they do without it! Not everybody has a craze for adventure.

TOM. Man is by instinct a lover, a hunter, a fighter, and none of those instincts are given much play at the warehouse!

AMANDA. Man is by instinct! Don't quote instinct to me! Instinct is something that people have got away from! It belongs to animals! Christian adults don't want it!

TOM. What do Christian adults want, then, Mother?

AMANDA. Superior things! Things of the mind and the spirit! Only animals have to satisfy instincts! Surely your aims are somewhat higher than theirs! Than monkeys—pigs—

TOM. I reckon they're not.

AMANDA. You're joking. However, that isn't what I wanted to discuss.

TOM *(rising)*. I haven't much time.

AMANDA *(pushing his shoulders)*. Sit down.

TOM. You want me to punch in red at the warehouse, Mother?

AMANDA. You have five minutes. I want to talk about Laura.

(LEGEND: "PLANS AND PROVISIONS.")

TOM. All right! What about Laura?

AMANDA. We have to be making some plans and provisions for her. She's older than you, two years, and nothing has happened. She just drifts along doing nothing. It frightens me terribly how she just drifts along.

TOM. I guess she's the type that people call home girls.

AMANDA. There's no such type, and if there is, it's a pity! That is unless the home is hers, with a husband!

TOM. What?

AMANDA. Oh, I can see the handwriting on the wall as plain as I see the nose in front of my face! It's terrifying!

More and more you remind me of your father! He was out all hours without explanation!—Then *left*! *Good-bye*!

And me with the bag to hold. I saw that letter you got from the Merchant Marine. I know what you're dreaming of. I'm not standing here blindfolded.

Very well, then. Then *do* it!

But not till there's somebody to take your place.

TOM. What do you mean?

AMANDA. I mean that as soon as Laura has got somebody to take care of her, married, a home of her own, independent—why, then you'll be free to go wherever you please, on land, on sea, whichever way the wind blows you!

But until that time you've got to look out for your sister. I don't say me because I'm old and don't matter! I say for your sister because she's young and dependent.

I put her in business college—a dismal failure! Frightened her so it made her sick at the stomach.

I took her over to the Young People's League at the church. Another fiasco. She spoke to nobody, nobody spoke to her. Now all she does is fool with those pieces of glass and play those worn-out records. What kind of a life is that for a girl to lead?

TOM. What can I do about it?

AMANDA. Overcome selfishness!
Self, self, self is all that you ever think of!

(TOM *springs up and crosses to get his coat. It is ugly and bulky. He pulls on a cap with earmuffs.*)

Where is your muffler? Put your wool muffler on!

(*He snatches it angrily from the closet and tosses it around his neck and pulls both ends tight.*)

Tom! I haven't said what I had in mind to ask you.

TOM. I'm too late to—

AMANDA (*catching his arm—very importunately. Then shyly*). Down at the warehouse, aren't there some—nice young men?

TOM. No!

AMANDA. There *must* be—*some*. . . .

TOM. Mother—

(*Gesture.*)

AMANDA. Find out one that's clean-living —doesn't drink and—ask him out for sister!

TOM. What?

AMANDA. For *sister*! To *meet*! Get *acquainted*!

TOM (*stamping to door*). Oh, my go-osh!

AMANDA. Will you? (*He opens door. Imploringly.*) Will you? (*He starts down.*) Will you? *Will* you, dear?

TOM (*calling back*). YES!

(AMANDA *closes the door hesitantly and with a troubled but faintly hopeful expression.*)

(SCREEN IMAGE: GLAMOR MAGAZINE COVER.)

(*Spot* AMANDA *at phone.*)

AMANDA. Ella Cartwright? This is Amanda Wingfield!

How are you, honey?

How is that kidney condition?

(*Count five.*)

*Horrors!*

(*Count five.*)

You're a Christian martyr, yes, honey, that's what you are, a Christian martyr! Well, I just now happened to notice in my little red book that your subscription to the *Companion* has just run out! I knew that you wouldn't want to miss out on the wonderful serial starting in this new issue. It's by Bessie Mae Hopper, the first thing she's written since *Honeymoon for Three*.

Wasn't that a strange and interesting story? Well, this one is even lovelier, I believe. It has a sophisticated, society back- ground. It's all about the horsey set on Long Island!

FADE OUT

# SCENE V

LEGEND ON SCREEN: "ANNUNCIATION." *Fade with music.*
*It is early dusk of a spring evening. Supper has just been finished in the Wingfield apartment.* AMANDA *and* LAURA *in light-colored dresses are removing dishes from the table, in the upstage area, which is shadowy, their movements formalized almost as a dance or ritual, their moving forms as pale and silent as moths.*
TOM, *in white shirt and trousers, rises from the table and crosses toward the fire-escape.*

AMANDA *(as he passes her).* Son, will you do me a favor?

TOM. What?

AMANDA. Comb your hair! You look so pretty when your hair is combed! *(*TOM *slouches on sofa with evening paper. Enormous caption "Franco Triumphs.")* There is only one respect in which I would like you to emulate your father.

TOM. What respect is that?

AMANDA. The care he always took of his appearance. He never allowed himself to look untidy. *(He throws down the paper and crosses to fire-escape.)* Where are you going?

TOM. I'm going out to smoke.

AMANDA. You smoke too much. A pack a day at fifteen cents a pack. How much would that amount to in a month? Thirty times fifteen is how much, Tom? Figure it out and you will be astounded at what you could save. Enough to give you a night-school course in accounting at Washington U! Just think what a wonderful thing that would be for you, Son!

*(*TOM *is unmoved by the thought.)*

TOM. I'd rather smoke. *(He steps out on landing, letting the screen door slam.)*

AMANDA *(sharply).* I know! That's the tragedy of it. . . . *(Alone, she turns to look at her husband's picture.)*

*(*DANCE MUSIC: "ALL THE WORLD IS WAITING FOR THE SUNSHINE!")*

TOM *(to the audience).* Across the alley from us was the Paradise Dance Hall. On evenings in spring the windows and doors were open and the music came outdoors. Sometimes the lights were turned out except for a large glass sphere that hung from the ceiling. It would turn slowly about and filter the dusk with delicate rainbow colors. Then the orchestra played a waltz or a tango, something that had a slow and sensuous rhythm. Couples would come outside, to the relative privacy of the alley. You could see them kissing behind ash-pits and telephone poles.

This was the compensation for lives that passed like mine, without any change or adventure.

Adventure and change were imminent in this year. They were waiting around the corner for all these kids.

Suspended in the mist over Berchtesgaden, caught in the folds of Chamberlain's umbrella—

In Spain there was Guernica!

But here there was only hot swing music and liquor, dance halls, bars, and movies, and sex that hung in the gloom like a chandelier and flooded the world with brief, deceptive rainbows. . . .

All the world was waiting for bombardments!

*(*AMANDA *turns from the picture and comes outside.)*

AMANDA *(sighing).* A fire-escape landing's a poor excuse for a porch. *(She spreads a newspaper on a step and sits down, gracefully and demurely as if she were settling into a swing on a Mississippi veranda.)* What are you looking at?

TOM. The moon.

AMANDA. Is there a moon this evening?

TOM. It's rising over Garfinkel's Delicatessen.

AMANDA. So it is! A little silver slipper of a moon. Have you made a wish on it yet?

TOM. Um-hum.

AMANDA. What did you wish for?

TOM. That's a secret.

AMANDA. A secret, huh? Well, I won't tell mine either. I will be just as mysterious as you.

TOM. I bet I can guess what yours is.

AMANDA. Is my head so transparent?

TOM. You're not a sphinx.

AMANDA. No, I don't have secrets. I'll tell you what I wished for on the moon. Success and happiness for my precious children! I wish for that whenever there's a moon, and when there isn't a moon, I wish it, too.

TOM. I thought perhaps you wished for a gentleman caller.

AMANDA. Why do you say that?

TOM. Don't you remember asking me to fetch one?

AMANDA. I remember suggesting that it would be nice for your sister if you brought home some nice young man from the warehouse. I think that I've made that suggestion more than once.

TOM. Yes, you have made it repeatedly.

AMANDA. Well?

TOM. We are going to have one.

AMANDA. *What?*

TOM. A gentleman caller!

(THE ANNUNCIATION IS CELEBRATED WITH MUSIC.)

(AMANDA *rises.*)

(IMAGE ON SCREEN: CALLER WITH BOUQUET.)

AMANDA. You mean you have asked some nice young man to come over?

TOM. Yep. I've asked him to dinner.

AMANDA. You really did?

TOM. I did!

AMANDA. You did, and did he—*accept?*

TOM. He did!

AMANDA. Well, well—well, well! That's —lovely!

TOM. I thought that you would be pleased.

AMANDA. It's definite, then?'

TOM. Very definite.

AMANDA. Soon?

TOM. Very soon.

AMANDA. For heaven's sake, stop putting on and tell me some things, will you?

TOM. What things do you want me to tell you?

AMANDA. *Naturally* I would like to know when he's *coming!*

TOM. He's coming tomorrow.

AMANDA. *Tomorrow?*

TOM. Yep. Tomorrow.

AMANDA. But, Tom!

TOM. Yes, Mother?

AMANDA. Tomorrow gives me no time!

TOM. Time for what?

AMANDA. Preparations! Why didn't you phone me at once, as soon as you asked him, the minute that he accepted? Then, don't you see, I could have been getting ready!

TOM. You don't have to make any fuss.

AMANDA. Oh, Tom, Tom, Tom, of course I have to make a fuss! I want things nice, not sloppy! Not thrown together. I'll certainly have to do some fast thinking, won't I?

TOM. I don't see why you have to think at all.

AMANDA. You just don't know. We can't have a gentleman caller in a pig-sty! All my wedding silver has to be polished, the monogrammed table linen ought to be laundered! The windows have to be washed and fresh curtains put up. And how about clothes? We have to *wear* something, don't we?

TOM. Mother, this boy is no one to make a fuss over!

AMANDA. Do you realize he's the first young man we've introduced to your sister? It's terrible, dreadful, disgraceful that poor little sister has never received a single gentleman caller! Tom, come inside! *(She opens the screen door.)*

TOM. What for?

AMANDA. I want to ask you some things.

TOM. If you're going to make such a fuss, I'll call it off, I'll tell him not to come!

AMANDA. You certainly won't do anything of the kind. Nothing offends people worse than broken engagements. It simply means I'll have to work like a Turk! We won't be brilliant, but we will pass inspection. Come on inside. *(*TOM *follows, groaning.)* Sit down.

TOM. Any particular place you would like me to sit?

AMANDA. Thank heavens I've got that new sofa! I'm also making payments on a floor lamp I'll have sent out! And put the chintz covers on, they'll brighten things up! Of course I'd hoped to have these walls repapered. . . . What is the young man's name?

TOM. His name is O'Connor.

AMANDA. That, of course, means fish—tomorrow is Friday! I'll have that salmon loaf—with Durkee's dressing! What does he do? He works at the warehouse?

TOM. Of course! How else would I—

AMANDA. Tom, he—doesn't drink?

TOM. Why do you ask me that?

AMANDA. Your father *did!*

TOM. Don't get started on that!

AMANDA. He *does* drink, then?

TOM. Not that I know of!

AMANDA. Make sure, be certain! The last thing I want for my daughter's a boy who drinks!

TOM. Aren't you being a little bit premature? Mr. O'Connor has not yet appeared on the scene!

AMANDA. But will tomorrow. To meet your sister, and what do I know about his character? Nothing! Old maids are better off than wives of drunkards!

TOM. Oh, my God!

AMANDA. Be still!

TOM *(leaning forward to whisper)*. Lots of fellows meet girls whom they don't marry!

AMANDA. Oh, talk sensibly, Tom—and don't be sarcastic! *(She has gotten a hairbrush.)*

TOM. What are you doing?

AMANDA. I'm brushing that cow-lick down! What is this young man's position at the warehouse?

TOM *(submitting grimly to the brush and the interrogation)*. This young man's position is that of a shipping clerk, Mother.

AMANDA. Sounds to me like a fairly responsible job, the sort of a job *you* would be in if you just had more *get-up*. What is his salary? Have you any idea?

TOM. I would judge it to be approximately eighty-five dollars a month.

AMANDA. Well—not princely, but—

TOM. Twenty more than I make.

AMANDA. Yes, how well I know! But for a family man, eighty-five dollars a month is not much more than you can just get by on. . . .

TOM. Yes, but Mr. O'Connor is not a family man.

AMANDA. He might be, mightn't he? Some time in the future?

TOM. I see. Plans and provisions.

AMANDA. You are the only young man that I know of who ignores the fact that the future becomes the present, the present the past and the past turns into everlasting regret if you don't plan for it!

TOM. I will think that over and see what I can make of it.

AMANDA. Don't be supercilious with your Mother! Tell me some more about this— what do you call him?

TOM. James D. O'Connor. The D. is for Delaney.

AMANDA. Irish on *both* sides! *Gracious!* And doesn't drink?

TOM. Shall I call him up and ask him right this minute?

AMANDA. The only way to find out about those things is to make discreet inquiries at the proper moment. When I was a girl in Blue Mountain and it was suspected that a young man drank, the girl whose attentions he had been receiving, if any girl *was,* would sometimes speak to the minister of his church, or rather her father would if her father was living, and sort of feel out on the young man's character. That is the way such things are discreetly handled to keep a young woman from making a tragic mistake!

TOM. Then how did you happen to make a tragic mistake?

AMANDA. That innocent look of your father's had everyone fooled!

He *smiled*—the world was *enchanted!*

No girl can do worse than put herself at the mercy of a handsome appearance!

I hope that Mr. O'Connor is not too good-looking.

TOM. No, he's not too good-looking. He's covered with freckles and hasn't too much of a nose.

AMANDA. He's not right-down homely, though?

TOM. Not right-down homely. Just medium homely, I'd say.

AMANDA. Character's what to look for in a man.

TOM. That's what I've always said, Mother.

AMANDA. You never said anything of the kind and I suspect you would never give it a thought.

TOM. Don't be so suspicious of me.

AMANDA. At least I hope he's the type that's up and coming.

TOM. I think he really goes in for self-improvement.

AMANDA. What reason have you to think so?

TOM. He goes to night school.

AMANDA *(beaming)*. Splendid! What does he do, I mean study?

TOM. Radio engineering and public speaking!

AMANDA. Then he has visions of being advanced in the world!

Any young man who studies public speaking is aiming to have an executive job some day!

And radio engineering? A thing for the future!

Both of these facts are very illuminating. Those are the sort of things that a mother should know concerning any young man who comes to call on her daughter. Seriously or—not.

TOM. One little warning. He doesn't know about Laura. I didn't let on that we had dark ulterior motives. I just said, why don't you come and have dinner with us? He said okay and that was the whole conversation.

AMANDA. I bet it was! You're eloquent as an oyster.

However, he'll know about Laura when he gets here. When he sees how lovely and sweet and pretty she is, he'll thank his lucky stars he was asked to dinner.

TOM. Mother, you mustn't expect too much of Laura.

AMANDA. What do you mean?

TOM. Laura seems all those things to you and me because she's ours and we love her. We don't even notice she's crippled any more.

AMANDA. Don't say crippled! You know that I never allow that word to be used!

TOM. But face facts, Mother. She is and—that's not all—

AMANDA. What do you mean "not all"?

TOM. Laura is very different from other girls.

AMANDA. I think the difference is all to her advantage.

TOM. Not quite all—in the eyes of others—strangers—she's terribly shy and lives in a world of her own and those things make her seem a little peculiar to people outside the house.

AMANDA. Don't say peculiar.

TOM. Face the facts. She is.

(THE DANCE-HALL MUSIC CHANGES TO A TANGO THAT HAS A MINOR AND SOMEWHAT OMINOUS TONE.)

AMANDA. In what way is she peculiar—may I ask?

TOM (*gently*). She lives in a world of her own—a world of—little glass ornaments, Mother. . . . (*Gets up.* AMANDA *remains holding brush, looking at him, troubled.*) She plays old phonograph records and—that's about all— (*He glances at himself in the mirror and crosses to door.*)

AMANDA (*sharply*). Where are you going?

TOM. I'm going to the movies. (*Out screen door.*)

AMANDA. Not to the movies, every night to the movies! (*Follows quickly to screen door.*) I don't believe you always go to the movies! (*He is gone.* AMANDA *looks worriedly after him for a moment. Then vitality and optimism return and she turns from the door. Crossing to portieres.*) Laura! Laura! (LAURA *answers from kitchenette.*)

LAURA. Yes, Mother.

AMANDA. Let those dishes go and come in front! (LAURA *appears with dish towel. Gaily.*) Laura, come here and make a wish on the moon!

(SCREEN IMAGE: MOON.)

LAURA (*entering*). Moon—moon?

AMANDA. A little silver slipper of a moon. Look over your left shoulder, Laura, and make a wish!

(LAURA *looks faintly puzzled as if called out of sleep.* AMANDA *seizes her shoulders and turns her at an angle by the door.*)

Now!

Now, darling, *wish!*

LAURA. What shall I wish for, Mother?

AMANDA (*her voice trembling and her eyes suddenly filling with tears*). Happiness! Good fortune!

(*The violin rises and the stage dims out.*)

CURTAIN

# SCENE VI

IMAGE: HIGH SCHOOL HERO.

TOM. And so the following evening I brought Jim home to dinner. I had known Jim slightly in high school. In high school Jim was a hero. He had tremendous Irish good nature and vitality with the scrubbed and polished look of white chinaware. He seemed to move in a continual spotlight. He was a star in basketball, captain of the debating club, president of the senior class and the glee club and he sang the male lead in the annual light operas. He was always running or bounding, never just walking. He seemed always at the point of defeating the law of gravity. He was shooting with such velocity through his adolescence that you would logically expect him to arrive at nothing short of the White House by the time he was thirty. But Jim apparently ran into more interference after his graduation from Soldan. His speed had definitely slowed. Six years after he left high school he was holding a job that wasn't much better than mine.

(IMAGE: CLERK.)

He was the only one at the warehouse with whom I was on friendly terms. I was valuable to him as someone who could remember his former glory, who had seen him win basketball games and the silver cup in debating. He knew of my secret practice of retiring to a cabinet of the wash-room to work on poems when business was slack in the warehouse. He called me Shakespeare. And while the other boys in the warehouse regarded me with suspicious hostility, Jim took a humorous attitude toward me. Gradually his attitude affected the others, their hostility wore off and they also began to smile at me as people smile at an oddly fashioned dog who trots across their path at some distance.

I knew that Jim and Laura had known each other at Soldan, and I had heard Laura speak admiringly of his voice. I didn't know if Jim remembered her or not. In high school Laura had been as unobtrusive as Jim had been astonishing. If he did remember Laura, it was not as my sister, for when I asked him to dinner, he grinned and said, "You know, Shakespeare, I never thought of you as having folks!"

He was about to discover that I did. . . .

(LIGHT *up* STAGE.)

(LEGEND ON SCREEN: "THE ACCENT OF A COMING FOOT.")

(*Friday evening. It is about five o'clock of a late spring evening which comes "scattering poems in the sky."*)

(*A delicate lemony light is in the Wingfield apartment.*)

(AMANDA *has worked like a Turk in preparation for the gentleman caller. The results are astonishing. The new floor lamp with its rose-silk shade is in place, a colored paper lantern conceals the broken light fixture in the ceiling, new billowing white curtains are at the windows, chintz covers are on chairs and sofa, a pair of new sofa pillows make their initial appearance.*)

(*Open boxes and tissue paper are scattered on the floor.*)

(LAURA *stands in the middle with lifted arms while* AMANDA *crouches before her, adjusting the hem of the new dress, devout and ritualistic. The dress is colored and designed by memory. The arrangement of* LAURA's *hair is changed; it is softer and more becoming. A fragile, unearthly prettiness has come out in* LAURA: *she is like a piece of translucent glass touched by light, given a momentary radiance, not actual, not lasting.*)

AMANDA (*impatiently*). Why are you trembling?

LAURA. Mother, you've made me so nervous!

AMANDA. How have I made you nervous?

LAURA. By all this fuss! You make it seem so important!

AMANDA. I don't understand you, Laura. You couldn't be satisfied with just sitting home, and yet whenever I try to arrange something for you, you seem to resist it. (*She gets up.*)

Now take a look at yourself.

No, wait! Wait just a moment—I have an idea!

LAURA. What is it now?

(AMANDA *produces two powder puffs which she wraps in handkerchiefs and stuffs in* LAURA's *bosom.*)

LAURA. Mother, what are you doing?

AMANDA. They call them "Gay Deceivers"!

LAURA. I won't wear them!

AMANDA. You will!

LAURA. Why should I?

AMANDA. Because, to be painfully honest, your chest is flat.

LAURA. You make it seem like we were setting a trap.

AMANDA. All pretty girls are a trap, a pretty trap, and men expect them to be.

(LEGEND: "A PRETTY TRAP.")

Now look at yourself, young lady. This is the prettiest you will ever be!

I've got to fix myself now! You're going to be surprised by your mother's appearance! (*She crosses through portieres, humming gaily.*)

(LAURA *moves slowly to the long mirror and stares solemnly at herself.*)

(*A wind blows the white curtains inward in a slow, graceful motion and with a faint, sorrowful sighing.*)

AMANDA (*off stage*). It isn't dark enough yet. (*She turns slowly before the mirror with a troubled look.*)

(LEGEND ON SCREEN: "THIS IS MY SISTER: CELEBRATE HER WITH STRINGS!" MUSIC.)

AMANDA (*laughing, off*). I'm going to show you something. I'm going to make a spectacular appearance!

LAURA. What is it, Mother?

AMANDA. Possess your soul in patience—you will see!

Something I've resurrected from that old trunk! Styles haven't changed so terribly much after all. . . .

(*She parts the portieres.*)

Now just look at your mother!

(*She wears a girlish frock of yellowed voile with a blue silk sash. She carries a*

*bunch of jonquils—the legend of her
youth is nearly revived. Feverishly.)*

This is the dress in which I led the cotil-
lion. Won the cakewalk twice at Sunset
Hill, wore one spring to the Governor's
ball in Jackson!

See how I sashayed around the ballroom,
Laura?

*(She raises her skirt and does a mincing
step around the room.)*

I wore it on Sundays for my gentlemen
callers! I had it on the day I met your
father—

I had malaria fever all that spring. The
change of climate from East Tennessee to
the Delta—weakened resistance—I had a
little temperature all the time—not enough
to be serious—just enough to make me
restless and giddy!—Invitations poured in
—parties all over the Delta!—"Stay in
bed," said Mother, "you have fever!"—but
I just wouldn't.—I took quinine but kept
on going, going!—Evenings, dances!—
Afternoons, long, long rides! Picnics—
lovely!—So lovely, that country in May.—
All lacy with dogwood, literally flooded
with jonquils!—That was the spring I
had the craze for jonquils. Jonquils became an absolute obsession. Mother said,
"Honey, there's no room for jonquils." And still I kept on bringing in
more jonquils. Whenever, wherever I saw
them, I'd say, "Stop! Stop! I see jonquils!"
I made the young men help me gather the
jonquils! It was a joke, Amanda and her
jonquils! Finally there were no more vases
to hold them, every available space was
filled with jonquils. No vases to hold
them? All right, I'll hold them myself!
And then I— *(She stops in front of the
picture.* MUSIC.*)* met your father!

Malaria fever and jonquils and then—this
—boy. . . .

*(She switches on the rose-colored lamp.)*

I hope they get here before it starts to rain.

*(She crosses upstage and places the jon-
quils in bowl on table.)*

I gave your brother a little extra change so
he and Mr. O'Connor could take the
service car home.

LAURA *(with altered look).* What did you
say his name was?

AMANDA. O'Connor.

LAURA. What is his first name?

AMANDA. I don't remember. Oh, yes, I do.
It was—Jim!

*(*LAURA *sways slightly and catches hold of
a chair.)*

(LEGEND ON SCREEN: "NOT JIM!")

LAURA *(faintly).* Not—Jim!

AMANDA. Yes, that was it, it was Jim! I've
never known a Jim that wasn't nice!

(MUSIC: OMINOUS.)

LAURA. Are you sure his name is Jim
O'Connor?

AMANDA. Yes. Why?

LAURA. Is he the one that Tom used to
know in high school?

AMANDA. He didn't say so. I think he just
got to know him at the warehouse.

LAURA. There was a Jim O'Connor we
both knew in high school— *(Then, with
effort.)* If that is the one that Tom is
bringing to dinner—you'll have to excuse
me, I won't come to the table.

AMANDA. What sort of nonsense is this?

LAURA. You asked me once if I'd ever liked
a boy. Don't you remember I showed you
this boy's picture?

AMANDA. You mean the boy you showed
me in the year book?

LAURA. Yes, that boy.

AMANDA. Laura, Laura, were you in love
with that boy?

LAURA. I don't know, Mother. All I know
is I couldn't sit at the table if it was him!

AMANDA. It won't be him! It isn't the least
bit likely. But whether it is or not, you
will come to the table. You will not be
excused.

LAURA. I'll have to be, Mother.

AMANDA. I don't intend to humor your
silliness, Laura. I've had too much from
you and your brother, both!

So just sit down and compose yourself
till they come. Tom has forgotten his key
so you'll have to let them in, when they
arrive.

LAURA *(panicky).* Oh, Mother, *you* answer the door!

AMANDA *(lightly).* I'll be in the kitchen—busy!

LAURA. Oh, Mother, please answer the door, don't make me do it!

AMANDA *(crossing into kitchenette).* I've got to fix the dressing for the salmon. Fuss, fuss—silliness!—over a gentleman caller!

*(Door swings shut.* LAURA *is left alone.)*

(LEGEND: "TERROR!")

*(She utters a low moan and turns off the lamp—sits stiffly on the edge of the sofa, knotting her fingers together.)*

(LEGEND ON SCREEN: "THE OPENING OF A DOOR!")

*(*TOM *and* JIM *appear on the fire-escape steps and climb to landing. Hearing their approach,* LAURA *rises with a panicky gesture. She retreats to the portieres.)*

*(The doorbell.* LAURA *catches her breath and touches her throat. Low drums.)*

AMANDA *(calling).* Laura, sweetheart! The door!

*(*LAURA *stares at it without moving.)*

JIM. I think we just beat the rain.

TOM. Uh-huh. *(He rings again, nervously.* JIM *whistles and fishes for a cigarette.)*

AMANDA *(very, very gaily).* Laura, that is your brother and Mr. O'Connor! Will you let them in, darling?

*(*LAURA *crosses toward kitchenette door.)*

LAURA *(breathlessly).* Mother—you go to the door!

*(*AMANDA *steps out of kitchenette and stares furiously at* LAURA. *She points imperiously at the door.)*

LAURA. Please, please!

AMANDA *(in a fierce whisper).* What is the matter with you, you silly thing?

LAURA *(desperately).* Please, you answer it, *please!*

AMANDA. I told you I wasn't going to humor you, Laura. Why have you chosen this moment to lose your mind?

LAURA. Please, please, please, you go!

AMANDA. You'll have to go to the door because I can't!

LAURA *(despairingly).* I can't either!

AMANDA. *Why?*

LAURA. I'm *sick!*

AMANDA. I'm sick, too—of your nonsense! Why can't you and your brother be normal people? Fantastic whims and behavior!

*(*TOM *gives a long ring.)*

Preposterous goings on! Can you give me one reason— *(Calls out lyrically.)* COMING! JUST ONE SECOND!—why you should be afraid to open a door? Now you answer it, Laura!

LAURA. Oh, oh, oh . . . *(She returns through the portieres. Darts to the victrola and winds it frantically and turns it on.)*

AMANDA. Laura Wingfield, you march right to that door!

LAURA. Yes—yes, Mother!

*(A faraway, scratchy rendition of "Dardanella" softens the air and gives her strength to move through it. She slips to the door and draws it cautiously open.)*

*(*TOM *enters with the caller,* JIM O'CONNOR.)

TOM. Laura, this is Jim. Jim, this is my sister, Laura.

JIM *(stepping inside).* I didn't know that Shakespeare had a sister!

LAURA *(retreating stiff and trembling from the door).* How—how do you do?

JIM *(heartily extending his hand).* Okay!

*(*LAURA *touches it hesitantly with hers.)*

JIM. Your hand's *cold,* Laura!

LAURA. Yes, well—I've been playing the victrola. . . .

TOM *(disinterest).* Yeah? *(Lights cigarette and crosses back to fire-escape door.)*

JIM. Where are *you* going?

TOM. I'm going out on the terrace.

JIM *(goes after him).* You know, Shakespeare—I'm going to sell you a bill of goods!

TOM. What goods?

JIM. A course I'm taking.

TOM. Huh?

JIM. In public speaking! You and me, we're not the warehouse type.

TOM. Thanks—that's good news.
But what has public speaking got to do with it?

JIM. It fits you for—executive positions!

TOM. Awww.

JIM. I tell you it's done a helluva lot for me.

(IMAGE: EXECUTIVE AT DESK.)

TOM. In what respect?

JIM. In every! Ask yourself what is the difference between you an' me and men in the office down front? Brains?—No!—Ability?—No! Then what? Just one little thing—

TOM. What is that one little thing?

JIM. Primarily it amounts to—social poise! Being able to square up to people and hold your own on any social level!

AMANDA (off stage). Tom?

TOM. Yes, Mother?

AMANDA. Is that you and Mr. O'Connor?

TOM. Yes, Mother.

AMANDA. Well, you just make yourselves comfortable in there.

TOM. Yes, Mother.

AMANDA. Ask Mr. O'Connor if he would like to wash his hands.

JIM. Aw, no—no—thank you—I took care of that at the warehouse. Tom—

TOM. Yes?

JIM. Mr. Mendoza was speaking to me about you.

TOM. Favorably?

JIM. What do you think?

TOM. Well—

JIM. You're going to be out of a job if you don't wake up.

TOM. I am waking up—

JIM. You show no signs.

TOM. The signs are interior.

(IMAGE ON SCREEN: THE SAILING VESSEL WITH JOLLY ROGER AGAIN.)

TOM. I'm planning to change. (He leans over the rail speaking with quiet exhilaration. The incandescent marquees and signs of the first-run movie houses light his face from across the alley. He looks like a voyager.) I'm right at the point of committing myself to a future that doesn't include the warehouse and Mr. Mendoza or even a night-school course in public speaking.

JIM. What are you gassing about?

TOM. I'm tired of the movies.

JIM. Movies!

TOM. Yes, movies! Look at them— (A wave toward the marvels of Grand Avenue.) All of those glamorous people—having adventures—hogging it all, gobbling the whole thing up! You know what happens? People go to the movies instead of moving! Hollywood characters are supposed to have all the adventures for everybody in America, while everybody in America sits in a dark room and watches them have them! Yes, until there's a war. That's when adventure becomes available to the masses! Everyone's dish, not only Gable's! Then the people in the dark room come out of the dark room to have some adventures themselves—Goody, goody!—It's our turn now, to go to the South Sea Island—to make a safari—to be exotic, far-off!—But I'm not patient. I don't want to wait till then. I'm tired of the movies and I am about to move!

JIM (incredulously). Move?

TOM. Yes.

JIM. When?

TOM. Soon!

JIM. Where? Where?

(THEME THREE MUSIC SEEMS TO ANSWER THE QUESTION, WHILE TOM THINKS IT OVER. HE SEARCHES AMONG HIS POCKETS.)

TOM. I'm starting to boil inside. I know I seem dreamy, but inside—well, I'm boiling!—Whenever I pick up a shoe, I shudder a little thinking how short life is and what I am doing!—Whatever that means, I know it doesn't mean shoes—except as something to wear on a traveler's feet! (Finds paper.) Look—

JIM. What?

TOM. I'm a member.

JIM *(reading)*. The Union of Merchant Seamen.

TOM. I paid my dues this month, instead of the light bill.

JIM. You will regret it when they turn the lights off.

TOM. I won't be here.

JIM. How about your mother?

TOM. I'm like my father. The bastard son of a bastard! See how he grins? And he's been absent going on sixteen years!

JIM. You're just talking, you drip. How does your mother feel about it?

TOM. Shhh!—Here comes Mother! Mother is not acquainted with my plans!

AMANDA *(enters portieres)*. Where are you all?

TOM. On the terrace, Mother.

*(They start inside. She advances to them.* TOM *is distinctly shocked at her appearance. Even* JIM *blinks a little. He is making his first contact with girlish Southern vivacity and in spite of the night-school course in public speaking is somewhat thrown off the beam by the unexpected outlay of social charm.)*

*(Certain responses are attempted by* JIM *but are swept aside by* AMANDA's *gay laughter and chatter.* TOM *is embarrassed but after the first shock* JIM *reacts very warmly. Grins and chuckles, is altogether won over.)*

(IMAGE: AMANDA AS A GIRL.)

AMANDA *(coyly smiling, shaking her girlish ringlets)*. Well, well, well, so this is Mr. O'Connor. Introductions entirely unnecessary. I've heard so much about you from my boy. I finally said to him, Tom—good gracious!—why don't you bring this paragon to supper? I'd like to meet this nice young man at the warehouse!—Instead of just hearing him sing your praises so much!

I don't know why my son is so stand-offish —that's not Southern behavior!

Let's sit down and—I think we could stand a little more air in here! Tom, leave the door open. I felt a nice fresh breeze a moment ago. Where has it gone to?

Mmm, so warm already! And not quite summer, even. We're going to burn up when summer really gets started.

However, we're having—we're having a very light supper. I think light things are better fo' this time of year. The same as light clothes are. Light clothes an' light food are what warm weather calls fo.' You know our blood gets so thick during th' winter—it takes a while fo' us to *adjust* ou'selves!—when the season changes . . .

It's come so quick this year. I wasn't prepared. All of a sudden—heavens! Already summer!—I ran to the trunk an' pulled out this light dress— Terribly old! Historical almost! But feels so good— so good an' co-ol, y' know. . . .

TOM. Mother—

AMANDA. Yes, honey?

TOM. How about—supper?

AMANDA. Honey, you go ask Sister if supper is ready! You know that Sister is in full charge of supper!

Tell her you hungry boys are waiting for it.

*(To* JIM.)

Have you met Laura?

JIM. She—

AMANDA. Let you in? Oh, good, you've met already! It's rare for a girl as sweet an' pretty as Laura to be domestic! But Laura is, thank heavens, not only pretty but also very domestic. I'm not at all. I never was a bit. I never could make a thing but angel-food cake. Well, in the South we had so many servants. Gone, gone, gone. All vestige of gracious living! Gone completely! I wasn't prepared for what the future brought me. All of my gentlemen callers were sons of planters and so of course I assumed that I would be married to one and raise my family on a large piece of land with plenty of servants. But man proposes—and woman accepts the proposal!—To vary that old, old saying a little bit—I married no planter! I married a man who worked for the telephone company!—That gallantly smiling gentleman over there! *(Points to the picture.)* A telephone man who—fell in love with long-distance!—Now he travels and I don't even know where!—But what am I going on for about my—tribulations?

Tell me yours—I hope you don't have any! Tom?

TOM *(returning)*. Yes, Mother?

AMANDA. Is supper nearly ready?

TOM. It looks to me like supper is on the table.

AMANDA. Let me look— *(She rises prettily and looks through portieres.)* Oh, lovely! —But where is Sister?

TOM. Laura is not feeling well and she says that she thinks she'd better not come to the table.

AMANDA. What?—Nonsense!—Laura? Oh, Laura!

LAURA *(off stage, faintly)*. Yes, Mother.

AMANDA. You really must come to the table. We won't be seated until you come to the table!

Come in, Mr. O'Connor. You sit over there, and I'll—

Laura? Laura Wingfield!

You're keeping us waiting, honey! We can't say grace until you come to the table!

*(The back door is pushed weakly open and* LAURA *comes in. She is obviously quite faint, her lips trembling, her eyes wide and staring. She moves unsteadily toward the table.)*

(LEGEND: "TERROR!")

*(Outside a summer storm is coming abruptly. The white curtains billow inward at the windows and there is a sorrowful murmur and deep blue dusk.)*

(LAURA *suddenly stumbles—she catches at a chair with a faint moan.)*

TOM. Laura!

AMANDA. Laura!

*(There is a clap of thunder.)*

(LEGEND: "AH!")

*(Despairingly.)*

Why, Laura, you *are* sick, darling! Tom, help your sister into the living room, dear! Sit in the living room, Laura—rest on the sofa.

Well!

*(To the gentleman caller.)*

Standing over the hot stove made her ill! —I told her that it was just too warm this evening, but—

*(*TOM *comes back in.* LAURA *is on the sofa.)*

Is Laura all right now?

TOM. Yes.

AMANDA. What *is* that? Rain? A nice cool rain has come up!

*(She gives the gentleman caller a frightened look.)*

I think we may—have grace—now . . .

*(*TOM *looks at her stupidly.)*

Tom, honey—you say grace!

TOM. Oh . . .

"For these and all thy mercies—"

*(They bow their heads,* AMANDA *stealing a nervous glance at* JIM. *In the living room* LAURA, *stretched on the sofa, clenches her hand to her lips, to hold back a shuddering sob.)*

God's Holy Name be praised—

THE SCENE DIMS OUT

# SCENE VII

A Souvenir.

*Half an hour later. Dinner is just being finished in the upstage area which is concealed by the drawn portieres.*

*As the curtain rises* LAURA *is still huddled upon the sofa, her feet drawn under her, her head resting on a pale blue pillow, her eyes wide and mysteriously watchful. The new floor lamp with its shade of rose-colored silk gives a soft, becoming light to her face, bringing out the fragile, unearthly prettiness which usually escapes attention. There is a steady murmur of rain, but it is slackening and stops soon after the scene begins; the air outside becomes pale and luminous as the moon breaks out.*

*A moment after the curtain rises, the lights in both rooms flicker and go out.*

JIM. Hey, there, Mr. Light Bulb!

(AMANDA *laughs nervously.*)

(LEGEND: "SUSPENSION OF A PUBLIC SERV-
ICE.")

AMANDA. Where was Moses when the lights
went out? Ha-ha. Do you know the answer
to that one, Mr. O'Connor?

JIM. No, Ma'am, what's the answer?

AMANDA. In the dark!

(JIM *laughs appreciatively.*)

Everybody sit still. I'll light the candles.
Isn't it lucky we have them on the table?
Where's a match? Which of you gentle-
men can provide a match?

JIM. Here.

AMANDA. Thank you, sir.

JIM. Not at all, Ma'am!

AMANDA. I guess the fuse has burnt out.
Mr. O'Connor, can you tell a burnt-out
fuse? I know I can't and Tom is a total
loss when it comes to mechanics.

(SOUND: GETTING UP: VOICES RECEDE A LIT-
TLE TO KITCHENETTE.)

Oh, be careful you don't bump into something. We don't want our gentleman caller
to break his neck. Now wouldn't that be
a fine howdy-do?

JIM. Ha-ha!

Where is the fuse-box?

AMANDA. Right here next to the stove. Can
you see anything?

JIM. Just a minute.

AMANDA. Isn't electricity a mysterious
thing?

Wasn't it Benjamin Franklin who tied a
key to a kite?

We live in such a mysterious universe,
don't we? Some people say that science
clears up all the mysteries for us. In my
opinion it only creates more!

Have you found it yet?

JIM. No, Ma'am. All these fuses look okay
to me.

AMANDA. Tom!

TOM. Yes, Mother?

AMANDA. That light bill I gave you several days ago. The one I told you we got
the notices about?

(LEGEND: "HA!")

TOM. Oh.—Yeah.

AMANDA. You didn't neglect to pay it by
any chance?

TOM. Why, I—

AMANDA. Didn't! I might have known it!

JIM. Shakespeare probably wrote a poem
on that light bill, Mrs. Wingfield.

AMANDA. I might have known better than
to trust him with it! There's such a high
price for negligence in this world!

JIM. Maybe the poem will win a ten-dollar
prize.

AMANDA. We'll just have to spend the re-
mainder of the evening in the nineteenth
century, before Mr. Edison made the
Mazda lamp!

JIM. Candlelight is my favorite kind of
light.

AMANDA. That shows you're romantic! But
that's no excuse for Tom.

Well, we got through dinner. Very considerate of them to let us get through
dinner before they plunged us into everlasting darkness, wasn't it, Mr. O'Connor?

JIM. Ha-ha!

AMANDA. Tom, as a penalty for your care-
lessness you can help me with the dishes.

JIM. Let me give you a hand.

AMANDA. Indeed you will not!

JIM. I ought to be good for something.

AMANDA. Good for something? (*Her tone
is rhapsodic.*)

*You?* Why, Mr. O'Connor, nobody, *nobody's* given me this much entertainment
in years—as you have!

JIM. Aw, now, Mrs. Wingfield!

AMANDA. I'm not exaggerating, not one
bit! But Sister is all by her lonesome. You
go keep her company in the parlor!

I'll give you this lovely old candelabrum
that used to be on the altar at the church
of the Heavenly Rest. It was melted a little
out of shape when the church burnt down.
Lightning struck it one spring. Gypsy

Jones was holding a revival at the time and he intimated that the church was destroyed because the Episcopalians gave card parties.

JIM. Ha-ha.

AMANDA. And how about you coaxing Sister to drink a little wine? I think it would be good for her! Can you carry both at once?

JIM. Sure. I'm Superman!

AMANDA. Now, Thomas, get into this apron!

*(The door of kitchenette swings closed on* AMANDA's *gay laughter; the flickering light approaches the portieres.)*

*(*LAURA *sits up nervously as he enters. Her speech at first is low and breathless from the almost intolerable strain of being alone with a stranger.)*

*(*THE LEGEND: "I DON'T SUPPOSE YOU REMEMBER ME AT ALL!")*

*(In her first speeches in this scene, before* JIM's *warmth overcomes her paralyzing shyness,* LAURA's *voice is thin and breathless as though she has just run up a steep flight of stairs.)*

*(*JIM's *attitude is gently humorous. In playing this scene it should be stressed that while the incident is apparently unimportant, it is to* LAURA *the climax of her secret life.)*

JIM. Hello, there, Laura.

LAURA *(faintly)*. Hello. *(She clears her throat.)*

JIM. How are you feeling now? Better?

LAURA. Yes. Yes, thank you.

JIM. This is for you. A little dandelion wine. *(He extends it toward her with extravagant gallantry.)*

LAURA. Thank you.

JIM. Drink it—but don't get drunk!

*(He laughs heartily.* LAURA *takes the glass uncertainly; laughs shyly.)*

Where shall I set the candles?

LAURA. Oh—oh, anywhere . . .

JIM. How about here on the floor? Any objections?

LAURA. No.

JIM. I'll spread a newspaper under to catch the drippings. I like to sit on the floor. Mind if I do?

LAURA. Oh, no.

JIM. Give me a pillow?

LAURA. What?

JIM. A pillow!

LAURA. Oh . . . *(Hands him one quickly.)*

JIM. How about you? Don't you like to sit on the floor?

LAURA. Oh—yes.

JIM. Why don't you, then?

LAURA. I—will.

JIM. Take a pillow! *(*LAURA *does. Sits on the other side of the candelabrum.* JIM *crosses his legs and smiles engagingly at her.)* I can't hardly see you sitting way over there.

LAURA. I can—see you.

JIM. I know, but that's not fair, I'm in the limelight. *(*LAURA *moves her pillow closer.)* Good! Now I can see you! Comfortable?

LAURA. Yes.

JIM. So am I. Comfortable as a cow! Will you have some gum?

LAURA. No, thank you.

JIM. I think that I will indulge, with your permission. *(Musingly unwraps it and holds it up.)* Think of the fortune made by the guy that invented the first piece of chewing gum. Amazing, huh? The Wrigley Building is one of the sights of Chicago.—I saw it summer before last when I went up to the Century of Progress. Did you take in the Century of Progress?

LAURA. No, I didn't.

JIM. Well, it was quite a wonderful exposition. What impressed me most was the Hall of Science. Gives you an idea of what the future will be in America, even more wonderful than the present time is! *(Pause. Smiling at her.)* Your brother tells me you're shy. Is that right, Laura?

LAURA. I—don't know.

JIM. I judge you to be an old-fashioned

type of girl. Well, I think that's a pretty good type to be. Hope you don't think I'm being too personal—do you?

LAURA *(hastily, out of embarrassment)*. I believe I *will* take a piece of gum, if you —don't mind. *(Clearing her throat.)* Mr. O'Connor, have you—kept up with your singing?

JIM. Singing? Me?

LAURA. Yes. I remember what a beautiful voice you had.

JIM. When did you hear me sing?

(VOICE OFF STAGE IN THE PAUSE.)

VOICE *(off stage)*.

O blow, ye winds, heigh-ho,
A-roving I will go!
I'm off to my love
With a boxing glove—
Ten thousand miles away!

JIM. You say you've heard me sing?

LAURA. Oh, yes! Yes, very often . . . I— don't suppose—you remember me—at all?

JIM *(smiling doubtfully)*. You know I have an idea I've seen you before. I had that idea soon as you opened the door. It seemed almost like I was about to remember your name. But the name that I started to call you—wasn't a name! And so I stopped myself before I said it.

LAURA. Wasn't it—Blue Roses?

JIM *(springs up. Grinning)*. Blue Roses! —My gosh, yes—Blue Roses!

That's what I had on my tongue when you opened the door!

Isn't it funny what tricks your memory plays? I didn't connect you with high school somehow or other.

But that's where it was; it was high school. I didn't even know you were Shakespeare's sister!

Gosh, I'm sorry.

LAURA. I didn't expect you to. You—barely knew me!

JIM. But we did have a speaking acquaintance, huh?

LAURA. Yes, we—spoke to each other.

JIM. When did you recognize me?

LAURA. Oh, right away!

JIM. Soon as I came in the door?

LAURA. When I heard your name I thought it was probably you. I knew that Tom used to know you a little in high school. So when you came in the door—

Well, then I was—sure.

JIM. Why didn't you *say* something, then?

LAURA *(breathlessly)*. I didn't know what to say, I was—too surprised!

JIM. For goodness' sakes! You know, this sure is funny!

LAURA. Yes! Yes, isn't it, though . . .

JIM. Didn't we have a class in something together?

LAURA. Yes, we did.

JIM. What class was that?

LAURA. It was—singing—Chorus!

JIM. Aw!

LAURA. I sat across the aisle from you in the Aud.

JIM. Aw.

LAURA. Mondays, Wednesdays and Fridays.

JIM. Now I remember—you always came in late.

LAURA. Yes, it was so hard for me, getting upstairs. I had that brace on my leg—it clumped so loud!

JIM. I never heard any clumping.

LAURA *(wincing at the recollection)*. To me it sounded like—thunder!

JIM. Well, well, well, I never even noticed.

LAURA. And everybody was seated before I came in. I had to walk in front of all those people. My seat was in the back row. I had to go clumping all the way up the aisle with everyone watching!

JIM. You shouldn't have been self-conscious.

LAURA. I know, but I was. It was always such a relief when the singing started.

JIM. Aw, yes, I've placed you now! I used to call you Blue Roses. How was it that I got started calling you that?

LAURA. I was out of school a little while with pleurosis. When I came back you asked me what was the matter. I said I had pleurosis—you thought I said Blue Roses. That's what you always called me after that!

JIM. I hope you didn't mind.

LAURA. Oh, no—I liked it. You see, I wasn't acquainted with many—people. . . .

JIM. As I remember you sort of stuck by yourself.

LAURA. I—I—never have had much luck at—making friends.

JIM. I don't see why you wouldn't.

LAURA. Well, I—started out badly.

JIM. You mean being—

LAURA. Yes, it sort of—stood between me—

JIM. You shouldn't have let it!

LAURA. I know, but it did, and—

JIM. You were shy with people!

LAURA. I tried not to be but never could—

JIM. Overcome it?

LAURA. No, I—I never could!

JIM. I guess being shy is something you have to work out of kind of gradually.

LAURA (sorrowfully). Yes—I guess it—

JIM. Takes time!

LAURA. Yes—

JIM. People are not so dreadful when you know them. That's what you have to remember! And everybody has problems, not just you, but practically everybody has got some problems.

You think of yourself as having the only problems, as being the only one who is disappointed. But just look around you and you will see lots of people as disappointed as you are. For instance, I hoped when I was going to high school that I would be further along at this time, six years later, than I am now— You remember that wonderful write-up I had in *The Torch?*

LAURA. Yes! (She rises and crosses to table.)

JIM. It said I was bound to succeed in anything I went into! (LAURA returns with the annual.) Holy Jeez! *The Torch!* (He accepts it reverently. They smile across it

with mutual wonder. LAURA crouches beside him and they begin to turn through it. LAURA's shyness is dissolving in his warmth.)

LAURA. Here you are in *The Pirates of Penzance!*

JIM (wistfully). I sang the baritone lead in that operetta.

LAURA (rapidly). So—beautifully!

JIM (protesting). Aw—

LAURA. Yes, yes—beautifully—beautifully!

JIM. You heard me?

LAURA. All three times!

JIM. No!

LAURA. Yes!

JIM. All three performances?

LAURA (looking down). Yes.

JIM. Why?

LAURA. I—wanted to ask you to—autograph my program.

JIM. Why didn't you ask me to?

LAURA. You were always surrounded by your own friends so much that I never had a chance to.

JIM. You should have just—

LAURA. Well, I—thought you might think I was—

JIM. Thought I might think you was—what?

LAURA. Oh—

JIM (with reflective relish). I was beleaguered by females in those days.

LAURA. You were terribly popular!

JIM. Yeah—

LAURA. You had such a—friendly way—

JIM. I was spoiled in high school.

LAURA. Everybody—liked you!

JIM. Including you?

LAURA. I—yes, I—I did, too— (She gently closes the book in her lap.)

JIM. Well, well, well!—Give me that program, Laura. (She hands it to him. He signs it with a flourish.) There you are—better late than never!

LAURA. Oh, I—what a—surprise!

JIM. My signature isn't worth very much right now.

But some day—maybe—it will increase in value!

Being disappointed is one thing and being discouraged is something else. I am disappointed but I am not discouraged.

I'm twenty-three years old.

How old are you?

LAURA. I'll be twenty-four in June.

JIM. That's not old age!

LAURA. No, but—

JIM. You finished high school?

LAURA *(with difficulty)*. I didn't go back.

JIM. You mean you dropped out?

LAURA. I made bad grades in my final examinations. *(She rises and replaces the book and the program. Her voice strained.)* How is—Emily Meisenbach getting along?

JIM. Oh, that kraut-head!

LAURA. Why do you call her that?

JIM. That's what she was.

LAURA. You're not still—going with her?

JIM. I never see her.

LAURA. It said in the Personal Section that you were—engaged!

JIM. I know, but I wasn't impressed by that—propaganda!

LAURA. It wasn't—the truth?

JIM. Only in Emily's optimistic opinion!

LAURA. Oh—

(LEGEND: "WHAT HAVE YOU DONE SINCE HIGH SCHOOL?")

*(JIM lights a cigarette and leans indolently back on his elbows smiling at LAURA with a warmth and charm which lights her inwardly with altar candles. She remains by the table and turns in her hands a piece of glass to cover her tumult.)*

JIM *(after several reflective puffs on a cigarette)*. What have you done since high school? *(She seems not to hear him.)*

Huh? *(LAURA looks up.)* I said what **have** you done since high school, Laura?

LAURA. Nothing much.

JIM. You must have been doing something these six long years.

LAURA. Yes.

JIM. Well, then, such as what?

LAURA. I took a business course at business college—

JIM. How did that work out?

LAURA. Well, not very—well—I had to drop out, it gave me—indigestion—

*(JIM laughs gently.)*

JIM. What are you doing now?

LAURA. I don't do anything—much. Oh, please don't think I sit around doing nothing! My glass collection takes up a good deal of time. Glass is something you have to take good care of.

JIM. What did you say—about glass?

LAURA. Collection I said—I have one— *(She clears her throat and turns away again, acutely shy.)*

JIM *(abruptly)*. You know what I judge to be the trouble with you?

Inferiority complex! Know what that is? That's what they call it when someone low-rates himself!

I understand it because I had it, too. Although my case was not so aggravated as yours seems to be. I had it until I took up public speaking, developed my voice, and learned that I had an aptitude for science. Before that time I never thought of myself as being outstanding in any way whatsoever!

Now I've never made a regular study of it, but I have a friend who says I can analyze people better than doctors that make a profession of it. I don't claim that to be necessarily true, but I can sure guess a person's psychology, Laura! *(Takes out his gum.)* Excuse me, Laura. I always take it out when the flavor is gone. I'll use this scrap of paper to wrap it in. I know how it is to get it stuck on a shoe.

Yep—that's what I judge to be your principal trouble. A lack of confidence in yourself as a person. You don't have the proper amount of faith in yourself. I'm basing that fact on a number of your remarks and also on certain observations I've made. For instance that clumping you thought was so awful in high school. You say that you even dreaded to walk into class. You see what you did? You dropped out of school, you gave up an education because of a clump, which as far as I know was practically non-existent! A little physical defect is what you have. Hardly noticeable even! Magnified thousands of times by imagination!

You know what my strong advice to you is? Think of yourself as *superior* in some way!

LAURA. In what way would I think?

JIM. Why, man alive, Laura! Just look about you a little. What do you see? A world full of common people! All of 'em born and all of 'em going to die!

Which of them has one-tenth of your good points! Or mine! Or anyone else's, as far as that goes—Gosh!

Everybody excels in some one thing. Some in many!

*(Unconsciously glances at himself in the mirror.)*

All you've got to do is discover in *what!* Take me, for instance.

*(He adjusts his tie at the mirror.)*

My interest happens to lie in electro-dynamics. I'm taking a course in radio engineering at night school, Laura, on top of a fairly responsible  job at the warehouse. I'm taking that course and studying public speaking.

LAURA. Ohhhh.

JIM. Because I believe in the future of television!

*(Turning back to her.)*

I wish to be ready to go up right along with it. Therefore I'm planning to get in on the ground floor. In fact I've already made the right connections and all that remains is for the industry itself to get under way! Full steam—

*(His eyes are starry.)*

Knowledge—Zzzzzp! Money—Zzzzzzp! —Power!

That's the cycle democracy is built on!

*(His attitude is convincingly dynamic. LAURA stares at him, even her shyness eclipsed in her absolute wonder. He suddenly grins.)*

I guess you think I think a lot of myself!

LAURA. No—o-o-o, I—

JIM. Now how about you? Isn't there something you take more interest in than anything else?

LAURA. Well, I do—as I said—have my—glass collection—

*(A peal of girlish laughter from the kitchen.)*

JIM. I'm not right sure I know what you're talking about.

What kind of glass is it?

LAURA. Little articles of it, they're ornaments mostly!

Most of them are little animals made out of glass, the tiniest little animals in the world. Mother calls them a glass menagerie!

Here's an example of one, if you'd like to see it!

This one is one of the oldest. It's nearly thirteen.

*(MUSIC: "THE GLASS MENAGERIE.")*

*(He stretches out his hand.)*

Oh, be careful—if you breathe, it breaks!

JIM. I'd better not take it. I'm pretty clumsy with things.

LAURA. Go on, I trust you with him!

*(Places it in his palm.)*

There now—you're holding him gently! Hold him over the light, he loves the light! You see how the light shines through him?

JIM. It sure does shine!

LAURA. I shouldn't be partial, but he is my favorite one.

JIM. What kind of a thing is this one supposed to be?

LAURA. Haven't you noticed the single horn on his forehead?

JIM. A unicorn, huh?

LAURA. Mmm-hmmm!

JIM. Unicorns, aren't they extinct in the modern world?

LAURA. I know!

JIM. Poor little fellow, he must feel sort of lonesome.

LAURA *(smiling)*. Well, if he does he doesn't complain about it. He stays on a shelf with some horses that don't have horns and all of them seem to get along nicely together.

JIM. How do you know?

LAURA *(lightly)*. I haven't heard any arguments among them!

JIM *(grinning)*. No arguments, huh? Well, that's a pretty good sign! Where shall I set him?

LAURA. Put him on the table. They all like a change of scenery once in a while!

JIM *(stretching)*. Well, well, well, well— Look how big my shadow is when I stretch!

LAURA. Oh, oh, yes—it stretches across the ceiling!

JIM *(crossing to door)*. I think it's stopped raining. *(Opens fire-escape door.)* Where does the music come from?

LAURA. From the Paradise Dance Hall across the alley.

JIM. How about cutting the rug a little, Miss Wingfield?

LAURA. Oh, I—

JIM. Or is your program filled up? Let me have a look at it. *(Grasps imaginary card.)* Why, every dance is taken! I'll just have to scratch some out. (WALTZ MUSIC: "LA GOLONDRINA.") Ahhh, a waltz! *(He executes some sweeping turns by himself then holds his arms toward LAURA.)*

LAURA *(breathlessly)*. I—can't dance!

JIM. There you go, that inferiority stuff!

LAURA. I've never danced in my life!

JIM. Come on, try!

LAURA. Oh, but I'd step on you!

JIM. I'm not made out of glass.

LAURA. How—how—how do we start?

JIM. Just leave it to me. You hold your arms out a little.

LAURA. Like this?

JIM. A little bit higher. Right. Now don't tighten up, that's the main thing about it —relax.

LAURA *(laughing breathlessly)*. It's hard not to.

JIM. Okay.

LAURA. I'm afraid you can't budge me.

JIM. What do you bet I can't? *(He swings her into motion.)*

LAURA. Goodness, yes, you can!

JIM. Let yourself go, now, Laura, just let yourself go.

LAURA. I'm—

JIM. Come on!

LAURA. Trying!

JIM. Not so stiff— Easy does it!

LAURA. I know but I'm—

JIM. Loosen th' backbone! There now, that's a lot better.

LAURA. Am I?

JIM. Lots, lots better! *(He moves her about the room in a clumsy waltz.)*

LAURA. Oh, my!

JIM. Ha-ha!

LAURA. Oh, my goodness!

JIM. Ha-ha-ha! *(They suddenly bump into the table.* JIM *stops.)* What did we hit on?

LAURA. Table.

JIM. Did something fall off it? I think—

LAURA. Yes.

JIM. I hope it wasn't the little glass horse with the horn!

LAURA. Yes.

JIM. Aw, aw, aw. Is it broken?

LAURA. Now it is just like all the other horses.

JIM. It's lost its—

LAURA. Horn! It doesn't matter. Maybe it's a blessing in disguise.

JIM. You'll never forgive me. I bet that that was your favorite piece of glass.

LAURA. I don't have favorites much. It's no tragedy, Freckles. Glass breaks so easily.

No matter how careful you are. The traffic jars the shelves and things fall off them.

JIM. Still I'm awfully sorry that I was the cause.

LAURA (smiling). I'll just imagine he had an operation.

The horn was removed to make him feel less—freakish!

(They both laugh.)

Now he will feel more at home with the other horses, the ones that don't have horns. . . .

JIM. Ha-ha, that's very funny!

(Suddenly serious.)

I'm glad to see that you have a sense of humor.

You know—you're—well—very different! Surprisingly different from anyone else I know!

(His voice becomes soft and hesitant with a genuine feeling.)

Do you mind me telling you that?

(LAURA is abashed beyond speech.)

I mean it in a nice way . . .

(LAURA nods shyly, looking away.)

You make me feel sort of—I don't know how to put it!

I'm usually pretty good at expressing things, but—

This is something that I don't know how to say!

(LAURA touches her throat and clears it—turns the broken unicorn in her hands.) (Even softer.)

Has anyone ever told you that you were pretty?

(PAUSE: MUSIC.)

(LAURA looks up slowly, with wonder, and shakes her head.)

Well, you are! In a different way from anyone else.

And all the nicer because of the difference, too.

(His voice becomes low and husky. LAURA turns away, nearly faint with the novelty of her emotions.)

I wish that you were my sister. I'd teach you to have some confidence in yourself. The different people are not like other people, but being different is nothing to be ashamed of. Because other people are not such wonderful people. They're one hundred times one thousand. You're one times one! They walk all over the earth. You just stay here. They're common as—weeds, but—you—well, you're—Blue Roses!

(IMAGE ON SCREEN: BLUE ROSES.)

(MUSIC CHANGES.)

LAURA. But blue is wrong for—roses . . .

JIM. It's right for you!—You're—pretty!

LAURA. In what respect am I pretty?

JIM. In all respects—believe me! Your eyes —your hair—are pretty! Your hands are pretty!

(He catches hold of her hand.)

You think I'm making this up because I'm invited to dinner and have to be nice. Oh, I could do that! I could put on an act for you, Laura, and say lots of things without being very sincere. But this time I am. I'm talking to you sincerely. I happened to notice you had this inferiority complex that keeps you from feeling comfortable with people. Somebody needs to build your confidence up and make you proud instead of shy and turning away and—blushing—

Somebody—ought to—

Ought to—kiss you, Laura!

(His hand slips slowly up her arm to her shoulder.)

(MUSIC SWELLS TUMULTUOUSLY.)

(He suddenly turns her about and kisses her on the lips.)

(When he releases her, LAURA sinks on the sofa with a bright, dazed look.)

(JIM backs away and fishes in his pocket for a cigarette.)

(LEGEND ON SCREEN: "SOUVENIR.")

Stumble-john!

(He lights the cigarette, avoiding her look.)

(There is a peal of girlish laughter from AMANDA in the kitchen.)

(LAURA slowly raises and opens her hand

*It still contains the little broken glass animal. She looks at it with a tender, bewildered expression.*)

Stumble-john!

I shouldn't have done that— That was way off the beam.

You don't smoke, do you?

(*She looks up, smiling, not hearing the question.*)

(*He sits beside her a little gingerly. She looks at him speechlessly—waiting.*)

(*He coughs decorously and moves a little farther aside as he considers the situation and senses her feelings, dimly, with perturbation.*)

(*Gently.*) Would you—care for a—mint?

(*She doesn't seem to hear him but her look grows brighter even.*)

Peppermint—Life-Saver?

My pocket's a regular drug store—wherever I go . . .

(*He pops a mint in his mouth. Then gulps and decides to make a clean breast of it. He speaks slowly and gingerly.*)

Laura, you know, if I had a sister like you, I'd do the same thing as Tom. I'd bring out fellows and—introduce her to them. The right type of boys of a type to—appreciate her.

Only—well—he made a mistake about me. Maybe I've got no call to be saying this. That may not have been the idea in having me over. But what if it was?

There's nothing wrong about that. The only trouble is that in my case—I'm not in a situation to—do the right thing.

I can't take down your number and say I'll phone.

I can't call up next week and—ask for a date.

I thought I had better explain the situation in case you—misunderstood it and—hurt your feelings. . . .

(*Pause.*)

(*Slowly, very slowly,* LAURA'S *look changes, her eyes returning slowly from his to the ornament in her palm.*)

(AMANDA *utters another gay laugh in the kitchen.*)

LAURA (*faintly*). You—won't call again?

JIM. No, Laura, I can't.

(*He rises from the sofa.*)

As I was just explaining, I've—got strings on me.

Laura, I've—been going steady!

I go out all of the time with a girl named Betty. She's a home-girl like you, and Catholic, and Irish, and in a great many ways we—get along fine.

I met her last summer on a moonlight boat trip up the river to Alton, on the *Majestic.* Well—right away from the start it was— love!

(LEGEND: LOVE!)

(LAURA *sways slightly forward and grips the arm of the sofa. He fails to notice, now enrapt in his own comfortable being.*)

Being in love has made a new man of me!

(*Leaning stiffly forward, clutching the arm of the sofa,* LAURA *struggles visibly with her storm. But* JIM *is oblivious, she is a long way off.*)

The power of love is really pretty tremendous!

Love is something that—changes the whole world, Laura!

(*The storm abates a little and* LAURA *leans back. He notices her again.*)

It happened that Betty's aunt took sick, she got a wire and had to go to Centralia. So Tom—when he asked me to dinner—I naturally just accepted the invitation, not knowing that you—that he—that I—

(*He stops awkwardly.*)

Huh—I'm a stumble-john!

(*He flops back on the sofa.*)

(*The holy candles in the altar of* LAURA'S *face have been snuffed out. There is a look of almost infinite desolation.*)

(JIM *glances at her uneasily.*)

I wish that you would—say something.

(*She bites her lip which was trembling and then bravely smiles. She opens her hand again on the broken glass ornament. Then she gently takes his hand and raises it level with her own. She carefully places the unicorn in the palm of his hand, then pushes his fingers closed upon it.)* What are you—doing that for? You want me to have him?—Laura? *(She nods.)* What for?

LAURA. A—souvenir . . . *(She rises unsteadily and crouches beside the victrola to wind it up.)*

(LEGEND ON SCREEN: "THINGS HAVE A WAY OF TURNING OUT SO BADLY!")

(OR IMAGE: "GENTLEMAN CALLER WAVING GOOD-BYE!—GAILY.")

*(At this moment* AMANDA *rushes brightly back in the front room. She bears a pitcher of fruit punch in an old-fashioned cut-glass pitcher and a plate of macaroons. The plate has a gold border and poppies painted on it.)*

AMANDA. Well, well, well! Isn't the air delightful after the shower? I've made you children a little liquid refreshment. *(Turns gaily to the gentleman caller.)*

Jim, do you know that song about lemonade?

"Lemonade, lemonade
  Made in the shade and stirred with a
    spade—
  Good enough for any old maid!"

JIM *(uneasily)*. Ha-ha! No—I never heard it.

AMANDA. Why, Laura! You look so serious!

JIM. We were having a serious conversation.

AMANDA. Good! Now you're better acquainted!

JIM *(uncertainly)*. Ha-ha! Yes.

AMANDA. You modern young people are much more serious-minded than my generation. I was so gay as a girl!

JIM. You haven't changed, Mrs. Wingfield.

AMANDA. Tonight I'm rejuvenated! The gaiety of the occasion, Mr. O'Connor! *(She tosses her head with a peal of laughter. Spills lemonade.)*

Oooo! I'm baptizing myself!

JIM. Here—let me—

AMANDA *(setting the pitcher down)*. There

now. I discovered we had some maraschino cherries. I dumped them in, juice and all!

JIM. You shouldn't have gone to that trouble, Mrs. Wingfield.

AMANDA. Trouble, trouble? Why, it was loads of fun!

Didn't you hear me cutting up in the kitchen? I bet your ears were burning! I told Tom how outdone with him I was for keeping you to himself so long a time! He should have brought you over much, much sooner! Well, now that you've found your way, I want you to be a frequent caller! Not just occasional but all the time. Oh, we're going to have a lot of gay times together! I see them coming!

Mmm, just breathe that air! So fresh, and the moon's so pretty!

I'll skip back out—I know where my place is when young folks are having a—serious conversation!

JIM. Oh, don't go out, Mrs. Wingfield. The fact of the matter is I've got to be going.

AMANDA. Going, now? You're joking! Why, it's only the shank of the evening, Mr. O'Connor!

JIM. Well, you know how it is.

AMANDA. You mean you're a young workingman and have to keep workingmen's hours. We'll let you off early tonight. But only on the condition that next time you stay later.

What's the best night for you? Isn't Saturday night the best night for you workingmen?

JIM. I have a couple of time-clocks to punch, Mrs. Wingfield. One at morning, another one at night!

AMANDA. My, but you *are* ambitious! You work at night, too?

JIM. No, Ma'am, not work but—Betty!

*(He crosses deliberately to pick up his hat. The band at the Paradise Dance Hall goes into a tender waltz.)*

AMANDA. Betty? Betty? Who's—Betty!

*(There is an ominous cracking sound in the sky.)*

JIM. Oh, just a girl. The girl I go steady with! (*He smiles charmingly. The sky falls.*)

(LEGEND: "THE SKY FALLS.")

AMANDA (*a long-drawn exhalation*). Ohhhh . . . Is it a serious romance, Mr. O'Connor?

JIM. We're going to be married the second Sunday in June.

AMANDA. Ohhhh—how nice!

Tom didn't mention that you were engaged to be married.

JIM. The cat's not out of the bag at the warehouse yet.

You know how they are. They call you Romeo and stuff like that. (*He stops at the oval mirror to put on his hat. He carefully shapes the brim and the crown to give a discreetly dashing effect.*)

It's been a wonderful evening, Mrs. Wingfield. I guess this is what they mean by Southern hospitality.

AMANDA. It really wasn't anything at all.

JIM. I hope it don't seem like I'm rushing off. But I promised Betty I'd pick her up at the Wabash depot, an' by the time I get my jalopy down there her train'll be in. Some women are pretty upset if you keep 'em waiting.

AMANDA. Yes, I know— The tyranny of women!

(*Extends her hand.*)

Good-bye, Mr. O'Connor.

I wish you luck—and happiness—and success! All three of them, and so does Laura! —Don't you, Laura?

LAURA. Yes!

JIM (*taking her hand*). Good-bye, Laura. I'm certainly going to treasure that souvenir. And don't you forget the good advice I gave you.

(*Raises his voice to a cheery shout.*)

So long, Shakespeare!

Thanks again, ladies— Good night!

(*He grins and ducks jauntily out.*)

(*Still bravely grimacing, AMANDA closes the door on the gentleman caller. Then she turns back to the room with a puzzled expression. She and LAURA don't dare to face each other. LAURA crouches beside the victrola to wind it.*)

AMANDA (*faintly*). Things have a way of turning out so badly.

I don't believe that I would play the victrola.

Well, well—well—

Our gentleman caller was engaged to be married!

Tom!

TOM (*from back*). Yes, Mother?

AMANDA. Come in here a minute. I want to tell you something awfully funny.

TOM (*enters with macaroon and a glass of the lemonade*). Has the gentleman caller gotten away already?

AMANDA. The gentleman caller has made an early departure.

What a wonderful joke you played on us!

TOM. How do you mean?

AMANDA. You didn't mention that he was engaged to be married.

TOM. Jim? Engaged?

AMANDA. That's what he just informed us.

TOM. I'll be jiggered! I didn't know about that.

AMANDA. That seems very peculiar.

TOM. What's peculiar about it?

AMANDA. Didn't you call him your best friend down at the warehouse?

TOM. He is, but how did I know?

AMANDA. It seems extremely peculiar that you wouldn't know your best friend was going to be married!

TOM. The warehouse is where I work, not where I know things about people!

AMANDA. You don't know things anywhere! You live in a dream; you manufacture illusions!

(*He crosses to door.*)

Where are you going?

TOM. I'm going to the movies.

AMANDA. That's right, now that you've had

us make such fools of ourselves. The effort, the preparations, all the expense! The new floor lamp, the rug, the clothes for Laura! All for what? To entertain some other girl's fiancé!

Go to the movies, go! Don't think about us, a mother deserted, an unmarried sister who's crippled and has no job! Don't let anything interfere with your selfish pleasure!

Just go, go, go—to the movies!

TOM. All right, I will! The more you shout about my selfishness to me the quicker I'll go, and I won't go to the movies!

AMANDA. Go, then! Then go to the moon— you selfish dreamer!

*(TOM smashes his glass on the floor. He plunges out on the fire-escape, slamming the door. LAURA screams—cut by door.)*

*(Dance-hall music up. TOM goes to the rail and grips it desperately, lifting his face in the chill white moonlight penetrating the narrow abyss of the alley.)*

*(LEGEND ON SCREEN: "AND SO GOOD-BYE . . .")*

*(TOM's closing speech is timed with the interior pantomime. The interior scene is played as though viewed through sound-proof glass. AMANDA appears to be making a comforting speech to LAURA who is huddled upon the sofa. Now that we cannot hear the mother's speech, her silliness is gone and she has dignity and tragic beauty. LAURA's dark hair hides her face until at the end of the speech she lifts it to smile at her mother. AMANDA's gestures are slow and graceful, almost dance-like, as she comforts the daughter. At the end of her speech she glances a moment at the father's picture—then withdraws through the portieres. At close of TOM's speech, LAURA blows out the candles, ending the play.)*

TOM. I didn't go to the moon, I went much further—for time is the longest distance between two places—

Not long after that I was fired for writing a poem on the lid of a shoe-box.

I left Saint Louis. I descended the steps of this fire-escape for a last time and followed, from then on, in my father's footsteps, attempting to find in motion what was lost in space—

I traveled around a great deal. The cities swept about me like dead leaves, leaves that were brightly colored but torn away from the branches.

I would have stopped, but I was pursued by something.

It always came upon me unawares, taking me altogether by surprise. Perhaps it was a familiar bit of music. Perhaps it was only a piece of transparent glass—

Perhaps I am walking along a street at night, in some strange city, before I have found companions. I pass the lighted window of a shop where perfume is sold. The window is filled with pieces of colored glass, tiny transparent bottles in delicate colors, like bits of a shattered rainbow.

Then all at once my sister touches my shoulder. I turn around and look into her eyes . . .

Oh, Laura, Laura, I tried to leave you behind me, but I am more faithful than I intended to be!

I reach for a cigarette, I cross the street, I run into the movies or a bar, I buy a drink, I speak to the nearest stranger— anything that can blow your candles out!

*(LAURA bends over the candles.)*

—for nowadays the world is lit by lightning! Blow out your candles, Laura—and so good-bye. . . .

*(She blows the candles out.)*

THE SCENE DISSOLVES

# 1945-46

The Circle's first citation to a musical was the only affirmative action that came out of the meeting on April 2, 1946. This honor was bestowed on the Rodgers-Hammerstein *Carousel* after it had been named on the nominating play ballot and then ruled out for the official vote because it was based on a foreign work.

Ten votes were needed to designate a grand winner, but the highest rating was only seven, given to the politically topical *State of the Union* by Howard Lindsay and Russel Crouse. Garson Kanin's *Born Yesterday,* a long-run powerhouse at the box office, received five votes, and one each went to Elmer Rice's *Dream Girl* and Harry Brown's *A Sound of Hunting. Home of the Brave* and *Deep Are the Roots* also figured in the trial ballot.

There was no better luck in the foreign category. Eleven members declined to pick a play. Five balloted for the *Antigone* of Jean Anouilh and Lewis Galantiere and one for Terence Rattigan's *O Mistress Mine.* The first of these was a vehicle for Katharine Cornell and the Lunts frolicked in the second.

Eleven members affirmed the citation to *Carousel,* three voted for *Lute Song* by Will Irwin and the late Sidney Howard, who adapted it from a Chinese classic, and three did not vote.

*State of the Union* was honored by the Pulitzer people.

There were a number of highlights to the season even though it was not especially distinguished. Oscar Hammerstein presented a fine revival of the great musical, *Show Boat,* which he and the composer Jerome Kern had written for Florenz Ziegfeld eighteen years earlier. Kern, who was to have been coproducer with Hammerstein, died in November, 1945, while in New York getting the production ready.

Spencer Tracy returned uneasily to the stage, after some fifteen years of movie stardom, in *The Rugged Path,* the first play turned out by Robert E. Sherwood in five years. The venture was not a success. Walter Huston did what was to prove to be his last New York stage work in *Apple of His Eye,* a minor bucolic piece. Bobby Clark, king of the musical clowns, cavorted attractively in Molière's *The Would-Be Gentleman.* Irving Berlin's most successful musical, *Annie Get Your Gun,* starred Ethel Merman. The Old Vic Repertory Company from London, headed by Laurence Olivier and Ralph Richardson, scored a hearty triumph in a late spring engagement in five classics.

*State of the Union* lasted 765 performances; *Born Yesterday,* 1,643.

# 1946-47

Two years and two months after his four-performance introduction as a Broadway playwright with *The Man Who Had All the Luck*, Arthur Miller won the grand prize with his second produced play, *All My Sons*, on April 21, 1947.

This reviewer always has regarded *All My Sons* as a highly overrated work and vastly inferior to the runner-up, Eugene O'Neill's *The Iceman Cometh*, for all that the latter was greatly overwritten and would have been much more effective in about half of its marathon length. Yet Miller did not have much trouble winning under the complicated preferential voting, used for the first time by the Circle.

An unsigned test ballot gave *All My Sons* twelve votes; *The Iceman Cometh*, seven; Lillian Hellman's *Another Part of the Forest*, an antedated sequel to *The Little Foxes*, four; Maxwell Anderson's *Joan of Lorraine*, one; and *Brigadoon*, a musical, one. The *Iceman Cometh* dropped one vote and *Joan of Lorraine* picked up one on the second, signed ballot. Since *All My Sons* did not have the required simple majority, the preferential vote was then taken to reach a decision. This resulted in 86 points for *All My Sons*, 80 for *The Iceman Cometh*, 72 for *Another Part of the Forest*, 55 for *Joan of Lorraine* and 53 for *Brigadoon*.

The foreign citation was won by Jean-Paul Sartre's *No Exit*, with sixteen votes to four for Konstantin Simonov's *The Whole World Over*.

*Brigadoon* won the musical citation from a rather large field but not until the preferential system was invoked. It wound up with 89 points to 73 for *Finian's Rainbow*, 65 for *Annie Get Your Gun*, 56 for *Call Me Mister* and 47 for *Street Scene* which had been supplied with songs by Kurt Weill.

*The Iceman Cometh* was the first O'Neill play the Circle ever had a chance to consider. The noted playwright's last previous production was *Days without End*, presented on January 8, 1934. After that one, he announced he would be out of circulation for several years because he was going to concentrate on completing a cycle of nine related dramas before he would let anything else of his be produced. His absence from the theatre was prolonged probably six years more than he had planned by (1) a wasting illness that stayed with him until his death on November 27, 1953, and held his writing in his last dozen years to a trickle and (2) his disinclination to have anything produced during World War II.

*The Iceman Cometh* was written six years before it was produced and was not one of the cycle of nine plays O'Neill had outlined. Broadway saw no other new play of his in his lifetime, although *A Moon for the Misbegotten* was tried out on the road by the Theatre Guild for several weeks early in 1947. It was decided not to bring it to New York because the casting was not satisfactory. Almost every season some producer is reported to be on the verge of producing this play anew, but this hasn't occurred at this writing. Random House published the text in 1952.

An ambitious effort of the season was the American Repertory Theatre, Inc., in which Cheryl Crawford, Eva Le Gallienne and Margaret Webster were prime movers. It presented *Henry VIII, What Every Woman Knows, John Gabriel Borkman, Androcles and the Lion, Pound on Demand, Yellow Jack* and *Alice in Wonderland*. The organization gave a total of 248 performances. However, the theatre's economic realities, so difficult for repertory to lick these days, cause it to fail.

*All My Sons* played 142 performances; *The Iceman Cometh*, 136.

# All My Sons

## By ARTHUR MILLER

Presented by Harold Clurman, Elia Kazan, and Walter Fried (in association with Herbert H. Harris) at the Coronet Theatre, New York City, January 29, 1947, with the following cast:

| | |
|---|---|
| JOE KELLER | *Ed Begley* |
| KATE KELLER | *Beth Merrill* |
| CHRIS KELLER | *Arthur Kennedy* |
| ANN DEEVER | *Lois Wheeler* |
| GEORGE DEEVER | *Karl Malden* |
| DR. JIM BAYLISS | *John McGovern* |
| SUE BAYLISS | *Peggy Meredith* |
| FRANK LUBEY | *Dudley Sadler* |
| LYDIA LUBEY | *Hope Cameron* |
| BERT | *Eugene Steiner* |

---

## SCENE

Act I—Backyard of the Keller home in the outskirts of an American town. August. of our era. Ten o'clock Sunday morning.

Act II—Same. That evening as twilight falls.

Act III—Same. Two o'clock the following morning.

---

## ACT ONE

*The back yard of the Keller home in the outskirts of an American town. August of our era.*

*The stage is hedged on* R. *and* L. *by tall, closely planted poplars which lend the yard a secluded atmosphere. Upstage is filled with the back of the house and its open, unroofed porch which extends into the yard some six feet. The house is two stories high and has seven rooms. It would have cost perhaps fifteen thousand in the early twenties when it was built. Now it is nicely painted, looks tight and comfortable, and the yard is green with sod, here and there plants whose season is gone. At the* R., *beside the house, the entrance of the driveway can be seen, but the poplars cut off view of its continuation downstage. In the* L. *corner, downstage, stands the four-foot high stump of a slender apple tree whose upper trunk and branches lie toppled beside it, fruit still clinging to its branches.*

*Downstage* R. *is a small, trellised arbor, shaped like a sea-shell, with a decorative bulb hanging from its forward-curving roof. Garden chairs and a table are scattered about. A garbage pail on the ground next to the porch steps, a wire leaf-burner near it.*

*On the rise: It is early Sunday morning. Joe Keller is sitting in the sun reading the want ads of the Sunday paper, the other sections of which lie neatly on the ground beside him. Behind his back, inside the arbor, Doctor Jim Bayliss is reading part of the paper at the table.*

*Keller is nearing sixty. A heavy man of stolid mind and build, a business man these many years, but with the imprint of the machine-shop worker and boss still upon him. When he reads, when he speaks, when he listens, it is with the terrible concentration of the uneducated man for whom there is still wonder in many commonly known things, a man whose judgments must be dredged out of experience and a peasant-like common sense. A man among men.*

*Doctor Bayliss is nearly forty. A wry self-controlled man, an easy talker, but with a wisp of sadness that clings even to his self-effacing humor.*

*At curtain, Jim is standing at* L., *staring at the broken tree. He taps a pipe on it, blows through the pipe, feels in his pockets for tobacco, then speaks.*

———

JIM. Where's your tobacco?

KELLER. I think I left it on the table. *(Jim goes slowly to table on the arbor, finds a pouch, and sits there on the bench, filling his pipe)* Gonna rain tonight.

JIM. Paper says so?

KELLER. Yeah, right here.

JIM. Then it can't rain.

*(Frank Lubey enters, through a small space between the poplars. Frank is thirty-two but balding. A pleasant, opinionated man, uncertain of himself, with a tendency toward peevishness when crossed, but always wanting it pleasant and neighborly. He rather saunters in, leisurely, nothing to do. He does not notice Jim in the arbor. On his greeting, Jim does not bother looking up.)*

FRANK. Hya.

KELLER. Hello, Frank. What's doin'?

FRANK. Nothin'. Walking off my breakfast. *(Looks up at the sky)* That beautiful? Not a cloud.

KELLER *(looks up)* Yeah, nice.

FRANK. Every Sunday ought to be like this.

KELLER *(indicating the sections beside him)*. Want the paper?

FRANK. What's the difference, it's all bad news. What's today's calamity?

KELLER. I don't know, I don't read the news part any more. It's more interesting in the want ads.

FRANK. Why, you trying to buy something?

KELLER. No, I'm just interested. To see what people want, y'know? For instance, here's a guy is lookin' for two Newfoundland dogs. Now what's he want with two Newfoundland dogs?

FRANK. That is funny.

KELLER. Here's another one. Wanted—Old Dictionaries. High prices paid. Now what's a man going to do with an old dictionary?

FRANK. Why not? Probably a book collector.

KELLER. You mean he'll make a living out of that?

FRANK. Sure, there's a lot of them.

KELLER *(shakes his head)*. All the kind of business goin' on. In my day, either you were a lawyer, or a doctor, or you worked in a shop. Now . . .

FRANK. Well, I was going to be a forester once.

KELLER. Well, that shows you; in my day, there was no such thing. *(Scanning the page, sweeping it with his hand)* You look at a page like this you realize how ignorant you are. *(Softly, with wonder, as he scans page)* Psss!

FRANK *(noticing tree)*. Hey, what happened to your tree?

KELLER. Ain't that awful? The wind must've got it last night. You heard the wind, didn't you?

FRANK. Yeah, I got a mess in my yard, too. *(Goes to tree)* What a pity. *(Turns to Keller)* What'd Kate say?

KELLER. They're all asleep yet. I'm just waiting for her to see it.

FRANK *(struck)*. You know?—it's funny.

KELLER. What?

FRANK. Larry was born in August. He'd been twenty-seven this month. And his tree blows down.

KELLER *(touched)*. I'm surprised you remember his birthday, Frank. That's nice.

FRANK. Well, I'm working on his horoscope.

KELLER. How can you make him a horoscope? That's for the future, ain't it?

FRANK. Well, what I'm doing is this, see. Larry was reported missing on November 25th, right?

KELLER. Yeah?

FRANK. Well, then, we assume that if he was killed it was on November 25th. Now, what Kate wants . . .

KELLER. Oh, Kate asked you to make a horoscope?

FRANK. Yeah, what she wants to find out is whether November 25th was a favorable day for Larry.

KELLER. What is that, favorable day?

FRANK. Well, a favorable day for a person is a fortunate day, according to his stars. In other words it would be practically impossible for him to have died on his favorable day.

KELLER. Well, was that his favorable day?—November 25th?

FRANK. That's what I'm working on to find out. It takes time! See, the point is, if November 25th was his favorable day, then it's completely possible he's alive somewhere, because . . . I mean it's possible. *(He notices Jim now. Jim is looking at him as though at an idiot. To Jim—*

*with an uncertain laugh)* I didn't even see you.

KELLER *(to Jim)*. Is he talkin' sense?

JIM. Him? He's all right. He's just completely out of his mind, that's all.

FRANK *(peeved)*. The trouble with you is, you don't *believe* in anything.

JIM. And your trouble is that you believe in *anything*. You didn't see my kid this morning, did you?

FRANK. No.

KELLER. Imagine? He walked off with his thermometer. Right out of his bag.

JIM *(gets up)*. What a problem. One look at a girl and he takes her temperature. *(Goes to driveway, looks upstage toward street)*

FRANK. That boy's going to be a real doctor; he's smart.

JIM. Over my dead body he'll be a doctor. A good beginning, too.

FRANK. Why? It's an honorable profession.

JIM *(looks at him tiredly)*. Frank, will you stop talking like a civics book? *(Keller laughs)*

FRANK. Why, I saw a movie a couple of weeks ago, reminded me of you. There was a doctor in that picture . . .

KELLER. Don Ameche!

FRANK. I think it was, yeah. And he worked in his basement discovering things. That's what you ought to do; you could help humanity, instead of . . .

JIM. I would love to help humanity on a Warner Brothers salary.

KELLER *(points at him, laughing)*. That's very good, Jim.

JIM *(looks toward house)*. Well, where's the beautiful girl was supposed to be here?

FRANK *(excited)*. Annie came?

KELLER. Sure, sleepin' upstairs. We picked her up on the one o'clock train last night. Wonderful thing. Girl leaves here, a scrawny kid. Couple of years go by, she's a regular woman. Hardly recognized her, and she was running in and out of this yard all her life. That was a very happy family used to live in your house, Jim.

JIM. Like to meet her. The block can use a pretty girl. In the whole neighborhood there's not a damned thing to look at. *(Enter Sue, Jim's wife. She is rounding forty, an overweight woman who fears it. On seeing her Jim wryly adds:)* . . . Except my wife, of course.

SUE *(in same spirit)*. Mrs. Adams is on the phone, you dog.

JIM *(to Keller)*. Such is the condition which prevails—*(Going to his wife)* my love, my light. . . .

SUE. Don't sniff around me. *(Points to their house)* And give her a nasty answer. I can smell her perfume over the phone.

JIM. What's the matter with her now?

SUE. I don't know, dear. She sounds like she's in terrible pain—unless her mouth is full of candy.

JIM. Why don't you just tell her to lay down?

SUE. She enjoys it more when you tell her to lay down. And when are you going to see Mr. Hubbard?

JIM. My dear; Mr. Hubbard is not sick, and I have better things to do than to sit there and hold his hand.

SUE. It seems to me that for ten dollars you could hold his hand.

JIM *(to Keller)*. If your son wants to play golf tell him I'm ready. Or if he'd like to take a trip around the world for about thirty years. *(He exits)*

KELLER. Why do you needle him? He's a doctor, women are supposed to call him up.

SUE. All I said was Mrs. Adams is on the phone. Can I have some of your parsley?

KELLER. Yeah, sure. *(She goes to parsley box and pulls some parsley)* You were a nurse too long, Susie. You're too . . . too . . . realistic.

SUE *(laughing, points at him)*. Now you said it! *(Enter Lydia Lubey. She is a robust, laughing girl of twenty-seven.)*

LYDIA. Frank, the toaster . . . *(Sees the others)* Hya.

KELLER. Heilo!

LYDIA *(to Frank)*. The toaster is off again.

FRANK. Well, plug it in, I just fixed it.

LYDIA *(kindly, but insistently)*. Please, dear, fix it back like it was before.

FRANK. I don't know why you can't learn to turn on a simple thing like a toaster! *(Frank exits.)*

SUE *(laughs)*. Thomas Edison.

LYDIA *(apologetically)*. He's really very handy. *(She sees broken tree)* Oh, did the wind get your tree?

KELLER. Yeah, last night.

LYDIA. Oh, what a pity. Annie get in?

KELLER. She'll be down soon. Wait'll you meet her, Sue, she's a knockout.

SUE. I should've been a man. People are always introducing me to beautiful women. *(To Joe)* Tell her to come over later; I imagine she'd like to see what we did with her house. And thanks. *(Sue exits.)*

LYDIA. Is she still unhappy, Joe?

KELLER. Annie? I don't suppose she goes around dancing on her toes, but she seems to be over it.

LYDIA. She going to get married? Is there anybody . . . ?

KELLER. I suppose . . . say, it's a couple years already. She can't mourn a boy forever.

LYDIA. It's so strange . . . Annie's here and not even married. And I've got three babies. I always thought it'd be the other way around.

KELLER. Well, that's what a war does. I had two sons, now I got one. It changed all the tallies. In my day when you had sons it was an honor. Today a doctor could make a million dollars if he could figure out a way to bring a boy into the world without a trigger finger.

LYDIA. You know, I was just reading . . . *(Enter Chris Keller from house, stands in doorway)*

LYDIA. Hya, Chris . . . *(Frank shouts from offstage)*

FRANK. Lydia, come in here! If you want the toaster to work don't plug in the malted mixer.

LYDIA *(embarrassed, laughs)*. Did I . . . ?

FRANK. And the next time I fix something don't tell me I'm crazy! Now come in here!

LYDIA *(to Keller)*. I'll never hear the end of this one.

KELLER *(calling to Frank)*. So what's the difference? Instead of toast have a malted!

LYDIA. Sh! sh! *(She exits, laughing)* *(Chris watches her off. He is thirty-two; like his father, solidly built, a listener. A man capable of immense affection and loyalty. He has a cup of coffee in one hand, part of a doughnut in other.)*

KELLER. You want the paper?

CHRIS. That's all right, just the book section. *(He bends down and pulls out part of paper on porch floor)*

KELLER. You're always reading the book section and you never buy a book.

CHRIS (*coming down to settee*). I like to keep abreast of my ignorance. (*He sits on settee*)

KELLER. What is that, every week a new book comes out?

CHRIS. Lot of new books.

KELLER. All different.

CHRIS. All different.

KELLER (*shakes his head, puts knife down on bench, takes oilstone up to the cabinet*). Psss! Annie up yet?

CHRIS. Mother's giving her breakfast in the dining-room.

KELLER (*looking at broken tree*). See what happened to the tree?

CHRIS (*without looking up*). Yeah.

KELLER. What's Mother going to say? (*Bert runs on from driveway. He is about eight. He jumps on stool, then on Keller's back*)

BERT. You're finally up.

KELLER (*swinging him around and putting him down*). Ha! Bert's here! Where's Tommy? He's got his father's thermometer again.

BERT. He's taking a reading.

CHRIS. What!

BERT. But it's only oral.

KELLER. Oh, well, there's no harm in oral. So what's new this morning, Bert?

BERT. Nothin'. (*He goes to broken tree, walks around it*)

KELLER. Then you couldn't've made a complete inspection of the block. In the beginning, when I first made you a policeman you used to come in every morning with something new. Now, nothin's ever new.

BERT. Except some kids from Thirtieth Street. They started kicking a can down the block, and I made them go away because you were sleeping.

KELLER. Now you're talkin', Bert. Now you're on the ball. First thing you know I'm liable to make you a detective.

BERT (*pulls him down by the lapel and whispers in his ear*). Can I see the jail now?

KELLER. Seein' the jail ain't allowed, Bert. You know that.

BERT. Aw, I betcha there isn't even a jail. I don't see any bars on the cellar windows.

KELLER. Bert, on my word of honor there's a jail in the basement. I showed you my gun, didn't I?

BERT. But that's a hunting gun.

KELLER. That's an arresting gun!

BERT. Then why don't you ever arrest anybody? Tommy said another dirty word to Doris yesterday, and you didn't even demote him.

KELLER (*he chuckles and winks at Chris, who is enjoying all this*). Yeah, that's a dangerous character, that Tommy. (*Beckons him closer*) What word does he say?

BERT (*backing away quickly in great embarrassment*). Oh, I can't say that.

KELLER (*grabs him by the shirt and pulls him back*). Well, gimme an idea.

BERT. I can't. It's not a nice word.

KELLER. Just whisper it in my ear. I'll close my eyes. Maybe I won't even hear it.

BERT (*on tiptoe, puts his lips to Keller's ear, then in unbearable embarrassment steps back*). I can't, Mr. Keller.

CHRIS (*laughing*). Don't make him do that.

KELLER. Okay, Bert. I take your word. Now go out, and keep both eyes peeled.

BERT (*interested*). For what?

KELLER. For what! Bert, the whole neighborhood is depending on you. A policeman don't ask questions. Now peel them eyes!

BERT (*mystified, but willing*). Okay. (*He runs off stage back of arbor*)

KELLER (*calling after him*). And mum's the word, Bert.

BERT (*stops and sticks his head through the arbor*). About what?

KELLER. Just in general. Be v-e-r-y careful.

BERT (*nods in bewilderment*). Okay. (*Bert exits.*)

KELLER (*laughs*). I got all the kids crazy!

CHRIS. One of these days, they'll all come in here and beat your brains out.

KELLER. What's she going to say? Maybe we ought to tell her before she sees it.

CHRIS. She saw it.

KELLER. How could she see it? I was the first one up. She was still in bed.

CHRIS. She was out here when it broke.

KELLER. When?

CHRIS. About four this morning. (*Indicating window above them*) I heard it cracking and I woke up and looked out.

She was standing right here when it cracked.

KELLER. What was she doing out here four in the morning?

CHRIS. I don't know. When it cracked she ran back into the house and cried in the kitchen.

KELLER. Did you talk to her?

CHRIS. No, I . . . I figured the best thing was to leave her alone. *(Pause)*

KELLER *(deeply touched)*. She cried hard?

CHRIS. I could hear her right through the floor of my room.

KELLER *(slight pause)*. What was she doing out here at that hour? *(Chris silent. An undertone of anger showing)* She's dreaming about him again. She's walking around at night.

CHRIS. I guess she is.

KELLER. She's getting just like after he died. *(Slight pause)* What's the meaning of that?

CHRIS. I don't know the meaning of it. *(Slight pause)* But I know one thing, Dad. We've made a terrible mistake with Mother.

KELLER. What?

CHRIS. Being dishonest with her. That kind of thing always pays off, and now it's paying off.

KELLER. What do you mean, dishonest?

CHRIS. You know Larry's not coming back and I know it. Why do we allow her to go on thinking that we believe with her?

KELLER. What do you want to do, argue with her?

CHRIS. I don't want to argue with her, but it's time she realized that nobody believes Larry is alive any more. *(Keller simply moves away, thinking, looking at the ground)* Why shouldn't she dream of him, walk the nights waiting for him? Do we contradict her? Do we say straight out that we have no hope any more? That we haven't had any hope for years now?

KELLER *(frightened at the thought)*. You can't say that to her.

CHRIS. We've got to say it to her.

KELLER. How're you going to prove it? Can you prove it?

CHRIS. For God's sake, three years! Nobody comes back after three years. It's insane.

KELLER. To you it is, and to me. But not to her. You can talk yourself blue in the face, but there's no body and there's no grave, so where are you?

CHRIS. Sit down, Dad. I want to talk to you.

KELLER *(looks at him searchingly a moment, and sitting . . .)*. The trouble is the Goddam newspapers. Every month some boy turns up from nowhere, so the next one is going to be Larry, so . . .

CHRIS. All right, all right, listen to me. *(Slight pause. Keller sits on settee)* You know why I asked Annie here, don't you?

KELLER *(he knows, but . . .)*. Why?

CHRIS. You know.

KELLER. Well, I got an idea, but . . . What's the story?

CHRIS. I'm going to ask her to marry me. *(Slight pause)*

KELLER *(nods)*. Well, that's only your business, Chris.

CHRIS. You know it's not only my business.

KELLER. What do you want me to do? You're old enough to know your own mind.

CHRIS *(asking, annoyed)*. Then it's all right, I'll go ahead with it?

KELLER. Well, you want to be sure Mother isn't going to . . .

CHRIS. Then it isn't just my business.

KELLER. I'm just sayin'. . . .

CHRIS. Sometimes you infuriate me, you know that? Isn't it your business, too, if I tell this to Mother and she throws a fit about it? You have such a talent for ignoring things.

KELLER. I ignore what I gotta ignore. The girl is Larry's girl . . .

CHRIS. She's not Larry's girl.

KELLER. From Mother's point of view he is not dead and you have no right to take his girl. *(Slight pause)* Now you can go on from there if you know where to go, but I'm tellin' you I don't know where to go. See? I don't know. Now what can I do for you?

CHRIS. I don't know why it is, but every time I reach out for something I want, I have to pull back because other people will suffer. My whole bloody life, time after time after time.

KELLER. You're a considerate fella, there's nothing wrong in that.

CHRIS. To hell with that.

KELLER. Did you ask Annie yet?

CHRIS. I wanted to get this settled first.

KELLER. How do you know she'll marry you? Maybe she feels the same way Mother does?

CHRIS. Well, if she does, then that's the end of it. From her letters I think she's forgotten him. I'll find out. And then we'll thrash it out with Mother? Right? Dad, don't avoid me.

KELLER. The trouble is, you don't see enough women. You never did.

CHRIS. So what? I'm not fast with women.

KELLER. I don't see why it has to be Annie. . . .

CHRIS. Because it is.

KELLER. That's a good answer, but it don't answer anything. You haven't seen her since you went to war. It's five years.

CHRIS. I can't help it. I know her best. I was brought up next door to her. These years when I think of someone for my wife, I think of Annie. What do you want, a diagram?

KELLER. I don't want a diagram . . . I . . . I'm . . . She thinks he's coming back, Chris. You marry that girl and you're pronouncing him dead. Now what's going to happen to Mother? Do you know? I don't! (Pause)

CHRIS. All right, then, Dad.

KELLER (thinking Chris has retreated). Give it some more thought.

CHRIS. I've given it three years of thought. I'd hoped that if I waited, Mother would forget Larry and then we'd have a regular wedding and everything happy. But if that can't happen here, then I'll have to get out.

KELLER. What the hell is this?

CHRIS. I'll get out. I'll get married and live some place else. Maybe in New York.

KELLER. Are you crazy?

CHRIS. I've been a good son too long, a good sucker. I'm through with it.

KELLER. You've got a business here, what the hell is this?

CHRIS. The business! The business doesn't inspire me.

KELLER. Must you be inspired?

CHRIS. Yes. I like it an hour a day. If I have to grub for money all day long at least at evening I want it beautiful. I want a family, I want some kids, I want to build something I can give myself to. Annie is in the middle of that. Now . . . where do I find it?

KELLER. You mean . . . (Goes to him) Tell me something, you mean you'd leave the business?

CHRIS. Yes. On this I would.

KELLER (pause). Well . . . you don't want to think like that.

CHRIS. Then help me stay here.

KELLER. All right, but . . . but don't think like that. Because what the hell did I work for? That's only for you, Chris, the whole shootin' match is for you!

CHRIS. I know that, Dad. Just you help me stay here.

KELLER (puts a fist up to Chris' jaw). But don't think that way, you hear me?

CHRIS. I am thinking that way.

KELLER (lowering his hand). I don't understand you, do I?

CHRIS. No, you don't. I'm a pretty tough guy.

KELLER. Yeah, I can see that. (Mother appears on porch. She is in her early fifties, a woman of uncontrolled inspirations, and an overwhelming capacity for love)

MOTHER. Joe?

CHRIS (going toward porch). Hello, Mom.

MOTHER (indicating house behind her. To Keller). Did you take a bag from under the sink?

KELLER. Yeah, I put it in the pail.

MOTHER. Well, get it out of the pail. That's my potatoes. (Chris bursts out laughing—goes up into alley)

KELLER (laughing). I thought it was garbage.

MOTHER. Will you do me a favor, Joe? Don't be helpful.

KELLER. I can afford another bag of potatoes.

MOTHER. Minnie scoured that pail in boiling water last night. It's cleaner than your teeth.

KELLER. And I don't understand why, after I worked forty years and I got a maid, why I have to take out the garbage.

MOTHER. If you would make up your mind that every bag in the kitchen isn't full of garbage you wouldn't be throwing out my vegetables. Last time it was the onions. (Chris comes on, hands her bag)

KELLER. I don't like garbage in the house.

MOTHER. Then don't eat. (She goes into the kitchen with bag)

CHRIS. That settles you for today.

KELLER. Yeah, I'm in last place again. I don't know, once upon a time I used to think that when I got money again I would have a maid and my wife would take it easy. Now I got money, and I got a maid, and my wife is workin' for the maid. *(He sits in one of the chairs. Mother comes out on last line. She carries a pot of stringbeans)*

MOTHER. It's her day off, what are you crabbing about?

CHRIS *(to Mother)*. Isn't Annie finished eating?

MOTHER *(looking around preoccupiedly at yard)*. She'll be right out. *(Moves)* That wind did some job on this place. *(Of the tree)* So much for that, thank God.

KELLER *(indicating chair beside him)*. Sit down, take it easy.

MOTHER *(she presses her hand to top of her head)*. I've got such a funny pain on the top of my head.

CHRIS. Can I get you an aspirin?

MOTHER *(picks a few petals off ground, stand there smelling them in her hand, then sprinkles them over plants)*. No more roses. It's so funny . . . everything decides to happen at the same time. This month is his birthday; his tree blows down, Annie comes. Everything that happened seems to be coming back. I was just down the cellar, and what do I stumble over? His baseball glove. I haven't seen it in a century.

CHRIS. Don't you think Annie looks well?

MOTHER. Fine. There's no question about it. She's a beauty . . . I still don't know what brought her here. Not that I'm not glad to see her, but . . .

CHRIS. I just thought we'd all like to see each other again. *(Mother just looks at him, nodding ever so slightly—almost as though admitting something)* And I wanted to see her myself.

MOTHER *(her nods halt. To Keller)*. The only thing is I think her nose got longer. But I'll always love that girl. She's one that didn't jump into bed with somebody else as soon as it happened with her fella.

KELLER *(as though that were impossible for Annie)*. Oh, what're you . . .?

MOTHER. Never mind. Most of them didn't wait till the telegrams were opened. I'm just glad she came, so you can see I'm not *completely* out of my mind. *(Sits, and rapidly breaks stringbeans in the pot)*

CHRIS. Just because she isn't married doesn't mean she's been mourning Larry.

MOTHER *(with an undercurrent of observation)*. Why then isn't she?

CHRIS *(a little flustered)*. Well . . . it could've been any number of things.

MOTHER *(directly at him)*. Like what, for instance?

CHRIS *(embarrassed, but standing his ground)*. I don't know. Whatever it is. Can I get you an aspirin? *(Mother puts her hand to her head)*

MOTHER *(she gets up and goes aimlessly toward the trees on rising)*. It's not like a headache.

KELLER. You don't sleep, that's why. She's wearing out more bedroom slippers than shoes.

MOTHER. I had a terrible night. *(She stops moving)* I never had a night like that.

CHRIS *(looks at Keller)*. What was it, Mom? Did you dream?

MOTHER. More, more than a dream.

CHRIS *(hesitantly)*. About Larry?

MOTHER. I was fast asleep, and . . . *(Raising her arm over the audience)* Remember the way he used to fly low past the house when he was in training? When we used to see his face in the cockpit going by? That's the way I saw him. Only high up. Way, way up, where the clouds are. He was so real I could reach out and touch him. And suddenly he started to fall. And crying, crying to me . . . Mom, Mom! I could hear him like he was in the room. Mom! . . . it was his voice! If I could touch him I knew I could stop him, if I could only . . . *(Breaks off, allowing her outstretched hand to fall)* I woke up and it was so funny . . . The wind . . . it was like the roaring of his engine. I came out here . . . I must've still been half asleep. I could hear that roaring like he was going by. The tree snapped right in front of me . . . and I like . . . came awake. *(She is looking at tree. She suddenly realizes something, turns with a reprimanding finger shaking slightly at Keller)* See? We should never have planted that tree. I said so in the first place; it was too soon to plant a tree for him.

CHRIS *(alarmed)*. Too soon!

MOTHER *(angering)*. We rushed into it. Everybody was in such a hurry to bury him. I *said* not to plant it yet *(To Keller)* I *told* you to . . .!

CHRIS. Mother, Mother! *(She looks into his face)* The wind blew it down. What significance has that got? What are you talking about? Mother, please . . . Don't go through it all again, will you? It's no good, it doesn't accomplish anything. I've been thinking, y'know?—maybe we ought to put our minds to forgetting him?

MOTHER. That's the third time you've said that this week.

CHRIS. Because it's not right; we never took up our lives again. We're like at a railroad station waiting for a train that never comes in.

MOTHER *(presses top of her head)*. Get me an aspirin, heh?

CHRIS. Sure, and let's break out of this, heh, Mom? I thought the four of us might go out to dinner a couple of nights, maybe go dancing out at the shore.

MOTHER. Fine. *(To Keller)* We can do it tonight.

KELLER. Swell with me!

CHRIS. Sure, let's have some fun. *(To Mother)* You'll start with this aspirin. *(He goes up and into house with new spirit. Her smile vanishes)*

MOTHER *(with an accusing undertone)*. Why did he invite her here?

KELLER. Why does that bother you?

MOTHER. She's been in New York three and a half years, why all of a sudden . . .?

KELLER. Well, maybe . . . maybe he just wanted to see her . . .

MOTHER. Nobody comes seven hundred miles "just to see."

KELLER. What do you mean? He lived next door to the girl all his life, why shouldn't he want to see her again? *(Mother looks at him critically)* Don't look at me like that, he didn't tell me any more than he told you.

MOTHER *(a warning and a question)*. He's not going to marry her.

KELLER. How do you know he's even thinking of it?

MOTHER. It's got that about it.

KELLER *(sharply watching her reaction)*. Well? So what?

MOTHER *(alarmed)*. What's going on here, Joe?

KELLER. Now listen, kid . . .

MOTHER *(avoiding contact with him)*. She's not his girl, Joe; she knows she's not.

KELLER. You can't read her mind.

MOTHER. Then why is she still single? New York is full of men, why isn't she married? *(Pause)* Probably a hundred people told her she's foolish, but she's waited.

KELLER. How do you know why she waited?

MOTHER. She knows what I know, that's why. She's faithful as a rock. In my worst moments, I think of her waiting, and I know again that I'm right.

KELLER. Look, it's a nice day. What are we arguing for?

MOTHER *(warningly)*. Nobody in this house dast take her faith away, Joe. Strangers might. But not his father, not his brother.

KELLER *(exasperated)*. What do you want me to do? What do you want?

MOTHER. I want you to act like he's coming back. Both of you. Don't think I haven't noticed you since Chris invited her. I won't stand for any nonsense.

KELLER. But, Kate . . .

MOTHER. Because if he's not coming back, then I'll kill myself! Laugh. Laugh at me. *(She points to tree)* But why did that happen the very night she came back? Laugh, but there are meanings in such things. She goes to sleep in his room and his memorial breaks in pieces. Look at it; look. *(She sits on bench.)* Joe . . .

KELLER. Calm yourself.

MOTHER. Believe with me, Joe. I can't stand all alone.

KELLER. Calm yourself.

MOTHER. Only last week a man turned up in Detroit, missing longer than Larry. You read it yourself.

KELLER. All right, all right, calm yourself.

MOTHER. You above all have got to believe, you . . .

KELLER *(rises)*. Why me above all?

MOTHER. . . . Just don't stop believing . . .

KELLER. What does that mean, me above all? *(Bert comes rushing on)*

BERT. Mr. Keller! Say, Mr. Keller . . . *(Pointing up driveway)* Tommy just said it again!

KELLER *(not remembering any of it)*. Said what? . . . Who? . . .

BERT. The dirty word.

KELLER. Oh. Well . . .

BERT. Gee, aren't you going to arrest him? I warned him.

MOTHER *(with suddenness).* Stop that, Bert. Go home. *(Bert backs up, as she advances)* There's no jail here.

KELLER *(as though to say, "Oh-what-the-hell-let-him-believe-there-is").* Kate . . .

MOTHER *(turning on Keller furiously).* There's no jail here! I want you to stop that jail business! *(He turns, shamed, but peeved)*

BERT *(past her to Keller).* He's right across the street . . .

MOTHER. Go home, Bert. *(Bert turns around and goes up driveway. She is shaken. Her speech is bitten off, extremely urgent)* I want you to stop that, Joe. That whole jail business!

KELLER *(alarmed, therefore angered).* Look at you, look at you shaking.

MOTHER *(trying to control herself, moving about clasping her hands).* I can't help it.

KELLER. What have I got to hide? What the hell is the matter with you, Kate?

MOTHER. I didn't say you had anything to hide, I'm just telling you to stop it! Now stop it! *(As Ann and Chris appear on porch. Ann is twenty-six, gentle but despite herself capable of holding fast to what she knows. Chris opens door for her)*

ANN. Hya, Joe! *(She leads off a general laugh that is not self-conscious because they know one another too well)*

CHRIS *(bringing Ann down, with an outstretched, chivalric arm).* Take a breath of that air, kid. You never get air like that in New York.

MOTHER *(genuinely overcome with it).* Annie, where did you get that dress!

ANN. I couldn't resist. I'm taking it right off before I ruin it. *(Swings around)* How's that for three weeks' salary?

MOTHER *(to Keller).* Isn't she the most . . . ? *(To Ann)* It's gorgeous, simply gor . . .

CHRIS *(to Mother).* No kidding, now, isn't she the prettiest gal you ever saw?

MOTHER *(caught short by his obvious admiration, she finds herself reaching out for a glass of water and aspirin in his hand, and . . .).* You gained a little weight, didn't you, darling? *(She gulps pill and drinks)*

ANN. It comes and goes.

KELLER. Look how nice her legs turned out!

ANN *(she runs to fence).* Boy, the poplars got thick, didn't they?

KELLER *(moves to settee and sits).* Well, it's three years, Annie. We're gettin' old, kid.

MOTHER. How does Mom like New York? *(Ann keeps looking through trees)*

ANN *(a little hurt).* Why'd they take our hammock away?

KELLER. Oh, no, it broke. Couple of years ago.

MOTHER. What broke? He had one of his light lunches and flopped into it.

ANN *(she laughs and turns back toward Jim's yard . . .).* Oh, excuse me! *(Jim has come to fence and is looking over it. He is smoking a cigar. As she cries out, he comes on around on stage)*

JIM. How do you do. *(To Chris)* She looks very intelligent!

CHRIS. Ann, this is Jim . . . Doctor Bayliss.

ANN *(shaking Jim's hand).* Oh, sure, he writes a lot about you.

JIM. Don't you believe it. He likes everybody. In the Battalion he was known as Mother McKeller.

ANN. I can believe it . . . You know—? *(To Mother)* It's so strange seeing him come out of that yard. *(To Chris)* I guess I never grew up. It almost seems that Mom and Pop are in there now. And you and my brother doing Algebra, and Larry trying to copy my home-work. Gosh, those dear dead days beyond recall.

JIM. Well, I hope that doesn't mean you want me to move out?

SUE *(calling from offstage).* Jim, come in here! Mr. Hubbard is on the phone!

JIM. I told you I don't want . . .

SUE *(commandingly sweet).* Please, dear! Please!

JIM *(resigned).* All right, Susie. *(Trailing off)* All right, all right . . . *(To Ann)* I've only met you, Ann, but if I may offer you a piece of advice— When you marry, never—even in your mind—never count your husband's money.

SUE *(from offstage).* Jim?!

JIM. At once! *(Turns and goes off)* At once. *(He exits)*

MOTHER *(Ann is looking at her. She speaks meaningfully).* I told her to take up the guitar. It'd be a common interest for them. *(They laugh)* Well, he loves the guitar!

ANN *(as though to overcome Mother,*

*she becomes suddenly lively, crosses to Keller on settee, sits on his lap).* Let's eat at the shore tonight! Raise some hell around here, like we used to before Larry went!

MOTHER *(emotionally).* You think of him! You see? *(Triumphantly)* She thinks of him!

ANN *(with an uncomprehending smile).* What do you mean, Kate?

MOTHER. Nothing. Just that you . . . remember him, he's in your thoughts.

ANN. That's a funny thing to say; how could I help remembering him?

MOTHER *(it is drawing to a head the wrong way for her; she starts anew. She rises and comes to Ann).* Did you hang up your things?

ANN. Yeah . . . *(To Chris)* Say, you've sure gone in for clothes. I could hardly find room in the closet.

MOTHER. No, don't you remember? That's Larry's room.

ANN. You mean . . . they're Larry's?

MOTHER. Didn't you recognize them?

ANN *(slowly rising, a little embarrassed).* Well, it never occurred to me that you'd . . . I mean the shoes are all shined.

MOTHER. Yes, dear. *(Slight pause. Ann can't stop staring at her. Mother breaks it by speaking with the relish of gossip, putting her arm around Ann and walking with her)* For so long I've been aching for a nice conversation with you, Annie. Tell me something.

ANN. What?

MOTHER. I don't know. Something nice.

CHRIS *(wryly).* She means do you go out much?

MOTHER. Oh, shut up.

KELLER. And are any of them serious?

MOTHER *(laughing, sits in her chair).* Why don't you both choke?

KELLER. Annie, you can't go into a restaurant with that woman any more. In five minutes thirty-nine strange people are sitting at the table telling her their life story.

MOTHER. If I can't ask Annie a personal question . . .

KELLER. Askin' is all right, but don't beat her over the head. You're beatin' her, you're beatin' her. *(They are laughing)*

ANN *(to Mother. Takes pan of beans off stool, puts them on floor under chair and sits).* Don't let them bulldoze you. Ask me anything you like. What do you want to know, Kate? Come on, let's gossip.

MOTHER *(to Chris and Keller).* She's the only one is got any sense. *(To Ann)* Your mother . . . she's not getting a divorce, heh?

ANN. No, she's calmed down about it now. I think when he gets out they'll probably live together. In New York, of course.

MOTHER. That's fine. Because your father is still . . . I mean he's a decent man after all is said and done.

ANN. I don't care. She can take him back if she likes.

MOTHER. And you? You . . . *(Shakes her head negatively)* . . . go out much? *(Slight pause)*

ANN *(delicately).* You mean am I still waiting for him?

MOTHER. Well, no, I don't expect you to wait for him but . . .

ANN *(kindly).* But that's what you mean, isn't it?

MOTHER. . . . Well . . . yes.

ANN. Well, I'm not, Kate.

MOTHER *(faintly).* You're not?

ANN. Isn't it ridiculous? You don't really imagine he's . . . ?

MOTHER. I know, dear, but don't say it's ridiculous, because the papers were full of it; I don't know about New York, but there was half a page about a man missing even longer than Larry, and he turned up from Burma.

CHRIS *(coming to Ann).* He couldn't have wanted to come home very badly, Mom.

MOTHER. Don't be so smart.

CHRIS. You can have a helluva time in Burma.

ANN *(rises and swings around in back of Chris).* So I've heard.

CHRIS. Mother, I'll bet you money that you're the only woman in the country who after three years is still . . .

MOTHER. You're sure?

CHRIS. Yes, I am.

MOTHER. Well, if you're sure then you're sure. *(She turns her head away an instant)* They don't say it on the radio but I'm sure that in the dark at night they're still waiting for their sons.

CHRIS. Mother, you're absolutely—

MOTHER *(waving him off).* Don't be so damned smart! Now stop it! *(Slight pause)* There are just a few things you *don't* know. All of you. And I'll tell you one of them, Annie. Deep, deep in your heart you've always been waiting for him.

ANN *(resolutely)*. No, Kate.

MOTHER *(with increasing demand)*. But deep in your heart, Annie!

CHRIS. She ought to know, shouldn't she?

MOTHER. Don't let them tell you what to think. Listen to your heart. Only your heart.

ANN. Why does your heart tell you he's alive?

MOTHER. Because he has to be.

ANN. But why, Kate?

MOTHER *(going to her)*. Because certain things have to be, and certain things can never be. Like the sun has to rise, it has to be. That's why there's God. Otherwise anything could happen. But there's God, so certain things can never happen. I would know, Annie—just like I knew the day he *(Indicates Chris)* went into that terrible battle. Did he write me? Was it in the papers? No, but that morning I couldn't raise my head off the pillow. Ask Joe. Suddenly, I knew. I knew! And he was nearly killed that day. Ann, you *know* I'm right!

ANN *(she stands there in silence, then turns trembling, going upstage)*. No, Kate.

MOTHER. I have to have some tea. *(Frank appears, carrying ladder)*

FRANK. Annie! *(Coming down)* How are you, gee whiz!

ANN *(taking his hand)*. Why, Frank, you're losing your hair.

KELLER. He's got responsibility.

FRANK. Gee whiz!

KELLER. Without Frank the stars wouldn't know when to come out.

FRANK *(laughs. To Ann)*. You look more womanly. You've matured. You . . .

KELLER. Take it easy, Frank, you're a married man.

ANN *(as they laugh)*. You still haberdashering?

FRANK. Why not? Maybe I too can get to be president. How's your brother? Got his degree, I hear.

ANN. Oh, George has his own office now!

FRANK. Don't say! *(Funereally)* And your dad? Is he . . . ?

ANN *(abruptly)*. Fine. I'll be in to see Lydia.

FRANK *(sympathetically)*. How about it, does Dad expect a parole soon?

ANN *(with growing ill-ease)*. I really don't know, I . . .

FRANK *(staunchly defending her father for her sake)*. I mean because I feel, y' know, that if an intelligent man like your father is put in prison, there ought to be a law that says either you execute him, or let him go after a year.

CHRIS *(interrupting)*. Want a hand with that ladder, Frank?

FRANK *(taking cue)*. That's all right, I'll . . . *(Picks up ladder)* I'll finish the horoscope tonight, Kate. *(Embarrassed)* See you later, Ann, you look wonderful. *(He exits. They look at Ann)*

ANN *(to Chris, sits slowly on stool)*. Haven't they stopped talking about Dad?

CHRIS *(comes down and sits on arm of chair)*. Nobody talks about him any more.

KELLER *(rises and comes to her)*. Gone and forgotten, kid.

ANN. Tell me. Because I don't want to meet anybody on the block if they're going to . . .

CHRIS. I don't want you to worry about it.

ANN *(to Keller)*. Do they still remember the case, Joe? Do they talk about you?

KELLER. The only one still talks about it is my wife.

MOTHER. That's because you keep on playing policeman with the kids. All their parents hear out of you is jail, jail, jail.

KELLER. Actually what happened was that when I got home from the penitentiary the kids got very interested in me. You know kids. I was *(Laughs)* like the expert on the jail situation. And as time passed they got it confused and . . . I ended up a detective. *(Laughs)*

MOTHER. Except that *they* didn't get it confused. *(To Ann)* He hands out police badges from the Post Toasties boxes. *(They laugh)*

ANN *(wondrously at them, happily. She rises and comes to Keller, putting her arm around his shoulder)*. Gosh, it's wonderful to hear you laughing about it.

CHRIS. Why, what'd you expect?

ANN. The last thing I remember on this block was one word—"Murderers!" Remember that, Kate? . . . Mrs. Hammond standing in front of our house and yelling that word . . . She's still around, I suppose?

MOTHER. They're all still around.

KELLER. Don't listen to her. Every Sat-

urday night the whole gang is playin' poker in this arbor. All the ones who yelled
murderer takin' my money now.

MOTHER. Don't, Joe; she's a sensitive
girl, don't fool her. (To Ann) They still
remember about Dad. It's different with
him— (Indicates Joe) —he was exoner-
ated, your father's still there. That's why I
wasn't so enthusiastic about your coming.
Honestly, I know how sensitive you are,
and I told Chris, I said . . .

KELLER. Listen, you do like I did and
you'll be all right. The day I come home, I
got out of my car;—but not in front of
the house . . . on the corner. You should've
been here, Annie, and you too, Chris;
you'd-a seen something. Everybody knew
I was getting out that day; the porches
were loaded. Picture it now; none of them
believed I was innocent. The story was, I
pulled a fast one getting myself exoner-
ated. So I get out of my car, and I walk
down the street. But very slow. And with
a smile. The beast! I was the beast; the guy
who sold cracked cylinder heads to the
Army Air Force; the guy who made
twenty-one P-40's crash in Australia. Kid,
walkin' down the street that day I was
guilty as hell. Except I wasn't, and there
was a court paper in my pocket to prove
I wasn't, and I walked . . . past . . . the
porches. Result? Fourteen months later I
had one of the best shops in the state
again, a respected man again; bigger than
ever.

CHRIS (with admiration). Joe McGuts.

KELLER (now with great force). That's
the only way you lick 'em is guts! (To
Ann) The worst thing you did was to
move away from here. You made it tough
for your father when he gets out. That's
why I tell you, I like to see him move back
right on this block.

MOTHER (pained). How could they move
back?

KELLER. It ain't gonna end till they
move back! (To Ann) Till people play
cards with him again, and talk with him,
and smile with him—you play cards with
a man you know he can't be a murderer.
And the next time you write him I like
you to tell him just what I said. (Ann
simply stares at him) You hear me?

ANN (surprised). Don't you hold anything against him?

KELLER. Annie, I never believed in cru-
cifying people.

ANN (mystified). But he was your partner, he dragged you through the mud . . .

KELLER. Well, he ain't my sweetheart,
but you gotta forgive, don't you?

ANN. You, either, Kate? Don't you feel
any . . . ?

KELLER (to Ann). The next time you
write Dad . . .

ANN. I don't write him.

KELLER (struck). Well, every now and
then you . . .

ANN (a little shamed, but determined).
No, I've never written to him. Neither has
my brother. (To Chris) Say, do you feel
this way, too?

CHRIS. He murdered twenty-one pilots.

KELLER. What the hell kinda talk is
that?

MOTHER. That's not a thing to say about
a man.

ANN. What else can you say? When they
took him away I followed him, went to
him every visiting day. I was crying all
the time. Until the news came about
Larry. Then I realized. It's wrong to pity
a man like that. Father or no father,
there's only one way to look at him. He
knowingly shipped out parts that would
crash an airplane. And how do you know
Larry wasn't one of them?

MOTHER. I was waiting for that. (Going
to her) As long as you're here, Annie, I
want to ask you never to say that again.

ANN. You surprise me. I thought you'd
be mad at him.

MOTHER. What your father did had
nothing to do with Larry. Nothing.

ANN. But we can't know that.

MOTHER (striving for control). As long
as you're here!

ANN (perplexed). But, Kate . . .

MOTHER. Put that out of your head!

KELLER. Because . . .

MOTHER (quickly to Keller). That's all,
that's enough. (Places her hand on her
head) Come inside now, and have some
tea with me. (She turns and goes up steps)

KELLER (to Ann). The one thing you . . .

MOTHER (sharply). He's not dead, so
there's no argument! Now come!

KELLER (angrily). In a minute! (Mother
turns and goes into house) Now look,
Annie . . .

CHRIS. All right, Dad, forget it.

KELLER. No, she dasn't feel that way.
Annie . . .

CHRIS. I'm sick of the whole subject, now cut it out.

KELLER. You want her to go on like this? *(To Ann)* Those cylinder heads went into P-40's only. What's the matter with you? You know Larry never flew a P-40.

CHRIS. So who flew those P-40's, pigs?

KELLER. The man was a fool, but don't make a murderer out of him. You got no sense? Look what it does to her! *(To Ann)* Listen, you gotta appreciate what was doin' in that shop in the war. The both of you! It was a madhouse. Every half hour the Major callin' for cylinder heads, they were whippin' us with the telephone. The trucks were hauling them away hot, damn near. I mean just try to see it human, see it human. All of a sudden a batch comes out with a crack. That happens, that's the business. A fine, hairline crack. All right, so . . . so he's a little man, your father, always scared of loud voices. What'll the Major say?—Half a day's production shot. . . . What'll I say? You know what I mean? Human. *(He pauses)* So he takes out his tools and he . . . covers over the cracks. All right . . . that's bad, it's wrong, but that's what a little man does. If I could have gone in that day I'd a told him—junk 'em, Herb, we can afford it. But alone he was afraid. But I know he meant no harm. He believed they'd hold up a hundred percent. That's a mistake, but it ain't murder. You mustn't feel that way about him. You understand me? It ain't right.

ANN *(she regards him a moment)*. Joe, let's forget it.

KELLER. Annie, the day the news came about Larry he was in the next cell to mine . . . Dad. And he cried, Annie . . . he cried half the night.

ANN *(touched)*. He shoulda cried all night. *(Slight pause)*

KELLER *(almost angered)*. Annie, I do not understand why you . . . !

CHRIS *(breaking in—with nervous urgency)*. Are you going to stop it?!

ANN. Don't yell at him. He just wants everybody happy.

KELLER *(clasps her around waist, smiling)*. That's my sentiments. Can you stand steak?

CHRIS. And champagne!

KELLER. Now you're operatin'! I'll call Swanson's for a table! Big time tonight, Annie!

ANN. Can't scare me.

KELLER *(to Chris, pointing at Ann)*. I like that girl. Wrap her up. *(They laugh. Goes up porch)* You got nice legs, Annie! . . . I want to see everybody drunk tonight. *(Pointing to Chris)* Look at him, he's blushin'! *(He exits, laughing, into house)*

CHRIS *(calling after him)*. Drink your tea, Casanova. *(He turns to Ann)* Isn't he a great guy?

ANN. You're the only one I know who loves his parents.

CHRIS. I know. It went out of style, didn't it?

ANN *(with a sudden touch of sadness)*. It's all right. It's a good thing. *(She looks about)* You know? It's lovely here. The air is sweet.

CHRIS *(hopefully)*. You're not sorry you came?

ANN. Not sorry, no. But I'm . . . not going to stay . . .

CHRIS. Why?

ANN. In the first place, your mother as much as told me to go.

CHRIS. Well . . .

ANN. You saw that . . . and then you . . . you've been kind of . . .

CHRIS. What?

ANN. Well . . . kind of embarrassed ever since I got here.

CHRIS. The trouble is I planned on kind of sneaking up on you over a period of a week or so. But they take it for granted that we're all set.

ANN. I knew they would. Your mother anyway.

CHRIS. How did you know?

ANN. From *her* point of view, why else would I come?

CHRIS. Well . . . would you want to? *(Ann still studies him)* I guess you know this is why I asked you to come.

ANN. I guess this is why I came.

CHRIS. Ann, I love you. I love you a great deal. *(Finally)* I love you. *(Pause. She waits)* I have no imagination . . . that's all I know to tell you. *(Ann, waiting, ready)* I'm embarrassing you. I didn't want to tell it to you here. I wanted some place we'd never been; a place where we'd be brand new to each other. . . . You feel it's wrong here, don't you? This yard, this chair? I want you to be ready for me. I don't want to win you away from anything.

ANN *(putting her arms around him)*. Oh, Chris, I've been ready a long, long time!

CHRIS. Then he's gone forever. You're sure.

ANN. I almost got married two years ago.

CHRIS. . . . why didn't you?

ANN. You started to write to me . . . *(Slight pause)*

CHRIS. You felt something that far back?

ANN. Every day since!

CHRIS. Ann, why didn't you let me know?

ANN. I was waiting for you, Chris. Till then you never wrote. And when you did, what did you say? You sure can be ambiguous, you know.

CHRIS *(he looks toward house, then at her, trembling)*. Give me a kiss, Ann. Give me a . . . *(They kiss)* God, I kissed you, Annie, I kissed Annie. How long, how long I've been waiting to kiss you!

ANN. I'll never forgive you. Why did you wait all these years? All I've done is sit and wonder if I was crazy for thinking of you.

CHRIS. Annie, we're going to live now! I'm going to make you so happy. *(He kisses her, but without their bodies touching)*

ANN *(a little embarrassed)*. Not like that you're not.

CHRIS. I kissed you . . .

ANN. Like Larry's brother. Do it like you, Chris. *(He breaks away from her abruptly)* What is it, Chris?

CHRIS. Let's drive some place . . . I want to be alone with you.

ANN. No . . . what is it, Chris, your mother?

CHRIS. No . . . nothing like that . . .

ANN. Then what's wrong? . . . Even in your letters, there was something ashamed.

CHRIS. Yes. I suppose I have been. But it's going from me.

ANN. You've got to tell me—

CHRIS. I don't know how to start. *(He takes her hand. He speaks quietly, factually at first)*

ANN. It wouldn't work this way. *(Slight pause)*

CHRIS. It's all mixed up with so many other things. . . . You remember, overseas, I was in command of a company?

ANN. Yeah, sure.

CHRIS. Well, I lost them.

ANN. How many?

CHRIS. Just about all.

ANN. Oh, gee!

CHRIS. It takes a little time to toss that off. Because they weren't just men. For instance, one time it'd been raining several days and this kid came to me, and gave me his last pair of dry socks. Put them in my pocket. That's only a little thing . . . but . . . that's the kind of guys I had. They didn't die; they killed themselves for each other. I mean that exactly; a little more selfish and they'd 've been here today. And I got an idea—watching them go down. Everything was being destroyed, see, but it seemed to me that one new thing was made. A kind of . . . responsibility. Man for man. You understand me? —To show that, to bring that on to the earth again like some kind of a monument and everyone would feel it standing there, behind him, and it would make a difference to him. *(Pause)* And then I came home and it was incredible. I . . . there was no meaning in it here; the whole thing to them was a kind of a— bus accident. I went to work with Dad, and that rat-race again. I felt . . . what you said . . . ashamed somehow. Because nobody was changed at all. It seemed to make suckers out of a lot of guys. I felt wrong to be alive, to open the bank-book, to drive the new car, to see the new refrigerator. I mean you can take those things out of a war, but when you drive that car you've got to know that it came out of the love a man can have for a man, you've got to be a little better because of that. Otherwise what you have is really loot, and there's blood on it. I didn't want to take any of it. And I guess that included you.

ANN. And you still feel that way?

CHRIS. I want you now, Annie.

ANN. Because you mustn't feel that way any more. Because you have a right to whatever you have. Everything, Chris, understand that? To me, too . . . And the money, there's nothing wrong in your money. Your father put hundreds of planes in the air, you should be proud. A man should be paid for that . . .

CHRIS. Oh Annie, Annie . . . I'm going to make a fortune for you!

KELLER *(offstage)*. Hello . . . Yes. Sure.

ANN *(laughing softly)*. What'll I do with

a fortune . . . ? *(They kiss. Keller enters from house)*

KELLER *(thumbing toward house)*. Hey, Ann, your brother . . . *(They step apart shyly. Keller comes down, and wryly . . .)* What is this, Labor Day?

CHRIS *(waving him away, knowing the kidding will be endless)*. All right, all right . . .

ANN. You shouldn't burst out like that.

KELLER. Well, nobody told me it was Labor Day. *(Looks around)* Where's the hot dogs?

CHRIS *(loving it)*. All right. You said it once.

KELLER. Well, as long as I know it's Labor Day from now on, I'll wear a bell around my neck.

ANN *(affectionately)*. He's so subtle!

CHRIS. George Bernard Shaw as an elephant.

KELLER. George!—hey, you kissed it out of my head—your brother's on the phone.

ANN *(surprised)*. My brother?

KELLER. Yeah, George. Long distance.

ANN. What's the matter, is anything wrong?

KELLER. I don't know, Kate's talking to him. Hurry up, she'll cost him five dollars.

ANN *(she takes a step upstage, then comes down toward Chris)*. I wonder if we ought to tell your mother yet? I mean I'm not very good in an argument.

CHRIS. We'll wait till tonight. After dinner. Now don't get tense, just leave it to me.

KELLER. What're you telling her?

CHRIS. Go ahead, Ann. *(With misgivings, Ann goes up and into house)* We're getting married, Dad. *(Keller nods indecisively)* Well, don't you say anything?

KELLER *(distracted)*. I'm glad, Chris, I'm just . . . George is calling from Columbus.

CHRIS. Columbus!

KELLER. Did Annie tell you he was going to see his father today?

CHRIS. No, I don't think she knew anything about it.

KELLER *(asking uncomfortably)*. Chris! You . . . you think you know her pretty good?

CHRIS *(hurt and apprehensive)*. What kind of a question . . . ?

KELLER. I'm just wondering. All these years George don't go to see his father. Suddenly he goes . . . and she comes here.

CHRIS. Well, what about it?

KELLER. It's crazy, but it comes to my mind. She don't hold nothin' against me, does she?

CHRIS *(angry)*. I don't know what you're talking about.

KELLER *(a little more combatively)*. I'm just talkin'. To his last day in court the man blamed it all on me; and this is his daughter. I mean if she was sent here to find out something?

CHRIS *(angered)*. Why? What is there to find out?

ANN *(on phone, offstage)*. Why are you so excited, George? What happened there?

KELLER. I mean if they want to open up the case again, for the nuisance value, to hurt us?

CHRIS. Dad . . . how could you think that of her? *(Together)*

ANN *(still on phone)*. But what did he say to you, for God's sake?

KELLER. It couldn't be, heh. You know.

CHRIS. Dad, you amaze me . . .

KELLER *(breaking in)*. All right, forget it, forget it. *(With great force, moving about)* I want a clean start for you, Chris. I want a new sign over the plant—Christopher Keller, Incorporated.

CHRIS *(a little uneasily)*. J. O. Keller is good enough.

KELLER. We'll talk about it. I'm going to build you a house, stone, with a driveway from the road. I want you to spread out, Chris, I want you to use what I made for you . . . *(He is close to him now)* . . . I mean, with joy, Chris, without shame . . . with joy.

CHRIS *(touched)*. I will, Dad.

KELLER *(with deep emotion)*. . . . . Say it to me.

CHRIS. Why?

KELLER. Because sometimes I think you're . . . ashamed of the money.

CHRIS. No, don't feel that.

KELLER. Because it's good money, there's nothing wrong with that money.

CHRIS *(a little frightened)*. Dad, you don't have to tell me this.

KELLER *(with overriding affection and self-confidence now. He grips Chris by the back of the neck, and with laughter between his determined jaws)*. Look, Chris, I'll go to work on Mother for you. We'll get her so drunk tonight we'll all get married! *(Steps away, with a wide gesture of his arm)* There's gonna be a wedding, kid, like there never was seen! Champagne, tuxedoes . . . !

*(He breaks off as Ann's voice comes out loud from the house where she is still talking on phone.)*

ANN. Simply because when you get excited you don't control yourself. . . . *(Mother comes out of house)* Well, what did he tell you for God's sake? *(Pause)* All right, come then. *(Pause)* Yes, they'll all be here. Nobody's running away from you. And try to get hold of yourself, will you? *(Pause)* All right, all right. Goodbye. *(There is a brief pause as Ann hangs up receiver, then comes out of kitchen)*

CHRIS. Something happen?

KELLER. He's coming here?

ANN. On the seven o'clock. He's in Columbus. *(To Mother)* I told him it would be all right.

KELLER. Sure, fine! Your father took sick?

ANN *(mystified)*. No, George didn't say he was sick. I . . . *(Shaking it off)* I don't know, I suppose it's something stupid, you know my brother . . . *(She comes to Chris)* Let's go for a drive, or something . . .

CHRIS. Sure. Give me the keys, Dad.

MOTHER. Drive through the park. It's beautiful now.

CHRIS. Come on, Ann. *(To them)* Be back right away.

ANN *(as she and Chris exit up driveway)*. See you. *(Mother comes down toward Keller, her eyes fixed on him)*

KELLER. Take your time. *(To Mother)* What does George want?

MOTHER. He's been in Columbus since this morning with Steve. He's gotta see Annie right away, he says.

KELLER. What for?

MOTHER. I don't know. *(She speaks with warning)* He's a lawyer now, Joe. George is a lawyer. All these years he never even sent a postcard to Steve. Since he got back from the war, not a postcard.

KELLER. So what?

MOTHER *(her tension breaking out)*. Suddenly he takes an airplane from New York to see him. An airplane!

KELLER. Well? So?

MOTHER *(trembling)*. Why?

KELLER. I don't read minds. Do you?

MOTHER. Why, Joe? What has Steve suddenly got to tell him that he takes an airplane to see him?

KELLER. What do I care what Steve's got to tell him?

MOTHER. You're sure, Joe?

KELLER *(frightened, but angry)*. Yes, I'm sure.

MOTHER *(she sits stiffly in a chair)*. Be smart now, Joe. The boy is coming. Be smart.

KELLER *(desperately)*. Once and for all, did you hear what I said? I said I'm sure!

MOTHER *(she nods weakly)*. All right, Joe. *(He straightens up)* Just . . . be smart. *(Keller, in hopeless fury, looks at her, turns around, goes up to porch and into house, slamming screen door violently behind him. Mother sits in chair downstage, stiffly, staring, seeing.)*

CURTAIN

## ACT TWO

*As twilight falls, that evening.*

*On the rise, Chris is discovered sawing the broken-off tree, leaving stump standing alone. He is dressed in good pants, white shoes, but without a shirt. He disappears with tree up the alley when Mother appears on porch. She comes down and stands watching him. She has on a dressing-gown, carries a tray of grape-juice drink in a pitcher, and glasses with sprigs of mint in them.*

MOTHER *(calling up alley)*. Did you have to put on good pants to do that? *(She comes downstage and puts tray on table in the arbor. Then looks around uneasily, then feels pitcher for coolness. Chris enters from alley brushing off his hands)* You notice there's more light with that thing gone?

CHRIS. Why aren't you dressing?

MOTHER. It's suffocating upstairs. I made a grape drink for Georgie. He always liked grape. Come and have some.

CHRIS *(impatiently)*. Well, come on, get dressed. And what's Dad sleeping so much for? *(He goes to table and pours a glass of juice)*

MOTHER. He's worried. When he's worried he sleeps. *(Pauses. Looks into his eyes)* We're dumb, Chris. Dad and I are stupid people. We don't know anything. You've got to protect us.

CHRIS. You're silly; what's there to be afraid of?

MOTHER. To his last day in court Steve never gave up the idea that Dad made him do it. If they're going to open the case again I won't live through it.

CHRIS. George is just a damn fool, Mother. How can you take him seriously?

MOTHER. That family hates us. Maybe even Annie. . . .

CHRIS. Oh, now, Mother . . .

MOTHER. You think just because you like everybody, they like you!

CHRIS. All right, stop working yourself up. Just leave everything to me.

MOTHER. When George goes home tell her to go with him.

CHRIS (*noncommittally*). Don't worry about Annie.

MOTHER. Steve is her father, too.

CHRIS. Are you going to cut it out? Now, come.

MOTHER (*going upstage with him*). You don't realize how people can hate, Chris, they can hate so much they'll tear the world to pieces. . . . (*Ann, dressed up, appears on porch*)

CHRIS. Look! She's dressed already. (*As he and Mother mount porch*) I've just got to put on a shirt.

ANN (*in a preoccupied way*). Are you feeling well, Kate?

MOTHER. What's the difference, dear. There are certain people, y'know, the sicker they get the longer they live. (*She goes into house*)

CHRIS. You look nice.

ANN. We're going to tell her tonight.

CHRIS. Absolutely, don't worry about it.

ANN. I wish we could tell her now. I can't stand scheming. My stomach gets hard.

CHRIS. It's not scheming, we'll just get her in a better mood.

MOTHER (*offstage, in the house*). Joe, are you going to sleep all day!

ANN (*laughing*). The only one who's relaxed is your father. He's fast asleep.

CHRIS. I'm relaxed.

ANN. Are you?

CHRIS. Look. (*He holds out his hand and makes it shake*) Let me know when George gets here. (*He goes into the house. She moves aimlessly, and then is drawn toward tree stump. She goes to it, hesitantly touches broken top in the hush of her thoughts. Offstage Lydia calls, "Johnny! Come get your supper!" Sue enters, and halts, seeing Ann*)

SUE. Is my husband . . . ?

ANN (*turns, startled*). Oh!

SUE. I'm terribly sorry.

ANN. It's all right, I . . . I'm a little silly about the dark.

SUE (*looks about*). It is getting dark.

ANN. Are you looking for your husband?

SUE. As usual. (*Laughs tiredly*) He spends so much time here, they'll be charging him rent.

ANN. Nobody was dressed so he drove over to the depot to pick up my brother.

SUE. Oh, your brother's in?

ANN. Yeah, they ought to be here any minute now. Will you have a cold drink?

SUE. I will, thanks. (*Ann goes to table and pours*) My husband. Too hot to drive me to beach.—Men are like little boys; for the neighbors they'll always cut the grass.

ANN. People like to do things for the Kellers. Been that way since I can remember.

SUE. It's amazing. I guess your brother's coming to give you away, heh?

ANN (*giving her drink*). I don't know. I suppose.

SUE. You must be all nerved up.

ANN. It's always a problem getting yourself married, isn't it?

SUE. That depends on your shape, of course. I don't see why you should have had a problem.

ANN. I've had chances—

SUE. I'll bet. It's romantic . . . it's very unusual to me, marrying the brother of your sweetheart.

ANN. I don't know. I think it's mostly that whenever I need somebody to tell me the truth I've always thought of Chris. When he tells you something you know it's so. He relaxes me.

SUE. And he's got money. That's important, you know.

ANN. It wouldn't matter to me.

SUE. You'd be surprised. It makes all the difference. I married an interne. On my salary. And that was bad, because as soon as a woman supports a man he owes her something. You can never owe somebody without resenting them. (*Ann laughs*) That's true, you know.

ANN. Underneath, I think the doctor is very devoted.

SUE. Oh, certainly. But it's bad when a

man always sees the bars in front of him. Jim thinks he's in jail all the time.

ANN. Oh . . .

SUE. That's why I've been intending to ask you a small favor, Ann . . . it's something very important to me.

ANN. Certainly, if I can do it.

SUE. You can. When you take up housekeeping, try to find a place away from here.

ANN. Are you fooling?

SUE. I'm very serious. My husband is unhappy with Chris around.

ANN. How is that?

SUE. Jim's a successful doctor. But he's got an idea he'd like to do medical research. Discover things. You see?

ANN. Well, isn't that good?

SUE. Research pays twenty-five dollars a week minus laundering the hair shirt. You've got to give up your life to go into it.

ANN. How does Chris?

SUE *(with growing feeling)*. Chris makes people want to be better than it's possible to be. He does that to people.

ANN. Is that bad?

SUE. My husband has a family, dear. Every time he has a session with Chris he feels as though he's compromising by not giving up everything for research. As though Chris or anybody else isn't compromising. It happens with Jim every couple of years. He meets a man and makes a statue out of him.

ANN. Maybe he's right. I don't mean that Chris is a statue, but . . .

SUE. Now darling, you know he's not right.

ANN. I don't agree with you. Chris . . .

SUE. Let's face it, dear. Chris is working with his father, isn't he? He's taking money out of that business every week in the year.

ANN. What of it?

SUE. You ask me what of it?

ANN. I certainly do. *(She seems about to burst out)* You oughtn't cast aspersions like that, I'm surprised at you.

SUE. You're surprised at me!

ANN. He'd never take five cents out of that plant if there was anything wrong with it.

SUE. You know that.

ANN. I know it. I resent everything you've said.

SUE *(moving toward her)*. You know what I resent, dear?

ANN. Please, I don't want to argue.

SUE. I resent living next door to the Holy Family. It makes me look like a bum, you understand?

ANN. I can't do anything about that.

SUE. Who is he to ruin a man's life? Everybody knows Joe pulled a fast one to get out of jail.

ANN. That's not true!

SUE. Then why don't you go out and talk to people? Go on, talk to them. There's not a person on the block who doesn't know the truth.

ANN. That's a lie. People come here all the time for cards and . . .

SUE. So what? They give him credit for being smart. I do, too, I've got nothing against Joe. But if Chris wants people to put on the hair shirt let him take off his broadcloth. He's driving my husband crazy with that phony idealism of his, and I'm at the end of my rope on it! *(Chris enters on porch, wearing shirt and tie now. She turns quickly, hearing. With a smile)* Hello, darling. How's Mother?

CHRIS. I thought George came.

SUE. No, it was just us.

CHRIS *(coming down to them)*. Susie, do me a favor, heh? Go up to Mother and see if you can calm her. She's all worked up.

SUE. She still doesn't know about you two?

CHRIS *(laughs a little)*. Well, she senses it, I guess. You know my mother.

SUE *(going up to porch)*. Oh, yeah, she's psychic.

CHRIS. Maybe there's something in the medicine chest.

SUE. I'll give her one of everything. *(On porch)* Don't worry about Kate; couple of drinks, dance her around a little . . . she'll love Ann. *(To Ann)* Because you're the female version of him. *(Chris laughs)* Don't be alarmed, I said version. *(She goes into house)*

CHRIS. Interesting woman, isn't she?

ANN. Yeah, she's very interesting.

CHRIS. She's a great nurse, you know, she . . .

ANN *(in tension, but trying to control it)*. Are you still doing that?

CHRIS *(sensing something wrong, but still smiling)*. Doing what?

ANN. As soon as you get to know somebody you find a distinction for them. How do you know she's a great nurse?

CHRIS. What's the matter, Ann?

ANN. The woman hates you. She despises you!

CHRIS. Hey . . . what's hit you?

ANN. Gee, Chris . . .

CHRIS. What happened here?

ANN. You never . . . Why didn't you tell me?

CHRIS. Tell you what?

ANN. She says they think Joe is guilty.

CHRIS. What difference does it make what they think?

ANN. I don't care what they think, I just don't understand why you took the trouble to deny it. You said it was all forgotten.

CHRIS. I didn't want you to feel there was anything wrong in you coming here, that's all. I know a lot of people think my father was guilty, and I assumed there might be some question in your mind.

ANN. But I never once said I suspected him.

CHRIS. Nobody says it.

ANN. Chris, I know how much you love him, but it could never . . .

CHRIS. Do you think I could forgive him if he'd done that thing?

ANN. I'm not here out of a blue sky, Chris. I turned my back on my father, if there's anything wrong here now . . .

CHRIS. I know that, Ann.

ANN. George is coming from Dad, and I don't think it's with a blessing.

CHRIS. He's welcome here. You've got nothing to fear from George.

ANN. Tell me that . . . just tell me that.

CHRIS. The man is innocent, Ann. Remember he was falsely accused once and it put him through hell. How would you behave if you were faced with the same thing again? Annie, believe me, there's nothing wrong for you here, believe me, kid.

ANN. All right, Chris, all right. *(They embrace as Keller appears quietly on porch. Ann simply studies him)*

KELLER. Every time I come out here it looks like Playland! *(They break and laugh in embarrassment)*

CHRIS. I thought you were going to shave?

KELLER *(sitting on bench)*. In a minute. I just woke up, I can't see nothin'.

ANN. You look shaved.

KELLER. Oh, no. *(Massages his jaw)* Gotta be extra special tonight. Big night, Annie. So how's it feel to be a married woman?

ANN *(laughs)*. I don't know, yet.

KELLER *(to Chris)*. What's the matter, you slippin'? *(He takes a little box of apples from under the bench as they talk)*

CHRIS. The great roué!

KELLER. What is that, roué?

CHRIS. It's French.

KELLER. Don't talk dirty. *(They laugh)*

CHRIS *(to Ann)*. You ever meet a bigger ignoramus?

KELLER. Well, somebody's got to make a living.

ANN *(as they laugh)*. That's telling him.

KELLER. I don't know, everybody's gettin' so Goddam educated in this country there'll be nobody to take away the garbage. *(They laugh)* It's gettin' so the only dumb ones left are the bosses.

ANN. You're not so dumb, Joe.

KELLER. I know, but you go into our plant, for instance. I got so many lieutenants, majors and colonels that I'm ashamed to ask somebody to sweep the floor. I gotta be careful I'll insult somebody. No kiddin'. It's a tragedy: you stand on the street today and spit, you're gonna hit a college man.

CHRIS. Well, don't spit.

KELLER *(breaks apple in half, passing it to Ann and Chris)*. I mean to say, it's comin' to a pass. *(He takes a breath)* I been thinkin', Annie . . . your brother, George. I been thinkin' about your brother George. When he comes I like you to *brooch* something to him.

CHRIS. Broach.

KELLER. What's the matter with brooch?

CHRIS *(smiling)*. It's not English.

KELLER. When I went to night school it was brooch.

ANN *(laughing)*. Well, in day school it's broach.

KELLER. Don't surround me, will you? Seriously, Ann . . . You say he's not well. George, I been thinkin', why should he knock himself out in New York with that cut-throat competition, when I got so many friends here; I'm very friendly with some big lawyers in town. I could set George up here.

ANN. That's awfully nice of you, Joe.

KELLER. No, kid, it ain't nice of me. I want you to understand me. I'm thinking of Chris. (*Slight pause*) See . . . this is what I mean. You get older, you want to feel that you . . . accomplished something. My only accomplishment is my son. I ain't brainy. That's all I accomplished. Now, a year, eighteen months, your father'll be a free man. Who is he going to come to, Annie? His baby. You. He'll come, old, mad, into your house.

ANN. That can't matter any more, Joe.

KELLER. I don't want that to come between us. (*Gestures between Chris and himself*)

ANN. I can only tell you that that could never happen.

KELLER. You're in love now, Annie, but believe me, I'm older than you and I know —a daughter is a daughter, and a father is a father. And it could happen. (*He pauses*) I like you and George to go to him in prison and tell him . . . "Dad, Joe wants to bring you into the business when you get out."

ANN (*surprised, even shocked*). You'd have him as a partner?

KELLER. No, no partner. A good job. (*Pause. He sees she is shocked, a little mystified. He gets up, speaks more nervously*) I want him to know, Annie . . . while he's sitting there I want him to know that when he gets out he's got a place waitin' for him. It'll take his bitterness away. To know you got a place . . . it sweetens you.

ANN. Joe, you owe him nothing.

KELLER. I owe him a good kick in the teeth, but he's your father. . . .

CHRIS. Then kick him in the teeth! I don't want him in the plant, so that's that! You understand? And besides, don't talk about him like that. People misunderstand you!

KELLER. And I don't understand why she has to crucify the man.

CHRIS. Well, it's her father, if she feels . . .

KELLER. No, no . . .

CHRIS (*almost angrily*). What's it to you? Why . . . ?

KELLER (*a commanding outburst in high nervousness*). A father is a father! (*As though the outburst had revealed him, he looks about, wanting to retract it. His hand goes to his cheek*) I better . . . I better shave. (*He turns and a smile is on his face. To Ann*) I didn't mean to yell at you, Annie.

ANN. Let's forget the whole thing, Joe.

KELLER. Right. (*To Chris*) She's likeable.

CHRIS (*a little peeved at the man's stupidity*). Shave, will you?

KELLER. Right again.

(*As he turns to porch Lydia comes hurrying from her house.*)

LYDIA. I forgot all about it . . . (*Seeing Chris and Ann*) Hya. (*To Joe*) I promised to fix Kate's hair for tonight. Did she comb it yet?

KELLER. Always a smile, hey, Lydia?

LYDIA. Sure, why not?

KELLER (*going up on porch*). Come on up and comb my Katie's hair. (*Lydia goes up on porch*) She's got a big night, make her beautiful.

LYDIA. I will.

KELLER (*he holds door open for her and she goes into kitchen. To Chris and Ann*). Hey, that could be a song. (*He sings softly*)

"Come on up and comb my Katie's hair . . .

Oh, come on up, 'cause she's my lady fair—"

(*To Ann*) How's that for one year of night school? (*He continues singing as he goes into kitchen*)

"Oh, come on up, come on up, and comb my lady's hair—"

(*Jim Bayliss rounds corner of driveway, walking rapidly. Jim crosses to Chris, motions him and pulls him down excitedly. Keller stands just inside kitchen door, watching them.*)

CHRIS. What's the matter? Where is he?

JIM. Where's your mother?

CHRIS. Upstairs, dressing.

ANN (*crossing to them rapidly*). What happened to George?

JIM. I asked him to wait in the car. Listen to me now. Can you take some advice? (*They wait*) Don't bring him in here.

ANN. Why?

JIM. Kate is in bad shape, you can't explode this in front of her.

ANN. Explode what?

JIM. You know why he's here, don't try to kid it away. There's blood in his eye; drive him somewhere and talk to him alone.

(*Ann turns to go up drive, takes a couple of steps, sees Keller and stops. He goes quietly on into house.*)

CHRIS *(shaken, and therefore angered)*. Don't be an old lady.

JIM. He's come to take her home. What does that mean? *(To Ann)* You know what that means. Fight it out with him some place else.

ANN *(she comes back down toward Chris)*. I'll drive . . . him somewhere.

CHRIS *(goes to her)*. No.

JIM. Will you stop being an idiot?

CHRIS. Nobody's afraid of him here. Cut that out! *(He starts for driveway, but is brought up short by George, who enters there. George is Chris' age, but a paler man, now on the edge of his self-restraint. He speaks quietly, as though afraid to find himself screaming. An instant's hesitation and Chris steps up to him, hand extended, smiling)* Helluva way to do; what're you sitting out there for?

GEORGE. Doctor said your mother isn't well, I . . .

CHRIS. So what? She'd want to see you, wouldn't she? We've been waiting for you all afternoon. *(He puts his hand on George's arm, but George pulls away, coming across toward Ann)*

ANN *(touching his collar)*. This is filthy, didn't you bring another shirt? *(George breaks away from her, and moves down, examining the yard. Door opens, and he turns rapidly, thinking it is Kate, but it's Sue. She looks at him, he turns away and moves to fence. He looks over it at his former home. Sue comes down stage)*

SUE *(annoyed)*. How about the beach, Jim?

JIM. Oh, it's too hot to drive.

SUE. How'd you get to the station—Zeppelin?

CHRIS. This is Mrs. Bayliss, George. *(Calling, as George pays no attention, staring at house)* George! *(George turns)* Mrs. Bayliss.

SUE. How do you do.

GEORGE *(removing his hat)*. You're the people who bought our house, aren't you?

SUE. That's right. Come and see what we did with it before you leave.

GEORGE *(he walks down and away from her)*. I liked it the way it was.

SUE *(after a brief pause)*. He's frank, isn't he?

JIM *(pulling her off)*. See you later. . . . Take it easy, fella. *(They exit)*

CHRIS *(calling after them)*. Thanks for driving him! *(Turning to George)* How about some grape juice? Mother made it especially for you.

GEORGE *(with forced appreciation)*. Good old Kate, remembered my grape juice.

CHRIS. You drank enough of it in this house. How've you been, George?—Sit down.

GEORGE *(he keeps moving)*. It takes me a minute. *(Looking around)* It seems impossible.

CHRIS. What?

GEORGE. I'm back here.

CHRIS. Say, you've gotten a little nervous, haven't you?

GEORGE. Yeah, toward the end of the day. What're you, big executive now?

CHRIS. Just kind of medium. How's the law?

GEORGE. I don't know. When I was studying in the hospital it seemed sensible, but outside there doesn't seem to be much of a law. The trees got thick, didn't they? *(Points to stump)* What's that?

CHRIS. Blew down last night. We had it there for Larry. You know.

GEORGE. Why, afraid you'll forget him?

CHRIS *(starts for George)*. Kind of a remark is that?

ANN *(breaking in, putting a restraining hand on Chris)*. When did you start wearing a hat?

GEORGE *(discovers hat in his hand)*. Today. From now on I decided to look like a lawyer, anyway. *(He holds it up to her)* Don't you recognize it?

ANN. Why? Where . . . ?

GEORGE. Your father's . . . he asked me to wear it.

ANN. . . . How is he?

GEORGE. He got smaller.

ANN. Smaller?

GEORGE. Yeah, little. *(Holds out his hand to measure)* He's a little man. That's what happens to suckers, you know. It's good I went to him in time—another year there'd be nothing left but his smell.

CHRIS. What's the matter, George, what's the trouble?

GEORGE. The trouble? The trouble is when you make suckers out of people once, you shouldn't try to do it twice.

CHRIS. What does that mean?

GEORGE *(to Ann)*. You're not married yet, are you?

ANN. George, will you sit down and stop—?

GEORGE. Are you married yet?

ANN. No, I'm not married yet.

GEORGE. You're not going to marry him.

ANN. Why am I not going to marry him?

GEORGE. Because his father destroyed your family.

CHRIS. Now look, George . . .

GEORGE. Cut it short, Chris. Tell her to come home with me. Let's not argue, you know what I've got to say.

CHRIS. George, you don't want to be the voice of God, do you?

GEORGE. I'm . . .

CHRIS. That's been your trouble all your life, George, you dive into things. What kind of a statement is that to make? You're a big boy now.

GEORGE. I'm a big boy now.

CHRIS. Don't come bulling in here. If you've got something to say, be civilized about it.

GEORGE. Don't civilize me!

ANN. Shhh!

CHRIS (ready to hit him). Are you going to talk like a grown man or aren't you?

ANN (quickly, to forestall an outburst). Sit down, dear. Don't be angry, what's the matter? (He allows her to seat him, looking at her) Now what happened? You kissed me when I left, now you . . .

GEORGE (breathlessly). My life turned upside down since then. I couldn't go back to work when you left. I wanted to go to Dad and tell him you were going to be married. It seemed impossible not to tell him. He loved you so much . . . (He pauses) Annie . . . we did a terrible thing. We can never be forgiven. Not even to send him a card at Christmas. I didn't see him once since I got home from the war! Annie, you don't know what was done to that man. You don't know what happened.

ANN (afraid). Of course I know.

GEORGE. You can't know, you wouldn't be here. Dad came to work that day. The night foreman came to him and showed him the cylinder heads . . . they were coming out of the process with defects. There was something wrong with the process. So Dad went directly to the phone and called here and told Joe to come down right away. But the morning passed. No sign of Joe. So Dad called again. By this time he had over a hundred defectives. The Army was screaming for stuff and

Dad didn't have anything to ship. So Joe told him . . . on the phone he told him to weld, cover up the cracks in any way he could, and ship them out.

CHRIS. Are you through now?

GEORGE (surging up at him). I'm not through now! (Back to Ann) Dad was afraid. He wanted Joe there if he was going to do it. But Joe can't come down . . . he's sick. Sick! He suddenly gets the flu! Suddenly! But he promised to take responsibility. Do you understand what I'm saying? On the telephone you can't have responsibility! In a court you can always deny a phone call and that's exactly what he did. They knew he was a liar the first time, but in the appeal they believed that rotten lie and now Joe is a big shot and your father is the patsy. (He gets up) Now what're you going to do? Eat his food, sleep in his bed? Answer me; what're you going to do?

CHRIS. What're you going to do, George?

GEORGE. He's too smart for me, I can't prove a phone call.

CHRIS. Then how dare you come in here with that rot?

ANN. George, the court . . .

GEORGE. The court didn't know your father! But you know him. You know in your heart Joe did it.

CHRIS (whirling him around). Lower your voice or I'll throw you out of here!

GEORGE. She knows. She knows.

CHRIS (to Ann). Get him out of here, Ann. Get him out of here.

ANN. George, I know everything you've said. Dad told that whole thing in court, and they . . .

GEORGE (almost a scream). The court did not know him, Annie!

ANN. Shhh!—But he'll say anything, George. You know how quick he can lie.

GEORGE (turning to Chris, with deliberation). I'll ask you something, and look me in the eye when you answer me.

CHRIS. I'll look you in the eye.

GEORGE. You know your father . . .

CHRIS. I know him well.

GEORGE. And he's the kind of boss to let a hundred and twenty-one cylinder heads be repaired and shipped out of his shop without even knowing about it?

CHRIS. He's that kind of boss.

GEORGE. And that's the same Joe Keller who never left his shop without first going around to see that all the lights were out.

CHRIS (*with growing anger*). The same Joe Keller.

GEORGE. The same man who knows how many minutes a day his workers spend in the toilet.

CHRIS. The same man.

GEORGE. And my father, that frightened mouse who'd never buy a shirt without somebody along—that man would dare do such a thing on his own?

CHRIS. On his own. And because he's a frightened mouse this is another thing he'd do;—throw the blame on somebody else because he's not man enough to take it himself. He tried it in court but it didn't work, but with a fool like you it works!

GEORGE. Oh, Chris, you're a liar to yourself!

ANN (*deeply shaken*). Don't talk like that!

CHRIS (*sits facing George*). Tell me, George. What happened? The court record was good enough for you all these years, why isn't it good now? Why did you believe it all these years?

GEORGE (*after a slight pause*). Because you believed it. . . . That's the truth, Chris. I believed everything, because I thought you did. But today I heard it from his mouth. From his mouth it's altogether different than the record. Anyone who knows him, and knows your father, will believe it from his mouth. Your Dad took everything we have. I can't beat that. But she's one item he's not going to grab. (*He turns to Ann*) Get your things. Everything they have is covered with blood. You're not the kind of a girl who can live with that. Get your things.

CHRIS. Ann . . . you're not going to believe that, are you?

ANN (*she goes to him*). You know it's not true, don't you?

GEORGE. How can he tell you? It's his father. (*To Chris*) None of these things ever even cross your mind?

CHRIS. Yes, they crossed my mind. Anything can cross your mind!

GEORGE. *He knows*, Annie. He knows!

CHRIS. The Voice of God!

GEORGE. Then why isn't your name on the business? Explain that to her!

CHRIS. What the hell has that got to do with . . .?

GEORGE. Annie, why isn't his name on it?

CHRIS. Even when I don't own it!

GEORGE. Who're you kidding? Who gets it when he dies? (*To Ann*) Open your eyes, you know the both of them, isn't that the first thing they'd do, the way they love each other?—J. O. Keller & Son? (*Pause. Ann looks from him to Chris*) I'll settle it. Do you want to settle it, or are you afraid to?

CHRIS. . . . What do you mean?

GEORGE. Let me go up and talk to your father. In ten minutes you'll have the answer. Or are you afraid of the answer?

CHRIS. I'm not afraid of the answer. I know the answer. But my mother isn't well and I don't want a fight here now.

GEORGE. Let me go to him.

CHRIS. You're not going to start a fight here now.

GEORGE (*to Ann*). What more do you want!!! (*There is a sound of footsteps in the house*)

ANN (*turns her head suddenly toward house*). Someone's coming.

CHRIS (*to George, quietly*). You won't say anything now.

ANN. You'll go soon. I'll call a cab.

GEORGE. You're coming with me.

ANN. And don't mention marriage, because we haven't told her yet.

GEORGE. You're coming with me.

ANN. You understand? Don't . . . George, you're not going to start anything now! (*She hears footsteps*) Shsh!

(*Mother enters on porch. She is dressed almost formally, her hair is fixed. They are all turned toward her. On seeing George she raises both hands, comes down toward him.*)

MOTHER. Georgie, Georgie.

GEORGE (*he has always liked her*). Hello, Kate.

MOTHER (*she cups his face in her hands*). They made an old man out of you. (*Touches his hair*) Look, you're gray.

GEORGE (*her pity, open and unabashed, reaches into him, and he smiles sadly*). I know, I . . .

MOTHER. I told you when you went away, don't try for medals.

GEORGE (*he laughs, tiredly*). I didn't try, Kate. They made it very easy for me.

MOTHER (*actually angry*). Go on. You're all alike. (*To Ann*) Look at him, why did you say he's fine? He looks like a ghost.

GEORGE *(relishing her solicitude)*. I feel all right.

MOTHER. I'm sick to look at you. What's the matter with your mother, why don't she feed you?

ANN. He just hasn't any appetite.

MOTHER. If he ate in my house he'd have an appetite. *(To Ann)* I pity your husband! *(To George)* Sit down. I'll make you a sandwich.

GEORGE *(sits with an embarrassed laugh)*. I'm really not hungry.

MOTHER. Honest to God, it breaks my heart to see what happened to all the children. How we worked and planned for you, and you end up no better than us.

GEORGE *(with deep feeling for her)*. You . . . you haven't changed at all, you know that, Kate?

MOTHER. None of us changed, Georgie. We all love you. Joe was just talking about the day you were born and the water got shut off. People were carrying basins from a block away—a stranger would have thought the whole neighborhood was on fire? *(They laugh. She sees the juice. To Ann)* Why didn't you give him some juice!

ANN *(defensively)*. I offered it to him.

MOTHER *(scoffingly)*. You offered it to him! *(Thrusting glass into George's hand)* Give it to him! *(To George, who is laughing)* And now you're going to sit here and drink some juice . . . and look like something!

GEORGE *(sitting)*. Kate, I feel hungry already.

CHRIS *(proudly)*. She could turn Mahatma Ghandi into a heavyweight!

MOTHER *(to Chris, with great energy)*. Listen, to hell with the restaurant! I got a ham in the icebox, and frozen strawberries, and avocados, and . . .

ANN. Swell, I'll help you!

GEORGE. The train leaves at eight-thirty, Ann.

MOTHER *(to Ann)*. You're leaving?

CHRIS. No, Mother, she's not . . .

ANN *(breaking through it, going to George)*. You hardly got here; give yourself a chance to get acquainted again.

CHRIS. Sure, you don't even know us any more.

MOTHER. Well, Chris, if they can't stay, don't . . .

CHRIS. No, it's just a question of George, Mother, he planned on . . .

GEORGE *(he gets up politely, nicely, for Kate's sake)*. Now wait a minute, Chris . . .

CHRIS *(smiling and full of command, cutting him off)*. If you want to go, I'll drive you to the station now, but if you're staying, no arguments while you're here.

MOTHER *(at last confessing the tension)*. Why should he argue? *(She goes to him, and with desperation and compassion, stroking his hair)* Georgie and us have no argument. How could we have an argument, Georgie? We all got hit by the same lightning, how can you . . .? Did you see what happened to Larry's tree, Georgie? *(She has taken his arm, and unwillingly he moves across stage with her)* Imagine? While I was dreaming of him in the middle of the night, the wind came along and . . . *(Lydia enters on porch. As soon as she sees him)*

LYDIA. Hey, Georgie! Georgie! Georgie! Georgie! Georgie! *(She comes down to him eagerly. She has a flowered hat in her hand, which Kate takes from her as she goes to George)*

GEORGE *(they shake hands eagerly, warmly)*. Hello, Laughy. What'd you do, grow?

LYDIA. I'm a big girl now.

MOTHER *(taking hat from her)*. Look what she can do to a hat!

ANN *(to Lydia, admiring the hat)*. Did you make that?

MOTHER. In ten minutes! *(She puts it on)*

LYDIA *(fixing it on her head)*. I only rearranged it.

GEORGE. You still make your own clothes?

CHRIS *(of Mother)*. Ain't she classy! All she needs now is a Russian wolfhound.

MOTHER *(moving her head)*. It feels like somebody is sitting on my head.

ANN. No, it's beautiful, Kate.

MOTHER *(kisses Lydia—to George)*. She's a genius! You should've married her. *(They laugh)* This one can feed you!

LYDIA *(strangely embarrassed)*. Oh, stop that, Kate.

GEORGE *(to Lydia)*. Didn't I hear you had a baby?

MOTHER. You don't hear so good. She's got three babies.

GEORGE *(a little hurt by it—to Lydia)*. No kidding, three?

LYDIA. Yeah, it was one, two, three—You've been away a long time, Georgie.

GEORGE. I'm beginning to realize.

MOTHER *(to Chris and George)*. The trouble with you kids is you *think* too much.

LYDIA. Well, we think, too.

MOTHER. Yes, but not all the time.

GEORGE *(with almost obvious envy)*. They never took Frank, heh?

LYDIA *(a little apologetically)*. No, he was always one year ahead of the draft.

MOTHER. It's amazing. When they were calling boys twenty-seven Frank was just twenty-eight, when they made it twenty-eight he was just twenty-nine. That's why he took up astrology. It's all in when you were born, it just goes to show.

CHRIS. What does it go to show?

MOTHER *(to Chris)*. Don't be so intelligent. Some superstitions are very nice! *(To Lydia)* Did he finish Larry's horoscope?

LYDIA. I'll ask him now, I'm going in. *(To George, a little sadly, almost embarrassed)* Would you like to see my babies? Come on.

GEORGE. I don't think so, Lydia.

LYDIA *(understanding)*. All right. Good luck to you, George.

GEORGE. Thanks. And to you . . . And Frank. *(She smiles at him, turns and goes off to her house. George stands staring after her)*

LYDIA *(as she runs off)*. Oh, Frank!

MOTHER *(reading his thoughts)*. She got pretty, heh?

GEORGE *(sadly)*. Very pretty.

MOTHER *(as a reprimand)*. She's beautiful, you damned fool!

GEORGE *(looks around longingly; and softly, with a catch in his throat)*. She makes it seem so nice around here.

MOTHER *(shaking her finger at him)*. Look what happened to you because you wouldn't listen to me! I told you to marry that girl and stay out of the war!

GEORGE *(laughs at himself)*. She used to laugh too much.

MOTHER. And you didn't laugh enough. While you were getting mad about Fascism Frank was getting into her bed.

GEORGE *(to Chris)*. He won the war, Frank.

CHRIS. All the battles.

MOTHER *(in pursuit of this mood)*. The day they started the draft, Georgie, I told you you loved that girl.

CHRIS *(laughs)*. And truer love hath no man!

MOTHER. I'm smarter than any of you.

GEORGIE *(laughing)*. She's wonderful!

MOTHER. And now you're going to listen to me, George. You had big principles, Eagle Scouts the three of you; so now I got a tree, and this one *(Indicating Chris)* when the weather gets bad he can't stand on his feet; and that big dope *(Pointing to Lydia's house)* next door who never reads anything but Andy Gump has three children and his house paid off. Stop being a philosopher, and look after yourself. Like Joe was just saying—you move back here, he'll help you get set, and I'll find you a girl and put a smile on your face.

GEORGE. Joe? Joe wants me here?

ANN *(eagerly)*. He asked me to tell you, and I think it's a good idea.

MOTHER. Certainly. Why must you make believe you hate us? Is that another principle?—that you have to hate us? You don't hate us, George, I know you, you can't fool me, I diapered you. *(Suddenly, to Ann)* You remember Mr. Marcy's daughter?

ANN *(laughing, to George)*. She's got you hooked already! *(George laughs, is excited)*

MOTHER. You look her over, George; you'll see she's the most beautiful . . .

CHRIS. She's got warts, George.

MOTHER *(to Chris)*. She hasn't got warts! *(To George)* So the girl has a little beauty mark on her chin . . .

CHRIS. And two on her nose.

MOTHER. You remember. Her father's the retired police inspector.

CHRIS. Sergeant, George.

MOTHER. He's a very kind man!

CHRIS. He looks like a gorilla.

MOTHER *(to George)*. He never shot anybody.

*(They all burst out laughing, as Keller appears in doorway. George rises abruptly, stares at Keller, who comes rapidly down to him.)*

KELLER *(the laughter stops. With strained joviality)*. Well! Look who's here! *(Extending his hand)* Georgie, good to see ya.

GEORGE *(shakes hands—somberly)*. How're you, Joe?

KELLER. So-so. Gettin' old. You comin' out to dinner with us?

GEORGE. No, got to be back in New York.

ANN. I'll call a cab for you. *(She goes up into the house)*

KELLER. Too bad you can't stay, George. Sit down. *(To Mother)* He looks fine.

MOTHER. He looks terrible.

KELLER. That's what I said, you look terrible, George. *(They laugh)* I wear the pants and she beats me with the belt.

GEORGE. I saw your factory on the way from the station. It looks like General Motors.

KELLER. I wish it was General Motors, but it ain't. Sit down, George. Sit down. *(Takes cigar out of his pocket)* So you finally went to see your father, I hear?

GEORGE. Yes, this morning. What kind of stuff do you make now?

KELLER. Oh, little of everything. Pressure cookers, an assembly for washing machines. Got a nice, flexible plant now. So how'd you find Dad? Feel all right?

GEORGE *(searching Keller, he speaks indecisively)*. No, he's not well, Joe.

KELLER *(lighting his cigar)*. Not his heart again, is it?

GEORGE. It's everything, Joe. It's his soul.

KELLER *(blowing out smoke)*. Uh huh—

CHRIS. How about seeing what they did with your house?

KELLER. Leave him be.

GEORGE *(to Chris, indicating Keller)*. I'd like to talk to him.

KELLER. Sure, he just got here. That's the way they do, George. A little man makes a mistake and they hang him by the thumbs; the big ones becomes ambassadors. I wish you'd-a told me you were going to see Dad.

GEORGE *(studying him)*. I didn't know you were interested.

KELLER. In a way, I am. I would like him to know, George, that as far as I'm concerned, any time he wants, he's got a place with me. I would like him to know that.

GEORGE. He hates your guts, Joe. Don't you know that?

KELLER. I imagined it. But that can change, too.

MOTHER. Steve was never like that.

GEORGE. He's like that now. He'd like to take every man who made money in the war and put him up against a wall.

CHRIS. He'll need a lot of bullets.

GEORGE. And he'd better not get any.

KELLER. That's a sad thing to hear.

GEORGE *(with bitterness dominant)*. Why? What'd you expect him to think of you?

KELLER *(the force of his nature rising, but under control)*. I'm sad to see he hasn't changed. As long as I know him, twenty-five years, the man never learned how to take the blame. You know that, George.

GEORGE *(he does)*. Well, I . . .

KELLER. But you do know it. Because the way you come in here you don't look like you remember it. I mean like in 1937 when we had the shop on Flood Street. And he damn near blew us all up with that heater he left burning for two days without water. He wouldn't admit that was his fault, either. I had to fire a mechanic to save his face. You remember that.

GEORGE. Yes, but . . .

KELLER. I'm just mentioning it, George. Because this is just another one of a lot of things. Like when he gave Frank that money to invest in oil stock.

GEORGE *(distressed)*. I know that, I . . .

KELLER *(driving in, but restrained)*. But it's good to remember those things, kid. The way he cursed Frank because the stock went down. Was that Frank's fault? To listen to him Frank was a swindler. And all the man did was give him a bad tip.

GEORGE *(gets up, moves away)*. I know those things . . .

KELLER. Then remember them, remember them. *(Ann comes out of house)* There are certain men in the world who rather see everybody hung before they'll take blame. You understand me, George? *(They stand facing each other, George trying to judge him)*

ANN *(coming downstage)*. The cab's on its way. Would you like to wash?

MOTHER *(with the thrust of hope)*. Why must he go? Make the midnight, George.

KELLER. Sure, you'll have dinner with us!

ANN. How about it? Why not? We're eating at the lake, we could have a swell time.

GEORGE *(long pause, as he looks at Ann, Chris, Keller, then back to her)*. All right.

MOTHER. Now you're talking.

CHRIS. I've got a shirt that'll go right with that suit.

MOTHER. Size fifteen and a half, right, George?

GEORGE. Is Lydia . . .? I mean—Frank and Lydia coming?

MOTHER. I'll get you a date that'll make her look like a . . . *(She starts upstage)*

GEORGE *(laughs)*. No, I don't want a date.

CHRIS. I know somebody just for you! Charlotte Tanner! *(He starts for the house)*

KELLER. Call Charlotte, that's right.

MOTHER. Sure, call her up. *(Chris goes into house)*

ANN. You go up and pick out a shirt and tie.

GEORGE *(he stops, looks around at them and the place)*. I never felt at home anywhere but here. I feel so . . . *(He nearly laughs, and turns away from them)* Kate, you look so young, you know? You didn't change at all. It . . . rings an old bell. *(Turns to Keller)* You too, Joe, you're amazingly the same. The whole atmosphere is.

KELLER. Say, I ain't got time to get sick.

MOTHER. He hasn't been laid up in fifteen years. . . .

KELLER. Except my flu during the war.

MOTHER. Huhh?

KELLER. My flu, when I was sick during . . . the war.

MOTHER. Well, sure . . . *(To George)* I mean except for that flu. *(George stands perfectly still)* Well, it slipped my mind, don't look at me that way. He wanted to go to the shop but he couldn't lift himself off the bed. I thought he had pneumonia.

GEORGE. Why did you say he's never . . .?

KELLER. I know how you feel, kid, I'll never forgive myself. If I could've gone in that day I'd never allow Dad to touch those heads.

GEORGE. She said you've never been sick.

MOTHER. I said he was sick, George.

GEORGE *(going to Ann)*. Ann, didn't you hear her say . . .?

MOTHER. Do you remember every time you were sick?

GEORGE. I'd remember pneumonia. Especially if I got it just the day my partner was going to patch up cylinder heads . . . What happened that day, Joe?

FRANK *(enters briskly from driveway, holding Larry's horoscope in his hand. He comes to Kate)*. Kate! Kate!

MOTHER. Frank, did you see George?

FRANK *(extending his hand)*. Lydia told me, I'm glad to . . . you'll have to pardon me. *(Pulling Mother over)* I've got something amazing for you, Kate, I finished Larry's horoscope.

MOTHER. You'd be interested in this, George. It's wonderful the way he can understand the . . .

CHRIS *(entering from house)*. George, the girl's on the phone . . .

MOTHER *(desperately)*. He finished Larry's horoscope!

CHRIS. Frank, can't you pick a better time than this?

FRANK. The greatest men who ever lived believed in the stars!

CHRIS. Stop filling her head with that junk!

FRANK. Is it junk to feel that there's a greater power than ourselves? I've studied the stars of his life! I won't argue with you, I'm telling you. Somewhere in this world your brother is alive!

MOTHER *(instantly to Chris)*. Why isn't it possible?

CHRIS. Because it's insane.

FRANK. Just a minute now. I'll tell you something and you can do as you please. Just let me say it. He was supposed to have died on November twenty-fifth. But November twenty-fifth was his favorable day.

CHRIS. Mother!

MOTHER. Listen to him!

FRANK. It was a day when everything good was shining on him, the kind of day he should've married on. You can laugh at a lot of it, I can understand you laughing. But the odds are a million to one that a man won't die on his favorable day. That's known, that's known, Chris!

MOTHER. Why isn't it possible, why isn't it possible, Chris!

GEORGE *(to Ann)*. Don't you understand what she's saying? She just told you to go. What are you waiting for now?

CHRIS. Nobody can tell her to go. *(A car horn is heard)*

MOTHER *(to Frank)*. Thank you, darling, for your trouble. Will you tell him to wait, Frank?

FRANK *(as he goes)*. Sure thing.

MOTHER (*calling out*). They'll be right out, driver!

CHRIS. She's not leaving, Mother.

GEORGE. You heard her say it, he's never been sick!

MOTHER. He misunderstood me, Chris! (*Chris looks at her, struck*)

GEORGE (*to Ann*). He simply told your father to kill pilots, and covered himself in bed!

CHRIS. You'd better answer him, Annie. Answer him.

MOTHER. I packed your bag, darling . . .

CHRIS. What?

MOTHER. I packed your bag. All you've got to do is close it.

ANN. I'm not closing anything. He asked me here and I'm staying till he tells me to go. (*To George*) Till Chris tells me!

CHRIS. That's all! Now get out of here, George!

MOTHER (*to Chris*). But if that's how he feels . . .

CHRIS. That's all, nothing more till Christ comes, about the case or Larry as long as I'm here! (*To Ann*) Now get out of here, George!

GEORGE (*to Ann*). You tell me. I want to hear you tell me.

ANN. Go, George!

(*They disappear up the driveway, Ann saying "Don't take it that way, Georgie! Please don't take it that way."*)

CHRIS (*turns to his mother*). What do you mean, you packed her bag? How dare you pack her bag?

MOTHER. Chris . . .

CHRIS. How dare you pack her bag?

MOTHER. She doesn't belong here.

CHRIS. Then I don't belong here.

MOTHER. She's Larry's girl.

CHRIS. And I'm his brother and he's dead, and I'm marrying his girl.

MOTHER. Never, never in this world!

KELLER. You lost your mind?

MOTHER. You have nothing to say!

KELLER (*cruelly*). I got plenty to say. Three and a half years you been talking like a maniac—

MOTHER (*she smashes him across the face*). Nothing. You have nothing to say. Now I say. He's coming back, and everybody has got to wait.

CHRIS. Mother, Mother . . .

MOTHER. Wait, wait . . .

CHRIS. How long? How long?

MOTHER (*rolling out of her*). Till he comes; forever and ever till he comes!

CHRIS (*as an ultimatum*). Mother, I'm going ahead with it.

MOTHER. Chris, I've never said no to you in my life, now I say no!

CHRIS. You'll never let him go till I do it.

MOTHER. I'll never let him go and you'll never let him go . . .!

CHRIS. I've let him go. I've let him go a long . . .

MOTHER (*with no less force, but turning from him*). Then let your father go. (*Pause. Chris stands transfixed*)

KELLER. She's out of her mind.

MOTHER. Altogether! (*To Chris, but not facing them*) Your brother's alive, darling, because if he's dead, your father killed him. Do you understand me now? As long as you live, that boy is alive. God does not let a son be killed by his father. Now you see, don't you? Now you see. (*Beyond control, she hurries up and into house*)

KELLER (*Chris has not moved. He speaks insinuatingly, questioningly*). She's out of her mind.

CHRIS (*a broken whisper*). Then . . . you did it?

KELLER (*the beginning of plea in his voice*). He never flew a P-40—

CHRIS (*struck. Deadly*). But the others.

KELLER (*insistently*). She's out of her mind. (*He takes a step toward Chris, pleadingly*)

CHRIS (*unyielding*). Dad . . . you did it?

KELLER. He never flew a P-40, what's the matter with you?

CHRIS (*still asking, and saying*). Then you did it. To the others.

(*Both hold their voices down.*)

KELLER (*afraid of him, his deadly insistence*). What's the matter with you? What the hell is the matter with you?

CHRIS (*quietly, incredibly*). How could you do that? How?

KELLER. What's the matter with you!

CHRIS. Dad . . . Dad, you killed twenty-one men!

KELLER. What, killed?

CHRIS. You killed them, you murdered them.

KELLER (*as though throwing his whole nature open before Chris*). How could I kill anybody?

CHRIS. Dad! Dad!

KELLER *(trying to hush him)*. I didn't kill anybody!

CHRIS. Then explain it to me. What did you do? Explain it to me or I'll tear you to pieces!

KELLER *(horrified at his overwhelming fury)*. Don't, Chris, don't . . .

CHRIS. I want to know what you did, now what did you do? You had a hundred and twenty cracked engine-heads, now what did you do?

KELLER. If you're going to hang me then I . . .

CHRIS. I'm listening. God Almighty, I'm listening!

KELLER *(their movements now are those of subtle pursuit and escape. Keller keeps a step out of Chris' range as he talks)*. You're a boy, what could I do! I'm in business, a man is in business; a hundred and twenty cracked, you're out of business; you got a process, the process don't work you're out of business; you don't know how to operate, your stuff is no good; they close you up, they tear up your contracts, what the hell's it to them? You lay forty years into a business and they knock you out in five minutes, what could I do, let them take forty years, let them take my life away? *(His voice cracking)* I never thought they'd install them. I swear to God. I thought they'd stop 'em before anybody took off.

CHRIS. Then why'd you ship them out?

KELLER. By the time they could spot them I thought I'd have the process going again, and I could show them they needed me and they'd let it go by. But weeks passed and I got no kick-back, so I was going to tell them.

CHRIS. Then why didn't you tell them?

KELLER. It was too late. The paper, it was all over the front page, twenty-one went down, it was too late. They came with handcuffs into the shop, what could I do? *(He sits on bench)* Chris . . . Chris, I did it for you, it was a chance and I took it for you. I'm sixty-one years old, when would I have another chance to make something for you? Sixty-one years old you don't get another chance, do ya?

CHRIS. You even knew they wouldn't hold up in the air.

KELLER. I didn't say that . . .

CHRIS. But you were going to warn them not to use them . . .

KELLER. But that don't mean . . .

CHRIS. It means you knew they'd crash.

KELLER. It don't mean that.

CHRIS. Then you *thought* they'd crash.

KELLER. I was afraid maybe . . .

CHRIS. You were afraid maybe! God in heaven, what kind of a man are you? Kids ·were hanging in the air by those heads. You knew that!

KELLER. For you, a business for you!

CHRIS *(with burning fury)*. For me! Where do you live, where have you come from? For me!—I was dying every day and you were killing my boys and you did it for me? What the hell do you think I was thinking of, the Goddam business? Is that as far as your mind can see, the business? What is that, the world—the business? What the hell do you mean, you did it for me? Don't you have a country? Don't you live in the world? What the hell are you? You're not even an animal, no animal kills his own, what are you? What must I do to you? I ought to tear the tongue out of your mouth, what must I do? *(With his fist he pounds down upon his father's shoulder. He stumbles away, covering his face as he weeps)* What must I do, Jesus God, what must I do?

KELLER. Chris . . . My Chris . . .

CURTAIN

## ACT THREE

*Two o'clock the following morning, Mother is discovered on the rise, rocking ceaselessly in a chair, staring at her thoughts. It is an intense, slight, sort of rocking. A light shows from upstairs bedroom, lower floor windows being dark. The moon is strong and casts its bluish light.*

*Presently Jim, dressed in jacket and hat, appears, and seeing her, goes up beside her.*

———

JIM. Any news?

MOTHER. No news.

JIM *(gently)*. You can't sit up all night, dear, why don't you go to bed?

MOTHER. I'm waiting for Chris. Don't worry about me, Jim, I'm perfectly all right.

JIM. But it's almost two o'clock.

MOTHER. I can't sleep. *(Slight pause)* You had an emergency?

JIM *(tiredly).* Somebody had a headache and thought he was dying. *(Slight pause)* Half of my patients are quite mad. Nobody realizes how many people are walking around loose, and they're cracked as coconuts. Money. Money-money-money-money. You say it long enough it doesn't mean anything. *(She smiles, makes a silent laugh)* Oh, how I'd love to be around when that happens!

MOTHER *(shakes her head).* You're so childish, Jim! Sometimes you are.

JIM *(looks at her a moment).* Kate. *(Pause)* What happened?

KATE. I told you. He had an argument with Joe. Then he got in the car and drove away.

JIM. What kind of an argument?

MOTHER. An argument, Joe . . . he was crying like a child, before.

JIM. They argued about Ann?

MOTHER *(slight hesitation).* No, not Ann. Imagine? *(Indicates lighted window above)* She hasn't come out of that room since he left. All night in that room.

JIM *(looks at window, then at her).* What'd Joe do, tell him?

MOTHER *(she stops rocking).* Tell him what?

JIM. Don't be afraid, Kate, I know. I've always known.

MOTHER. How?

JIM. It occurred to me a long time ago.

MOTHER. I always had the feeling that in the back of his head, Chris . . . almost knew. I didn't think it would be such a shock.

JIM *(gets up).* Chris would never know how to live with a thing like that. It takes a certain talent . . . for lying. You have it, and I do. But not him.

MOTHER. What do you mean . . . he's not coming back?

JIM. Oh, no, he'll come back. We all come back, Kate. These private little revolutions always die. The compromise is always made. In a peculiar way. Frank is right—every man does have a star. The star of one's honesty. And you spend your life groping for it, but once it's out it never lights again. I don't think he went very far. He probably just wanted to be alone to watch his star go out.

MOTHER. Just as long as he comes back.

JIM. I wish he wouldn't, Kate. One year I simply took off, went to New Orleans; for two months I lived on bananas and milk, and studied a certain disease. It was beautiful. And then she came, and she cried. And I went back home with her. And now I live in the usual darkness; I can't find myself; it's even hard sometimes to remember the kind of man I wanted to be. I'm a good husband; Chris is a good son—he'll come back.

*(Keller comes out on porch in dressing-gown and slippers. He goes upstage—to alley. Jim goes to him.)*

JIM. I have a feeling he's in the park. I'll look around for him. Put her to bed, Joe; this is no good for what she's got. *(Jim exits up driveway)*

KELLER *(coming down).* What does he want here?

MOTHER. His friend is not home.

KELLER *(his voice is husky. Comes down to her).* I don't like him mixing in so much.

MOTHER. It's too late, Joe. He knows.

KELLER *(apprehensively).* How does he know?

MOTHER. He guessed a long time ago.

KELLER. I don't like that.

MOTHER *(laughs dangerously, quietly into the line).* What you don't like . . .

KELLER. Yeah, what I don't like.

MOTHER. You can't bull yourself through this one, Joe, you better be smart now. This thing—this thing is not over yet.

KELLER *(indicating lighted window above).* And what is she doing up there? She don't come out of the room.

MOTHER. I don't know, what is she doing? Sit down, stop being mad. You want to live? You better figure out your life.

KELLER. She don't know, does she?

MOTHER. She saw Chris storming out of here. It's one and one—she knows how to add.

KELLER. Maybe I ought to talk to her?

MOTHER. Don't ask me, Joe.

KELLER *(almost an outburst).* Then who do I ask? But I don't think she'll do anything about it.

MOTHER. You're asking me again.

KELLER. I'm askin' you. What am I, a stranger? I thought I had a family here. What happened to my family?

MOTHER. You've got a family. I'm simply telling you that I have no strength to think anymore.

KELLER. You have no strength. The minute there's trouble you have no strength.

MOTHER. Joe, you're doing the same thing again; all your life whenever there's trouble you yell at me and you think that settles it.

KELLER. Then what do I do? Tell me, talk to me, what do I do?

MOTHER. Joe . . . I've been thinking this way. If he comes back . . .

KELLER. What do you mean "if"? . . . he's comin' back!

MOTHER. I think if you sit him down and you . . . explain yourself. I mean you ought to make it clear to him that you know you did a terrible thing. *(Not looking into his eyes)* I mean if he saw that you realize what you did. You see?

KELLER. What ice does that cut?

MOTHER *(a little fearfully)*. I mean if you told him that you want to pay for what you did.

KELLER *(sensing . . . quietly)*. How can I pay?

MOTHER. Tell him . . . you're willing to go to prison. *(Pause)*

KELLER *(struck, amazed)*. I'm willing to . . . ?

MOTHER *(quickly)*. You wouldn't go, he wouldn't ask you to go. But if you told him you wanted to, if he could feel that you wanted to pay, maybe he would forgive you.

KELLER. He would forgive me! For what?

MOTHER. Joe, you know what I mean.

KELLER. I don't know what you mean! You wanted money, so I made money. What must I be forgiven? You wanted money, didn't you?

MOTHER. I didn't want it that way.

KELLER. I didn't want it that way, either! What difference is it what you want? I spoiled the both of you. I should've put him out when he was ten like I was put out, and make him earn his keep. Then he'd know how a buck is made in this world. Forgiven! I could live on a quarter a day myself, but I got a family so I . . .

MOTHER. Joe, Joe . . . it don't excuse it that you did it for the family.

KELLER. It's got to excuse it!

MOTHER. There's something bigger than the family to him.

KELLER. Nothin' is bigger!

MOTHER. There is to him.

KELLER. There's nothin' he could do that I wouldn't forgive. Because he's my son. Because I'm his father and he's my son.

MOTHER. Joe, I tell you . . .

KELLER. Nothin's bigger than that. And you're goin' to tell him, you understand? I'm his father and he's my son, and if there's something bigger than that I'll put a bullet in my head!

MOTHER. You stop that!

KELLER. You heard me. Now you know what to tell him. *(Pause. He moves from her—halts)* But he wouldn't put me away though . . . He wouldn't do that . . . Would he?

MOTHER. He loved you, Joe, you broke his heart.

KELLER. But to put me away . . .

MOTHER. I don't know. I'm beginning to think we don't really know him. They say in the war he was such a killer. Here he was always afraid of mice. I don't know him. I don't know what he'll do.

KELLER. Goddam, if Larry was alive he wouldn't act like this. He understood the way the world is made. He listened to me. To him the world had a forty-foot front, it ended at the building line. This one, everything bothers him. You make a deal, overcharge two cents, and his hair falls out. He don't understand money. Too easy, it came too easy. Yes, sir. Larry. That was a boy we lost. Larry. Larry. *(He slumps on chair in front of her)* What am I gonna do, Kate . . .

MOTHER. Joe, Joe, please . . . you'll be all right, nothing is going to happen . . .

KELLER *(desperately, lost)*. For you, Kate, for both of you, that's all I ever lived for . . .

MOTHER. I know, darling, I know . . . *(Ann enters from house. They say nothing, waiting for her to speak.)*

ANN. Why do you stay up? I'll tell you when he comes.

KELLER *(rises, goes to her)*. You didn't eat supper, did you? *(To Mother)* Why don't you make her something?

MOTHER. Sure, I'll . . .

ANN. Never mind, Kate, I'm all right. *(They are unable to speak to each other)* There's something I want to tell you. *(She starts, then halts)* I'm not going to do anything about it. . . .

MOTHER. She's a good girl! *(To Keller)* You see? She's a . . .

ANN. I'll do nothing about Joe, but you're going to do something for me.

*(Directly to Mother)* You made Chris feel guilty with me. Whether you wanted to or not, you've crippled him in front of me. I'd like you to tell him that Larry is dead and that you know it. You understand me? I'm not going out of here alone. There's no life for me that way. I want you to set him free. And then I promise you, everything will end, and we'll go away, and that's all.

KELLER. You'll do that. You'll tell him.

ANN. I know what I'm asking, Kate. You had two sons. But you've only got one now.

KELLER. You'll tell him . . .

ANN. And you've got to say it to him so he knows you mean it.

MOTHER. My dear, if the boy was dead, it wouldn't depend on my words to make Chris know it. . . . The night he gets into your bed, his heart will dry up. Because he knows and you know. To his dying day he'll wait for his brother! No, my dear, no such thing. You're going in the morning, and you're going alone. That's your life, that's your lonely life. *(She goes to porch, and starts in)*

ANN. Larry is dead, Kate.

MOTHER *(she stops)*. Don't speak to me.

ANN. I said he's dead. I know! He crashed off the coast of China November twenty-fifth! His engine didn't fail him. But he died. I know . . .

MOTHER. How did he die? You're lying to me. If you know, how did he die?

ANN. I loved him. You know I loved him. Would I have looked at anyone else if I wasn't sure? That's enough for you.

MOTHER *(moving on her)*. What's enough for me? What're you talking about? *(She grasps Ann's wrists)*

ANN. You're hurting my wrists.

MOTHER. What are you talking about! *(Pause. She stares at Ann a moment, then turns and goes to Keller)*

ANN. Joe, go in the house . . .

KELLER. Why should I . . .

ANN. Please go.

KELLER. Lemme know when he comes. *(Keller goes into house)*

MOTHER *(sees Ann take a letter from her pocket)*. What's that?

ANN. Sit down . . . *(Mother moves left to chair, but does not sit)* First you've got to understand. When I came, I didn't have any idea that Joe . . . I had nothing against him or you. I came to get married. I hoped . . . So I didn't bring this to hurt you. I thought I'd show it to you only if there was no other way to settle Larry in your mind.

MOTHER. Larry? *(Snatches letter from Ann's hand)*

ANN. He wrote it to me just before he— *(Mother opens and begins to read letter)* I'm not trying to hurt you, Kate. You're making me do this, now remember you're —Remember. I've been so lonely, Kate . . . I can't leave here alone again. *(A long, low moan comes from Mother's throat as she reads)* You made me show it to you. You wouldn't believe me. I told you a hundred times, why wouldn't you believe me!

MOTHER. Oh, my God . . .

ANN *(with pity and fear)*. Kate, please, please . . .

MOTHER. My God, my God . . .

ANN. Kate, dear, I'm so sorry . . . I'm so sorry.

*(Chris enters from driveway. He seems exhausted.)*

CHRIS. What's the matter . . . ?

ANN. Where were you? . . . you're all perspired. *(Mother doesn't move)* Where were you?

CHRIS. Just drove around a little. I thought you'd be gone.

ANN. Where do I go? I have nowhere to go.

CHRIS *(to Mother)*. Where's Dad?

ANN. Inside lying down.

CHRIS. Sit down, both of you. I'll say what there is to say.

MOTHER. I didn't hear the car . . .

CHRIS. I left it in the garage.

MOTHER. Jim is out looking for you.

CHRIS. Mother . . . I'm going away. There are a couple of firms in Cleveland, I think I can get a place. I mean, I'm going away for good. *(To Ann alone)* I know what you're thinking, Annie. It's true. I'm yellow. I was made yellow in this house because I suspected my father and I did nothing about it, but if I knew that night when I came home what I know now, he'd be in the district attorney's office by this time, and I'd have brought him there. Now if I look at him, all I'm able to do is cry.

MOTHER. What are you talking about? What else can you do?

CHRIS. I could jail him! I could jail him, if I were human any more. But I'm like everybody else now. I'm practical now. You made me practical.

MOTHER. But you have to be.

CHRIS. The cats in that alley are practical, the bums who ran away when we were fighting were practical. Only the dead ones weren't practical. But now I'm practical, and I spit on myself. I'm going away. I'm going now.

ANN *(goes up to him)*. I'm coming with you. . . .

CHRIS. No, Ann.

ANN. Chris, I don't ask you to do anything about Joe.

CHRIS. You do, you do . . .

ANN. I swear I never will.

CHRIS. In your heart you always will.

ANN. Then do what you have to do!

CHRIS. Do what? What is there to do? I've looked all night for a reason to make him suffer.

ANN. There's reason, there's reason!

CHRIS. What? Do I raise the dead when I put him behind bars? Then what'll I do it for? We used to shoot a man who acted like a dog, but honor was real there, you were protecting something. But here? This is the land of the great big dogs, you don't love a man here, you eat him! That's the principle; the only one we live by—it just happened to kill a few people this time, that's all. The world's that way, how can I take it out on him? What sense does that make? This is a zoo, a zoo!

ANN *(to Mother)*. You know what he's got to do! Tell him!

MOTHER. Let him go.

ANN. I won't let him go. You'll tell him what he's got to do . . .

MOTHER. Annie!

ANN. Then I will!

*(Keller enters from house. Chris sees him, goes down near arbor.)*

KELLER. What's the matter with you? I want to talk to you.

CHRIS. I've got nothing to say to you.

KELLER *(taking his arm)*. I want to talk to you!

CHRIS *(pulling violently away from him)*. Don't do that, Dad. I'm going to hurt you if you do that. There's nothing to say, so say it quick.

KELLER. Exactly what's the matter? What's the matter? You got too much money? Is that what bothers you?

CHRIS *(with an edge of sarcasm)*. It bothers me.

KELLER. If you can't get used to it, then throw it away. You hear me? Take every cent and give it to charity, throw it in the sewer. Does that settle it? In the sewer, that's all. You think I'm kidding? I'm tellin' you what to do, if it's dirty then burn it. It's your money, that's not my money. I'm a dead man, I'm an old dead man, nothing's mine. Well, talk to me!— what do you want to do!

CHRIS. It's not what I want to do. It's what you want to do.

KELLER. What should I want to do? *(Chris is silent)* Jail? You want me to go to jail? If you want me to go, say so! Is that where I belong?—then tell me so! *(Slight pause)* What's the matter, why can't you tell me? *(Furiously)* You say everything else to me, say that! *(Slight pause)* I'll tell you why you can't say it. Because you know I don't belong there. Because you know! *(With growing emphasis and passion, and a persistent tone of desperation)* Who worked for nothin' in that war? When they work for nothin', I'll work for nothin'. Did they ship a gun or a truck outa Detroit before they got their price? Is that clean? It's dollars and cents, nickels and dimes; war and peace, it's nickels and dimes, what's clean? Half the Goddam country is gotta go if I go! That's why you can't tell me.

CHRIS. That's exactly why.

KELLER. Then . . . why am *I* bad?

CHRIS. *I* know you're no worse than most men but I thought you were better. I never saw you as a man. I saw you as my father. *(Almost breaking)* I can't look at you this way, I can't look at myself!

*(He turns away unable to face Keller. Ann goes quickly to Mother, takes letter from her and starts for Chris. Mother instantly rushes to intercept her.)*

MOTHER. Give me that!

ANN. He's going to read it! *(She thrusts letter into Chris' hand)* Larry. He wrote it to me the day he died. . . .

KELLER. Larry!?

MOTHER. Chris, it's not for you. *(He starts to read)* Joe . . . go away . . .

KELLER *(mystified, frightened)*. Why'd she say, Larry, what . . . ?

MOTHER *(she desperately pushes him toward alley, glancing at Chris)*. Go to the street, Joe, go to the street! *(She comes down beside Keller)* Don't, Chris . . .

*(Pleading from her whole soul)* Don't tell him . . .

CHRIS *(quietly)*. Three and one half years . . . talking, talking. Now you tell me what you must do. . . . This is how he died, now tell me where you belong.

KELLER *(pleading)*. Chris, a man can't be a Jesus in this world!

CHRIS. I know all about the world. I know the whole crap story. Now listen to this, and tell me what a man's got to be! *(Reads)* "My dear Ann: . . ." You listening? He wrote this the day he died. Listen, don't cry . . . listen! "My dear Ann: It is impossible to put down the things I feel. But I've got to tell you something. Yesterday they flew in a load of papers from the States and I read about Dad and your father being convicted. I can't express myself. I can't tell you how I feel— I can't bear to live any more. Last night I circled the base for twenty minutes before I could bring myself in. How could he have done that? Every day three or four men never come back and he sits back there doing business. . . . I don't know how to tell you what I feel . . . I can't face anybody . . . I'm going out on a mission in a few minutes. They'll probably report me missing. If they do, I want you to know that you mustn't wait for me. I tell you, Ann, if I had him here now I could kill him—" *(Keller grabs letter from Chris' hand and reads it. After a long pause)* Now blame the world. Do you understand that letter?

KELLER *(he speaks almost inaudibly)*. I think I do. Get the car. I'll put on my jacket. *(He turns and starts slowly for the house. Mother rushes to intercept him)*

MOTHER. Why are you going? You'll sleep, why are you going?

KELLER. I can't sleep here. I'll feel better if I go.

MOTHER. You're so foolish. Larry was your son too, wasn't he? You know he'd never tell you to do this.

KELLER *(looking at letter in his hand)*. Then what is this if it isn't telling me? Sure, he was my son. But I think to him they were all my sons. And I guess they were, I guess they were. I'll be right down. *(Exits into house)*

MOTHER *(to Chris, with determination)*. You're not going to take him!

CHRIS. I'm taking him.

MOTHER. It's up to you, if you tell him to stay he'll stay. Go and tell him!

CHRIS. Nobody could stop him now.

MOTHER. You'll stop him! How long will he live in prison?—are you trying to kill him?

CHRIS *(holding out letter)*. I thought you read this!

MOTHER *(of Larry, the letter)*. The war is over! Didn't you hear?—it's over!

CHRIS. Then what was Larry to you? A stone that fell into the water? It's not enough for him to be sorry. Larry didn't kill himself to make you and Dad sorry.

MOTHER. What more can we be!

CHRIS. You can be better! Once and for all you can know there's a universe of people outside and you're responsible to it, and unless you know that, you threw away your son because that's why he died. *(A shot is heard in the house. They stand frozen for a brief second. Chris starts for porch, pauses at step, turns to Ann.)*

CHRIS. Find Jim! *(He goes on into the house and Ann runs up driveway. Mother stands alone, transfixed)*

MOTHER *(softly, almost moaning)*. Joe . . . Joe . . . Joe . . . Joe . . . *(Chris comes out of house, down to Mother's arms)*

CHRIS *(almost crying)*. Mother, I didn't mean to . . .

MOTHER. Don't dear. Don't take it on yourself. Forget now. Live. *(Chris stirs as if to answer)* Shhh . . . *(She puts his arms down gently and moves toward porch)* Shhh . . . *(As she reaches porch steps she begins sobbing, as*

THE CURTAIN FALLS

# 1947-48

This was the first season for the simplified voting method whereby the play with the most votes wins, but as it turned out there wouldn't have been any difficulty under any of the previous systems.

Tennessee Williams' *A Streetcar Named Desire* won all by itself, getting seventeen votes to two for *Mister Roberts* by Thomas Heggen and Joshua Logan and one each for William Wister Haines's *Command Decision* and the Robinson Jeffers adaptation of *Medea* in which Judith Anderson gave such an outstanding performance. Williams also won the Pulitzer prize.

The foreign citation went to Terence Rattigan's *The Winslow Boy*, which received ten votes to five for *The Respectful Prostitute* by Jean-Paul Sartre, three for *The Old Lady Says "No!"* by Denis Johnston, two for *Where Stars Walk* by Michael MacLiammoir and one for *Galileo* by Bertold Brecht.

There was no musical selection at the meeting on March 31, 1948.

*A Streetcar Named Desire* had such a success that it cemented Williams' position as a leading dramatist. He had followed *The Glass Menagerie* with a collaboration entitled *You Touched Me!* which did nothing for him. To borrow from Percy Hammond's estimate of Maxwell Anderson's *Winterset*, I still say *Streetcar* is spinach despite the trimmings. The play also "made" Marlon Brando as an actor in the eyes of those who are not too difficult to please.

Sid Caesar made his first (and at this date his only) Broadway appearance as a leading player in *Make Mine Manhattan*, a revue, and Mrs. Gertrude Berg, the famous Molly Goldberg of radio, appeared in a play for the first time, her own *Me and Molly*, derived from her radio series, *The Goldbergs*. Dublin's Gate Theatre company made its first trip here, presenting three plays to a sad lack of appreciation although its *The Old Lady Says "No!"* and *Where Stars Walk*, new only in the sense that they had never been done here, picked up votes in the competition for the foreign play citation.

The season was as notable for its closings as for its openings because it brought an end to the careers of *Life With Father* and *Oklahoma!*

*Life with Father* closed on July 12, 1947, with the long-run championship safely in its custody. Its record was 3,224 performances as against *Tobacco Road's* 3,182.

*Oklahoma!* closed on May 28, 1948, with 2,248 performances in the books. This placed it fourth in the list of all long-run attractions, behind *Abie's Irish Rose*, and it played 323 more performances than the Number 2 musical, *South Pacific*. In fact, an international long-run record is claimed for it in the musical field. It played 10 more performances than did *Chu Chin Chow*, a London champion of the World War I period.

*A Streetcar Named Desire* achieved 855 performances; *Mister Roberts*, 1,157.

# A Streetcar Named Desire

## *By* TENNESSEE WILLIAMS

Presented by Irene M. Selznick at the Ethel Barrymore Theatre, New York City, December 3, 1947, with the following cast:

| | |
|---|---|
| NEGRO WOMAN | *Gee Gee James* |
| EUNICE HUBBEL | *Peg Hillias* |
| STANLEY KOWALSKI | *Marlon Brando* |
| STELLA KOWALSKI | *Kim Hunter* |
| STEVE HUBBEL | *Rudy Bond* |
| HAROLD MITCHELL (Mitch) | *Karl Malden* |
| MEXICAN WOMAN | *Edna Thomas* |
| BLANCHE DU BOIS | *Jessica Tandy* |
| PABLO GONZALES | *Nick Dennis* |
| A YOUNG COLLECTOR | *Vito Christi* |
| A STRANGE WOMAN | *Ann Dere* |
| A STRANGE MAN | *Richard Garrick* |

---

## SCENE

The action of the play takes place in the spring, summer and early fall in New Orleans. It is performed with intermissions after Scene Four and Scene Six.

---

## SCENE ONE

*The exterior of a two-story corner building on a street in New Orleans which is named Elysian Fields and runs between the L & N tracks and the river. The section is poor but, unlike corresponding sections in other American cities, it has a raffiish charm. The houses are mostly white frame, weathered gray, with rickety outside stairs and galleries and quaintly ornamented gables. This building contains two flats, upstairs and down. Faded white stairs ascend to the entrances of both.*

*It is first dark of an evening early in May. The sky that shows around the dim white building is a peculiarly tender blue, almost a turquoise, which invests the scene with a kind of lyricism and gracefully attenuates the atmosphere of decay. You can almost feel the warm breath of the brown river beyond the river warehouses with their faint redolences of bananas and coffee. A corresponding air is evoked by the music of Negro entertainers at a barroom around the corner. In this part of New Orleans you are practically always just around the corner, or a few doors down the street, from a tinny piano being played with the infatuated fluency of brown fingers. This "blue piano" expresses the spirit of the life which goes on here.*

*Two women, one white and one colored, are taking the air on the steps of the building. The white woman is Eunice, who occupies the upstairs flat; the colored woman a neighbor, for New Orleans is a cosmopolitan city where there is a relatively warm and easy intermingling of races in the old part of town.*

*Above the music of the "blue piano" the voices of people on the street can be heard overlapping.*

———

*(Two men come around the corner, Stanley Kowalski and Mitch. They are about twenty-eight or thirty years old, roughly dressed in blue denim work clothes. Stanley carries his bowling jacket and a red-stained package from a butcher's. They stop at the foot of the steps.)*

STANLEY *(bellowing)*. Hey, there! Stella, baby!

*(Stella comes out on the first floor landing, a gentle young woman, about twenty-five, and of a background obviously quite different from her husband's.)*

STELLA *(mildly)*. Don't holler at me like that. Hi, Mitch.

STANLEY. Catch!

STELLA. What?

STANLEY. Meat!

*(He heaves the package at her. She cries out in protest but manages to catch it: then she laughs breathlessly. Her husband and his companion have already started back around the corner.)*

STELLA *(calling after him)*. Stanley! Where are you going?

STANLEY. Bowling!

STELLA. Can I come watch?

STANLEY. Come on. *(He goes out)*

STELLA. Be over soon. *(To the white woman)* Hello, Eunice. How are you?

EUNICE. I'm all right. Tell Steve to get him a poor boy's sandwich 'cause nothing's left here.

*(They all laugh; the colored woman does not stop. Stella goes out.)*

NEGRO WOMAN. What was that package he th'ew at 'er? *(She rises from steps, laughing louder)*

EUNICE. You hush, now!

NEGRO WOMAN. Catch *what!*

*(She continues to laugh. Blanche comes around the corner, carrying a valise. She looks at a slip of paper, then at the building, then again at the slip and again at the building. Her expression is one of shocked disbelief. Her appearance is incongruous in this setting. She is daintily dressed in a white suit with a fluffy bodice, necklace and earrings of pearl, white gloves and hat, looking as if she were arriving at a summer tea or cocktail party in the garden district. She is about five years older than Stella. Her delicate beauty must avoid a strong light. There is something about her uncertain manner, as well as her white clothes, that suggests a moth.)*

EUNICE *(finally)*. What's the matter, honey? Are you lost?

BLANCHE *(with faintly hysterical humor)*. They told me to take a streetcar named Desire, and then transfer to one called Cemeteries and ride six blocks and get off at—Elysian Fields!

EUNICE. That's where you are now.

BLANCHE. At Elysian Fields?

EUNICE. This here is Elysian Fields.

BLANCHE. They mustn't have—understood—what number I wanted . . .

EUNICE. What number you lookin' for?

*(Blanche wearily refers to the slip of paper.)*

BLANCHE. Six thirty-two.

EUNICE. You don't have to look no further.

BLANCHE *(uncomprehendingly).* I'm looking for my sister, Stella DuBois. I mean— Mrs. Stanley Kowalski.

EUNICE. That's the party.—You just did miss her, though.

BLANCHE. This—can this be—her home?

EUNICE. She's got the downstairs here and I got the up.

BLANCHE. Oh. She's—out?

EUNICE. You noticed that bowling alley around the corner?

BLANCHE. I'm—not sure I did.

EUNICE. Well, that's where she's at, watchin' her husband bowl. *(There is a pause)* You want to leave your suitcase here an' go find her?

BLANCHE. No.

NEGRO WOMAN. I'll go tell her you come.

BLANCHE. Thanks.

NEGRO WOMAN. You welcome. *(She goes out)*

EUNICE. She wasn't expecting you?

BLANCHE. No. No, not tonight.

EUNICE. Well, why don't you just go in and make yourself at home till they get back.

BLANCHE. How could I—do that?

EUNICE. We own this place so I can let you in.

*(She gets up and opens the downstairs door. A light goes on behind the blind, turning it light blue. Blanche slowly follows her into the downstairs flat. The surrounding areas dim out as the interior is lighted.*

*(Two rooms can be seen, not too clearly defined. The one first entered is primarily a kitchen but contains a folding bed to be used by Blanche. The room beyond this is a bedroom. Off this room is a narrow door to a bathroom.)*

EUNICE *(defensively, noticing Blanche's look).* It's sort of messed up right now but when it's clean it's real sweet.

BLANCHE. Is it?

EUNICE. Uh-huh, I think so. So you're Stella's sister?

BLANCHE. Yes. *(Wanting to get rid of her)* Thanks for letting me in.

EUNICE. *Por nada,* as the Mexicans say, *por nada!* Stella spoke of you.

BLANCHE. Yes?

EUNICE. I think she said you taught school.

BLANCHE. Yes.

EUNICE. And you're from Mississippi, huh?

BLANCHE. Yes.

EUNICE. She showed me a picture of your home-place, the plantation.

BLANCHE. Belle Reve?

EUNICE. A great big place with white columns.

BLANCHE. Yes . . .

EUNICE. A place like that must be awful hard to keep up.

BLANCHE. If you will excuse me, I'm just about to drop.

EUNICE. Sure, honey. Why don't you set down?

BLANCHE. What I meant was I'd like to be left alone.

EUNICE *(offended).* Aw. I'll make myself scarce, in that case.

BLANCHE. I didn't mean to be rude, but—

EUNICE. I'll drop by the bowling alley an' hustle her up. *(She goes out the door)*

*(Blanche sits in-a chair very stiffly with her shoulders slightly hunched and her legs pressed close together and her hands tightly clutching her purse as if she were quite cold. After a while the blind look goes out of her eyes and she begins to look slowly around. A cat screeches. She catches her breath with a startled gesture. Suddenly she notices something in a half opened closet. She springs up and crosses to it, and removes a whiskey bottle. She pours a half tumbler of whiskey and tosses it down. She carefully replaces the bottle and washes out the tumbler at the sink. Then she resumes her seat in front of the table.)*

BLANCHE *(faintly to herself).* I've got to keep hold of myself!

*(Stella comes quickly around the corner of the building and runs to the door of the downstairs flat.)*

STELLA *(calling out joyfully).* Blanche!

*(For a moment they stare at each other. Then Blanche springs up and runs to her with a wild cry.)*

BLANCHE. Stella, oh, Stella, Stella! Stella for Star!

*(She begins to speak with feverish vivacity as if she feared for either of them to stop and think. They catch each other in a spasmodic embrace.)*

BLANCHE. Now, then, let me look at you. But don't you look at me, Stella, no, no, no, not till later, not till I've bathed and rested! And turn that over-light off! Turn that off! I won't be looked at in this merciless glare! *(Stella laughs and complies)* Come back here now! Oh, my baby! Stella! Stella for Star! *(She embraces her again)* I thought you would never come back to this horrible place! What am I saying? I didn't mean to say that. I meant to be nice about it and say—Oh, what a convenient location and such—Ha-a-ha! Precious lamb! You haven't said a *word* to me.

STELLA. You haven't given me a chance to, honey! *(She laughs, but her glance at Blanche is a little anxious)*

BLANCHE. Well, now you talk. Open your pretty mouth and talk while I look around for some liquor! I know you must have some liquor on the place! Where could it be, I wonder? Oh, I spy, I spy! *(She rushes to the closet and removes the bottle; she is shaking all over and panting for breath as she tries to laugh. The bottle nearly slips from her grasp.)*

STELLA *(noticing)*. Blanche, you sit down and let me pour the drinks. I don't know what we've got to mix with. Maybe a coke's in the icebox. Look'n see, honey, while I'm —

BLANCHE. No coke, honey, not with my nerves tonight— Where—where—where is—?

STELLA. Stanley? Bowling! He loves it. They're having a—found some soda!—tournament . . .

BLANCHE. Just water, baby, to chase it! Now don't get worried, your sister hasn't turned into a drunkard, she's just all shaken up and hot and tired and dirty! You sit down, now, and explain this place to me! What are you doing in a place like this?

STELLA. Now, Blanche—

BLANCHE. Oh, I'm not going to be hypocritical, I'm going to be honestly critical about it! Never, never, never in my worst dreams could I picture— Only Poe! Only Mr. Edgar Allan Poe!—could do it justice! Out there I suppose is the ghoul-haunted woodland of Weir! *(She laughs)*

STELLA. No, honey, those are the L & N tracks.

BLANCHE. No, now seriously, putting joking aside. Why didn't you tell me, why

didn't you write me, honey, why didn't you let me know?

STELLA *(carefully, pouring herself a drink)*. Tell you what, Blanche?

BLANCHE. Why, that you had to live in these conditions!

STELLA. Aren't you being a little intense about it? It's not that bad at all! New Orleans isn't like other cities.

BLANCHE. This has got nothing to do with New Orleans. You might as well say —forgive me, blessed baby! *(She suddenly stops short)* The subject is closed!

STELLA *(a little drily)*. Thanks.
*(During the pause, Blanche stares at her. She smiles at Blanche.)*

BLANCHE *(looking down at her glass, which shakes in her hand)*. You're all I've got in the world, and you're not glad to see me!

STELLA *(sincerely)*. Why, Blanche, you know that's not true.

BLANCHE. No?—I'd forgotten how quiet you were.

STELLA. You never did give me a chance to say much, Blanche. So I just got in the habit of being quiet around you.

BLANCHE *(vaguely)*. A good habit to get into . . . *(Then, abruptly)* You haven't asked me how I happened to get away from the school before the spring term ended.

STELLA. Well, I thought you'd volunteer that information—if you wanted to tell me.

BLANCHE. You thought I'd been fired?

STELLA. No, I—thought you might have —resigned . . .

BLANCHE. I was so exhausted by all I'd been through my—nerves broke. *(Nervously tamping cigarette)* I was on the verge of—lunacy, almost! So Mr. Graves— Mr. Graves is the high school superintendent—he suggested I take a leave of absence. I couldn't put all of those details into the wire . . . *(She drinks quickly)* Oh, this buzzes right through me and feels so *good!*

STELLA. Won't you have another?

BLANCHE. No, one's my limit.

STELLA. Sure?

BLANCHE. You haven't said a word about my appearance.

STELLA. You look just fine.

BLANCHE. God love you for a liar! Daylight never exposed so total a ruin! But you—you've put on some weight, yes, you're just as plump as a little partridge! And it's so becoming to you!

STELLA. Now, Blanche—

BLANCHE. Yes, it is, it is or I wouldn't say it! You just have to watch around the hips a little. Stand up.

STELLA. Not now.

BLANCHE. You hear me? I said stand up! *(Stella complies reluctantly)* You messy child, you, you've spilt something on that pretty white lace collar! About your hair— you ought to have it cut in a feather bob with your dainty features. Stella, you have a maid, don't you?

STELLA. No. With only two rooms it's—

BLANCHE. What? *Two* rooms, did you say?

STELLA. This one and—*(She is embarrassed)*

BLANCHE. The other one? *(She laughs sharply. There is an embarrassed silence)* I am going to take just one little tiny nip more, sort of to put the stopper on, so to speak. . . . Then put the bottle away so I won't be tempted. *(She rises)* I want you to look at *my* figure! *(She turns around)* You know I haven't put on one ounce in ten years, Stella? I weigh what I weighed the summer you left Belle Reve. The summer Dad died and you left us . . .

STELLA *(a little wearily)*. It's just incredible, Blanche, how well you're looking.

BLANCHE *(they both laugh uncomfortably)*. But, Stella, there's only two rooms, I don't see where you're going to put me!

STELLA. We're going to put you in here.

BLANCHE. What kind of bed's this—one of those collapsible things? *(She sits on it)*

STELLA. Does it feel all right?

BLANCHE *(dubiously)*. Wonderful, honey. I don't like a bed that gives much. But there's no door between the two rooms, and Stanley—will it be decent?

STELLA. Stanley is Polish, you know.

BLANCHE. Oh, yes. They're something like Irish, aren't they?

STELLA. Well—

BLANCHE. Only not so—highbrow? *(They both laugh again in the same way)* I brought some nice clothes to meet all your lovely friends in.

STELLA. I'm afraid you won't think they are lovely.

BLANCHE. What are they like?

STELLA. They're Stanley's friends.

BLANCHE. Polacks?

STELLA. They're a mixed lot, Blanche.

BLANCHE. Heterogeneous—types?

STELLA. Oh, yes. Yes, types is right!

BLANCHE. Well—anyhow—I brought nice clothes and I'll wear them. I guess you're hoping I'll say I'll put up at a hotel, but I'm not going to put up at a hotel. I want to be *near* you, got to be *with* somebody, I *can't* be *alone*! Because—as you must have noticed—I'm—*not* very *well* . . . *(Her voice drops and her look is frightened)*

STELLA. You seem a little bit nervous or overwrought or something.

BLANCHE. Will Stanley like me, or will I be just a visiting in-law, Stella? I couldn't stand that.

STELLA. You'll get along fine together, if you'll just try not to—well—compare him with men that we went out with at home.

BLANCHE. Is he so—different?

STELLA. Yes. A different species.

BLANCHE. In what way; what's he like?

STELLA. Oh, you can't describe someone you're in love with! Here's a picture of him! *(She hands a photograph to Blanche)*

BLANCHE. An officer?

STELLA. A Master Sergeant in the Engineers' Corps. Those are decorations!

BLANCHE. He had those on when you met him?

STELLA. I assure you I wasn't just blinded by all the brass.

BLANCHE. That's not what I—

STELLA. But of course there were things to adjust myself to later on.

BLANCHE. Such as his civilian background! *(Stella laughs uncertainly)* How did he take it when you said I was coming?

STELLA. Oh, Stanley doesn't know yet.

BLANCHE *(frightened)*. You—haven't told him?

STELLA. He's on the road a good deal.

BLANCHE. Oh. Travels?

STELLA. Yes.

BLANCHE. Good. I mean—isn't it?

STELLA *(half to herself)*. I can hardly stand it when he is away for a night . . .

BLANCHE. Why, Stella!

STELLA. When he's away for a week I nearly go wild!

BLANCHE. Gracious!

STELLA. And when he comes back I cry on his lap like a baby . . . *(She smiles to herself)*

BLANCHE. I guess that is what is meant by being in love . . . *(Stella looks up with a radiant smile)* Stella—

STELLA. What?

BLANCHE *(in an uneasy rush)*. I haven't asked you the things you probably thought I was going to ask. And so I'll expect you to be understanding about what *I* have to tell *you*.

STELLA. What, Blanche? *(Her face turns anxious)*

BLANCHE. Well, Stella—you're going to reproach me, I know that you're bound to reproach me—but before you do—take into consideration—you left! I stayed and struggled! You came to New Orleans and looked out for yourself! I stayed at Belle Reve and tried to hold it together! I'm not meaning this in any reproachful way, but *all* the burden descended on *my* shoulders.

STELLA. The best I could do was make my own living, Blanche.

*(Blanche begins to shake again with intensity.)*

BLANCHE. I know, I know. But you are the one that abandoned Belle Reve, not I! I stayed and fought for it, bled for it, almost died for it!

STELLA. Stop this hysterical outburst and tell me what's happened? What do you mean fought and bled? What kind of—

BLANCHE. I knew you would, Stella. I knew you would take this attitude about it!

STELLA. About—what?—please!

BLANCHE *(slowly)*. The loss—the loss . . .

STELLA. Belle Reve? Lost, is it? No!

BLANCHE. Yes, Stella.

*(They stare at each other across the yellow-checked linoleum of the table. Blanche slowly nods her head and Stella looks slowly down at her hands folded on the table. The music of the "blue piano" grows louder. Blanche touches her handkerchief to her forehead.)*

STELLA. But how did it go? What happened?

BLANCHE *(springing up)*. You're a fine one to ask me how it went!

STELLA. Blanche!

BLANCHE. You're a fine one to sit there *accusing me* of it!

STELLA. *Blanche!*

BLANCHE. I, I, *I* took the blows in my face and my body! All of those deaths! The long parade to the graveyard! Father, mother! Margaret, that dreadful way! So big with it, it couldn't be put in a coffin! But had to be burned like rubbish! You just came home in time for the funerals, Stella. And funerals are pretty compared to deaths. Funerals are quiet, but deaths—not always. Sometimes their breathing is hoarse, and sometimes it rattles, and sometimes they even cry out to you, "Don't let me go!" Even the old, sometimes, say, "Don't let me go." As if you were able to stop them! But funerals are quiet, with pretty flowers. And, oh, what gorgeous boxes they pack them away in! Unless you were there at the bed when they cried out, "Hold me!" you'd never suspect there was the struggle for breath and bleeding. You didn't dream, but I saw! *Saw! Saw!* And now you sit there telling me with your eyes that I let the place go! How in hell do you think all that sickness and dying was paid for? Death is expensive, Miss Stella! And old Cousin Jessie's right after Margaret's, hers! Why, the Grim Reaper had put up his tent on our doorstep! . . . Stella. Belle Reve was his headquarters! Honey—that's how it slipped through my fingers! Which of them left us a fortune? Which of them left a cent of insurance even? Only poor Jessie—one hundred to pay for her coffin. That was all, Stella! And I with my pitiful salary at the school. Yes, accuse me! Sit there and stare at me, thinking I let the place go! *I* let the place go? Where were *you!* In bed with your—Polack!

STELLA *(springing)*. Blanche! You be still! That's enough! *(She starts out)*

BLANCHE. Where are you going?

STELLA. I'm going into the bathroom to wash my face.

BLANCHE. Oh, Stella, Stella, you're crying!

STELLA. Does that surprise you?

BLANCHE. Forgive me—I didn't mean to—

*(The sound of men's voices is heard. Stella goes into the bathroom, closing the door behind her. When the men appear, and Blanche realizes it must be Stanley returning, she moves uncertainly from the bathroom door to the dressing table, looking apprehensively towards the front door. Stanley enters, followed by Steve and Mitch. Stanley pauses near his door, Steve by the foot of the spiral stair, and Mitch is slightly above and to the right of them,*

about to go out. *As the men enter, we
hear some of the following dialogue.)*

STANLEY. Is that how he got it?

STEVE. Sure that's how he got it. He hit
the old weather-bird for 300 bucks on a
six-number-ticket.

MITCH. Don't tell him those things; he'll
believe it.

*(Mitch starts out.)*

STANLEY *(restraining Mitch).* Hey,
Mitch—come back here.

*(Blanche, at the sound of voices, retires in
the bedroom. She picks up Stanley's photo
from dressing table, looks at it, puts it
down. When Stanley enters the apartment,
she darts and hides behind the screen at
the head of bed.)*

STEVE *(to Stanley and Mitch).* Hey, are
we playin' poker tomorrow?

STANLEY. Sure—at Mitch's.

MITCH *(hearing this, returns quickly to
the stair rail).* No—not at my place. My
mother's still sick!

STANLEY. Okay, at my place . . . *(Mitch
starts out again)* But you bring the beer!
*(Mitch pretends not to hear—calls out
"Goodnight all," and goes out, singing.
Eunice's voice is heard, above.)*

EUNICE. Break it up down there! I made
the spaghetti dish and ate it myself.

STEVE *(going upstairs).* I told you and
phoned you we was playing. *(To the men)*
Jax beer!

EUNICE. You never phoned me once.

STEVE. I told you at breakfast—and
phoned you at lunch . . .

EUNICE. Well, never mind about that.
You just get yourself home here once in a
while.

STEVE. You want it in the papers?

*(More laughter and shouts of parting come
from the men. Stanley throws the screen
door of the kitchen open and comes in. He
is of medium height, about five feet eight
or nine, and strongly, compactly built.
Animal joy in his being is implicit in all
his movements and attitudes. Since earliest
manhood the center of his life has been
pleasure with women, the giving and taking of it, not with weak indulgence, de-
pendently, but with the power and pride
of a richly feathered male bird among
hens. Branching out from this complete
and satisfying center are all the auxiliary
channels of his life, such as his heartiness
with men, his appreciation of rough humor, his love of good drink and food and*
games, *his car, his radio, everything that
is his, that bears his emblem of the gaudy
seed-bearer. He sizes women up at a
glance, with sexual classification, crude
images flashing into his mind and deter-
mining the way he smiles at them.)*

BLANCHE *(drawing involuntarily back
from his stare).* You must be Stanley. I'm
Blanche.

STANLEY. Stella's sister?

BLANCHE. Yes.

STANLEY. H'lo. Where's the little
woman?

BLANCHE. In the bathroom.

STANLEY. Oh. Didn't know you were
coming in town.

BLANCHE. I—uh—

STANLEY. Where you from, Blanche?

BLANCHE. Why, I—live in Laurel.

*(He has crossed to the closet and removed
the whiskey bottle.)*

STANLEY. In Laurel, huh? Oh, yeah.
Yeah, in Laurel, that's right. Not in my
territory. Liquor goes fast in hot weather.
*(He holds the bottle to the light to ob-
serve its depletion)* Have a shot?

BLANCHE. No, I—rarely touch it.

STANLEY. Some people rarely touch it,
but it touches them often.

BLANCHE *(faintly).* Ha-ha.

STANLEY. My clothes're stickin' to me.
Do you mind if I make myself comfortable? *(He starts to remove his shirt)*

BLANCHE. Please, please do.

STANLEY. Be comfortable is my motto.

BLANCHE. It's mine, too. It's hard to stay
looking fresh. I haven't washed or even
powdered my face and—here you are!

STANLEY. You know you can catch cold
sitting around in damp things, especially
when you been exercising hard like bowling is. You're a teacher, aren't you?

BLANCHE. Yes.

STANLEY. What do you teach, Blanche?

BLANCHE. English.

STANLEY. I never was a very good English student. How long you here for,
Blanche?

BLANCHE. I—don't know yet.

STANLEY. You going to shack up here?

BLANCHE. I thought I would if it's not
inconvenient for you all.

STANLEY. Good.

BLANCHE. Traveling wears me out.

STANLEY. Well, take it easy.

*(A cat screeches near the window. Blanche
springs up.)*

BLANCHE. What's that?

STANLEY. Cats . . . Hey, Stella!

STELLA (*faintly, from the bathroom*). Yes, Stanley.

STANLEY. Haven't fallen in, have you? (*He grins at Blanche. She tries unsuccessfully to smile back. There is a silence*) I'm afraid I'll strike you as being the unrefined type. Stella's spoke of you a good deal. You were married once, weren't you? (*The music of the polka rises up, faint in the distance.*)

BLANCHE. Yes. When I was quite young.

STANLEY. What happened?

BLANCHE. The boy—the boy died. (*She sinks back down*) I'm afraid I'm—going to be sick!

(*Her head falls on her arms.*)

## SCENE TWO

*It is six o'clock the following evening. Blanche is bathing. Stella is completing her toilette. Blanche's dress, a flowered print, is laid out on Stella's bed.*

*Stanley enters the kitchen from outside, leaving the door open on the perpetual "blue piano" around the corner.*

STANLEY. What's all this monkey doings?

STELLA. Oh, Stan! (*She jumps up and kisses him which he accepts with lordly composure*) I'm taking Blanche to Galatoire's for supper and then to a show, because it's your poker night.

STANLEY. How about my supper, huh? I'm not going to no Galatoire's for supper!

STELLA. I put you a cold plate on ice.

STANLEY. Well, isn't that just dandy!

STELLA. I'm going to try to keep Blanche out till the party breaks up because I don't know how she would take it. So we'll go to one of the little places in the Quarter afterwards and you'd better give me some money.

STANLEY. Where is she?

STELLA. She's soaking in a hot tub to quiet her nerves. She's terribly upset.

STANLEY. Over what?

STELLA. She's been through such an ordeal.

STANLEY. Yeah?

STELLA. Stan, we've—lost Belle Reve!

STANLEY. The place in the country?

STELLA. Yes.

STANLEY. How?

STELLA (*vaguely*). Oh, it had to be—sacrificed or something. (*There is a pause while Stanley considers. Stella is changing into her dress*) When she comes in be sure to say something nice about her appearance. And, oh! Don't mention the baby. I haven't said anything yet, I'm waiting until she gets in a quieter condition.

STANLEY (*ominously*). So?

STELLA. And try to understand her and be nice to her, Stan.

BLANCHE (*singing in the bathroom*). "From the land of the sky blue water, They brought a captive maid!"

STELLA. She wasn't expecting to find us in such a small place. You see I'd tried to gloss things over a little in my letters.

STANLEY. So?

STELLA. And admire her dress and tell her she's looking wonderful. That's important with Blanche. Her little weakness!

STANLEY. Yeah. I get the idea. Now let's skip back a little to where you said the country place was disposed of.

STELLA. Oh!—yes . . .

STANLEY. How about that? Let's have a few more details on that subjeck.

STELLA. It's best not to talk much about it until she's calmed down.

STANLEY. So that's the deal, huh? Sister Blanche cannot be annoyed with business details right now!

STELLA. You saw how she was last night.

STANLEY. Uh-hum, I saw how she was. Now let's have a gander at the bill of sale.

STELLA. I haven't seen any.

STANLEY. She didn't show you no papers, no deed of sale or nothing like that, huh?

STELLA. It seems like it wasn't sold.

STANLEY. Well, what in hell was it then, give away? To charity?

STELLA. Shhh! She'll hear you.

STANLEY. I don't care if she hears me. Let's see the papers!

STELLA. There weren't any papers, she didn't show any papers, I don't care about papers.

STANLEY. Have you ever heard of the Napoleonic code?

STELLA. No, Stanley, I haven't heard of the Napoleonic code and if I have, I don't see what it—

STANLEY. Let me enlighten you on a point or two, baby.

STELLA. Yes?

STANLEY. In the state of Louisiana we have the Napoleonic code according to which what belongs to the wife belongs to the husband and vice versa. For instance if I had a piece of property, or you had a piece of property—

STELLA. My head is swimming!

STANLEY. All right. I'll wait till she gets through soaking in a hot tub and then I'll inquire if *she* is acquainted with the Napoleonic code. It looks to me like you have been swindled, baby, and when you're swindled under the Napoleonic code I'm swindled *too*. And I don't like to be *swindled*.

STELLA. There's plenty of time to ask her questions later but if you do now she'll go to pieces again. I don't understand what happened to Belle Reve but you don't know how ridiculous you are being when you suggest that my sister or I or anyone of our family could have perpetrated a swindle on anyone else.

STANLEY. Then where's the money if the place was sold?

STELLA. Not sold—*lost, lost!* (He stalks into bedroom, and she follows him) Stanley!

(He pulls open the wardrobe trunk standing in middle of room and jerks out an armful of dresses.)

STANLEY. Open your eyes to this stuff! You think she got them out of a teacher's pay?

STELLA. Hush!

STANLEY. Look at these feathers and furs that she come here to preen herself in! What's this here? A solid-gold dress, I believe! And this one! What is these here? Fox-pieces! (He blows on them) Genuine fox fur-pieces, a half a mile long! Where are your fox-pieces, Stella? Bushy snow-white ones, no less! Where are your white fox-pieces?

STELLA. Those are inexpensive summer furs that Blanche has had a long time.

STANLEY. I got an acquaintance who deals in this sort of merchandise. I'll have him in here to appraise it. I'm willing to bet you there's thousands of dollars invested in this stuff here!

STELLA. Don't be such an idiot, Stanley!

(He hurls the furs to the daybed. Then he jerks open small drawer in the trunk and pulls up a fist-full of costume jewelry.)

STANLEY. And what have we here? The treasure chest of a pirate!

STELLA. Oh, Stanley!

STANLEY. Pearls! Ropes of them! What is this sister of yours, a deep-sea diver? Bracelets of solid gold, too! Where are your pearls and gold bracelets?

STELLA. Shhh! Be still, Stanley!

STANLEY. And diamonds! A crown for an empress!

STELLA. A rhinestone tiara she wore to a costume ball.

STANLEY. What's rhinestone?

STELLA. Next door to glass.

STANLEY. Are you kidding? I have an acquaintance that works in a jewelry store. I'll have him in here to make an appraisal of this. Here's your plantation, or what was left of it, here!

STELLA. You have no idea how stupid and horrid you're being! Now close that trunk before she comes out of the bathroom!

(He kicks the trunk partly closed and sits on the kitchen table.)

STANLEY. The Kowalskis and the DuBois have different notions.

STELLA (angrily). Indeed they have, thank heavens—*I'm* going outside. (She snatches up her white hat and gloves and crosses to the outside door) You come out with me while Blanche is getting dressed.

STANLEY. Since when do you give me orders?

STELLA. Are you going to stay here and insult her?

STANLEY. You're damn tootin' I'm going to stay here.

(Stella goes out to the porch. Blanche comes out of the bathroom in a red satin robe.)

BLANCHE (airily). Hello, Stanley! Here I am, all freshly bathed and scented, and feeling like a brand new human being!

(He lights a cigarette.)

STANLEY. That's good.

BLANCHE (drawing the curtains at the window). Excuse me while I slip on my pretty new dress!

STANLEY. Go right ahead, Blanche.

(She closes the drapes between the rooms.)

BLANCHE. I understand there's to be a little card party to which we ladies are cordially *not* invited!

STANLEY (ominously). Yeah?

(Blanche throws off her robe and slips into a flowered print dress.)

BLANCHE. Where's Stella?

STANLEY. Out on the porch.

BLANCHE. I'm going to ask a favor of you in a moment.

STANLEY. What could that be, I wonder?

BLANCHE. Some buttons in back! You may enter! *(He crosses through drapes with a smoldering look)* How do I look?

STANLEY. You look all right.

BLANCHE. Many thanks! Now the buttons!

STANLEY. I can't do nothing with them.

BLANCHE. You men with your big clumsy fingers. May I have a drag on your cig?

STANLEY. Have one for yourself.

BLANCHE. Why, thanks! . . . It looks like my trunk has exploded.

STANLEY. Me an' Stella were helping you unpack.

BLANCHE. Well, you certainly did a fast and thorough job of it!

STANLEY. It looks like you raided some stylish shops in Paris.

BLANCHE. Ha-ha! Yes—clothes are my passion!

STANLEY. What does it cost for a string of fur-pieces like that?

BLANCHE. Why, those were a tribute from an admirer of mine!

STANLEY. He must have had a lot of—admiration!

BLANCHE. Oh, in my youth I excited some admiration. But look at me now! *(She smiles at him radiantly)* Would you think it possible that I was once considered to be—attractive?

STANLEY. Your looks are okay.

BLANCHE. I was fishing for a compliment, Stanley.

STANLEY. I don't go in for that stuff.

BLANCHE. What—stuff?

STANLEY. Compliments to women about their looks. I never met a woman that didn't know if she was good-looking or not without being told, and some of them give themselves credit for more than they've got. I once went out with a doll who said to me, "I am the glamorous type, I am the glamorous type!" I said, "So what?"

BLANCHE. And what did she say then?

STANLEY. She didn't say nothing. That shut her up like a clam.

BLANCHE. Did it end the romance?

STANLEY. It ended the conversation—that was all. Some men are took in by this Hollywood glamor stuff and some men are not.

BLANCHE. I'm sure you belong in the second category.

STANLEY. That's right.

BLANCHE. I cannot imagine any witch of a woman casting a spell over you.

STANLEY. That's—right.

BLANCHE. You're simple, straightforward and honest, a little bit on the primitive side I should think. To interest you a woman would have to—*(She pauses with an indefinite gesture)*

STANLEY *(slowly)*. Lay . . . her cards on the table.

BLANCHE *(smiling)*. Well, I never cared for wishy-washy people. That was why, when you walked in here last night, I said to myself—"My sister has married a man!" —Of course that was all that I could tell about you.

STANLEY *(booming)*. Now let's cut the re-bop!

BLANCHE *(pressing hands to her ears* Ouuuuu!

STELLA *(calling from the steps)*. Stanley! You come out here and let Blanche finish dressing!

BLANCHE. I'm through dressing, honey.

STELLA. Well, you come out, then.

STANLEY. Your sister and I are having a little talk.

BLANCHE *(lightly)*. Honey, do me a favor. Run to the drugstore and get me a lemon-coke with plenty of chipped ice in it!—Will you do that for me, Sweetie?

STELLA *(uncertainly)*. Yes. *(She goes around the corner of the building)*

BLANCHE. The poor little thing was out there listening to us, and I have an idea she doesn't understand you as well as I do. . . . All right; now, Mr. Kowalski, let us proceed without any more double-talk. I'm ready to answer all questions. I've nothing to hide. What is it?

STANLEY. There is such a thing in this state of Louisiana as the Napoleonic code, according to which whatever belongs to my wife is also mine—and vice versa.

BLANCHE. My, but you have an impressive judicial air!

*(She sprays herself with her atomizer; then playfully sprays him with it. He seizes the atomizer and slams it down on the dresser. She throws back her head and laughs.)*

STANLEY. If I didn't know that you was my wife's sister I'd get ideas about you!

BLANCHE. Such as what!

STANLEY. Don't play so dumb. You know!

BLANCHE (*she puts the atomizer on the table*). All right. Cards on the table. That suits me. (*She turns to Stanley*) I know I fib a good deal. After all, a woman's charm is fifty per cent illusion, but when a thing is important I tell the truth, and this is the truth: I haven't cheated my sister or you or anyone else as long as I have lived.

STANLEY. Where's the papers? In the trunk?

BLANCHE. Everything that I own is in that trunk.

(*Stanley crosses to the trunk, shoves it roughly open and begins to open compartments.*)

BLANCHE. What in the name of heaven are you thinking of! What's in the back of that little boy's mind of yours? That I am absconding with something, attempting some kind of treachery on my sister? —Let me do that! It will be faster and simpler . . . (*She crosses to the trunk and takes out a box*) I keep my papers mostly in this tin box. (*She opens it*)

STANLEY. What's them underneath? (*He indicates another sheaf of paper*)

BLANCHE. These are love-letters, yellowing with antiquity, all from one boy. (*He snatches them up. She speaks fiercely*) Give those back to me!

STANLEY. I'll have a look at them first!

BLANCHE. The touch of your hands insults them!

STANLEY. Don't pull that stuff!

(*He rips off the ribbon and starts to examine them. Blanche snatches them from him, and they cascade to the floor.*)

BLANCHE. Now that you've touched them I'll burn them!

STANLEY (*staring, baffled*). What in hell are they?

BLANCHE (*on the floor, gathering them up*). Poems a dead boy wrote. I hurt him the way that you would like to hurt me, but you can't! I'm not young and vulnerable any more. But my young husband was and I—never mind about that! Just give them back to me!

STANLEY. What do you mean by saying you'll have to burn them?

BLANCHE. I'm sorry, I must have lost my head for a moment. Everyone has something he won't let others touch because of their—intimate nature . . . (*She now seems faint with exhaustion and she sits down with the strong box and puts on a pair of glasses and goes methodically through a large stack of papers*) Ambler & Ambler. Hmmmmm. . . . Crabtree. . . . More Ambler & Ambler.

STANLEY. What is Ambler & Ambler?

BLANCHE. A firm that made loans on the place.

STANLEY. Then it *was* lost on a mortgage?

BLANCHE (*touching her forehead*). That must've been what happened.

STANLEY. I don't want no ifs, ands or buts! What's all the rest of them papers? (*She hands him the entire box. He carries it to the table and starts to examine the papers.*)

BLANCHE (*picking up a large envelope containing more papers*). There are thousands of papers, stretching back over hundreds of years, affecting Belle Reve as, piece by piece, our improvident grandfathers and father and uncles and brothers exchanged the land for their epic fornications—to put it plainly! (*She removes her glasses with an exhausted laugh*) The four-letter word deprived us of our plantation, till finally all that was left—and Stella can verify that!—was the house itself and about twenty acres of ground, including a graveyard, to which now all but Stella and I have retreated. (*She pours the contents of the envelope on the table*) Here all of them are, all papers! I hereby endow you with them! Take them, peruse them— commit them to memory, even! I think it's wonderfully fitting that Belle Reve should finally be this bunch of old papers in your big, capable hands! . . . I wonder if Stella's come back with my lemon-coke . . . (*She leans back and closes her eyes*)

STANLEY. I have a lawyer acquaintance who will study these out.

BLANCHE. Present them to him with a box of aspirin tablets.

STANLEY (*becoming somewhat sheepish*). You see, under the Napoleonic code—a man has to take an interest in his wife's affairs—especially now that she's going to have a baby.

(*Blanche opens her eyes. The "blue piano" sounds louder.*)

BLANCHE. Stella? Stella going to have a

baby? *(Dreamily)* I didn't know she was going to have a baby!

*(She gets up and crosses to the outside door. Stella appears around the corner with a carton from the drugstore.)*

*(Stanley goes into the bedroom with the envelope and the box.)*

*(The inner rooms fade to darkness and the outside wall of the house is visible. Blanche meets Stella at the foot of the steps to the sidewalk.)*

BLANCHE. Stella, Stella for star! How lovely to have a baby! It's all right. Everything's all right.

STELLA. I'm sorry he did that to you.

BLANCHE. Oh, I guess he's just not the type that goes for jasmine perfume, but maybe he's what we need to mix with our blood now that we've lost Belle Reve. We thrashed it out. I feel a bit shaky, but I think I handled it nicely, I laughed and treated it all as a joke. *(Steve and Pablo appear, carrying a case of beer)* I called him a little boy and laughed and flirted. Yes, I was flirting with your husband! *(As the men approach)* The guests are gathering for the poker party. *(The two men pass between them, and enter the house)* Which way do we go now, Stella—this way?

STELLA. No, this way. *(She leads Blanche away)*

BLANCHE *(laughing)*. The blind are leading the blind!

*(A tamale vendor is heard calling.)*

VENDOR'S VOICE. Red-hot!

## SCENE THREE

THE POKER NIGHT

*There is a picture of Van Gogh's of a billiard-parlor at night. The kitchen now suggests that sort of lurid nocturnal brilliance, the raw colors of childhood's spectrum. Over the yellow linoleum of the kitchen table hangs an electric bulb with a vivid green glass shade. The poker players—Stanley, Steve, Mitch and Pablo—wear colored shirts, solid blues, a purple, a red-and-white check, a light green, and they are men at the peak of their physical manhood, as coarse and direct and powerful as the primary colors. There are vivid slices of watermelon on the table, whiskey bottles and glasses. The bedroom is relatively dim with only the light that spills between the portieres and through the wide window on the street.*

*For a moment, there is absorbed silence as a hand is dealt.*

———

STEVE. Anything wild this deal?

PABLO. One-eyed jacks are wild.

STEVE. Give me two cards.

PABLO. You, Mitch?

MITCH. I'm out.

PABLO. One.

MITCH. Anyone want a shot?

STANLEY. Yeah, me.

PABLO. Why don't somebody go to the Chinaman's and bring back a load of chop suey?

STANLEY. When I'm losing you want to eat! Ante up! Openers? Openers! Get y'r ass off the table, Mitch. Nothing belongs on a poker table but cards, chips and whiskey. *(He lurches up and tosses some watermelon rinds to the floor)*

MITCH. Kind of on your high horse, ain't you?

STANLEY. How many?

STEVE. Give me three.

STANLEY. One.

MITCH. I'm out again. I oughta go home pretty soon.

STANLEY. Shut up.

MITCH. I gotta sick mother. She don't go to sleep until I come in at night.

STANLEY. Then why don't you stay home with her?

MITCH. She says to go out, so I go, but I don't enjoy it. All the while I keep wondering how she is.

STANLEY. Aw, for the sake of Jesus, go home, then!

PABLO. What've you got?

STEVE. Spade flush.

MITCH. You all are married. But I'll be alone when she goes.—I'm going to the bathroom.

STANLEY. Hurry back and we'll fix you a sugar-tit.

MITCH. Aw, go rut. *(He crosses through the bedroom into the bathroom)*

STEVE *(dealing a hand)*. Seven card stud. *(Telling his joke as he deals)* This ole farmer is out in back of his house sittin' down th'owing corn to the chickens when all at once he hears a loud cackle and this young hen comes lickety split around the side of the house with the rooster right behind her and gaining on her fast.

STANLEY (*impatient with the story*). Deal!

STEVE. But when the rooster catches sight of the farmer th'owing the corn he puts on the brakes and lets the hen get away and starts pecking corn. And the old farmer says, "Lord God, I hopes I never gits *that* hongry!"

(*Steve and Pablo laugh. The sisters appear around the corner of the building.*)

STELLA. The game is still going on.

BLANCHE. How do I look?

STELLA. Lovely, Blanche.

BLANCHE. I feel so hot and frazzled. Wait till I powder before you open the door. Do I look done in?

STELLA. Why no. You are as fresh as a daisy.

BLANCHE. One that's been picked a few days.

(*Stella opens the door and they enter.*)

STELLA. Well, well, well. I see you boys are still at it!

STANLEY. Where you been?

STELLA. Blanche and I took in a show. Blanche, this is Mr. Gonzales and Mr. Hubbell.

BLANCHE. Please don't get up.

STANLEY. Nobody's going to get up, so don't be worried.

STELLA. How much longer is this game going to continue?

STANLEY. Till we get ready to quit.

BLANCHE. Poker is so fascinating. Could I kibitz?

STANLEY. You could not. Why don't you women go up and sit with Eunice?

STELLA. Because it is nearly two-thirty. (*Blanche crosses into the bedroom and partially closes the portieres*) Couldn't you call it quits after one more hand?

(*A chair scrapes. Stanley gives a loud whack of his hand on her thigh.*)

STELLA (*sharply*). That's not fun, Stanley.

(*The men laugh. Stella goes into the bedroom.*)

STELLA. It makes me so mad when he does that in front of people.

BLANCHE. I think I will bathe.

STELLA. Again?

BLANCHE. My nerves are in knots. Is the bathroom occupied?

STELLA. I don't know.

(*Blanche knocks. Mitch opens the door and comes out, still wiping his hands on a towel.*)

BLANCHE. Oh!—good evening.

MITCH. Hello. (*He stares at her*)

STELLA. Blanche, this is Harold Mitchell. My sister, Blanche DuBois.

MITCH (*with awkward courtesy*). How do you do, Miss DuBois.

STELLA. How is your mother now, Mitch?

MITCH. About the same, thanks. She appreciated your sending over that custard. —Excuse me, please.

(*He crosses slowly back into the kitchen, glancing back at Blanche and coughing a little shyly. He realizes he still has the towel in his hands and with an embarrassed laugh hands it to Stella. Blanche looks after him with a certain interest.*)

BLANCHE. That one seems—superior to the others.

STELLA. Yes, he is.

BLANCHE. I thought he had a sort of sensitive look.

STELLA. His mother is sick.

BLANCHE. Is he married?

STELLA. No.

BLANCHE. Is he a wolf?

STELLA. Why, Blanche! (*Blanche laughs*) I don't think he would be.

BLANCHE. What does—what does he do? (*She is unbuttoning her blouse*)

STELLA. He's on the precision bench in the spare parts department. At the plant Stanley travels for.

BLANCHE. Is that something much?

STELLA. No. Stanley's the only one of his crowd that's likely to get anywhere.

BLANCHE. What makes you think Stanley will?

STELLA. Look at him.

BLANCHE. I've looked at him.

STELLA. Then you should know.

BLANCHE. I'm sorry, but I haven't noticed the stamp of genius even on Stanley's forehead.

(*She takes off the blouse and stands in her pink silk brassiere and white skirt in the light through the portieres. The game has continued in undertones.*)

STELLA. It isn't on his forehead and it isn't genius.

BLANCHE. Oh. Well, what is it, and where? I would like to know.

STELLA. It's a drive that he has. You're standing in the light, Blanche!

BLANCHE. Oh, am I!

(*She moves out of the yellow streak of*

*light. Stella has removed her dress and put on a light blue satin kimono.)*

STELLA *(with girlish laughter).* You ought to see their wives.

BLANCHE *(laughingly).* I can imagine. Big, beefy things, I suppose.

STELLA. You know that one upstairs? *(More laughter)* One time *(laughing)* the plaster—*(laughing)* cracked—

STANLEY. You hens cut out that conversation in there!

STELLA. You can't hear us.

STANLEY. Well, you can hear me and I said to hush up!

STELLA. This is my house and I'll talk as much as I want to!

BLANCHE. Stella, don't start a row.

STELLA. He's half drunk!—I'll be out in a minute.

*(She goes into the bathroom. Blanche rises and crosses leisurely to a small white radio and turns it on.)*

STANLEY. Awright, Mitch, you in?

MITCH. What? Oh!—No, I'm out!

*(Blanche moves back into the streak of light. She raises her arms and stretches, as she moves indolently back to the chair.*

*(Rhumba music comes over the radio. Mitch rises at the table.)*

STANLEY. Who turned that on in there?

BLANCHE. I did. Do you mind?

STANLEY. Turn it off!

STEVE. Aw, let the girls have their music.

PABLO. Sure, that's good, leave it on!

STEVE. Sounds like Xavier Cugat!

*(Stanley jumps up and, crossing to the radio, turns it off. He stops short at the sight of Blanche in the chair. She returns his look without flinching. Then he sits again at the poker table.*

*(Two of the men have started arguing hotly.)*

STEVE. I didn't hear you name it.

PABLO. Didn't I name it, Mitch?

MITCH. I wasn't listenin'.

PABLO. What were you doing, then?

STANLEY. He was looking through them drapes. *(He jumps up and jerks roughly at curtains to close them)* Now deal the hand over again and let's play cards or quit. Some people get ants when they win. *(Mitch rises as Stanley returns to his seat.)*

STANLEY *(yelling).* Sit down!

MITCH. I'm going to the "head. Deal me out.

PABLO. Sure he's got ants now Seven

five-dollar bills in his pants pocket folded up tight as spitballs.

STEVE. Tomorrow you'll see him at the cashier's window getting them changed into quarters.

STANLEY. And when he goes home he'll deposit them one by one in a piggy bank his mother give him for Christmas. *(Dealing)* This game is Spit in the Ocean. *(Mitch laughs uncomfortably and continues through the portieres. He stops just inside.)*

BLANCHE *(softly).* Hello! The Little Boys' Room is busy right now.

MITCH. We've—been drinking beer.

BLANCHE. I hate beer.

MITCH. It's—a hot weather drink.

BLANCHE. Oh, I don't think so; it always makes me warmer. Have you got any cigs? *(She has slipped on the dark red satin wrapper)*

MITCH. Sure.

BLANCHE. What kind are they?

MITCH. Luckies.

BLANCHE. Oh, good. What a pretty case. Silver?

MITCH. Yes. Yes; read the inscription.

BLANCHE. Oh, is there an inscription? I can't make it out. *(He strikes a match and moves closer)* Oh! *(Reading with feigned difficulty)*

"And if God choose,
I shall but love thee better—after—death!"

Why, that's from my favorite sonnet by Mrs. Browning!

MITCH. You know it?

BLANCHE. Certainly I do!

MITCH. There's a story connected with that inscription.

BLANCHE. It sounds like a romance.

MITCH. A pretty sad one.

BLANCHE. Oh?

MITCH. The girl's dead now.

BLANCHE *(in a tone of deep sympathy).* Oh!

MITCH. She knew she was dying when she give me this. A very strange girl, very sweet—very!

BLANCHE. She must have been fond of you. Sick people have such deep, sincere attachments.

MITCH. That's right, they certainly do.

BLANCHE. Sorrow makes for sincerity, I think.

MITCH. It sure brings it out in people.

BLANCHE. The little there is belongs to people who have experienced some sorrow.

MITCH. I believe you are right about that.

BLANCHE. I'm positive that I am. Show me a person who hasn't known any sorrow and I'll show you a shuperficial— Listen to me! My tongue is a little—thick! You boys are responsible for it. The show let out at eleven and we couldn't come home on account of the poker game so we had to go somewhere and drink. I'm not accustomed to having more than one drink. Two is the limit—and *three! (She laughs)* Tonight I had three.

STANLEY. Mitch!

MITCH. Deal me out. I'm talking to Miss—

BLANCHE. DuBois.

MITCH. Miss DuBois?

BLANCHE. It's a French name. It means woods and Blanche means white, so the two together mean white woods. Like an orchard in spring! You can remember it by that.

MITCH. You're French?

BLANCHE. We are French by extraction. Our first American ancestors were French Huguenots.

MITCH. You are Stella's sister, are you not?

BLANCHE. Yes, Stella is my precious little sister. I call her little in spite of the fact she's somewhat older than I. Just slightly. Less than a year. Will you do something for me?

MITCH. Sure. What?

BLANCHE. I bought this adorable little colored paper lantern at a Chinese shop on Bourbon. Put it over the light bulb! Will you, please?

MITCH. Be glad to.

BLANCHE. I can't stand a naked light bulb, any more than I can a rude remark or a vulgar action.

MITCH *(adjusting the lantern)*. I guess we strike you as being a pretty rough bunch.

BLANCHE. I'm very adaptable—to circumstances.

MITCH. Well, that's a good thing to be. You are visiting Stanley and Stella?

BLANCHE. Stella hasn't been so well lately, and I came down to help her for a while. She's very rundown.

MITCH. You're not—?

BLANCHE. Married? No, no. I'm an old maid schoolteacher!

MITCH. You may teach school but you're certainly not an old maid.

BLANCHE. Thank you, sir! I appreciate your gallantry!

MITCH. So you are in the teaching profession?

BLANCHE. Yes. Ah, yes . . .

MITCH. Grade school or high school or—

STANLEY *(bellowing)*. Mitch!

MITCH. Coming!

BLANCHE. Gracious, what lung-power! . . . I teach high school. In Laurel.

MITCH. What do you teach? What subject?

BLANCHE. Guess!

MITCH. I bet you teach art or music? *(Blanche laughs delicately)* Of course I could be wrong. You might teach arithmetic.

BLANCHE. Never arithmetic, sir; never arithmetic! *(With a laugh)* I don't even know my multiplication tables! No, I have the misfortune of being an English instructor. I attempt to instill a bunch of bobby-soxers and drugstore Romeos with reverence for Hawthorne and Whitman and Poe!

MITCH. I guess that some of them are more interested in other things.

BLANCHE. How very right you are! Their literary heritage is not what most of them treasure above all else! But they're sweet things! And in the spring, it's touching to notice them making their first discovery of love! As if nobody had ever known it before! *(The bathroom door opens and Stella comes out. Blanche continues talking to Mitch)* Oh! Have you finished? Wait—I'll turn on the radio.

*(She turns the knobs on the radio and it begins to play "Wien, Wien, nur du allein." Blanche waltzes to the music with romantic gestures. Mitch is delighted and moves in awkward imitation like a dancing bear.*

*(Stanley stalks fiercely through the portieres into the bedroom. He crosses to the small white radio and snatches it off the table. With a shouted oath, he tosses the instrument out the window.)*

STELLA. *Drunk—drunk—animal thing, you! (She rushes through to the poker table)* All of you—please go home! If any of you have one spark of decency in you—

BLANCHE *(wildly)*. Stella, watch out, he's—

*(Stanley charges after Stella.)*

MEN *(feebly)*. Take it easy, Stanley. Easy, fellow.—Let's all—

STELLA. You lay your hands on me and I'll—

(*She backs out of sight. He advances and disappears. There is the sound of a blow. Stella cries out. Blanche screams and runs into the kitchen. The men rush forward and there is grappling and cursing. Something is overturned with a crash.*)

BLANCHE (*shrilly*). My sister is going to have a baby!

MITCH. This is terrible.

BLANCHE. Lunacy, absolute lunacy!

MITCH. Get him in here, men.

(*Stanley is forced, pinioned by the two men, into the bedroom. He nearly throws them off. Then all at once he subsides and is limp in their grasp.*)

(*They speak quietly and lovingly to him and he leans his face on one of their shoulders.*)

STELLA (*in a high, unnatural voice, out of sight*). I want to go away, I want to go away!

MITCH. Poker shouldn't be played in a house with women.

(*Blanche rushes into the bedroom.*)

BLANCHE. I want my sister's clothes! We'll go to that woman's upstairs!

MITCH. Where is the clothes?

BLANCHE (*opening the closet*). I've got them! (*She rushes through to Stella*) Stella, Stella, precious! Dear, dear little sister, don't be afraid!

(*With her arms around Stella, Blanche guides her to the outside door and upstairs.*)

STANLEY (*dully*). What's the matter; what's happened?

MITCH. You just blew your top, Stan.

PABLO. He's okay, now.

STEVE. Sure, my boy's okay!

MITCH. Put him on the bed and get a wet towel.

PABLO. I think coffee would do him a world of good, now.

STANLEY (*thickly*). I want water.

MITCH. Put him under the shower!

(*The men talk quietly as they lead him to the bathroom.*)

STANLEY. Let the rut go of me, you sons of bitches!

(*Sounds of blows are heard. The water goes on full tilt.*)

STEVE. Let's get quick out of here!

(*They rush to the poker table and sweep up their winnings on their way out.*)

MITCH (*sadly but firmly*). Poker should not be played in a house with women.

(*The door closes on them and the place is still. The Negro entertainers in the bar around the corner play "Paper Doll" slow and blue. After a moment Stanley comes out of the bathroom dripping water and still in his clinging wet polka dot drawers.*)

STANLEY. Stella! (*There is a pause*) My baby doll's left me! (*He breaks into sobs. Then he goes to the phone and dials, still shuddering with sobs*) Eunice? I want my baby! (*He waits a moment; then he hangs up and dials again*) Eunice! I'll keep on ringin' until I talk with my baby!

(*An indistinguishable shrill voice is heard. He hurls phone to floor. Dissonant brass and piano sounds as the rooms dim out to darkness and the outer walls appear in the night light. The "blue piano" plays for a brief interval.*)

(*Finally, Stanley stumbles half-dressed out to the porch and down the wooden steps to the pavement before the building. There he throws back his head like a baying hound and bellows his wife's name: "Stella! Stella, sweetheart! Stella!"*)

STANLEY. Stell-*lahhhhh!*

EUNICE (*calling down from the door of her upper apartment*). Quit that howling out there an' go back to bed!

STANLEY. I want my baby down here. Stella, Stella!

EUNICE. She ain't comin' down so you quit! Or you'll git th' law on you!

STANLEY. Stella!

EUNICE. You can't beat on a woman an' then call 'er back! She won't come! And her goin' t' have a baby! . . . You stinker! You whelp of a Polack, you! I hope they do haul you in and turn the fire hose on you, same as the last time!

STANLEY (*humbly*). Eunice, I want my girl to come down with me!

EUNICE. Hah! (*She slams her door*)

STANLEY (*with heaven-splitting violence*). STELL-LAHHHHH!

(*The low-tone clarinet moans. The door upstairs opens again. Stella slips down the rickety stairs in her robe. Her eyes are glistening with tears and her hair loose about her throat and shoulders. They stare at each other. Then they come together with low animal moans. He falls to his knees on the steps and presses his face to her belly, curving a little with maternity. Her eyes go blind with tenderness as she catches his head and raises him level with her. He snatches the screen door open and lifts her off her feet and bears her into the dark flat.*

*(Blanche comes out on the upper landing in her robe and slips fearfully down the steps.)*

BLANCHE. Where is my little sister? Stella? Stella?

*(She stops before the dark entrance of her sister's flat. Then catches her breath as if struck. She rushes down to the walk before the house. She looks right and left as if for a sanctuary.*

*(The music fades away. Mitch appears from around the corner.)*

MITCH. Miss DuBois?

BLANCHE. Oh!

MITCH. All quiet on the Potomac now?

BLANCHE. She ran downstairs and went back in there with him.

MITCH. Sure she did.

BLANCHE. I'm terrified!

MITCH. Ho-ho! There's nothing to be scared of. They're crazy about each other.

BLANCHE. I'm not used to such—

MITCH. Naw, it's a shame this had to happen when you just got here. But don't take it serious.

BLANCHE. Violence! Is so—

MITCH. Set down on the steps and have a cigarette with me.

BLANCHE. I'm not properly dressed.

MITCH. That don't make no difference in the Quarter.

BLANCHE. Such a pretty silver case.

MITCH. I showed you the inscription, didn't I?

BLANCHE. Yes. *(During the pause she looks up at the sky)* There's so much—so much confusion in the world . . . *(He coughs diffidently)* Thank you for being so kind! I need kindness now.

## SCENE FOUR

*It is early the following morning. There is a confusion of street cries like a choral chant.*

*Stella is lying down in the bedroom. Her face is serene in the early morning sunlight. One hand rests on her belly, rounding slightly with new maternity. From the other dangles a book of colored comics. Her eyes and lips have that almost* narcotized tranquility that is in the faces of Eastern idols.

*The table is sloppy with remains of breakfast and the debris of the preceding night, and Stanley's gaudy pyjamas lie across the threshold of the bathroom. The outside door is slightly ajar on a sky of summer brilliance.*

*Blanche appears at this door. She has spent a sleepless night and her appearance entirely contrasts with Stella's. She presses her knuckles nervously to her lips as she looks through the door, before entering.*

———

BLANCHE. Stella?

STELLA *(stirring lazily)*. Hmmh?

*(Blanche utters a moaning cry and runs into the bedroom, throwing herself down beside Stella in a rush of hysterical tenderness.)*

BLANCHE. Baby, my baby sister!

STELLA *(drawing away from her)*. Blanche, what is the matter with you?

*(Blanche straightens up slowly and stands beside the bed looking down at her sister with knuckles pressed to her lips.)*

BLANCHE. He's left?

STELLA. Stan? Yes.

BLANCHE. Will he be back?

STELLA. He's gone to get the car greased. Why?

BLANCHE. Why! I've been half crazy, Stella! When I found out you'd been insane enough to come back in here after what happened—I started to rush in after you!

STELLA. I'm glad you didn't.

BLANCHE. What were you thinking of? *(Stella makes an indefinite gesture)* Answer me! What? What?

STELLA. Please, Blanche! Sit down and stop yelling.

BLANCHE. All right, Stella. I will repeat the question quietly now. How could you come back in this place last night? Why, you must have slept with him!

*(Stella gets up in a calm and leisurely way.)*

STELLA. Blanche, I'd forgotten how excitable you are. You're making much too much fuss about this.

BLANCHE. Am I?

STELLA. Yes, you are, Blanche. I know how it must have seemed to you and I'm awful sorry it had to happen, but it wasn't anything as serious as you seem to take it. In the first place, when men are drinking and playing poker anything can happen. It's always a powder-keg. He didn't know what he was doing. . . . He was as good as a lamb when I came back and he's really very, very ashamed of himself.

BLANCHE. And that—that makes it all right?

STELLA. No, it isn't all right for anybody to make such a terrible row, but—people do sometimes. Stanley's always smashed things. Why, on our wedding night—soon as we came in here—he snatched off one of my slippers and rushed about the place smashing the light-bulbs with it.

BLANCHE. He did—*what?*

STELLA. He smashed all the light-bulbs with the heel of my slipper! *(She laughs)*

BLANCHE. And you—you *let* him? Didn't *run,* didn't *scream?*

STELLA. I was—sort of—thrilled by it. *(She waits for a moment)* Eunice and you had breakfast?

BLANCHE. Do you suppose I wanted any breakfast?

STELLA. There's some coffee left on the stove.

BLANCHE. You're so—matter of fact about it, Stella.

STELLA. What other can I be? He's taken the radio to get it fixed. It didn't land on the pavement so only one tube was smashed.

BLANCHE. And you are standing there smiling!

STELLA. What do you want me to do?

BLANCHE. Pull yourself together and face the facts.

STELLA. What are they, in your opinion?

BLANCHE. In my opinion? You're married to a madman!

STELLA. No!

BLANCHE. Yes, you are, your fix is worse than mine is! Only you're not being sensible about it. I'm going to *do* something. Get hold of myself and make myself a new life!

STELLA. Yes?

BLANCHE. But you've given in. And that isn't right, you're not old! You can get out.

STELLA *(slowly and emphatically).* I'm not in anything I want to get out of.

BLANCHE *(incredulously).* What—Stella?

STELLA. I said I am not in anything that I have a desire to get out of. Look at the mess in this room! And those empty bottles! They went through two cases last night! He promised this morning that he

was going to quit having these poker parties, but you know how long such a promise is going to keep. Oh, well, it's his pleasure, like mine is movies and bridge. People have got to tolerate each other's habits, I guess.

BLANCHE. I don't understand you. *(Stella turns toward her)* I don't understand your indifference. Is this a Chinese philosophy you've—cultivated?

STELLA. Is what—what?

BLANCHE. This shuffling about and mumbling—"One tube smashed—beer-bottles—mess in the kitchen!"—as if nothing out of the ordinary has happened! *(Stella laughs uncertainly, and picking up the broom, twirls it in her hands)*

BLANCHE. Are you deliberately shaking that thing in my face?

STELLA. No.

BLANCHE. Stop it. Let go of that broom. I won't have you cleaning up for him!

STELLA. Then who's going to do it? Are you?

BLANCHE. I? I!

STELLA. No, I didn't think so.

BLANCHE. Oh, let me think, if only my mind would function! We've got to get hold of some money, that's the way out!

STELLA. I guess that money is always nice to get hold of.

BLANCHE. Listen to me. I have an idea of some kind. *(Shakily she twists a cigarette into her holder)* Do you remember Shep Huntleigh? *(Stella shakes her head)* Of course you remember Shep Huntleigh. I went out with him at college and wore his pin for a while. Well—

STELLA. Well?

BLANCHE. I ran into him last winter. You know I went to Miami during the Christmas holidays?

STELLA. No.

BLANCHE. Well, I did. I took the trip as an investment, thinking I'd meet someone with a million dollars.

STELLA. Did you?

BLANCHE. Yes. I ran into Shep Huntleigh—I ran into him on Biscayne Boulevard, on Christmas Eve, about dusk . . . getting into his car—Cadillac convertible; must have been a block long!

STELLA. I should think it would have been—inconvenient in traffic!

BLANCHE. You've heard of oil-wells?

STELLA. Yes—remotely.

BLANCHE. He has them, all over Texas.

Texas is literally spouting gold in his pockets.

STELLA. My, my.

BLANCHE. Y'know how indifferent I am to money. I think of money in terms of what it does for you. But he could do it, he could certainly do it!

STELLA. Do what, Blanche?

BLANCHE. Why—set us up in a—shop!

STELLA. What kind of a shop?

BLANCHE. Oh, a—shop of some kind! He could do it with half what his wife throws away at the races.

STELLA. He's married?

BLANCHE. Honey, would I be here if the man weren't married? *(Stella laughs a little. Blanche suddenly springs up and crosses to phone. She speaks shrilly)* How do I get Western Union?—Operator! Western Union!

STELLA. That's a dial phone, honey.

BLANCHE. I can't dial, I'm too—

STELLA. Just dial O.

BLANCHE. O?

STELLA. Yes, "O" for Operator! *(Blanche considers a moment; then she puts the phone down)*

BLANCHE. Give me a pencil. Where is a slip of paper? I've got to write it down first—the message, I mean . . . *(She goes to the dressing table, and grabs up a sheet of Kleenex and an eyebrow pencil for writing equipment)* Let me see now . . . *(She bites the pencil)* "Darling Shep. Sister and I are in desperate situation."

STELLA. I beg your pardon!

BLANCHE. "Sister and I in desperate situation. Will explain details later. Would you be interested in—?" *(She bites the pencil again)* "Would you be—interested—in . . ." *(She smashes the pencil on the table and springs up)* You never get anywhere with direct appeals!

STELLA *(with a laugh)*. Don't be so ridiculous, darling!

BLANCHE. But I'll think of something, I've *got* to think of—*some*thing! Don't, don't laugh at me, Stella! Please, please don't—I—I want you to look at the contents of my purse! Here's what's in it! *(She snatches her purse open)* Sixty-five measly cents in coin of the realm!

STELLA *(crossing to bureau)*. Stanley doesn't give me a regular allowance, he likes to pay bills himself, but—this morning he gave me ten dollars to smooth things over. You take five of it, Blanche, and I'll keep the rest.

BLANCHE. Oh, no. No, Stella.

STELLA *(insisting)*. I kno.. ..ow it helps your morale just having a little pocket-money on you.

BLANCHE. No, thank you—I'll take to the streets!

STELLA. Talk sense! How did you happen to get so low on funds?

BLANCHE. Money just goes—it goes places. *(She rubs her forehead)* Sometime today I've got to get hold of a bromo!

STELLA. I'll fix you one now.

BLANCHE. Not yet—I've got to keep thinking!

STELLA. I wish you'd just let things go, at least for a—while . . .

BLANCHE. Stella, I can't live with him! You can, he's your husband. But how could I stay here with him, after last night, with just those curtains between us?

STELLA. Blanche, you saw him at his worst last night.

BLANCHE. On the contrary, I saw him at his best! What such a man has to offer is animal force and he gave a wonderful exhibition of that! But the only way to live with such a man is to—go to bed with him! And that's your job—not mine!

STELLA. After you've rested a little, you'll see it's going to work out. You don't have to worry about anything while you're here. I mean—expenses . . .

BLANCHE. I have to plan for us both, to get us both—out!

STELLA. You take it for granted that I am in something that I want to get out of.

BLANCHE. I take it for granted that you still have sufficient memory of Belle Reve to find this place and these poker players impossible to live with.

STELLA. Well, you're taking entirely too much for granted.

BLANCHE. I can't believe you're in earnest.

STELLA. No?

BLANCHE. I understand how it happened —a little. You saw him in uniform, an officer, not here but—

STELLA. I'm not sure it would have made any difference where I saw him.

BLANCHE. Now don't say it was one of those mysterious electric things between people! If you do I'll laugh in your face.

STELLA. I am not going to say anything more at all about it!

BLANCHE. All right, then, don't!

STELLA. But there are things that happen between a man and a woman in the dark —that sort of make everything else seem —unimportant. *(Pause)*

BLANCHE. What you are talking about is brutal desire—just—Desire!—the name of that rattle-trap streetcar that bangs through the Quarter, up one old narrow street and down another . . .

STELLA. Haven't you ever ridden on that streetcar?

BLANCHE. It brought me here.—Where I'm not wanted and where I'm ashamed to be . . .

STELLA. Then don't you think your superior attitude is a bit out of place?

BLANCHE. I am not being or feeling at all superior, Stella. Believe me I'm not! It's just this. This is how I look at it. A man like that is someone to go out with—once —twice—three times when the devil is in you. But live with? Have a child by?

STELLA. I have told you I love him.

BLANCHE. Then I tremble for you! I just —*tremble* for you. . . .

STELLA. I can't help your trembling if you insist on trembling!

*(There is a pause.)*

BLANCHE. May I—speak—*plainly?*

STELLA. Yes, do. Go ahead. As plainly as you want to.

*(Outside, a train approaches. They are silent till the noise subsides. They are both in the bedroom.*

*(Under cover of the train's noise Stanley enters from outside. He stands unseen by the women, holding some packages in his arms, and overhears their following conversation. He wears an undershirt and grease-stained seersucker pants.)*

BLANCHE. Well—if you'll forgive me— he's *common!*

STELLA. Why, yes, I suppose he is.

BLANCHE. Suppose! You can't have forgotten that much of our bringing up, Stella, that you just *suppose* that any part of a gentleman's in his nature! *Not one particle, no!* Oh, if he was just—*ordinary!* Just *plain*—but good and wholesome, but —*no.* There's something downright—*bestial*—about him! You're hating me saying this, aren't you?

STELLA *(coldly).* Go on and say it all, Blanche.

BLANCHE. He acts like an animal, has an animal's habits! Eats like one, moves like one, talks like one! There's even something —sub-human—something not quite to the stage of humanity yet! Yes, something— ape-like about him, like one of those pictures I've seen in—anthropological studies! Thousands and thousands of years have passed him right by, and there he is— Stanley Kowalski—survivor of the stone age! Bearing the raw meat home from the kill in the jungle! And you—*you* here— *waiting* for him! Maybe he'll strike you or maybe grunt and kiss you! That is, if kisses have been discovered yet! Night falls and the other apes gather! There in the front of the cave, all grunting like him, and swilling and gnawing and hulking! His poker night!—you call it—this party of apes! Somebody growls—some creature snatches at something—the fight is on! *God!* Maybe we are a long way from being made in God's image, but Stella—my sister—there has been *some* progress since then! Such things as art—as poetry and music—such kinds of new light have come into the world since then! In some kinds of people some tenderer feelings have had some little beginning! That we have got to make *grow!* And *cling* to, and hold as our flag! In this dark march toward whatever it is we're approaching. . . . *Don't—don't hang back with the brutes!*

*(Another train passes outside. Stanley hesitates, licking his lips. Then suddenly he turns stealthily about and withdraws through front door. The women are still unaware of his presence. When the train has passed he calls through the closed front door.)*

STANLEY. Hey! Hey, Stella!

STELLA *(who has listened gravely to Blanche).* Stanley!

BLANCHE. Stell, I—

*(But Stella has gone to the front door. Stanley enters casually with his packages.)*

STANLEY. Hiyuh, Stella. Blanche back?

STELLA. Yes, she's back.

STANLEY. Hiyuh, Blanche. *(He grins at her)*

STELLA. You must've got under the car.

STANLEY. Them darn mechanics at Fritz's don't know their ass fr'm— *Hey!* *(Stella has embraced him with both arms, fiercely, and full in the view of Blanche. He laughs and clasps her head to him. Over her head he grins through the curtains at Blanche.*

*(As the lights fade away, with a lingering

brightness on their embrace, the music of the "blue piano" and trumpet and drums is heard.)

## SCENE FIVE

*Blanche is seated in the bedroom fanning herself with a palm leaf as she reads over a just completed letter. Suddenly she bursts into a peal of laughter. Stella is dressing in the bedroom.*

STELLA. What are you laughing at, honey?

BLANCHE. Myself, myself, for being such a liar! I'm writing a letter to Shep. *(She picks up the letter)* "Darling Shep. I am spending the summer on the wing, making flying visits here and there. And who knows, perhaps I shall take a sudden notion to *swoop* down on *Dallas!* How would you feel about that? Ha-ha!" *(She laughs nervously and brightly, touching her throat as if actually talking to Shep)* "Forewarned is forearmed, as they say!"— How does that sound?

STELLA. Uh-huh . . .

BLANCHE *(going on nervously).* "Most of my sister's friends go north in the summer but some have homes on the Gulf and there has been a continued round of entertainments, teas, cocktails, and luncheons—"

*(A disturbance is heard upstairs at the Hubbells' apartment.)*

STELLA. Eunice seems to be having some trouble with Steve.

*(Eunice's voice shouts in terrible wrath.)*

EUNICE. I heard about you and that blonde!

STEVE. That's a damn lie!

EUNICE. You ain't pulling the wool over my eyes! I wouldn't mind if you'd stay down at the Four Deuces, but you always going up.

STEVE. Who ever seen me up?

EUNICE. I seen you chasing her 'round the balcony—I'm gonna call the vice squad!

STEVE. Don't you throw that at me!

EUNICE *(shrieking).* You hit me! I'm gonna call the police!

*(A clatter of aluminum striking a wall is heard, followed by a man's angry roar, shouts and overturned furniture. There is a crash; then a relative hush.)*

BLANCHE *(brightly).* Did he *kill* her?

*(Eunice appears on the steps in daemonic disorder.)*

STELLA. No! She's coming downstairs.

EUNICE. Call the police, I'm going to call the police! *(She rushes around the corner)* *(They laugh lightly. Stanley comes around the corner in his green and scarlet silk bowling shirt. He trots up the steps and bangs into the kitchen. Blanche registers his entrance with nervous gestures.)*

STANLEY. What's a matter with Eun-uss?

STELLA. She and Steve had a row. Has she got the police?

STANLEY. Naw. She's gettin' a drink.

STELLA. That's much more practical!

*(Steve comes down nursing a bruise on his forehead and looks in the door.)*

STEVE. She here?

STANLEY. Naw, naw. At the Four Deuces.

STEVE. That rutting hunk! *(He looks around the corner a bit timidly, then turns with affected boldness and runs after her)*

BLANCHE. I must jot that down in my notebook. Ha-ha! I'm compiling a notebook of quaint little words and phrases I've picked up here.

STANLEY. You won't pick up nothing here you ain't heard before.

BLANCHE. Can I count on that?

STANLEY. You can count on it up to five hundred.

BLANCHE. That's a mighty high number. *(He jerks open the bureau drawer, slams it shut and throws shoes in a corner. At each noise Blanche winces slightly. Finally she speaks)* What sign were you born under?

STANLEY *(while he is dressing).* Sign?

BLANCHE. Astrological sign. I bet you were born under Aries. Aries people are forceful and dynamic. They dote on noise! They love to bang things around! You must have had lots of banging around in the army and now that you're out, you make up for it by treating inanimate objects with such a fury!

*(Stella has been going in and out of closet during this scene. Now she pops her head out of the closet.)*

STELLA. Stanley was born just five minutes after Christmas.

BLANCHE. Capricorn—the Goat!

STANLEY. What sign were *you* born under?

BLANCHE. Oh, my birthday's next month,

the fifteenth of September; that's under Virgo.

STANLEY. What's Virgo?

BLANCHE. Virgo is the Virgin.

STANLEY (*contemptuously*). Hah! (*He advances a little as he knots his tie*) Say, do you happen to know somebody named Shaw?

(*Her face expresses a faint shock. She reaches for the cologne bottle and dampens her handkerchief as she answers carefully.*)

BLANCHE. Why, everybody knows somebody named Shaw!

STANLEY. Well, this somebody named Shaw is under the impression he met you in Laurel, but I figure he must have got you mixed up with some other party because this other party is someone he met at a hotel called the Flamingo.

(*Blanche laughs breathlessly as she touches the cologne-dampened handkerchief to her temples.*)

BLANCHE. I'm afraid he does have me mixed up with this "other party." The Hotel Flamingo is not the sort of establishment I would dare to be seen in!

STANLEY. You know of it?

BLANCHE. Yes, I've seen it and smelled it.

STANLEY. You must've got pretty close if you could smell it.

BLANCHE. The odor of cheap perfume is penetrating.

STANLEY. That stuff you use is expensive?

BLANCHE. Twenty-five dollars an ounce! I'm nearly out. That's just a hint if you want to remember my birthday! (*She speaks lightly but her voice has a note of fear*)

STANLEY. Shaw must've got you mixed up. He goes in and out of Laurel all the time so he can check on it and clear up any mistake.

(*He turns away and crosses to the portieres. Blanche closes her eyes as if to faint. Her hand trembles as she lifts the handkerchief again to her forehead.*

(*Steve and Eunice come around the corner. Steve's arm is around Eunice's shoulder and she is sobbing luxuriously and he is cooing love-words. There is a murmur of thunder as they go slowly upstairs in a tight embrace.*)

STANLEY (*to Stella*). I'll wait for you at the Four Deuces!

STELLA. Hey! Don't I rate one kiss?

STANLEY. Not in front of your sister.

(*He goes out. Blanche rises from her chair. She seems faint; looks about her with an expression of almost panic.*)

BLANCHE. Stella! What have you heard about me?

STELLA. Huh?

BLANCHE. What have people been telling you about me?

STELLA. Telling?

BLANCHE. You haven't heard any—unkind—gossip about me?

STELLA. Why, no, Blanche, of course not!

BLANCHE. Honey, there was—a good deal of talk in Laurel.

STELLA. About *you*, Blanche?

BLANCHE. I wasn't so good the last two years or so, after Belle Reve had started to slip through my fingers.

STELLA. All of us do things we—

BLANCHE. I never was hard or self-sufficient enough. When people are soft—soft people have got to shimmer and glow—they've got to put on soft colors, the colors of butterfly wings, and put a—paper lantern over the light. . . . It isn't enough to be soft. You've got to be soft *and attractive*. And I—I'm fading now! I don't know how much longer I can turn the trick.

(*The afternoon has faded to dusk. Stella goes into the bedroom and turns on the light under the paper lantern. She holds a bottled soft drink in her hand.*)

BLANCHE. Have you been listening to me?

STELLA. I don't listen to you when you are being morbid! (*She advances with the bottled coke*)

BLANCHE (*with abrupt change to gaiety*). Is that coke for me?

STELLA. Not for anyone else!

BLANCHE. Why, you precious thing, you! Is it just coke?

STELLA (*turning*). You mean you want a shot in it!

BLANCHE. Well, honey, a shot never does a coke any harm! Let me! You mustn't wait on me!

STELLA. I like to wait on you, Blanche. It makes it seem more like home. (*She goes into the kitchen, finds a glass and pours a shot of whiskey into it*)

BLANCHE. I have to admit I love to be waited on . . . (*She rushes into the bedroom. Stella goes to her with the glass. Blanche suddenly clutches Stella's free hand with a moaning sound and presses the hand to her lips. Stella is embarrassed by her show of emotion. Blanche speaks in a choked voice)* You're—you're so *good* to me! And I—

STELLA. Blanche.

BLANCHE. I know, I won't! You hate me to talk sentimental! But honey, *believe* I feel things more than I *tell* you! I *won't* stay long! I won't, I *promise* I—

STELLA. Blanche!

BLANCHE *(hysterically).* I won't, I promise, *I'll* go! Go *soon!* I will *really!* I *won't* hang around until he—throws me out . . .

STELLA. Now will you stop talking foolish?

BLANCHE. Yes, honey. Watch how you pour—that fizzy stuff foams over!

*(Blanche laughs shrilly and grabs the glass, but her hand shakes so it almost slips from her grasp. Stella pours the coke into the glass. It foams over and spills. Blanche gives a piercing cry.)*

STELLA *(shocked by the cry).* Heavens!

BLANCHE. Right on my pretty white skirt!

STELLA. Oh . . . Use my hanky. Blot gently.

BLANCHE *(slowly recovering).* I know—gently—gently . . .

STELLA. Did it stain?

BLANCHE. Not a bit. Ha-ha! Isn't that lucky? *(She sits down shakily, taking a grateful drink. She holds the glass in both hands and continues to laugh a little)*

STELLA. Why did you scream like that?

BLANCHE. I don't know why I screamed! *(Continuing nervously)* Mitch—Mitch is coming at seven. I guess I am just feeling nervous about our relations. *(She begins to talk rapidly and breathlessly)* He hasn't gotten a thing but a goodnight kiss, that's all I have given him, Stella. I want his respect. And men don't want anything they get too easy. But on the other hand men lose interest quickly. Especially when the girl is over—thirty. They think a girl over thirty ought to—the vulgar term is—"put out." . . . And I—I'm not "putting out." Of course he—he doesn't know—I mean I haven't informed him—of my real age!

STELLA. Why are you sensitive about your age?

BLANCHE. Because of hard knocks my vanity's been given. What I mean is—he thinks I'm sort of—prim and proper, you know! *(She laughs out sharply)* I want to *deceive* him enough to make him—want me . . .

STELLA. Blanche, do you want *him?*

BLANCHE. I want to *rest!* I want to breathe quietly again! Yes—I *want* Mitch . . . *very badly!* Just think! If it happens! I can leave here and not be anyone's problem . . .

*(Stanley comes around the corner with a drink under his belt.)*

STANLEY *(bawling).* Hey, Steve! Hey, Eunice! Hey, Stella!

*(There are joyous calls from above. Trumpet and drums are heard from around the corner.)*

STELLA *(kissing Blanche impulsively).* It *will* happen!

BLANCHE *(doubtfully).* It will?

STELLA. It *will!* *(She goes across into the kitchen, looking back at Blanche)* It will, honey, it will. . . . But don't take another drink! *(Her voice catches as she goes out the door to meet her husband)*

*(Blanche sinks faintly back in her chair with her drink. Eunice shrieks with laughter and runs down the steps. Steve bounds after her with goat-like screeches and chases her around corner. Stanley and Stella twine arms as they follow, laughing. (Dusk settles deeper. The music from the Four Deuces is slow and blue.)*

BLANCHE. Ah, me, ah, me, ah, me . . .

*(Her eyes fall shut and the palm leaf fan drops from her fingers. She slaps her hand on the chair arm a couple of times. There is a little glimmer of lightning about the building.*

*(A Young Man comes along the street and rings the bell.)*

BLANCHE. Come in.

*(The Young Man appears through the portieres. She regards him with interest.)*

BLANCHE. Well, well! What can I do for *you?*

YOUNG MAN. I'm collecting for *The Evening Star.*

BLANCHE. I didn't know that stars took up collections.

YOUNG MAN. It's the paper.

BLANCHE. I know, I was joking—feebly! Will you—have a drink?

YOUNG MAN. No, ma'am. No, thank you, I can't drink on the job.

BLANCHE. Oh, well, now, let's see. . . . No, I don't have a dime! I'm not the lady of the house. I'm her sister from Mississippi. I'm one of those poor relations you've heard about.

YOUNG MAN. That's all right. I'll drop by later. (*He starts to go out. She approaches a little*)

BLANCHE. Hey! (*He turns back shyly. She puts a cigarette in a long holder*) Could you give me a light? (*She crosses toward him. They meet at the door between the two rooms*)

YOUNG MAN. Sure. (*He takes out a lighter*) This doesn't always work.

BLANCHE. It's temperamental? (*It flares*) Ah!—thank you. (*He starts away again*) Hey! (*He turns again, still more uncertainly. She goes close to him*) Uh—what time is it?

YOUNG MAN. Fifteen of seven, ma'am.

BLANCHE. So late? Don't you just love these long rainy afternoons in New Orleans when an hour isn't just an hour—but a little piece of eternity dropped into your hands—and who knows what to do with it? (*She touches his shoulders*) You—uh—didn't get wet in the rain?

YOUNG MAN. No, ma'am. I stepped inside.

BLANCHE. In a drugstore? And had a soda?

YOUNG MAN. Uh-huh.

BLANCHE. Chocolate?

YOUNG MAN. No, ma'am. Cherry.

BLANCHE (*laughing*). Cherry!

YOUNG MAN. A cherry soda.

BLANCHE. You make my mouth water. (*She touches his cheek lightly, and smiles. Then she goes to the trunk*)

YOUNG MAN. Well, I'd better be going—

BLANCHE. (*stopping him*). Young man! (*He turns. She takes a large, gossamer scarf from the trunk and drapes it about her shoulders.*)

(*In the ensuing pause, the "blue piano" is heard. It continues through the rest of this scene and the opening of the next. The young man clears his throat and looks yearningly at the door.*)

Young man! Young, young, young man! Has anyone ever told you that you look like a young Prince out of the Arabian Nights?

(*The Young Man laughs uncomfortably and stands like a bashful kid. Blanche speaks softly to him.*)

Well, you do, honey lamb! Come here. I want to kiss you, just once, softly and sweetly on your mouth!

(*Without waiting for him to accept, she crosses quickly to him and presses her lips to his.*)

Now run along, now, quickly! It would be nice to keep you, but I've got to be good—and keep my hands off children.

(*He stares at her a moment. She opens the door for him and blows a kiss at him as he goes down the steps with a dazed look. She stands there a little dreamily after he has disappeared. Then Mitch appears around the corner with a bunch of roses.*)

BLANCHE (*gaily*). Look who's coming! My Rosenkavalier! Bow to me first . . . now present them! Ahhhh—Merciiii!

(*She looks at him over them, coquettishly pressing them to her lips. He beams at her self-consciously.*)

## SCENE SIX

*It is about two A.M. on the same evening. The outer wall of the building is visible. Blanche and Mitch come in. The utter exhaustion which only a neurasthenic personality can know is evident in Blanche's voice and manner. Mitch is stolid but depressed. They have probably been out to the amusement park on Lake Pontchartrain, for Mitch is bearing, upside down, a plaster statuette of Mae West, the sort of prize won at shooting-galleries and carnival games of chance.*

---

BLANCHE (*stopping lifelessly at the steps*). Well—(*Mitch laughs uneasily*) Well . . .

MITCH. I guess it must be pretty late—and you're tired.

BLANCHE. Even the hot tamale man has deserted the street, and he hangs on till the end. (*Mitch laughs uneasily again*) How will you get home?

MITCH. I'll walk over to Bourbon and catch an owl-car.

BLANCHE (*laughing grimly*). Is that streetcar named Desire still grinding along the tracks at this hour?

MITCH (*heavily*). I'm afraid you haven't gotten much fun out of this evening, Blanche.

BLANCHE. I spoiled it for *you*.

MITCH. No, you didn't, but I felt all the time that I wasn't giving you much—entertainment.

BLANCHE. I simply couldn't rise to the occasion. That was all. I don't think I've ever tried so hard to be gay and made such a dismal mess of it. I get ten points for trying!—I *did* try.

MITCH. Why did you try if you didn't feel like it, Blanche?

BLANCHE. I was just obeying the law of nature.

MITCH. Which law is that?

BLANCHE. The one that says the lady must entertain the gentleman—or no dice! See if you can locate my door-key in this purse. When I'm so tired my fingers are all thumbs!

MITCH *(rooting in her purse)*. This it?

BLANCHE. No, honey, that's the key to my trunk which I must soon be packing.

MITCH. You mean you are leaving here soon?

BLANCHE. I've outstayed my welcome.

MITCH. This it?

*(The music fades away.)*

BLANCHE. Eureka! Honey, you open the door while I take a last look at the sky. *(She leans on the porch rail. He opens the door and stands awkwardly behind her)* I'm looking for the Pleiades, the Seven Sisters, but these girls are not out tonight. Oh, yes they are, there they are! God bless them! All in a bunch going home from their little bridge party. . . . Y' get the door open? Good boy! I guess you—want to go now . . .

*(He shuffles and coughs a little.)*

MITCH. Can I—uh—kiss you—good-night?

BLANCHE. Why do you always ask me if you may?

MITCH. I don't know whether you want me to or not.

BLANCHE. Why should you be so doubtful?

MITCH. That night when we parked by the lake and I kissed you, you—

BLANCHE. Honey, it wasn't the kiss I objected to. I liked the kiss very much. It was the other little—familiarity—that I—felt obliged to—discourage. . . . I didn't resent it! Not a bit in the world! In fact, I was somewhat flattered that you—desired me! But, honey, you know as well as I do that a single girl, a girl alone in the world, has got to keep a firm hold on her emotions or she'll be lost!

MITCH *(solemnly)*. Lost?

BLANCHE. I guess you are used to girls that like to be lost. The kind that get lost immediately, on the first date!

MITCH. I like you to be exactly the way that you are, because in all my—experience—I have never known anyone like you.

*(Blanche looks at him gravely; then she bursts into laughter and then claps a hand to her mouth.)*

MITCH. Are you laughing at me?

BLANCHE. No, honey. The lord and lady of the house have not yet returned, so come in. We'll have a night-cap. Let's leave the lights off. Shall we?

MITCH. You just—do what you want to.

*(Blanche precedes him into the kitchen. The outer wall of the building disappears and the interiors of the two rooms can be dimly seen.)*

BLANCHE *(remaining in the first room)*. The other room's more comfortable—go on in. This crashing around in the dark is my search for some liquor.

MITCH. You want a drink?

BLANCHE. I want *you* to have a drink! You have been so anxious and solemn all evening, and so have I; we have both been anxious and solemn and now for these few last remaining moments of our lives together—I want to create—*joie de vivre!* I'm lighting a candle.

MITCH. That's good.

BLANCHE. We are going to be very Bohemian. We are going to pretend that we are sitting in a little artists' cafe on the Left Bank in Paris! *(She lights a candle stub and puts it in a bottle)* Je suis la Dame aux Camellias! Vous êtes—Armand! Understand French?

MITCH *(heavily)*. Naw. Naw, I—

BLANCHE. *Voulez-vous couchez avec moi ce soir? Vous ne comprenez pas? Ah, quelle dommage!*—I mean it's a damned good thing. . . . I've found some liquor! Just enough for two shots without any dividends, honey . . .

MITCH *(heavily)*. That's—good.

*(She enters the bedroom with the drinks and the candle.)*

BLANCHE. Sit down! Why don't you take off your coat and loosen your collar?

MITCH. I better leave it on.

BLANCHE. No. I want you to be comfortable.

MITCH. I am ashamed of the way I perspire. My shirt is sticking to me.

BLANCHE. Perspiration is healthy. If people didn't perspire they would die in five minutes. *(She takes his coat from him)* This is a nice coat. What kind of material is it?

MITCH. They call that stuff alpaca.

BLANCHE. Oh. Alpaca.

MITCH. It's very lightweight alpaca.

BLANCHE. Oh. Lightweight alpaca.

MITCH. I don't like to wear a wash-coat even in summer because I sweat through it.

BLANCHE. Oh.

MITCH. And it don't look neat on me. A man with a heavy build has got to be careful of what he puts on him so he don't look too clumsy.

BLANCHE. You are not too heavy.

MITCH. You don't think I am?

BLANCHE. You are not the delicate type. You have a massive bone-structure and a very imposing physique.

MITCH. Thank you. Last Christmas I was given a membership to the New Orleans Athletic Club.

BLANCHE. Oh, good.

MITCH. It was the finest present I ever was given. I work out there with the weights and I swim and I keep myself fit. When I started there, I was getting soft in the belly but now my belly is hard. It is so hard now that a man can punch me in the belly and it don't hurt me. Punch me! Go on! See? *(She pokes lightly at him)*

BLANCHE. Gracious. *(Her hand touches her chest)*

MITCH. Guess how much I weigh, Blanche?

BLANCHE. Oh, I'd say in the vicinity of— one hundred and eighty?

MITCH. Guess again.

BLANCHE. Not that much?

MITCH. No. More.

BLANCHE. Well, you're a tall man and you can carry a good deal of weight without looking awkward.

MITCH. I weigh two hundred and seven pounds and I'm six feet one and one half inches tall in my bare feet—without shoes on. And that is what I weigh stripped.

BLANCHE. Oh, my goodness, me! It's awe-inspiring.

MITCH *(embarrassed)*. My weight is not a very interesting subject to talk about. *(He hesitates for a moment)* What's yours?

BLANCHE. My weight?

MITCH. Yes.

BLANCHE. Guess!

MITCH. Let me lift you.

BLANCHE. Samson! Go on, lift me. *(He comes behind her and puts his hands on her waist and raises her lightly off the ground)* Well?

MITCH. You are light as a feather.

BLANCHE. Ha-ha! *(He lowers her but keeps his hands on her waist. Blanche speaks with an affectation of demureness)* You may release me now.

MITCH. Huh?

BLANCHE *(gaily)*. I said unhand me, sir. *(He fumblingly embraces her. Her voice sounds gently reproving)* Now, Mitch. Just because Stanley and Stella aren't at home is no reason why you shouldn't behave like a gentleman.

MITCH. Just give me a slap whenever I step out of bounds.

BLANCHE. That won't be necessary. You're a natural gentleman, one of the very few that are left in the world. I don't want you to think that I am severe and old maid schoolteacherish or anything like that. It's just—well—

MITCH. Huh?

BLANCHE. I guess it is just that I have— old-fashioned ideals! *(She rolls her eyes, knowing he cannot see her face. Mitch goes to the front door. There is a considerable silence between them. Blanche sighs and Mitch coughs self-consciously)*

MITCH *(finally)*. Where's Stanley and Stella tonight?

BLANCHE. They have gone out. With Mr. and Mrs. Hubbell upstairs.

MITCH. Where did they go?

BLANCHE. I think they were planning to go to a midnight prevue at Loew's State.

MITCH. We should all go out together some night.

BLANCHE. No. That wouldn't be a good plan.

MITCH. Why not?

BLANCHE. You are an old friend of Stanley's?

MITCH. We was together in the Two-forty-first.

BLANCHE. I guess he talks to you frankly?

MITCH. Sure.

BLANCHE. Has he talked to you about me?

MITCH. Oh—not very much.

BLANCHE. The way you say that, I suspect that he has.

MITCH. No, he hasn't said much.

BLANCHE. But what he *has* said. What would you say his attitude toward me was?

MITCH. Why do you want to ask that?

BLANCHE. Well—

MITCH. Don't you get along with him?

BLANCHE. What do you think?

MITCH. I don't think he understands you.

BLANCHE. That is putting it mildly. If it weren't for Stella about to have a baby, I wouldn't be able to endure things here.

MITCH. He isn't—nice to you?

BLANCHE. He is insufferably rude. Goes out of his way to offend me.

MITCH. In what way, Blanche?

BLANCHE. Why, in every conceivable way.

MITCH. I'm surprised to hear that.

BLANCHE. Are you?

MITCH. Well, I—don't see how anybody could be rude to you.

BLANCHE. It's really a pretty frightful situation. You see, there's no privacy here. There's just these portieres between the two rooms at night. He stalks through the rooms in his underwear at night. And I have to ask him to close the bathroom door. That sort of commonness isn't necessary. You probably wonder why I don't move out. Well, I'll tell you frankly. A teacher's salary is barely sufficient for her living-expenses. I didn't save a penny last year and so I had to come here for the summer. That's why I have to put up with my sister's husband. And he has to put up with me, apparently so much against his wishes. . . . Surely he must have told you how much he hates me!

MITCH. I don't think he hates you.

BLANCHE. He hates me. Or why would he insult me? The first time I laid eyes on him I thought to myself, that man is my executioner! That man will destroy me, unless—

MITCH. Blanche—

BLANCHE. Yes, honey?

MITCH. Can I ask you a question?

BLANCHE. Yes. What?

MITCH. How old are you?

*(She makes a nervous gesture.)*

BLANCHE. Why do you want to know?

MITCH. I talked to my mother about you and she said, "How old is Blanche?" And I wasn't able to tell her. *(There is another pause)*

BLANCHE. You talked to your mother about me?

MITCH. Yes.

BLANCHE. Why?

MITCH. I told my mother how nice you were, and I liked you.

BLANCHE. Were you sincere about that?

MITCH. You know I was.

BLANCHE. Why did your mother want to know my age?

MITCH. Mother is sick.

BLANCHE. I'm sorry to hear it. Badly?

MITCH. She won't live long. Maybe just a few months.

BLANCHE. Oh.

MITCH. She worries because I'm not settled.

BLANCHE. Oh.

MITCH. She wants me to be settled down before she—*(His voice is hoarse and he clears his throat twice, shuffling nervously around with his hands in and out of his pockets)*

BLANCHE. You love her very much, don't you?

MITCH. Yes.

BLANCHE. I think you have a great capacity for devotion. You will be lonely when she passes on, won't you? *(Mitch clears his throat and nods)* I understand what that is.

MITCH. To be lonely?

BLANCHE. I loved someone, too, and the person I loved I lost.

MITCH. Dead? *(She crosses to the window and sits on the sill, looking out. She pours herself another drink)* A man?

BLANCHE. He was a boy, just a boy, when I was a very young girl. When I was sixteen, I made the discovery—love. All at once and much, much too completely. It was like you suddenly turned a blinding light on something that had always been half in shadow, that's how it struck the world for me. But I was unlucky. Deluded. There was something different about the boy, a nervousness, a softness and tenderness which wasn't like a man's, although he wasn't the least bit effeminate looking—still—that thing was there. . . . He came to me for help. I didn't know that. I didn't find out anything till after our marriage when we'd run away and come back and all I knew was I'd failed him in some mysterious way and wasn't able to give the help he needed but couldn't speak of! He was in the quicksands and clutching at me—but I wasn't holding him out, I was slipping in with him! I didn't know that. I didn't know anything except I loved him unendurably but without being able to help him or help myself. Then I found out. In the worst of all possible ways. By coming suddenly into a room that I thought was empty—which wasn't empty, but had two people in it . . . the boy I had married and an older man who had been his friend for years . . .

*(A locomotive is heard approaching outside. She claps her hands to her ears and crouches over. The headlight of the locomotive glares into the room as it thunders past. As the noise recedes she straightens slowly and continues speaking.)*

Afterwards we pretended that nothing had been discovered. Yes, the three of us drove out to Moon Lake Casino, very drunk and laughing all the way.

*(Polka music sounds, in a minor key faint with distance.)*

We danced the Varsouviana! Suddenly in the middle of the dance the boy I had married broke away from me and ran out of the casino. A few moments later—a shot!

*(The Polka stops abruptly.)*

*(Blanche rises stiffly. Then, the Polka resumes in a major key.)*

I ran out—all did!—all ran and gathered about the terrible thing at the edge of the lake! I couldn't get near for the crowding. Then somebody caught my arm. "Don't go any closer! Come back! You don't want to see!" See? See what! Then I heard voices say—Allan! Allan! The Grey boy! He'd stuck the revolver into his mouth, and fired—so that the back of his head had been—blown away!

*(She sways and covers her face.)*

It was because—on the dance-floor—unable to stop myself—I'd suddenly said—"I saw! I know! You disgust me . . ." And then the searchlight which had been turned on the world was turned off again and never for one moment since has there been any light that's stronger than this—kitchen—candle . . .

*(Mitch gets up awkwardly and moves toward her a little. The Polka music increases. Mitch stands beside her.)*

MITCH *(drawing her slowly into his arms).* You need somebody. And I need somebody, too. Could it be—you and me, Blanche?

*(She stares at him vacantly for a moment. Then with a soft cry huddles in his embrace. She makes a sobbing effort to speak but the words won't come. He kisses her forehead and her eyes and finally her lips. The Polka tune fades out. Her breath is drawn and released in long, grateful sobs.)*

BLANCHE. Sometimes—there's God—so quickly!

## SCENE SEVEN

*It is late afternoon in mid-September.*

*The portieres are open and a table is set for a birthday supper, with cake and flowers.*

*Stella is completing the decorations as Stanley comes in.*

———

STANLEY. What's all this stuff for?

STELLA. Honey, it's Blanche's birthday.

STANLEY. She here?

STELLA. In the bathroom.

STANLEY *(mimicking).* "Washing out some things"?

STELLA. I reckon so.

STANLEY. How long she been in there?

STELLA. All afternoon.

STANLEY *(mimicking).* "Soaking in a hot tub"?

STELLA. Yes.

STANLEY. Temperature 100 on the nose, and she soaks herself in a hot tub.

STELLA. She says it cools her off for the evening.

STANLEY. And you run out an' get her cokes, I suppose? And serve 'em to Her Majesty in the tub? *(Stella shrugs)* Set down here a minute.

STELLA. Stanley, I've got things to do.

STANLEY. Set down! I've got th' dope on your big sister, Stella.

STELLA. Stanley, stop picking on Blanche.

STANLEY. That girl calls *me* common!

STELLA. Lately you been doing all you can think of to rub her the wrong way, Stanley, and Blanche is sensitive and you've got to realize that Blanche and I grew up under very different circumstances than you did.

STANLEY. So I been told. And told and

told and told! You know she's been feeding us a pack of lies here?

STELLA. No, I don't, and—

STANLEY. Well, she has, however. But
now the cat's out of the bag! I found out
some things!

STELLA. What—things?

STANLEY. Things I already suspected.
But now I got proof from the most reliable sources—which I have checked on!
(*Blanche is singing in the bathroom a saccharine popular ballad which is used con-
trapuntally with Stanley's speech.*)

STELLA (*to Stanley*). Lower your voice!

STANLEY. Some canary-bird, huh!

STELLA. Now please tell me quietly what
you think you've found out about my sister.

STANLEY. Lie Number One: All this
squeamishness she puts on! You should
just know the line she's been feeding to
Mitch. He thought she had never been
more than kissed by a fellow! But Sister
Blanche is no lily! Ha-ha! Some lily she is!

STELLA. What have you heard and who
from?

STANLEY. Our supply-man down at the
plant has been going through Laurel for
years and he knows all about her and everybody else in the town of Laurel knows
all about her. She is as famous in Laurel
as if she was the President of the United
States, only she is not respected by any
party! This supply-man stops at a hotel
called the Flamingo.

BLANCHE (*singing blithely*). "Say, it's
only a paper moon, Sailing over a cardboard sea—But it wouldn't be make-believe If you believed in me!"

STELLA. What about the—Flamingo?

STANLEY. She stayed there, too.

STELLA. My sister lived at Belle Reve.

STANLEY. This is after the home-place
had slipped through her lily-white fingers!
She moved to the Flamingo! A second-
class hotel which has the advantage of not
interfering in the private social life of the
personalities there! The Flamingo is used
to all kinds of goings-on. But even the
management of the Flamingo was impressed by Dame Blanche! In fact they
was so impressed by Dame Blanche that
they requested her to turn in her room-
key—for permanently! This happened a
couple of weeks before she showed here.

BLANCHE (*singing*). "It's a Barnum and

Bailey world, Just as phony as it can
be—

But it wouldn't be make-believe If you
believed in me!"

STELLA. What—contemptible—lies!

STANLEY. Sure, I can see how you would
be upset by this. She pulled the wool over
your eyes as much as Mitch's!

STELLA. It's pure invention! There's not
a word of truth in it and if I were a man
and this creature had dared to invent such
things in my presence—

BLANCHE (*singing*). "Without your love,
It's a honky-tonk parade!

Without your love,

It's a melody played In a penny ar-
cade . . ."

STANLEY. Honey, I told you I thoroughly checked on these stories! Now wait
till I'm finished. The trouble with Dame
Blanche was that she couldn't put on her
act any more in Laurel! They got wised
up after two or three dates with her and
then they quit, and she goes on to another,
the same old line, same old act, same old
hooey! But the town was too small for
this to go on forever! And as time went
by she became a town character. Regarded
as not just different but downright loco—
nuts. (*Stella draws back*) And for the last
year or two she has been washed up like
poison. That's why she's here this summer, visiting royalty, putting on all this
act—because she's practically told by the
mayor to get out of town! Yes, did you
know there was an army camp near Laurel and your sister's was one of the places
called "Out-of-Bounds"?

BLANCHE. "It's only a paper moon, Just
as phony as it can be—

But it wouldn't be make-believe If you
believed in me!"

STANLEY. Well, so much for her being
such a refined and particular type of girl.
Which brings us to Lie Number Two.

STELLA. I don't want to hear any more!

STANLEY. She's not going back to teach
school! In fact I am willing to bet you
that she never had no idea of returning to
Laurel! She didn't resign temporarily from
the high school because of her nerves! No,
siree, Bob! She didn't. They kicked her
out of that high school before the spring
term ended—and I hate to tell you the reason that step was taken! A seventeen-year-
old boy—she'd gotten mixed up with!

BLANCHE. "It's a Barnum and Bailey

world, Just as phony as it can be—"
*(In the bathroom the water goes on loud;
little breathless cries and peals of laughter
are heard as if a child were frolicking in
the tub.)*

STELLA. This is making me—sick!

STANLEY. The boy's dad learned about it
and got in touch with the high school
superintendent. Boy, oh, boy, I'd like to
have been in that office when Dame
Blanche was called on the carpet! I'd like
to have seen her trying to squirm out of
that one! But they had her on the hook
good and proper that time and she knew
that the jig was all up! They told her she
better move on to some fresh territory.
Yep, it was practickly a town ordinance
passed against her!

*(The bathroom door is opened and
Blanche thrusts her head out, holding a
towel about her hair.)*

BLANCHE. Stella!

STELLA *(faintly)*. Yes, Blanche?

BLANCHE. Give me another bath-towel
to dry my hair with. I've just washed it.

STELLA. Yes, Blanche. *(She crosses in a
dazed way from the kitchen to the bathroom door with a towel)*

BLANCHE. What's the matter, honey?

STELLA. Matter? Why?

BLANCHE. You have such a strange expression on your face!

STELLA. Oh—*(She tries to laugh)* I guess
I'm a little tired!

BLANCHE. Why don't you bathe, too,
soon as I get out?

STANLEY *(calling from the kitchen)*.
How soon is that going to be?

BLANCHE. Not so terribly long! Possess
your soul in patience!

STANLEY. It's not my soul, it's my kidneys I'm worried about!

*(Blanche slams the door. Stanley laughs
harshly. Stella comes slowly back into the
kitchen.)*

STANLEY. Well, what do you think of it?

STELLA. I don't believe all of those stories
and I think your supply-man was mean
and rotten to tell them. It's possible that
some of the things he said are partly true.
There are things about my sister I don't
approve of—things that caused sorrow at
home. She was always—flighty!

STANLEY. Flighty!

STELLA. But when she was young, very
young, she married a boy who wrote poetry. . . . He was extremely good-looking.
I think Blanche didn't just love him but
worshipped the ground he walked on!
Adored him and thought him almost too
fine to be human! But then she found
out—

STANLEY. What?

STELLA. This beautiful and talented
young man was a degenerate. Didn't your
supply-man give you that information?

STANLEY. All we discussed was recent
history. That must have been a pretty long
time ago.

STELLA. Yes, it was—a pretty long time
ago . . .

*(Stanley comes up and takes her by the
shoulders rather gently. She gently withdraws from him. Automatically she starts
sticking little pink candles in the birthday
cake.)*

STANLEY. How many candles you putting in that cake?

STELLA. I'll stop at twenty-five.

STANLEY. Is company expected?

STELLA. We asked Mitch to come over
for cake and ice-cream.

*(Stanley looks a little uncomfortable. He
lights a cigarette from the one he has just
finished.)*

STANLEY. I wouldn't be expecting Mitch
over tonight.

*(Stella pauses in her occupation with
candles and looks slowly around at Stanley.)*

STELLA. *Why?*

STANLEY. Mitch is a buddy of mine. We
were in the same outfit together—Two-
forty-first Engineers. We work in the same
plant and now on the same bowling team.
You think I could face him if—

STELLA. Stanley Kowalski, did you—did
you repeat what that—?

STANLEY. You're goddam right I told
him! I'd have that on my conscience the
rest of my life if I knew all that stuff and
let my best friend get caught!

STELLA. Is Mitch through with her?

STANLEY. Wouldn't you be if—?

STELLA. I said, *Is Mitch through with
her?*

*(Blanche's voice is lifted again, serenely as
a bell. She sings "But it wouldn't be make
believe if you believed in me.")*

STANLEY. No, I don't think he's necessarily through with her—just wised up!

STELLA. Stanley, she thought Mitch was
—going to—going to marry her. I was
hoping so, too.

STANLEY. Well, he's not going to marry her. Maybe he *was,* but he's not going to jump in a tank with a school of sharks— now! *(He rises)* Blanche! Oh, Blanche! Can I please get in my bathroom? *(There is a pause)*

BLANCHE. Yes, indeed, sir! Can you wait one second while I dry?

STANLEY. Having waited one hour I guess one second ought to pass in a hurry.

STELLA. And she hasn't got her job? Well, what will she do!

STANLEY. She's not stayin' here after Tuesday. You know that, don't you? Just to make sure I bought her ticket myself. A bus-ticket!

STELLA. In the first place, Blanche wouldn't go on a bus.

STANLEY. She'll go on a bus and like it.

STELLA. No, she won't, no, she won't, Stanley!

STANLEY. *She'll go!* Period. P.S. She'll go *Tuesday!*

STELLA *(slowly).* What'll — she — do? What on earth will she—*do!*

STANLEY. Her future is mapped out for her.

STELLA. What do you mean?

*(Blanche sings.)*

STANLEY. Hey, canary bird! Toots! Get *OUT* of the *BATHROOM!*

*(The bathroom door flies open and Blanche emerges with a gay peal of laughter, but as Stanley crosses past her, a frightened look appears in her face, almost a look of panic. He doesn't look at her but slams the bathroom door shut as he goes in.)*

BLANCHE *(snatching up a hair-brush).* Oh, I feel so good after my long, hot bath, I feel so good and cool and—rested!

STELLA *(sadly and doubtfully from the kitchen).* Do you, Blanche?

BLANCHE *(brushing her hair vigorously).* Yes, I do, so refreshed! *(She tinkles her highball glass)* A hot bath and a long, cold drink always give me a brand new outlook on life! *(She looks through the portieres at Stella, standing between them, and slowly stops brushing)* Something has happened!—What is it?

STELLA *(turning away quickly).* Why, nothing has happened, Blanche.

BLANCHE. You're lying! Something has! *(She stares fearfully at Stella, who pretends to be busy at the table. The distant piano goes into a hectic breakdown.)*

## SCENE EIGHT

*Three-quarters of an hour later.*

*The view through the big windows is fading gradually into a still-golden dusk. A torch of sunlight blazes on the side of a big water-tank or oil-drum across the empty lot toward the business district which is now pierced by pinpoints of lighted windows or windows reflecting the sunset.*

*The three people are completing a dismal birthday supper. Stanley looks sullen. Stella is embarrassed and sad.*

*Blanche has a tight, artificial smile on her drawn face. There is a fourth place at the table which is left vacant.*

———

BLANCHE *(suddenly).* Stanley, tell us a joke, tell us a funny story to make us all laugh. I don't know what's the matter, we're all so solemn. Is it because I've been stood up by my beau? *(Stella laughs feebly)* It's the first time in my entire experience with men, and I've had a good deal of all sorts, that I've actually been stood up by anybody! Ha-ha! I don't know how to take it. . . . Tell us a funny little story, Stanley! Something to help us out.

STANLEY. I didn't think you liked my stories, Blanche.

BLANCHE. I like them when they're amusing but not indecent.

STANLEY. I don't know any refined enough for your taste.

BLANCHE. Then let me tell one.

STELLA. Yes, you tell one, Blanche. You used to know lots of good stories.

*(The music fades.)*

BLANCHE. Let me see, now. . . . I must run through my repertoire! Oh, yes—I love parrot stories! Do you all like parrot stories? Well, this one's about the old maid and the parrot. This old maid, she had a parrot that cursed a blue streak and knew more vulgar expressions than Mr. Kowalski!

STANLEY. Huh.

BLANCHE. And the only way to hush the parrot up was to put the cover back on its cage so it would think it was night and go back to sleep. Well, one morning the old maid had just uncovered the parrot for the day—when who should she see coming up the front walk but the preacher! Well, she rushed back to the parrot and slipped the cover back on the cage and then she let in the preacher. And the parrot was perfectly still, just as quiet as a mouse, but just as she was asking the preacher how much sugar he wanted in his coffee—the parrot broke the silence with a loud—*(She whistles)*—and said— "God *damn*, but that was a short day!" *(She throws back her head and laughs. Stella also makes an ineffectual effort to seem amused. Stanley pays no attention to the story but reaches way over the table to spear his fork into the remaining chop which he eats with his fingers.)*

BLANCHE. Apparently Mr. Kowalski was not amused.

STELLA. Mr. Kowalski is too busy making a pig of himself to think of anything else!

STANLEY. That's right, baby.

STELLA. Your face and your fingers are disgustingly greasy. Go and wash up and then help me clear the table.
*(He hurls a plate to the floor.)*

STANLEY. That's how I'll clear the table! *(He seizes her arm)* Don't ever talk that way to me! "Pig—Polack—disgusting— vulgar—greasy!"—them kind of words have been on your tongue and your sister's too much around here! What do you two think you are? A pair of queens? Remember what Huey Long said—"Every Man Is a King!" And I am the king around here, so don't forget it! *(He hurls a cup and saucer to the floor)* My place is cleared! You want me to clear your places? *(Stella begins to cry weakly. Stanley stalks out on the porch and lights a cigarette.*
*(The Negro entertainers around the corner are heard.)*

BLANCHE. What happened while I was bathing? What did he tell you, Stella?

STELLA. Nothing, nothing, nothing!

BLANCHE. I think he told you something about Mitch and me! You know why Mitch didn't come but you won't tell me! *(Stella shakes her head helplessly)* I'm going to call him!

STELLA. I wouldn't call him, Blanche.

BLANCHE. I am, I'm going to call him on the phone.

STELLA *(miserably)*. I wish you wouldn't.

BLANCHE. I intend to be given some explanation from someone!
*(She rushes to the phone in the bedroom. Stella goes out on the porch and stares re-*proachfully at her husband. He grunts and turns away from her.)*

STELLA. I hope you're pleased with your doings. I never had so much trouble swallowing food in my life, looking at that girl's face and the empty chair! *(She cries quietly)*

BLANCHE *(at the phone)*. Hello. Mr. Mitchell, please. . . . Oh. . . . I would like to leave a number if I may. Magnolia 9047. And say it's important to call. . . . Yes, very important. . . . Thank you. *(She remains by the phone with a lost, frightened look)*
*(Stanley turns slowly back toward his wife and takes her clumsily in his arms.)*

STANLEY. Stell, it's gonna be all right after she goes and after you've had the baby. It's gonna be all right again between you and me the way that it was. You remember that way that it was? Them nights we had together? God, honey, it's gonna be sweet when we can make noise in the night the way that we used to and get the colored lights going with nobody's sister behind the curtains to hear us! *(Their upstairs neighbors are heard in bellowing laughter at something. Stanley chuckles)* Steve an' Eunice. . . .

STELLA. Come on back in. *(She returns to the kitchen and starts lighting the candles on the white cake)* Blanche?

BLANCHE. Yes. *(She returns from the bedroom to the table in the kitchen)* Oh, those pretty, pretty little candles! Oh, don't burn them, Stella.

STELLA. I certainly will.
*(Stanley comes back in.)*

BLANCHE. You ought to save them for baby's birthdays. Oh, I hope candles are going to glow in his life and I hope that his eyes are going to be like candles, like two blue candles lighted in a white cake!

STANLEY *(sitting down)*. What poetry!

BLANCHE *(she pauses reflectively for a moment)*. I shouldn't have called him.

STELLA. There's lots of things could have happened.

BLANCHE. There's no excuse for it, Stella. I don't have to put up with insults. I won't be taken for granted.

STANLEY. Goddamn, it's hot in here with the steam from the bathroom.

BLANCHE. I've said I was sorry three times. *(The piano fades out)* I take hot baths for my nerves. Hydro-therapy, they call it. You healthy Polack, without a nerve in your body, of course you don't know what anxiety feels like!

STANLEY. I am not a Polack. People from Poland are Poles, not Polacks. But what I am is a one hundred percent American, born and raised in the greatest country on earth and proud as hell of it, so don't ever call me a Polack.

(*The phone rings. Blanche rises expectantly.*)

BLANCHE. Oh, that's for me, I'm sure.

STANLEY. *I'm* not sure. Keep your seat. (*He crosses leisurely to phone*) H'lo. Aw, yeh, hello, Mac.

(*He leans against wall, staring insultingly in at Blanche. She sinks back in her chair with a frightened look. Stella leans over and touches her shoulder.*)

BLANCHE. Oh, keep your hands off me, Stella. What is the matter with you? Why do you look at me with that pitying look?

STANLEY (*bawling*). Q U I E T  I N THERE!—We've got a noisy woman on the place.—Go on, Mac. At Riley's? No, I don't wanta bowl at Riley's. I had a little trouble with Riley last week. I'm the team-captain, ain't I? All right, then, we're not gonna bowl at Riley's, we're gonna bowl at the West Side or the Gala! All right, Mac. See you! (*He hangs up and returns to the table. Blanche fiercely controls herself, drinking quickly from her tumbler of water. He doesn't look at her but reaches in a pocket. Then he speaks slowly and with false amiability*) Sister Blanche, I've got a little birthday remembrance for you.

BLANCHE. Oh, have you, Stanley? I wasn't expecting any, I—I don't know why Stella wants to observe my birthday! I'd much rather forget it—when you— reach twenty-seven! Well—age is a subject that you'd prefer to—ignore!

STANLEY. Twenty-seven?

BLANCHE (*quickly*). What is it? Is it for me?

(*He is holding a little envelope toward her.*)

STANLEY. Yes, I hope you like it!

BLANCHE. Why, why—Why, it's a—

STANLEY. Ticket! Back to Laurel! On the Greyhound! Tuesday! (*The Varsouviana music steals in softly and continues playing. Stella rises abruptly and turns her back. Blanches tries to smile. Then she tries to laugh. Then she gives both up and springs from the table and runs into the next room. She clutches her throat and

then runs into the bathroom. Coughing, gagging sounds are heard*) Well!

STELLA. You didn't need to do that.

STANLEY. Don't forget all that I took off her.

STELLA. You needn't have been so cruel to someone alone as she is.

STANLEY. Delicate piece she is.

STELLA. She is. She was. You didn't know Blanche as a girl. Nobody, nobody, was tender and trusting as she was. But people like you abused her, and forced her to change. (*He crosses into the bedroom, ripping off his shirt, and changes into a brilliant silk bowling shirt. She follows him*) Do you think you're going bowling now?

STANLEY. Sure.

STELLA. You're not going bowling. (*She catches hold of his shirt*) Why did you do this to her?

STANLEY. I done nothing to no one. Let go of my shirt. You've torn it.

STELLA. I want to know why. Tell me why.

STANLEY. When we first met, me and you, you thought I was common. How right you was, baby. I was common as dirt. You showed me the snapshot of the place with the columns. I pulled you down off them columns and how you loved it, having them colored lights going! And wasn't we happy together, wasn't it all okay till she showed here? (*Stella makes a slight movement. Her look goes suddenly inward as if some interior voice had called her name. She begins a slow, shuffling progress from the bedroom to the kitchen, leaning and resting on the back of the chair and then on the edge of a table with a blind look and listening expression. Stanley, finishing with his shirt, is unaware of her reaction*) And wasn't we happy together? Wasn't it all okay? Till she showed here. Hoity-toity, describing me as an ape. (*He suddenly notices the change in Stella*) Hey, what is it, Stel? (*He crosses to her*)

STELLA (*quietly*). Take me to the hospital.

(*He is with her now, supporting her with his arm, murmuring indistinguishably as they go outside.*)

## SCENE NINE

*A while later that evening. Blanche is*

*seated in a tense hunched position in a bedroom chair that she has re-covered with diagonal green and white stripes. She has on her scarlet satin robe. On the table beside chair is a bottle of liquor and a glass. The rapid, feverish polka tune, the "Varsouviana," is heard. The music is in her mind; she is drinking to escape it and the sense of disaster closing in on her, and she seems to whisper the words of the song. An electric fan is turning back and forth across her.*

*Mitch comes around the corner in work clothes: blue denim shirt and pants. He is unshaven. He climbs the steps to the door and rings. Blanche is startled.*

———

BLANCHE. Who is it, please?

MITCH *(hoarsely)*. Me. Mitch. *(The polka tune stops.)*

BLANCHE. Mitch!—Just a minute. *(She rushes about frantically, hiding the bottle in a closet, crouching at the mirror and dabbing her face with cologne and powder. She is so excited that her breath is audible as she dashes about. At last she rushes to the door in the kitchen and lets him in)* Mitch!—Y'know, I really shouldn't let you in after the treatment I have received from you this evening! So utterly uncavalier! But hello, beautiful! *(She offers him her lips. He ignores it and pushes past her into the flat. She looks fearfully after him as he stalks into the bedroom)* My, my, what a cold shoulder! And such uncouth apparel! Why, you haven't even shaved! The unforgivable insult to a lady! But I forgive you. I forgive you because it's such a relief to see you. You've stopped that polka tune that I had caught in my head. Have you ever had anything caught 'in your head? No, of course you haven't, you dumb angel-puss, you'd never get anything awful caught in your head!

*(He stares at her while she follows him while she talks. It is obvious that he has had a few drinks on the way over.)*

MITCH. Do we have to have that fan on?

BLANCHE. No!

MITCH. I don't like fans.

BLANCHE. Then let's turn it off, honey. I'm not partial to them! *(She presses the switch and the fan nods slowly off. She clears her throat uneasily as Mitch plumps himself down on the bed in the bedroom and lights a cigarette)* I don't know what

there is to drink. I—haven't investigated.

MITCH. I don't want Stan's liquor.

BLANCHE. It isn't Stan's. Everything here isn't Stan's. Some things on the premises are actually mine! How is your mother? Isn't your mother well?

MITCH. Why?

BLANCHE. Something's the matter tonight, but never mind. I won't cross-examine the witness. I'll just— *(She touches her forehead vaguely. The polka tune starts up again)*—pretend I don't notice anything different about you! That—music again . . .

MITCH. What music?

BLANCHE. The "Varsouviana"! The polka tune they were playing when Allan— Wait! *(A distant revolver shot is heard. Blanche seems relieved)* There now, the shot! It always stops after that. *(The polka music dies out again)* Yes, now it's stopped.

MITCH. Are you boxed out of your mind?

BLANCHE. I'll go and see what I can find in the way of— *(She crosses into the closet, pretending to search for the bottle)* Oh, by the way, excuse me for not being dressed. But I'd practically given you up! Had you forgotten your invitation to supper?

MITCH. I wasn't going to see you any more.

BLANCHE. Wait a minute. I can't hear what you're saying and you talk so little that when you do say something, I don't want to miss a single syllable of it. . . . What am I looking around here for? Oh, yes—liquor! We've had so much excitement around here this evening that I *am* boxed out of my mind! *(She pretends suddenly to find the bottle. He draws his foot up on the bed and stares at her contemptuously)* Here's something. Southern Comfort! What is that, I wonder?

MITCH. If you don't know, it must belong to Stan.

BLANCHE. Take your foot off the bed. It has a light cover on it. Of course you boys don't notice things like that. I've done so much with this place since I've been here.

MITCH. I bet you have.

BLANCHE. You saw it before I came. Well, look at it now! This room is almost —dainty! I want to keep it that way. I wonder if this stuff ought to be mixed with something? Ummm, it's sweet, so sweet! It's terribly, terribly sweet! Why, it's a *liqueur,* I believe! Yes, that's what it *is,* a liqueur! *(Mitch grunts)* I'm afraid you won't like it, but try it, and maybe you will.

MITCH. I told you already I don't want none of his liquor and I mean it. You ought to lay off his liquor. He says you been lapping it up all summer like a wild-cat!

BLANCHE. What a fantastic statement! Fantastic of him to say it, fantastic of you to repeat it! I won't descend to the level of such cheap accusations to answer them, even!

MITCH. Huh.

BLANCHE. What's in your mind? I see something in your eyes!

MITCH *(getting up).* It's dark in here.

BLANCHE. I like it dark. The dark is comforting to me.

MITCH. I don't think I ever seen you in the light. *(Blanche laughs breathlessly)* That's a fact!

BLANCHE. Is it?

MITCH. I've never seen you in the after-noon.

BLANCHE. Whose fault is that?

MITCH. You never want to go out in the afternoon.

BLANCHE. Why, Mitch, you're at the plant in the afternoon!

MITCH. Not Sunday afternoon. I've asked you to go out with me sometimes on Sun-days but you always make an excuse. You never want to go out till after six and then it's always some place that's not lighted much.

BLANCHE. There is some obscure mean-ing in this but I fail to catch it.

MITCH. What it means is I've never had a real good look at you, Blanche. Let's turn the light on here. !

BLANCHE *(fearfully).* Light? Which light? What for?

MITCH. This one with the paper thing on it. *(He tears the paper lantern off the light bulb. She utters a frightened gasp)*

BLANCHE. What did you do that for?

MITCH. So I can take a look at you good and plain!

BLANCHE. Of course you don't really mean to be insulting!

MITCH. No, just realistic.

BLANCHE. I don't want realism. I want magic! *(Mitch laughs)* Yes, yes, magic! I try to give that to people. I misrepresent things to them. I don't tell truth, I tell what *ought* to be truth. And if that is sin-ful, then let me be damned for it!—*Don't turn the light on!*

*(Mitch crosses to the switch. He turns the light on and stares at her. She cries out and covers her face. He turns the light off again.)*

MITCH *(slowly and bitterly).* I don't mind you being older than what I thought. But all the rest of it—Christ! That pitch about your ideals being so old-fashioned and all the malarkey that you've dished out all summer. Oh, I knew you weren't sixteen any more. But I was a fool enough to believe you was straight.

BLANCHE. Who told you I wasn't—"straight"? My loving brother-in-law. And you believed him.

MITCH. I called him a liar at first. And then I checked on the story. First I asked our supply-man who travels through Lau-rel. And then I talked directly over long-distance to this merchant.

BLANCHE. Who is this merchant?

MITCH. Kiefaber.

BLANCHE. The merchant Kiefaber of Laurel! I know the man. He whistled at me. I put him in his place. So now for revenge he makes up stories about me.

MITCH. Three people, Kiefaber, Stanley and Shaw, swore to them!

BLANCHE. Rub-a-dub-dub, three men in a tub! And such a filthy tub!

MITCH. Didn't you stay at a hotel called The Flamingo?

BLANCHE. Flamingo? No! Tarantula was the name of it! I stayed at a hotel called The Tarantula Arms!

MITCH *(stupidly).* Tarantula?

BLANCHE. Yes, a big spider! That's where I brought my victims. *(She pours herself another drink)* Yes, I had many intimacies with strangers. After the death of Allan—intimacies with strangers was all I seemed able to fill my empty heart with. . . . I think it was panic, just panic, that drove me from one to another, hunting for some protection—here and there, in the most unlikely places—even, at last, in a seven-teen-year-old boy but—somebody wrote the superintendent about it—"This woman is morally unfit for her position!" *(She throws back her head with convulsive sobbing laughter. Then she repeats the statement, gasps, and drinks)* True? Yes I suppose—unfit somehow—anyway. . . So I came here. There was nowhere else I could go. I was played out. You know what played out is? My youth was suddenly gone up the water-spout, and—I met you. You said you needed somebody. Well, I needed somebody, too. I thanked God for you, because you seemed to be gentle—a cleft in the rock of the world that I could hide in! But I guess I was asking, hoping—too much! Kiefaber, Stanley and Shaw have tied an old tin can to the tail of the kite.

*(There is a pause. Mitch stares at her dumbly.)*

MITCH. You lied to me, Blanche.

BLANCHE. Don't say I lied to you.

MITCH. Lies, lies, inside and out, all lies.

BLANCHE. Never inside, I didn't lie in my heart . . .

*(A vendor comes around the corner. She is a blind Mexican woman in a dark shawl, carrying bunches of those gaudy tin flowers that lower class Mexicans display at funerals and other festive occasions. She is calling barely audibly. Her figure is only faintly visible outside the building.)*

MEXICAN WOMAN. Flores. Flores. Flores para los muertos. Flores. Flores.

BLANCHE. What? Oh! Somebody outside . . . *(She goes to the door, opens it and stares at the Mexican Woman)*

MEXICAN WOMAN *(she is at the door and offers Blanche some of her flowers)*. Flores? Flores para los muertos?

BLANCHE *(frightened)*. No, no! Not now! Not now! *(She darts back into the apartment, slamming the door)*

MEXICAN WOMAN *(she turns away and starts to move down the street)*. Flores para los muertos.

*(The polka tune fades in.)*

BLANCHE *(as if to herself)*. Crumble and fade and—regrets—recriminations . . . "If you'd done this, it wouldn't've cost me that!"

MEXICAN WOMAN. Corones para los muertos. Corones . . .

BLANCHE. Legacies! Huh . . . And other things such as bloodstained pillow-slips—"Her linen needs changing"—"Yes, Mother. But couldn't we get a colored girl to do it?" No, we couldn't of course. Everything gone but the—

MEXICAN WOMAN. Flores.

BLANCHE. Death—I used to sit here and she used to sit over there and death was as close as you are. . . . We didn't dare even admit we had ever heard of it!

MEXICAN WOMAN. Flores para los muertos, flores—flores . . .

BLANCHE. The opposite is desire. So do you wonder? How could you possibly wonder! Not far from Belle Reve, before we had lost Belle Reve, was a camp where they trained young soldiers. On Saturday nights they would go in town to get drunk—

MEXICAN WOMAN *(softly)*. Corones . . .

BLANCHE. —and on the way back they would stagger onto my lawn and call—"Blanche! Blanche!"—The deaf old lady remaining suspected nothing. But sometimes I slipped outside to answer their calls. . . . Later the paddy-wagon would gather them up like daisies . . . the long way home . . .

*(The Mexican Woman turns slowly and drifts back off with her soft mournful cries. Blanche goes to the dresser and leans forward on it. After a moment, Mitch rises and follows her purposefully. The polka music fades away. He places his hands on her waist and tries to turn her about.)*

BLANCHE. What do you want?

MITCH *(fumbling to embrace her)*. What I been missing all summer.

BLANCHE. Then marry me, Mitch!

MITCH. I don't think I want to marry you any more.

BLANCHE. No?

MITCH *(dropping his hands from her waist)*. You're not clean enough to bring in the house with my mother.

BLANCHE. Go away, then. *(He stares at her)* Get out of here quick before I start screaming fire! *(Her throat is tightening with hysteria)* Get out of here quick before I start screaming fire. *(He still remains staring. She suddenly rushes to the big window with its pale blue square of the soft summer light and cries wildly)* Fire! Fire! Fire!

*(With a startled gasp, Mitch turns and goes out the outer door, clatters awkwardly down the steps and around the corner of the building. Blanche staggers back from the window and falls to her knees. The distant piano is slow and blue.)*

## SCENE TEN

*It is a few hours later that night.*
*Blanche has been drinking fairly steadily since Mitch left. She has dragged her*

*wardrobe trunk into the center of the bedroom. It hangs open with flowery dresses thrown across it. As the drinking and packing went on, a mood of hysterical exhilaration came into her and she has decked herself out in a somewhat soiled and crumpled white satin evening gown and a pair of scuffed silver slippers with brilliants set in their heels.*

*Now she is placing the rhinestone tiara on her head before the mirror of the dressing-table and murmuring excitedly as if to a group of spectral admirers.*

———

BLANCHE. How about taking a swim, a moonlight swim at the old rock-quarry? If anyone's sober enough to drive a car! Ha-ha! Best way in the world to stop your head buzzing! Only you've got to be careful to dive where the deep pool is—if you hit a rock you don't come up till tomorrow . . .

*(Tremblingly she lifts the hand mirror for a closer inspection. She catches her breath and slams the mirror face down with such violence that the glass cracks. She moans a little and attempts to rise.)*

*(Stanley appears around the corner of the building. He still has on the vivid green silk bowling shirt. As he rounds the corner the honky-tonk music is heard. It continues softly throughout the scene.)*

*(He enters the kitchen, slamming the door. As he peers in at Blanche, he gives a low whistle. He has had a few drinks on the way and has brought some quart beer bottles home with him.)*

BLANCHE. How is my sister?

STANLEY. She is doing okay.

BLANCHE. And how is the baby?

STANLEY *(grinning amiably)*. The baby won't come before morning so they told me to go home and get a little shut-eye.

BLANCHE. Does that mean we are to be alone in here?

STANLEY. Yep. Just me and you, Blanche. Unless you got somebody hid under the bed. What've you got on those fine feathers for?

BLANCHE. Oh, that's right. You left before my wire came.

STANLEY. You got a wire?

BLANCHE. I received a telegram from an old admirer of mine.

STANLEY. Anything good?

BLANCHE. I think so. An invitation.

STANLEY. What to? A fireman's ball?

BLANCHE *(throwing back her head)*. A cruise of the Caribbean on a yacht!

STANLEY. Well, well. What do you know?

BLANCHE. I have never been so surprised in my life.

STANLEY. I guess not.

BLANCHE. It came like a bolt from the blue!

STANLEY. Who did you say it was from?

BLANCHE. An old beau of mine.

STANLEY. The one that give you the white fox-pieces?

BLANCHE. Mr. Shep Huntleigh. I wore his ATO pin my last year at college. I hadn't seen him again until last Christmas. I ran in to him on Biscayne Boulevard. Then—just now—this wire—inviting me on a cruise of the Caribbean! The problem is clothes. I tore into my trunk to see what I have that's suitable for the tropics!

STANLEY. And come up with that—gorgeous—diamond—tiara?

BLANCHE. This old relic? Ha-ha! It's only rhinestones.

STANLEY. Gosh. I thought it was Tiffany diamonds. *(He unbuttons his shirt)*

BLANCHE. Well, anyhow, I shall be entertained in style.

STANLEY. Uh-huh. It goes to show, you never know what is coming.

BLANCHE. Just when I thought my luck had begun to fail me—

STANLEY. Into the picture pops this Miami millionaire.

BLANCHE. This man is not from Miami. This man is from Dallas.

STANLEY. This man is from Dallas?

BLANCHE. Yes, this man is from Dallas where gold spouts out of the ground!

STANLEY. Well, just so he's from somewhere! *(He starts removing his shirt)*

BLANCHE. Close the curtains before you undress any further.

STANLEY *(amiably)*. This is all I'm going to undress right now. *(He rips the sack off a quart beer-bottle)* Seen a bottle-opener? *(She moves slowly toward the dresser, where she stands with her hands knotted together)* I used to have a cousin who could open a beer-bottle with his teeth. *(Pounding the bottle cap on the corner of table)* That was his only accomplishment, all he could do—he was just a human bottle-opener. And then one time, at a wedding party, he broke his front teeth off! After that he was so ashamed of himself he used t' sneak out of the house when company came . . . *(The bottle cap pops off and a geyser of foam shoots up. Stanley laughs happily, holding up the bottle over his head)* Ha-ha! Rain from heaven! *(He extends the bottle toward her)* Shall we bury the hatchet and make it a loving-cup? Huh?

BLANCHE. No, thank you.

STANLEY. Well, it's a red letter night for us both. You having an oil-millionaire and me having a baby.

*(He goes to the bureau in the bedroom and crouches to remove something from the bottom drawer.)*

BLANCHE *(drawing back)*. What are you doing in here?

STANLEY. Here's something I always break out on special occasions like this. The silk pyjamas I wore on my wedding night!

BLANCHE. Oh.

STANLEY. When the telephone rings and they say, "You've got a son!" I'll tear this off and wave it like a flag! *(He shakes out a brilliant pyjama coat)* I guess we are both entitled to put on the dog. *(He goes back to the kitchen with the coat over his arm)*

BLANCHE. When I think of how divine it is going to be to have such a thing as privacy once more—I could weep with joy!

STANLEY. This millionaire from Dallas is not going to interfere with your privacy any?

BLANCHE. It won't be the sort of thing you have in mind. This man is a gentleman and he respects me. *(Improvising feverishly)* What he wants is my companionship. Having great wealth sometimes makes people lonely! A cultivated woman, a woman of intelligence and breeding, can enrich a man's life—immeasurably! I have those things to offer, and this doesn't take them away. Physical beauty is passing. A transitory possession. But beauty of the mind and richness of the spirit and tenderness of the heart—and I have all of those things—aren't taken away, but grow! Increase with the years! How strange that I should be called a destitute woman! When I have all of these treasures locked in my heart. *(A choked sob comes from her)* I think of myself as a very, very rich woman! But I have been foolish—casting my pearls before swine!

STANLEY. Swine, huh?

BLANCHE. Yes, swine! Swine! And I'm thinking not only of you but of your friend, Mr. Mitchell. He came to see me tonight. He dared to come here in his work-clothes! And to repeat slander to me, vicious stories that he had gotten from you! I gave him his walking papers . . .

STANLEY. You did, huh?

BLANCHE. But then he came back. He returned with a box of roses to beg my forgiveness! He implored my forgiveness. But some things are not forgivable. Deliberate cruelty is not forgivable. It is the one unforgivable thing in my opinion and it is the one thing of which I have never, never been guilty. And so I told him, I said to him, "Thank you," but it was foolish of me to think that we could ever adapt ourselves to each other. Our ways of life are too different. Our attitudes and our backgrounds are incompatible. We have to be realistic about such things. So farewell, my friend! And let there be no hard feelings . . .

STANLEY. Was this before or after the telegram came from the Texas oil millionaire?

BLANCHE. What telegram? No! No, after! As a matter of fact, the wire came just as—

STANLEY. As a matter of fact there wasn't no wire at all!

BLANCHE. Oh, oh!

STANLEY. There isn't no millionaire! And Mitch didn't come back with roses 'cause I know where he is—

BLANCHE. Oh!

STANLEY. There isn't a goddam thing but imagination!

BLANCHE. Oh!

STANLEY. And lies and conceit and tricks!

BLANCHE. Oh!

STANLEY. And look at yourself! Take a look at yourself in that worn-out Mardi Gras outfit, rented for fifty cents from some rag-picker! And with the crazy crown on! What queen do you think you are?

BLANCHE. Oh—God . . .

STANLEY. I've been on to you from the start! Not once did you pull any wool over this boy's eyes! You come in here and sprinkle the place with powder and spray perfume and cover the light-bulb with a paper lantern, and lo and behold the place has turned into Egypt and you are the

Queen of the Nile! Sitting on your throne and swilling down my liquor! I say—*Ha!* —*Ha!* Do you hear me? *Ha—ha—ha!* (*He walks into the bedroom*)

BLANCHE. Don't come in here! (*Lurid reflections appear on the walls around Blanche. The shadows are of a grotesque and menacing form. She catches her breath, crosses to the phone and jiggles the hook. Stanley goes into the bathroom and closes the door*) Operator, operator! Give me long-distance, please. . . . I want to get in touch with Mr. Shep Huntleigh of Dallas. He's so well-known he doesn't require any address. Just ask anybody who—Wait! —No, I couldn't find it right now. . . . Please understand. I—No! No, wait! . . . One moment! Someone is—Nothing! Hold on, please!

(*She sets the phone down and crosses warily into the kitchen. The night is filled with inhuman voices like cries in a jungle. (The shadows and lurid reflections move sinuously as flames along the wall spaces. (Through the back wall of the rooms, which have become transparent, can be seen the sidewalk. A prostitute has rolled a drunkard. He pursues her along the walk, overtakes her and there is a struggle. A policeman's whistle breaks it up. The figures disappear.*

(*Some moments later the Negro Woman appears around the corner with a sequined bag which the prostitute had dropped on the walk. She is rooting excitedly through it.*

(*Blanche presses her knuckles to her lips and returns slowly to the phone. She speaks in a hoarse whisper.*)

BLANCHE. Operator! Operator! Never mind long-distance. Get Western Union. There isn't time to be—Western—Western Union! (*She waits anxiously*) Western Union? Yes! I—want to— Take down this message! "In desperate, desperate circumstances! Help me! Caught in a trap. Caught in—" *Oh!*

(*The bathroom door is thrown open and Stanley comes out in the brilliant silk pyjamas. He grins at her as he knots the tasseled sash about his waist. She gasps and backs away from the phone. He stares at her for a count of ten. Then a clicking becomes audible from the telephone, steady and rasping.*)

STANLEY. You left th' phone off th' hook. (*He crosses to it deliberately and sets it*

back on the hook. *After he has replaced it, he stares at her again, his mouth slowly curving into a grin, as he weaves between Blanche and the outer door.*

(*The barely audible "blue piano" begins to drum up louder. The sound of it turns into the roar of an approaching locomotive. Blanche crouches, pressing her fists to her ears until it has gone by.*)

BLANCHE (*finally straightening*). Let me —let me get by you!

STANLEY. Get by me? Sure. Go ahead. (*He moves back a pace in the doorway*)

BLANCHE. You—you stand over there! (*She indicates a further position*)

STANLEY (*grinning*). You got plenty of room to walk by me now.

BLANCHE. Not with you there! But I've got to get out somehow!

STANLEY. You think I'll interfere with you? Ha-ha!

(*The "blue piano" goes softly. She turns confusedly and makes a faint gesture. The inhuman jungle voices rise up. He takes a step toward her, biting his tongue which protrudes between his lips.*)

STANLEY (*softly*). Come to think of it— maybe you wouldn't be bad to—interfere with . . .

(*Blanche moves backward through the door into the bedroom.*)

BLANCHE. Stay back! Don't you come toward me another step or I'll—

STANLEY. What?

BLANCHE. Some awful thing will happen! It will!

STANLEY. What are you putting on now? (*They are now both inside the bedroom.*)

BLANCHE. I warn you, don't, I'm in danger!

(*He takes another step. She smashes a bottle on the table and faces him, clutching the broken top.*)

STANLEY. What did you do that for?

BLANCHE. So I could twist the broken end in your face!

STANLEY. I bet you would do that!

BLANCHE. I would! I will if you—

STANLEY. Oh! So you want some roughhouse! All right, let's have some roughhouse! (*He springs toward her, overturning the table. She cries out and strikes at him with the bottle top but he catches her wrist*) Tiger—tiger! Drop the bottle-top! Drop it! We've had this date with each other from the beginning!

(*She moans. The bottle-top falls. She sinks*

*to her knees. He picks up her inert figure and carries her to the bed. The hot trumpet and drums from the Four Deuces sound loudly.)*

## SCENE ELEVEN

*It is some weeks later. Stella is packing Blanche's things. Sound of water can be heard running in the bathroom.*

*The portieres are partly open on the poker players—Stanley, Steve, Mitch and Pablo—who sit around the table in the kitchen. The atmosphere of the kitchen is now the same raw, lurid one of the disastrous poker night.*

*The building is framed by the sky of turquoise. Stella has been crying as she arranges the flowery dresses in the open trunk.*

*Eunice comes down the steps from her flat above and enters the kitchen. There is an outburst from the poker table.*

STANLEY. Drew to an inside straight and made it, by God.

PABLO. *Maldita sea tu suerto!*

STANLEY. Put it in English, greaseball.

PABLO. I am cursing your rutting luck.

STANLEY (*prodigiously elated*). You know what luck is? Luck is believing you're lucky. Take at Salerno. I believed I was lucky. I figured that four out of five would not come through but I would . . . and I did. I put that down as a rule. To hold front position in this rat-race you've got to believe you are lucky.

MITCH. You . . . you . . . you. . . . Brag . . . brag . . . bull . . . bull.

*(Stella goes into the bedroom and starts folding a dress.)*

STANLEY. What's the matter with him?

EUNICE (*walking past the table*). I always did say that men are callous things with no feelings, but this does beat anything. Making pigs of yourselves. (*She comes through the portieres into the bedroom*)

STANLEY. What's the matter with her?

STELLA. How is my baby?

EUNICE. Sleeping like a little angel. Brought you some grapes. (*She puts them on a stool and lowers her voice*) Blanche?

STELLA. Bathing.

EUNICE. How is she?

STELLA. She wouldn't eat anything but asked for a drink.

EUNICE. What did you tell her?

STELLA. I—just told her that—we'd made arrangements for her to rest in the country. She's got it mixed in her mind with Shep Huntleigh.

*(Blanche opens the bathroom door slightly.)*

BLANCHE. Stella.

STELLA. Yes, Blanche?

BLANCHE. If anyone calls while I'm bathing take the number and tell them I'll call right back.

STELLA. Yes.

BLANCHE. That cool yellow silk—the bouclé. See if it's crushed. If it's not too crushed I'll wear it and on the lapel that silver and turquoise pin in the shape of a seahorse. You will find them in the heart-shaped box I keep my accessories in. And Stella . . . Try and locate a bunch of artificial violets in that box, too, to pin with the seahorse on the lapel of the jacket.

*(She closes the door. Stella turns to Eunice.)*

STELLA. I don't know if I did the right thing.

EUNICE. What else could you do?

STELLA. I couldn't believe her story and go on living with Stanley.

EUNICE. Don't ever believe it. Life has got to go on. No matter what happens, you've got to keep on going.

*(The bathroom door opens a little.)*

BLANCHE (*looking out*). Is the coast clear?

STELLA. Yes, Blanche. (*To Eunice*) Tell her how well she's looking.

BLANCHE. Please close the curtains before I come out.

STELLA. They're closed.

STANLEY. —How many for you?

PABLO. —Two.

STEVE. —Three.

*(Blanche appears in the amber light of the door. She has a tragic radiance in her red satin robe following the sculptural lines of her body. The "Varsouviana" rises audibly as Blanche enters the bedroom.)*

BLANCHE (*with faintly hysterical vivacity*). I have just washed my hair.

STELLA. Did you?

BLANCHE. I'm not sure I got the soap out.

EUNICE. Such fine hair!

BLANCHE (*accepting the compliment*). It's a problem. Didn't I get a call?

STELLA. Who from, Blanche?

BLANCHE. Shep Huntleigh . . .

STELLA. Why, not yet, honey!

BLANCHE. How strange! I—

*(At the sound of Blanche's voice, Mitch's arm supporting his cards has sagged and his gaze is dissolved into space. Stanley slaps him on the shoulder.)*

STANLEY. Hey, Mitch, come to!

*(The sound of this new voice shocks Blanche. She makes a shocked gesture, forming his name with her lips. Stella nods and looks quickly away. Blanche stands quite still for some moments—the silverbacked mirror in her hand and a look of sorrowful perplexity as though all human experience shows on her face. Blanche finally speaks but with sudden hysteria.)*

BLANCHE. What's going on here?

*(She turns from Stella to Eunice and back to Stella. Her rising voice penetrates the concentration of the game. Mitch ducks his head lower but Stanley shoves back his chair as if about to rise. Steve places a restraining hand on his arm.)*

BLANCHE *(continuing)*. What's happened here? I want an explanation of what's happened here.

STELLA *(agonizingly)*. Hush! Hush!

EUNICE. Hush! Hush! Honey.

STELLA. Please, Blanche.

BLANCHE. Why are you looking at me like that? Is something wrong with me?

EUNICE. You look wonderful, Blanche. Don't she look wonderful?

STELLA. Yes.

EUNICE. I understand you are going on a trip.

STELLA. Yes, Blanche *is*. She's going on a vacation.

EUNICE. I'm green with envy.

BLANCHE. Help me, help me get dressed!

STELLA *(handing her dress)*. Is this what you—

BLANCHE. Yes, it will do! I'm anxious to get out of here—this place is a trap!

EUNICE. What a pretty blue jacket.

STELLA. It's lilac colored.

BLANCHE. You're both mistaken. It's Della Robbia blue. The blue of the robe in the old Madonna pictures. Are these grapes washed?

*(She fingers the bunch of grapes which Eunice had brought in.)*

EUNICE. Huh?

BLANCHE. Washed, I said. Are they washed?

EUNICE. They're from the French Market.

BLANCHE. That doesn't mean they've been washed. *(The cathedral bells chime)* Those cathedral bells—they're the only clean thing in the Quarter. Well, I'm going now. I'm ready to go.

EUNICE *(whispering)*. She's going to walk out before they get here.

STELLA. Wait, Blanche.

BLANCHE. I don't want to pass in front of those men.

EUNICE. Then wait'll the game breaks up.

STELLA. Sit down and . . .

*(Blanche turns weakly, hesitantly about. She lets them push her into a chair.)*

BLANCHE. I can smell the sea air. The rest of my time I'm going to spend on the sea. And when I die, I'm going to die on the sea. You know what I shall die of? *(She plucks a grape)* I shall die of eating an unwashed grape one day out on the ocean. I will die—with my hand in the hand of some nice-looking ship's doctor, a very young one with a small blond mustache and a big silver watch. "Poor lady," they'll say, "the quinine did her no good. That unwashed grape has transported her soul to heaven." *(The cathedral chimes are heard)* And I'll be buried at sea sewn up in a clean white sack and dropped overboard—at noon—in the blaze of summer—and into an ocean as blue as *(Chimes again)* my first lover's eyes!

*(A Doctor and a Matron have appeared around the corner of the building and climbed the steps to the porch. The gravity of their profession is exaggerated—the unmistakable aura of the state institution with its cynical detachment. The Doctor rings the doorbell. The murmur of the game is interrupted.)*

EUNICE *(whispering to Stella)*. That must be them.

*(Stella presses her fists to her lips.)*

BLANCHE *(rising slowly)*. What is it?

EUNICE *(affectedly casual)*. Excuse me while I see who's at the door.

STELLA. Yes.

*(Eunice goes into the kitchen.)*

BLANCHE *(tensely)*. I wonder if it's for me.

*(A whispered colloquy takes place at the door.)*

EUNICE *(returning, brightly)*. Someone is calling for Blanche.

BLANCHE. It *is* for me, then! *(She looks fearfully from one to the other and then to the portieres. The "Varsouviana" faintly plays)* Is it the gentleman I was expecting from Dallas?

EUNICE. I think it is, Blanche.

BLANCHE. I'm not quite ready.

STELLA. Ask him to wait outside.

BLANCHE. I . . .

*(Eunice goes back to the portieres. Drums sound very softly.)*

STELLA. Everything packed?

BLANCHE. My silver toilet articles are still out.

STELLA. Ah!

EUNICE *(returning)*. They're waiting in front of the house.

BLANCHE. They! Who's "they"?

EUNICE. There's a lady with him.

BLANCHE. I cannot imagine who this "lady" could be! How is she dressed?

EUNICE. Just—just a sort of a—plain-tailored outfit.

BLANCHE. Possibly she's—*(Her voice dies out nervously)*

STELLA. Shall we go, Blanche?

BLANCHE. Must we go through that room?

STELLA. I will go with you.

BLANCHE. How do I look?

STELLA. Lovely.

EUNICE *(echoing)*. Lovely.

*(Blanche moves fearfully to the portieres. Eunice draws them open for her. Blanche goes into the kitchen.)*

BLANCHE *(to the men)*. Please don't get up. I'm only passing through.

*(She crosses quickly to outside door. Stella and Eunice follow. The poker players stand awkwardly at the table—all except Mitch, who remains seated, looking down at the table. Blanche steps out on a small porch at the side of the door. She stops short and catches her breath.)*

DOCTOR. How do you do?

BLANCHE. You are not the gentleman I was expecting. *(She suddenly gasps and starts back up the steps. She stops by Stella, who stands just outside the door, and speaks in a frightening whisper)* That man isn't Shep Huntleigh.

*(The "Varsouviana" is playing distantly. (Stella stares back at Blanche. Eunice is holding Stella's arm. There is a moment of silence—no sound but that of Stanley steadily shuffling the cards.*

*(Blanche catches her breath again and slips*

back into the flat. She enters the flat with a peculiar smile, her eyes wide and brilliant. As soon as her sister goes past her, Stella closes her eyes and clenches her hands. Eunice throws her arms comfortingly about her. Then she starts up to her flat. Blanche stops just inside the door. Mitch keeps staring down at his hands on the table, but the other men look at her curiously. At last she starts around the table toward the bedroom. As she does, Stanley suddenly pushes back his chair and rises as if to block her way. The Matron follows her into the flat.)*

STANLEY. Did you forget something?

BLANCHE *(shrilly)*. Yes! Yes, I forgot something!

*(She rushes past him into the bedroom. Lurid reflections appear on the walls in odd, sinuous shapes. The "Varsouviana" is filtered into a weird distortion, accompanied by the cries and noises of the jungle. Blanche seizes the back of a chair as if to defend herself.)*

STANLEY *(sotto voce)*. Doc, you better go in.

DOCTOR *(sotto voce, motioning to the Matron)*. Nurse, bring her out.

*(The Matron advances on one side, Stanley on the other. Divested of all the softer properties of womanhood, the Matron is a peculiarly sinister figure in her severe dress. Her voice is bold and toneless as a firebell.)*

MATRON. Hello, Blanche.

*(The greeting is echoed and re-echoed by other mysterious voices behind the walls, as if reverberated through a canyon of rock.)*

STANLEY. She says that she forgot something.

*(The echo sounds in threatening whispers.)*

MATRON. That's all right.

STANLEY. What did you forget, Blanche?

BLANCHE. I—I—

MATRON. It don't matter. We can pick it up later.

STANLEY. Sure. We can send it along with the trunk.

BLANCHE *(retreating in panic)*. I don't know you—I don't know you. I want to be—left alone—please!

MATRON. Now, Blanche!

ECHOES *(rising and falling)*. Now, Blanche—now, Blanche—now, Blanche!

STANLEY. You left nothing here but spilt

talcum and old empty perfume bottles—unless it's the paper lantern you want to take with you. You want the lantern?

*(He crosses to dressing table and seizes the paper lantern, tearing it off the light bulb, and extends it toward her. She cries out as if the lantern was herself. The Matron steps boldly toward her. She screams and tries to break past the Matron. All the men spring to their feet. Stella runs out to the porch, with Eunice following to comfort her, simultaneously with the confused voices of the men in the kitchen. Stella rushes into Eunice's embrace on the porch.)*

STELLA. Oh, my God, Eunice, help me! Don't let them do that to her, don't let them hurt her! Oh, God, oh, please God, don't hurt her. What are they doing to her? What are they doing? *(She tries to break from Eunice's arms)*

EUNICE. No, honey, no, no, honey. Stay here. Don't go back in there. Stay with me and don't look.

STELLA. What have I done to my sister? Oh, God, what have I done to my sister?

EUNICE. You done the right thing, the only thing you could do. She couldn't stay here; there wasn't no other place for her to go.

*(While Stella and Eunice are speaking on the porch the voices of the men in the kitchen overlap them. Mitch has started toward the bedroom. Stanley crosses to block him. Stanley pushes him aside. Mitch lunges and strikes at Stanley. Stanley pushes Mitch back. Mitch collapses at the table, sobbing.)*

*(During the preceding scenes, the Matron catches hold of Blanche's arm and prevents her flight. Blanche turns wildly and scratches at the Matron. The heavy woman pinions her arms. Blanche cries out hoarsely and slips to her knees.)*

MATRON. These fingernails have to be trimmed. *(The Doctor comes into the room and she looks at him)* Jacket, Doctor?

DOCTOR. Not unless necessary.

*(He takes off his hat and now he becomes personalized. The inhuman quality goes. His voice is gentle and reassuring as he crosses to Blanche and crouches in front of her. As he speaks her name, her terror subsides a little. The lurid reflections fade from the walls, the inhuman cries and noises die out and her own hoarse crying is calmed.)*

DOCTOR. Miss DuBois. *(She turns her face to him and stares at him with desperate pleading. He smiles; then he speaks to the Matron)* It won't be necessary.

BLANCHE *(faintly)*. Ask her to let go of me.

DOCTOR *(to the Matron)*. Let go.

*(The Matron releases her. Blanche extends her hands toward the Doctor. He draws her up gently and supports her with his arm and leads her through the portieres.)*

BLANCHE *(holding tight to his arm)*. Whoever you are—I have always depended on the kindness of strangers.

*(The poker players stand back as Blanche and the Doctor cross the kitchen to the front door. She allows him to lead her as if she were blind. As they go out on the porch, Stella cries out her sister's name from where she is crouched a few steps up on the stairs.)*

STELLA. Blanche! Blanche, Blanche!

*(Blanche walks on without turning, followed by the Doctor and the Matron. They go around the corner of the building.*

*(Eunice descends to Stella and places the child in her arms. It is wrapped in a pale blue blanket. Stella accepts the child, sobbingly. Eunice continues downstairs and enters the kitchen where the men, except for Stanley, are returning silently to their places about the table. Stanley has gone out on the porch and stands at the foot of the steps looking at Stella.)*

STANLEY *(a bit uncertainly)*. Stella?

*(She sobs with inhuman abandon. There is something luxurious in her complete surrender to crying now that her sister is gone.)*

STANLEY *(voluptuously, soothingly)*. Now, honey. Now, love. Now, now, love. *(He kneels beside her and his fingers find the opening of her blouse)* Now, now, love. Now, love. . . .

*(The luxurious sobbing, the sensual murmur fade away under the swelling music of the "blue piano" and the muted trumpet.)*

STEVE. This game is seven-card stud.

CURTAIN

# 1948-49

Arthur Miller matched Tennessee Williams and Maxwell Anderson as a two-time Circle winner with *Death of a Salesman*, which was quite an improvement over *All My Sons*, although by no means "the great American play" that some seemed to regard it in the heat of its newness.

There was no contest. *Death of a Salesman* received twenty-three votes as against two for Anderson's *Anne of the Thousand Days*, one for Williams' *Summer and Smoke* and one for Robert E. McEnroe's *The Silver Whistle*. Miller also won the Pulitzer prize.

*The Madwoman of Chaillot* by the late French playwright Jean Giraudoux, in an adaptation by Maurice Valency, won the foreign citation without difficulty. It received twenty-two votes to three for *Edward, My Son* by Robert Morley and Noel Langley and two for *The Victors* by Jean-Paul Sartre in a Thornton Wilder adaptation.

The Rodgers-Hammerstein *South Pacific* received the musical citation on eighteen votes to six for *Kiss Me, Kate* by Cole Porter and Samuel and Bella Spewack and one for *Love Life* by Alan Jay Lerner and Kurt Weill.

The meeting was held on April 12, 1949.

*South Pacific* was destined to continue through 1,925 performances to become, at this writing, number five in the long-run list. It put the finishing touch to making Mary Martin the great star that she is today, and it introduced to Broadway from opera the veteran basso, Ezio Pinza.

Two attractions ranking high in the long-run list closed during the season—*Harvey* with 1,775 performances and *Annie Get Your Gun* with 1,147. At this writing *Harvey* is sixth in the list and the musical comedy is sixteenth.

It was at this meeting that the Circle voted not to have the usual cocktail party for the winner. Kermit Bloomgarden and Walter Fried, producers of *Death of a Salesman*, felt prosperous enough to take up the slack by giving a party at "21" after the performance of the night of April 23. The critics, of course, were invited and thoroughly enjoyed the novelty of not having to pick up the check. Unfortunately, no subsequent winning producer has felt inclined to duplicate this generous gesture.

*Death of a Salesman* ran 742 performances.

# Death of a Salesman

## By ARTHUR MILLER

Presented by Kermit Bloomgarden and Walter Fried at the Morosco Theatre, New York City, February 10, 1949, with the following cast:

| | |
|---|---|
| WILLY LOMAN | Lee J. Cobb |
| LINDA | Mildred Dunnock |
| BIFF | Arthur Kennedy |
| HAPPY | Cameron Mitchell |
| BERNARD | Don Keefer |
| THE WOMAN | Winnifred Cushing |
| CHARLEY | Howard Smith |
| UNCLE BEN | Thomas Chalmers |
| HOWARD WAGNER | Alan Hewitt |
| JENNY | Ann Driscoll |
| STANLEY | Tom Pedi |
| MISS FORSYTHE | Constance Ford |
| LETTA | Hope Cameron |

## SCENE

The action takes place in Willy Loman's house and yard and in various places he visits in the New York and Boston of today.

## ACT ONE

*A melody is heard, played upon a flute. It is small and fine, telling of grass and trees and the horizon. The curtain rises.*

*Before us is the Salesman's house. We are aware of towering, angular shapes behind it, surrounding it on all sides. Only the blue light of the sky falls upon the house and forestage; the surrounding area shows an angry glow of orange. As more light appears, we see a solid vault of apartment houses around the small, fragile-seeming home. An air of the dream clings to the place, a dream rising out of reality. The kitchen at center seems actual enough, for there is a kitchen table with three chairs, and a refrigerator. But no other fixtures are seen. At the back of the kitchen there is a draped entrance, which leads to the living-room. To the right of the kitchen, on a level raised two feet, is a bedroom furnished only with a brass bedstead and a straight chair. On a shelf over the bed a silver athletic trophy stands. A window opens onto the apartment house at the side.*

*Behind the kitchen, on a level raised six and a half feet, is the boys' bedroom, at present barely visible. Two beds are dimly seen, and at the back of the room a dormer window. (This bedroom is above the unseen living-room.) At the left a stairway curves up to it from the kitchen.*

*The entire setting is wholly or, in some places, partially transparent. The roof-line of the house is one-dimensional; under and over it we see the apartment buildings. Before the house lies an apron, curving beyond the forestage into the orchestra. This forward area serves as the back yard as well as the locale of all Willy's imaginings and of his city scenes. Whenever the action is in the present the actors observe the imaginary wall-lines, entering the house only through its door at the left. But in the scenes of the past these boundaries are broken, and characters enter or leave a room by stepping "through" a wall onto the forestage.*

*From the right, Willy Loman, the Salesman, enters, carrying two large sample cases. The flute plays on. He hears but is not aware of it. He is past sixty years of age, dressed quietly. Even as he crosses the stage to the doorway of the house, his exhaustion is apparent. He unlocks the door, comes into the kitchen, and thankfully lets his burden down, feeling the soreness of his palms. A word-sigh escapes his lips—it might be "Oh, boy, oh, boy." He closes the door, then carries his cases out into the living-room, through the draped kitchen doorway.*

*Linda, his wife, has stirred in her bed at the right. She gets out and puts on a robe, listening. Most often jovial, she has developed an iron repression of her exceptions to Willy's behavior—she more than loves him, she admires him, as though his mercurial nature, his temper, his massive dreams and little cruelties, served her only as sharp reminders of the turbulent longings within him, longings which she shares but lacks the temperament to utter and follow to their end.*

———

LINDA (*hearing Willy outside the bedroom, calls with some trepidation*). Willy!

WILLY. It's all right. I came back.

LINDA. Why? What happened? (*Slight pause*) Did something happen, Willy?

WILLY. No, nothing happened.

LINDA. You didn't smash the car, did you?

WILLY (*with casual irritation*). I said nothing happened. Didn't you hear me?

LINDA. Don't you feel well?

WILLY. I'm tired to the death. (*The flute has faded away. He sits on the bed beside her, a little numb*) I couldn't make it. I just couldn't make it, Linda.

LINDA (*very carefully, delicately*). Where were you all day? You look terrible.

WILLY. I got as far as a little above Yonkers. I stopped for a cup of coffee. Maybe it was the coffee.

LINDA. What?

WILLY (*after a pause*). I suddenly couldn't drive any more. The car kept going off onto the shoulder, y'know?

LINDA (*helpfully*). Oh. Maybe it was the steering again. I don't think Angelo knows the Studebaker.

WILLY. No, it's me, it's me. Suddenly I realize I'm goin' sixty miles an hour and I don't remember the last five minutes. I'm—I can't seem to—keep my mind to it.

LINDA. Maybe it's your glasses. You never went for your new glasses.

WILLY. No, I see everything. I came back ten miles an hour. It took me nearly four hours from Yonkers.

LINDA (*resigned*). Well, you'll just have

to take a rest, Willy, you can't continue this way.

WILLY. I just got back from Florida.

LINDA. But you didn't rest your mind. Your mind is overactive, and the mind is what counts, dear.

WILLY. I'll start out in the morning. Maybe I'll feel better in the morning. (*She is taking off his shoes*) These goddam arch supports are killing me.

LINDA. Take an aspirin. Should I get you an aspirin? It'll soothe you.

WILLY (*with wonder*). I was driving along, you understand? And I was fine. I was even observing the scenery. You can imagine, me looking at scenery, on the road every week of my life. But it's so beautiful up there, Linda, the trees are so thick, and the sun is warm. I opened the windshield and just let the warm air bathe over me. And then all of a sudden I'm goin' off the road! I'm tellin' ya, I absolutely forgot I was driving. If I'd've gone the other way over the white line I might've killed somebody. So I went on again—and five minutes later I'm dreamin' again, and I nearly— (*He presses two fingers against his eyes*) I have such thoughts, I have such strange thoughts.

LINDA. Willy, dear. Talk to them again. There's no reason why you can't work in New York.

WILLY. They don't need me in New York. I'm the New England man. I'm vital in New England.

LINDA. But you're sixty years old. They can't expect you to keep traveling every week.

WILLY. I'll have to send a wire to Portland. I'm supposed to see Brown and Morrison tomorrow morning at ten o'clock to show the line. Goddammit, I could sell them! (*He starts putting on his jacket*)

LINDA (*taking the jacket from him*). Why don't you go down to the place tomorrow and tell Howard you've simply got to work in New York? You're too accommodating, dear.

WILLY. If old man Wagner was alive I'd a been in charge of New York now! That man was a prince, he was a masterful man. But that boy of his, that Howard, he don't appreciate. When I went north the first time, the Wagner Company didn't know where New England was!

LINDA. Why don't you tell those things to Howard, dear?

WILLY (*encouraged*). I will, I definitely will. Is there any cheese?

LINDA. I'll make you a sandwich.

WILLY. No, go to sleep. I'll take some milk. I'll be up right away. The boys in?

LINDA. They're sleeping. Happy took Biff on a date tonight.

WILLY (*interested*). That so?

LINDA. It was so nice to see them shaving together, one behind the other, in the bathroom. And going out together. You notice? The whole house smells of shaving lotion.

WILLY. Figure it out. Work a lifetime to pay off a house. You finally own it, and there's nobody to live in it.

LINDA. Well, dear, life is a casting off. It's always that way.

WILLY. No, no, some people—some people accomplish something. Did Biff say anything after I went this morning?

LINDA. You shouldn't have criticized him, Willy, especially after he just got off the train. You mustn't lose your temper with him.

WILLY. When the hell did I lose my temper? I simply asked him if he was making any money. Is that a criticism?

LINDA. But, dear, how could he make any money?

WILLY (*worried and angered*). There's such an undercurrent in him. He became a moody man. Did he apologize when I left this morning?

LINDA. He was crestfallen, Willy. You know how he admires you. I think if he finds himself, then you'll both be happier and not fight any more.

WILLY. How can he find himself on a farm? Is that a life? A farmhand? In the beginning, when he was young, I thought, well, a young man, it's good for him to tramp around, take a lot of different jobs. But it's more than ten years now and he has yet to make thirty-five dollars a week!

LINDA. He's finding himself, Willy.

WILLY. Not finding yourself at the age of thirty-four is a disgrace!

LINDA. Shh!

WILLY. The trouble is he's lazy, goddammit!

LINDA. Willy, please!

WILLY. Biff is a lazy bum!

LINDA. They're sleeping. Get something to eat. Go on down.

WILLY. Why did he come home? I

would like to know what brought him home.

LINDA. I don't know. I think he's still lost, Willy. I think he's very lost.

WILLY. Biff Loman is lost. In the greatest country in the world a young man with such—personal attractiveness, gets lost. And such a hard worker. There's one thing about Biff—he's not lazy.

LINDA. Never.

WILLY (*with pity and resolve*). I'll see him in the morning; I'll have a nice talk with him. I'll get him a job selling. He could be big in no time. My God! Remember how they used to follow him around in high school? When he smiled at one of them their faces lit up. When he walked down the street . . . (*He loses himself in reminiscences*)

LINDA (*trying to bring him out of it*). Willy, dear, I got a new kind of American-type cheese today. It's whipped.

WILLY. Why do you get American when I like Swiss?

LINDA. I just thought you'd like a change—

WILLY. I don't want a change! I want Swiss cheese. Why am I always being contradicted?

LINDA (*with a covering laugh*). I thought it would be a surprise.

WILLY. Why don't you open a window in here, for God's sake?

LINDA (*with infinite patience*). They're all open, dear.

WILLY. The way they boxed us in here. Bricks and windows, windows and bricks.

LINDA. We should've bought the land next door.

WILLY. The street is lined with cars. There's not a breath of fresh air in the neighborhood. The grass don't grow any more, you can't raise a carrot in the back yard. They should've had a law against apartment houses. Remember those two beautiful elm trees out there? When I and Biff hung the swing between them?

LINDA. Yeah, like being a million miles from the city.

WILLY. They should've arrested the builder for cutting those down. They massacred the neighborhood. (*Lost*) More and more I think of those days, Linda. This time of year it was lilac and wisteria. And then the peonies would come out, and the daffodils. What fragrance in this room!

LINDA. Well, after all, people had to move somewhere.

WILLY. No, there's more people now.

LINDA. I don't think there's more people. I think—

WILLY. There's more people! That's what's ruining this country! Population is getting out of control. The competition is maddening! Smell the stink from that apartment house! And another one on the other side . . . How can they whip cheese? (*On Willy's last line, Biff and Happy raise themselves up in their beds, listening.*)

LINDA. Go down, try it. And be quiet.

WILLY (*turning to Linda, guiltily*). You're not worried about me, are you, sweetheart?

BIFF. What's the matter?

HAPPY. Listen!

LINDA. You've got too much on the ball to worry about.

WILLY. You're my foundation and my support, Linda.

LINDA. Just try to relax, dear. You make mountains out of molehills.

WILLY. I won't fight with him any more. If he wants to go back to Texas, let him go.

LINDA. He'll find his way.

WILLY. Sure. Certain men just don't get started till later in life. Like Thomas Edison, I think. Or B. F. Goodrich. One of them was deaf. (*He starts for the bedroom doorway*) I'll put my money on Biff.

LINDA. And, Willy—if it's warm Sunday we'll drive in the country. And we'll open the windshield, and take lunch.

WILLY. No, the windshields don't open on the new cars.

LINDA. But you opened it today.

WILLY. Me? I didn't. (*He stops*) Now isn't that peculiar! Isn't that remarkable— (*He breaks off in amazement and fright as the flute is heard distantly*)

LINDA. What, darling?

WILLY. That is the most remarkable thing.

LINDA. What, dear?

WILLY. I was thinking of the Chevvy. (*Slight pause*) Nineteen twenty-eight . . . when I had that red Chevvy—(*Breaks off*) That's funny? I coulda sworn I was driving that Chevvy today.

LINDA. Well, that's nothing. Something must've reminded you.

WILLY. Remarkable. Ts. Remember those days? The way Biff used to simonize that car? The dealer refused to believe there was eighty thousand miles on it. (*He shakes his head*) Heh! (*To Linda*) Close your eyes, I'll be right up. (*He walks out of the bedroom*)

HAPPY (*to Biff*). Jesus, maybe he smashed up the car again!

LINDA (*calling after Willy*). Be careful on the stairs, dear! The cheese is on the middle shelf! (*She turns, goes over to the bed, takes his jacket, and goes out of the bedroom*)

(*Light has risen on the boys' room. Unseen, Willy is heard talking to himself, "Eighty thousand miles," and a little laugh. Biff gets out of bed, comes downstage a bit, and stands attentively. Biff is two years older than his brother Happy, well built, but in these days bears a worn air and seems less self-assured. He has succeeded less, and his dreams are stronger and less acceptable than Happy's. Happy is tall, powerfully made. Sexuality is like a visible color on him, or a scent that many women have discovered. He, like his brother, is lost, but in a different way, for he has never allowed himself to turn his face toward defeat and is thus more confused and hard-skinned, although seemingly more content.*)

HAPPY (*getting out of bed*). He's going to get his license taken away if he keeps that up. I'm getting nervous about him, y'know, Biff?

BIFF. His eyes are going.

HAPPY. No, I've driven with him. He sees all right. He just doesn't keep his mind on it. I drove into the city with him last week. He stops at a green light and then it turns red and he goes. (*He laughs*)

BIFF. Maybe he's color-blind.

HAPPY. Pop? Why he's got the finest eye for color in the business. You know that.

BIFF (*sitting down on his bed*). I'm going to sleep.

HAPPY. You're not still sour on Dad, are you, Biff?

BIFF. He's all right, I guess.

WILLY (*underneath them, in the living-room*). Yes, sir, eighty thousand miles—eighty-two thousand!

BIFF. You smoking?

HAPPY (*holding out a pack of cigarettes*). Want one?

BIFF (*taking a cigarette*). I can never sleep when I smell it.

WILLY. What a simonizing job, heh!

HAPPY (*with deep sentiment*). Funny, Biff, y'know? Us sleeping in here again? The old beds. (*He pats his bed affectionately*) All the talk that went across those two beds, huh? Our whole lives.

BIFF. Yeah. Lotta dreams and plans.

HAPPY (*with a deep and masculine laugh*). About five hundred women would like to know what was said in this room. (*They share a short laugh*)

BIFF. Remember that big Betsy something—what the hell was her name—over on Bushwick Avenue?

HAPPY (*combing his hair*). With the collie dog!

BIFF. That's the one. I got you in there, remember?.

HAPPY. Yeah, that was my first time—I think. Boy, there was a pig! (*They laugh, almost crudely*) You taught me everything I know about women. Don't forget that.

BIFF. I bet you forgot how bashful you used to be. Especially with girls.

HAPPY. Oh, I still am, Biff.

BIFF. Oh, go on.

HAPPY. I just control it, that's all. I think I got less bashful and you got more so. What happened, Biff? Where's the old humor, the old confidence? (*He shakes Biff's knee. Biff gets up and moves restlessly about the room*) What's the matter?

BIFF. Why does Dad mock me all the time?

HAPPY. He's not mocking you, he—

BIFF. Everything I say there's a twist of mockery on his face. I can't get near him.

HAPPY. He just wants you to make good, that's all. I wanted to talk to you about Dad for a long time, Biff. Something's—happening to him. He—talks to himself.

BIFF. I noticed that this morning. But he always mumbled.

HAPPY. But not so noticeable. It got so embarrassing I sent him to Florida. And you know something? Most of the time he's talking to you.

BIFF. What's he say about me?

HAPPY. I can't make it out.

BIFF. What's he say about me?

HAPPY. I think the fact that you're not settled, that you're still kind of up in the air . . .

BIFF. There's one or two other things depressing him, Happy.

HAPPY. What do you mean?

BIFF. Never mind. Just don't lay it all to me.

HAPPY. But I think if you just got started —I mean—is there any future for you out there?

BIFF. I tell ya, Hap, I don't know what the future is. I don't know—what I'm supposed to want.

HAPPY. What do you mean?

BIFF. Well, I spent six or seven years after high school trying to work myself up. Shipping clerk, salesman, business of one kind or another. And it's a measly manner of existence. To get on that subway on the hot mornings in summer. To devote your whole life to keeping stock, or making phone calls, or selling or buying. To suffer fifty weeks of the year for the sake of a two-week vacation, when all you really desire is to be outdoors, with your shirt off. And always to have to get ahead of the next fella. And still—that's how you build a future.

HAPPY. Well, you really enjoy it on a farm? Are you content out there?

BIFF (*with rising agitation*). Hap, I've had twenty or thirty different kinds of jobs since I left home before the war, and it always turns out the same. I just realized it lately. In Nebraska where I herded cattle, and the Dakotas, and Arizona, and now in Texas. It's why I came home now, I guess, because I realized it. This farm I work on, it's spring there now, see? And they've got about fifteen new colts. There's nothing more inspiring or—beautiful than the sight of a mare and a new colt. And it's cool there now, see? Texas is cool now, and it's spring. And whenever spring comes to where I am, I suddenly get the feeling, my God, I'm not gettin' anywhere! What the hell am I doing, playing around with horses, twenty-eight dollars a week! I'm thirty-four years old, I oughta be makin' my future. That's when I come running home. And now, I get here, and I don't know what to do with myself. (*After a pause*) I've always made a point of not wasting my life, and everytime I come back here I know that all I've done is to waste my life.

HAPPY. You're a poet, you know that, Biff? You're a—you're an idealist!

BIFF. No, I'm mixed up very bad. Maybe I oughta get married. Maybe I oughta get stuck into something. Maybe that's my trouble. I'm like a boy. I'm not married, I'm not in business, I just—I'm like a boy.

Are you content, Hap? You're a success, aren't you? Are you content?

HAPPY. Hell, no!

BIFF. Why? You're making money, aren't you?

HAPPY (*moving about with energy, expressiveness*). All I can do now is wait for the merchandise manager to die. And suppose I get to be merchandise manager? He's a good friend of mine, and he just built a terrific estate on Long Island. And he lived there about two months and sold it, and now he's building another one. He can't enjoy it once it's finished. And I know that's just what I would do. I don't know what the hell I'm workin' for. Sometimes I sit in my apartment—all alone. And I think of the rent I'm paying. And it's crazy. But then, it's what I always wanted. My own apartment, a car, and plenty of women. And still, goddammit, I'm lonely.

BIFF (*with enthusiasm*). Listen, why don't you come out West with me?

HAPPY. You and I, heh?

BIFF. Sure, maybe we could buy a ranch. Raise cattle, use our muscles. Men built like we are should be working out in the open.

HAPPY (*avidly*). The Loman Brothers, heh?

BIFF (*with vast affection*). Sure, we'd be known all over the counties!

HAPPY (*enthralled*). That's what I dream about, Biff. Sometimes I want to just rip my clothes off in the middle of the store and outbox that goddam merchandise manager. I mean I can outbox, outrun, and outlift anybody in that store, and I have to take orders from those common, petty sons-of-bitches till I can't stand it any more.

BIFF. I'm tellin' you, kid, if you were with me I'd be happy out there.

HAPPY (*enthused*). See, Biff, everybody around me is so false that I'm constantly lowering my ideals . . .

BIFF. Baby, together we'd stand up for one another, we'd have someone to trust.

HAPPY. If I were around you—

BIFF. Hap, the trouble is we weren't brought up to grub for money. I don't know how to do it.

HAPPY. Neither can I!

BIFF. Then let's go!

HAPPY. The only thing is—what can you make out there?

BIFF. But look at your friend. Builds an estate and then hasn't the peace of mind to live in it.

HAPPY. Yeah, but when he walks into the store the waves part in front of him. That's fifty-two thousand dollars a year coming through the revolving door, and I got more in my pinky finger than he's got in his head.

BIFF. Yeah, but you just said—

HAPPY. I gotta show some of those pompous, self-important executives over there that Hap Loman can make the grade. I want to walk into the store the way he walks in. Then I'll go with you, Biff. We'll be together yet, I swear. But take those two we had tonight. Now weren't they gorgeous creatures?

BIFF. Yeah, yeah, most gorgeous I've had in years.

HAPPY. I get that any time I want, Biff. Whenever I feel disgusted. The only trouble is, it gets like bowling or something. I just keep knockin' them over and it doesn't mean anything. You still run around a lot?

BIFF. Naa. I'd like to find a girl—steady, somebody with substance.

HAPPY. That's what I long for.

BIFF. Go on! You'd never come home.

HAPPY. I would! Somebody with character, with resistance! Like Mom, y'know? You're gonna call me a bastard when I tell you this. That girl Charlotte I was with tonight is engaged to be married in five weeks. (*He tries on his new hat*)

BIFF. No kiddin'!

HAPPY. Sure, the guy's in line for the vice-presidency of the store. I don't know what gets into me, maybe I just have an overdeveloped sense of competition or something, but I went and ruined her, and furthermore I can't get rid of her. And he's the third executive I've done that to. Isn't that a crummy characteristic? And to top it all, I go to their weddings! (*Indignantly, but laughing*) Like I'm not supposed to take bribes. Manufacturers offer me a hundred-dollar bill now and then to throw an order their way. You know how honest I am, but it's like this girl, see. I hate myself for it. Because I don't want the girl, and, still, I take it and—I love it!

BIFF. Let's go to sleep.

HAPPY. I guess we didn't settle anything, heh?

BIFF. I just got one idea that I think I'm going to try.

HAPPY. What's that?

BIFF. Remember Bill Oliver?

HAPPY. Sure, Oliver is very big now. You want to work for him again?

BIFF. No, but when I quit he said something to me. He put his arm on my shoulder and he said, "Biff, if you ever need anything, come to me."

HAPPY. I remember that. That sounds good.

BIFF. I think I'll go to see him. If I could get ten thousand or even seven or eight thousand dollars I could buy a beautiful ranch.

HAPPY. I bet he'd back you. 'Cause he thought highly of you, Biff. I mean, they all do. You're well liked, Biff. That's why I say to come back here, and we both have the apartment. And I'm tellin' you, Biff, any babe you want . . .

BIFF. No, with a ranch I could do the work I like and still be something. I just wonder though. I wonder if Oliver still thinks I stole that carton of basketballs.

HAPPY. Oh, he probably forgot that long ago. It's almost ten years. You're too sensitive. Anyway, he didn't really fire you.

BIFF. Well, I think he was going to. I think that's why I quit. I was never sure whether he knew or not. I know he thought the world of me, though. I was the only one he'd let lock up the place.

WILLY (*below*). You gonna wash the engine, Biff?

HAPPY. Shh! (*Biff looks at Happy, who is gazing down, listening. Willy is mumbling in the parlor*)

HAPPY. You hear that? (*They listen. Willy laughs warmly*)

BIFF (*growing angry*). Doesn't he know Mom can hear that?

WILLY. Don't get your sweater dirty, Biff! (*A look of pain crosses Biff's face*)

HAPPY. Isn't that terrible? Don't leave again, will you? You'll find a job here. You gotta stick around. I don't know what to do about him, it's getting embarrassing.

WILLY. What a simonizing job!

BIFF. Mom's hearing that!

WILLY. No kiddin', Biff, you got a date? Wonderful!

HAPPY. Go on to sleep. But talk to him in the morning, will you?

BIFF (*reluctantly getting into bed*). With her in the house. Brother!

HAPPY (*getting into bed*). I wish you'd have a good talk with him.

(*The light on their room begins to fade.*)

BIFF (*to himself, in bed*). That selfish, stupid . . .

HAPPY. Sh . . . Sleep, Biff.

(*Their light is out. Well before they have finished speaking, Willy's form is dimly seen below in the darkened kitchen. He opens the refrigerator, searches in there and takes out a bottle of milk. The apartment houses are fading out, and the entire house and surroundings become covered with leaves. Music insinuates itself as the leaves appear.*)

WILLY. Just wanna be careful with those girls, Biff, that's all. Don't make any promises. No promises of any kind. Because a girl, y'know, they always believe what you tell 'em, and you're very young, Biff, you're too young to be talking seriously to girls.

(*Light rises on the kitchen. Willy, talking, shuts the refrigerator door and comes downstage to the kitchen table. He pours milk into a glass. He is totally immersed in himself, smiling faintly.*)

WILLY. Too young entirely, Biff. You want to watch your schooling first. Then when you're all set, there'll be plenty of girls for a boy like you. (*He smiles broadly at a kitchen chair*) That so? The girls pay for you? (*He laughs*) Boy, you must really be makin' a hit.

(*Willy is gradually addressing—physically —a point offstage, speaking through the wall of the kitchen, and his voice has been rising in volume to that of a normal conversation.*)

WILLY. I been wondering why you polish the car so careful. Ha! Don't leave the hubcaps, boys. Get the chamois to the hubcaps. Happy, use newspapers on the windows, it's the easiest thing. Show him how to do it, Biff! You see, Happy? Pad it up, use it like a pad. That's it, that's it, good work. You're doin' all right, Hap. (*He pauses, then nods in approbation for a few seconds, then looks upward*) Biff, first thing we gotta do when we get time is clip that big branch over the house. Afraid it's gonna fall in a storm and hit the roof. Tell you what. We get a rope and sling her around, and then we climb up there with a couple of saws and take her down. Soon as you finish the car, boys, I wanna see ya. I got a surprise for you, boys.

BIFF (*offstage*). Whatta ya got, Dad?

WILLY. No, you finish first. Never leave a job till you're finished—remember that. (*Looking toward the "big trees"*) Biff, up in Albany I saw a beautiful hammock. I think I'll buy it next trip, and we'll hang it right between those two elms. Wouldn't that be something? Just swingin' there under those branches. Boy, that would be . . .

(*Young Biff and Young Happy appear from the direction Willy was addressing. Happy carries rags and a pail of water. Biff, wearing a sweater with a block "S," carries a football.*)

BIFF (*pointing in the direction of the car offstage*). How's that, Pop, professional?

WILLY. Terrific. Terrific job, boys. Good work, Biff.

HAPPY. Where's the surprise, Pop?

WILLY. In the back seat of the car.

HAPPY. Boy! (*He runs off*)

BIFF. What is it, Dad? Tell me, what'd you buy?

WILLY (*laughing, cuffs him*). Never mind, something I want you to have.

BIFF (*turns and starts off*). What is it, Hap?

HAPPY (*offstage*). It's a punching bag!

BIFF. Oh, Pop!

WILLY. It's got Gene Tunney's signature on it!

(*Happy runs onstage with a punching bag.*)

BIFF. Gee, how'd you know we wanted a punching bag?

WILLY. Well, it's the finest thing for the timing.

HAPPY (*lies down on his back and pedals with his feet*). I'm losing weight, you notice, Pop?

WILLY (*to Happy*). Jumping rope is good too.

BIFF. Did you see the new football I got?

WILLY (*examining the ball*). Where'd you get a new ball?

BIFF. The coach told me to practice my passing.

WILLY. That so? And he gave you the ball, heh?

BIFF. Well, I borrowed it from the locker room. (*He laughs confidentially*)

WILLY (*laughing with him at the theft*). I want you to return that.

HAPPY. I told you he wouldn't like it!

BIFF (*angrily*). Well, I'm bringing it back!

WILLY (*stopping the incipient argument, to Happy*). Sure, he's gotta practice with a regulation ball, doesn't he? (*To Biff*) Coach'll probably congratulate you on your initiative!

BIFF. Oh, he keeps congratulating my initiative all the time, Pop.

WILLY. That's because he likes you. If somebody else took that ball there'd be an uproar. So what's the report, boys, what's the report?

BIFF. Where'd you go this time, Dad? Gee, we were lonesome for you.

WILLY (*pleased, puts an arm around each boy and they come down to the apron*). Lonesome, heh?

BIFF. Missed you every minute.

WILLY. Don't say? Tell you a secret, boys. Don't breathe it to a soul. Someday I'll have my own business, and I'll never have to leave home any more.

HAPPY. Like Uncle Charley, heh?

WILLY. Bigger than Uncle Charley! Because Charley is not liked. He's liked, but he's not—well liked.

BIFF. Where'd you go this time, Dad?

WILLY. Well, I got on the road, and I went north to Providence. Met the Mayor.

BIFF. The Mayor of Providence!

WILLY. He was sitting in the hotel lobby.

BIFF. What'd he say?

WILLY. He said, "Morning!" And I said, "You got a fine city here, Mayor." And then he had coffee with me. And then I went to Waterbury. Waterbury is a fine city. Big clock city, the famous Waterbury clock. Sold a nice bill there. And then Boston—Boston is the cradle of the Revolution. A fine city. And a couple of other towns in Mass., and on to Portland and Bangor and straight home!

BIFF. Gee, I'd love to go with you sometime, Dad.

WILLY. Soon as summer comes.

HAPPY. Promise?

WILLY. You and Hap and I, and I'll show you all the towns. America is full of beautiful towns and fine, upstanding people. And they know me, boys, they know me up and down New England. The finest people. And when I bring you fellas up, there'll be open sesame for all of us, 'cause one thing, boys: I have friends. I can park my car in any street in New England, and the cops protect it like their own. This summer, heh?

BIFF and HAPPY (*together*). Yeah! You bet!

WILLY. We'll take our bathing suits.

HAPPY. We'll carry your bags, Pop!

WILLY. Oh, won't that be somethin'! Me comin' into the Boston stores with you boys carryin' my bags. What a sensation! (*Biff is prancing around, practicing passing the ball.*)

WILLY. You nervous, Biff, about the game?

BIFF. Not if you're gonna be there.

WILLY. What do they say about you in school, now that they made you captain?

HAPPY. There's a crowd of girls behind him everytime the classes change.

BIFF (*taking Willy's hand*). This Saturday, Pop, this Saturday—just for you, I'm going to break through for a touchdown.

HAPPY. You're supposed to pass.

BIFF. I'm takin' one play for Pop. You watch me, Pop, and when I take off my helmet, that means I'm breakin' out. Then you watch me crash through that line!

WILLY (*kisses Biff*). Oh, wait'll I tell this in Boston!

(*Bernard enters in knickers. He is younger than Biff, earnest and loyal, a worried boy.*)

BERNARD. Biff, where are you? You're supposed to study with me today.

WILLY. Hey, looka Bernard. What're you lookin' so anemic about, Bernard?

BERNARD. He's gotta study, Uncle Willy. He's got Regents next week.

HAPPY (*tauntingly, spinning Bernard around*). Let's box, Bernard!

BERNARD. Biff! (*He gets away from Happy*) Listen, Biff, I heard Mr. Birnbaum say that if you don't start studyin' math he's gonna flunk you, and you won't graduate. I heard him!

WILLY. You better study with him, Biff. Go ahead now.

BERNARD. I heard him!

BIFF. Oh, Pop, you didn't see my sneakers! (*He holds up a foot for Willy to look at*)

WILLY. Hey, that's a beautiful job of printing!

BERNARD (*wiping his glasses*). Just because he printed University of Virginia on his sneakers doesn't mean they've got to graduate him, Uncle Willy!

WILLY (*angrily*). What're you talking about? With scholarships to three universities they're gonna flunk him?

BERNARD. But I heard Mr. Birnbaum say—

WILLY. Don't be a pest, Bernard! (*To his boys*) What an anemic!

BERNARD. Okay, I'm waiting for you in my house, Biff.

(*Bernard goes off. The Lomans laugh.*)

WILLY. Bernard is not well liked, is he?

BIFF. He's liked, but he's not well liked.

HAPPY. That's right, Pop.

WILLY. That's just what I mean. Bernard can get the best marks in school, y'understand, but when he gets out in the business world, y'understand, you are going to be five times ahead of him. That's why I thank Almighty God you're both built like Adonises. Because the man who makes an appearance in the business world, the man who creates personal interest, is the man who gets ahead. Be liked and you will never want. You take me, for instance. I never have to wait in line to see a buyer. "Willy Loman is here!" That's all they have to know, and I go right through.

BIFF. Did you knock them dead, Pop?

WILLY. Knocked 'em cold in Providence, slaughtered 'em in Boston.

HAPPY (*on his back, pedaling again*). I'm losing weight, you notice, Pop?

(*Linda enters, as of old, a ribbon in her hair, carrying a basket of washing.*)

LINDA (*with youthful energy*). Hello, dear!

WILLY. Sweetheart!

LINDA. How'd the Chevvy run?

WILLY. Chevrolet, Linda, is the greatest car ever built. (*To the boys*) Since when do you let your mother carry wash up the stairs?

BIFF. Grab hold there, boy!

HAPPY. Where to, Mom?

LINDA. Hang them up on the line. And you better go down to your friends, Biff. The cellar is full of boys. They don't know what to do with themselves.

BIFF. Ah, when Pop comes home they can wait!

WILLY (*laughs appreciatively*). You better go down and tell them what to do, Biff.

BIFF. I think I'll have them sweep out the furnace room.

WILLY. Good work, Biff.

BIFF (*goes through wall-line of kitchen to doorway at back and calls down*). Fellas! Everybody sweep out the furnace room! I'll be right down!

VOICES. All right! Okay, Biff!

BIFF. George and Sam and Frank, come out back! We're hangin' up the wash! Come on, Hap, on the double! (*He and Happy carry out the basket*)

LINDA. The way they obey him!

WILLY. Well, that's training, the training. I'm tellin' you, I was sellin' thousands and thousands, but I had to come home.

LINDA. Oh, the whole block'll be at that game. Did you sell anything?

WILLY. I did five hundred gross in Providence and seven hundred gross in Boston.

LINDA. No! Wait a minute, I've got a pencil. (*She pulls pencil and paper out of her apron pocket*) That makes your commission . . . Two hundred—my God! Two hundred and twelve dollars!

WILLY. Well, I didn't figure it yet, but . . .

LINDA. How much did you do?

WILLY. Well, I—I did—about a hundred and eighty gross in Providence. Well, no —it came to—roughly two hundred gross on the whole trip.

LINDA (*without hesitation*). Two hundred gross. That's . . . (*She figures*)

WILLY. The trouble was that three of the stores were half closed for inventory in Boston. Otherwise I woulda broke records.

LINDA. Well, it makes seventy dollars and some pennies. That's very good.

WILLY. What do we owe?

LINDA. Well, on the first there's sixteen dollars on the refrigerator—

WILLY. Why sixteen?

LINDA. Well, the fan belt broke, so it was a dollar eighty.

WILLY. But it's brand new.

LINDA. Well, the man said that's the way it is. Till they work themselves in, y'know. (*They move through the wall-line into the kitchen.*)

WILLY. I hope we didn't get stuck on that machine.

LINDA. They got the biggest ads of any of them!

WILLY. I know, it's a fine machine. What else?

LINDA. Well, there's nine-sixty for the washing machine. And for the vacuum cleaner there's three and a half due on the fifteenth. Then the roof, you got twenty-one dollars remaining.

WILLY. It don't leak, does it?

LINDA. No, they did a wonderful job. Then you owe Frank for the carburetor.

WILLY. I'm not going to pay that man! That goddam Chevrolet, they ought to prohibit the manufacture of that car!

LINDA. Well, you owe him three and a half. And odds and ends, comes to around a hundred and twenty dollars by the fifteenth.

WILLY. A hundred and twenty dollars! My God, if business don't pick up I don't know what I'm gonna do!

LINDA. Well, next week you'll do better.

WILLY. Oh, I'll knock 'em dead next week. I'll go to Hartford. I'm very well liked in Hartford. You know, the trouble is, Linda, people don't seem to take to me. (*They move onto the forestage.*)

LINDA. Oh, don't be foolish.

WILLY. I know it when I walk in. They seem to laugh at me.

LINDA. Why? Why would they laugh at you? Don't talk that way, Willy.

(*Willy moves to the edge of the stage. Linda goes into the kitchen and starts to darn stockings.*)

WILLY. I don't know the reason for it, but they just pass me by. I'm not noticed.

LINDA. But you're doing wonderful, dear. You're making seventy to a hundred dollars a week.

WILLY. But I gotta be at it ten, twelve hours a day. Other men—I don't know—they do it easier. I don't know why—I can't stop myself—I talk too much. A man oughta come in with a few words. One thing about Charley. He's a man of few words, and they respect him.

LINDA. You don't talk too much, you're just lively.

WILLY (*smiling*). Well, I figure, what the hell, life is short, a couple of jokes. (*To himself*) I joke too much! (*The smile goes*)

LINDA. Why? You're—

WILLY. I'm fat. I'm very—foolish to look at, Linda. I didn't tell you, but Christmas time I happened to be calling on F. H. Stewarts, and a salesman I know, as I was going in to see the buyer I heard him say something about—walrus. And I—I cracked him right across the face. I won't take that. I simply will not take that. But they do laugh at me. I know that.

LINDA. Darling . . .

WILLY. I gotta overcome it. I know I gotta overcome it. I'm not dressing to advantage, maybe.

LINDA. Willy, darling, you're the handsomest man in the world—

WILLY. Oh, no, Linda.

LINDA. To me you are. (*Slight pause*) The handsomest.

(*From the darkness is heard the laughter of a woman. Willy doesn't turn to it, but it continues through Linda's lines.*)

LINDA. And the boys, Willy. Few men are idolized by their children the way you are.

(*Music is heard as behind a scrim, to the left of the house. The Woman, dimly seen, is dressing.*)

WILLY (*with great feeling*). You're the best there is, Linda, you're a pal, you know that? On the road—on the road I want to grab you sometimes and just kiss the life outa you.

(*The laughter is loud now, and he moves into a brightening area at the left, where The Woman has come from behind the scrim and is standing, putting on her hat, looking into a "mirror" and laughing.*)

WILLY. 'Cause I get so lonely—especially when business is bad and there's nobody to talk to. I get the feeling that I'll never sell anything again, that I won't make a living for you, or a business, a business for the boys. (*He talks through The Woman's subsiding laughter; The Woman primps at the "mirror"*) There's so much I want to make for—

THE WOMAN. Me? You didn't make me, Willy. I picked you.

WILLY (*pleased*). You picked me?

THE WOMAN (*who is quite proper-looking, Willy's age*). I did. I've been sitting at that desk watching all the salesmen go by, day in, day out. But you've got such a sense of humor, and we do have such a good time together, don't we?

WILLY. Sure, sure. (*He takes her in his arms*) Why do you have to go now?

THE WOMAN. It's two o'clock . . .

WILLY. No, come on in! (*He pulls her*)

THE WOMAN. . . . my sisters'll be scandalized. When'll you be back?

WILLY. Oh, two weeks about. Will you come up again?

THE WOMAN. Sure thing. You do make me laugh. It's good for me. (*She squeezes his arm, kisses him*) And I think you're a wonderful man.

WILLY. You picked me, heh?

THE WOMAN. Sure. Because you're so sweet. And such a kidder.

WILLY. Well, I'll see you next time I'm in Boston.

THE WOMAN. I'll put you right through to the buyers.

WILLY (*slapping her bottom*). Right. Well, bottoms up!

THE WOMAN (*slaps him gently and laughs*). You just kill me, Willy. (*He suddenly grabs her and kisses her roughly*) You kill me. And thanks for the stockings. I love a lot of stockings. Well, good night.

WILLY. Good night. And keep your pores open!

THE WOMAN. Oh, Willy!

(*The Woman bursts out laughing, and Linda's laughter blends in. The Woman disappears into the dark. Now the area at the kitchen table brightens. Linda is sitting where she was at the kitchen table, but now is mending a pair of her silk stockings.*)

LINDA. You are, Willy. The handsomest man. You've got no reason to feel that—

WILLY (*coming out of The Woman's dimming area and going over to Linda*). I'll make it all up to you. Linda, I'll—

LINDA. There's nothing to make up, dear. You're doing fine, better than—

WILLY (*noticing her mending*). What's that?

LINDA. Just mending my stockings. They're so expensive—

WILLY (*angrily, taking them from her*). I won't have you mending stockings in this house! Now throw them out!

(*Linda puts the stockings in her pocket.*)

BERNARD (*entering on the run*). Where is he? If he doesn't study!

WILLY (*moving to the forestage, with great agitation*). You'll give him the answers!

BERNARD. I do, but I can't on a Regents! That's a state exam! They're liable to arrest me!

WILLY. Where is he? I'll whip him, I'll whip him!

LINDA. And he'd better give back that football, Willy, it's not nice.

WILLY. Biff! Where is he? Why is he taking everything?

LINDA. He's too rough with the girls, Willy. All of the mothers are afraid of him!

WILLY. I'll whip him!

BERNARD. He's driving the car without a license!

(*The Woman's laugh is heard.*)

WILLY. Shut up!

LINDA. All the mothers—

WILLY. Shut up!

BERNARD (*backing quietly away and out*). Mr. Birnbaum says he's stuck up.

WILLY. Get outa here!

BERNARD. If he doesn't buckle down he'll flunk math! (*He goes off*)

LINDA. He's right, Willy, you've gotta—

WILLY (*exploding at her*). There's nothing the matter with him! You want him to be a worm like Bernard? He's got spirit, personality . . .

(*As he speaks, Linda, almost in tears, exits into the living-room. Willy is alone in the kitchen, wilting and staring. The leaves are gone. It is night again, and the apartment houses look down from behind.*)

WILLY. Loaded with it. Loaded! What is he stealing? He's giving it back, isn't he? Why is he stealing? What did I tell him? I never in my life told him anything but decent things.

(*Happy in pajamas has come down the stairs; Willy suddenly becomes aware of Happy's presence.*)

HAPPY. Let's go now, come on.

WILLY (*sitting down at the kitchen table*). Huh! Why did she have to wax the floors herself? Everytime she waxes the floors she keels over. She knows that!

HAPPY. Shh! Take it easy. What brought you back tonight?

WILLY. I got an awful scare. Nearly hit a kid in Yonkers. God! Why didn't I go to Alaska with my brother Ben that time! Ben! That man was a genius, that man was success incarnate! What a mistake! He begged me to go.

HAPPY. Well, there's no use in—

WILLY. You guys! There was a man started with the clothes on his back and ended up with diamond mines!

HAPPY. Boy, some day I'd like to know how he did it.

WILLY. What's the mystery? The man knew what he wanted and went out and got it! Walked into a jungle, and comes out, the age of twenty-one, and he's rich! The world is an oyster, but you don't crack it open on a mattress!

HAPPY. Pop, I told you I'm gonna retire you for life.

WILLY. You'll retire me for life on seventy goddam dollars a week? And your women and your car and your apartment, and you'll retire me for life! Christ's sake, I couldn't get past Yonkers today! Where are you guys, where are you? The woods are burning! I can't drive a car!

*(Charley has appeared in the doorway. He is a large man, slow of speech, laconic, immovable. In all he says, despite what he says, there is pity, and, now, trepidation. He has a robe over pajamas, slippers on his feet. He enters the kitchen.)*

CHARLEY. Everything all right?

HAPPY. Yeah, Charley, everything's . . .

WILLY. What's the matter?

CHARLEY. I heard some noise. I thought something happened. Can't we do something about the walls? You sneeze in here, and in my house hats blow off.

HAPPY. Let's go to bed, Dad. Come on. *(Charley signals to Happy to go.)*

WILLY. You go ahead, I'm not tired at the moment.

HAPPY *(to Willy)*. Take it easy, huh? *(He exits)*

WILLY. What're you doin' up?

CHARLEY *(sitting down at the kitchen table opposite Willy)*. Couldn't sleep good. I had a heartburn.

WILLY. Well, you don't know how to eat.

CHARLEY. I eat with my mouth.

WILLY. No, you're ignorant. You gotta know about vitamins and things like that.

CHARLEY. Come on, let's shoot. Tire you out a little.

WILLY *(hesitantly)*. All right. You got cards?

CHARLEY *(taking a deck from his pocket)*. Yeah, I got them. Someplace. What is it with those vitamins?

WILLY *(dealing)*. They build up your bones. Chemistry.

CHARLEY. Yeah, but there's no bones in a heartburn.

WILLY. What are you talkin' about? Do you know the first thing about it?

CHARLEY. Don't get insulted.

WILLY. Don't talk about something you don't know anything about.

*(They are playing. Pause.)*

CHARLEY. What're you doin' home?

WILLY. A little trouble with the car.

CHARLEY. Oh. *(Pause)* I'd like to take a trip to California.

WILLY. Don't say.

CHARLEY. You want a job?

WILLY. I got a job, I told you that. *(After a slight pause)* What the hell are you offering me a job for?

CHARLEY. Don't get insulted.

WILLY. Don't insult me.

CHARLEY. I don't see no sense in it. You don't have to go on this way.

WILLY. I got a good job. *(Slight pause)* What do you keep comin' in here for?

CHARLEY. You want me to go?

WILLY *(after a pause, withering)*. I can't understand it. He's going back to Texas again. What the hell is that?

CHARLEY. Let him go.

WILLY. I got nothin' to give him, Charley, I'm clean, I'm clean.

CHARLEY. He won't starve. None of them starve. Forget about him.

WILLY. Then what have I got to remember?

CHARLEY. You take it too hard. To hell with it. When a deposit bottle is broken you don't get your nickel back.

WILLY. That's easy enough for you to say.

CHARLEY. That ain't easy for me to say.

WILLY. Did you see the ceiling I put up in the living-room?

CHARLEY. Yeah, that's a piece of work. To put up a ceiling is a mystery to me. How do you do it?

WILLY. What's the difference?

CHARLEY. Well, talk about it.

WILLY. You gonna put up a ceiling?

CHARLEY. How could I put up a ceiling?

WILLY. Then what the hell are you bothering me for?

CHARLEY. You're insulted again.

WILLY. A man who can't handle tools is not a man. You're disgusting.

CHARLEY Don't call me disgusting, Willy.

*(Uncle Ben, carrying a valise and an umbrella, enters the forestage from around the right corner of the house. He is a stolid man, in his sixties, with a mustache and an authoritative air. He is utterly certain of his destiny, and there is an aura of far places about him. He enters exactly as Willy speaks.)*

WILLY. I'm getting awfully tired, Ben.

*(Ben's music is heard. Ben looks around at everything.)*

CHARLEY. Good, keep playing; you'll sleep better. Did you call me Ben?

*(Ben looks at his watch.)*

WILLY. That's funny. For a second there you reminded me of my brother Ben.

BEN. I only have a few minutes. *(He strolls, inspecting the place. Willy and Charley continue playing)*

CHARLEY. You never heard from him again, heh? Since that time?

WILLY. Didn't Linda tell you? Couple of weeks ago we got a letter from his wife in Africa. He died.

CHARLEY. That so.

BEN *(chuckling)*. So this is Brooklyn, eh?

CHARLEY. Maybe you're in for some of his money.

WILLY. Naa, he had seven sons. There's just one opportunity I had with that man . . .

BEN. I must make a train, William. There are several properties I'm looking at in Alaska.

WILLY. Sure, sure! If I'd gone with him to Alaska that time, everything would've been totally different.

CHARLEY. Go on, you'd froze to death up there.

WILLY. What're you talking about?

BEN. Opportunity is tremendous in Alaska, William. Surprised you're not up there.

WILLY. Sure, tremendous.

CHARLEY. Heh?

WILLY. There was the only man I ever met who knew the answers.

CHARLEY. Who?

BEN. How are you all?

WILLY *(taking a pot, smiling)*. Fine, fine.

CHARLEY. Pretty sharp tonight.

BEN. Is Mother living with you?

WILLY. No, she died a long time ago.

CHARLEY. Who?

BEN. That's too bad. Fine specimen of a lady, Mother.

WILLY *(to Charley)*. Heh?

BEN. I'd hoped to see the old girl.

CHARLEY. Who died?

BEN. Heard anything from Father, have you?

WILLY *(unnerved)*. What do you mean, who died?

CHARLEY *(taking a pot)*. What're you talkin' about?

BEN *(looking at his watch)*. William, it's half-past eight!

WILLY *(as though to dispel his confusion he angrily stops Charley's hand)*. That's my build!

CHARLEY. I put the ace—

WILLY. If you don't know how to play the game I'm not gonna throw my money away on you!

CHARLEY *(rising)*. It was my ace, for God's sake!

WILLY. I'm through, I'm through!

BEN. When did Mother die?

WILLY. Long ago. Since the beginning you never knew how to play cards.

CHARLEY *(picks up the cards and goes to the door)*. All right! Next time I'll bring a deck with five aces.

WILLY. I don't play that kind of game!

CHARLEY *(turning to him)*. You ought to be ashamed of yourself!

WILLY. Yeah?

CHARLEY. Yeah! *(He goes out)*

WILLY *(slamming the door after him)*. Ignoramus!

BEN *(as Willy comes toward him through the wall-line of the kitchen)*. So you're William.

WILLY *(shaking Ben's hand)*. Ben! I've been waiting for you so long! What's the answer? How did you do it?

BEN. Oh, there's a story in that.

*(Linda enters the forestage, as of old, carrying the wash basket.)*

LINDA. Is this Ben?

BEN *(gallantly)*. How do you do, my dear.

LINDA. Where've you been all these years? Willy's always wondered why you—

WILLY *(pulling Ben away from her impatiently)*. Where is Dad? Didn't you follow him? How did you get started?

BEN. Well, I don't know how much you remember.

WILLY. Well, I was just a baby, of course, only three or four years old—

BEN. Three years and eleven months.

WILLY. What a memory, Ben!

BEN. I have many enterprises, William, and I have never kept books.

WILLY. I remember I was sitting under the wagon in—was it Nebraska?

BEN. It was South Dakota, and I gave you a bunch of wild flowers.

WILLY. I remember you walking away down some open road.

BEN *(laughing)*. I was going to find Father in Alaska.

WILLY. Where is he?

BEN. At that age I had a very faulty view of geography, William. I discovered after a few days that I was heading due south, so instead of Alaska, I ended up in Africa.

LINDA. Africa!

WILLY. The Gold Coast!

BEN. Principally diamond mines.

LINDA. Diamond mines!

BEN. Yes, my dear. But I've only a few minutes—

WILLY. No! Boys! Boys! *(Young Biff and Happy appear)* Listen to this. This is your Uncle Ben, a great man! Tell my boys, Ben!

BEN. Why, boys, when I was seventeen I walked into the jungle, and when I was twenty-one I walked out. *(He laughs)* And by God I was rich.

WILLY *(to the boys)*. You see what I been talking about? The greatest things can happen!

BEN *(glancing at his watch)*. I have an appointment in Ketchikan Tuesday week.

WILLY. No, Ben! Please tell about Dad. I want my boys to hear. I want them to know the kind of stock they spring from. All I remember is a man with a big beard, and I was in Mamma's lap, sitting around a fire, and some kind of high music.

BEN. His flute. He played the flute.

WILLY. Sure, the flute, that's right!

*(New music is heard, a high, rollicking tune.)*

BEN. Father was a very great and a very wild-hearted man. We would start in Boston, and he'd toss the whole family into the wagon, and then he'd drive the team right across the country; through Ohio, and Indiana, Michigan, Illinois, and all the Western states. And we'd stop in the towns and sell the flutes that he'd made on the way. Great inventor, Father. With one gadget he made more in a week than a man like you could make in a lifetime.

WILLY. That's just the way I'm bringing them up, Ben—rugged, well liked, all-around.

BEN. Yeah? *(To Biff)* Hit that, boy—hard as you can. *(He pounds his stomach)*

BIFF. Oh, no, sir!

BEN *(taking boxing stance)*. Come on, get to me! *(He laughs)*

WILLY. Go to it, Biff! Go ahead, show him!

BIFF. Okay! *(He cocks his fists and starts in)*

LINDA *(to Willy)*. Why must he fight, dear?

BEN *(sparring with Biff)*. Good boy! Good boy!

WILLY. How's that, Ben, heh?

HAPPY. Give him the left, Biff!

LINDA. Why are you fighting?

BEN. Good boy! *(Suddenly comes in, trips Biff, and stands over him, the point of his umbrella poised over Biff's eye)*

LINDA. Look out, Biff!

BIFF. Gee!

BEN *(patting Biff's knee)*. Never fight fair with a stranger, boy. You'll never get out of the jungle that way. *(Taking Linda's hand and bowing)* It was an honor and a pleasure to meet you, Linda.

LINDA *(withdrawing her hand coldly, frightened)*. Have a nice—trip.

BEN *(to Willy)*. And good luck with your—what do you do?

WILLY. Selling.

BEN. Yes. Well . . . *(He raises his hand in farewell to all)*

WILLY. No, Ben, I don't want you to think . . . *(He takes Ben's arm to show him)* It's Brooklyn, I know, but we hunt too.

BEN. Really, now.

WILLY. Oh, sure, there's snakes and rabbits and—that's why I moved out here. Why, Biff can fell any one of these trees in no time! Boys! Go right over to where they're building the apartment house and get some sand. We're gonna rebuild the entire front stoop right now! Watch this, Ben!

BIFF. Yes, sir! On the double, Hap!

HAPPY *(as he and Biff run off)*. I lost weight, Pop, you notice?

*(Charley enters in knickers, even before the boys are gone.)*

CHARLEY. Listen, if they steal any more from that building the watchman'll put the cops on them!

LINDA *(to Willy)*. Don't let Biff . . .

*(Ben laughs lustily.)*

WILLY. You shoulda seen the lumber they brought home last week. At least a dozen six-by-tens worth all kinds a money.

CHARLEY. Listen, if that watchman—

WILLY. I gave them hell, understand. But I got a couple of fearless characters there.

CHARLEY. Willy, the jails are full of fearless characters.

BEN *(clapping Willy on the back, with a laugh at Charley)*. And the stock exchange, friend!

WILLY *(joining in Ben's laughter)*. Where are the rest of your pants?

CHARLEY. My wife bought them.

WILLY. Now all you need is a golf club and you can go upstairs and go to sleep. (*To Ben*) Great athlete! Between him and his son Bernard they can't hammer a nail!

BERNARD (*rushing in*). The watchman's chasing Biff!

WILLY (*angrily*). Shut up! He's not stealing anything!

LINDA (*alarmed, hurrying off left*). Where is he? Biff, dear! (*She exits*)

WILLY (*moving toward the left, away from Ben*). There's nothing wrong. What's the matter with you?

BEN. Nervy boy. Good!

WILLY (*laughing*). Oh, nerves of iron, that Biff!

CHARLEY. Don't know what it is. My New England man comes back and he's bleedin', they murdered him up there.

WILLY. It's contacts, Charley, I got important contacts!

CHARLEY (*sarcastically*). Glad to hear it, Willy. Come in later, we'll shoot a little casino. I'll take some of your Portland money. (*He laughs at Willy and exits*)

WILLY (*turning to Ben*). Business is bad, it's murderous. But not for me, of course.

BEN. I'll stop by on my way back to Africa.

WILLY (*longingly*). Can't you stay a few days? You're just what I need, Ben, because I—I have a fine position here, but I—well, Dad left when I was such a baby and I never had a chance to talk to him and I still feel—kind of temporary about myself.

BEN. I'll be late for my train.

(*They are at opposite ends of the stage.*)

WILLY. Ben, my boys—can't we talk? They'd go into the jaws of hell for me, see, but I—

BEN. William, you're being first-rate with your boys. Outstanding, manly chaps.

WILLY (*hanging on to his words*). Oh, Ben, that's good to hear! Because sometimes I'm afraid that I'm not teaching them the right kind of—Ben, how should I teach them?

BEN (*giving great weight to each word, and with a certain vicious audacity*). William, when I walked into the jungle, I was seventeen. When I walked out I was twenty-one. And, by God, I was rich! (*He goes off into the darkness around the right corner of the house*)

WILLY. . . . was rich! That's just the spirit I want to imbue them with! To walk into a jungle! I was right! I was right! I was right!

(*Ben is gone, but Willy is still speaking to him as Linda, in nightgown and robe, enters the kitchen, glances around for Willy, then goes to the door of the house, looks out and sees him. Comes down to his left. He looks at her.*)

LINDA. Willy, dear? Willy?

WILLY. I was right!

LINDA. Did you have some cheese? (*He can't answer*) It's very late, darling. Come to bed, heh?

WILLY (*looking straight up*). Gotta break your neck to see a star in this yard.

LINDA. You coming in?

WILLY. Whatever happened to that diamond watch fob? Remember? When Ben came from Africa that time? Didn't he give me a watch fob with a diamond in it?

LINDA. You pawned it, dear. Twelve, thirteen years ago. For Biff's radio correspondence course.

WILLY. Gee, that was a beautiful thing. I'll take a walk.

LINDA. But you're in your slippers.

WILLY (*starting to go around the house at the left*). I was right! I was! (*Half to Linda, as he goes, shaking his head*) What a man! There was a man worth talking to. I was right!

LINDA (*calling after Willy*). But in your slippers, Willy!

(*Willy is almost gone when Biff, in his pajamas, comes down the stairs and enters the kitchen.*)

BIFF. What is he doing out there?

LINDA. Sh!

BIFF. God Almighty, Mom, how long has he been doing this?

LINDA. Don't, he'll hear you.

BIFF. What the hell is the matter with him?

LINDA. It'll pass by morning.

BIFF. Shouldn't we do anything?

LINDA. Oh, my dear, you should do a lot of things, but there's nothing to do, so go to sleep.

(*Happy comes down the stairs and sits on the steps.*)

HAPPY. I never heard him so loud, Mom.

LINDA. Well, come around more often; you'll hear him. (*She sits down at the table and mends the lining of Willy's jacket)*

BIFF. Why didn't you ever write me about this, Mom?

LINDA. How would I write to you? For over three months you had no address.

BIFF. I was on the move. But you know I thought of you all the time. You know that, don't you, pal?

LINDA. I know, dear, I know. But he likes to have a letter. Just to know that there's still a possibility for better things.

BIFF. He's not like this all the time, is he?

LINDA. It's when you come home he's always the worst.

BIFF. When I come home?

LINDA. When you write you're coming, he's all smiles, and talks about the future, and—he's just wonderful. And then the closer you seem to come, the more shaky he gets, and then, by the time you get here, he's arguing, and he seems angry at you. I think it's just that maybe he can't bring himself to—open up to you. Why are you so hateful to each other? Why is that?

BIFF *(evasively)*. I'm not hateful, Mom.

LINDA. But you no sooner come in the door than you're fighting!

BIFF. I don't know why, I mean to change. I'm tryin', Mom, you understand?

LINDA. Are you home to stay now?

BIFF. I don't know. I want to look around, see what's doin'.

LINDA. Biff, you can't look around all your life, can you?

BIFF. I just can't take hold, Mom. I can't take hold of some kind of a life.

LINDA. Biff, a man is not a bird, to come and go with the springtime.

BIFF. Your hair . . . *(He touches her hair)* Your hair got so gray.

LINDA. Oh, it's been gray since you were in high school. I just stopped dyeing it, that's all.

BIFF. Dye it again, will ya? I don't want my pal looking old. *(He smiles)*

LINDA. You're such a boy! You think you can go away for a year and . . . You've got to get it into your head now that one day you'll knock on this door and there'll be strange people here—

BIFF. What are you talking about? You're not even sixty, Mom.

LINDA. But what about your father?

BIFF *(lamely)*. Well, I meant him too.

HAPPY. He admires Pop.

LINDA. Biff, dear, if you don't have any feeling for him, then you can't have any feeling for me.

BIFF. Sure I can, Mom.

LINDA. No. You can't just come to see me, because I love him. *(With a threat, but only a threat, of tears)* He's the dearest man in the world to me, and I won't have anyone making him feel unwanted and low and blue. You've got to make up your mind now, darling, there's no leeway any more. Either he's your father and you pay him that respect, or else you're not to come here. I know he's not easy to get along with—nobody knows that better than me—but . . .

WILLY *(from the left, with a laugh)*. Hey, hey, Biffo!

BIFF *(starting to go out after Willy)*. What the hell is the matter with him? *(Happy stops him)*

LINDA. Don't—don't go near him!

BIFF. Stop making excuses for him! He always, always wiped the floor with you! Never had an ounce of respect for you.

HAPPY. He's always had respect for—

BIFF. What the hell do you know about it?

HAPPY *(surlily)*. Just don't call him crazy!

BIFF. He's got no character—Charley wouldn't do this. Not in his own house—spewing out that vomit from his mind.

HAPPY. Charley never had to cope with what he's got to.

BIFF. People are worse off than Willy Loman. Believe me, I've seen them!

LINDA. Then make Charley your father, Biff. You can't do that, can you? I don't say he's a great man. Willy Loman never made a lot of money. His name was never in the paper. He's not the finest character that ever lived. But he's a human being, and a terrible thing is happening to him. So attention must be paid. He's not to be allowed to fall into his grave like an old dog. Attention, attention must be finally paid to such a person. You called him crazy—

BIFF. I didn't mean—

LINDA. No, a lot of people think he's lost his—balance. But you don't have to be very smart to know what his trouble is. The man is exhausted.

HAPPY. Sure!

LINDA. A small man can be just as exhausted as a great man. He works for a company thirty-six years this March, opens up unheard-of territories to their trademark, and now in his old age they take his salary away.

HAPPY (*indignantly*). I didn't know that, Mom.

LINDA. You never asked, my dear! Now that you get your spending money someplace else you don't trouble your mind with him.

HAPPY. But I gave you money last—

LINDA. Christmas time, fifty dollars! To fix the hot water it cost ninety-seven fifty! For five weeks he's been on straight commission, like a beginner, an unknown!

BIFF. Those ungrateful bastards!

LINDA. Are they any worse than his sons? When he brought them business, when he was young, they were glad to see him. But now his old friends, the old buyers that loved him so and always found some order to hand him in a pinch—they're all dead, retired. He used to be able to make six, seven calls a day in Boston. Now he takes his valises out of the car and puts them back and takes them out again and he's exhausted. Instead of walking he talks now. He drives seven hundred miles, and when he gets there no one knows him any more, no one welcomes him. And what goes through a man's mind, driving seven hundred miles home without having earned a cent? Why shouldn't he talk to himself? Why? When he has to go to Charley and borrow fifty dollars a week and pretend to me that it's his pay? How long can that go on? How long? You see what I'm sitting here and waiting for? And you tell me he has no character? The man who never worked a day but for your benefit? When does he get the medal for that? Is this his reward—to turn around at the age of sixty-three and find his sons, who he loved better than his life, one a philandering bum—

HAPPY. Mom!

LINDA. That's all you are, my baby! (*To Biff*) And you! What happened to the love you had for him? You were such pals! How you used to talk to him on the phone every night! How lonely he was till he could come home to you!

BIFF. All right, Mom. I'll live here in my room, and I'll get a job. I'll keep away from him, that's all.

LINDA. No, Biff. You can't stay here and fight all the time.

BIFF. He threw me out of this house, remember that.

LINDA. Why did he do that? I never knew why.

BIFF. Because I know he's a fake and he doesn't like anybody around who knows!

LINDA. Why a fake? In what way? What do you mean?

BIFF. Just don't lay it all at my feet. It's between me and him—that's all I have to say. I'll chip in from now on. He'll settle for half my pay check. He'll be all right. I'm going to bed. (*He starts for the stairs*)

LINDA. He won't be all right.

BIFF (*turning on the stairs, furiously*). I hate this city and I'll stay here. Now what do you want?

LINDA. He's dying, Biff.

(*Happy turns quickly to her, shocked.*)

BIFF (*after a pause*). Why is he dying?

LINDA. He's been trying to kill himself.

BIFF (*with great horror*). How?

LINDA. I live from day to day.

BIFF. What're you talking about?

LINDA. Remember I wrote you that he smashed up the car again? In February?

BIFF. Well?

LINDA. The insurance inspector came. He said that they have evidence. That all these accidents in the last year—weren't—weren't—accidents.

HAPPY. How can they tell that? That's a lie.

LINDA. It seems there's a woman . . . (*She takes a breath as*)

⎧ BIFF (*sharply but contained*). What woman?

⎩ LINDA (*simultaneously*). . . . and this woman . . .

LINDA. What?

BIFF. Nothing. Go ahead.

LINDA. What did you say?

BIFF. Nothing. I just said what woman?

HAPPY. What about her?

LINDA. Well, it seems she was walking down the road and saw his car. She says that he wasn't driving fast at all, and that he didn't skid. She says he came to that little bridge, and then deliberately smashed into the railing, and it was only the shallowness of the water that saved him.

BIFF. Oh, no, he probably just fell asleep again.

LINDA. I don't think he fell asleep.

BIFF. Why not?

LINDA. Last month . . . (*With great difficulty*) Oh, boys, it's so hard to say a thing like this! He's just a big stupid man to you, but I tell you there's more good in him than in many other people. (*She chokes, wipes her eyes*) I was looking for a fuse. The lights blew out, and I went down the cellar. And behind the fuse box —it happened to fall out—was a length of rubber pipe—just short.

HAPPY. No kidding?

LINDA. There's a little attachment on the end of it. I knew right away. And sure enough, on the bottom of the water heater there's a new little nipple on the gas pipe.

HAPPY (*angrily*). That—jerk.

BIFF. Did you have it taken off?

LINDA. I'm—I'm ashamed to. How can I mention it to him? Every day I go down and take away that little rubber pipe. But, when he comes home, I put it back where it was. How can I insult him that way? I don't know what to do. I live from day to day, boys. I tell you, I know every thought in his mind. It sounds so old-fashioned and silly, but I tell you he put his whole life into you and you've turned your backs on him. (*She is bent over in the chair, weeping, her face in her hands*) Biff, I swear to God! Biff, his life is in your hands!

HAPPY (*to Biff*). How do you like that damned fool!

BIFF (*kissing her*). All right, pal, all right. It's all settled now. I've been remiss. I know that, Mom. But now I'll stay, and I swear to you, I'll apply myself. (*Kneeling in front of her, in a fever of self-reproach*) It's just—you see, Mom, I don't fit in business. Not that I won't try. I'll try, and I'll make good.

HAPPY. Sure you will. The trouble with you in business was you never tried to please people.

BIFF. I know, I—

HAPPY. Like when you worked for Harrison's. Bob Harrison said you were tops, and then you go and do some damn fool thing like whistling whole songs in the elevator like a comedian.

BIFF (*against Happy*). So what? I like to whistle sometimes.

HAPPY. You don't raise a guy to a responsible job who whistles in the elevator!

LINDA. Well, don't argue about it now.

HAPPY. Like when you'd go off and swim in the middle of the day instead of taking the line around.

BIFF (*his resentment rising*). Well, don't you run off? You take off sometimes, don't you? On a nice summer day?

HAPPY. Yeah, but I cover myself!

LINDA. Boys!

HAPPY. If I'm going to take a fade the boss can call any number where I'm supposed to be and they'll swear to him that I just left. I'll tell you something that I hate to say, Biff, but in the business world some of them think you're crazy.

BIFF (*angered*). Screw the business world!

HAPPY. All right, screw it! Great, but cover yourself!

LINDA. Hap, Hap!

BIFF. I don't care what they think! They've laughed at Dad for years, and you know why? Because we don't belong in this nuthouse of a city! We should be mixing cement on some open plain, or— or carpenters. A carpenter is allowed to whistle! (*Willy walks in from the entrance of the house, at left.*)

WILLY. Even your grandfather was better than a carpenter. (*Pause. They watch him*) You never grew up. Bernard does not whistle in the elevator, I assure you.

BIFF (*as though to laugh Willy out of it*). Yeah, but you do, Pop.

WILLY. I never in my life whistled in an elevator! And who in the business world thinks I'm crazy?

BIFF. I didn't mean it like that, Pop. Now don't make a whole thing out of it, will ya?

WILLY. Go back to the West! Be a carpenter, a cowboy, enjoy yourself!

LINDA. Willy, he was just saying—

WILLY. I heard what he said!

HAPPY (*trying to quiet Willy*). Hey, Pop, come on now . . .

WILLY (*continuing over Happy's line*). They laugh at me, heh? Go to Filene's, go to the Hub, go to Slattery's, Boston. Call out the name Willy Loman and see what happens! Big shot!

BIFF. All right, Pop.

WILLY. Big!

BIFF. All right!

WILLY. Why do you always insult me?

BIFF. I didn't say a word. (*To Linda*) Did I say a word?

LINDA. He didn't say anything, Willy.

WILLY (*going to the doorway of the living-room*). All right, good night, good night.

LINDA. Willy, dear, he just decided . . .

WILLY (*to Biff*). If you get tired hanging around tomorrow, paint the ceiling I put up in the living-room.

BIFF. I'm leaving early tomorrow.

HAPPY. He's going to see Bill Oliver, Pop.

WILLY (*interestedly*). Oliver? For what?

BIFF (*with reserve, but trying, trying*). He always said he'd stake me. I'd like to go into business, so maybe I can take him up on it.

LINDA. Isn't that wonderful?

WILLY. Don't interrupt. What's wonderful about it? There's fifty men in the City of New York who'd stake him. (*To Biff*) Sporting goods?

BIFF. I guess so. I know something about it and—

WILLY. He knows something about it! You know sporting goods better than Spalding, for God's sake! How much is he giving you?

BIFF. I don't know, I didn't even see him yet, but—

WILLY. Then what're you talkin' about?

BIFF (*getting angry*). Well, all I said was I'm gonna see him, that's all!

WILLY (*turning away*). Ah, you're counting your chickens again.

BIFF (*starting left for the stairs*). Oh, Jesus, I'm going to sleep!

WILLY (*calling after him*). Don't curse in this house!

BIFF (*turning*). Since when did you get so clean?

HAPPY (*trying to stop them*). Wait a . . .

WILLY. Don't use that language to me! I won't have it!

HAPPY (*grabbing Biff, shouts*). Wait a minute! I got an idea. I got a feasible idea. Come here, Biff, let's talk this over now, let's talk some sense here. When I was down in Florida last time, I thought of a great idea to sell sporting goods. It just came back to me. You and I, Biff—we have a line, the Loman Line. We train a couple of weeks, and put on a couple of exhibitions, see?

WILLY. That's an idea!

HAPPY. Wait! We form two basketball teams, see? Two water-polo teams. We play each other. It's a million dollars' worth of publicity. Two brothers, see? The Loman Brothers. Displays in the Royal Palms—all the hotels. And banners over the ring and the basketball court: "Loman Brothers." Baby, we could sell sporting goods!

WILLY. That is a one-million-dollar idea!

LINDA. Marvelous!

BIFF. I'm in great shape as far as that's concerned.

HAPPY. And the beauty of it is, Biff, it wouldn't be like a business. We'd be out playin' ball again . . .

BIFF (*enthused*). Yeah, that's . . .

WILLY. Million-dollar . . .

HAPPY. And you wouldn't get fed up with it, Biff. It'd be the family again. There'd be the old honor, and comradeship, and if you wanted to go off for a swim or somethin'—well, you'd do it! Without some smart cooky gettin' up ahead of you!

WILLY. Lick the world! You guys together could absolutely lick the civilized world.

BIFF. I'll see Oliver tomorrow. Hap, if we could work that out . . .

LINDA. Maybe things are beginning to—

WILLY (*wildly enthused, to Linda*). Stop interrupting! (*To Biff*) But don't wear sport jacket and slacks when you see Oliver.

BIFF. No, I'll—

WILLY. A business suit, and talk as little as possible, and don't crack any jokes.

BIFF. He did like me. Always liked me.

LINDA. He loved you!

WILLY (*to Linda*). Will you stop? (*To Biff*) Walk in very serious. You are not applying for a boy's job. Money is to pass. Be quiet, fine, and serious. Everybody likes a kidder, but nobody lends him money.

HAPPY. I'll try to get some myself, Biff. I'm sure I can.

WILLY. I see great things for you kids. I think your troubles are over. But remember, start big and you'll end big. Ask for fifteen. How much you gonna ask for?

BIFF. Gee, I don't know—

WILLY. And don't say "Gee." "Gee" is a boy's word. A man walking in for fifteen thousand dollars does not say "Gee!"

BIFF. Ten, I think, would be top though.

WILLY. Don't be so modest. You always started too low. Walk in with a big laugh. Don't look worried. Start off with a couple of your good stories to lighten things up.

It's not what you say, it's how you say it—because personality always wins the day.

LINDA. Oliver always thought the highest of him—

WILLY. Will you let me talk?

BIFF. Don't yell at her, Pop, will ya?

WILLY (*angrily*). I was talking, wasn't I?

BIFF. I don't like you yelling at her all the time, and I'm tellin' you, that's all.

WILLY. What're you, takin' over this house?

LINDA. Willy—

WILLY (*turning on her*). Don't take his side all the time, goddammit!

BIFF (*furiously*). Stop yelling at her!

WILLY (*suddenly pulling on his cheek, beaten down, guilt ridden*). Give my best to Bill Oliver—he may remember me. (*He exits through the living-room doorway*)

LINDA (*her voice subdued*). What'd you have to start that for? (*Biff turns away*) You see how sweet he was as soon as you talked hopefully? (*She goes over to Biff*) Come up and say good night to him. Don't let him go to bed that way.

HAPPY. Come on, Biff, let's buck him up.

LINDA. Please, dear. Just say good night. It takes so little to make him happy. Come. (*She goes through the living-room doorway, calling upstairs from within the living-room*) Your pajamas are hanging in the bathroom, Willy!

HAPPY (*looking toward where Linda went out*). What a woman! They broke the mold when they made her. You know that, Biff?

BIFF. He's off salary. My God, working on commission!

HAPPY. Well, let's face it: he's no hot-shot selling man. Except that sometimes, you have to admit, he's a sweet personality.

BIFF (*deciding*). Lend me ten bucks, will ya? I want to buy some new ties.

HAPPY. I'll take you to a place I know. Beautiful stuff. Wear one of my striped shirts tomorrow.

BIFF. She got gray. Mom got awful old. Gee, I'm gonna go in to Oliver tomorrow and knock him for a—

HAPPY. Come on up. Tell that to Dad. Let's give him a whirl. Come on.

BIFF (*steamed up*). You know, with ten thousand bucks, boy!

HAPPY (*as they go into the living-room*). That's the talk, Biff, that's the first time I've heard the old confidence out of you!

(*From within the living-room, fading off*) You're gonna live with me, kid, and any babe you want just say the word . . . (*The last lines are hardly heard. They are mounting the stairs to their parents' bedroom*)

LINDA (*entering her bedroom and addressing Willy, who is in the bathroom. She is straightening the bed for him*). Can you do anything about the shower? It drips.

WILLY (*from the bathroom*). All of a sudden everything falls to pieces! Goddam plumbing, oughta be sued, those people. I hardly finished putting it in and the thing . . . (*His words rumble off*)

LINDA. I'm just wondering if Oliver will remember him. You think he might?

WILLY (*coming out of the bathroom in his pajamas*). Remember him? What's the matter with you, you crazy? If he'd've stayed with Oliver he'd be on top by now! Wait'll Oliver gets a look at him. You don't know the average caliber any more. The average young man today—(*He is getting into bed*)—is got a caliber of zero. Greatest thing in the world for him was to bum around.

(*Biff and Happy enter the bedroom. Slight pause.*)

WILLY (*stops short, looking at Biff*). Glad to hear it, boy.

HAPPY. He wanted to say good night to you, sport.

WILLY (*to Biff*). Yeah. Knock him dead, boy. What'd you want to tell me?

BIFF. Just take it easy, Pop. Good night. (*He turns to go*)

WILLY (*unable to resist*). And if anything falls off the desk while you're talking to him—like a package or something—don't you pick it up. They have office boys for that.

LINDA. I'll make a big breakfast—

WILLY. Will you let me finish? (*To Biff*) Tell him you were in the business in the West. Not farm work.

BIFF. All right, Dad.

LINDA. I think everything—

WILLY (*going right through her speech*). And don't undersell yourself. No less than fifteen thousand dollars.

BIFF (*unable to bear him*). Okay. Good night, Mom. (*He starts moving*)

WILLY. Because you got a greatness in you, Biff, remember that. You got all kinds a greatness . . . (*He lies back, exhausted. Biff walks out*)

LINDA (*calling after Biff*). Sleep well, darling!

HAPPY. I'm gonna get married, Mom. I wanted to tell you.

LINDA. Go to sleep, dear.

HAPPY (*going*). I just wanted to tell you.

WILLY. Keep up the good work. (*Happy exits*) God . . . remember that Ebbets Field game? The championship of the city?

LINDA. Just rest. Should I sing to you?

WILLY. Yeah. Sing to me. (*Linda hums a soft lullaby*) When that team came out—he was the tallest, remember?

LINDA. Oh, yes. And in gold.

(*Biff enters the darkened kitchen, takes a cigarette, and leaves the house. He comes downstage into a golden pool of light. He smokes, staring at the night.*)

WILLY. Like a young god. Hercules—something like that. And the sun, the sun all around him. Remember how he waved to me? Right up from the field, with the representatives of three colleges standing by? And the buyers I brought, and the cheers when he came out—Loman, Loman, Loman! God Almighty, he'll be great yet. A star like that, magnificent, can never really fade away!

(*The light on Willy is fading. The gas heater begins to glow through the kitchen wall, near the stairs, a blue flame beneath red coils.*)

LINDA (*timidly*). Willy dear, what has he got against you?

WILLY. I'm so tired. Don't talk any more. (*Biff slowly returns to the kitchen. He stops, stares toward the heater.*)

LINDA. Will you ask Howard to let you work in New York?

WILLY. First thing in the morning. Everything'll be all right.

(*Biff reaches behind the heater and draws out a length of rubber tubing. He is horrified and turns his head toward Willy's room, still dimly lit, from which the strains of Linda's desperate but monotonous humming rise.*)

WILLY (*staring through the window into the moonlight*). Gee, look at the moon moving between the buildings!

(*Biff wraps the tubing around his hand and quickly goes up the stairs.*)

**CURTAIN**

## ACT TWO

*Music is heard, gay and bright. The curtain rises as the music fades away. Willy, in shirt sleeves, is sitting at the kitchen table, sipping coffee, his hat in his lap. Linda is filling his cup when she can.*

WILLY. Wonderful coffee. Meal in itself.

LINDA. Can I make you some eggs?

WILLY. No. Take a breath.

LINDA. You look so rested, dear.

WILLY. I slept like a dead one. First time in months. Imagine, sleeping till ten on a Tuesday morning. Boys left nice and early, heh?

LINDA. They were out of here by eight o'clock.

WILLY. Good work!

LINDA. It was so thrilling to see them leaving together. I can't get over the shaving lotion in this house!

WILLY (*smiling*). Mmm—

LINDA. Biff was very changed this morning. His whole attitude seemed to be hopeful. He couldn't wait to get downtown to see Oliver.

WILLY. He's heading for a change. There's no question, there simply are certain men that take longer to get—solidified. How did he dress?

LINDA. His blue suit. He's so handsome in that suit. He could be a—anything in that suit!

(*Willy gets up from the table. Linda holds his jacket for him.*)

WILLY. There's no question, no question at all. Gee, on the way home tonight I'd like to buy some seeds.

LINDA (*laughing*). That'd be wonderful. But not enough sun gets back there. Nothing'll grow any more.

WILLY. You wait, kid, before it's all over we're gonna get a little place out in the country, and I'll raise some vegetables, a couple of chickens . . .

LINDA. You'll do it yet, dear.

(*Willy walks out of his jacket. Linda follows him.*)

WILLY. And they'll get married, and come for a weekend. I'd build a little guest house. 'Cause I got so many fine tools, all I'd need would be a little lumber and some peace of mind.

LINDA (*joyfully*). I sewed the lining . . .

WILLY. I could build two guest houses,

so they'd both come. Did he decide how much he's going to ask Oliver for?

LINDA (*getting him into the jacket*). He didn't mention it, but I imagine ten or fifteen thousand. You going to talk to Howard today?

WILLY. Yeah, I'll put it to him straight and simple. He'll just have to take me off the road.

LINDA. And Willy, don't forget to ask for a little advance, because we've got the insurance premium. It's the grace period now.

WILLY. That's a hundred . . . ?

LINDA. A hundred and eight, sixty-eight. Because we're a little short again.

WILLY. Why are we short?

LINDA. Well, you had the motor job on the car . . .

WILLY. That goddam Studebaker!

LINDA. And you got one more payment on the refrigerator . . .

WILLY. But it just broke again!

LINDA. Well, it's old, dear.

WILLY. I told you we should've bought a well-advertised machine. Charley bought a General Electric and it's twenty years old and it's still good, that son-of-a-bitch.

LINDA. But, Willy—

WILLY. Whoever heard of a Hastings refrigerator. Once in my life I would like to own something outright before it's broken! I'm always in a race with the junkyard! I just finished paying for the car and it's on its last legs. The refrigerator consumes belts like a goddam maniac. They time those things. They time them so when you finally paid for them, they're used up.

LINDA (*buttoning up his jacket as he unbuttons it*). All told, about two hundred dollars would carry us, dear. But that includes the last payment on the mortgage. After this payment, Willy, the house belongs to us.

WILLY. It's twenty-five years!

LINDA. Biff was nine years old when we bought it.

WILLY. Well, that's a great thing. To weather a twenty-five-year mortgage is—

LINDA. It's an accomplishment.

WILLY. All the cement, the lumber, the reconstruction I put in this house! There ain't a crack to be found in it any more.

LINDA. Well, it served its purpose.

WILLY. What purpose? Some stranger'll come along, move in, and that's that. If only Biff would take this house, and raise a family . . . (*He starts to go*) Good-by, I'm late.

LINDA (*suddenly remembering*). Oh, I forgot! You're supposed to meet them for dinner.

WILLY. Me?

LINDA. At Frank's Chop House on Forty-eighth near Sixth Avenue.

WILLY. Is that so! How about you?

LINDA. No, just the three of you. They're gonna blow you to a big meal!

WILLY. Don't say! Who thought of that?

LINDA. Biff came to me this morning, Willy, and he said, "Tell Dad, we want to blow him to a big meal." Be there six o'clock. You and your two boys are going to have dinner.

WILLY. Gee whiz! That's really somethin'. I'm gonna knock Howard for a loop, kid. I'll get an advance, and I'll come home with a New York job. Goddammit, now I'm gonna do it!

LINDA. Oh, that's the spirit, Willy!

WILLY. I will never get behind a wheel the rest of my life!

LINDA. It's changing, Willy, I can feel it changing!

WILLY. Beyond a question. G'by, I'm late. (*He starts to go again*)

LINDA (*calling after him as she runs to the kitchen table for a handkerchief*). You got your glasses?

WILLY (*feels for them, then comes back in*). Yeah, yeah, got my glasses.

LINDA (*giving him the handkerchief*). And a handkerchief.

WILLY. Yeah, handkerchief.

LINDA. And your saccharine?

WILLY. Yeah, my saccharine.

LINDA. Be careful on the subway stairs. (*She kisses him, and a silk stocking is seen hanging from her hand. Willy notices it.*)

WILLY. Will you stop mending stockings? At least while I'm in the house. It gets me nervous. I can't tell you. Please. (*Linda hides the stocking in her hand as she follows Willy across the forestage in front of the house.*)

LINDA. Remember, Frank's Chop House.

WILLY (*passing the apron*). Maybe beets would grow out there.

LINDA (*laughing*). But you tried so many times.

WILLY. Yeah. Well, don't work hard today. (*He disappears around the right corner of the house*)

LINDA. Be careful!

(*As Willy vanishes, Linda waves to him. Suddenly the phone rings. She runs across the stage and into the kitchen and lifts it.*)

LINDA. Hello? Oh, Biff! I'm so glad you called, I just . . . Yes, sure, I just told him. Yes, he'll be there for dinner at six o'clock, I didn't forget. Listen, I was just dying to tell you. You know that little rubber pipe I told you about? That he connected to the gas heater? I finally decided to go down the cellar this morning and take it away and destroy it. But it's gone! Imagine? He took it away himself, it isn't there! (*She listens*) When? Oh, then you took it. Oh nothing, it's just that I'd hoped he'd taken it away himself. Oh, I'm not worried, darling, because this morning he left in such high spirits, it was like the old days! I'm not afraid any more. Did Mr. Oliver see you? . . . Well, you wait there then. And make a nice impression on him, darling. Just don't perspire too much before you see him. And have a nice time with Dad. He may have big news too! . . . That's right, a New York job. And be sweet to him tonight, dear. Be loving to him. Because he's only a little boat looking for a harbor. (*She is trembling with sorrow and joy*) Oh, that's wonderful, Biff, you'll save his life. Thanks, darling. Just put your arm around him when he comes into the restaurant. Give him a smile. That's the boy . . . Good-by, dear. . . . You got your comb? . . . That's fine. Good-by, Biff dear. (*In the middle of her speech, Howard Wagner, thirty-six, wheels in a small typewriter table on which is a wire-recording machine and proceeds to plug it in. This is on the left forestage. Light slowly fades on Linda as it rises on Howard. Howard is intent on threading the machine and only glances over his shoulder as Willy appears.*)

WILLY. Pst! Pst!

HOWARD. Hello, Willy, come in.

WILLY. Like to have a little talk with you, Howard.

HOWARD. Sorry to keep you waiting. I'll be with you in a minute.

WILLY. What's that, Howard?

HOWARD. Didn't you ever see one of these? Wire recorder.

WILLY. Oh. Can we talk a minute?

HOWARD. Records things. Just got delivery yesterday. Been driving me crazy, the most terrific machine I ever saw in my life. I was up all night with it.

WILLY. What do you do with it?

HOWARD. I bought it for dictation, but you can do anything with it. Listen to this. I had it home last night. Listen to what I picked up. The first one is my daughter. Get this. (*He flicks the switch and "Roll Out the Barrel" is heard being whistled*) Listen to that kid whistle.

WILLY. That is lifelike, isn't it?

HOWARD. Seven years old. Get that tone.

WILLY. Ts, ts. Like to ask a little favor if you . . .

(*The whistling breaks off, and the voice of Howard's daughter is heard.*)

HIS DAUGHTER. "Now you, Daddy."

HOWARD. She's crazy for me! (*Again the same song is whistled*) That's me! Ha! (*He winks*)

WILLY. You're very good!

(*The whistling breaks off again. The machine runs silent for a moment.*)

HOWARD. Sh! Get this now, this is my son.

HIS SON. "The capital of Alabama is Montgomery; the capital of Arizona is Phoenix; the capital of Arkansas is Little Rock; the capital of California is Sacramento . . ." (*And on, and on*)

HOWARD (*holding up five fingers*). Five years old, Willy!

WILLY. He'll make an announcer some day!

HIS SON (*continuing*). "The capital . . ."

HOWARD. Get that—alphabetical order! (*The machine breaks off suddenly*) Wait a minute. The maid kicked the plug out.

WILLY. It certainly is a—

HOWARD. Sh, for God's sake!

HIS SON. "It's nine o'clock, Bulova watch time. So I have to go to sleep."

WILLY. That really is—

HOWARD. Wait a minute! The next is my wife.

(*They wait.*)

HOWARD'S VOICE. "Go on, say something." (*Pause*) "Well, you gonna talk?"

HIS WIFE. "I can't think of anything."

HOWARD'S VOICE. "Well, talk—it's turning."

HIS WIFE (*shyly, beaten*). "Hello." (*Silence*) "Oh, Howard, I can't talk into this . . ."

HOWARD (*snapping the machine off*). That was my wife.

WILLY. That is a wonderful machine. Can we—

HOWARD. I tell you, Willy, I'm gonna

take my camera, and my bandsaw, and all my hobbies, and out they go. This is the most fascinating relaxation I ever found.

WILLY. I think I'll get one myself.

HOWARD. Sure, they're only a hundred and a half. You can't do without it. Supposing you wanna hear Jack Benny, see? But you can't be at home at that hour. So you tell the maid to turn the radio on when Jack Benny comes on, and this automatically goes on with the radio . . .

WILLY. And when you come home you . . .

HOWARD. You can come home twelve o'clock, one o'clock, any time you like, and you get yourself a Coke and sit yourself down, throw the switch, and there's Jack Benny's program in the middle of the night!

WILLY. I'm definitely going to get one. Because lots of time I'm on the road, and I think to myself, what I must be missing on the radio!

HOWARD. Don't you have a radio in the car?

WILLY. Well, yeah, but who ever thinks of turning it on?

HOWARD. Say, aren't you supposed to be in Boston?

WILLY. That's what I want to talk to you about, Howard. You got a minute? *(He draws a chair in from the wing)*

HOWARD. What happened? What're you doing here?

WILLY. Well . . .

HOWARD. You didn't crack up again, did you?

WILLY. Oh, no. No . . .

HOWARD. Geez, you had me worried there for a minute. What's the trouble?

WILLY. Well, tell you the truth, Howard. I've come to the decision that I'd rather not travel any more.

HOWARD. Not travel! Well, what'll you do?

WILLY. Remember, Christmas time, when you had the party here? You said you'd try to think of some spot for me here in town.

HOWARD. With us?

WILLY. Well, sure.

HOWARD. Oh, yeah, yeah. I remember. Well, I couldn't think of anything for you, Willy.

WILLY. I tell ya, Howard. The kids are all grown up, y'know. I don't need much any more. If I could take home—well, sixty-five dollars a week, I could swing it.

HOWARD. Yeah, but Willy, see I—

WILLY. I tell ya why, Howard. Speaking frankly and between the two of us, y'know —I'm just a little tired.

HOWARD. Oh, I could understand that, Willy. But you're a road man, Willy, and we do a road business. We've only got a half-dozen salesmen on the floor here.

WILLY. God knows, Howard, I never asked a favor of any man. But I was with the firm when your father used to carry you in here in his arms.

HOWARD. I know that, Willy, but—

WILLY. Your father came to me the day you were born and asked me what I thought of the name of Howard, may he rest in peace.

HOWARD. I appreciate that, Willy, but there just is no spot here for you. If I had a spot I'd slam you right in, but I just don't have a single solitary spot.
*(He looks for his lighter. Willy has picked it up and gives it to him. Pause.)*

WILLY *(with increasing anger)*. Howard, all I need to set my table is fifty dollars a week.

HOWARD. But where am I going to put you, kid?

WILLY. Look, it isn't a question of whether I can sell merchandise, is it?

HOWARD. No, but it's a business, kid, and everybody's gotta pull his own weight.

WILLY *(desperately)*. Just let me tell you a story, Howard—

HOWARD. 'Cause you gotta admit, business is business.

WILLY *(angrily)*. Business is definitely business, but just listen for a minute. You don't understand this. When I was a boy —eighteen, nineteen—I was already on the road. And there was a question in my mind as to whether selling had a future for me. Because in those days I had a yearning to go to Alaska. See, there were three gold strikes in one month in Alaska, and I felt like going out. Just for the ride, you might say.

HOWARD *(barely interested)*. Don't say.

WILLY. Oh, yeah, my father lived many years in Alaska. He was an adventurous man. We've got quite a little streak of self-reliance in our family. I thought I'd go out with my older brother and try to locate him, and maybe settle in the North with the old man. And I was almost decided to go, when I met a salesman in the

Parker House. His name was Dave Single-man. And he was eighty-four years old, and he'd drummed merchandise in thirty-one states. And old Dave, he'd go up to his room, y'understand, put on his green velvet slippers—I'll never forget—and pick up his phone and call the buyers, and without ever leaving his room, at the age of eighty-four, he made his living. And when I saw that, I realized that selling was the greatest career a man could want. 'Cause what could be more satisfying than to be able to go, at the age of eighty-four, into twenty or thirty different cities, and pick up a phone, and be remembered and loved and helped by so many different people? Do you know? when he died—and by the way he died the death of a salesman, in his green velvet slippers in the smoker of the New York, New Haven and Hartford, going into Boston—when he died, hundreds of salesmen and buyers were at his funeral. Things were sad on a lotta trains for months after that. (*He stands up. Howard has not looked at him*) In those days there was personality in it, Howard. There was respect, and comradeship, and gratitude in it. Today, it's all cut and dried, and there's no chance for bringing friendship to bear —or personality. You see what I mean? They don't know me any more.

HOWARD (*moving away, to the right*). That's just the thing, Willy.

WILLY. If I had forty dollars a week— that's all I'd need. Forty dollars, Howard.

HOWARD. Kid, I can't take blood from a stone, I—

WILLY (*desperation is on him now*). Howard, the year Al Smith was nominated, your father came to me and—

HOWARD (*starting to go off*). I've got to see some people, kid.

WILLY (*stopping him*). I'm talking about your father! There were promises made across this desk! You mustn't tell me you've got people to see—I put thirty-four years into this firm, Howard, and now I can't pay my insurance! You can't eat the orange and throw the peel away— a man is not a piece of fruit! (*After a pause*) Now pay attention. Your father— in 1928 I had a big year. I averaged a hundred and seventy dollars a week in commissions.

HOWARD (*impatiently*). Now, Willy, you never averaged—

WILLY (*banging his hand on the desk*).

I averaged a hundred and seventy dollars a week in the year of 1928; and your father came to me—or rather, I was in the office here—it was right over this desk— and he put his hand on my shoulder—

HOWARD (*getting up*). You'll have to excuse me, Willy. I gotta see some people. Pull yourself together. (*Going out*) I'll be back in a little while.

(*On Howard's exit, the light on his chair grows very bright and strange.*)

WILLY. Pull myself together! What the hell did I say to him? My God, I was yelling at him! How could I! (*Willy breaks off, staring at the light, which occupies the chair, animating it. He approaches this chair, standing across the desk from it*) Frank, Frank, don't you remember what you told me that time? How you put your hand on my shoulder, and Frank . . . (*He leans on the desk and as he speaks the dead man's name he accidentally switches on the recorder, and instantly*)

HOWARD'S SON. ". . . of New York is Albany. The capital of Ohio is Cincinnati, the capital of Rhode Island is . . ." (*The recitation continues*)

WILLY (*leaping away with fright, shouting*). Ha! Howard! Howard! Howard!

HOWARD (*rushing in*). What happened?

WILLY (*pointing at the machine, which continues nasally, childishly, with the capital cities*). Shut it off! Shut it off!

HOWARD (*pulling the plug out*). Look, Willy . . .

WILLY (*pressing his hands to his eyes*). I gotta get myself some coffee. I'll get some coffee . . .

(*Willy starts to walk out. Howard stops him.*)

HOWARD (*rolling up the cord*). Willy, look . . .

WILLY. I'll go to Boston.

HOWARD. Willy, you can't go to Boston for us.

WILLY. Why can't I go?

HOWARD. I don't want you to represent us. I've been meaning to tell you for a long time now.

WILLY. Howard, are you firing me?

HOWARD. I think you need a good long rest, Willy.

WILLY. Howard—

HOWARD. And when you feel better, come back, and we'll see if we can work something out.

WILLY. But I gotta earn money, Howard. I'm in no position to—

HOWARD. Where are your sons? Why don't your sons give you a·hand?

WILLY. They're working on a very big deal.

HOWARD. This is no time for false pride, Willy. You go to your sons and tell them that you're tired. You've got two great boys, haven't you?

WILLY. Oh, no question, no question, but in the meantime . . .

HOWARD. Then that's that, heh?

WILLY. All right, I'll go to Boston to-morrow.

HOWARD. No, no.

WILLY. I can't throw myself on my sons. I'm not a cripple!

HOWARD. Look, kid, I'm busy this morning.

WILLY (grasping Howard's arm). Howard, you've got to let me go to Boston!

HOWARD (hard, keeping himself under control). I've got a line of people to see this morning. Sit down, take five minutes, and pull yourself together, and then go home, will ya? I need the office, Willy. (He starts to go, turns, remembering the recorder, starts to push off the table holding the recorder) Oh, yeah. Whenever you can this week, stop by and drop off the samples. You'll feel better, Willy, and then come back and we'll talk. Pull yourself together, kid, there's people outside.

(Howard exits, pushing the table off left. Willy stares into space, exhausted. Now the music is heard—Ben's music—first distantly, then closer, closer. As Willy speaks, Ben enters from the right. He carries valise and umbrella.)

WILLY. Oh, Ben, how did you do it? What is the answer? Did you wind up the Alaska deal already?

BEN. Doesn't take much time if you know what you're doing. Just a short business trip. Boarding ship in an hour. Wanted to say good-by.

WILLY. Ben, I've got to talk to you.

BEN (glancing at his watch). Haven't the time, William.

WILLY (crossing the apron to Ben). Ben, nothing's working out. I don't know what to do.

BEN. Now, look here, William. I've bought timberland in Alaska and I need a man to look after things for me.

WILLY. God, timberland! Me and my boys in those grand outdoors!

BEN. You've a new continent at your doorstep, William. Get out of these cities, they're full of talk and time payments and courts of law. Screw on your fists and you can fight for a fortune up there.

WILLY. Yes, yes! Linda, Linda!

(Linda enters, as of old, with the wash.)

LINDA. Oh, you're back?

BEN. I haven't much time.

WILLY. No, wait! Linda, he's got a proposition for me in Alaska.

LINDA. But you've got— (To Ben) He's got a beautiful job here.

WILLY. But in Alaska, kid, I could—

LINDA. You're doing well enough, Willy!

BEN (to Linda). Enough for what, dear?

LINDA (frightened of Ben and angry at him). Don't say those things to him! Enough to be happy right here, right now. (To Willy, while Ben laughs) Why must everybody conquer the world? You're well liked, and the boys love you, and some-day— (To Ben) —why, old man Wagner told him just the other day that if he keeps it up he'll be a member of the firm, didn't he, Willy?

WILLY. Sure, sure. I am building something with this firm, Ben, and if a man is building something he must be on the right track, mustn't he?

BEN. What are you building? Lay your hand on it. Where is it?

WILLY (hesitantly). That's true, Linda, there's nothing.

LINDA. Why? (To Ben) There's a man eighty-four years old—

WILLY. That's right, Ben, that's right. When I look at that man I say, what is there to worry about?

BEN. Bah!

WILLY. It's true, Ben. All he has to do is go into any city, pick up the phone, and he's making his living—and you know why?

BEN (picking up his valise). I've got to go.

WILLY (holding Ben back). Look at this boy!

(Biff, in his high school sweater, enters carrying suitcase. Happy carries Biff's shoulder guards, gold helmet, and football pants.)

WILLY. Without a penny to his name, three great universities are begging for him, and from there the sky's the limit, because it's not what you do, Ben. It's who you know and the smile on your face! It's contacts, Ben, contacts! The whole wealth of Alaska passes over the lunch table at the Commodore Hotel, and that's the wonder, the wonder of this country, that a man can end with diamonds here on the basis of being liked! (*He turns to Biff*) And that's why when you get out on that field today it's important. Because thousands of people will be rooting for you and loving you. (*To Ben, who has again begun to leave*) And Ben! when he walks into a business office his name will sound out like a bell and all the doors will open to him! I've seen it, Ben, I've seen it a thousand times! You can't feel it with your hand like timber, but it's there!

BEN. Good-by, William.

WILLY. Ben, am I right? Don't you think I'm right? I value your advice.

BEN. There's a new continent at your doorstep, William. You could walk out rich. Rich! (*He is gone*)

WILLY. We'll do it here, Ben! You hear me? We're gonna do it here!

(*Young Bernard rushes in. The gay music of the Boys is heard.*)

BERNARD. Oh, gee, I was afraid you left already!

WILLY. Why? What time is it?

BERNARD. It's half-past one!

WILLY. Well, come on, everybody! Ebbets Field next stop! Where's the pennants? (*He rushes through the wall-line of the kitchen and out into the living-room*)

LINDA (*to Biff*). Did you pack fresh underwear?

BIFF (*who has been limbering up*). I want to go!

BERNARD. Biff, I'm carrying your helmet, ain't I?

HAPPY. No, I'm carrying the helmet.

BERNARD. Oh, Biff, you promised me.

HAPPY. I'm carrying the helmet.

BERNARD. How am I going to get in the locker room?

LINDA. Let him carry the shoulder guards. (*She puts her coat and hat on in the kitchen*)

BERNARD. Can I, Biff? 'Cause I told everybody I'm going to be in the locker room.

HAPPY. In Ebbets Field it's the clubhouse.

BERNARD. I meant the clubhouse. Biff!

HAPPY. Biff!

BIFF (*grandly, after a slight pause*). Let him carry the shoulder guards.

HAPPY (*as he gives Bernard the shoulder guards*). Stay close to us now.

(*Willy rushes in with the pennants.*)

WILLY (*handing them out*). Everybody wave when Biff comes out on the field. (*Happy and Bernard run off*) You set now, boy?

(*The music has died away.*)

BIFF. Ready to go, Pop. Every muscle is ready.

WILLY (*at the edge of the apron*). You realize what this means?

BIFF. That's right, Pop.

WILLY (*feeling Biff's muscles*). You're comin' home this afternoon captain of the All-Scholastic Championship Team of the City of New York.

BIFF. I got it, Pop. And remember, pal, when I take off my helmet, that touchdown is for you.

WILLY. Let's go! (*He is starting out, with his arm around Biff, when Charley enters, as of old, in knickers*) I got no room for you, Charley.

CHARLEY. Room? For what?

WILLY. In the car.

CHARLEY. You goin' for a ride? I wanted to shoot some casino.

WILLY (*furiously*). Casino! (*Incredulously*) Don't you realize what today is?

LINDA. Oh, he knows, Willy. He's just kidding you.

WILLY. That's nothing to kid about!

CHARLEY. No, Linda, what's goin' on?

LINDA. He's playing in Ebbets Field.

CHARLEY. Baseball in this weather?

WILLY. Don't talk to him. Come on, come on! (*He is pushing them out*)

CHARLEY. Wait a minute, didn't you hear the news?

WILLY. What?

CHARLEY. Don't you listen to the radio? Ebbets Field just blew up.

WILLY. You go to hell! (*Charley laughs. Pushing them out*) Come on, come on! We're late.

CHARLEY (*as they go*). Knock a homer, Biff, knock a homer!

WILLY (*the last to leave, turning to Charley*). I don't think that was funny, Charley. This is the greatest day of his life.

CHARLEY. Willy, when are you going to grow up?

WILLY. Yeah, heh? When this game is

over, Charley, you'll be laughing out of the other side of your face. They'll be calling him another Red Grange. Twenty-five thousand a year.

CHARLEY (*kidding*). Is that so?

WILLY. Yeah, that's so.

CHARLEY. Well, then, I'm sorry, Willy. But tell me something.

WILLY. What?

CHARLEY. Who is Red Grange?

WILLY. Put up your hands. Goddam you, put up your hands!

(*Charley, chuckling, shakes his head and walks away, around the left corner of the stage. Willy follows him. The music rises to a mocking frenzy.*)

WILLY. Who the hell do you think you are, better than everybody else? You don't know everything, you big, ignorant, stupid . . . Put up your hands!

(*Light rises, on the right side of the forestage, on a small table in the reception room of Charley's office. Traffic sounds are heard. Bernard, now mature, sits whistling to himself. A pair of tennis rackets and an overnight bag are on the floor beside him.*)

WILLY (*offstage*). What are you walking away for? Don't walk away! If you're going to say something say it to my face! I know you laugh at me behind my back. You'll laugh out of the other side of your goddam face after this game. Touchdown! Touchdown! Eighty thousand people! Touchdown! Right between the goal posts. (*Bernard is a quiet, earnest, but self-assured young man. Willy's voice is coming from right upstage now. Bernard lowers his feet off the table and listens. Jenny, his father's secretary, enters.*)

JENNY (*distressed*). Say, Bernard, will you go out in the hall?

BERNARD. What is that noise? Who is it?

JENNY. Mr. Loman. He just got off the elevator.

BERNARD (*getting up*). Who's he arguing with?

JENNY. Nobody. There's nobody with him. I can't deal with him any more, and your father gets all upset everytime he comes. I've got a lot of typing to do, and your father's waiting to sign it. Will you see him?

WILLY (*entering*). Touchdown! Touch— (*He sees Jenny*) Jenny, Jenny, good to see you. How're ya? Workin'? Or still honest?

JENNY. Fine. How've you been feeling?

WILLY. Not much any more, Jenny. Ha, ha! (*He is surprised to see the rackets*)

BERNARD. Hello, Uncle Willy.

WILLY (*almost shocked*). Bernard! Well, look who's here! (*He comes quickly, guiltily, to Bernard and warmly shakes his hand*)

BERNARD. How are you? Good to see you.

WILLY. What are you doing here?

BERNARD. Oh, just stopped by to see Pop. Get off my feet till my train leaves. I'm going to Washington in a few minutes.

WILLY. Is he in?

BERNARD. Yes, he's in his office with the accountant. Sit down.

WILLY (*sitting down*). What're you going to do in Washington?

BERNARD. Oh, just a case I've got there, Willy.

WILLY. That so? (*Indicating the rackets*) You going to play tennis there?

BERNARD. I'm staying with a friend who's got a court.

WILLY. Don't say. His own tennis court. Must be fine people, I bet.

BERNARD. They are, very nice. Dad tells me Biff's in town.

WILLY (*with a big smile*). Yeah, Biff's in. Working on a very big deal, Bernard.

BERNARD. What's Biff doing?

WILLY. Well, he's been doing very big things in the West. But he decided to establish himself here. Very big. We're having dinner. Did I hear your wife had a boy?

BERNARD. That's right. Our second.

WILLY. Two boys! What do you know

BERNARD. What kind of a deal has Bi got?

WILLY. Well, Bill Oliver—very big sporting-goods man—he wants Biff very badly. Called him in from the West. Long distance, carte blanche, special deliveries. Your friends have their own private tennis court?

BERNARD. You still with the old firm, Willy?

WILLY (*after a pause*). I'm—I'm overjoyed to see how you made the grade, Bernard, overjoyed. It's an encouraging thing to see a young man really—really— Looks very good for Biff—very—(*He breaks off, then*) Bernard—(*He is so full of emotion, he breaks off again*)

BERNARD. What is it, Willy?

WILLY (*small and alone*). What—what's the secret?

BERNARD. What secret?

WILLY. How—how did you? Why didn't he ever catch on?

BERNARD. I wouldn't know that, Willy.

WILLY (*confidentially, desperately*). You were his friend, his boyhood friend. There's something I don't understand about it. His life ended after that Ebbets Field game. From the age of seventeen nothing good ever happened to him.

BERNARD. He never trained himself for anything.

WILLY. But he did, he did. After high school he took so many correspondence courses. Radio mechanics; television; God knows what, and never made the slightest mark.

BERNARD (*taking off his glasses*). Willy, do you want to talk candidly?

WILLY (*rising, faces Bernard*). I regard you as a very brilliant man, Bernard. I value your advice.

BERNARD. Oh, the hell with the advice, Willy. I couldn't advise you. There's just one thing I've always wanted to ask you. When he was supposed to graduate, and the math teacher flunked him—

WILLY. Oh, that son-of-a-bitch ruined his life.

BERNARD. Yeah, but, Willy, all he had to do was go to summer school and make up that subject.

WILLY. That's right, that's right.

BERNARD. Did you tell him not to go to summer school?

WILLY. Me? I begged him to go. I ordered him to go!

BERNARD. Then why wouldn't he go?

WILLY. Why? Why! Bernard, that question has been trailing me like a ghost for the last fifteen years. He flunked the subject, and laid down and died like a hammer hit him!

BERNARD. Take it easy, kid.

WILLY. Let me talk to you—I got nobody to talk to. Bernard, Bernard, was it my fault? Y'see? It keeps going around in my mind, maybe I did something to him. I got nothing to give him.

BERNARD. Don't take it so hard.

WILLY. Why did he lay down? What is the story there? You were his friend!

BERNARD. Willy, I remember, it was June, and our grades came out. And he'd flunked math.

WILLY. That son-of-a-bitch!

BERNARD. No, it wasn't right then. Biff just got very angry, I remember, and he was ready to enroll in summer school.

WILLY (*surprised*). He was?

BERNARD. He wasn't beaten by it at all. But then, Willy, he disappeared from the block for almost a month. And I got the idea that he'd gone up to New England to see you. Did he have a talk with you then?

(*Willy stares in silence.*)

BERNARD. Willy?

WILLY (*with a strong edge of resentment in his voice*). Yeah, he came to Boston. What about it?

BERNARD. Well, just that when he came back—I'll never forget this, it always mystifies me. Because I'd thought so well of Biff, even though he'd always taken advantage of me. I loved him, Willy, y'know? And he came back after that month and took his sneakers—remember those sneakers with "University of Virginia" printed on them? He was so proud of those, wore them every day. And he took them down in the cellar, and burned them up in the furnace. We had a fist fight. It lasted at least half an hour. Just the two of us, punching each other down the cellar, and crying right through it. I've often thought of how strange it was that I knew he'd given up his life. What happened in Boston, Willy?

(*Willy looks at him as at an intruder.*)

BERNARD. I just bring it up because you asked me.

WILLY (*angrily*). Nothing. What do you mean, "What happened?" What's that got to do with anything?

BERNARD. Well, don't get sore.

WILLY. What are you trying to do, blame it on me? If a boy lays down is that my fault?

BERNARD. Now, Willy, don't get—

WILLY. Well, don't—don't talk to me that way! What does that mean, "What happened?"

(*Charley enters. He is in his vest, and he carries a bottle of bourbon.*)

CHARLEY. Hey, you're going to miss that train. (*He waves the bottle*)

BERNARD. Yeah, I'm going. (*He takes the bottle*) Thanks, Pop. (*He picks up his rackets and bag*) Good-by, Willy, and don't worry about it. You know, "If at first you don't succeed . . ."

WILLY. Yes, I believe in that.

BERNARD. But sometimes, Willy, it's better for a man just to walk away.

WILLY. Walk away?

BERNARD. That's right.

WILLY. But if you can't walk away?

BERNARD (*after a slight pause*). I guess that's when it's tough. (*Extending his hand*) Good-by, Willy.

WILLY (*shaking Bernard's hand*). Good-by, boy.

CHARLEY (*an arm on Bernard's shoulder*). How do you like this kid? Gonna argue a case in front of the Supreme Court.

BERNARD (*protesting*). Pop!

WILLY (*genuinely shocked, pained and happy*). No! The Supreme Court!

BERNARD. I gotta run. 'By, Dad!

CHARLEY. Knock 'em dead, Bernard!

(*Bernard goes off.*)

WILLY (*as Charley takes out his wallet*). The Supreme Court! And he didn't even mention it!

CHARLEY (*counting out money on the desk*). He don't have to—he's gonna do it.

WILLY. And you never told him what to do, did you? You never took any interest in him.

CHARLEY. My salvation is that I never took any interest in anything. There's some money—fifty dollars. I got an accountant inside.

WILLY. Charley, look . . . (*With difficulty*) I got my insurance to pay. If you can manage it—I need a hundred and ten dollars.

(*Charley doesn't reply for a moment; merely stops moving.*)

WILLY. I'd draw it from my bank, but Linda would know, and I . . .

CHARLEY. Sit down, Willy.

WILLY (*moving toward the chair*). I'm keeping an account of everything, remember. I'll pay every penny back. (*He sits*)

CHARLEY. Now listen to me, Willy.

WILLY. I want you to know I appreciate . . .

CHARLEY (*sitting down on the table*). Willy, what're you doin'? What the hell is goin' on in your head?

WILLY. Why? I'm simply . . .

CHARLEY. I offered you a job. You can make fifty dollars a week. And I won't send you on the road.

WILLY. I've got a job.

CHARLEY. Without pay? What kind of a job is a job without pay? (*He rises*) Now, look, kid, enough is enough. I'm no genius but I know when I'm being insulted.

WILLY. Insulted!

CHARLEY. Why don't you want to work for me?

WILLY. What's the matter with you? I've got a job.

CHARLEY. Then what're you walkin' in here every week for?

WILLY (*getting up*). Well, if you don't want me to walk in here—

CHARLEY. I am offering you a job.

WILLY. I don't want your goddam job!

CHARLEY. When the hell are you going to grow up?

WILLY (*furiously*). You big ignoramus, if you say that to me again I'll rap you one! I don't care how big you are! (*He's ready to fight*)

(*Pause.*)

CHARLEY (*kindly, going to him*). How much do you need, Willy?

WILLY. Charley, I'm strapped, I'm strapped. I don't know what to do. I was just fired.

CHARLEY. Howard fired you?

WILLY. That snotnose. Imagine that? I named him. I named him Howard.

CHARLEY. Willy, when're you gonna realize that them things don't mean anything? You named him Howard, but you can't sell that. The only thing you got in this world is what you can sell. And the funny thing is that you're a salesman, and you don't know that.

WILLY. I've always tried to think otherwise, I guess. I always felt that if a man was impressive, and well liked, that nothing—

CHARLEY. Why must everybody like you? Who liked J. P. Morgan? Was he impressive? In a Turkish bath he'd look like a butcher. But with his pockets on he was very well liked. Now listen, Willy, I know you don't like me, and nobody can say I'm in love with you, but I'll give you a job because—just for the hell of it, put it that way. Now what do you say?

WILLY. I—I just can't work for you, Charley.

CHARLEY. What're you, jealous of me?

WILLY. I can't work for you, that's all, don't ask me why.

CHARLEY (*angered, takes out more bills*). You been jealous of me all your life, you damned fool! Here, pay your insurance.

(*He puts the money in Willy's hand*)

WILLY. I'm keeping strict accounts.

CHARLEY. I've got some work to do. Take care of yourself. And pay your insurance.

WILLY (*moving to the right*). Funny, y'know? After all the highways, and the trains, and the appointments, and the years, you end up worth more dead than alive.

CHARLEY. Willy, nobody's worth nothin' dead. (*After a slight pause*) Did you hear what I said?

(*Willy stands still, dreaming.*)

CHARLEY. Willy!

WILLY. Apologize to Bernard for me when you see him. I didn't mean to argue with him. He's a fine boy. They're all fine boys, and they'll end up big—all of them. Someday they'll all play tennis together. Wish me luck, Charley. He saw Bill Oliver today.

CHARLEY. Good luck.

WILLY (*on the verge of tears*). Charley, you're the only friend I got. Isn't that a remarkable thing? (*He goes out*)

CHARLEY. Jesus!

(*Charley stares after him a moment and follows. All light blacks out. Suddenly raucous music is heard, and a red glow rises behind the screen at right. Stanley, a young waiter, appears, carrying a table, followed by Happy, who is carrying two chairs*)

STANLEY (*putting the table down*). That's all right, Mr. Loman. I can handle it myself. (*He turns and takes the chairs from Happy and places them at the table*)

HAPPY (*glancing around*). Oh, this is better.

STANLEY. Sure, in the front there you're in the middle of all kinds of noise. Whenever you got a party, Mr. Loman, you just tell me and I'll put you back here. Y'know, there's a lotta people they don't like it private, because when they go out they like to see a lotta action around them because they're sick and tired to stay in the house by theirself. But I know you, you ain't from Hackensack. You know what I mean?

HAPPY (*sitting down*). So how's it coming, Stanley?

STANLEY. Ah, it's a dog's life. I only wish during the war they'd a took me in the Army. I coulda been dead by now.

HAPPY. My brother's back, Stanley.

STANLEY. Oh, he come back, heh? From the Far West.

HAPPY. Yeah, big cattle man, my brother, so treat him right. And my father's coming too.

STANLEY. Oh, your father too!

HAPPY. You got a couple of nice lobsters?

STANLEY. Hundred per cent, big.

HAPPY. I want them with the claws.

STANLEY. Don't worry, I don't give you no mice. (*Happy laughs*) How about some wine? It'll put a head on the meal.

HAPPY. No. You remember, Stanley, that recipe I brought you from overseas? With the champagne in it?

STANLEY. Oh, yeah, sure. I still got it tacked up yet in the kitchen. But that'll have to cost a buck apiece anyways.

HAPPY. That's all right.

STANLEY. What'd you, hit a number or somethin'?

HAPPY. No, it's a little celebration. My brother is—I think he pulled off a big deal today. I think we're going into business together.

STANLEY. Great! That's the best for you. Because a family business, you know what I mean?—that's the best.

HAPPY. That's what I think.

STANLEY. 'Cause what's the difference? Somebody steals? It's in the family. Know what I mean? (*Sotto voce*) Like this bartender here. The boss is goin' crazy what kinda leak he's got in the cash register. You put it in but it don't come out.

HAPPY (*raising his head*). Sh!

STANLEY. What?

HAPPY. You notice I wasn't lookin' right or left, was I?

STANLEY. No.

HAPPY. And my eyes are closed.

STANLEY. So what's the—?

HAPPY. Strudel's comin'.

STANLEY (*catching on, looks around*). Ah, no, there's no—

(*He breaks off as a furred, lavishly dressed girl enters and sits at the next table. Both follow her with their eyes.*)

STANLEY. Geez, how'd ya know?

HAPPY. I got radar or something. (*Staring directly at her profile*) Oooooooo . . . Stanley.

STANLEY. I think that's for you, Mr. Loman.

HAPPY. Look at that mouth. Oh, God. And the binoculars.

STANLEY. Geez, you got a life, Mr. Loman.

HAPPY. Wait on her.

STANLEY (*going to the girl's table*). Would you like a menu, ma'am?

GIRL. I'm expecting someone, but I'd like a—

HAPPY. Why don't you bring her—excuse me, miss, do you mind? I sell champagne, and I'd like you to try my brand. Bring her a champagne, Stanley.

GIRL. That's awfully nice of you.

HAPPY. Don't mention it. It's all company money. (*He laughs*)

GIRL. That's a charming product to be selling, isn't it?

HAPPY. Oh, gets to be like everything else. Selling is selling, y'know.

GIRL. I suppose.

HAPPY. You don't happen to sell, do you?

GIRL. No, I don't sell.

HAPPY. Would you object to a compliment from a stranger? You ought to be on a magazine cover.

GIRL (*looking at him a little archly*). I have been.

(*Stanley comes in with a glass of champagne.*)

HAPPY. What'd I say before, Stanley? You see? She's a cover girl.

STANLEY. Oh, I could see, I could see.

HAPPY (*to the Girl*). What magazine?

GIRL. Oh, a lot of them. (*She takes the drink*) Thank you.

HAPPY. You know what they say in France, don't you? "Champagne is the drink of the complexion"—Hya, Biff!

(*Biff has entered and sits with Happy.*)

BIFF. Hello, kid. Sorry I'm late.

HAPPY. I just got here. Uh, Miss—?

GIRL. Forsythe.

HAPPY. Miss Forsythe, this is my brother.

BIFF. Is Dad here?

HAPPY. His name is Biff. You might've heard of him. Great football player.

GIRL. Really? What team?

HAPPY. Are you familiar with football?

GIRL. No, I'm afraid I'm not.

HAPPY. Biff is quarterback with the New York Giants.

GIRL. Well, that is nice, isn't it? (*She drinks*)

HAPPY. Good health.

GIRL. I'm happy to meet you.

HAPPY. That's my name. Hap. It's really Harold, but at West Point they called me Happy.

GIRL (*now really impressed*). Oh, I see. How do you do? (*She turns her profile*)

BIFF. Isn't Dad coming?

HAPPY. You want her?

BIFF. Oh, I could never make that.

HAPPY. I remember the time that idea would never come into your head. Where's the old confidence, Biff?

BIFF. I just saw Oliver—

HAPPY. Wait a minute. I've got to see that old confidence again. Do you want her? She's on call.

BIFF. Oh, no. (*He turns to look at the Girl*)

HAPPY. I'm telling you. Watch this. (*Turning to the Girl*) Honey? (*She turns to him*) Are you busy?

GIRL. Well, I am . . . but I could make a phone call.

HAPPY. Do that, will you, honey? And see if you can get a friend. We'll be here for a while. Biff is one of the greatest football players in the country.

GIRL (*standing up*). Well, I'm certainly happy to meet you.

HAPPY. Come back soon.

GIRL. I'll try.

HAPPY. Don't try, honey, try hard.

(*The Girl exits. Stanley follows, shaking his head in bewildered admiration.*)

HAPPY. Isn't that a shame now? A beautiful girl like that? That's why I can't get married. There's not a good woman in a thousand. New York is loaded with them, kid!

BIFF. Hap, look—

HAPPY. I told you she was on call!

BIFF (*strangely unnerved*). Cut it out, will ya? I want to say something to you.

HAPPY. Did you see Oliver?

BIFF. I saw him all right. Now look, I want to tell Dad a couple of things and I want you to help me.

HAPPY. What? Is he going to back you?

BIFF. Are you crazy? You're out of your goddam head, you know that?

HAPPY. Why? What happened?

BIFF (*breathlessly*). I did a terrible thing today, Hap. It's been the strangest day I ever went through. I'm all numb, I swear.

HAPPY. You mean he wouldn't see you?

BIFF. Well, I waited six hours for him, see? All day. Kept sending my name in.

Even tried to date his secretary so she'd get me to him, but no soap.

HAPPY. Because you're not showin' the old confidence, Biff. He remembered you, didn't he?

BIFF (*stopping Happy with a gesture*). Finally, about five o'clock, he comes out. Didn't remember who I was or anything. I felt like such an idiot, Hap.

HAPPY. Did you tell him my Florida idea?

BIFF. He walked away. I saw him for one minute. I got so mad I could've torn the walls down! How the hell did I ever get the idea I was a salesman there? I even believed myself that I'd been a salesman for him! And then he gave me one look and—I realized what a ridiculous lie my whole life has been! We've been talking in a dream for fifteen years. I was a shipping clerk.

HAPPY. What'd you do?

BIFF (*with great tension and wonder*). Well, he left, see. And the secretary went out. I was all alone in the waiting-room. I don't know what came over me, Hap. The next thing I know I'm in his office—paneled walls, everything. I can't explain it. I—Hap, I took his fountain pen.

HAPPY. Geez, did he catch you?

BIFF. I ran out. I ran down all eleven flights. I ran and ran and ran.

HAPPY. That was an awful dumb—what'd you do that for?

BIFF (*agonized*). I don't know, I just—wanted to take something, I don't know. You gotta help me, Hap, I'm gonna tell Pop.

HAPPY. You crazy? What for?

BIFF. Hap, he's got to understand that m not the man somebody lends that kind of money to. He thinks I've been spiting him all these years and it's eating him up.

HAPPY. That's just it. You tell him something nice.

BIFF. I can't.

HAPPY. Say you got a lunch date with Oliver tomorrow.

BIFF. So what do I do tomorrow?

HAPPY. You leave the house tomorrow and come back at night and say Oliver is thinking it over. And he thinks it over for a couple of weeks, and gradually it fades away and nobody's the worse.

BIFF. But it'll go on forever!

HAPPY. Dad is never so happy as when he's looking forward to something!

(*Willy enters.*)

HAPPY. Hello, scout!

WILLY. Gee, I haven't been here in years! (*Stanley has followed Willy in and sets a chair for him. Stanley starts off but Happy stops him.*)

HAPPY. Stanley!

(*Stanley stands by, waiting for an order.*)

BIFF (*going to Willy with guilt, as to an invalid*). Sit down, Pop. You want a drink?

WILLY. Sure, I don't mind.

BIFF. Let's get a load on.

WILLY. You look worried.

BIFF. N-no. (*To Stanley*) Scotch all around. Make it doubles.

STANLEY. Doubles, right. (*He goes*)

WILLY. You had a couple already, didn't you?

BIFF. Just a couple, yeah.

WILLY. Well, what happened, boy? (*Nodding affirmatively, with a smile*) Everything go all right?

BIFF (*takes a breath, then reaches out and grasps Willy's hand*). Pal . . . (*He is smiling bravely, and Willy is smiling too*) I had an experience today.

HAPPY. Terrific, Pop.

WILLY. That so? What happened?

BIFF (*high, slightly alcoholic, above the earth*). I'm going to tell you everything from first to last. It's been a strange day. (*Silence. He looks around, composes himself as best he can, but his breath keeps breaking the rhythm of his voice*) I had to wait quite a while for him, and—

WILLY. Oliver?

BIFF. Yeah, Oliver. All day, as a matter of cold fact. And a lot of—instances—facts, Pop, facts about my life came back to me. Who was it, Pop? Who ever said I was a salesman with Oliver?

WILLY. Well, you were.

BIFF. No, Dad, I was a shipping clerk.

WILLY. But you were practically—

BIFF (*with determination*). Dad, I don't know who said it first, but I was never a salesman for Bill.Oliver.

WILLY. What're you talking about?

BIFF. Let's hold on to the facts tonight, Pop. We're not going to get anywhere bullin' around. I was a shipping clerk.

WILLY (*angrily*). All right, now listen to me—

BIFF. Why don't you let me finish?

WILLY. I'm not interested in stories about the past or any crap of that kind because the woods are burning, boys, you understand? There's a big blaze going on all around. I was fired today.

BIFF (*shocked*). How could you be?

WILLY. I was fired, and I'm looking for a little good news to tell your mother, because the woman has waited and the woman has suffered. The gist of it is that I haven't got a story left in my head, Biff. So don't give me a lecture about facts and aspects. I am not interested. Now what've you got to say to me?

(*Stanley enters with three drinks. They wait until he leaves.*)

WILLY. Did you see Oliver?

BIFF. Jesus, Dad!

WILLY. You mean you didn't go up there?

HAPPY. Sure he went up there.

BIFF. I did. I—saw him. How could they fire you?

WILLY (*on the edge of his chair*). What kind of a welcome did he give you?

BIFF. He won't even let you work on commission?

WILLY. I'm out! (*Driving*) So tell me, he gave you a warm welcome?

HAPPY. Sure, Pop, sure!

BIFF (*driven*). Well, it was kind of—

WILLY. I was wondering if he'd remember you. (*To Happy*) Imagine, man doesn't see him for ten, twelve years and gives him that kind of a welcome!

HAPPY. Damn right!

BIFF (*trying to return to the offensive*). Pop, look—

WILLY. You know why he remembered you, don't you? Because you impressed him in those days.

BIFF. Let's talk quietly and get this down to the facts, huh?

WILLY (*as though Biff had been interrupting*). Well, what happened? It's great news, Biff. Did he take you into his office or'd you talk in the waiting-room?

BIFF. Well, he came in, see, and—

WILLY (*with a big smile*). What'd he say? Betcha he threw his arm around you.

BIFF. Well, he kinda—

WILLY. He's a fine man. (*To Happy*) Very hard man to see, y'know.

HAPPY (*agreeing*). Oh, I know.

WILLY (*to Biff*). Is that where you had the drinks?

BIFF. Yeah, he gave me a couple of—no, no!

HAPPY (*cutting in*). He told him my Florida idea.

WILLY. Don't interrupt. (*To Biff*) How'd he react to the Florida idea?

BIFF. Dad, will you give me a minute to explain?

WILLY. I've been waiting for you to explain since I sat down here! What happened? He took you into his office and what?

BIFF. Well—I talked. And—and he listened, see.

WILLY. Famous for the way he listens, y'know. What was his answer?

BIFF. His answer was—(*He breaks off, suddenly angry*) Dad, you're not letting me tell you what I want to tell you!

WILLY (*accusing, angered*). You didn't see him, did you?

BIFF. I did see him!

WILLY. What'd you insult him or something? You insulted him, didn't you?

BIFF. Listen, will you let me out of it, will you just let me out of it!

HAPPY. What the hell!

WILLY. Tell me what happened!

BIFF (*to Happy*). I can't talk to him!

(*A single trumpet note jars the ear. The light of green leaves stains the house, which holds the air of night and a dream. Young Bernard enters and knocks on the door of the house.*)

YOUNG BERNARD (*frantically*). Mrs. Loman, Mrs. Loman!

HAPPY. Tell him what happened!

BIFF (*to Happy*). Shut up and leave me alone!

WILLY. No, no! You had to go and flunk math!

BIFF. What math? What're you talking about?

YOUNG BERNARD. Mrs. Loman, Mrs. Loman!

(*Linda appears in the house, as of old.*)

WILLY (*wildly*). Math, math, math!

BIFF. Take it easy, Pop!

YOUNG BERNARD. Mrs. Loman!

WILLY (*furiously*). If you hadn't flunked you'd've been set by now!

BIFF. Now, look, I'm gonna tell you what happened, and you're going to listen to me.

YOUNG BERNARD. Mrs. Loman!

BIFF. I waited six hours—

HAPPY. What the hell are you saying?

BIFF. I kept sending in my name but he wouldn't see me. So finally he . . . (*He continues unheard as light fades low on the restaurant*)

YOUNG BERNARD. Biff flunked math!

LINDA. No!

YOUNG BERNARD. Birnbaum flunked him! They won't graduate him!

LINDA. But they have to. He's gotta go to the university. Where is he? Biff! Biff!

YOUNG BERNARD. No, he left. He went to Grand Central.

LINDA. Grand—You mean he went to Boston!

YOUNG BERNARD. Is Uncle Willy in Boston?

LINDA. Oh, maybe Willy can talk to the teacher. Oh, the poor, poor boy!

(*Light on house area snaps out.*)

BIFF (*at the table, now audible, holding up a gold fountain pen*). . . . so I'm washed up with Oliver, you understand? Are you listening to me?

WILLY (*at a loss*). Yeah, sure. If you hadn't flunked—

BIFF. Flunked what? What're you talking about?

WILLY. Don't blame everything on me! I didn't flunk math—you did! What pen?

HAPPY. That was awful dumb, Biff, a pen like that is worth—

WILLY (*seeing the pen for the first time*). You took Oliver's pen?

BIFF (*weakening*). Dad, I just explained it to you.

WILLY. You stole Bill Oliver's fountain pen!

BIFF. I didn't exactly steal it! That's just what I've been explaining to you!

HAPPY. He had it in his hand and just then Oliver walked in, so he got nervous and stuck it in his pocket!

WILLY. My God, Biff!

BIFF. I never intended to do it, Dad!

OPERATOR'S VOICE. Standish Arms, good evening!

WILLY (*shouting*). I'm not in my room!

BIFF (*frightened*). Dad, what's the matter? (*He and Happy stand up*)

OPERATOR. Ringing Mr. Loman for you!

WILLY. I'm not there, stop it!

BIFF (*horrified, gets down on one knee before Willy*). Dad, I'll make good, I'll make good. (*Willy tries to get to his feet. Biff holds him down*) Sit down now.

WILLY. No, you're no good, you're no good for anything.

BIFF. I am, Dad, I'll find something else, you understand? Now don't worry about

anything. (*He holds up Willy's face*) Talk to me, Dad.

OPERATOR. Mr. Loman does not answer. Shall I page him?

WILLY (*attempting to stand, as though to rush and silence the Operator*). No, no, no!

HAPPY. He'll strike something, Pop.

WILLY. No, no . . .

BIFF (*desperately, standing over Willy*). Pop, listen! Listen to me! I'm telling you something good. Oliver talked to his partner about the Florida idea. You listening? He—he talked to his partner, and he came to me . . . I'm going to be all right, you hear? Dad, listen to me, he said it was just a question of the amount!

WILLY. Then you . . . got it?

HAPPY. He's gonna be terrific, Pop!

WILLY (*trying to stand*). Then you got it, haven't you? You got it! You got it!

BIFF (*agonized, holds Willy down*). No, no. Look, Pop, I'm supposed to have lunch with them tomorrow. I'm just telling you this so you'll know that I can still make an impression, Pop. And I'll make good somewhere, but I can't go tomorrow, see?

WILLY. Why not? You simply—

BIFF. But the pen, Pop!

WILLY. You give it to him and tell him it was an oversight!

HAPPY. Sure, have lunch tomorrow!

BIFF. I can't say that—

WILLY. You were doing a crossword puzzle and accidentally used his pen!

BIFF. Listen, kid, I took those balls years ago, now I walk in with his fountain pen? That clinches it, don't you see? I can't face him like that! I'll try elsewhere.

PAGE'S VOICE. Paging Mr. Loman!

WILLY. Don't you want to be anything?

BIFF. Pop, how can I go back?

WILLY. You don't want to be anything, is that what's behind it?

BIFF (*now angry at Willy for not crediting his sympathy*). Don't take it that way! You think it was easy walking into that office after what I'd done to him? A team of horses couldn't have dragged me back to Bill Oliver!

WILLY. Then why'd you go?

BIFF. Why did I go? Why did I go! Look at you! Look at what's become of you!

(*Off left, The Woman laughs.*)

WILLY. Biff, you're going to go to that lunch tomorrow, or—

BIFF. I can't go. I've got no appointment!

HAPPY. Biff, for . . . !

WILLY. Are you spiting me?

BIFF. Don't take it that way! Goddammit!

WILLY (*strikes Biff and falters away from the table*). You rotten little louse! Are you spiting me?

THE WOMAN. Someone's at the door, Willy!

BIFF. I'm no good, can't you see what I am?

HAPPY (*separating them*). Hey, you're in a restaurant! Now cut it out, both of you! (*The girls enter*) Hello, girls, sit down.

(*The Woman laughs, off left.*)

MISS FORSYTHE. I guess we might as well. This is Letta.

THE WOMAN. Willy, are you going to wake up?

BIFF (*ignoring Willy*). How're ya, miss, sit down. What do you drink?

MISS FORSYTHE. Letta might not be able to stay long.

LETTA. I gotta get up very early tomorrow. I got jury duty. I'm so excited! Were you fellows ever on a jury?

BIFF. No, but I been in front of them! (*The girls laugh*) This is my father.

LETTA. Isn't he cute? Sit down with us, Pop.

HAPPY. Sit him down, Biff!

BIFF (*going to him*). Come on, slugger, drink us under the table. To hell with it! Come on, sit down, pal.

(*On Biff's last insistence, Willy is about to sit.*)

THE WOMAN (*now urgently*). Willy, are you going to answer the door!

(*The Woman's call pulls Willy back. He starts right, befuddled.*)

BIFF. Hey, where are you going?

WILLY. Open the door.

BIFF. The door?

WILLY. The washroom . . . the door . . . where's the door?

BIFF (*leading Willy to the left*). Just go straight down.

(*Willy moves left.*)

THE WOMAN. Willy, Willy, are you going to get up, get up, get up, get up?

(*Willy exits left.*)

LETTA. I think it's sweet you bring your daddy along.

MISS FORSYTHE. Oh, he isn't really your father!

BIFF (*at left, turning to her resentfully*). Miss Forsythe, you've just seen a prince walk by. A fine, troubled prince. A hard-working, unappreciated prince. A pal, you understand? A good companion. Always for his boys.

LETTA. That's so sweet.

HAPPY. Well, girls, what's the program? We're wasting time. Come on, Biff. Gather round. Where would you like to go?

BIFF. Why don't you do something for him?

HAPPY. Me!

BIFF. Don't you give a damn for him, Hap?

HAPPY. What're you talking about? I'm the one who—

BIFF. I sense it, you don't give a good goddam about him. (*He takes the rolled-up hose from his pocket and puts it on the table in front of Happy*) Look what I found in the cellar, for Christ's sake. How can you bear to let it go on?

HAPPY. Me? Who goes away? Who runs off and—

BIFF. Yeah, but he doesn't mean anything to you. You could help him—I can't! Don't you understand what I'm talking about? He's going to kill himself, don't you know that?

HAPPY. Don't I know it! Me!

BIFF. Hap, help him! Jesus . . . help him . . . Help me, help me, I can't bear to look at his face! (*Ready to weep, he hurries out, up right*)

HAPPY (*staring after him*). Where are you going?

MISS FORSYTHE. What's he so mad about?

HAPPY. Come on, girls, we'll catch up with him.

MISS FORSYTHE (*as Happy pushes her out*). Say, I don't like that temper of his!

HAPPY. He's just a little overstrung, he'll be all right!

WILLY (*off left, as The Woman laughs*). Don't answer! Don't answer!

LETTA. Don't you want to tell your father—

HAPPY. No, that's not my father. He's just a guy. Come on, we'll catch Biff, and, honey, we're going to paint this town! Stanley, where's the check! Hey, Stanley!

(*They exit. Stanley looks toward left.*)

STANLEY (*calling to Happy indignantly*). Mr. Loman! Mr. Loman!

(*Stanley picks up a chair and follows them off. Knocking is heard off left. The Woman enters, laughing. Willy follows her. She is in a black slip; he is buttoning his shirt. Raw, sensuous music accompanies their speech.*)

WILLY. Will you stop laughing? Will you stop?

THE WOMAN. Aren't you going to answer the door? He'll wake the whole hotel.

WILLY. I'm not expecting anybody.

THE WOMAN. Whyn't you have another drink, honey, and stop being so damn self-centered?

WILLY. I'm so lonely.

THE WOMAN. You know you ruined me, Willy? From now on, whenever you come to the office, I'll see that you go right through to the buyers. No waiting at my desk any more, Willy. You ruined me.

WILLY. That's nice of you to say that.

THE WOMAN. Gee, you are self-centered! Why so sad? You are the saddest, self-centeredest soul I ever did see-saw. (*She laughs. He kisses her*) Come on inside, drummer boy. It's silly to be dressing in the middle of the night. (*As knocking is heard*) Aren't you going to answer the door?

WILLY. They're knocking on the wrong door.

THE WOMAN. But I felt the knocking. And he heard us talking in here. Maybe the hotel's on fire!

WILLY (*his terror rising*). It's a mistake.

THE WOMAN. Then tell him to go away!

WILLY. There's nobody there.

THE WOMAN. It's getting on my nerves, Willy. There's somebody standing out there and it's getting on my nerves!

WILLY (*pushing her away from him*). All right, stay in the bathroom here, and don't come out. I think there's a law in Massachusetts about it, so don't come out. It may be that new room clerk. He looked very mean. So don't come out. It's a mistake, there's no fire.

(*The knocking is heard again. He takes a few steps away from her, and she vanishes into the wing. The light follows him, and now he is facing Young Biff, who carries a suitcase. Biff steps toward him. The music is gone.*)

BIFF. Why didn't you answer?

WILLY. Biff! What are you doing in Boston?

BIFF. Why didn't you answer? I've been knocking for five minutes, I called you on the phone—

WILLY. I just heard you. I was in the bathroom and had the door shut. Did anything happen home?

BIFF. Dad—I let you down.

WILLY. What do you mean?

BIFF. Dad . . .

WILLY. Biffo, what's this about? (*Putting his arm around Biff*) Come on, let's go downstairs and get you a malted.

BIFF. Dad, I flunked math.

WILLY. Not for the term?

BIFF. The term. I haven't got enough credits to graduate.

WILLY. You mean to say Bernard wouldn't give you the answers?

BIFF. He did, he tried, but I only got a sixty-one.

WILLY. And they wouldn't give you four points?

BIFF. Birnbaum refused absolutely. I begged him, Pop, but he won't give me those points. You gotta talk to him before they close the school. Because if he saw the kind of man you are, and you just talked to him in your way, I'm sure he'd come through for me. The class came right before practice, see, and I didn't go enough. Would you talk to him? He'd like you, Pop. You know the way you could talk.

WILLY. You're on. We'll drive right back.

BIFF. Oh, Dad, good work! I'm sure he'll change it for you!

WILLY. Go downstairs and tell the clerk I'm checkin' out. Go right down.

BIFF. Yes, sir! See, the reason he hates me, Pop—one day he was late for class so I got up at the blackboard and imitated him. I crossed my eyes and talked with a lithp.

WILLY (*laughing*). You did? The kids like it?

BIFF. They nearly died laughing.

WILLY. Yeah? What'd you do?

BIFF. The thquare root of thixthy twee is . . . (*Willy bursts out laughing; Biff joins him*) And in the middle of it he walked in!

(*Willy laughs and The Woman joins in offstage.*)

WILLY (*without hesitation*). Hurry downstairs and—

BIFF. Somebody in there?

WILLY. No, that was next door.

(*The Woman laughs offstage.*)

BIFF. Somebody got in your bathroom!

WILLY. No, it's the next room, there's a party—

THE WOMAN (*enters, laughing. She lisps this*). Can I come in? There's something in the bathtub, Willy, and it's moving! (*Willy looks at Biff, who is staring open-mouthed and horrified at The Woman.*)

WILLY. Ah—you better go back to your room. They must be finished painting by now. They're painting her room so I let her take a shower here. Go back, go back . . , (*He pushes her*)

THE WOMAN (*resisting*). But I've got to get dressed, Willy, I can't—

WILLY. Get out of here! Go back, go back . . . (*Suddenly striving for the ordinary*) This is Miss Francis, Biff, she's a buyer. They're painting her room. Go back, Miss Francis, go back . . .

THE WOMAN. But my clothes, I can't go out naked in the hall!

WILLY (*pushing her offstage*). Get outa here! Go back, go back!

(*Biff slowly sits down on his suitcase as the argument continues offstage.*)

THE WOMAN. Where's my stockings? You promised me stockings, Willy!

WILLY. I have no stockings here!

THE WOMAN. You had two boxes of size nine sheers for me, and I want them!

WILLY. Here, for God's sake, will you get outa here!

THE WOMAN (*enters holding a box of stockings*). I just hope there's nobody in the hall. That's all I hope. (*To Biff*) Are you football or baseball?

BIFF. Football.

THE WOMAN (*angry, humiliated*). That's me too. G'night. (*She snatches her clothes from Willy, and walks out*)

WILLY (*after a pause*). Well, better get going. I want to get to the school first thing in the morning. Get my suits out of the closet. I'll get my valises. (*Biff doesn't move*) What's the matter? (*Biff remains motionless, tears falling*) She's a buyer. Buys for J. H. Simmons. She lives down the hall—they're painting. You don't imagine—(*He breaks off. After a pause*) Now listen, pal, she's just a buyer. She sees merchandise in her room and they have to keep it looking just so . . . (*Pause. Assuming command*) All right, get my suits. (*Biff doesn't move*) Now stop crying and do as I say. I gave you an order. Biff, I gave you an order! Is

that what you do when I give you an order? How dare you cry! (*Putting his arm around Biff*) Now look, Biff, when you grow up you'll understand ᷄᷄᷄ ᷄᷄ ᷄out these things. You mustn't—you mustn't over-emphasize a thing like this. I'll see Birnbaum first thing in the morning.

BIFF. Never mind.

WILLY (*getting down beside Biff*). Never mind! He's going to give you those points. I'll see to it.

BIFF. He wouldn't listen to you.

WILLY. He certainly will listen to me. You need those points for the U. of Virginia.

BIFF. I'm not going there.

WILLY. Heh? If I can't get him to change that mark you'll make it up in summer school. You've got all summer to—

BIFF (*his weeping breaking from him*). Dad . . .

WILLY (*infected by it*). Oh, my boy . . .

BIFF. Dad . . .

WILLY. She's nothing to me, Biff. I was lonely, I was terribly lonely.

BIFF. You—you gave her Mama's stockings! (*His tears break through and he rises to go*)

WILLY (*grabbing for Biff*). I gave you an order!

BIFF. Don't touch me, you—liar!

WILLY. Apologize for that!

BIFF. You fake! You phony little fake! You fake! (*Overcome, he turns quickly and weeping fully goes out with his suitcase. Willy is left on the floor on his knees*)

WILLY. I gave you an order! Biff, come back here or I'll beat you! Come back here! I'll whip you!

(*Stanley comes quickly in from the right and stands in front of Willy.*)

WILLY (*shouts at Stanley*). I gave you an order . . .

STANLEY. Hey, let's pick it up, pick it up, Mr. Loman. (*He helps Willy to his feet*) Your boys left with the chippies. They said they'll see you home.

(*A second waiter watches some distance away.*)

WILLY. But we were supposed to have dinner together.

(*Music is heard, Willy's theme.*)

STANLEY. Can you make it?

WILLY. I'll—sure, I can make it. (*Sud-*

*denly concerned about his clothes*) Do I— I look all right?

STANLEY. Sure, you look all right. (*He flicks a speck off Willy's lapel*)

WILLY. Here—here's a dollar.

STANLEY. Oh, your son paid me. It's all right.

WILLY (*putting it in Stanley's hand*). No, take it. You're a good boy.

STANLEY. Oh, no, you don't have to . . .

WILLY. Here—here's some more, I don't need it any more. (*After a slight pause*) Tell me—is there a seed store in the neighborhood?

STANLEY. Seeds? You mean like to plant? (*As Willy turns, Stanley slips the money back into his jacket pocket.*)

WILLY. Yes. Carrots, peas . . .

STANLEY. Well, there's hardware stores on Sixth Avenue, but it may be too late now.

WILLY (*anxiously*). Oh, I'd better hurry. I've got to get some seeds. (*He starts off to the right*) I've got to get some seeds, right away. Nothing's planted. I don't have a thing in the ground.

(*Willy hurries out as the light goes down. Stanley moves over to the right after him, watches him off. The other waiter has been staring at Willy.*)

STANLEY (*to the waiter*). Well, whatta you looking at?

(*The waiter picks up the chairs and moves off right. Stanley takes the table and follows him. The light fades on this area. There is a long pause, the sound of the flute coming over. The light gradually rises on the kitchen, which is empty. Happy appears at the door of the house, followed by Biff. Happy is carrying a large bunch of long-stemmed roses. He enters the kitchen, looks around for Linda. Not seeing her, he turns to Biff, who is just outside the house door, and makes a gesture with his hands, indicating "Not here, I guess." He looks into the living-room and freezes. Inside, Linda, unseen, is seated, Willy's coat on her lap. She rises ominously and quietly and moves toward Happy, who backs up into the kitchen, afraid.*)

HAPPY. Hey, what're you doing up? (*Linda says nothing but moves toward him implacably*) Where's Pop? (*He keeps backing to the right, and now Linda is in full view in the doorway to the living-room*) Is he sleeping?

LINDA. Where were you?

HAPPY (*trying to laugh it off*). We met two girls, Mom, very fine types. Here, we brought you some flowers. (*Offering them to her*) Put them in your room, Ma.

(*She knocks them to the floor at Biff's feet. He has now come inside and closed the door behind him. She stares at Biff, silent.*)

HAPPY. Now what'd you do that for? Mom, I want you to have some flowers—

LINDA (*cutting Happy off, violently to Biff*). Don't you care whether he lives or dies?

HAPPY (*going to the stairs*). Come upstairs, Biff.

BIFF (*with a flare of disgust, to Happy*). Go away from me! (*To Linda*) What do you mean, lives or dies? Nobody's dying around here, pal.

LINDA. Get out of my sight! Get out of here!

BIFF. I wanna see the boss.

LINDA. You're not going near him!

BIFF. Where is he? (*He moves into the living-room and Linda follows*)

LINDA (*shouting after Biff*). You invite him for dinner. He looks forward to it all day—(*Biff appears in his parents' bedroom, looks around, and exits*)—and then you desert him there. There's no stranger you'd do that to!

HAPPY. Why? He had a swell time with us. Listen, when I—(*Linda comes back into the kitchen*)—desert him I hope I don't outlive the day!

LINDA. Get out of here!

HAPPY. Now look, Mom . . .

LINDA. Did you have to go to women tonight? You and your lousy rotten whores! (*Biff re-enters the kitchen.*)

HAPPY. Mom, all we did was follow Biff around trying to cheer him up! (*To Biff*) Boy, what a night you gave me!

LINDA. Get out of here, both of you, and don't come back! I don't want you tormenting him any more. Go on now, get your things together! (*To Biff*) You can sleep in his apartment. (*She starts to pick up the flowers and stops herself*) Pick up this stuff, I'm not your maid any more. Pick it up, you bum, you!

(*Happy turns his back to her in refusal. Biff slowly moves over and gets down on his knees, picking up the flowers.*)

LINDA. You're a pair of animals! Not one, not another living soul would have had the cruelty to walk out on that man in a restaurant!

BIFF (*not looking at her*). Is that what he said?

LINDA. He didn't have to say anything. He was so humiliated he nearly limped when he came in.

HAPPY. But, Mom, he had a great time with us—

BIFF (*cutting him off violently*). Shut up!

(*Without another word, Happy goes upstairs.*)

LINDA. You! You didn't even go in to see if he was all right!

BIFF (*still on the floor in front of Linda, the flowers in his hand; with self-loathing*). No. Didn't. Didn't do a damned thing. How do you like that, heh? Left him babbling in a toilet.

LINDA. You louse. You . . .

BIFF. Now you hit it on the nose! (*He gets up, throws the flowers in the wastebasket*) The scum of the earth, and you're looking at him!

LINDA. Get out of here!

BIFF. I gotta talk to the boss, Mom. Where is he?

LINDA. You're not going near him. Get out of this house!

BIFF (*with absolute assurance, determination*). No. We're gonna have an abrupt conversation, him and me.

LINDA. You're not talking to him!

(*Hammering is heard from outside the house, off right. Biff turns toward the noise.*)

LINDA (*suddenly pleading*). Will you please leave him alone?

BIFF. What's he doing out there?

LINDA. He's planting the garden!

BIFF (*quietly*). Now? Oh, my God!

(*Biff moves outside, Linda following. The light dies down on them and comes up on the center of the apron as Willy walks into it. He is carrying a flashlight, a hoe, and a handful of seed packets. He raps the top of the hoe sharply to fix it firmly, and then moves to the left, measuring off the distance with his foot. He holds the flashlight to look at the seed packets, reading off the instructions. He is in the blue of night.*)

WILLY. Carrots . . . quarter-inch apart. Rows . . . one-foot rows. (*He measures it off*) One foot. (*He puts down a package and measures off*) Beets. (*He puts down another package and measures again*) Let-

tuce. (*He reads the package, puts it down*) One foot—(*He breaks off as Ben appears at the right and moves slowly down to him*) What a proposition, ts, ts. Terrific, terrific. 'Cause she's suffered, Ben, the woman has suffered. You understand me? A man can't go out the way he came in, Ben, a man has got to add up to something. You can't, you can't—(*Ben moves toward him as though to interrupt*) You gotta consider, now. Don't answer so quick. Remember, it's a guaranteed twenty-thousand-dollar proposition. Now look, Ben, I want you to go through the ins and outs of this thing with me. I've got nobody to talk to, Ben, and the woman has suffered, you hear me?

BEN (*standing still, considering*). What's the proposition?

WILLY. It's twenty thousand dollars on the barrelhead. Guaranteed, gilt-edged, you understand?

BEN. You don't want to make a fool of yourself. They might not honor the policy.

WILLY. How can they dare refuse? Didn't I work like a coolie to meet every premium on the nose? And now they don't pay off? Impossible!

BEN. It's called a cowardly thing, William.

WILLY. Why? Does it take more guts to stand here the rest of my life ringing up a zero?

BEN (*yielding*). That's a point, William. (*He moves, thinking, turns*) And twenty thousand—that *is* something one can feel with the hand, it is there.

WILLY (*now assured, with rising power*). Oh, Ben, that's the whole beauty of it! I see it like a diamond, shining in the dark, hard and rough, that I can pick up and touch in my hand. Not like—like an appointment! This would not be another damned-fool appointment, Ben, and it changes all the aspects. Because he thinks I'm nothing, see, and so he spites me. But the funeral—(*Straightening up*) Ben, that funeral will be massive! They'll come from Maine, Massachusetts, Vermont, New Hampshire! All the old-timers with the strange license plates—that boy will be thunder-struck, Ben, because he never realized—I am known! Rhode Island, New York, New Jersey—I am known, Ben, and he'll see it with his eyes once and for all. He'll see what I am, Ben! He's in for a shock, that boy!

BEN (*coming down to the edge of the garden*). He'll call you a coward.

WILLY (*suddenly fearful*). No, that would be terrible.

BEN. Yes. And a damned fool.

WILLY. No, no, he mustn't. I won't have that! (*He is broken and desperate*)

BEN. He'll hate you, William.

(*The gay music of the Boys is heard.*)

WILLY. Oh, Ben, how do we get back to all the great times? Used to be so full of light, and comradeship, the sleigh-riding in winter, and the ruddiness on his cheeks. And always some kind of good news coming up, always something nice coming up ahead. And never even let me carry the valises in the house, and simonizing, simonizing that little red car! Why, why can't I give him something and not have him hate me?

BEN. Let me think about it. (*He glances at his watch*) I still have a little time. Remarkable proposition, but you've got to be sure you're not making a fool of yourself. (*Ben drifts off upstage and goes out of sight. Biff comes down from the left.*)

WILLY (*suddenly conscious of Biff, turns and looks up at him, then begins picking up the packages of seeds in confusion*). Where the hell is that seed? (*Indignantly*) You can't see nothing out here! They boxed in the whole goddam neighborhood!

BIFF. There are people all around here. Don't you realize that?

WILLY. I'm busy. Don't bother me.

BIFF (*taking the hoe from Willy*). I'm saying good-by to you, Pop. (*Willy looks at him, silent, unable to move*) I'm not coming back any more.

WILLY. You're not going to see Oliver tomorrow?

BIFF. I've got no appointment, Dad.

WILLY. He put his arm around you, and you've got no appointment?

BIFF. Pop, get this now, will you? Everytime I've left it's been a fight that sent me out of here. Today I realized something about myself and I tried to explain it to you and I—I think I'm just not smart enough to make any sense out of it for you. To hell with whose fault it is or anything like that. (*He takes Willy's arm*) Let's just wrap it up, heh? Come on in, we'll tell Mom. (*He gently tries to pull Willy to left*)

WILLY (*frozen, immobile, with guilt in his voice*). No, I didn't want to see her.

BIFF. Come on! (*He pulls again, and Willy tries to pull away*)

WILLY (*highly nervous*). No, no, I don't want to see her.

BIFF (*tries to look into Willy's face, as if to find the answer there*). Why don't you want to see her?

WILLY (*more harshly now*). Don't bother me, will you?

BIFF. What do you mean, you don't want to see her? You don't want them calling you yellow, do you? This isn't your fault; it's me, I'm a bum. Now come inside. (*Willy strains to get away*) Did you hear what I said to you?

(*Willy pulls away and quickly goes by himself into the house. Biff follows.*)

LINDA (*to Willy*). Did you plant, dear?

BIFF (*at the door, to Linda*). All right, we had it out. I'm going and I'm not writing any more.

LINDA (*going to Willy in the kitchen*). I think that's the best way, dear. 'Cause there's no use drawing it out, you'll just never get along.

(*Willy doesn't respond.*)

BIFF. People ask where I am and what I'm doing, you don't know, and you don't care. That way it'll be off your mind and you can start brightening up again. All right? That clears it, doesn't it? (*Willy is silent, and Biff goes to him*) You gonna wish me luck, scout? (*He extends his hand*) What do you say?

LINDA. Shake his hand, Willy.

WILLY (*turning to her, seething with hurt*). There's no necessity to mention the pen at all, y'know.

BIFF (*gently*). I've got no appointment, Dad.

WILLY (*erupting fiercely*). He put his arm around . . . ?

BIFF. Dad, you're never going to see what I am, so what's the use of arguing? If I strike oil I'll send you a check. Meantime, forget I'm alive.

WILLY (*to Linda*). Spite, see?

BIFF. Shake hands, Dad.

WILLY. Not my hand.

BIFF. I was hoping not to go this way.

WILLY. Well, this is the way you're going. Good-by.

(*Biff looks at him a moment, then turns sharply and goes to the stairs.*)

WILLY (*stops him with*). May you rot in hell if you leave this house!

BIFF (*turning*). Exactly what is it that you want from me?

WILLY. I want you to know, on the train, in the mountains, in the valleys, wherever you go, that you cut down your life for spite!

BIFF. No, no.

WILLY. Spite, spite, is the word of your undoing! And when you're down and out, remember what did it. When you're rotting somewhere beside the railroad tracks, remember, and don't you dare blame it on me!

BIFF. I'm not blaming it on you!

WILLY. I won't take the rap for this, you hear?

(*Happy comes down the stairs and stands on the bottom step, watching.*)

BIFF. That's just what I'm telling you!

WILLY (*sinking down into a chair at the table, with full accusation*). You're trying to put a knife in me—don't think I don't know what you're doing!

BIFF. All right, phony! Then let's lay it on the line. (*He whips the rubber tube out of his pocket and puts it on the table*)

HAPPY. You crazy—

LINDA. Biff! (*She moves to grab the hose, but Biff holds it down with his hand*)

BIFF. Leave it there! Don't move it!

WILLY (*not looking at it*). What is that?

BIFF. You know goddam well what that is.

WILLY (*caged, wanting to escape*). I never saw that.

BIFF. You saw it. The mice didn't bring it into the cellar! What is this supposed to do, make a hero out of you? This supposed to make me sorry for you?

WILLY. Never heard of it.

BIFF. There'll be no pity for you, you hear it? No pity!

WILLY (*to Linda*). You hear the spite!

BIFF. No, you're going to hear the truth —what you are and what I am!

LINDA. Stop it!

WILLY. Spite!

HAPPY (*coming down toward Biff*). You cut it now!

BIFF (*to Happy*). The man don't know who we are! The man is gonna know! (*To Willy*) We never told the truth for ten minutes in this house!

HAPPY. We always told the truth!

BIFF (*turning on him*). You big blow, are you the assistant buyer? You're one of the two assistants to the assistant, aren't you?

HAPPY. Well, I'm practically—

BIFF. You're practically full of it! We all are! And I'm through with it! (*To Willy*) Now hear this, Willy, this is me.

WILLY. I know you!

BIFF. You know why I had no address for three months? I stole a suit in Kansas City and I was in jail. (*To Linda, who is sobbing*) Stop crying, I'm through with it. (*Linda turns away from them, her hands covering her face.*)

WILLY. I suppose that's my fault!

BIFF. I stole myself out of every good job since high school!

WILLY. And whose fault is that?

BIFF. And I never got anywhere because you blew me so full of hot air I could never stand taking orders from anybody! That's whose fault it is!

WILLY. I hear that!

LINDA. Don't, Biff!

BIFF. It's goddam time you heard that! I had to be boss big shot in two weeks, and I'm through with it!

WILLY. Then hang yourself! For spite, hang yourself!

BIFF. No! Nobody's hanging himself, Willy! I ran down eleven flights with a pen in my hand today. And suddenly I stopped, you hear me? And in the middle of that office building, do you hear this? I stopped in the middle of that building and I saw—the sky. I saw the things that I love in this world. The work and the food and time to sit and smoke. And I looked at the pen and said to myself, what the hell am I grabbing this for? Why am I trying to become what I don't want to be? What am I doing in an office, making a contemptuous, begging fool of myself, when all I want is out there, waiting for me the minute I say I know who I am! Why can't I say that, Willy? (*He tries to make Willy face him, but Willy pulls away and moves to the left*)

WILLY (*with hatred, threateningly*). The door of your life is wide open!

BIFF. Pop, I'm a dime a dozen, and so are you!

WILLY (*turning on him now in an uncontrolled outburst*). I am not a dime a dozen! I am Willy Loman, and you are Biff Loman!

(*Biff starts for Willy, but is blocked by*

*Happy. In his fury, Biff seems on the verge of attacking his father.*)

BIFF. I am not a leader of men, Willy, and neither are you. You were never anything but a hard-working drummer who landed in the ash can like all the rest of them! I'm one dollar an hour, Willy! I tried seven states and couldn't raise it. A buck an hour! Do you gather my meaning? I'm not bringing home any prizes any more, and you're going to stop waiting for me to bring them home!

WILLY (*directly to Biff*). You vengeful, spiteful mutt!

(*Biff breaks from Happy. Willy, in fright, starts up the stairs. Biff grabs him.*)

BIFF (*at the peak of his fury*). Pop, I'm nothing! I'm nothing, Pop. Can't you understand that? There's no spite in it any more. I'm just what I am, that's all.

(*Biff's fury has spent itself, and he breaks down, sobbing, holding on to Willy, who dumbly fumbles for Biff's face.*)

WILLY (*astonished*). What're you doing? What're you doing? (*To Linda*) Why is he crying?

BIFF (*crying, broken*). Will you let me go, for Christ's sake? Will you take that phony dream and burn it before something happens? (*Struggling to contain himself, he pulls away and moves to the stairs*) I'll go in the morning. Put him—put him to bed. (*Exhausted, Biff moves up the stairs to his room*)

WILLY (*after a long pause, astonished, elevated*). Isn't that—isn't that remarkable? Biff—he likes me!

LINDA. He loves you, Willy.

HAPPY (*deeply moved*). Always did, Pop.

WILLY. Oh, Biff! (*Staring wildly*) He cried! Cried to me. (*He is choking with his love, and now cries out his promise*) That boy—that boy is going to be magnificent!

(*Ben appears in the light just outside the kitchen.*)

BEN. Yes, outstanding, with twenty thousand behind him.

LINDA (*sensing the racing of his mind, fearfully, carefully*). Now come to bed, Willy. It's all settled now.

WILLY (*finding it difficult not to rush out of the house*). Yes, we'll sleep. Come on. Go to sleep, Hap.

BEN. And it does take a great kind of a man to crack the jungle.

(*In accents of dread, Ben's idyllic music starts up.*)

HAPPY (*his arm around Linda*). I'm getting married, Pop, don't forget it. I'm changing everything. I'm gonna run that department before the year is up. You'll see, Mom. (*He kisses her*)

BEN. The jungle is dark but full of diamonds, Willy.

(*Willy turns, moves, listening to Ben.*)

LINDA. Be good. You're both good boys, just act that way, that's all.

HAPPY. 'Night, Pop. (*He goes upstairs*)

LINDA (*to Willy*). Come, dear.

BEN (*with greater force*). One must go in to fetch a diamond out.

WILLY (*to Linda, as he moves slowly along the edge of the kitchen, toward the door*). I just want to get settled down, Linda. Let me sit alone for a little.

LINDA (*almost uttering her fear*). I want you upstairs.

WILLY (*taking her in his arms*). In a few minutes, Linda. I couldn't sleep right now. Go on, you look awful tired. (*He kisses her*)

BEN. Not like an appointment at all. A diamond is rough and hard to the touch.

WILLY. Go on now. I'll be right up.

LINDA. I think this is the only way, Willy.

WILLY. Sure, it's the best thing.

BEN. Best thing!

WILLY. The only way. Everything is gonna be—go on, kid, get to bed. You look so tired.

LINDA. Come right up.

WILLY. Two minutes.

(*Linda goes into the living-room, then reappears in her bedroom. Willy moves just outside the kitchen door.*)

WILLY. Loves me. (*Wonderingly*) Always loved me. Isn't that a remarkable thing? Ben, he'll worship me for it!

BEN (*with promise*). It's dark there, but full of diamonds.

WILLY. Can you imagine that magnificence with twenty thousand dollars in his pocket?

LINDA (*calling from her room*). Willy! Come up!

WILLY (*calling into the kitchen*). Yes! Yes. Coming! It's very smart, you realize that, don't you, sweetheart? Even Ben sees it. I gotta go, baby. 'By! 'By! (*Going over to Ben, almost dancing*) Imagine? When the mail comes he'll be ahead of Bernard again!

BEN. A perfect proposition all around.

WILLY. Did you see how he cried to me? Oh, if I could kiss him, Ben!

BEN. Time, William, time!

WILLY. Oh, Ben, I always knew one way or another we were gonna make it, Biff and I!

BEN (*looking at his watch*). The boat. We'll be late. (*He moves slowly off into the darkness*)

WILLY (*elegiacally, turning to the house*). Now when you kick off, boy, I want a seventy-yard boot, and get right down the field under the ball, and when you hit, hit low and hit hard, because it's important, boy. (*He swings around and faces the audience*) There's all kinds of important people in the stands, and the first thing you know . . . (*Suddenly realizing he is alone*) Ben, Ben, where do I . . . ? (*He makes a sudden movement of search*) Ben, how do I . . .?

LINDA (*calling*). Willy, you coming up?

WILLY (*uttering a gasp of fear, whirling about as if to quiet her*). Sh! (*He turns around as if to find his way; sounds, faces, voices seem to be swarming in upon him and he flicks at them, crying*) Sh! Sh! (*Suddenly music, faint and high, stops him. It rises in intensity, almost to an unbearable scream. He goes up and down on his toes, and rushes off around the house*) Shhh!

LINDA. Willy?

(*There is no answer. Linda waits. Biff gets up off his bed. He is still in his clothes. Happy sits up. Biff stands listening.*)

LINDA (*with real fear*). Willy, answer me! Willy!

(*There is the sound of a car starting and moving away at full speed.*)

LINDA. No!

BIFF (*rushing down the stairs*). Pop!

(*As the car speeds off, the music crashes down in a frenzy of sound, which becomes the soft pulsation of a single cello string. Biff slowly returns to his bedroom. He and Happy gravely don their jackets. Linda slowly walks out of her room. The music has developed into a death march. The leaves of day are appearing over everything. Charley and Bernard, somberly dressed, appear and knock on the kitchen door. Biff and Happy slowly descend the stairs to the kitchen as Charley and Ber-*

*nard enter. All stop a moment when Linda, in clothes of mourning, bearing a little bunch of roses, comes through the draped doorway into the kitchen. She goes to Charley and takes his arm. Now all move toward the audience, through the wall-line of the kitchen. At the limit of the apron, Linda lays down the flowers, kneels, and sits back on her heels. All stare down at the grave.*)

## REQUIEM

CHARLEY. It's getting dark, Linda.

(*Linda doesn't react. She stares at the grave.*)

BIFF. How about it, Mom? Better get some rest, heh? They'll be closing the gate soon.

(*Linda makes no move. Pause.*)

HAPPY (*deeply angered*). He had no right to do that. There was no necessity for it. We would've helped him.

CHARLEY (*grunting*). Hmmm.

BIFF. Come along, Mom.

LINDA. Why didn't anybody come?

CHARLEY. It was a very nice funeral.

LINDA. But where are all the people he knew? Maybe they blame him.

CHARLEY. Naa. It's a rough world, Linda. They wouldn't blame him.

LINDA. I can't understand it. At this time especially. First time in thirty-five years we were just about free and clear. He only needed a little salary. He was even finished with the dentist.

CHARLEY. No man only needs a little salary.

LINDA. I can't understand it.

BIFF. There were a lot of nice days. When he'd come home from a trip; or on Sundays, making the stoop; finishing the cellar; putting on the new porch; when he built the extra bathroom; and put up the garage. You know something, Charley, there's more of him in that front stoop than in all the sales he ever made.

CHARLEY. Yeah, he was a happy man with a batch of cement.

LINDA. He was so wonderful with his hands.

BIFF. He had the wrong dreams. All, all, wrong.

HAPPY (*almost ready to fight Biff*). Don't say that!

BIFF. He never knew who he was.

CHARLEY (*stopping Happy's movement and reply. To Biff*). Nobody dast blame this man. You don't understand: Willy was a salesman. And for a salesman, there is no rock bottom to the life. He don't put a bolt to a nut, he don't tell you the law or give you medicine. He's the man way out there in the blue riding on a smile and a shoeshine. And when they start not smiling back—that's an earthquake. And then you get yourself a couple of spots on your hat, and you're finished. Nobody dast blame this man. A salesman is got to dream, boy. It comes with the territory.

BIFF. Charley, the man didn't know who he was.

HAPPY (*infuriated*). Don't say that!

BIFF. Why don't you come with me, Happy?

HAPPY. I'm not licked that easily. I'm staying right in this city, and I'm gonna beat this racket! (*He looks at Biff, his chin set*) The Loman Brothers!

BIFF. I know who I am, kid.

HAPPY. All right, boy. I'm gonna show you and everybody else that Willy Loman did not die in vain. He had a good dream. It's the only dream you can have—to come out number-one man. He fought it out here, and this is where I'm gonna win it for him.

BIFF (*with a hopeless glance at Happy, bends toward his mother*). Let's go, Mom.

LINDA. I'll be with you in a minute. Go on, Charley. (*He hesitates*) I want to, just for a minute. I never had a chance to say good-by.

(*Charley moves away, followed by Happy. Biff remains a slight distance up and left of Linda. She sits there, summoning herself. The flute begins, not far away, playing behind her speech.*)

LINDA. Forgive me, dear. I can't cry. I don't know what it is, but I can't cry. I don't understand it. Why did you ever do that? Help me, Willy, I can't cry. It seems to me that you're just on another trip. I keep expecting you. Willy, dear, I can't cry. Why did you do it? I search and search and I search, and I can't understand it, Willy. I made the last payment on the house today. Today, dear. And there'll be nobody home. (*A sob rises in her throat*) We're free and clear. (*Sobbing more fully, released*) We're free. (*Biff comes slowly toward her*) We're free . . . We're free . . . (*Biff lifts her to her feet and moves up right with her in his arms. Linda sobs quietly. Bernard and Charley come together and follow them, followed by Happy. Only the music of the flute is left on the darkening stage as over the house the hard towers of the apartment buildings rise into sharp focus, and*)

**THE CURTAIN FALLS**

# 1949-50

Again there was not much competition. Carson McCullers, a prominent novelist of the decayed magnolia school, had turned her 1946 novel, *The Member of the Wedding*, into her first produced play, and the Circle gave it seventeen votes to four for *Come Back, Little Sheba*, by William Inge, another first-time playwright. The voting occurred on April 4, 1950.

Others which received consideration were Gian-Carlo Menotti's opera *The Consul*, whose libretto was widely admired, three votes, and *The Innocents* by William Archibald, adapted from the Henry James story, *The Turn of the Screw*, one vote.

*The Cocktail Party* by expatriate T. S. Eliot, a mystical, sometimes puzzling but somehow satisfying play, won the foreign citation with no trouble. It received twenty votes to four for Jean Giraudoux's *The Enchanted*.

Menotti's *The Consul* picked up the musical citation with twenty votes to three each for *Lost in the Stars* by Maxwell Anderson and the late Kurt Weill, and *Regina*, a distinguished musical version of *The Little Foxes* turned out by Marc Blitzstein.

*The Cocktail Party* was regarded by some as a prime argument for establishment of a one-play award regardless of nationality. There was no doubt that it was the most interesting drama of the season.

As a matter of fact, *The Member of the Wedding* was not distinguished at all for the dramatic skill of its author or what she had to say. It was a triumph for two actresses, and the greasepaint apparently blinded a number of the brethren. The players in question were Julie Harris and that great singer of the blues, Ethel Waters.

People close to the theatre had had an eye on Miss Harris for a few seasons as she appeared in several minor or better parts in some unsuccessful plays. It appeared that she might be out of the ordinary, and she proved it quickly and lastingly in *The Member of the Wedding*. Playing a girl of twelve—her own age was twenty-five at the time—she was completely engaging, convincing and heartbreaking. The first-nighters experienced one of the most beautiful things the stage can offer—the seemingly spontaneous flowering of a new career. Miss Waters, not exactly a stranger to the serious drama—there had been a memorable performance in *Mamba's Daughters* ten years earlier—was merely superb.

As a play, Inge's *Come Back, Little Sheba* was excellent theatre, much superior to *The Member of the Wedding* if not to *The Cocktail Party*, and it also had two superlative performances, by Shirley Booth and Sidney Blackmer.

The Pulitzer prize went to the Rodgers-Hammerstein-Joshua Logan musical, *South Pacific*. Although it had opened in time for the Circle to consider it as part of the 1948–49 season, it came in after the Pulitzer deadline which is March 31 each year.

Katharine Hepburn returned to the stage in a picturesque revival of *As You Like It*, Jean Arthur also returned after a long career in motion pictures in the title role of a fine revival of *Peter Pan* in which Boris Karloff was a capital Captain Hook. Helen Hayes appeared in a not too successful Louisiana version of Chekhov's *The Cherry Orchard* fashioned by Joshua Logan and entitled *The Wisteria Trees*.

For those who like to know where the future stars come from, Grace Kelly made her first Broadway appearance in a revival of Strindberg's *The Father* with Raymond Massey, and Wally Cox was seen as a monologist in a short-lived revue called *Dance Me a Song*. And Carol Channing became an overnight star playing Lorelei Lee in the musical version of Anita Loos's *Gentlemen Prefer Blondes*.

*The Member of the Wedding* lasted 501 performances; *The Cocktail Party*, 409; *Come Back, Little Sheba*, 190; *The Consul*, 269.

# The Member of the Wedding

## By CARSON McCULLERS

Presented by Robert Whitehead, Oliver Rea and Stanley Martineau at the Empire Theatre, New York City, January 5, 1950, with the following cast:

| | |
|---|---|
| BERENICE SADIE BROWN | Ethel Waters |
| FRANKIE ADDAMS | Julie Harris |
| JOHN HENRY WEST | Brandon de Wilde |
| JARVIS | James Holden |
| JANICE | Janet de Gore |
| ROYAL ADDAMS | William Hansen |
| MRS. WEST | Margaret Barker |
| HELEN FLETCHER | Mitzie Blake |
| DORIS | Joan Shepard |
| MURIEL | Phyllis Love |
| SIS LAURA | Phyllis Walker |
| T. T. WILLIAMS | Harry Bolden |
| HONEY CAMDEN BROWN | Henry Scott |
| BARNEY McKEAN | Jimmy Dutton |

## SCENE

Act I—A Friday in August, late afternoon.

Act II—Afternoon of the next day.

Act III—Scene 1—The wedding day, afternoon of the next day following Act II. Scene 2—4 a.m. the following morning. Scene 3—Late afternoon, the following November.

### Time—1945.

### Place—A small town in Georgia.

*Reprinted by permission of New Directions Books, published by James Laughlin, 333 Sixth Avenue, New York, N. Y. All rights reserved.*

## ACT ONE

*A part of a Southern back yard and kitchen. At stage left there is a scuppernong arbor. A sheet, used as a stage curtain, hangs raggedly at one side of the arbor. There is an elm tree in the yard. The kitchen has in the center a table with chairs. The walls are drawn with child drawings. There is a stove to the right and a small coal heating stove with coal scuttle in rear center of kitchen. The kitchen opens on the left into the yard. At the interior right a door leads to a small inner room. A door at the left leads into the front hall. The lights go on dimly, with a dreamlike effect, gradually revealing the family in the yard and Berenice Sadie Brown in the kitchen. Berenice, the cook, is a stout, motherly Negro woman with an air of great capability and devoted protection. She is about forty-five years old. She has a quiet, flat face and one of her eyes is made of blue glass. Sometimes, when her socket bothers her, she dispenses with the false eye and wears a black patch. When we first see her she is wearing the patch and is dressed in a simple print work dress and apron.*

*Frankie, a gangling girl of twelve with blonde hair cut like a boy's, is wearing shorts and a sombrero and is standing in the arbor gazing adoringly at her brother Jarvis and his fiancée Janice. She is a dreamy, restless girl, and periods of energetic activity alternate with a rapt attention to her inward world of fantasy. She is thin and awkward and very much aware of being too tall. Jarvis, a good-looking boy of twenty-one, wearing an army uniform, stands by Janice. He is awkward when he first appears because this is his betrothal visit. Janice, a young, pretty, fresh-looking girl of eighteen or nineteen, is charming but rather ordinary, with brown hair done up in a small knot. She is dressed in her best clothes and is anxious to be liked by her new family. Mr. Addams, Frankie's father, is a deliberate and absent-minded man of about forty-five. A widower of many years, he has become set in his habits. He is dressed conservatively, and there is about him an old-fashioned look and manner. John Henry, Frankie's small cousin, aged seven, picks and eats any scuppernongs he can reach. He is a delicate, active boy and wears gold-rimmed spectacles which give him an oddly judicious look. He is blond and sun-burned and when we first see him he is wearing a sun-suit and is barefooted.*

———

*(Berenice Sadie Brown is busy in the kitchen.)*

JARVIS. Seems to me like this old arbor has shrunk. I remember when I was a child it used to seem absolutely enormous. When I was Frankie's age, I had a vine swing here. Remember, Papa?

FRANKIE. It don't seem so absolutely enormous to me, because I am so tall.

JARVIS. I never saw a human grow so fast in all my life. I think maybe we ought to tie a brick to your head.

FRANKIE *(hunching down in obvious distress)*. Oh, Jarvis! Don't.

JANICE. Don't tease your little sister. I don't think Frankie is too tall. She probably won't grow much more. I had the biggest portion of my growth by the time I was thirteen.

FRANKIE. But I'm just twelve. When I think of all the growing years ahead of me, I get scared.

*(Janice goes to Frankie and puts her arms around her comfortingly. Frankie stands rigid, embarrassed and blissful.)*

JANICE. I wouldn't worry.

*(Berenice comes from the kitchen with a tray of drinks. Frankie rushes eagerly to help her serve them.)*

FRANKIE. Let me help.

BERENICE. Them two drinks is lemonade for you and John Henry. The others got liquor in them.

FRANKIE. Janice, come sit down on the arbor seat. Jarvis, you sit down too.

*(Jarvis and Janice sit close together on the wicker bench in the arbor. Frankie hands the drinks around, then perches on the ground before Janice and Jarvis and stares adoringly at them.)*

FRANKIE. It was such a surprise when Jarvis wrote home you are going to be married.

JANICE. I hope it wasn't a bad surprise.

FRANKIE. Oh, Heavens no! *(With great feeling)* As a matter of fact . . . *(She strokes Janice's shoes tenderly and Jarvis' army boot)* If only you knew how I feel.

MR. ADDAMS. Frankie's been bending my ears ever since your letter came, Jarvis. Going on about weddings, brides, grooms, etc.

JANICE. It's lovely that we can be married at Jarvis' home.

MR. ADDAMS. That's the way to feel, Janice. Marriage is a sacred institution.

FRANKIE. Oh, it will be beautiful.

JARVIS. Pretty soon we'd better be shoving off for Winter Hill. I have to be back in barracks tonight.

FRANKIE. Winter Hill is such a lovely, cold name. It reminds me of ice and snow.

JANICE. You know it's just a hundred miles away, darling.

JARVIS. Ice and snow indeed! Yesterday the temperature on the parade ground reached 102.

*(Frankie takes a palmetto fan from the table and fans first Janice, then Jarvis.)*

JANICE. That feels so good, darling. Thanks.

FRANKIE. I wrote you so many letters, Jarvis, and you never, never would answer me. When you were stationed in Alaska, I wanted so much to hear about Alaska. I sent you so many boxes of home-made candy, but you never answered me.

JARVIS. Oh, Frankie. You know how it is . . .

FRANKIE *(sipping her drink)*. You know this lemonade tastes funny. Kind of sharp and hot. I believe I got the drinks mixed up.

JARVIS. I was thinking my drink tasted mighty sissy. Just plain lemonade—no liquor at all.

*(Frankie and Jarvis exchange their drinks. Jarvis sips his.)*

JARVIS. This is better.

FRANKIE. I drank a lot. I wonder if I'm drunk. It makes me feel like I had four legs instead of two. I think I'm drunk. *(She gets up and begins to stagger around in imitation of drunkenness)* See! I'm drunk! Look, Papa, how drunk I am! *(Suddenly she turns a handspring; then there is a blare of music from the club house gramophone off to the right)*

JANICE. Where does the music come from? It sounds so close.

FRANKIE. It is. Right over there. They have club meetings and parties with boys on Friday nights. I watch them here from the yard.

JANICE. It must be nice having your club house so near.

FRANKIE. I'm not a member now. But they are holding an election this afternoon, and maybe I'll be elected.

JOHN HENRY. Here comes Mama.

*(Mrs. West, John Henry's mother, crosses the yard from the right. She is a vivacious, blonde woman of about thirty-three. She is dressed in sleazy, rather dowdy summer clothes.)*

MR. ADDAMS. Hello, Pet. Just in time to meet our new family member.

MRS. WEST. I saw you out here from the window.

JARVIS *(rising, with Janice)*. Hi, Aunt Pet. How is Uncle Eustace?

MRS. WEST. He's at the office.

JANICE *(offering her hand with the engagement ring on it)*. Look, Aunt Pet. May I call you Aunt Pet?

MRS. WEST *(hugging her)*. Of course, Janice. What a gorgeous ring!

JANICE. Jarvis just gave it to me this morning. He wanted to consult his father and get it from his store, naturally.

MRS. WEST. How lovely.

MR. ADDAMS. A quarter carat—not too flashy but a good stone.

MRS. WEST *(to Berenice, who is gathering up the empty glasses)*. Berenice, what have you and Frankie been doing to my John Henry? He sticks over here in your kitchen morning, noon and night.

BERENICE. We enjoys him and Candy seems to like it over here.

MRS. WEST. What on earth do you do to him?

BERENICE. We just talks and passes the time of day. Occasionally plays cards.

MRS. WEST. Well, if he gets in your way just shoo him home.

BERENICE. Candy don't bother nobody.

JOHN HENRY *(walking around barefooted in the arbor)*. These grapes are so squelchy when I step on them.

MRS. WEST. Run home, darling, and wash your feet and put on your sandals.

JOHN HENRY. I like to squelch on the grapes.

*(Berenice goes back to the kitchen.)*

JANICE. That looks like a stage curtain. Jarvis told me how you used to write plays and act in them out here in the arbor. What kind of shows do you have?

FRANKIE. Oh, crook shows and cowboy shows. This summer I've had some cold shows—about Esquimos and explorers— on account of the hot weather.

JANICE. Do you ever have romances?

FRANKIE. Naw . . . *(With bravado)* I had crook shows for the most part. You see I never believed in love until now. *(Her look lingers on Janice and Jarvis. She hugs Janice and Jarvis, bending over them from back of the bench)*

MRS. WEST. Frankie and this little friend of hers gave a performance of "The Vagabond King" out here last spring.

*(John Henry spreads out his arms and imitates the heroine of the play from memory, singing in his high childish voice.*

JOHN HENRY. Never hope to bind me. Never hope to know. *(Speaking)* Frankie was the king-boy. I sold the tickets.

MRS. WEST. Yes, I have always said that Frankie has talent.

FRANKIE. Aw, I'm afraid I don't have much talent.

JOHN HENRY. Frankie can laugh and kill people good. She can die, too.

FRANKIE *(with some pride)*. Yeah, I guess I die all right.

MR. ADDAMS. Frankie rounds up John Henry and those smaller children, but by the time she dresses them in the costumes, they're worn out and won't act in the show.

JARVIS *(looking at his watch)*. Well, it's time we shove off for Winter Hill—Frankie's land of icebergs and snow—where the temperature goes up to 102. *(Jarvis takes Janice's hand. He gets up and gazes fondly around the yard and the arbor. He pulls her up and stands with his arm around her, gazing around him at the arbor and yard.)*

JARVIS. It carries me back—this smell of mashed grapes and dust. I remember all the endless summer afternoons of my childhood. It does carry me back.

FRANKIE. Me too. It carries me back, too.

MR. ADDAMS *(putting one arm around Janice and shaking Jarvis' hand)*. Merciful Heavens! It seems I have two Methuselahs in my family! Does it carry you back to your childhood too, John Henry?

JOHN HENRY. Yes, Uncle Royal.

MR. ADDAMS. Son, this visit was a real pleasure. Janice, I'm mighty pleased to see my boy has such lucky judgment in choosing a wife.

FRANKIE. I hate to think you have to go. I'm just now realizing you're here.

JARVIS. We'll be back in two days. The wedding is Sunday.

*(The family move around the house toward the street. John Henry enters the kitchen through the back door. There are the sounds of "good-byes" from the front yard.)*

JOHN HENRY. Frankie was drunk. She drank a liquor drink.

BERENICE. She just made out like she was drunk—pretended.

JOHN HENRY. She said, "Look, Papa, how drunk I am," and she couldn't walk.

FRANKIE'S VOICE. Good-bye, Jarvis. Good-bye, Janice.

JARVIS' VOICE. See you Sunday.

MR. ADDAMS' VOICE. Drive carefully, son. Good-bye, Janice.

JANICE'S VOICE. Good-bye and thanks, Mr. Addams. Good-bye, Frankie darling.

ALL THE VOICES. Good-bye! Good-bye!

JOHN HENRY. They are going now to Winter Hill.

*(There is the sound of the front door opening, then of steps in the hall. Frankie enters through the hall.)*

FRANKIE. Oh, I can't understand it! The way it all just suddenly happened.

BERENICE. Happened? Happened?

FRANKIE. I have never been so puzzled.

BERENICE. Puzzled about what?

FRANKIE. The whole thing. They are so beautiful.

BERENICE *(after a pause)*. I believe the sun done fried your brains.

JOHN HENRY *(whispering)* Me too.

BERENICE. Look here at me. You jealous.

FRANKIE. Jealous?

BERENICE. Jealous because your brother's going to be married.

FRANKIE *(slowly)*. No. I just never saw any two people like them. When they walked in the house today it was so queer.

BERENICE. You jealous. Go and behold yourself in the mirror. I can see from the color of your eyes.

*(Frankie goes to the mirror and stares. She draws up her left shoulder, shakes her head, and turns away.)*

FRANKIE *(with feeling)*. Oh! They were the two prettiest people I ever saw. I just can't understand how it happened.

BERENICE. Whatever ails you?—actin' so queer.

FRANKIE. I don't know. I bet they have a good time every minute of the day.

JOHN HENRY. Less us have a good time.

FRANKIE. Us have a good time? Us? *(She rises and walks around the table)*

BERENICE. Come on. Less have a game of three-handed bridge.

*(They sit down at the table, shuffle the cards, deal, and play a game.)*

FRANKIE. Oregon, Alaska, Winter Hill, the wedding. It's all so queer.

BERENICE. I can't bid, never have a hand these days.

FRANKIE. A spade.

JOHN HENRY. I want to bid spades. That's what I was going to bid.

FRANKIE. Well, that's your tough luck. I bid them first.

JOHN HENRY. Oh, you fool jackass! It's not fair!

BERENICE. Hush quarreling, you two. *(She looks at both their hands)* To tell the truth, I don't think either of you got such a grand hand to fight over the bid about. Where is the cards? I haven't had no kind of a hand all week.

FRANKIE. I don't give a durn about it. It is immaterial with me. *(There is a long pause. She sits with her head propped on her hand, her legs wound around each other)* Let's talk about them—and the wedding.

BERENICE. What you want to talk about?

FRANKIE. My heart feels them going away—going farther and farther away— while I am stuck here by myself.

BERENICE. You ain't here by yourself. By the way, where's your Pa?

FRANKIE. He went to the store. I think about them, but I remembered them more as a feeling than as a picture.

BERENICE. A feeling?

FRANKIE. They were the two prettiest people I ever saw. Yet it was like I couldn't see all of them I wanted to see. My brains couldn't gather together quick enough to take it all in. And then they were gone.

BERENICE. Well, stop commenting about it. You don't have your mind on the game.

FRANKIE *(playing her cards, followed by John Henry)*. Spades are trumps and you got a spade. I have some of my mind on the game.

*(John Henry puts his donkey necklace in his mouth and looks away.)*

FRANKIE. Go on, cheater.

BERENICE. Make haste.

JOHN HENRY. I can't. It's a king. The only spade I got is a king, and I don't want to play my king under Frankie's ace. And I'm not going to do it either.

FRANKIE *(throwing her cards down on the table)*. See, Berenice, he cheats!

BERENICE. Play your king, John Henry. You have to follow the rules of the game.

JOHN HENRY. My king. It isn't fair.

FRANKIE. Even with this trick, I can't win.

BERENICE. Where is the cards? For three days I haven't had a decent hand. I'm beginning to suspicion something. Come on less us count these old cards.

FRANKIE. We've worn these old cards out. If you would eat these old cards, they would taste like a combination of all the dinners of this summer together with a sweaty-handed, nasty taste. Why, the jacks and the queens are missing.

BERENICE. John Henry, how come you do a thing like that? So that's why you asked for the scissors and stole off quiet behind the arbor. Now, Candy, how come you took our playing cards and cut out the pictures?

JOHN HENRY. Because I wanted them. They're cute.

FRANKIE. See? He's nothing but a child. It's hopeless. Hopeless!

BERENICE. Maybe so.

FRANKIE. We'll just have to put him out of the game. He's entirely too young.

*(John Henry whimpers.)*

BERENICE. Well, we can't put Candy out of the game. We gotta have a third to play. Besides, by the last count he owes me close to three million dollars.

FRANKIE. Oh, I am sick unto death. *(She sweeps the cards from the table, then gets up and begins walking around the kitchen. John Henry leaves the table and picks up a large blonde doll on the chair in the corner)* I wish they'd taken me with them to Winter Hill this afternoon. I wish tomorrow was Sunday instead of Saturday.

BERENICE. Sunday will come.

FRANKIE. I doubt it. I wish I was going somewhere for good. I wish I had a hundred dollars and could just light out and never see this town again.

BERENICE. It seems like you wish for a lot of things.

FRANKIE. I wish I was somebody else except me.

JOHN HENRY *(holding the doll)*. You serious when you gave me the doll a while ago?

FRANKIE. It gives me a pain just to think about them.

BERENICE. It is a known truth that gray-eyed people are jealous.

*(There are sounds of children playing in the neighboring yard.)*

JOHN HENRY. Let's go out and play with the children.

FRANKIE. I don't want to.

JOHN HENRY. There's a big crowd, and they sound like they having a mighty good time. Less go.

FRANKIE. You got ears. You heard me.

JOHN HENRY. I think maybe I better go home.

FRANKIE. Why, you said you were going to spend the night. You just can't eat dinner and then go off in the afternoon like that.

JOHN HENRY. I know it.

BERENICE. Candy, Lamb, you can go home if you want to.

JOHN HENRY. But less go out, Frankie. They sound like they having a lot of fun.

FRANKIE. No, they're not. Just a crowd of ugly, silly children. Running and hollering and running and hollering. Nothing to it.

JOHN HENRY. Less go!

FRANKIE. Well, then I'll entertain you. What do you want to do? Would you like for me to read to you out of The Book of Knowledge, or would you rather do something else?

JOHN HENRY. I rather do something else. *(He goes to the back door, and looks into the yard. Several young girls of thirteen or fourteen, dressed in clean print frocks, file slowly across the back yard)* Look. Those big girls.

FRANKIE *(running out into the yard).* Hey, there. I'm mighty glad to see you. Come on in.

HELEN. We can't. We were just passing through to notify our new member.

FRANKIE *(overjoyed).* Am I the new member?

DORIS. No, you're not the one the club elected.

FRANKIE. Not elected?

HELEN. Every ballot was unanimous for Mary Littlejohn.

FRANKIE. Mary Littlejohn! You mean that girl who just moved in next door? That pasty fat girl with those tacky pigtails? The one who plays the piano all day long?

DORIS. Yes. The club unanimously elected Mary.

FRANKIE. Why, she's not even cute.

HELEN. She is too; and, furthermore, she's talented.

FRANKIE. I think it's sissy to sit around the house all day playing classical music.

DORIS. Why, Mary is training for a concert career.

FRANKIE. Well, I wish to Jesus she would train somewhere else.

DORIS. You don't have enough sense to appreciate a talented girl like Mary.

FRANKIE. What are you doing in my yard? You're never to set foot on my Papa's property again. *(Frankie shakes Helen)* Son-of-a-bitches. I could shoot you with my Papa's pistol.

JOHN HENRY *(shaking his fists).* Son-of-a-bitches.

FRANKIE. Why didn't you elect me? *(She goes back into the house)* Why can't I be a member?

JOHN HENRY. Maybe they'll change their mind and invite you.

BERENICE. I wouldn't pay them no mind. All my life I've been wantin' things that I ain't been gettin'. Anyhow those club girls is fully two years older than you.

FRANKIE. I think they have been spreading it all over town that I smell bad. When I had those boils and had to use that black bitter-smelling ointment, old Helen Fletcher asked me what was that funny smell I had. Oh, I could shoot every one of them with a pistol.

*(Frankie sits with her head on the table. John Henry approaches and pats the back of Frankie's neck.)*

JOHN HENRY. I don't think you smell so bad. You smell sweet, like a hundred flowers.

FRANKIE. The son-of-a-bitches. And there was something else. They were telling nasty lies about married people. When I think of Aunt Pet and Uncle Eustace! And my own father! The nasty lies! I don't know what kind of fool they take me for.

BERENICE. That's what I tell you. They too old for you.

*(John Henry raises his head, expands his nostrils and sniffs at himself. Then Frankie goes into the interior bedroom and returns with a bottle of perfume.)*

FRANKIE. Boy! I bet I use more perfume than anybody else in town. Want some on you, John Henry? You want some, Berenice? (She sprinkles perfume)*

JOHN HENRY. Like a thousand flowers.

BERENICE. Frankie, the whole idea of a club is that there are members who are included and the non-members who are not included. Now what you ought to do is to round you up a club of your own. And you could be the president yourself. *(There is a pause)*

FRANKIE. Who would I get?

BERENICE. Why, those little children you hear playing in the neighborhood.

FRANKIE. I don't want to be the president of all those little young left-over people.

BERENICE. Well, then enjoy your misery. That perfume smells so strong it kind of makes me sick.

*(John Henry plays with the doll at the kitchen table and Frankie watches.)*

FRANKIE. Look here at me, John Henry. Take off those glasses. *(John Henry takes off his glasses)* I bet you don't need those glasses. *(She points to the coal scuttle)* What is this?

JOHN HENRY. The coal scuttle.

FRANKIE *(taking a shell from the kitchen shelf)*. And this?

JOHN HENRY. The shell we got at Saint Peter's Bay last summer.

FRANKIE. What is that little thing crawling around on the floor?

JOHN HENRY. Where?

FRANKIE. That little thing crawling around near your feet.

JOHN HENRY. Oh. *(He squats down)* Why, it's an ant. How did that get in here?

FRANKIE. If I were you I'd just throw those glasses away. You can see good as anybody.

BERENICE. Now quit picking with John Henry.

FRANKIE. They don't look becoming. *(John Henry wipes his glasses and puts them back on)* He can suit himself. I was only telling him for his own good. *(She walks restlessly around the kitchen)* I bet Janice and Jarvis are members of a lot of clubs. In fact, the army is kind of like a club.

*(John Henry searches through Berenice's pocketbook.)*

BERENICE. Don't root through my pocketbook like that, Candy. Ain't a wise policy to search folks' pocketbooks. They might think you trying to steal their money.

JOHN HENRY. I'm looking for your new glass eye. Here it is. *(He hands Berenice the glass eye)* You got two nickels and a dime.

*(Berenice takes off her patch, turns away and inserts the glass eye.)*

BERENICE. I ain't used to it yet. The socket bothers me. Maybe it don't fit properly.

JOHN HENRY. The blue glass eye looks very cute.

FRANKIE. I don't see why you had to get that eye. It has a wrong expression—let alone being blue.

BERENICE. Ain't anybody ask your judgment, wise-mouth.

JOHN HENRY. Which one of your eyes do you see out of the best?

BERENICE. The left eye, of course. The glass eye don't do me no seeing good at all.

JOHN HENRY. I like the glass eye better. It is so bright and shiny—a real pretty eye. Frankie, you serious when you gave me this doll a while ago?

FRANKIE. Janice and Jarvis. It gives me this pain just to think about them.

BERENICE. It is a known truth that gray-eyed people are jealous.

FRANKIE. I told you I wasn't jealous. I couldn't be jealous of one of them without being jealous of them both. I 'sociate the two of them together. Somehow they're just so different from us.

BERENICE. Well, I were jealous when my foster-brother, Honey, married Clorina. I sent a warning I could tear the ears off her head. But you see I didn't. Clorina's got ears just like anybody else. And now I love her.

FRANKIE *(stopping her walking suddenly)*. J.A.—Janice and Jarvis. Isn't that the strangest thing?

BERENICE. What?

FRANKIE. J.A.—Both their names begin with "J.A."

BERENICE. And? What about it?

FRANKIE *(walking around the kitchen table)*. If only my name was Jane. Jane or Jasmine.

BERENICE. I don't follow your frame of mind.

FRANKIE. Jarvis and Janice and Jasmine. See?

BERENICE. No. I don't see.

FRANKIE. I wonder if it's against the law to change your name. Or add to it.

BERENICE. Naturally. It's against the law.

FRANKIE (*impetuously*). Well, I don't care. F. Jasmine Addams.

JOHN HENRY (*approaching with the doll*). You serious when you give me this? (*He pulls up the doll's dress and pats her*) I will name her Belle.

FRANKIE. I don't know what went on in Jarvis' mind when he brought me that doll. Imagine bringing me a doll! I had counted on Jarvis bringing me something from Alaska.

BERENICE. Your face when you unwrapped that package was a study.

FRANKIE. John Henry, quit pickin' at the doll's eyes. It makes me so nervous. You hear me! (*He sits the doll up*) In fact, take the doll somewhere out of my sight.

JOHN HENRY. Her name is Lily Belle. (*John Henry goes out and props the doll up on the back steps. There is the sound of an unseen Negro singing from the neighboring yard.*)

FRANKIE (*going to the mirror*). The big mistake I made was to get this close crew cut. For the wedding, I ought to have long brunette hair. Don't you think so?

BERENICE. I don't see how come brunette hair is necessary. But I warned you about getting your head shaved off like that before you did it. But nothing would do but you shave it like that.

FRANKIE (*stepping back from the mirror and slumping her shoulders*). Oh, I am so worried about being so tall. I'm twelve and five-sixth years old and already five feet five and three-fourths inches tall. If I keep on growing like this until I'm twenty-one, I figure I will be nearly ten feet tall.

JOHN HENRY (*re-entering the kitchen*). Lily Belle is taking a nap on the back steps. Don't talk so loud, Frankie.

FRANKIE (*after a pause*). I doubt if they ever get married or go to a wedding. Those freaks.

BERENICE. Freaks. What freaks you talking about?

FRANKIE. At the fair. The ones we saw there last October.

JOHN HENRY. Oh, the freaks at the fair! (*He holds out an imaginary skirt and begins to skip around the room with one finger resting on the top of his head*) Oh, she was the cutest little girl I ever saw. I never saw anything so cute in my whole life. Did you, Frankie?

FRANKIE. No. I don't think she was cute.

BERENICE. Who is that he's talking about?

FRANKIE. That little old pin-head at the fair. A head no bigger than an orange. With the hair shaved off and a big pink bow at the top. Bow was bigger than the head.

JOHN HENRY. Shoo! She was too cute.

BERENICE. That little old squeezed-looking midget in them little trick evening clothes. And that giant with the hang-jaw face and them huge loose hands. And that morphidite! Half man—half woman. With that tiger skin on one side and that spangled skirt on the other.

JOHN HENRY. But that little-headed girl was cute.

FRANKIE. And that wild colored man they said came from a savage island and ate those real live rats. Do you think they make a very big salary?

BERENICE. How would I know? In fact, all them freak folks down at the fair every October just gives me the creeps.

FRANKIE (*after a pause, and slowly*). Do I give you the creeps?

BERENICE. You?

FRANKIE. Do you think I will grow into a freak?

BERENICE. You? Why certainly not, I trust Jesus!

FRANKIE (*going over to the mirror, and looking at herself*). Well, do you think I will be pretty?

BERENICE. Maybe. If you file down them horns a inch or two.

FRANKIE (*turning to face Berenice, and shuffling one bare foot on the floor*). Seriously.

BERENICE. Seriously, I think when you fill out you will do very well. If you behave.

FRANKIE. But by Sunday, I want to do something to improve myself before the wedding.

BERENICE. Get clean for a change. Scrub your elbows and fix yourself nice. You will do very well.

JOHN HENRY. You will be all right if you file down them horns.

FRANKIE (*raising her right shoulder and turning from the mirror*). I don't know what to do. I just wish I would die.

BERENICE. Well, die then!

JOHN HENRY. Die.

FRANKIE *(suddenly exasperated)*. Go home! *(There is a pause)* You heard me! *(She makes a face at him and threatens him with the fly swatter. They run twice around the table)* Go home! I'm sick and tired of you, you little midget.

*(John Henry goes out, taking the doll with him.)*

BERENICE. Now what makes you act like that? You are too mean to live.

FRANKIE. I know it. *(She takes a carving knife from the table drawer)* Something about John Henry just gets on my nerves these days. *(She puts her left ankle over her right knee and begins to pick with the knife at a splinter in her foot)* I've got a splinter in my foot.

BERENICE. That knife ain't the proper thing for a splinter.

FRANKIE. It seems to me that before this summer I used always to have such a good time. Remember this spring when Evelyn Owen and me used to dress up in costumes and go down town and shop at the five-and-dime? And how every Friday night we'd spend the night with each other either at her house or here? And then Evelyn Owen had to go and move away to Florida. And now she won't even write to me.

BERENICE. Honey, you are not crying, is you? Don't that hurt you none?

FRANKIE. It would hurt anybody else except me. And how the wisteria in town was so blue and pretty in April but somehow it was so pretty it made me sad. And how Evelyn and me put on that show the Glee Club did at the High School Auditorium? *(She raises her head and beats time with the knife and her fist on the table, singing loudly with sudden energy)* Sons of toil and danger! Will you serve a stranger! And bow down to Burgundy! *(Berenice joins in on "Burgundy." Frankie pauses, then begins to pick her foot again, humming the tune sadly)*

BERENICE. That was a nice show you children copied in the arbor. You will meet another girl friend you like as well as Evelyn Owen. Or maybe Mr. Owen will move back into town. *(There is a pause)* Frankie, what you need is a needle.

FRANKIE. I don't care anything about my feet. *(She stomps her foot on the floor*

*and lays down the knife on the table)* It was just so queer the way it happened this afternoon. The minute I laid eyes on the pair of them I had this funny feeling. *(She goes over and picks up a saucer of milk near the cat-hole in back of the door and pours the milk in the sink)* How old were you, Berenice, when you married your first husband?

BERENICE. I were thirteen years old.

FRANKIE. What made you get married so young for?

BERENICE. Because I wanted to.

FRANKIE. You never loved any of your four husbands but Ludie.

BERENICE. Ludie Maxwell Freeman was my only true husband. The other ones were just scraps.

FRANKIE. Did you marry with a veil every time?

BERENICE. Three times with a veil.

FRANKIE *(pouring milk into the saucer and returning the saucer to the cat-hole)*. If only I just knew where he is gone. Ps, ps, ps . . . Charles, Charles.

BERENICE. Quit worrying yourself about that old alley cat. He's gone off to hunt a friend.

FRANKIE. To hunt a friend?

BERENICE. Why certainly. He roamed off to find himself a lady friend.

FRANKIE. Well, why don't he bring his friend home with him? He ought to know I would be only too glad to have a whole family of cats.

BERENICE. You done seen the last of that old alley cat.

FRANKIE *(crossing the room)*. I ought to notify the police force. They will find Charles.

BERENICE. I wouldn't do that.

FRANKIE *(at the telephone)*. I want the police force, please . . . Police force? . . . I am notifying you about my car . . . Cat! He's lost. He is almost pure Persian.

BERENICE. As Persian as I is.

FRANKIE. But with short hair. A lovely color of gray with a little white spot on his throat. He answers to the name of Charles, but if he don't answer to that, he might come if you call "Charlina." . . . My name is Miss F. Jasmine Addams and the address is 124 Grove Street.

BERENICE *(giggling as Frankie re-enters)*. Gal, they going to send around here and tie you up and drag you off to Milledgeville. Just picture them fat blue police

chasing tomcats around alleys and hollering, "Oh Charles! Oh come here, Charlina!" Merciful Heavens.

FRANKIE. Aw, shut up!

*(Outside a voice is heard calling in a
drawn-out chant, the words almost indistinguishable: "Lot of okra, peas, fresh
butter beans . . .")*

BERENICE. The trouble with you is that
you don't have no sense of humor no
more.

FRANKIE *(disconsolately)*. Maybe I'd be
better off in jail.

*(The chanting voice continues and an
ancient Negro woman, dressed in a clean
print dress with several petticoats, the
ruffle of one of which shows, crosses the
yard. She stops and leans on a gnarled
stick.)*

FRANKIE. Here comes the old vegetable
lady.

BERENICE. Sis Laura is getting mighty
feeble to peddle this hot weather.

FRANKIE. She is about ninety. Other old
folks lose their faculties, but she found
some faculty. She reads futures, too.

BERENICE. Hi, Sis Laura. How is your
folks getting on?

SIS LAURA. We ain't much, and I feels
my age these days. Want any peas today?
*(She shuffles across the yard)*

BERENICE. I'm sorry, I still have some
left over from yesterday. Good-bye, Sis
Laura.

SIS LAURA. Good-bye. *(She goes off behind the house to the right, continuing
her chant)*

*(When the old woman is gone Frankie
begins walking around the kitchen.)*

FRANKIE. I expect Janice and Jarvis are
almost to Winter Hill by now.

BERENICE. Sit down. You make me nervous.

FRANKIE. Jarvis talked about Granny.
He remembers her very good. But when
I try to remember Granny, it is like her
face is changing—like a face seen under
water. Jarvis remembers Mother too, and
I don't remember her at all.

BERENICE. Naturally! Your mother died
the day that you were born.

FRANKIE *(standing with one foot on the
seat of the chair, leaning over the chair
back and laughing)*. Did you hear what
Jarvis said?

BERENICE. What?

FRANKIE *(after laughing more)*. They

were talking about whether to vote for
C. P. MacDonald. And Jarvis said, "Why
I wouldn't vote for that scoundrel if he
was running to be dogcatcher." I never
heard anything so witty in my life. *(There
is a silence during which Berenice watches
Frankie, but does not smile)* And you
know what Janice remarked. When Jarvis mentioned about how much I've
grown, she said she didn't think I looked
so terribly big. She said she got the major
portion of her growth before she was
thirteen. She said I was the right height
and had acting talent and ought to go to
Hollywood. She did, Berenice.

BERENICE. O.K. All right! She did!

FRANKIE. She said she thought I was a
lovely size and would probably not grow
any taller. She said all fashion models and
movie stars . . .

BERENICE. She did not. I heard her from
the window. She only remarked that you
probably had already got your growth.
But she didn't go on and on like that or
mention Hollywood.

FRANKIE. She said to me . . .

BERENICE. She said to you! This is a
serious fault with you, Frankie. Somebody
just makes a loose remark and then you
cozen it in your mind until nobody would
recognize it. Your Aunt Pet happened to
mention to Clorina that you had sweet
manners and Clorina passed it on to you.
For what it was worth. Then next thing
I know you are going all around and
bragging how Mrs. West thought you had
the finest manners in town and ought to
go to Hollywood, and I don't know what-
all you didn't say. And that is a serious
fault.

FRANKIE. Aw, quit preaching at me.

BERENICE. I ain't preaching. It's the
solemn truth and you know it.

FRANKIE. I admit it a little. *(She sits
down at the table and puts her forehead
on the palms of her hands. There is a
pause, and then she speaks softly)* What
I need to know is this. Do you think I
made a good impression?

BERENICE. Impression?

FRANKIE. Yes.

BERENICE. Well, how would I know?

FRANKIE. I mean, how did I act? What
did I do?

BERENICE. Why, you didn't do anything
to speak of.

FRANKIE. Nothing?

BERENICE. No. You just watched the pair of them like they was ghosts. Then, when they talked about the wedding, them ears of yours stiffened out the size of cabbage leaves . . .

FRANKIE (*raising her hand to her ears*). They didn't!

BERENICE. They did.

FRANKIE. Some day you going to look down and find that big fat tongue of yours pulled out by the roots and laying there before you on the table.

BERENICE. Quit talking so rude.

FRANKIE (*after a pause*). I'm so scared I didn't make a good impression.

BERENICE. What of it? I got a date with T. T. and he's supposed to pick me up here. I wish him and Honey would come on. You make me nervous.

(*Frankie sits miserably, her shoulders hunched. Then with a sudden gesture she bangs her forehead on the table. Her fists are clenched and she is sobbing.*)

BERENICE. Come on. Don't act like that.

FRANKIE (*her voice muffled*). They were so pretty. They must have such a good time. And they went away and left me.

BERENICE. Sit up. Behave yourself.

FRANKIE. They came and went away, and left me with this feeling.

BERENICE. Hosee! I bet I know something. (*She begins tapping with her heel: one, two, three—bang! After a pause, in which the rhythm is established, she begins singing*) Frankie's got a crush! Frankie's got a crush! Frankie's got a crush on the *wedding!*

FRANKIE. Quit!

BERENICE. Frankie's got a crush! Frankie's got a crush!

FRANKIE. You better quit! (*She rises suddenly and snatches up the carving knife*)

BERENICE. You lay down that knife.

FRANKIE. Make me. (*She bends the blade slowly*)

BERENICE. Lay it down, *Devil*. (*There is a silence*) Just throw it! You just!

(*After a pause Frankie aims the knife carefully at the closed door leading to the bedroom and throws it. The knife does not stick in the wall.*)

FRANKIE. I used to be the best knife thrower in this town.

BERENICE. Frances Addams, you goin' to try that stunt once too often.

FRANKIE. I warned you to quit pickin' with me.

BERENICE. You are not fit to live in a house.

FRANKIE. I won't be living in this one much longer; I'm going to run away from home.

BERENICE. And a good riddance to big old bag of rubbage.

FRANKIE. You wait and see. I'm leavin town.

BERENICE. And where do you think you are going?

FRANKIE (*gazing around the walls*). I don't know.

BERENICE. You're going crazy. That's where you going.

FRANKIE. No. (*Solemnly*) This coming Sunday after the wedding, I'm leaving town. And I swear to Jesus by my two eyes I'm never coming back here any more.

BERENICE (*going to Frankie and pushing her damp bangs back from her forehead*). Sugar? You serious?

FRANKIE (*exasperated*). Of course! Do you think I would stand here and say that swear and tell a story? Sometimes, Berenice, I think it takes you longer to realize a fact than it does anybody who ever lived.

BERENICE. But you say you don't know where you going. You going, but you don't know where. That don't make no sense to me.

FRANKIE (*after a long pause in which she again gazes around the walls of the room*). I feel just exactly like somebody has peeled all the skin off me. I wish I had some good cold peach ice cream. (*Berenice takes her by the shoulders*) (*During the last speech, T. T. Williams and Honey Camden Brown have been approaching through the back yard. T. T. is a large and pompous-looking Negro man of about fifty. He is dressed like a church deacon, in a black suit with a red emblem in the lapel. His manner is timid and over-polite. Honey is a slender, limber Negro boy of about twenty. He is quite light in color and he wears loud-colored, snappy clothes. He is brusque and there is about him an odd mixture of hostility and playfulness. He is very high-strung and volatile. They are trailed by John Henry. John Henry is dressed for afternoon in a clean white linen suit,*) *white shoes and socks. Honey carries a horn. They cross the back yard and knock at the back door. Honey holds his hand to his head.)*

FRANKIE. But every word I told you was the solemn truth. I'm leaving here after the wedding.

BERENICE *(taking her hands from Frankie's shoulders and answering the door).* Hello, Honey and T. T. I didn't hear you coming.

T. T. You and Frankie too busy discussing something. Well, your foster-brother, Honey, got into a ruckus standing on the sidewalk in front of the Blue Moon Café. Police cracked him on the haid.

BERENICE *(turning on the kitchen light).* What! *(She examines Honey's head)* Why, it's a welt the size of a small egg.

HONEY. Times like this I feel like I got to bust loose or die.

BERENICE. What were you doing?

HONEY. Nothing. I was just passing along the street minding my own business when this drunk soldier came out of the Blue Moon Café and ran into me. I looked at him and he gave me a push. I pushed him back and he raised a ruckus. This white M.P. came up and slammed me with his stick.

T. T. It was one of those accidents can happen to any colored person.

JOHN HENRY *(reaching for the horn).* Toot some on your horn, Honey.

FRANKIE. Please blow.

HONEY *(to John Henry, who has taken the horn).* Now, don't bother my horn, Butch.

JOHN HENRY. I want to toot it some. *(John Henry takes the horn, tries to blow it, but only succeeds in slobbering in it. He holds the horn away from his mouth and sings: "Too-ty-toot, too-ty-toot." Honey snatches the horn away from him and puts it on the sewing table.)*

HONEY. I told you not to touch my horn. You got it full of slobber inside and out. It's ruined! *(He loses his temper, grabs John Henry by the shoulders and shakes him hard)*

BERENICE *(slapping Honey).* Satan! Don't you dare touch that little boy! I'm going to stomp out your brains!

HONEY. You ain't mad because John Henry is a little boy. It's because he's a white boy. John Henry knows he needs a good shake. Don't you, Butch?

BERENICE. Ornery—no good!

*(Honey lifts John Henry and swings him, then reaches in his pocket and brings out some coins.)*

HONEY. John Henry, which would you rather have—the nigger money or the white money?

JOHN HENRY. I rather have the dime. *(He takes it)* Much obliged. *(He goes out and crosses the yard to his house)*

BERENICE. You troubled and beat down and try to take it out on a little boy. You and Frankie just alike. The club girls don't elect her and she turns on John Henry too. When folks are lonesome and left out, they turn so mean. T. T., do you wish a small little quickie before we start?

T. T. *(looking at Frankie and pointing toward her).* Frankie ain't no tattle-tale. Is you? *(Berenice pours a drink for T. T.)*

FRANKIE *(disdaining his question).* That sure is a cute suit you got on, Honey. Today I heard somebody speak of you as Lightfoot Brown. I think that's such a grand nickname. It's on account of your travelling—to Harlem, and all the different places where you have run away, and your dancing. Lightfoot! I wish somebody would call me Lightfoot Addams.

BERENICE. It would suit me better if Honey Camden had brick feets. As it is, he keeps me so anxious-worried. C'mon, Honey and T. T. Let's go! *(Honey and T. T. go out)*

FRANKIE. I'll go out into the yard. *(Frankie, feeling excluded, goes out into the yard. Throughout the act the light in the yard has been darkening steadily. Now the light in the kitchen is throwing a yellow rectangle in the yard.)*

BERENICE. Now Frankie, you forget all that foolishness we were discussing. And if Mr. Addams don't come home by good dark, you go over to the Wests'. Go play with John Henry.

HONEY AND T. T. *(from outside).* So long!

FRANKIE. So long, you all. Since when have I been scared of the dark? I'll invite John Henry to spend the night with me.

BERENICE. I thought you were sick and tired of him.

FRANKIE. I am.

BERENICE *(kissing Frankie).* Good night, Sugar!

FRANKIE. Seems like everybody goes off and leaves me. *(She walks toward the Wests' yard, calling, with cupped hands)* John Henry. John Henry.

JOHN HENRY'S VOICE. What do you want, Frankie?

FRANKIE. Come over and spend the night with me.

JOHN HENRY'S VOICE. I can't.

FRANKIE. Why?

JOHN HENRY. Just because.

FRANKIE. Because why? *(John Henry does not answer)* I thought maybe me and you could put up my Indian tepee and sleep out here in the yard. And have a good time. *(There is still no answer)* Sure enough. Why don't you stay and spend the night?

JOHN HENRY *(quite loudly).* Because, Frankie. I don't want to.

FRANKIE *(angrily).* Fool Jackass! Suit yourself! I only asked you because you looked so ugly and so lonesome.

JOHN HENRY *(skipping toward the arbor).* Why, I'm not a bit lonesome.

FRANKIE *(looking at the house).* I wonder when that Papa of mine is coming home. He always comes home by dark. I don't want to go into that empty, ugly house all by myself.

JOHN HENRY. Me neither.

FRANKIE *(standing with outstretched arms, and looking around her).* I think something is wrong. It is too quiet. I have a peculiar warning in my bones. I bet you a hundred dollars it's going to storm.

JOHN HENRY. I don't want to spend the night with you.

FRANKIE. A terrible, terrible dog-day storm. Or maybe even a cyclone.

JOHN HENRY. Huh.

FRANKIE. I bet Jarvis and Janice are now at Winter Hill. I see them just plain as I see you. Plainer. Something is wrong. It is too quiet.

*(A clear horn begins to play a blues tune in the distance.)*

JOHN HENRY. Frankie?

FRANKIE. Hush! It sounds like Honey. *(The horn music becomes jazzy and spangling, then the first blues tune is repeated. Suddenly, while still unfinished, the music stops. Frankie waits tensely.)*

FRANKIE. He has stopped to bang the spit out of his horn. In a second he will finish. *(After a wait)* Please, Honey, go on finish!

JOHN HENRY *(softly).* He done quit now.

FRANKIE *(moving restlessly).* I told Berenice that I was leavin' town for good and she did not believe me. Sometimes I honestly think she is the biggest fool that ever drew breath. You try to impress something on a big fool like that, and it's just like talking to a block of cement. I kept on telling and telling and telling her. I told her I had to leave this town for good because it is inevitable. Inevitable.

*(Mr. Addams enters the kitchen from the house, calling: "Frankie, Frankie.")*

MR. ADDAMS *(calling from the kitchen door).* Frankie, Frankie.

FRANKIE. Yes, Papa.

MR. ADDAMS *(opening the back door).* You had supper?

FRANKIE. I'm not hungry.

MR. ADDAMS. Was a little later than I intended, fixing a timepiece for a railroad man. *(He goes back through the kitchen and into the hall, calling: "Don't leave the yard!")*

JOHN HENRY. You want me to get the weekend bag?

FRANKIE. Don't bother me, John Henry. I'm thinking.

JOHN HENRY. What you thinking about?

FRANKIE. About the wedding. About my brother and the bride. Everything's been so sudden today. I never believed before about the fact that the earth turns at the rate of about a thousand miles a day. I didn't understand why it was that if you jumped up in the air you wouldn't land in Selma or Fairview or somewhere else instead of the same back yard. But now it seems to me I feel the world going around very fast. *(Frankie begins turning around in circles with arms outstretched. John Henry copies her. They both turn)* I feel it turning and it makes me dizzy.

JOHN HENRY. I'll stay and spend the night with you.

FRANKIE *(suddenly stopping her turning).* No. I just now thought of something.

JOHN HENRY. You just a little while ago was begging me.

FRANKIE. I know where I'm going.

*(There are sounds of children playing in the distance.)*

JOHN HENRY. Let's go play with the children, Frankie.

FRANKIE. I tell you I know where I'm going. It's like I've known it all my life. Tomorrow I will tell everybody.

JOHN HENRY. Where?

FRANKIE (dreamily). After the wedding I'm going with them to Winter Hill. I'm going off with them after the wedding.

JOHN HENRY. You serious?

FRANKIE. Shush, just now I realized something. The trouble with me is that for a long time I have been just an "I" person. All other people can say "we." When Berenice says "we" she means her lodge and church and colored people. Soldiers can say "we" and mean the army. All people belong to a "we" except me.

JOHN HENRY. What are we going to do?

FRANKIE. Not to belong to a "we" makes you too lonesome. Until this afternoon I didn't have a "we," but now after seeing Janice and Jarvis I suddenly realize something.

JOHN HENRY. What?

FRANKIE. I know that the bride and my brother are the "we" of me. So I'm going with them, and joining with the wedding. This coming Sunday when my brother and the bride leave this town, I'm going with the two of them to Winter Hill. And after that to whatever place that they will ever go. (There is a pause) I love the two of them so much and we belong to be together. I love the two of them so much because they are the *we* of me.

THE CURTAIN FALLS.

## ACT TWO

*The scene is the same: the kitchen of the Addams home. Berenice is cooking. John Henry sits on the stool, blowing soap bubbles with a spool. It is the afternoon of the next day.*

———

(*The front door slams and Frankie enters from the hall.*)

BERENICE. I been phoning all over town trying to locate you. Where on earth have you been?

FRANKIE. Everywhere. All over town.

BERENICE. I been so worried I got a good mind to be seriously mad with you. Your Papa came home to dinner today. He was mad when you didn't show up. He's taking a nap now in his room.

FRANKIE. I walked up and down Main Street and stopped in almost every store. Bought my wedding dress and silver shoes. Went around by the mills. Went all over the complete town and talked to nearly everybody in it.

BERENICE. What for, pray tell me?

FRANKIE. I was telling everybody about the wedding and my plans. (*She takes off her dress and remains barefooted in her slip*)

BERENICE. You mean just people on the street? (*She is creaming butter and sugar for cookies*)

FRANKIE. Everybody. Storekeepers. The monkey and monkey-man. A soldier. Everybody. And you know the soldier wanted to join with me and asked me for a date this evening. I wonder what you do on dates.

BERENICE. Frankie, I honestly believe you have turned crazy on us. Walking all over town and telling total strangers this big tale. You know in your soul this mania of yours is pure foolishness.

FRANKIE. Please call me F. Jasmine. I don't wish to have to remind you any more. Everything good of mine has got to be washed and ironed so I can pack them in the suitcase. (*She brings in a suitcase and opens it*) Everybody in town believes that I'm going. All except Papa. He's stubborn as an old mule. No use arguing with people like that.

BERENICE. Me and Mr. Addams has some sense.

FRANKIE. Papa was bent over working on a watch when I went by the store. I asked him could I buy the wedding clothes and he said charge them at MacDougals. But he wouldn't listen to any of my plans. Just sat there with his nose to the grindstone and answered with—kind of grunts. He never listens to what I say. (*There is a pause*) Sometimes I wonder if Papa loves me or not.

BERENICE. Course he loves you. He is just a busy widowman—set in his ways.

FRANKIE. Now I wonder if I can find some tissue paper to line this suitcase.

BERENICE. Truly, Frankie, what makes you think they want you taggin' along with them? Two is company and three is a crowd. And that's the main thing about a wedding. Two is company and three is a crowd.

FRANKIE. You wait and see.

BERENICE. Remember back to the time of the flood. Remember Noah and the Ark.

FRANKIE. And what has that got to do with it?

BERENICE. Remember the way he admitted them creatures.

FRANKIE. Oh, shut up your big old mouth!

BERENICE. Two by two. He admitted them creatures two by two.

FRANKIE *(after a pause)*. That's all right. But you wait and see. They will take me.

BERENICE. And if they don't?

FRANKIE *(turning suddenly from washing her hands at the sink)*. If they don't, I will kill myself.

BERENICE. Kill yourself, how?

FRANKIE. I will shoot myself in the side of the head with the pistol that Papa keeps under his handkerchiefs with Mother's picture in the bureau drawer.

BERENICE. You heard what Mr. Addams said about playing with that pistol. I'll just put this cookie dough in the icebox. Set the table and your dinner is ready. Set John Henry a plate and one for me. *(Berenice puts the dough in the icebox. Frankie hurriedly sets the table. Berenice takes dishes from the stove and ties a napkin around John Henry's neck)* I have heard of many a peculiar thing. I have knew men to fall in love with girls so ugly that you wonder if their eyes is straight.

JOHN HENRY. Who?

BERENICE. I have knew women to love veritable satans and thank Jesus when they put their split hooves over the threshold. I have knew boys to take it into their heads to fall in love with other boys. You know Lily Mae Jenkins?

FRANKIE. I'm not sure. I know a lot of people.

BERENICE. Well, you either know him or you don't know him. He prisses around in a girl's blouse with one arm akimbo. Now this Lily Mae Jenkins fell in love with a man name Juney Jones. A man, mind you. And Lily Mae turned into a girl. He changed his nature and his sex and turned into a girl.

FRANKIE. What?

BERENICE. He did. To all intents and purposes. *(Berenice is sitting in the center chair at the table. She says grace)* Lord, make us thankful for what we are about to receive to nourish our bodies. Amen.

FRANKIE. It's funny I can't think who you are talking about. I used to think I knew so many people.

BERENICE. Well, you don't need to know Lily Mae Jenkins. You can live without knowing him.

FRANKIE. Anyway, I don't believe you.

BERENICE. I ain't arguing with you. What was we speaking about?

FRANKIE. About peculiar things.

BERENICE. Oh, yes. As I was just now telling you I have seen many a peculiar thing in my day. But one thing I never knew and never heard tell about. No, siree. I never in all my days heard of anybody falling in love with a wedding. *(There is a pause)* And thinking it all over I have come to a conclusion.

JOHN HENRY. How? How did that boy change into a girl? Did he kiss his elbow? *(He tries to kiss his elbow)*

BERENICE. It was just one of them things, Candy Lamb. Yep, I have come to the conclusion that what you ought to be thinking about is a beau. A nice little white boy beau.

FRANKIE. I don't want any beau. What would I do with one? Do you mean something like a soldier who would maybe take me to the Idle Hour?

BERENICE. Who's talking about soldiers? I'm talking about a nice little white boy beau your own age. How 'bout that little old Barney next door?

FRANKIE. Barney MacKean! That nasty Barney!

BERENICE. Certainly! You could make out with him until somebody better comes along. He would do.

FRANKIE. You are the biggest crazy in this town.

BERENICE. The crazy calls the sane the crazy.

*(Barney MacKean, a boy of twelve, shirtless and wearing shorts, and Helen Fletcher, a girl of twelve or fourteen, cross the yard from the left, go through the arbor and out on the right. Frankie and John Henry watch them from the window.)*

FRANKIE. Yonder's Barney now with Helen Fletcher. They are going to the alley behind the Wests' garage. They do something bad back there. I don't know what it is.

BERENICE. If you don't know what it is, how come you know it is bad?

FRANKIE. I just know it. I think maybe they look at each other and peepee or something. They don't let anybody watch them.

JOHN HENRY. I watched them once.

FRANKIE. What do they do?

JOHN HENRY. I saw. They don't peepee.

FRANKIE. Then what do they do?

JOHN HENRY. I don't know what it was. But I watched them. How many of them did you catch, Berenice? Them beaus?

BERENICE. How many? Candy Lamb, how many hairs is in this plait? You're talking to Miss Berenice Sadie Brown.

FRANKIE. I think you ought to quit worrying about beaus and be content with T. T. I bet you are forty years old.

BERENICE. Wise-mouth. How do you know so much? I got as much right as anybody else to continue to have a good time as long as I can. And as far as that goes, I'm not so old as some peoples would try and make me. I ain't changed life yet.

JOHN HENRY. Did they all treat you to the picture show, them beaus?

BERENICE. To the show, or one thing or another. Wipe off your mouth.

*(There is the sound of piano tuning.)*

JOHN HENRY. The piano tuning man.

BERENICE. Ye Gods, I seriously believe this will be the last straw.

JOHN HENRY. Me too.

FRANKIE. It makes me sad. And jittery too. *(She walks around the room)* They tell me that when they want to punish the crazy people in Milledgeville, they tie them up and make them listen to piano tuning. *(She puts the empty coal scuttle on her head and walks around the table)*

BERENICE. We could turn on the radio and drown him out.

FRANKIE. I don't want the radio on. *(She goes into the interior room and takes off her dress, speaking from inside)* But I advise you to keep the radio on after I leave. Some day you will very likely hear us speak over the radio.

BERENICE. Speak about what, pray tell me?

FRANKIE. I don't know exactly what about. But probably some eye witness account about something. We will be asked to speak.

BERENICE. I don't follow you. What are we going to eye witness? And who will ask you to speak?

JOHN HENRY *(excitedly)*. What, Frankie? Who is speaking on the radio?

FRANKIE. When I said *we*, you thought I meant you and me and John Henry West. To speak over the world radio. I have never heard of anything so funny since I was born.

JOHN HENRY *(climbing up to kneel on the seat of the chair)*. Who? What?

FRANKIE. Ha! Ha! Ho! Ho! Ho! Ho! *(Frankie goes around punching things with her fist, and shadow boxing. Berenice raises her right hand for peace. Then suddenly they all stop. Frankie goes to the window, and John Henry hurries there also and stands on tiptoe with his hands on the sill. Berenice turns her head to see what has happened. The piano is still. Three young girls in clean dresses are passing before the arbor. Frankie watches them silently at the window.)*

JOHN HENRY *(softly)*. The club of girls.

FRANKIE. What do you son-of-a-bitches mean crossing my yard? How many times must I tell you not to set foot on my Papa's property?

BERENICE. Just ignore them and make like you don't see them pass.

FRANKIE. Don't mention those crooks to me.

*(T. T. and Honey approach by way of the back yard. Honey is whistling a blues tune.)*

BERENICE. Why don't you show me the new dress? I'm anxious to see what you selected. *(Frankie goes into the interior room. T. T. knocks on the door. He and Honey enter)* Why T. T., what you doing around here this time of day?

T. T. Good afternoon, Miss Berenice. I'm here on a sad mission.

BERENICE *(startled)*. What's wrong?

T. T. It's about Sis Laura Thompson. She suddenly had a stroke and died.

BERENICE. What! Why she was by here just yesterday. We just ate her peas. They in my stomach right now, and her lyin' dead on the cooling board this minute. The Lord works in strange ways.

T. T. Passed away at dawn this morning.

FRANKIE (*putting her head in the doorway*). Who is it that's dead?

BERENICE. Sis Laura, Sugar. That old vegetable lady.

FRANKIE (*unseen, from the interior room*). Just to think—she passed by yesterday.

T. T. Miss Berenice, I'm going around to take up a donation for the funeral. The policy people say Sis Laura's claim has lapsed.

BERENICE. Well, here's fifty cents. The poor old soul.

T. T. She was brisk as a chipmunk to the last. The Lord had appointed the time for her. I hope I go that way.

FRANKIE (*from the interior room*). I've got something to show you all. Shut your eyes and don't open them until I tell you. (*She enters the room dressed in an orange satin evening dress with silver shoes and stockings*) These are the wedding clothes. (*Berenice, T. T. and John Henry stare*)

JOHN HENRY. Oh, how pretty!

FRANKIE. Now tell me your honest opinion. (*There is a pause*) What's the matter? Don't you like it, Berenice?

BERENICE. No. It don't do.

FRANKIE. What do you mean? It don't do.

BERENICE. Exactly that. It just don't do. (*She shakes her head while Frankie looks at the dress*)

FRANKIE. But I don't see what you mean. What is wrong?

BERENICE. Well, if you don't see it I can't explain it to you. Look there at your head, to begin with. (*Frankie goes to the mirror*) You had all your hair shaved off like a convict and now you tie this ribbon around this head without any hair. Just looks peculiar.

FRANKIE. But I'm going to wash and try to stretch my hair tonight.

BERENICE. Stretch your hair! How you going to stretch your hair? And look at them elbows. Here you got on a grown woman's evening dress. And that brown crust on your elbows. The two things just don't mix. (*Frankie, embarrassed, covers her elbows with her hands. Berenice is still shaking her head*) Take it back down to the store.

T. T. The dress is too growny looking.

FRANKIE. But I can't take it back. It's bargain basement.

BERENICE. Very well then. Come here. Let me see what I can do.

FRANKIE (*going to Berenice, who works with the dress*). I think you're just not accustomed to seeing anybody dressed up.

BERENICE. I'm not accustomed to seein' a human Christmas tree in August.

JOHN HENRY. Frankie's dress looks like a Christmas tree.

FRANKIE. Two-faced Judas! You just now said it was pretty. Old double-faced Judas! (*The sounds of piano tuning are heard again*) Oh, that piano tuner!

BERENICE. Step back a little now.

FRANKIE (*looking in the mirror*). Don't you honestly think it's pretty? Give me your candy opinion.

BERENICE. I never knew anybody so unreasonable! You ask me my candy opinion, I give you my candy opinion. You ask me again, and I give it to you again. But what you want is not my honest opinion, but my good opinion of something I know is wrong.

FRANKIE. I only want to look pretty.

BERENICE. Pretty is as pretty does. Ain't that right, T. T.? You will look well enough for anybody's wedding. Excepting your own. (*Mr. Addams enters through the hall door.*)

MR. ADDAMS. Hello, everybody. (*To Frankie*) I don't want you roaming around the streets all morning and not coming home at dinner time. Looks like I'll have to tie you up in the back yard.

FRANKIE. I had business to tend to. Papa, look!

MR. ADDAMS. What is it, Miss Picklepriss?

FRANKIE. Sometimes I think you have turned stone blind. You never even noticed my new dress.

MR. ADDAMS. I thought it was a show costume.

FRANKIE. Show costume! Papa, why is it you don't ever notice what I have on or pay any serious mind to me? You just walk around like a mule with blinders on, not seeing or caring.

MR. ADDAMS. Never mind that now. (*To T. T. and Honey*) I need some help down at my store. My porter failed me again. I wonder if you or Honey could help me next week.

T. T. I will if I can, sir, Mr. Addams.

What days would be convenient for you, sir?

MR. ADDAMS. Say Wednesday afternoon.

T. T. Now, Mr. Addams, that's one afternoon I promised to work for Mr. Finny, sir. I can't promise anything, Mr. Addams. But if Mr. Finny changes his mind about needing me, I'll work for you, sir.

MR. ADDAMS. How about you, Honey?

HONEY (shortly). I ain't got the time.

MR. ADDAMS. I'll be so glad when the war is over and you biggety, worthless niggers get back to work. And, furthermore, you *sir* me! Hear me!

HONEY (reluctantly). Yes—sir.

MR. ADDAMS. I getter go back to the store now and get my nose down to the grindstone. You stay home, Frankie. (He goes out through the hall door)

JOHN HENRY. Uncle Royal called Honey a nigger. Is Honey a nigger?

BERENICE. Be quiet now, John Henry. (To Honey) Honey, I got a good mind to shake you till you spit. Not saying *sir* to Mr. Addams, and acting so impudent.

HONEY. T. T. said sir enough for a whole crowd of niggers. But for folks that calls me nigger, I got a real good nigger razor. (He takes a razor from his pocket. Frankie and John Henry crowd close to look. When John Henry touches the razor, Honey says) Don't touch it, Butch, it's sharp. Liable to hurt yourself.

BERENICE. Put up that razor, Satan! I worry myself sick over you. You going to die before your appointed span.

JOHN HENRY. Why is Honey a nigger?

BERENICE. Jesus knows.

HONEY. I'm so tensed up. My nerves been scraped with a razor. Berenice, loan me a dollar.

BERENICE. I ain't handing you no dollar, worthless, to get high on them reefer cigarettes.

HONEY. Gimme, Berenice, I'm so tensed up and miserable. The nigger hole. I'm sick of smothering in the nigger hole. I can't stand it no more.

(Relenting, Berenice gets her pocketbook from the shelf, opens it, and takes out some change.)

BERENICE. Here's thirty cents. You can buy two beers.

HONEY. Well, thankful for tiny, infinitesimal favors. I better be dancing off now.

T. T. Same here. I still have to make a good deal of donation visits this afternoon. (Honey and T. T. go to the door)

BERENICE. So long, T. T. I'm counting on you for tomorrow and you too, Honey.

FRANKIE and JOHN HENRY. So long.

T. T. Good-bye, you all. Good-bye. (He goes out, crossing the yard)

BERENICE. Poor ole Sis Laura. I certainly hope that when my time comes I will have kept up my policy. I dread to think the church would ever have to bury me. When I die.

JOHN HENRY. Are you going to die, Berenice?

BERENICE. Why, Candy, everybody has to die.

JOHN HENRY. Everybody? Are you going to die, Frankie?

FRANKIE. I doubt it. I honestly don't think I'll ever die.

JOHN HENRY. What is "die"?

FRANKIE. It must be terrible to be nothing but black, black, black.

BERENICE. Yes, baby.

FRANKIE. How many dead people do you know? I know six dead people in all. I'm not counting my mother. There's William Boyd who was killed in Italy. I knew him by sight and name. An' that man who climbed poles for the telephone company. An' Lou Baker. The porter at Finny's place who was murdered in the alley back of Papa's store. Somebody drew a razor on him and the alley people said that his cut throat shivered like a mouth and spoke ghost words to the sun.

JOHN HENRY. Ludie Maxwell Freeman is dead.

FRANKIE. I didn't count Ludie; it wouldn't be fair. Because he died just before I was born. (To Berenice) Do you think very frequently about Ludie?

BERENICE. You know I do. I think about the five years when me and Ludie was together, and about all the bad times I seen since. Sometimes I almost wish I had never knew Ludie at all. It leaves you too lonesome afterward. When you walk home in the evening on the way from work, it makes a little lonesome quinch come in you. And you take up with too many sorry men to try to get over the feeling.

FRANKIE. But T. T. is not sorry.

BERENICE. I wasn't referring to T. T. He is a fine upstanding colored gentleman, who has walked in a state of grace all his life.

FRANKIE. When are you going to marry with him?

BERENICE. I ain't going to marry with him.

FRANKIE. But you were just now saying . . .

BERENICE. I was saying how sincerely I respect T. T. and sincerely regard T. T. *(There is a pause)* But he don't make me shiver none.

FRANKIE. Listen, Berenice, I have something queer to tell you. It's something that happened when I was walking around town today. Now I don't exactly know how to explain what I mean.

BERENICE. What is it?

FRANKIE *(now and then pulling her bangs or lower lip)*. I was walking along and I passed two stores with a alley in between. The sun was frying hot. And just as I passed this alley, I caught a *glimpse* of something in the corner of my left eye. A dark double shape. And this glimpse brought to my mind—so sudden and clear—my brother and the bride that I just stood there and couldn't hardly bear to look and see what it was. It was like they were there in that alley, although I knew that they are in Winter Hill almost a hundred miles away. *(There is a pause)* Then I turn slowly and look. And you know what was there? *(There is a pause)* It was just two colored boys. That was all. But it gave me such a queer feeling.

*(Berenice has been listening attentively. She stares at Frankie, then draws a package of cigarettes from her bosom and lights one.)*

BERENICE. Listen at me! Can you see through these bones in my forehead? *(She points to her forehead)* Have you, Frankie Addams, been reading my mind? *(There is a pause)* That's the most remarkable thing I ever heard of.

FRANKIE. What I mean is that . . .

BERENICE. I know what you mean. You mean right here in the corner of your eye. *(She points to her eye)* You suddenly catch something there. And this cold shiver run all the way down you. And you whirl around. And you stand there facing Jesus knows what. But not Ludie, not who you want. And for a minute you feel like you been dropped down a well.

FRANKIE. Yes. That is it. *(Frankie reaches for a cigarette and lights it, coughing a bit)*

BERENICE. Well, that is mighty remarkable. This is a thing been happening to me all my life. Yet just now is the first time I ever heard it put into words. *(There is a pause)* Yes, that is the way it is when you are in love. A thing known and not spoken.

FRANKIE *(patting her foot)*. Yet I always maintained I never believed in love. I didn't admit it and never put any of it in my shows.

JOHN HENRY. I never believed in love.

BERENICE. Now I will tell you something. And it is to be a warning to you. You hear me, John Henry. You hear me, Frankie.

JOHN HENRY. Yes. *(He points his forefinger)* Frankie is smoking.

BERENICE *(squaring her shoulders)*. Now I am here to tell you I was happy. There was no human woman in all the world more happy than I was in them days. And that includes everybody. You listening to me, John Henry? It includes all queens and millionaires and first ladies of the land. And I mean it includes people of all color. You hear me, Frankie? No human woman in all the world was happier than Berenice Sadie Brown.

FRANKIE. The five years you were married to Ludie.

BERENICE. From that autumn morning when I first meet him on the road in front of Campbell's Filling Station until the very night he died, November, the year 1933.

FRANKIE. The very year and the very month I was born.

BERENICE. The coldest November I ever seen. Every morning there was frost and puddles were crusted with ice. The sunshine was pale yellow like it is in winter time. Sounds carried far away, and I remember a hound dog that used to howl toward sundown. And everything I seen come to me as a kind of sign.

FRANKIE. I think it is a kind of sign I was born the same year and the same month he died.

BERENICE. And it was a Thursday towards six o'clock. About this time of day. Only November. I remember I went to the passage and opened the front door. Dark was coming on; the old hound was howling far away. And I go back in the room and lay down on Ludie's bed. I lay myself down over Ludie with my arms spread out and my face on his face. And I pray that the Lord would contage my strength to him. And I ask the Lord to let it be anybody, but not let it be Ludie. And I lay there and pray for a long time. Until night.

JOHN HENRY. How? *(In a higher, wailing voice)* How, Berenice?

BERENICE. That night he died. I tell you he died. Ludie! Ludie Freeman! Ludie Maxwell Freeman died! *(She hums)*

FRANKIE *(after a pause)*. It seems to me I feel sadder about Ludie than any other dead person. Although I never knew him. I know I ought to cry sometimes about my mother, or anyhow Granny. But it looks like I can't. But Ludie—maybe it was because I was born so soon after Ludie died. But you were starting out to tell some kind of a warning.

BERENICE *(looking puzzled for a moment)*. Warning? Oh, yes! I was going to tell you how this thing we was talking about applies to me. *(As Berenice begins to talk Frankie goes to a shelf above the refrigerator and brings back a fig bar to the table)* It was the April of the following year that I went one Sunday to the church where the congregation was strange to me. I had my forehead down on the top of the pew in front of me, and my eyes were open—not peeping around in secret, mind you, but just open. When suddenly this shiver ran all the way through me. I had caught sight of something from the corner of my eye. And I looked slowly to the left. There on the pew, just six inches from my eyes, was this *thumb*.

FRANKIE. What thumb?

BERENICE. Now I have to tell you. There was only one small portion of Ludie Freeman which was not pretty. Every other part about him was handsome and pretty as anyone would wish. All except this right thumb. This one thumb had a mashed, chewed appearance that was not pretty. You understand?

FRANKIE. You mean you suddenly saw Ludie's thumb when you were praying?

BERENICE. I mean I seen *this* thumb. And as I knelt there just staring at this thumb, I begun to pray in earnest. I prayed out loud! Lord, manifest! Lord, manifest!

FRANKIE. And did He—manifest?

BERENICE. Manifest, my foot! *(Spitting)* You know who that thumb belonged to?

FRANKIE. Who?

BERENICE. Why, Jamie Beale. That big old no-good Jamie Beale. It was the first time I ever laid eyes on him.

FRANKIE. Is that why you married him? Because he had a mashed thumb like Ludie's?

BERENICE. Lord only knows. I don't. I guess I felt drawn to him on account of that thumb. And then one thing led to another. First thing I know I had married him.

FRANKIE. Well, I think that was silly. To marry him just because of that thumb.

BERENICE. I'm not trying to dispute with you. I'm just telling you what actually happened. And the very same thing occurred in the case of Henry Johnson.

FRANKIE. You mean to sit there and tell me Henry Johnson had one of those mashed thumbs too?

BERENICE. No. It was not the thumb this time. It was the coat. *(Frankie and John Henry look at each other in amazement. After a pause Berenice continues)* Now when Ludie died, them policy people cheated me out of fifty dollars so I pawned everything I could lay hands on, and I sold my coat and Ludie's coat. Because I couldn't let Ludie be put away cheap.

FRANKIE. Oh! Then you mean Henry Johnson bought Ludie's coat and you married him because of it?

BERENICE. Not exactly. I was walking down the street one evening when I suddenly seen this shape appear before me. Now the shape of this boy ahead of me was so similar to Ludie through the shoulders and the back of the head that I almost dropped dead there on the sidewalk. I followed and run behind him. It was Henry Johnson. Since he lived in the country and didn't come into town, he had chanced to buy Ludie's coat and from the back view it looked like he was Ludie's ghost or Ludie's twin. But how I married him I don't exactly know, for, to begin with, it was clear that he did not have his share of sense. But you let a boy hang around you and you get fond of him. Anyway, that's how I married Henry Johnson.

FRANKIE. He was the one went crazy on you. Had eatin' dreams and swallowed the corner of the sheet. *(There is a pause)* But I don't understand the point of what you was telling. I don't see how that about

Jamie Beale and Henry Johnson applies to me.

BERENICE. Why, it applies to evervbody and it is a warning.

FRANKIE. But how?

BERENICE. Why, Frankie, don't you see what I was doing? I loved Ludie and he was the first man I loved. Therefore I had to go and copy myself forever afterward. What I did was to marry off little pieces of Ludie whenever I come across them. It was just my misfortune they all turned out to be the wrong pieces. My intention was to repeat me and Ludie. Now don't you see?

FRANKIE. I see what you're driving at. But I don't see how it is a warning applied to me.

BERENICE. You don't! Then I'll tell you. *(Frankie does not nod or answer. The piano tuner plays an arpeggio)* You and that wedding tomorrow. That is what I am warning about. I can see right through them two gray eyes of yours like they was glass. And what I see is the saddest piece of foolishness I ever knew.

JOHN HENRY *(in a low voice)*. Gray eyes is glass.

*(Frankie tenses her brows and looks steadily at Berenice.)*

BERENICE. I see what you have in mind. Don't think I don't. You see something unheard of tomorrow, and you right in the center. You think you going to march to the preacher right in between your brother and the bride. You think you going to break into that wedding, and then Jesus knows what else.

FRANKIE. No. I don't see myself walking to the preacher with them.

BERENICE. I see through them eyes. Don't argue with me.

JOHN HENRY *(repeating softly)*. Gray eyes is glass.

BERENICE. But what I'm warning is this. If you start out falling in love with some unheard-of thing like that, what is going to happen to you? If you take a mania like this, it won't be the last time and of that you can be sure. So what will become of you? Will you be trying to break into weddings the rest of your days?

FRANKIE. It makes me sick to listen to people who don't have any sense. *(She sticks her fingers in her ears and hums)*

BERENICE. You just settin' yourself this fancy trap to catch yourself in trouble. And you know it.

FRANKIE. They will take me. You wait and see.

BERENICE. Well, I been trying to reason seriously. But I see it is no use.

FRANKIE. You are just jealous. You are just trying to deprive me of all the pleasure of leaving town.

BERENICE. I am just trying to head this off. But I still see it is no use.

JOHN HENRY. Gray eyes is glass.

*(The piano is played to the seventh note of the scale and this is repeated.)*

FRANKIE *(singing)*. Do, ray, mee, fa, sol, la, tee, do. Tee. Tee. It could drive you wild. *(She crosses to the screen door and slams it)* You didn't say anything about Willis Rhodes. Did he have a mashed thumb or a coat or something? *(She returns to the table and sits down)*

BERENICE. Lord, now that really was something.

FRANKIE. I only know he stole your furniture and was so terrible you had to call the Law on him.

BERENICE. Well, imagine this! Imagine a cold bitter January night. And me laying all by myself in the big parlor bed. Alone in the house because everybody else had gone for the Saturday night. Me, mind you, who hates to sleep in a big empty bed all by myself at any time. Past twelve o'clock on this cold, bitter January night. Can you remember winter time, John Henry? *(John Henry nods)* Imagine! Suddenly there comes a sloughing sound and a tap, tap, tap. So Miss Me . . . *(She laughs uproariously and stops suddenly, putting her hand over her mouth)*

FRANKIE. What? *(Leaning closer across the table and looking intently at Berenice)* What happened?

*(Berenice looks from one to the other, shaking her head slowly. Then she speaks in a changed voice.)*

BERENICE. Why, I wish you would look yonder. I wish you would look. *(Frankie glances quickly behind her, then turns back to Berenice)*

FRANKIE. What? What happened?

BERENICE. Look at them two little pitchers and them four big ears. *(Berenice gets up suddenly from the table)* Come on, chillin, less us roll out the dough for the cookies tomorrow. *(Berenice clears the table and begins washing dishes at the sink)*

FRANKIE. If it's anything I mortally despise, it's a person who starts out to tell something and works up people's interest, and then stops.

BERENICE *(still laughing)*. I admit it. And I am sorry. But it was just one of them things I suddenly realized I couldn't tell you and John Henry.

*(John Henry skips up to the sink.)*

JOHN HENRY *(singing)*. Cookies! Cookies! Cookies!

FRANKIE. You could have sent him out of the room and told me. But don't think I care a particle about what happened. I just wish Willis Rhodes had come in about that time and slit your throat. *(She goes out into the hall)*

BERENICE *(still chuckling)*. That is a ugly way to talk. You ought to be ashamed. Here, John Henry, I'll give you a scrap of dough to make a cookie man. *(Berenice gives John Henry some dough. He climbs up on a chair and begins to work with it. Frankie enters with the evening newspaper. She stands in the doorway, then puts the newspaper on the table.)*

FRANKIE. I see in the paper where we dropped a new bomb—the biggest one dropped yet. They call it a atom bomb. I intend to take two baths tonight. One long soaking bath and scrub with a brush. I'm going to try to scrape this crust off my elbows. Then let out the dirty water and take a second bath.

BERENICE. Hooray, that's a good idea. I will be glad to see you clean.

JOHN HENRY. I will take two baths.

*(Berenice has picked up the paper and is sitting in a chair against the pale white light of the window. She holds the newspaper open before her and her head is twisted down to one side as she strains to see what is printed there.)*

FRANKIE. Why is it against the law to change your name?

BERENICE. What is that on your neck? I thought it was a head you carried on that neck. Just think. Suppose I would suddenly up and call myself Mrs. Eleanor Roosevelt. And you would begin naming yourself Joe Louis. And John Henry here tried to pawn himself off as Henry Ford.

FRANKIE. Don't talk childish; that is not the kind of changing I mean. I mean from

a name that doesn't suit you to a name you prefer. Like I changed from Frankie to F. Jasmine.

BERENICE. But it would be a confusion. Suppose we all suddenly change to entirely different names. Nobody would ever know who anybody was talking about. The whole world would go crazy.

FRANKIE. I don't see what that has to do with it.

BERENICE. Because things accumulate around your name. You have a name and one thing after another happens to you and things have accumulated around the name.

FRANKIE. But what has accumulated around my old name? *(Berenice does not reply)* Nothing! See! My name just didn't mean anything. Nothing ever happened to me.

BERENICE. But it will. Things will happen.

FRANKIE. What?

BERENICE. You pin me down like that and I can't tell you truthfully. If I could, I wouldn't be sitting here in this kitchen right now, but making a fine living on Wall Street as a wizard. All I can say is that things will happen. Just what, I don't know.

FRANKIE. Until yesterday, nothing ever happened to me.

*(John Henry crosses to the door and puts on Berenice's hat and shoes, takes her pocketbook and walks around the table twice.)*

BERENICE. John Henry, take off my hat and my shoes and put up my pocketbook. Thank you very much. *(John Henry does so)*

FRANKIE. Listen, Berenice. Doesn't it strike you as strange that I am I and you are you? Like when you are walking down a street and you meet somebody. And you are you. And he is him. Yet when you look at each other, the eyes make a connection. Then you go off one way. And he goes off another way. You go off into different parts of town, and maybe you never see each other again. Not in your whole life. Do you see what I mean?

BERENICE. Not exactly.

FRANKIE. That's not what I meant to say anyway. There are all these people here in town I don't even know by sight or name. And we pass alongside each other and don't have any connection. And they don't know me and I don't know them. And now I'm leaving town and there are all these people I will never know.

BERENICE. But who do you want to know?

FRANKIE. Everybody. Everybody in the world.

BERENICE. Why, I wish you would listen to that. How about people like Willis Rhodes? How about them Germans? How about them Japanese?

*(Frankie knocks her head against the door jamb and looks up at the ceiling.)*

FRANKIE. That's not what I mean. That's not what I'm talking about.

BERENICE. Well, what *is* you talking about?

*(A child's voice is heard outside, calling: "Batter up! Batter up!")*

JOHN HENRY *(in a low voice)*. Less play out, Frankie.

· FRANKIE. No. You go. *(After a pause)* This is what I mean.

*(Berenice waits, and when Frankie does not speak again, says:)*

BERENICE. What on earth is wrong with you?

FRANKIE *(after a long pause, then suddenly, with hysteria)*. Boyoman! Manoboy! When we leave Winter Hill we're going to more places than you ever thought about or even knew existed. Just where we will go first I don't know, and it don't matter. Because after we go to that place we're going on to another. Alaska, China, Iceland, South America. Traveling on trains. Letting her rip on motorcycles. Flying around all over the world in airplanes. Here today and gone tomorrow. All over the world. It's the damn truth. Boyoman! *(She runs around the table)*

BERENICE. Frankie!

FRANKIE. And talking of things happening. Things will happen so fast we won't hardly have time to realize them. Captain Jarvis Addams wins highest medals and is decorated by the President. Miss F. Jasmine Addams breaks all records. Mrs. Janice Addams elected Miss United Nations in beauty contest. One thing after another happening so fast we don't hardly notice them.

BERENICE. Hold still, fool.

FRANKIE *(her excitement growing more and more intense)*. And we will meet them. Everybody. We will just walk up to people and know them right away. We will be walking down a dark road and see a lighted house and knock on the door and strangers will rush to meet us and say: "Come in! Come in!" We will know decorated aviators and New York people and movie stars. We will have thousands and thousands of friends. And we will belong to so many clubs that we can't even keep track of all of them. We will be members of the whole world. Boyoman! Manoboy!

*(Frankie has been running round and round the table in wild excitement and when she passes the next time Berenice catches her slip so quickly that she is caught up with a jerk.)*

BERENICE. Is you gone raving wild? *(She pulls Frankie closer and puts her arm around her waist)* Sit here in my lap and rest a minute. *(Frankie sits in Berenice's lap. John Henry comes close and jealously pinches Frankie)* Leave Frankie alone. She ain't bothered you.

JOHN HENRY. I'm sick.

BERENICE. Now no, you ain't. Be quiet and don't grudge your cousin a little bit love.

JOHN HENRY *(hitting Frankie)*. Old mean bossy Frankie.

BERENICE. What she doing so mean right now? She just laying here wore out. *(They continue sitting. Frankie is relaxed now)*

FRANKIE. Today I went to the Blue Moon—this place that all the soldiers are so fond of and I met a soldier—a redheaded boy.

BERENICE. What is all this talk about the Blue Moon and soldiers?

FRANKIE. Berenice, you treat me like a child. When I see all these soldiers milling around town I always wonder where they came from and where they are going.

BERENICE. They were born and they going to die.

FRANKIE. There are so many things about the world I do not understand.

BERENICE. If you did understand you would be God. Didn't you know that?

FRANKIE. Maybe so. *(She stares and stretches herself on Berenice's lap, her long legs sprawled out beneath the kitchen table)* Anyway, after the wedding I won't have to worry about things any more.

BERENICE. You don't have to now. Nobody requires you to solve the riddles of the world.

FRANKIE *(looking at newspaper)*. The paper says this new atom bomb is worth twenty thousand tons of T.N.T.

BERENICE. Twenty thousand tons? And there ain't but two tons of coal in the coal house—all that coal.

FRANKIE. The paper says the bomb is a very important science discovery.

BERENICE. The figures these days have got too high for me. Read in the paper about ten million peoples killed. I can't crowd that many people in my mind's eye.

JOHN HENRY. Berenice, is the glass eye your mind's eye?

*(John Henry has climbed up on the back rungs of Berenice's chair and has been hugging her head. He is now holding her ears.)*

BERENICE. Don't yank my head back like that, Candy. Me and Frankie ain't going to float up through the ceiling and leave you.

FRANKIE. I wonder if you have ever thought about this? Here we are—right now. This very minute. Now. But while we're talking right now, this minute is passing. And it will never come again. Never in all the world. When it is gone, it is gone. No power on earth could bring it back again.

JOHN HENRY *(beginning to sing)*.
I sing because I'm happy,
I sing because I'm free,
For His eye is on the sparrow,
And I know He watches me.

BERENICE *(singing)*.
Why should I feel discouraged?
Why should the shadows come?
Why should my heart be lonely,
Away from heaven and home?
For Jesus is my portion,
My constant friend is He,
For His eye is on the sparrow,
And I know He watches me.
So, I sing because I'm happy.

*(John Henry and Frankie join on the last three lines.)*

I sing because I'm happy,
I sing because I'm free,
For His eye is on the sparrow,
And I know He watches . . .

BERENICE. Frankie, you got the sharpest set of human bones I ever felt.

THE CURTAIN FALLS

# ACT THREE

## SCENE ONE

*The scene is the same: the kitchen. It is the day of the wedding. When the curtain rises Berenice, in her apron, and T. T. Williams in a white coat have just finished preparations for the wedding refreshments. Berenice has been watching the ceremony through the half-open door leading into the hall. There are sounds of congratulations offstage, the wedding ceremony having just finished.*

———

BERENICE *(to T. T. Williams)*. Can't see much from this door. But I can see Frankie. And her face is a study. And John Henry's chewing away at the bubble gum that Jarvis bought him. Well, sounds like it's all over. They crowding in now to kiss the bride. We better take this cloth off the sandwiches. Frankie said she would help you serve.

T. T. From the way she's been acting, I don't think we can count much on her.

BERENICE. I wish Honey was here. I'm so worried about him since what you told me. It's going to storm. It's a mercy they didn't decide to have the wedding in the back yard like they first planned.

T.T. I thought I'd better not minch the matter. Honey was in a bad way when I saw him this morning.

BERENICE. Honey Camden don't have too large a share of judgment as it is, but when he gets high on them reefers, he's got on more judgment than a four-year-old child. Remember that time he swung at the police and nearly got his eyes beat out?

T. T. Not to mention six months on the road.

BERENICE. I haven't been so anxious in all my life. I've got two people scouring Sugarville to find him. *(In a fervent voice)* God, you took Ludie but please watch over my Honey Camden. He's all the family I got.

T. T. And Frankie behaving this way about the wedding. Poor little critter.

BERENICE. And the sorry part is that she's perfectly serious about all this foolishness. *(Frankie enters the kitchen through the hall door)* Is it all over? *(T. T. crosses to the icebox with sandwiches)*

FRANKIE. Yes. And it was such a pretty wedding I wanted to cry.

BERENICE. You told them yet?

FRANKIE. About my plans—no, I haven't yet told them.

*(John Henry comes in and goes out.)*

BERENICE. Well, you better hurry up and do it, for they going to leave the house right after the refreshments.

FRANKIE. Oh, I know it. But something just seems to happen to my throat; every time I tried to tell them, different words came out.

BERENICE. What words?

FRANKIE. I asked Janice how come she didn't marry with a veil. *(With feeling)* Oh, I'm so embarrassed. Here I am all dressed up in this tacky evening dress. Oh, why didn't I listen to you! I'm so ashamed. *(T. T. goes out with a platter of sandwiches.)*

BERENICE. Don't take everything so strenuous like.

FRANKIE. I'm going in there and tell them now! *(She goes)*

JOHN HENRY *(coming out of the interior bedroom, carrying several costumes).* Frankie sure gave me a lot of presents when she was packing the suitcase. Berenice, she gave me all the beautiful show costumes.

BERENICE. Don't set so much store by all those presents. Come tomorrow morning and she'll be demanding them back again.

JOHN HENRY. And she even gave me the shell from the Bay. *(He puts the shell to his ear and listens)*

BERENICE. I wonder what's going on up there. *(She goes to the door and opens it and looks through)*

T. T. *(returning to the kitchen).* They all complimenting the wedding cake. And drinking the wine punch.

BERENICE. What's Frankie doing? When she left the kitchen a minute ago she was going to tell them. I wonder how they'll take this total surprise. I have a feeling like you get just before a big thunder storm.

*(Frankie enters, holding a punch cup.)*

BERENICE. You told them yet?

FRANKIE. There are all the family around and I can't seem to tell them. I wish I had written it down on the typewriter beforehand. I try to tell them and the words just—die.

BERENICE. The words just die because the very idea is so silly.

FRANKIE. I love the two of them so much. Janice put her arms around me and said she had always wanted a little sister. And she kissed me. She asked me again what grade I was in school. That's the third time she's asked me. In fact, that's the main question I've been asked at the wedding.

*(John Henry comes in, wearing a fairy costume, and goes out. Berenice notices Frankie's punch and takes it from her.)*

FRANKIE. And Jarvis was out in the street seeing about this car he borrowed for the wedding. And I followed him out and tried to tell him. But while I was trying to reach the point, he suddenly grabbed me by the elbows and lifted me up and sort of swung me. He said: "Frankie, the lankie, the alaga fankie, the tee-legged, toe-legged, bow-legged Frankie." And he gave me a dollar bill.

BERENICE. That's nice.

FRANKIE. I just don't know what to do. I have to tell them and yet I don't know how to.

BERENICE. Maybe when they're settled, they will invite you to come and visit with them.

FRANKIE. Oh no! I'm going *with* them. *(Frankie goes back into the house. There are louder sounds of voices from the interior. John Henry comes in again.)*

JOHN HENRY. The bride and the groom are leaving. Uncle Royal is taking their suitcases out to the car.

*(Frankie runs to the interior room and returns with her suitcase. She kisses Berenice.)*

FRANKIE. Good-bye, Berenice. Good-bye, John Henry. *(She stands a moment and looks around the kitchen)* Farewell, old ugly kitchen. *(She runs out)*

*(There are sounds of good-byes as the wedding party and the family guests move out of the house to the sidewalk. The voices get fainter in the distance. Then, from the front sidewalk there is the sound of disturbance. Frankie's voice is heard, diminished by distance, although she is speaking loudly.)*

FRANKIE'S VOICE. That's what I am telling you. *(Indistinct protesting voices are heard)*

MR. ADDAMS' VOICE *(indistinctly).* Now be reasonable, Frankie.

FRANKIE'S VOICE *(screaming).* I have to go. Take me! Take me!

JOHN HENRY (*entering excitedly*). Frankie is in the wedding car and they can't get her out. (*He runs out but soon returns*) Uncle Royal and my Daddy are having to haul and drag old Frankie. She's holding onto the steering wheel.

MR. ADDAMS' VOICE. You march right along here. What in the world has come into you? (*He comes into the kitchen with Frankie who is sobbing*) I never heard of such an exhibition in my life. Berenice, you take charge of her. (*Frankie flings herself on the kitchen chair and sobs with her head in her arms on the kitchen table.*)

JOHN HENRY. They put old Frankie out of the wedding. They hauled her out of the wedding car.

MR. ADDAMS (*clearing his throat*). That's sufficient, John Henry. Leave Frankie alone. (*He puts a caressing hand on Frankie's head*) What makes you want to leave your old papa like this? You've got Janice and Jarvis all upset on their wedding day.

FRANKIE. I love them so!

BERENICE (*looking down the hall*). Here they come. Now please be reasonable, Sugar.

(*The bride and groom come in. Frankie keeps her face buried in her arms and does not look up. The bride wears a blue suit with a white flower corsage pinned at the shoulder.*)

JARVIS. Frankie, we came to tell you good-bye. I'm sorry you're taking it like this.

JANICE. Darling, when we are settled we want you to come for a nice visit with us. But we don't yet have any place to live. (*She goes to Frankie and caresses her head. Frankie jerks*) Won't you tell us good-bye now?

FRANKIE (*with passion*). We! When you say *we,* you only mean you and Jarvis. And I am not included. (*She buries her head in her arms again and sobs*)

JANICE. Please, darling, don't make us unhappy on our wedding day. You know we love you.

FRANKIE. See! *We*—when you say we, I am not included. It's not fair.

JANICE. When you come visit us you must write beautiful plays, and we'll all act in them. Come, Frankie, don't hide your sweet face from us. Sit up. (*Frankie raises her head slowly and stares with a*

look *of wonder and misery*) Good-bye, Frankie, darling.

JARVIS. So long, now, kiddo.

(*They go out and Frankie still stares at them as they go down the hall. She rises, crosses towards the door and falls on her knees.*)

FRANKIE. Take me! Take me!

(*Berenice puts Frankie back on her chair.*)

JOHN HENRY. They put Frankie out of the wedding. They hauled her out of the wedding car.

BERENICE. Don't tease your cousin, John Henry.

FRANKIE. It was a frame-up all around.

BERENICE. Well, don't bother no more about it. It's over now. Now cheer up.

FRANKIE. I wish the whole world would die.

BERENICE. School will begin now in only three more weeks and you'll find another bosom friend like Evelyn Owens you so wild about.

JOHN HENRY (*seated below the sewing machine*). I'm sick, Berenice. My head hurts.

BERENICE. No you're not. Be quiet, I don't have the patience to fool with you.

FRANKIE (*hugging her hunched shoulders*). Oh, my heart feels so cheap!

BERENICE. Soon as you get started in school and have a chance to make these here friends, I think it would be a good idea to have a party.

FRANKIE. These baby promises rasp on my nerves.

BERENICE. You could call up the society editor of the *Evening Journal* and have the party written up in the paper. And that would make the fourth time your name has been published in the paper.

FRANKIE (*with a trace of interest*). When my bike ran into that automobile, the paper called me Fankie Addams, F-A-N-K-I-E. (*She puts her head down again*)

JOHN HENRY. Frankie, don't cry. This evening we can put up the tepee and have a good time.

FRANKIE. Oh, hush up your mouth.

BERENICE. Listen to me. Tell me what you would like and I will try to do it if it is in my power.

FRANKIE. All I wish in the world, is for no human being ever to speak to me as long as I live.

BERENICE. Bawl, then, misery.

*(Mr. Addams enters the kitchen, carrying Frankie's suitcase, which he sets in the middle of the kitchen floor. He cracks his finger joints. Frankie stares at him resentfully, then fastens her gaze on the suitcase.)*

MR. ADDAMS. Well, it looks like the show is over and the monkey's dead.

FRANKIE. You think it's over, but it's not.

MR. ADDAMS. You want to come down and help me at the store tomorrow? Or polish some silver with the shammy rag? You can even play with those old watch springs.

FRANKIE *(still looking at her suitcase)*. That's my suitcase I packed. If you think it's all over, that only shows how little you know. *(T. T. comes in)* If I can't go with the bride and my brother as I was meant to leave this town, I'm going anyway. Somehow, anyhow, I'm leaving town. *(Frankie raises up in her chair)* I can't stand this existence—this kitchen—this town—any longer! I will hop a train and go to New York. Or hitch rides to Hollywood, and get a job there. If worse comes to worse, I can act in comedies. *(She rises)* Or I could dress up like a boy and join the Merchant Marines and run away to sea. Somehow, anyhow, I'm running away.

BERENICE. Now, quiet down—

FRANKIE *(grabbing the suitcase and running into the hall)*. Please, Papa, don't try to capture me.

*(Outside the wind starts to blow.)*

JOHN HENRY *(from the doorway)*. Uncle Royal, Frankie's got your pistol in her suitcase.

*(There is the sound of running footsteps and of the screen door slamming.)*

BERENICE. Run, catch her.

*(T. T. and Mr. Addams rush into the hall, followed by John Henry.)*

MR. ADDAMS' VOICE. Frankie! Frankie! Frankie!

*(Berenice is left alone in the kitchen. Outside the wind is higher and the hall door is blown shut. There is a rumble of thunder, then a loud clap. Thunder and flashes of lightning continue. Berenice is seated in her chair, when John Henry comes in.)*

JOHN HENRY. Uncle Royal is going with my Daddy, and they are chasing her in our car. *(There is a thunder clap)* The thunder scares me, Berenice.

BERENICE *(taking him in her lap)*. Ain't nothing going to hurt you.

JOHN HENRY. You think they're going to catch her?

BERENICE *(putting her hand to her head)*. Certainly. They'll be bringing her home directly. I've got such a headache. Maybe my eye socket and all these troubles.

JOHN HENRY *(with his arms around Berenice)*. I've got a headache, too. I'm sick, Berenice.

BERENICE. No, you ain't. Run along, Candy. I ain't got the patience to fool with you now.

*(Suddenly the lights go out in the kitchen, plunging it in gloom. The sound of wind and storm continues and the yard is a dark storm-green.)*

JOHN HENRY. Berenice!

BERENICE. Ain't nothing. Just the lights went out.

JOHN HENRY. I'm scared.

BERENICE. Stand still, I'll just light a candle. *(Muttering)* I always keep one around, for such like emergencies. *(She opens a drawer)*

JOHN HENRY. What makes the lights go out so scarey like this?

BERENICE. Just one of them things, Candy.

JOHN HENRY. I'm scared. Where's Honey?

BERENICE. Jesus knows. I'm scared, too. With Honey snow-crazy and loose like this—and Frankie run off with a suitcase and her Papa's pistol. I feel like every nerve had been picked out of me.

JOHN HENRY *(holding out his seashell and stroking Berenice)*. You want to listen to the ocean?

THE CURTAIN FALLS

SCENE TWO

*The scene is the same. There are still signs in the kitchen of the wedding: punch glasses and the punch bowl on the drainboard. It is four o'clock in the morning. As the curtain rises, Berenice and Mr. Addams are alone in the kitchen. There is a crepuscular glow in the yard.*

MR. ADDAMS. I never was a believer in corporal punishment. Never spanked

Frankie in my life, but when I lay my hands on her . . .

BERENICE. She'll show up soon—but I know how you feel. What with worrying about Honey Camden, John Henry's sickness and Frankie, I've never lived through such a anxious night. (She looks through the window. It is dawning now)

MR. ADDAMS. I'd better go and find out the last news of John Henry, poor baby. (He goes through the hall door)

(Frankie comes into the yard and crosses to the arbor. She looks exhausted and almost beaten. Berenice has seen her from the window, rushes into the yard and grabs her by the shoulders and shakes her.)

BERENICE. Frankie Addams, you ought to be skinned alive. I been worried.

FRANKIE. I've been so worried too.

BERENICE. Where have you been this night? Tell me everything.

FRANKIE. I will, but quit shaking me.

BERENICE. Now tell me the A and the Z of this.

FRANKIE. When I was running around the dark scarey streets, I begun to realize that my plans for Hollywood and the Merchant Marines were child plans that would not work. I hid in the alley behind Papa's store, and it was dark and I was scared. I opened the suitcase and took out Papa's pistol. (She sits down on her suitcase) I vowed I was going to shoot myself. I said I was going to count three and on three pull the trigger. I counted one—two—but I didn't count three—because at the last minute, I changed my mind.

BERENICE. You march right along with me. You going to bed.

FRANKIE. Oh, Honey Camden!

(Honey Camden Brown, who has been hiding behind the arbor, has suddenly appeared.)

BERENICE. Oh, Honey, Honey. (They embrace)

HONEY. Shush, don't make any noise; the law is after me.

BERENICE (in a whisper). Tell me.

HONEY. Mr. Wilson wouldn't serve me so I drew a razor on him.

BERENICE. You kill him?

HONEY. Didn't have no time to find out. I been runnin' all night.

FRANKIE. Lightfoot, if you drew a razor on a white man, you'd better not let them catch you.

BERENICE. Here's six dolla's. If you can get to Fork Falls and then to Atlanta. But be careful slippin' through the white folks' section. They'll be combing the county looking for you.

HONEY (with passion). Don't cry, Berenice.

BERENICE. Already I feel that rope.

HONEY. Don't you dare cry. I know now all my days have been leading up to this minute. No more "boy this—boy that"— no bowing, no scraping. For the first time, I'm free and it makes me happy. (He begins to laugh hysterically)

BERENICE. When they catch you, they'll string you up.

HONEY (beside himself, brutally). Let them hang me—I don't care. I tell you I'm glad. I tell you I'm happy. (He goes out behind the arbor)

FRANKIE (calling after him). Honey, remember you are Lightfoot. Nothing can stop you if you want to run away.

(Mrs. West, John Henry's mother, comes into the yard.)

MRS. WEST. What was all that racket? John Henry is critically ill. He's got to have perfect quiet.

FRANKIE. John Henry's sick, Aunt Pet?

MRS. WEST. The doctors say he has meningitis. He must have perfect quiet.

BERENICE. I haven't had time to tell you yet. John Henry took sick sudden last night. Yesterday afternoon when I complained of my head, he said he had a headache too and thinking he copies me I said, "Run along, I don't have the patience to fool with you." Looks like a judgment on me. There won't be no more noise, Mrs. West.

MRS. WEST. Make sure of that. (She goes away)

FRANKIE (putting her arm around Berenice). Oh, Berenice, what can we do?

BERENICE (stroking Frankie's head). Ain't nothing we can do but wait.

FRANKIE. The wedding—Honey—John Henry—so much has happened that my brain can't hardly gather it in. Now for the first time I realize that the world is certainly—a sudden place.

BERENICE. Sometimes sudden, but when you are waiting, like this, it seems so slow.

THE CURTAIN FALLS

SCENE THREE

*The scene is the same: the kitchen and arbor. It is months later, a November day, about sunset.*

*The arbor is brittle and withered. The elm tree is bare except for a few ragged leaves. The yard is tidy and the lemonade stand and sheet stage curtain are now missing. The kitchen is neat and bare and the furniture has been removed. Berenice, wearing a fox fur, is sitting in a chair with an old suitcase and doll at her feet. Frankie enters.*

FRANKIE. Oh, I am just mad about these Old Masters.

BERENICE. Humph!

FRANKIE. The house seems so hollow. Now that the furniture is packed. It gives me a creepy feeling in the front. That's why I came back here.

BERENICE. Is that the only reason why you came back here?

FRANKIE. Oh, Berenice, you know. I wish you hadn't given quit notice just because Papa and I are moving into a new house with Uncle Eustace and Aunt Pet out in Limewood.

BERENICE. I respect and admire Mrs. West but I'd never get used to working for her.

FRANKIE. Mary is just beginning this Rachmaninoff Concerto. She may play it for her debut when she is eighteen years old. Mary playing the piano and the whole orchestra playing at one and the same time, mind you. Awfully hard.

BERENICE. Ma-ry Littlejohn.

FRANKIE. I don't know why you always have to speak her name in a tinged voice like that.

BERENICE. Have I ever said anything against her? All I said was that she is too lumpy and marshmallow white and it makes me nervous to see her just setting there sucking them pigtails.

FRANKIE. Braids. Furthermore, it is no use our discussing a certain party. You could never possibly understand it. It's just not in you.

*(Berenice looks at her sadly, with faded stillness, then pats and strokes the fox fur.)*

BERENICE. Be that as it may. Less us not fuss and quarrel this last afternoon.

FRANKIE. I don't want to fuss either.

Anyway, this is not our last afternoon. I will come and see you often.

BERENICE. No, you won't, baby. You'll have other things to do. Your road is already strange to me.

*(Frankie goes to Berenice, pats her on the shoulder, then takes her fox fur and examines it.)*

FRANKIE. You still have the fox fur that Ludie gave you. Somehow this little fur looks so sad—so thin and with a sad little fox-wise face.

BERENICE *(taking the fur back and continuing to stroke it).* Got every reason to be sad. With what has happened in these two last months. I just don't know what I have done to deserve it. *(She sits, the fur in her lap, bent over with her forearms on her knees and her hands limply dangling)* Honey gone and John Henry, my little boy gone.

FRANKIE. You did all you could. You got poor Honey's body and gave him a Christian funeral and nursed John Henry.

BERENICE. It's the way Honey died and the fact that John Henry had to suffer so. Little soul!

FRANKIE. It's peculiar—the way it all happened so fast. First Honey caught and hanging himself in the jail. Then later in that same week, John Henry died and then I met Mary. As the irony of fate would have it, we first got to know each other in front of the lipstick and cosmetics counter at Woolworth's. And it was the week of the fair.

BERENICE. The most beautiful September I ever seen. Countless white and yellow butterflies flying around them autumn flowers—Honey dead and John Henry suffering like he did and daisies, golden weather, butterflies—such strange death weather.

FRANKIE. I never believed John Henry would die. *(There is a long pause. She looks out the window)* Don't it seem quiet to you in here? *(There is another, longer pause)* When I was a little child I believed that out under the arbor at night there would come three ghosts and one of the ghosts wore a silver ring. *(Whispering)* Occasionally when it gets so quiet like this I have a strange feeling. It's like John Henry is hovering somewhere in this kitchen—solemn looking and ghost-grey.

A BOY'S VOICE *(from the neighboring yard).* Frankie, Frankie.

FRANKIE *(calling to the boy)*. Yes, Barney. *(To Berenice)* Clock stopped. *(She shakes the clock)*

THE BOY'S VOICE. Is Mary there?

FRANKIE *(to Berenice)*. It's Barney MacKean. *(To the boy, in a sweet voice)* Not yet. I'm meeting her at five. Come on in, Barney, won't you?

BARNEY. Just a minute.

FRANKIE *(to Berenice)*. Barney puts me in mind of a Greek god.

BERENICE. What? Barney puts you in mind of a what?

FRANKIE. Of a Greek god. Mary remarked that Barney reminded her of a Greek god.

BERENICE. It looks like I can't understand a thing you say no more.

FRANKIE. You know, those old-timey Greeks worship those Greek gods.

BERENICE. But what has that got to do with Barney MacKean?

FRANKIE. On account of the figure.

*(Barney MacKean, a boy of thirteen, wearing a football suit, bright sweater and cleated shoes, runs up the back steps into the kitchen.)*

BERENICE. Hi, Greek god Barney. This afternoon I saw your initials chalked down on the front sidewalk. M.L. loves B.M.

BARNEY. If I could find out who wrote it, I would rub it out with their faces. Did you do it, Frankie?

FRANKIE *(drawing herself up with sudden dignity)*. I wouldn't do a kid thing like that. I even resent you asking me. *(She repeats the phrase to herself in a pleased undertone)* Resent you asking me.

BARNEY. Mary can't stand me anyhow.

FRANKIE. Yes she can stand you. I am her most intimate friend. I ought to know. As a matter of fact she's told me several lovely compliments about you. Mary and I are riding on the moving van to our new house. Would you like to go?

BARNEY. Sure.

FRANKIE. O.K. You will have to ride back with the furniture 'cause Mary and I are riding on the front seat with the driver. We had a letter from Jarvis and Janice this afternoon. Jarvis is with the Occupation Forces in Germany and they took a vacation trip to Luxembourg. *(She repeats in a pleased voice)* Luxembourg. Berenice, don't you think that's a lovely name?

BERENICE. It's kind of a pretty name, but it reminds me of soapy water.

FRANKIE. Mary and I will most likely pass through Luxembourg when we—are going around the world together.

*(Frankie goes out followed by Barney and Berenice sits in the kitchen alone and motionless. She picks up the doll, looks at it and hums the first two lines of "I Sing Because I'm Happy." In the next house the piano is heard again, as the curtain falls.)*

# 1950-51

For some reason that no one ever will be able to explain satisfactorily to this writer, Sidney Kingsley's *Darkness at Noon* did not win the Circle's award hands down on April 3, 1951. It received ten votes to an uncomfortably close eight for *Billy Budd*, an interesting but not nearly so impressive a work by Louis O. Coxe and Robert Chapman, who adapted it from Herman Melville's novel about discipline in the Royal Navy of 1798.

Trailing these two badly were *The Rose Tattoo* by Tennessee Williams, three votes; *The Autumn Garden* by Lillian Hellman, three; *The Country Girl* by Clifford Odets, one. There was no Pulitzer award.

Broadway's first long play by Christopher Fry, Britain's new "genius" of the poetic drama, easily won the foreign citation. *The Lady's Not for Burning*, in which John Gielgud gave a fine performance, received twenty-three votes to one for *Black Chiffon* by Lesley Storm and one for *The House of Bernarda Alba* by Federico Garcia Lorca.

There were two outstanding musicals, *Guys and Dolls*, with libretto by Jo Swerling and Abe Burrows and songs by Frank Loesser, and *The King and I* by Richard Rodgers and Oscar Hammerstein. A proposal before the Circle that joint recognition be given them was narrowly defeated, after which *Guys and Dolls* was selected, seventeen to seven.

It was a season in which Michael Todd presented a stage full of showgirls taking a bubble bath in the revue *Peep Show;* Cole Porter's good score failed to save *Out of This World;* John Patrick's *The Curious Savage* was curiously unappreciated; John van Druten's *Bell, Book and Candle* was popular, with Rex Harrison and Lilli Palmer heading the cast; the always admirable Cyril Ritchard showed in *The Relapse* how Restoration comedy should be played; Arthur Schwartz turned out a fine period score for *A Tree Grows in Brooklyn;* a rare revival of *King Lear*, with Louis Calhern doing a good job in the title role, failed to capture the public; a Circle member, Wolcott Gibbs, wrote a mildly amusing comedy entitled *Season in the Sun* which, for some odd reason, seemed to enchant a majority of his colleagues and ran for a profitable 367 performances; and Irving Berlin brought out into the open a matter of steadily growing importance with the presidential election still two years away when he included in his score for *Call Me Madam* a song entitled *They Like Ike.*

*Mister Roberts* earned itself a place high on the long-run list by running up 1,157 performances before closing on January 6, 1951.

*Darkness at Noon* wound up with 186 performances, *Billy Budd* with 105, *The Lady's Not for Burning* with 151, *Guys and Dolls* with 1,200 and *The King and I* with 1,246.

# Darkness At Noon

## By SIDNEY KINGSLEY

### Based on the Novel by ARTHUR KOESTLER

Presented by The Playwrights' Company at the Alvin Theatre, New York City, January 13, 1951, with the following cast:

| | |
|---|---|
| RUBASHOV | Claude Rains |
| GUARD | Robert Keith, Jr. |
| 402 | Philip Coolidge |
| 302 | Richard Seff |
| 202 | Allan Rich |
| LUBA | Kim Hunter |
| GLETKIN | Walter J. Palance |
| 1st STORM TROOPER | Adams MacDonald |
| RICHARD | Herbert Ratner |
| YOUNG GIRL | Virginia Howard |
| 2nd STORM TROOPER | Johnson Hayes |
| IVANOFF | Alexander Scourby |
| BOGROV | Norman Roland |
| HRUTSCH | Robert Crozier |
| ALBERT | Daniel Polis |
| LUIGI | Will Kuluva |
| PABLO | Henry Beckman |
| ANDRE | Geoffrey Barr |
| BARKEEPER | Tony Ancona |
| SECRETARY | Lois Nettleton |
| PRESIDENT | Maurice Gosfield |

*Soldiers, sailors, judges, jurors*

---

## SCENE

First Hearing—A Prison—March, 1937.
Second Hearing—The same—Five weeks later.
Third Hearing—The same—One week later.

The action of the play oscillates dialectically between the Material world of a Russian prison during the harsh days of March, 1937, and the Ideal realms of the spirit as manifested in Rubashov's memories and thoughts moving freely through space and time.

---

ACT ONE

*March, 1937*

*Granite and iron! The corridor of an ancient Russian prison buried deep underground. To the left, set into a soaring, Byzantine arch, is a thick, iron portcullis. Beyond it, visible through the bars, a steep flight of stone steps curves up out of sight. To the right a tier of cells forms an ominous column of sweating granite, towering up to vanish in the shadows above. A Guard with rifle and bayonet paces the corridor. He halts as the iron portcullis slides up to the clangor of chains, revealing an Officer and a Prisoner. The Prisoner, N. S. Rubashov, is a short, stocky, smooth-shaven, bespectacled man in his early fifties. His head is large beyond the proportions of his body, and characterized by an expanse of forehead. His eyes are set far apart and mongoloid in cast. He carries himself very erect and with fierce authority. The Guard opens the door of a cell, throws a switch in the corridor which turns on the light, and the Prisoner is pushed inside. The door clangs behind him. The heavy metallic sound of bolts being closed and a key turned. The Prisoner surveys his cell slowly: a solid, windowless cubicle with an iron bed and a straw mattress, nothing else. There is no day here, no night; it is a timeless dank grave for the living corpse. He reaches into his pocket automatically for cigarettes, then he remembers, turns to the judas-hole and observes the eye of the Guard staring at him.*

———

RUBASHOV. Comrade guard! *(He turns his empty pockets inside out)* They've taken away my cigarettes, too! Can you get me a cigarette?

GUARD *(harshly)*. It's late, go to bed.

RUBASHOV. I've been dragged out of a sick-bed. I have a fever. I need some cigarettes.

GUARD *(mutters)*. Your mother! *(Turns out the light in the cell, leaving the Prisoner lit only by the light streaming through the judas-hole. The Guard goes off)*

RUBASHOV *(rubs his inflamed cheek, shakes his head, sighs, looks about, takes off his coat, slowly, painfully; throws it on the cot, murmurs to himself)*. So, it's come. You're to die, Rubashov. Well, the old guard is gone! *(He sits on the bed; rolls up his coat for a pillow, murmuring to himself)* For golden lads and girls all must as chimney sweepers come to dust. *(He takes off his spectacles, places them on the floor, and lies back, staring grimly at the ceiling)* Yes. The old guard is gone. *(He sighs again, repeats mechanically)* For golden lad and girls all must . . . *(A ticking sound is heard. Three ticks, then a pause, then three more ticks. He sits up, listening)* . . . as chimney sweepers . . . *(The ticking becomes louder. He picks up his spectacles, rises, glances at the judas-hole to make certain he is not being observed, places his ear to one wall, taps on it with his spectacles, listens, then tries another wall. Returning to the wall left, he listens, murmurs "Ah," taps three times. The answering taps become louder. He repeats the series, placing his ear to the wall; the taps now come in a different series, louder, rapid, more excited)* Easy! Slow . . . Slow. *(He taps slowly, deliberately. The answering taps slow down)* That's better . . . *(He counts the taps)* 5-3, W; 2-3, H; 3-5, O. "Who?" *(The Prisoner smiles and addresses himself softly to the wall)* Direct enough, aren't you, Comrade?

*(The lights come up in the adjoining cell, the wall dissolves, the Prisoner in 402 appears. He is verminous, caked with filth, his hair matted, his old Tsarist uniform in rags, but he has somehow preserved his monocle and the tatters of an old illusion. He strokes his moustache and swaggers about as if he were still a perfumed dandy.)*

402 *(As he taps on the wall, his lips unconsciously form the words and utter them. In their communications by tapping, all the prisoners unconsciously voice the messages as they tap them through)*. Who are you? *(Pause, as Rubashov shakes his head but doesn't answer. Taps again)* Is it day or night outside?

RUBASHOV *(glances again at the judas-hole, taps)*. 4:00 A.M.

402 *(taps)*. What day?

RUBASHOV *(taps)*. Tuesday.

402 *(taps)*. Month?

RUBASHOV *(taps)*. March . . .

402 *(taps)*. Year?

RUBASHOV *(taps)*. 1937.

402 *(taps)*. The weather?

RUBASHOV *(taps)*. Snowing.

402 *(to himself)*. Snow. *(Taps)* Who are you?

RUBASHOV *(to himself)*. Well, why not? *(He taps)* Nicolai Semonovitch Rubashov.

402 *(straightens up with a cry)*. Rubashov? *(He bursts into wild ugly laughter. He taps)* The wolves are devouring each other! *(Crosses over to the opposite wall. Taps three times, and listens, his ear to the wall. The cell above lights up and the occupant rises painfully from his cot. He is a young man, thin, with a white ghostlike face, bruises and burns on it, and a split lip. He crosses with effort to the wall, taps three times, then listens as 402 taps)* New prisoner. Rubashov.

302 *(taps)*. Nicolai Rubashov?

402 *(laughing hoarsely as he taps)*. N. S. Rubashov. Ex-Commissar of the People, ex-Member of the Central Committee, ex-General of the Red Army, Bearer of the Order of the Red Banner. Pass it along.

302 *(crouches, stunned, cries out suddenly)*. Oh! Father, Father, what have I done? . . . *(He crosses to the opposite wall, taps three times. An answering tap is heard. The cell above lights up; 202, a peasant with insane eyes, puts his head to the floor as 302 taps)*

302 *(taps)*. N. S. Rubashov arrested. Pass it along.

202. Rubashov? Well, well! *(Crosses to other wall, taps)* N. S. Rubashov arrested. Pass it along.

*(The tiers of cells darken and vanish, leaving only Rubashov visible, leaning against the wall, staring into space. The taps echo and re-echo throughout the prison, to the whispering accompaniment: "N. S. Rubashov arrested! N. S. Rubashov arrested!" The whispers grow into the roar of a mighty throng calling out, "Rubashov! Rubashov!" Rubashov's voice is heard, young and triumphant, addressing the crowd.)*

RUBASHOV'S VOICE. Comrades! *(The tumult subsides)* Proletarians, soldiers and sailors of the Revolution. The great, terrible and joyful day has arrived! *(The crowd roars. Rubashov, listening to the past, head bowed, paces his cell slowly)* Eight months ago the chariot of the blood-stained and mire-bespattered Romanov monarchy was tilted over at one blow. *(The oceanic roar of the crowd)* The gray, stuttering Provisional Government of bourgeois democracy was already dead and only waiting for the broom of History to sweep its putrid corpse into the sewer. In the name of the Revolutionary Committee I now declare the Provisional Government overthrown. *(The roar swells)* Power to the Soviets! Land to the peasants! Bread to the hungry! Peace to all the peoples! *(The victorious shouts of "Rubashov! Rubashov!" mount to a crescendo, fade away and die, leaving only the blanketed stillness of the cell and Rubashov listening to his memories. Three taps from 402's wall arouse him. He responds, ear to the wall. The wall dissolves, revealing 402.)*

402 *(taps, gloating)*. Serves you right.

RUBASHOV *(to himself)*. What is this? *(Taps)* Who are you?

402 *(taps)*. None of your damned business . . .

RUBASHOV *(taps)*. As you like.

402 *(taps)*. Long live His Majesty, the Tsar!

RUBASHOV. So that's it. *(Taps)* I thought you birds extinct.

402 *(beats out the rhythm with his shoe)*. Long live the Tsar!

RUBASHOV *(grins sardonically, taps)*. Amen! Amen!

402 *(taps)*. Swine!

RUBASHOV *(amused, taps out)*. Didn't quite understand.

402 *(in a frenzy, hammers out)*. Dirty swine . . .

RUBASHOV *(taps)*. Not interested in your family tree.

402 *(fury suddenly passes, taps out slowly)*. Why have you been locked up?

RUBASHOV *(taps)*. I don't know. *(Pause)*

402 *(taps)*. Anything happened? Big? Assassination? War?

RUBASHOG *(taps)*. No. Can you lend me tobacco?

402 *(taps)*. For you? I'd be castrated first.

RUBASHOV *(taps)*. Good idea.

*(402 walks away, lies down on his cot. The lights fade out on him.)*

RUBASHOV *(paces his cell, counting off the steps)*. 1-2-3-4-5- and a half . . . *(He wheels back)* 1-2-3-4 . . . *(Strange ghostly voices are dimly heard)* It starts. So soon. *(The vague outline of ghostly faces hover above him)* The waking, walking dreams. *(Other ghostly faces appear in space)* Yes, you sailors of Kronstadt—I shall pay . . . And you nameless ones. *(The face of a little hunchback appears, smoking a pipe and smiling)* And Comrade Luigi. *(Some plates appear dancing in space—then a big moon-face of a man, juggling them, grinning)* And Pablo. *(The luminous face of a young woman appears in space. A striking face; large, soft brown eyes; dark hair; white skin)* And Luba. *(The voices and faces fade away)* My debts will be paid—my debts will be paid.

*(The young woman materializes. The cell becomes the office of the Commissar of the Iron Works. Huge graphs hang on the walls. Through the window, a vista of factory chimneys and the skeletons of incompleted buildings may be seen. The young woman is bent over her notebook, taking down dictation. Rubashov walks up and down, dictating. In the pauses, she raises her head, and her soft, round eyes follow his wanderings through the room. There is wonder and worship in the way she looks at him. She wears a white peasant blouse, embroidered with little flowers at the high neck. Her body is generously formed and voluptuous.)*

RUBASHOV *(dictates)*. "To meet the Five-Year Plan we must step up our tempo. A twelve-hour day if necessary. Tempo! Tempo!" *(The girl tosses her head as she writes, and her dangling earrings attract his attention. He frowns. Her head buried in her notebook, she does not observe this)* ". . . The Unions will dismiss workers who come late and deprive all laggards of their food cards . . ." *(She quickly reaches down to scratch her ankle, and he notices she is wearing high-heeled slippers. He frowns again)* ". . . In the building of a new, hitherto undreamt-of Communist state, we must be guided by one rule, dash, the end justifies the means, period. Relentlessly, exclamation point." *(The girl bobs her head, the earrings sway. He suddenly growls)* Why do you wear those earrings? And those high heels? With a peasant blouse. Ridiculous! *(The girl looks up)* What's your name?

LUBA. Loshenko.

RUBASHOV. Loshenko?

LUBA. Yes, Comrade Commissar. Luba Loshenko. *(Her voice is low and hoarse, but gentle)*

RUBASHOV. And how long have you been working here?

LUBA. For you, Comrade Commissar?

RUBASHOV *(growls)*. Yes, for me. Of course, for me.

LUBA. Three weeks.

RUBASHOV. Three? Really? Well, Comrade Loshenko, don't dress up like a ceremonial elephant in the office!

LUBA. Yes, Comrade Commissar, I'm sorry.

RUBASHOV. You weren't wearing those earrings yesterday?

LUBA. No, Comrade Commissar, I wasn't.

RUBASHOV. Then what are you getting dressed up for now? What's the occasion? This is an office. We've work to do. Ridiculous . . . Where was I?

LUBA *(glances at her notebook)*. "The end justifies the means, period. Relentlessly, exclamation point."

RUBASHOV. Mm! *(He picks up some papers from the desk, glances at them)* "You liberals sitting on a cloud, dangling your feet in the air . . ." *(He turns and looks at her; she is watching him, but quickly turns back to her notebook)* You—you've really very pretty little ears. Why do you ruin them with those survivals of barbaric culture? *(She plucks off the earrings)* That's better. And don't look so frightened. I'm not going to eat you. What do you people in this office think I am? An ogre? I don't eat little children.

LUBA *(looks at him)*. I'm not frightened.

RUBASHOV. You're not?

LUBA. No.

RUBASHOV *(surprised)*. Humph! Good! Good! Where was I?

LUBA *(scans her notebook)*. "Sitting on a cloud, dangling your feet in the air."

RUBASHOV. Ah! *(She looks up at him and smiles. In spite of himself he returns her smile)* Yes . . . *(Then soberly again)* "You liberals are wrong." *(He begins to pace)* "And those who are wrong will pay . . . !" *(The image of the girl fades; the office vanishes, and he is back in his cell)* Yes, Luba, I will pay. I will pay my debt to you, above all. . . . *(Three taps are heard from 402's wall. He turns to the wall, fiercely)* But not you. I owe you nothing. How many of your people have I killed? No matter. You taught us to hate. *(Three taps from 402)* You stood over us with the knout and the hangman. *(Three taps from 402)* Your police made us fear this world, your priests the next, you poured melted lead down our throats, you massacred us in Moscow, you slit the bellies of our partisans in Siberia and stuffed them with grain. No! *(Crossing to the wall)* You? I owe no debt to you. *(Three taps from 402. Rubashov places his ear to the wall, taps curtly)* What do you want?

402 *(appears, tapping).* I'm sending you tobacco.

RUBASHOV *(after a long pause, taps).* Thanks. *(Sighs, murmurs to the wall)* Do I owe you a debt too? We at least acted in the name of humanity. Mm. But doesn't that double our debt? *(He shakes his head, cynically)* What is this, Rubashov? A breath of religious madness? *(A feverish chill shakes him. He puts on his coat)*

402 *(rattles his door, peers through the judas-hole, calls).* Guard! Guard! *(The Guard is heard shuffling across the corridor)*

GUARD *(through the bars of the judas-hole).* What do you want?

402. Could you take this tobacco to cell 400?

GUARD. No.

402. I'll give you a hundred rubles.

GUARD. I'll give you my butt in your face.

402 *(walks away).* For two rubles he'd cut his mother's throat.

GUARD *(returns to the judas-hole, menacingly).* What did you say?

402 *(cringes, whining).* Nothing! I said nothing. *(The Guard shuffles off. 402 crosses to wall, taps)* You're in for it.

RUBASHOV *(on sudden impulse goes to the iron door of his cell, bangs on it, shouting).* Guard! Guard! *(The Guard is heard approaching down the corridor)*

GUARD. Quiet! You're waking everyone. *(His shadow appears in the judas-hole)*

RUBASHOV *(peremptorily commands).* Tell the Commandant I must speak to him.

GUARD *(cackles).* Oh, sure.

RUBASHOV. At once!

GUARD. Who do you think you are?

RUBASHOV. Read your Party history.

GUARD. I know who you are.

RUBASHOV. Then don't ask idiotic questions.

GUARD. You're Number 400, in solitary, and you're probably going to be taken down in the cellar and shot. Now don't give me any more trouble or you'll get a butt in your face.

RUBASHOV. You try it and we'll see who'll be shot. *(The Guard hesitates. Rubashov again hammers on the door)*

GUARD. You're waking everyone. Stop that or I'll report you.

RUBASHOV. Do so! Report me! At once!

GUARD. I will. *(He goes)*

*(Rubashov continues to hammer on the cell door. The lights come up in the cell tier, bringing the other prisoners into vision. They have been listening to this exchange through the judas-hole. 302 turns from the door and seats himself on his cot. Slowly, painfully, he begins to tap the signal to 402.)*

*(402 stands on his cot, responds and listens.)*

302 *(taps).* Outside?

402 *(taps).* It's morning, 4:00 A.M., Tuesday. March. Snowing.

302 *(taps).* Send Rubashov my greetings.

402 *(taps).* Who shall I say?

302 *(taps).* Just say an old friend.

*(402 crosses to Rubashov, summons him with a tap. Rubashov rises and listens at the wall as 402 taps: 302 sends greetings.)*

RUBASHOV *(taps).* What's his name?

402 *(taps).* Won't say. Just old friend. He was tortured last week.

RUBASHOV *(taps).* Why?

402 *(taps).* Political divergencies.

RUBASHOV. Your kind?

402 *(taps).* No, your kind.

RUBASHOV *(taps).* How many prisoners here?

402 *(taps).* Thousands. Come and go.

RUBASHOV *(taps).* Your kind?

402 *(taps).* No. Yours. I'm extinct. Ha! Ha!

RUBASHOV *(taps).* Ha! Ha! *(Footsteps approaching ring out in the corridor. He taps quickly)* Someone's coming.

*(402 vanishes. Rubashov throw himself on the cot.)*

*(A huge, young man in an officer's uniform enters. His shaven head, his deep-set, expressionless eyes, and his jutting, Slavic cheek-bones give him the appearance of a death's head. His stiff uniform creaks, as do his boots. The officer who arrested Rubashov and the guard are visible in the doorway. The young man enters the cell which becomes smaller through his presence. His name is Gletkin.)*

GLETKIN *(fixes Rubashov with a cold stare).* Were you the one banging on the door? *(He looks about)* This cell needs cleaning. *(To Rubashov)* You know the regulations? *(He glances behind the door, turns to the guard)* He has no mop. Get him a mop! *(The Guard hurries off)*

RUBASHOV. Are you the Commandant here?

GLETKIN. No. Why were you banging on the door?

RUBASHOV. Why am I under arrest? Why have I been dragged out of a sick-bed? Why have I been brought here?

GLETKIN. If you wish to argue with me you'll have to stand up.

RUBASHOV. If you're not the Commandant, I haven't the slightest desire to argue with you . . . or even to speak to you for that matter.

GLETKIN. Then don't bang on the door again—or the usual disciplinary measures will have to be applied. *(Turns to the arresting officer)* When was the prisoner brought in?

ARRESTING OFFICER. Ten minutes ago.

GLETKIN *(glances at his watch, sternly)*. His arrest was ordered for three A.M. sharp. What happened?

ARRESTING OFFICER. The car broke down.

GLETKIN. That's inexcusable. It's the Commandant's new car, and it was in perfect condition. This looks very suspicious. *(He takes out a note-book and writes in it)* Send the driver up to my office at once!

RUBASHOV. It's not his fault. It wasn't sabotage.

GLETKIN *(writes, without glancing up)*. How do you know it wasn't?

RUBASHOV. Make allowances.

GLETKIN. For what?

RUBASHOV. Our roads.

GLETKIN *(puts away the note-book and measures Rubashov impersonally)*. What's the matter with our roads?

RUBASHOV. They're primitive cow paths.

GLETKIN. Very critical, aren't we? I suppose the roads in the bourgeois countries are better?

RUBASHOV *(looks at Gletkin, smiles cynically)*. Young man, have you ever been outside of our country?

GLETKIN. No. I don't have to . . . to know. And I don't want to hear any fairy tales.

RUBASHOV. Fairy tales? *(Sits up)* Have you read any of my books or articles?

GLETKIN. In the Komsomol Youth I read your political-education pamphlets. In their time I found them useful.

RUBASHOV. How flattering! And did you find any fairy tales in them?

GLETKIN. That was fifteen years ago. *(Pause)*. Don't think that gives you any privileges now! *(The Guard appears, flapping a dirty rag. Gletkin takes it, throws it at Rubashov's feet)* When the morning bugle blows, you will clean up your cell. You know the rules. You've been in prison before?

RUBASHOV. Yes. Many of them. But this is my first experience under my own people. *(He rubs his inflamed jaw)*

GLETKIN. Do you wish to go on sick call?

RUBASHOV. No, thanks. I know prison doctors.

GLETKIN. Then you're not really sick?

RUBASHOV. I have an abscess. It'll burst itself.

GLETKIN *(without irony)*. Have you any more requests?

RUBASHOV. Tell your superior officer I want to talk to him and stop wasting my time!

GLETKIN. Your time has run out, Rubashov! *(He starts to go, pulling the door behind him)*

RUBASHOV *(murmurs in French)*. Plus un singe monte . . .

GLETKIN *(re-enters quickly)*. Speak in your own tongue! Are you so gone you can't even think any longer except in a filthy, foreign language?

RUBASHOV *(sharply, with military authority)*. Young man, there's nothing wrong with the French language as such. Now, tell them I'm here and let's have a little Bolshevik discipline! *(Gletkin stiffens, studies Rubashov coldly, turns and goes, slamming the iron door. The jangle of the key in the lock; his footsteps as he marches off down the corridor. Suddenly Rubashov bounds to the door. He shouts through the judas-hole)* And get me some cigarettes! Damn you! *(Rubs his inflamed cheek, ruefully. To himself)* Now, why did you do that, Rubashov? What does this young man think of you? "Worn-out old intellectual! Self-appointed Messiah! Dares to question the party line! Ripe for liquidation . . ." There you go again, Rubashov—the old disease. *(Paces)* 4 . . . 5. Revolutionaries shouldn't see through other people's eyes. Or should they? How can you change the world if you identify yourself with everybody? How else can you change it? *(Paces)* 3 . . . 4. *(He pauses, frowning, searching his memory)* What is it about this young man? Something? *(Paces)* 3 . . . 4. Why do I recall a religious painting? A Pietà, a dead Christ in Mary's arms? Of course—Germany. The Museum, Leipzig, 1933. *(Slowly the prison becomes a museum in Germany. A large painting of the Pietà materializes. An S.S. Officer in black uniform and swastika arm-band is staring at the Pietà. His face, though different from Gletkin's in features, has the same, cold, fanatical expression. Rubashov, catalogue in hand, walks slowly down, studying a row of invisible paintings front; then he crosses over, studies the Pietà. The S.S. Officer glances at him with hard searching eyes, then goes.)* *(A middle-aged man with a sensitive face, sunken cheeks, enters, looks alternately at the catalogue he is holding and the paintings in space. He halts next to Rubashov, squinting to make out the title.)*

MAN *(softly, reading)*. "Christ Crowned With Thorns."

RUBASHOV *(turns, front, nods)*. Titian.

MAN *(to Rubashov)*. What page is it in your catalogue, please? *(Rubashov, without looking at him, hands over his catalogue. Man glances at it, looks about hurriedly, returns it, whispers hoarsely)* Be very careful. They're everywhere.

RUBASHOV. I know. You're late, Comrade Richard.

RICHARD. I went a round-about way.

RUBASHOV. Give me your report.

RICHARD. It's bad.

RUBASHOV. Give it to me.

RICHARD. Since the Reichstag fire, they've turned the tables on us. It's a massacre. All Germany is a shambles. Two weeks ago we had six hundred and twelve cells here—today there are fifty-two left. The Party is a thousand-headed mass of bleeding flesh. Two of my group jumped out of a window last night in order to avoid arrest! *(His lips start to tremble; his entire body is suddenly convulsed)*

RUBASHOV *(sharply)*. Control yourself! *(Glances about)* You're one of the leaders here. If you go on this way, what can we expect of the other comrades?

RICHARD *(controls himself with an effort)*. I'm sorry.

RUBASHOV. For a man who has written such heroic plays of the proletariat, this is surprising.

RICHARD. This is a bad moment for me. My wife, Comrade Truda, was arrested two days ago. The Storm Troopers took her and I haven't heard since.

RUBASHOV. Where were you at the time?

RICHARD. Across the street, on a roof. *(His voice becomes shrill as he begins to lose control again. A stutter creeps into his speech)* I w-w-watched them take her away.

RUBASHOV *(glances around to see if they are observed, motions Richard to the bench under the Pietà)*. Sit down. *(They both sit on the bench)* We have a big job here. We have to pull the Party together. We have to stiffen its backbone. This is only a temporary phase.

RICHARD. We carry on, Comrade. We work day and night. We distribute literature in the factories and house to house.

RUBASHOV. I've seen some of these pamphlets. Who wrote them?

RICHARD. I did.

RUBASHOV. You did?

RICHARD. Yes. Why?

RUBASHOV. They're not quite satisfactory, Comrade Richard.

RICHARD. In what respect?

RUBASHOV. A bit off the line. We sense a certain sympathy with the Liberals and the Social Democrats.

RICHARD. The Storm Troopers are . . . *(The stammer again creeps into his speech)* Sl . . . sl . . . slaughtering them, too, like animals in the street.

RUBASHOV. Let them! How does that affect us? In that respect the Nazis are clearing the way for us by wiping out this trash and saving us the trouble.

RICHARD. Trash?

RUBASHOV. The Liberals are our most treacherous enemies. Historically, they have always betrayed us.

RICHARD. But that's inhuman, man. You comrades back there act as if nothing had happened here. Try and understand! We're living in a j . . . j . . . jungle. All of us. We call ourselves "dead men on ho . . . holiday."

RUBASHOV. The party leadership here carries a great responsibility and those who go soft now are betraying it. You're playing into the enemies' hands!

RICHARD. I . . . ?

RUBASHOV. Yes, Comrade Richard, you.

RICHARD. What is this? I suppose Truda betrayed the Party, too?

RUBASHOV. If you go on this way . . . *(Suddenly, urgently)* Speak quietly, and don't turn your head to the door! *(A tall young man in the uniform of a Storm Trooper has entered the room with a girl and they stand nearby, studying their catalogues and the pictures. The S.S. Officer whispers to the girl. She titters. Rubashov rises; in a low calm voice).* Go on talking.

RICHARD *(rises, glances at his catalogue, talking rapidly).* Roger van der Weyden, the elder, 1400 to 1464. He's probably Van Eyck's most famous pupil.

RUBASHOV. His figures are somewhat angular.

RICHARD. Yes, but look at the heads. There's real power there. And look at the depth of physiognomy. *(Again the stammer)* Compare h . . . h . . . him with the other masters; you'll see his coloring is softer . . . and I . . . I . . . lighter. *(His eyes stray to the S.S. Officer in panic and hatred)*

RUBASHOV. Did you stammer as a child? *(Sharply)* Don't look over there!

RICHARD *(looks away quickly).* S . . . sometimes.

RUBASHOV. Breathe slowly and deeply several times. *(Richard obeys. The girl with the Storm Trooper giggles shrilly, and the pair move slowly toward the exit. In passing, they both turn their heads toward Richard and Rubashov. The Storm Trooper says something to the girl. She replies in a low voice. They leave, the girl's giggling audible as their footsteps recede)*

RICHARD *(softly, to himself).* Truda used to laugh at my stutter. She had a funny little laugh.

RUBASHOV *(motioning Richard to reseat himself).* You must give me your promise to write only according to the lines laid down by the Comintern.

RICHARD *(sitting).* Understand one thing, Comrade: Some of my colleagues write easily. I don't. I write out of torment; I write what I believe and feel in here. I have no choice—I write what I must, because I must. Even if I'm wrong, I must write what I believe. That's how we arrive at the truth.

RUBASHOV. We have already arrived at the truth. Objective truth. And with us Art is its weapon. I'm amazed at you, Comrade Richard. You're seeking the truth for the sake of your own ego! What kind of delusion is this? The individual is nothing! The Party is everything! And its policy as laid down by the Comintern must be like a block of polished granite. One conflicting idea is dangerous. Not one crack in its surface is to be tolerated. Nothing! Not a mustard seed must be allowed to sprout in it and split our solidarity! The "me," the "I" is a grammatical fiction. *(He takes out his watch, glances at it)* My time is up. *(He puts his watch back in his pocket, rises)* You know what's expected of you. Keep on the line. We will send you further instructions.

RICHARD *(rises).* I don't think I can do it.

RUBASHOV. Why not?

RICHARD. I don't believe in their policy.

RUBASHOV. Against our enemies, we're implacable!

RICHARD. That means . . . ?

RUBASHOV. You know what it means.

RICHARD. You'd t . . . turn me over to the Nazis?

RUBASHOV. Those who are not with us are against us.

RICHARD. Then what's the difference between us and them? Our people here are going over to them by the tens of thousands. It's an easy step. Too easy. *(A pause. He speaks almost inaudibly)* Who can say what your Revolution once meant to me? The end of all injustice. Paradise! And my Truda now lies bleeding in some S.S. cellar. She may be dead even now Yes. In my heart—I know she's dead.

RUBASHOV *(buttons his coat).* We'll have to break this off now. We'd better go separately. You leave first, I'll follow.

RICHARD. What are my instructions?

RUBASHOV. There are none. There's nothing more to be said.

RICHARD. And that's all?

RUBASHOV. Yes, that's all! *(Walks off into the shadows)*

RICHARD *(groans).* Christ!

*(Richard, the Pietà, and the Museum vanish, leaving Rubashov alone, pacing his cell. A tap from 402 brings him across*

*to 402's wall. Rubashov taps three times.)*

402 *(becomes visible, tapping).* I've a very important question.

RUBASHOV *(taps).* What?

402 *(taps).* Promise answer?

RUBASHOV *(taps).* Your question?

402 *(taps).* When did you last sleep with a woman?

RUBASHOV *(groans; after a long pause, laughs sardonically).* Now what would you like? *(Taps)* Three weeks ago.

402 *(taps).* Tell me about it.

RUBASHOV. Ach! *(Turns away)*

402 *(taps).* Tell me! Tell me! What were her breasts like?

RUBASHOV *(to the wall).* I suppose I have to humor you. *(He taps)* Snowy, fitting into champagne glasses. *(Murmurs to the wall)* Is that your style?

402 *(taps).* Go on. Details. Her thighs.

RUBASHOV *(taps).* Thighs like wild mares. *(To the wall)* How's that?

402. Good fellow! *(Taps)* Go on! More!

RUBASHOV *(taps).* That's all. You idiot —I'm teasing you.

402 *(taps).* Go on, go on. Details, please.

*(Suddenly the joke goes stale. Rubashov's face clouds as a haunting memory rises to torment him. Soft strains of distant music are heard. His hand brushes his face as if to wipe away the memory.)*

RUBASHOV *(taps).* No more.

402 *(taps).* Go on, please. Please!

RUBASHOV *(to himself).* No more. No more. *(He lies down on his cot, throws his coat over him, brooding. The music rises)*

402 *(taps)* Please! *(On his knees, pleading)* Please! *(Moans and taps)* Please! *(He buries his head in his cot, pleading inaudibly as the lights fade out on him)* *(The lights in Rubashov's cell dim. The music swells to the strains of a piano recording of Beethoven's "Appassionata." As the lights come up, the cell dissolves and becomes Luba Loshenko's bedroom. Rubashov's cot becomes part of a large double bed. At the edge of the bed Luba, clad only in her chemise, sits smoking, dreamily staring into space, listening to the music which is coming from a small gramophone on the table nearby.)*

LUBA. So tomorrow I'll have a new boss.

RUBASHOV. Yes.

LUBA. I'll hate him.

RUBASHOV. No. He'll be all right. *(They listen in silence. He smiles, musing)* This music is dangerous.

LUBA. You'll be gone long?

RUBASHOV. I don't know.

LUBA. I'll miss you terribly *(She hums the melody of the music)*

RUBASHOV *(taking out a cigarette).* Get me a match, will you, Luba?

LUBA *(smiles, rises, walks to the table, picks up some matches, crosses to him, swaying to the music).* I love this. It always makes me feel like crying. *(She lights his cigarette)*

RUBASHOV *(smiling).* Do you enjoy that?

LUBA. Crying? *(She blows out the match, laughs)* Sometimes.

RUBASHOV. Our racial weakness.

LUBA. What?

RUBASHOV. Tears and mysticism.

LUBA. You mean the Slavic soul?

RUBASHOV *(smiling cynically).* The soul? Soul?

LUBA. I believe in it.

RUBASHOV. I know you do.

LUBA. Petty bourgeois?

RUBASHOV. Yes, Luba, you are. *(He looks at her fondly, leans over, pulls her to him, kisses her throat. The music rises)* This music is dangerous. *(They listen in silence a while. She goes to the gramophone and winds it. She leans against the wall near Rubashov)*

LUBA. When I was a little girl in the Pioneer Youth I would start crying at the most unexpected moments.

RUBASHOV. You? In the Pioneer Youth? You, Luba?

LUBA. You're surprised? I wasn't in very long. I wasn't good material. *(Rubashov smiles)* I would cry suddenly for no reason at all.

RUBASHOV. But there was a reason?

LUBA. I don't know. *(She smokes for a moment)* Yes, I do. Our primer books made little Pavelik such a hero. All of us children wanted to turn our mothers and fathers over to the G.P.U. to be shot.

RUBASHOV. Was there anything to turn them in for?

LUBA *(laughs gently).* No. Nothing. But I would picture myself doing it anyway and becoming a great national hero like Pavelik. Then I would burst out crying. I loved my parents very much. Of course no one knew why I was crying. So I was expelled, and my political career ended at the age of nine! *(Rubashov smiles. Luba hums the melody)* My father loved this. He and mother used to play it over and over and over.

RUBASHOV. Where are they now?

LUBA. They died in the famine after the Revolution. My father was a doctor.

RUBASHOV. Have you any family left?

LUBA. One brother. He's a doctor too. He's married. My sister-in-law is very nice. She's a Polish woman . . . an artist. *(Luba picks up a small painting, crosses to Rubashov, kneels at his side)* She painted this picture. It's their baby. A little boy. Two years old. Isn't he fat?

RUBASHOV *(studies it)*. Yes, he is fat. *(He puts it aside, looks at Luba)* Why don't you get married, Luba, and have some fat babies of your own? Isn't there a young man at the office . . . ?

LUBA. Yes.

RUBASHOV. I thought so. And he wants to marry you?

LUBA *(rests her cheek on his knee, lovingly caresses his hand)*. Yes, he does.

RUBASHOV. Well . . . ?

LUBA. No!

RUBASHOV. Why not?

LUBA. I don't love him.

RUBASHOV. Mm, I see, I see. *(A pause)*

LUBA *(suddenly)*. You can do anything you wish with me.

RUBASHOV *(studies her)*. Why did you say that? *(Luba shrugs her shoulders)* You don't reproach me?

LUBA. Oh, no, no, no! Why should I? *(The music swells and fills the room)*

RUBASHOV. This music is dangerous. When you listen to this and you realize human beings can create such beauty, you want to pat them on the head. That's bad. They'll only bite your hand off.

LUBA *(takes his hand, and kisses it)*. Like this?

RUBASHOV *(gently)*. Luba, you know, with us, there can never be anything more.

LUBA. I don't expect anything more. Did I give you the impression I expected anything more?

RUBASHOV. No. You've been very kind, Luba, and sweet. *(Pause)* I may be gone a long time. I may never see you again.

LUBA. Where are you going?

RUBASHOV *(hands her the painting)*. Wherever the Party sends me.

LUBA *(rises)*. I understand. I'm not ask-ing anything. Only, wherever you go, I'll be thinking of you. I'll be with you in my mind always!

RUBASHOV *(snuffs out cigarette)*. But this is exactly what I don't want.

LUBA *(turns toward him)*. You don't?

RUBASHOV. No Luba, no!

LUBA *(quietly)*. Oh! *(She crosses slowly to the gramophone)*

*(Suddenly the phantasmagoria of Luba and the bedroom vanish as the lights are switched on in the cell. The jangle of the key in the lock. The door flies open. A young Guard enters.)*

GUARD. All right! Get up. Come with me.

RUBASHOV. Are you taking me to your Commandant?

GUARD. Don't ask questions! Do as you're told.

RUBASHOV. Very well. *(Rises)* All the posters show our young people smiling. *(He puts on his overcoat)* Have you ever smiled?

GUARD *(humorlessly)*. Yes.

RUBASHOV. Wonderful! When? On what occasion short of an execution?

*(The Guard grimly motions him out. They go. The light is switched off in his cell, as the lights come up on the prison tier.)*

402 *(crosses to 302's wall and taps)*. They've taken him up.

302 *(taps)*. So soon?

402 *(taps)*. Pass it on.

302 *(taps)*. They've taken Rubashov up. Pass it on.

202 *(taps)*. I hope they give him a bad time.

302 *(taps)*. Oh, no! He was a friend of the people.

202 *(taps)*. Yes. *(His eyes bulge wildly as he addresses an imaginary group about him)* They're all friends of the people. Didn't they free us? Look at us. Free as birds! Everything's all right, Comrades. The land belongs to us! But, the bread belongs to them. The rivers are ours! But the fish are theirs. The forests are ours, but not the wood! That's for them. Everything's for them. *(He crosses taps)* They've taken Rubashov up! Pass it on!

*(The taps echo and re-echo throughout the prison: "Rubashov taken up," "Rubashov taken up." The lights dim and the prisoners in the honeycomb of cells vanish behind the scrim, leaving only a*

*huge pillar of granite and iron shrouded in shadows. The lights come up on an office in the prison. A barred window reveals dawn, and snow falling, outside. The bayonet of a guard cuts back and forth across the window like a metronome. On the wall, over the desk, is a portrait of The Leader seen vaguely in shadow. The rest of the wall is empty except for faded patches where other pictures have been hung and removed. Seated at the desk, smoking a long Kremlin cigarette, is a middle-aged man in officer's uniform. He is rough, heavy-set, jowly, graying at the temples, a face once handsome, now dissipated and cynical. He is grimly examining some papers, carelessly dribbling cigarette ashes over his jacket. There is a knock at the door. The officer, Ivanoff, calls out, "Come in." The Guard enters with Rubashov.)*

IVANOFF *(gruffly, to the Guard)*. Shut the door. *(Exit the Guard. Ivanoff rises, shakes his head at Rubashov, laughs; then familiarly)*. Kolya!

RUBASHOV. Well . . . !

IVANOFF. Surprised?

RUBASHOV. Nothing surprises me any more. *(Ivanoff laughs, opens a drawer, takes out a box of cigarettes, limps across the room to him)* Are you the Commandant here?

IVANOFF *(shaking his head)*. I'm your investigator.

RUBASHOV. That makes it difficult.

IVANOFF. Not at all. Not if we're intelligent . . . which we are. *(Offers him the box of cigarettes)* Cigarette? *(Rubashov pauses)*

RUBASHOV. Have hostilities begun yet?

IVANOFF. Why?

RUBASHOV. You know the etiquette.

IVANOFF. Take one! *(Forces the box into his hand)* Put them in your pocket, keep them.

RUBASHOV. All right. *(He takes a cigarette, and puts the box in his pocket)* We'll call this an unofficial prelude.

IVANOFF. Why so aggressive?

RUBASHOV. Did I arrest you? Or did you people arrest me?

IVANOFF. You people? *(Shakes his head, lights his own cigarette)* What's happened to you, Kolya? What a falling off is here! *(Sighs)* Ekh! Ekh!

RUBASHOV. Why have I been arrested?

IVANOFF *(gives Rubashov a match, geni-*ally*)*. Later. Sit down. Light your cigarette. Relax. *(He limps to the door, closes the judas-hole, and locks it. Rubashov sits down)* I saw you last three years ago.

RUBASHOV *(smoking his cigarette with relish)*. Where?

IVANOFF. Moscow. *(As he talks he crosses up to the window and pulls the chain, letting down the iron shutters)* You were speaking. You'd just escaped from the German prison. They gave you a bad time, didn't they? They didn't dull your edge, though. *(Crosses back to Rubashov)* Good speech, plenty of bite. I was proud of my old General.

RUBASHOV. Why didn't you come back stage?

IVANOFF. You were surrounded by all the big wigs.

RUBASHOV *(dryly)*. Mm, a fine assortment of opportunists, bureaucrats, and variegated pimps. *(Ivanoff grins, shakes his head, hobbles to his desk. Rubashov points to his leg)* Your leg's very good. I hadn't even noticed.

IVANOFF *(nods, smiles, sits on the desk, tapping his legs)*. Automatic joints, rustless chromium plating. I can swim, ride, drive a car, dance, make love. You see how right you were? And how stupid I was.

RUBASHOV. You were young and emotional, that's all. Tell me, Sascha, does the amputated foot still itch?

IVANOFF *(laughs)*. The big toe. In rainy weather.

RUBASHOV *(smoking)*. Curious.

IVANOFF *(lowers his lids, squints at Rubashov, blows a smoke ring)*. Not at all. Doesn't your recent amputation itch?

RUBASHOV. Mine?

IVANOFF *(calmly, blowing smoke rings)*. When did you cut yourself off from the Party? How long have you been a member of the organized opposition?

RUBASHOV *(throws his cigarette away, grinds it out under his foot)*. The unofficial part is over.

IVANOFF *(rises, stands over him)*. Don't be so aggressive, Nicolai!

RUBASHOV *(takes off his glasses, rubs his eyes)*. I'm tired, and I'm sick and I don't care to play any games with you. Why have I been arrested?

IVANOFF *(cynically, crossing back to his desk-chair)*. Supposing you tell me why.

RUBASHOV *(bounds to his feet, furious)*.

Stop this nonsense now! Who do you think you're dealing with? What are the charges against me?

IVANOFF (*shrugs his shoulders, leans back in his chair*). What difference does that make?

RUBASHOV. I demand that you either read the charges—or dismiss me at once!

IVANOFF (*blows a smoke ring*). Let's be sensible, shall we? Legal subtleties are all right for others, but for the likes of you and myself? (*He taps his cigarette ash off into the tray*) Why put on an act? When did you ever trouble about formal charges? At Kronstadt? (*He rises, confronts Rubashov*) After all—remember—I served under you. I know you.

RUBASHOV. No man fights a war without guilt. You don't win battles with rose water and silk gloves.

IVANOFF. Not our kind of battles, no!

RUBASHOV (*heatedly*). A bloodless revolution is a contradiction in terms. Illegality and violence are like dynamite in the hands of a true revolutionary—weapons of the class struggle.

IVANOFF. Agreed.

RUBASHOV. But, you people have used the weapons of the Revolution to strangulate the Revolution! You've turned the Terror *against* the people. You've begun the blood bath of the Thermidor. (*He controls himself, speaks quietly*) And that's something quite different, my onetime friend and comrade. (*Sits*)

IVANOFF. Damn it, Kolya. I'd hate to see you shot.

RUBASHOV (*polishing his glasses, smiles sarcastically*). Very touching of you. And exactly why do you people wish to shoot me?

IVANOFF (*flares up*). "You people!" Again. What the hell's happened to you? It used to be "we."

RUBASHOV (*on his feet again*). Yes, it used to be. But who is the "we" today? (*He points to the picture on the wall*) The Boss? The Iron Man and his machine? Who is the "we"? Tell me.

IVANOFF. The people, the masses . . .

RUBASHOV. Leave the masses out. You don't understand them any more. Probably I don't either. Once we worked with them. We knew them. We made history with them. We were part of them. For one little minute we started them on what promised to be a new run of dignity for man. But that's gone! Dead! And buried. There they are. (*He indicates the faded patches of wallpaper*) Faded patches on the wall. The old guard. Our old comrades. Where are they? Slaughtered! Your pock-marked leader has picked us off one by one till no one's left except a few broken-down men like myself, and a few careerist prostitutes like you!

IVANOFF. And when did you arrive at this morbid conclusion?

RUBASHOV. I didn't arrive at it. It was thrust on me.

IVANOFF. When? On what occasion would you say?

RUBASHOV. On the occasion when I came back from the Nazi slaughter house, when I looked about for my old friends, when all I could find of them were those (*Again he waves his spectacles at the telltale patches*) faded patches on every wall in every house in the land.

IVANOFF (*nods his head, murmurs reasonably*). Mm, hm! I see. That's logical. And that, of course, was when you . . . (*The telephone rings. Ivanoff picks up the receiver, barks*) I'm busy . . . (*And hangs up*) When you joined the organized opposition . . .

RUBASHOV (*slowly, deliberately*). You know as well as I do, I never joined the organized opposition.

IVANOFF. Kolya! Please! We both grew up in the tradition.

RUBASHOV (*sharply*). I never joined the opposition.

IVANOFF. Why not? You mean you sat by with your arms folded? You thought we were leading the Revolution to destruction and you did nothing? (*Shakes his head*)

RUBASHOV. Perhaps I was too old and used up.

IVANOFF (*sits back again, clucks with good-natured disbelief*). Ekh, ekh, ekh!

RUBASHOV (*shrugging his shoulders*). Believe what you will.

IVANOFF. In any event, we have all the proofs.

RUBASHOV. Proofs of what? Sabotage?

IVANOFF. That, of course.

RUBASHOV. Of course.

IVANOFF. If that were all.

RUBASHOV. There's more?

IVANOFF (*nods*). And worse. (*Rises*) Attempted murder.

RUBASHOV. Ah! And who am I supposed to have attempted to murder?

IVANOFF. Not personally. You instigated the act. Naturally.

RUBASHOV. Naturally.

IVANOFF. I told you we have proofs. *(Picks up a sheaf of typewritten pages and waves them under his nose)*

RUBASHOV. For instance?

IVANOFF. Confessions.

RUBASHOF. Whose?

IVANOFF. For one, the man who was to do the killing.

RUBASHOV. Congratulations. And who was it I instigated to murder whom?

IVANOFF. Indiscreet question.

RUBASHOV. May I read the confession? *(Rubashov reaches out for the papers. Ivanoff smiles, draws them out of his reach)* May I be confronted with the man? *(Ivanoff smiles again, shakes his head)* Who the hell would I want to murder?

IVANOFF. You've been sitting there for ten minutes telling me. *(He opens a drawer, drops in the sheaf of papers)* The man you tried to murder is the Leader. *(He slams the drawer shut)* Our Leader.

RUBASHOV *(takes off his glasses, leans forward, speaks deliberately, between his teeth)*. Do you really believe this nonsense? *(He studies Ivanoff)* Or are you only pretending to be an idiot? *(He suddenly laughs knowingly)* You don't believe it.

IVANOFF *(sits slowly, adjusting his prosthetic leg)*. Put yourself in my place. Our positions could very easily be reversed. Ask yourself that question—and you have the answer. *(Ivanoff rubs his thigh at the amputation line, stares moodily at the false leg)* I was always so proud of my body. Then to wake, to find a stump in a wire cage. I can smell that hospital room. I can see it as if it were happening now: you sitting there by my bed, soothing, reasoning, scolding, and I crying because they had just amputated my leg. *(He turns to Rubashov)* Remember how I begged you to lend me your pistol? Remember how you argued with me for three hours, till you persuaded me that suicide was petty bourgeois romanticism? *(He rises, his voice suddenly harsh)* Today the positions are reversed. Now it's you who want to throw yourself into the

abyss. Well, I'm not going to let you. Then we'll be quits.

RUBASHOV *(putting on his glasses, studies Ivanoff for a second, with an ironic smile)*. You want to save me? You've a damned curious way of doing it. I am unimpressed by your bogus sentimentality. You've already tricked me into talking my head off my shoulders. Let it go at that!

IVANOFF *(beams)*. I had to make you explode now, or you'd have exploded at the wrong time. Haven't you even noticed? *(Gestures about the room)* No stenographer! *(He crosses back to his desk, opens a drawer)* You're behaving like an infant. A romantic infant. Now you know what we're going to do? *(Extracts a dossier out of the drawer)*

RUBASHOV *(grimly)*. No, what are we going to do?

IVANOFF. We are going to concoct a nice little confession.

RUBASHOV. Ah!

IVANOFF. For the public trial.

RUBASHOV *(nods his head in amused comprehension)*. So that's it? There's to be a public trial? And I'm to make a nice little confession?

IVANOFF. Let me finish . . .

RUBASHOV *(biting out each word)*. That is to say, I'm to transform myself into a grinning chimpanzee in a zoo? I'm to beat my breast and spit at myself in a mirror, so the People can laugh and say, "The Old Guard—how ridiculous!" I'm to pick at my own excrement and put it in my own mouth, so the People can say, "The Old Guard—how disgusting!" No, Sascha, no! You've got the wrong man.

IVANOFF *(drawling with exaggerated patience)*. Let me finish. *(The patience vanishes. He shouts at Rubashov)* Which are we to save? Your dignity or your head? *(He controls his impatience, begins to talk rapidly, thinking out the plan in his own mind, as he paces to and fro)* You make this confession now. You admit developing a deviation. You joined such and such an opposition bloc. You give us their names. (They've all been shot by now, anyway, so nothing's lost.) However, when you learned of their terroristic plans, you were shocked. You broke off with them. You see?

RUBASHOV. Yes, I see.

IVANOFF. Your case then goes to public

trial. We refute the murder charge completely. Even so, you'll get twenty years. But in two, perhaps three years, a reprieve. In five years you'll be back in the ring again. And that is all that matters. *(He stops and nods cheerfully at Rubashov)*

RUBASHOV. No, I'm sorry.

IVANOFF *(his smile fades, he lights a fresh cigarette, speaks slowly, dryly).* Then your case will be taken out of my hands. You'll be tried in secret session administratively. You know what that means?

RUBASHOV. Yes. The rubber ball in my mouth, the bullet in the back of the neck.

IVANOFF *(shakes out the match, blows a perfect smoke ring, and smiles).* The methods follow logically. You just disappear into thin air. As far as your followers are concerned, no demonstrations. How can they? Perhaps you're off on a mission? Perhaps you've run away? Hidden somewhere? Suspicious, of course. But what does that matter? N. S. Rubashov has vanished. Pf! Quietly! Forever! That's your alternative. *(The phone rings. Ivanoff picks up the receiver)* Look here, I'm . . . What? Oh! Yes? Yes. I see. I'll investigate at once. *(He hangs up, turns to Rubashov, chuckles, and nods his head)* You fox! Oh, you old fox! *(He picks up the phone, presses a button. An answering voice responds)* Gletkin? Ivanoff. Come to my office at once! The Rubashov arrest. You bungled it, that's what. Yes. At once! *(He hangs up. Turns again to Rubashov)* Very adroit.

RUBASHOV. Really? What have I done now?

IVANOFF. You've no idea?

RUBASHOV. I have a small notion. Nuisance tactics! Of no real importance. You overestimate them.

*(Gletkin enters; crosses above the desk, salutes stiffly. Ivanoff returns the salute.)*

IVANOFF. I have just received a phone call from the prosecutor's office. Your men were instructed to arrest Citizen Rubashov as quietly as possible. What the hell went wrong?

GLETKIN. I'm interrogating the arresting officers now. The prisoner refused them entrance and barricaded his door against them.

IVANOFF. So they shot off the lock?

RUBASHOV *(with mock indignation).* Woke up the whole neighborhood.

GLETKIN *(not glancing at him).* There was no alternative.

RUBASHOV *(over his shoulder to Gletkin).* There were five alternatives. You need some lessons in elementary tactics. *(Stung, Gletkin turns toward Rubashov.)*

IVANOFF *(quickly, commanding).* Go on!

GLETKIN. Then he refused to accompany them on his feet. They were forced to pick him up and carry him out bodily, screaming like a woman.

RUBASHOV. Wrong! Roaring like a bear. A wounded bear. And they tore my pants. *(Gletkin stands there, straight as a ramrod, his eyes expressionless, in perfect control now.)*

IVANOFF. Your instructions were to treat him with care. You will see that the prisoner gets cigarettes and medical attention.

RUBASHOV. Not unless you furnish an outside physician. I know these prison doctors.

GLETKIN. That is against regulations.

IVANOFF *(to Rubashov).* We'll see what can be done. *(To Gletkin)* Wait outside. *(Exit Gletkin)* You'll be given every consideration. Pencil and paper, if you wish . . .

RUBASHOV. Many thanks, but it won't work. I've had my bellyful of this farce. *(He rises)* Kindly have me taken to my cell.

IVANOFF. As you like. *(He picks up the phone, presses a button, and barks)* Guard! *(He hangs up)* I didn't expect you to confess at once. Take your time. You have plenty of time. Think it over. When you are ready to confess, send me a note. *(The men stare at each other. Ivanoff smiles)* You will. I'm sure you will.

RUBASHOV. Never, Sascha. That's final! *(The door is opened. The Guard enters.)*

IVANOFF. The next decade will decide the fate of the world in our era. Don't you want to be here to see it? *(Rubashov glances at Ivanoff, then turns and goes off with the Guard)*

*(As soon as Rubashov leaves, Ivanoff drops his monumental calm, rises and calls out irritably, "Gletkin!" As Gletkin enters, Ivanoff speaks quickly and harshly, hobbling up and down nervously.)*

IVANOFF. By now all Moscow knows. Make a full report. Send the arresting officers over to Headquarters. *(Indicates the chair)* Sit down. *(Gletkin sits)* Now, look here! I want it clearly understood. This is no ordinary prisoner. We can't afford any more bungling. When you handle this man you dance on eggs! The political and historical importance of these trials is enormous. And N. S. Rubashov is the key figure. We must have his confession. Those are our orders. From the top.

GLETKIN. Then why not turn him over to me? I'll bring you his confession in three days.

IVANOFF. Thanks! And you'll carry N. S. Rubashov to the witness stand in pieces? Wonderful. No, your harsh methods won't work here. Not with this man. *(Lights a fresh cigarette, calms down)* He'll confess. There's enough of the old Bolshevik left in him. He'll confess. You're to leave him in peace. I don't want him disturbed. He's to have paper, pencils, cigarettes, extra rations . . .

GLETKIN. Why?

IVANOFF. To accelerate the processes of thought. He has to work this out alone. *(Taps his head)* In here.

GLETKIN. This approach, in my opinion, is all wrong.

IVANOFF *(looks at Gletkin with veiled amusement)*. You don't like him? You had a little trouble with him a few minutes ago, didn't you?

GLETKIN. That has nothing to do with it.

IVANOFF. Old Rubashov can still spit a sword! What'd he do? Cut you up the middle?

GLETKIN *(coldly)*. His personality has nothing to do with it. I hope I'm a better Party member than that. I never allow likes or dislikes to interfere with my judgment.

IVANOFF. Very commendable.

GLETKIN. Only, since this confession is so important to the Party, I consider your method wrong. This won't get you results. I know how to handle these old-timers. They're all rotten at the core. They're all infected with the Western leprosy. If you want a confession, turn him over to me.

IVANOFF. You young people amuse me. You know everything, don't you? The Nazis captured this man, broke his leg, smashed his jaw, killed him and brought him to life again—I don't know how many times—but they couldn't extract one admission out of him. And finally, he escaped. And you're going to break him for

me in three days? *(Musing)* No! If he confesses it won't be out of cowardice. *(To Gletkin)* Your methods won't work with him. He's made out of a material, the more you hammer it, the tougher it gets.

GLETKIN. I don't agree. My experience with these old counter-revolutionaries proves otherwise. The human nervous system at best can only stand so much—and when they have these bourgeois flaws in them, a little pressure—in the right places —and they split like rotten logs.

IVANOFF *(laughs softly, shakes his head)*. I'd hate to fall into your hands.

GLETKIN. It's my experience that every human nervous system has a breaking point under pain. It's only necessary to find the lever, the special pain . . .

IVANOFF *(abruptly and harshly)*. That'll do!

GLETKIN *(rises stiffly)*. You asked me.

IVANOFF *(pause)*. Comrade Gletkin, in the early days . . . *(He goes to his desk, opens a drawer, takes out a bottle and several glasses. He fills the glasses, pushes one over to Gletkin)* . . . before you were born, we started the Revolution with the illusion that some day we were going to abolish prisons and substitute flower gardens. Ekh, ekh! Maybe, some day. *(He tosses off his drink)*

GLETKIN. Why are you all so cynical?

IVANOFF. Cynical? *(Turns and surveys him)* Please explain that remark!

GLETKIN. I'd rather not, if you don't mind.

IVANOFF. I do mind. Explain it.

GLETKIN *(picks up the glass, drains it)*. I notice you older men always talk as if only the past were glorious . . . or some distant future. But we're already far ahead of any other country, here and now! As for the past, we have to crush it. The quicker, the better.

IVANOFF. I see. *(He sits, shaking his head, amused)* In your eyes, then, I am the cynic?

GLETKIN. Yes, I think so. *(He crosses to the table, sets down the glass, abruptly)*

IVANOFF. Well, that may be. As for Rubashov, my instructions remain. He's to be left alone, and he will become his own torturer.

GLETKIN. I don't agree.

IVANOFF. He'll confess. *(He catches the expression in Gletkin's face, then sharply)*

You're to leave him alone! That's an order.

GLETKIN. As you command. *(Clicks his heels, jerks to attention, wheels about and marches out as if on parade. Ivanoff curls his lip in disgust, pours himself a stiff drink, sighs heavily, and drinks . . . as the scene fades out)*

*(The lights come up on all the cells. Rubashov is seated on his cot, smoking, wrapped in thought. The other prisoners are passing communications down the grapevine.)*

202 *(taps)*. All the prisoners ask Rubashov not to confess. Die in silence.

302 *(taps)*. Prisoners ask Rubashov not to confess. Die in silence.

*(402 crosses to Rubashov's wall and signals. Rubashov raises his head, pauses, slowly rises, glances at the judas-hole, then crosses to the wall, responds to the signal.)*

402 *(taps)*. Prisoners ask you not to give in. Don't let them make you go on trial.

RUBASHOV *(pause, then taps)*. How was 302 tortured?

402 *(taps)*. Steam.

*(Rubashov, grimly, puffs at his lit cigarette, till it glows, blows off the ashes, presses the live coal into the back of his hand, and holds it there without flinching, staring stoically at the blue wisps of smoke that curl up from his burning flesh. Finally, he grinds out the cigarette, tosses it away.)*

402 *(taps again)*. You'll die in silence? You'll die in silence?

RUBASHOV *(taps wearily)*. I will. Tell them. I will.

402 *(taps)*. My respects. You're a man! *(He crosses, taps on 302's wall)* Rubashov will die in silence. Pass it on.

302 *(taps)*. Rubashov will die in silence. Pass it on.

*(The news is tapped through the prison and a murmur like a wind rises and falls: "Rubashov will die in silence . . . Rubashov will die in silence . . ." The lights fade, and the prisoners in the tier vanish.)*

*(Rubashov, staring at the scorched hand, crosses to his cot, sits, nods his head, and murmurs: As chimney sweepers come to dust . . . to dust . . . to dust . . . The lights fade on him.)*

**CURTAIN**

## ACT TWO

SCENE: *Rubashov's cell, five weeks later.*

AT RISE: *Darkness. Bars of light from the judas-hole illumine Rubashov's feverish face. His eyes are closed; he is dreaming evil dreams. He breathes heavily, moaning and tossing about fitfully on his cot. Ghostly images hover over and around him; ghostly voices whisper hollowly: "Rubashov! Rubashov!" Echoes of the past—Richard's voice calling: "Christ crowned with thorns!", Luba's voice, rich and low, "You can do anything you want with me." The nameless ones appear and disappear, whispering, "Rubashov, Rubashov."*

*Rubashov, dreaming, raises his head, his eyes shut, and cries out:* Death is no mystery to us. There's nothing exalted about it. It's the logical solution to political divergencies. *His head falls back again, turning from side to side, moaning.*

*The lights come up in the corridor. A sound of heels on a stone floor. Gletkin enters from a door right, coming up from the execution cellar; he is followed by a young fellow officer. They move toward Rubashov's cell, talking inaudibly. Ivanoff enters through the gate, glimpses them, stops short, then calls out sharply: "Gletkin!" Gletkin halts, turns to face Ivanoff.*

IVANOFF *(hobbles down to Gletkin, scrutinizing him suspiciously)*. What are you up to?

GLETKIN *(very correct)*. I don't understand you, Comrade.

IVANOFF. No. I'm sure you don't. Have you been at my prisoner?

GLETKIN. Been at him?

IVANOFF *(irritably)*. Laid your hands on him. You understand that, don't you?

GLETKIN. I haven't seen Citizen Rubashov for five weeks. However, I am informed, in the line of duty, his fever is worse. I suggest it would be advisable I bring him to the prison doctor.

IVANOFF *(blows a smoke ring, then slowly, measuring his words)*. Keep away from him. And keep that prison doctor away from him. *(Sharply)* My orders still stand.

GLETKIN. Very well, Comrade. They'll be obeyed.

*(Ivanoff snorts, blows smoke into his face*

*then turns and limps off. They watch him
go. The Young Officer turns to Gletkin
who has taken out his note-book and is
writing in it.)*

YOUNG OFFICER. Comrade Ivanoff's
nerves are wearing thin.

GLETKIN. I'm afraid this prisoner is
proving stubborn. I told them when they
brought him in that I could break him.

YOUNG OFFICER. Easily.

GLETKIN. Comrade Ivanoff wants to use
psychological methods only.

YOUNG OFFICER *(scornfully)*. These old
bookworms of the Revolution!

GLETKIN. Tonight I'm using psychological methods. *(Closes his note-book,
puts it away)* I'll break this prisoner.

YOUNG OFFICER. Against orders?

GLETKIN. No. I won't so much as go
near his cell. But *(Glances at his watch)*
inside an hour he'll be ready to confess.

YOUNG OFFICER. How?

GLETKIN *(enigmatically)*. It'll be very
interesting.

*(Rubashov wakes, sits up with a sudden
start, listening. The lights in the tier of
cells come up.)*

*(402 sits up abruptly, wakening suddenly,
also listens, frozen. 302 and 202 also
awaken—suddenly and listen to the
ominous stillness. The lights fade on Gletkin and the Young Officer.)*

*(The prisoners rise, one by one, and be-
gin to pace nervously to and fro like
caged animals. Once in a while one of
them will pause, listen, and then continue
to pace. Rubashov rises, wipes the perspiration from his face with the sleeve of
his coat, listens, then crosses to 402's wall,
taps, waits, and 402 responds.)*

RUBASHOV *(taps)*. Did I wake you?

402 *(taps)*. No.

RUBASHOV *(taps)*. Something's happening . . .

402 *(taps)*. You feel it too?

RUBASHOV *(taps)*. What?

402 *(taps)*. Don't know. Something.
How's your fever?

RUBASHOV *(taps)*. Not good.

402 *(taps)*. Try to sleep. *(Overhead
302 taps signal)* Wait! *(Crosses over to
302's segment of wall, and answers the
signal)*

302 *(taps)*. Who is Bogrov?

402 *(taps)*. Don't know. *(Returns, taps)*
Who is Bogrov?

RUBASHOV *(taps)*. Mischa Bogrov?

402 *(taps)*. No first name.

RUBASHOV *(taps)*. I know a Mischa Bogrov. Why?

402 *(taps)*. Name tapped through.

RUBASHOV *(taps)*. He arrested?

402 *(taps)*. Don't know. Name Bogrov.
That is all.

RUBASHOV *(taps)*. What connection?

402 *(taps)*. Don't know.

RUBASHOV *(to himself)*. Curious.

*(The lights fade on the other prisoners as
they start to pace nervously. Rubashov,
alone, thinking, smiles, murmurs: Mischa.
He sits on his cot, shaking his head.
Mischa!)*

*(A chorus of men singing is faintly heard.
It grows louder. The bronze of a flickering campfire. Russian soldiers and marines
of the Revolution, in conglomerate uni-
forms, half-military, half-civilian, laden
with assorted weapons, dangling stick
grenades and daggers, are gathered around
the fire, smoking, warming their hands,
singing. General Rubashov, his face shining with reflected firelight, shakes his
head and beats out the tune as a big, snub-
nosed, sandy-haired marine with thick
shoulders and an enchanting smile, sings
out in a mellow, ringing voice:*

"In the dawn's light, faintly gleaming
Stand the ancient Kremlin walls;
And the land, no longer dreaming,
Now awakes as morning calls.
Though the winds are coldly blowing,
Streets begin to hum with noise;
And the sun with splendor glowing
Greets the land with all its joys.
We'll shout aloud for we are proud;
Our power is invincible.
We'll ne'er disband, we'll always stand
Together for dear Moscow's land."

*The marine punctuates the finish by toss-
ing his hat in the air. The others applaud
and shout: "Bravo Mischa! Bravo Mischa
Bogrov!")*

MISCHA *(laughs, crosses to Rubashov, un-
hooks from his belt a curved, elaborately
chased, silver-handled dagger)*. Kolya . . .

RUBASHOV. Yes, Mischa?

BOGROV *(presenting the dagger to him)*.
Here, I want you to have this. To remember me.

RUBASHOV *(laughs)*. You may need it,
yourself.

BOGROV *(shakes his head, grins. There is
something of the good-natured, ingenuous
child in this big man)*. No. The Civil

War is over. No more killing. Now we go home. We build a new life. *(He extends the gift again)* Please, take it.

RUBASHOV *(accepts it)*. All right, Mischa. Thank you. Now, I have something for you. Can you guess?

BOGROV *(thinks hard, frowning, then his eyes open wide)*. Kolya, is it . . . Am I . . . They're . . . ?

RUBASHOV *(beaming, nods)*. Tomorrow you'll be a member of the Party.

BOGROV *(overcome with joy)*. Me? Me? Mischa Bogrov a member of the Party!

RUBASHOV. You've earned it. You fought well for the Revolution.

BOGROV. I'm ignorant, Kolya; I'm just a stupid peasant and I don't know enough yet—but I'd die for the Revolution.

RUBASHOV. We know that. Now you must learn the meaning of it. You must go to school. You must study, Mischa.

BOGROV. I will, I will. You'll see, you'll be very proud of me. Wherever I am, every year on this day, I'll send you a letter and I'll sign it. "Your Comrade, Faithful to the Grave." *(The soldiers call for more song. "Come on, Mischa. More!")* For you, I sing this just for you, Kolya.

BOGROV *(sings in a rich voice the chorus of "Red Moscow")*.
"We'll shout aloud for we are proud,
Our power is invincible.
We'll ne'er disband, we'll always stand
Together for dear Moscow's land."
*(Gradually Bogrov and the campfire and the men singing with him fade away as do their voices, leaving Rubashov alone in his dank, silent, gray cell, nodding and humming the tune quietly to himself. Lights come up on 402 who is tapping on Rubashov's wall. Rubashov crosses to the wall, responds.)*

402 *(taps)*. What day?

RUBASHOV *(taps)*. Lost track.

402 *(taps)*. What you doing?

RUBASHOV *(taps)*. Dreaming.

402 *(taps)*. Sleeping?

RUBASHOV *(taps)*. Waking.

402 *(taps)*. Bad. What dreams?

RUBASHOV *(taps)*. My life.

402 *(taps)*. You won't confess?

RUBASHOV *(taps)*. I told you no.

402 *(taps)*. Die in silence is best. *(Pause)*

RUBASHOV *(to himself, sardonically)*. Yes. Die in silence! Fade into darkness!

Easily said. Die in silence! Vanish without a word! Easily said.

402 *(taps)*. Walking?

RUBASHOV *(taps)*. Yes.

402 *(taps)*. Careful of blisters. Walking dreams bad for feet. I walked twelve hours in cell once. Wore out shoes. *(He laughs hoarsely)* Didn't mind. *(He licks his lips, rolls his eyes, and moans voluptuously)* Mm! I was dreaming women. Ah-h-h! Question: When is woman best? Answer: After hot bath, well soaped all over, slippery. Ha! Ha! *(His laughter is tinctured with agony and madness)* Ha! Ha! *(He stops, listens. The want of a response from Rubashov makes him suddenly angry)* What's matter? You didn't laugh. Joke!

RUBASHOV *(shrugs his shoulders, taps)*. Ha! Ha!

402 *(bursts into laughter again, taps)*. Ha! Ha! Funny, ha!

RUBASHOV *(taps)*. Funny.

402 *(taps)*. How many women you love? *(Pause)* How many?

RUBASHOV *(taps)*. None.

402 *(taps)*. Why not?

RUBASHOV *(taps)*. My work. No time.

402 *(taps)*. You and Revolution. Some love affair! Don't you fellows have sex?

RUBASHOV *(taps)*. Oh, yes.

402 *(taps)*. What you use it for? Write in snow? Ha! Ha! *(He doubles up with laughter, plucking at the lean flesh on his arms and thighs)* Good joke?

RUBASHOV *(taps)*. Not good.

402 *(soured, taps)*. No sense humor No wonder. Your women are half men! Your women have moustaches. You killed the beauty of our women. Son of bitch, son of bitch, son of bitch!

RUBASHOV *(dryly, taps)*. Repeating yourself.

402 *(taps)*. Confess. Never in love? Once?

RUBASHOV *(taps)* No. Never. *(He sighs heavily, frowns, thinking. 402 vanishes)*
*(A gray-haired man, Hrutsch, materializes, sighing heavily and clutching his breast over the heart.)*

HRUTSCH *(laughs timidly)*. It's nothing. My heart skips about a bit.
*(The cell fades away. Hrutsch is standing at the desk in the office of the Commissariat of the Iron Works. The vista outside the window reveals the new-com-*

*pleted factory buildings. Hrutsch is obviously frightened and nervous.)*

HRUTSCH *(squeezes his speech out in short spasmodic gasps).* Yes, the files are ready for you, and of course you'll want to see the charts. *(He turns to the darkness. Luba Loshenko materializes, standing there with the charts in her hand, staring at Rubashov with large luminous eyes and parted lips. She hands the charts to Hrutsch, but her eyes never leave Rubashov)* Ah, here we are. Now, anything you want explained, our secretary here knows them backwards. *(He observes them staring at each other)* You remember Comrade Loshenko? *(Hands the charts to Rubashov)*

RUBASHOV *(leaning heavily on a cane, steps forward. He walks with a slight limp).* Yes. How have you been, Comrade Loshenko?

LUBA. Very well, thank you, Comrade Rubashov. Welcome back home.

HRUTSCH. Many changes since you've been gone. The factories are completed.

RUBASHOV *(depositing the charts on the desk).* You haven't filled your quota. Iron is off 23 per cent, steel 38 per cent.

HRUTSCH. Yes, yes, the sabotage is a problem. *(He sighs, clutches his heart. He laughs apologetically, indicating his heart)* Every once in a while it just starts hammering . . . I should complain—look at him. The stories you could tell, Comrade Rubashov? Those Nazis! What they did to you! And he escapes, comes home, and right to work. Wonderful spirit. Wonderful. What an example to us! *(He laughs feebly, pants, holding his heart)* Of course, as for us filling the new quota, mechanically it can't be. It's physically . . .

RUBASHOV *(coldly, impersonal).* Those are the orders.

HRUTSCH *(again the fear rises; he essays a feeble smile).* Well, if those are the orders, it will just have to be done, won't it?

RUBASHOV. Yes. I'll send for you. *(He dismisses him. Hrutsch goes quickly. Rubashov turns. He looks at Luba in silence, smiles)*

LUBA. I wondered if I'd ever see you again.

RUBASHOV. It was a question whether anyone would.

LUBA. I know. My prayers were answered. I prayed for you.

RUBASHOV. To which god?

LUBA. I did. I prayed.

RUBASHOV. The same little bourgeoise, Luba. Are you married yet?

LUBA. No.

RUBASHOV. Why not? *(Luba shrugs her shoulders)* Any babies?

LUBA. No. *(Luba laughs)* You've no idea of the excitement here when we read that you were alive and home. We saw a picture of you when you arrived at Moscow, and our Leader had his arm around you. I was so proud. *(There is an embarrassed pause)*

RUBASHOV *(glances at the charts).* Hrutsch is in trouble.

LUBA. Poor man, it's not his fault.

RUBASHOV. Whose fault is it?

LUBA. No one's. The men are overworked, and . . . *(She stops herself abruptly)*

RUBASHOV. Go on.

LUBA *(shakes her head).* That's all. Who am I to tell you?

RUBASHOV. Go on! Go on!

LUBA *(a sudden outpouring).* They're frightened. Last week more than forty workers were taken away by the G.P.U.

RUBASHOV. Well, we have to have discipline. Socialism isn't going to drop down on us from your nice neat heaven.

LUBA. Yes, but the machines don't know that. The machines break down, too.

RUBASHOV. Why?

LUBA. The same reason. They're overworked.

RUBASHOV *(sighs).* Problems. *(He puts the charts away, turns to her)* Tell me about yourself. Any lovers?

LUBA *(seriously).* No.

RUBASHOV *(teasing her).* No? Why not? Put on those old earrings and find yourself a lover.

LUBA. I thought you were dead and I didn't want to go on living. I found that out. I wouldn't want to live in a world without knowing you were somewhere in it.

RUBASHOV. Come here. *(Luba goes to him. He puts his arms around her and kisses her)*

LUBA *(begins to tremble and cry).* I thought you were dead. I thought the Nazis had killed you.

RUBASHOV *(burying his face in her hair).* I'm hard to kill.

LUBA. But they hurt you so. Your poor legs—they broke them?

RUBASHOV. The pieces grow together.

LUBA. Was it awful?

RUBASHOV. I forget. *(Holds her at arm's length, studies her face)* It's good to see you again, Luba.

LUBA. Do you mean that?

RUBASHOV *(impersonally)*. Yes. *(He turns from her, picks up the charts)* I have some dictation. Get your pad and pencil. And call in Hrutsch. I'm afraid we're going to have to get rid of that milksop. *(Crossing away from her into the shadows)*

LUBA *(very quietly)*. Yes, Comrade Commissar.

*(The memory scene fades. Rubashov, alone, leaning against the stone wall, sighs heavily. Three taps are heard. He responds.)*

402 *(appears, taps)*. Sad!

RUBASHOV *(taps)*. What?

402 *(taps)*. You! Never in love. To die without ever being in love. Sad!

*(A chill seizes Rubashov; he groans, puts his hand to his swollen cheek, and shivers.)*

RUBASHOV *(taps)*. Good night.

402 *(taps)*. What's wrong?

RUBASHOV *(taps)*. My fever's back.

402 *(taps)*. Again? Maybe you should try the prison doctor?

RUBASHOV *(taps)*. No, thanks.

402 *(taps)*. Don't blame you. A butcher!

*(They both turn from the wall, pace a few steps, and simultaneously freeze, listening, listening as if the silence itself contained some unheard and unholy sound.)*

RUBASHOV *(crosses to 402, taps)*. What's that?

402 *(taps)*. You felt it again?

RUBASHOV *(taps)*. In the air . . .

402 *(taps)*. Yes . . . *(The lights fade on 402)*

*(Rubashov wipes his feverish brow with the back of his sleeve and slowly paces to and fro; to himself:* What if the Leader is right? In spite of everything. In spite of the dirt and blood and lies. Suppose the Leader is right? *A chill shakes him. He puts on his coat, continues to pace.* Suppose the true foundations of the future are being built here? History has always been an inhumane and unscrupulous builder, mixing its mortar of lies and blood and filth. *He shivers again, pulls his coat tighter.* Well, what of it, Rubashov? Be logical. Haven't you always lived under the compulsion of working things out to their final conclusions? *He accelerates his pacing, counting the steps:* 1 . . . 2 . . . 3 . . . 4 . . . 5 . . . and a half; 1 . . . 2 . . . 3 . . . 4 . . . 5 and a half. *He stops abruptly as a thought strikes him:* Yes. Yes.*)*

*(A sound of distant laughter. Slowly the figures of some dockworkers materialize, sitting at a small iron table in a pub on the waterfront of the Marseilles docks. They are eating bread and cheese and drinking wine, talking loudly and laughing good-naturedly. A big stocky man wearing a sailor's sweater and stocking cap is seated next to a little hunchback who wears a sailor's cap and a seaman's pea-jacket. Next to the little hunchback sits a third dockworker. The big man is juggling some apples and the others are watching and roaring with laughter. On the wall over the table is a militant poster demanding sanctions against Mussolini for his rape of Ethiopia. Benito's caricature dominates the scene: the jutting jaw, the pop-eyes, the little fez on the shaved dome.)*

*(Rubashov, accompanied by Albert, a sharp-featured, young French intellectual, with long expressive hands which are forever gesturing, and a mincing, epicene manner, approaches the table. The little hunchback sees them and rises.)*

ALBERT *(waving to him)*. Comrade Luigi, head of the Dockworkers' Union. This is the comrade from Moscow.

LUIGI *(smiles and extends his hand)*. We're honored. We're honored. *(He shakes Rubashov's hand vigorously)* Please sit down. *(He motions to the big dockworker)* Comrade Pablo, business manager of the union.

PABLO *(shakes hands)*. How do you like the job we're doing here?

RUBASHOV. You've the strongest dockworkers' union in Europe.

PABLO. Nothing'll get by us. We'll strangle Il Duce.

LUIGI *(introduces the third dockworker)*. Comrade André, our secretary.

ANDRE. Comrade. *(They shake hands. Rubashov and Albert sit)*

PABLO. Those Italian ships out there will rot before we call off this strike.

LUIGI. Drink?

RUBASHOV. Coffee, black.

ALBERT. A double fine.

PABLO *(calls off)*. One coffee, black. One double fine.

VOICE *(off)*. Coming.

PABLO *(pointing off, shouts a warning to Luigi)*. Luigi, look—Here comes that cat again.

ANDRE. Meow! Meow!

LUIGI *(jumping to his feet in panic, growls at the unseen cat)*. Get out! Fft— out! *(He throws a spoon across the floor. The cat obviously flees. André and Pablo collapse in their chairs, holding their sides, filling the café with booming laughter. Luigi looks at them, shakes his head, laughs sheepishly)*

PABLO *(to Rubashov)*. Luigi don't like cats.

ANDRE. But they love him. They come to him like a bowl of cream.

LUIGI. They got no reason to. *(The three laugh. Luigi's laughter becomes a racking cough. The Waiter enters and sets the drinks on the table. They are silent until he leaves)*

ANDRE. When Luigi escaped from Italy he lived by killing cats.

PABLO. And selling their skins.

LUIGI. I had no papers. I couldn't get a job.

RUBASHOV. You're Italian?

LUIGI. I'm a man without a country. *(He spits at Benito's caricature)* Three years ago I escaped. Benito was after me. I got here in France. No passport. The French police arrest me. Take me at night to the Belgian border. "We catch you here again, God help you!" In Belgium the Belgian police arrest me . . . "No passport?" Take me to the French border. Kick me back here into France. Six times back and forth. Luigi, the human football. *(He grimaces. His two comrades laugh appreciatively)* A man without a country. *(They laugh louder and slap him on the back. He laughs)* Well, I can laugh now, too, thanks to Pablo. I meet him in jail. He gets me passport. Finds me this job with the union. I'm alive again, I belong.

PABLO *(leans across the table confidentially to Rubashov)*. If you need any passports, I have a man will make you anything. A real artist.

RUBASHOV *(nods)*. Thanks. I'll remember that.

ALBERT *(half rises, significantly)*. The comrade from Moscow has a message for us.

LUIGI. For us? *(They all lean forward, intent)*

RUBASHOV. In connection with this strike.

PABLO. Ah! The strike? Don't worry. Nothing'll get by us.

LUIGI. Sh, Pablo! *(To Rubashov)* Your message?

RUBASHOV. As you know, our strength in the Soviet Union is the strength of the revolutionary movement all over the world.

PABLO *(hits the table with his fist)*. You can count on us!

LUIGI. Sh, Pablo! *(To Rubashov)*. The strike?

RUBASHOV. The Italian shipyards are completing two destroyers and a cruiser for us.

ALBERT. For the Motherland of the Revolution!

RUBASHOV. The Italian Government has informed Moscow if we want these ships this strike must be called off at once.

PABLO. What?

ANDRE. You want us to call off this strike?
*(The dockworkers look at each other, stunned, bewildered.)*

LUIGI. But Moscow called on the world for sanctions!

ALBERT. The comrade from over there has explained this is in the interest of the defense of the Motherland of the Revolution.

PABLO *(angrily)*. But the Fascists are taking on supplies to make war.

ANDRE. To kill Ethiopian workers!

LUIGI. To make slaves of them.

ALBERT. Comrades, sentimentality gets us nowhere.

LUIGI *(gesticulates with his dirty handkerchief)*. But this isn't right; we can't do this! It isn't fair, it isn't just, it isn't . . .

RUBASHOV *(quickly, sharply)*. It isn't according to the rules laid down by the Marquis of Queensberry? No, it isn't. But revolutions aren't won by "fair play" morality. That's fine in the lulls of history, but in the crises, there is only one rule: The end justifies the means.

LUIGI. No, there are principles; the whole world looks to you back there for an example. . . . (*He coughs violently into the handkerchief*)

ANDRE (*pointing at the scarlet stains on Luigi's handkerchief*). You see? Blood. He spits blood. Benito gave him that. And took two brothers in exchange. If you knew . . .

LUIGI. That doesn't matter.

PABLO. This is just scabbing.

ANDRE. I vote to continue the strike.

PABLO. Strike.

LUIGI. Strike. The meeting is closed. (*He stands up*)

RUBASHOV (*rises quickly, decisively*). No, it isn't! I'm in authority now. We have a job to be done here and it will be done.

ALBERT. In spite of agents provocateurs. (*Pablo reaches over, grabs Albert by the lapels of his coat, and shakes him*)

LUIGI (*rises*). No, Pablo, stop that! Stop! (*Pablo releases Albert. Luigi addresses Albert*) Provocateurs? For who, in God's name?

ALBERT (*furious, his voice shrill*). For the Fascists.

PABLO. Because we won't load their ships? You hear, Comrades. That's a joke —a rotten joke, isn't it?

LUIGI (*softly*). No, it's not a joke, Pablo; it's rotten, but it's not a joke. (*He looks up at the caricature of Mussolini*) The joke is Benito brought me into socialism, me and my two brothers. We lived in Forli, 1911. Italy was starting a war with Tripoli. There was a big antiwar meeting, banners, posters. Benito took the platform. Benito, the humble socialist, in a dirty black suit and a bow tie. (*He imitates the crowd*) "Bravo, Benito!" (*He mimics the gestures and facial expressions of Mussolini*) "Fellow workers, militarism is our enemy! We hate war!" (*He becomes the crowd*) "Bravo, Benito!" (*Again he is Mussolini*) "We don't want iron discipline, we don't want colonial adventures! We want bread and schools and freedom." "Bravo, Benito!" (*He angrily admonishes the invisible crowd*) "Don't applaud me! Don't follow me. I hate fetishism. Follow my words!" (*Softly, nodding to himself*) Benito. (*He leans on the table; to Rubashov*) We followed his words; my two brothers and I. Ten years later he gives my brothers the castor-oil treatment. To some that sounds like a joke, too. You know what happens when a quart of castor oil is poured down your throat? It tears your intestines to pieces, like you put them in a butcher's grinder, to little pieces. Two brothers I had. Not like me.. Well-formed, beautiful, like Michelangelo carved them out of Carrara marble—one a David and one a Moses. I, the ugly one, I escaped. (*Softly, tenderly*) Two brothers I had . . . and now, (*fiercely*) Mother of God, I'm a Fascist! (*He coughs convulsively into his handkerchief*) Back where I started with Benito. (*He spits at the caricature of Mussolini*)

PABLO (*fervently*). I swear to God it's all true.

ANDRE. Luigi's not a Fascist!

ALBERT (*rises, gesticulating with the long slender hands*). Now, Comrades, you're thinking mechanistically. Dialectically, the fact is that, whoever does not serve the long-distance aims of the Party is an enemy of the Party and therefore, even though he may think himself subjectively an anti-Fascist, he is in fact objectively a Fascist . . .

PABLO (*ironically seizes some dishes, tosses them into the air, juggles them, catches them, then proffers them to Albert with an ironic bow*). Here! You do it better than I.

RUBASHOV (*rising*). The ships are to be unloaded tomorrow.

LUIGI. Over my dead body.

PABLO. And mine.

ANDRE. And mine.

RUBASHOV. You can tear up your cards! (*Silence*) The meeting is adjourned. (*Indicating the phone*) Albert. (*Albert nods, crosses to the phone, picks it up*)

LUIGI (*to the others*). Come. (*The three men leave, Luigi coughing as he does*)

ALBERT (*at phone*). André, Pablo, Luigi. Yes. Publish their pictures in tomorrow's press. Front page. Agents provocateurs. Any Party member who even talks to them will be dismissed at once.

RUBASHOV. Their passports!

ALBERT. Ah, of course. (*On phone*) Also notify the French police their papers here are forged. Arrange for their immediate arrest and deportation. (*He hangs up, grins smugly*) That'll do it! Now little Luigi is really a man without a country!

RUBASHOV (*stonily*). Yes. (*Albert laughs. Rubashov turns a withering look of re-*

*vulsion on him, and then, unable to endure it, shouts at him)* What the hell are you laughing at? What's so funny? *(Albert's laughter dies in his throat. He looks pained and puzzled. With an exclamation of disgust Rubashov walks away)*
*(The scene fades. Rubashov is back in his cell, pacing nervously.)*

RUBASHOV. Yes . . . We lived under the compulsion of working things out to their final conclusions. I thought and acted as I had to; I destroyed people I was fond of; I gave power to others I disliked . . . Well—History put you in that position, Rubashov. What else could you do? . . . But, I've exhausted the credit she gave me. Was I right? Was I wrong? I don't know. . . . The fact is, Rubashov, you no longer believe in your infallibility. That's why you're lost.

*(A tapping. Rubashov crosses to the wall and replies. The lights come up on 402.)*

402 *(taps)*. Knew something was happening.

RUBASHOV *(taps)*. Explain.

402 *(taps)*. Executions.

RUBASHOV *(to himself)*. Executions? *(Taps)* Who?

402 *(taps)*. Don't know.

RUBASHOV *(taps)*. What time?

402 *(taps)*. Soon. Pass it on.

RUBASHOV *(goes to another wall of his cell, taps, receives an answering click, then he taps out the message)*. Executions soon. Pass it on. *(To himself, pacing)* Perhaps this time it is you, Rubashov. Well, so long as they do it quickly. *(He stops, rubs his swollen cheek thoughtfully)* But is that right? You can still save yourself. One word—"Confess." *(Fiercely)* What does it matter what you say or what you sign? Isn't the important thing to go on? Isn't that all that matters?—To go on? *(An agonized look appears on his face, as an unbidden memory rises)*

*(Faint strains of music. Luba's voice humming the melody of the "Appassionata." The prison vanishes. We are in Luba's room. It is a bright Sunday afternoon. The sun is pouring through the window, flooding the room with golden warmth. Luba, kneeling, is snipping sprays of apple blossoms from a large bough spread out on a cloth laid on the floor. She is pruning the twigs preparatory to arranging them in a vase on the table. She hums*

*happily. Rubashov enters, stands, watching her. She turns.)*

LUBA. Oh! I didn't hear you come in. *(She rises, goes to him, holding out the flowers as an offering)*

RUBASHOV *(touches them)*. Beautiful! Where did you get them?

LUBA. I took a long walk this morning in the country. They were lying on the ground. The branch had broken off an old apple tree. *(Luba notices that Rubashov's face is strained and lined with fatigue)* You look tired.

RUBASHOV. I am. I've been walking too.

LUBA. Not in the country?

RUBASHOV. No.

LUBA *(crosses to the table, arranges the flowers in the vase)*. If you want to walk you should go out to the country. *(Disposing of the flowers, she opens a drawer, takes out a bar of chocolate and hands it to him)* Yesterday was my lucky day.

RUBASHOV. Chocolate?

LUBA *(triumphantly)*. Two bars. I ate one. They were the last in the store. I stood in line three hours. I had to battle for them, but I won.

RUBASHOV *(softly, under the strain of some deep emotion)*. Thank you.

LUBA *(kneels, cutting more sprays off the branch, reminiscing)*. We had some apple trees at home. On Sundays we'd help Father prune them. There was one huge old tree so gnarled and full of bumps. We had a special affection for that tree. Tch, the pains Father took to save it. We called it his "patient." *(Rises with the blooms)* One spring morning he took us out to look at the "patient." It was blossom time. The other apple trees didn't have many blossoms that year—but the "patient" . . . You've never seen so many blossoms on one tree. It took our breath away. The tree was all covered with blossoms like snow. Then Father said, "I'm going to lose my patient."

RUBASHOV. Why'd he say that?

LUBA. An apple tree puts out its most beautiful bloom just before it dies.

RUBASHOV. I didn't know that.

LUBA. It's true. The next year the "patient" was gone.

RUBASHOV. Oh!

LUBA. When I'm working at the factory, everything seems matter-of-fact; but whenever I go out to the country, the world suddenly becomes full of mystery.

*(Luba looks at Rubashov. He sits slowly, a strained expression on his face)* What is it? What's wrong?

RUBASHOV *(shakes his head)*. Troubles.

LUBA. At the factory?

RUBASHOV *(tastes the chocolate)*. There too. All over. Upheavals. *(He glances at the chocolate evasively)* This chocolate is made of soya beans. Tastes almost like real chocolate. *(He sighs, pauses)* Luba...

LUBA. Yes?

RUBASHOV *(carefully places the chocolate on the table, speaks softly, deliberately)*. Orders came in late yesterday, after you left. You'll have to report back to Moscow. *(Luba's hand, lifting a spray of blossoms to the vase, freezes in mid-air)* You're to leave tonight.

LUBA. Tonight?

RUBASHOV *(evading her glance)*. Those are the orders. There's a train at ten o'clock.

LUBA *(trying desperately to control her mounting terror)*. Why am I being sent back there?

RUBASHOV. They're investigating the files and production records.

LUBA. How long will I be gone?

RUBASHOV. I don't know that, Luba.

LUBA. Why didn't you tell me last night?

RUBASHOV. I wanted to find out what it is about.

LUBA. But I've so much work at the office to clean up. So many . . .

RUBASHOV *(rises)*. It's hurried, I know. But that's the way the Bureau does things.

LUBA. What have I done wrong?

RUBASHOV. Nothing.

LUBA. Has my work been unsatisfactory?

RUBASHOV. It's been excellent.

LUBA *(the terror in her voice now)*. Then why am I being sent back?

RUBASHOV *(patiently, soothingly)*. I told you, they're examining the books.

LUBA *(dully wiping her wet hands on a cloth)*. Someone else will take on my job here?

RUBASHOV. Only while you're gone.

LUBA *(turns to Rubashov, childishly)*. I don't want to go.

RUBASHOV. You have to, Luba.

LUBA *(crossing to Rubashov, pleading)*. Can't you help me?

RUBASHOV. You understand, I have ene-mies. It would look bad for you, if I interceded.

LUBA. For me?

RUBASHOV. For both of us. As if I wanted to conceal something.

LUBA *(her love and her fear for him taking precedent, she studies him)*. You're not in any trouble?

RUBASHOV. No.

LUBA. You're sure?

RUBASHOV. Yes. *(There is a long pause)*

LUBA *(very simply and directly)*. They're not going to arrest me?

RUBASHOV. Of course not.

LUBA. I'm frightened. *(She sits, looks about helplessly, a trapped animal)*

RUBASHOV *(goes to her, places his hands soothingly on her shoulders)*. There's no need to be. If they should interrogate you, tell them the truth. You have nothing to fear. Just tell them the truth.

LUBA *(whispers)*. I'm frightened *(Suddenly the waves of panic explode, and she cries out)* I'm not going to Moscow. I just won't go.

RUBASHOV *(quickly, trying to control the panic)*. Then it would look as if you had done something wrong, wouldn't it?

LUBA *(turns to Rubashov, hysterically)*. But I haven't, I haven't.

RUBASHOV. I know that, Luba.

LUBA *(her hysteria mounting, her body trembling, her voice becoming shrill)*. Oh God! I want to run away. I want to hide! I want to run away.

RUBASHOV *(grips her arms tightly)*. Nothing's going to happen to you. Understand? There are no charges against you. Nothing's going to happen. Nothing, nothing! *(He holds her tight and kisses her. She clings to him with all her strength, wildly, passionately returning his embrace. Then she goes limp, withdraws, looks at him, smiles sadly, shakes her head)*

LUBA. I'm sorry. I'm stupid. *(She turns to gather up the flowers from the floor)* I'll be all right. *(Kneeling)* Ten o'clock?

RUBASHOV. Ten o'clock.

LUBA. The tickets? And my travel warrant? *(Rubashov plucks them out of his pocket and hands them to her. She takes them quietly. She rises, and, tonelessly)* I'll have to pack now.

RUBASHOV. Yes. I'll go.

LUBA. Not yet.

RUBASHOV. It would be best . . . for both of us, at this time.

LUBA. Yes, I suppose so. (*She looks at the bouquet of blossoms in her hands*) Wouldn't it be wonderful if we could just say "No" to them? If we could come and go as we wished, all of us?

RUBASHOV. But we can't, Luba. That would be anarchy. We haven't the right. (*He crosses into the shadows*)

LUBA (*almost inaudibly*). No. of course not. We haven't the right.

(*Luba, flowers, room and sunlight, all fade away, leaving Rubashov alone in his dank cell, talking to himself.*)

RUBASHOV. And have *I* the right to say "No"? Even now? Have I the right to leave—to walk out, to die out of mere tiredness, personal disgust and vanity? Have I this right?

(*The lights come up in the other cells. The prisoners, ears to the wall, are listening for the news. 202 has just received a message. He crosses to 302's wall.*)

202 (*taps*). They're reading death sentence to him now. Pass it on. (*He shuttles back to the other post to listen*)

302 (*crosses, taps on 402's wall*). They're reading death sentence to him now. Pass it on. (*Shuttles back to listen*)

402 (*taps*). They're reading death sentence now. Pass it on.

RUBASHOV (*taps*). Who is he? (*But 402 has crossed back to listen to the next message. Rubashov crosses to the rear wall, taps*) They're reading death sentence to him now. Pass it on. (*Rubashov crosses back to 402's wall to listen*)

202 (*crosses to wall, taps to 302*). They are bringing him, screaming and hitting out. Pass it on. (*202 returns to his other post, listening*)

302 (*crosses, taps to 402*). They are bringing him, screaming and hitting out. Pass it on. (*302 returns to his other post*)

402 (*taps to Rubashov*). They are bringing him, screaming and hitting out. Pass it on.

RUBASHOV (*taps, urgently*). Who is he? (*But 402 has gone back to the opposite wall to listen for more news. Rubashov shuffles over to the rear wall and taps*) They are bringing him screaming and hitting out. Pass it on. (*Then he moves back to 402's wall and taps insistently*) Who is he? (*402 crosses to Rubashov's wall, listening. Rubashov, very clearly*) What's his name?

402 (*taps*). Mischa Bogrov.

RUBASHOV (*suddenly becomes faint; wipes the sweat from his forehead and for a moment braces himself against the wall; walks slowly to the rear wall and leans heavily against it as he taps through to 402*) Mischa Bogrov, former sailor on Battleship Potemkin, Commander of the Baltic Fleet, bearer of Order of Red Banner, led to execution! Pass it on.

202 (*taps*). Now! (*He crosses to the door and starts drumming on the iron surface*)

302 (*taps*). Now! (*He crosses to the door and starts drumming on the iron surface*)

402 (*taps*). Now! (*He crosses to the door and starts drumming on the iron surface*)

RUBASHOV (*taps*). Now! (*Drags himself across the cell and starts drumming on the door's iron surface*)

(*The prison becomes vibrant with the low beat of subdued drumming. The men in the cells who form the acoustic chain stand behind their doors like a guard of honor in the dark, create a deceptive resemblance to the muffled solemn sound of the roll of drums, carried by the wind from the distance. At the far end of the corridor, the grinding of iron doors becomes louder. A bunch of keys jangle. The iron door is shut again. The drumming rises to a steady, muffled crescendo. Sliding and squealing sounds approach quickly, a moaning and whimpering like the whimpering of a child is heard. Shadowy figures enter the field of vision. Two dimly lit figures, both in uniform, drag between them a third whom they hold under their arms. The middle figure hangs slack and yet with doll-like stiffness in their grasp, stretched out its full length, face turned to the ground, belly arched downwards, the legs trailing after, the shoes scraping on the toes. Whitish strands of hair hang over the face, the mouth is open. As they turn the corner of the corridor and open the trap-door to the cellar, we see that this tortured, mangled face is Bogrov's. Gletkin now appears, whispers in his ear. Bogrov straightens up, looks about, flings off his captors for a moment and moans out some vowels.*)

BOGROV. Oo . . . a . . . ah; Oo . . . a

. . . ah! *(Then with a mighty effort, he articulates the word and bellows out)* Rubashov; Rubashov!

RUBASHOV *(pounds on his door like a madman, screaming).* Mischa! Mischa! *(The other prisoners accelerate their drumming. Bogrov is dragged through the cellar-door; it clangs shut, and we can hear his voice as he is being dragged down to the execution cellar, growing fainter and fainter, calling "Rubashov! Rubashov!" Gradually the drumming dies down, the other prisoners vanish, a deep terrible silence settles on the prison. Rubashov stands in the middle of his cell, clutching his stomach to prevent himself from vomiting. He staggers to his cot, collapses on it, and is enveloped by complete darkness.)*
*(There is a long silence. From somewhere above a prisoner cries out, "Arise, ye wretched of the earth!")*
*(The electric light in Rubashov's cell is suddenly turned on. Ivanoff is standing next to his bed with a bottle of brandy and a glass. Rubashov, his eyes glazed, is staring, unseeing, into space.)*

IVANOFF. You feel all right?

RUBASHOV. It's hot! Open the window! *(He looks up at Ivanoff)* Who are you?

IVANOFF. Would you like some brandy? *(Rubashov's eyes follow him, dull, uncomprehending. Ivanoff pours a drink, extends it to Rubashov. Sits next to him)* Drink this. *(Ivanoff holds the glass, feeding the drink to Rubashov)*

RUBASHOV *(finishes the drink, looks at him).* You been arrested too?

IVANOFF. No. I only came to visit you. *(He places the bottle and the glass on the floor)* I think you're ill. Are you in pain?

RUBASHOV. No.

IVANOFF. Your cheek is swollen. I think, you've a fever.

RUBASHOV. Give me a cigarette. *(Ivanoff gives him a cigarette, lights it for him. Rubashov inhales the smoke deeply, hungrily. After a few moments of this, his eyes come into focus, his breathing becomes a little more regular, and he looks at Ivanoff who is patiently blowing smoke rings)* What time is it?

IVANOFF. Two thirty A.M.

RUBASHOV. How long have I been here?

IVANOFF. Five weeks tomorrow.

RUBASHOV *(examines Ivanoff. He is be-ginning to think quite clearly now).* What are you doing here?

IVANOFF. I want to talk to you. Some more brandy? *(Picks up the bottle)*

RUBASHOV *(the iron creeping into his voice).* No, thank you.

IVANOFF. Lie down. Rest!

RUBASHOV *(sits up, spits out).* You pimp! Get out of here. You're a pimp like all the rest of them! You disgust me—you and your filthy tricks.

IVANOFF. Tricks? *(Pours a drink)*

RUBASHOV *(raging).* You drag him by my cell—Bogrov—or what you've left of him, and when my bowels are split open, a savior appears with a bottle of brandy. You think I can be taken in by a cheap trick like that? You think you can wheedle a confession out of me with a bottle of brandy?

IVANOFF *(smiles and shows his gold teeth).* You really believe that I have such a primitive mind?

RUBASHOV. Take your whorish mind the hell out of here! It stinks! It's choking me.

IVANOFF *(drinks).* Very well. I'll go if you want me to.

RUBASHOV. You cannot begin to understand how you disgust me. All of you.

IVANOFF. But first, you must listen to me for one second.

RUBASHOV. I don't want to hear any more . . .

IVANOFF *(outshouts him).* I'm afraid you'll have to! *(Pause, gently)* Now listen—logically and calmly, if you can. First, to remove any doubts, Bogrov has already been shot!
*(There is a long silence as Rubashov absorbs this news, then:)*

RUBASHOV *(low, strangulated).* Good!

IVANOFF. He was also tortured for several days.

RUBASHOV. That was obvious.

IVANOFF. It was meant to be. But not by me. *(Sits next to Rubashov, placing the bottle on the floor)* I'm going to put my life in your hands, Kolya. *(Rubashov looks at him)* If you mention what I tell you, to anyone, I am done for. This filthy trick, as you call it, was arranged by my young colleague, Gletkin, against my instructions. I would never make this mistake, not out of concern for you, but because it's bad psychology. You've recently been suffering humanitarian scruples? A scene with Bogrov could only intensify them. Obvious? Only a fool like Gletkin makes such mistakes. He's been urging me to use his methods on you too!

RUBASHOV. You can torture me; it will get you no results.

IVANOFF. Won't it? *(He smiles cynically, reaches for the bottle)* You don't know Gletkin. *(He fills the glass, studies it)* He's something new in the world—the Neanderthal Man! He came after the flood. He had no umbilical cord to the past. He was born without a navel. He doesn't approve of us old apes in general, and of *you* in particular. *(He shakes his head at Rubashov)* It seems the other day you showed him your behind. He didn't like that. *(Ominously)* He wants to lay his big hands on you.

RUBASHOV. I'm quite prepared to die.

IVANOFF. But I'm not prepared to let you die. Your martyrdom, Kolya, will consist of not being allowed to become a martyr. That's not why you're here. We need you, and we need you logical, because when you've thought the whole thing out clearly, then, but only then, will you make your confession. Am I right?

RUBASHOV. Go away, it's no use.

IVANOFF. Do you believe that I'm telling you the truth? *(Pause)* Do you?

RUBASHOV. Yes . . . I suppose so.

IVANOFF. Then why do you want me to go? *(He bends forward, pushing his face into Rubashov's, mockingly)* Because you are afraid of me, because my way of reasoning is your way and you're afraid of the echoes in your own head.

RUBASHOV *(impatiently)*. I've had enough of this reasoning. We've been running amok with it for thirty years. Enough.

IVANOFF. Get thee behind me, Satan. *(Rises, goes to the door, peers out the judas-hole, turns back)* In the old days temptation was carnal. It took the form of little naked women running around shaking their things in your face. Today it's cerebral. It takes the form of naked reason pushing facts in your face. Values change. *(He drinks)*

RUBASHOV. Why was Bogrov tortured?

IVANOFF. He was stubborn like you.

RUBASHOV. Did you hear him whimpering?

IVANOFF. No, I didn't hear it. But I've heard and seen others. *(He wheels on Rubashov, stabbing an accusing finger at him)* And so have you! And so have you,

my General! *(He hobbles to Rubashov, face thrust forward, accusingly)* What of it? A conscience is as unsuited to a revolutionary as a double chin. Since when did N. S. Rubashov develop this bourgeois conscience? Hm? When? *(Pause)* Shall I tell you? The day, the hour, the minute? Nine months, two weeks ago—at 3:10 A.M.—when your little secretary, Luba Loshenko, was shot! *(He sits next to Rubashov)* You were sleeping with her, weren't you? Now she's dead. So you're making the world a metaphysical brothel for your emotions. What have the shape of Luba Loshenko's breasts or Bogrov's whimperings to do with the new world we're creating?

RUBASHOV. Bogrov's dead, she's dead. You can afford a little pity.

IVANOFF. I have many vices:—I drink; for a time, as you know, I took drugs; but so far I've avoided the vice of pity. One drop of that and a revolutionary's lost. *(He fills his glass)* The great temptation! To renounce violence, to make peace with ourselves . . . Hm? *(He drinks)* I prefer my synthetic ecstasy in a glass. You get over it in the morning.

RUBASHOV *(after a long silence, shakes his head, murmurs sadly.)* Our golden dream! *(Then savagely)* What a stinking mess we've made of it.

IVANOFF *(setting down the glass, articulates carefully).* Have we? *(He lights a fresh cigarette)* We've taken the land from the landlords. *(He blows a smoke ring)* We've freed them from industrial exploitation. *(He blows another)* For the first time in history a revolution is functional.

RUBASHOV. Functional? *(He jumps to his feet, furious)* So functional in taking the land, in one year, we let five million farmers and their families die of starvation! 'Deliberately. So functional *(He begins to pace up and down)* in freeing the people from industrial exploitation we sent ten million of them to forced labor under worse conditions than galley slaves. *(He plucks off his spectacles nervously and waves them at Ivanoff)* So functional, to settle a difference of opinion, the omnipotent Leader knows only one argument— Death!—whether it's a matter of submarines, manure, or the party-line in Indo-China. Death! *(He replaces his spectacles and glares at Ivanoff)*

IVANOFF *(rises, belligerently).* That

woman has really given you softening of the brain! What of the millions who die of starvation in China and India, of tuberculosis in rice fields, cotton plantations . . . ?

RUBASHOV. In negatives we agree. Where has it led us?

IVANOFF. Well, where?

RUBASHOV. Our standard of living is lower than the most backward country in Europe. Labor conditions are harder; discipline's more inhuman. Our country is run by the police. *(Again he plucks off the glasses for emphasis)* We've torn the living skin off our people and left them standing with bare tissues, muscles and nerves quivering.

IVANOFF. Well, and what of it? *(With warmth and conviction)* Don't you find that wonderful? Has anything more wonderful ever happened in history? We're tearing the old skin off mankind and giving it a new one! That's not an occupation for people with weak nerves, but there was a time it filled you with enthusiasm.

RUBASHOV. I know.

IVANOFF. Look at the pamphlets put out by the antivivisectionists. When you read how some poor cur, who has just had his liver cut out, whines and licks his tormentor's hand, it breaks your heart. But if we listened to these sentimentalists we'd have no cures for typhus, cholera, diphtheria . . .

RUBASHOV. I know, I know. *(He turns away, sits, moodily)*

IVANOFF *(following him, persistently)*. Of course you do. Better than I. And you still insist on being a martyr? *(He waits for an answer. Finally he throws up his hands and growls in disgust)* All right. Have it your way. *(He picks up the bottle and glass)* If you must throw yourself into the dust-bin of history, I can't stop you. Go. Let Gletkin have you. You're his. *(He turns to the door, pauses, turns back. His voice becomes soft)* Only tell me, why? Why are you so in love with death? It stinks! Why do you want to die?

RUBASHOV *(hoarsely)*. I don't want to die. No one does.

IVANOFF. You act as if you do.

RUBASHOV. It's a fake. *(He clutches his throat)* From here up, I'm resigned. From here down, I'm frightened.

IVANOFF. Yet I offer you your life.

RUBASHOV. On what terms?

IVANOFF. The only terms that matter. To go on being useful. *(He places the bottle on the floor and fumbles in his pocket)*

RUBASHOV. To act the fool in public trial? No, thanks. The terms are too high.

IVANOFF *(taking out an official communication, pushes it under Rubashov's nose)*. Here's a confidential report I received today. *(Rubashov takes it, glances at it)* Read between the lines.

RUBASHOV *(dryly)*. I need no instructions, thank you. *(Studies the document)*

IVANOFF. What do you see?

RUBASHOV. War! It's coming.

IVANOFF. How soon?

RUBASHOV. Depends on how we play our cards. Perhaps years, perhaps months.

IVANOFF. The last war gave us Russia, Kolya; the next gives us the world. Or does it?

RUBASHOV. It could, if . . .

IVANOFF. If . . . ? Good! *(He sits next to him)* There's a breach in the Party, in the whole country; the people are restless, dissatisfied; our economy is in pieces. The breach must be mended first; and you, and those who think like you, must mend it!

RUBASHOV. Hence the trials! *(Hands him back the document, contemptuously)* They're better than the opera or the theater.

IVANOFF. The goal, Kolya. It's coming. Nearer. Listen. You can hear it on the wind. And when that day comes . . .

RUBASHOV. The Gletkins take over.

IVANOFF. They're brutes. They don't count.

RUBASHOV *(plucking off his spectacles and glaring at Ivanoff)*. Who made them brutes? We did! Their Byzantine leader worship is frightening. Their cultivated ignorance is disgusting.

IVANOFF. Would they have been any use to us any other way?

RUBASHOV. You'd trust our revolution to them?

IVANOFF. Why do you think I'm risking my neck to save you? It's your brain I want to save. When the day comes, your brain will be needed. We'll get rid of them. You'll be needed more than ever!

RUBASHOV *(studies him, replaces his spectacles, shakes his head)*. If I thought that . . .

IVANOFF *(strongly)*. Think it! Think it! *(He watches Rubashov wrestle with the thought, then leans forward, and softly)*

What other choice have you? To become a Christian martyr? For the Western democracies?

RUBASHOV (rises, angrily). What are you talking about, "the Western democracies"? What have I to do with those decadent humanists—those phantoms of religion and superstition?

IVANOFF (pressing his point, sharpening his irony). Do you want their liberal press, that hated your guts while you were alive, to sanctify you after your death?

RUBASHOV. The liberal press? Those puking jackals of holy property? What have I to do with them? I'd rather be two feet of manure in a Russian field. (He nervously polishes the glasses with his shirt)

IVANOFF. Nevertheless they'll put you in a stained-glass window. Saint Rubashov—the martyr for the Western world! Is that what you want?

(Rubashov looks at him, looks away, ponders, replaces the. spectacles, sighs. For a long time he stands there, head bowed, wrapped in thought. Ivanoff watches him patiently.)

RUBASHOV (finally, wearily). I'll think it over.

IVANOFF (triumphantly picks up his bottle, rises, and going to the judas-hole, calls). Guard! (He turns back to Rubashov, beaming) You old war-horse. You've had an attack of nerves. (The Guard opens door) But that's over now. Go to bed. Get some sleep. You'll need a clear head tomorrow when we make up your statement.

RUBASHOV (frowning). I said I'll think it over.

IVANOFF (nods, laughs). Good night, Kolya.

RUBASHOV. Good night, Sascha.

(Ivanoff goes. Rubashov stands, thinking, thinking. In the corridor Ivanoff sees Gletkin, leaning against the wall, watching Rubashov's cell.)

IVANOFF (crosses to Gletkin, with supreme contempt). What genius inspired you tonight? (Pause. He blows a smoke ring) It's all right. He'll confess. But I had to sweat blood to repair the damage you did. You are all still suffering from personal feelings. In his place you'd be even more stubborn.

GLETKIN. I have some backbone, which he hasn't.

IVANOFF. But you're an idiot! For that answer alone, you ought to be shot before he is! (He blows a cloud of cigarette smoke directly into Gletkin's face, shows his gold teeth in a grin of utter disdain, and hobbles off down the corridor) (Gletkin stands there as if he were made of stone, the face completely without expression, then he raises his hand and waves aside the fumes of smoke with a sudden, quick gesture.)

DIM-OUT AND CURTAIN

## ACT THREE

SCENE: Rubashov's cell; several days later.

AT RISE: Rubashov seated on the cot, his shoes off, his coat thrown over his shoulders, a pad of blank paper on his knee, is writing intently, completely absorbed. He pauses, chews his pencil, studies the page, writes rapidly. Alongside him is a stack of completed pages. The tensions and the fever appear to have abated. As he writes, three taps are heard from 402's wall. He ignores them. Three more taps. Then three more. He glances up, annoyed, but continues to work. The taps now flow rapidly and insistently in a staccato stream. With an exclamation of annoyance, Rubashov tears off the page he has just completed, lays it carefully on the pile next to him, rises and, crossing to the wall, taps. The lights come up on 402.

——

402 (taps). I tried to talk to you all day. Why didn't you answer?

RUBASHOV (taps). I've been busy.

402 (taps). How?

RUBASHOV (taps). Writing.

402 (taps). What?

RUBASHOV (taps). A new theory.

402 (taps). What about?

RUBASHOV (smiling ironically, taps). The immaturity of the masses. The historical necessity for dictatorship.

402 (taps). Repeat!

RUBASHOV (taps). Never mind.

402 (taps). What's happened?

RUBASHOV (taps). I'm waiting for word. Upstairs.

402 (taps). Why?

RUBASHOV (taps). I am confessing.

402 (pauses, stunned by this volte-face, then angrily, taps). I'd rather hang.

RUBASHOV *(cynically, taps).* Each in his own way.

402 *(taps slowly).* I thought you an exception. Have you no honor?

RUBASHOV *(taps).* Our ideas of honor differ.

402 *(taps).* Honor is to live and die for your beliefs.

RUBASHOV *(taps).* I am living for mine.

402 *(taps louder and more sharply).* Honor is decency.

RUBASHOV *(taps slowly, calmly).* What is decency?

402 *(very excited, taps).* Something your kind will never understand.

RUBASHOV *(taps).* We have replaced decency by reason.

402 *(taps).* What reason?

RUBASHOV *(taps).* Pure Reason.

402 *(taps).* You're pure son of bitch.

RUBASHOV *(amused, chuckles and taps).* Flattery does not impress me.

402 *(taps).* I'll never talk to you again. *(The scene is interrupted by a jangling sound. The door of Rubashov's cell is thrown open. A Young Officer enters.)*

OFFICE. Put on your shoes!

RUBASHOV. Well! It's about time! *(Crosses to the cot, sits and proceeds to put on his shoes, leisurely)* I've been waiting on Commissar Ivanoff for several days.

OFFICE. Put on your shoes, and come with me.

RUBASHOV. You might have timed it a little more considerately. But, I suppose you Neanderthal men only come out after midnight.

OFFICE. Don't talk so much. Just put on your shoes and hurry up.

RUBASHOV *(looks at the Officer, smiles, shakes' his head as he ties the laces).* Brutes! *(He rises, the Officer motions him out with a jerk of the head. Rubashov goes, remarking over his shoulder)* But then you wouldn't be any use to us if you weren't, would you? *(Exit. The Officer frowns, follows him out. The lights in the cell dim out)*

402 *(watching at the judas-hole).* Son of a bitch! *(He crosses up to 302's wall, taps)* *(The lights come up in the tier above. 302 is pacing. He stops at the sound of tapping, crosses, and listens.)*

402 *(taps).* Rubashov is a filthy coward.

302 *(taps).* You're wrong. He's brave. My father told me.

402 *(taps).* Your father is mistaken . . .

302 *(taps).* What's he done?

402 *(taps).* He's saving his skin. He's confessing. They've taken him up now.

302 *(taps).* Oh, my God! Pray for me.

402 *(taps).* For you?

302 *(taps).* Yes, for me. *(He crosses, taps on 202's wall. The lights come up on 202, who responds and listens. 302 taps)* Rubashov confessing. Pass it on.

202 *(groans, crosses to opposite wall, taps).* Rubashov confessing. Pass it on . . . *(The tappings multiply and the murmur "Rubashov confessing, Rubashov confessing," echoes back and forth through the prison. The cells dim out slowly as the lights come up on Ivanoff's office. Seated at the desk, his chair wheeled around, his back to us is a man in uniform, apparently Ivanoff. Rubashov enters, accompanied by the Guard. There is a faint ironic smile on Rubashov's lips as he enters. The man seated at the desk swings his chair round to face Rubashov. It's not Ivanoff, it's Gletkin! He looks at Rubashov, stony-faced. The smile on Rubashov's lips vanishes, he pauses in his stride, looks about quickly. Near Gletkin a grim-lipped young woman, obviously a secretary, sits, sharpening her pencils.)*

GLETKIN *(rises, waves the Guard out).* Shut the door! *(The Guard goes, shutting the door behind him. Gletkin turns to a heavy floor lamp nearby and switches it on. There is a humming sound, and a fierce, white light strikes Rubashov full in the eyes. He jerks his face away as if he'd been struck, then turns back to face Gletkin, squinting and shielding his eyes with his hand. Gletkin sits, picks up some official documents)* We will proceed with your examination. You wish to make a full confession?

RUBASHOV *(takes off his glasses and wipes his eyes).* Yes. To Commissar Ivanoff. Not to you.

GLETKIN. You will make your confession to me, here and now, or this investigation is closed, and you will be sentenced at once. Those are my orders from above. *(Rubashov puts on his spectacles and tries to meet Gletkin's gaze, but the harsh light blinds him. He removes his glasses again)* You have your choice. Which is it?

RUBASHOV *(avoiding the light).* I am ready to make a statement.

GLETKIN. Sit there.

RUBASHOV. On one condition. *(He turns to Gletkin firmly, even though he has to almost shut his eyes)* Turn off that dazzle-light! Save these devices for gangsters.

GLETKIN *(calmly)*. You're in no position to make conditions. The fact is you are charged with being the worst kind of "gangster."

RUBASHOV *(controls his anger)*. Exactly what are these charges? Please read them to me. Up till now this hasn't been done.

GLETKIN. Very well. Sit here! *(Rubashov sits in the chair upon which the dazzle-light has been trained. Gletkin reads the official statement in a rapid monotone)* "Enemy of the people, Nicolai Semono-vitch Rubashov, you are charged with be-ing a counter-revolutionary in the pay of hostile, foreign governments; of having, at the instigation of their agents, committed such acts of treason and wreckage as to cause vital shortages—undermining the military power of the U.S.S.R. You are also charged with having incited an accom-plice to attempt the assassination of the Leader of the Party. I.e., you are charged with crimes covered by Articles 58-1A; 58-2; 58-7; 58-9 and 58-11 of the Criminal Code." *(He drops the official papers and looks up)* You've heard the charges? You plead guilty?

RUBASHOV *(turns to face him, shielding his eyes with his hand)*. I plead guilty to having fallen out of step with historical necessity. I plead guilty to bourgeois senti-mentality. I plead guilty to having wanted an immediate alleviation of the Terror, and extension of freedom to the masses. *(The secretary who is writing this in shorthand smiles contemptuously. Ruba-shov glances at her)* Don't be cynical, young woman. *(To Gletkin)* I now realize fully that the regime is right and I am wrong. The times demand a tightening of the dictatorship; any sentimental aberra-tions at the present moment in history could become suicide. In this sense can you call me a counter-revolutionary, but in this sense only. With the insane charges made in the accusation I have nothing to do. I deny them categorically.

GLETKIN. Have you finished?

RUBASHOV. I deny that I, Rubashov, ever plotted against my country. I deny that I am in the pay of a foreign government. I deny any act of sabotage. I deny ever having taken the least part in any act of terror against the Leader of the Party. *(To the stenographer, quietly)* Have you all that, young woman?

GLETKIN. Have you finished?

RUBASHOV. I have finished.

GLETKIN. Wipe your lips then. They're slimy with lies. Lies! Lies! Vomit! *(He snatches a thick dossier off the desk, and cracks Rubashov across the face with it)* The statement you have just made is vomit. Enough nobility! Enough postur-ing! Enough strutting! What we demand of you is not high talk, but a full confes-sion of your real crimes!

RUBASHOV *(his hand to his face, breath-ing hard, biting back the indignation, fighting for control)*. I cannot confess to crimes I have not committed.

GLETKIN *(pressing a button the desk)*. Oh, no, that you cannot. *(The Guard en-ters, bringing in 302, whose eyes at once fix on Gletkin, and who moves and talks like a sleepwalker. There is something in his manner of the helpless child, desper-ately eager to be "good" and to please. Gletkin dismisses the Guard with a nod, then points to a spot on the floor)* Step over here. *(Immediately 302 nods and shuffles over to stand correctly as desig-nated. Gletkin crosses above the desk. To Rubashov)* Do you know this person? *(Pause. Harshly)* You will please pay at-tention! Do you know this person?

RUBASHOV. The light's in my eyes.

GLETKIN *(softly)*. Stand up! *(Rubashov hesitates. Gletkin roars)* Stand up! *(Ruba-shov rises)* Step over there! *(He points to 302. Rubashov walks up closer)* Do you recognize him now?

RUBASHOV *(shielding his eyes from the blinding light, scrutinizes 302, then shakes his head)*. No.

GLETKIN. You've never met him before?

RUBASHOV *(hesitates)*. Mm . . . No.

GLETKIN. You hesitated. Why?

RUBASHOV *(studies 302's face)*. I don't place him.

GLETKIN. Your memory was once pro-verbial in the Party. *(A long pause)* You refuse to answer?

RUBASHOV. I do not refuse to answer. I simply do not place him.

GLETKIN. Good. Sit down. *(Rubashov sits. Gletkin turns to 302)* Help Citizen Rubashov's memory. Where did you last meet him?

302. Citizen Rubashov instigated me to

murder the Leader of the Party by poison . . .

GLETKIN (*irritably*). I didn't ask you that. I asked you where you last met him.

RUBASHOV (*smiles grimly, and mutters*). Wrong lever.

GLETKIN (*turns on him, snaps*). What?

RUBASHOV. The automatic barrel organ played the wrong tune.

GLETKIN (*ominously*). I warn you. Remember where you are. We want none of your so-called wit. (*Nods to 302*)

302. I met Citizen Rubashov in Brussels.

GLETKIN. Can you remember the date?

302. Distinctly. It was on the 17th anniversary of the Revolution. At his apartment!

RUBASHOV (*studying 302, suddenly puts his hands to his forehead*). Yes, of course. The date is correct. I didn't recognize Joseph Kieffer. (*To Gletkin*) Congratulations!

GLETKIN. You admit you knew him then? You met him on the day and occasion aforementioned?

RUBASHOV (*his eyes glued to the terrible spectacle of 302's mangled, ghost-like mask*). I've just told you that. If you'd informed me at once that he was the son of my unfortunate friend, Professor Kieffer, I'd have identified him sooner.

GLETKIN (*turns to 302*). How did this meeting come about?

302. After the reception at the Legation my father took me up to Citizen Rubashov's apartment.

GLETKIN (*nods*). Go on.

302. He and my father hadn't seen each other for years. They talked about the early days of the Revolution.

GLETKIN. They were drinking?

302. Yes. They drank and talked. (*A far-away look and a gentle smile illumine his face at the memory*) In the last few years I've never seen my father in such a good mood.

GLETKIN (*quietly*). That was three months before the discovery of your father's counter-revolutionary crimes and his execution!

(*302 darts a glance at him, licks his lips, and stands there dumb. Rubashov turns to Gletkin on a sudden impulse, but, blinded by the light, he shuts his eyes and turns slowly away, taking off his spectacles and wiping them on his sleeve. The secretary's*

*pencil scratches on the paper and stops. After a long pause 302 regains himself.*)

302. Yes.

GLETKIN. Proceed! Repeat their conversation. Only essentials.

302. He said . . .

GLETKIN. Rubashov?

302. Yes. Rubashov said, since the Boss sat on the Party with his broad posterior, the air underneath was no longer breathable. He said they must hold tight and wait the hour.

GLETKIN. What did he mean by that? "Wait the hour"?

302. The hour in which the Leader would be eliminated. (*Rubashov smiles*)

GLETKIN. These reminiscences seem to amuse you.

RUBASHOV. Two old friends get a little drunk, talk carelessly, and you make a conspiracy.

GLETKIN. So Rubashov spoke of the hour in which the Leader of the Party would be eliminated? How eliminated?

302. My father said some day the Party would force him to resign.

GLETKIN. And Rubashov?

302. Laughed. He said the Boss had made the Party bureaucracy his puppets. He said the Boss could only be removed by force.

RUBASHOV. By this I meant political action.

GLETKIN. As opposed to what?

RUBASHOV. Individual terrorism.

GLETKIN. In other words, you preferred civil war?

RUBASHOV. No, mass action.

GLETKIN. Which leads to civil war. Is that the distinction on which you place so much value?

RUBASHOV (*loses patience, shouting*). I cannot think straight with that damned light in my eyes.

GLETKIN (*outshouts him*). I can't change the lighting in this room to suit you. (*To 302, quietly*) So Rubashov said they had to use violence? (*302 nods*) And his wild talk, plus the alcohol he'd fed you, inflamed you?

302 (*after a pause*). I didn't drink, but he—yes, he made a deep impression on me.

GLETKIN. And later that evening he outlined his plan for you to murder the Leader? (*302 is silent. He blinks into the light. Rubashov raises his head. A pause, during which one hears only the lamp humming)* Would you like your memory refreshed?

302 *(quivers as though struck by a whip)*. It didn't happen that evening, but next morning.

RUBASHOV *(to Gletkin)*. I believe the defendant has the right to ask questions.

GLETKIN *(fiercely)*. You have no rights here! *(He leans forward to make some notations, and after a brief pause, without looking up)* Go ahead; ask your questions.

RUBASHOV *(rises, steps toward 302, very gently)*. Now, Joseph, if I remember correctly, your father received the Order of Lenin the day after the celebration of the 17th anniversary of the Revolution.

302 *(whispers)*. Yes.

RUBASHOV *(gently)*. So that is correct. If I again remember rightly, Joseph, you were with him at the time he received it. *(302 nods)* And as I recall it, the Order was presented at Moscow. Right, Joseph? *(302 nods. Rubashov pauses, turns to Gletkin)* Professor Kieffer took a midnight plane and young Kieffer went with him. This alleged instigation to murder never took place because at the alleged moment young Kieffer was hundreds of miles away, high in the clouds.

*(The secretary's pencil comes to a sudden standstill. She turns to Gletkin. 302, his face twisting with bewilderment and fear, also looks to Gletkin.)*

GLETKIN *(calmly)*. Have you any more questions?

RUBASHOV. That is all for the present. *(Sits)*

GLETKIN. Now, Joseph— *(Rises, assumes Rubashov's gentleness, even exaggerates it, crosses to 302)* —did you leave with your father? Or did you, in fact, join him later after your rendezvous with Rubashov?

302 *(almost a sob of relief)*. After! I joined my father later.

GLETKIN. In time to be with him for the presentation?

302. Yes. Yes.

GLETKIN *(nods, turns to Rubashov)*. Have you any more questions?

RUBASHOV. No.

GLETKIN *(turns to 302)*. You may go.

302. Thank you . . .

GLETKIN *(calls)*. Guard!

*(A uniformed Guard enters and leads 302 out. At the door 302 turns his head once*

more to Rubashov. Rubashov meets 302's imploring glance for a second, then turns away. Exit 302.)*

RUBASHOV *(angrily)*. Poor devil! What have you done to him?

GLETKIN *(who has walked away, the full diameter of the room, turns, bellowing)*. What can be done to you. *(And with incredible speed for such a huge man he hurls himself across the room, grabs Rubashov by the throat and pulls him to his feet)* We have many ways of making a man tell the truth.

RUBASHOV *(quickly)*. Very well, what do you want me to sign? *(Gletkin relaxes his grip)* If you torture me I will sign anything you place before me. I will say anything you wish me to say at once. But tomorrow I will recant. At the public trial I'll stand up in open court and I'll cry out for all the world to hear, "They are drowning the Revolution in blood. Tyranny is afoot. She strides over our dead bodies." You've become quite pale. It would end your career, wouldn't it? You hold me by the throat, young man, but I hold you by the throat too. Remember that!

GLETKIN *(slowly releasing Rubashov)*. Why do you make this so personal?

RUBASHOV. Death, even in an impersonal cause, is a personal matter. Death and promotions. *(Sits)*

GLETKIN. I am here only to serve the Party. I am nothing. *(He sits at the desk, gathering up his papers)* The personal element in this case has been removed along with your friend Ivanoff.

RUBASHOV *(his face clouding, apprehensively)*. Removed?

GLETKIN. There'll be no partial confessions; there'll be no bargains. We promise you nothing.

RUBASHOV. What's happened to Ivanoff?

GLETKIN. Enemy of the people Ivanoff was executed early this morning.

RUBASHOV *(after a long pause, nods to himself, murmurs)*. I see. *(Looks up at Gletkin)* Why? Was it because of me?

GLETKIN. Perhaps.

RUBASHOV. Perhaps he thought I was innocent.

GLETKIN. Then he shouldn't have conducted your investigation.

RUBASHOV *(sighs heavily, murmurs)*. Go, Sascha. Go, in peace!

GLETKIN. He was corrupt, like so many

of your old guard, and his counter-revolutionary action in your examination . . .

RUBASHOV *(jumps to his feet, all his pent-up feelings exploding).* Counter-revolutionary? You ignorant young ass! What the hell do you know about the Revolution *or* the old guard? When you were peeing in your diapers we were working and fighting and studying and writing one thing: Revolution! Revolution! Half our lives we lived like moles—underground; we rotted away in every prison in Europe; we knew poverty, we knew persecution, we knew starvation, but every living second we dreamed and built the Revolution with our blood and our bones! And now you have the gall to sit there and *(He waves his hand to the faded patches on the wall)* spit at these, the heroes of your boyhood? Are you insane? Do you really believe that we have all suddenly become venal and corrupt?

GLETKIN *(leans forward, rising slowly, his face apoplectic).* Quiet! You washed-out, disgusting, rotten old man! You didn't make the Revolution—the Revolution made you. You adventurers rode along, scum on the flood of the people's uprising. But don't make any mistake! You never fooled our Leader! He used you, because he had to use whatever was at hand, but he knew you were defective. That's why our Leader has taken such pains with us. We have learned to recognize your defectiveness by the smell of you. You were needed for a while like the white-collared intelligentsia after the Revolution. But a new generation is at the helm now and your day is over. Understand! There'll be no bargains! You, we offer nothing! You are going to die! The only question is whether you'll die uselessly, or whether you will confess and perform a last service for the Party. But, die you will, you understand?

RUBASHOV *(stares at him. Something dies; something of the will, and the battle, and the spirit go out of Rubashov forever. He suddenly becomes a very tired, sick old man. He nods, whispers hoarsely)* I understand.

GLETKIN *(harshly, triumphant).* Then let's have no more arrogance. *(He pushes a button, picks up the phone)* Next witness! *(The lights flicker, and as Rubashov slowly sits the scene vanishes)*

*(The lights come up on the tier of cells.*

*We see 402 and the wraith-like 302. They are eating their meager supper of black bread and cabbage soup.)*

302 *(taps to 402).* Is Rubashov back yet?

402 *(taps).* No.

302 *(taps).* How long?

402 *(taps).* They've had him upstairs—it must be ten hours now.

302 *(taps).* I wonder are they torturing him now.

402 *(taps).* Why should they? He's confessed.

302 *(taps).* They want more than that from him.

402 *(taps).* What more is there?

302 *(taps).* There's more. I hope he understood. I think he did. I looked into his eyes before I left. He seemed to understand. My father used to talk so well of him. *(Suddenly overcome, to himself)* Oh, my father, my father!

402 *(taps).* Eat your supper.

*(The lights fade and the prisoners vanish. The lights come up again, revealing the office. A new Interrogator and Secretary have replaced Gletkin and the Young Woman. As the scene appears the Interrogator, red-eyed, perspiration-soaked, purple-faced, is standing over Rubashov, hammering away at him. On the verge of fainting from fatigue, white-faced as the ghosts that haunt him, Rubashov exerts every ounce of will power to resist the fanatical onslaught. The Secretary is also washed out with fatigue, his hair in disarray, his tie loosened.)*

INTERROGATOR *(bellowing).* Is this true? Answer yes or no!

RUBASHOV. I can't . . .

INTERROGATOR. Yes or no!

RUBASHOV. Partially . . .

INTERROGATOR *(harshly).* Yes or no! Yes or no!

RUBASHOV *(wearily).* Yes . . . Yes.

INTERROGATOR *(grunts).* Yes. Good. *(Returns to the chair at the desk, seats himself)* And now we return to the Kieffer episode. *(Picks up the documents)* You admit this conversation with Professor Kieffer? *(Pause. He glances up; Rubashov's eyes have closed, his head, fallen, rests on his chest. The Interrogator shouts)* You will pay attention!

RUBASHOV *(opens his eyes, raises his head).* What?

INTERROGATOR. Don't you feel well?

RUBASHOV. I'm all right.

INTERROGATOR *(with quiet threat).* Would you like me to call in the doctor?

RUBASHOV *(quickly, alert again).* No.

INTERROGATOR. Stand up! *(Rubashov pulls himself to his feet)* Straight! Head up! Hands at your sides! At attention! *(Rubashov obeys)* Perhaps that will keep you awake. You admit this conversation? *(Pause)* Yes or no!

RUBASHOV. There were conversations.

INTERROGATOR. I didn't ask you about conversations, I ask you about this one.

RUBASHOV. In Hegel's philosophy, every yes has a no and every no has a yes.

INTERROGATOR. You're not here as a philosopher, you're here as a criminal. You'd better not talk about Hegel's philosophy. It'd be better first of all for Hegel. Do you admit this conversation? Yes or no.

RUBASHOV. Yes.

*(The door opens, Gletkin and his Secretary enter briskly. They are fresh and rested. She has changed her dress. Gletkin carries an armful of books, with slips inserted.)*

INTERROGATOR. Yes. Good.

RUBASHOV. But I deny your conclusions.

GLETKIN *(interrupting).* That is to say you admit everything except the logical consequence of your admissions? *(He nods to the seated Secretary, who folds his notebook and rises. Gletkin's Secretary occupies the chair and proceeds to make notes)*

INTERROGATOR. Stop this crude lying!

RUBASHOV. I'm not lying, young man.

GLETKIN *(crosses to the desk).* You've been here for ten hours poisoning the air with your Jesuit tactics. What do you expect to gain by this?

RUBASHOV. Gain? Nothing?

GLETKIN *(touches the Interrogator who nods, rises).* Then admit your crimes and get it over with!

RUBASHOV. Admit to crimes I didn't commit? Even Danton in the French Revolution was allowed to defend himself.

INTERROGATOR *(now up out of the chair).* And what happened to the French Revolution?

GLETKIN *(sliding into the seat, leaning across the desk, without interrupting the interrogation. The effect is of a well-oiled machine)* Powdered pigtails declaiming about personal honor! All that mattered to Danton and Company was to go with a swan song. Is that what you want? *(The*

*Interrogator and the male Secretary exit, stretching, yawning wearily)*

RUBASHOV. I certainly don't want to go howling like a wolf in the night.

GLETKIN. Whether it does good or harm to the Cause, that doesn't matter?

RUBASHOV. My whole life has been a single purpose: to serve the Cause.

GLETKIN. There's only one way you can serve it now. A full confession in open court. A voluntary confession of all these crimes.

RUBASHOV *(sways, leans on the desk to support himself).* I've pleaded guilty to a false and harmful policy. Isn't that enough?

GLETKIN. Our country today is the bastion of the new era. Everything depends on our keeping the bastion intact, keeping the country solidly united.

RUBASHOV. How does it unite the country? How does it serve the Party that her members have to grovel in the dust? The name N. S. Rubashov is a piece of Party history. By dragging me in the mud you besmirch the Revolution. I—

GLETKIN. I, I, me, me, I! *(He picks up one of the books, opening it to a marked page)* Do you recognize this book?

RUBASHOV *(puts on his glasses. His hands are trembling. It takes him some time to focus his vision as he peers at the book).* Yes.

GLETKIN. Who wrote it?

RUBASHOV. I did.

GLETKIN *(reads from the page).* "With us the objective result is everything. With us objective good faith is of no interest. Those who prove wrong will pay!" You said that?

RUBASHOV *(his body sags again).* Yes.

GLETKIN. Well, you are wrong.

*(The ghost-like image of Richard appears, pointing a finger at Rubashov.)*

RUBASHOV *(staring into space, nods).* Yes.

GLETKIN. And you will pay.

*(The phantom of Richard vanishes.)*

RUBASHOV. I am paying.

GLETKIN. With your life!

RUBASHOV. My life has been the Party. My life would be worthless unless I could go on working for it. *(His knees buckle, he sways, about to collapse)*

GLETKIN. Sit down! *(Rubashov sinks to the chair)* There's only one way you can serve the Party now. As an example to the masses. *(He opens another book, reading from it)* "For the masses, what is right must be gilded, what is wrong must be black as pitch." You wrote that?

RUBASHOV. Yes.

GLETKIN. Even if we let you go on liv-ing—as you say—what would you have to live for?

RUBASHOV *(to himself)*. Nothing. A man without a country. *(The ghostly image of Luigi appears, smiling, gesticulating)* Like little Luigi.

GLETKIN. Who?

*(Luigi's phantom vanishes.)*

RUBASHOV *(shakes his head)*. Never mind.

GLETKIN. You admit your guilt?

RUBASHOV. In thought.

GLETKIN. In thought? *(Holds up a book)* And this?

RUBASHOV. Yes. Mine too.

GLETKIN *(reads)*. "The consequences of our thinking will be felt unto the seventh generation. Hence a wrong thought from us is more criminal than a wrong deed from others." You wrote that?

RUBASHOV. Yes. I wrote it.

GLETKIN. Then, when you say you are not guilty, aren't you thinking mechan-istically, Citizen Rubashov? *(Albert's im-age appears. He is waving his hands with the ridiculously exaggerated gestures. Pab-lo's image appears, juggling plates) (Rubashov laughs softly.)*

GLETKIN. What are you laughing at? *(The phantoms of Pablo and Albert van-ish.)*

RUBASHOV *(startled, looks up)*. Was I laughing?

GLETKIN. Yes.

RUBASHOV *(passes his hand over his forehead)*. I wasn't conscious of it.

GLETKIN. Do you usually do things you're not conscious of?

RUBASHOV. No. Not often.

GLETKIN. These acts of sabotage, for ex-ample.

RUBASHOV. I deny them.

GLETKIN. Perhaps you committed them unconsciously.

RUBASHOV. I didn't commit them at all.

GLETKIN. These factories had great losses.

RUBASHOV. Yes.

GLETKIN. Sabotage is a weapon of the class struggle.

RUBASHOV. Yes. But I didn't employ it.

GLETKIN. You've advocated its use again and again?

RUBASHOV. Yes. But I didn't employ it here.

GLETKIN. Didn't you? *(Pause. He looks through the papers)* The case of the woman Luba Loshenko. She was your secretary? Correct?

RUBASHOV. Yes.

GLETKIN. And you were sleeping with her. *(Rubashov straightens up)*. Correct? *(Silence)* Shall I give you the place, dates, conversations? *(He waves the dossier)* They're all here.

RUBASHOV *(almost inaudible)*. Yes, I was sleeping with her.

GLETKIN. Speak up!

RUBASHOV *(loudly)*. Yes. I admit the re-lationship.

GLETKIN. You admit it?

RUBASHOV. I said yes.

GLETKIN. She was tried and shot for sabotage, correct?

RUBASHOV *(wildly)*. She was innocent.

GLETKIN. Innocent? *(He rises)*

RUBASHOV. Yes.

GLETKIN. She had no political motives? Is that when you mean?

RUBASHOV. Precisely.

GLETKIN. Precisely. She was an ordinary young woman, infatuated—blindly, stu-pidly, the slave and tool of one man who, however, did have considerable political motives—you!

RUBASHOV. What motives?

GLETKIN. You hated the Revolution, and you taught her to hate us.

RUBASHOV *(desperately)*. That's not true. She was innocent.

GLETKIN. Why didn't you say so at the time?

RUBASHOV. You know as well as I there wasn't anything I could do to save her.

GLETKIN. So you did nothing?

RUBASHOV. Nothing.

GLETKIN. You were silent.

RUBASHOV. I was silent.

GLETKIN. To save your own neck!

RUBASHOV. To go on working.

GLETKIN. Without a neck one cannot work; hence, to save your own neck. And this silence of yours was finally respon-sible for her execution. Correct?

RUBASHOV. So I was informed.

GLETKIN. For your further information, I was one of her interrogators.

RUBASHOV *(raises his head)*. You?

GLETKIN *(thumbs through the transcript).* I have here a transcript of her interrogation. I think it might interest you. Ninth day. Tenth day. Yes, here we have it. This Loshenko woman was surprising. These thin delicate ones sometimes really stand up. Listen! *(He reads)* Interrogator: "Under whose orders?" Loshenko: "No one's . . ."

*(Luba's image appears in space, bowed, drenched with pain. She shakes her head slowly, moving her lips silently at first, then her trembling voice becomes barely audible, grows stronger, finally topping and supplanting Gletkin's voice. Gletkin continues to read from the transcript.)*

LUBA. No one's. I've told you a hundred times there were no orders.

GLETKIN. Stop lying.

LUBA. No matter what I say you don't believe me. Oh, God! I'm so tired.

GLETKIN. I want the truth.

LUBA. I've told you the truth, over and over and over and over. I'm so tired, I can't . . .

GLETKIN. Who gave you these instructions?

LUBA. No one.

GLETKIN. You sabotaged without instructions?

LUBA. No, no, no. You're twisting my words.

GLETKIN. That's what you said.

LUBA. I didn't say that! I said I didn't do these things and no one asked me to.

GLETKIN. We've all the proofs.

LUBA. What are you trying to make me say?

GLETKIN. Stop shielding Rubashov!

LUBA. I'm not shielding anyone.

GLETKIN. You're shielding Rubashov.

LUBA. A man like that doesn't need shielding. A man like that . . .

GLETKIN. You were sleeping with him, weren't you?

LUBA. I loved him.

GLETKIN. You loved him?

LUBA. Yes.

GLETKIN. You'd do anything he asked you?

LUBA. He wouldn't ask me to commit crimes.

GLETKIN. Idiot! This man has used you.

LUBA. No!

GLETKIN. He's made a fool of you.

LUBA. No!

GLETKIN. And now when you need him, where is he? Where is he?

LUBA. Oh, God, God, make them leave me alone!

GLETKIN. God is dead, Luba Loshenko! God is dead.

LUBA. What do you want of me?

GLETKIN. Rubashov's making you responsible for his guilt.

LUBA. He's not.

GLETKIN. Use your head! He's refused to testify for you.

LUBA. I don't believe that.

GLETKIN. Here are the proofs! Look, look!

LUBA. I don't want to look.

GLETKIN. He was asked to testify and he's refused.

LUBA. I don't believe that. I don't believe you . . . I don't believe you . . .

RUBASHOV *(staring into space, murmurs).* I had no choice, Luba. Don't you see? I had no choice. I couldn't have saved you. It was only a trap to destroy my usefulness. *(The Secretary rises, leans forward to catch Rubashov's words and writes them down)* I tried! I went everywhere—to my friends in high places. They said no, nothing will help.

GLETKIN *(reads on).* Save yourself! This is your last chance, Luba Loshenko! You admit these acts of sabotage.

LUBA. I can't admit them because there weren't any. There was no sabotage. There were only tired men and sick men and frightened men.

GLETKINS *(slaps his hand as he reads).* You stupid bitch! *(Luba's image recoils as if she'd been struck)* All right! Then you'll be shot in the back of your neck!

LUBA. What are you doing to us? What are you doing to us? We're not stones, we're not machines! We're human beings. We feel, we think, we see, we dream, we're a part of God. Why have you done this to us? You say God is dead, but you've made your own god out of darkness, out of misery and lies and pain! Why? Why are you doing this to us?

RUBASHOV *(stands up unsteadily, staring into space, calls out).* This was not the way it was to be.

*(Gletkin glances quickly at Rubashov who is no longer aware of his surroundings, nods to the Secretary. She rises and leans closer to Rubashov, taking down his words.)*

LUBA. You've made a prison . . . out of our wonderful country—a prison.

RUBASHOV. We wanted to build a new and better world.

LUBA. You've put chains on our people. Chains. In their hearts, inside their skulls. Why? Why?

RUBASHOV. I don't understand why myself. Our principles were right.

LUBA. Our people are more miserable than before the Revolution.

RUBASHOV. We diagnosed the disease, but wherever we applied the healing knife . . .

LUBA. Our people are covered with sores.

RUBASHOV. Our will was pure. We should have been loved by the people . . .

LUBA. They hate you.

RUBASHOV. Why? Why are we so hated? We brought truth.

LUBA. In your mouths everything becomes a lie.

RUBASHOV. We brought living life . . .

LUBA. The trees in the forest wither.

RUBASHOV. I sang of hope.

LUBA. Your tongues stammer and bark.

RUBASHOV. Yes, yes, and every premise of unimpeachable truth has led me to this final weird and ghostly game. Why? Why?

LUBA. Kolya! Kolya, darling! Wherever you are . . . (*She vanishes and only her voice is heard crying "Kolya! Kolya!"*)

RUBASHOV. Luba! Luba! What have I done? What have I done? (*He whispers*) Guilty, guilty, guilty! (*Then, very simply*) I'm going to faint. (*He slides gently and quietly out of the chair and falls to the floor*)

GLETKIN (*rings for his colleague, snaps his fingers at his Secretary*). The ammonia! (*The Secretary rushes across to the table, opens a drawer, takes out a bottle of ammonia and hands it to him. Gletkin, on one knee, slaps Rubashov's face and administers the restorative. The door is thrown open and the other Interrogator enters*)

GLETKIN (*nods, indicating Rubashov's crumpled body*). We've got him. We've got the lever. (*The sharp fumes of the ammonia begin to revive Rubashov*) Stand him up! (*The other Interrogator lifts Rubashov to his feet and holds him there, limp as a rag-doll. Gletkin waves the ammonia bottle under his nose until he responds, then, putting one huge hand gently on his shoulder, speaks softly, caressingly*) You haven't eaten your food today, Comrade Rubashov. Would you like some hot soup?

RUBASHOV (*murmurs*). Sleep. I must sleep.

GLETKIN. You understand, Comrade Rubashov, what the Party expects of you.

RUBASHOV. Yes.

GLETKIN. This is the last service you can perform for the Party.

RUBASHOV. I must sleep. Sleep.

GLETKIN. Very well. (*To Guard*) Take him back to his cell. (*To Rubashov, gently*) I'll see that you are not disturbed.

RUBASHOV (*like a child, eagerly*). Thank you, Comrade Gletkin. (*The Guard takes Rubashov out*)

GLETKIN (*to the Interrogator*). In exactly twenty minutes wake him up and bring him back here. I'll interrogate him till midnight, you take him till five A.M., and I'll take him again at five. (*Blinks his eyes, avoids the dazzle-light*) This Loshenko thing—that's the lever. Work it around in his belly. Keep returning to it. It's simply a question of time now. (*The Interrogator nods, feels his aching back, and goes, yawning. Gletkin snaps off the dazzle-light*)

SECRETARY. Congratulations, Comrade Gletkin.

GLETKIN (*sits down to his desk, stretches his legs, pleased*). It's just a matter of constitution.

(*The scene fades out. The lights come up. The Supreme Court of the U.S.S.R. This scene is another memory in the mind of the brooding Rubashov after the event has occurred. The President, bathed in a hot white light, is seated at a long covered table, three judges to his left, three to his right. The rest are shadowy figures.*)

PRESIDENT. Comrade Judges, you have heard the evidence against Citizen Rubashov. Comrade Procurateur of the U.S.S.R. has summed up for the prosecution. Accused Rubashov step forward. (*Rubashov appears in the white light before the judge's bench. The Guard brings on a microphone and sets it in front of Rubashov*) Accused Rubashov may make his last plea.

RUBASHOV (*bending a little, speaking into the microphone, in a dead voice*). Citizen Judges. Covered with shame, trampled in the dust, about to die—let me serve my final purpose. Let my horrible story demonstrate how the slightest deflection from the Party line must inevitably drag one down into counter-revolutionary banditry. If I ask myself today: "For what am I dying?" I am confronted by absolute nothingness. Therefore, on the threshold of my final hour, I bend my knees to my country and to my people. The political masquerade is over. We were dead long before the Public Prosecutor demanded our heads. With this my task is ended. I have paid my debts. To ask for mercy would be derision. You must hate me, and you must kill me! I have nothing more to say. *(He stands with lowered head. The Guard removes the microphone)*

PRESIDENT. I will announce the sentence of the Military Collegium of the Supreme Court. *(He reads)* "The Sentence. The Military Collegium of the Supreme Court of the U.S.S.R. sentences N. S. Rubashov to the supreme penalty—to be shot, with the confiscation of all his personal property . . ."

*(His voice trails off. The lights fade. The court vanishes. Only Rubashov remains, sitting in his cell, wrapped in meditation, his head between his hands, his brow furrowed, his face old and gray as if all the blood had been drained out of him. An insistent tapping. 402 comes into view, tapping three times, waiting, and gently repeating the code.)*

RUBASHOV *(coming out of his reverie, rises feebly, crosses unsteadily to the wall, taps)*. Yes?

402 *(taps)*. I thought 302 behaved quite well. He went like a brave man.

RUBASHOV *(taps)*. Yes.

402 *(taps)*. You still have about ten minutes. What are you doing?

RUBASHOV *(taps)*. I'm thinking.

402 *(taps)*. Thinking's bad. You won't show the white feather! We know you're a man. A man. *(Pause)* Do you still remember "Breasts fit champagne glasses!" Ha! Ha! What a man you are! *(Rubashov listens for a sound from the corridor. 402 senses his thoughts)* Don't listen. I'll tell you in time when they are coming. *(Pause)* What would you do if you were pardoned?

RUBASHOV *(thinks, taps)*. I'd study astronomy.

402 *(taps)*. Ha! Ha! Me too, perhaps. But they say other stars are perhaps also inhabited. That would spoil it. *(Pause)* May I give you some advice?

RUBASHOV *(taps)*. Yes.

402 *(taps)*. But don't take it wrong. Technical suggestion of an old soldier. Empty your bladder. Is always better in such case. The spirit is willing but the flesh is weak. Ha! Ha!

RUBASHOV *(smiles, taps)*. Thanks. *(Pause)*

402 *(taps)*. Why astronomy?

RUBASHOV *(taps)*. As a boy I loved to watch the stars. I wanted to solve the riddle of the universe.

402 *(taps)*. Why? Talk to me.

RUBASHOV *(to himself)*. Recently I read they have discovered the Universe is finite. Forty years pass and I read that. If the Public Prosecutor had asked, "Defendant Rubashov, what about the Infinite?," I would not have been able to answer. Perhaps there is my real guilt.

402 *(taps)*. It's too late to worry about guilt.

RUBASHOV *(taps)*. How can I die till I find out what I'm dying for? *(Pause, taps)* Sorry! Tell me, what are your prospects?

402 *(taps slowly)*. Eighteen years more. Not quite. Only six thousand five hundred thirty days. *(Pause)* Think of it. Another six thousand five hundred thirty days without a woman. I envy you really. My brain is turning to water. I have returned to the habits of my childhood. I loathe myself!

RUBASHOV *(to the wall)*. Oh, you poor, poor devil! *(To the entire prison, to all Russia)* All of you! My hundred and eighty million fellow prisoners, what have I done to you? What have I created? If History is all calculation, Rubashov, give me the sum of a hundred and eighty million nightmares. Quickly calculate me the pressure of a hundred and eighty million cravings. Where in your mathematics, Rubashov, is the human soul? At the very beginning you forgot what you were searching for?

*(Footsteps ring out in the corridor.)*

402 *(taps)*. They're coming. *(The footsteps grow louder)* What a shame. We were having such a pleasant talk.

RUBASHOV *(taps)*. You've helped me a lot. Thanks.

402 *(taps)*. Farewell. I envy you, I envy you.

*(The door of Rubashov's cell is thrown open with a clang. Gletkin enters.)*

GLETKIN. Enemy of the People Nicolai Semonovitch Rubashov, before you are executed, have you any last wish? *(A long pause)*

RUBASHOV. One. *(He tries to catch Gletkin's eyes)* If I could only make you understand where in the very beginning we failed.

GLETKIN. These are your last words. Don't waste them.

RUBASHOV *(passionately)*. You don't build a Paradise out of concrete. My son . . .

GLETKIN *(quickly, distastefully)*. I am not your son.

RUBASHOV *(after a long pause, sadly)*. Yes, you are. That's the horror. *(He shakes his head, bitterly)* The means have become the end; and darkness has come over the land.

GLETKIN. Have you any last wish?

RUBASHOV. To die.

*(Gletkin motions him to walk. Rubashov moves slowly out of the cell; Gletkin takes out his pistol, cocks it and follows. The Guard opens the gate to the cellar, a shaft of light coming up catches them. 402 begins to drum on the door. From all over the prison comes the hollow muffled drumming, which mounts higher and higher as Rubashov and Gletkin descend, and the iron gate clangs behind them. The drumming reaches a climax as the curtain falls slowly.)*

# 1951-52

Quite the most charming, the most memorable thing about this season was a fantasy of childhood entitled *Mrs. McThing,* written by Mary Chase, author of the equally memorable *Harvey.* But it didn't win the Circle award which went, on April 2, 1952, to *I Am a Camera* by John van Druten.

Van Druten's play received ten votes to five for *Mrs. McThing.* Three each went to Joseph Kramm's meritorious *The Shrike* and Paul Osborn's stodgy *Point of No Return,* based on the John P. Marquand novel; two to Maxwell Anderson's *Barefoot in Athens* and one to a first play by novelist Truman Capote, *The Grass Harp,* a precious and ineffectual work that seemed to have some appeal for a certain coterie. *The Shrike* took the Pulitzer prize.

Christopher Fry's pretentious and empty *Venus Observed* was given the foreign citation with fifteen votes, to eight for Jan de Hartog's *Fourposter,* a two-character work which had a highly profitable 632 performances, thanks largely to the excellent playing of the husband-wife team of Hume Cronyn and Jessica Tandy.

The revival of the Rodgers-Hart *Pal Joey,* which had 374 performances in 1940–41 in its original presentation, was voted to be the best "new musical" through a curious lapse of memory regarding the rules. It received twenty votes; *Three Wishes for Jamie* and *Paint Your Wagon* received one each. It was a shame that the latter was so heavy-footed; it had one of the better scores in recent years by Alan Jay Lerner and Frederick Loewe, the team that provided such wonderful songs for *Brigadoon.*

An unusual step was taken in voting a special citation as "a distinguished and original contribution to the theatre" to the unorthodox presentation of the *Don Juan in Hell* (third) act of Bernard Shaw's *Man and Superman.* This exceptionally long and delightful but not essential "dream" act is nearly always omitted in any presentation of the play.

This special citation was to the First Drama Quartet, the creation of one of its members, actor Charles Laughton, and Paul Gregory, an enterprising young entrepreneur whose impact on the stage was to grow in following seasons. Laughton, Sir Cedric Hardwicke, Charles Boyer and Agnes Moorehead "read" *Don Juan in Hell* while seated before microphones; there were no costumes, no scenery. It was tremendous intellectual theatre, and, of all things, a smashing financial success.

Louis Kronenberger's effort to vote for it as the best new foreign play—on the grounds that it had never been performed here before—was voted down, and the special recognition followed.

*Mrs. McThing* was distinguished by the acting of Helen Hayes, and Julie Harris, playing a disillusioned sophisticate of the early 1930's, gave a glow to van Druten's award-winner.

Mae West revived her durable *Diamond Lil,* Audrey Hepburn leaped to almost immediate stardom in her first bid in *Gigi,* Eugene O'Neill received some belated revival interest with the presentation of *Anna Christie* and *Desire under the Elms, The Male Animal* was highly successful in a splendid revival, and Katharine Cornell found comfort in a revival of Somerset Maugham's *The Constant Wife.*

*I Am a Camera* ran 214 performances; *Mrs. McThing,* 350; *The Shrike,* 161, although it could have continued much longer had its star, director and producer, José Ferrer, been able to stay with it; *Venus Observed,* 86; *Pal Joey,* 540; *Don Juan in Hell,* 105 in a purposely limited engagement.

# I Am a Camera

## By JOHN VAN DRUTEN

Adapted from "The Berlin Stories" of Christopher Isherwood

Presented by Gertrude Macy, in association with Walter Starcke, at the Empire Theatre, New York City, November 28, 1951, with the following cast:

| | |
|---|---|
| CHRISTOPHER ISHERWOOD . . . . . | *William Prince* |
| FRAULEIN SCHNEIDER . . . . . . | *Olga Fabian* |
| FRITZ WENDEL . . . . . . . . . | *Martin Brooks* |
| SALLY BOWLES . . . . . . . . . | *Julie Harris* |
| NATALIA LANDAUER . . . . . . | *Marian Winters* |
| CLIVE MORTIMER . . . . . . . | *Edward Andrews* |
| MRS. WATSON-COURTNEIDGE . . . | *Catherine Willard* |

## SCENE

The play is in three acts and seven scenes. The set, throughout, is a room in Fraülein Schneider's flat in Berlin in 1930, before the rise of the Hitler regime.

Act I—Scene 1—A summer afternoon. Scene 2—Three months later.

Act II—Scene 1—A week later. Scene 2—Five days later.

Act III—Scene 1—Two days later. Scene 2—Three days later. Scene 3—Three days later.

Library of Congress Catalogue Card Number: 52-5920

*Reprinted by permission of Random House, Inc.*

## ACT ONE

### Scene I

Scene: *The scene throughout is a room in Fräulein Schneider's flat in Berlin around 1930.*

*The bed is hidden, or partially so, behind curtains upstage. The door to the hall is in the right wall. Windows in the left wall.*

*The room is excessively German and middle-class. There is a tall, tiled stove with an angel on it. A washstand by the curtains, like a Gothic shrine. A best chair like a bishop's throne. Antlers make a kind of hatstand by the door. There is a small table for tea. A backless sofa, and an ottoman. A large table by the window piled with books, papers and notebooks. There are one or two good Medici prints on the walls, between heavy German engravings.*

Time: *A summer afternoon. When the curtain rises, the stage is dark except for a light on Christopher Isherwood, seated alone at the table. He is in his twenties, English and untidy. He wears flannel trousers, very dirty, and a shirt. (He wears this throughout the play. The only change will be in his tie.) He is writing and smoking. Then he stops and reads over what he has written.*

---

CHRIS (*reading aloud*). "In the last few days, there has been a lot of Nazi rioting in the streets, here in Berlin. They are getting bolder, more arrogant." (*He stops*) No, that's all wrong. (*He crumples the page and throws it aside*)

That's not the right way to start. It's sheer journalism. I must explain who it is who is telling all this—a typical beachcomber of the big city. He comes to Berlin for the week end, stays on, runs out of money, starts giving English lessons. Now he sits in a rented room, waiting for something to happen—something that will help him understand what his life is all about. (*Rises, pouring beer into a glass*)

When Lord Tennyson wanted to write a poem, they say he used to put himself into a mystic trance by just repeating his own name. Alfred Tennyson. Christopher Isherwood. Christopher Isherwood. Christopher Isherwood. I like the sound of my name.

"Alone among the writers of his generation, Christopher Isherwood can be said to have achieved true greatness." Shut up, idiot. The only book I ever published got five reviews, all bad, and sold two hundred and thirty-three copies to date. And I haven't even started this new one, though I've been here six months already. (*Sits at the table again*) Well, you're going to start now, this minute. You're not leaving this chair until you do. Write "Chapter One." (*Does so*) Good. Now begin. Create something. Anything. (*He writes, then reads*)

"I am a camera, with it's shutter open, quite passive. Some day all of this will have to be developed, printed, fixed."

(*The lights come up on the room. There is a knock on the door.*)

Who's that?

FRÄULEIN SCHNEIDER (*off*). It is I, Herr Issyvoo.

CHRIS. Come in, Fräulein.

(*She comes in. She is a large, bosomy, German woman. She carries a lace tea-cloth.*)

FRÄULEIN SCHNEIDER. I bring you this tea-cloth. When you are having a lady guest, you can trust Schneiderschen to make things elegant. Now, where do you want all of these things to go, Herr Issyvoo?

CHRIS. Oh, put them on the floor.

FRÄULEIN SCHNEIDER. But you cannot put things on the floor.

CHRIS. There are a lot of things there already.

FRÄULEIN SCHNEIDER. But they must not stay there, not if a lady is coming. It does not look good at all.

CHRIS. You'd better put them on the bed. She won't be looking at the bed.

FRÄULEIN SCHNEIDER. And how do you know that, Herr Issyvoo? A handsome young man like you?

CHRIS. Fräulein Schneider, I'm surprised at you.

FRÄULEIN SCHNEIDER (*with a big laugh*). Oh, Herr Issyvoo, I have been young, too. Young and saucy (*rather archly, she takes the things to the bed behind the curtains*).

CHRIS. I suppose you had a great many admirers, Fräulein Schneider?

FRÄULEIN SCHNEIDER. Oh, I had dozens, Herr Issyvoo. But only one Friend. (*She returns for more stuff*) Eleven years we were together. Then he died. And it was after that that I became fat. The bosom, you know. It grew and it grew. I think it is still growing. And it is such a weight to carry about with you. It is like carrying a suitcase. *Two* suitcases. And it is sad that it should all have grown after he died. He was a man for bosoms. It would have made him so happy. And now it does no one any good. This young lady you are expecting—she is very attractive?

CHRIS. She is one of my pupils. She wanted to see where I lived. Though when I say she is one of my pupils, it isn't true. She's the only one I have left. The others have all gone away for the summer. Fräulein Schneider, I have got to have a talk with you.

FRÄULEIN SCHNEIDER. Ja, Herr Issyvoo?

CHRIS. I don't think I can go on living here.

FRÄULEIN SCHNEIDER. What? Oh, Herr Issyvoo, you are not going to leave me? Are you not comfortable here?

CHRIS. Yes, I am very comfortable. It's just that I can't afford it.

FRÄULEIN SCHNEIDER. Oh, that can wait.

CHRIS. No. It's been waiting too long. I haven't paid you for two months—not properly. I've got it here. (*Takes money from wallet*) I was just wondering—that little room across the passage—just across the passage—that's not let.

FRÄULEIN SCHNEIDER. But it is so small, Herr Issyvoo. Why, I can hardly get into it myself. And what do I do with this room? With the summer coming on, I shall never find a tenant for it.

CHRIS. Oh, I'm sure you will. And until you do, why don't you live in it yourself, instead of the sitting room?

FRÄULEIN SCHNEIDER (*setting tea-cloth*). I like the sitting room. I can look onto the corner and see what's going on. And believe me, Herr Issyvoo, there is plenty. Those women—they are as old as I am—almost—and they stand there and whisper to all the men who pass by—Komm, Süsser. And believe me, Herr Issyvoo, they come. Sometimes I think I shall adopt that profession myself.

CHRIS. Can I rent the other room, Fräulein Schneider? What do you charge for it?

FRÄULEIN SCHNEIDER. I have charged twenty-eight marks when times were good.

CHRIS. I can't afford twenty-eight.

FRÄULEIN SCHNEIDER (*ruffling his hair*). Ach, du armer Junger. But of course you can rent it. I will not have you leave. You rent it for twenty marks.

CHRIS. You're very sweet, Fräulein Schneider.

FRÄULEIN SCHNEIDER. Sweet? Ja. Once I was sweet. Sweet as a sugar cake. Now I am sweet like a fat old bun. And soon you make a great deal of money with your stories that you are always writing, and you take this room again, and everyone is happy once more.

CHRIS. I'll buy you a fur coat.

FRÄULEIN SCHNEIDER. And then I become one of the ladies. Only I will not go up and down the street. I sit at my window in my fur coat and call out, "Komm, Süsser." Komm to the third floor. And then I open the coat a little—just a little—and what do you think I have on underneath? Nothing! I have nothing on underneath. (*Bell rings*) Ach Gott, there is the bell. It will be your young lady.

CHRIS. You need not tell her that I am leaving this room.

FRÄULEIN SCHNEIDER (*on her way out*). But of course not, Herr Issyvoo. You can trust me perfectly. And I will bring you serviettes for your coffee. Most ladylike. Ladies appreciate these things.

(*She goes out. Chris starts to tidy the room.*)

FRÄULEIN SCHNEIDER'S VOICE (*off*). Nein, nein, Herr Wendel. Sie können nicht hinein gehen. Herr Issyvoo erwartet heute eine Dame.

FRITZ'S VOICE. Aber ich muss mit ihm sprechen. Christopher. Christopher.

CHRIS (*going to door*). Fritz.

FRITZ'S VOICE. Fräulein Schneider says I cannot come in. She says you expect a lady.

CHRIS. Yes, I do. But that's all right. Come in, Fritz. (*Fritz enters. Young and dark. Fräulein Schneider stands behind*) Do you want some coffee? One of my pupils is coming.

FRITZ. But yes, I would like some coffee. *Black* coffee.

CHRIS. Will you make enough for three, Fräulein Schneider?

FRÄULEIN SCHNEIDER. You are too good,

Herr Issyvoo. You entertain whoever comes. No matter whoever. (*She goes out*)

FRITZ. I do not think your landlady likes me. And that is with me all right. Ultimately, I do not like her, too. In fact, I think the world is lousy.

CHRIS. Is business bad?

FRITZ. It is terrible. Lousy and terrible. Or I pull off a new deal in the next month, or I go as a gigolo.

CHRIS. Either—or. I'm sorry. That's just force of habit.

FRITZ. I am speaking a lousy English just now. Sally says maybe she will give me a few lessons.

CHRIS. Who is Sally?

FRITZ. She is a friend of mine. Eventually she is coming around here this afternoon. I want that you should know each other.

CHRIS. Is she a girl friend of yours?

FRITZ. Not yet. But she is wonderful, Chris.

CHRIS. Who is she? What does she do?

FRITZ. She is an actress. She sings at the Lady Windermere. Hot stuff, believe me. Ultimately she has a bit of French in her. Her mother was French.

CHRIS. I wonder what Natalia will think of her. Natalia Landauer is the pupil I am expecting.

FRITZ. Landauer? Of the big department store?

CHRIS. Her father owns it. It's the family business.

FRITZ. But they must be enormously wealthy.

CHRIS. Oh, yes, they're stinking rich.

FRITZ. And are you going to marry her?

CHRIS (*laughing*). Me? No, of course not.

FRITZ. Do you not want her?

CHRIS. Not a bit. Except as a pupil.

FRITZ. Then if I should meet her and perhaps make a pass after her, you would not mind?

CHRIS. But you haven't even seen her.

FRITZ. Why would that make a difference? I tell you, Chris, I need money. Maybe then her father will take a liking from me, and give me a job in the business. If I marry her, a partnership, perhaps.

CHRIS. What makes you think she'd have you?

FRITZ. All women will have me if I want them.

CHRIS. Not Sally, apparently.

FRITZ. Sally has been too busy. With other men. But one day she will be free, and then I will ultimately get my look in.

CHRIS (*teasing him*). Perhaps *you* won't be free. Perhaps you will be all tied up with Natalia.

FRITZ (*seriously*). Yes, business must come first, ultimately. I suppose she is a Jewess?

CHRIS. Oh, yes.

FRITZ. Well, there is always something. And you know, Chris, I am very broadminded.

(*Bell rings.*)

CHRIS. That will be Natalia.

FRITZ. How do I look, Chris? How is my hair? (*He gets out a comb and mirror*) Um Gotteswillen . . . a gray hair. No, that is too much. (*He pulls it out*) You see, Chris dear, I must marry soon. You will help me to arrange the marriage settlement?

(*Voices off.*)

SALLY'S VOICE. Herr Isherwood ist er zu Hause?

FRITZ. That is Sally. Chris, put on your coat.

CHRIS. Why?

FRITZ. She is a lady. Very elegant.

FRÄULEIN'S VOICE. He is not here. He is not to house.

SALLY'S VOICE. But he must be. He is expecting me. Isn't Herr Wendel here?

FRITZ (*going to the door while Chris gets his coat from the cupboard*). Sally—liebling . . .

SALLY'S VOICE. Fritz, darling. The old lady said there was nobody here.

FRITZ. Come in. (*Sally comes in. She is young and attractive. She wears black silk with a small cape over her shoulders, and a page boy's cap stuck jauntily on one side of her head. Her fingernails are painted emerald green. Fräulein Schneider stands again in the doorway*) Sally, this is Christopher. Christopher, this is Sally. Sally Bowles.

CHRIS. How do you do?

SALLY. I'm terribly glad to meet you.

CHRIS. Make coffee for four, will you, Fräulein Schneider?

SALLY. Oh, not for me. I'm allergic to coffee. I come out in the most sinister spots if I drink it before dinner.

CHRIS (*to Fräulein Schneider*) Just for three, then. (*Fräulein Schneider goes*)

SALLY. I always have Prairie Oysters for breakfast. Don't you adore them? Eggs with Worcester Sauce all sort of wooshed up together. I simply live on them. Actually, I suppose I couldn't have a whiskey and soda, could I? I'm simply dead.

CHRIS. I'm afraid I haven't got any whiskey.

SALLY. I thought you were English.

CHRIS. I am. But I'm also poor.

SALLY. Oh, so am I. Terribly poor. But I always have whiskey. I mean, I think one must. Do you have anything? I mean, anything besides coffee?

CHRIS. I think I've got a little spot of gin.

SALLY. Dear old Mother's ruin. Gin will be wonderful. (*Chris gets gin out of cupboard*) Am I terribly late, Fritz darling?

FRITZ. No, you are beautifully on time.

SALLY. I thought I wasn't going to be able to come at all. I had a most frantic row with my landlady. Finally, I just said Pig, and swept out.

CHRIS. What would you like in this—or this in?

SALLY. Have you got anything?

CHRIS (*helplessly*). No, I don't think I have.

SALLY. Then I'll just have it straight.

CHRIS. I'm afraid it will have to be in a tooth glass.

SALLY. That will be wonderful. Give me one of your marvelous cigarettes, Fritz darling. Do you ever smoke any of Fritz's cigarettes? They're absolutely devastating. I'm sure they're full of opium, or something. They always make me feel terribly sensual.

CHRIS (*handing her the glass*). Here you are.

SALLY. Thank you so much. This looks wonderful (*Sips it*) Oh, it is. It's got an extraordinary taste. Like peppermint.

CHRIS. Oh, I'm afraid I can't have washed out the glass properly. That must be toothpaste. I'm so sorry.

SALLY. I think it is wonderful. Have some, Fritz. Taste it. Perhaps we can all make a fortune selling mint-flavored gin.

FRITZ (*tasting*). It is extremely interesting.

SALLY (*to Chris*). You have some, too.

CHRIS (*tasting*). It really isn't bad.

FRITZ. What for was your row with your landlady?

SALLY. Oh, it was absolutely awful. You should have heard the things she called me. I mean—well, I suppose in a way I may be a bit of a tart. . . . I mean, in a nice way—but one doesn't like to be called that. Just because I brought a man home with me last night. And, anyway, I'm terribly in love with him.

FRITZ. Anyone I know?

SALLY. You'll never guess. Klaus.

FRITZ. Klaus? Your accompanist, Klaus?

SALLY. Yes. He was always just like part of the piano to me. And then last night he was absolutely astonishing. Just like a faun, or something. He made me feel like a most marvelous nymph, miles away from anywhere, in the middle of the forest. And then the landlady came in and made the most boring remarks, so I simply can't go back. I shall have to find a new room. (*To Chris*) I don't suppose you know of any, do you?

CHRIS. A room?

SALLY. Something like this, perhaps. I suppose there aren't any more in this flat?

CHRIS. Well, there is this one.

FRITZ. Why, are you leaving?

CHRIS. I'm leaving this room. I can't afford it any more.

SALLY. Is it terribly expensive?

CHRIS. I pay fifty marks a month. That includes breakfast.

SALLY (*rising*). But that's nothing. I pay eighty for mine. This is very nice. (*She looks around*) Is that your bed? Oh, I think that's sweet—all hidden away like that. (*She looks behind the curtains*) Oh, that's where you keep things.

CHRIS (*laughing*). Only when I have visitors.

SALLY. You mean I could really have this? How soon?

CHRIS. As soon as you like. I've only got to move across the hall. It won't take me a minute. And I know Fräulein Schneider is very anxious to let it.

SALLY. What is she like? I mean, is she going to make trouble if I bring men home occasionally? I mean, it would only be very occasionally, because I do think one ought to go to the man's rooms, if one can. I mean, it doesn't look so much as if one was sort of expecting it. And men feel very keenly about that sort of thing. And it won't be men, anyway. It'll only be Klaus. I've decided to be absolutely faithful to him. I really have. She wouldn't mind that, would she, or would she?

CHRIS. If she can let the room, I'm sure she wouldn't mind anything.

SALLY. I say, am I shocking you, talking like this?

CHRIS. Not a bit. No one ever shocks me when they try to.

SALLY (*rather sharply*). Why do you say I'm trying to shock you?

CHRIS. I have an idea you like to try and shock everyone. Why do you paint your fingernails green?

SALLY. I think it's pretty. Don't you?

CHRIS. Suppose you thought it was pretty to paint dirty pictures on them, would you do that, too?

SALLY. Yes. You know, that's rather a good idea. Not dirty pictures exactly, but sort of *stimulating* ones. I must get someone to do it for me. Is he really unshockable, Fritz, or is he just pretending?

FRITZ. Oh, no. Chris is quite unshockable. I have tried many times, but ultimately I cannot do it.

CHRIS. But—there is a young lady coming this afternoon who *is* shockable. So would you mind awfully being just a bit more careful what you say? She's one of my pupils, and I do rather need her.

SALLY. Oh, but darling, of course. I'll be terribly ladylike.

CHRIS. And don't let her know I'm going to move out of here, do you mind? She'd probably start cutting down on my terms.

SALLY. I won't breathe a word.
(*Bell rings.*)

CHRIS. That must be her now.

SALLY. You'd better put the gin away.

CHRIS. Oh, yes, thanks.

SALLY. I'm afraid there isn't time for me to clean my nails. I'll try and keep my fists clenched.

NATALIA'S VOICE. Herr Isherwood?

FRÄULEIN SCHNEIDER'S VOICE. Ja, gnädiges Fräulein. Er erwartet Sie. Bitte sehr. (*She*

opens the door and ushers in Natalia)

FRÄULEIN SCHNEIDER. Bitte. Hier ist die Dame die Sie erwartet haben, Herr Issyvoo. (*She goes. Natalia is about twenty-two—correctly dressed, very German, formal and decided*)

CHRIS. Natalia. These are friends of mine. Miss Bowles, Fräulein Landauer, and Mr. Wendel. Fräulein Landauer.

FRITZ. Sehr erfreut, gnädiges Fräulein.

CHRIS. I think we'd better speak English. Fräulein Landauer speaks wonderful English.

FRITZ. I am charmed, dearest Miss.
(*Natalia shakes hands with Sally, noticing her nails.*)

SALLY (*concealing them*). How do you do?

NATALIA. I am well. I have just had a cold, but it is better now.

SALLY (*doing her best*). Oh, I'm so sorry. Colds are beastly things, aren't they? One's head gets all stopped up.

NATALIA. This was a cold in the chest. It was not in my head. All the plegm was here. (*She points to her chest*)

SALLY. All the what?

NATALIA. The plegm that comes into the tubes.

CHRIS. Phlegm. You pronounce the "h."

NATALIA. Oh. Then why do you say phthisis—what the Lady of the Camellias had—and not pronounce the "h" there, too? (*A pause while she waits for an answer*)

CHRIS. Well . . .

NATALIA. There must be a reason. You give it to me, please.

CHRIS. I don't know it. But you don't say p-tisis, either.

NATALIA. Then you should say "lem," and leave it right out as in thisis. I have lem in my chest. Is it not so? It is not an exact language, your English.

SALLY. What *is* phthisis?

NATALIA. It is consumption. From the lungs. They are consumed in phlegm.

SALLY. Do you mind not going on about it? I think I'm going to be sick.
(*Fräulein Schneider enters with the coffee, and then returns with a cake-stand and paper napkins.*)

NATALIA. But why should it make you sick? You do not have it.

SALLY. All stories about illness make me

want to throw up. I saw a movie about syphilis the other night that was too awful. I couldn't let a man touch me for almost a week. Is it true you can get it from kissing?

FRITZ. Oh, yes—and your King, Henry the Eighth, caught it from letting Cardinal Wolsey whisper to him.

NATALIA. That is not, I think, founded in fact. But kissing, most decidedly yes. And from towels. And cups. I hope these have been cleaned properly.

CHRIS (*flippantly*). Oh, yes. Fräulein Schneider always boils them every day.

SALLY. I mean, you can't ask every man to run out and have tests and things before you let him touch you. I mean, there isn't time, and he'd be off in a nip to someone much less particular.

(NATALIA *freezes. Chris comes in hastily.*)

CHRIS. Natalia, let me give you some coffee.

SALLY (*rising*). Oh, Fräulein. Could I have a talk with your landlady, Chris darling?

CHRIS. There's plenty of time.

SALLY. Oh, we'll talk outside. Won't we, Fräulein darling? We'll have secrets together. (*To Natalia*) If you'll excuse me.

NATALIA. But most obligingly.

SALLY (*to Fräulein Schneider*). Komm, liebes Fräulein, wir werden haben Geheimnesse zusammen. (*They go out together*)

FRITZ (*to Natalia, while Fritz passes coffee*). You will allow me to pass you a cake, dearest Miss? They are jam tarts.

NATALIA. I thank you, no. I do not eat between meals. And Miss is not the correct way to address a lady in English. No sugar, neither. Just plain black coffee.

FRITZ. That, too, is how I like it. Black, black, black, like Othello.

NATALIA. You tell me, please, about Fräulein Bowles. She is a remarkable girl.

FRITZ. She is a night-club artist. Very talented.

NATALIA. Where does she perform?

FRITZ. At a club calling the Lady Windermere. You know perhaps the play from Oscar Villder, calling *Lady Windermere's Fan?*

NATALIA (*correcting him*). Called *Lady Windermere's Fan*. But of course I know

it. I have read it, both in English and in German. I think it is better in German. But the club I do not know.

FRITZ. Would you let me take you to it one night, to hear Sally sing?

CHRIS. Do you think it is quite the right place for Fräulein Landauer?

NATALIA. But why not?

CHRIS. Oh, I don't know. I just thought . . .

NATALIA. You thought what, please?

CHRIS. I don't know, really.

NATALIA. You don't know. Then I cannot help you.

CHRIS. I thought it might be just a bit—Bohemian.

NATALIA. Then I must see it. I accept your invitation, my dear sir. When shall we go?

FRITZ. We could go tonight, if you are free.

NATALIA. I can be free. You will come and fetch me at a quarter to nine.

FRITZ. Oh, but it doesn't start until after midnight. Sally never goes on until one o'clock.

NATALIA. Then you fetch me please at a quarter to midnight. I will give you my address. You will come, too, Christopher, and we will be a party to hear your girl friend sing.

CHRIS. She is not my girl friend.

NATALIA. No? Then what is she, please?

CHRIS. She's—just a friend.

NATALIA. I see. And she is not a girl?

CHRIS. Yes, but . . .

NATALIA. Then why is she not a girl friend?

FRITZ. Girl friend means something more than a friend who is a girl, Fräulein.

NATALIA. So? What does it mean?

FRITZ. It means a sweetheart.

NATALIA. Ah, so. I did not know. Then I am not a girl friend of yours, Christopher?

CHRIS (*feebly*). Unfortunately—no . . .

NATALIA. You do not mean that, Christopher. You say it only to be polite.

FRITZ. He ought to mean it.

NATALIA (*ever so slightly coquettish*). You think, Herr Wendel?

FRITZ. I think very much.

NATALIA. And you too, are polite.

FRITZ. No, I am never polite. I am only sincere.

(SALLY *returns.*)

SALLY. It's all fixed up, Chris. The poor old thing was almost in tears of gratitude.

NATALIA. And why was she so grateful?

SALLY. Because I'm moving in here.

CHRIS (*hurriedly*). Sally! We are all coming to hear you sing tonight.

SALLY. Tonight? Oh, but, my dear, I shall be exhausted. I didn't sleep a wink last night.

NATALIA. You had rather I come some other evening?

SALLY. Oh, I expect it will be all right. Only don't let the proprietor bother you. He's quite a darling, really, but he takes dope quite a lot, and sometimes it doesn't agree with him. He pinches people. It doesn't mean anything.

NATALIA (*stiffly*). I think now that I must go.

FRITZ. Please, if I may accompany you?

NATALIA. My dear young man, I am not sixty years old, and I can go home un-molested all by myself.

CHRIS (*quoting*). Bin weder Fräulein, weder schön, kann ungeleitet nach Hause gehen.

SALLY. What is that?

NATALIA. It is from *Faust*.

CHRIS. It means, "I am not a virgin, and I am not beautiful, and I can go home alone."

FRITZ (*earnestly*). Oh, but that is not true. None of it is true. Not in this case.

SALLY (*eagerly*). You mean you think Fräulein Landauer *is* a virgin? How do you know?

NATALIA. You are filled with interesting curiosity, Fräulein Bowles, but I must pull myself away. I say good-bye.

SALLY. Good-bye.

NATALIA. Good-bye, Christopher. I think I will talk to your landlady on my way out. I do not like these rooms, and she is charg-ing you too much. (*She goes out with Fritz*)

SALLY (*after a moment*). I don't think that girl liked me very much, did she?

CHRIS. No, I don't think she really did.

SALLY. I'm sure I don't know why. I was doing my best. It won't make any difference to you, will it? To your lessons, I mean?

CHRIS. No, I don't think so. She's very

broad-minded in an intellectual sort of way. She'll probably decide it's her duty to un-derstand you.

SALLY. What on earth was Fritz up to? I can't think what got into him, dancing about like that. He isn't after her, is her?

CHRIS. She's very rich, you know. And Fritz is very broke.

SALLY. Do you think he'll get anywhere with her?

CHRIS. I've always understood from him that women find him attractive.

SALLY. I shouldn't think *she* would, with his going on like that. I should think his best way with a girl of that kind would be to make a pounce.

CHRIS. I can't imagine anyone pouncing on Natalia.

SALLY. No, dear. That's why it would be so effective.

CHRIS. I believe you're right. You know, that's quite wonderful of you, Sally.

SALLY. It seems very simple to me. Give me the rest of that gin, will you, Chris? There's just a little left. Then you won't have to pack the bottle.

CHRIS (*getting it*). Sure.

SALLY. And you're going to be right across the hall. I took a look at the room. It's not very nice. But you can use this any time you like, you know, and then if I'm low—or you are—we can just sob on each other's bosoms. I say, Fräulein Schneider's got a big one, hasn't she? Like an opera singer, or that woman in the music halls who can make hers jump. Can Fräulein Schneider do that?

CHRIS. We might train her.

SALLY (*looking at the paper on the table*). Chapter One. Are you writing a novel?

CHRIS. Starting one.

SALLY (*reading*). "I am a camera, with its shutter open, quite passive." Do you mean this is a story written by a camera?

CHRIS (*laughing*). No, it's written by me. I'm the camera.

SALLY. How do you mean?

CHRIS. I'm the one who sees it all. I don't take part. I don't really even think. I just sort of photograph it. Ask questions, maybe. How long have you been in Ger-many?

SALLY. About two months.

CHRIS. And your mother is French. (*She*

*looks blank*) Fritz told me she was.

SALLY (*irritated*). Fritz is an idiot. He's always inventing things. Mother's a bit County, but she's an absolute darling. I simply worship her. I'm afraid Daddy's side of the family comes out in me. You'd love Daddy. He doesn't care a damn for anyone. It was he who said I could go to London and learn acting. You see, I couldn't bear school, so I got myself expelled.

CHRIS. How did you do that?

SALLY. I told the headmistress I was going to have a baby.

CHRIS. Oh, rot, Sally, you didn't.

SALLY. Yes, I did. So they got a doctor to examine me, and then when they found out there was nothing the matter they were most frightfully disappointed. And the headmistress said that a girl who could even think of anything so disgusting couldn't possibly be let stay on. So I went to London. And that's where things started happening.

CHRIS. What sort of things?

SALLY. Oh—things. I had a wonderful, voluptuous little room—with no chairs— that's how I used to seduce men. One of them told me I'd do better in Berlin. What do you think, Chris?

CHRIS. I think you're doing fine. I think you're wonderful, Sally.

SALLY. Do you, Chris dear? I think you're wonderful, too. We're going to be real good friends, aren't we?

CHRIS (*rather slowly*). Do you know, I believe we are. Real good friends.

SALLY. You know, Chris, you were quite right about my wanting to shock people. I do, and I don't know why. I do think you were clever to notice it. And, Chris, there's one thing more. I'm not sure if you'll understand or not. I did tell Fritz my mother was French. I suppose I wanted to impress him.

CHRIS. What's so impressive about a French mother?

SALLY. I suppose it's like whores calling themselves French names to excite men. I'm a bit mad like that sometimes, Chris. You must be patient with me.

CHRIS. I will, Sally.

SALLY. And you'll swear on your honor not to tell Fritz? And if you do, I can cut your throat? (*Stands over him, mock-bullying him with a paper knife*)

CHRIS. From ear to ear. Sally, was that all true just now, what you told me about your family?

SALLY. Yes, of course it was. Well, most of it. (*Puts paper knife down*) Only, Chris, you mustn't ever ask me questions. If I want to tell you anything, I will. But I've got to be free.

CHRIS (*amused*). Very well, Sally.

SALLY. I've got to have a free soul. You know, I think I'm really rather a strange and extraordinary person, Chris.

CHRIS. So do I, Sally. (*Copying her tone*) Quite extraordinary. (*He starts to laugh. She joins in. Their laughter grows louder. She embraces him*)

SALLY. Oh, Chris, you are awful. (*Releasing herself, she picks up her handbag and starts for the door*) Look, darling, I must go. I'll be back in an hour with all my things, and you can help me unpack. So long, Chris.

CHRIS. So long, Sally.

(*She leaves.*)

CHRIS. Well, I'd better start moving out of here. I bet Fräulein Schneider's pleased. Sally is just the kind of person she goes for. (*Takes two personal pictures from the wall and puts them on the table*) How do I know that? How do I know what kind of a person Sally is? I suppose that's what's so fascinating about her. People who talk like that about themselves *ought* to be lying. But I don't believe she is. And yet she's that mysterious thing my family calls a lady, too. (*Looks out of the window*) Look at her. She's even flirting with the taxi-driver. And she knows I'm watching her. Oh, my God. (*He laughs*) I've got to put that down right away. (*He sits at the desk and starts to write in a notebook*) Let's make notes. How would you describe her? Sally Bowles was a girl of about . . . I wonder how old she is. Her face is young, but her hands look terribly old. And they were dirty, too. Dirty as a little girl's hands. (*He writes again*) Sally's hands were like the old hands of a dirty little girl.

CURTAIN

## ACT ONE

### SCENE II

TIME: *About three months later.*
SCENE: *The scene is very slightly changed. A few feminine touches. A doll or two. Some bottles and jars are spread out on the table. The Medici prints are missing, and a couple of other pictures, very sentimental, are in their places. A pair of silk stockings and a pair of panties on a hanger, drying. When the curtain rises, Fräulein Schneider is tidying up the room. There is a knock on the door.*

————

FRÄULEIN SCHNEIDER. Ja, herein.
(*Chris enters.*)

CHRIS. Oh, is Sally not here?

FRÄULEIN SCHNEIDER. No, Herr Issyvoo, she has gone out. And so late she was getting up. It's not as if she were working nights any more. I don't think she is well, Herr Issyvoo.

CHRIS. Do you know where she keeps my thermometer, Fräulein Schneider? I want to take my temperature.

FRÄULEIN SCHNEIDER. What, again?

CHRIS. I've got pains in my back. I think I've got a slipped disk.

FRÄULEIN SCHNEIDER. I thought it was your stomach.

CHRIS. That was yesterday.

FRÄULEIN SCHNEIDER (*feeling his head*). You have no temperature.

CHRIS. I'm not so sure. I'd like to see, if I can find the thermometer.

FRÄULEIN SCHNEIDER (*looking for it*). I saw her using it only yesterday to stir those Prairie Oysters with. Ah, here it is. I think there is still a little egg on it, but it's on the case.

CHRIS. Thank you. (*He opens thermometer and shakes it down*) Has the afternoon post come yet?

FRÄULEIN SCHNEIDER. It will be here soon now. There was nothing for her this morning. (*Chris puts the thermometer in his mouth*) I begin to worry for Fräulein Sally. That friend Klaus of hers. Six weeks he has been away now in England and only one letter has he written. (*Bell rings*) There is the bell. (*She goes to answer it*)

FRITZ'S VOICE. Ist Fräulein Bowles zu Hause?

FRÄULEIN SCHNEIDER. Nein, Herr Wendel.

Aber Herr Issyvoo ist da. In ihren Zimmer. Gehen Sie nur hinein.
(*Fritz enters.*)

FRITZ. Hello, Chris. Are you ill?

CHRIS. I don't know yet. Sit down.

FRITZ. What's the matter?

CHRIS. My legs don't seem to work properly.

FRITZ. That can be locomotor ataxia.

CHRIS. I know. That's what I'm afraid of.

(*Fritz sits beside him, and tests his knee for reflex action. The first time nothing happens. They both look worried.* FRITZ *tries again, and Chris's leg reacts*)

FRITZ (*pushing Chris's leg away*). There is nothing the matter with you.

CHRIS. (*removing the thermometer*). I think it's just over normal. (*Shakes thermometer down*) I think I'll take some aspirin. How are you, Fritz? How's Natalia?

FRITZ. Christopher, I cannot get anywhere with that girl. I have spent money on her. Money I have not got. I meet her parents. I write her poems. Poems from Heinrich Heine, and always she recognizes them, and then she laughs at me. It is not even the money any more. But when she will not let me make love to her, it drives me ultimately mad. I kiss her, and it is like my aunt. And, Chris, she has a wonderful body, and it is untouched. By me or anybody.

CHRIS. Sally said you ought to pounce on her.

FRITZ. But no one could pounce on Natalia.

CHRIS. Sally said that's why it would be so effective. Knock her down, or something. Throw her on a couch and ravish her.

FRITZ. You do not mean that, Chris.

CHRIS. You don't seem to be doing any good the usual way. How do you ordinarily manage with women?

FRITZ. I have only to uncurl my little finger, and purr a little, and they come running. I think perhaps I try. I can after all do myself no harm. She is away now. I write to her every day. Now I will write no more. I wait for her to come home, and then I will pounce, and I will ravish, and I will snarl.

CHRIS. Good.

FRITZ. And what is with you, Chris? You still live in that dark, tiny prison of a room?

CHRIS. Oh, yes.

FRITZ. And can you get anyone else in the room at the same time?

CHRIS. Oh, yes. If they're fond of me.

FRITZ. Do you have any love-life now?

CHRIS. I have a little. Now and then.

FRITZ. And you will not talk about it. Not ever. You are so reticent. If Sally did not ultimately have a French mother, she would not talk about it, either.

CHRIS. A what? (*Remembering*) Oh . . . yes.

FRITZ. She is a strange girl. Half of her is so ultimately frank, and half is so sentimental. (*He takes a picture from the wall*) This picture. She has it with her everywhere. It is called "The Kitten's Awakening." It is childish.

(*Sally enters. She is rather smarter than when we last saw her—a new and rather unsuitable hat. She carries several packages. She looks tired.*)

SALLY. Oh, hello, Chris. Hello, Fritz.

FRITZ. Hello, Sally. We were just admiring your picture.

SALLY. Oh, "The Kitten's Awakening." I've had that ever since I was a child. It's a dead kitten waking up in Heaven—with angel kittens around. Chris makes awful fun of it. But I think it's rather sweet.

FRITZ. It is very sweet.

SALLY. Goodness, it's hot out, and it's late September already.

CHRIS. You are very dressy today.

SALLY. I am? Oh, this hat. Yes, it's new. (*She takes it off*) Clive bought it for me. I don't like it much, but it cost so much money. Let's have a Prairie Oyster. Will you, Chris?

CHRIS. Not for me. I think they affect my legs.

SALLY. Fritz?

FRITZ. I would like to try one.

SALLY. I'll make them. Chris doesn't really know how. (*She starts to do so, getting the eggs and things from under the washstand, and mixing them in two tooth glasses*)

FRITZ. And who is this Clive who gives you hats?

SALLY. He's an American. Chris and I met him a week ago at the Troika bar. We were both sitting alone, having a beer each because we were both so bloody miserable, and he was sitting next to us, and he ordered champagne for us all, and we didn't separate till four the next morning. And ever since then we've hardly been apart, have we, Chris?

CHRIS. He's so rich, we daren't let him out of our sight.

FRITZ. And he is here just on vacation?

CHRIS. He lives on vacation. I've never seen anyone drink so much. He's unhappy, he says. But I've never really found out why. Have you, Sally?

SALLY. Yes, dear. It's his wives. There have been four of them, and they none of them liked him. And, before that, it was his peculiar grandfathers. They both raised him six months each. One was a Baptist, and the other lived in Paris. So, no wonder it split him! He's sort of lost faith in everything, and I think Chris and I are putting it back, in bits. That's why I feel all right about letting Clive give us things. There's a dozen pairs of silk stockings in there, Chris. And absolutely gallons of Chanel 5. Oh, and some shirts for you. Some silk shirts.

CHRIS. Good God.

SALLY. The colors are a bit outrageous, but they're the best silk. Where's something to stir this with? Oh, this pen will do. (*She picks up a fountain pen and stirs the Oysters*) There. (*She hands one over to Fritz, who chokes over it. She gulps her own*) Oh, that's marvelous. I feel better already. How are you, Fritz? You know, Natalia came to see me several times, as though she were doing District Visiting and I were a fallen woman or something. But she seems to have stopped.

FRITZ. She is away with her parents. She comes back next week, and then there is a surprise for her. Chris has told me your advice—that I should pounce on her —and I am going to take it. (*He takes another sip of his drink*)

SALLY. What's the matter? Don't you like your Prairie Oyster?

FRITZ. It is a little painful. You drink them all down at once?

SALLY. Yes, they're better that way. Especially when you are not feeling well. They sort of come back at you.

CHRIS. Aren't you feeling well, Sally?

SALLY. Not really.

FRITZ. You would like me to go?

SALLY. Fritz darling—would you mind terribly? I would like to lie down a bit.

FRITZ. But of course. With me there are no compliments. Sally, you lie down. Then you feel better. I go now. You take her to dinner, Chris, and cheer her up.

CHRIS. I'll try. Good-bye, Fritz. (*Fritz goes*) Sally, are you really feeling ill? (*He gets her slippers, and helps her on with them*)

SALLY. Not so much ill, as just wanting to get rid of him. Fritz is sweet. I mean, he's an old friend, but I thought if I had to go on being bright any longer that I'd die. I've got something to tell you, Chris.

CHRIS. What is it?

SALLY. Chris, I went to the doctor this afternoon, and—I'm going to have a baby.

CHRIS. Oh, my God!

SALLY. I've been afraid of it for a long time, only I wouldn't think about it. I kept pretending it wasn't true. Then yesterday I was sick, and then I fainted this morning. And that's what made me go.

CHRIS. Is it Klaus's child?

SALLY. Yes.

CHRIS. Does he know?

SALLY (*sharply*). No, he doesn't.

CHRIS. Well, you're going to tell him, aren't you?

SALLY. I don't know. Chris, I haven't heard from him for weeks and weeks. I wrote to him last week, the nicest letter I could, and he hasn't answered. Not a word. You didn't like him, did you?

CHRIS. I didn't really know him. I didn't think he was good enough for you.

SALLY. That's sweet of you.

CHRIS. But you're going to tell him this, now?

SALLY. No. Not if he doesn't write to me. It's awful, Chris. I do want to marry him, and have a family. But I can't beg him. And that's what it would be like. I mean, I mayn't be up to much, but I do have some pride.

CHRIS. Well, what then—if he doesn't write?

SALLY. I don't know. That's what scares

me. It's silly, Chris . . . it happens to other girls. Almost all other girls. But I am scared. Do you suppose they all are, too? (*A knock at the door.*)

FRÄULEIN SCHNEIDER'S VOICE. It is I, Fräulein Sally. The post is here.

CHRIS (*sotto voce*). She's been keeping an eye out for it.

SALLY. Come in.

FRÄULEIN SCHNEIDER (*entering*). There is a letter for you. The one you want. From England.

SALLY. Oh, thank you.

FRÄULEIN SCHNEIDER. Ja, Fräulein. (*She hands it to her, and waits. Sally starts to undo her packages. Fräulein Schneider gives up and goes out. Sally waits for her to leave. Then she rips the letter open. Chris stands by. She reads it. Her face changes*)

CHRIS. What's the matter?

SALLY. It's what I thought. He's throwing me over.

CHRIS. Oh, no.

SALLY. Right over. With a whole lot of stuff about how badly he's behaved to me. (*She hands Chris the first page. He reads it. She goes on with the second*) Apparently there's someone else. An English girl. A Lady Gore-Eckersley. He says she is wonderful. She's a virgin. A Communist Virgin. (*She lays the letter down*) Well, those are two things no one could ever say of *me*.

CHRIS. (*going to her, putting his arms around her*). Oh, Sally, I'm sorry.

SALLY (*leaning against him*). It's silly, isn't it?

CHRIS. It is a kind of bloody letter.

SALLY. I'm afraid he's rather a bloody person, really. Oh, Chris, I am a lousy picker. Always the duds who'll do me in.

CHRIS. I won't, Sally.

SALLY. I know. I suppose that's why I haven't been interested in you that way.

CHRIS. Sally, you'll have to tell Klaus. He'll have to help you.

SALLY. He'd only run away. Leave no address. Besides, it's just as much my fault as his.

CHRIS. Well, what are you going to do?

SALLY. I knew this was going to happen. I can't have the baby, Chris. It's awful because I want to. But not unless I'm married, and can look after it.

CHRIS (*after a second*). I'll marry you, Sally.

SALLY. Oh, Chris, what good would that do? Klaus's child—and I'd be a rotten sort of mother. Just a betrayed whore.

CHRIS (*sharply*). Sally, for God's sake, stop calling yourself that. You know you're not.

SALLY (*bitterly*). Yes, I am. Just that. A whore who's fallen in love with a swine, because he's her type, and then got caught. That's all. Just a whore and a fool. (*She starts to cry*)

CHRIS. Sally, stop crying.

SALLY. I've got to find someone.

CHRIS. Won't this doctor . . . ?

SALLY. No. He was quite shocked when I told him I wasn't married.

CHRIS. Then we'll get someone. Maybe we should ask Fräulein Schneider.

SALLY. Do you think *she'd* know anyone?

CHRIS. She knows just about everything, I've always thought. I'll call her. (*Opens door*) Fräulein Schneider. Fräulein. Can you come in here? (*He comes back*) It will be all right, Sally. I promise you.

(FRÄULEIN SCHNEIDER *enters.*)

FRÄULEIN SCHNEIDER. You called for me, Herr Issyvoo?

CHRIS. Yes. We need your advice. Do you want to tell her, Sally?

SALLY (*her back to them*). No. You do it.

CHRIS. Well, you see, Fräulein Schneider, Sally is in a little bit of trouble . . .

FRÄULEIN SCHNEIDER. Ja?

CHRIS. She's going to have a baby.

FRÄULEIN SCHNEIDER. Um Gotteswillen.

CHRIS. So you see . . .

FRÄULEIN SCHNEIDER. But then this Herr Klaus, he will come back and marry her.

CHRIS. Well, you see, he isn't awfully anxious to. You see . . .

SALLY (*angrily*). It isn't that at all, Chris. You never can tell anything right. It's I who doesn't want him, Fräulein. I don't ever want to see him again.

FRÄULEIN SCHNEIDER. Ach, so . . .

CHRIS. So you see, we want to get—er—to get rid of the baby. The point is—do you know anyone?

FRÄULEIN SCHNEIDER. Yes, I do. There was a young lady living here once, and she went to the doctor.

SALLY. For the same thing?

FRÄULEIN SCHNEIDER. Exactly the same thing.

SALLY. And was it all right?

FRÄULEIN SCHNEIDER. It was quite all right. I have his address and telephone number still. I kept it just in case it should ever happen again.

SALLY (*trying to be easy over it*) I suppose it happens quite often, really?

FRÄULEIN SCHNEIDER. It can always happen. It is just bad luck.

SALLY. I'm glad you know someone.

FRÄULEIN SCHNEIDER. He is rather expensive. It is a certificate he has to give that your health will not let you have the risk of childbirth. It costs money, that certificate.

SALLY. How much?

FRÄULEIN SCHNEIDER. For this other young lady, it was three hundred marks.

CHRIS. Three hundred!

FRÄULEIN SCHNEIDER. We could make it a little cheaper, I think, if we argued. Maybe two hundred and fifty.

CHRIS. That's still an awful lot.

SALLY. I know it is. But I've got to do it, Chris. I really have. You'd better ring up the doctor, Fräulein, and see if he can see us.

FRÄULEIN SCHNEIDER. You like that I come with you?

SALLY. Oh, would you? That would be marvelous. Where—where does he do it?

FRÄULEIN SCHNEIDER. There is a nursing home. You stay there two or three days, and then you come back here and rest. In maybe ten days, no more, it is all forgotten. I go telephone. (*She goes out, gaily*)

SALLY. It's like a treat to *her*.

CHRIS. It'll be all right, Sally. I know it will. The other girl was all right.

SALLY. There's something so *degrading* about it, as well as dangerous. Oh, damn! Isn't it idiotic? All the men I've had—and there have been quite a lot—and this has to happen to me. It's awful, too, when you think about it—that there's something alive inside of you—that you can't have. That you mustn't have. It's like finding out that all the old rules are true, after all. But I've got to go through with it.

CHRIS. Sally, two hundred and fifty marks. And the home will probably cost a bit of money, too. I've started making a little more now, too. If I can help you . . .

SALLY. Oh, Chris, you are an angel. I'll pay you back. I swear I will. And you know, I think maybe you had better come with us. We'll say you're the father. I think it looks better to have him along.

CHRIS. Yes, Sally, of course I'll come with you.

SALLY. Oh, Chris, I don't know what I'd do without you. (*He holds her. Bell rings*) Oh, damn, there's the bell. If it's anyone for me, I'm not home. I won't see anyone. (*Opens the door, and goes down the passage*) Fräulein Schneider, I'm not . . . Oh, hello, Clive.

CLIVE's VOICE. Hello, there. I just thought I'd come and look you up.

SALLY (*returning*). Yes, of course. Come in.

(*Clive enters. He is in his late thirties, large, American, blond and drunkish.*)

CLIVE. Well, hello, Chris, you son of a gun.

CHRIS. Hello, Clive.

CLIVE. (*to Sally*). I've never seen your place before. I thought I'd come and take a gander at it. I brought you these. (*He presents an enormous box of very expensive flowers*)

SALLY. Oh, Clive, how wonderful of you. Look, Chris, from that terribly expensive shop on the Linden.

CHRIS. Goodness.

CLIVE. So this is where you live, eh? Just one room? Say, it's not very grand, is it? Can't you do better than this?

SALLY. I—er—I have in my time. This is just temporary.

CLIVE. Oh, sure. Sure.

CHRIS (*defensive*). What's the matter with it?

CLIVE. Well, it's not exactly *de luxe,* do you think?

CHRIS (*as before*). I think it's fine.

CLIVE. Oh, sure. Sure. I wasn't casting any slurs. I just thought maybe something a bit larger. More modern. But it's okay. Say, I bet your rooms are bigger.

SALLY. Oh, yes, they're much bigger. They're wonderful.

CLIVE. Where are they?

CHRIS. Just across the hall.

CLIVE. Mind if I take a look?

(*Sally starts to gesture wildly at Chris not to show his room.*)

CHRIS. Well—er—they're rather untidy just now.

CLIVE. That's all right with me.

(*Sally repeats her gesture.*)

CHRIS. There are some things lying around that—well, that I wouldn't want anyone to see.

CLIVE. Say, what are those?

CHRIS. Just some personal things.

CLIVE. Boy, that's what I'd like to look at.

CHRIS. I'm awfully sorry, but I don't think . . .

CLIVE. You mean, you've got someone in there?

CHRIS. Well, er . . .

CLIVE. Why don't you come right out and say it, feller? Don't beat about the bush. Go on back to her. I'll understand.

CHRIS (*again on a gesture from Sally*). Well, she's—er—asleep just now.

CLIVE. And, boy, I bet she needs it. Well, say, now what have you got in the way of liquor?

SALLY. We've got some gin.

CHRIS. Not much.

SALLY. I'm afraid we're out of whiskey.

CLIVE. Say, you need some stores. I'll send you in a cellar. Now, look, what are we going to do? I've been all by myself all day, and it's driving me nuts. There's a place I've heard of out on the Wannsee. The Regina Palast Garten. I thought we might drive out there for dinner.

SALLY. The three of us.

CLIVE (*to Chris*). If you're free.

(*Sally nods at Chris.*)

CHRIS. Oh, yes, I'll be free.

CLIVE. Is that a good place?

CHRIS. I've always heard it was.

CLIVE. But you've never been there?

CHRIS. It's much too expensive for us.

CLIVE. Well, fine. Only is it *really* a good place? Can we have a good time there? The real McCoy?

SALLY. It's about the best place there is.

CLIVE. Oh, well, swell, then. That's great. That's the *real* thing. Well, shall we go?

SALLY. I can't go yet.

CLIVE. Why, what have you got on?

(*Fräulein Schneider enters.*)

FRÄULEIN SCHNEIDER. Fräulein Sally, can I speak to you a moment, please?

CLIVE. That's all right. You speak up. No secrets here. No secrets in front of Uncle Clive.

SALLY. Have you talked to the—to the man, Fräulein?

FRÄULEIN SCHNEIDER. He says he can see you right away.

SALLY. Oh—oh, thanks.

FRÄULEIN SCHNEIDER. It takes twenty minutes from here. I think maybe you should go now.

SALLY. Oh, yes, I will. You get your hat and coat, Fräulein, and I'll be ready.

FRÄULEIN SCHNEIDER. Ja, Fräulein. (*She goes*)

CLIVE. What man is this?

SALLY. It's just a man about a job. A sort of audition.

CLIVE. I'll drive you there.

SALLY. I don't think you'd better. I mean, it's not a very big job, and it would look a little funny if I were to arrive in a Dusenberg car.

CLIVE. It would make them pay you more.

SALLY. Look, Clive, it's awfully sweet of you, but I think we'd better go by bus.

CLIVE. You take your landlady on auditions with you?

SALLY. Sometimes. She gives me confidence.

CLIVE. Well, then, Chris and I will go to the Adlon, and sit in the bar and wait for you. He can bring his girl along, if he wants to.

CHRIS. Oh, no, that's all right. But—I've got to go out, too.

CLIVE. Not with Sally?

CHRIS. No, but I have to go—and then come back here for just a minute. Why don't we all meet later at the Adlon?

CLIVE. I'll send my car back here for you. Six o'clock?

SALLY. That would be wonderful. And thank you so much for these.

CLIVE. Well, good luck. I hope you get the job.

SALLY. I do, too. At least, I—I think I do.

CLIVE. We'll celebrate tonight, if you do. And if you don't, well then, we'll tie a bun on anyway, just to forget it all. So either way, you can't lose. So long, Chris, you sexy old bastard. See you both later. (*He goes*)

SALLY. Oh, Chris, I thought we were never going to get rid of him.

CHRIS. Yes, so did I. You know, he is an extraordinary man.

SALLY. But he's awfully sweet, really. Perhaps when this is over, I can devote myself to him. I've always thought I'd like to have a really rich man for a lover. I wouldn't want more than three thousand a year—pounds, I mean—and a flat and a decent car. Or maybe I could marry him, and then I might reform him. I could, you know, I really could.

CHRIS. Sally, do you really think you could reform anyone?

SALLY. Oh, Chris, don't. Don't pull me down again. I feel awful.

CHRIS. I'm sorry, Sally. And don't worry about reforming people. You're sweet. You really are.

SALLY. Thank you, Chris. Even if you don't mean it.

CHRIS. But I do. And now we'd better get going.

SALLY. Yes, I suppose so. (*Chris helps Sally on with her shoes*) I suppose we should put these flowers in water. They cost such a lot. I'll just put them in the bath for now. Then I'll see if Fräulein Schneider is ready, and come back for my hat. (*She goes to the door, and turns to Chris*) Thank you for offering to marry me. (*She exits*)

CHRIS (*her slippers in his hand*). And this is the kind of thing we used to make dirty jokes about at school. The facts of life. And here we go to prove they're not true, or that you can duck them. (*Drops the slippers*) And then we'll get pounds and pounds spent on us for dinner. And drink too much. And try to believe that none of it matters anyway. (*Gets a cigarette from his pocket*) And soon, as Fräulein Schneider said, we'll forget the whole thing. It'll seem like another of those nasty dreams. And we won't believe or remember a thing about it. Either of us. (*He starts to put the cigarette in his mouth. Then he stops, and looks at the door*) Or will we?

**CURTAIN**

## ACT TWO

### Scene I

SCENE: *About a week later. Chris is alone, sitting on the ottoman pasting photographs in an album. The sofa has been moved to the window and the table to the center of the room. The large chair has been placed at the right of the table. There is another chair to the left of the table.*

CHRIS (*arranges some photographs, then stops*). This awful, obscene laziness. I ought to be flogged. Where has the time gone to? Jittering helplessly over the bad news in the papers, staring half-drunk at my reflection in the mirrors of bars, skimming crime-novels, hunting for sex. This place stinks of my failure.

(*Sally comes back into the room. She wears a robe and looks pale and ill.*)

CHRIS. Are you all right?

SALLY. Yes, I'm all right. Just. Goodness, if it takes all that effort, just to go across the hall. (*Passing behind Chris, she ruffles his hair*) How's all your locomotor ataxia, Chris?

CHRIS. Oh, that's gone. I must have imagined it. (*Feeling his left side*) But, you know, I think I've got appendicitis.

SALLY (*settling down to a half-finished Solitaire*). If you have, you just die of it. Don't let them operate on you. You know, Chris, what I would really like would be some champagne. Some really cold champagne.

CHRIS. I'm afraid we haven't got any of that.

SALLY. Clive ought to have sent us whole baskets of it. I do think it was odd his disappearing like he did. Where do you think he went, Chris?

CHRIS. I wonder if he didn't go off on an opium jag.

SALLY. That's quite possible. I never thought of that. Oh dear, I've known a lot of opium fiends, and you never could really rely on them. And then what happens to my career?

CHRIS. Do you really think he's going to do anything about that?

SALLY. He says he's going to put up all the money for a show for me. All I've got to do now is find the show. And then find *him* again. But until he shows up we don't get any champagne, and I do want some. I want some terribly, now I've thought about it.

CHRIS. I'd buy you some, if I could, Sally. But you know we really are desperately broke.

SALLY. You know, Chris, in some ways now I wish I had had that kid. The last day or two, I've been sort of feeling what it would be like to be a mother. Do you know, last night I sat here for a long time by myself, and held this teddy-bear in my arms, and imagined it was my baby? I felt a most marvelous sort of shut-off feeling from all the rest of the world. I imagined how it would grow up, and how after I'd put it to bed at nights, I'd go out and make love to filthy old men to get money to pay for its clothes and food.

CHRIS. You mean, a baby would be your purpose in life?

SALLY. Yes, I wouldn't think of myself at all. Just it. It must be rather wonderful never to think of yourself, just of someone else. I suppose that's what people mean by religion. Do you think I could be a nun, Chris? I really rather think I could. All pale and pious, singing sort of faint and lovely hymns all day long.

CHRIS. I think you'd get tired of it. You'd better just marry and have a child.

SALLY. I feel as if I'd lost faith in men. Even you, Christopher, if you were to go out into the street now and be run over by a taxi . . . I should be sorry in a way, of course, but I shouldn't really care a damn.

CHRIS (*laughing*). Thank you, Sally.

SALLY (*moving to him*). I didn't mean that, of course, darling—at least, not personally. You mustn't mind what I say when I'm like this. I can see now why people say operations like that are wrong. They are. You know, the whole business of having children is all wrong. It's a most wonderful thing, and it ought to be the result of something very rare and special and sort of privileged, instead of just *that!* What are you grinning about?

CHRIS. Well, that's what it's supposed to be. The result of something rare and special. That's what *that's* supposed to be.

SALLY. Oh, goodness, is it? Yes, I suppose it *is* supposed to be. Oh, is *that* why people say it's wrong to do it when you're not married, or terribly deeply in love?

CHRIS. Yes, of course it is.

SALLY. Well, why didn't anyone ever *tell* me?

CHRIS. I expect they did, and you didn't believe them.

SALLY. Did *you* believe them when they told you?

CHRIS. No, Sally.

SALLY. But you think they're right?

CHRIS. I suppose I do.

SALLY. Then why can't we do things that we know are right?

CHRIS. I don't know, Sally. But it seems we can't. Do you really think you're going to stop having sex just because of this? Forever?

SALLY. No, I don't suppose I do.

CHRIS. I don't think we'll ever quite trust things, in the long run.

SALLY. I trust you, Chris. I'm terribly fond of you.

CHRIS. I'm fond of you too, Sally.

SALLY. And you're not in love with me, are you?

CHRIS. No, I'm not in love with you.

SALLY. I'm awfully glad. I wanted you to like me from the first minute we met. But I'm glad you're not in love with me. Somehow or other, I couldn't possibly be in love with you. . . . So, if you had been, everything would have spoiled. Hold my hand, Chris, and let's swear eternal friendship.

CHRIS (*taking her hand*). I swear eternal friendship.

SALLY. So do I. (*The bell rings*) Oh dear, I wonder who that is. I hope it's no one for us. Chris, suppose it was Klaus?

CHRIS. What would you do?

SALLY. I'd be very good and noble about it. I wouldn't tell him anything—about the child, or anything. I'd just forgive him, beautifully.

(*Fräulein Schneider enters.*)

FRÄULEIN SCHNEIDER. It is Fräulein Landauer to see you, Fräulein.

(*Natalia enters.*)

CHRIS. Hello, Natalia.

NATALIA. Fräulein Bowles, I am but just back from the country and I have only just heard that you have not been well. So I have hurried in to see you.

SALLY. That's very nice of you.

NATALIA (*turning*). Oh, hello, Christopher.

CHRIS. Hello, Natalia.

NATALIA (*to Sally*). I bring you these few flowers.

SALLY. Oh, thank you so much. Chris . . . (*He takes them*)

NATALIA. What is, please, that has been the matter with you?

CHRIS (*quickly*). Oh, just a little ulcer, that's all. They had to cut it out.

NATALIA. Where was the ulcer?

SALLY. Inside.

NATALIA. But, of course, it was inside. Where, please, inside?

SALLY. I don't really know. In here, somewhere.

NATALIA. And who, please, was it who cut it out for you?

SALLY. The doctor.

NATALIA. But yes, it was the doctor. I did not think it was the sewing-lady. What doctor is it you go to?

SALLY. A doctor . . . (*She checks herself*) I forget his name. What was it, Chris?

CHRIS. A Doctor—Mayer.

NATALIA. I do not know of him. All of my uncles are doctors. You should have gone to one of them. I will ask one of them to come and examine you.

SALLY. Oh, I'm quite all right again now. Would you like some coffee or anything?

NATALIA. Yes, I think that I would like some coffee.

SALLY. Will you get it, Chris?

NATALIA. And Christopher, if you could stay away for just a little while, it would be nice, too. I have something that I wish to say to Fräulein Bowles.

CHRIS. Yes, of course. (*He goes out*)

NATALIA. Tell me, Fräulein, please, have you seen Fritz Wendel lately?

SALLY. No, I haven't.

NATALIA. I come back from the country two days before yesterday. He comes to call on me that evening. Fräulein, I think I have done you perhaps an injustice.

SALLY. Oh?

NATALIA. I have always think of you as a young lady who has no control of herself, and I have been disdainful of you therefrom. I am sorry. I do not think I quite understood.

SALLY. How do you mean?

NATALIA. I have think always that I have control of myself. Please, you will not laugh at me if I tell you something that is very personal to me?

SALLY. No, of course I won't.

NATALIA. I do not know of anyone else to whom I can go for some advice. Fräulein Bowles, Fritz Wendel has made love to me, and I have not taken him seriously, because it is all too formal, too discreet. Then, two nights before last, it is all changed. He throws aside his formality, and it is quite different. I have never known a man like that. And it has disturbed me. I cannot sleep for it. And that is not like me.

SALLY. But what am I supposed to tell you?

NATALIA. I wish to know, please, if I should marry him. My parents tell me no. They care for me. They think only of me, and they do not care for him. And he is not Jewish, and they wish that I should marry a Jewish man. I have always wished so, myself. Now I do not care. Only I think perhaps there is something of Herr Wendel's life that I do not know, that perhaps you do. And that therefore I should not marry him. You will tell me, please?

SALLY. Yes, I . . . I think perhaps there is.

NATALIA. What, please?

SALLY. I . . . I don't think I can tell you, exactly. But I don't really think he's your kind. I don't really think you ought to marry him—not if you ask me like that, point-blank.

NATALIA. I do not think so, too. But I think if I do not, that perhaps I will kill myself.

SALLY. Oh, no, you won't.

NATALIA. I do not think you know me. I do not think I know myself. (*She begins to cry*)

SALLY. Oh, there's nothing to cry about. (*Natalia goes on*) Oh, don't. Please don't. You'll have me crying, too. I'm most frightfully weak still, and I cry over almost anything.

NATALIA (*still crying*). I am sorry. I did not know that love was like this. It is not what the poets have said. It is awful, and it is degrading.

SALLY. Yes, I know. It is. It's absolutely awful when it really hits you. But you mustn't give in to it, really, you mustn't. I know that sounds silly coming from me.

But what do you think has been the matter with me? I was going to have a baby, and the chap let me down, and I had to get rid of it.

NATALIA (*turning, amazed*). Oh, I am sorry. I did not know.

SALLY. And marriage isn't going to make it any better if it's not the right man. And I really don't think Fritz is. For you.

NATALIA. You think, then, that I must be strong?

SALLY. Yes, I do.

NATALIA. I think so, too. But um Gotteswillen, what is there to *do* with one's life, all of a sudden?

SALLY. You could become a nun. Do they have Jewish nuns? (*Chris taps on the door.*)

CHRIS'S VOICE. The coffee is all ready.

NATALIA. You may come in now. (*She turns her back, and straightens her face. Chris comes in with coffee.*)

CHRIS. I only brought one cup. Sally doesn't take it, and I think I'm getting allergic to it, too.

NATALIA. You are very kind, but I do not think now that I have time. (*She turns*) So, Christopher, we will start our lessons again now? I think now that I will perhaps take more. I will take two every day. You can manage that?

CHRIS. Yes, I can manage it. But that is an awful lot for you. It's an awful lot to do.

NATALIA. I need an awful lot to do. Goodbye, Fräulein. I thank you, and I come again. (*She goes out, rather hurriedly*)

CHRIS. What was all that about?

SALLY (*very nobly and remotely*). That was something personal. That poor girl is terribly unhappy.

CHRIS. What about?

SALLY (*as before*). This is something between women. (*Chris giggles*) It is. I've given her some advice. Some very good advice.

CHRIS. You gave Fritz some advice, too.

SALLY. Oh, I did, didn't I? Oh, that was awful. Because it paid off. I'm never going to be funny and flippant again. I'm going to be dead serious, and take everyone's problems to heart. I am, Chris. I wish you wouldn't sit there, and snigger like that. You don't know how silly it makes you look.

(*Bell rings offstage.*)

CHRIS. I'm a bit on your nerves, aren't I, Sally?

SALLY. Yes, you are. Oh, it's not only you. It's everyone. I'm on my own nerves.

FRÄULEIN SCHNEIDER (*opening door*). Fräulein Sally, hier ist der Herr Americaner. Bitte, mein Herr. Bitte sehr.

(*Clive comes in. He carries a basket of champagne.*)

CLIVE. Well, hello, hello, hello there.

SALLY. Well, hello, Clive.

CHRIS. Hello.

(*Handshakes are performed.*)

SALLY. We thought you'd forgotten all about us.

CLIVE. Oh, for God's sake, no. Say, I've only just heard you'd been sick. Why didn't you let me know?

SALLY. You weren't around.

CLIVE. What was the matter with you, anyway?

SALLY. I had an operation.

CLIVE. Oh gee, that's tough. How are you feeling now?

SALLY. Better. Much better. Now that I've seen you.

CLIVE. Well, that's fine. Feel like coming out to dinner tonight?

SALLY. I can't do that. It's all I can do to get to the bathroom.

CLIVE. Ah, come on. Do you good.

CHRIS. She can't, Clive. She really can't walk yet.

CLIVE. Oh, hell, anyone can walk if they want to.

CHRIS. No, she mustn't. Really.

CLIVE. Well, let's have dinner up here, then. All of us. I brought you some champagne.

SALLY. Oh, Clive, how wonderful of you. I was just saying to Chris that what I'd like best in the world would be some champagne.

CLIVE. Well, let's have it. It's still good and cold. I only just got it. Open it, will you, Chris, there's a good feller?

CHRIS. I'll just get another glass from my room. (*He goes out*)

CLIVE. Well, let's take a look at you. Gee, you're a pale little lady. We'll have to pack you off some place to perk you up a bit. Where would you like to go?

SALLY. I don't really know, Clive. I think maybe I ought to stay here for my career.

CLIVE (*vaguely*). Your career?

SALLY. Yes, the theatre.

CLIVE. Oh, sure, sure.

SALLY. I mean, if I am going to do a play, we ought to start thinking and planning a bit quite soon.

CLIVE. Oh, plenty of time for that. Get you well first. (*Chris returns with a tooth glass, and gets two more from the wash-stand.*)

SALLY. I'll be all right in a few days.

CLIVE. Get you really well.

SALLY. No, but Clive, I do think . . .

CLIVE. You leave that all to me. Leave that all to Uncle Clive. (*To Chris*) Say, are those the best glasses you can manage?

CHRIS. I think Fräulein Schneider may have some others.

SALLY. Don't bother, darling. All I want is the champagne. Open it, won't you?

CHRIS. All right. (*He starts to do so*)

SALLY. Where have you been, Clive?

CLIVE. Been?

SALLY. You've been away somewhere, haven't you?

CLIVE. Ah, just for a day or two.

SALLY. It's ten days.

CLIVE. Is it? Yeah, it may have been. I can never keep track of time when I'm on a bat. You know, this is a funny city. Driving here, just now, we ran right into a bit of shooting.

CHRIS. Shooting?

CLIVE. Seemed just like Chicago.

SALLY. Who was shooting at whom?

CLIVE. I don't know. Just shooting. Couple of people in the street, I guess. I thought I saw a fellow lying there, and a lot of people running in the opposite direction.

CHRIS. Where was this?

CLIVE. I don't know. Right in front of one of the big department stores. Birnbaum's, I think, where we bought you those fancy undies.

CHRIS. That's a Jewish store. That would be Nazi rioting, I imagine.

CLIVE. Say, who are these Nazis, anyway? I keep reading the word in the papers, when I look at them, and I never know who they are referring to. Are the Nazis the same as the Jews?

CHRIS. No—they're—well, they're more or less the opposite.

(*The champagne bottle is opened.*)

SALLY. Oh, that looks wonderful.

CLIVE. And there's a funeral going on today, too.

SALLY. Darling, isn't there always?

CLIVE. No, but this is the real thing. This is a real elegant funeral. It's been going on for over an hour. With banners and streamers, and God knows what all. I wonder who the guy was? He must have been a real swell.

CHRIS (*passing glasses*). He was an old liberal leader. They put him in prison once for trying to stop the war. So now everybody loves him.

SALLY. Oh, this is marvelous. Just what the doctor ordered. Let's drink to Clive. Our best friend.

CHRIS. To Clive.

(*They drink.*)

CLIVE. Well, thank you both. I'll drink to the pair of you. Two real good playmates. (*He does so*)

SALLY. You know, I think there's something almost sacred about champagne. The taste and the look of it. Like holy wine, or something. I think it's absolutely right that it's as expensive as it is. It makes one appreciate it more, like something really special. Like : ..

CHRIS. Like—*that!*

SALLY. Yes, exactly like *that.*

CLIVE. What's *that?*

SALLY (*vaguely noble*). Oh—love, and that sort of thing.

CLIVE. You know, kids, this is a pretty dreary sort of town. I've been here three weeks, and I'm getting kind of fed up with it.

SALLY (*alarmed*). You're not going away?

CLIVE. I was kinda thinking of it.

SALLY. Oh, no, Clive. You mustn't.

CLIVE (*suddenly*). What do you say we *all* go? All three of us.

CHRIS. But where?

CLIVE. Where would you like to go?

CHRIS (*as in a game*). Anywhere in the world?

CLIVE. Anywhere in the world.

CHRIS. I think I'd like to go to India.

SALLY. Oh no, it's all so terribly unsanitary. I want to go somewhere terrifically mysterious and sinister, and full of history. I'd like to go to Egypt.

CLIVE. We can do both. Say, what do you say—we take off from here as soon as Sally's well enough? Take the Orient Express.

SALLY. That's such a lovely name.

CLIVE. Take it as far as Athens. Then we can fly to Egypt. Then back to Marseilles. From there we can get a boat to South America. Then Tahiti. Singapore. Japan.

CHRIS. You know, you manage to say those names as though they were stations on the subway.

SALLY. Well, he's been to them all heaps of times, haven't you, Clive darling?

CLIVE. Sure. Sure, I have. But I'd kind of get a kick out of showing them to you two kids. And then we can end up in California.

CHRIS. You don't mean it, do you, Clive? Just take off and go—just like that?

SALLY. But of course, Chris. Why ever not? This is sheer absolute heaven.

CHRIS. And what happens to your stage career?

SALLY. Oh, that can wait. Or we can pick it up again in California. I'm sure Clive knows all the movie magnates, don't you, Clive?

CLIVE. I know quite a few of them.

SALLY. I mean, you could get me on the films like that, if you wanted to?

CLIVE. Oh, I guess so. Well, what about it? When shall we take off? You won't need more than a week, will you? You can rest on the train.

SALLY. I can rest anywhere.

CLIVE. How's about a week from today?

SALLY. I think it would be marvelous.

CLIVE (*to Chris*). All right with you?

CHRIS (*sitting down, helplessly*). Yes, I— I guess so.

CLIVE. Okay, that's that, then. And, look, if we're going to have dinner up here, I'd better go get us a few things. What would you like? Some caviar, to start with?

SALLY. Oh, I'd adore that.

CLIVE. Then some soup. Some green turtle, maybe. And a partridge. With salad, of course. And I guess some of that chestnut ice cream with whipped cream all over it. And some fruit—some peaches.

SALLY. Get something for Fräulein Schneider.

CHRIS. Get her a pineapple. It's her idea of real luxury.

CLIVE. I think maybe we'd better get some new china, too, and some decent glasses.

CHRIS. Well, if we're going away next week . . .

CLIVE. Oh heck, you can present them to your landlady to make up for your rent. I'll go get them.

SALLY. Why don't you send your driver?

CLIVE. Heck no, this is kinda fun. Something to do. I'll be right back. I'll get some real good brandy, too—half a dozen bottles—and we'll make a real picnic of it. So long, kids. (*He goes out. A long silence*)

SALLY. Isn't life extraordinary? Just when you think you've really touched bottom, something always turns up.

CHRIS. Do you think he means it?

SALLY. Yes, of course he does. You know, Chris, I really do adore him. I mean that. I really do.

CHRIS. I know. I've watched you doing it.

SALLY. You're looking all stunned. What's the matter?

CHRIS. I feel stunned. Doesn't it stun you when someone comes along and just whirls you right out of the whole flux of your life?

SALLY. No, dear, not a bit. Besides, my life hasn't got a flux. And I don't think yours has, either.

CHRIS. No, you're right, it hasn't.

SALLY. Well, then?

CHRIS. But what will become of us?

SALLY. We shall have a wonderful time.

CHRIS. And then?

SALLY. I don't know. Oh, stop bothering with it, Chris. You always spoil things so.

CHRIS. We shall never come back.

SALLY. I don't want to come back.

CHRIS. I suppose you'll marry him.

SALLY. Of course I will.

CHRIS. And I? What will I be?

SALLY. You'll be sort of a private secretary, or something.

CHRIS. Without any duties. You know, Sally, I can suddenly see myself ten years from now—in flannels and black-and-white shoes, pouring out drinks in the lounge of a Californian hotel. I'll be a bit glassy in the eyes, and a lot heavier round the jowls.

SALLY. You'll have to take a lot of exercise, that's all.

CHRIS (*going to the window*). You were both quite right. We've got nothing to do with these Germans down there—or the

shooting, or the funeral, with the dead man in his coffin, or the words on the banners. You know, in a few days, we shall have forfeited all kinship with about ninety-nine per cent of the world's population. The men and women who earn their livings, and insure their lives, and are anxious about the future of their children.

SALLY. It's the only way to live. Isn't there something in the Bible about "Take no thought for the morrow"? That's exactly what it means.

CHRIS. I think in the Middle Ages, people must have felt like this when they believed they had sold themselves to the devil.

SALLY. Well, you needn't come, if you don't want to.

CHRIS. Oh no, I shall come. It's a funny feeling. Sort of exhilarating. Not really unpleasant. And yet, I'm sort of scared, too. If I do this, I'm lost. And yet I'm going to do it.

SALLY. Darling, is there any more in that bottle of champagne?

CHRIS. Sure.

SALLY (*pouring*). Chris, this is the end of one life, and the beginning of another. Two weeks from now, we'll probably be floating down the Nile, with the desert all round us in the moonlight, and all those marvelous sensual Arabs watching us from the tops of the pyramids. And then there'll be India. And a Maharajah will offer me my weight in diamonds if I'll spend one night in his harem.

CHRIS. You'd better put on some weight. Will you do it?

SALLY. Well, not unless he's one of the kind who looks like a sort of mixture of Valentino and Buddha. If you know what I mean.

CHRIS. Well, not exactly. What will I be doing all this time?

SALLY. Oh, you'll be looking simply marvelous and sexy in jodhpurs and an explorer's hat. And then there'll be feasts on volcanoes in the South Seas, and cocktails with Garbo. (*She pours more drinks*) Chris, what is it they say in German when you're going on a journey, and they want to wish you luck?

CHRIS. Hals and Beinbruch.

SALLY. What does that mean?

CHRIS. Neck and leg-break. It's supposed

to stop you having them.

SALLY. That's wonderful. (*Raising her glass*) Neck and leg-break, Chris.

CHRIS. Neck and leg-break.

(*They drink.*)

CURTAIN

## ACT TWO

### SCENE II

SCENE: *Five days later. When the curtain rises, Chris is seated at the table finishing some coffee. There are one or two dress boxes lying around, and an open suitcase in front of the bed.*

_____

(*Fräulein Schneider enters, carrying a large package*)

FRÄULEIN SCHNEIDER. Herr Issyvoo, there is a box for you from Landauer's store. I bring it in here, because the man has not come yet to repair the ceiling in your room. I think perhaps it is the news that has stopped him.

CHRIS. What news?

FRÄULEIN SCHNEIDER. They have closed the National Bank. I heard it this morning, and I couldn't believe it. I went down to see. And, Herr Issyvoo, it is true. The bank is closed at the corner of the Nollendorf Platz. There will be thousands ruined, I shouldn't wonder. Such times we live in! It was bad during the war. Then they promise us it will be better. And now it is almost worse again. It is the Jews. I know it is the Jews.

CHRIS. Fräulein Schneider, how can it be? You don't know what you are saying.

FRÄULEIN SCHNEIDER. They are too clever. And you buy things at Landauer's store. That is a Jewish store. What did you buy?

CHRIS (*opening the parcel*). I bought a suit. It's—it's a tropical suit. (*Then, with determination*) Fräulein Schneider, there is something that I have got to tell you. I should have told you before. Fräulein Sally and I are going away. We're going—well, right round the world. We're leaving on Thursday.

FRÄULEIN SCHNEIDER. *This* Thursday? The day after tomorrow?

CHRIS. Yes, I'm afraid so. We'll pay you till the end of the month, of course.

FRÄULEIN SCHNEIDER. But, Herr Issyvoo, this is dreadful. Both of you going away, and my other rooms empty, too. And now with the banks closing—what shall I do?

CHRIS. I'm terribly sorry, but there are other tenants. There must be.

FRÄULEIN SCHNEIDER. How shall I live? And you tell me now, at the last minute!

CHRIS. I know. I'm sorry, but—you can have all that new china and glass we have.

FRÄULEIN SCHNEIDER (*in an outburst*). Never, never did I think it would come to this. To live on other people—to become fond of them, as I have on you. To help Fräulein Sally, take her to the doctor—and then to have you walk out like this, as though I were nothing but a landlady to whom you can fling the rent.

CHRIS (*helplessly*). Fräulein Schneider, it's not that. . . .

FRÄULEIN SCHNEIDER. And now I am an old woman, and nobody will care what becomes of me. I can go drown myself in the Spree. (*She is crying now. Chris touches her*)

CHRIS. Oh, please, Fräulein Schneider . . .

FRÄULEIN SCHNEIDER (*springing up*). No, do not touch me. It is the Judas touch.

(*Sally comes in. She wears a new, light suit, carries another dress box. She is very gay.*)

SALLY. What on earth's going on?

CHRIS. I've just broken it to Fräulein Schneider that we're leaving. I am afraid that she is rather upset.

FRÄULEIN SCHNEIDER. Upset? Yes, I am upset. You go off on a trip of the whole world. You can afford to do that. But me, I have had to wait for my money, because you were too hard up sometimes to pay me. And now you throw me the china and the glass as a tip. The china and the glass . . . I will throw them from the windows after your taxi as you go away. That is what I think from your china and your glass. And from you, too. (*She goes out*)

SALLY. You're quite right, Chris. She *is* upset. What did you have to tell her for?

CHRIS. Well, I thought we had to. It's only two days now. You know, that was sort of awful what she said, about our being able to afford this trip.

SALLY. I don't see why.

CHRIS. It doesn't seem wrong to you—to let Clive pay it all?

SALLY. Well, we couldn't do it, if he

didn't. And he *wants* to. I mean, we didn't *ask* for it.

(*The bell rings.*)

CHRIS. I didn't feel that I could quite explain that to Fräulein Schneider.

SALLY. I've got an absolutely exquisite negligee. I must show it to you. (*She opens the box, and takes out a fluffy pink negligee*) Look, isn't it simply marvelous?

CHRIS. But, Sally, what are you going to need that for?

SALLY. Darling, to lie around in.

CHRIS. Where?

SALLY. Anywhere. I expect we'll do lots of lying around.

(*Fraulein Schneider, quite grim now, announces.*)

FRÄULEIN SCHNEIDER. Herr Wendel. (*Fritz enters. Fräulein Schneider retires*)

FRITZ. Well, then, hello, you.

SALLY. Hello. Look, Fritz, don't you think this is wonderful? (*She shows the negligee, jumping on the ottoman to do so*)

FRITZ. But, yes. That is extremely seductive. It is for a part in the movies?

SALLY. No, it's to wear. We're going away, Fritz. Clive is taking us. All around the world. We're leaving on Thursday.

FRITZ. You say again, please.

CHRIS. We're going round the world.

FRITZ. The two of you. (*They nod*) With Clive?

CHRIS. I know, Fritz. It doesn't sound likely. But he did ask us.

SALLY. Chris, do we have any of that champagne left?

CHRIS. Oh, yes, there are still about four bottles. You know he brought a dozen.

SALLY. Let's open one.

CHRIS (*getting it*). It isn't cold.

SALLY. That's all right. I'm terribly thirsty, and we've just got time before his car arrives to fetch us to lunch. (*Chris gets a bottle and glasses from the washstand*) How are you, Fritz?

FRITZ. I am not good. I am not good at all.

SALLY. Oh, dear, what's the trouble now?

FRITZ. I would like to tell you. Can I, please?

SALLY. Yes, of course.

FRITZ. You remember, Chris, the advice you give me from Natalia. I attempt it. I think it goes well. And then I go again

to see her, and she sends me a note. She will not see me, she will never see me again. (*Sally turns away in embarrassment*) I beg. I plead. I go again. At last she see me. She tell me it is all over. (*Chris opens the bottle and pours*) And she shows me a note that her father has received.

SALLY. From whom?

FRITZ. It is not signed. But it say, Herr Landauer, beware. We are going to settle the score with all you dirty Jews. We give you twenty-four hours to leave Germany. If not, you are dead men.

CHRIS (*stopping pouring*). Good God! When was this?

FRITZ. This was last night. And she say that with that sort of thing she cannot think now from anything else, and I am to go away and never come back. And when I try to comfort her, and tell her that it is some silly schoolboy who writes it, she scream at me that I do not understand. That I am like all the others. That her father is worried sick, and her mother is falling all the time ohnmächtig . . .

SALLY. What is that?

CHRIS. Fainting.

FRITZ. Ja, she is falling fainting, and now will I go, please. Please. Please. Please. So I go.

SALLY (*embarrassed*). Well . . . Chris, isn't that champagne ready yet?

CHRIS (*roused*). Oh, yes.

SALLY. Well, let's have it. Here, Fritz. Here's how.

CHRIS. How.

FRITZ (*sadly*). How.

SALLY. Oh, this is wonderful. Even warm, it is wonderful.

CHRIS. What is Herr Landauer going to do?

SALLY. I should think he is going away, isn't he?

FRITZ. No, he will not go away. He wants that Natalia and her mother should go. And Natalia will not. I think her mother will go to Paris. But Natalia will stay by her father.

SALLY. If it was me, I'd fly like a bird. If I could afford it. And I'm sure they can. I mean, what is the point of staying, with that sort of thing going on?

FRITZ. I do not know. (*He drinks again, then suddenly flings his glass from him with a melodramatic gesture*) Verfluchter Kerl! (*He buries his head in his hands*)

SALLY. Fritz, what on earth's the matter?

CHRIS. What is it?

FRITZ. It is I. Please, can I tell you something else? Can I tell you both something?

SALLY. Yes, of course.

FRITZ. It is something I have never told anyone in my life before. But now I must make confession. I am a Jew.

SALLY (*quite unperturbed*). Well?

FRITZ. That does not surprise you?

SALLY. I sort of had an idea you were, especially when you made so much fuss about not being. And then I forgot all about it. But so what?

FRITZ. So what? I have lied and pretended. Even to Natalia I have lied.

CHRIS. If you were so keen on getting her, I should have thought that was the very thing to tell her.

SALLY. Her parents wanted her to marry a Jew.

FRITZ. I know. I know. She has told me that. And still I could not say it. I think I wanted it even more, that no one should ever know. Even now, I cannot be one from the Landauers, and have letters like that written to me. I am ashamed from myself, but it is so. And now I have told you, and now you know me for what I am. And it is not nice. It is not nice at all. (*A long pause*) Well, you say something, please.

SALLY. Fritz, I think you are taking it all too seriously. I mean, it is your own business.

FRITZ. I do not think it is any more. But still I cannot speak.

(*Bell rings.*)

SALLY. That'll be the car. Clive's car. Quick, let's have another drop of champagne. Fritz?

FRITZ. No, I do not want any more.

SALLY. Come on, it'll do you good. Here . . . (*She offers him her glass. He pushes it away*) Oh, well, have it your own way.

CHRIS (*touching Fritz*). Fritz, I am terribly sorry. (*Fräulein Schneider enters with a note. She gives it to Sally and goes out again*) I know it's not for me to give you any advice. I don't think I could, anyhow. But don't you think maybe you should tell Natalia that . . .

SALLY (*who has opened the note and read it*). But . . . but . . . (*she cannot speak*)

CHRIS. What is it, Sally?

SALLY. Oh, it's nothing. Look, Fritz, we've got to go out to lunch . . .

CHRIS (*shocked*). But, Sally . . .

SALLY (*sharply*). Well, we have. And right away. Fritz, I'm not trying to get rid of you, but we do have to go.

FRITZ. Ja. Ja, of course.

SALLY. I'm most terribly sorry. And please, please come back. Come back soon.

FRITZ. But you are going away.

SALLY. Oh . . . yes . . . Well, come tomorrow.

FRITZ. I will see. Good-bye, Sally. Good-bye, Chris. I think maybe now I go pray a little. But in what church? I do not know. (*He goes out*)

CHRIS. Really, Sally, that was a little cruel. Fritz really is in trouble . . .

SALLY. Yes, well, so are we. Real trouble. Read that. (*She hands him the note. He reads it*)

CHRIS. Good God!

SALLY. Read it aloud, will you? I want to be sure I got it right.

CHRIS (*reading*). "Dear Sally and Chris, I can't stick this damned town any longer. I'm off to the States. Hoping to see you sometime. Clive. These are in case I forgot anything." (*He looks in the envelope*) Three hundred marks. (*A long pause*) Well!

SALLY. I should think you might be able to say something better than "well."

CHRIS. I said "well" when it happened. I can't think of anything else to say, now it isn't going to.

SALLY. Do you think it's true?

CHRIS. Do you want to call up the hotel and see? See if he's gone?

SALLY. You call. I don't want him to think I'm running after him.

CHRIS. I feel rather the same way.

SALLY. We could ask Fräulein Schneider to call. (*Opens door*) Fräulein Schneider . . . Fräulein Schneider . . .

CHRIS. What are you going to tell her?

SALLY. Nothing. Just ask her to call.

CHRIS. And if he's gone . . . ?

SALLY. Well, we should have to tell her in the end. That just shows why you shouldn't have told her now.

(*Fräulein Schneider enters.*)

FRÄULEIN SCHNEIDER. You called for me?

SALLY (*over-sweetly*). Yes, Schneider-schen. Will you be a liebling, and call the Adlon Hotel, and ask for Mr. Mortimer?

FRÄULEIN SCHNEIDER. You want to speak to him?

SALLY. No, I don't. I just want you to ask for him. And if he *is* there—well, say we'll be a little late for lunch. And then come and tell us.

(FRÄULEIN SCHNEIDER goes without a word.)

CHRIS. You know he's gone, don't you?

SALLY. I suppose I do, really. But we've got to be sure. Do you think he did it on purpose? Just to get us all steamed up, and then let us down like this?

CHRIS. I think he just got fed up.

SALLY. And what about us?

CHRIS. I don't imagine he even remembered us—or not for more than a minute. I think that's the way he lives. And that he leaves every town and every set of acquaintances just that way.

SALLY. Easy come, easy go.

CHRIS. Yes.

SALLY. We were easy come, all right. But, Chris, don't you think it was outrageous? I mean, really outrageous?

CHRIS. Sally, I don't think we've got too much right to have an opinion anyway, about the whole thing.

SALLY. And what have we got out of it?

CHRIS. Not much. But it didn't last very long.

SALLY. I don't think we're much good as gold-diggers, are we, darling? (*They begin to laugh. Fräulein Schneider returns*)

FRÄULEIN SCHNEIDER. Herr Mortimer has left, Fräulein. He has gone back to the United States.

SALLY. I see. Thank you.

CHRIS. And, Fräulein Schneider, we won't be going away—after all.

FRÄULEIN SCHNEIDER (*overjoyed*). Ah, Herr Issyvoo, you mean that?

CHRIS. Yes, I do.

FRÄULEIN SCHNEIDER. Oh, but that is good. That is wonderful. Neither of you? Not Fräulein Sally, either?

SALLY. No, neither of us.

FRÄULEIN SCHNEIDER. Then, that is a miracle. Oh, but I am happy. I am happy.

(*She seizes Sally by the waist, and starts to dance*)

SALLY (*releasing herself*). Yes, I'm sure you're happy, Fräulein. But not now, please. I'd like you to leave us alone.

FRÄULEIN SCHNEIDER (*repentant*). But, of course. Forgive me, Fräulein Sally. I go now. (*She leaves*)

CHRIS. Do you want to come out and have some lunch?

SALLY. I don't think I could eat any.

CHRIS. I don't, either.

SALLY. Well, there we are. We've got three hundred marks.

CHRIS. What are you going to do with them?

SALLY. We'll divide them.

CHRIS. No, you take them. They were sent to you.

SALLY. They were meant for both of us. Halves, Chris.

CHRIS. Well, thank you.

(*She halves the money.*)

SALLY. I shall take this negligee back.

CHRIS. I'll take this suit back, too.

SALLY (*changing into mules and opening the jacket of her suit*). And we shall have to find some work. There was a man who wrote to me the other day about a job in Frankfurt. I never answered him, because I thought we'd be gone. I'll go and see him this afternoon. (*Starting to go through her address book*) He's a horrible old man, and he's always trying to go to bed with me, but I've got to make some money, somehow—I suppose. I've got his address here somewhere.

CHRIS. I'll have to put my advertisement in the paper again. English lessons given.

SALLY (*finding something else*). Oh, and there's this. Do you want to earn some money, Chris?

CHRIS. You know I do. I need to. (*Puts suit box on floor*)

SALLY (*pouring champagne*). Well, there's a man who's starting a magazine. It's going to be terribly highbrow with lots of marvelous modern photographs—you know, girls' heads reflected upside down in inkpots. (*Passing drinks*) Here, Chris. It's silly to waste it. Well, he wanted me to write an article in the first number on the English girl. I forgot all about it, and I haven't an idea what to say, so why don't you do it for me? I'll give you the money.

CHRIS. That's fine. Thank you. But you must have part. How soon do you want it done?

SALLY. I should give it him in a day or two at the latest.

CHRIS. How long is it to be?

SALLY. Oh, I don't know. About *that long.* (*She gesticulates, then gets a book*) Here's a dictionary, in case there are any words you can't spell.

CHRIS (*taking it, amused*). Good.

SALLY (*her arms around his neck*). Oh, Chris, I do like you. You're like a marvelous brother.

CHRIS. I feel the same thing. But, you know, Sally, we've been delivered from something. From the Devil. I know it's disappointing, in a way. . . . That's where the old plays and operas were wrong. . . . There ought to be a sort of disappointment chorus at the end. But it is another chance.

SALLY. Yes, I know. It couldn't have gone on forever. Clive wasn't the type. He'd have ditched us somewhere, and that would have been far worse.

CHRIS. It would have been worse still if he hadn't ditched us.

SALLY. He never meant to play straight with us. You're right. He was the Devil.

CHRIS. I didn't mean that. The Devil was in *us.* Sally, how about our trying to reform, and change our way of life a bit?

SALLY. What's wrong with our way of life?

CHRIS. Just about everything. Isn't it?

SALLY. I suppose so. Not getting any work. Not even trying to. That operation. The lies I've written Mother. The way I haven't written her at all for weeks now.

CHRIS. Me, too. Can't we reform, Sally?

SALLY. Yes, we can. I'll tell you something, Chris. Something I've just decided.

CHRIS. What's that?

SALLY. I'm sick of being a whore. I'm never going to look at another man with money, as long as I live. (*He laughs*) What's funny about that?

CHRIS. Nothing. It's a beginning, anyway.

SALLY. What are *you* going to begin on?

CHRIS. I'm going to start work tomorrow morning.

SALLY (*carried away*). We're both going to begin. We're going to be good. Oh, Chris, isn't it wonderful?

CHRIS (*smiling*). Yes, Sally.

SALLY. We're going to be quite, quite different people. We're even going to look wonderful, too. People will turn around and stare at us in the street, because our eyes will be shining like diamonds.

CHRIS. Diamonds—without any rings under them.

SALLY (*very gaily*). And think how we'll feel in the mornings. Imagine what it will be like to wake up without coughing, or feeling even the least little bit sick.

CHRIS. We'll have appetites like wolves. Ravening wolves.

SALLY. Don't you suppose we ought to diet? Eat just nuts and things?

CHRIS. All right. And we'll give up smoking in bed . . .

SALLY. And drinking before breakfast.

CHRIS (*shocked*). Sally, do you?

SALLY. We must have a time-table. What time shall we get up?

CHRIS. Eight o'clock.

SALLY. Half-past seven.

CHRIS. All right.

SALLY. We shall take cold baths. You have yours first.

CHRIS. And do exercises.

SALLY. Then we'll have breakfast together, and talk German. Nothing but German.

CHRIS. Ja. Jawohl.

SALLY. Then we should study something. Do you think we could learn a useful trade?

CHRIS. We'll weave from eight-thirty to nine. And then spend an hour making small, hand-painted boxes.

SALLY (*laughing hard*). And then it'll be time for you to start your novel, while I practice Interpretive Dancing. You know, with shawls and things . . .

CHRIS. Sally, joking aside. You are serious about all this, aren't you?

SALLY. Of course I am. Terribly serious. (*She gets the address book*) I'm going to start calling up everyone I know.

CHRIS. What for?

SALLY. To see what's going on. And then, one decent piece of luck . . .

CHRIS (*urgently*). Oh, no, Sally. That isn't what we need. A piece of good luck today—a piece of bad luck tomorrow—

always at the mercy of *things* again . . .

SALLY. One *is*. That's life. It's all accident.

CHRIS (*as before*). Accidents are only the result of things one's done. Things that one is.

SALLY. Why, I could go to a party tonight, and I could meet the most wonderful man, who'd make all the difference to my whole life and my career . . . (*She breaks off, looking at him*) What's the matter? Why do you look like that?

CHRIS (*slowly*). Sally, you weren't seri-out. You didn't mean a word of it.

SALLY. Yes, I did. I meant every word. I'm going to be quite different. But there's no reason why I shouldn't go out. I don't have to shut myself up in prison. That isn't what you want, is it?

CHRIS. No, Sally, of course not. But . . .

SALLY (*angrily*). Well, then, stop looking so disapproving. You're almost as bad as Mother. She never stopped nagging at me. That's why I had to lie to her. I always lie to people, or run away from them, if they won't accept me as I am.

CHRIS. I know you do, Sally.

SALLY (*putting on an act*). I think I'm really rather a strange and extraordinary person, Chris. (*Pause*) What's the matter? You laughed at me the first time I told you that. Can't you laugh now? Come on. (*She starts to laugh, not too brightly. He starts a moment later, still more feebly. The laughter dies. She tries again—it fails. They move slowly away from each other.*)

CURTAIN

## ACT THREE

### SCENE I

SCENE: *Two days later. The room is untidy. A half-used coffee tray is on the table with a glass of brandy. The bed is unmade, and clothes are strewn around the room. Fräulein Schneider is tidying up. There is a knock on the door.*

———

CHRIS'S VOICE. Sally, may I come in?

FRÄULEIN SCHNEIDER. Come in, Herr Issyvoo. (*Chris comes in*) Fräulein Sally is telephoning.

CHRIS. She's up very late.

FRÄULEIN SCHNEIDER. She was in very late last night.

CHRIS. I left a manuscript in here for her yesterday afternoon.

FRÄULEIN SCHNEIDER. She did not come back until almost six this morning. I think maybe she drank a little too much. Her clothes are all over the floor. And she had only half her coffee this morning and some brandy too. It is not good so early.

(*Sally enters. She is wearing a robe, and looks hung-over.*)

SALLY. Oh, hello, Chris.

CHRIS. Hello, Sally.

SALLY. Leave all that stuff for now, Fräulein. I'm going to wear it. I'm going out quite soon. You can do the room then.

FRÄULEIN SCHNEIDER. Very good, Fräulein. (*She goes.*)

CHRIS. I haven't seen you for a day and a half.

SALLY. I know. I've missed you, Chris.

CHRIS. I've missed you, too. I say, you don't look too well this morning.

SALLY. I've got a terrible hangover.

CHRIS. What were you doing last night?

SALLY. I was out with some people. I've been out both nights. I've been an awful fool, Chris. But don't scold me, please.

CHRIS. What have you been up to?

SALLY. Oh, not *that*.

CHRIS. I wasn't thinking of that!

SALLY. But we never stopped going around. And then I got drunk and sentimental the first night, and I telephoned Mother in London.

CHRIS. Good God, what for?

SALLY. I suddenly felt like it. But we had the most awful connection, and I couldn't hear a word. And last night was worse. We went to the most boring places. Oh, Chris, I need someone to stop me. I really do. I wish I'd stayed home with you.

CHRIS. Well, thank you, Sally.

SALLY. But you're awfully nice to come back to.

CHRIS. You're nice to have come back. I say, that sounds like a popular song.

SALLY. Oh, it does. Maybe we could write it together and make a fortune. (*She improvises a tune*) "You're awfully nice to come back to."

CHRIS (*doing the same*). "You're awfully nice to come back."

SALLY AND CHRIS (*singing together*) "You're awfully nice to come back to . . ."

SALLY (*her arms around him*). I do think we belong together. Much more than if we'd ever had an affair. That little quarrel we had didn't mean anything, did it?

CHRIS. I don't think two people can live as close as we do, and not have them.

SALLY. But it was that that sent me out on that idiotic binge.

CHRIS (*pause*). Did you read the article I left you?

SALLY. The what, dear?

CHRIS. My article.

SALLY (*vaguely*). Oh, yes, I—looked at it.

CHRIS. Well?

SALLY (*too brightly*). I'm terribly sorry, Chris. But it won't do.

CHRIS. Why, what's wrong with it?

SALLY. It's not nearly snappy enough.

CHRIS. Snappy?

SALLY. But it's all right, Christopher. I've got someone else to do it.

CHRIS. Oh? Who?

SALLY. Kurt Rosenthal. I called him this morning.

CHRIS. Who's he?

SALLY. Really, Chris, I thought you took an interest in the cinema. He's miles the best young scenario writer. He earns pots of money.

CHRIS. Then why's he doing this?

SALLY. As a favor to me. He said he'd dictate it while he's shaving, and send it round to the editor's flat.

CHRIS. Well, journalism isn't really in my line. But I think you might have let me know.

SALLY. I didn't think you'd want to be bothered.

CHRIS. And *he* would?

SALLY (*starting to dress*). He doesn't make such a fuss about writing as you do. He's writing a novel in his spare time. He's so terribly busy, he can only dictate it while he's having a bath.

CHRIS (*bitterly*). I bet that makes it wonderful.

SALLY. He read me the first few chapters. Honestly, I think it's the best novel I've ever read.

CHRIS. But that doesn't add up to very many, does it?

SALLY (*her tone sharpening, from his*).

He's the kind of author I really admire. And he's not stuck up, either. Not like one of these young men who, because they've written one book, start talking about art, and imagining they're the most wonderful authors in the world.

CHRIS. Just who are you talking about, Sally?

SALLY (*brushing her hair*). Well, you do, Chris. You know you do. And it's silly to get jealous.

CHRIS (*angrily*). Jealous? Who's jealous?

SALLY. There's no need to get upset, either.

CHRIS (*furious*). I am not upset. You don't like my article. All right, you needn't go on about it. I can't think why I expected you to, with that snappy little bird-brain of yours. Or your rich, successful friends either, from whom you seem to have got all this stuff about me.

SALLY (*equally angry*). Would you like to know what my friends said about you?

CHRIS. No, I wouldn't.

SALLY. Well, I'll tell you. They said you were ruining me. That I'd lost all my sparkle and my effervescence. And that it was all due to you. I've let you eat me up, just sitting here, pouring myself into you.

CHRIS. Oh, is that what you've been doing?

SALLY. It's all you want. You're like a vampire. If you don't have someone around you, you sit about in bars waiting to devour someone.

CHRIS. Your friends said that?

SALLY. My friends are a lot better than the tatty people you run around with. All your friends seem to be interested in, is just flopping into bed.

CHRIS. And since when have you had anything against bed?

SALLY. I haven't anything. So long as it leads somewhere.

CHRIS. You mean not just for the fun of it.

SALLY. That's disgusting. That's like animals. But, you know, Chris, I'll tell you something. I've outgrown you.

CHRIS (*turns to her*). You've *what*?

SALLY. I've gone beyond you. I'd better move away from here.

CHRIS. All right. When?

SALLY. The sooner the better, I should think.

CHRIS. That's fine with me.

SALLY. Good.

CHRIS. So, this is the end for us?

SALLY. Yes. If you want it that way. We'll probably bump into each other somewhere, sometime, I expect.

CHRIS. Well, call me sometime, and ask me around for a cocktail.

SALLY (*pausing*). I never know whether you're being serious, or not.

CHRIS. Try it and find out, if your friends will spare you the time.

SALLY (*throwing it at him*). You know, you make me sick. Good-bye, Chris.

CHRIS (*alone*). What a little bitch she is! Well, I've always know that from the start. No, that's not true. I've flattered myself she was fond of me. Nothing would please me better than to see her whipped. Really whipped. Not that I care a curse what she thinks of my article . . . Well, not much. My literary conceit is proof against anything she could say. It's her criticism of myself. The awful, sexual flair women have for taking the stuffing out of men. It's no good telling myself that Sally had the vocabulary and mind of a twelve-year-old schoolgirl. . . . I mismanaged our interview, right from the beginning. I should have been wonderful, convincing, fatherly, mature. I made the one fatal mistake. I let her see I was jealous. Vulgarly jealous. I feel prickly all over with shame. Friends, indeed! Well, I certainly won't see her again, after all this. Never. Never!

(*Sally returns, very shattered.*)

SALLY. Chris, something awful's happened. Guess who I met in the street, right outside. I met Mother.

CHRIS. Whose mother?

SALLY. Mine.

CHRIS. I thought you said she was in London.

SALLY. She was. But that call of mine upset her. I suppose I did sound a bit drunk. Anyway, she jumped to conclusions, and into an aeroplane. Chris, you're going to have to do something for me. I've been writing her now and then . . . . I mean, they do send me money from time to time. I've never had the nerve to tell you, but I sort of gave her to understand—when I first moved in here—that we were engaged.

CHRIS. That who was engaged?

SALLY. You and I. To be married.

CHRIS. Sally, you didn't!

SALLY. Well, I needed someone who sounded like a good, steady influence—and you were the best I could think of. She's in the sitting-room. I told her this place was all untidy, but she'll be in in a minute. Oh, and her name isn't Mrs. Bowles. It's Mrs. Watson-Courtneidge. That's my real name. Only you can't imagine the Germans pronouncing it.

CHRIS. And I'm supposed to stand by and pretend? Oh, no, Sally.

SALLY. Chris, you've got to. You owe it to me.

CHRIS. For what? For letting me eat you up? I'm sorry. And I'm going to my room.

SALLY (*getting in his way*). If you don't, I'll tell her the most awful things about you.

CHRIS. I'm afraid I don't care. Tell her what you like.

SALLY (*pleading*). Chris, you can't do this to me.

CHRIS. After the things you just said to me? That I made you sick.

SALLY. That was just an expression.

CHRIS. No, Sally. We're through. Quite through.

SALLY. Well, we still can be, after she goes home. Only, help me keep her happy. Don't believe everything I said at first about Mother. She isn't easy. Please, darling. Please!

(*Her arms are around his neck. He struggles to disengage himself. Then Mrs. Watson-Courtneidge comes in. She is a middle-aged English lady, in tweeds. She carries a coat.*)

MRS. WATSON-COURTNEIDGE (*catching sight of the embrace*). Excuse me.

SALLY (*extricating herself*). Oh . . .

MRS. WATSON-COURTNEIDGE. I hope this is Mr. Isherwood.

SALLY. Yes. Christopher.

MRS. WATSON-COURTNEIDGE. I'm Mother.

CHRIS. I imagined that.

MRS. WATSON-COURTNEIDGE. Well—don't I deserve a kiss, too?

CHRIS (*as Sally looks pleadingly at him*). Oh—yes, of course. (*A kiss is performed*)

MRS. WATSON-COURTNEIDGE. You're not a bit like I imagined you.

CHRIS. Oh, really. How did you imagine me?

MRS. WATSON-COURTNEIDGE. Oh, quite different. So this is your room, Sally. Yes, I can see why you said it was untidy.

SALLY. I got up very late this morning. Fräulein Schneider hasn't really had time to do it.

MRS. WATSON-COURTNEIDGE. I don't imagine she does it very well at the best of times. I've just been having a little talk with her. I can't say I like her very much. And why does she sleep in the sitting-room?

CHRIS. So that she can watch the corner.

MRS. WATSON-COURTNEIDGE. And what happens on the corner?

CHRIS. Oh—*that*!

SALLY. Chris!

MRS. WATSON-COURTNEIDGE. I beg your pardon?

CHRIS (*vaguely*). This and that.

MRS. WATSON-COURTNEIDGE. I should think she'd be much better occupied, looking after . . . (*Dusting the table with her fingers*) that and this! (*She picks up the brandy glass*) Sally, you haven't been drinking brandy, I hope.

SALLY. That's Chris's glass.

MRS. WATSON-COURTNEIDGE. On *your* breakfast tray? Where do *you* live, Mr. Isherwood?

CHRIS. Just across the hall.

MRS. WATSON-COURTNEIDGE (*dryly*). How convenient!

SALLY. What do you mean by that, Mother?

MRS. WATSON-COURTNEIDGE. Sally, dear, I'm not asking for details. There are things one doesn't choose to know. But tell me, you two, when are you getting married?

SALLY. I don't know, Mother. We're happy as—we are. Aren't we, Chris?

CHRIS (*grimly*). Just as we are.

MRS. WATSON-COURTNEIDGE. I can well believe it. But sooner or later, these things have to be—well, shall we say, tidied up. There are some questions I would like to ask you, Mr. Isherwood.

CHRIS. Yes?

MRS. WATSON-COURTNEIDGE. I've read your book.

CHRIS. Oh, really?

MRS. WATSON-COURTNEIDGE. After Sally wrote me the title, I got it from the library—with a good deal of trouble. It's an odd book. Was it a success?

CHRIS. No. Not really.

MRS. WATSON-COURTNEIDGE. That doesn't altogether surprise me. I take it you don't live on your writing?

CHRIS. No. Hardly. (*Warningly*) Sally!

MRS. WATSON-COURTNEIDGE. What do you live on?

CHRIS. I teach English.

MRS. WATSON-COURTNEIDGE. And is that sufficient?

CHRIS. I get by.

MRS. WATSON-COURTNEIDGE. Can two get by?

CHRIS. I'm inclined to doubt it. (*As before, but more so*) Sally!

MRS. WATSON-COURTNEIDGE. Well that is not my concern. That will be Sally's father's.

CHRIS (*getting no response from Sally*). Well, now if you'll excuse me, Sally . . .

MRS. WATSON-COURTNEIDGE. Are you not lunching with us?

SALLY. Yes, of course he is.

CHRIS. Sally, I can't.

SALLY. Yes, you can. You were lunching with me.

CHRIS. Look, I think there's something we ought to clear up.

SALLY. *No!*

MRS. WATSON-COURTNEIDGE. What is that? (*Silence a moment. Then Chris gives way.*)

CHRIS. I haven't got any decent clothes.

SALLY. You've got your blue suit.

CHRIS. It's almost in rags by daylight.

MRS. WATSON-COURTNEIDGE. My dear Mr. Isherwood, it's not your clothes we want, it's your company. I know all about your background. Anything you wear will be all right, so long as it is clean.

CHRIS. Well, that's part of the point.

SALLY (*pushing him out*). Go and change, Chris. We'll wait here for you.

CHRIS (*after a look at her*). I won't be a minute. (*He goes*)

MRS. WATSON-COURTNEIDGE. He's an odd young man, Sally.

SALLY. Oh, I don't know, Mother.

MRS. WATSON-COURTNEIDGE. Tell me, that strange telephone call of yours—how much was Mr. Isherwood involved in it?

SALLY. Involved?

MRS. WATSON-COURTNEIDGE. Had you had a few too many cocktails because of some—well—little quarrel with him?

SALLY. Oh, no, Mother. Chris and I never quarrel.

MRS. WATSON-COURTNEIDGE. Well, in any case, I think you two have been together quite enough for the moment. You had better move into the hotel with me.

SALLY (*protesting*). No, Mother, I . . .

MRS. WATSON-COURTNEIDGE. Sally, don't answer back. You always answer back. I've begun to realize that things are a little more complicated than I had imagined. Hasn't Mr. Isherwood suggested any date for your wedding?

SALLY. No, Mother, I don't think he has.

MRS. WATSON-COURTNEIDGE. I'm not suggesting he will let you down. He's a gentleman. That's one comfort. But . . .

SALLY (*urgently*). Mother, you've got entirely the wrong idea about Chris and me. We aren't . . .

MRS. WATSON-COURTNEIDGE (*interrupting her*). Sally, that is something you might have had to say to your grandmother. You don't have to say it to me.

SALLY. But, Mother . . .

MRS. WATSON-COURTNEIDGE (*as before*). Mother's quite broad-minded.

SALLY (*giving way*). Well, all right, but don't rush him. Don't try and force him, or anything.

MRS. WATSON-COURTNEIDGE. Trust Mother! I see you still have that picture. You had that in the nursery. "The Kitten's Awakening." I'm glad you still have that. The old things are still the best, after all, aren't they?

SALLY (*subdued*). Yes, Mother.

MRS. WATSON-COURTNEIDGE (*embracing her*). We must get you back to them.

CURTAIN

## ACT THREE

### SCENE II

SCENE: *The same. Afternoon. About three days later.*

AT RISE: *Fritz is on stage. Fräulein Schneider is setting a tray of coffee for him. The old pictures are back on the walls. The room is again as in Scene I.*

———

FRÄULEIN SCHNEIDER. He is always back around this time, Herr Wendel. You cannot have to wait long.

FRITZ. I am glad that Christopher could move back into this room again. Will he stay on here?

FRÄULEIN SCHNEIDER. Oh, I hope. He is doing better now. Starting new lessons. It is true they are almost all to the Jews, but even so there is at least some good that comes from them that way. (*Fritz does not answer*) Is it true, Herr Wendel, that they will take the money away from the Jews, and drive them all out?

FRITZ. I have no idea.

FRÄULEIN SCHNEIDER. It would be a good thing. Do you not agree with me?

FRITZ. I don't really know.

FRÄULEIN SCHNEIDER. But you must know, Herr Wendel. That is what the speakers all say. Everyone must know, and everyone must agree and only then can Germany be saved.

(*Voices heard offstage.*)

CHRIS's VOICE. Go right in there, Natalia. Are you sure you're all right?

NATALIA's VOICE. Oh, yes, I thank you. I am all right.

CHRIS's VOICE. And then come to my room. It's the old room. (*He comes in. He is a little more messed up than usual*) Oh, hello, Fritz. I didn't know you were here. (*Fräulein Schneider goes out*)

FRITZ. Was that Natalia's voice I heard outside?

CHRIS. Yes, she's gone to the bathroom. I must wash my hands.

FRITZ. What is the matter?

CHRIS. There was a bit of trouble. (*He pours water into the basin*)

FRITZ. But what is it all about?

CHRIS (*washing his hands*). I was walking with Natalia after her lesson. We ran into a bunch of toughs. Nazis, of course. They were holding a street meeting. And Natalia insisted on joining in.

FRITZ. Joining in?

CHRIS. Yes, she got quite fierce. She made a speech. She was almost like Joan of Arc. I was quite astonished.

FRITZ. She is wonderful, that girl.

CHRIS. And she was hit in the face with a stone.

FRITZ. Um Gotteswillen.

CHRIS. It wasn't serious. At least, I don't think it was. I wanted her to go to a doctor, but she wouldn't. I think she is a bit shaken, that's all. And this place was nearer than her home. I brought her here.

FRITZ. It is better perhaps if your landlady does not see her.

CHRIS. Why?

FRITZ. She is not very partial to the Jews, your landlady.

CHRIS. Yes, I know. But she doesn't know what she is talking about.

FRITZ. She knows as much as most people.

CHRIS. And that is the tragedy. (*Chris takes a series of Band-Aids, and starts to put them on his hands rather excessively*)

FRITZ. What is with your hands? Were you in it too?

CHRIS. Well, after Natalia started, I couldn't really keep out of it. Trying to get her away.

FRITZ. Natalia should not stay here.

CHRIS. She'll stay as long as her father stays.

FRITZ. She would go if she married.

CHRIS. I doubt that.

FRITZ (*urgently*). But she ought to go! Christopher, I know now I am in love with Natalia. I have not seen her, but I am in love with her.

(*Natalia enters. There is a small scar, newly washed, on her face.*)

NATALIA. So, Christopher, I think now . . . (*She see Fritz, and stops*) Oh, Fritz.

FRITZ. Ja, Natalia.

NATALIA. Christopher did not tell me you were here.

FRITZ. He did not know.

CHRIS. Let me give you some brandy, Natalia.

NATALIA. I do not think so.

CHRIS. Yes, but I do think so. You need something. And it's quite good brandy. It's part of—quite a good loot. I'm going to have some.

FRITZ (*to Natalia*). Please, may I see your face?

NATALIA (*turning*). There is nothing there.

FRITZ (*kneeling*). I would like to see, please. It is clean? You have washed it? You have washed it thoroughly?

NATALIA. I have washed it thoroughly.

CHRIS. Would you like to put a Band-Aid on it?

NATALIA. On my face?

CHRIS. I think you should. You can get blood poisoning.

NATALIA. And a bandage will help that?

CHRIS. I have some iodine. I can put that on for you.

NATALIA. Not on my face, I thank you.

FRITZ. You let me put one of these on. Just a very small one. Like so. (*He holds one up*)

NATALIA (*touched, but unwilling to show it*). I can put it on myself.

FRITZ. I know, but let me do it, please. You drink your brandy, and let me do it. (*He starts to do so*)

CHRIS (*looking at his hands*). You know, I wonder if I shouldn't take these Band-Aids off, and put on some iodine. I could get gangrene.

NATALIA. No, Christopher, you could not.

CHRIS. You never know. Then they amputate your hands. And you can't write or type any more. (*He tears off the Band-Aids and paints on iodine*)

FRITZ (*finishing his job*). There. (*He seems to feel a little faint*) Now I take some brandy. (*He and Natalia gulp some, hastily*)

NATALIA. And now I think I go home.

FRITZ. You let me take you, please.

NATALIA. My dear young man, I . . .

FRITZ (*finishing for her*). I am not yet sixty years old, and I can go home unmolested.

NATALIA. I prefer that I go alone.

FRITZ. I would like that you let me take you.

NATALIA. And if we run into another of these street riots?

FRITZ. I would still like to take you. (*Chris raises his head. The two men exchange glances. Fritz nods very gently*) I tell it now.

CHRIS. Let him take you, Natalia. I would feel better.

NATALIA. Very well. I see you tomorrow, Christopher. At the usual hour.

CHRIS. Yes, of course. Good-bye, Natalia. I admired you very much this afternoon.

FRITZ. I, too.

NATALIA. I cannot see why. Come. (*She goes out with Fritz*)

(*Chris looks after them, then picks up the Band-Aids and the iodine, and resumes his painting.*)

CHRIS. It doesn't look too good. (*He splashes on some more iodine*)

(*Fräulein Schneider comes in.*)

FRÄULEIN SCHNEIDER. I take the coffee tray. What is with your hands, Herr Issyvoo?

CHRIS. I think they may be poisoned.

FRÄULEIN SCHNEIDER. But how did you come to hurt them?

CHRIS. It was in a street riot.

FRÄULEIN SCHNEIDER. An anti-Jewish riot?

CHRIS. Yes.

FRÄULEIN SCHNEIDER. And you were attacking the Jews.

CHRIS. No, I was doing the other thing. I was defending them.

FRÄULEIN SCHNEIDER. But that is not right, Herr Issyvoo. The Jews are at the bottom of all the trouble.

CHRIS (*sharply*). Fräulein Schneider, I think I've heard enough of that this afternoon. Let's not talk about it any more.

FRÄULEIN SCHNEIDER. But that is wrong, Herr Issyvoo. We must all talk about it. That is what the speakers say. Germany must come first.

CHRIS (*turning angrily*). And what does that mean? How can any country come first that does things like that? Suppose I push this in your face (*He thrusts his fist near her face, and she retreats*) because Germany must come first—and I'm strong enough to do it, and to hurt you? What does that prove?

FRÄULEIN SCHNEIDER. But, Herr Issyvoo . . .

CHRIS. I've always been fond of you. Now I'm ashamed of you. And everything you say is horrible and dangerous and abominable. And now please go away.

FRÄULEIN SCHNEIDER (*angrily*). You will see, Herr Issyvoo. You will see.

(*Bell rings.*)

CHRIS. I know that talking like this makes me almost as bad as you. Or perhaps worse. Because I've got intelligence—I hope—and you've just been listening to things. Now go and answer the bell. (*She goes. He cries out in exasperation to himself*) God, what is one supposed to do? (*He examines his hands again*) I wonder if I've broken anything. It feels awfully loose. (*He flexes his thumb*) Ought that to move like that, or oughtn't it?

(*Sally comes in. She wears the coat her mother was carrying in the previous scene.*)

SALLY. Hello, Chris.

CHRIS. Well, fancy seeing you again, without your mother.

(*Mrs. Watson-Courtneidge comes in.*)

CHRIS. Oh, hello, Mrs. Watson-Courtneidge!

MRS. WATSON-COURTNEIDGE. Good afternoon, Christopher.

CHRIS. And how are things with you two?

MRS. WATSON-COURTNEIDGE. They're very well. Sally has been making me very happy.

CHRIS. I see you've dressed her up in your clothes.

SALLY (*defensively*). What's wrong with that? Mother's got very good taste.

CHRIS. But it's hardly *your* taste, is it?

MRS. WATSON-COURTNEIDGE (*lifting the glass*). Brandy again?

CHRIS (*defiantly*). Yes.

MRS. WATSON-COURTNEIDGE. I see. What's the matter with your hands?

CHRIS. I hurt them. I was in a fight.

SALLY. Good gracious, you! What was the fight about?

CHRIS. Jews.

MRS. WATSON-COURTNEIDGE. Why were you fighting about *them?*

CHRIS. I don't like seeing people being pushed around. (*To Sally*) Or made to pretend they're what they're not.

MRS. WATSON-COURTNEIDGE. Oh, I see. Well, now, Christopher, there's something I want to tell you. I'm taking Sally home.

CHRIS. Oh? And what do *you* say about that, Sally?

SALLY. Mother's quite right, Chris. She really is. I ought to go home. To my past, and my roots and things. They're very important to a girl.

CHRIS. Sally, don't. Don't let her!

SALLY. Let her what?

CHRIS. You're disappearing, right in front of my eyes.

MRS. WATSON-COURTNEIDGE. I hope the girl you knew *is* disappearing. I want you to come, too, Christopher. Then you can meet Sally's father, and, if he approves of you, he will find you a job of some sort. Then you can be married from our house at the end of next month. That will give me time to arrange Sally's trousseau.

CHRIS. Look, Sally, haven't you told your mother yet?

SALLY (*miserably*). No, not yet.

MRS. WATSON-COURTNEIDGE. Told me what?

CHRIS. Sally, I think you should.

SALLY (*desperately*). No, Chris, not now.

CHRIS. Yes, now. Mrs. Courtneidge, there's something I have to tell you. Sally and I are no longer engaged. She sent me a note this morning, to break it off.

MRS. WATSON-COURTNEIDGE. Sally, you never told me.

SALLY (*very relieved*). I wanted to speak to Chris first.

MRS. WATSON-COURTNEIDGE. This is all a little sudden.

CHRIS. I don't think it's very sudden, really. We had a sort of quarrel the morning you arrived, and we never really made it up since.

MRS. WATSON-COURTNEIDGE. I thought you never quarreled.

CHRIS. Who said that?

MRS. WATSON-COURTNEIDGE. Sally did. Are you sure about this, Sally?

SALLY. Well, yes, Mother, as a matter of fact, I am. I don't think Chris and I are really suited to each other.

MRS. WATSON-COURTNEIDGE. Neither do I. But I didn't expect you to realize it. Well, this alters everything. I will not expect *you* to come back to England, Christopher.

CHRIS. Good.

MRS. WATSON-COURTNEIDGE. But I'm very glad that Sally has been able to see the truth for herself. I was afraid that she had changed almost too much. That *you* had changed her.

SALLY (*to Chris*). See?

MRS. WATSON-COURTNEIDGE (*to Sally*). Now you'll come back and settle down again, and quite soon all of this will be forgotten. I'm sure it will seem like a rather bitter experience, but one gets over everything in the right surroundings.

SALLY (*subdued again*). Yes, Mother.

MRS. WATSON-COURTNEIDGE. She has been very good about you, Christopher. She has continued to deny everything that I am absolutely sure has taken place. I think that shows a very fine character.

CHRIS. No doubt that was due to *your* influence.

MRS. WATSON-COURTNEIDGE. Perhaps you'll forgive me if I say a few things to you, Christopher. I think someone should say them, and Sally's father isn't here to do so. Perhaps that's lucky for you. He's not a patient man, and he adores Sally. I know he'd think that anyone who'd harmed her richly deserved a sound horse-whipping.

CHRIS. Now, listen, Mrs. Courtneidge . . .

MRS. WATSON-COURTNEIDGE. I have no intention of listening to you, Mr. Isherwood. Sally has done quite enough of that, already. She's a very sweet, simple girl, but she's too easily influenced.

CHRIS (*with meaning*). Yes, I know.

MRS. WATSON-COURTNEIDGE. Perhaps you think I'm a simple woman, too. Perhaps you think I haven't noticed that, while you've dragged me to the opera and all the museums, you have never introduced me to a single one of your friends. I can well imagine why.

CHRIS. Look, do we have to go into all this?

MRS. WATSON-COURTNEIDGE (*sharply*). Yes, I think we do. It's people like you who are ruining the world. Unprincipled drifters who call themselves authors, never write a word, and then vote Labor on the slightest provocation. No wonder we're headed for socialism. You live in foreign countries, and you let yourself get involved in obscure political issues that are no concern of yours . . .

SALLY (*suddenly*). Yes, they are.

MRS. WATSON-COURTNEIDGE (*surprised*). Sally!

SALLY. Some sort of principles are, and I'm very glad to see he has some, and that there is something he is willing to fight for, instead of just sitting around.

CHRIS. Now, Sally, wait a minute. . . .

SALLY. I know. I've told you a lot of the same things, myself. But I don't like to hear Mother say them. Certainly not to you. You don't know Chris, Mother. You don't understand him. He's a very fine person. He's been wonderful to me. He has. He's done a lot for me, and he's tried to do more. And he's an artist. Well—potentially. All artists need time. He's going to write a wonderful book one day, that'll sell millions of copies—or a lot of short stories all about Germany or something—which will tell the world wonderful things about life and people and everything—and then you'll feel very silly for the things you've just said.

MRS. WATSON-COURTNEIDGE. I thought you'd just broken off your engagement.

SALLY. Yes, I have. But I'm not going to stand here and let you nag at him like that. He doesn't chase around after horrible, influential people, and I bet he wouldn't take a job from Father if he offered him one. He's got too much pride. And character. It just wants—working up, that's all. And now let's go.

MRS. WATSON-COURTNEIDGE (*staggered*). Well . . . I'll say good-bye, Christopher. We shall be leaving tomorrow, or the next day. I don't imagine that we'll meet again. And I prefer that you and Sally did not see each other again, either. Shall we go, Sally?

SALLY. Yes, Mother.

(*They leave, Sally refusing to look back at Chris.*)

CHRIS. Well. Really! (*He goes to the table, and the brandy bottle, then stops*) No, I won't. I *will* have some principles!

CURTAIN

## ACT THREE

### SCENE III

TIME: *Three days later. Evening.*

SCENE: *A large trunk is open in the middle of the floor. Chris is putting things into it and sorting others from the closet.*

———

CHRIS. Where did I ever get all these things? This shirt—I can't possibly have bought it. No, I didn't, of course. I remember. It was at that party at the Lithuanian sculptor's, where a whole bottle of crème de menthe got spilled over mine. These **are** Clive's silk ones. I don't suppose I'll ever wear them, but you never know. This pair of drawers. No, really, they're too far gone. Out! (*He throws them away. Enter Sally. She is dressed as in the first scene*)

SALLY. Chris!

CHRIS. Sally! I thought you'd gone. I thought you'd gone home.

SALLY. No. Mother left this morning.

CHRIS. And you're not going?

SALLY. Not home. Oh, Chris, it was

ghastly getting rid of Mother. But I knew I had to, after that scene here.

CHRIS. How did you do it?

SALLY (*giggling*). I did something awful. I got a friend in London to send her an anonymous telegram telling her Daddy was having an affair. That sent her off in a mad whirl. But Daddy will forgive me. Besides, it's probably true—and I don't blame him. I told Mother I'd follow her when I got some business settled. And something will turn up to stop it. It always does, for me. I'm all right, Chris. I'm back again.

CHRIS (*smiling*). Yes. I can see you are.

SALLY. Is there anything to drink?

CHRIS. There's just a little gin, that's all.

SALLY. I'd love a little gin. In a tooth glass. Flavored with peppermint. Where are you off to?

CHRIS. I *am* going home.

SALLY. When?

CHRIS. Tomorrow night. I'm going to Fritz and Natalia's wedding in the afternoon.

SALLY. Wedding? How did that happen?

CHRIS. Fritz told Natalia about himself, and that did it. And now he doesn't have to pretend any more. Come with me, Sally. They'd love to see you.

SALLY. Oh, I'd like to, but I won't be here.

CHRIS. Where will you be?

SALLY. I'm leaving for the Riviera tonight.

CHRIS. With whom?

SALLY. For a picture.

CHRIS. Well, fine. Is it a good part?

SALLY. I don't really know. I expect so. You haven't got a drink, Chris. Have a drop of this. Make it a loving cup. (*He takes a sip*) Why are you going away, Chris?

CHRIS. Because I'll never write as long as I'm here. And I've got to write. It's the only thing I give a damn about. I don't regret the time I've spent here. I wouldn't have missed a single hangover of it. But now I've got to put it all down—what I think about it. And live by it, too, if I can. Thank you for the idea about that book, Sally. The short stories. I think maybe that will work out.

SALLY. Oh, I hope so. I do want you to be good, Chris.

CHRIS. I am going to try, Sally. Now, tell me about you and this job that you don't seem to know anything about. Or care about. Who's the man, Sally?

SALLY. Man?

CHRIS. Oh, come off it.

SALLY (*giggling a little*). Well, there is a man. He's wonderful, Chris. He really is.

CHRIS. Where did you meet him?

SALLY. Two days ago. Just after we left here. He saw us in the street. . . . Mother and me, I mean—and our eyes met—his and mine, I mean—and he sort of followed us. To a tea shop, where he sat and gazed at me. And back to the hotel. And at the restaurant. He had the table next to us, and he kept sort of hitching his foot around my chair. And he passed me a note in the fruit-basket. Only Mother got it by mistake. But it was in German. I told her it was from a movie agent. And I went over and talked to him, and he *was!* Then we met later. He's quite marvelous, Chris. He's got a long, black beard. Well, not really long. I've never been kissed by a beard before. I thought it would be awful. But it isn't. It's quite exciting. Only he doesn't speak much German. He's a Yugoslavian. That's why I don't know much about the picture. But I'm sure it will be all right. He'll write in something. And now I've got to run.

CHRIS. Oh, Sally, *must* you? Must you go on like this? Why don't you go home, too? Come back with me. I mean it, Sally. My family'll give me some money if I'm home. Or I'll get a job. I'll see that you're all right.

SALLY. It wouldn't be any good, Chris. I'd run away from you, too. The moment anything attractive came along. It's all right for you. You're a writer. You really are. I'm not even an actress, really. I'd love to see my name in lights, but even if I had a first-night tomorrow, if something exciting turned up, I'd go after it. I can't help it. That's me. I'm sentimental enough to hope that one day I'll meet the perfect man, and marry him and have an enormous family and be happy, but until then—well, that's how I am. You know that really, don't you?

CHRIS. Yes, Sally, I'm afraid I do.

SALLY. Afraid? Oh, Chris, am I too awful—for *me*, I mean?

CHRIS. No, Sally. I'm very fond of you.

SALLY. I do hope you are. Because I am of you. Was it true about eternal friendship that we swore?

CHRIS. Yes, of course it was. Really true. Tell me, do you have an address?

SALLY. No, I don't. But I'll write. I really will. Postcards and everything. And you write to me. Of course, you'll be writing all sorts of things—books and things—that I can read. Will you dedicate one to me?

CHRIS. The very first one.

SALLY. Oh, good. Perhaps that'll be my only claim to fame. Well—good-bye for now, Chris. Neck and leg-break.

CHRIS. Neck and leg-break. (*They go into each other's arms*)

SALLY (*starts to go, then turns to Chris*). I do love you. (*She goes, swiftly*)

CHRIS (*stares after her, for a moment*). I love you too, Sally. And it's so damned stupid that that's not enough to keep two people together. (*He starts to move toward the window. The lights begin to dim*) The camera's taken all its pictures, and now it's going away to develop them. I wonder how Sally will look when I've developed her? I haven't got an end for her yet, but there probably isn't one. She'll just go on and on, as she always has—somewhere. (*He looks out of the window*) There she goes now. Into the photograph. She's just going around the corner. (*He watches as the curtain starts to fall*) Don't forget those postcards, Sally.

**CURTAIN**

# 1952 - 53

William Inge finally made it with *Picnic,* an inferior play to *Come Back, Little Sheba.* The Circle gave it eleven votes to four for *The Crucible* by Arthur Miller, two for *Camino Real* by Tennessee Williams and one for *The Climate of Eden* by Moss Hart, adapted from Edgar Mittelhölzer's novel, *Shadows Move Among Them. Picnic* also won the Pulitzer prize.

An indication that it was scarcely an outstanding season could be seen in the failure of four of the critics to vote for anything. These sporadic abstentions, by the way, still bring an occasional protest at the meetings, usually from John Chapman, who comments plaintively that he thought matters had been arranged so everyone had to vote. George Jean Nathan especially goes right on refraining much of the time.

*The Love of Four Colonels* by Peter Ustinov won the foreign citation with thirteen votes. Eight went to Frederick Knott's *Dial M for Murder,* an excellent thriller in which Maurice Evans was seen in one of his few non-classical efforts.

*Wonderful Town,* the musical version of the long-run comedy success of 1940–41, *My Sister Eileen,* won the musical citation with twenty votes as against one for *Hazel Flagg.*

The awards were voted on April 14, 1953.

It was this critic's opinion that *Picnic* was a script of some merit that might have been more appealing in presentation had it not been directed to the teeth by Joshua Logan. He and Elia Kazan have shown a distressing tendency to try and brand their productions with the hot iron of their techniques. There is an old and sage theatrical truism about "the art that hides art," and the best direction always is that which is not obvious and obtrusive.

*Picnic* ran 477 performances; *The Love of Four Colonels,* 141.

# Picnic

## By WILLIAM INGE

Presented by The Theatre Guild and Joshua Logan at the Music Box Theatre, New York City, February 19, 1953, with the following cast:

| | |
|---|---|
| HELEN POTTS | *Ruth McDevitt* |
| HAL CARTER | *Ralph Meeker* |
| MILLIE OWENS | *Kim Stanley* |
| BOMBER | *Morris Miller* |
| MADGE OWENS | *Janice Rule* |
| FLO OWENS | *Peggy Conklin* |
| ROSEMARY SYDNEY | *Eileen Heckart* |
| ALAN SEYMOUR | *Paul Newman* |
| IRMA KRONKITE | *Reta Shaw* |
| CHRISTINE SCHOENWALDER | *Elizabeth Wilson* |
| HOWARD BEVANS | *Arthur O'Connell* |

## SCENE

The action of the play takes place in a small Kansas town in the yard shared by Flo Owens and Helen Potts.

Act  I—Early morning, Labor Day.

Act  II—Late the same afternoon.

Act III—Scene 1—Very early the following morning. Scene 2—A few hours later.

## ACT ONE

*The action of the play is laid on the porches and in the yards of two small houses that sit close beside each other in a small Kansas town. The house at the right belongs to Mrs. Flora Owens, a widow lady of about forty who lives there with her two young daughters, Madge and Millie. The audience sees only a section of the house, from the doorstep and the front door extending to the back door, a porch lining all of the house that we see.*

*The house at the left is inhabited by Mrs. Helen Potts, another but older widow lady who lives with her aged and invalid mother. Just the back of her house is visible, with steps leading up to the back door. Down farther is a woodshed, attached to the house by the roof. The space between woodshed and house forms a narrow passageway leading to the rest of Mrs. Potts' property. The yard between the houses is used interchangeably by members of both houses for visiting and relaxation.*

*Both houses are humble dwellings built with no other pretension than to provide comfortable shelter for their occupants. The ladies cannot always afford to keep their houses painted, but they work hard to maintain a tidy appearance, keeping the yards clean, watching the flower beds, supplying colorful slip covers for the porch furniture.*

*Behind the houses is a stretch of picket fence with a gateway leading from the sidewalk into the yard between the houses. Beyond the fence, in the distance, is the panorama of a typical small Midwestern town, including a grain elevator, a railway station, a great silo and a church steeple, all blessed from above by a high sky of innocent blue.*

*The curtain rises on an empty, sunlit stage. It is early morning in late summer, Labor Day, and autumn has just begun to edge the green landscape with a rim of brown. Dew is still on the landscape and mist rises from the earth in the distance. Mrs. Potts appears on her back porch, at left. She is a merry, dumpy little woman close to sixty. She comes down the steps and stands before the woodshed, waiting for Hal Carter to follow. Hal comes out carrying a basket of trash on his shoulder,*

*an exceedingly handsome, husky youth dressed in T-shirt, dungarees and cowboy boots. In a past era he would have been called a vagabond, but Hal today is usually referred to as a bum. Mrs. Potts speaks to him.*

———

MRS. POTTS. You just had a big breakfast. Wouldn't you like to rest a while before you go to work?

HAL. *(managing to sound cheerful).* Work's good for my digestion, Mam.

MRS. POTTS. Now, stop being embarrassed because you asked for breakfast.

HAL. I never did it before.

MRS. POTTS. What's the difference? We all have misfortune part of the time.

HAL. Seems to me, Mam, like I have it lots of the time.

*(Then they laugh together. Mrs. Potts leads him off through the passageway. In a moment, Millie Owens bursts out of the kitchen door of the house, right. She is a wiry kid of sixteen, boisterous and assertive, but likable when one begins to understand that she is trying to disguise her basic shyness. Her secret habit is to come outside after breakfast and enjoy her morning cigarette where her mother will not see her. She is just lighting up when Bomber, the newsboy, appears at the back gate and slings a paper noisily against the house. This gives Millie a chance to assail him.)*

MILLIE. Hey, Crazy, wanta knock the house down?

BOMBER. *(a tough kid about Millie's age).* I don't hear you.

MILLIE. If you ever break a window, you'll hear me.

BOMBER. Go back to bed.

MILLIE. Go blow your nose.

BOMBER *(with a look at the upper window of the house which presumably marks Madge's room).* Go back to bed and tell your pretty sister to come out. It's no fun lookin' at you. *(Millie ignores him. Bomber doesn't intend to let her)* I'm talkin' to *you*, Goonface!

MILLIE *(jumping to her feet and tearing into Bomber with flying fists).* You take that back, you ornery bastard. You take that back.

BOMBER *(laughing, easily warding off her blows).* Listen to Goonface! She cusses just like a man.

MILLIE (*goes after him with doubled fists*). I'll kill you, you ornery bastard! I'll *kill* you!

BOMBER (*dodging her fists*). Lookit Mrs. Tar-zan! Lookit Mrs. Tar-zan!

(*Madge comes out of the back door. She is an unusually beautiful girl of eighteen, who seems to take her beauty very much for granted. She wears sandals and a simple wash dress. She has just shampooed her hair and is now scrubbing her head with a towel.*)

MADGE. Who's making so much noise?

BOMBER (*with a shy grin*). Hi, Madge!

MADGE. Hi, Bomber.

BOMBER. I hope I didn't wake you, Madge, or bother you or anything.

MADGE. Nothing bothers me.

BOMBER (*warming up*). Hey, Madge, a bunch of us guys are chippin' in on a hot-rod—radio and everything. I get it every Friday night.

MADGE. I'm not one of those girls that jump in a hot-rod every time you boys turn a corner and honk. If a boy wants a date with me, he can come to the door like a gentleman and ask if I'm in.

MILLIE. Alan Seymour sends her flowers every time they go out.

BOMBER (*to Madge*). I can't send you flowers, Baby—but I can *send* you!

MILLIE. Listen to him braggin'.

BOMBER (*persisting*). Lemme pick you up some night after Seymour brings you home.

MADGE (*a trifle haughty*). That wouldn't be fair to Alan. We go steady.

MILLIE. Don't you know what "steady" means, stupid?

BOMBER. I seen you riding around in his Cadillac like you was a duchess. Why do good-looking girls havé to be so stuck on themselves?

MADGE (*jumps up, furious*). I'm not stuck on myself! You take that back, Bomber Gutzel!

BOMBER (*still persisting*). Lemme pick you up some night! Please! (*Madge walks away to evade him but Bomber is close behind her*) We'll get some cans of beer and go down to the river road and listen to music on the radio.

(*Hal Carter has come on from right and put a rake in the woodshed. He observes the scene between Madge and Bomber.*)

MILLIE (*laughing at Bomber*). Wouldn't that be romantic!

BOMBER (*grabbing Madge's arm*). C'mon, Madge, give a guy a break!

HAL (*to Bomber*). On your way, lover boy!

BOMBER (*turning*). Who're *you*?

HAL. What's that matter? I'm bigger'n you are.

(*Bomber looks at Hal, feels a little inadequate, and starts off.*)

MILLIE (*calling after Bomber*). Go peddle your papers! (*Gives Bomber a raspberry as he disappears with papers.*)

HAL (*to Millie*). Got a smoke, kid? (*Millie gives Hal a cigarette, wondering who he is*) Thanks, kid.

MILLIE. You workin' for Mrs. Potts?

HAL. Doin' a few jobs in the yard.

MILLIE. She give you breakfast?

HAL (*embarrassed about it*). Yah.

MADGE. Millie! Mind your business.

HAL (*turning to Madge, his face lighting*). Hi.

MADGE. Hi.

(*Madge and Hal stand looking at each other, awkward and self-conscious. Flo, the mother, comes out almost immediately, as though she had sensed Hal's presence. Flo carries a sewing basket in one arm and a party dress over the other. She is a rather impatient little woman who has worked hard for ten years or more to serve as both father and mother to her girls. One must feel that underneath a certain hardness in her character there is a deep love and concern for the girls. She regards Hal suspiciously.*)

FLO. Young man, this is *my* house. Is there something you want?

HAL. Just loafin', Mam.

FLO. This is a busy day for us. We have no time to loaf.

(*There is a quick glance between Hal and Flo, as though each sized up the other as a potential threat.*)

HAL. You the mother?

FLO. Yes. You better run along now.

HAL. Like you say, Lady. It's your house. (*With a shrug of the shoulders, he saunters off stage.*)

FLO. Has Helen Potts taken in another tramp?

MADGE. I don't see why he's a tramp just because Mrs. Potts gave him breakfast.

FLO. I'm going to speak to her about the way she takes in every Tom, Dick and Harry!

MADGE. He wasn't doing any harm.

FLO. I bet he'd like to. (*Sits on the porch and begins sewing on party dress. To Madge*) Have you called Alan this morning?

MADGE. I haven't had time.

MILLIE. He's coming by pretty soon to take us swimming.

FLO (*to Madge*). Tell him they're expecting a big crowd at the park this evening, so he'd better use his father's influence at the City Hall to reserve a table. Oh, and tell him to get one down by the river, close to a Dutch oven.

MADGE. He'll think I'm being bossy.

FLO. Alan is the kind of man who doesn't mind if a woman's bossy.

(*A train whistle in the distance. Madge listens.*)

MADGE. Whenever I hear that train coming to town, I always get a little feeling of excitement—in here. (*Hugging her stomach.*)

MILLIE. Whenever I hear it, I tell myself I'm going to get on it some day and go to New York.

FLO. That train just goes as far as Tulsa.

MILLIE. In Tulsa I could catch another train.

MADGE. I always wonder, maybe some wonderful person is getting off here, just by accident, and he'll come into the dime store for something and see me behind the counter, and he'll study me very strangely and then decide I'm just the person they're looking for in Washington for an important job in the Espionage Department. (*She is carried away*) Or maybe he wants me for some great medical experiment that'll save the whole human race.

FLO. Things like that don't happen in dime stores. (*Changing the subject*) Millie, would you take the milk inside?

MILLIE (*as she exits into kitchen with milk.*) Awwww.

FLO (*after a moment*). Did you and Alan have a good time on your date last night?

MADGE. Uh-huh.

FLO. What'd you do?

MADGE. We went over to his house and he played some of his classical records.

FLO (*after a pause*). Then what'd you do?

MADGE. Drove over to Cherryvale and had some barbecue.

FLO (*a hard question to ask*). Madge, does Alan ever—make love?

MADGE. When we drive over to Cherryvale we always park the car by the river and get real romantic.

FLO. Do you let him kiss you? After all, you've been going together all summer.

MADGE. Of course I let him.

FLO. Does he ever want to go beyond kissing?

MADGE (*embarrassed*). Mom!

FLO. I'm your mother, for heaven's sake! These things have to be talked about. Does he?

MADGE. Well—yes.

FLO. Does Alan get mad if you—won't?

MADGE. No.

FLO (*to herself, puzzled*). He doesn't . . .

MADGE. Alan's not like *most* boys. He doesn't wanta do anything he'd be sorry for.

FLO. Do *you* like it when he kisses you?

MADGE. Yes.

FLO. You don't sound very enthusiastic.

MADGE. What do you expect me to do— pass out every time Alan puts his arm around me?

FLO. No, you don't have to pass out. (*Gives Madge the dress she has been sewing on*) Here. Hold this dress up in front of you. (*She continues*) It'd be awfully nice to be married to Alan. You'd live in comfort the rest of your life, with charge accounts at all the stores, automobiles and trips. You'd be invited by all his friends to parties in their homes and at the Country Club.

MADGE (*a confession*). Mom, I don't feel right with those people.

FLO. Why not? You're as good as they are.

MADGE. I know, Mom, but all of Alan's friends talk about college and trips to Europe. I feel left out.

FLO. You'll get over those feelings in time. Alan will be going back to school in a few weeks. You better get busy.

MADGE. Busy what?

FLO. A pretty girl doesn't have long—just a few years. Then she's the equal of kings and she can walk out of a shanty like this and live in a palace with a doting husband who'll spend his life making her happy.

MADGE (*to herself*). I know.

FLO. Because once, *once* she was young and pretty. If she loses her chance then, she might as well throw all her prettiness away. (*Giving Madge the dress*)

MADGE (*holding the dress before her as FLO checks length*). I'm only eighteen.

FLO. And next summer you'll be nineteen, and then twenty, and then twenty-one, and then the years'll start going by so fast you'll lose count of them. First thing you know, you'll be forty, still selling candy at the dime store.

MADGE. You don't have to get morbid.

MILLIE (*comes out with sketch book, sees Madge holding dress before her*). Everyon around here gets to dress up and go places except me.

MADGE. Alan said he'd try to find you a date for the picnic tonight.

MILLIE. I don't want Alan asking any of these crazy boys in town to take me anywhere.

MADGE. Beggars can't be choosers!

MILLIE. You shut up.

FLO. Madge, that was mean. There'll be dancing at the pavilion tonight. Millie should have a date, too.

MADGE. If she wants a date, why doesn't she dress up and act decent?

MILLIE. Cause I'm gonna dress and act the way I want to, and if you don't like it you know what you can do!

MADGE. Always complaining because she doesn't have any friends, but she smells so bad people don't want to be near her!

FLO. Girls, don't fight.

MILLIE (*ignoring Flo*). La-de-da! Madge is the pretty one—but she's so dumb they almost had to burn the schoolhouse down to get *her* out of it! (*She mimics Madge*)

MADGE. That's not so!

MILLIE. Oh, isn't it? You never would have graduated if it hadn't been for Jumpin' Jeeter.

FLO (*trying at least to keep up with the scrap*). Who's Jumpin' Jeeter?

MILLIE. Teaches history. Kids call him Jumpin' Jeeter cause he's so *jumpy* with all the pretty girls in his classes. He was flunking Madge till she went in his room and cried, and said . . . (*Resorting again to mimicry*) "I just don't know what I'll do if I don't pass history!"

MADGE. Mom, she's making that up.

MILLIE. Like fun I am! You couldn't even pass Miss Sydney's course in shorthand and you have to work in the dime store!

MADGE (*the girls know each other's most sensitive spots*). You *are* a goon!

FLO (*giving up*). Oh, girls!

MILLIE (*furious*). Madge, you slut! You take that back or I'll kill you! (*She goes after Madge, who screams and runs on the porch.*)

FLO. Girls! What will the neighbors say! (*Millie gets hold of Madge's hair and yanks. Flo has to intercede*)

MILLIE. No one can call me goon and get by with it!

FLO. You called her worse names!

MILLIE. It doesn't hurt what names I call her! She's pretty, so names don't bother her at all! She's pretty, so nothing else matters. (*She storms inside*)

FLO. Poor Millie!

MADGE (*raging at the injustice*). All I ever hear is "poor Millie," and poor Millie won herself a scholarship for four whole years of college!

FLO. A girl like Millie can need confidence in other ways. (*This quiets Madge. There is a silence*)

MADGE (*subdued*). Mom, do you love Millie more than me?

FLO. Of course not!

MADGE. Sometimes you act like you did.

FLO (*with warmth, trying to effect an understanding*). You were the first born. Your father thought the sun rose and set in you. He used to carry you on his shoulder for all the neighborhood to see. But things were different when Millie came.

MADGE. How?

FLO (*with misgivings*). They were just —different. Your father wasn't home much. The night Millie was born he was with a bunch of his wild friends at the road house.

MADGE. I loved Dad.

FLO (*a little bitterly*). Oh, everyone loved your father.

MADGE. Did you?

FLO (*after a long pause of summing up*). Some women are humiliated to love a man.

MADGE. Why?

FLO (*thinking as she speaks*). Because— a woman is weak to begin with, I suppose, and sometimes—her love for him makes her feel—almost helpless. And maybe she fights him—'cause her love makes her seem so dependent.

(*There is another pause. Madge ruminates.*)

MADGE. Mom, what good is it to be pretty?

FLO. What a question!

MADGE. I mean it.

FLO. Well—pretty things are rare in this life.

MADGE. But what good are they?

FLO. Well—pretty things—like flowers and sunsets and rubies—and pretty girls, too—they're like billboards telling us life is good.

MADGE. But where do *I* come in?

FLO. What do you mean?

MADGE. Maybe I get tired being looked at.

FLO. Madge!

MADGE. Well, maybe I do!

FLO. Don't talk so selfish!

MADGE. I don't care if I *am* selfish. It's no good just being pretty. It's no good!

HAL (*comes running on from passageway*). Mam, is it all right if I start a fire?

FLO (*jumps to see Hal*). What?

HAL. The nice lady, she said it's a hot enough day already and maybe you'd object.

FLO (*matter-of-factly*). I guess we can stand it.

HAL. Thank you, Mam. (*Hal runs off*)

FLO (*looking after him*). He just moves right in whether you want him to or not!

MADGE. I knew you wouldn't like him when I first saw him.

FLO. Do *you?*

MADGE. I don't like him or dislike him. I just wonder what he's like.

(*Rosemary Sydney makes a sudden, somewhat cavalier entrance out of the front door. She is a roomer, probably as old as Flo but would never admit it. Her hair is plastered to her head with wave-set and she wears a flowered kimono.*)

ROSEMARY. Anyone mind if an old-maid schoolteacher joins their company?

FLO. Sit down, Rosemary.

ROSEMARY. Mail come yet?

FLO. No mail today. It's Labor Day.

ROSEMARY. I forgot. I thought I might be gettin' a letter from that man I met at the high-school picnic last spring. (*A bawdy laugh*) Been wantin' to marry me ever since. A nice fellow and a peck of fun, but I don't have time for any of 'em when they start gettin' serious on me.

FLO. You schoolteachers are mighty independent!

(*Millie wanders out of kitchen, reading a book.*)

ROSEMARY. Shoot! I lived this long without a man. I don't see what's to keep me from getting *on* without one.

FLO. What about Howard?

ROSEMARY. Howard's just a friend-boy— not a boy friend. (*Madge and Millie giggle at this. Rosemary sniffs the air*) I smell smoke.

FLO. Helen Potts is having her leaves burned. Smells kind of good, doesn't it?

ROSEMARY (*seeing Hal off stage*). Who's the young man?

FLO. Just another no-good Helen Potts took in.

ROSEMARY (*very concerned*). Mrs. Owens, he's working over there with his shirt off. I don't think that's right in the presence of ladies.

FLO (*as Millie runs to look*). Get away from there, Millie!

MILLIE (*returning to doorstep*). Gee whiz! I go swimming every day and the boys don't have on half as much as he does now.

FLO. Swimming's different!

MILLIE. Madge, can I use your manicure set, just for kicks?

MADGE. If you promise not to get it messy. (*Millie picks up the set and begins to experiment*)

FLO (*looking off at Hal*). Look at him showing off!

ROSEMARY (*turning away with propriety*). Who does he think is interested? (*She continues to massage her face*)

FLO (*to Rosemary*). What's that you're rubbing in?

ROSEMARY. Ponsella Three-Way Tissue Cream. Makes a good base for your make-up.

FLO. There was an article in *The Reader's Digest* about some woman who got skin poisoning from using all those face creams.

ROSEMARY. Harriett Bristol—she's the American History teacher—she got ahold of some of that beauty clay last winter and it darn near took her skin off. All we girls thought she had leprosy! (*She manages one more glance back at Hal*)

MILLIE (*laboring over her manicure*). Made, how do you do your right hand?

MADGE. If you were nicer to people, mabe people would do something nice for *you* some time.

ROSEMARY. You got a beau, Millie?

MILLIE. No!

ROSEMARY. You can't kid me! Girls don't paint their fingernails unless they think some boy is gonna take notice.

FLO. Madge, will you try this dress on now, dear? (*Madge goes inside with the dress*)

MRS. POTTS (*appears on her back porch, carrying a bundle of wet laundry*). Flo!

FLO (*calling back, a noise like an owl*). Hoooo!

MRS. POTTS. Are you going to be using the clothesline this morning?

FLO. I don't think so.

MRS. POTTS' MOTHER (*an aged and quivering voice that still retains its command, issuing from the upper window of the house, left*). Helen! Helen!

MRS. POTTS (*calling back*). I'm hanging out the clothes, Mama. I'll be right back. (*She goes busily off stage through the passageway*)

FLO (*confidentially to Rosemary*). Poor Helen! She told me sometimes she has to get up *three* times a night to take her mother to the bathroom.

ROSEMARY. Why doesn't she put her in an old ladies' home?

FLO. None of 'em will take her. She's too mean.

ROSEMARY. She must be mean—if that story is true.

FLO. It *is* true! Helen and the Potts boy ran off and got married. Helen's mother caught her that very day and had the marriage annulled!

ROSEMARY. (*With a shaking of her head*). She's Mrs. Potts in name only.

FLO. Sometimes I think she keeps the boy's name just to defy the old lady. (*Alan's car is heard approaching. It stops and the car door slams.*)

MILLIE (*putting down her book*). Hi, Alan! (*Jumps up, starts inside*) Oh, boy! I'm gonna get my suit!

FLO (*calling after Millie*). See if Madge is decent. (*Alan comes on downstage, right*) Good morning, Alan!

ALAN. Morning, Mrs. Owens . . . Miss Sydney. (*Rosemary doesn't bother to speak, usually affecting indifference to men*)

MRS. POTTS (*coming back on from the passageway*). Have you girls seen the handsome young man I've got working for me?

ROSEMARY. I think it's a disgrace, his parading around, naked as an Indian.

MRS. POTTS (*protectingly*). I *told* him to take his shirt off.

FLO. Helen Potts, I wish you'd stop taking in all sorts of riffraff!

MRS. POTTS. He isn't riffraff. He's been to several colleges.

FLO. College—and he begs for breakfast!

MRS. POTTS. He's working for his breakfast! Alan, he said he knew you at the university.

ALAN (*with no idea whom she's talking about*). Who?

MILLIE (*coming out the front door*). We going swimming, Alan?

ALAN. You bet.

FLO. Alan, why don't you go up and see Madge? Just call from the bottom of the stairs.

ALAN (*goes inside, calling*). Hey, Delilah!

FLO (*seeing that Millie is about to follow Alan inside*). Millie! (*Millie gets the idea that Madge and Alan are to be left alone. She sulks.*)

ROSEMARY (*to Flo, confidentially*). Do you think Alan's going to marry Madge?

*Flo* (*she's usually a very truthful woman*). I hadn't thought much about it.

MRS. POTTS (*after a moment, drying her neck with handkerchief*). It's so hot and still this time of year. When it gets this way I'd welcome a good strong wind.

FLO. I'd rather wipe my brow than get blown away.

MRS. POTTS (*looking off at Hal, full of smiling admiration*). Look at him lift that big old washtub like it was so much tissue paper!

MRS. POTTS' MOTHER (*off stage, again*). Helen! Helen!

MRS. POTTS (*patient but firm*). I'm visiting Flo, Mama. You're all right. You don't need me.

FLO. What did you feed him?

MRS. POTTS. Biscuits.

FLO. You went to all that trouble?

MRS. POTTS. He was *so* hungry. I gave him ham and eggs and all the hot coffee he could drink. Then he saw a piece of cherry pie in the icebox and he wanted that, too!

ROSEMARY (*laughs bawdily*). Sounds to me like Mrs. Potts had herself a new boy friend!

MRS. POTTS (*rising, feeling injured*). I don't think that's very funny.

FLO. Helen, come on. Sit down.

ROSEMARY. Shoot, Mrs. Potts, I'm just a tease.

FLO. Sit down, Helen.

MRS. POTTS (*still touchy*). I *could* sit on my own porch, but I hate for the neighbors to see me there all alone.

(*Madge and Alan come out together, Madge in her new dress. They march out hand in hand in a mock ceremony as though they were marching down the aisle.*)

ROSEMARY (*consolingly*). Mrs. Potts, if I said anything to offend you . . .

FLO (*Signals Rosemary to be quiet, points to Madge and Alan*). Bride and groom! Look, everybody! Bride and groom! (*To Madge*) How does it feel Madge? (*Laughs at her unconscious joke*) I mean the dress.

MADGE (*crossing to her mother*). I love it, except it's a little tight in places.

MRS. POTTS (*all eyes of admiration*). Isn't Madge the pretty one!

ALAN (*turning to Millie*). What are you reading, Millie?

MILLIE. *The Ballad of the Sad Café* by Carson McCullers. It's wonderful!

ROSEMARY (*shocked*). Good Lord, Mrs. Owens, you let your daughter read filthy books like that?

FLO. Filthy?

ROSEMARY. Everyone in it is some sort of degenerate!

MILLIE. That's not so!

ROSEMARY. The D.A.R.'s had it banned from the public library.

MRS. POTTS (*eliminating herself from the argument*). I don't read much.

FLO. Millie, give me that book!

MILLIE (*tenaciously*). No!

ALAN. Mrs. Owens, I don't wanta interfere, but that book is on the reading list at college. For the course in the modern novel.

FLO (*full of confusion*). Oh, dear! What's a person to believe?

(*Millie takes the book from Flo. Alan's word about such matters is apparently final.*)

ROSEMARY. Well, those college professors don't have any morals!

(*Millie and Alan shake hands.*)

FLO. Where Millie comes by her tastes, I'll never know.

MADGE (*as Flo inspects her dress*). Some of the pictures she has over her bed *scare* me.

MILLIE. Those pictures are by Picasso, and he's a great artist.

MADGE. A woman with seven eyes. Very pretty.

MILLIE (*delivering her ultimatum*). Pictures don't have to be *pretty*!

(*A sudden explosion from Mrs. Potts' back-yard. The women are startled.*)

FLO. Helen!

MRS. POTTS (*jumping up, alarmed*). I'll go see what it is.

FLO. Stay here. He must have had a gun!

VOICE OFF STAGE. Helen! Helen!

FLO (*grabbing Mrs. Potts' arm*). Don't go over there, Helen! Your mother's old. She has to go soon anyway!

MRS. POTTS (*running off stage*). Pshaw! I'm not afraid.

ALAN (*looking off at Hal*). Who did that guy say he was? (*No one hears Alan*).

MRS. POTTS (*coming back and facing Flo*). I was a bad girl.

FLO. What *is* it, Helen?

MRS. POTTS. I threw the *new* bottle of cleaning fluid into the trash.

FLO. You're the limit! Come on, Madge, let's finish that dress.

(*Flo and Madge go into the house. Rosemary looks at her watch and then goes into the house also.*)

MRS. POTTS. Come help me, Millie. The young man ran into the clothesline.

(*She and Millie hurry off stage. Alan stands alone, trying to identify Hal who comes on from Mrs. Potts'. Hal is bare-chested now, wearing his T-shirt wrapped about his neck. Alan finally recognizes him and is overjoyed at seeing him.*)

ALAN. Where did *you* come from?

HAL (*loud and hearty*). Kid!

ALAN. Hal Carter!

HAL. I was comin' over to see you a little later.

ALAN (*recalling some intimate roughhouse greeting from their college days*). How's the old outboard motor?

HAL (*with the eagerness of starting a game*). Want a ride?

ALAN (*springing to Hal, clasping his legs around Hal's waist, hanging by one hand wrapped about Hal's neck, as though riding some sort of imagined machine*). Gassed up? (*With his fingers, he twists Hal's nose as if it were a starter. Hal makes the sputtering noise of an outboard motor and swings Alan about the stage, Alan holding on like a bronco-buster. They laugh uproariously together*) Ahoy, brothers! Who's winkin', blinkin', and stinkin'? (*Alan drops to the ground, both of them still laughing uproariously with the recall of carefree, college days*)

HAL. That used to wake the whole damn fraternity.

ALAN. The last time I saw you, you were on your way to Hollywood to become a movie hero.

HAL (*with a shrug of his shoulders*). Oh, that!

ALAN. What do you mean, "Oh that"? Isn't that what I loaned you the hundred bucks for?

HAL. Sure, Seymour.

ALAN. Well, what happened?

HAL (*he'd rather the subject had not been brought up*). Things just didn't work out.

ALAN. I tried to warn you, Hal. Every year some talent scout promised screen tests to all the athletes.

HAL. Oh, I got the test okay! I was about to have a big career. They were gonna call me Brush Carter. How d'ya like that?

ALAN. Yeah?

HAL. Yah! They took a lotta pictures of me with my shirt off. Real rugged. Then they dressed me up like the Foreign Legion. Then they put me in a pair of tights—and they gave me a big hat with a plume, and had me makin' with the sword play. (*Pantomimes a duel*) Touché, mug! (*Returning the sword to its scabbard*) It was real crazy!

ALAN (*a little skeptical*). Did they give you any lines to read?

HAL. Yah, that part went okay. It was my teeth.

ALAN. Your teeth?

HAL. Yah! Out there, you gotta have a certain kind of teeth or they can't use you. Don't ask me why. This babe said they'd have to pull all my teeth and give me new ones, so naturally . . .

ALAN. Wait a minute. What babe?

HAL. The babe that got me the test. She wasn't a babe exactly. She was kinda beat up—but not bad. (*He sees Alan's critical eye*) Jesus, Seymour, a guy's gotta get along somehow.

ALAN. Uh-huh. What are you doing here?

HAL (*a little hurt*). Aren't you glad to see me?

ALAN. Sure, but fill me in.

HAL. Well—after I left Hollywood I took a job on a ranch in Nevada. You'da been proud of me, Seymour. In bed every night at ten, up every morning at six. No liquor —no babes. I saved up two hundred bucks!

ALAN (*holding out a hand*). Oh! I'll take half.

HAL. Gee, Seymour, I wish I had it, but I got rolled.

ALAN. Rolled? *You?*

HAL (*he looks to see that no one can overhear*). Yeah, I was gonna hitchhike to Texas to get in a big oil deal. I got as far as Phoenix when two babes pull up in this big yellow convertible. And one of these dames slams on the brakes and hollers, "Get in, stud!" So I got in. Seymour, it was crazy. They had a shakerful of martinis right there in the car!

MRS. POTTS (*appears on her porch, followed by Millie. Mrs. Potts carries a cake*). Oh, talking over old times? Millie helped me ice the cake.

HAL. Any more work, Mam?

MRS. POTTS. No. I feel I've been more than paid for the breakfast.

HAL. 'Spose there's any place I could wash up

MILLIE. We got a shower in the basement. Come on, I'll show you.

ALAN (*holding Hal*). He'll be there in a minute. (*Mrs. Potts and Millie exit into the Owens house*) Okay, so they had a shakerful of martinis!

HAL. And one of these babes was smokin' the weed!

ALAN (*with vicarious excitement*). Nothing like that ever happens to me! Go on!

HAL. Seymour, you wouldn't believe it, the things those two babes started doin' to me.

ALAN. Were they good-looking?

HAL. What do you care?

ALAN. Makes the story more interesting. Tell me what happened.

HAL. Well, you know *me*, Seymour. I'm an agreeable guy.

ALAN. Sure.

HAL. So when they parked in front of this tourist cabin, I said, "Okay, girls, if I gotta pay for the ride, this is the easiest way I know." (*He shrugs*) But, gee, they musta thought I was Superman.

ALAN. You mean—*both* of them?

HAL. Sure.

ALAN. Golly!

HAL. Then I said, "Okay, girls, the party's over—let's get goin.'" Then this dame on the weed, she sticks a gun in my back. She says, "This party's goin' on till *we* say it's over, Buck!" You'da thought she was Humphrey Bogart!

ALAN. Then what happened?

HAL. Finally I passed out! And when I woke up, the dames was gone and so was my two hundred bucks! I went to the police and they wouldn't believe me—they said my whole story was wishful thinking! How d'ya like *that*!

ALAN (*thinking it over*). Mmmm.

HAL. Women are gettin' desperate, Seymour.

ALAN. *Are* they?

HAL. Well, that did it. Jesus, Seymour, what's a poor bastard like me ever gonna do?

ALAN. You don't sound like you had such a hard time.

HAL. I got thinking of you, Seymour, at school—how you always had things under control.

ALAN. Me?

HAL. Yah. Never cut classes—understood the lectures—took notes! (*Alan laughs*) What's so funny?

ALAN. The hero of the campus, and he envied me!

HAL. Yah! Big hero, between the goal posts. You're the only guy in the whole fraternity ever treated me like a human being.

ALAN (*with feeling for Hal*). I know.

HAL. Those other snob bastards always watchin' to see which fork I used.

ALAN. You've got an inferiority complex. You imagined those things.

HAL. In a pig's eye!

ALAN (*delicately*). What do you hear about your father?

HAL (*grave*). It finally happened . . . before I left for Hollywood.

ALAN. What?

HAL (*with a solemn hurt*). He went on his last bender. The police scraped him up off the sidewalk. He died in jail.

ALAN (*moved*). Gee, I'm sorry to hear that, Hal.

HAL. The old lady wouldn't even come across with the dough for the funeral. They had to bury him in Pauper's Row.

ALAN. What happened to the filling station?

HAL. He left it to me in his will, but the old lady was gonna have him declared insane so she could take over. I let her have it. Who cares?

ALAN (*rather depressed by Hal's story*). Gee, Hal, I just can't believe people really do things like that.

HAL. Don't let *my* stories cloud up your rosy glasses.

ALAN. Why didn't you come to see me, when you got to town?

HAL. I didn't want to walk into your palatial mansion lookin' like a bum. I wanted to get some breakfast in my belly and pick up a little change.

ALAN. That wouldn't have made any difference.

HAL. I was hoping maybe you and your old man, between you, might fix me up with a job.

ALAN. What kind of a job, Hal?

HAL. What kinda jobs you got?

ALAN. What kind of job did you have in mind?

HAL (*this is his favorite fantasy*). Oh, something in a nice office where I can wear a tie and have a sweet little secretary and talk over the telephone about enterprises and things. (*As Alan walks away skeptically*) I've always had the feeling, if I just had the chance, I could set the world on fire.

ALAN. Lots of guys have that feeling, Hal.

HAL (*with some desperation*). I gotta get some place in this world, Seymour, I *got* to.

ALAN (*with a hand on Hal's shoulder*). Take it easy.

HAL. This is a free country, and I got just as much rights as the next fellow. Why can't I get along?

ALAN. Don't worry, Hal. I'll help you out as much as I can. (*Mrs. Potts comes out the Owens' back door*) Sinclair is hiring new men, aren't they, Mrs. Potts?

MRS. POTTS. Yes, Alan. Carey Hamilton needs a hundred new men for the pipeline.

HAL (*Had dared to hope for more*). Pipeline?

ALAN. If you wanta be president of the company, Hal, I guess you'll just have to work hard and be patient.

HAL (*clenching his fists together, so eager is he for patience*). Yah. That's something I gotta learn. Patience! (*He hurries inside the Owens' back door now.*)

MRS. POTTS. I feel sorry for young men today.

ROSEMARY (*coming out the front door, very proud of the new outfit she is wearing, a fall suit and an elaborate hat*). Is this a private party I'm crashin'?

MRS. POTTS (*with some awe of Rosemary's finery*). My, you're dressed up!

ROSEMARY. 'S my new fall outfit. Got it in Kansas City. Paid twenty-two-fifty for the hat.

MRS. POTTS. You schoolteachers do have nice things.

ROSEMARY. And don't have to ask anybody when we wanta get 'em, either.

FLO (*coming out back door with Madge*). Be here for lunch today, Rosemary?

ROSEMARY. No. There's a welcome-home party down at the hotel. Lunch and bridge for the new girls on the faculty.

MADGE. Mom, can't I go swimming, too?

FLO. Who'll fix lunch? I've got a million things to do.

MADGE. It wouldn't kill Millie if she ever did any cooking.

FLO. No, but it might kill the rest of us. (*Now we hear the voices of Irma Kronkite and Christine Schoenwalder, who are coming by for Rosemary. They think it playful to call from a distance.*)

IRMA. Rosemary! Let's get going, girl! (*As they come into sight, Irma turns to Christine*) You'll love Rosemary Sydney. She's a peck of fun! Says the craziest things.

ROSEMARY (*with playful suspiciousness*). What're you saying about me, Irma Kronkite?

(*They run to hug each other like eager sisters who had not met in a decade.*)

IRMA. Rosemary Sydney!

ROSEMARY. Irma Kronkite! How was your vacation?

IRMA. I worked like a slave. But I had fun, too. I don't care if I *never* get that Masters. I'm not going to be a slave *all* my life.

CHRISTINE (*shyly*). She's been telling me about all the wicked times she had in New York—and *not* at Teachers College, if I may add.

IRMA (*to Rosemary*). Kid, this is Christine Schoenwalder, taking Mabel Fremont's place in Feminine Hygiene. (*Rosemary and Christine shake hands*) Been a hot summer, Mrs. Owens?

FLO. The worst I can remember.

MRS. POTTS (*As Rosemary brings Christine up on porch*). Delighted to know you, Christine. Welcome back, Irma.

IRMA. Are you working now, Madge?

MADGE. Yes.

FLO (*taking over for Madge*). Yes, Madge has been working downtown this summer— just to keep busy. (*Now Hal and Millie burst out the kitchen door, engaged in a noisy and furious mock fist-fight. Hal is still bare-chested, his T-shirt still around his neck, and the sight of him is something of a shock to the ladies*) Why, when did he . . .

ALAN (*seizing Hal for an introduction*). Mrs. Owens, this is my friend, Hal Carter. Hal is a fraternity brother.

MRS. POTTS (*nudging Flo*). What did I tell you, Flo?

FLO (*stunned*). Fraternity brother! Really?

(*Making the best of it*) Any friend of Alan's is a friend of ours. (*She offers Hal her hand*)

HAL. Glad to make your acquaintance, Mam.

ALAN (*embarrassed for him*). Hal, don't you have a shirt?

HAL. It's all sweaty, Seymour. (*Alan nudges him. Hal realizes he has said the wrong thing and reluctantly puts on the T-shirt*)

ROSEMARY (*collecting Irma and Christine*). Girls, we better get a hustle on.

CHRISTINE (*to Irma*). Tell them about what happened in New York, kid.

IRMA (*the center of attention*). I went to the Stork Club!

ROSEMARY. How did *you* get to the Stork Club?

IRMA. See, there was this fellow in my Educational Statistics class . . .

ROSEMARY (*continuing the joke*). I *knew* there was a *man* in it.

IRMA. Now, girl! It was nothing serious. He was just a good sport, that's all. We made a bet that the one who made the lowest grade on the *final* had to take the other to the Stork Club—and *I* lost! (*The teachers go off noisily laughing, as Flo and Mrs. Potts watch them*)

ALAN (*calling to Hal, at back of stage playing with Millie*). Wanta go swimming, Hal? I've got extra trunks in the car.

HAL. Why not?

MRS. POTTS (*in a private voice*). Flo, let's ask the young man on the picnic. He'd be a date for Millie.

FLO. That's right, but . . .

MRS. POTTS (*taking it upon herself*). Young man, Flo and I are having a picnic for the young people. You come, too, and be an escort for Millie.

HAL. Picnic?

MRS. POTTS. Yes.

HAL. I don't think it's right, me bargin' in this way.

MRS. POTTS. Nonsense. A picnic's no fun without lots and lots of young people.

ALAN (*bringing Hal down center*). Hal, I want you to meet Madge.

MADGE. Oh, we've met already. That is, we *saw* each other.

HAL. Yah, we saw each other.

ALAN (*to Madge*). Hal sees every pretty girl.

MADGE (*pretending to protest*). Alan.

ALAN. Well, you're the prettiest girl in town, aren't you? (*To Hal*) The Chamber of Commerce voted her Queen of Neewollah last year.

HAL. I don't dig.

MILLIE. She was Queen of Neewollah. Neewollah is Halloween spelled backwards.

MRS. POTTS (*joining in*). Every year they have a big coronation ceremony in Memorial Hall, with all kinds of artistic singing and dancing.

MILLIE. Madge had to sit through the whole ceremony till they put a crown on her head.

HAL (*impressed*). Yah?

MADGE. I got awfully tired.

MILLIE. The Kansas City *Star* ran color pictures in their Sunday magazine.

MADGE. Everyone expected me to get real conceited, but I didn't.

HAL. You didn't?

MILLIE. It'd be pretty hard to get conceited about *those* pictures.

MADGE (*humorously*). The color got blurred and my mouth was printed right in the middle of my forehead.

HAL (*sympathetic*). Gee, that's too bad.

MADGE (*philosophically*). Things like that are bound to happen.

MILLIE (*to Hal*). I'll race you to the car.

HAL (*starting off with Millie*). Isn't your sister goin' with us?

MILLIE. Madge has to cook lunch.

HAL. Do you mean *she cooks?*

MILLIE. Sure! Madge cooks and sews and does all those things that women do. (*They race off, Millie getting a head start through the gate and Hal scaling the fence to get ahead of her*)

FLO (*in a concerned voice*). Alan!

ALAN. Yes?

FLO. How did a boy like him get into college?

ALAN. On a football scholarship. He made a spectacular record in a little high school down in Arkansas.

FLO. But a fraternity! Don't those boys have a little more . . . breeding?

ALAN. I guess they're *supposed* to, but fraternities like to pledge big athletes—for the publicity. And Hal could have been All-American . . .

MRS. POTTS (*delighted*). All-American!

ALAN. . . . if he'd only studied.

FLO. But how did the other boys feel about him?

ALAN (*reluctantly*). They didn't like him, Mrs. Owens. They were pretty rough on him. Every time he came into a room, the other fellows seemed to *bristle*. I didn't like him either, at first. Then we shared a room and I got to know him better. Hal's really a nice guy. About the best friend I ever had.

FLO (*more to the point*). Is he wild?

ALAN. Oh—not really. He just . . .

FLO. Does he drink?

ALAN. A little. (*Trying to minimize*) Mrs. Owens, Hal pays attention to me. I'll see he behaves.

FLO. I wouldn't want anything to happen to Millie.

MADGE. Millie can take care of herself. You pamper her.

FLO. Maybe I do. Come on, Helen. (*As she and Mrs. Potts go in through the back door*) Oh, dear, why can't things be simple?

ALAN (*after Flo and Mrs. Potts leave*). Madge, I'm sorry I have to go back to school this fall. It's Dad's idea.

MADGE. I thought it was.

ALAN. Really, Madge, Dad likes you very much. I'm sure he does. (*But Alan himself doesn't sound convinced*)

MADGE. Well—he's always very polite.

ALAN. I'll miss you, Madge.

MADGE. There'll be lots of pretty girls at college.

ALAN. Honestly, Madge, my entire four years I never found a girl I liked.

MADGE. I don't believe that.

ALAN. It's true. They're all so affected, if you wanted a date with them you had to call them a month in advance.

MADGE. Really?

ALAN. Madge, it's hard to say, but I honestly never believed that a girl like you could care for me.

MADGE (*touched*). Alan . . .

ALAN. I—I hope you do care for me, Madge. (*He kisses her*)

HAL (*comes back on stage somewhat apologetically. He is worried about something and tries to get Alan's attention*) Hey, Seymour . . .

ALAN (*annoyed*). What's the matter,

Hal? Can't you stand to see anyone else kiss a pretty girl?

HAL. What the hell, Seymour!

ALAN (*an excuse to be angry*). Hal, will you watch your language!

MADGE. Alan! It's all right.

HAL. I'm sorry. (*Beckons Alan to him*)

ALAN (*crossing to him*). What's the trouble?

(*Madge walks away, sensing that Hal wants to talk privately.*)

HAL. Look, Seymour, I—I never been on a picnic.

ALAN. What're you talking about? Everybody's been on a picnic.

HAL. Not me. When I was a kid, I was too busy shooting craps or stealing milk bottles.

ALAN. Well, there's a first time for everything.

HAL. I wasn't brought up proper like *you*. I won't know how to act around all these *women*.

ALAN. Women aren't anything new in *your* life.

HAL. But these are—*nice* women. What if I say the wrong word or maybe my stomach growls? I feel *funny*.

ALAN. You're a psycho!

HAL. OK, but if I do anything wrong, you gotta try to overlook it. (*He runs off stage. Alan laughs. Then Alan returns to Madge*)

ALAN. We'll be by about five, Madge.

MADGE. OK.

ALAN (*beside her, tenderly*). Madge, after we have supper tonight maybe you and I can get away from the others and take a boat out on the river.

MADGE. All right, Alan.

ALAN. I want to see if you look *real* in the moonlight.

MADGE. Alan! Don't say that!

ALAN. Why? I don't care if you're real or not. You're the prettiest girl I ever saw.

MADGE. Just the same, I'm real. (*As Alan starts to kiss her, the noise of an automobile horn is heard*)

HAL (*hollering lustily from off stage*). Hey, Seymour—get the lead outa your pants! (*Alan goes off, irritated. Madge watches them as they drive away. She waves to them.*)

FLO (*inside*). Madge! Come on inside now.

MADGE. All right, Mom. (*As she starts in, there is a train whistle in the distance. Madge hears it and stands listening*)

## ACT TWO

*It is late afternoon, the same day. The sun is beginning to set and fills the atmosphere with radiant orange. When the curtain goes up, Millie is on the porch alone. She has permitted herself to "dress up" and wears a becoming, feminine dress in which she cannot help feeling a little strange. She is quite attractive. Piano music can be heard off stage, somewhere past Mrs. Potts' house, and Millie stands listening to it for a moment. Then she begins to sway to the music and in a moment is dancing a strange, impromptu dance over the porch and yard. The music stops suddenly and Millie's mood is broken. She rushes upstage and calls off, left.*

———

MILLIE. Don't quit now Ernie! (*She cannot hear Ernie's reply*) Huh? (*Madge enters from kitchen. Millie turns to Madge*) Ernie's waiting for the rest of the band to practice. They're going to play out at the park tonight.

MADGE (*crossing to center and sitting on chair*). I don't know why you couldn't have helped us in the kitchen.

MILLIE (*lightly, giving her version of the sophisticated belle*). I had to dress for the ball.

MADGE. I had to make the potato salad and stuff the eggs and make three dozen bread-and-butter sandwiches.

MILLIE (*in a very affected accent*). I had to *bathe*—and dust my limbs with powder—and slip into my frock . . .

MADGE. Did you clean out the bathtub?

MILLIE. Yes, I cleaned out the bathtub. (*She becomes very selfconscious*) Madge, how do I look? Now tell me the truth.

MADGE. You look very pretty.

MILLIE. I feel sorta funny.

MADGE. You can have the dress if you want it.

MILLIE. Thanks. (*A pause*) Madge, how do you talk to boys?

MADGE. Why, you just talk, silly.

MILLIE. How d'ya think of things to say?

MADGE. I don't know. You just say whatever comes into your head.

MILLIE. Supposing nothing ever comes into my head?

MADGE. You talked with him all right this morning.

MILLIE. But now I've got a *date* with him, and it's *different*!

MADGE. You're crazy.

MILLIE. I think he's a big show-off. You should have seen him this morning on the high diving board. He did real graceful swan dives, and a two and a half gainer, and a back flip—and kids stood around clapping. He just ate it up.

MADGE (*her mind elsewhere*). I think I'll paint my toenails tonight and wear sandals.

MILLIE. And he was braggin' all afternoon how he used to be a deep-sea diver off Catalina Island.

MADGE. Honest?

MILLIE. And he says he used to make hundreds of dollars doin' parachute jumps out of a balloon. Do you believe it?

MADGE. I don't see why not.

MILLIE. You never hear Alan bragging that way.

MADGE. Alan never jumped out of a balloon.

MILLIE. Madge, I think he's girl crazy.

MADGE. You think every boy you see is something horrible.

MILLIE. Alan took us into the Hi Ho for Cokes and there was a gang of girls in the back booth — Juanita Badger and her gang. (*Madge groans at hearing this name*) When they saw him, they started giggling and tee-heeing and saying all sorts of crazy things. Then Juanita Badger comes up to me and whispers, "He's the cutest thing I ever saw." Is he, Madge?

MADGE (*not willing to go overboard*). I certainly wouldn't say he was "the cutest thing I ever *saw*."

MILLIE. Juanita Badger's an old floozy. She sits in the back row at the movie so the guys that come in will see her and sit with her. One time she and Rubberneck Krauss were asked by the management to leave—and they weren't just kissin', either!

MADGE (*proudly*). I never even speak to Juanita Badger.

MILLIE. Madge, do you think he'll like me?

MADGE. Why ask me all these questions? You're supposed to be the smart one.

MILLIE. I don't really care. I just wonder.

FLO (*coming out of kitchen*). Now I tell myself I've got two beautiful daughters.

MILLIE (*embarrassed*). Be quiet, Mom!

FLO. Doesn't Millie look pretty, Madge?

MADGE. When she isn't picking her nose.

FLO. Madge! (*To Millie*) She doesn't want anyone to be pretty but her.

MILLIE. You're just saying I'm pretty because you're my mom. People we love are always pretty, but people who're pretty to begin with, everybody loves *them*.

FLO. Run over and show Helen Potts how nice you look.

MILLIE (*in a wild parody of herself*). Here comes Millie Owens, the great beauty of all time! Be prepared to swoon when you see her! (*She climbs up over the side of Mrs. Potts' porch and disappears.*)

FLO (*sits on chair on porch*). Whatever possessed me to let Helen Potts ask that young hoodlum to take Millie on the picnic?

MADGE. Hal?

FLO. Yes, Hal, or whatever his name is. He left every towel in the bathroom black as dirt. He left the seat up, too.

MADGE. It's not going to hurt anyone just to be nice to him.

FLO. If there's any drinking tonight, you put a stop to it.

MADGE. I'm not going to be a wet blanket.

FLO. If the boys feel they have to have a few drinks, there's nothing you can do about it, but you can keep Millie from taking any.

MADGE. She wouldn't pay any attention to me.

FLO (*changing the subject*). You better be getting dressed. And don't spend the whole evening admiring yourself in the mirror.

MADGE. Mom, don't make fun of me.

FLO. You shouldn't object to being kidded if it's well meant.

MADGE. It seems like—when I'm looking in the mirror that's the only way I can prove to myself I'm alive.

FLO. Madge! You puzzle me.

(*The three schoolteachers come on, downstage right, making a rather tired return from their festivity. After their high-spirited exit in Act One, their present mood seems glum, as though they had expected from the homecoming some fulfillment that had not been realized.*)

IRMA. We've brought home your wayward girl, Mrs. Owens!

FLO (*turning from Madge*). Hello, girls! Have a nice party?

IRMA. It wasn't a real party. Each girl paid for her own lunch. Then we played bridge all afternoon. (*Confidentially to Rosemary*) I get tired playing bridge.

FLO. Food's good at the hotel, isn't it?

IRMA. Not very. But they serve it to you nice, with honest-to-goodness napkins. Lord, I hate paper napkins!

CHRISTINE. I had a French-fried pork chop and it was mostly fat. What'd you girls have?

ROSEMARY. I had the stuffed peppers.

IRMA. I had the Southern-fried chicken.

CHRISTINE. Linda Sue Breckenridge had pot roast of veal and there was only one little hunk of meat in it. All we girls at her table made her call the waiter and complain.

ROSEMARY. Well, I should hope so!

IRMA. Good for you! (*There is a pause*) I thought by this time someone might have noticed my new dress.

ROSEMARY. I was going to say something, kid, and then I . . . uh . . .

IRMA. Remember that satin-back crepe I had last year?

ROSEMARY. Don't tell me!

IRMA. Mama remodeled it for me while I was at Columbia. I feel like I had a brand-new outfit. (*Smarting*) But nobody said anything all afternoon!

CHRISTINE. It's—chic.

IRMA (*This soothes Irma a bit and she beams. But now there is an awkward pause wherein no one can think of any more to say.*) Well—we better run along, Christine. Rosemary has a date. (*To Rosemary*) We'll come by for you in the morning. Don't be late. (*She goes upstage and waits at the gate for Christine.*)

CHRISTINE (*crossing to Rosemary*). Girl, I want to tell you, in one afternoon I feel I've known you my whole life.

ROSEMARY (*with assurance of devotion*). I look upon you as an old friend already.

CHRISTINE (*overjoyed*). Aw . . .

ROSEMARY (*as Christine and Irma go off*). Good-bye girls!

FLO (*to Rosemary*). What time's Howard coming by?

ROSEMARY. Any minute now.

MADGE. Mom, is there any hot water?

FLO. You'll have to see.

MADGE (*crosses to door, then turns to Rosemary*). Miss Sydney, would you mind terribly if I used some of your Shalimar?

ROSEMARY. Help yourself!

MADGE. Thanks. (*She goes inside*)

ROSEMARY. Madge thinks too much about the boys, Mrs. Owens.

FLO (*disbelieving*). Madge?

(*The conversation is stopped by the excited entrance of Mrs. Potts from her house. She is followed by Millie who carries another cake.*)

MRS. POTTS. It's a *miracle*, that's what it is! I never knew Millie could look so pretty. It's just like a movie I saw once with Betty Grable—or was it Lana Turner? Anyway, she played the part of a secretary to some very important business man. She wore glasses and did her hair real plain and men didn't pay any attention to her at all. Then one day she took off her glasses and her hair real plain and men wanted to marry her right away! Now all the boys are going to fall in love with Millie!

ROSEMARY. Millie have a date tonight?

FLO. Yes, I'm sorry to say.

MRS. POTTS. Why, Flo!

ROSEMARY. Who is he, Millie? Tell your Aunt Rosemary.

MILLIE. Hal.

ROSEMARY. Who?

FLO. The young man over at Helen's turned out to be a friend of Alan's.

ROSEMARY. Oh, *him!*

(*Millie exits into kitchen.*)

FLO. Helen, have you gone to the trouble of baking another cake?

MRS. POTTS. An old lady like me, if she wants any attention from the young men on a picnic, all she can do is bake a cake!

FLO (*rather reproving*). Helen Potts!

MRS. POTTS. I feel sort of excited, Flo. I think we plan picnics just to give ourselves an excuse—to let something thrilling happen in our lives.

FLO. Such as what?

MRS. POTTS. I don't know.

MADGE (*bursting out the door*). Mom, Millie makes me furious! Every time she takes a bath, she fills the whole tub. There isn't any hot water at all.

FLO. You should have thought of it earlier.

ROSEMARY (*hears Howard's car drive up and stop*). It's him! It's him!

MRS. POTTS. Who? Oh, it's Howard. Hello, Howard!

ROSEMARY (*sitting down again*). If he's been drinking, I'm not going out with him.

HOWARD (*as he comes on through gate*). Howdy, ladies.

(*Howard is a small, thin man, rapidly approaching middle age. A small-town businessman, he wears a permanent smile of greeting which, most of the time, is pretty sincere.*)

FLO. Hello, Howard.

HOWARD. You sure look nice, Rosemary.

ROSEMARY (*her tone of voice must tell a man she is independent of him*). Seems to me you might have left your coat on.

HOWARD. Still too darn hot, even if it is September. Good evening, Madge.

MADGE. Hi, Howard.

FLO. How are things over in Cherryvale, Howard?

HOWARD. Good business. Back to school and everybody buying.

FLO. When business is good, it's good for everyone.

MILLIE (*comes out of kitchen, stands shyly behind Howard*). Hi, Howard!

HOWARD (*turning around, making a discovery*). Hey, Millie's a good-lookin' kid. I never realized it before.

MILLIE (*crossing to Flo, apprehensive*). Mom, what time did the fellows say they'd be here?

FLO. At five-thirty. You've asked me a dozen times. (*There is a sound of approaching automobiles, and Flo looks off stage, right*) Alan's brought *both* cars!

(*Millie runs into the house.*)

MRS. POTTS (*to Flo*). Some day *you'll* be riding around in that big Cadillac, Ladybug.

ALAN (*coming on from right*). Everyone ready?

FLO. Come sit down, Alan.

ROSEMARY (*like a champion hostess*). The more the merrier!

ALAN. I brought both cars. I thought we'd let Hal and Millie bring the baskets out in the Ford. Hal's parking it now. (*To Madge, who is sitting up on Mrs. Potts' porch railing*) Hello, Beautiful!

MADGE. Hello, Alan!

ALAN (*calling off stage*). Come on, Hal.

FLO. Is he a careful driver, Alan?

(*This question does not get answered. Hal comes running on, tugging uncomfortably at the shoulders of his jacket and hollering in a voice that once filled the locker rooms.*)

HAL. Hey, Seymour! Hey, I'm a big man, Seymour. I'm a lot huskier than you are. I can't wear your jacket.

ALAN. Then take it off.

MRS. POTTS. Yes. I like to see a man comfortable.

HAL (*with a broad smile of total confidence*). I never could wear another fellow's clothes. See, I'm pretty big through the shoulders. (*He demonstrates the fact*) I should have all my clothes tailor-made. (*He now swings his arms in appreciation of their new freedom. Mrs. Potts is admiring, the other women speculative*)

ALAN (*wanting to get over the formalities*). Hey—uh—Hercules, you've met Mrs. Owens . . .

HAL. Sure! (*Flo nods at him*)

ALAN. . . . and I believe you met Mrs. Potts this morning.

HAL (*throwing his arms around her*). Oh, she's my best girl!

MRS POTTS (*giggling like a girl*). I baked a Lady Baltimore cake!

HAL (*expansively as though making an announcement of public interest*). This little lady, she took pity on me when I was practically starving. I ran into some hard luck when I was travelin'. Some characters robbed me of every cent I had.

ALAN (*interrupting*). And—er—this is Rosemary Sydney, Hal. Miss Sydney teaches shorthand and typing in the local high school.

ROSEMARY (*offering her hand*). Yes, I'm an old-maid schoolteacher.

HAL (*with unnecessary earnestness*). I have every respect for schoolteachers, Mam. It's a lotta hard work and not much pay. (*Rosemary cannot decide whether or not this is a compliment*)

ALAN. And this is Howard Bevans, Hal. Mr. Bevans is a friend of Miss Sydney.

HOWARD (*as they shake hands*). I run a little shop over in Cherryvale. Notions, novelties and school supplies. You and Alan drive over some time and get acquainted. (*Millie enters and stands on the porch, pretending to be nonchalant and at ease.*)

HAL (*to Howard, earnestly*). Sir, we'll come over as soon as we can fit it into our schedule. (*He spies Millie*) Hey kid! (*He does an elaborate imitation of a swan dive and lands beside her on the porch*) You got a little more tan today, didn't you? (*He turns to the others*) You folks shoulda seen Millie this morning. She did a fine jackknife off the high diving board!

MILLIE (*breaking away, sitting on steps*). Cut it out!

HAL. What'sa matter, kid? Think I'm snowin' you under? (*Back to the whole group*) I wouldn't admit this to many people, but she does a jack-knife almost as good as me! (*Realizes that this sounds bragging so goes on to explain*) You see, I was diving champion on the West Coast, so I know what I'm talking about! (*He laughs to reassure himself and sit beside Millie on doorstep*)

FLO (*after a moment*). Madge, you should be getting dressed.

ALAN. Go on upstairs and get beautiful for us.

MADGE. Mom, can I wear my new dress?

FLO. No. I made you that dress to save for dances this fall.

(*The attention returns now to Hal, and Madge continues to sit, unnoticed, watching him.*)

ROSEMARY (*to Hal*). Where'd you get those boots?

HAL. I gues maybe I should apologize for the way I look. But you see, those characters I told you about made off with all my clothes, too.

MRS. POTTS. What a pity!

HAL. You see, I didn't want you folks to think you were associatin' with a bum. (*He laughs uncomfortably*)

MRS. POTTS (*intuitively, she says what is*

*needed to save his ego*). Clothes don't make the man.

HAL. That's what I tell myself, Mam.

FLO. Is your mother taken care of, Helen?

MRS. POTTS. Yes, Flo, I've got a baby sitter for her. (*All laugh*)

FLO. Then let's start packing the baskets. (*She goes into kitchen. Mrs. Potts starts after her, but Hal's story holds her and she sits down again*)

HAL (*continuing his explanation to Rosemary*). See, Mam, my old man left me these boots when he died.

ROSEMARY (*impishly*). That all he left you—just a pair of boots?

HAL. He said, "Son, the man of the house needs a pair of boots 'cause he's gotta do a lot of kickin'.

Your wages all are spent.
The landlord wants his rent.
You go to your woman for solace,
And she fills you fulla torment."

(*Hal smiles and explains proudly*) That's a little poem he made up. He says, "Son, there'll be times when the only thing you got to be proud of is the fact you're a man. So wear your boots so people can hear you comin', and keep your fists doubled up so they'll know you mean business when you get there." (*He laughs*) My old man, he was a corker!

ALAN (*laughing*). Hal's always so shy of people before he meets them. Then you can't keep him still!

(*Suddenly Hal's eye catches Madge, perched on Mrs. Potts' porch.*)

HAL. Hi!

MADGE. Hi!

(*Now they both look away from each other, a little guiltily.*)

HOWARD. What line of business you in, Son?

HAL (*he begins to expand with importance*). I'm about to enter the oil business, sir. (*He sits on the chair, center stage*)

HOWARD. Oh!

HAL. You see, while my old man was no aristocratic millionaire or anything, he had some very important friends who were very big men—in their own way. One of them wanted me to take a position with this oil company down in Texas, but . . .

ALAN (*matter-of-factly*). Dad and I have found a place for Hal on the pipeline.

HAL. Gee, Seymour, I think you oughta let *me* tell the story.

ALAN (*knowing he might as well let Hal go on*). Sorry, Hal.

HAL (*with devout earnestness to all*). You, see, I've decided to start in from the very bottom, 'cause that way I'll learn things lots better—even if I don't make much money for a while.

MRS. POTTS (*comes through again*). Money isn't everything.

HAL. That's what I tell myself, Mam. Money isn't everything. I've learned that much. And I sure do appreciate Alan and his old . . . (*Thinks a moment and substitutes* father *for* man) *father* . . . giving me this opportunity.

MRS. POTTS. I think that's wonderful. (*She has every faith in him.*)

HOWARD. It's a good business town. A young man can go far.

HAL. Sir! I intend to go *far*.

ROSEMARY (*her two-bits' worth*). A young man, coming to town, he's gotta be a good mixer.

MRS. POTTS. Wouldn't it be nice if he could join the Country Club and play golf?

ALAN. He won't be able to afford that.

ROSEMARY. The bowling team's a rowdy gang.

MRS. POTTS. And there's a young men's Bible class at the Baptist Church.

(*Hal's head has been spinning with these plans for his future. Now he reassures them.*)

HAL. Oh, I'm gonna join clubs and go to church and do all those things.

FLO (*coming out of the kitchen*). Madge! Are you still here?

MADGE (*running across to the front door of her own house*). If everyone will pardon me, I'll get dressed. (*She goes inside*)

FLO. It's about time.

ALAN (*calling after Madge*). Hurry it up, will you, Delilah?

MILLIE. You oughta see the way Madge primps. She uses about six kinds of face cream and dusts herself all over with powder, and rubs perfume underneath her ears to make her real mysterious. It takes her half an hour just to get her lipstick on. She won't be ready for hours.

FLO. Come on, Helen. Alan, we'll need a man to help us chip the ice and put the baskets in the car. (*Mrs. Potts goes inside.*)

HAL (*generously*). I'll help you, Mam.

FLO (*she simply cannot accept him*). No, thank you, Alan won't mind.

ALAN (*to Hal as he leaves*). Mind your manners, Hal. (*He and Flo start in*)

MILLIE (*uncertain how to proceed with Hal on her own, she runs to Flo*). Mom!

FLO. Millie, show the young man your drawings.

MILLIE (*to Hal*). Wanta see my art?

HAL. You mean to tell me you can draw pictures?

MILLIE (*Gets her sketch book and shows it to Hal. Flo and Alan go inside*). That's Mrs. Potts.

HAL (*impressed*). Looks just like her.

MILLIE. I just love Mrs. Potts. When I go to heaven, I expect everyone to be just like her.

HAL. Hey, kid, wanta draw me?

MILLIE. Well, I'll try.

HAL. I had a job as a model once. (*Strikes a pose*) How's this? (*Millie shakes her head*) Here's another. (*Sits on stump in another pose*) Okay?

MILLIE. Why don't you just try to look natural?

HAL. Gee, that's hard. (*But he shakes himself into a natural pose finally. Millie starts sketching him. Rosemary and Howard sit together on the doorstep. The sun now is beginning to set, filling the stage with an orange glow that seems almost aflame*)

ROSEMARY (*grabs Howard's arm*). Look at that sunset, Howard!

HOWARD. Pretty, isn't it?

ROSEMARY. That's the most flaming sunset I ever did see.

HOWARD. If you painted it in a picture, no one'd believe you.

ROSEMARY. It's like the daytime didn't want to end, isn't it?

HOWARD (*not fully aware of what she means*). Oh—I don't know.

ROSEMARY. Like the daytime didn't wanta end, like it was gonna put up a big scrap and maybe set the world on fire—to keep the nighttime from creepin' on.

HOWARD. Rosemary . . . you're a poet.

HAL (*as Millie sketches him he begins to relax and reflect on his life*). You know, there comes a time in every man's life when he's gotta settle down. A little town like this, this is the place to settle down in, where people are easygoin' and sincere.

ROSEMARY. No, Howard, I don't think there ought to be any drinking, while Millie's here.

HAL (*turns at the mention of drink*). What's that?

ROSEMARY. We were just talkin'.

HAL (*back to Millie*). What'd you do this afternoon, kid?

MILLIE. Read a book.

HAL (*impressed*). You mean, you read a *whole* book in one afternoon?

MILLIE. Sure. Hold still.

HAL. I'm a son of a gun. What was it about?

MILLIE. There wasn't much story. It's just the way you feel when you read it— kind of warm inside and sad and amused— all at the same time.

HAL. Yeah—sure. (*After a moment*) I wish I had more time to read books. (*Proudly*) That's what I'm gonna do when I settle down. I'm gonna read all the better books—and listen to all the better music. A man owes it to himself. (*Millie continues sketching*) I used to go with a girl who read books. She joined the Book-of-the-Month Club and they had her readin' books all the time! She wouldn't any more finish one book than they'd send her another!

ROSEMARY (*as Howard walks off*). Howard, where you goin'?

HOWARD. I'll be right back, Honey. (*Rosemary follows him to gate and watches him while he is off stage.*)

HAL (*as Millie hands him the sketch*). Is that *me*? (*Admiring it*) I sure do admire people who are artistic. Can I keep it?

MILLIE. Sure. (*Shyly*) I write poetry, too. I've written poems I've never shown to a living soul.

HAL. Kid, I think you must be some sort of a genius.

ROSEMARY (*calling off to Howard*). Howard, leave that bottle right where it is!

HAL (*jumps at the word bottle*). Did she say "bottle"?

ROSEMARY (*coming down to Hal*). He's been down to the hotel, buying bootleg whiskey off those good-for-nothing porters!

HOWARD (*coming back, holding out a bottle*). Young man, maybe you'd like a swig of this.

HAL. Hot damn! (*He takes a drink*)

ROSEMARY. Howard, put that away.

HOWARD. Millie's not gonna be shocked if she sees someone take a drink. Are you, Millie?

MILLIE. Gosh, no!

ROSEMARY. What if someone'd come by and tell the School Board? I'd lose my job quick as you can say Jack Robinson.

HOWARD. Who's gonna see you, Honey? Everyone in town's at the park, havin' a picnic.

ROSEMARY. I don't care. Liquor's against the law in this state, and a person oughta abide by the law. (*To Hal*) Isn't that what· you say, young fellow?

HAL (*eager to agree*). Oh, sure! A person oughta abide by the law.

HOWARD. Here, Honey, have one.

ROSEMARY. No, Howard, I'm not gonna touch a drop.

HOWARD. Come on, Honey, have one little drink just for *me*.

ROSEMARY (*beginning to melt*). Howard, you oughta be ashamed of yourself.

HOWARD (*innocent*). I don't see why.

ROSEMARY. I guess I know why you want me to take a drink.

HOWARD. Now, Honey, that's not so. I just think you should have a good time like the rest of us. (*To Hal*) Schoolteachers gotta right to live. Isn't that what you say, young fella?

HAL. Sure, schoolteachers got a right to live.

ROSEMARY (*taking the bottle*). Now, Millie, don't you tell any of the kids at school.

MILLIE. What do you take me for?

ROSEMARY (*looking around her*). Anyone coming?

HOWARD. Coast is clear.

ROSEMARY (*takes a hearty drink, and makes a lugubrious face*). Whew! I want some water!

HOWARD. Millie, why don't you run in the house and get us some?

ROSEMARY. Mrs. Owens'd suspect something. I'll get a drink from the hydrant! (*She runs off to Mrs. Potts' yard*)

HOWARD. Millie, my girl, I'd like to offer *you* one, but I s'pose your old lady'd raise Ned.

MILLIE. What Mom don't know won't hurt her! (*She reaches for the bottle*)

HAL (*grabs the bottle first*). No, kid. you lay off the stuff! (*He takes another drink*)

ROSEMARY (*calling from off stage*). Howard, come help me! I see a snake!

HOWARD. You go, Millie. She don't see no snake. (*Millie goes off. As Hal takes another drink, he sees a light go on in Madge's window. Howard follows Hal's gaze*) Look at her there, powdering her arms. You know, every time I come over here I look forward just to seein' her. I tell myself, "Bevans, old boy, you can look at that all you want, but you couldn't touch it with a ten-foot pole."

HAL (*with some awe of her*). She's the kind of girl a guy's gotta *respect*.

HOWARD. Look at her, putting lipstick on that cute kisser. Seems to me, when the good Lord made a girl as pretty as she is, he did it for a reason, and it's about time she found out what that reason is. (*He gets an idea*) Look, son, if you're agonizin', I know a couple of girls down at the hotel.

HAL. Thanks, but I've given up that sorta thing.

HOWARD. I think that's a very fine attitude.

HAL. Besides, I never had to pay for it.

ROSEMARY (*entering, followed by Millie*). Lord, I thought I was going to faint!

MILLIE (*laughing at Rosemary's excitability*). It was just a piece of garden hose.

ROSEMARY (*regarding the two men suspiciously*). What're you two talking about?

HOWARD. Talkin' about the weather, Honey. Talkin' about the weather.

ROSEMARY. I bet.

MILLIE (*seeing Madge in the window*). Hey, Madge, why don't you charge admission? (*Madge's curtains close*)

ROSEMARY. Shoot! When I was a girl I was just as good-looking as she is!

HOWARD. Of course you were, Honey.

ROSEMARY (*taking the bottle*). I had boys callin' me all the time. But if my father had ever caught me showing off in front of the window he'd have tanned me with a razor strap. (*takes a drink*) Cause I was brought up strict by a God-fearing man. (*Takes another*)

MILLIE (*music has started in the back-*

*ground*). Hey, hit it, Ernie! (*Explaining to Hal*) It's Ernie Higgins and His Happiness Boys. They play at all the dances around here.

ROSEMARY (*beginning to sway rapturously*). Lord, I like that music! Come dance with me, Howard.

HOWARD. Honey, I'm no good at dancin'.

ROSEMARY. That's just what you menfolks tell yourselves to get out of it. (*Turns to Millie*) Come dance with me, Millie! (*She pulls Millie up onto the porch and they push the chairs out of the way*)

MILLIE. I gotta lead! I gotta lead.

(*Rosemary and Millie dance together in a trim, automatic way that keeps time to the music but little else. Both women seem to show a little arrogance in dancing together, as though boasting to the men of their independence. Their rhythm is accurate but uninspired. Howard and Hal watch, laughing.*)

HOWARD. S'posin' Hal and I did that.

ROSEMARY. Go ahead for all I care. (*Howard turns to Hal and, laughing, they start dancing together, Hal giving his own version of a coy female. Rosemary is irritated by this*) Stop it!

HOWARD. I thought we were doin' very nicely. (*Rosemary grabs Howard and pulls him up on the porch*)

HAL. Come and dance with me, Millie!

MILLIE. Well—I never danced with boys. I always have to lead.

HAL. Just relax and do the steps I do. Come on and try. (*They dance together but Millie has an awkward feeling of uncertainty that shows in her dancing. Howard, dancing with Rosemary, has been cutting up*)

ROSEMARY. Quit clowning, Howard, and dance with me.

HOWARD. Honey, you don't get any fun out of dancing with *me*.

ROSEMARY. The band's playin'. You gotta dance with *someone*. (*They resume an uncertain toddle*)

MILLIE (*to Hal*). Am I too bad?

HAL. Naw! You just need a little practice.

ROSEMARY (*while dancing*). Lord, I love to dance. At school, kids all called me the Dancin' Fool. Went somewhere dancin' every night!

MRS. POTTS (*coming out of kitchen, she sits and watches the dancers. Flo and Alan appear and stand in doorway watching*). I can't stay in the kitchen while there's dancing!

HAL (*stops the dancing to deliver the needed instructions*). Now look, kid, you gotta remember *I'm* the man, and you gotta do the steps *I* do.

MILLIE. I keep wantin' to do the steps I make up myself.

HAL. The man's gotta take the lead, kid, as long as he's able. (*They resume dancing*)

MRS. POTTS. You're doing fine, Millie!

MILLIE (*as she is whirled around*). I feel like Rita Hayworth!

(*Flo and Alan go into the house.*)

ROSEMARY (*her youth returns in reverie*). One night I went dancin' at a big Valentine party. I danced so hard I swooned! That's when they called me the Dancin' Fool.

HAL (*stops dancing for a moment*). I'll show you a new step, kid. I learned this in L. A. Try it. (*He nimbly executes a somewhat more intricate step*)

MRS. POTTS. Isn't he graceful?

MILLIE. Gee, that looks hard.

HAL. Takes a little time. Give it a try! (*Millie tries to do it, but it is too much for her*)

MILLIE (*giving up*). I'm sorry, I just can't seem to get it.

HAL. Watch close, kid. If you learn this step you'll be the sharpest kid in town. See? (*He continues his demonstration*)

MILLIE (*observing but baffled*). Yah—but . . .

HAL. Real loose, see? You give it a little of this—and give it a little of that. (*He snaps his fingers, keeping a nimble, sensitive response to the rhythm*)

MILLIE. Gee, I wish *I* could do that. (*Now the music changes to a slower, more sensuous rhythm. Hal and Millie stop dancing and listen*)

ROSEMARY (*who has been watching Hal enviously*). That's the way to dance, Howard! That's the way.

(*Hal begins to dance to the slower rhythm and Millie tries to follow him. Now Madge comes out the front door, wearing her new dress. Although the dress is indeed "too fussy" for a picnic, she is ravishing. She stands watching Hal and Millie.*)

HOWARD (*drifting from Rosemary*). You

sure look pretty, Madge.

MADGE. Thank you, Howard.

HOWARD. Would you like a little dance? (*She accepts, and they dance together on the porch. Rosemary is dancing by herself on the porch, upstage, and does not notice them*)

MRS. POTTS (*seeing Madge and Howard dancing*). More dancers! We've turned the backyard into a ballroom!

ROSEMARY (*snatching Howard from Madge*). Thought you couldn't dance. (*Madge goes down into the yard and watches Hal and Millie.*)

MRS. POTTS (*to Madge*). The young man is teaching Millie a new step.

MADGE. Oh, that's fun. I've been trying to teach it to Alan. (*She tries the step herself and does it as well as Hal*)

MRS. POTTS. Look, everyone! Madges does it, too!

HAL (*turns around and sees Madge dancing*). Hey! (*Some distance apart, snapping their fingers to the rhythm, their bodies respond without touching. Then they dance slowly toward each other and Hal takes her in his arms. The dance has something of the nature of a primitive rite that would mate the two young people. The others watch rather solemnly*)

MRS. POTTS (*finally*). It's like they were *made* to dance together, isn't it? (*This remark breaks the spell. Millie moves to Mrs. Potts' steps and sits quietly in the background, beginning to inspect the bottle of whiskey.*)

ROSEMARY (*impatiently to Howard*). Can't *you* dance that way?

HOWARD. Golly, Honey, I'm a businessman.

ROSEMARY (*dances by herself, kicking her legs in the air. Millie takes an occasional drink from the whiskey bottle during the following scene, unobserved by the others*). I danced so hard one night, I swooned! Right in the center of the ballroom!

HOWARD (*amused and observing*). Rosemary's got pretty legs, hasn't she?

ROSEMARY (*this strikes her as hilarious*). That's just like you men, can't talk about anything but women's legs.

HOWARD (*a little offended to be misinterpreted*). I just noticed they had a nice shape.

ROSEMARY (*laughing uproariously*). How would you like it if we women went around talkin' 'bout *your* legs all the time?

HOWARD (*ready to be a sport, stands and lifts his trousers to his knees*). All right! There's *my* legs if you wanna talk about them.

ROSEMARY (*she explodes with laughter*). Never saw anything so ugly. Men's big hairy legs! (*Rosemary goes over to Hal, yanking him from Madge possessively*) Young man, let's see your legs.

HAL (*not knowing what to make of his seizure*). Huh?

ROSEMARY. We passed a new rule here to-night. Every man here's gotta show his legs.

HAL. Mam, I got on boots.

HOWARD. Let the young man alone, Rosemary. He's dancin' with Madge.

ROSEMARY. Now it's his turn to dance with *me*. (*To Hal*) I may be an old-maid schoolteacher, but *I* can keep up with you. Ride 'em cowboy! (*A little tight, stimulated by Hal's physical presence, she abandons convention and grabs Hal closely to her, plastering a cheek next to his and holding her hips fast against him. One can sense that Hal is embarrassed and repelled*)

HAL (*wanting to object*). Mam, I . . .

ROSEMARY. I used to have a boy friend was a cowboy. Met him in Colorado when I went out there to get over a case of flu. He was in love with me, 'cause I was an older woman and had some sense. Took me up in the mountains one night and made love. Wanted me to marry me right there on the mountain top. Said God'd be our preacher, the moon our best man. Ever hear such talk?

HAL (*trying to get away*). Mam, I'd like another li'l drink now.

ROSEMARY (*jerking him closer to her*). Dance with me, young man. Dance with me. I can keep up with you. You know what? You remind me of one of those ancient statues. There was one in the school library until last year. He was a Roman gladiator. All he had on was a shield. (*She gives him a bawdy laugh*) A shield over his arm. That was all he had on. All we girls felt insulted, havin' to walk past that statue every time we went to the library. We got up a petition and made the principal do something about it. (*She laughs hilariously during her narration*) You know what he did? He got the school janitor to fix things right. He got a chisel and made that statue decent. (*Another bawdy laugh*) Lord, those ancient people were depraved.

HAL (*he seldom has been made so uncomfortable*). Mam, I guess I just don't feel like dancin'.

ROSEMARY (*sobering from her story, grabs for Hal, catching him by the shirt*). Where you goin'?

HAL. Mam, I . . .

ROSEMARY (*commanding him imploringly*). Dance with me, young man. Dance with me.

HAL. I . . . I . . . (*He pulls loose from her grasp but her hand, still clutching, tears off a strip of his shirt as he gets away. Howard intervenes.*)

HOWARD. He wants to dance with Madge, Rosemary. Let 'em alone. They're young people.

ROSEMARY (*in a hollow voice*). Young? What do you mean, they're *young*?

MILLIE (*a sick groan from the background*). Oh, I'm sick.

MRS. POTTS. Millie!

MILLIE. I wanna die. (*All eyes are on Millie now as she runs over to the kitchen door*)

MADGE. Millie!

HOWARD. What'd the little Dickens do? Get herself tight?

HAL. Take it easy, kid.

ROSEMARY (*she has problems of her own. She gropes blindly across the stage, suffering what has been a deep humiliation*). I suppose that's something wonderful—they're young.

MADGE (*going to Millie*). Let's go inside, Millie.

MILLIE (*turning on Madge viciously*). I hate you!

MADGE (*hurt*). Millie!

MILLIE (*sobbing*). Madge is the pretty one—Madge is the pretty one. (*Millie dashes inside the kitchen door, Mrs. Potts behind her*)

MADGE (*to herself*). What did she have to do that for?

HOWARD (*examining the bottle*). She must have had several good snifters.

ROSEMARY (*pointing a finger at Hal. She has found vengeance*). It's all *his* fault, Howard.

HOWARD. Now, Honey . . .

ROSEMARY (*to Hal, defiantly and accusingly*). Millie was your date. You shoulda been looking after her. But you were too busy making eyes at Madge.

HOWARD. Honey . . .

ROSEMARY. And you're no better than he is, Madge. You should be ashamed.

FLO (*flies out on the porch in a fury*). Who fed whiskey to my Millie?

ROSEMARY (*pointing fanatically at Hal*). He did, Mrs. Owens! It's all his fault! (*Flo glares at Hal.*)

HOWARD (*trying to straighten things out*). Mrs. Owens, it was this way . . .

FLO. My Millie is too young to be drinking whiskey!

ROSEMARY. Oh, he'd have fed her whiskey and taken his pleasure with the child and then skidaddled!

HOWARD (*trying to bring them to reason*). Now listen, everyone. Let's . . .

ROSEMARY. I know what I'm doing, Howard! And I don't need any advice from *you*. (*Back at Hal.*) You been stomping around here in those boots like you owned the place, thinking every woman you saw was gonna fall madly in love. But here's one woman didn't pay you any mind.

HOWARD. The boy hasn't done anything, Mrs. Owens!

ROSEMARY (*facing Hal, drawing closer with each accusation*). Aristocratic millionaire, my foot! You wouldn't know an aristocratic millionaire if he spit on you. Braggin' about your father, and I bet he wasn't any better'n you are.

(*Hal is as though paralyzed. Howard still tries to reason with Flo.*)

HOWARD. None of us saw Millie drink the whiskey.

ROSEMARY (*closer to Hal*). You think just cause you're a man, you can walk in here and make off with whatever you like. You think just cause you're young you can push other people aside and not pay them any mind. You think just cause you're strong you can show your muscles and nobody'll know what a pitiful specimen you are. But you won't stay young forever, didja ever thinka that? What'll become of you then? You'll end your life in the gutter and it'll serve you right, 'cause the gutter's where you came from and the gutter's where you belong. (*She has thrust her face into Hal's and is spitting her final words at him before Howard finally grabs her, almost as though to protect her from herself, and holds her arms at her sides, pulling her away*)

HOWARD. Rosemary, shut your damn mouth. (*Hal withdraws to the far edge of the porch, no one paying any attention to him now, his reaction to the attack still a mystery.*)

MRS. POTTS (*comes out of kitchen*). Millie's going to be perfectly all right, Flo. Alan held her head and let her be sick. She's going to be perfectly all right, now.

FLO (*a general announcement, clear and firm*). I want it understood by everyone that there's to be no more drinking on this picnic.

HOWARD. It was all my fault, Mrs. Owens. My fault.

(*Alan escorts a sober Millie out on the porch.*)

MRS. POTTS. Here's Millie now, good as new. And we're all going on the picnic and forget it.

ALAN (*quick to accuse Hal*). Hal, what's happened? (*Hal does not respond*)

FLO (*to Alan*). Millie will come with us, Alan.

ALAN. Sure, Mrs. Owens. Hal, I told you not to drink! (*Hal is still silent*)

FLO. Madge, why did you wear your new dress?

MADGE (*as though mystified at herself*). I don't know. I just put it on.

FLO. Go upstairs and change, this minute. I mean it! You come later with Rosemary and Howard! (*Madge runs inside*)

MRS. POTTS. Let's hurry. All the tables will be taken.

ALAN. Mr. Bevans, tell Madge I'll see her out there. Hal, the baskets are all in the Ford. Get goin'. (*Hal doesn't move. Alan hurries off*)

FLO. Millie, darling, are you feeling better? (*Flo and Millie go off through alley, right*)

MRS. POTTS (*to Hal*). Young man, you can follow us and find the way.

(*Mrs. Potts follows the others off. We hear the Cadillac drive off. Hal is sitting silent and beaten on the edge of the porch.*)

*Howard and Rosemary are on the lawn by Mrs. Potts' house.*)

HOWARD. He's just a boy, Rosemary. You talked awful.

ROSEMARY. What made me do it, Howard? What made me act that way?

HOWARD. You gotta remember, men have got feelings, too—same as women. (*To Hal*) Don't pay any attention to her, young man. She didn't mean a thing.

ROSEMARY (*has gone up to the gate*). I don't want to go on the picnic, Howard. This is my last night of vacation and I want to have a good time.

HOWARD. We'll go for a ride, Honey.

ROSEMARY. I want to drive into the sunset, Howard! I want to drive into the sunset! (*She runs off toward the car, Howard following. Howard's car drives away. Hal sits on the porch, defeated. Madge soon comes out in another dress. She comes out very quietly and he makes no recognition of her presence. She sits on a bench on the porch and finally speaks in a soft voice.*)

MADGE. You're a wonderful dancer . . .

HAL (*hardly audible*). Thanks.

MADGE. . . . and I can tell a lot about a boy by dancing with him. Some boys, even though they're very smart, or very successful in some other way, when they take a girl in their arms to dance, they're sort of awkward and a girl feels sort of uncomfortable.

HAL (*he keeps his head down, his face in his hands*). Yah.

MADGE. But when you took me in your arms—to dance—I had the most relaxed feeling, that you knew what you were doing, and I could follow every step of the way.

HAL. Look, Baby, I'm in a pretty bad mood. (*He stands suddenly and walks away from her, his hands thrust into his pockets. He is uncomfortable to be near her, for he is trembling with insult and rage*)

MADGE. You mustn't pay any attention to Miss Sydney. (*Hal is silent*) Women like her make me mad at the whole female sex.

HAL. Look, Baby, why don't you beat it?

MADGE (*she is aware of the depth of his feelings*). What's the matter?

HAL (*gives up and begins to shudder, his shoulders heaving as he fights to keep from bawling*). What's the use, Baby? I'm a bum. She saw through me like a God-damn X-ray machine. There's just no place in the world for a guy like me.

MADGE. There's got to be.

HAL (*with self-derision*). Yah?

MADGE. Of course. You're young, and—you're very entertaining. I mean—you say all sorts of witty things, and I just loved listening to you talk. And you're strong and—you're very goodlooking. I bet Miss Sydney thought so, too, or she wouldn't have said those things.

HAL. Look, Baby, lemme level with you. When I was fourteen, I spent a year in the reform school. How ya like that?

MADGE. Honest?

HAL. Yah!

MADGE. What for?

HAL. For stealin' another guy's motorcycle. Yah! I *stole* it. I stole it 'cause I wanted to get on the damn thing and go so far away, so fast, that no one'd ever catch up with me.

MADGE. I think—lots of boys feel that way at times.

HAL. Then my old lady went to the authorities. (*He mimics his "old lady"*) "I've done everything I can with the boy. I can't do anything more." So off I go to the God-damn reform school.

MADGE (*with all the feeling she has*). Gee!

HAL. Finally some welfare league hauls me out and the old lady's sorry to see me back. Yah! she's got herself a new boy friend and I'm in the way.

MADGE. It's awful when parents don't get along.

HAL. I never told that to another soul, not even Seymour.

MADGE (*at a loss*). I—I wish there was something I could say—or *do*.

HAL. Well—that's the Hal Carter story, but no one's ever gonna make a movie of it.

MADGE (*to herself*). Most people would be awfully shocked.

HAL (*looking at her, then turning away cynically*). There you are, Baby. If you wanta faint—or get sick—or run in the house and lock the doors—go ahead. I aint stoppin' you. (*There is a silence. Then Madge, suddenly and impulsively, takes his face in her hands and kisses him. Then she returns her hands to her lap and feels embarrassed. Hal looks at her in amazement*)

Baby! What'd you do?

MADGE. I . . . I'm proud you told me.

HAL (*with humble appreciation*). Baby!

MADGE. I . . . I get so tired of being told I'm pretty.

HAL (*folding her in his arms caressingly*). Baby, Baby, Baby.

MADGE (*resisting him, jumping to her feet*). Don't. We have to go. We have all the baskets in our car and they'll be waiting. (*Hal gets up and walks slowly to her, their eyes fastened and Madge feeling a little thrill of excitement as he draws nearer*) Really—we have to be going. (*Hal takes her in his arms and kisses her passionately. Then Madge utters his name in a voice of resignation*) Hal!

HAL. Just be quiet, Baby.

MADGE. Really . . . We have to go. They'll be waiting.

HAL (*picking her up in his arms and starting off. His voice is deep and firm*). We're not goin' on no God-damn picnic.

CURTAIN

## ACT THREE

### SCENE I

*It is after midnight. A great harvest moon shines in the sky, a deep, murky blue. The moon is swollen and full and casts a pale light on the scene below. Soon we hear Howard's Chevrolet chugging to a stop by the house, then Howard and Rosemary come on, Rosemary first. Wearily, a groggy depression having set in, she makes her way to the doorstep and drops there, sitting limp. She seems preoccupied at first and her responses to Howard are mere grunts.*

———

HOWARD. Here we are, Honey. Right back where we started from.

ROSEMARY (*her mind elsewhere*). Uhh.

HOWARD. You were awful nice to me tonight, Rosemary.

ROSEMARY. Uhh.

HOWARD. Do you think Mrs. Owens suspects anything?

ROSEMARY. I don't care if she does.

HOWARD. A *businessman's* gotta be careful of talk. And after all, you're a schoolteacher. (*Fumbling to get away*) Well, I better be gettin' back to Cherryvale. I gotta open up the store in the morning. Good night, Rosemary.

ROSEMARY. Uhh.

HOWARD (*he pecks at her cheek with a kiss*). Good night. Maybe I should say, good morning. (*He starts off*)

ROSEMARY (*just coming to*). Where you goin', Howard?

HOWARD. Honey, I gotta get home.

ROSEMARY. You can't go off without me.

HOWARD. Honey, talk sense.

ROSEMARY. You can't go off without me. Not tonight. *That's* sense.

HOWARD (*a little nervous*). Honey, be reasonable.

ROSEMARY. Take me with you.

HOWARD. What'd people say?

ROSEMARY (*almost vicious*). To *hell* with what people'd say!

HOWARD (*shocked*). Honey!

ROSEMARY. What'd people say if I thumbed my nose at them? What'd people say if I walked down the street and showed 'em my pink panties? What do I care what people say?

HOWARD. Honey, you're not yourself tonight.

ROSEMARY. Yes, I am. I'm more myself than I ever was. Take me with you, Howard. If you don't I don't know what I'll do with myself. I mean it.

HOWARD. Now look, Honey, you better go upstairs and get some sleep. You gotta start school in the morning. We'll talk all this over Saturday.

ROSEMARY. Maybe you won't be back Saturday. Maybe you won't be back ever again.

HOWARD. Rosemary, you know better than that.

ROSEMARY. Then what's the next thing in store for me? To be nice to the next man, then the next—till there's no one left to care whether I'm nice to him or not. Till I'm ready for the grave and don't have anyone to take me there.

HOWARD (*in an attempt to be consoling*). Now, Rosemary!

ROSEMARY. You can't let that happen to me, Howard. I won't let you.

HOWARD. I don't understand. When we first started going together, you were the best sport I ever saw, always good for a laugh.

ROSEMARY (*in a hollow voice*). I can't laugh any more.

HOWARD. We'll talk it over Saturday.

ROSEMARY. We'll talk it over *now*.

HOWARD (*squirming*) Well—Honey—I . . .

ROSEMARY. You said you were gonna marry me, Howard. You said when I got back from my vacation, you'd be waitin' with the preacher.

HOWARD. Honey, I've had an awful busy summer and . . .

ROSEMARY. Where's the preacher, Howard? Where is he?

HOWARD (*walking away from her*). Honey, I'm forty-two years old. A person forms certain ways of livin', then one day it's too late to change.

ROSEMARY (*grabbing his arm and holding him*). Come back here, Howard. I'm no spring chicken either. Maybe I'm a little older than you think *I* am. I've formed my ways too. But they can be changed. They *gotta* be changed. It's no good livin' like this, in rented rooms, meetin' a bunch of old maids for supper every night, then comin' back home alone.

HOWARD. *I* know how it is, Rosemary. My life's no bed of roses either.

ROSEMARY. Then why don't you do something about it?

HOWARD. I figure—there's some bad things about every life.

ROSEMARY. There's too much bad about mine. Each year, I keep tellin' myself, is the last. Something'll happen. Then nothing ever does—except I get a little crazier all the time.

HOWARD (*hopelessly*). Well . . .

ROSEMARY. A *well's* a hole in the ground, Howard. Be careful you don't fall in.

HOWARD. I wasn't tryin' to be funny.

ROSEMARY. . . . and all this time you just been leadin' me on.

HOWARD (*defensive*). Rosemary, that's not *so!* I've not been leading you *on*.

ROSEMARY. I'd like to know what else you call it.

HOWARD. Well—can't we talk about it Saturday? I'm dead tired and I got a busy week ahead, and . . .

ROSEMARY (*she grips him by the arm and looks straight into his eyes*). You **gotta** marry me, Howard.

HOWARD (*tortured*). Well—Honey, I can't marry you *now*.

ROSEMARY. You can be over here in the morning.

HOWARD. Sometimes you're unreasonable.

ROSEMARY. You gotta marry me.

HOWARD. What'll you do about your job?

ROSEMARY. Alvah Jackson can take my place till they get someone new from the agency.

HOWARD. I'll have to pay Fred Jenkins to take care of the store for a few days.

ROSEMARY. Then get him.

HOWARD. Well . . .

ROSEMARY. I'll be waitin' for you in the morning, Howard.

HOWARD (*after a few moments' troubled thought*). No.

ROSEMARY (*a muffled cry*). Howard!

HOWARD. I'm not gonna marry anyone that says, "You gotta marry me, Howard." I'm not gonna. (*He is silent. Rosemary weeps pathetic tears. Slowly Howard reconsiders*) If a woman wants me to marry her—she can at least say "please."

ROSEMARY (*beaten and humble*). Please marry me, Howard.

HOWARD. Well—you got to give me time to think it over.

ROSEMARY (*desperate*). Oh, God! Please marry me, Howard. Please . . . (*She sinks to her knees*) Please . . . please . . .

HOWARD (*embarrassed by her suffering humility*). Rosemary . . . I . . . I gotta have some time to think it over. You go to bed now and get some rest. I'll drive over in the morning and maybe we can talk it over before you go to school. I . . .

ROSEMARY. You're not just tryin' to get out of it, Howard?

HOWARD. I'll be over in the morning, Honey.

ROSEMARY. Honest?

HOWARD. Yah. I gotta go to the courthouse anyway. We'll talk it over then.

ROSEMARY. Oh, God, please marry me, Howard. Please.

HOWARD (*trying to get away*). Go to bed, Honey. I'll see you in the morning.

ROSEMARY. Please, Howard!

HOWARD. I'll see you in the morning. Good night, Rosemary. (*Starting off*)

ROSEMARY (*in a meek voice*). Please!

HOWARD. Good night, Rosemary.

ROSEMARY (*after he is gone*). Please. (*Rosemary stands alone on the doorstep. We hear the sound of Howard's car start up and drive off, chugging away in the distance. Rosemary is drained of energy. She pulls herself together and goes into the house. The stage is empty for several moments. Then Madge runs on from the back, right. Her face is in her hands. She is sobbing. Hal follows fast behind. He reaches her just as she gets to the door, and grabs her by the wrist. She resists him furiously.*)

HAL. Baby . . . you're not sorry, are you? (*There is a silence. Madge sobs*)

MADGE. Let me go.

HAL. Please, Baby. If I thought I'd done anything to make you unhappy, I . . . I'd almost wanta die.

MADGE. I . . . I'm so ashamed.

HAL. Don't say that, Baby.

MADGE. I didn't even know what was happening, and then . . . all of a sudden, it seems like my whole life was changed.

HAL (*with bitter self-disparagement*). I oughta be taken out and hung. I'm just a no-good bum. That schoolteacher was right. I oughta be in the gutter.

MADGE. Don't talk that way.

HAL. Times like this, I hate myself, Baby.

MADGE. I guess . . . it's no more your fault than mine.

HAL. Sometimes I do pretty impulsive things. (*Madge starts inside*) Will I see you tomorrow?

MADGE. I don't know.

HAL. Gee, I almost forgot. I start a new job tomorrow.

MADGE. I have to be at the dime store at nine.

HAL. What time you through?

MADGE. Five.

HAL. Maybe I could see you then, huh? Maybe I could come by and . . .

MADGE. I've got a date with Alan—if he'll still speak to me.

HAL (*a new pain*). Jesus, I'd forgot all about Seymour.

MADGE. So had I.

HAL. I can't go back to his house. What'll I do?

MADGE. Maybe Mrs. Potts could . . .

HAL. I'll take the car back to where we were, stretch out in the front seat and get a little sleep. (*He thinks a moment*) Baby, how you gonna handle your old lady?

MADGE (*with a slight tremor*). I . . . I don't know.

HAL (*in a funk again*). Jesus, I oughta be shot at sunrise.

MADGE. I . . . I'll think of something to tell her.

HAL (*awkward*). Well—good night.

MADGE. Good night. (*She starts again*)

HAL. Baby—would you kiss me good night . . . maybe? Just one more time.

MADGE. I don't think I better.

HAL. Please!

MADGE. It . . . It'd just start things all over again. Things I better forget.

HAL. Pretty please!

MADGE. Promise not to hold me?

HAL. I'll keep my hands to my side. Swear to God!

MADGE. Well . . . (*Slowly she goes toward him, takes his face in her hands and kisses him. The kiss lasts. Hal's hands become nervous and finally find their way around her. Their passion is revived. Then Madge utters a little shriek, tears herself away from Hal and runs into the house, sobbing*) Don't. You *promised*. I never want to see you again. I might as well be dead. (*She runs inside the front door, leaving Hal behind to despise himself. He beats his fists together, kicks the earth with his heel, and starts off, hating the day he was born*)

CURTAIN

## ACT THREE

### SCENE II

*It is very early the next morning. Millie sits on the doorstep smoking a cigarette. She wears a fresh wash dress in honor of the first day of school. Flo breaks out of the front door. She is a frantic woman. Millie puts out her cigarette quickly. Flo has not even taken the time to dress. She wears an old robe over her nightdress. She speaks to Millie.*

FLO. Were you awake when Madge got in?

MILLIE. No.

FLO. Did she say anything to you this morning?

MILLIE. No.

FLO. Dear God! I couldn't get two words out of her last night, she was crying so hard. Now she's got the door locked.

MILLIE. I bet I know what happened.

FLO. You don't know anything, Millie Owens. And if anyone says anything to you, you just . . . (*Now she sniffs the air*) Have you been smoking?

MRS. POTTS (*coming down her backsteps*). Did Madge tell you what happened?

FLO. The next time you take in tramps, Helen Potts, I'll thank you to keep them on your own side of the yard.

MRS. POTTS. Is Madge all right?

FLO. Of course she's all right. She got out of the car and left that hoodlum alone. That's what she did.

MRS. POTTS. Have you heard from Alan?

FLO. He said he'd be over this morning.

MRS. POTTS. Where's the young man?

FLO. I know where he should be! He should be in the penitentiary, and that's where he's going if he shows up around here again!

ROSEMARY (*sticking her head out front door*). Has anyone seen Howard?

FLO (*surprised*). Howard? Why, no, Rosemary!

ROSEMARY (*nervous and uncertain*). He said he might be over this morning. Mrs. Owens, I'm storing my summer clothes in the attic. Could someone help me?

FLO. We're busy, Rosemary.

MRS. POTTS. I'll help you, Rosemary. (*She looks at Flo, then goes up on porch*)

ROSEMARY. Thanks, Mrs. Potts. (*Goes inside*)

FLO (*to Mrs. Potts*). She's been running around like a chicken with its head off all morning. Something's *up!* (*Mrs. Potts goes inside. Flo turns to Millie*) You keep watch for Alan. (*Flo goes inside. Now we hear the morning voices of Irma and Christine, coming by for Rosemary*)

IRMA. Girl, I hope Rosemary is ready. I promised the principal that I'd be there early to help with registration.

CHRISTINE. How do I look, Irma?

IRMA. It's a cute dress. Let me fix it in the back. (*Irma adjusts the hang of the dress as Christine stands patiently*)

CHRISTINE. I think a teacher should dress up first day of school, to give the students a good first impression.

IRMA (*going up on the porch*). Good morning, Millie!

MILLIE. Hi.

IRMA. Is Rosemary ready?

MILLIE. Go on up if you want to.

CHRISTINE (*to Millie*). We missed seeing Madge on the picnic last night.

MILLIE. So did a lot of other people.

IRMA (*gives Christine a significant look*). Come on, Christine. I bet we have to get that sleepy girl out of bed.

(*They go inside front door. Bomber rides on, gets off his bicycle, throws a paper on Mrs. Potts' steps, then on Flo's back porch. Then he climbs up on Mrs. Potts' porch so he can look across into Madge's room.*)

BOMBER. Hey, Madge! Wanta go dancin'? Let me be next, Madge!

MILLIE. You shut up, Crazy.

BOMBER. My brother seen 'em parked under the bridge. Alan Seymour was lookin' for 'em all over town. She always put on a lot of airs, but I knew she liked guys. (*He sees Alan approaching from beyond the Owens' house, and leaves quickly*)

MILLIE. Some day I'm really gonna kill that ornery bastard. (*She turns and sees Alan*)

ALAN. Could I see Madge?

MILLIE. I'll call her, Alan. (*Calls up to Madge's window*) Madge! Alan's here! (*Back to Alan*) She prob'ly has to dress.

ALAN. I'll wait.

MILLIE (*she sits on the stump and turns to him very shyly*). I . . . I always liked you, Alan. Didn't you know it?

ALAN (*with some surprise*). *Like* me?

MILLIE (*nods her head*). It's awfully hard to show someone you like them, isn't it?

ALAN (*with just a little bitterness*). It's easy for *some* people.

MILLIE. It makes you feel like such a sap. I don't know why.

ALAN (*rather touched*). I . . . I'm glad you like me, Millie.

MILLIE (*one can sense her loneliness*). I don't expect you to do anything about it. I just wanted to tell you.

(*Howard comes bustling on through the gate, very upset. He addresses Millie.*)

HOWARD. Could I see Rosemary?

MILLIE. My gosh, Howard, what are you doing here?

HOWARD. I think she's expecting me.

MILLIE. You better holler at the bottom of the stairs—(*Howard is about to go in the door, but turns back at this*) all the others are up there, too.

HOWARD (*he looks very grave*). The others?

MILLIE. Mrs. Potts and Miss Kronkite and Miss Schoenwalder.

HOWARD. Golly, I gotta see her alone.

ROSEMARY (*calling from inside*). Howard! (*Inside, to all the women*) It's Howard! He's here!

HOWARD (*knowing he is stuck*). Golly! (*We hear a joyful babble of women's voices from inside. Howard gives one last pitiful look at Millie, then goes in. Millie follows him in and Alan is left alone in the yard. After a moment, Madge comes out the kitchen door. She wears a simple dress, and her whole being appears chastened. She is inscrutable in her expression.*)

MADGE. Hello, Alan.

ALAN (*very moved by seeing her*). Madge!

MADGE. I'm sorry about last night.

ALAN. Madge, whatever happened—it wasn't your fault. I know what Hal's like when he's drinking. But I've got Hal taken care of now! He won't be bothering you again!

MADGE. Honest?

ALAN. At school I spent half my life getting him out of jams. I knew he'd had a few tough breaks, and I always tried to be sorry for the guy. But this is the thanks I get.

MADGE (*still noncommittal*). Where is he now?

HAL. Don't worry about Hal! I'll take it on myself now to offer you his official goodbye!

MADGE (*one still cannot decipher her feelings*). Is he gone?

FLO (*running out kitchen door. She is dressed now*). Alan, I didn't know you were here!

(*Now we hear shouts from inside the house. Millie comes out, throwing rice over her shoulder at all the others, who are laughing and shouting so that we only hear bits of the following.*)

MRS. POTTS. Here comes the bride! Here comes the bride!

IRMA. May all your troubles be little ones!

CHRISTINE. You're getting a wonderful

girl, Howard Bevans!

IRMA. Rosemary is getting a fine man!

CHRISTINE. They don't come any better'n Rosemary!

MRS. POTTS. Be happy!

IRMA. May all your troubles be little ones!

MRS. POTTS. Be happy forever and ever! (*Now they are all out on the porch and we see that Howard carries two suitcases. His face has an expression of complete confusion. Rosemary wears a fussy going-away outfit.*)

IRMA (*to Rosemary*). Girl, are you wearing something old?

ROSEMARY. An old pair of nylons but they're as good as new.

CHRISTINE. And that's a brand-new outfit she's got on. Rosemary, are you wearing something blue? I don't see it!

ROSEMARY (*daringly*). And you're not gonna! (*They all laugh, and Rosemary begins a personal inventory*) Something borrowed! I don't have anything to borrow! (*Now we see Hal's head appear from the edge of the woodshed. He watches for a moment when he can be sure of not being observed, then darts into the shed.*)

FLO. Madge, you give Rosemary something to borrow. It'll mean good luck for you. Go on, Madge! (*She takes Alan's arm and pulls him toward the steps with her*) Rosemary, Madge has something for you to borrow!

MADGE (*crossing to the group by steps*). You can borrow my handkerchief, Miss Sydney.

ROSEMARY. Thank you, Madge. (*She takes the handkerchief*) Isn't Madge pretty, girls?

IRMA AND CHRISTINE. Oh, yes! Yes, indeed! (*Madge turns and leaves the group, going toward Mrs. Potts' house.*)

ROSEMARY (*during the above*). She's modest! A girl as pretty as Madge can sail through life without a care! (*Alan turns from the group to join Madge. Flo then turns and crosses toward Madge. Rosemary follows Flo*) Mrs. Owens I left my hot-water bottle in the closet and my curlers are in the bathroom. You and the girls can have them. I stored the rest of my things in the attic. Howard and I'll come and get 'em after we settle down. Cherryvale's not so far away. we can be good friends, same as before. (*Hal sticks his head through woodshed door and catches Madge's eye. Madge is startled.*)

FLO. I hate to mention it now, Rosemary, but you didn't give us much notice. Do you know anyone I could rent the room to?

IRMA (*to Rosemary*). Didn't you tell her about Linda Sue Breckenridge?

ROSEMARY. Oh, yes! Linda Sue Breckenridge—she's the sewing teacher!

IRMA (*a positive affirmation to them all*). And she's a darling girl!

ROSEMARY. She and Mrs. Bendix had a fight. Mrs. Bendix wanted to charge her twenty cents for her orange juice in the morning and none of us girls ever paid more'n fifteen. Did we, girls?

IRMA AND CHRISTINE (*in staunch support*). No! Never! I certainly never did!

ROSEMARY. Irma, you tell Linda Sue to get in touch with Mrs. Owens.

IRMA. I'll do that very thing.

FLO. Thank you, Rosemary.

HOWARD. Rosemary, we still got to pick up the license . . .

ROSEMARY (*to Irma and Christine, all of them blubbering*) Good-bye, girls! We've had some awfully jolly times together! (*Irma, Christine and Rosemary embrace*)

HOWARD (*a little restless*). Come on, Honey! (*Alan takes the suitcases from Howard*)

HOWARD (*to Alan*). A man's gotta settle down some time.

ALAN. Of course.

HOWARD. And folks'd rather do business with a married man!

ROSEMARY (*to Madge and Alan*). I hope both of you are going to be as happy as Howard and I will be. (*Turns to Mrs. Potts*) You've been a wonderful friend, Mrs. Potts!

MRS. POTTS. I wish you all sorts of happiness, Rosemary.

ROSEMARY. Good-bye, Millie. You're going to be a famous author some day and I'll be proud I knew you.

MILLIE. Thanks, Miss Sydney.

HOWARD (*to Rosemary*). All set?

ROSEMARY. All set and rarin' to go! (*A sudden thought*) Where we goin'?

HOWARD (*after an awkward pause*). Well . . . I got a cousin who runs a tourist camp in the Ozarks. He and his wife could put us up for free.

ROSEMARY. Oh, I love the Ozarks! (*She grabs Howard's arm and pulls him off stage.*

*Alan carries the suitcase off stage. Irma, Christine, Mrs. Potts and Millie follow them, all throwing rice and calling after them)*

ALL *(as they go off).* The Ozarks are lovely this time of year!

Be happy!

May all your troubles be little ones!

You're getting a wonderful girl!

You're getting a wonderful man!

FLO *(alone with Madge).* Madge, what happened last night? You haven't told me a word.

MADGE. Let me alone, Mom.

ROSEMARY *(off stage).* Mrs. Owens aren't you going to tell us good-bye?

FLO *(exasperated).* Oh, dear! I've been saying good-bye to her all morning.

ALAN *(appearing in the gateway).* Mrs. Owens, Miss Sydney wants to give you her house keys.

MRS. POTTS *(behind Alan).* Come on, Flo!

FLO *(hurrying off).* I'm coming. I'm coming. *(She follows Alan and Mrs. Potts to join the noisy shivaree in the background. Now Hal appears from the woodshed. His clothes are drenched and cling plastered to his body. He is barefoot and there is blood on his T-shirt. He stands before Madge)*

HAL. Baby!

MADGE *(backing from him).* You shouldn't have come here.

HAL. Look, Baby, I'm in a jam.

MADGE. Serves you right.

HAL. Seymour's old man put the cops on my tail. Accused me of stealin' the car. I had to knock one of the bastards cold and swim the river to get away. If they ever catch up with me, it'll be too bad.

MADGE *(things are in a slightly different light now).* You were born to get in trouble.

HAL. Baby, I just *had* to say good-bye.

MADGE *(still not giving away her feelings).* Where are you going?

HAL. The freight train's by pretty soon. I'll hop a ride. I done it lotsa times before.

MADGE. What're you gonna do?

HAL. I got some friends in Tulsa. I can always get a job hoppin' bells at the Hotel Mayo. Jesus, I hate to say good-bye.

MADGE *(not knowing what her precise feelings are).* Well . . . I don't know what else there is to do.

HAL. Are you still mad, Baby?

MADGE *(evasively).* I . . . I never knew a

boy like you.

*(The shivaree is quieting down now, and Howard and Rosemary can be heard driving off as the others call. Flo returns, stopping in the gateway, seeing Hal.)*

FLO. Madge!

*(Now Alan comes running on.)*

ALAN *(incensed).* Hal, what're you doing here?

*(Mrs. Potts and Millie come on, followed by Irma and Christine.)*

MRS. POTTS. It's the young man!

HAL. Look, Seymour, I didn't swipe your lousy car. Get that straight!

ALAN. You better get out of town if you know what's good for you.

HAL. I'll go when I'm ready.

MRS. POTTS. Go? I thought you were going to stay here and settle down.

HAL. No'm. I'm not gonna settle down.

ALAN *(tearing into Hal savagely).* You'll go *now.* What do you take me for?

HAL *(holding Alan off, not wanting a fight).* Look, Kid, I don't wanta fight with you. You're the only friend I ever had.

ALAN. We're not friends any more. I'm not scared of you. *(Alan plows into Hal, but Hal is far beyond him in strength and physical alertness. He fastens Alan's arms quickly behind him and brings him to the ground. Irma and Christine watch excitedly from the gateway. Mrs. Potts is apprehensive. Alan cries out in pain)* Let me go, you God-damn tramp! Let me go!

FLO *(to Hal).* Take your hands off him, this minute.

*(But Alan has to admit he is mastered. Hal releases him and Alan retires to Mrs. Potts' back doorstep, sitting there, holding his hands over his face, feeling the deepest humiliation. A train whistle is heard in the distance. Hal hurries to Madge's side.)*

HAL *(to Madge).* Baby, aren't you gonna say good-bye?

FLO *(to Irma and Christine).* You better run along, girls. This is no side show we're running. *(They depart in a huff)*

MADGE *(keeping her head down, not wanting to look at Hal).* . . . Good-bye . . .

HAL. Please don't be mad, Baby. You were sittin' there beside me lookin' so pretty, sayin' all those sweet things, and I . . . I thought you liked me, too, Baby. Honest I did.

MADGE. It's all right. I'm not mad.

HAL. Thanks. Thanks a lot.

FLO (*like a barking terrier*). Young man, if you don't leave here this second, I'm going to call the police and have you put where you belong. (*Madge and Hal do not even hear*)

MADGE. And I . . . I *did* like you . . . the first time I saw you.

FLO (*incensed*). Madge!

HAL (*beaming*). Honest? (*Madge nods*) I kinda thought you did.

(*All has been worth it now for Hal. Millie watches skeptically from doorstep. Mrs. Potts looks on lovingly from the back. Flo at times concerns herself with Alan, then with trying to get rid of Hal.*)

FLO. Madge, I want you inside the house this minute. (*Madge doesn't move*)

HAL. Look, Baby, I never said it before. I never could. It made me feel like such a freak, but I . . .

MADGE. What?

HAL. I'm nuts about you, Baby. I mean it.

MADGE. You make love to lots of girls . . .

HAL. A few.

MADGE. . . . just like you made love to me last night.

HAL. Not like last night, Baby. Last night was . . . (*Gropes for the word*) inspired.

MADGE. Honest?

HAL. The way you sat there, knowin' just how I felt. The way you held my hand and talked.

MADGE. I couldn't stand to hear Miss Sydney treat you that way. After all, you're a man.

HAL. And you're a woman, Baby, whether you know it or not. You're a real, live woman.

(*A police siren is heard stirring up the distance. Flo, Mrs. Potts and Millie are alarmed.*)

MILLIE. Hey, it's the cops.

MRS. POTTS. I'll know how to take care of them. (*Mrs. Potts hurries off, right, Millie watching. Hal and Madge have not moved. They stand looking into each other's eyes. Then Hal speaks*)

HAL. Do—do you love me?

MADGE (*tears forming in her eyes*). What good is it if I do?

HAL. I'm a poor bastard, Baby. I've gotta claim the things in this life that're mine.

Kiss me good-bye. (*He grabs her and kisses her*) Come with me, Baby. They gimme a room in the basement of the hotel. It's kinda crummy but we could share it till we found something better.

FLO (*outraged*). Madge! Are you out of your senses?

MADGE. I couldn't.

(*The train whistles in the distance.*)

FLO. Young man, you'd better get on that train as fast as you can.

HAL (*to Madge*). When you hear that train pull outa town and know I'm on it, your little heart's gonna be busted, cause you love me, God damn it! You love me, you love me, you love me. (*He stamps one final kiss on her lips, then runs off to catch his train. Madge falls in a heap when he releases her. Flo is quick to console Madge*)

FLO. Get up, girl.

MADGE. Oh, Mom!

FLO. Why did this have to happen to you?

MADGE. I *do* love him! I *do!*

FLO. Hush, girl. Hush. The neighbors are on their porches, watching.

MADGE. I never knew what the feeling was. Why didn't someone tell me?

MILLIE (*peering off at the back*). He made it. He got on the train.

MADGE (*a cry of deep regret*). Now I'll never see him again.

FLO. Madge, believe me, that's for the best.

MADGE. Why? Why?

FLO. At least you didn't marry him.

MADGE (*a wail of anguish*). Oh, Mom, what can you do with the love you feel? Where is there you can take it?

FLO (*beaten and defeated*). I . . . I never found out.

(*Madge goes into the house, crying. Mrs. Potts returns, carrying Hal's boots. She puts them on the porch.*)

MRS. POTTS. The police found these on the river bank.

ALAN (*on Mrs. Potts' steps, rises*). Girls have always liked Hal. Months after he'd left the fraternity, they still called. "Is Hal there?" "Does anyone know where Hal's gone?" Their voices always sounded so forlorn.

FLO. Alan, come to dinner tonight. I'm having sweet-potato pie and all the things you like.

ALAN. I'll be gone, Mrs. Owens.

FLO. Gone?

ALAN. Dad's been wanting me to take him up to Michigan on a fishing trip. I've been stalling him, but now I . . .

FLO. You'll be back before you go to school, won't you?

ALAN. I'll be back Christmas, Mrs. Owens.

FLO. Christmas! Alan, go inside and say good-bye to Madge!

ALAN (*recalling his past love*). Madge is beautiful. It made me feel so proud—just to *look* at her—and tell myself she's mine.

FLO. See her one more time, Alan!

ALAN (*his mind is made up*). No! I'll be home Christmas. I'll run over then and —say hello. (*He runs off*)

FLO (a *cry of loss*). Alan!

MRS. POTTS (*consolingly*). He'll be back, Flo. He'll be back.

MILLIE (*waving good-bye*). Good-bye Alan!

FLO (*getting life started again*). You better get ready for school, Millie.

MILLIE (*going to doorstep, rather sad*). Gee, I almost forgot. (*She goes inside. Flo turns to Mrs. Potts*)

FLO. You—you liked the young man, didn't you, Helen? Admit it.

MRS. POTTS. Yes, I did.

FLO (*belittlingly*). Hmm.

MRS. POTTS. With just Mama and me in the house, I'd got so used to things as they were, everything so prim, occasionally a hairpin on the floor, the geranium in the window, the smell of Mama's medicines . . .

FLO. I'll keep things as they are in *my* house, thank you.

MRS. POTTS. Not when a man is there, Flo. He walked through the door and suddenly everything was different. He clomped through the tiny rooms like he was still in the great outdoors, he talked in a booming voice that shook the ceiling. Everything he did reminded me there was a man in the house, and it seemed good.

FLO (*skeptically*). Did it?

MRS. POTTS. And that reminded *me* . . . I'm a woman, and that seemed good, too. (*Now Millie comes swaggering out the front door, carrying her schoolbooks.*)

MILLIE (*disparagingly*). Madge is in love with that crazy guy. She's in there crying her eyes out.

FLO. Mind your business and go to school.

MILLIE. I'm never gonna fall in love. Not me.

MRS. POTTS. Wait till you're a little older before you say that, Millie-girl.

MILLIE. I'm old enough already. Madge can *stay* in this jerkwater town and marry some ornery guy and raise a lot of dirty kids. When I graduate from college I'm going to New York, and write novels that'll shock people right out of their senses.

MRS. POTTS. You're a talented girl, Millie.

MILLIE (*victoriously*). I'll be so great and famous—I'll never have to fall in love.

A BOY'S VOICE (*from off stage, heckling Millie*). Hey, Goongirl!

MILLIE (*spotting him in the distance*). It's Poopdeck McCullough. He thinks he's so smart.

BOY'S VOICE. Hey Goongirl! Come kiss me. I wanna be sick.

MILLIE (*her anger roused*). If he thinks he can get by with that, he's crazy. (*She finds a stick with which to chastise her offender.*)

FLO. Millie! Millie! You're a grown girl now. (*Millie thinks better of it, drops the stick and starts off*)

MILLIE. See you this evening. (*She goes off*)

FLO (*wanting reassurance*). Alan *will* be back, don't you think so, Helen?

MRS. POTTS. Of course he'll be back, Flo. He'll be back at Christmas time and take her to the dance at the Country Club, and they'll get married and live happily ever after.

FLO. I hope so.

(*Suddenly Madge comes out the front door. She wears a hat and carries a small cardboard suitcase. There is a look of firm decision on her face. She walks straight to the gateway.*)

FLO (*stunned*). Madge!

MADGE. I'm going to Tulsa, Mom.

MRS. POTTS (*to herself*). For heaven sake!

MADGE. Please don't get mad. I'm not doing it to be spiteful.

FLO (*holding her head*). As a live and breathe!

MADGE. I know how you feel, but I don't know what else to do.

FLO (*anxiously*). Now look, Madge, Alan's coming back Christmas. He'll take you to the dance at the Club. I'll make another new dress for you, and . . .

MADGE. I'm going, Mom.

FLO (*frantic*). Madge! Listen to what I've got to say . . .

MADGE. My bus leaves in a few minutes.

FLO. He's no good. He'll never be able to support you. When he does have a job, he'll spend all his money on booze. After a while, there'll be other women.

MADGE. I've thought of all those things.

MRS. POTTS. You don't love someone cause he's perfect, Flo.

FLO. Oh, God!

BOYS' VOICES (*in the distance*). Hey, Madge! Hey, Beautiful! You're the one for me!

MRS. POTTS. Who are those boys?

MADGE. Some of the gang, in their hotrod. (*Kisses Mrs. Potts*) Good-bye, Mrs. Potts. I'll miss you almost as much as Mom.

FLO (*tugging at Madge, trying to take the suitcase from her*). Madge, now listen to me. I can't let you . . .

MADGE. It's no use, Mom. I'm going. Don't worry. I've got ten dollars I was saving for a pair of pumps, and I saw ads in the Tulsa *World*. There's lots of jobs as waitresses.

Tell Millie good-bye for me, Mom. Tell her I never meant it all those times I said I hated her.

FLO (*wailing*). Madge . . . Madge . . .

MADGE. Tell her I've always been very proud to have such a smart sister. (*She runs off now, Flo still tugging at her, then giving up and standing by the gatepost, watching Madge in the distance*)

FLO. Helen, could I stop her?

MRS. POTTS. Could anyone have stopped you, Flo? (*Flo gives Mrs. Potts a look of realization.*)

BOYS' VOICES. Hey Madge! You're the one for me!

FLO (*still watching Madge in the distance*). She's so young. There are so many things I meant to tell her, and never got around to it.

MRS. POTTS. Let her learn them for herself, Flo.

MRS. POTTS' MOTHER. Helen! Helen!

MRS. POTTS. Be patient, Mama. (*Starts up the stairs to her back porch. Flo still stands in the gateway, watching in the distance*)

CURTAIN

# 1953-54

There was never much doubt that *The Teahouse of the August Moon* would win the Circle award rather easily at the meeting on April 13, 1954. The Pulitzer prize came three weeks later.

This play by John Patrick, a writer of increasing stature during the past decade even if his box-office success left considerable to be desired, was one of the theatre's most delightful works in years. It was based on the novel by Vern Sneider dealing with the American occupation work on the island of Okinawa, with sly and wry comments on the attempt to reconcile democracy with colonial administration.

The Circle gave Patrick's play fourteen votes. Four went to *The Caine Mutiny Court Martial* by Herman Wouk, two to *Tea and Sympathy* by Robert Anderson, and one each to *The Girl on the Via Flaminia* by Alfred Hayes and *The Ladies of the Corridor* by Dorothy Parker and Arnaud d'Usseau.

Jean Giraudoux's *Ondine*, in an adaptation by Maurice Valency, won the foreign citation with sixteen votes. T. S. Eliot's *The Confidential Clerk* received five votes.

The Circle honored a most unusual musical, *The Golden Apple*, which had libretto and lyrics by John Latouche and music by Jerome Moross. Three votes went to the Fields-Schwartz *By the Beautiful Sea* and one each to *John Murray Anderson's Almanac* and a new version of the Bertold Brecht-Kurt Weill *The Threepenny Opera* fashioned by Marc Blitzstein.

The Circle voted down proposals to give special citations to the Phoenix Theatre, a new off Broadway house with uptown standards except for salaries, and to Victor Borge, the pianist-comedian who presented himself in a one-man show that was to accomplish the incredible feat of spanning at least two seasons.

The off-Broadway influence was the outstanding feature of the season. Since World War II there had been an increasing number of such operations, mainly centered in Greenwich Village. While a majority of them were and still are on a semi-professional basis, a few began to stand out and demand the respectful attention of the first-string critics.

*The Golden Apple*, for example, was the last of four productions of the first season at the Phoenix. Although it was to move to Broadway shortly afterward, at the time the Circle voted it was still downtown. Before the vote on a musical was taken, the members agreed that there was nothing in the rules to prevent them from considering an off-Broadway production for an award; a "New York production" is the requirement.

*The Threepenny Opera* was presented in the small Theatre de Lys in Greenwich Village, but it also was done with first-class professionals.

Similarly *The Girl on the Via Flaminia* originated in the highly regarded Circle in the Square in the Village, but it had been moved to Broadway by the time the critics voted.

Earlier in the season, a somewhat imperfect but strong and provocative play by Calder Willingham, *End as a Man*, a better drama than most of the Broadway output, opened at the de Lys and then was moved uptown. It served to bring to Broadway for the first time a very young and very forceful and versatile actor named Ben Gazzara.

*Teahouse* began its third Broadway year on October 15, 1955; *Ondine* was performed 156 times; *The Golden Apple* had 173 performances.

# The Teahouse of the
# August Moon

## By JOHN PATRICK

### Adapted from the novel by Vern Sneider

Presented by Maurice Evans, in association with George Schaefer, at the Martin Beck Theatre, New York City, October 15, 1953, with the following cast:

| | |
|---|---|
| SAKINI | David Wayne |
| SERGEANT GREGOVICH | Harry Jackson |
| COL. WAINWRIGHT PURDY III | Paul Ford |
| CAPTAIN FISBY | John Forsythe |
| OLD WOMAN | Naoe Kondo |
| OLD WOMAN'S DAUGHTER | Mara Kim |
| THE DAUGHTER'S CHILDREN | Moy Moy Thom, Joyce Chen, Kenneth Wong |
| LADY ASTOR | Saki |
| ANCIENT MAN | Kame Ishikawa |
| MR. HOKAIDA | Chuck Morgan |
| MR. OMURA | Kuraji Seida |
| MR. SUMATA | Kaie Deei |
| MR. SUMATA'S FATHER | Kikuo Hiromura |
| MR. SEIKO | Haim Winant |
| MISS HIGA JIGA | Shizu Moriya |
| MR. KEORA | Yuki Shimoda |
| MR. OSHIRA | William Hansen |
| VILLAGERS | Jerry Fujikawa, Frank Ogawa, Richard Akagi, Lawrence Kim, Norman Chi |
| LADIES' LEAGUE FOR DEMOCRATIC ACTION | Vivian Thom, Naoe Kondo, Mary Ann Reeve, Mara Kim |
| LOTUS BLOSSOM | Mariko Niki |
| CAPTAIN MCLEAN | Larry Gates |

## SCENE

Act I—Scene 1—Okinawa. Colonel Purdy's office, GHQ. Scene 2—Outside Captain Fisby's quarters, GHQ. Scene 3—Tobiki Village.

Act II—Scene 1—Tobiki Village. Scene 2—Captain Fisby's office, Tobiki. Scene 3—The same. Scene 4—Tobiki Village.

Act III—Scene 1—The Teahouse of the August Moon. Scene 2—Captain Fisby's office, Tobiki. Scene 3—The Teahouse of the August Moon.

Library of Congress Catalogue Card Number: 54-10486

## ACT ONE

### Scene I

*Directly behind the house curtain is a second curtain consisting of four panels of split bamboo. Each of these sections can be raised and lowered individually.*

At rise: *As the house lights dim, the Oriental strains from a stringed instrument can be heard playing softly in the background. A pool of light picks up Sakini standing framed against the bamboo backing. He wears a pair of tattered shorts and a native shirt. His shoes, the gift of a G.I., are several sizes too large. His socks are also too large and hang in wrinkles over his ankles. He is an Okinawan who might be any age between thirty and sixty. In repose his face betrays age, but the illusion is shattered quickly by his smile of childlike candor.*

*With hands together in prayer-like supplication, he walks down to the footlights and bows to the audience center in solemn ritual. Then he bows from the waist—to the left and to the right.*

*Straightening up, he examines the audience seated before him with open curiosity. The music ceases. As it ceases, Sakini begins to work his jaws vigorously.*

———

sakini. Tootie-fruitie. (*He takes the gum from his mouth and, wrapping it carefully in a piece of paper, puts it in a matchbox and restores it to a pocket in his shirt*) Most generous gift of American sergeant. (*He resumes his original posture of dignity*)
Lovely ladies, kind gentlemen:
Please to introduce myself.
Sakini by name.
Interpreter by profession.
Education by ancient dictionary.
Okinawan by whim of gods.
History of Okinawa reveal distinguished record of conquerors.
We have honor to be subjugated in fourteenth century by Chinese pirates.
In sixteenth century by English missionaries.
In eighteenth century by Japanese war lords.
And in twentieth century by American Marines.
Okinawa very fortunate.

Culture brought to us. . . . Not have to leave home for it.
Learn many things.
Most important that rest of world not like Okinawa.
World filled with delightful variation.
Illustration.
In Okinawa . . . no locks on doors.
Bad manners not to trust neighbors.
In America . . . lock and key big industry.
Conclusion?
Bad manners good business.
In Okinawa . . . wash self in public bath with nude lady quite proper.
Picture of nude lady in private home . . . quite improper.
In America . . . statue of nude lady in park win prize.
But nude lady in flesh in park win penalty.
Conclusion?
Pornography question of geography.
But Okinawans most eager to be educated by conquerors.
Deep desire to improve friction.
Not easy to learn.
Sometimes painful.
But pain makes man think.
Thought makes man wise.
Wisdom makes life endurable.
So . . . (*He crosses back to the left of the first of the panels*)
We tell little story to demonstrate splendid example of benevolent assimilation of democracy by Okinawa.

(*He claps his hands, signaling the stagehand to raise the first of the four panels. Flush against the curtain is revealed a sign nailed onto a denuded palm stump. It points toward the other side of the stage and reads:* Col. Wainwright Purdy iii.)
Boss by name of Colonel Purdy—Three.
Number three after name indicate he is a son of a son of a son.

(*He steps to the next panel and claps again. The screen rolls up revealing a laundry line tied to a second denuded stump. As these panels are raised the background is revealed in sections. It includes a jeep parked against a pile of empty gasoline drums, trees ripped of foliage by recent gunfire—all creating an impression of general destruction. There are several articles of wearing apparel hanging on the laundry line, foremost of which is a pair of khaki pants size forty.*)

Colonel Purdy, Three, displays splendid example of cleanliness for native population to follow. But native population cannot follow. Native not *have* two pairs of pants.

(*He then claps for the next screen to rise, revealing more of the laundry. To the extreme right is seen the outside of Colonel Purdy's Quonset office. Nailed on the post holding the other end of the line is a sign reading:* OFFICERS' LAUNDRY ONLY.)

Colonel Purdy put up many signs. This exceedingly civilized. Make it very easy for uncivilized to know what *not* to do. Here laundry of officer not to fraternize with laundry of enlisted man.

(*Sakini now signals for the last panel to be raised, revealing the inside of the hut. Colonel Purdy's vacant desk is beside the door. A sign denotes his proprietorship. Another sign admonishes the visitor to* THINK! *The office is small and sparse. A bulletin board for "Daily Orders" hangs on the upstage wall. Against this wall is the desk of Sergeant Gregovich. Behind a sign denoting his rating sits the Sergeant. His posture is frozen—as if awaiting a signal to come to life. Sakini crosses down center to explain to his audience.*)

This gentleman honorable Sergeant Gregovich—assistant to Colonel Purdy. Not son of a son of a son. (*He turns toward the Sergeant*) Play has begun, Sergeant. (*Gregovich now comes to life. He begins to chew his gum vigorously and to look about the office. He rises and crosses down to Colonel Purdys' desk. He gets down on his hands and knees in front of the desk and reaches under it*) Oh, you know what he is doing? Explanation. Colonel Purdy great student of history. Every month wife of Colonel Purdy send him magazine called *Adventure Magazine.* Cover has picture of pirate with black patch over eye. Everybody try to steal magazine. Colonel hide under desk so he can read first. (*Gregovich rises triumphantly with the magazine*) But Sergeant always find. Smart mouse. (*Gregovich returns to his desk and buries himself behind the pages of the magazine. At this point Colonel Purdy himself enters from the left. As his laundry has indicated, he is a man of* proportions. *The worries of the world in general and the Army of Occupation in particular weigh heavily on his shoulders. He stops to glance at the nearest official sign. He takes out a small notebook to make an entry. Sakini's presence is not recognized until indicated*) This gentleman exalted boss—Colonel Purdy, Three. Subject of sovereign American city of Pottawattamie, Michigan. (*Colonel Purdy hiccups and taps his chest*) Also subject to indignity of indigestion. Colonel Purdy explain this by saying—

PURDY (*clears his throat and says to himself*). An occupational disorder of the Army of Occupation. (*He taps his chest again and puts the notebook away*)

SAKINI. Colonel Purdy very wise man. Always hit nail on head.

Every morning, look at sky—(*Colonel Purdy puts his hands on his hips and glances skyward*) And make prophecy.

PURDY. It's not going to rain today.

SAKINI. And you know what? Not rain. Of course, not rain here this time of year in whole history of Okinawa. But Colonel not make mistake. (*Colonel Purdy goes down the laundry line and stops to button the top of a pair of shorts*) Colonel Purdy gentleman of propriety. (*Purdy goes back to count articles of clothing*) And precision. Always count laundry.

PURDY (*counts aloud*). Un—deux—trois.

SAKINI. Explanation. Army teach Colonel French for invasion of Europe. Then send to Okinawa instead.

PURDY. . . . quatre—cinq—six—sept. (*He beams with satisfaction*)

SAKINI. Very good. Colonel count in French and not notice one pair shorts missing in Okinawa.

PURDY (*his expression quickly changes*). What? (*He goes down the line and counts again in English*) One, two, three, four, five, six, seven! (*He inhales deeply for an explosion*)

SAKINI (*rushes down to the footlights*). Oh—ladies please close ears unless want to hear unladylike oath. (*He puts his hands over his own ears*)

PURDY (*explodes*). Damitohell! Damitohell! Damitohell!

SAKINI. Now Colonel yell loud for Sakini. But Sakini hide. Pretend to be asleep. (*He promptly curls up on the ground beside the office, with his back to the Colonel*)

PURDY. Sakini! (*Sakini snores. Purdy strides over to tower above him*) Sakini!

SAKINI (*rises quickly*). Oh—oh. Good morning, boss. You sure surprise me.

PURDY. *Where* is the boy that does my laundry!

SAKINI. Bring laundry back and go home to sleep, boss.

PURDY. I want you to find out why my laundry comes back every week with one piece missing!

SAKINI. Gets lost, boss.

PURDY. I *know* it gets lost. What I want to find out is *how* it gets lost.

SAKINI. Very simple. Boy takes laundry to top of mountain stream and throws in water. Then runs down hill fast as dickens to catch laundry at bottom. Sometimes not run fast enough.

PURDY. (*heaves a martyr's sigh*) No wonder you people were subjugated by the Japanese. If you're not sleeping you're running away from work. Where is your "get-up-and-go"?

SAKINI. Guess "get-up-and-go" went. (*Sakini starts to sit on the ground*)

PURDY. Well, get up and go over to the mess and see if Captain Fisby has arrived. If he has, tell him to report to me at once. Hurry! (*As Sakini starts across the stage Purdy looks with annoyance at the G.I. socks that hang down over Sakini's ankles*) Sakini!

SAKINI (*stops*). Yes, boss?

PURDY. You're a civilian employee in the pay of the United States Army. And should dress accordingly. *Pull Your Socks Up!*

SAKINI. Yes, boss. (*He leans over and pulls up his socks—not a great improvement*) Anything else, boss?

PURDY. That will be all. (*Sakini ambles across the stage so slowly that the Colonel explodes in exasperation*) Is that as *fast* as you can walk!

SAKINI. Oh no, boss. But if walk any faster—socks fall down.

(*As Sakini exits, Colonel Purdy closes his eyes and counts to ten in vehement French. Purdy remains arrested in this position. Sakini re-enters downstage. He signals the closing of the panels left, shutting out the Colonel*)

SAKINI. Introduction now over. Kindly direct attention to office. (*He leans out toward the footlights and calls across stage*) Oh, Honorable Sergeant—ready now to continue.

(*Sergeant Gregovich again comes to life. He glances out the office door and quickly hides the Adventure Magazine. He stands at attention as Colonel Purdy enters. Sakini exits into the wings.*)

GREGOVICH. Good morning, sir.

PURDY. At ease. (*Colonel Purdy sits down behind his desk and begins searching through the papers on it*) I'm thinking of getting rid of that interpreter. He doesn't set a good example.

GREGOVICH. We've got to have someone around that speaks the language, sir.

PURDY. You're quite right, Sergeant. You're quite right. It isn't often I make a mistake, but when I do—

GREGOVICH. It's a beaut?

PURDY (*stiffly*). I wasn't going to say that. I was going to say—I admit it.

GREGOVICH. Sorry, sir.

PURDY. We've got a new officer reporting this morning. He's been transferred to us from "Psychological Warfare." (*Benevolently*) I don't suppose you happen to know who *they* are?

GREGOVICH. Aren't they something at the rear of the Rear Echelon?

PURDY. They're just the cream of the Army's geniuses. They're just the brains behind the fighting heart. Every man jack of them has a mind like a steel trap. And we are lucky to be getting one of their officers.

GREGOVICH. I'll watch my step, sir.

PURDY. While we're waiting for Captain Fisby, I want you to make a note of some new signs I want painted.

GREGOVICH (*takes up a pad*). The painter hasn't finished the ones you ordered yesterday, sir.

PURDY. There's only one answer to that. Put on another sign painter. Now. I noticed the men were dancing with each other in the canteen the other night.

GREGOVICH. Yes, sir. (*He writes on his pad*) "No dancing allowed."

PURDY (*annoyed*). I didn't say that, Gregovich! I don't object to the men dancing. I want them to enjoy themselves.

But it doesn't set a good example for the natives to see noncoms dancing with enlisted men. So have a sign posted saying, "Sergeants Are Forbidden to Dance with Privates."

GREGOVICH. Yes, sir.

PURDY. Have another sign put up beside that clear pool of water just below the falls—"For Officers Only."

GREGOVICH. Where will the men bathe, sir?

PURDY. There is another pool just below it they can use.

GREGOVICH. If you'll pardon me, sir— they're not going to like that. They'll be bathing in water the officers have already bathed in.

PURDY. That's a valid objection, Gregovich. We don't wany to do anything unreasonable. (*He concentrates for a moment*) How far is the second pool below the first?

GREGOVICH. About three hundred yards.

PURDY (*satisfied*). Then it's quite all right. Water purifies itself every two hundred feet.

GREGOVICH. Do you think that will satisfy the men, sir?

PURDY. I don't see why it shouldn't. It satisfies science. Well, you might as well take those memos to the sign painter now.

GREGOVICH. Yes, sir. (*He goes out. As soon as he is gone, Colonel Purdy moves around to the front of his desk and feels under it for his* Adventure Magazine. *When he fails to find it, he kneels down on all fours to peer under the desk. Sakini enters and looks around. He steps over and taps the nearest part of Colonel Purdy—his ample rear end.*)

SAKINI. Sakini here, boss.

PURDY (*glances around indignantly*). Don't *ever* put your finger on an officer!

SAKINI. Not right, boss?

PURDY. No! If you want to announce your presence—knock! (*He peers under the desk again*) Can't you natives learn anything about custom? (*Sakini stands unhappily a moment, then leans forward and knocks gently on the Colonel. Purdy rises in wrath*) What do you think you're doing?

SAKINI. Not know, boss. Do what you ask.

PURDY (*moves behind his desk*). Every-thing in this Godforsaken country conspires to annoy me. (*He turns to Sakini*) Well, where is Captain Fisby?

SAKINI (*points out the door*). He come now. I run ahead. (*He points to his ankles*) Socks fall down. (*He then steps back to allow Captain Fisby to enter. Captain Fisby is in his late twenties, nice-looking and rather on the earnest side. He is nervous and eager to make a good impression. He salutes smartly*)

CAPTAIN FISBY. Captain Fisby reporting, sir.

PURDY (*returns the salute*). Welcome to Team 147, Captain. (*He puts out his hand*)

FISBY (*shakes hands*). Thank you, sir.

PURDY. I can't tell you how glad I am to have you, Captain. Frankly, we're so desperate for officer personnel I'd be glad to see you even if you had two heads. (*Sakini breaks into gales of laughter. Purdy turns to him icily.*) That will be all, Sakini. You can wait outside.

SAKINI (*bows*). I sit by door. Not sleep! (*He exits*)

PURDY. Sit down, Captain, sit down. (*Fisby sits facing Purdy*) Have you unpacked?

FISBY (*proudly*). Yes *sir!* I got in last night and unpacked at once.

PURDY. Well, that's too bad, because you'll have to pack again. I'm sending you to Tobiki at once. We need a man of your caliber up there right away. (*He laughs with forced heartiness*)

FISBY (*forces a laugh in return*). Thank you.

PURDY. I'm informed, Captain, that you requested this transfer from "Psychological Warfare" to *my* outfit. May I say that I am honored.

FISBY. Well—in all fairness, sir—I think I should tell you . . . the information is only partly true.

PURDY (*pauses*). You *didn't* request this transfer to me?

FISBY. I was *requested* to request it, sir.

PURDY. Oh. (*He blinks to aid his digestion of this information*) May I ask why?

FISBY. Well, my propaganda to undermine enemy morale always seemed to undermine the staff's morale instead, sir.

PURDY. *How* did you get into "Psychological Warfare" in the *first* place?

FISBY. I had been requested to request a transfer.

PURDY. From what?

FISBY. Paymaster General's office.

PURDY. What was your duty there?

FISBY. I was in charge of the payroll computation machine until—until— (*he flounders unhappily*)

PURDY. Until *what*?

FISBY. Well, sir, machines have always been my mortal enemies. I don't think they're inanimate at all. I think they're full of malice and ill will. They—

PURDY. I *asked* you what happened, Captain.

FISBY. Well, this computation machine made a mistake of a quarter of a million dollars on the payroll. Unfortunately, the men were paid *before* the mistake was discovered.

PURDY. What did they do to you?

FISBY. For a while I was given a job licking envelopes.

PURDY. Then you asked for a transfer?

FISBY. No, sir, I developed an allergy to glue.

PURDY. How many outfits in this man's army have you been in, Captain?

FISBY. How many are there, sir?

PURDY. Never mind. I admit disappointment but not defeat. I'd thought you were given to me in recognition of my work here. Frankly, I expect to be made a general soon, and I want that star for my wife's crown. Naturally, that's very hush-hush.

FISBY (*nods*). Naturally. Maybe I just wasn't cut out to be a soldier.

PURDY. Captain, none of us was cut out to be a soldier. But we do the job. We adjust. We adapt. We roll with the punch and bring victory home in our teeth. Do you know what *I* was before the war?

FISBY (*hesitates unhappily*). A football coach?

PURDY. I was the Purdy Paper Box Company of Pottawattamie. What did I know about foreigners? But my job is to teach these natives the meaning of democracy, and they're going to learn democracy if I have to shoot every one of them.

FISBY. I'm sure your wife wouldn't want her star that way, sir.

PURDY. What did you do before the war?

FISBY. I was an associate professor at Muncie.

PURDY. What did you teach?

FISBY. The humanities.

PURDY. Captain, you are finally getting a job you're qualified by training to handle—teaching these natives how to act human.

FISBY. The humanities isn't quite that, sir.

PURDY. If you can teach one thing you can teach another. Your job at Tobiki will be to teach the natives democracy and make them self-supporting. Establish some sort of industry up there.

FISBY. Is there a general plan?

PURDY. There is a specific plan. (*He extends a document the size of a telephone book*) Washington has drawn up full instructions pertaining to the welfare and recovery of these native villages. *This* is Plan B. Consider it your *Bible*, Captain.

FISBY. I'll study it carefully, sir. There might be some questions I'd like to ask you.

PURDY (*points to Plan B*). Washington has anticipated all your questions.

FISBY. But I was thinking—

PURDY. You don't even have to think, Captain. This document relieves you of that responsibility.

FISBY. But in dealing with the natives, sir—

PURDY (*interrupts*). It's all covered in Section Four: "Orienting the Oriental." How is your Luchuan?

FISBY. I don't know, sir. What is it?

PURDY. It's the native dialect. Well, I can see you'll need an interpreter. (*His eyes light up and he slaps his desk*) I have just the man for you! (*He turns and calls out the door*) Sakini!

FISBY. I could study the dialect, sir.

PURDY. No need. We won the war. I'll give you my own interpreter.

FISBY. Oh, I wouldn't want to deprive you of—

PURDY. I insist. (*Sakini enters. He bows—and then remembers. He leans forward and politely knocks on the desk.*)

SAKINI. Sakini present. Socks up. Not sleeping.

PURDY. Sakini, this is Captain Fisby.

FISBY. Hello, Sakini.

SAKINI (*bows, then turns to Purdy*). We meet already. (*He smiles in comradeship*) You forget, boss?

PURDY (*covers his face, counts to ten, then looks up*). I am assigning you to Captain Fisby. He's going to take charge of a village at the top of Okinawa—a village called Tobiki.

SAKINI. Oh! Tobiki very nice place, boss. But not at top of Okinawa. At bottom.

PURDY. Don't tell me where the villages under my command are located. I happen to have looked at the map.

SAKINI. So sorry, boss. But I happen to get born in Tobiki. Is at bottom.

PURDY (*whips a map out of his desk*). Then it's time you learned where you were born. I also happen to give a course in map reading.

SAKINI (*looks at map*). So sorry, boss. But map upside down.

FISBY (*looks at map*). He's right.

PURDY (*looks at map—turns it around*). Why in hell doesn't the Army learn how to draw a map properly! (*Turns to Sakini*) That will be all, Sakini. Find Sergeant Gregovich and have him assign a jeep to Captain Fisby. Then load supplies and the captain's gear in the jeep. You will be leaving at once. I'll send rice rations later.

SAKINI (*takes the Colonel's hand and pumps it*). Oh, thank you, boss. You very kind to send me home. I mention you in prayer to gods. (*He turns to Fisby*) I wait at jeep for you, Captain. (*He starts to run, then slows down quickly*) Very happy, sir. Socks up. (*He goes out. Purdy turns wearily to Fisby*)

PURDY. I sometimes think we Occupation Teams have it tougher than combat troops. (*He quickly holds up a protesting hand*) Granted they have it rough for a while. But we have the killing daily grind, with no glory in it.

FISBY. Yes, sir, I know what you mean. Life itself is a battlefield with its own obscure heroes.

PURDY (*looks at Fisby wtih surprise*). I consider that poetry, Captain.

FISBY. I'm afraid it's just prose, sir. And it isn't mine, it's Victor Hugo's.

PURDY (*corrected*). Oh, yes. Victor Hugo! How I loved *Tale of Two Cities*.

FISBY. Isn't that Dickens, sir?

PURDY. I guess I was thinking of the movie. Well! To get back to Tobiki. Your first job when you get there will be to establish a municipal government and build a school.

FISBY. A school?

PURDY. It's all in Plan B. I'll see that cement and lumber are sent down to you. Plan B calls for the schoolhouse to be pentagon-shaped.

FISBY. If you say so, sir.

PURDY. When the school is built, you will organize a Ladies' League for Democratic Action. You will deliver a series of lectures on democracy as outlined in the outline. Captain, this is a chance for you to make a name for yourself.

FISBY. I will, sir. You see, I feel that I've personally delayed victory at least a year, and I have to vindicate myself.

PURDY. That's the kind of talk I like to hear from my officers. Well, I won't detain you then. (*He rises*) My only order to you is: Put that village on the map.

FISBY. Yes, sir.

PURDY. Send me a bimonthly Progress Report—in triplicate.

FISBY. Yes, sir.

PURDY. Don't duplicate your work.

FISBY. No, sir.

PURDY. Fire those natives wtih the Spirit of Occupation.

FISBY. Yes, sir.

PURDY. And remember—that the eyes of Washington are on our Occupation Teams. And the eyes of the world are on Washington.

FISBY. I'll keep the eyes in mind, sir.

PURDY. Good-bye, Captain. (*Fisby salutes smartly and goes out. Purdy stands for a moment, moved by the vastness of the canvas. Then he turns to his desk*) Where the hell is my *Adventure Magazine!*

THE SCENE BLACKS OUT QUICKLY

SCENE II

SCENE: *Outside Captain Fisby's quarters.*
TIME: *Few minutes later.*
AT RISE: *Captain Fisby and Sakini enter from left and cross before the panels, all of which are now down.*

———

SAKINI. Everything all ready, boss. We go to Tobiki now?

FISBY. I guess so. Well, wish me luck, Sakini. I'm going out to spread the gospel of Plan B.

SAKINI. You already lucky, boss. You got me.

FISBY (*smiles*). Thanks . . . do you know the road?

SAKINI. No road, boss—just path for wagon cart and goat.

FISBY. Will a jeep make it?

SAKINI. We find out, boss.

FISBY. Naturally. How long will it take us?

SAKINI. Oh—not know until we arrive, boss.

FISBY. Naturally. Well, we might as well get started. I'll drive and you give directions.

SAKINI. Oh, very happy to go home.

FISBY. Where is the jeep?

SAKINI. Right here, boss. (*He turns and claps his hands. The panels go up. The laundry line has been removed and the jeep pulled down center. The jeep is piled with Fisby's belongings. Perched high on the top of this pyramid sits a very old and very wrinkled native woman. Sakini pays no attention to her as he goes around the jeep test-kicking the tires. And the old woman sits disinterested and aloof from what goes on below her*)

FISBY. Hey, wait a minute! What's she doing up there? (*He points to her. The old woman sits with hands folded serenely, looking straight ahead*)

SAKINI. She nice old lady hear we go to Tobiki village. She think she go along to visit grandson.

FISBY. Oh, she does. Well, you explain that I'm very sorry but she'll have to take a bus.

SAKINI. No buses to Tobiki. People very poor—can only travel on generosity.

FISBY. I'm sorry, but it's against regulations.

SAKINI. She not fall off, boss. She tied on.

FISBY. Well, untie her and get her down. She'll just have to find some other way to visit her grandson.

SAKINI. Her grandson mayor of Tobiki village. You make him lose face if you kick old grandmother off jeep.

FISBY. She's the mayor's grandmother?

SAKINI. Oh yes, boss.

FISBY. Well, since she's already tied on, I guess we can take her. (*He looks at the bundles*) Are all those *mine*?

SAKINI. Oh, no. Most of bundles belong to old lady. She think she visit three or four months so she bring own bed and cooking pots.

FISBY. Well, tell her to yell out if she sees any low branches coming. (*He starts to get in*) Let's get started.

SAKINI. Oh, can't go yet, boss.

FISBY. Why not?

SAKINI. Old lady's daughter not here.

FISBY (*glances at watch*). We can't wait for a lot of good-byes, Sakini!

SAKINI (*looking behind Fisby*). Oh, she come now—right on dot you bet.

(*Captain Fisby turns to witness a squat young native woman come on pushing a wheelbarrow loaded with bundles. She stops long enough to bow low to Fisby—then begins to tie bundles onto the jeep.*)

FISBY. Sakini, can't the old lady leave some of that stuff behind?

SAKINI. Not her things, boss. Belong to daughter.

FISBY. Wait a minute. Is the daughter planning on going with us, too?

SAKINI. Old lady very old. Who take care of her on trip?

FISBY. Well, I—(*The daughter takes the wheelbarrow and hurries off*) Hey—you come back! Sakini—tell her to come back. We can't carry any more bundles.

SAKINI (*calmly*). Oh, she not go to get bundles, boss. She go to get children.

FISBY. Come here, Sakini. Now look—this sort of thing is always happening to me and I have to put a stop to it some place. This time I'm determined to succeed. It's not that I don't *want* to take them. But you can see for yourself, *there's no room left for kids!*

SAKINI. But daughter not go without children and old lady not go without daughter. And if old lady not go, mayor of Tobiki be mad at you. (*Turns to see the daughter hurry back with three children in tow. They all bow politely to Fisby. Their mother then piles them on the hood of the jeep*)

FISBY. For Pete's sake, Sakini, how does she expect me to see how to drive!

SAKINI. Old lady got very good eyesight. She sit on top and tell us when to turn.

(*At this point one of the children climbs off the hood and points off stage.*)

CHILD. A! Wasureta!

DAUGHTER. Wasureta? Nanisa?

CHILD. Fija dayo. (*The child dashes off-stage*)

FISBY. Now, where's *he* going?

SAKINI (*to daughter*). Doshtano?

DAUGHTER. Fija turete kurendes!

SAKINI (*to Fisby*). He go to get goat.

FISBY. A goat!

SAKINI. Can't go and leave poor goat behind.

DAUGHTER (*waves gaily to the old woman on top of the jeep*). Okasan daijobu! (*She climbs the pyramid of bundles to settle beside her*)

NOTE: The Luchuan dialect used throughout the play is merely a phonetic approximation.

FISBY. Well, right here is where we start seeing who's going to lose face. No goat is going to travel on this jeep.

SAKINI. You not like goats, boss?

FISBY. It has nothing to do with whether I like goats or not. I'm positive the Colonel wouldn't like it.

SAKINI. But children not go without goat, mother not go without children, old lady not go without daughter—

FISBY (*repeats with Sakini*). —and if old lady not go the mayor of Tobiki be mad at you! (*Fisby sees the goat being led on by the small boy*) Oh, no!

SAKINI. Everybody here, boss. Goat not got children. Goat unmarried lady goat.

FISBY. All right, all right. Put it on the hood with the kids. (*The goat is placed on the hood and held by the children*) We've got to get started or we'll never get off the ground.

SAKINI. All ready to go, boss. You get in now. Nobody else going.

(*But before Fisby can climb in an old man comes hurrying in and, without looking to the right or left, climbs on the back of the jeep and settles down.*)

FISBY. Now who the hell is he?

SAKINI (*looks at old man*). Now who the hell is he? (*Back to Fisby*) Not know, boss, never see before.

FISBY. Is he a relation of theirs?

SAKINI (*to the woman on top of the jeep*). Kore dare?

MOTHER. Mitakoto nai hito desu.

SAKINI. She say she never see him before, boss.

FISBY. Well, ask him what he's doing here!

SAKINI (*goes to the old man*). Ojisan, doshtano?

OLD MAN. Washimo notte ikuyo.

SAKINI. He say he see people going somewhere on trip and he think maybe he like to go somewhere, too.

FISBY. Tell him to get off and get off quick!

SAKINI. Dame dayo, ojisan, orina, orina!

OLD MAN (*angrily*). Fija noserunnera washimo noruyo!

SAKINI. He say why not take him? You take goat. He say maybe you think he not as good as goat?

FISBY. Look, Sakini, explain to him that the eyes of the world are on Washington and the eyes of Washington are on me. I can't be responsible for—

(*But before this can be translated, Colonel Purdy stalks on and comes to an abrupt halt.*)

PURDY. Captain Fisby?

FISBY. Yes, sir.

PURDY. What in the name of Occupation do you think you're doing!

FISBY. It's hard to explain, sir. . . . I, ah . . . ah . . .

(*As he founders, the old lady on top of the bundles comes to life. She looks down and screams shrilly.*)

OLD LADY. Yakamashii oyajijana, hayo *iko, iko!*

PURDY. What is *she* saying?

SAKINI. She say . . . tell fat old man to shut up so we can get started!

(*As Colonel Purdy's jaw drops, the panels drop also.*)

BLACKOUT

## SCENE III

SCENE: *Tobiki village.*

TIME: *Ten days later.*

AT RISE: *All the bamboo panels are down. Sakini walks in front of them to the center of the stage from the wings.*

———

SAKINI (*bows*). Distance from Headquarters to Tobiki village by map . . . two inches.

By horse . . . three days.

By foot . . . four days.

By jeep . . . ten days.

Explanation:

Captain want to go to Tobiki.

Children want to go ocean. Never see ocean.

We see ocean.

Captain want to go to Tobiki.

Old lady's daughter want to visit Awasi.

We go Awasi.

Old lady make second mistake.

Captain demand we go Tobiki.

Ancient man have cousin in Yatoda.

We go Yatoda.

Damn fool old lady not know one road from another.

Now we arrive Tobiki.

Tobiki welcome rice and democracy. (*He claps his hands for the panels to be raised, then walks into the scene. The destitute village of Tobiki is revealed with its sagging huts and its ragged villagers grouped in the square just outside of Captain Fisby's office. This is a small bamboo structure with a thatched roof. It has a makeshift desk and field telephone. There is a cot crowded against the upper wall. Fisby, his glasses on, sits studying Plan B. He puts the document down, and, taking off his glasses, calls to Sakini*)

FISBY. Sakini!

SAKINI. Right here, boss. Not asleep, boss.

FISBY. Good. According to Plan B, my first job here is to hold a public meeting.

SAKINI. Public waiting in public square . . . eager to meet new boss, boss.

FISBY. Good. Now, Plan B calls for a lecture on the ABC's of democracy. (*He turns to Sakini*) Make sure they understand that I come as a friend of the people. That we intend to lift the yoke of oppression from their shoulders.

SAKINI. Oh, they like that, boss. This their favorite speech.

FISBY. What do you mean, their favorite speech?

SAKINI. Oh, Japanese say same things when they come, boss. Then take everything.

FISBY. Well, we're not here to *take* anything.

SAKINI. They got nothing left to take away, boss.

FISBY (*annoyed*). Well, if they *did* have, we wouldn't take it. We're here to *give* them something.

SAKINI. Oh, not get angry, boss. We not mind. After eight centuries we get used to it. When friends come now, we hide things quick as the dickens.

FISBY (*rises, a little upset*). Well, I guess it's up to me to convince them we really are friends. Let's meet the villagers. (*He picks up his papers*) And let them meet Plan B. (*As they step out the door to the office, the villagers rise and bow respectfully in unison. Fisby surveys them*)

SAKINI (*introducing Fisby*). Amerikano Taisho-san, Captain Fisby.

FISBY (*bows in return*). Well, we might as well get started, Sakini. (*He finds a box and stands on it. He glances into Plan B and clears his throat*) Citizens of Tobiki village. I—

SAKINI (*interrupts him*). Sorry, boss. Can't begin lecture yet.

FISBY. Why not?

SAKINI. Not good manners. People bring you gifts. You must accept gifts first.

FISBY. But I'm here to bring gifts from my government to them.

SAKINI. Very rude to make people feel poor, boss.

FISBY. I don't want to make anyone feel poor, but—

SAKINI. You make them lose face if you refuse, boss. They not accept democracy from you.

FISBY. All right. All right, then. Say to them that I'll accept their gifts in the name of the United States Occupation Forces.

SAKINI (*turns to the villagers*). Soreja moratte okuyo!

(*Mr. Hokaida, an enormous villager in tattered peasant clothes, steps forward.*)

MR. HOKAIDA (*bows diffidently and offers his present to Fisby*). Amerika-san, korewo dozo.

SAKINI. This Mr. Hokaida, boss. He give you fine present.

FISBY. Thank you. Thank you very much. (*He takes it and turns to Sakini puzzled*) What is it?

SAKINI. You not know?

FISBY. No.

SAKINI. Oh, where you been all your life, boss?

FISBY. Living without one of these, I guess.

SAKINI. Is very splendid cricket cage, boss.

FISBY. What's it used for?

SAKINI. Keep cricket in.

FISBY. Why?

SAKINI. So Fortune smile on you. Cricket very good luck.

FISBY. But there's no cricket in it.

SAKINI. Bad luck to give cricket. You must catch your own fortune. No one can get it for you.

FISBY (*considers this*). Thank him and tell him I'll keep my eye out for a cricket.

SAKINI. Ya, arigato. (*Mr. Hokadia bows away as an ancient native steps forward and bows*) This Mr. Omura. He bring you gift of chopsticks.

MR. OMURA. Korede mainichi gochiso wo, dozo.

SAKINI. He say: May only food of gods touch your lips.

(*As Fisby bows, Mr. Sumata, a nervous citizen in a torn straw hat, pushes his way toward Sakini.*)

MR. SUMATA. Sugu modotte kuruyo!

SAKINI. Doshtandes?

MR. SUMATA. Ima sugu presento motte kuruyo. (*he turns and runs hurriedly off stage right*)

FISBY. What was that?

SAKINI. That Mr. Sumata. He have present at home for you. He say not go away until he get.

(*A rather handsome young Tobikian, Mr. Seiko, now steps forward and extends a pair of wooden sandals.*)

MR. SEIKO. Dozo korewo chakini.

SAKINI. This Mr. Seiko. He brings you geta.

FISBY. Geta?

SAKINI. Wooden sandals. Very comfortable for tired feet. He say: May you walk in prosperity.

FISBY. Tell him I shall walk in the—the cool—meadow—of—of pleasant memories. Is that all right?

SAKINI. Oh, that's very pretty, boss. (*He turns to Mr. Seiko*) Ya, arigato, Seiko-san.

MR. SEIKO (*beams, bows, and backs away*). Iya, kosi no itari desu.

SAKINI. He say you do him honor. (*Here a chunky, flat-faced, aggressive young woman with heavy glasses pushes forward with her present*) Oh, this Miss Higa Jiga—unmarried lady. She bring you three eggs.

FISBY. Tell her I shall eat them for breakfast. (*He bows to her*)

SAKINI. Captain-san, daisuki desu.

MISS HIGA JIGA. Kame no tamago desu. (*She bows away*)

SAKINI. She say she hope you enjoy turtle eggs.

FISBY (*grins and bows to her*). She'll never know.

SAKINI. You very big success. They sure like you already. (*Another villager steps forward and offers a gift*) This Mr. Keora. He bring you another cricket cage. Minus cricket.

FISBY. Say to him—that my prospects of good fortune are doubled. (*He looks rather pleased with himself*)

SAKINI. Kagowa futatsu de, un wa bai!

MR. KEORA. Hoho! Naka naka shiteki desna! (*He bows away*)

SAKINI. He say you are inspired poet.

FISBY (*modestly*). It's all in getting the hang of it.

SAKINI (*introducing the next citizen, a very old man leaning on a stick*). This old man Mr. Oshira. He bring you fine lacquered cup he make himself.

FISBY. Tell him I'm forever in his debt for such a beautiful gift.

OSHIRA. You are most welcome, Captain.

FISBY (*turns to him in surprise*). You speak English!

SAKINI. Mr. Oshira teach me English when I am little boy in Tobiki.

OSHIRA. In my youth I work in Manila. How is Mr. McKinley?

FISBY (*puzzled for a moment*). Who? Oh—President McKinley. I'm afraid someone shot him.

OSHIRA. I am sad.

FISBY. It was a long time ago.

OSHIRA. Yes, a long time. (*He indicates the cup*) May August moon fill your cup.

FISBY. May I ask, why an August moon?

OSHIRA. All moons good, but August moon little older, little wiser.

FISBY. Did Sakini say you made this cup yourself?

OSHIRA. Oh, yes. I learned from my father before me who learned from his father before him. Is our heritage.

SAKINI. Look, boss, this cup thin as paper,

carved from one block of wood. Then painted many times with red lacquer.

FISBY. And did you paint the gold fish inside?

OSHIRA (*nods*). It is imperfect.

SAKINI. When Mr. Oshira little boy, he work ten years to learn how to paint a gold fish exactly like his papa paint.

FISBY. It's just beautiful! Can you still make things like this?

OSHIRA. One does not forget.

FISBY. Sakini, here's an industry we can start right away. This is a lost art. (*Turns to Oshira*) Is there any way we could mass-produce these?

OSHIRA. Mass-produce?

FISBY. You know—set up machines and turn them out by the gross.

OSHIRA (*shakes his head*). I take pride in making one cup at time, Captain. How can I take pride in work of machine?

FISBY. How many of these could you turn out in a day?

OSHIRA. If I work hard, maybe one or two a week.

FISBY (*disappointed*). Well, it's a start. Make as many as you can. We'll send them up to the American Post Exchange and sell them as fast as you can turn them out.

OSHIRA. I shall do my best. The swiftness of my youth has deserted me, sir. (*He bows and moves back*) But I shall make fewer mistakes.

FISBY (*excitedly*). Sakini, tell Mr. Omura to make up a batch of chopsticks. Have everybody get to work making cricket cages, wooden sandals and—(*Pointing*)—these straw hats. We'll put this village in the souvenir business.

SAKINI. We all make money, boss?

FISBY. If they can turn out enough of these things, I guarantee the recovery of Tobiki village. Tell them.

SAKINI. Kore dondon tskuru yoni . . . (*There is a general exchange of chatter and approval*) They say they make everything fast as the dickens, boss.

FISBY. Good. We're in business. Now ask them if they'd mind postponing the rest of the gifts until later. I'd like to tell them what *we're* planning for *them*.

SAKINI. Sa, sono hanashi shiyo.

CITIZENS. No agerumono naiyo! Hanashi wo kiko.

SAKINI. They say sure. They got no more presents anyhow.

FISBY. Good. First I want to tell them about the school we're going to build for their children. All set to translate?

SAKINI. All set.

FISBY. All right. (*He consults Plan B*). Plan B says the direct approach is most effective. This is it. (*He steps back up on a box and looks forcefully at his listeners. Then he points a dramatic finger at them*) Do you want to be ignorant?

SAKINI (*also points a finger*). Issho bakaja dame daro?

(*The citizens make a noise that sounds like "Hai."*)

FISBY. What did they say?

SAKINI. They say "Yes."

FISBY. What do you mean, "yes"? They *want* to be ignorant?

SAKINI. No, boss. But in Luchuan "yes" means "no." They say "yes," they *not* want to be ignorant.

FISBY. Oh. (*He turns back to his rapt audience and assumes his forensic posture*) Do you want your *children* to be ignorant?

SAKINI. Issho kodomotachi mo bakaja dame daro?

(*The villagers respond quickly with a noise that sounds like "Iie."*)

FISBY. What did they say then?

SAKINI. They say "No."

FISBY. "No" they do, or "No" they don't?

SAKINI. Yes, they not want no ignorant children.

FISBY. Good. (*He turns back to the villagers*) Then this is what my government is planning to do for you. First there will be daily issues of rice for everyone.

SAKINI. Mazu kome no hykyu!

(*The villagers cheer.*)

FISBY. We will build a fine new school here for your children. (*Then recalling Colonel Purdy's dictum*) Pentagon-shaped.

SAKINI. Gakko taterundayo katachi wa— (*He flounders*) Ah—Pentagon.

(*The citizens look at each other, puzzled.*)

MISS HIGA JIGA. Nandesutte?

SAKINI. Pentagon.

MISS HIGA JIGA. Sore wa nandesuka?

SAKINI. They say what is Pentagon? Never hear before.

FISBY. Never heard of the *Pentagon*!

SAKINI. No, boss.

FISBY. Well, they certainly do need a school here. The Pentagon is—is—(*He looks down at their eager faces*) Well, it really means five-sided.

SAKINI. Kabega itsutsusa, ii, ni, san, yon, go. (*Holds up five fingers. There is a burst of laughter from the Citizens*)

MISS HIGA JIGA (*giggling*). Ara, gokakuno kodomo nante arimasenyo.

SAKINI. They say no children in Tobiki got five sides.

FISBY. The *school* will be five-sided—like a building in Washington.

SAKINI (*explains*). Chigauyo, chigauyo, onaji mono arundes yo, Washington ni. (*There is a decided reaction of approval. Sakini turns back to Fisby*) They very impressed.

FISBY (*continuing*). Everyone will learn about democracy.

SAKINI. Mazu minsho shugi bera-bera bera-bera.

MISS HIGA JIGA. Minshu shugi bera-bera bera-bera?

SAKINI. They say: Explain what is democracy. They know what rice is.

FISBY. Oh. (*He scratches his head*) Well, it's a system of self-determination. It's—It's the right to make the wrong choice.

SAKINI. Machigattemo iindayo.
(*They look up blankly, silently.*)

FISBY. I don't think we're getting the point over. Explain that if I don't like the way Uncle Sam treats me, I can write the President himself and tell him so.

SAKINI. Daitoryo ni tegami kaitemo iinosa.
(*The Villagers all laugh heartily.*)

MISS HIGA JIGA. Masaka soonakoto!

SAKINI (*triumphantly*). They say: But do you *send* the letters?

FISBY. Let's get on with the lecture. (*He turns back to the citizens and reads from Plan B*) Tell them hereafter all men will be free and equal. . . .

SAKINI. Subete, jiyuu, to byodo, de ar, de ar.

FISBY (*increases his tempo and volume*). Without discrimination . . .

SAKINI (*taking Fisby's tone*). Sabetsu taigoo haishi de ar.

FISBY. The will of the majority will rule!

SAKINI. Subete minna de kime, de ar!

FISBY (*finishing with a flourish*). And Tobiki village will take its place in the brotherhood of democratic peoples the world over!

SAKINI (*rising to new demagogic heights*). Koshite, Tobiki, jiyuu, Okinawa, byodo sabetsu, taigu—haishi, jiyuu, byodo de ar, de ar. (*A great burst of applause greets Sakini's performance. He turns to Fisby*) We going over big, boss.

FISBY (*agrees with a nod*). Now to get this village organized. Is the mayor here?

SAKINI (*points*). Mr. Omura is mayor, boss. (*Mr. Omura steps forward*) He only one in Tobiki with white coat.

FISBY (*glances at the worn, ragged coat*). It looks to me as if you'll have to get a new coat or a new mayor soon.

SAKINI. Better keep mayor, boss. Impossible to get white coat.

FISBY. Well, since we've got a mayor, we only have to find a Chief of Agriculture and a Chief of Police. That's going to present a problem.

FISBY. No problem, boss. You just look over gifts and see who give you best gift. Then you give him best job.

FISBY. Sakini, that is *not* the democratic way. The people themselves must choose the man best qualified. Tell them they are to elect their own Chief of Agriculture.

SAKINI. Sah! Senkyo desu. Mazu Chief of Agriculture.

WOMEN VILLAGERS (*push Mr. Sieko forward shouting*). Seiko-san, Seiko-san ga ii, Seiko-san!

SAKINI. They say they elect Mr. Seiko. He best qualified for agriculture.

FISBY. He's an experienced farmer?

SAKINI. No, boss. He's artist. He draw lovely picture of golden wheat stalk with pretty green butterfly.

FISBY. Drawing pictures of wheat doesn't make him a wheat expert.

SAKINI. Wheat not grow here anyhow, boss. Only sweet potatoes.

FISBY. All right, all right! If he's their choice.

SEIKO. Ano! Watashimo shiroi koto wo.

SAKINI. He say do he get white coat like the mayor?

FISBY. Tell him I'll get him a helmet that says "Chief of Agriculture" on it.

SAKINI. Yoshi, yoshi, kammuri ageruyo. (*Seiko bows and backs away.*)

FISBY. Next we want to elect a Chief of Police.

SAKINI. Kondowa Chief of Police.

VILLAGERS (*clamor and push the fat Mr. Hokaida forward*). Hokaida-san. Soda, soda. Hokaida-san.

FISBY. What are *his* qualifications for office?

SAKINI. People afraid of him. He champion wrestler.

(*Mr. Hokaida flexes his muscles.*)

FISBY. Well, no one can say this isn't self-determination.

MR. HOKAIDA. Washime ano kammuri wo.

SAKINI. He say do he get helmet too?

FISBY (*nods*). I'll requisition another helmet.

SAKINI. Agemasuyo.

MR. HOKAIDA (*bows smiling*). Ya, doomo.

FISBY. Now for the ladies. We intend to organize a Ladies' League for Democratic Action. We'll want to elect a League President.

SAKINI. Oh, ladies never vote before—they like that. (*He turns to the Ladies*) Kondowa Ladies' League for Democratic Action!

(*This announcement is greeted by excited chatter. The Ladies push Miss Higa Jiga forward.*)

LADIES. Higa-Jiga-san—Higa-Jiga-san!

SAKINI. They say they elect Miss Higa Jiga. They think she make classy president.

MISS HIGA JIGA (*points to her head*). Ano, watashi nimo ano booshio . . .

FISBY (*laughs*). All right, I'll see that she gets a helmet, too. Now ask them if they have any question they'd like to ask *me*.

SAKINI. Sa, nanka kikitai koto ga attara.

OLD WOMAN. Sakini-san, ima nanji kaina?

SAKINI. They say they like to know what time is it?

FISBY (*puzzled*). Time? (*Glances at his watch*) Quarter of five, why?

SAKINI. They say they got to hurry then. They not like to miss sunset. This is time of day they sit in pine grove, sip tea and watch sun go down.

FISBY. All right, thank them and tell them they can go have tea in the pine grove.

SAKINI. Ya, minna kaette mo iiyo.

(*They bow and, chattering happily among themselves, go off right. Fisby gathers up his gifts.*)

FISBY. How do you think we did, Sakini?

SAKINI. They cooperate, boss. Future look very rosy.

FISBY. Where do you think I can find a cricket?

SAKINI. One come along. May have one in house now and not know it.

FISBY. Well, I'll take these things in and get started on my Progress Report. (*He goes into the office hut*)

SAKINI. I take a little snooze then. Public speaking very exhausting.

FISBY (*as he goes inside*). I think I handled it pretty well. (*He sits down at his desk. He examines his gifts and then, putting on his glasses, begins to study Plan B again. After a moment, Mr. Sumata enters from the right. He carries a couple of battered suitcases. He is followed by Lotus Blossom, a petite and lovely geisha girl in traditional costume. When they are about center stage, young Mr. Seiko runs up after the geisha girl. She turns to him*)

SEIKO. Ano, chotto . . .

LOTUS BLOSSOM. Ara! Nani?

SUMATA (*steps in front of Seiko and points an angry finger under his nose*). Dame, dame, atchi ike.

(*Seiko bows head and retreats. Mr. Sumata then turns to Sakini*) Amerika-san doko?

SAKINI (*indicates the office*). Asco.

SUMATA (*indicates geisha girl*). Kore tsurete kitandayo.

SAKINI. Oh? Do-sunno?

SUMATA. Kore Taisho-san ni agetainja. (*He bows and goes off quickly, almost running. The Geisha remains with Sakini. Sakini smiles and steps inside the office. He stands behind Fisby.*)

SAKINI. You busy, boss?

FISBY (*without turning around to him*). Yes, but what is it?

SAKINI. Mr. Sumata leave present for you, boss.

FISBY. Put it on the shelf where it'll be out of the way.

SAKINI (*glances back outside*). Not able to do, boss. Present get mad.

FISBY (*turns around*). What's this about, Sakini?

SAKINI (*motions to the Geisha, who steps inside smiling. She bows*). Here you are, boss.

FISBY (*rising*). Who is *she*?

SAKINI. Souvenir.

FISBY. What are you talking about?

SAKINI. Present from Mr. Sumata.

FISBY. Wait a minute. Is he kidding? I can't accept a human present.

SAKINI. Oh, human present very lovely. Introducing Lotus Blossom, geisha girl first class. (*He turns to Lotus Blossom*) Amerika-san no Captain Fisby.

LOTUS BLOSSOM (*smiling happily*). Ara, ii otokomaene! Watashi sukidawa.

SAKINI. She say she very happy to belong to handsome captain. She say she serve you well.

FISBY. She's not going to serve me at all. You get that Mr. Sumata and tell him I'm returning his present.

SAKINI. Impossible to do, boss. Mr. Sumata leave present and go up mountains to visit cousin. He say good-bye and wish you much success in Tobiki.

LOTUS BLOSSOM (*sweetly*). Watashi kokoni sumun desho?

SAKINI. She say, where do you want her to stay, boss?

FISBY. You tell her I don't care where she stays. She can't stay here.

SAKINI (*shocked*). Where she go then? She got no home. Mr. Sumata already gone away.

FISBY. Well, find her a place for the time being.

SAKINI (*grins*). Plenty of room in my house, boss. Just me and my grandpapa.

FISBY. No, I can't do that. Sit her over on that box until I can think where to put her.

SAKINI. You can put her in business, boss.

FISBY. You keep a civil tongue in your head, Sakini.

LOTUS BLOSSOM (*comes over to Fisby, whom she has been watching with great interest*). Okimono to ozohri motte kimasune.

SAKINI. She like to put on your sandals and kimono for you. She trained to please you, boss.

FISBY. I know what she's trained to do. And I don't need any translation. (*He sits down at his desk again*) Sakini . . . take my supplies out of the shack and bring them over here. We'll set her up there where I can keep an eye on her.

SAKINI. Not very democratic, boss. You make her lose face if she not make you comfortable, boss. She think she bad geisha girl.

FISBY. You tell her . . . I've got some face to save, too . . . so she can just forget this Oriental hanky-panky.

SAKINI. Anta irantesa!

LOTUS BLOSSOM (*waves him away*). Ara, nani ittennoyo. Imasara ikettatte ikarenai desho.

FISBY. Well, what did she say?

SAKINI. She say for me to go on home to grandpapa . . . she first-class geisha girl . . . she know her business. Good night, boss.

(*Fisby stands eyeing Lotus Blossom as Sakini goes out. The lights go down quickly. During the brief blackout, the two center panels are lowered, shutting out the village street. The office of Colonel Purdy is swung into place in the last panel right. The lights come up on Purdy twisting the bell on his field telephone.*)

PURDY. What do you mean . . . there's no answer? Well, keep trying. I'm not the kind of a man to take "no answer" for an answer.

(*The lights come up on the opposite side of the stage in Fisby's office. Fisby is holding onto his jacket buttons. Lotus Blossom stands in front of him holding out his robe. She is gently persistent and puzzled at his reticence.*)

FISBY. It's *not* a kimono . . . it's a bath-robe. And I don't *want* to put it on.

LOTUS BLOSSOM (*reaches to unbutton his jacket*). Sa! Shizukani shimasho ne.

FISBY. No, it's against regulations. (*Phone rings. He takes the robe away from Lotus Blossom and sits on it. Then he picks up the phone*) Hello!

PURDY. (*jumps*). You don't have to shout. I can hear you. This is Colonel Purdy.

FISBY (*leaps to his feet and pushes Lotus Blossom behind him as if to hide her*). Yes, sir.

PURDY. Just thought I'd check up on you. How are things going?

(*Lotus Blossom begins to fan her master.*)

FISBY. Well, everything seems to be under control at the moment. (*He sits down and takes out a cigarette. Lotus Blossom promptly lights it for him*)

PURDY. Anything *I* can do for you?

FISBY (*pauses*). I can't think of anything, sir.

PURDY. I realize it's bound to get lonely for you down there . . . so you know what I'm going to do, my boy?

FISBY (*Lotus Blossom gets the geta and kneels before him. Fisby watches her apprehensively and asks*). What are you going to do?

PURDY. I'll tell you. I'm going to send you some of my old *Adventure Magazines*.

FISBY (*as Lotus Blossom starts to take off his shoes*). No, *no*. I don't want them. (*Into the phone*) I mean . . . yes . . . thank you. (*He rises and twists about trying to pull his foot away from Lotus Blossom*) I'd like something to read.

PURDY. How are you getting along with the natives?

FISBY (*his leg over the chair*). The problem here, sir, is a very old one. It seems to be a question of who's going to lose face.

PURDY. I understand. As Mrs. Purdy says, "East is East and West is West, and there can be no Twain." But you're making progress?

FISBY. Nothing I'd like to put on paper, sir. (*Lotus Blossom gets his shoes off and slips the sandals on*)

PURDY. Well, when things get moving down there, send in a detailed Progress Report.

FISBY. If that's what you want, sir. (*Lotus Blossom recovers the robe. She reaches out to unbutton his jacket*)

PURDY. You'll find these people lack the capacity for sustained endeavor. Don't hesitate to build a fire under them.

FISBY (*struggling to keep his jacket on*). That won't be necessary, sir.

PURDY. Don't forget . . . the eyes of Washington are on you, Fisby.

FISBY (*as Lotus Blossom tries to pull his jacket over his head*). I hope not, sir.

PURDY (*ponders*). Fisby, it just occurred to me. Have you given any thought to physical education?

FISBY. If I may say so, sir . . . (*Lotus Blossom gets one arm out*) I consider the suggestion . . . (*He hugs the other sleeve*) a masterpiece of timeliness. (*He gets down on one knee*)

PURDY. Thank you, my boy. (*Pauses*) Could you use a deck of cards? Hello? Hello, Fisby . . . you're getting weak.

(*As Fisby looks back at the telephone and nods in complete agreement, the two scenes black out simultaneously. The panels fall. A spot picks up Sakini as he steps from the wings.*)

SAKINI. Discreet place to stop now and sip soothing cup of jasmine tea.
Conclusion?
Not yet.
Continuation shortly.
Lotus Blossom not lose face! (*He bows*)

THE CURTAIN FALLS


ACT TWO

SCENE I

SCENE: *Tobiki village.*
TIME: *A few days later.*
AT RISE: *All the panels are down. Sakini enters from the wings and crosses down to the footlights center. He bows to the audience.*

————

SAKINI. Lovely ladies, kind gentlemen:
Most traveled person in history of world is summer sun.
Each day must visit each man no matter where he live on globe.
Always welcome visitor.
Not bring gossip.
Not stay too long.
Not depart leaving bad taste of rude comment.
But summer sun never tell topside of world what bottomside like.
So bottomside must speak for self.
We continue with little story of Tobiki.
Center of industry.
Seat of democracy. (*He beams.*)
Home of geisha girl. (*He goes to the right proscenium arch as all the panels are raised, revealing the empty street outside of Fisby's office. Fisby enters, starts across stage, Sakini falling in step behind him*)
Was wondering what happened to you, boss?

FISBY (*stops*). I went down to inspect the sweet-potato fields. Sakini, no one was there. The potatoes were piled up, but no one was working.

SAKINI. Very hot day, boss.

FISBY. But I can't find my Chief of Agriculture: Or the Mayor, or the Chief of Police. Where is everybody?

SAKINI. Lotus Blossom leave belongings over at Awasi—got no way to bring things here. So—everybody take wheelbarrow to help move Lotus Blossom to Tobiki.

FISBY. And has she got so many things that it takes my entire staff to move her to this village?

SAKINI. No, boss, but Chief of Police not trust Chief of Agriculture, and Mayor not trust Mr. Oshira, so all go.

FISBY. Mr. Oshira? That old man!

SAKINI. He's old, boss, but not dead.

FISBY. A fine way for officials to behave! You tell them I want to see them the moment they come back. (*He starts for his office*) A fine thing!

SAKINI. Nothing to worry about, boss. They not beat your time. You own Lotus Blossom.

FISBY. I do *not* own her. It's a question of—of—(*He sits down at his desk*) Well, this sort of nonsense isn't going to stop my work. (*He shifts the papers on his desk*) I intend to get started on that schoolhouse today. We've got the materials, so all we need now is some good carpenters. (*He turns to Sakini who has followed him inside*) Who is the best carpenter in the village?

SAKINI. Mr. Sumata.

FISBY. Fine. Get hold of him. Wait a minute! Isn't he the joker who gave me Lotus Blossom?

SAKINI. Mr. Sumata has finger in lots of pies, boss.

FISBY. Well, since he's vanished, who is the next best carpenter?

SAKINI. Father of Mr. Sumata.

FISBY. Where is he?

SAKINI. Go on vacation with Mr. Sumata.

FISBY (*beginning to get annoyed*). Well, who is the *third* best carpenter then?

SAKINI. No more, boss. Only Sumata and son. They have what you call monopoly.

FISBY. There's something fishy about their disappearing.

(*Miss Higa Jiga, wearing a red helmet with flowers, followed by several other Ladies, comes storming across the stage to the office door. Sakini hears them and goes to the door.*)

MISS HIGA JIGA (*angrily*). Watashitachi sabetsu taigu desyo!

FISBY (*goes to the door also*). What's the matter with her?

SAKINI. Miss Higa Jiga say do you know what we got in this village, boss? Discrimination.

FISBY (*wearily*). Where?

(*Sakini turns to Miss Higa Jiga.*)

MISS HIGA JIGA (*indignantly*). Watashitachi hykyu matte itara Lotus Blossom ga kite clarku ga anata desuka ma dozo kochirae watashitachi nijikan mo machi mashita yo.

SAKINI. She say that Ladies' League for Democratic Action wait in line for rice rations. Along come Lotus Blossom and ration clerks say, "Oh, how do you do. Oh, please don't stand in line. You come inside and have cup of tea." Then clerks shut up warehouse and leave Ladies' League waiting in sun two hours.

FISBY. It's things like this that undermine the democratic ideal. You tell Miss Higa Jiga I intend to do something about it. (*He storms into his office*)

SAKINI (*turns to Miss Higa Jiga*). Nantoka shimasuyo.

FISBY. I can see right now we're going to have to get rid of the disrupting factor in our recovery. (*He picks up the field telephone and twists the handle*) Get me Major McEvoy at Awasi.

SAKINI (*follows Fisby inside*). What are you going to do, boss?

FISBY. This village isn't big enough for Plan B and a geisha girl.

SAKINI. Oh, boss, Tobiki never have geisha girl before. We like very much.

FISBY. *She has to go.* (*Then into the telephone*) Major McEvoy? Captain Fisby at Tobiki. I have a request from one of my people to transfer to your village. Yes, it's a female citizen. Profession? Well . . . (*He looks at Sakini*)

SAKINI. Oh, please not send her away, boss. Not democratic.

FISBY. As a matter of fact her name *is* Lotus Blossom. *How* did *you* know? What do you mean, what am I trying to put over on you? Oh, you did? (*He hangs up. Then he glares at Sakini*)

SAKINI (*with great innocence*). He knows Lotus Blossom, boss?

FISBY. Very well. She was at Awasi and damn near wrecked his whole plan for recovery. She's been booted out of every village by every commander on the island.

SAKINI. Oh, poor little Lotus Blossom.

FISBY. Poor little Lotus Blossom my eye. She upsets every village she's in.

SAKINI. Not her fault she beautiful, boss.

FISBY. No wonder that Mr. Sumata disappeared. The major paid him a hundred yen to get her out of his village.

SAKINI (*eagerly*). You keep her now, boss?

FISBY. I have to. (*He points a finger at Sakini*) Well, she's not going to get away with causing dissension in *my* village! (*Miss Higa Jiga, weary of waiting outside, storms in.*)

MISS HIGA JIGA. Doshte itadakemasno Daitoryo ni tegami wo kakimasawayo.

FISBY (*pleads*). Tell her to go away.

SAKINI. She say she waiting for some democratic action. She say if she don't get it, she thinks she write this Uncle Sam you talk about.

FISBY. Now, look. I don't want complaints going into Headquarters. Tell her discrimination is being eliminated.

SAKINI. Sabetsu yamemasyo.

MISS HIGA JIGA. Yamenakutemo iinoyo, watashitachi nimo wakete itadakeba.

SAKINI. Miss Higa Jiga say please not eliminate discrimination. She say just give her some too.

FISBY. And just what does she mean by that?

SAKINI. She say Lotus Blossom unfair competition.

FISBY. Granted.

SAKINI. She say you promise everybody going to be equal.

FISBY. I intend to keep my word.

SAKINI. Well, she say she can't be equal unless she has everything Lotus Blossom has.

FISBY. What Lotus Blossom's got, the Government doesn't issue.

SAKINI (*taking a piece of paper which Miss Higa Jiga waves*). She make list, boss. Shall I read, boss?

FISBY. Go ahead.

SAKINI. She wants you to get her and ladies in League following items:

A. Red stuff to put on lips like geisha.

B. Stuff that smell pretty—

FISBY. Now, *just* wait a minute. What would H.Q. think if I requisitioned lipstick?

SAKINI (*hands list back to Miss Higa Jiga*). Dame desuyo.

MISS HIGA JIGA. Jaa Daitoryo ni tegami wo dashimaswa.

SAKINI. She say she sorry, but now she guess she just have to write this letter to Uncle Samuel after all.

FISBY (*throws up his hands*). All right. *All Right!* Tell her I'll call up the post exchange at Awasi and see if they have any shaving powder and toilet water.

SAKINI. Ya, katte agemasuyo.

MISS HIGA JIGA (*beams*). Ano wasure naidene bobby pin.

SAKINI. She say, not forget bobby pins for hair.

FISBY. I think I might have been happier in the submarine command.

MISS HIGA JIGA (*stops as she is about to go*). Mohitotsu onegai watashitachi mo mina geisha ni.

SAKINI. She say one more thing. Can you get Lotus Blossom to teach Ladies' League all to be geisha girls?

FISBY (*leaps to his feet*). Teach the innocent women of this village to be—*No!* (*Miss Higa Jiga shrugs and goes outside. As Fisby sinks back at his desk, Miss Higa Jiga talks excitedly to the women gathered outside. They run off giggling. Fisby sits at his desk and picks up Plan B*) Plan B! (*He thumbs through its pages*) Let's just see if Washington anticipated this. (*He buries his chin in his hands. Sakini sits quietly watching him. Outside in the village street, Lotus Blossom enters and starts daintily toward the office. She has only gotten halfway when Seiko overtakes her*)

SEIKO (*panting*). Ano, chotto.

LOTUS BLOSSOM (*stops and looks at him archly*). Nani?

SEIKO (*takes a chrysanthemum bud from his waist*). Ano korewo dozo.

LOTUS BLOSSOM (*takes it indifferently*). Ara, so arigato.

SEIKO (*strikes his heart passionately*). Boku no, kono, hato, o.

LOTUS BLOSSOM (*flicks her finger*). Anato no hahto? Ara shinzo ne.

SEIKO (*disembowels himself with an imaginary knife*). Harakitte shinimas.

LOTUS BLOSSOM (*yawns*). Imagoro sonnano hayaranai noyo.

SEIKO (*points toward Fisby's office*). Soka Amerika-san ga iinoka?

LOTUS BLOSSOM (*haughtily*). Nandeste! Sonnakoto yokeina osowa.

SEIKO (*laughs derisively*). Nanda rashamon janaika.

LOTUS BLOSSOM (*backs him up with an angry finger*). Watashimo kotoni kansho shinaideyo.

SEIKO (*bows his head*). Gomen nasai iisugi deshta.

LOTUS BLOSSOM (*points away*). Atchi, itte. (*Seiko sighs, turns and plods off toward the sweet-potato fields, crushed and dejected. Lotus Blossom tidies her hair and continues to the office. She calls in coyly*) Fuisbee-san!

SAKINI (*rises and looks out the door*). Oh, what do you think, boss? Lotus Blossom back. She come to see you.

FISBY. *And high time.* (*He turns to face the door as Lotus Blossom enters and bows*) Where have *you* been all day? Never mind, I know—upsetting the agricultural horse cart.

LOTUS BLOSSOM. Fu-san no kao nikkori nasaruto totemo kawaii wa.

SAKINI. She say sun burst through the clouds now that you smile on her.

FISBY. I'm not smiling. (*She hands him Seiko's chrysanthemum bud.*)

SAKINI. Oh, boss, you know what she give you?

FISBY. The works.

SAKINI. When lady give gentleman chrysanthemum bud, in Okinawa that means her heart is ready to unfold.

FISBY. Well, this is one bud that's not going to flower.

LOTUS BLOSSOM (*offering a box she has brought*). Kore otsukemono yo. Dozo.

SAKINI. She say, you like to eat some tsukemono? Tsukemono nice thing to eat between meals.

FISBY. No.

LOTUS BLOSSOM (*takes geta and kneels beside him*). Dozo ohaki osobase.

FISBY. Tell her to *leave my feet* alone.

LOTUS BLOSSOM (*studies Fisby*). Kasa kaburu. Nisshabyo nanoyo.

SAKINI. She worried about you, boss. She say, when you go in hot sun, should wear *kasa*—that straw hat—on head.

FISBY. Tell her never mind about my feet or my head. I want her to stop interfering with the recovery program. To stop causing rebellion and making the men—ah—ah—discontented.

SAKINI (*turns to Lotus Blossom*). Jama shicha dame dayo.

LOTUS BLOSSOM (*smiles*). Fu-san ocha ikaga?

SAKINI. She say: You want some tea?

FISBY (*throwing himself down on his cot*). No.

LOTUS BLOSSOM. Shami demo hikimasho-ka?

SAKINI. She say: You want some music?

FISBY. No.

LOTUS BLOSSOM (*giggles*). Ara Fu-santara yaiteruno.

SAKINI. She say: You jealous, boss?

FISBY (*mirthlessly*). Ha!

LOTUS BLOSSOM. Honto ni doshita no?

SAKINI. She say: You want to tell her your troubles, boss?

FISBY. Why should I tell her my troubles?

SAKINI. She geisha girl, that's her *business*, boss.

FISBY. Some business.

LOTUS BLOSSOM. Shoga naiwane. Mah soshite irasshai yo.

SAKINI. She say she hear about lack of co-operation here. She feel very bad. She say she want to help because you best boss she ever had. You not make her work and you not take money from her.

FISBY (*sits up on his cot*). Did the other men who owned her . . . hire her out and then take money from her?

SAKINI. Oh, sure.

FISBY. Well, where I come from we have a name for men who—who—do *that* sort of thing.

SAKINI. You have geisha business in America, too?

FISBY (*rises*). No! Sakini, you give her to understand I have no intention of putting her to—to work.

SAKINI. Why not, boss? She pay all her dues to Geisha Guild. She member in good standing.

FISBY. You mean they've got a union for this sort of thing?

SAKINI. Geisha girl have to be protected, boss. Must keep up rates.

FISBY. This is the most immoral thing

I've ever heard of. Haven't you people any sense of shame?

SAKINI. We bad not to be ashamed, boss?

FISBY. Obviously, there is a fundamental difference between us that can't be reconciled. I don't say that where I come from there's no such thing as prostitution. But, by God, we don't have unions, set rates and collect dues!

SAKINI. But geisha girl not prostitute, boss.

FISBY. At least we have the decency— (*he stops*) What do you mean, geisha girls aren't prostitutes? Everybody knows what they do.

SAKINI. Then everybody wrong, boss.

FISBY. Well, what do they get paid for, then?

SAKINI. Hard to explain fundamental difference. Poor man like to feel rich. Rich man like to feel wise. Sad man like to feel happy. All go to geisha house and tell troubles to geisha girl. She listen politely and say, "Oh, that's too bad." She very pretty. She make tea, she sing, she dance, and pretty soon troubles go away. Is not worth something, boss?

FISBY. And that's *all* they do?

SAKINI. Very ancient and honorable profession.

FISBY. Look, Sakini, I apologize. I guess I jumped the gun. And I'm glad you explained. It sort of puts a new light on things. (*He turns to Lotus Blossom and grins*)

LOTUS BLOSSOM. Ara, kyuni nikkorisite, mada okotteru no.

SAKINI. She say: Why are you smiling at her all of a sudden? You mad or something?

FISBY. Tell her that I'm a dope. That I have a coconut for a head.

SAKINI. No use, boss. She not believe.

FISBY. Then will you ask her if she'd be kind enough to give geisha lessons to the Ladies' League for Democratic Action?

SAKINI. Odori ya shami Ladies' League ni oshiete?

LOTUS BLOSSOM. Er iiwa, demo kumiaiaga kowaiwane.

SAKINI. She say Geisha Guild closed shop, but she teach if you not report her. (*At this point the men of the village come across the square and stop before the office. Lotus Blossom goes to the door. Immediately there are ohs and ahs from the men.*)

FISBY. What is that?

SAKINI. Sound like Okinawan wolf call, boss.

FISBY. Well, let's find out. (*He goes outside to face the group, followed by Sakini*) Ask what's the matter.

SAKINI. Doshtano?

MR. KEORA. Minna gakko nanka yori chaya ga ii soda.

SAKINI. They say they just held meeting in democratic fashion and majority agree on resolution. They want you to build them cha ya.

FISBY. A what?

SAKINI. Cha ya. That's teahouse, boss.

FISBY. A teahouse?

SAKINI. Yes, boss. They say now that this village have geisha girl just like big city, they should have teahouse like big city too.

FISBY. But I can't build them a teahouse . . . I have no authority to do that.

SAKINI. But you tell them will of majority is law. You going to break law?

FISBY. They're going to get a school . . . that's enough.

SAKINI. But majority too old to go to school . . . they want teahouse.

FISBY. There is no provision in Plan B for a teahouse.

LOTUS BLOSSOM. Ano . . . ochaya sae tatereba mondai naija nai no.

SAKINI. Lotus blossom say teahouse in Tobiki make recovery program work. Everybody make geta and cricket cages like crazy so they can spend money at teahouse.

FISBY. I haven't got any materials to build a teahouse.

SAKINI. Zairyo ga naiyo.

LOTUS BLOSSOM. Ara, kinoo renga ya zaimoku takusan kite orimashitayo.

SAKINI. She say Army truck come yesterday and leave beautiful brick and lovely paint.

FISBY. For the new *schoolhouse*. Tell them . . . it just can't be done.

SAKINI. Dame, dame, dame desuyo! (*Fisby looks down into the disappointed faces of the villagers.*)

VILLAGERS. Achara-san, iijiwaru dane.

SAKINI. They say you very mean to them after *all* the nice presents they give you.

FISBY. I'm sorry.

SAKINI. They very sorry too, boss. You know why?

FISBY. I think I do.

SAKINI. No, boss. When you leave here . . . Tobiki be forgotten village. Not have park, not have statue . . . not even lovely jail. Tobiki like to be proud. Teahouse give them face.

FISBY. It's going to be a fine schoolhouse. Five sides.

OSHIRA. May I speak, Captain-san?

FISBY. Of course, Mr. Oshira.

OSHIRA. There are lovely teahouses in the big cities. But the men of Tobiki have never been inside them. We are too poor and our clothes are too ragged. All of my life I have dreamed of visiting a teahouse where paper lanterns cast a light in the lotus pond and bamboo bells hanging in the pines tinkle as the breezes brush them. But this picture is only in my heart . . . I may never see it. I am an old man, sir. I shall die soon. It is evil for the soul to depart this world laden with envy or regret. Give us our teahouse, sir. Free my soul for death.

FISBY (unhappily). But . . . we haven't got any carpenters!

SAKINI (calls over the heads of the group). Oi! Daiku-san! Daiku-san! (Mr. Sumata and his father come trotting across the stage carrying their carpenter boxes. Sakini turns to Fisby) Oh, what you think? Mr. Sumata and his papa just come down from mountains!

FISBY (gives Sakini a penetrating but defeated look). All right. All right! I haven't got a chance. I guess Uncle Sam is going into the teahouse business. (He turns and goes back into his office, followed by Lotus Blossom. He picks up Plan B. Sakini announces the decision from the steps)

SAKINI. Cha ya, tatete iiyo! (There is an outburst of cheers from the villagers. It sounds very much like "Fisby-san, Banzai, Uncle Sam, Banzai!" Inside Fisby begins tearing up Plan B. Lotus Blossom kneels before him, geta in hand. Fisby extends his feet and smiles down at her. The cheering outside continues. As the panels descend—

THE SCENE BLACKS OUT QUICKLY

SCENE 2

SCENE: *Colonel Purdy's office.*
TIME: *Few weeks later.*
AT RISE: *The right panel is lifted. A light*

*picks up Colonel Purdy. He sits at his desk fuming over a report. The rest of the stage remains dark. He calls Gregovich on his office inter-com.*

———

PURDY. Gregovich!

GREGOVICH'S VOICE. Yes, sir?

PURDY. Get me Captain Fisby at Tobiki.

GREGOVICH. Yes, sir. (*The extreme left panel rises leaving the intervening panels lowered. Fisby sits with his feet propped up on his desk. He is wearing his bathrobe "kimono." Lotus Blossom stands at his side fanning him. Over the scene, the sound of hammering and sawing can be heard. Over this the phone can be heard to ring. Fisby lifts the receiver.*)

FISBY. Captain Fisby.

PURDY. Colonel Purdy.

FISBY (*over noise*). Who?

PURDY. Colonel Purdy!

FISBY. I can't hear you. Hold on a minute. (*He turns to Lotus Blossom*) See if you can stop that hammering on the teahouse for a minute. (*He goes through the motions. Lotus Blossom nods understandingly and goes out*)

PURDY. What's going on down there, Fisby?

FISBY (*as the noises cease*). Now, who is it?

PURDY. Colonel Purdy.

FISBY (*wraps his robe about his legs quickly*). Oh, good afternoon, Colonel.

PURDY. I want to talk to you about your Progress Report.

FISBY. I sent it in.

PURDY. I have it. I have it right in front of be. I've read it twice. Now, suppose *you* tell *me* what it says.

FISBY. What would you like to have me explain, sir?

PURDY. I'd like you to explain why there's nothing in here about the schoolhouse. Didn't you get the lumber?

FISBY (*uneasily*). Yes, sir . . . it's being used right now. But we'll need some more, I'm afraid.

PURDY. I sent ample according to specifications. How big a structure are you building?

FISBY. Well . . . we ought to consider expansion. Populations increase.

PURDY. We don't need to consider expansion. Our troops will be out of here by the next generation. Which brings me to another point. (*He refers to the report*) What's this about six kids being born last week?

FISBY. Well, there wasn't much else to fill the Progress Report, sir.

PURDY. Then you've failed at your indoctrination. Don't you know yet that births are entered under "Population Increases"? They are not considered progress.

FISBY. But they weren't children, sir. They were kids . . . goats.

PURDY. There must be something wrong with this connection. It sounded just as if you said "goats."

FISBY. I did, sir. Kids . . . goats. You see, we're trying to increase the livestock herd down here. I thought . . .

PURDY. Goats! I don't care what you thought. Look here, Fisby. Suppose some congressman flew in to inspect our team. How would I explain such a report?

FISBY. Well, goats will breed, sir. Congress can't stop that. And I've been concerned with . . . .

PURDY. The population of civilians alone concerns us. I want to know exactly what progress you've made as outlined in Plan B.

FISBY. Well . . . I'm getting along fine with the people.

PURDY. In other words, nothing. Listen to me. Do you realize what Major McEvoy has accomplished in his village?

FISBY. No, sir.

PURDY. Well, I'll tell you. His fourth-graders know the alphabet through "M," and his whole village can sing "God Bless America" in English.

FISBY. Yes, sir. That's real progress, sir. I wish I could say the same.

PURDY. See that you do. I don't want any rotten apples in my barrel. Now . . . I want to know exactly what you have accomplished in the five weeks you've been down there.

FISBY. Well, sir . . . I've started an industry. I'm sending our first shipment out for sale this week.

PURDY. What are you making?

FISBY (*looks down at his feet*). Oh, getas and . . .

PURDY. Wait a minute . . . what in God's name is a *geta?*

FISBY. Not "a" geta . . . *getas* . . . you have to have two.

PURDY. Are you breeding some *other* kind of animal?

FISBY. You wear them on your feet, sir. Excellent for strengthening the metatarsal muscles. Then . . . I have a group busy building cricket cages. . . .

PURDY. Captain Fisby!

FISBY. Yes, sir.

PURDY. What kind of cages did you say?

FISBY. Cricket. Like in cricket on the hearth. I think we'll find a great market for them. Of course, we don't supply the crickets.

PURDY. Naturally not. Captain Fisby . . . have you been taking your salt pills?

FISBY. Yes, sir . . . I take them at cha ya . . . with my tea.

PURDY. Have you been going out in the sun without your helmet?

FISBY. I wear a kasa, sir . . . it's more practical . . . wind can blow through the straw.

PURDY. I see. I see. That will be all, Captain. (*He hangs up quickly*)

FISBY. Hello . . . hello . . . (*He hangs up and sits looking at the phone rather puzzled. The lights go down in his office and the panel descends. Colonel Purdy also sits looking at the phone in his office. He calls Sergeant Gregovich on the inter-com*)

PURDY. Sergeant! What is the name of that psychiatrist over at Awasi?

GREGOVICH. Captain McLean?

PURDY. Get him on the phone. My man at Tobiki has gone completely off his rocker!

THE SCENE BLACKS OUT QUICKLY

### SCENE 3

SCENE: *Captain Fisby's office.*

TIME: *A few days later.*

AT RISE: *The office is empty as the panel rises. After a moment Captain McLean enters. He is an intense, rather wild-eyed man in his middle forties. He glances about furtively, then begins to examine the papers on Fisby's desk. He makes several notes in a notebook. He picks up Fisby's cricket cage and is examining it intently when Fisby enters behind him. He halts upon seeing McLean. Fisby is wearing his blue bathrobe, his geta and a native straw hat.*

————

FISBY. Well, who are you?

MC LEAN (*gasps in surprise*). Oh, you startled me.

FISBY. Can I do anything for you? I'm Captain Fisby.

MC LEAN. I'm Captain McLean. There was no one here . . . so I came in.

FISBY (*he looks at his insignia*). Oh, medical corps. What brings you to Tobiki?

MC LEAN. Well, I'm—I'm on leave. Thought I'd spend it making some—some—ethnological studies. (*He adds quickly*) Of the natives.

FISBY. Well, you couldn't have come to a more interesting spot. Sit down, Captain.

MC LEAN (*sits*). Thank you. Would you have any objection to my spending a week or so making my studies, Captain?

FISBY. Not at all. Make yourself at home. I'll take that if it's in your way. (*He reaches out to relieve McLean of the cricket cage he still holds*)

MC LEAN (*glances at the cage in his hand and laughs awkwardly*). Oh, yes. I was just examining it.

FISBY (*pleased at his authority on the subject*). It's a cricket cage.

MC LEAN (*pauses*). You . . . like crickets?

FISBY. I haven't found one yet. But at least I've got the cage. I've got two . . . if you want one.

MC LEAN. Thank you, no. Thank you very much. (*He looks at Fisby's attire*) What happened to your uniform, Captain?

FISBY. It's around. I find getas and a kimono much more comfortable in this climate.

MC LEAN. But isn't that a bathrobe?

FISBY (*shrugs*). It passes for a kimono. Would you like to take off your shoes, Captain?

MC LEAN. Thank you . . . no. I'll keep them on if you don't mind.

FISBY. Can I offer you some tsukemono? You eat these during the day between meals. (*He extends a platter*) Tsukemono means fragrant things.

MC LEAN. I just had a chocolate bar, thank you. (*He rises and looks out the door*) May I ask what you're building down the road?

FISBY (*proudly*). That's my cha ya. (*He pops a few tsukemonos into his mouth*) It's really going to be something to write home about.

MC LEAN. Cha ya?

FISBY. Well, it just so happens, Captain, that I own a geisha girl. That might sound strange to you, but you get used to these things after a while. And if you have a geisha, you've got to have a cha ya. Sure you don't want some tsukemono?

MC LEAN. I really couldn't eat a thing. (*He glances out the door again*) May I ask what the men are doing down there wading in that irrigation ditch?

FISBY. They're not wading, they're building a lotus pond. You can't have a cha ya without a lotus pond.

MC LEAN (*sits opposite Fisby*). How have you felt lately, Fisby?

FISBY. McLean, I'll tell you something. I've never been happier. I feel reckless and free. And it all happened the moment I decided not to build that damned pentagon-shaped school.

MC LEAN. That what?

FISBY. The good colonel ordered me to build a pentagon-shaped schoolhouse down here. But the people wanted a teahouse. Believe it or not, someone gave me a geisha girl. So I'm giving this village what it wants. That must all sound pretty crazy to you, Mac.

MC LEAN. Well, yes and no.

FISBY. These are wonderful people with a strange sense of beauty. And hard-working . . . when there's a purpose. You should have seen them start out day before yesterday, great bundles of things they'd made piled high on their heads. Getas, cricket cages, lacquer ware—things to sell as souvenirs up north. Don't let anyone tell you these people are lazy.

MC LEAN. Oh. I see. I see.

FISBY. No, you don't. But you'll have a chance to study them.

MC LEAN. So you're building them a teahouse.

FISBY. Next thing I'm going to do for them is find out if this land here will grow anything besides sweet potatoes. I'm going to send for fertilizers and DDT and—

MC LEAN (*leaps to his feet*). Chemicals!

FISBY. Sure, why not?

MC LEAN. Do you want to poison these people?

FISBY. No, but—

MC LEAN. Now you've touched on a subject that is very close to me. For years I've planned to retire and buy a farm—raise specialties for big restaurants. So let me tell you this. Chemicals will kill all your earthworms, and earthworms aerate your soil.

FISBY. They do?

MC LEAN. Do you know an earthworm leaves castings eight times its own weight every day?

FISBY. That much!

MC LEAN. Organic gardening is the only thing. Nature's way—compost, manure, but no chemicals.

FISBY. Hey! You know a lot about this.

MC LEAN (*modestly*). I should. I've subscribed to all the farm journals for years.

FISBY. Say, you could help these people out while you're here—if you would. Do you think you could take over supervision—establish a sort of experimental station for them?

MC LEAN. Well, I—no—no—I haven't time.

FISBY. Take time. This is a chance for you to put some of your theories into practice.

MC LEAN (*haughtily*). They are not theories. They are proven facts.

FISBY. I'll give you a couple of men to help, and all you'd have to do is tell us how.

MC LEAN (*hesitates*). Is your soil acid or alkaline?

FISBY. Gosh, I don't know.

MC LEAN. Well, that's the very *first* thing you have to find out. Do you have bees?

FISBY. I haven't seen any.

MC LEAN (*shakes his head sadly*). People always underestimate the importance of bees for pollinating.

FISBY (*slaps him on the back*). Mac, you're just the man we've needed down here. You're a genius!

MC LEAN. I'll want plenty of manure.

FISBY. You'll get it.

MC LEAN. And I'll want to plan this program scientifically. I wish I had some of my books . . . and my seed catalogues. (*He measures from the floor*) I've got a stack of catalogues that high.

FISBY. Why don't you make a list, and I'll get the boys over at the airstrip to fly us in seeds from the States.

MC LEAN (*The gardener fever possesses the doctor as he begins to make his list*). Every spring I've made lists of seeds and never had any soil to put them in. And now . . . I could actually germinate. (*He writes*) Corn—Golden Bantam. (*Then adds enthusiastically*) And Country Gentleman! Hybrid.

FISBY. Why don't I just leave you with your list while I check on the lotus pond? (*McLean doesn't hear him*) Well, I'll be back for tea. We have tea in the pine grove and watch the sun go down. (*He goes out*)

MC LEAN (*continues with his list reading aloud*). Cucumbers—Extra Early Green Prolific. (*His enthusiasm mounts*) Radishes—Crimson Giant! (*The telephone begins to ring; he ignores it as he writes*) Tomatoes—Ponderosa Earliana. (*The telephone rings insistently*) Watermelon! (*He closes his eyes ecstatically*)

(*The panel on the opposite side of the stage revealing Colonel Purdy's office. The intervening panel remains down. Colonel Purdy sits at his desk jiggling his telephone hook.*)

PURDY. What's the matter with this connection! Ring again!

MC LEAN (*ignores the ringing*). Watermelon—All-American Gold Medal! (*He writes it down as the phone rings. He looks up impatiently and lifts the receiver*) Hello!

PURDY (*confidentially*). Who is this?

MC LEAN. This is Captain McLean.

PURDY. This is Colonel Purdy. Can you talk?

MC LEAN. Why not?

PURDY. I was anxious to hear your report on you-know-who.

MC LEAN. On *who*?

PURDY. *Captain Fisby!* The man I sent you down to examine.

MC LEAN. Oh. (*He weighs his problem quickly*) Oh. Well . . . I'll have to stay down here several weeks for some . . .

PURDY. Several weeks!

MC LEAN. Rome wasn't built in a day.

PURDY. What?

MC LEAN. I said, Rome wasn't built in a day.

PURDY (*digests this*). Well . . . you're the doctor.

MC LEAN. I'll send in a report . . . from time to time. I can tell you now I expect to work miracles down here.

PURDY. Splendid . . . splendid. Is there anything I can send? Some old *Adventure Magazines* or anything?

MC LEAN. There are a couple of books I'd like, but I don't think you could get them.

PURDY (*picks up pencil*). You name them.

MC LEAN. Well . . . one is *Principles of Pea Production*, and the other is *Do's and Don'ts of Cabbage Culture*. (*Purdy starts to write . . . then stops*) And do you think you could lay your hands on a soil test kit?

PURDY (*looks at earphone*). A what?

MC LEAN (*enunciating*). A soil test kit. I want to see if the soil is sour down here.

PURDY. Sour, did you say?

MC LEAN. Yes . . . if your soil is sour your seeds won't germinate. And I sure wish I had some bees.

PURDY. There *is* something wrong with this connection!

MC LEAN. I'm going to take time out here to build up the soil with manure.

PURDY (*unbelieving*). Did you say manure?

MC LEAN. I've lost faith in chemicals. You kill all your worms. I can tell you, when you kill a worm, Colonel . . . you're killing a friend. (*There is a long pause*) Hello . . . hello.

PURDY (*puts down the phone and turns to the squawk box*). Gregovich, where is Plan B!

GREGOVICH'S VOICE. What did you want, sir?

PURDY. I want to see who I send to analyze an analyst.

THE PANELS FALL QUICKLY ON EACH SIDE
OF THE STAGE

SCENE 4

SCENE: *Village square.*

TIME: *Few weeks later.*

AT RISE: *The panels rise to reveal the village square and Fisby's office. Natives are seated in the square, great bundles beside them. Others arrive and sink into positions of dejection. Fisby works at his desk. Sakini enters and looks at the villagers.*

———

SAKINI (*to Mr. Keora*). Doshtano?

KEORA. Hitotsu mo unremasenna.

SAKINI. Oh, oh . . . too bad. (*Sakini crosses and enters Fisby's office*) Boss!

FISBY. Yes?

SAKINI. Mr. Keora and everybody back from Big Koza.

FISBY. Good. Let's see how they made out. (*He steps outside followed by Sakini. He stops as he sees his villagers sitting dejectedly before their large bundles. He turns to Sakini*) What's the matter?

SAKINI. Mr. Keora very tired. Walk two days with bundle on back to sell straw hats to American soldiers at Big Koza. Nobody buy, so walk back. Too many damn hats now, boss.

FISBY. He couldn't sell *any*? (*Sakini shakes his head*) Why not?

SAKINI (*shrugs*). Soldiers not want. Soldiers say . . . what you think we are . . . hayseed? So come home.

FISBY (*sees old Mr. Oshira and crosses to him. Oshira rises*). Mr. Oshira . . . did you take your lacquer ware to Yatoda?

OSHIRA. Oh, yes . . . but come back . . . not go again.

FISBY. But I don't understand . . . The Navy always spends money.

OSHIRA. Sailors say, "Oh, pretty good . . . how much you want?" I say, "Twenty-five yen." They say, "Oh, too much . . . can get better in five-and-ten-cent store. Give you one nickel."

FISBY. Did you explain how many years it took you to learn how to turn out such work?

OSHIRA (*nods*). They say, "What you want us to do, cry?"

FISBY (*angrily*). Damn stupid morons! (*He turns back to Oshira*) Did you tell them that each cup was handmade?

OSHIRA. They say . . . not care. They say . . . at home have big machines that turn out ten cups every minute. They say . . . take nickel or jump in lake.

FISBY (*unhappily*). So you had to carry them all the way back?

SAKINI. Poor Mr. Oshira. No one want his lacquer ware.

FISBY. Well, he's wrong. He's a great artist and I'll buy everything he's made myself.

SAKINI. But you not able to buy everything from everybody in Tobiki, boss.

FISBY (*sits down on steps*). Tell them that they should all be proud of their work. And that I'm proud of all of them.

SAKINI. Gokro, gokro san.

FISBY. I'll think of something . . . I'll hit on an idea to bring money to this village yet.

SAKINI. Boss . . . you stop work on teahouse now?

FISBY. No! You'll get a teahouse if I give you nothing else.

SAKINI. They sure wish they could make some money to spend at teahouse, boss. Not like to go like beggars.

FISBY. Give me a little time, Sakini. (*As they sit around, each deep in his personal problems, McLean enters. His uniform is gone. He is wearing his bathrobe, a straw hat and geta.*)

MC LEAN. Fisby! You're just the man I want to see. Can I have a couple of boys to help me? The damn Japanese beetles are eating up my Chinese peas.

FISBY (*dispiritedly*). Sure . . . I'll get a couple for you.

MC LEAN (*looks around*). What's the matter?

FISBY. There's no market for our products.

MC LEAN. Oh . . . that's too bad. What are you going to do? (*He sits down*)

FISBY. Try to think of something.

OSHIRA. The world has left us behind. (*The villagers begin to rise and pick up their handiwork.*)

SEIKO. Amerika-san no seija naiyo. Sa, sa, kaette yakezake da!

SAKINI. They say . . . tell you not your fault no one wants to buy, boss. They say guess they go home now and get drunk.

FISBY. Tell them I don't blame them. If I had anything to drink . . . I'd do the same. (*As they start to file out, both McLean and Fisby have a delayed reaction. They leap to their feet together*) Wait a minute! (*The villagers stop*) What are they going to get drunk *on?*

SAKINI. They got nothing but brandy.

MC LEAN. Nothing but *brandy!*

FISBY. How did they manage to get brandy?

SAKINI. We make very fine brandy here, from sweet potatoes. Been making for generations.

FISBY. You make a brandy *yourselves?*

SAKINI. Oh, yes. We make for weddings and funerals.

FISBY (*looks at McLean*). What does it taste like?

SAKINI. You want some, boss? (*He turns to Hokaida*) Imozake, skoshi!

FISBY. Sakini, if this stuff is any good at all, we're in business. This is one thing I *know* our men will buy.

SAKINI. Oh . . . I think we not like to sell brandy. Only make for ceremony.

MC LEAN. It may not be any good anyhow. There are some things even the troops won't drink.

HOKAIDA (*returns with an earthen jug*). Hai, imozake. (*He hands the jug to Fisby*)

SAKINI. There you are, boss. You like taste now?

FISBY. I'd like to smell it first. (*He gives it a sniff and jerks his head back*)

MC LEAN. Obviously, it has a kick.

FISBY. How old is this brandy, Sakini?

SAKINI (*turns to Hokaida*). Kore itsuno?

HOKAIDA (*holds up seven fingers*). Issukan mae dayo.

FISBY. Seven years old?

SAKINI. Oh, no, boss. He make last week.

FISBY. It couldn't smell like that in only a week.

SAKINI. Is village secret. You try now?

FISBY (*hands it to McLean*). You try it, Mac. You're a medical man.

MC LEAN (*backs away*). You first.

FISBY. I insist. You're my guest.

MC LEAN. I waive the honor.

FISBY (*turns to Sakini*). Has anyone ever gone blind or died from this?

MC LEAN. He said they make it for funerals.

SAKINI. Oh, no, boss. We not blind. We not dead.

FISBY. There, you see.

MC LEAN. They've worked up an immunity over the years.

FISBY. Well, I don't want to kill any of my countrymen. Couldn't you make some sort of test, Doc? (*As McLeans considers this, the bleat of a goat is heard offstage. Fisby and McLean exchange looks and nod*) Sakini, get Lady Astor. (*To McLean*) That's Miss Higa Jiga's goat. She asked me to give it a classy name.

(*Sakini goes to get Lady Astor.*)

MC LEAN. I'm not sure what we'll prove. Goats have hardy stomachs.

SAKINI (*returns leading a goat*). Boss, you make guinea pig of goat?

FISBY. If this passes the goat-test, it's all right. No Marine would ever admit he had a weaker stomach than a goat.

MC LEAN. May I borrow this a moment? (*He takes Mr. Hokaida's red helmet and pours into it from the jug*)

SAKINI. Lady Astor very lucky goat.

FISBY. You hold her, Sakini. Proceed, Doctor . . . in the name of science. (*The goat sniffs the contents of the helmet*) We're either going to have an industry or goat meat for dinner.

(*Lady Astor begins to drink the concoction. They watch her lap up the liquor and lick her lips with relish.*)

MC LEAN (*stands back*). It doesn't seem to affect her. (*Draws his fingers back and forth in front of the goat's eyes*) Reflexes all right.

FISBY. Let's watch her a minute. The future of Tobiki and the health of the Army are at stake here. (*Fisby and McLean and the villagers stand watching the goat. Lady Astor is quite content. Fisby rises*) Well, here goes. (*He takes the jug and samples the contents himself. McLean watches him. Then he, too, tests from the jug. They look at each other and grin*) Whee! (*He dashes for his office*)

SAKINI (*follows*). What you going to do, boss?

FISBY. I am about to form the Co-opera-tive Brewing Company of Tobiki. (*Fisby is followed by Sakini, McLean, and some of the villagers. He picks up the phone*) Get me the Officers' Club at Awasi.

SAKINI. We going to make brandy, boss?

FISBY. I'll tell you in a minute. (*He turns back to telephone*) Hello . . . Officers' Club, Awasi. This is Captain Fisby at Tobiki. Oh, hello, Major, how are you? Major, when I was with your unit, you could never keep a supply of liquor in the club, and I stum-bled onto something and wondered if you'd be interested. Tobiki, as you know, is the heart of the brandy industry and— (*He takes the phone away from his ear as the word brandy is shouted back at him*) Yes . . . brandy. . . . (*He turns to McLean*) Doc, look up the word "sweet potato" and see if it has another fancier name. (*He turns back to the phone*) Yes . . . I'm here . . . yes . . . I could get you some if you could pay their price and keep the source secret. Oh, yes, it's been made here for generations. Why, you never tasted anything like it.

MC LEAN. The Haitian word for sweet potato is *b-a-t-a-t-a*. (*He spells it out*)

FISBY (*into the phone*). You've heard of Seven Star Batata, haven't you? Well, To-biki is where it's made. (*He turns to Mc-Lean*) The Seven Star did it.

SAKINI. Brandy much better if eight or ten days old, boss.

FISBY. We also have Eight Star and Ten Star. Well, naturally the Ten Star comes a little higher. It sells for— (*He looks at Sakini desperately. Sakini holds up ten fingers*) A hundred occupation yen a gal-lon.

SAKINI. I mean *ten* yen, boss.

FISBY. Delivered. All right, we'll send up five gallons in about a week. It'll be deliv-ered by our Department of Agriculture. You're welcome. (*He hangs up and turns to Sakini*) Sakini, if every family in Tobiki starts making brandy, how much can we turn out in a week?

SAKINI. Oh, maybe . . . forty . . . fifty gallons.

FISBY. Better aim for eighty. (*he lifts the receiver again*) I'd like to get the naval base at Big Koza, Officers' Club, Com-mander Myers.

SAKINI. Maybe if everybody build private stills, Tobiki can turn out hundred gallon.

FISBY. I'll know better after I talk to the Navy. (*He speaks into the phone*) Com-mander Myers? Captain Fisby at Tobiki. Commander, we've got a surplus of brandy down here and I was wondering . . . (*Again he takes the phone away from his ear as the word brandy is blasted back.*) Yes. Brandy. Ten Star Batata. Well, Lady Astor won't drink anything else. Oh . . . we could sup-ply you with as much as you want at a hundred yen a gallon. Fifteen gallons?

Right! It will be delivered Horse Cart Special in ten days. (*He hangs up and turns to the others crowding into his office*) Sakini, tell them to all start making brandy, and in a week or two everyone in this village is going to have more money than he ever dreamed of.

SAKINI. Ah, dondon kaseide sake tsukreba minna kanega mokaruyo!

MR. KEORA. Minna shiroi koto katte moii darone?

SAKINI. They say . . . if they work like the dickens, can they all have white coats like the mayor?

FISBY. Yes. I'll get the cloth somewhere. That's a promise. (*The telephone rings*) Waita minute. Hello? Well, word gets around fast. (*He picks up his order blank*) Twenty gallons? PX, GHQ, C.O.D. O.K. (*He hangs up*) Get to work, boys! (*As they turn to leave, Fisby suddenly leaps to his feet*) Wait! (*They stand frozen as he crouches and starts toward them. He slaps his hand on the floor and then rises triumphantly*) I got my cricket!
(*The villagers cheer for Fisby.*)

THE PANELS FALL QUICKLY

## ACT THREE

### SCENE 1

SCENE: *Teahouse of the August Moon.*

TIME: *Several weeks later.*

AT RISE: *All the panels are down. Sakini steps from the wings to address the audience.*

———

SAKINI (*bows*) Ability of Americans for mass production equaled only by American capacity for consumption.

Fortune often comes in back door while we look out front window.

Prosperity not only smile on Tobiki.

Prosperity giggle like silly girl.

Very strange.

Things we do best . . . not wanted.

Things we think least of . . . wanted most.

No conclusion.

Tobiki now village of beautiful houses.

But loveliest of all is Teahouse of August Moon.

(*He goes off extreme left, signaling for the panels to rise. Offstage the music of string instruments can be heard playing softly. The panels go up. The ugly thatched huts are gone. In the center of the stage, exquisite in its simplicity, stands the teahouse. Small bells tinkle from its pagoda roof. Soft lights glow through the colored paper panels. Dwarf pines edge the walk leading to a small bridge. An August moon hangs in the autumn sky. The silhouette of Lotus Blossom is framed in the center panel by the soft back lighting. She slides the panel open and steps into the almost bare center room of the teahouse. She crosses and lights the lanterns hanging from the eave extensions. As she goes through this ceremony, the Guests wander in. Before they enter the teahouse, they remove their shoes and rinse their fingers in the ceremonial bamboo basin. Then they enter and seat themselves on green floor mats. The Women are dressed in silk kimonos of varying hues and the majority of the men wear spotless white suits. Lotus Blossom bows to them and returns through the sliding door again. Fisby and McLean, followed by Sakini, enter. Sakini wears a white suit and the Americans wear their bathrobes and geta. They are greeted enthusiastically by the Guests.*)

———

SAKINI. I tell Lotus Blossom you here, boss. (*He disappears through the sliding panel in the center of the teahouse*)

FISBY (*as they walk around inspecting the grounds*). It's really something, isn't it?

MC LEAN. Where did they all get their white suits?

FISBY. They made them.

MC LEAN. Where'w they get the cloth?

FISBY. I got it from the naval base at Awasi for ten gallons of brandy. It's target cloth.

MC LEAN. Those kimonos aren't target cloth.

FISBY. Parachute silk. Six gallons' worth. (*Lotus Blossom enters, followed by Sakini. She hurries down to Fisby and bows. She extends a yellow chrysanthemum to him.*)

SAKINI. Chrysanthemum bud in full bloom, boss.

LOTUS BLOSSOM (*she bows as Fisby accepts the gift*). Hop-pee. (*Her eyes almost disappear in a great smile of pride*)

FISBY. What did she say?

SAKINI. I try like the dickens to teach her to say "happy birthday," but she can't say "birthday," boss.

LOTUS BLOSSOM. Hop-pee.

FISBY. Well . . . I'm floored! (*He bows to her*) Thank you, Lotus Blossom. (*To Sakini*) How did you know?

MC LEAN. I gave you away.

SAKINI. Everybody in village like to show appreciation, boss.

FISBY. I should have had a kimono made. When you said "formal," I thought this would do.

LOTUS BLOSSOM. Hop-pee. Hop-pee.

FISBY. And a hop-pee hop-pee to you.

GUESTS (*murmur in the background*). Hayaku oiwai hajimeyo, soda, soda.

SAKINI. Everybody impatient to get on with the party, boss.

LOTUS BLOSSOM. Hop-pee. (*She indicates the center mat*)

SAKINI. You sit down now, boss. Lotus Blossom going to dance in your honor.

FISBY. You hear that. . . . She's going to dance! (*Quickly sits down*) Sit down, you farmer. . . . This is in my honor.

MC LEAN. My, my! How am I going to stall Purdy so I can stay down here?

FISBY. I'll have a relapse for you. (*They turn to watch Lotus Blossom as she takes her position and the first notes are struck by the musicians present. Lotus Blossom performs for them a traditional dance of infinite grace and delicacy. She finishes, concluding her performance in front of Fisby, who rises and bows to her*) What a lovely little thing you are! This belongs to you. (*He returns the chrysanthemum with a flourish. Lotus Blossom accepts it and seats herself quickly on a mat and hides her head*)

SAKINI. Oh, boss . . . you know what you do!

FISBY. It called for flowers.

SAKINI. That mean you give your heart to her.

FISBY (*lightly*). Well, I do. We all do. (*Turns to Mc Lean*) Wasn't that beautiful, Mac!

MC LEAN. She can dance in my cha ya any day.

SAKINI. You sit beside Lotus Blossom now, boss. You guest of honor and referee.

FISBY (*starts to sit down*). Referee! I

thought this was a birthday party.

SAKINI. Lotus Blossom now putting on wrestling match for you, boss.

FISBY. *Wrestling* match?

LOTUS BLOSSOM (*stands and claps hands*). Sa, osumo hajime mashoyo. (*Immediately two men bring in four poles which they set up downstage center to mark a square. Each pole has colored cloth hanging from it.*)

MC LEAN. Who is wrestling? (*He sits next to Fisby*)

SAKINI. Wrestling match between Chief of Agriculture and Chief of Police.

FISBY (*to Lotus Blossom*). Hokaida and Seiko? (*She nods*)

SAKINI. Grudge fight, boss.

FISBY. Really?

SAKINI. Whoever win match get to haul sweet potatoes for Lotus Blossom.

FISBY (*watching the poles being set up, he indicates them to Lotus Blossom*). Why have they wrapped colored cloth around the poles?

LOTUS BLOSSOM. Kuro wa fuyu, Ao wa haru, Akaga natsu de, Shirowa akiyo. Wakkatta?

SAKINI. She explain, boss, that black cloth remind us of winter, green cloth remind us of spring, red is the summer and white the autumn.

LOTUS BLOSSOM (*claps her hands*). Osumo, osumo!

(*Mr. Hokaida, bare except for a pair of black shorts, enters and crosses to one corner of the ring, where he squats on his heels. An outburst of approval greets his entrance. He smiles with fatuous pleasure, and makes a desperate effort to hold in his fat stomach.*)

MC LEAN. Do his black shorts mean anything?

SAKINI. Just easy to clean.

(*Lotus Blossom claps her dainty hands again. Mr. Seiko enters, lean and wiry, also wearing black shorts and a sweat shirt reading U.S.S. Princeton.*)

FISBY. Where did he get *that?*

SAKINI. Sailor at naval base. Some class, eh? (*Mr. Seiko peels off the shirt to great applause and squats in the opposite corner. He glares across at Hokaida, who thrusts his jaw forward*) They waiting on you to give signal now, boss.

FISBY. Waiting on *me?*

SAKINI. Oh, yes . . . you are Honorable Referee.

LOTUS BLOSSOM (*hands her fan to Fisby*). Korede aizu shite kudasai.

FISBY. What do I do with this?

SAKINI. Now you cover face with fan.

FISBY. Why?

SAKINI. That mean you not take sides. Now you go to center of ring and drop fan from face.

MC LEAN. And get the hell out in a hurry.

FISBY. How many falls?

SAKIN. No falls, boss. First one to throw other out of ring—winner. (*Fisby covers his face with the fan and walks down center. The two wrestlers crouch, poised to leap, their eyes on the fan. Fisby whips the fan away from his face and dashes back out of range. The protagonists circle each other slowly. Suddenly all hell breaks loose. The teahouse guests cheer their favorite. The fat Mr. Hokaida picks up Mr. Seiko and subjects him to a series of head spins and thumpings. But he exhausts himself; and it is Seiko who ends by tossing Hokaida out of the ring. A cheer rises from the guests. Fisby sighs with relief*) Now the judges must decide who win.

FISBY. Decide! Is there any doubt?

(*The three judges confer. They then turn to Mr. Hokaida and bow.*)

SAKINI. Mr. Hokaida! The winner . . .

(*This startling announcement is greeted with approval. Seiko beats his head and wails.*)

FISBY. How *could* he be the winner! He was thrown out of the ring.

SAKINI. Maybe so, but judges all cousins of Mr. Hokaida.

FISBY. But the judges are wrong.

SAKINI (*confidentially*). We know who really win . . . but this way nobody lose face. (*Seiko and Hokaida exit.*)

LOTUS BLOSSOM. Sa kondo wa Fu-san no ban yo.

SAKINI. Lotus Blossom say guests now wish *you* to perform.

FISBY. Perform what?

SAKINI. They like now for you and doctor to sing song or something.

FISBY. Sing!

SAKINI. Must do, boss. Bad manners to refuse.

FISBY (*repeats in alarm*). Sing! (*He turns to McLean*) Get on your feet, Mac, we've got to sing something.

MC LEAN. What?

FISBY. We could sing the national anthem.

MC LEAN. No, we couldn't—I don't know the words.

FISBY. How about "Deep in the Heart of Texas"?

MC LEAN. Why not? There're no Texans here. (*They step forward*)

FISBY. Mac, let's have some fun. (*He turns to Sakini.*) Sakini, you tell them they must all help us. They must clap and sing "Deep in the Heart of Texas" every time *we* do.

SAKINI (*beaming*). Tewo tataite Deep in the Heart of Texas. (*Demonstrates clapping*) Koshte, Deep in the Heart of Texas. (*The Villagers chatter and agree with enthusiasm. Fisby and Mc Lean stand close together and begin singing. Each time they come to the designated phrase, Sakini gives a signal and the Villagers join in lustily. Lost in their eager concentration, no one observes the entrance of Colonel Purdy. He looks from the "kimono"-clad figures of Fisby and Mc Lean to the assemblage. As he shouts at Fisby, his voice is drowned out by the chorus of "Deep in the Heart of Texas." The song continues. Purdy signals off stage. Gregovich enters and is instructed by Colonel Purdy to end the objectionable noises.*)

GREGOVICH. Captain Fisby!

(*Again the voice coincides with the shouts of "Deep in the Heart of Texas" and is lost. Colonel Purdy stalks downstage center, followed by Gregovich.*)

PURDY. Captain Fisby! What in the name of Occupation is going on here?

(*Fisby gasps and backs away. Suddenly aware of his bathrobe, he stoops down to cover his bare legs. Mc Lean surrenders completely to panic. He runs to hide behind guests. The Guests, alarmed by the sudden intrusion, scatter in all directions. In the midst of this bedlam—*)

THE PANELS ARE LOWERED

## SCENE 2

SCENE: *Office of Captain Fisby.*
TIME: *Next morning.*

AT RISE: *The four bamboo panels are down. Sakini enters from the wings right and crosses down to the footlights.*

———

SAKINI (*bows*).
When present is blackest,
Future can only be brighter.
Okinawa invaded many times.
Not sink in ocean yet.
Survive Chinese.
Survive Japanese.
Survive missionaries and Americans.
Invaded by typhoon.
Invaded by locust.
Invaded by cockroach and sweet-potato moth.
Tobiki now invaded by Honorable Colonel.
Not sink in ocean.
(*He goes to the left side of the stage and raises the panels in front of Fisby's office. He then exits. Colonel Purdy is seated at Fisby's desk going through his papers. Fisby stands behind him nervously watching. Mc-Lean sits on the cot biting his nails. He rises.*)

PURDY (*without looking up*). Sit down! (*Mc Lean sits down again. Purdy turns to Fisby and glares at him*) Where are your bimonthly Progress Reports?

FISBY. I—I think they should be right here under the cricket cage, sir.

PURDY (*takes some papers from under the cage and glances at them*). These are all completely blank. (*He turns to Fisby*) Fisby, you can't convince me that you've been down here for two months doing absolutely nothing.

FISBY. O, no, sir. I mean yes, sir, I have not been doing "nothing."

PURDY. You're beginning to sound like a native.

MC LEAN (*rises*). The tendency is always to descend to the level of the environment, sir. It's a primary postulate of psychology.

PURDY (*turns on him*). Well, it's a primary regulation of the Army to make out reports! (*Back to Fisby*) Now, I want to know exactly what you've accomplished here from the moment you arrived.

FISBY. Well, let me think . . .

MC LEAN. Could I—

PURDY. Sit down! (*He turns to Fisby*) How many lectures have you delivered to the village children on democratic theory?

FISBY. Well, let me see.

PURDY. Four—five?

FISBY (*thinks*). Not that many, sir.

PURDY. Three?

MC LEAN (*hopefully*). Two?

FISBY. N-no.

PURDY. You only delivered *one* lecture?

FISBY. None, sir.

PURDY. Don't tell me you haven't delivered a single lecture!

FISBY. Yes, sir, I haven't delivered no lecture. I mean . . . any lecture.

PURDY. Did you organize a Ladies' League for Democratic Action?

FISBY (*beaming*). Yes, sir. I sure did. I did that all right!

PURDY. And how many lectures on democratic theory have you given *them*?

FISBY (*deflated again*). None, sir.

PURDY. You can't mean none. You must mean one or two.

FISBY. No, sir, none.

PURDY. I refuse to believe it.

FISBY. I'm glad, sir.

MC LEAN (*rises in desperation*). Sir, I *must* go.

PURDY. Where!

MC LEAN. My *seedlings* are wilting. I have to transplant them.

PURDY. Captain, you will pack your gear and transplant yourself to your unit at once.

MC LEAN. Yes, sir. (*He turns to Fisby*) They'll die. It's murder. (*He goes to the door and turns sadly to Fisby again*) Please take care of my beans. (*He exits*)

PURDY (*turns back to Fisby*). Now! Is the schoolhouse finished?

FISBY (*sighs*). No, sir.

PURDY. *Why* isn't it finished?

FISBY. It isn't finished, sir, because it isn't started.

PURDY. I have a splitting headache, Fisby. I ask you not to provoke me needlessly. Now, where is the schoolhouse?

FISBY. I never built it.

PURDY. Don't stand there and tell me you never built it. I sent the lumber down two months ago.

FISBY (*impressed*). Is it *that* long, sir?

PURDY. What did you do with the lumber I sent?

FISBY. Well, I built a teahouse.

PURDY (*stares at him*). I don't suppose you have any aspirin here?

FISBY. No, sir, I haven't.

PURDY. Now, sit down. Fisby. I want to be fair. (*Fisby sits down*) I'm a patient man. When I run into something that defies reason, I like to find the reason. (*Explodes*) What in the name of Occupation do you mean by saying you built a *teahouse* instead of a *schoolhouse!*

FISBY. It's a little hard to explain, sir. Everybody in the village wanted one . . . and Lotus Blossom needed it for her work.

PURDY. And just what is your relationship with this woman?

FISBY. Well, she was a present. So to speak. She's a geisha girl—after a fashion.

PURDY. You built this teahouse—this place for her to ply her trade—with lumber belonging to the Army of Occupation of the United States Government?

FISBY. Well, it just seemed like lumber at the time.

PURDY. Fisby, are you operating a house of prostitution here on Government rice?

FISBY. No, sir! Geishas aren't what you think.

PURDY. Don't tell me what to think. Army Intelligence warned me I'd find something mighty peculiar going on in Tobiki.

FISBY. What's Army Intelligence got to do with it, sir?

PURDY. You're not very cunning, Fisby. With all the Occupation money on the island finding its way to this village, did you think it wouldn't come to the attention of Intelligence?

FISBY. Oh.

PURDY. Why did you do it, Fisby, why!

FISBY. Well, Lotus Blossom had to have a place to teach the Ladies' League how to become geishas and—

PURDY. Fisby! You mean to say you've turned all the decent women of this village into professional . . . (*He slumps into the chair*) How could you sink to such depths, man!

FISBY. I was only giving in to what the majority wanted, sir.

PURDY. I don't doubt that statement—not at all. It is a sad thing that it took a war to convince me that most of the human race is degenerate. Thank God I come from a country where the air is clean, where the wind is fresh, where—

FISBY (*interrupts*). For heaven's sake, sir, would you please listen to me instead of yourself! There is not a thing goes on in that teahouse that your mother couldn't watch.

PURDY (*leaps to his feet and points a warning finger*). You be careful how you use my mother's name, Fisby.

FISBY. Well, *my* mother then. I swear there's nothing immoral about our teahouse.

PURDY. Then answer me this. What is bringing all that Occupation money to this particular village? There is only one thing that attracts that kind of money.

FISBY. Well, evidently there are two things.

PURDY. And if it isn't honor that you sell here, what is it?

FISBY (*sighs unhappily*). We . . . make things.

PURDY. What?

FISBY. Mats . . . and hats . . . and cricket cages.

PURDY. One hundred and fifty thousand yen finds its way to this village every month. You can't convince me that the American soldier is spending that much on "cricket cages."

FISBY. Well, naturally . . . not all of it. (*The telephone rings. Fisby looks at it apprehensively*)

PURDY. Answer it.

FISBY (*pauses*). It's nothing important, sir.

PURDY. It might be for me. Answer it.

FISBY (*airily*). Oh, it rings all day, sir. Pay no attention.

PURDY. Then I'll *answer* it! (*He picks up the telephone. Fisby covers his face*) Hello? *What* do you want? Who is this? Well, Commander Myers, I think you have the wrong connection. This is not a brewery. Yes . . . yes . . . yes! (*He turns to look at Fisby.*) Oh . . . I see. I see. I see. (*He hangs up. He turns to Fisby, who smiles weakly*)

FISBY. It was the only thing we could make that anyone wanted to buy, sir.

PURDY. Brandy! (*Sadly*) I don't know which is worse. Putting your country in the white slave trade or the wholesale liquor business. Congress will have to decide.

FISBY. We've the most prosperous village on the island, sir.

PURDY. This ends my Army career. I promised Mrs. Purdy I'd come out a general. You've broken a fine woman's heart, Fisby.

FISBY. You said to make the village self-supporting, sir.

PURDY. I didn't tell you to encourage lewdness and drunkenness. You've sullied the reputation of your nation and all the tears—

FISBY. All right, sir, shall I kill myself?

PURDY. Oh, don't minimize this. You don't know the enemy's genius for propaganda.

FISBY. Does anyone have to know, sir? We're doing all right.

PURDY (explodes). Yes, they have to know! I requested an investigation myself. I've notified the Inspector General. Now I'll have to radio the whole story to Washington.

FISBY. Oh.

PURDY (calmer). Well, what have you done with all this money you've made so dishonestly?

FISBY. Banked it in Seattle.

PURDY. Oh, that's despicable—making a personal fortune off the labor of these ignorant people.

FISBY. I haven't touched a cent for myself, sir. It's been deposited in the name of the Tobiki Co-operative. The whole village are equal partners. Share and share alike.

PURDY (leaps up). That's *Communism!*

FISBY. Is it?

PURDY (sinks down again). I'll be lucky to get out of this war a private. (He is a beaten man) Well, there is only one thing for me to do.

FISBY. What is that, sir?

PURDY. First, you are to consider yourself under technical arrest. You will proceed to H.Q. at once to await court-martial.

FISBY. Yes, sir.

PURDY (steps to the door). Gregovich! (He turns back to Fisby) I must go on to Awasi this afternoon on an inspection tour. But before I leave, I intend to wipe this stain from our country's honor.

(Sergeant Gregovich enters and salutes.)

GREGOVICH. You called, sir?

PURDY. I did. We have some business to attend to here before going on to Awasi.

GREGOVICH. Yes, sir. I'm glad to hear it. (He turns to Fisby) May I congratulate you on what you've done to this village, sir. It's a dream.

FISBY. Thank you, Sergeant.

PURDY. It is an alcoholic dream. It is one vast distillery. I want you to take a detail and some axes and smash every still in this village.

GREGOVICH. Destroy them?

PURDY. Beyond repair. I want you to take another detail and rip down that teahouse.

GREGOVICH. But, Colonel—

PURDY. Pile the lumber beside the warehouse. That is an order. Do you understand?

GREGOVICH. Yes, sir!

(As he turns to follow orders, Fisby sinks into his chair and the scene blacks out quickly.)

CURTAIN


SCENE 3

SCENE: *Teahouse of the August Moon.*
TIME: *A few hours later.*
AT RISE: *All the panels are down. Behind the scenes can be heard the destruction of the stills and the dismantling of the teahouse. Sakini comes out from the wings and crosses down to the footlights. He flinches at the sound of an ax falling on wood.*

———

SAKINI (sadly). Oh, no comment.
(He walks back into the wings as all the panels are raised simultaneously. Only the frame of the teahouse has been spared. The paper panels have disappeared, the pagoda roof is gone with its tinkling bells. There are no colored lanterns and no dwarf pines to grace the path. The bare supports stand stark and ugly. Resting at the edge of the frame is a wheelbarrow. Lotus Blossom is collecting the last of her possessions. She takes a brass brazier down to place in the wheelbarrow. Then she stands with her back to the audience surveying all that remains of the teahouse. Fisby comes on, and, seeing Lotus Blossom, hesitates. Then he crosses to stand beside her. He takes her hand, and the two of them stand looking at the ruins. Lotus Blossom walks to the center

*of the teahouse and sits on the bare floor. Fisby comes up and sits on the floor facing her. She goes through the ceremony of pouring him an imaginary cup of tea. Fisby accepts with mock formality. As he takes the cup and pretends to drink it, Lotus Blossom covers her face with her hands. Fisby sits watching her mutely.)*

SAKINI (*entering*). Jeep all loaded, boss.

FISBY. I'll be along in a minute.

SAKINI. Oh, pretty soon have nice schoolhouse here.

FISBY (*bitterly*). Pentagon-shaped.

SAKINI. Not be too bad. You take Lotus Blossom with you?

FISBY. No.

SAKINI. What happen to her then?

FISBY. What would have happened to her if we'd never come along?

SAKINI. Not know. Maybe someday she meet nice man and give up Geisha Guild.

FISBY. Ask her if there is anything I can do for her before I go.

SAKINI (*comes up to stand behind them*). Nanika iitai?

LOTUS BLOSSOM (*softly*). Fu-san, watashito kekkon shite chodai.

SAKINI (*scolding*). Sonna bakana koto.

LOTUS BLOSSOM (*persistent*). Iikara hayaku itte!

FISBY. What does she want?

SAKINI. Oh, that crazy Lotus Blossom. She want you to marry her.

FISBY. Why should she want to marry me?

SAKINI. She think you nicest man she ever see, boss.

FISBY. Tell her that I am clumsy, that I seem to have a gift for destruction. That I'd disillusion her as I have disillusioned her people.

SAKINI. Kokai suruyo.

LOTUS BLOSSOM. Ikitai noyo. Amerika ni. Ikitai noyo.

SAKINI. She say she think she like to go to America. There everybody happy. Sit around and drink tea while machines do work.

FISBY. She wouldn't like it, Sakini. I should hate to see her wearing sweaters and sport shoes and looking like an American looking like an Oriental.

SAKINI. But she want to be an American, boss. She never see an American she not

like, boss.

FISBY. Some of them wouldn't like her, Sakini. In the small town where I live, there'd be some who would make her unhappy.

SAKINI. Why, boss?

FISBY. She'd be different.

SAKINI. Dame dayo.

LOTUS BLOSSOM (*takes Fisby's hand*). Sonna koto naiwa, Amerikatte minshu shugi desumono ne.

SAKINI. She say not believe that. In America everybody love everybody. Everybody help everybody; that's democracy.

FISBY. No. That's faith. Explain to her that democracy is only a method—an ideal system for people to get together. But that unfortunately . . . the people who get together . . . are not always ideal.

SAKINI. That's very hard to explain, boss. She girl in love. She just want to hear pretty things.

FISBY. Then tell her that I love what she is, and that it would be wrong to change that. To impose my way of life on her.

SAKINI. Tassha dene!

FISBY. Tell her that I shall never forget her. Nor this village. Tell her that in the autumn of my life—on the other side of the world—when an August moon rises from the east, I will remember what was beautiful in my youth, and what I was wise enough to leave beautiful.

SAKINI. Issho wasurenai kara ne. Mangetsu no yoru niwa anata o omoidashimasu.

LOTUS BLOSSOM (*remains silent a moment*). Watashi mo Fu-san no koto issho wasurenaiwa. Fu-san no koto uta ni shite, Okinawaju ni hirome masu.

SAKINI. She say she always remember you, boss. She say she guess maybe she be what she is—first-class geisha girl. She want you to know she make up long song-story about you to sing in teahouse. And maybe hundred years from now, you be famous all over Okinawa.

FISBY (*rises*). I'd like that.

LOTUS BLOSSOM (*rises*). Iinoyo. Fu-san damedemo Seiko-san ga irun dakara.

SAKINI. She say, since you not marry her, maybe you suggest somebody here. (*Fisby laughs*) She say that Mr. Seiko been looking at her like sick goat. She say what you think of him?

FISBY. Well, he took an awful beating just so he could carry her sweet potatoes.

LOTUS BLOSSOM. Fu-san, Seiko-san iito omouno?

SAKINI. She say you think she ought to marry him?

FISBY. I think she ought to decide for herself.

(*And Mr. Seiko enters. He is dressed in his white suit and his hair is slicked down tight. He crosses to Lotus Blossom. They all turn to look at him.*)

SEIKO (*bows to Lotus Blossom*). A, boku, oshimasho.

SAKINI (*to Fisby*). Mr. Seiko tell Lotus Blossom he sure like to push her wheelbarrow for her.

LOTUS BLOSSOM. Iikara sakini itte chodai.

SAKINI. She say, oh, all right, but not to think that means she's his property.

(*Mr. Seiko beams like a schoolboy and, picking up the handles of the wheelbarrow, he trots off stage with Lotus Blossom's possessions. She turns to Fisby and hands him her fan.*)

LOTUS BLOSSOM. Korede aizu shite chodai. Soremade watashi dokonimo ikimasen kara.

SAKINI. She say she go now, but you still her boss. She not go until you give signal. (*Fisby takes the fan and puts it before his eyes. Without waiting for him to drop it, Lotus Blossom runs off right. When he lowers the fan, he knows she's gone. He sits down on the platform that had been the teahouse veranda*) You go now, boss?

FISBY. Shortly.

SAKINI. Since you not take Lotus Blossom, maybe you take me, boss?

FISBY. Major McEvoy is coming down to take charge. You'll work with him.

SAKINI. Would rather work with you.

FISBY. You'll like Major McEvoy.

SAKINI. I'll work for you for half price, boss.

FISBY. Major McEvoy will need your help in getting this village on its feet again.

SAKINI. You very hard man to bargain with, boss. If you want, I work for rice rations only.

FISBY. No.

SAKINI. You mean you going to make me work for *nothing,* boss?

FISBY. I mean *yes,* you're *not* going to work for me at all. And you belong here.

SAKINI. You know what I think happen when Americans leave Okinawa?

FISBY. What?

SAKINI (*grins*). I think maybe we use pentagon-shaped schoolhouse for teahouse. (*Fisby laughs. He gives Sakini a slap on the shoulder.*)

FISBY. Good-bye, Sakini, you're a rare rascal and I'll miss you.

SAKINI. Good-bye, boss. (*Fisby starts off left. He has gone halfway when Sakini calls*) Boss—

FISBY (*stops*). Yes?

SAKINI. You not failure.

FISBY (*laughs*). I'll tell you something, Sakini. I used to worry a lot about not being a big success. I must have felt as you people felt at always being conquered. Well, now I'm not so sure who's the conqueror and who the conquered.

SAKINI. Not understand, boss.

FISBY. It's just that I've learned from Tobiki the wisdom of gracious acceptance. I don't want to be a world leader. I'm making peace with myself somewhere between my ambitions and my limitations.

SAKINI. That's good?

FISBY. It's a step backward in the right direction. (*He throws Sakini a salute*) Take care. (*He walks off and Sakini watches him go. Then, with a sigh, Sakini turns to survey the skeleton of the teahouse. The silence is broken by the stormy entrance of Colonel Purdy*)

PURDY. Sakini! Where is Captain Fisby?

SAKINI (*points*). Just leaving, boss.

PURDY (*shouts*). Fisby! Fisby! (*Gestures frantically*) Come back here at once! (*He goes to the platform and sinks down gasping*) I'm not in shape—too much paper work. (*Fisby returns from the left*) Where in hell have you been, Fisby? I've been looking all over for you.

FISBY. I'm ready to leave, sir.

PURDY. You can't leave. You've got to stay here. You've got to help me, Fisby.

FISBY. Help doing what, sir?

PURDY. Pulling this village back together again. All hell has broken loose, Fisby. (*He sits down to wipe his brow*) Where is Gregovich!

FISBY. Breaking up the last of the stills, sir.

PURDY. Oh, *no!* (*He holds his head*)

FISBY. What's happened, sir?

PURDY. I radioed the report to Washington. Some fool senator misunderstood. He's using this village as an example of American "get-up-and-go" in the recovery program. The Pentagon is boasting. Congress is crowing. We're all over the papers.

FISBY. But that's wonderful, sir.

PURDY. No, it's not wonderful. A Congressional Committee is flying over to study our methods. They are bringing in photographers for a magazine spread. Today, Fisby, today!

FISBY. Oh, that's bad, sir.

PURDY (*wails*). Gregovich!

FISBY. Isn't there any way to stall them off, sir? Quarantine the place or something?

PURDY. You can't quarantine a congressman. They have immunity or something. (*He takes Fisby by the jacket*) Fisby, help me. I don't ask it for my sake. I ask it for Mrs. Purdy. I could be a brigadier yet. (*Before Fisby can answer, Gregovich comes in from the left and salutes.*)

GREGOVICH. You called, sir?

PURDY (*hurries over to him*). Gregovich! Gregovich! You haven't destroyed all the stills, have you, Gregovich? No, of course you haven't.

GREGOVICH. Yes, sir, I have. I carried out orders to the letter.

PURDY (*turns away shouting*). Why can't someone disobey orders once in a while! What has happened to the American spirit of rebellion! (*Gregovich hiccups, smiles sillily and folds up on the floor. Fisby and Purdy race over to kneel beside him.*) Sunstroke?

FISBY. Potato brandy.

PURDY. Sergeant, wake up. Do you hear me? That's an order.

FISBY. I'm afraid he's passed out, sir.

PURDY. It's desertion. I need every man. Gregovich, get to your feet! (*With Fisby's help he gets Gregovich to his feet*)

GREGOVICH. Sorry, sir.

PURDY. I want to ask you some questions. Stop weaving.

GREGOVICH. *You're* weaving, sir. *I'm* perfectly still.

PURDY. You smell like a brewery.

GREGOVICH. I fell in a vat.

PURDY. You got drunk.

GREGOVICH. No, sir. I fell in a vat.

Naturally, I had to open my mouth to yell for help.

PURDY. Go to the office and sober up at once.

GREGOVICH. Yes, sir. (*He salutes with a happy smile, jogs off*)

PURDY. I'm a sinking ship . . . scuttled by my own men.

(*He sinks. Sakini, who has been sitting with arms folded and a fatuous grin on his face, speaks up.*)

SAKINI. Colonel Purdy?

PURDY. Don't bother me.

SAKINI. Stills not all destroyed.

PURDY. I haven't got time to . . . What did you say?

SAKINI. We not born yesterday. Get sergeant drunk . . . and give him water barrels to break.

PURDY. Sakini, my friend, you're not just saying that to make me feel better?

SAKINI. Oh, stills all good as ever. Production not cease yet.

FISBY (*fondly*). You really are a rogue, Sakini.

PURDY. No . . . he's really an American. He has get-up-and-go.

FISBY. Sakini, if everybody in the village worked together . . . how long would it take to rebuild the teahouse?

PURDY. We don't ask the impossible.

SAKINI. Oh, maybe three minutes . . . maybe five.

PURDY. That's impossible.

SAKINI. We not destroy. Just take away and hide. You watch now, boss. (*He turns and calls*) Oi, mo iiyo, mo iiyo. (*From the wings, right and left, the Villagers step out*) Oi, haba, haba. (*The Villagers respond with happy cries and dash off*) Country that has been invaded many times soon master art of hiding things.

PURDY. You think we can pull it off, Sakini?

SAKINI. You watch now.

(*And even as he speaks, the sections of the teahouse are carried in and the swift work of putting them together progresses before our eyes. Music is heard in the background. The pagoda roof with its tinkling bells is lowered. The dwarf pines and the arched bridge are brought back. The colored panels are slipped into place and the lanterns are hung. Lotus Blossom comes on with flowers*) *which she arranges. Sakini snaps his fingers and the August moon is magically turned on in the sky. When the final lantern is hung, McLean comes in. He stops. His mouth falls open.)*

PURDY. Close your mouth, Captain— haven't you ever seen a cha ya before? (*He turns back to Fisby*) Fisby, this is a land of adventure . . . a land of jade and spices . . . of Chinese junks and river pirates. . . . Makes a man's blood pound.

FISBY. Colonel . . . I consider what you just said pure . . . (*He pauses*) . . . poetry.

PURDY. Thank you . . . thank you, boy. (*He sighs ectstatically*) It's the mystery of the Orient.

FISBY. It's beautiful. Simply beautiful.

PURDY. There's only one thing wrong. It needs a sign to tell people what it is. And I think we ought to put a sign up over there naming this Grace Purdy Avenue. And another sign . . .

FISBY. Colonel Purdy. Won't you have a cup of tea? (*He takes his arm. As he propels him toward the teahouse, he speaks over his shoulder to Sakini.*) Twenty Star for the colonel, Sakini.

(*As the bamboo panels begin to descend on the teahouse, Sakini steps down to the audience.*)

SAKINI. Little story now concluded.
History of world unfinished.
Lovely ladies . . . kind gentlemen—
Go home to ponder.
What was true at the beginning remains true.
Pain makes man think.
Thought makes man wise.
Wisdom makes life endurable.
Our play has ended.
May August moon bring gentle sleep. (*He bows*)

THE CURTAIN FALLS

# 1954-55

Tennessee Williams became the first three-time winner of a Critics' Circle prize with *Cat on a Hot Tin Roof*. This play also won him his second Pulitzer award.

The first nine months of the 1954–55 season offered a meager measure of American plays that could have been considered of prize-winning caliber. Had the decision to be made as of March 1, the contest would have been between *The Bad Seed*, Maxwell Anderson's dramatization of the late William March's novel, and *The Desperate Hours*, Joseph Hayes's dramatization of his own best-selling novel. If the standing of these two plays in the eventual Circle vote can be accepted as conclusive evidence, Hayes would have won.

In either case, there would have been a feeling that it had been a mediocre season. Both *The Bad Seed* and *The Desperate Hours*, while providing top theatrical entertainment and excitement, bore the mark of melodrama of a frankly extroverted type that, right or wrong, has a couple of strikes on it in the eyes of the deep-thinkers who deal in prize-giving.

Other than *The Desperate Hours* and *The Bad Seed*, there had been Robert Anderson's *All Summer Long*, which had nothing like the skill or impact of his earlier *Tea and Sympathy*; N. Richard Nash's *The Rainmaker*, with more claim than most to critical appreciation; *The Traveling Lady*, a disappointing effort by Horton Foote, one of those often-a-bridesmaid-but-never-a-bride playwrights; and *The Flowering Peach*, Clifford Odets' treatment of the Noah story, too sophomoric in conception.

The arrival on March 2 of William Inge's *Bus Stop*, a much better play in every respect than his prize-winning *Picnic* of 1952–53, took the critics off the hook, so to speak. This was a really respectable candidate. Twenty-two days later, along came *Cat on a Hot Tin Roof*, and, while it scarcely could be called respectable, it mesmerized just enough members of the Circle to win the award.

The vote was nine for *Cat* and eight for *Bus Stop*. *The Desperate Hours* received three votes; *The Bad Seed* and *The Rainmaker*, one each.

As though to contradict my earlier comment about melodrama, Agatha Christie's *Witness for the Prosecution* walked away with the foreign play citation, receiving ten votes to four each for Christopher Fry's *The Dark is Light Enough* (it wasn't) and Jean Anouilh's *Thieves' Carnival* (an off-Broadway production, by the way), and two each for Graham Greene's *The Living Room* and Guy Bolton's English version of Marcelle Maurette's French *Anastasia*.

The Circle's award to a musical went to Gian-Carlo Menotti's *The Saint of Bleecker Street*, which received eleven votes to six for *The Pajama Game*, three for *Plain and Fancy* and one each for *Fanny* and *Silk Stockings*.

Menotti presents something of a problem for the Circle. He doesn't write musicals; he writes operas. Yet they are given Broadway rather than operatic presentation. The Circle gave Menotti its award in 1949–50 for *The Consul*. But every season that he has a new opera on the boards there is some muttering among Circle members as to whether they're doing right by the authors of the regular type of musical in considering their works on the same plane with Menotti's. Frankly, it would seem they were not. Even if Menotti turned out a mediocre product, the prestige of opera would give him a certain psychological edge. The honest thing to do would be to rule him out, even at this late date.

Whether it is Menotti or Hammerstein, opera or regulation musical, the drama critics are not too comfortable with either. It might be just as well if the Circle dropped the musical category altogether. It isn't that the Circle ever has made an especially reprehensible selection in this department—after all, musicals have only been considered for ten seasons and there is always a limited number from which to choose.

But anyone who really knows the musical game—it's a very special one—and reads the reviews regularly over a couple of seasons has to come to the conclusion that the critics are not at knowledgeable ease in the medium. Even when they manage to come up with the right over-all estimate, more often than not they have arrived at it despite a number of misplaced judgments of the many elements involved, from the pulchritude of the chorus girls to the value of the music, especially the latter.

This season, incidentally, supplied about a third more musicals than has been customary in recent years—thirteen. The over-all production level, at fifty-six, was slightly under what has come to be normal in these restricted years. But, from a financial standpoint, it was considered an excellent season. Even plays that didn't last on Broadway long enough to make a profit, ended in the black through movie sales. Television bleached the red ink from the musical version of *Peter Pan,* an estimable production improperly geared finance-wise to make a profit. For a long time the money-makers have been approximately one in four productions; this season the rate was about one in three.

Almost the only extracurricular excitement of the season was provided by Williams' prize-winner, which certainly didn't suffer from the box-office standpoint as a result of it. The word got around quickly after opening night—it even had seeped in from the tryout engagement—that this was a "dirty" play. And it was—and is. Despite whatever high-minded intent anyone may find in it, the simple, unprejudiced truth is that no play that has achieved Broadway production ever has contained so much rough dialogue of a sexual nature. And this has nothing whatever to do with the fact that an important element of the drama is homosexuality. That theme in itself does not make for a "dirty" play.

The author simply seems to have reveled in seeing how much he could get away with—well beyond the demands of character, plot, situation and theme—like a small boy engaging in a exhibitionistic orgy with a piece of chalk on an outhouse wall. One item in the play that gained quick circulation was the extraneous introduction of the "elephant profile" smoking-car story in the third act.

The almost immediate result was that the city's license commissioner was reported interesting himself in the matter, although he has absolutely no censorship power as such—nor does anyone else in the city of New York where the drama is concerned. But the commissioner does control licenses of buildings such as theatres, and pressure can be brought on a theatre owner, whose property can suddenly become unremunerative if closed for an alleged infraction of any one of numerous, and often obscure, building, fire or safety regulations. This has happened. *Variety* quickly editorialized about what it felt was going to become another case of veiled, unauthorized censorship.

Whether conferences of interested parties were held or not—there were denials—the fact remains that, within two weeks, the elephant story had been dropped, two or three of the more vivid gutter words had been eliminated—and the box office hummed all the while. Williams explained at the time that he never had been convinced that the elephant story should have been kept in the play beyond the tryout date, implying that it would have been excised anyway. The incredible thing is that it ever was allowed to be in the script at all—not from the smut angle, but simply from the standpoint that it meant absolutely nothing to the play. In this connection it should be remembered that the author of a stage play, even one who does not have Williams' stature, has absolute control of the dialogue—if he wants to.

The "dirt" angle was interesting from a reportorial standpoint, but it did not have—or should not have had—any effect in the critical weighing of the play. This reviewer, an unreconstructed *Bus Stop* man, felt that, while *Cat* admittedly has two powerful scenes (which, by the way, are far from actor-proof), Williams does not have an integrated, purposeful drama. The two scenes mentioned make this all too apparent. It has nothing whatever of the poetic quality which some cite as a saving grace in other Williams works, even in such a hodgepodge as *Camino Real*. He couldn't have tried purposely and succeeded in assembling a more boring group of characters. He has nothing to say on human relationships or other profound subjects that has not been said many times and much better. And, finally, he has been in the same thematic and dramatic rut so long that he has become a very dull playwright indeed. He needs to come up for a long breath of fresh air.

The newness of the play, which was first published only a short time ago, precluded the printing of the full text of *Cat on a Hot Tin Roof* in this volume. What follows is a digest of the play, with dialogue excerpts.

# Cat on a Hot Tin Roof

## By TENNESSEE WILLIAMS

Presented by The Playwrights' Company at the Morosco Theatre, New York City, March 24, 1955, with the following cast:

| | |
|---|---|
| LACEY | *Maxwell Glanville* |
| SOOKEY | *Musa Williams* |
| MARGARET | *Barbara Bel Geddes* |
| BRICK | *Ben Gazzara* |
| MAE (Sister Woman) | *Madeleine Sherwood* |
| GOOPER (Brother Man) | *Pat Hingle* |
| BIG MAMA | *Mildred Dunnock* |
| DIXIE | *Pauline Hahn* |
| BUSTER | *Darryl Richard* |
| SONNY | *Seth Edwards* |
| TRIXIE | *Janice Dunn* |
| BIG DADDY | *Burl Ives* |
| REVEREND TOOKER | *Fred Stewart* |
| DOCTOR BAUGH | *R. G. Armstrong* |
| DAISY | *Eva Vaughan Smith* |
| BRIGHTIE | *Brownie McGhee* |
| SMALL | *Sonny Terry* |

---

## SCENE

The bed-sitting-room and section of the gallery of a plantation home in the Mississippi Delta. An evening in summer. The action is continuous, with two intermissions.

---

# Cat on a Hot Tin Roof

## (A Synopsized Version)

In a stage direction near the end of Act II, the author has interpolated an explanation of his intention which will be useful to have at the outset. It reads:

" . . . The bird that I hope to catch in the net of this play is not the solution of one man's psychological problem. I'm trying to catch the true quality of experience in a group of people, that cloudy, flickering, evanescent—fiercely charged!—interplay of live human beings in the thundercloud of a common crisis. Some mystery should be left in the revelation of character in a play, just as a great deal of mystery is always left in the revelation of character in life, even in one's own character to himself. This does not absolve the playwright of his duty to observe and probe as clearly and deeply as he *legitimately* can: but it should steer him away from 'pat' conclusions, facile definitions which make a play just a play, not a snare for the truth of human experience."

The author also gives specific instructions for the set designer as to the mood that should be established on sight by the bed-sitting-room along an upstairs gallery of a plantation home:

" . . . It is Victorian with a touch of the Far East. It hasn't changed much since it was occupied by the original owners of the place, Jack Straw and Peter Ochello, a pair of old bachelors who shared this room all their lives together. In other words, the room must evoke some ghosts; it is gently and poetically haunted by a relationship that must have involved a tenderness which was uncommon. . . . "

This is the room occupied by Brick, the younger son of the family, and his wife, Margaret, "a pretty young woman, with anxious lines in her face." Margaret has come to the room to change her dress, complaining through the bathroom door to Brick, who is taking a shower, that it was soiled during dinner by one of the five "no-neck monsters" who are the children of Brick's older brother, Gooper, a Memphis attorney, and his wife, Mae.

The children are "no-neck monsters," Margaret explains, because "their fat little heads are set on their fat little bodies without a bit of connection," a fact she deplores because they thus have no necks to wring.

But there are more important things disturbing the childless Margaret. The gathering of the clan is because it is Big Daddy's sixty-fifth birthday, and it is her idea that Gooper and Mae are attempting to cut Brick out of the multi-million-dollar estate that Big Daddy is going to relinquish soon because a clinic diagnosis has determined that he is rapidly succumbing to an inoperable cancer. Brick has become an alcoholic, one consequence of which is apparent when he emerges from the bathroom. He uses a crutch; one ankle has been broken and is in a cast. Gooper and Mae, Margaret says, are making too many veiled references to Rainbow Hill, a "place that's famous for treatin' alcoholics an' dope fiends in the movies." Brick observes that he's not in the movies.

MARGARET. No, and you don't take dope. Otherwise you're a perfect candidate for Rainbow Hill, Baby, and that's where they aim to ship you—over my dead body! Yep, over my dead body they'll ship you there, but nothing would please them better. Then Brother Man could get a-hold of the purse strings and dole out remittances to us, maybe get power-of-attorney and sign checks for us and cut off our credit wherever, whenever he wanted! Son-of-a-bitch!—How'd you like that, Baby?—Well, you've been doin' just about ev'rything in your power to bring it about, you've just been doin' ev'ry thing you can think of to aid and abet them in this scheme of theirs! Quittin' work, devoting yourself to the occupation of drinkin'!—Breakin' your ankle last night on the high school athletic field: doin what? Jumpin' hurdles? At two or three in the morning? Just fantastic! . . . But, Brick? You still have one big advantage!

BRICK (*wryly*). Did you *say* something, Maggie?

MARGARET. Big Daddy dotes on you honey. And he can't stand Brother Man and Brother Man's wife, that monster of fertility, Mae; she's downright odious to him! Know how I know? By little expressions that flicker over his face when that woman is holding fo'th on one of her choice topics such as—how she refused twilight sleep!—when the twins were delivered! Because she feels motherhood's an experience that a woman ought to experience fully!—in order to fully appreciate the wonder and beauty of it! HAH!—and how she made Brother Man come in an' stand beside her in the delivery room so he would not miss out on the "wonder and beauty" of it either!—producin' those no-neck monsters. Big Daddy shares my attitude toward those two! As for me, well—I give him a laugh now and then and he tolerates me. In fact! —I sometimes suspect that Big Daddy harbors a little unconscious "lech" fo' me. . . .

BRICK. What makes you think that Big Daddy has a lech for you, Maggie?

MARGARET. Way he always drops his eyes down my body when I'm talkin' to him, drops his eyes to my boobs an' licks his old chops! Ha ha!

BRICK. That kind of talk is disgusting.

MARGARET. Did anyone ever tell you that you're an ass-aching Puritan, Brick? I think it's mighty fine that that ole fellow, on the doorstep of death, still takes in my shape with what I think is deserved appreciation! . . .

As she proceeds with her toilet, Margaret chats wtih seeming irrelevancy about the birthday dinner, her sister-in-law, Mae, who was once a Memphis cotton carnival queen, and suddenly halts to turn on Brick and demand, "Why are you looking at me like that?" He disclaims looking at her at all, and part of the secret of her unhappiness spills out as she confesses that "living with someone you love can be lonelier—than living entirely *alone!*—if the one that y' love doesn't love you. . . . " But she vehemently rejects Brick's suggestion that maybe she would like to live alone.

Margaret returns to small talk again, commenting on the fact that Brick's drinking hasn't yet affected his physical appearance, although he says that he's beginning to get softer.

"Well, sooner or later it's bound to soften you up," Margaret comments. "It was just beginning to soften up Skipper when—"

Skipper is obviously a touchy subject. She breaks off with a brief apology, and resumes talking about Brick's good looks, his detached quality and his ability as a lover:

"You were a wonderful lover. . . . Such a wonderful person to go to bed with, and I think mostly because you were really indifferent to it. Isn't that right? Never had any anxiety about it, did it naturally, easily, slowly, with absolute confidence and perfect calm, more like opening a door for a lady or seating her at a table than giving expression to any longing for her. Your indifference made you wonderful at lovemaking—*strange!*—but true. . . . You know, if I thought you would never, never, *never* make love to me again—I would go downstairs to the kitchen and pick out the longest and sharpest knife I could find and stick it straight into my heart, I swear that I would! But one thing I don't have is the charm of the defeated, my hat is still in the ring, and I am determined to win!—What is the victory of a cat on a hot tin roof?—I wish I knew. . . . Just staying on it, I guess, as long as she can. . . . (*Croquet sounds from outside*) Later tonight I'm going to tell you I love you an' maybe by that time you'll be drunk enough to believe me. Yes, they're playing croquet. . . . Big Daddy is dying of cancer. . . . What were you thinking of when I caught you looking at me like that? Were you thinking of Skipper?"

Mention of the name causes Brick to rise quickly, go to the bar for another of the drinks he consumes almost without stopping. Again she apologizes, but adds that silence about a subject doesn't work, merely magnifies it, causing it to grow and fester.

Margaret tries to make Brick stop drinking until the party starts. She has to explain to him that it is Big Daddy's birthday party, and they get into a raised-voice argument over his refusal to sign a card to go with the present Margaret has purchased as Brick's gift to his father. Mae, who obviously has heard part of the argument, interrupts on the pretense of inquiring about "the invalid," and she and Margaret have a brief exchange of insults involving the "kiddies."

With Mae gone, Margaret tries to make Brick get dressed for the party, but he refuses, although making the concession of donning a pair of pajamas. She explodes again, begging for release from "this punishment," saying that *"I feel all the time like a cat on a hot tin roof."*

"Then jump off the roof," Brick advises, "jump off it, cats can jump off roofs and land on their four feet uninjured! . . . Do it!—fo' God's sake, do it. . . . Take a lover!"

"I can't see a man but you!" she replies. "Even with my eyes closed, I just see you! Why don't you get ugly, Brick, why don't you please get fat or ugly or something so I could stand it?"

She builds up to another passionate appeal that they revise the circumstances of their life together, grasps him by the shoulder for emphasis, and he breaks away. They are interrupted this time by Big Mama, who shouts from outside the door that she has wonderful news about Big Daddy. Brick retreats into the bathroom to leave Margaret alone with his mother, a short, stout woman of sixty who is bursting with the news that she shouts through the bathroom door that the clinic report on Big Daddy has been completely negative as to cancer—his only trouble is a spastic colon.

But Big Mama is not so filled with her news that she isn't interested in prying a bit into the Brick-Margaret situation. Margaret's remarks about the "no-necks" cause Big Mama to say that Margaret simply doesn't like children, which the young woman vehemently denies. She asks about Brick's drinking, pointing out that he did not drink until after he married Margaret, who retorts, *"THAT'S NOT FAIR!"*

"Fair or not fair," Big Mama retorts, "I want to ask you a question, one question: D'you make Brick happy in bed?"

"Why don't you ask him if he makes *me* happy in bed? . . . *It works both ways!"*

"Something's not right! You're childless and my son drinks! (*She points to bed*) When a marriage goes on the rocks, the rocks are *there,* right *there!"*

Big Mama's departure brings Brick out of the bathroom haven to fix himself another drink, while Margaret admires her body before the mirror, comments on her physical desirability to others and rejects Brick's renewed advice that she take a lover. She says she isn't going to give him an excuse to divorce her; he replies that he wouldn't divorce her for any reason. Brick suddenly recalls Big Mama's news about Big Daddy, and Margaret explains that Big Daddy really is dying of cancer, but that he and Big Mama will not be told the truth until after the birthday.

Margaret warms again to the subject of Gooper and Mae trying to do them out of the estate, pointing out that Big Daddy has never made a will. She recounts her background of a genteel family without money, her desire not to go through the rest of her life that way.

"You can be young without money but you can't be old without it," she says. "You've got to be old *with* money because to be old without it is just too awful, you've got to be one or the other, either *young* or *with money,* you can't be old and *without* it. . . ."

Again Margaret brings up the elusive subject of Skipper, and this time she persists despite Brick's demands that she drop it. Her mistake, she says, was in telling Brick the truth "about that thing with Skipper."

MARGARET. This time I'm going to finish what I have to say to you. Skipper and I made love, if love you could call it, because it made both of us feel a little bit closer to you. You see, you son of a bitch, you asked too much of people, of me, of him, of all the unlucky poor damned sons of bitches that happen to love you. . . . And so we made love to each other to dream it was you, both of us! . . .

(*Brick turns suddenly out upon the gallery and calls.*)

BRICK. Little girl! Hey, little girl!

LITTLE GIRL (*at a distance*). What, Uncle Brick?

BRICK. Tell the folks to come up!—Bring everybody upstairs!

MARGARET. I can't stop myself! I'd go on telling you this in front of them all, if I had to! . . . Because it's got to be told and you, you!—you never let me! (*She sobs, then controls herself, and continues almost calmly*) It was one of those beautiful, ideal things they tell about in the Greek legends, it couldn't be anything else, you being you, and that's what made it so sad, that's what made it so awful, because it was love that never could be carried through to anything satisfying or even talked about plainly. Brick, I tell you, you got to believe me, Brick, I *do* understand all about it! I—I think it was—*noble!* Can't you tell I'm sincere when I say I respect it? My only point, the only point that I'm making, is life has got to be allowed to continue even after the *dream* of life is—all—over. Why I remember when we double-dated at college, Gladys Fitzgerald and I and you and Skipper, it was more like a date between you and Skipper. Gladys and I were just sort of tagging along as if it was necessary to chaperone you!—to make a good public impression—

BRICK (*turns to face her, half lifting crutch*). Maggie, you want me to hit you with this crutch? Don't you know I could kill you with this crutch?

MARGARET. Good Lord, man, d'you think I'd care if you did?

BRICK. One man has one great good true thing in his life. One great good thing which is true!—I had friendship with Skipper.— You are naming it dirty!

MARGARET. I'm not naming it dirty! I am naming it clean.

BRICK. Not love with you, Maggie, but friendship with Skipper was that one great true thing, and you are naming it dirty!

MARGARET. Then you haven't been listenin', not understood what I'm saying! I'm naming it so damn clean that it killed poor Skipper!—You two had something that had to be kept on ice, yes, incorruptible, yes!— and death was the only icebox where you could keep it. . . .

BRICK. I married you, Maggie. Why would I marry you, Maggie, if I was—?

MARGARET. Brick, don't brain me yet, let me finish!—I know, believe me I know, that it was only Skipper that harbored even any *unconscious* desire for anything not perfectly pure between you two!—Now let me skip a little. You married me early that summer we graduated out of Ole Miss, and we were happy, weren't we, we were blissful, yes, hit heaven together ev'ry time that we loved! But that fall you and Skipper turned down wonderful offers of jobs in order to keep on bein' football heroes—pro-football heroes. You organized the Dixie Stars that fall, so you could keep on bein' team-mates forever! But somethin' was not right with it!—*Me included!*—between you. Skipper began hittin' the bottle . . . you got a spinal injury —couldn't play the Thanksgivin' game in Chicago, watched it on TV from a traction bed in Toledo. I joined Skipper. The Dixie Stars lost because poor Skipper was drunk. We drank together that night all night in the bar of the Blackstone and when cold day was comin' up over the Lake an' we were comin' out drunk to take a dizzy look at it, I said, "SKIPPER! STOP LOVIN' MY HUSBAND OR TELL HIM HE'S GOT TO LET YOU ADMIT IT TO HIM!"—one way or another! HE SLAPPED ME HARD ON THE MOUTH!—then turned and ran without stopping once, I am sure, all the way back into his room at the Blackstone. . . . When I came to his room that night, with a little scratch like a shy little mouse at his door, he made that pitiful, ineffectual little attempt to prove that what I had said wasn't true. . . . (*Brick strikes at her with crutch*) In this way, I destroyed him, by telling him truth that he and his world which he was born and raised in, yours and his world, had told him could not be told?—From then on Skipper was nothing at all but a receptacle for liquor and drugs. . . .

Brick misses her twice with two swings of the crutch as she talks, then hurls the crutch at her ineffectively, falling to the floor without its support as Dixie, one of the "no-necks," bursts in as part of a game of cowboys and Indians, breaking the tension. Margaret, exasperated, takes the girl's cap pistol and throws it through the gallery doors, causing the child to taunt her, "You're *jealous!*—You're just jealous because you can't have babies!"

Desperate at the taunt, Margaret appeals to Brick, telling him she has seen a gynecologist in Memphis, that she can have a child and that now is the right time of the month for her to conceive.

"But how in hell on earth," he responds, "do you imagine—that you're going to have a child by a man that can't stand you?"

"That's a problem that I will have to work out," she replies as the other members of the family approach their room in answer to Brick's earlier invitation.

## ACT II

They troop into the room—Big Daddy, a tall, fierce-looking, profane man; the Reverend Tooker; Gooper; Mae; the children; Doctor Baugh and Big Mama. Big Daddy engages in a certain amount of barbed raillery with the minister and Big Mama, showing an ill-disguised dislike for both; Negro servants bring in a huge birthday cake, ablaze with candles, and buckets of champagne; there is the usual "Happy Birthday" singing; Margaret brings out Brick's gift to his father, a cashmere robe, and is taunted by Gooper and Mae for having had to buy it herself because Brick never thought about getting his father a gift.

Big Mama has to thrill again over the fact that the medical report on Big Daddy was negative; Big Daddy kids Brick about his accident.

"Was it jumping or humping that you were doing out there?" he asks. "What were you doing out there at three A.M., layin' a woman on that cindertrack?" He rides over his wife's protests about talking so roughly in front o' the minister, continuing: "*QUIET*—I ast you, Brick, if you was cuttin' you'self a piece o' poon-tang last night on that cinder track? I thought maybe you were chasin' poon-tang on that track an' tripped over something in the heat of the chase—'sthat it?"

Big Mama's efforts to tone Big Daddy down rile him to the point of exclaiming to his wife: "You don't know a goddam thing and you never did!" He overrides her protests:

"Oh, yes, I do, oh, yes, I do, I mean it! I put up with a whole lot of crap around here because I thought I was dying. And you thought I was dying and you started taking over, well, you can stop taking over now, Ida, because I'm not gonna die, you can just stop now this business of taking over because you're not taking over because I'm not dying, I went through the laboratory and the goddam exploratory operation and there's nothing wrong with me but a spastic colon. And I'm not dying of cancer which you thought I was dying of. Ain't that so? Didn't you think that I was dying of cancer, Ida? Ain't that so, Ida? Didn't you have an idea I was dying of cancer and now you could take control of this place and everything on it? I got that impression, I seemed to get that impression. Your loud voice everywhere, your fat old body butting in here and there!"

Her admonishment for him to shush on account of the preacher, who by now has left the room, gets the retort, "Rut the goddam preacher."

Big Daddy continues his tirade, recounting how he started with nothing, worked his way up as overseer of the old Straw and Ochello plantation, became a partner and took it all over and made it much bigger when they passed on. His spastic colon, he reckons, is the result of disgust, brought on: . . . "By all the goddam lies and liars that I have had to put up with, and all the goddam hypocrisy that I lived with all these forty years that we been livin' together!"

"*In all these years you never believed that I loved you?*" Big Mama asks, sobbing. "*And I did, I did so much, I did love you!—I even loved your hate and your hardness, Big Daddy!*"

She rushes from the room as Big Daddy mumbles to himself, "*Wouldn't it be funny if that was true. . . .*"

Big Daddy calls Brick in from the gallery; obviously he wants to have a serious talk with his son. He introduces the matter of Brick not sleeping with Margaret, then shifts to the drink question. He wants to know why Brick drinks. They get nowhere —"*Why is it so damn hard for people to talk?*" Big Daddy finally exclaims.

Taking another tack, Big Daddy reminisces about a trip to Europe with Big Mama some years earlier—about how she bought up everything "in the European fire sale," the misery of the poor people abroad, his disgust with sex mores in Morocco. Brick comments on his talking jag, Big Daddy says he feels like talking because he had been too silent when he feared he might have cancer. He wants to know why Brick is so anxious to shut him up.

"Well, sir," Brick explains, "ever so often you say to me, Brick, I want to have a talk with you, but when we talk, it never materializes. Nothing is said. You sit in a chair and gas about this and that and I look like I listen. I try to look like I listen, but I don't listen, not much. Communication is —awful hard between people an'—somehow between you and me, it just don't—"

But Big Daddy is off on another angle— about the scare he's had, about the fear of death—how it is that of all the creatures only man lacks the comforting ignorance of mortality. Now that the load is lifted, he's going to live a little—he even accepts a drink from Brick; he is going to have some "pleasure with women." Big Mama passes through the room to answer the telephone in the hall and is reprimanded by her husband for the interruption.

"All I ask of that woman is that she leave me alone," he says. "But she can't admit to herself that she makes me sick. That comes of having slept with her too many years. Should of quit much sooner but that old woman she never got enough of it—and I was good in bed . . . I never should of wasted so much of it on her. . . . They say you got just so many and each one is numbered. Well, I got a few left in me, a few, and I'm going to pick me a good one to spend 'em on! I'm going to pick me a choice one, I don't care how much she costs, I'll smother her in—minks! Ha ha! I'll strip her naked and smother her in minks and choke her with diamonds! Ha ha! I'll strip her naked and choke her with diamonds and smother her with minks and hump her from hell to breakfast. *Ha aha ha ha ha!*"

Brick explains his restlessness by saying that he has not yet achieved the peace that comes sometime during his drinking day and night when he has absorbed enough liquor to cause a "click" in his head. The click is late today. This causes Big Daddy to realize more than ever before that he really does have an alcoholic on his hands,

and he probes to get at the reason. He pulls Brick's crutch from him, causing him to fall on his broken ankle.

Bargaining to get back the crutch so he can get another drink, Brick finally admits that he drinks because of "disgust," and Big Daddy naturally wants to know, "Disgust with what?" Given a drink, Brick starts a roundabout explanation about "mendacity," without pinning down who has been lying to him about what. Big Daddy knows all about mendacity:

"Hell! I could write a book on it! Don't you know that? I could write a book on it and still not cover the subject? Well, I could, I could write a goddam book on it and still not cover the subject anywhere near enough!!—Think of all the lies I got to put up with!—Pretenses! Ain't that mendacity? Having to protend stuff you don't think or feel or have any idea of? Having for instance to act like I care for Big Mama! —I haven't been able to stand the sight, sound or smell of that woman for forty years now!—even when I *laid* her!—regular as a piston. . . . Pretend to love that son of a bitch of a Gooper and his wife Mae and those five same screechers out there like parrots in a jungle? Jesus! Can't stand to look at 'em! Church!—it bores the Bejesus out of me but I go!—I go an' sit there and listen to the fool preacher! Clubs!—Elks! Masons! Rotary!—*crap! You* I *do* like for some reason, did always have some kind of real feeling for—affection—respect—yes, always. . . . You and being a success as a planter is all I ever had any devotion to in my whole life!—and that's the truth. . . . I don't know why, but it is! *I've* lived with mendacity!— Why can't *you* live with it? Hell, you *got* to live with it, there's nothing *else* to *live* with except mendacity, is there?"

Brick says there is also liquor. Big Daddy says he is dodging the issue, that his explanation of his drinking is "crap," then he hits the sore spot—"You started drinkin' when your friend Skipper died." Gooper and Mae had suggested there was something "not, well, exactly *normal* in your friendship. . . ."

This brings Brick out of his shell of detachment. He demands to know if Big Daddy is suggesting anything, who else is suggesting such a thing. His father tries to calm him, to tell him how he came to understand many things in his life.

BRICK. Oh, *you* think so, too, you call me your son and a queer. Oh! Maybe that's why you put Maggie and me in this room that was Jack Straw's and Peter Ochello's, in which that pair of old sisters slept in a double bed where both of 'em died!

BIG DADDY. *Now just don't go throwing rocks at—* (*There is an interruption by the Reverend Tooker, seeking directions to the lavatory*)—I seen all things and understood a lot of them, till 1910. Christ, the year that —I had worn my shoes through, hocked my —I hopped off a yellow dog freight car half a mile down the road, slept in a wagon of cotton outside the gin—Jack Straw an' Peter Ochello took me in. Hired me to manage this place which grew into this one.—When Jack Straw died—why, old Peter Ochello quit eatin' like a dog does when its master's dead, and died, too!

BRICK. Christ!

BIG DADDY. I'm just saying I understand such—

BRICK (*violently*). Skipper is dead. I have not quit eating!

BIG DADDY. No, but you started drinking. (*Brick wheels on his crutch and hurls his glass across the room shouting.*)

BRICK. YOU THINK SO, TOO? . . . You think so, too? You think so, too? You think me an' Skipper did, did, did!—*sodomy!*—together?

The son becomes almost hysterical in denouncing those who might think that his relationship with Skipper was "queer," while the father tries to calm him. "I told Mae an' Gooper—" Big Daddy begins.

"Frig Mae and Gooper, frig all dirty lies and liars!" Brick interrupts. "Skipper and me had a clean, true thing between us!— had a clean friendship, practically all our lives, till Maggie got the idea you're talking about. Normal? No!—It was too rare to be normal, any true thing between two people is too rare to be normal. Oh, once in a while he put his hand on my shoulder or I'd put mine on his, oh, maybe even, when we were touring the country in pro-football an' shared hotel-rooms we'd reach across the space between the two beds and shake hands to say goodnight, yeah, one or two times we—"

Big Daddy reminds Brick that nobody thinks that's not normal, but the son replies that they're mistaken if they don't because a pure and true thing is not normal. Big Daddy still insists on knowing why both Skipper and Brick cracked up, and Brick launches into the long explanation of the pro-football continuation of their college careers, how he married Maggie when she said "now or never," how Maggie went on with Skipper and the team when Brick was injured. . . .

BRICK. So! She took this time to work on poor dumb Skipper. He was a less than average student at Ole Miss, you know that, don't you?!—Poured in his mind the dirty, false idea that what we were, him and me, was a frustrated case of that ole pair of sisters that lived in this room, Jack Straw and Peter Ochello!—He, poor Skipper, went to bed with Maggie to prove it wasn't true, and when it didn't work out, he thought it *was* true!—Skipper broke in two like a rotten stick—nobody ever turned so fast to a lush,—or died of it so quick. . . . Now, are you satisfied?

BIG DADDY. Are *you* satisfied?

BRICK. With what?

BIG DADDY. That half-ass story?

BRICK. What's half-ass about it?

BIG DADDY. Something's left out of that story. What did you leave out?

BRICK. Yes!—I left out a long-distance call which I had from Skipper, in which he made a drunken confession to me and on which I hung up!—last time we spoke .to each other in our lives. . . .

BIG DADDY. You hung up?

BRICK. Hung up. Jesus! Well—

BIG DADDY. Anyhow now!—we have tracked down the lie with which you're disgusted and which you are drinking to kill your disgust with, Brick. You been passing the buck. This disgust with mendacity is disgust with yourself. *You!*—dug the grave of your friend and kicked him in it!—before you'd face truth with him!

BRICK. *His* truth, not *mine!*

BIG DADDY. His truth, okay! But you wouldn't face it with him!

BRICK. Who *can* face truth? Can *you?*

BIG DADDY. Now don't start passin' the rotten buck again, boy!

BRICK. *How about these birthday con-*

*gratulations, these many, many happy returns of the day, when ev'rybody but you knows there won't be any!*

Brick suddenly realizes the enormity of his disclosure. He tries to pass over it, but Big Daddy has grasped its significance and insists that he elaborate on it. The father grabs Brick's crutch. Had they been lying to him; did he have cancer?

"Mendacity is a system that we live in," Brick replies. "Liquor is one way out an' death's the other. . . .

"I'm sorry, Big Daddy. My head don't work any more and it's hard for me to understand how anybody could care if he lived or died or was dying or cared about anything but whether or not there was liquor left in the bottle and so I said what I said without thinking. In some ways I'm no better than the others, in some ways worse because I'm less alive. Maybe it's being alive that makes them lie, and being almost *not* alive makes me sort of accidentally truthful—I don't know but—anyway—we've been friends . . . And being friends is telling each other the truth. . . . You told *me!* I told *you!"*

"CHRIST — DAMN — ALL — LYING SONS OF — LYING BITCHES!" Big Daddy finally exclaims as he crosses to the door to go out. "Yes, all liars, all liars, all lying dying liars!—Lying! Dying! Liars!

## ACT III

Immediately after Big Daddy's departure, with Brick outside, Mae, the Reverend Tooker, Gooper, Big Mama, Margaret and Doctor Baugh make quick entrances. Big Mama is animated about the hearty meal Big Daddy put away on the assurance that he was in no danger; Mae and Gooper are anxious to get down to "the talk" now that Big Daddy isn't around. Big Mama is puzzled about the need for a conference. Margaret brings in Brick, but he returns to the gallery later.

Gradually the news is broken to Big Mama that her husband is doomed by cancer. In her grief, her first demand is for Brick, "my only son." This riles Gooper and Mae, but Big Mama retorts that "Goo-

per never liked Daddy." The doctor leaves a package of morphine, saying Big Daddy will be needing it soon, and departs in the wake of the minister. Big Mama tells Margaret that they must straighten out Brick so he can take hold of things, which brings more protests from Mae and Gooper. Mae brings in Gooper's briefcase. Margaret and her in-laws engage in an argument about Brick and the estate that ends in Big Mama screaming for them to stop and asking Margaret to sit with her.

"You jest won't let me do this in a nice way, will yah?" says Gooper. "Aw right— Mae and I have five kids with another one coming! I don't give a goddam if Big Daddy likes me or don't like me or did or never did or will or will never! I'm just appealing to a sense of common decency and fair play. I'll tell you the truth. I've resented Big Daddy's partiality to Brick ever since Brick was born, and the way I've been treated like I was just barely good enough to spit on and sometimes not even good enough for that. Big Daddy is dying of cancer, and it's spread all through him and it's attacked all his vital organs including the kidneys and right now he is sinking into uremia, and you all know what uremia is, it's poisoning of the whole system due to the failure of the body to eliminate its poisons. . . . I am asking for a square deal, and I expect to get one. But if I don't get one, if there's any peculiar shenanigans going on around here behind my back, or before me, well, I'm not a corporation lawyer for nothing. I know how to protect my own interests. . . ."

Brick is back now from the gallery, a little more vague from the drink than before, and becomes the center of bitter remarks by Mae and Gooper which Big Mama finally silences. Gooper explains that he has to be back in Memphis in the morning, so there is no time to lose in bringing up an important matter—outline of a trusteeship for the estate he has drawn up, the papers for which he takes from his briefcase.

BIG MAMA. Now you listen to me, all of you, you listen here! They's not going to be any more catty talk in my house! And Gooper, you put that away before I grab it out of your hand and tear it right up! I don't know what the hell's in it, and I don't want to know what the hell's in it. I'm talkin' in Big Daddy's language now; I'm his *wife,* not his *widow,* I'm still his *wife!* And I'm talkin' to you in his language an'—

GOOPER. Big Mama, what I have here is—

MAE. Gooper explained that it's just a plan. . . .

BIG MAMA. I don't care what you got there. Just put it back where it came from, an' don't let me see it again, not even the outside of the envelope of it! Is that understood? Basis! Plan! Preliminary! Design! I say—what is it Big Daddy always says when he's disgusted?

BRICK. Big Daddy says "crap" when he's disgusted.

BIG MAMA. That's right—*CRAP!* I say *CRAP* too, like Big Daddy!

MAE. Coarse language doesn't seem called for in this—

GOOPER. Somethin' in me is *deeply outraged* by hearin' you talk like this.

BIG MAMA. *Nobody's goin' to take nothin'!* —till Big Daddy let's go of it, and maybe, just possibly, not—not even then! No, not even then!

Big Mama gets a little maudlin over Brick again, as the conference shows signs of breaking up, and wishes that he could give Big Daddy a grandson before the old man dies.

"Everybody listen," Margaret suddenly commands . . . "I have an announcement to make . . . Brick and I are going to—*have a child!*"

Big Mama is ecstatic, rushing off to tell Big Daddy the news. Mae and Gooper do not believe the claim and are trying to trick more information out of Margaret when there is a great cry of pain from another part of the house. Big Daddy's agony has started; they leave.

Margaret thanks Brick for having kept still and saving her face. He is concerned over not yet having felt the "click." There is a slight argument about putting Brick's pillow on the sofa where he has been sleeping; Margaret wants to put it on the bed. Suddenly another drink brings the "click," and Brick wanders peacefully out onto the gallery singing to himself.

In a rush of decision, Margaret puts the pillow on the bed, goes to the liquor cabinet, gathers up the bottles and runs off with

them. Brick comes back in, picks up the pillow, and then is confronted by a smiling Margaret.

"Brick," she says, "I used to think that you were stronger than me and I didn't want to be overpowered by you. But now, since you've taken to liquor—you know what?—I guess it's bad, but now I'm stronger than you and I can love you more truly! Don't move that pillow. I'll move it right back if you do!"

She reminds him of her visit to the gynecologist and that right now is the time for her to conceive, and he wants to know how she can conceive by a man in love with his liquor.

She shows him that the liquor has disappeared and answers his question:

"By locking his liquor up and making him satisfy my desire before I unlock it."

The couple is interrupted briefly by the arrival of Big Mama, in a hurry to get the morphine and give Big Daddy some relief. "My son, Big Daddy's boy! Little Father!" she sobs over Brick as she runs out.

"And so tonight we're going to make the lie true," says Margaret, "and when that's done, I'll bring the liquor back here and we'll get drunk together, here, tonight, in this place that death has come into. . . . What do you say?"

"I don't say anything," Brick replies. "I guess there's nothing to say."

Margaret turns out the single bedside lamp.

"Oh, you weak people, you weak, beautiful people!—who give up.—What you want is someone to—take hold of you.—Gently, gently, with love! And—I *do* love you, Brick, I *do!*"

"Wouldn't it be funny if that was true?" Brick says, as the slowly falling curtain completes its descent.

---

Editor's Note: The published version of *Cat on a Hot Tin Roof,* issued by New Directions, includes an alternate Act III of slightly greater length than the above. It is labeled, "As played in New York production," a description that was completely accurate only for the first couple of weeks of the run. The "censorship" matter resulted in a few alterations thereafter. In a "note of explanation" to this alternate act, Williams

relates that the changes were the result of
the "creative influence" of the director, Elia
Kazan, who felt that the third act should
(1) not abandon so vital a character as Big
Daddy, (2) show Brick as having under-
gone "some apparent mutation" as a result
of the talk with his father in Act II, and (3)
present Margaret more definitely in a sympathetic light. The author says he was
wholeheartedly only for the third point but
made the changes because he didn't want to
risk losing Kazan's interest and his services
as director. The reception of the revised act
"more than justified, in my opinion, the
adjustments made to that (Kazan's) influence," Williams adds. However, the in-
clusion of the original third act in the published text would seem to indicate that the
playwright still prefers it.

## ALTERNATE ACT III

Big Daddy is seen leaving as at the end
of Act II, with the words, "Liars! Liars!
Liars!," trailing behind him. Margaret enters to ask Brick what has been going on;
he assures her that he didn't lie to his father,
that he has lied to no one but himself and
that the time has come to put him in Rainbow Hill. Big Daddy, he says, has gone
to bed.

Gooper, Mae, the Reverend Tooker and
Doctor Baugh are bustling in and out, sending servants in search of Big Mama for the
important conference. After she arrives, the
procedure is much the same as in the first
Act III, with some changes of dialogue
here and there. A sudden thunderstorm,
with much offstage scurrying by servants,
is introduced after the revelation of Big
Daddy's true condition, and as it passes
over Big Daddy enters from the gallery.
The storm didn't disturb him so much as
the loud talk he heard; he wants to know
what is going on.

BIG DADDY. What is that pregnant-lookin'
envelope you're puttin' back in your briefcase, Gooper?

GOOPER. That? Nothin', suh—nothin'
much of anythin' at all . . .

BIG DADDY. Nothin'? It looks like a whole

lot of nothing! You all know th' story about
th' young married couple—

GOOPER. Yes, sir!

BIG DADDY. Hello, Brick—

BRICK. Hello, Big Daddy.

BIG DADDY. Young married couple took
Junior out to th' zoo one Sunday, inspected
all of God's creatures in their cages, with
satisfaction.

GOOPER. Satisfaction.

BIG DADDY. This afternoon was a warm
afternoon in spring an' that ole elephant had
somethin' else on his mind which was
bigger'n peanuts. You know this story,
Brick?

BRICK. No, sir, I don't know it.

BIG DADDY. Y'see, in th' cage adjoinin'
they was a young female elephant in heat!

BIG MAMA. Oh, Big Daddy!

BIG DADDY. What's the matter, preacher's
gone, ain't he? All right. That female
elephant in the next cage was permeatin'
the atmosphere about her with a powerful
and excitin' odor of female fertility! Huh!
Ain't that a nice way to put it, Brick?

BRICK. Yes, sir, nothin' wrong with it.

BIG DADDY. Brick says the's nothin' wrong
with it.

BIG MAMA. Oh, Big Daddy!

BIG DADDY. So this ole bull elephant still
had a couple of fornications left in him.
He reared back his trunk an' got a whiff of
that elephant lady next door!—began to
paw at the dirt in his cage an' butt his head
against the separatin' partition and, first
thing y'know, there was a conspicuous
change in his *profile—very conspicuous!*
Ain't I tellin' this story in decent language,
Brick?

BRICK. Yes, sir, too ruttin' decent!

BIG DADDY. So, the little boy pointed at it
and said, "What's that?" His Mam said,
"Oh, that's — nothin'!" — His Papa said,
"She's spoiled!"

It is after this story that Margaret makes
the announcement of her "pregnancy" directly to Big Daddy, offering her "big present" on her knees before him.

*"Uh-huh, this girl has life in her body,
that's no lie!"* Big Daddy comments, accepting the announcement at face value. He
tells Gooper that he wants to see his lawyer
in the morning and, answering Brick as to
where he is going, says:

"Son, I'm goin' up on the roof to the belvedere on th' roof to look over my kingdom before I give up my kingdom—twenty-eight thousand acres of th' richest land this side of the Valley Nile!"

The recriminations by Gooper and Mae against Brick and Margaret are somewhat more extended than in the first ACT III, with Mae revealing that they have been able to hear from their adjoining room how Brick has spurned Margaret's advances. Brick speaks up for his wife and finally dismisses the other couple with:

"An' now if you will stop actin' as if Brick Pollitt was dead an' buried, invisible, not heard, an' go on back to your peep-hole in the wall—I'm drunk, and sleepy— not as alive as Maggie, but still alive. . . ."

Brick achieves his "click," Margaret grabs his pillow from him and throws it on the bed, then goes to the bar and tosses the bottles out onto the lawn, where breaking glass can be heard. She reminds Brick that she's the only one who can drive him to town for a new supply, and Brick says, "I admire you, Maggie."

He sits on the bed, she reaches up and turns out the light and kneels beside him, saying:

"Oh, you weak, beautiful people who give up with such grace. What you need is someone to take hold of you—gently, with love, and hand your life back to you, like something gold you let go of—and I can! I'm determined to do it—and nothing's more determined than a cat on a tin roof— is there? Is there, baby?"

She touches his cheek gently as the curtain falls.

EDITOR'S NOTE: In performance at the Morosco Theatre, New York City, the third act is not now precisely like either of the two outlined here. However, it more nearly resembles the alternate third act, with the same beginning and ending and with Big Daddy returning to the scene as the storm passes. He personally receives Margaret's pregnancy announcement, but he does not tell the elephant story.

This, because of the "censorship," has been replaced by Big Daddy's observation, after Gooper says there is nothing important in the envelope he is putting back in his briefcase, that there is a smell in the room— "a powerful and obnoxious odor of mendacity." He adds, "It smells like *Death!*"

There is another aspect of the performance at the Morosco that may confuse a playgoer who first has read the play. That is the emphasis resulting from numerous serious and joking references to Big Mama as a short, stout woman—she weighs 170 pounds, according to the description, and is often referred to as fat. Big Mama is played by Mildred Dunnock, who is of normal height and thin, almost on the frail side.

The answer to this is that Miss Dunnock is one of the finest character actresses in the theatre, she happened to be available when this play was being cast and it was decided that talent was more important than weight. In the alternate third act, the one reference to Big Mama's appearance fits the Dunnock appearance—where Big Daddy notices that his wife is crying and asks, "What's wrong with that long, thin woman over there, loaded with diamonds?"

# Appendix

ROSTER OF THE NEW YORK DRAMA CRITICS' CIRCLE, 1954–55

| | |
|---|---|
| Brooks Atkinson | *The New York Times* |
| Mark Barron | *Associated Press* |
| Whitney Bolton | *Morning Telegraph* |
| John Mason Brown | *The Saturday Review* |
| John Chapman | *Daily News* |
| Ethel Colby | *Journal of Commerce* |
| Robert Coleman | *Daily Mirror* |
| Richard Cooke | *Wall Street Journal* |
| Thomas R. Dash | *Women's Wear Daily* |
| George Freedley | *(Secretary of Circle)* |
| Jack Gaver | *United Press* |
| Wolcott Gibbs | *The New Yorker* |
| William Hawkins | *New York World-Telegram* |
| Henry Hewes | *The Saturday Review* |
| John Keating | *Cue* |
| Walter F. Kerr | *New York Herald Tribune* |
| Louis Kronenberger | *Time* |
| John McClain | *New York Journal-American* |
| Ward Morehouse | *North American Newspaper Alliance* |
| George Jean Nathan | *New York Journal-American* |
| Louis Sheaffer | *Brooklyn Eagle* |
| Joseph T. Shipley | *The New Leader* |
| Richard Watts, Jr. | *New York Post* |
| Thomas H. Wenning | *Newsweek* |

*Members Emeritus:* Howard Barnes, Robert Garland, John Gassner, Rosamond Gilder, Joseph Wood Krutch, Arthur Pollock, Stark Young.

## PRESIDENTS OF THE CIRCLE

| | | | |
|---|---|---|---|
| Brooks Atkinson | 1935–37 | Howard Barnes | 1943–45 |
| George Jean Nathan | 1937–39 | John Mason Brown | 1945–49 |
| Burns Mantle | 1939–40 | John Chapman | 1949–51 |
| Joseph Wood Krutch | 1940–41 | Gilbert Gabriel | 1951–52 |
| John Mason Brown | 1941–42 | Joseph T. Shipley | 1952–54 |
| John Anderson | 1942–43 | Walter F. Kerr | 1954–55 |

Among past members of the Circle not mentioned elsewhere in this volume have been: Mrs. Edith J. R. Isaacs, *Theatre Arts Monthly;* Grenville Vernon, *Commonweal;* Ruth Sedgwick, *Stage;* Vernon Rice, *Post;* Otis L. Guernsey, *Cue;* Harry Bull, *Town and Country;* John Lardner, *Star;* George Currie, *Eagle;* Thomas Fielder, *Cue;* Lawrence Perry, *North American Newspaper Alliance;* Jesse Zunser, *Cue;* Wilella Waldorf, *Post.*

# PULITZER PRIZE PLAYS

1918—*Why Marry?* by Jesse Lynch Williams

1919—No award

1920—*Beyond the Horizon* by Eugene O'Neill

1921—*Miss Lulu Bett* by Zona Gale

1922—*Anna Christie* by Eugene O'Neill

1923—*Icebound* by Owen Davis

1924—*Hell-Bent fer Heaven* by Hatcher Hughes

1925—*They Knew What They Wanted* by Sidney Howard

1926—*Craig's Wife* by George Kelly

1927—*In Abraham's Bosom* by Paul Green

1928—*Strange Interlude* by Eugene O'Neill

1929—*Street Scene* by Elmer Rice

1930—*The Green Pastures* by Marc Connelly

1931—*Alison's House* by Susan Glaspell

1932—*Of Thee I Sing* by George S. Kaufman, Morrie Ryskind, Ira and George Gershwin

1933—*Both Your Houses* by Maxwell Anderson

1934—*Men in White* by Sidney Kingsley

1935—*The Old Maid* by Zoë Akins

1936—*Idiot's Delight* by Robert E. Sherwood

1937—*You Can't Take It with You* by George S. Kaufman and Moss Hart

1938—*Our Town* by Thornton Wilder

1939—*Abe Lincoln in Illinois* by Robert E. Sherwood

1940—*The Time of Your Life* by William Saroyan

1941—*There Shall Be No Night* by Robert E. Sherwood

1942—No award

1943—*The Skin of Our Teeth* by Thornton Wilder

1944—No award

1945—*Harvey* by Mary Coyle Chase

1946—*State of the Union* by Howard Lindsay and Russel Crouse

1947—No award

1948—*A Streetcar Named Desire* by Tennessee Williams

1949—*Death of a Salesman* by Arthur Miller

1950—*South Pacific* by Richard Rodgers, Oscar Hammerstein II and Joshua Logan

1951—No award

1952—*The Shrike* by Joseph Kramm

1953—*Picnic* by William Inge

1954—*The Teahouse of the August Moon* by John Patrick

1955—*Cat on a Hot Tin Roof* by Tennessee Williams

# THE EDITOR AND HIS BOOK

JACK GAVER *was born in Tolono, Illinois, on February 20, 1906. Since the fall season of 1930, he has been the drama editor and theatrical critic for the United Press, one of America's three great news services. Before joining the United Press, he worked on newspapers in Hartford City, Indiana; Champaign, Urbana and Springfield, Illinois. Educated in the public schools of Indiana, Tennessee and Ohio, he spent three years at the University of Illinois, where he spent some time on the acting side of the footlights. His work as a newspaperman is his primary interest and he has worked on newspapers since high school. Married to Jessyca Gaver, the publisher of Writers' Newsletter, he makes his home in New York City. The Gavers have a daughter, Claudia, who is not yet old enough to be taken to the theatre. Jack Gaver is the author of two previous books,* There's Laughter In the Air *(Greenberg, 1945) and* Curtain Calls *(Dodd, Mead, 1949).*